Index to the
Bauer-Arndt-Gingrich

GREEK
LEXICON

Index to the
Bauer-Arndt-Gingrich
GREEK
LEXICON

by John R. Alsop

ZONDERVAN
PUBLISHING HOUSE OF THE ZONDERVAN CORPORATION
GRAND RAPIDS, MICHIGAN 49506

Index to the
Bauer, Arndt and Gingrich Greek Lexicon

© Summer Institute of Linguistics 1968
Wycliffe Bible Translators, Inc.

This edition by special arrangement with
Wycliffe Bible Translators, Inc.

Eighth printing   1977
ISBN 0-310-20011-3

Printed in the United States of America

INTRODUCTION

PURPOSE

With the publication of Arndt and Gingrich's A Greek- English Lexicon of the New Testament and Other Early Christian Literature, which is a translation and adaptation of Bauer's lexicon, English speaking students of the Greek New Testament have the first comprehensive New Testament lexicon since Thayer's in 1886. Since this Lexicon should be one of the first volumes consulted by Bible translators when beginning to exegete a passage, this index is presented to make the Lexicon more readily usable.

The Index will be a time saver for all Bible translators, from those who know little Greek to those who are proficient in Greek studies.   In an experiment performed by a proficient Greek student it was found that the amount of time spent in locating the specific references in the Lexicon was cut by more than half.   In the overall experiment, the median search time without the Index was 27 seconds per entry, whereas it was only 12 seconds when the Index was consulted.   The difference is greater for those who know little Greek.

The advantages, however, do not stop here.   When the translator needs to know how the lexicographer classifies an instance of some frequently used word, he often can find it only after a diligent and time- consuming search for the verse reference through three, four or more columns of closely packed entries; that is, if the particular reference is included at all as an example.   If he fails to find the reference after such a search he still cannot be sure that it was not there, because it is easy for the eye to skip over a verse reference when scanning through the columns.   With the Index the translator can immediately ascertain whether or not the word is cited, and he can turn to the correct section in the Lexicon rapidly.

The advantage for the translator who knows little Greek is obvious.   He can find entries in the Lexicon readily without having to struggle parsing the forms in the text to identify them.   Some deprecate this "short cut to the forms"; but let it be remembered that this Index was produced to meet the needs of over three hundred working Bible translation teams who are already burdened with obstacles enough in the ten- to thirty- year course of their work that any help is welcome.   It is not intended to be an aid to students who ought to be learning their principal parts and declensions themselves.   Furthermore, experience shows that those whose Greek is wobbly rarely bother to go through the steps needed to use any lexicon. By consulting the Index, these people can begin using a lexicon once again.

The Index was produced with the aid of an electronic computer. Without high speed data processing machinery for organizing, sorting, and printing the entries the Index would never have gone beyond wishful thinking.

DESCRIPTION OF THE INDEX

Page Headings

A facsimile of page 15 of the Index is reproduced on the adjacent page. This is a right-hand page. The Index page number is at the top of the page in the center of the heading. In the right-hand corner is MATTHEW 8.3. This indicates Matthew 8.3 is the last reference to be found on the right-hand page. A reference to the first entry found on the left page is placed in the left-hand corner of the heading of all left-hand (even numbered) pages. With these two entries listed at the upper corners of the open pages, it is easy to thumb through the Index quickly to locate the desired reference.

Book and Chapter

In the second column near the bottom of the page a chapter heading MATTHEW 8 is centered in the column. Each new chapter is introduced in this form. Chapter numbers and book names are found only in this heading, and in the headings at the top of the pages.

Verses

The verse references are indicated at the left of each column. After the chapter heading MATTHEW 8 the reader will find a '1' to the left of the column. That entry and the succeeding ones refer to verse one. The same is true for verse 2, etc.

When Arndt and Gingrich list the same Greek word two or more times in different parts of the same verse, an entry like that in verse 18 in the left-hand column of the facsimile will be found. After the regular entries to verse 18 there appears an 18A followed by an 18B. Each one has the same Greek entry. The same is true in verse 21 but only the second occurrence of OURANOS is singled out by the authors. In verse 22, SOS occurs three times, hence 22A, 22B, and 22C.

When the same Greek word occurs in the succeeding verse or verses, the kind of entry found under verse 21F applies. In this case KURIOS occurs in both verse 21 and verse 22 but is listed only once. The two words listed under 17FF occur also in the two succeeding verses.

The entry under verse 24-7 indicates that the Greek word OIKIA occurs in

17FF	KALOS 2A	GOOD	401B
17FF	KARPOS 1A	FRUIT	405C
18	KARPOS 1A	FRUIT	405C
	OUDE 1	AND NOT	595D
	POIEW 11Bη	DO	688A
18A	PHERW 2	BEAR	862D
18B	PHERW 2	BEAR	862D
19	EKKOPTW 1	CUT DOWN	241B
	M8 AII2B	NOT	518B
	POIEW 11Bη	DO	688A
	PUR 1B	FIRE	737D
20	ARA 4	THEN	103C
	EPIGINWSKW 2A	KNOW	291A
	KARPOS 2A	RESULT	405D
21	ALLA 1A	BUT, YET	37B
	BASILEIA 3G	KINGDOM	135A
	EISERCHOMAI 2A	COME	232B
	THEL8MA 1Cγ	WILL	355A
	OU 2A	NO	594B
	OURANOS 3	HEAVEN	599D
	PAT8R 3D«	FATHER	641D
	POIEW 11C«	DO	688C
21B	OURANOS 2A	HEAVEN	599B
21F	KURIOS 2Cβ	LORD	460D
22	DAIMONION 2	DEMON	168B
	DUNAMIS 4	MIRACLE	207B
	EKBALLW 1	DRIVE OUT	237A
	EKEINOS 2Bβ	THAT	239B
	EN 112	WHILE	259D
	H8MERA 3Bβ	DAY	348A
	HO,H8,TO III1H	THE	553B
	POIEW 11Bβ	DO	687C
	POLUS 12A«	MANY	694D
	PROPH8TEUW 1	PROPHESY	730A
22A	SOS 1	YOURS	766C
22B	POLUS 11A«	MANY	694A
22B	SOS 1	YOURS	766C
22C	SOS 1	YOURS	766C
23	ANOMIA 2	LAWLESSNESS	71B
	APOCHWREW	LEAVE	101D
	GINWSKW 7	ACKNOWLEDGE	160D
	ERGAZOMAI 2A	WORK	307D
	HO,H8,TO III1	THE	553B
	HOMOLOGEW 4	CONFESS	571B
	HOTI 2	THAT	593D
	OUDEPOTE	NEVER	596D
	TOTE 2	AT THAT TIME	831D
24	AN8R 4	MAN	66B
	LOGOS 1A6	WORD	478D
	OIKODOMEW 1A	BUILD	560D
	HOMOIOW 1	MAKE LIKE	570B
	HOMOIOW 2	COMPARE	570B
	HOSTIS 1A	WHOEVER	590D
	OUN 1A	THEREFORE	597B
	PAS 1Cγ	WHOEVER	637B
	PAS 1Cγ	WHOEVER	637C
	POIEW 11C«	DO	688C
	PHRONIMOS	THOUGHTFUL	874C
24F	PETRA 1A	ROCK	660A
24=7	OIKIA 1A	HOUSE	559D
25	ANEMOS 1A	WIND	64A
	BROCH8	RAIN	147B
	EKEINOS 2A	THAT	239B

25	ERCHOMAI 11C«	COME	311B
	THEMELIOW 1		356C
	LAY THE FOUNDATION OF		
	KATABAINW 1B	COME DOWN	409D
	HO,H8,TO III1H	THE	553B
	PIPTW 1Bβ	FALL	665C
	PNEW 1A	BLOW	686A
	POTAMOS 1	RIVER	701C
	PROSKOPTW 1B	STRIKE AGAINST	723C
	PROSPAIW	STRIKE	725A
	PROSPIPTW 2	FALL DOWN BEFORE	725B
26	AMMOS	SAND	45D
	AN8R 4	MAN	66B
	LOGOS 1A6	WORD	478D
	M8 AII2A	NOT	518B
	MWROS 1	FOOLISH	533B
	OIKODOMEW 1A	BUILD	560D
	HOMOIOW 1	MAKE LIKE	570B
	PAS 1Cγ	WHOEVER	637B
	POIEW 11C«	DO	688C
27	ANEMOS 1A	WIND	64A
	BROCH8	RAIN	147B
	EKEINOS 2A	THAT	239B
	ERCHOMAI 11C«	COME	311B
	KATABAINW 1B	COME DOWN	409D
	HO,H8,TO III1H	THE	553B
	PIPTW 1Bβ	FALL	665C
	PNEW 1A	BLOW	686A
	POTAMOS 1	RIVER	701C
	PROSKOPTW 1B	STRIKE AGAINST	723C
	PROSR8SSW 2	BURST UPON	725C
	PTWSIS	COLLAPSE	735B
28	GINOMAI 13F	TAKE PLACE	158C
	DIDACH8 3	TEACHING	191C
	EKPL8SSW 2	BE AMAZED	243D
	EPI III1Bγ	ON	287A
	LOGOS 1A6	WORD	478D
	HOTE 1B	WHEN	592C
	OCHLOS 1	CROWD	605D
	SUNTELEW 1	COMPLETE	799D
	TELEW 1	FINISH	818C
29	EXOUSIA 2	ABILITY	277D

MATTHEW 8

1	AKOLOUTHEW 2	ACCOMPANY	30D
	AUTOS 3A	(OBLIQUE CASE)	122D
	KATABAINW 1A«	COME DOWN	409B
	HO,H8,TO III1A«	THE	552B
	OROS	MOUNTAIN	586B
	OCHLOS 1	CROWD	605D
	POLUS 11Aβ	MANY	694B
2	EAN 11A	IF	210B
	THELW 2·	WISH	355D
	IDOU 1Bβ	BEHOLD	371C
	KATHARIZW 1B«	CLEANSE	388A
	KURIOS 2Cβ	LORD	460D
	LEGW 18A	SAY	470B
	LEPROS	LEPER	473A
	PROSERCHOMAI 1	APPROACH	720A
	PROSKUNEW 5	DO REVERENCE	724B
3	HAPTW 2B	TOUCH	102C
	EKTEINW 1	STRETCH OUT	244D

the verses included by the hyphen. This does not necessarily mean that all the verses include this word, although in this example they do. In Matthew 2, however, the reference for Herod is listed as 1-19, but the Greek word H8RWD8S is found only in verses 1, 3, 7, 12, 13, 15, 16, and 19.

Entries which refer to more than one occurrence of the word in a verse or succeeding verses are indented three spaces.

Greek Word

Following the verse number in each entry is the Greek word in its lexical form. Unfortunately the economic limitations of the project made it impossible to publish the Index with Greek entries written in Greek letters. Yet, one becomes accustomed to this transliteration of Greek in a very short time. The transliteration is straightforward except for a few characters as indicated below. Accents are not indicated. Rough breathing is represented by H.

$$
\begin{array}{rcl}
8 & = & \eta \\
TH & = & \theta \\
X & = & \xi \\
P & = & \pi \\
R & = & \rho \\
PH & = & \varphi \\
CH & = & \chi \\
PS & = & \psi \\
W & = & \omega
\end{array}
$$

Sections under Greek Words

The sections and subsections into which the authors divide discussions of a Greek word are indicated following the Greek word in the Index. (Many Greek words have only one meaning and these are not divided into sections.) The primary sectioning is usually indicated by the Arabic numbers 1, 2, 3, etc. The subsectioning of these are indicated in the Lexicon by the lower case letters, a through j, but since the character set of the computer does not include lower case letters these were represented in the Index by the upper case letters, A through J. In addition, under many Greek words these lower case letters were subdivided again. At this level each subdivision is indicated by letters of the Greek alphabet.

On some occasions the authors need more than three levels in their outline. When four levels are needed, the highest level is indicated by Roman numerals. This highest level is then divided by sections indicated with the Arabic numerals, etc. When five levels are desired, the highest level is indicated by the Roman letters, A, B, C, etc. These are then subdivided into sections headed by the Roman numerals, etc.

On rare occasions the subsections headed by Greek letters are further divided. On one occasion (under the Greek word PIPTW) the division is indicated by the Hebrew letters א (aleph) and ב (beth). Also in a few entries this same level is represented by Arabic numerals set in parentheses. Neither is included in the Index.

Page Numbers and Quadrants

On the right side of each column is the page number and quadrant where the entry will be found. Quadrant A is the upper half of the left-hand column. Quadrant B is the lower half of the left-hand column. Quadrant C is the upper half of the right-hand column; and quadrant D is the lower half of the right-hand column. In this way it is never necessary to search more than half a column to find a particular verse reference.

English Glosses

Next to the page number on the right side of the column is an English gloss which represents the Greek word. These glosses were included to help those who know little Greek find quickly the entry which interests them without referring to an interlinear Greek-English New Testament. Care was taken to choose fairly representative glosses. However, it would be impossible to give an adequate rendering for each entry in the space available. It cannot be overemphasized that the user of the Index should not rely on these English glosses as adequately conveying the meaning of the Greek word.

In some cases grammatical descriptors such as (PARTICLE) are indicated in lieu of an English gloss. These are enclosed in parentheses. In a few cases neither English gloss nor grammatical descriptor is indicated.

In order to simplify the preparation of the Index hyphens, apostrophes, and commas were removed from the English glosses.

EDITORIAL DECISIONS

Every verse reference to the New Testament in the 1957 edition of the Arndt-Gingrich Lexicon is included in the Index, with a few exceptions which fall into two classes. The first refers to verse references that illustrate the forms of a word. These are given in the introductory part of an entry before the entry is broken into sections. An example of this is found on page 41, quadrant C of the Lexicon under the Greek word HAMARTANW, to sin. The introductory paragraph includes nine verse references to the New Testament, but since these refer only to forms of the Greek word it was not deemed necessary to include them. There are some cases, however, where references in the introductory paragraph were included in the Index.

The other exceptions are the references to bibliographical materials such as the title of an article. These were omitted from the Index since they were already included in the body of the entry.

DUPLICATE ENTRIES

On many occasions there are duplicate verse references to a Greek word which occurs only once in the verse. These fall into two types. In the first type the authors were uncertain under which section or meaning the reference should be included so both sections are cited in the Lexicon and the Index. An example is found on page 4 of the Index under Matthew 3.2. BASILEIA, kingdom, occurs only once in the verse, yet it is referenced twice, once under Section 3A and the other under Section 3G.

In the second type the authors cited the reference twice within the same section. If the two references are on different page quadrants a second entry is included in the Index to refer to the new page quadrant. If both are in the same page quadrant, an asterisk precedes the entry, and the entry itself is not repeated. The reference may occur more than twice, but that is unlikely. (A few references which occurred a second time were not included. In addition, for some unknown reason, when the machine printed the Index it failed to recognize that some successive entries were identical and so printed out two identical lines rather than one line with an asterisk.)

Variant readings provide another source of multiple entries but they are under different Greek words. They are not identified in the Index as variant readings so the user must consult the Lexicon to identify them.

USE OF THE INDEX

The use of the Index is straightforward. The translator turns in the Index to the verse he is considering. The Greek words are listed there in Greek alphabetical order under the verse. He chooses either the Greek word of interest, or the corresponding English gloss. The page and quadrant where each entry is discussed is listed at the right of the column. He turns to the page quadrant of the Lexicon and searches there for the Greek word, the section and subsection, and finally (within a new highly limited space) the verse reference. After finding the verse reference he works outward to ascertain the general meaning of the word for that passage.

Take, for example, Romans 3.23. The entry is listed as follows:

23 HAMARTANW 1	SIN 41D
DOXA 1A	BRIGHTNESS 202D
DOXA 3	FAME 203A
HUSTEREW 2	TO MISS 857A

The first Greek word in the verse which is included in the Index is H8MARTON, sinned. The Greek student will immediately recognize this as corresponding to HAMARTANW in the Index. The untrained readily surmises that this is the desired entry since there is only one occurrence of some kind of 'sin' in the passage. This verse reference occurs on page 41, quadrant D; and it will be found in the outline under section 1.

One who knows Greek should have no trouble identifying HUSTEROUNTAI (the succeeding word in the Greek New Testament which occurs in the Index) as coming from HUSTEREW; but the novice may find this one difficult. Yet, since the verse is short, the process of elimination should narrow his choice to HUSTEREW. The English gloss TO MISS also helps. The verse reference is on page 857 in quadrant A under section 2 of the word.

The last Greek word in the verse that is referenced in the lexicon is DOX8S, or DOXA in the lexicon form. There are two entries with DOXA because there are two interpretations given in the Lexicon for the meaning of this Greek word in this context. One interpretation is found on page 202, quadrant D under section 1A. The other is on page 203, quadrant A under section 3.

USE OF THE LEXICON

The purpose of a lexicon is to cover the range of usage of a word as it occurs within a given body of literature. The body of literature covered by this Lexicon is the New Testament and other early Christian literature.

Once the translator has found the verse reference under a specific Greek word in the Lexicon he should consider the range of meaning that word has over all its subdivisions. In many instances the word has only one meaning; but when the meanings are multiple, he should give them much thought and choose for himself which area of meaning best fits the given verse and why. Thus he compares his judgment with that of the authors. In any case, he should consult the commentaries, versions, and other lexicons to see if there is general agreement. If there is not, the arguments of each must be weighed against the others. The decision should be made with reference to the work of as many scholars as possible.

Experimentation shows that working translators tend to spend about the same amount of time evaluating lexicon entries whether they use the Index or not. It is the proportion of time spent in thinking about what the lexicon says, as over against the dead time spent in finding the discussion of a word, that is striking. In the experiment mentioned at the beginning of the introduction, an experienced translator spent 65 per cent of his time trying to find references when he did not use the Index, and only 35 per cent of his time thinking about what he had found. With the Index the proportions were reversed. Although the actual time spent in reading the lexicon entries for content and drawing conclusions was the same as when he did not use the Index, the profitable proportion of his time shot up to 65 per cent, and searching occupied only 35 per cent of his time.

CAUTION

Two warnings must be repeated. First, the English glosses in the Index do not give the exact area of meaning for most verses. Always refer to the meanings found in the Lexicon.

Secondly, the opinions of Professors Bauer, Arndt, and Gingrich are not considered infallible. The classification of a Greek word in any one verse may not be upheld by other scholars. It is the user's responsibility to use the Index and the Lexicon advisedly and with good judgment.

PRODUCTION OF THE INDEX

Before the advent of modern data processing machinery a project as extensive as the Index would have taken years. With modern computing equipment, however, data processing of this nature can be performed in a short time.

It took one man-month to mark for the key punch operator all that was to be put on data cards. It took two man-months to key punch the 10,000 data cards, verify their accuracy, and correct them. These ten thousand punched cards carried the information necessary to build the 60,728 entries included in the Index. The machine required 45 minutes to read these 10,000 cards, build the 60,728 index lines, and write them all out on magnetic tape for further processing. An additional hour was required to print the entries line by line for proofreading. After corrections were prepared on other data cards it took 30 minutes for the machine to correct the mistaken records. Three hours were required to sort the lines according to book, chapter, verse and Greek form. Finally, it required one hour to build the 489 pages of the Index one by one in the memory of the machine and print them in the present form—seven and a half seconds per page.

At that stage, it was only necessary to photograph the printed output, prepare the offset masters, and print the Index.

That each individual page should be printed by the machine in the desired format follows the suggestion made by Dr. Joseph E. Grimes for the 1964 Bibliography of the Summer Institute of Linguistics. This alone saves a tremendous amount of typing, proofreading, and retyping. Unfortunately, due to the present design of printers for computing machinery, the type set of characters is limited.

ACKNOWLEDGEMENTS

The assistance of many people helped make this work possible. First of all, the Director of the Mexican Branch of Wycliffe Bible Translators, Dr. Benjamin F. Elson, and the Translation Coordinator, John Beekman, saw the need for the Index as a tool for better translations.

The task of selecting and marking the data to be key punched was reduced through the help of Dr. Grimes, Barbara Grimes, and Kent Gordon. My wife,

Jean Alsop key punched and corrected the ten thousand data cards used to feed the computer. Miss Audrey Johnson machine-verified those same data cards so as to discover as many errors as possible in the pre-machine stage. Dr. Grimes also helped organize the project and contributed valuable suggestions for preparing the computer program.

I am also grateful to the members of Wycliffe Bible Translators who spent hours checking the data output to remove as many errors as possible. It would be foolish to believe that all errors have been removed, but they have been reduced to a minimum (around one half of one per cent). I would appreciate hearing of any errors or omissions.

Finally I would like to thank Ing. Sergio Beltran, Director of the Centro de Cálculo Electrónico, of the Universidad Nacional Autónoma de Mexico, and his staff, for their cooperation. I would also like to thank the University of Chicago Press, publishers of the lexicon, for their permission to produce this Index.

John R. Alsop

Ixmiquilpan, Hidalgo
Mexico

April 18, 1964

INDEX

MATTHEW 1

1	ABRAAM	ABRAHAM	1D
	BIBLOS 1	BOOK	141A
	GENESIS 3	EXISTENCE	154A
	I8SOUS 3	JESUS CHRIST	374C
	CHRISTOS 2	ANOINTED ONE	895C
1A	HUIOS 2A	SON	842A
2	ABRAAM	ABRAHAM	1D
	ADELPHOS 1	BROTHER	15C
	IAKWB 1	JACOB	368A
	ISAAK	ISAAC	381C
2F	IOUDAS 1A	JUDAH	380C
2FF	GENNAW 1A	BEGET	154C
2-16	DE 1C	BUT, AND	170C
3	GENNAW 1A	BEGET	154C
	EK 3A	FROM	234A
	HESRWM	HEZRON	313D
	ZARA	ZERAH	336A
	THAMAR	TAMAR	351A
3A	PHARES	PEREZ	861B
3B	PHARES	PEREZ	861B
3F	ARAM	ARAM	103D
4	AMINADAB	AMMINADAB	45D
4A	NAASSWN	NAHSHON	534A
4B	NAASSWN	NAHSHON	534A
4F	SALA 1	SHELAH	747C
4F	SALMWN	SALMON	748B
5	BOES	BOAZ	144A
	EK 3A	FROM	234A
	IWB8D	OBED	385D
	RACHAB	RAHAB	742A
	ROUTH	RUTH	744D
5F	GENNAW 1A	BEGET	154C
5F	IESSAI	JESSE	374B
6	BASILEUS 1	KING	135D
	DAUID	DAVID	170B
	HO,H8,TO 117	THE	554C
	OURIAS	URIAH	600A
6F	SOLOMWN	SOLOMON	766C
7A	ABIA 1	ABIJAH	1C
7A	ROBOAM	REHOBOAM	744A
7B	ABIA 1	ABIJAH	1C
7B	ROBOAM	REHOBOAM	744A
8	AMASIAS	AMAZIAH	43D
	IWAS	JOASH	385D
	IWRAM	JORAM	386A
	IWSAPHAT	JEHOSHAPHAT	386B
	OCHOZIAS	AHAZIAH	606A
8F	OZIAS	UZZIAH	557D
9	ACHAZ	AHAZ	127C
	IWATHAM	JOTHAM	385B
9F	HEZEKIAS	HEZEKIAH	217A
10	AMWN	AMON	47C
	AMWS 2	AMOS	47C
	MANASS8S 2	MANASSEH	491B
10F	IWSIAS	JOSIAH	386D
11	ADELPHOS 1	BROTHER	15C
	EPI 12	UNDER	286B
	IECHONIAS	JECHONIAH	374B
	IWAKIM	JEHOIAKIM	385B
	METOIKESIA	DEPORTATION	515D
11F	BABULWN	BABYLON	129B
12	IECHONIAS	JECHONIAH	374B
	META BII2	AFTER	511C
	METOIKESIA	DEPORTATION	515D
	SALATHI8L	SHEALTIEL	747D
12F	ZOROBABEL	ZERUBBABEL	340A
13	ELIAKIM	ELIAKIM	250C
13A	ABIOUD	ABIUD	1D
13B	ABIOUD	ABIUD	1D
13F	AZWR	AZOR	19C
14	ACHIM	ACHIM	127D
14A	SADWK	ZADOK	747A
14B	SADWK	ZADOK	747A
14F	ELIOUD	ELIUD	250D
15	ELEAZAR	ELEAZAR	248C
	MATTHAN	MATTHAN	497A
15F	IAKWB 2	JACOB	368B
16	AN8R 1	MAN	65D
	IWS8PH 4	JOSEPH	386C
	LEGW II3	CALL	471B
	MARIA 1	MARY	492D
	MN8STEUW	BECOME ENGAGED	527C
17	ABRAAM	ABRAHAM	1D
	APO II3B	FROM	86C
	BABULWN	BABYLON	129B
	GENEA 3A	AGE	153C
	DAUID	DAVID	170B
	DEKATESSARES	FOURTEEN	173A
	OUN 1A	THEREFORE	597B
	PAS 1Dα	ALL	637C
17A	HEWS III1A	UNTIL	335B
17B	HEWS III1A	UNTIL	335B
18	GAST8R 2	WOMB	152A
	GENESIS 1	BIRTH	154A
	GENN8SIS	BIRTH	155A
	DE 2	BUT, AND	170C
	EK 3A	FROM	234A
	HEURISKW 2	FIND	325D
	ECHW I2J	HAVE	333C
8	2Dα	BEFORE	343C
	MARIA 1	MARY	492D
	M8T8R 1	MOTHER	521D

18 MN8STEUW	BECOME ENGAGED 527C
HOUTW 5	THUS 602D
PNEUMA 5Cβ	SPIRIT 683A
PRIN 1B	BEFORE 708A
SUNERCHOMAI 1B	ASSEMBLE 796A
CHRISTOS 2	ANOINTED ONE 895C
18~20 IWS8PH 4	JOSEPH 386C
19 AN8R 1	MAN 65D
APOLUW 2A	SEND AWAY 96A
BOULOMAI 2Aβ	DESIRE 145D
DEIGMATIZW	EXPOSE 171C
DIKAIOS 1A	UPRIGHT 194C
LATHRA 1	SECRETLY 463D
PARADEIGMATIZW	EXPOSE 619A
20 AGGELOS 2A	ANGEL 7B
GENNAW 1A	BEGET 154C
GUN8 3	BRIDE 167C
DAUID	DAVID 170B
EIMI III3	TO BE 224B
ENTHUMEOMAI	CONSIDER 265C
IDOU 1Bα	BEHOLD 371C
KATA II2A	DURING 407C
KURIOS 2A	LORD 460B
LEGW I8A	SAY 470B
*MARIA 1	MARY 492D
M8 AIII5A	NOT 518D
ONAR	DREAM 573A
PARALAMBANW 1	TAKE 625A
PNEUMA 5Cβ	SPIRIT 683A
SU 3	YOU 780A
HUIOS 1Bα	SON 841C
PHAINW 2C	APPEAR 859C
PHOBEW 1A	BE AFRAID 870D
21 AUTOS 2	THEY 122D
AUTOS 3Fβ	(OBLIQUE CASE) 123B
I8SOUS 3	JESUS CHRIST 374C
KAI I2B	AND 393A
KALEW I Aγ	CALL 400A
HO,H8,TO IIID	THE 552D
ONOMA I2A	NAME 574B
SWZW 2Aα	SAVE 806A
TIKTW 1	GIVE BIRTH 824C
HUIOS 1Aα	SON 841B
22 GINOMAI I3A	TAKE PLACE 157D
DE 2	BUT, AND 170D
DIA AIII2A	BY 179C
EIPON 4	SAY 225D
HINA II8	IN ORDER THAT 377C
HINA II2	IN ORDER THAT 378D
HOLOS 3	WHOLE 567D
PL8ROW 4A	MAKE FULL 677C
PROPH8T8S 1	PROPHET 730D
HUPO I Aα	BY 850D
23 GAST8R 2	WOMB 152A
EMMANOU8L	EMMANUEL 254B
ECHW I2J	HAVE 333C
THEOS 3A	GOD 357D
KAI I2A	AND 393A
KALEW I Aγ	CALL 400A
METHERM8NEUW	TRANSLATE 499D
META AIIICβ	WITH 510A
ONOMA I2A	NAME 574B
HOS,H8,HO I7A	(REL PRON) 588C

23 PARTHENOS 1	VIRGIN 632B
TIKTW 1	GIVE BIRTH 824C
HUIOS 1Aα	SON 841B
24 GUN8 3	BRIDE 167C
DE 2	BUT, AND 170C
DIEGEIRW	AROUSE 193A
EGEIRW 2A	AWAKEN 214A
IWS8PH 4	JOSEPH 386C
KURIOS 2A	LORD 460B
PARALAMBANW 1	TAKE 625A
POIEW I2Aα	DO 689A
PROSTASSW	COMMAND 725D
HUPNOS	SLEEP 850C
HWS I2B	AS 905C
25 GINWSKW 5	KNOW 160C
HEWS IIIBα	UNTIL 335C
I8SOUS 3	JESUS CHRIST 374C
KALEW I Aγ	CALL 400A
HO,H8,TO IIID	THE 552D
ONOMA I2A	NAME 574B
HOS,H8,HO IIIF	(REL PRON) 589A
OU 4A	NO 594D
PRWTOTOKOS 1	FIRSTBORN 734A
TIKTW 1	GIVE BIRTH 824C
HUIOS 1Aα	SON 841B

MATTHEW 2

1 ANATOL8 2B	EAST 62A
BASILEUS 1	KING 135D
B8THLEEM	BETHLEHEM 139C
GENNAW 2	BEAR 154D
EN IIA	IN 257C
EN II1B	WHILE 259D
H8MERA 4B	TIME 348B
IDOU 1Bα	BEHOLD 371C
HIEROSOLUMA 1A	JERUSALEM 373D
IOUDAIA 1	JUDAEA 379D
HO,H8,TO IIIAα	THE 552B
PARAGINOMAI 1	COME 618D
1B MAGOS 1	MAGI 486A
1~19 H8RWD8S 1	HEROD 349B
2 ANATOL8 1	RISING 61D
BASILEUS 2A	KING 135D
GAR 1E	FOR 151C
EIDON 1A	SEE 219C
ERCHOMAI IIAε	COME 310D
IOUDAIOS 2C	JEWISH 380B
POU 1A	WHERE 702D
PROSKUNEW 5	DO REVERENCE 724B
TIKTW 1	GIVE BIRTH 824C
3 BASILEUS 1	KING 135D
HIEROSOLUMA 1B	JERUSALEM 373D
META AII2	WITH 510C
PAS 1Aε	ALL 637C
TARASSW 2	STIR UP 813A
4 ARCHIEREUS 1B	HIGH PRIEST 112B
GENNAW 2	BEAR 154D
GRAMMATEUS 2	SCRIBES 165A
LAOS 3A	PEOPLE 468A
HO,H8,TO IIIOA	THE 555A
PARA I3C	FROM 615A
PAS 1Dα	ALL 637C

4	POU IB	WHERE	702D
	PUNTHANOMAI I	INQUIRE	737A
	SUNAGW 2	GATHER	790A
	CHRISTOS I	ANOINTED ONE	895B
5	IOUDAIA I	JUDAEA	379D
	HOUTW 2	THUS	602C
	PROPH8T8S i	PROPHET	730D
	SU IB	YOU	779D
5F	B8THLEEM	BETHLEHEM	139C
6	G8 4	LAND	156C
	EGW	I	216C
	ELACHISTOS 2A	SMALLEST	248B
	EN I4A	IN	258B
	EXERCHOMAI IBα	GO OUT	274C
	H8GEMWN I	PRINCE	344A
	H8GEOMAI I	LEAD	344B
	ISRA8L 2	ISRAEL	382B
	LAOS 3A	PEOPLE	468A
	HOSTIS 2A	WHOEVER	591A
	OUDAMWS	BY NO MEANS	595D
	POIMAINW 2Aβ	TEND	690B
6A	IOUDAS IC	JUDAH	380C
6B	IOUDAS IC	JUDAH	380C
7	AKRIBOW	ASCERTAIN	32C
	KALEW ID	CALL	400B
	LATHRA I	SECRETLY	463D
	MAGOS I	MAGI	486A
	HO,H8,TO IIIAα	THE	552B
	PARA I3C	FROM	615A
	TOTE 2	AT THAT TIME	831C
	PHAINW 2A	SHINE	859B
	CHRONOS	TIME	896B
8	AKRIBWS	ACCURATELY	32D
	APAGGELLW I	REPORT	78C
	B8THLEEM	BETHLEHEM	139C
	EGW	I	216C
	EIPON 2B	SAY	225C
	EXETAZW I	SCRUTINIZE	275A
	EPAN	WHEN	282B
	ERCHOMAI IIAζ	COME	310D
	HEURISKW IA	FIND	325A
	KAGW 3A	I ALSO	387A
	HOPWS 2Aα	IN ORDER THAT	580C
	PAIDION I	INFANT	609A
	*PEMPW I	SEND	647C
	PROSKUNEW 5	DO REVERENCE	724B
9	EIMI II9A	TO BE	223D
	EPANW 2A	ON	283A
	HEWS IIA	UNTIL	334D
	IDOU IBβ	BEHOLD	371C
	HIST8MI IIIA	STAND	383A
	HO,H8,TO I3	THE	552A
	HOS,H8,HO II	(REL PRON)	587A
	HOU IAβ	WHERE	594A
	PAIDION I	INFANT	609A
	POREUW I	PROCEED	699B
	PROAGW 2A	LEAD	709A
9F	EIDON IA	SEE	219C
10	EIDON IA	SEE	219D
	MEGAS 2Aγ	GREAT	499A
	SPHODRA	GREATLY	803D
	CHAIRW 1	REJOICE	881B
	CHAIRW I	REJOICE	881D

10	CHARA I	JOY	883D
11	ANOIGW IC	OPEN	70C
	DWRON I	GIFT	210A
	EIDON IA	SEE	219C
	ERCHOMAI IIAβ	COME	310B
	TH8SAUROS IAα	TREASURE BOX	362A
	KAI IIA	AND	392C
	LIBANOS	FRANKINCENSE	474D
	MARIA I	MARY	492D
	META AII4	WITH	510D
	M8T8R I	MOTHER	521D
	OIKIA IA	HOUSE	559D
	PAIDION I	INFANT	609A
	PIPTW IBα	FALL	665B
	PROSKUNEW 5	DO REVERENCE	724B
	PROSPHERW 2A	BRING (TO)	727A
	SMURNA	MYRRH	766A
	CHRUSOS	GOLD	897A
12	ALLOS IB	OTHER	39B
	ANACHWREW 2A	RETURN	63A
	KATA II2A	DURING	407C
	M8 AIII8β	NOT	518A
	HODOS IA	WAY	556B
	CHR8MATIZW IBα		894A
		IMPART A WARNING	
	CHWRA IB	COUNTRY	897C
12F	ONAR	DREAM	573A
13	AGGELOS 2A	ANGEL	7B
	AN 3D	(PARTICLE)	48C
	ANACHWREW I	GO AWAY	63A
	APOLLUMI IAα	RUIN	94C
	EIMI I3	TO BE	222B
	EKEI I	THERE	238C
	HEWS IIB	UNTIL	334D
	Z8TEW IAβ	SEEK	339B
	IDOU IBα	BEHOLD	371C
	IWS8PH 4	JOSEPH	386C
	KURIOS 2A	LORD	460B
	LEGW I8A	SAY	470B
	MELLW ICγ	INTEND	502B
	HO,H8,TO II4Bζ	THE	554A
	PHAINW 2C	APPEAR	859C
	PHEUGW I	FLEE	863C
13F	AIGUPTOS	EGYPT	21C
13F	EGEIRW 2B	RISE	214A
13F	M8T8R I	MOTHER	521D
13F	PAIDION I	INFANT	609A
13F	PARALAMBANW I	TAKE	624D
14	ANACHWREW 2B	WITHDRAW	63A
	NUX IB	NIGHT	548D
	HO,H8,TO I3	THE	552A
15	AIGUPTOS	EGYPT	21C
	DIA AIII2A	BY	179C
	EIMI I3	TO BE	222B
	EK IA	AWAY FROM	233C
	EKEI I	THERE	238C
	HEWS IIIA	UNTIL	335B
	HINA II2	IN ORDER THAT	378D
	KALEW ID	CALL	400C
	PL8ROW 4A	MAKE FULL	677C
	PROPH8T8S I	PROPHET	730D
	TELEUT8	END	818B
	HUIOS 2B	SON	842B

15	HUPO IA∝		BY	850D
16	AKRIBOW		ASCERTAIN	32C
	APO II3A		FROM	86C
	APOSTELLW ID		SEND AWAY	98C
	B8THLEEM		BETHLEHEM	139C
	DIET8S		TWO YEARS OLD	193D
	EMPAIZW 2		DECEIVE	255B
	THUMOW		MAKE ANGRY	366B
	KATA II5Aγ		ACCORDING TO	408B
	KATWTERW		BELOW	426C
	LIAN I		VERY	474C
	HORION		BOUNDARY	585A
	PAIS IA∝		CHILD	609A
	PARA I3C		FROM	615A
	PAS ID∝		ALL	637C
	TOTE 2		AT THAT TIME	831C
	HUPO IA∝		BY	850D
	CHRONOS		TIME	896B
16A	MAGOS I		MAGI	486A
16B	MAGOS I		MAGI	486A
17	EIPON 4		SAY	225D
	IEREMIAS		JEREMIAH	372C
	PL8ROW 4A		MAKE FULL	677C
	PROPH8T8S I		PROPHET	730D
	TOTE IA		AT THAT TIME	831C
18	EIMI I2		TO BE	222B
	THELW 2		WISH	355D
	THR8NOS		DIRGE	363D
	KLAIW 2		WEEP	434B
	KLAUTHMOS		WEEPING	434C
	ODURMOS		LAMENTATION	557C
	HOTI 3A		THAT	593D
	PARAKALEW 4		IMPLORE	623A
	POLUS II8β		MANY	694C
	RAMA		RAMA	741C
	RACH8L		RACHEL	742A
	TEKNON I8		CHILD	816B
	PHWN8 I		SOUND	878D
19	AGGELOS 2A		ANGEL	7B
	AIGUPTOS		EGYPT	21C
	DE 2		BUT, AND	170C
	IWS8PH 4		JOSEPH	386C
	KURIOS 2A		LORD	460C
	ONAR		DREAM	573A
	TELEUTAW		DIE	818B
	PHAINW 2C		APPEAR	859C
20	Z8TEW 2B6		SEEK	339D
	THN8SKW I		DIE	363A
	POREUW I		PROCEED	699A
	PSUCH8 IA8		SOUL LIFE	901C
20F	G8 4		LAND	156D
20F	EGEIRW 2B		RISE	214A
20F	ISRA8L 2		ISRAEL	382B
20F	M8T8R I		MOTHER	521D
20F	PAIDION I		INFANT	609A
20F	PARALAMBANW I		TAKE	624D
22	AKOUW 3E		LEARN	32A
	ANACHWREW 2B		WITHDRAW	63A
	ANTI I		OPPOSITE	72D
	BASILEUW IA		RULE	136D
	GALILAIA		GALILEE	149D
	EKEI 2		THERE	238D
	IOUDAIA I		JUDAEA	379D
22	MEROS I8γ		PART	507A
	ONAR		DREAM	573A
	PAT8R IA		FATHER	640C
	PHOBEW IA		BE AFRAID	870D
	CHR8MATIZW I8∝			894A
		IMPART A WARNING		
23	DIA AIII2A		BY	179C
	EIPON 4		SAY	225D
	EIS 9A		IN	229D
	KALEW IA6		CALL	400B
	KATOIKEW IA		LIVE	425B
	LEGW II3		CALL	471B
	NAZARA		NAZARETH	534A
	NAZWRAIOS		NAZARENE	534B
	HOPWS 2A∝		IN ORDER THAT	580C
	HOTI 2		THAT	593D
	PL8ROW 4A		MAKE FULL	677C
	POLIS I		CITY	692B
	PROPH8T8S I		PROPHET	730D

MATTHEW 3

I	BAPTIST8S		BAPTIST	132B
	DE 2		BUT, AND	170C
	EKEINOS 2B∝		THAT	239B
	EN IIA		IN	257C
	EN IIIB		WHILE	259D
	ER8MOS 2		DESERT	309A
	H8MERA 4B		TIME	348B
	IOUDAIA I		JUDAEA	379D
	IWAN(N)8S I		JOHN	385B
	PARAGINOMAI 2		COME	619A
IF	K8RUSSW 2Bβ		ANNOUNCE	432D
2	BASILEIA 3A		KINGDOM	134D
	BASILEIA 3G		KINGDOM	135B
	EGGIZW 5B		APPROACH	212D
	METANOEW	CHANGE ONES MIND		513B
	OURANOS IE		HEAVEN	598D
	OURANOS 3		HEAVEN	599D
2F	GAR IC		FOR	151B
3	BOAW 2		SHOUT	143D
	EIPON I		SAY	225B
	HETOIMAZW I		PREPARE	316B
	EUTHUS I		STRAIGHT	321B
	8SAIAS		ISAIAH	349C
	KURIOS 2C∝		LORD	460C
	HODOS IA		WAY	556B
	HOUTOS IAβ		THIS	601A
	POIEW II8ι		DO	688B
	PROPH8T8S I		PROPHET	730D
	TRIBOS		BEATEN PATH	834A
	PHWN8 2E		VOICE	879C
4	AGRIOS I		WILD	13B
	AKRIS		GRASSHOPPER	32D
	APO IVIB		FROM	87A
	AUTOS IH		EVEN	122C
	DE 3		BUT, AND	170D
	DERMATINOS	(MADE OF) LEATHER		174C
	ENDUMA I		GARMENT	263A
	ECHW II8		HAVE	332A
	ZWN8		BELT	342A
	THRIX I		HAIR	364C
	IWAN(N)8S I		JOHN	385B

4	KAM8LOS	CAMEL	402C
	MELI	HONEY	501C
	OSPHUS 1	WAIST	591D
	PERI 2Aβ	ABOUT	650D
	TROPH8 1	FOOD	835C
5	EKPOREUOMAI 1C	GO OUT	244A
	HIEROSOLUMA 1B	JERUSALEM	373D
	IOUDAIA 1	JUDAEA	379D
	HO,H8,TO II2B	THE	553B
	PAS 1Cα	ALL	637B
	*PERICHWROS	NEIGHBORING	659B
	TOTE 1A	AT THAT TIME	831C
5F	IORDAN8S	JORDAN	379C
6	HAMARTIA 1	SIN	42D
	BAPTIZW 2A	BAPTIZE	131B
	EXOMOLOGEW 2A	CONFESS	276C
	POTAMOS 1	RIVER	701B
	HUPO 1Aα	BY	850D
7	BAPTISMA 1	BAPTISM	132A
	GENN8MA	CHILD	155A
	EIDON 1B	SEE	219D
	EPI III1Bη	ON	289B
	ERCHOMAI I1Aβ	COME	310C
	ECHIDNA	VIPER	332A
	MELLW 2	IS DESTINED	502C
	ORG8 2B	ANGER	583A
	POLUS I2Aα	MANY	694D
	SADDOUKAIOS	SADDUCEE	747A
	TIS, TI 1Aα	WHICH	826C
	HUPODEIKNUMI 2	SHOW	852A
	PHARISAIOS	PHARISEE	861C
	PHEUGW 2	FLEE	863C
8	AXIOS 1B	WORTHY	77B
	KARPOS 2A	RESULT	405D
	METANOIA	REPENTANCE	514A
	OUN 1B	THEREFORE	597B
	OUN 3	THEREFORE	597D
	POIEW I1Bη	DO	688A
9	ABRAAM	ABRAHAM	1D
	DOKEW 1A	THINK	200D
	EGEIRW 1Aε	RAISE UP	213D
	EK 3A	FROM	234A
	EN I5B	IN	258D
	ECHW I2Bα	HAVE	332C
	THEOS 3A	GOD	357D
	LEGW I6	SAY	470A
	LITHOS 1A	STONE	475B
	M8 AIII5A	NOT	518D
	HOUTOS 2B	THIS	601D
	PAT8R 1B	FOREFATHER	640C
	TEKNON 2D	CHILD	816C
10	AXIN8	AX	77A
	BALLW 1B	THROW	130C
	DE 4A	BUT, AND	170D
	DENDRON	TREE	173B
	EKKOPTW 1	CUT DOWN	241B
	8D8 1A	ALREADY	344C
	KALOS 2A	GOOD	401B
	KARPOS 1A	FRUIT	405C
	KEIMAI 1B	LIE	428A
	M8 AII2B	NOT	518B
	OUN 3	THEREFORE	597D
	PAS 1Aα	EVERY EACH	636C

10	POIEW I1B8	DO	688A
	RIZA 1A	ROOT	743B
11	BASTAZW 3A	REMOVE	137A
	EIS 6A	BECAUSE OF	229B
	ERCHOMAI I1Aη	COME	311A
	HIKANOS 2	APPROPRIATE	375B
	ISCHUROS 1A	STRONG	384A
	MEN 1Aα	(PARTICLE)	503D
	METANOIA	REPENTANCE	514A
	OPISW 2B	AFTER	578D
	PNEUMA 5Cβ	SPIRIT	683A
	PUR 1B	FIRE	737D
	HUDWR 1	WATER	840D
	HUPOD8MA	SANDAL	852B
11A	BAPTIZW 2A	BAPTIZE	131B
11B	BAPTIZW 3B	BAPTIZE	131D
12	HALWN 2	WHAT WAS THRESHED	41A
	APOTH8K8	STOREHOUSE	90C
	ASBESTOS 1	INEXTINGUISHABLE	114A
	AUTOS 3D	(OBLIQUE CASE)	123A
	ACHURON	CHAFF	128D
	DIAKATHARIZW	CLEAN OUT	183A
	KAI I2A	AND	393A
	KATAKAIW	CONSUME	412A
	HOS,H8,HO I3A	(REL PRON)	587C
	PTUON	WINNOWING SHOVEL	735A
	PUR 1B	FIRE	737C
	SITOS	WHEAT	759D
	SUNAGW 1	GATHER	789D
	CHEIR 1	HAND	888B
13	APO IV1Aβ	FROM	86D
	EPI III1Aγ	ON	288B
	IORDAN8S	JORDAN	379C
	IWAN(N)8S 1	JOHN	385B
	HO,H8,TO II4Bζ	THE	554A
	PARAGINOMAI 1	COME	618D
	TOTE 2	AT THAT TIME	831C
	HUPO 1Aα	BY	850D
13F	BAPTIZW 2A	BAPTIZE	131B
14	DIAKWLUW	PREVENT	184C
	EGW	I	216C
	ERCHOMAI I1Aβ	COME	310C
	ECHW I2I	HAVE	333C
	KAI I2G	AND	393C
	SU 1A	YOU	779D
	CHREIA 1	NEED	893B
15	APOKRINOMAI 1	ANSWER	92D
	ARTI 2	NOW	109D
	APHI8MI 4	TOLERATE	126A
	DIKAIOSUN8 2A	RIGHTEOUSNESS	195C
	EIMI II4D	TO BE	223B
	HOUTW	THUS	602B
	PL8ROW 4B	MAKE FULL	677D
	PREPW	BE FITTING	706A
	TOTE 2	AT THAT TIME	831C
16	ANABAINW 1Aα	GO UP	49D
	ANOIGW 1B	OPEN	70C
	BAPTIZW 2A	BAPTIZE	131B
	EIDON 1A	SEE	219C
	EPI III1Aβ	ON	288A
	ERCHOMAI I2C	COME	311D
	EUTHUS	IMMEDIATELY	321B
	IDOU 1Bβ	BEHOLD	371C

16	KATABAINW 1B	COME DOWN 409C	6	EPI 11Aα	ON 285D
	OURANOS 2A	HEAVEN 599B		KATW 2	DOWNWARDS 426B
	PERISTERA	PIGEON 657D		MBPOTE 2Bα	(NEG PARTICLE) 521A
	PNEUMA 5A	SPIRIT 682C		POUS 1A	FOOT 703B
	HUDWR 1	WATER 840C		PROSKOPTW 1A	STRIKE AGAINST 723C
	HWSEI 1	AS 907D		SEAUTOU 3	YOURSELF 753A
17	AGAPBTOS 1	BELOVED 6B		SU 3	YOU 780A
	EUDOKEW 2A	WELL PLEASED 319C		HUIOS 2B	SON 842C
	IDOU 2	THERE IS 371D		CHEIR 1	HAND 888B
	OURANOS 2A	HEAVEN 599B		CHEIR 1	HAND 888C
	HOUTOS 1Aα	THIS 600D	6F	GRAPHW 2C	WRITE 165D
	HUIOS 2B	SON 842C	7	EKPEIRAZW	PUT TO THE TEST 243A
	PHWNB 2D	VOICE 879B		THEOS 3C	GOD 358A
				KURIOS 2A	LORD 460B
	MATTHEW 4			PALIN 4	AGAIN 611D
				PHBMI 1Bα	SAY 864A
1	ANAGW 1	LEAD 52D	8	BASILEIA 2	KINGDOM 134C
	DIABOLOS 2	THE SLANDERER 181A		DEIKNUMI 1A	SHOW 171D
	PEIRAZW 2D	TRY 646B		DIABOLOS 2	THE SLANDERER 181A
	PNEUMA 5Dα	SPIRIT 683A		DOXA 2	MAGNIFICENCE 203A
	TOTE 2	AT THAT TIME 831C		KOSMOS 4A	WORLD 447A
2	HBMERA 1A	DAY 346C		LIAN 2A	VERY 474C
	NBSTEUW	TO FAST 540B		OROS	MOUNTAIN 586B
	NUX 1D	NIGHT 549A		PALIN 2	AGAIN 611C
	PEINAW 1	HUNGER 645D		PARALAMBANW 1	TAKE 625A
	HUSTEROS 2A	LATER 857B		PAS 1Dα	ALL 637C
2A	TESSARAKONTA	FORTY 820D		HUPSBLOS 1	HIGH 857C
2B	TESSARAKONTA	FORTY 820D	9	DIDWMI 1A	GIVE 191D
3	ARTOS 1A	BREAD 110A		PAS 1Eβ	ALL 637D
	GINOMAI 14A	BECOME 158C		PIPTW 1Bα	FALL 665B
	EI 11A	IF 217D		PROSKUNEW 3	DO REVERENCE 724B
	EIPON 3C	SAY 225D	10	GRAPHW 2C	WRITE 165D
	HINA 111Aδ	IN ORDER THAT 378B		LATREUW	SERVE 468C
	LITHOS 1A	STONE 475B		LEGW 111B	ANSWER 470C
	HO,HB,TO 113A	THE 553C		MONOS 1Aβ	ONLY 529C
	PEIRAZW 2D	TRY 646B		OPISW 2Aα	BEHIND 578C
	PROSERCHOMAI 1	APPROACH 720A		PROSKUNEW	DO REVERENCE 723D
	HUIOS 2B	SON 842C		PROSKUNEW 2A	DO REVERENCE 724A
4	ANTHRWPOS 3B	MAN 68C		SATAN	ADVERSARY 752B
	APOKRINOMAI 1	ANSWER 92D		HUPAGW 1	GO AWAY 844B
	ARTOS 1A	BREAD 110A	10F	TOTE 2	AT THAT TIME 831D
	GRAPHW 2C	WRITE 165D	11	AGGELOS 2A	ANGEL 7D
	DIA A11	THROUGH 178C		APHIBMI 3A	LEAVE 125C
	EKPOREUOMAI 2	GO OUT 244A		DIABOLOS 2	THE SLANDERER 181A
	EPI 111Bγ	ON 287A		DIAKONEW 2	SERVE 183A
	ZAW 1C	LIVE 336D		IDOU 1Bβ	BEHOLD 371C
	MONOS 1Aγ	ONLY 529C		PROSERCHOMAI 1	APPROACH 720A
	HO,HB,TO 13	THE 552A	12	AKOUW 3E	LEARN 32A
	PAS 1Aγ	EVERY EACH 637A		ANACHWREW 2B	WITHDRAW 63A
	RBMA 1	WORD 743A		IWAN(N)BS 1	JOHN 385B
	STOMA 1B	MOUTH 777C		PARADIDWMI 1B	GIVE OVER 619D
5	HAGIOS 1Aα	DEDICATED TO GOD 9B	13	EIS 9A	IN 229D
	DIABOLOS 2	THE SLANDERER 181A		ZABOULWN	ZEBULUN 336A
	HIERON 2	TEMPLE 373B		KATALEIPW 2B	LEAVE BEHIND 414D
	HISTBMI 11Aα	PUT 382D		KATOIKEW 1A	LIVE 425B
	PALIN 2	AGAIN 611C		KAPHARNAOUM	CAPERNAUM 427C
	PARALAMBANW 1	TAKE 625A		NAZARA	NAZARETH 534A
	POLIS 1	CITY 692B		NEPHTHALIM	NAPHTALI 538D
	PTERUGION	END EDGE 734D		HORION	BOUNDARY 584D
	TOTE 2	AT THAT TIME 831C		PARATHALASSIOS	BY THE SEA 621B
6	AIRW 2	LIFT UP 24A	14	DIA A1112A	BY 179C
	BALLW 1B	LIE 130D		EIPON 4	SAY 225D
	ENTELLW	COMMAND 268A		BSAIAS	ISAIAH 349C

14 HINA II2	IN ORDER THAT	378D
PL8ROW 4A	MAKE FULL	677C
PROPH8T8S I	PROPHET	730D
15 GALILAIA	GALILEE	149C
ZABOULWN	ZEBULUN	336A
IORDAN8S	JORDAN	379C
NEPHTHALIM	NAPHTALI	538D
HODOS IA	WAY	556C
PERAN 2C	ON THE OTHER SIDE	649C
16 ANATELLW 2	RISE	61C
AUTOS 3C	(OBLIQUE CASE)	123A
EIDON IA	SEE	219C
THANATOS 2A	DEATH	352A
MEGAS 2AY	GREAT	499A
SKIA IA	SHADE	763A
SKOTIA 2	DARKNESS	764D
SKOTOS 2B	DARKNESS	765B
CHWRA 5	COUNTRY	897D
16A PHWS 3A	LIGHT	880B
16B PHWS 3A	LIGHT	880B
17 ARCHW 2Aα	BEGIN	113A
ARCHW 2C	BEGIN	113B
BASILEIA 3A	KINGDOM	134D
BASILEIA 3G	KINGDOM	135B
EGGIZW 5B	APPROACH	212D
K8RUSSW 2Bβ	ANNOUNCE	432D
METANOEW	CHANGE ONES MIND	513B
OURANOS 3	HEAVEN	599D
TOTE IA	AT THAT TIME	831C
18 ADELPHOS I	BROTHER	15C
HALIEUS	FISHERMAN	37A
AMPHIBL8STRON	CASTING NET	46D
ANDREAS	ANDREW	63B
BALLW IB	THROW	130C
GALILAIA	GALILEE	149D
DUO 4	TWO	208C
EIDON IA	SEE	219C
THALASSA 2	LAKE	351A
PARA IIIIA	ALONG	616A
PERIPATEW IC	GO ABOUT	654D
PETROS	PETER	661A
SIMWN I	SIMON	758C
19 HALIEUS	FISHERMAN	37A
ANTHRWPOS IAβ	MAN	67C
DEUTE 2	COME	175D
KAI I2F	AND	393C
OPISW 2Aβ	AFTER	578D
POIEW IIBı	DO	688B
20 APHI8MI 3A	LEAVE	125D
EUTHEWS	IMMEDIATELY	320D
KURIOS 2A	LORD	460B
20F DIKTUON	NET	197D
21 ADELPHOS I	BROTHER	15C
ALLOS 2	MORE	39C
DUO 4	TWO	208C
EIDON IA	SEE	219C
EKEITHEN	FROM THERE	238D
ZEBEDAIOS	ZEBEDEE	337D
IAKWBOS I	JAMES	368B
IWAN(N)8S 2	JOHN	385C
KALEW IE	CALL	400C
KATARTIZW IA	RESTORE	418D
PROBAINW I	GO ON	709C

21F PAT8R IA	FATHER	640C
21F PLOION 2	SHIP	679B
22 EUTHEWS	IMMEDIATELY	320D
23 AUTOS 3B	(OBLIQUE CASE)	123A
BASILEIA 3G	KINGDOM	135A
DIDASKW I	TEACH	191A
EUAGGELION IC	GOSPEL	318B
EUAGGELION 2Bα	GOSPEL	318B
THERAPEUW 2	HEAL	359D
KAI I5	AND	394A
K8RUSSW 2Bβ	ANNOUNCE	432C
LAOS IB	PEOPLE	467D
MALAKIA I	SICKNESS	489D
NOSOS I	DISEASE	545D
PAS IAβ	EVERY EACH	636D
PERIAGW 2	LEAD AROUND	651B
SUNAGWG8 2A		790C
	PLACE OF ASSEMBLY	
24 AKO8 2A	REPORT	30C
APERCHOMAI 3	GO	84A
BASANOS 2	TORMENT	134C
DAIMONIZOMAI		168A
	BE POSSESSED BY A DEMON	
ECHW III	BE	334B
THERAPEUW 2	HEAL	359C
KAKWS I	BADLY	399B
NOSOS I	DISEASE	545D
PARALUTIKOS	PARALYTIC	625D
PAS IDβ	ALL	637C
*POIKILOS I	DIVERSIFIED	690A
PROSPHERW IA	BRING (TO)	726D
SEL8NIAZOMAI	BE MOON STRUCK	754B
SUNECHW 5	DISTRESS	797A
SUNORIA	NEIGHBORING COUNTRY	799B
SURIA	SYRIA	801C
25 AKOLOUTHEW 2	ACCOMPANY	30D
APO IVIB	FROM	86D
GALILAIA	GALILEE	149D
DEKAPOLIS	DECAPOLIS	173A
IORDAN8S	JORDAN	379C
IOUDAIA I	JUDAEA	379D
OCHLOS I	CROWD	605D
PERAN 2C	ON THE OTHER SIDE	649C
POLUS IIAβ	MANY	694B

MATTHEW 5

1 ANABAINW IAα	GO UP	49C
EIDON IA	SEE	219D
KATHIZW 2Aα	SIT DOWN	390D
HO,H8,TO IIIAα	THE	552B
OROS	MOUNTAIN	586A
OCHLOS I	CROWD	605D
PROSERCHOMAI I	APPROACH	720A
2 ANOIGW IEα	OPEN	70D
DIDASKW 2A	TEACH	191A
STOMA IA	MOUTH	777B
3 BASILEIA 3A	KINGDOM	134D
EIMI IVI	TO BE	224D
OURANOS 3	HEAVEN	599D
PNEUMA 3B	SPIRIT	681C
PTWCHOS IC	BEGGING POOR	735D
3FF MAKARIOS IB	BLESSED	487D

3FF　HOTI 3A	THAT 593D	13A　HALAS 2	SALT 34C
4 AUTOS 2	THEY 122D	13B　HALAS I	SALT 34B
HO,H8,TO II3B	THE 553D	13F　SU ID	YOU 780A
PARAKALEW 4	IMPLORE 623A	14 EPANW 2A	ON 283A
PENTHEW I	BE SAD 648B	KEIMAI IB	LIE 427D
5 G8 4	LAND 156D	KOSMOS 5A	WORLD 447B
KLBRONOMEW 2	INHERIT 435D	KRUPTW IA	HIDE 455B
PENTHEW I	BE SAD 648B	OROS	MOUNTAIN 586B
PRAUS	HUMBLE 705D	POLIS I	CITY 692A
5FF　AUTOS 2	THEY 122D	PHWS 3B	LIGHT 880C
6 DIKAIOSUN8 2B	RIGHTEOUSNESS 195C	15 EPI IIIIA9	ON 288A
DIPSAW 3	THIRST 199D	KAI I2F	AND 393C
HO,H8,TO II3B	THE 553D	KAIW IA	LIGHT 397A
PEINAW 2	HUNGER 645D	LAMPW IA	SHINE 467B
CHORTAZW 2B	FEED 892B	LUCHNIA	LAMPSTAND 484B
7 ELEEW	HAVE MERCY 249B	LUCHNOS I	LAMP 484C
ELE8MWN	MERCIFUL 249C	MODIOS	A PECK MEASURE 527D
8 THEOS 3A	GOD 357D	HO,H8,TO II5	THE 554B
KATHAROS 3A	CLEAN 389A	OIKIA IA	HOUSE 560A
KARDIA IB6	HEART 404D	OUDE I	AND NOT 595D
HORAW IAY	SEE 581D	PAS IDY	ALL 637D
9 EIR8NOPOIOS	THE PEACE MAKER 227A	TITH8MI IIA9	PUT 823D
KALEW IA6	CALL 400B	HUPO 2A«	UNDER 851A
HUIOS ICY	SON 841D	16 ANTHRWPOS IA6	PEOPLE 67C
10 BASILEIA 3A	KINGDOM 134D	DOXAZW I	PRAISE 203C
DIKAIOSUN8 4	RIGHTEOUSNESS 196C	EMPROSTHEN 2C	IN FRONT 256C
DIWKW 2	PERSECUTE 200B	ERGON ICP	DEED 308A
EIMI IVI	TO BE 224D	KALOS 2B	GOOD 401B
HO,H8,TO II3B	THE 553D	LAMPW 2	SHINE 467B
OURANOS 3	HEAVEN 599D	HOPWS 2A«	IN ORDER THAT 580C
IOF　HENEKA	BECAUSE OF 264B	OURANOS 2A	HEAVEN 599B
II EIPON I	SAY 225D	HOUTW IB	THUS 602B
KATA I2B9	DOWN 406D	PAT8R 3C«	FATHER 641C
MAKARIOS IB	BLESSED 488A	PHWS 3B	LIGHT 880C
ONEIDIZW I	REPROACH 573A	17 ALLA IA	BUT, YET 37B
HOTAN IB	WHEN 592A	ERCHOMAI IIAη	COME 311A
PON8ROS IB9	WICKED 697D	8　IA9	OR 342B
PON8ROS 2C	WICKED 698A	M8　AIII5A	NOT 518D
PSEUDOMAI I	LIE 900A	NOMIZW 2	THINK 543B
IIF　DIWKW 2	PERSECUTE 200B	NOMOS 4A	LAW 545A
12 AGALLIAW	BE GLAD 3D	PL8ROW 4B	MAKE FULL 677D
MISTHOS 2A	REWARD 525B	PROPH8T8S I	PROPHET 731A
OURANOS 2D	HEAVEN 599D	17A　*KATALUW IC	ANNUL 415C
POLUS IIB«	MANY 694C	17B　KATALUW IC	ANNUL 415C
PRO 2	BEFORE 708D	18 AM8N 2	AMEN 45B
PROPH8T8S I	PROPHET 730D	G8　5A	EARTH 156D
CHAIRW I	REJOICE 881B	GINOMAI I3A	TAKE PLACE 157D
13 HALAS 2	SALT 34C	HEIS IC	ONE 230A
HALIZW	TO SALT 37A	HEWS IIB	UNTIL 334D
ANTHRWPOS IA6	PEOPLE 67C	8　IC	NOR 343A
BALLW IB	THROW 130C	IWTA	IOTA 386D
G8　5B	EARTH 156D	KERAIA	HOOK 429D
EI　VI8A	IF NOT 219A	M8　DIA	NOT 519B
EIS 5	FOR 229B	NOMOS 3	LAW 544D
EN IIIIA	BY 260A	NOMOS 4B	LAW 545A
EXW IB	OUTSIDE 279A	OURANOS IA«	HEAVEN 598B
ETI IB9	STILL 316A	18A　PARERCHOMAI IB«	631C
ISCHUW 2A	BE STRONG 384C	PASS AWAY	
KATAPATEW IA	TRAMPLE 416D	18B　PARERCHOMAI IB«	631C
M8　AII	NOT 517C	PASS AWAY	
MWRAINW 2	BECOME TASTELESS 533A	19 AN　2A	(PARTICLE) 48A
OUDEIS 2B«	NOTHING 596C	BASILEIA 3G	KINGDOM 135B
TIS, TI IB«	WHICH 826D	EAN II	IF 211A

19	HEIS 1Aβ	ONE 230A
	ENTOL8 2Aβ	COMMAND 268C
	LUW 4	DESTROY 485C
	MEGAS 2Bα	GREAT 499B
	OUN 5	THEREFORE 597D
	HOUTOS 1Aε	THIS 601B
	HOUTOS 2B	THIS 601D
	HOUTW 1B	THUS 602B
	POIEW IICα	DO 688C
19A	ELACHISTOS 2A	SMALLEST 248B
19A	KALEW 1A6	CALL 400B
19B	ELACHISTOS 2A	SMALLEST 248B
19B	KALEW 1A6	CALL 400B
19F	BASILEIA 3A	KINGDOM 134D
19F	OURANOS 3	HEAVEN 599D
20	BASILEIA 3G	KINGDOM 135A
	BASILEIA 3G	KINGDOM 135B
	GRAMMATEUS 2	SCRIBES 165A
	DIKAIOSUN8 2A	RIGHTEOUSNESS 195C
	EAN 13B	IF 210D
	EISERCHOMAI 2A	COME 232B
	LEGW IIIE	DECLARE 471A
	M8 AII	NOT 517C
	M8 DIA	NOT 519B
	PERISSEUW 1Aβ	BE LEFT OVER 656C
	POLUS II2C	MANY 696A
	PHARISAIOS	PHARISEE 861C
21	ARCHAIOS 2	ANCIENT 111A
	ENOCHOS 2A	SUBJECT TO 267B
	OU 4B	NO 594D
21A	PHONEUW	MURDER 872C
21F	ANTHRWPOKTONOS	MURDERER 67B
21F	KRISIS 2	COURT 454A
22	GEENNA	HELL 152C
	EIK8 1	WITHOUT CAUSE 221A
	EIPON 1	SAY 225C
	EIS 7	TO 229C
	*ENOCHOS 2C	GUILTY 267C
	LEGW IIIE	DECLARE 471A
	MWROS 1	FOOLISH 533B
	MWROS 3	FOOLISH 533B
	HO,H8,TO II3B	THE 553D
	ORGIZW	BE ANGRY 583B
	PAS ICγ	WHOEVER 637B
	PUR 1B	FIRE 737C
	RAKA	FOOL 741B
	SUNEDRION 2	SANHEDRIN 794A
22A	ENOCHOS 2A	SUBJECT TO 267B
22B	ENOCHOS 2A	SUBJECT TO 267B
22FF	ADELPHOS 4	NEIGHBOR 16B
22FF	EGW	I 216A
23	ECHW I7A	HAVE 334A
	KAKEI 1	AND THERE 397C
	KATA I2Bγ	DOWN 406D
	MIMN8SKOMAI 1A6	REMEMBER 524B
	OUN 5	THEREFORE 597D
	TIS, TI 1Bα	ANY ONE 828A
23F	DWRON 2	GIFT 210C
23F	THUSIAST8RION 1A	ALTAR 367B
23F	PROSPHERW 2A	BRING (TO) 727A
24	APHI8MI 3A	LEAVE 125D
	DIALLASSOMAI	185A
	BECOME RECONCILED	
24	DWRON 2	GIFT 210C
	EKEI 1	THERE 238C
	EMPROSTHEN 2A	IN FRONT 256C
	PRWTOS 2A	FIRST 733D
	TOTE 2	AT THAT TIME 831D
	HUPAGW 2	GO AWAY 844A
25	ANTIDIKOS	OPPONENT 73C
	EN IIB	IN 257D
	EUNOEW	BE WELL DISPOSED 323C
	KAI I2E	AND 393C
	KRIT8S 1Aα	JUDGE 454C
	META AIIICα	WITH 510A
	M8POTE 2Bα	(NEG PARTICLE) 521A
	HODOS 1B	WAY 556C
	PARADIDWMI 1B	GIVE OVER 619D
	TACHUS 2B	QUICK 814D
	HUP8RET8S	SERVANT 850C
	PHULAK8 3	GUARD 875D
26	AM8N 2	AMEN 45B
	AN 3D	(PARTICLE) 48C
	APODIDWMI 2	GIVE BACK 90A
	DIDWMI	GIVE 191D
	EKEITHEN	FROM THERE 238D
	EXERCHOMAI 1Aη	GO OUT 274B
	ESCHATOS 3B	LAST 314A
	HEWS IIB	UNTIL 334D
	KODRANT8S	PENNY 438A
	LEGW IIID	ASSURE 470D
	M8 DIA	NOT 519B
27	ARCHAIOS 2	ANCIENT 111A
	MOICHEUW 1	COMMIT ADULTERY 528B
	OU 4B	NO 594D
	PALIN 3	AGAIN 611D
28	BLEPW 3	SEE 143B
	GUN8 2	WIFE 167C
	EN IIE	IN 257D
	EPITHUMEW	DESIRE 293A
	8D8 2	ALREADY 344D
	KARDIA 1Bε	HEART 405A
	LEGW IIIE	DECLARE 471A
	MOICHEUW 2B	COMMIT ADULTERY 528B
	PAS ICγ	WHOEVER 637B
	PROS III3B	TOWARD 717B
29	BALLW 1B	THROW 130C
	GEENNA	HELL 152C
	DEXIOS 1	RIGHT 173C
	EXAIREW 1	TAKE OUT 271B
	OPHTHALMOS 1	EYE 604B
29F	APOLLUMI 2B	BE LOST 95A
29F	BALLW 1B	THROW 130C
29F	EI IIA	IF 217D
29F	HINA IIIB	IN ORDER THAT 378C
29F	MELOS 1	MEMBER 502D
29F	M8 AI2	NOT 517C
29F	HOLOS 2A	WHOLE 567C
29F	SKANDALIZW 1A	760B
	CAUSE TO FALL	
29F	SUMPHERW 2A	788A
	HELP	
29F	SWMA 1B	BODY 806D
30	GEENNA	HELL 152C
	DEXIOS 1	RIGHT 173C
	EKKOPTW 1	CUT OFF 241B

30	CHEIR I	HAND	888A
31	APOSTASION		97D
	CERTIFICATE OF DIVORCE		
	DE IC	BUT, AND	170C
	DIDWMI 2	GIVE	192C
31F	APOLUW 2A	SEND AWAY	96A
31F	GUN8 2	WIFE	167C
32	GAMEW IA	MARRY	150A
	EAN II	IF	211A
	LEGW IIIE	DECLARE	471A
	LOGOS IAє	MATTER	478D
	LOGOS 2D	REASON	479D
	MOICHEUW 2B	COMMIT ADULTERY	528B
	*PAREKTOS 2	OUTSIDE	630C
	PAS ICγ	WHOEVER	637B
	POIEW IIB θ	DO	688A
	PORNEIA I	PROSTITUTION	700A
32A	MOICHAW I	COMMIT ADULTERY	528A
32B	MOICHAW I	COMMIT ADULTERY	528A
33	APODIDWMI I	GIVE AWAY	90A
	ARCHAIOS 2	ANCIENT	111A
	DIO	THEREFORE	197D
	EPIORKEW 2	BREAK ONES OATH	296D
	KURIOS 2A	LORD	460B
	HORKOS	OATH	585B
	OU 4B	NO	594D
	PALIN 3	AGAIN	611D
34	THEOS 3A	GOD	357D
	THRONOS IB	THRONE	364D
	LEGW IIIC	ORDER	470D
	M8 AIIIBβ	NOT	517D
	HOLWS	GENERALLY SPEAKING AND NOT	568A
			521D
34F	M8TE	TAKE AN OATH	568D
34F	OMNUW		
34F	OURANOS IAβ	HEAVEN	598B
34FF	EN IV5	IN	260D
35	BASILEUS 2B	KING	136A
	G8 5A	EARTH	156D
	EIS 6B	SWEAR BY	229B
	OMNUW	TAKE AN OATH	569A
	POLIS I	CITY	692B
	POUS IB	FOOT	703C
	HUPOPODION	FOOTSTOOL	854D
36	HEIS IC	ONE	230A
	8 IAє	OR	342B
	THRIX 2	HAIR	364C
	KEPHAL8 IA	HEAD	431A
	LEUKOS 2	WHITE	473C
	MELAS	BLACK	501A
	OMNUW	TAKE AN OATH	569A
	POIEW IIB	DO	688B
37	EK 3C	FROM	234B
	LOGOS IAβ	WORD	478B
	NAI 5	YES	535A
	OU I	NO	594B
	PERISSOS 3	EXTRAORDINARY	657B
	PON8ROS 2B	WICKED	698A
38	ANTI 2	FOR	73A
	ODOUS	TOOTH	557D
	OPHTHALMOS I	EYE	604B
39	ALLOS 3	THE OTHER	39D
	ANTHIST8MI I	SET AGAINST	66C
	DEXIOS I	RIGHT	173C

39	EIS IC	IN	227C
	KAI III	ALSO	394A
	LEGW IIIC	ORDER	470D
	M8 AIIIBβ	NOT	517D
	HOSTIS IA	WHOEVER	590D
	PON8ROS 2A	WICKED	697D
	RAPIZW	STRIKE WITH A CLUB	741D
	SIAGWN	CHEEK	757A
	STREPHW IAє	TURN	778D
40	AUTOS 3C	(OBLIQUE CASE)	123A
	APHI8MI 3A	LEAVE	125D
	THELW I	WISH	355C
	HIMATION 2	GARMENT	377A
	KAI III	ALSO	394A
	KRINW 4Aβ	JUDGE	452D
	LAMBANW IC	TAKE	465C
	CHITWN	SHIRT	890C
41	AGGAREUW	REQUISITION	6D
	HEIS IAє	ONE	230A
	META AIIIA	WITH	509D
	MILION	MILE	523D
	HOSTIS IC	WHOEVER	590D
	HUPAGW 2	GO AWAY	844C
42	AITEW	ASK	25B
	APO IV2A	FROM	87A
	APOSTREPHW 3A	TURN AWAY	100A
	DAN(E)IZW 2	BORROW	169D
	M8 AIII5A	NOT	518D
43	AGAPAW IAє	LOVE	4B
	MISEW I	HATE	524C
	HO,H8,TO II6	THE	554B
	PL8SION IB	NEAR	678D
43F	ECHTHROS 2Bβ	THE ENEMY	331D
44	AGAPAW IAє	LOVE	4C
	DIWKW 2	PERSECUTE	200B
	EP8REAZW	MISTREAT	285C
	KALWS 3	WELL	402B
	LEGW IIIC	ORDER	470D
	N8STEUW	TO FAST	540C
	POIEW I2Aβ	DO	689D
	PROSEUCHOMAI	PRAY	721A
45	AGATHOS IBє	GOOD	3A
	ADIKOS I	UNJUST	17D
	ANATELLW I	CAUSE TO SPRING UP	61C
	BRECHW 2A	SEND RAIN	147A
	GINOMAI I4A	BECOME	158C
	DIKAIOS IB	UPRIGHT	194D
	EPI IIIIAβ	ON	288A
	H8LIOS	THE SUN	346B
	HO,H8,TO IIID	THE	552D
	HOPWS 2Aє	IN ORDER THAT	580C
	OURANOS 2A	HEAVEN	599B
	PAT8R 3Cє	FATHER	641C
	PON8ROS 2A	WICKED	697D
	HUIOS ICγ	SON	841D
46	AGAPAW IAє	LOVE	4C
	HAMARTWLOS 2	SINNER	43D
	AUTOS 4B	THE SAME	123B
	EAN IIB	IF	210B
	MISTHOS 2A	REWARD	525B
	OUCHI 3	NOT	603A
	POIEW IIBє	DO	687D
	TELWN8S	TAX COLLECTOR	820B

46	TIS, TI 2		WHICH	827B
46F	KAI II2		EVEN	394B
47	HAMARTWLOS 2		SINNER	43D
	ASPAZOMAI IA		GREET	116B
	EAN IIB		IF	210B
	ETHNIKOS		GENTILE	217B
	MONOS 2B		ONLY	529D
	OUCHI 3		NOT	603A
	PERISSOS I	EXTRAORDINARY	657A
	TIS, TI 2		WHICH	827B
47A	POIEW IIBε		DO	687D
47B	POIEW IIBε		DO	687D
48	OUN IB		THEREFORE	597B
	OURANIOS		HEAVENLY	598A
	PAT8R 3Cα		FATHER	641C
	SU IA		YOU	779D
	HWS II4A		SO	906B
48A	TELEIOS 2D		PERFECT	817B
48B	TELEIOS 2E		PERFECT	817B

MATTHEW 6

I	GE 3Bα		OTHERWISE	152B
	DE IA		BUT, AND	170C
	DOSIS 2		GIVING	204A
	EMPROSTHEN 2C		IN FRONT	256C
	THEAOMAI ICβ		SEE	353D
	M8 AII		NOT	517C
	M8 AIIIA		NOT	517D
	MISTHOS 2A		REWARD	525B
	OURANOS 2A		HEAVEN	599B
	PARA IIIBγ		BESIDE	615C
	PAT8R 3Cα		FATHER	641C
	POIEW IICβ		DO	688C
	PROS III3A		TOWARD	717A
	PROSECHW IB	PAY ATTENTION TO	721D
IF	ANTHRWPOS IA6		PEOPLE	67C
IF	DIKAIOSUN8 2A			195C
	RIGHTEOUSNESS			
2	AM8N 2		AMEN	45B
	APECHW I	RECEIVE IN FULL	84B
	EMPROSTHEN 2E		IN FRONT	256D
	LEGW IIID		ASSURE	470D
	MISTHOS 2A		REWARD	525B
	HOPWS 2Aα		IN ORDER THAT	580C
	HOTAN IA		WHEN	592A
	OUN 5		THEREFORE	597D
	RUM8		LANE	744D
	SALPIZW	SOUND THE TRUMPET	748C
	SUNAGWG8 2A			790C
	PLACE OF ASSEMBLY			
	HUPOKRIT8S		HYPOCRITE	853A
	HWSPER 2		(JUST) AS	908A
2A	POIEW IICβ		DO	688C
2B	POIEW I2Aα		DO	689A
2F	ELE8MCSUN8			249B
	CHARITABLE GIVING			
3	ARISTEROS		WEAPONS	106B
	DEXIOS 2A		RIGHT	173D
	M8 AIII4		NOT	518D
	HO,H8,TO II2B		THE	553C
3A	POIEW IICβ		DO	688C
4	APODIDWMI 3		RECOMPENSE	90A

4	AUTOS 2		THEY	122D
	BLEPW IC		SEE	143A
	ELE8MOSUN8	CHARITABLE GIVING	249B
	HO,H8,TO II2A		THE	553B
	HOPWS 2Aα		IN ORDER THAT	580C
	PAT8R 3Cα		FATHER	641C
	PHANEROS 2		CLEAR	860B
4A	KRUPTOS 2B		HIDDEN	455A
4B	KRUPTOS 2B		HIDDEN	455A
5	AM8N 2		AMEN	45B
	ANTHRWPOS IA6		PEOPLE	67C
	APECHW I	RECEIVE IN FULL	84B
	GWNIA		CORNER	167D
	EIMI II9B		TO BE	224A
	EN IIB		IN	257D
	LEGW IIID		ASSURE	470D
	MISTHOS 2A		REWARD	525B
	HOPWS 2Aα		IN ORDER THAT	580C
	HOPWS 2Aβ		IN ORDER THAT	580D
	OU 4B		NO	594D
	PLATEIA		WIDE ROAD	672D
	SUNAGWG8 2A			790C
	PLACE OF ASSEMBLY			
	HUPOKRIT8S		HYPOCRITE	853A
	PHAINW 2C		APPEAR	859C
	PHILEW IB		LOVE LIKE	867A
5F	HOTAN IA		WHEN	592A
5-7	PROSEUCHOMAI		PRAY	720D
6	APODIDWMI 3		RECOMPENSE	90A
	BLEPW IC		SEE	143A
	DE IA		BUT, AND	170C
	EISERCHOMAI IAβ		COME	231D
	THURA IA		DOOR	366B
	KLEIW I		SHUT	435A
	SU IA		YOU	779D
	TAMEION 2		STOREROOM	811B
	PHANEROS 2		CLEAR	860B
6A	KRUPTOS 2B		HIDDEN	455B
6A	PAT8R 3Cα		FATHER	641C
6B	KRUPTOS 2B		HIDDEN	455B
6B	PAT8R 3Cα		FATHER	641C
6B	PROSEUCHOMAI		PRAY	721A
7	BATTALOGEW		BABBLE	137B
	DOKEW ID		THINK	201A
	ETHNIKOS		GENTILE	217B
	EISAKOUW 2A		LISTEN TO	231C
	EN III3A		BECAUSE OF	260C
	POLULOGIA		WORDINESS	693D
	HWSPER 2		(JUST) AS	908A
8	AITEW		ASK	25B
	ANOIGW IEα		OPEN	70D
	ECHW I2I		HAVE	333C
	OIDA IG		KNOW	558C
	HOMOIOW I		MAKE LIKE	570B
	OUN IB		THEREFORE	597B
	PRO 2		BEFORE	708D
	CHREIA I		NEED	893B
9	HAGIAZW 3		TO REVERENCE	9A
	LITHOS IA		STONE	475B
	ONOMA I4B		NAME	574D
	OUN IB		THEREFORE	597B
	OURANOS 2A		HEAVEN	599B
	HOUTW 2		THUS	602C

9	PAT8R 3C«	FATHER	641C
	SU IA	YOU	779D
10	BASILEIA 3G	KINGDOM	135B
	G8 5A	EARTH	156D
	GINOMAI I2A	CREATED	157C
	EPI IIA«	ON	285C
	ERCHOMAI I2B	COME	311C
	THEL8MA IA	WILL	354D
	KAI II3	ALSO	394B
	OURANOS IA∅	HEAVEN	598B
	HWS III	SO	905D
10-12	HO,H8,TO IIID	THE	552D
11	ARTOS 2	FOOD	110C
	EPIOUSIOS	CONTINUAL	296D
	S8MERON	TODAY	756B
12	KATHA	JUST AS	387B
	OPHEILET8S 2C«	DEBTOR	603B
	OPHEIL8MA 2	DEBT	603C
	HWS II4A	SO	906B
	HWS IIIIB	SO	906C
12A	APHI8MI 2	CANCEL	125C
12B	APHI8MI 2	CANCEL	125C
13	AIWN IB	TIME	26D
	AM8N I	AMEN	45A
	DOXA IA	GLORY	202D
	DUNAMIS I	POWER	206C
	EIS 4A	INTO	228B
	EISPHERW 2	BRING IN	233A
	PEIRASMOS 2B	TEST	646C
	PON8RIA	WICKEDNESS	697A
	*PON8ROS 2B	WICKED	698A
	RUOMAI	SAVE	744D
14	ANTHRWPOS IA6	PEOPLE	67C
	EAN IIB	IF	210B
	OURANIOS	HEAVENLY	598A
	PARAPTWMA I	TRANSGRESSION	627B
	PAT8R 3C«	FATHER	641C
14F	APHI8MI 2	FORGIVE	125C
15	DE IA	BUT, AND	170C
	EAN I3B	IF	210D
	M8 AII	NOT	517C
	OUDE 2	AND NOT	595D
	PAT8R 3C«	FATHER	641C
15A	PARAPTWMA I	TRANSGRESSION	627B
15B	PARAPTWMA 2B	TRANSGRESSION	627B
16	AM8N 2	AMEN	45B
	APECHW I	RECEIVE IN FULL	84B
	APHANIZW	RENDER INVISIBLE	124B
	GINOMAI III	BE	159B
	DE IC	BUT, AND	170C
	M8 AIII3A	NOT	518C
	MISTHOS 2A	REWARD	525B
	HOTAN IA	WHEN	592A
	SKUTHRWPOS	SULLEN LOOK	765C
	HUPOKRIT8S	HYPOCRITE	853A
	PHAINW 2C	APPEAR	859D
16F	PROSWPON IA	FACE	728A
16-18	N8STEUW	TO FAST	540C
17	ALEIPHW I	ANOINT	34D
	DE IA	BUT, AND	170C
	KEPHAL8 IA	HEAD	431A
	NIPTW 2B	WASH	542B
17	SU IA	YOU	779D
18	ANTHRWPOS IA6	PEOPLE	67C
	APODIDWMI 3	RECOMPENSE	90A
	BLEPW IC	SEE	143A
	KRUPTOS 2B	HIDDEN	455B
	KRUPHIOS	HIDDEN	455D
	M8 AI2	NOT	517C
	HOPWS 2A«	IN ORDER THAT	580C
	PHAINW 2C	APPEAR	859D
	PHANEROS 2	CLEAR	860B
18A	KRUPHAIOS	HIDDEN	455D
18A	PAT8R 3C«	FATHER	641C
18B	KRUPHAIOS	HIDDEN	455D
18B	PAT8R 3C«	FATHER	641C
19	G8 5A	EARTH	156D
	EPI IIA«	ON	285C
	TH8SAURIZW I	STORE UP	362A
	TH8SAUROS 2A	TREASURE	362B
	M8 AIII3A	NOT	518C
19F	APHANIZW	RENDER INVISIBLE	124B
19F	BRWSIS 2	CORROSION	147D
19F	DIORUSSW	DIGS THROUGH	198B
19F	KLEPT8S	THIEF	435B
19F	KLEPTW	STEAL	435C
19F	HOPOU IA«	WHERE	579C
19F	S8S	MOTH	756D
20	TH8SAURIZW 2A	STORE UP	362A
	TH8SAUROS 2B«	TREASURE	362B
	OUDE I	AND NOT	595D
	OURANOS 2D	HEAVEN	599D
	OUTE	NOT	600C
21	EKEI I	THERE	238C
	TH8SAUROS 2	TREASURE	362B
	KAI III	ALSO	394A
	KARDIA IB«	HEART	405A
	HOPOU IA«	WHERE	579C
22	HAPLOUS	SINCERE	85C
	LUCHNOS 2	LAMP	484C
	OPHTHALMOS I	EYE	604B
	PHWTEINOS	SHINING	880D
22F	HOLOS 2A	WHOLE	567C
22F	SWMA IB	BODY	806D
23	EI IIA	IF	217D
	EI VII0	IF	219A
	OPHTHALMOS I	EYE	604B
	PON8ROS IA«	SICK	697B
	POSOS I	HOW GREAT	701A
	SKOTEINOS	DARK	764C
	SU 2	YOU	780A
	PHWS IB«	LIGHT	880A
23A	SKOTOS 2B	DARKNESS	765B
23B	SKOTOS 2B	DARKNESS	765B
24	AGAPAW IA«	LOVE	4C
	ANTECHW I	CLING TO	72D
	DOULEUW 2A	SERVE	204B
	DOULEUW 2B	SERVE	204B
	DUNAMAI IA	ABLE	206B
	DUO 3	TWO	208C
	HEIS 5D	ONE	231B
	HETEROS IA	OTHER	315A
	8 IB	OR	342D
	THEOS 3B	GOD	357D
	KATAPHRONEW I	SCORN	421C

24	KURIOS IAβ	LORD	460A
	MAMWNAS	MAMMON	491A
	MISEW I	HATE	524C
	OU 4A	NO	594D
	OUDEIS 2A	NO ONE	596B
25	DIA BII2	THEREFORE	180B
	ENDUMA I	GARMENT	263A
	ENDUW 2A	DRESS	263C
	ESTHIW IA	EAT	312C
	LEGW IIIC	ORDER	470D
	MERIMNAW I	HAVE ANXIETY	506A
	M8 AIII3A	NOT	518C
	M8DE IA	AND NOT	519C
	OUCHI 3	NOT	603A
	PINW I	DRINK	664B
	POLUS II2C	MANY	696A
	TROPH8 I	FOOD	835C
25A	SWMA IB	BODY	806D
25A	PSUCH8 IAβ	SOUL LIFE	901C
25B	SWMA IB	BODY	806D
25B	PSUCH8 IAβ	SOUL LIFE	901C
26	APOTH8K8	STOREHOUSE	90C
	AUTOS 3A	(OBLIQUE CASE)	122D
	DIAPHERW 2B	BE SUPERIOR	189C
	EMBLEPW 2	LOOK AT	254A
	EMBLEPW I	LOOK AT	254A
	THERIZW I	REAP	359D
	KAI I2G	AND	393C
	MALLON I	MORE	490B
	OU 4C	NO	594D
	OUDE I	AND NOT	595D
	OURANIOS	HEAVENLY	598A
	OURANOS ID	HEAVEN	598D
	PAT8R 3Cα	FATHER	641C
	PETEINON	BIRD	660A
	SPEIRW IAα	SOW	768C
	SUNAGW I	GATHER	789D
	TREPHW I	FEED	833B
26B	SU IA	YOU	779D
27	EK 4Aβ	FROM	235B
	EPI IIIIBβ	TO	288D
	H8LIKIA IA	AGE	345D
	H8LIKIA 2	BODILY STATURE	346A
	MERIMNAW I	HAVE ANXIETY	506A
	P8CHUS	FOREARM	662D
	PROSTITH8MI IA	ADD	726B
	TIS, TI IAα	WHICH	826D
28	AGROS I	FIELD	13D
	AUXANW 3	GROW	121C
	ENDUMA I	GARMENT	263A
	KATAMANTHANW	OBSERVE	415D
	KOPIAW 2	BECOME WEARY	444B
	KRINON	LILY	452A
	MERIMNAW I	HAVE ANXIETY	506A
	N8THW	SPIN	539B
	XAINW	COMB	549B
	OUDE I	AND NOT	595D
	PWS 2A	HOW	739D
	TIS, TI 3A	WHICH	827B
29	DOXA 2	MAGNIFICENCE	203A
	HEIS IAβ	ONE	230A
	EN I4B	IN	258B
	OUDE 3	NOT EVEN	596A

29	PERIBALLW IBε	THROW AROUND	651D
	SOLOMWN	SOLOMON	766C
30	AGROS I	FIELD	13D
	AMPHIENNUMI	CLOTHE	46D
	AURION 2	SOON	121D
	BALLW IB	THROW	130C
	EI III	IF	218C
	KLIBANOS	OVEN	437B
	MALLON 2B	MORE	490C
	OLIGOPISTOS	OF LITTLE FAITH	566B
	OU 4C	NO	594D
	HOUTW IB	THUS	602B
	POLUS I2Cα	MANY	695B
	S8MERON	TODAY	756C
	CHORTOS	GRASS	892B
31	ESTHIW IA	EAT	312C
	MERIMNAW I	HAVE ANXIETY	506A
	OUN IB	THEREFORE	597B
	PERIBALLW IBε	THROW AROUND	651D
	PINW I	DRINK	664B
32	HAPAS 2	ALL	81A
	ETHNOS 2	GENTILES	217C
	EPIZ8TEW 2A	STRIVE FOR	292D
	OIDA IE	KNOW	558C
	OURANIOS	HEAVENLY	598A
	PAS IEβ	ALL	637D
	PAT8R 3Cα	FATHER	641C
	CHR8ZW	NEED	893D
33	BASILEIA 3B	KINGDOM	134D
	BASILEIA 3G	KINGDOM	135A
	DE ID	BUT, AND	170C
	DIKAIOSUN8 2B	RIGHTEOUSNESS	195C
	Z8TEW 2A	SEEK	339C
	PAS IEβ	ALL	638A
	PROSTITH8MI 2	ADD	726C
	PRWTOS 2C	FIRST	734A
34	ARKETOS	SUFFICIENT	106C
	EIS 2Aβ	FOR	228A
	H8MERA 2	DAY	346D
	KAKIA 2	TROUBLE	397D
34A	AURION I	TOMORROW	121D
34A	MERIMNAW I	HAVE ANXIETY	506B
34B	AURION I	TOMORROW	121D
34B	MERIMNAW 2		506B
		BE CONCERNED ABOUT	

MATTHEW 7

I	HINA IIC	IN ORDER THAT	377C
	M8 AI2	NOT	517C
	M8 AIII3A	NOT	518C
IA	KRINW 6A	JUDGE	453B
IB	KRINW 4Bα	JUDGE	452D
2	KRIMA 6	JUDGMENT	452A
	METREW 2	GIVE OUT	516B
	METRON IA	MEASURE	516C
2A	KRINW 6A	JUDGE	453B
2A	HOS,H8,HO I5B	(REL PRON)	588B
2B	KRINW 4Bα	JUDGE	452D
2B	HOS,H8,HO I5B	(REL PRON)	588B
3	BLEPW IA	SEE	142D
	KATANOEW I	NOTICE	416A
	SOS I	YOURS	766C

Ref	Greek		English	
3	TIS, TI 3A		WHICH	827B
3FF	ADELPHOS 4		NEIGHBOR	16B
3FF	DOKOS		BEAM	202A
3FF	KARPHOS		SPECK	406B
3FF	OPHTHALMOS 1		EYE	604B
4	APO 12		FROM	85D
	APHI8MI 4		TOLERATE	126A
	8	1D6	OR	343B
	IDOU 1B8		BEHOLD	371C
	PWS 1C		HOW	739C
4F	EKBALLW 3		TAKE OUT	237B
5	DIABLEPW 2		SEE CLEARLY	180D
	PRWTOS 2A		FIRST	733D
	TOTE 2		AT THAT TIME	831D
	HUPOKRIT8S		HYPOCRITE	853A
6	HAGIOS 2Aα		WHAT IS HOLY	9D
	BALLW 1B		THROW	130C
	DIDWMI 1A		GIVE	191D
	EMPROSTHEN 2A		IN FRONT	256C
	EN III1A		BY	260A
	KAI 12E		AND	393C
	KATAPATEW 1A		TRAMPLE	416D
	KUWN 1		DOG	462B
	MARGARIT8S 2		PEARL	492C
	M8DE 1B		AND NOT	519D
	M8POTE 28γ		(NEG PARTICLE)	521B
	HO,H8,TO II2A		THE	553B
	POUS 1A		FOOT	703B
	R8GNUMI 1		TEAR	742C
	STREPHW 2Aα		TURN	778D
	CHOIROS		SWINE	891C
7	KAI 12F		AND	393C
7F	AITEW		ASK	25C
7F	ANOIGW 1A		OPEN	70B
7F	HEURISKW 1A		FIND	325A
7F	Z8TEW 1A8		SEEK	339B
7F	KROUW		STRIKE	454D
8	GAR 1D		FOR	151B
	LAMBANW 2		RECEIVE	466B
	PAS 1Cγ		WHOEVER	637B
9	AITEW		ASK	25B
	ANTHRWPOS 3Aζ		MAN	68C
	ARTOS 1A		BREAD	110A
	EPIDIDWMI 1		GIVE	292B
	8	1D6	OR	343B
	HUIOS 1Aα		SON	841B
9F	M8 C1		NOT	519A
10	AITEW		ASK	25B
	8	1D8	OR	343A
	ICHTHUS		FISH	385A
	OPHIS 1		SNAKE	604D
11	AGATHOS 1A8		GOOD	2D
	AITEW		ASK	25B
	DIDWMI 1A		GIVE	191D
	DOMA		GIFT	202C
	EI III		IF	218C
	EIMI II8		TO BE	223D
	EPIDIDWMI 1		GIVE	292B
	MALLON 2B		MORE	490C
	OIDA 3		KNOW	558D
	OURANOS 2A		HEAVEN	599B
	PAT8R 3Cα		FATHER	641C
	PON8ROS 1B8α		WICKED	697C
11	POSOS 1		HOW GREAT	701A
	SU 1C		YOU	779D
	TEKNON 1Aα		CHILD	815D
12	ANTHRWPOS 1A6		PEOPLE	67C
	THELW 1		WISH	355C
	HINA III1Aα		IN ORDER THAT	378A
	NOMOS 4A		LAW	545A
	HOSOS 2		HOW GREAT	590C
	HOUTOS 1Aη		THIS	601B
	PAS 1Eγ		ALL	638A
	PROPH8T8S 1		PROPHET	731A
	SU 1C		YOU	779D
12A	POIEW IID8		DO	688D
13	APAGW 3		LEAD AWAY	79A
	APWLEIA 2		DESTRUCTION	103A
	EISERCHOMAI 1F		COME	232B
	EISERCHOMAI 2A		COME	232B
	EURUCHWROS		BROAD	326B
	HODOS 2A		WAY	556D
	HOTI 3B		THAT	594A
	PLATUS		BROAD	673A
	POLUS IIAα		MANY	694B
13A	DIA AII		THROUGH	178C
13A	PUL8 2		GATE	736C
13B	DIA AII		THROUGH	178C
13B	PUL8 2		GATE	736C
13F	STENOS		NARROW	773D
14	APAGW 3		LEAD AWAY	79A
	HEURISKW 1A		FIND	325A
	ZW8 2B8		LIFE	341C
	THLIBW 2B		BECOME NARROW	362C
	HODOS 2A		WAY	556D
	OLIGOS 1B		FEW	566C
	PUL8 2		GATE	736C
	STENOS		NARROW	774A
	TIS, TI 3B		WHICH	827C
15	HARPAX 1		RAPACIOUS	108D
	EN I4B		IN	258B
	ENDUMA 2		GARMENT	263A
	ERCHOMAI IIA8		COME	310C
	ESWTHEN 2		INSIDE	314C
	LUKOS 2		WOLF	482D
	HOSTIS 2B		WHOEVER	591A
	PROBATON 1		SHEEP	710A
	PROSECHW 1B		PAY ATTENTION TO	721D
	PSEUDOPROPH8T8S		FALSE PROPHET	900B
16	AKANTHA		THORN PLANT	29A
	EPIGINWSKW 2A		KNOW	291A
	8	1D8	NOR	343A
	KARPOS 2A		RESULT	405D
	M8TI		(INTERROG PARTICLE)	522A
	STAPHUL8		BUNCH OF GRAPES	773D
	SUKON		RIPE FIG	784A
	SULLEGW		COLLECT	784D
	TRIBOLOS		THISTLE	833D
16-20	APO IV2B		FROM	87A
17	HOUTW		THUS	602B
17A	POIEW IIB8η		DO	688A
17B	POIEW IIB8η		DO	688A
17F	AGATHOS 1A8		GOOD	2D
17F	PON8ROS 1Aγ		SICK	697C
17F	SAPROS 1		DECAYED	749C
17FF	DENDRON		TREE	173C

17FF KALOS 2A	GOOD	401B
17FF KARPOS 1A	FRUIT	405C
18 KARPOS 1A	FRUIT	405C
OUDE 1	AND NOT	595D
POIEW IIBη	DO	688A
18A PHERW 2	BEAR	862D
18B PHERW 2	BEAR	862D
19 EKKOPTW 1	CUT DOWN	241B
M8 AII2B	NOT	518B
POIEW IIBη	DO	688A
PUR 1B	FIRE	737D
20 ARA 4	THEN	103C
EPIGINWSKW 2A	KNOW	291A
KARPOS 2A	RESULT	405D
21 ALLA 1A	BUT, YET	37B
BASILEIA 3G	KINGDOM	135A
EISERCHOMAI 2A	COME	232B
THEL8MA 1Cγ	WILL	355A
OU 2A	NO	594B
OURANOS 3	HEAVEN	599D
PAT8R 3Dα	FATHER	641D
POIEW IICα	DO	688C
21B OURANOS 2A	HEAVEN	599B
21F KURIOS 2Cβ	LORD	460D
22 DAIMONION 2	DEMON	168B
DUNAMIS 4	MIRACLE	207B
EKBALLW 1	DRIVE OUT	237A
EKEINOS 2Bβ	THAT	239B
EN II2	WHILE	259D
H8MERA 3Bβ	DAY	348A
HO,H8,TO IIIH	THE	553B
POIEW IIBβ	DO	687C
POLUS I2Aα	MANY	694D
PROPH8TEUW 1	PROPHESY	730B
22A SOS 1	YOURS	766C
22B POLUS IIAα	MANY	694A
22B SOS 1	YOURS	766C
22C SOS 1	YOURS	766C
23 ANOMIA 2	LAWLESSNESS	71B
APOCHWREW	LEAVE	101D
GINWSKW 7	ACKNOWLEDGE	160D
ERGAZOMAI 2A	WORK	307B
HO,H8,TO IIII	THE	553B
HOMOLOGEW 4	CONFESS	571B
HOTI 2	THAT	593D
OUDEPOTE	NEVER	596D
TOTE 2	AT THAT TIME	831D
24 AN8R 4	MAN	66B
LOGOS 1A6	WORD	478D
OIKODOMEW 1A	BUILD	560D
HOMOIOW 1	MAKE LIKE	570B
HOMOIOW 2	COMPARE	570B
HOSTIS 1A	WHOEVER	590D
OUN 1A	THEREFORE	597B
PAS 1Cγ	WHOEVER	637B
PAS 1Cγ	WHOEVER	637C
POIEW IICα	DO	688C
PHRONIMOS	THOUGHTFUL	874C
24F PETRA 1A	ROCK	660A
24=7 OIKIA 1A	HOUSE	559D
25 ANEMOS 1A	WIND	64A
BROCH8	RAIN	147B
EKEINOS 2A	THAT	239B

25 ERCHOMAI IICα	COME	311B
THEMELIOW 1		356C
LAY THE FOUNDATION OF		
KATABAINW 1B	COME DOWN	409D
HO,H8,TO IIIH	THE	553B
PIPTW 1Bβ	FALL	665C
PNEW 1A	BLOW	686A
POTAMOS 1	RIVER	701C
PROSKOPTW 1B	STRIKE AGAINST	723C
PROSPAIW	STRIKE	725A
PROSPIPTW 2	FALL DOWN BEFORE	725B
26 AMMOS	SAND	45D
AN8R 4	MAN	66B
LOGOS 1A6	WORD	478D
M8 AII2A	NOT	518B
MWROS 1	FOOLISH	533B
OIKODOMEW 1A	BUILD	560D
HOMOIOW 1	MAKE LIKE	570B
PAS 1Cγ	WHOEVER	637B
POIEW IICα	DO	688C
27 ANEMOS 1A	WIND	64A
BROCH8	RAIN	147B
EKEINOS 2A	THAT	239B
ERCHOMAI IICα	COME	311B
KATABAINW 1B	COME DOWN	409D
HO,H8,TO IIIH	THE	553B
PIPTW 1Bβ	FALL	665C
PNEW 1A	BLOW	686A
POTAMOS 1	RIVER	701C
PROSKOPTW 1B	STRIKE AGAINST	723C
PROSR8SSW 2	BURST UPON	725C
PTWSIS	COLLAPSE	735B
28 GINOMAI I3F	TAKE PLACE	158C
DIDACH8 3	TEACHING	191C
EKPL8SSW 2	BE AMAZED	243D
EPI IIIBγ	ON	287A
LOGOS 1A6	WORD	478D
HOTE 1B	WHEN	592C
OCHLOS 1	CROWD	605D
SUNTELEW 1	COMPLETE	799D
TELEW 1	FINISH	818C
29 EXOUSIA 2	ABILITY	277D

MATTHEW 8

1 AKOLOUTHEW 2	ACCOMPANY	30D
AUTOS 3A	(OBLIQUE CASE)	122D
KATABAINW 1Aα	COME DOWN	409B
HO,H8,TO IIIAα	THE	552B
OROS	MOUNTAIN	586B
OCHLOS 1	CROWD	605D
POLUS IIAβ	MANY	694B
2 EAN IIA	IF	210B
THELW 2	WISH	355D
IDOU 1Bβ	BEHOLD	371C
KATHARIZW 1Bα	CLEANSE	388A
KURIOS 2Cβ	LORD	460D
LEGW I8A	SAY	470B
LEPROS	LEPER	473A
PROSERCHOMAI 1	APPROACH	720A
PROSKUNEW 5	DO REVERENCE	724B
3 HAPTW 2B	TOUCH	102C
EKTEINW 1	STRETCH OUT	244D

3   EUTHEWS   IMMEDIATELY 320D
    LEGW I8A   SAY 470B
    LEPRA   LEPROSY 473A
3A   KATHARIZW I8α   CLEANSE 388A
3B   KATHARIZW I8β   CLEANSE 388A
4   DEIKNUMI IA   SHOW 171D
    DWRON 2   GIFT 210C
    EIS 4F   (PURPOSE) 228D
    HIEREUS I8α   PRIEST 372C
    LEGW IIIC   ORDER 470D
    MARTURION IA   TESTIMONY 494D
    M8DEIS 2A   NO 520A
    MWUS8S   MOSES 533D
    HORAW 2B   SEE 582B
    PROSTASSW   COMMAND 725D
    PROSPHERW 2A   BRING (TO) 727A
    SEAUTOU 3   YOURSELF 753A
    HUPAGW 2   GO AWAY 844C
5   EISERCHOMAI IAα   COME 231D
    HEKATONTARCH8S   CENTURION 236C
    KAPHARNAOUM   CAPERNAUM 427C
    PARAKALEW 3   IMPLORE 622D
    PROSERCHOMAI I   APPROACH 720A
6   BALLW I8   LIE 130C
    BASANIZW 2A   TORMENT 134A
    DEINWS   TERRIBLY 172B
    KURIOS 2Cβ   LORD 460D
    OIKIA IA   HOUSE 560A
    PAIS IA8   CHILD 609C
    PARALUTIKOS   PARALYTIC 625D
7   ERCHOMAI IIAζ   COME 310D
    THERAPEUW 2   HEAL 359C
    LEGW I3   SAY 469D
8   APOKRINOMAI I   ANSWER 92D
    EIPON 2A   SAY 225C
    EISERCHOMAI IG   COME 232B
    HEKATONTARCH8S   CENTURION 236C
    IAOMAI I   HEAL 369A
    HIKANOS 2   APPROPRIATE 375B
    HINA IIICβ   IN ORDER THAT 378C
    KAI I2F   AND 393C
    KURIOS 2Cβ   LORD 460D
    LOGOS IAα   WORD 478B
    PAIS IA8   CHILD 609C
    STEG8   ROOF 773B
    HUPO 2Aα   UNDER 851A
    PH8MI I8α   SAY 864A
9   GAR I8   FOR 151A
    DOULOS IA   SLAVE 204D
    EMAUTOU 3   MYSELF 253B
    EXOUSIA 4A   AUTHORITY 278A
    ERCHOMAI IIAα   COME 310B
    LEGW IIIC   ORDER 470D
    POREUW I   PROCEED 699B
    STRATIWT8S I   SOLDIER 778B
    TASSW I8   PLACE 813C
9A   HUPO 2B   UNDER 851B
9B   HUPO 2B   UNDER 851B
10 AM8N 2   AMEN 45B
    EIPON I   SAY 225C
    HEURISKW I8   FIND 325B
    THAUMAZW IAα   WONDER 352D
    ISRA8L 2   ISRAEL 382B

10 LEGW IIID   ASSURE 470D
    OUDEIS 2A   NO ONE 596B
    PARA II2D   BESIDE 615D
    PISTIS 28α   FAITH 668D
    TOSOUTOS IA8   SO GREAT 831B
11 ABRAAM   ABRAHAM 2A
    ANAKLINW 2   RECLINE 55D
    ANATOL8 2B   EAST 62A
    APO IVIA8   FROM 86D
    BASILEIA 3G   KINGDOM 135B
    DUSM8   WEST 209A
    H8KW IA   HAVE COME 345B
    IAKWB I   JACOB 368B
    ISAAK   ISAAC 381C
    LEGW IIIE   DECLARE 471A
    META AII2   WITH 510B
    OURANOS 3   HEAVEN 599D
    POLUS I2Aα   MANY 694D
12 BASILEIA 3G   KINGDOM 135B
    BRUGMOS   GNASHING 147B
    EKBALLW I   DRIVE OUT 236D
    EKEI I   THERE 238C
    EXERCHOMAI IAη   GO OUT 274B
    EXWTEROS 2   FARTHEST 279C
    KLAUTHMOS   WEEPING 434D
    ODOUS   TOOTH 557B
    SKOTOS I   DARKNESS 765A
    HUIOS IC6   SON 842A
13 GINOMAI I3Bβ   TAKE PLACE 158A
    EIPON I   SAY 225C
    HEKATONTARCH8S   CENTURION 236C
    EN II2   WHILE 259D
    IAOMAI I   HEAL 369A
    HO,H8,TO IIIH   THE 553B
    PAIS IA8   CHILD 609C
    PISTEUW 2C   BELIEVE 667C
    HUGIAINW I   BE HEALTHY 839D
    HUPAGW I   GO AWAY 844B
    HWRA 3   TIME OF DAY 905A
    HWS I2B   AS 905C
14 BALLW I8   LIE 130C
    EIDON I8   SEE 219D
    ERCHOMAI IIA8   COME 310B
    KAI I5   AND 394A
    OIKIA IA   HOUSE 559D
    PENTHERA   MOTHER IN LAW 648B
    PURESSW   SUFFER WITH A FEVER 738B
15 HAPTW 2B   TOUCH 102C
    APHI8MI 3A   LEAVE 125C
    DIAKONEW 2   SERVE 183A
    EGEIRW 2B   RISE 214A
    PURETOS   FEVER 738B
    CHEIR I   HAND 888A
16 GINOMAI IIBγ   COME ABOUT 157C
    DAIMONIZOMAI   168A
        BE POSSESSED BY A DEMON
    EKBALLW I   DRIVE OUT 237A
    ECHW III   BE 334B
    THERAPEUW 2   HEAL 359C
    KAKWS I   BADLY 399B
    LOGOS IAα   WORD 478B
    OPSIOS 2   LATE 606C
    PNEUMA 4C   SPIRIT 682A

16	POLUS IIA∝	MANY 694A
	PROSPHERW IA	BRING (TO) 726D
17	ASTHENEIA IA	WEAKNESS 114D
	BASTAZW 3A	REMOVE 137A
	EIPON 4	SAY 225D
	8SAIAS	ISAIAH 349C
	LAMBANW IB	TAKE 465C
	NOSOS I	DISEASE 545D
	HOPWS 2A∝	IN ORDER THAT 580C
	PL8ROW 4A	MAKE FULL 677C
	PROPH8T8S I	PROPHET 730D
18	APERCHOMAI 2	GO 84A
	KELEUW	COMMAND 428C
	HO,H8,TO II6	THE 554B
	PERAN I	ON THE OTHER SIDE 649C
	PERI 2A8	ABOUT 651A
19	AKOLOUTHEW 3	FCLLOW 30D
	DIDASKALOS	TEACHER 190D
	EAN II	IF 211A
	EIPON I	SAY 225C
	HEIS 3B	SOMEONE 230D
	HOPOU I8β	WHERE 579D
	PROSERCHOMAI I	APPROACH 720A
20	ALWP8X I	FOX 41B
	DE IA	BUT, AND 170C
	KATASK8NWSIS 2	NEST 419D
	KEPHAL8 IA	HEAD 431B
	KLINW IB	LAY DOWN 437C
	HO,H8,TO IIII	THE 555A
	OURANOS ID	HEAVEN 598D
	PETEINON	BIRD 660A
	POU IB	WHERE 703A
	HUIOS 2C	SON 843A
	PHWLEOS	DEN 878B
21	APERCHOMAI IA	GO AWAY 83D
	EIPON I	SAY 225C
	EPITREPW I	ALLOW 303C
	HETEROS IB∝	ANOTHER 315A
	KURIOS 2Cβ	LORD 460D
	MATH8T8S 2B∝	DISCIPLE 487A
	PAT8R IA	FATHER 640C
	PRWTOS 2A	FIRST 733C
21F	THAPTW	BURY 352C
22	APHI8MI 4	TOLERATE 126A
	HEAUTOU 4	ONESELF 211D
	NEKROS 2B	DEAD 537B
23	EIS IA∝	INTO 227B
	EMBAINW	GO IN 253C
	KAI I5	AND 394A
24	AUTOS IB	SELF 122B
	GINOMAI IIB∝	COME ABOUT 157B
	THALASSA 2	LAKE 351A
	IDOU I8β	BEHOLD 371C
	KATHEUDW I	SLEEP 389C
	KALUPTW I	COVER 402A
	KUMA	WAVE 458B
	MEGAS 2AY	GREAT 499A
	SEISMOS	SHAKING 753D
	HUPO IA8	BY 850D
	HWSTE 2Aβ	THEREFORE 908C
25	APOLLUMI 2A∝	PERISH 94D
	EGEIRW IA∝	WAKE 213C
	KURIOS 2Cβ	LORD 460D
25	SWZW IA	SAVE 805D
26	GAL8N8	CALM 149C
	GINOMAI IIB∝	COME ABOUT 157B
	DEILOS	COWARDLY 172A
	EGEIRW 2B	RISE 214A
	EPITIMAW I	REBUKE 303B
	LEGW IIIB	ANSWER 470C
	MEGAS 2AY	GREAT 499A
	OLIGOPISTOS	OF LITTLE FAITH 566B
	TOTE 2	AT THAT TIME 831D
26F	ANEMOS IA	WIND 64A
26F	SEISMOS	SHAKING 753D
27	ANTHRWPOS IA8	PEOPLE 67C
	THAUMAZW IA∝	WONDER 352D
	HOTI IC	THAT 593B
	POTAPOS	WHAT SORT 701C
	HUPAKOUW I	LISTEN TO 845B
28	GADAR8NOS	GADARENE 148B
	GERAS8NOS	GERASENE 155D
	GERGES8NOS	GERGESENE 155D
	DAIMONIZOMAI	168A
	BE POSSESSED BY A DEMON	
	DIA AII	THROUGH 178C
	DUO IA	TWO 208B
	EXERCHOMAI IA∝	GO OUT 273D
	ERCHOMAI IIA8	COME 310C
	ISCHUW 2B	BE STRONG 384C
	KAI I5	AND 394A
	LIAN 2A	VERY 474C
	M8 AI3	NOT 517C
	MN8MEION 2	TOMB 526C
	HO,H8,TO II6	THE 554B
	HODOS IA	WAY 556B
	PARERCHOMAI IA∝	GO BY 631B
	PERAN I	ON THE OTHER SIDE 649C
	TIS, TI IAY	ANY ONE 827D
	HUPANTAW	GO TO MEET 845C
	CHALEPOS	HARD 882C
	CHWRA IB	COUNTRY 897C
	HWSTE 2Aβ	THEREFORE 908C
29	BASANIZW 2A	TORMENT 134A
	EGW	I 216C
	ERCHOMAI IIAY	COME 310C
	IDOU I8β	BEHOLD 371C
	KAIROS 4	TIME 396B
	KRAZW 2A	CALL 448D
	PRO 2	BEFORE 708C
	TIS, TI IB∝	WHICH 827B
	HUIOS 2B	SON 842C
	HWDE I	HERE 903B
30	BOSKW 2	FEED 144D
	DE 2	BUT, AND 170C
	MAKRAN IA∝	FAR 488D
	POLUS IIA∝	MANY 694A
30=2	AGEL8	HERD 8C
30=2	CHOIROS	SWINE 891C
31	DAIMWN	DEMON 168D
	EI IIA	IF 217D
	PARAKALEW 3	IMPLORE 622D
32	APERCHOMAI 2	GO 84A
	APOTHN8SKW IA8	DIE 91A
	IDOU I8β	BEHOLD 371C
	KATA IIA	DOWN 406B

32	KR8MNOS	BANK 451B
	HORMAW	RUSH DOWN 585C
	PAS IC«	ALL 637B
	HUDWR I	WATER 840C
	HUPAGW 2	GO AWAY 844C
33	APAGGELLW I	REPORT 78C
	APERCHOMAI 2	GO 83D
	BOSKW I	FEED 144D
	DAIMONIZOMAI	168A
	BE POSSESSED BY A DEMON	
	KAI I3	AND 393D
	HO,H8,TO II7	THE 554C
	POLIS I	CITY 692A
	PHEUGW I	FLEE 863C
34	EIDON IA	SEE 219D
	EIS 4F	(PURPOSE) 228D
	EXERCHOMAI IA«	GO OUT 274B
	IDOU IB8	BEHOLD 371C
	METABAINW IA«	PASS OVER 511D
	HOPWS 2B	IN ORDER THAT 580D
	HORION	BOUNDARY 584D
	PARAKALEW 3	IMPLORE 622D
	PAS IC«	ALL 637B
	POLIS 3	CITY 692C
	SUNANT8SIS	MEETING 792B
	HUPANT8SIS	COMING TO MEET 845C

MATTHEW 9

1	DIAPERAW	CROSS 186C
	EMBAINW	GO IN 253C
	ERCHOMAI IIA8	COME 310B
	IDIOS 2C	ONES OWN 370C
	KAI I5	AND 394A
	PLOION 2	SHIP 679B
	POLIS I	CITY 692A
2	HAMARTIA I	SIN 42C
	APHI8MI 2	FORGIVE 125C
	BALLW IB	LIE 130C
	EIDON 3	NOTICE 220A
	EPI IIA«	ON 285C
	THARSEW	BE CHEERFUL 352C
	IDOU IB8	BEHOLD 371C
	KLIN8	COUCH 437C
	PISTIS 2B«	FAITH 668D
	PROSPHERW IA	BRING (TO) 727A
	TEKNON 2A	CHILD 816B
2A	PARALUTIKOS	PARALYTIC 625D
2B	PARALUTIKOS	PARALYTIC 625D
3	BLASPH8MEW 2B«	BLASPHEME 142A
	EIPON 5	SAY 225D
	IDOU IB8	BEHOLD 371C
	TIS, TI IA«	ANY ONE 827C
4	EIPON 3B	SAY 225D
	ENTHUMEOMAI	CONSIDER 265C
	ENTHUM8SIS	THOUGHT 265D
	HINATI	WHY 379B
	KARDIA IB8	HEART 404C
	OIDA IB	KNOW 558B
	PON8ROS 2C	WICKED 698A
5	APHI8MI 2	FORGIVE 125C
	GAR IF	WHAT 151C
	EUKOPOS	EASY 322A
5	PERIPATEW IC	GO ABOUT 655A
	TIS, TI IBr	WHICH 827A
5F	HAMARTIA I	SIN 42C
5F	EGEIRW IB	RAISE UP 214A
6	AIRW IA	LIFT UP 23D
	APHI8MI 2	FORGIVE 125C
	EXOUSIA 3	AUTHORITY 278A
	EPI IIA«	ON 285C
	KLIN8	COUCH 437C
	OIDA IE	KNOW 558C
	OIKOS IA«	HOUSE 563A
	PARALUTIKOS	PARALYTIC 625D
	SU 3	YOU 780A
	HUIOS 2C	SON 843A
	HUPAGW 2	GO AWAY 844C
7	APERCHOMAI 2	GO 83D
	EGEIRW 2B	RISE 214A
	EIS IA«	INTO 227B
	OIKOS IA«	HOUSE 563A
8	DIDWMI IB8	GIVE 192B
	DOXAZW I	PRAISE 203C
	EIDON IA	SEE 219D
	EXOUSIA 2	ABILITY 277D
	OCHLOS I	CROWD 605D
	TOIOUTOS 2A8	SUCH A KIND 829A
	PHOBEW IA	BE AFRAID 870B
9	AKOLOUTHEW 3	FOLLOW 30D
	ANTHRWPOS 3A8	MAN 68B
	ANIST8MI 2D	RISE 69D
	EIDON IB	SEE 219D
	EKEITHEN	FROM THERE 238D
	EPI IIIIA5	ON 288C
	KATH8MAI IA«	SIT 390B
	KAI I5	AND 394A
	LEGW II3	CALL 471B
	LEUI 4	LEVI 473B
	PARAGW 2B	BRING IN 619A
	TELWNION	TAX OFFICE 820B
10	ANAKEIMAI 2	BE AT TABLE 55C
	GINOMAI I3F	TAKE PLACE 158B
	ERCHOMAI IIA5	COME 310D
	KAI I2B	AND 393A
	OIKIA IA	HOUSE 560A
	POLUS IIA«	MANY 694A
	SUGKEIMAI	RECLINE TOGETHER 781B
	SUNANAKEIMAI	EAT WITH 792A
10F	HAMARTWLOS 2	SINNER 43D
10F	TELWN8S	TAX COLLECTOR 820B
11	DIA BII2	WHY 180B
	DIDASKALOS	TEACHER 190D
	EIDON IA	SEE 219D
	ESTHIW IC	EAT 313A
	META AII2	WITH 510C
	PHARISAIOS	PHARISEE 861C
12	IATROS I	PHYSICIAN 369C
	ISCHUW I	BE STRONG 384C
	KAKWS I	BADLY 399B
	CHREIA I	NEED 893B
12A	ECHW I2I	HAVE 333C
12B	ECHW III	BE 334B
13	ALLA IB	BUT, YET 37C
	HAMARTWLOS 2	SINNER 43C
	GAR IB	FOR 151B

13 GAR IE	FOR	151C
DIKAIOS IB	UPRIGHT	194D
EIMI II3	TO BE	222D
ELEOS I	MERCY	249C
THELW 4B	WISH	356A
THUSIA 2A	SACRIFICE	366D
KALEW 2	CALL	400D
MANTHANW I	LEARN	491C
METANOIA	REPENTANCE	514A
POREUW I	PROCEED	699B
14 DIA BII2	WHY	180B
LEGW IIIA	ASK	470C
N8STEUW	TO FAST	540C
PROSERCHOMAI I	APPROACH	720A
PHARISAIOS	PHARISEE	861C
14A MATH8T8S 2A	DISCIPLE	486D
14A POLUS I2Bβ	MANY	695B
15 APAIRW	TAKE AWAY	79A
DUNAMAI IA	ABLE	206B
EPI III2B	ON	289B
ERCHOMAI IIBα	COME	311B
H8MERA 4B	TIME	348B
M8 CI	NOT	519A
N8STEUW	TO FAST	540B
NUMPHWN 2	BRIDAL CHAMBER	547C
HOSOS I	HOW GREAT	590B
HOTAN IB	WHEN	592B
PENTHEW I	BE SAD	648B
HUIOS IC6	SON	842A
15A NUMPHIOS	BRIDEGROOM	547B
15B NUMPHIOS	BRIDEGROOM	547B
15C NUMPHIOS	BRIDEGROOM	547B
16 AGNAPHOS	UNSHRUNKEN	10D
AIRW 4	TAKE AWAY	24B
GINOMAI IIBβ	COME ABOUT	157B
EPI IIIAβ	ON	286D
EPIBALLW IB	LAY ON	289D
EPIBL8MA	A PATCH	290B
HIMATION I	GARMENT	377A
OUDEIS 2A	NO ONE	596B
PALAIOS I	OLD	610C
PL8RWMA IB	THAT WHICH FILLS	678A
RAKOS 2	PATCH	741B
SCHISMA I	SPLIT	805B
CHEIRWN	WORSE	889B
17 AMPHOTEROI I	BOTH	47A
APOLLUMI 2Aβ	PASS AWAY	94D
ASKOS	WINESKIN	116A
BALLW 2B	PUT	130D
GE 3Bβ	OTHERWISE	152B
DE IA	BUT, AND	170C
EKCHEW I	POUR OUT	246D
KAINOS I	NEW	394D
M8 AII	NOT	517C
NEOS IAα	NEW	537D
OINOS I	WINE	565A
OUDE I	AND NOT	595D
PALAIOS I	OLD	610C
R8GNUMI I	TEAR	742C
SUNT8REW I	PROTECT	800B
18 ALLA 6	NOW	38B
ARTI I	NOW	109D
ARCHWN 2A	AUTHORITIES	113C

18 EPITITH8MI IAα	PUT UPON	302D
ERCHOMAI IIAζ	COME	310D
ZAW IAβ	LIVE	336C
THUGAT8R I	DAUGHTER	365B
IDOU IBα	BEHOLD	371C
LEGW IIBα	SAY	469C
LEGW I8A	SAY	470B
PROSERCHOMAI I	APPROACH	720A
PROSKUNEW 5	DO REVERENCE	724B
TELEUTAW	DIE	818B
19 AKOLOUTHEW I	FOLLOW	30C
EGEIRW 2B	RISE	214A
20 HAIMORROEW	HEMORRHAGE	23A
HAPTW 2B	TOUCH	102D
GUN8 I	WOMAN	167B
DWDEKA	TWELVE	209B
ETOS	YEAR	317A
ECHW I2F	HAVE	333B
IDOU IBβ	BEHOLD	371C
KRASPEDON I	EDGE	449B
OPISTHEN IA	FROM BEHIND	578B
20F HIMATION 2	GARMENT	377A
21 HAPTW 2B	TOUCH	102D
EAN IIB	IF	210B
EN I5B	IN	258D
LEGW I6	SAY	470A
MONOS 2A	ONLY	529D
SWZW IC	SAVE	806A
22 EIPON 2B	SAY	225C
THARSEW	BE CHEERFUL	352C
THUGAT8R 2A	DAUGHTER	365B
HO,H8,TO IIIH	THE	553B
PISTIS 2Bα	FAITH	668D
STREPHW 2Aα	TURN	778D
HWRA 3	TIME OF DAY	905A
22A SWZW IC	SAVE	806A
22B SWZW IC	SAVE	806A
23 ARCHWN 2A	AUTHORITIES	113C
AUL8T8S	FLUTE PLAYER	121A
THORUBEW 2	BE TROUBLED	363C
OIKIA IA	HOUSE	559D
OCHLOS I	CROWD	605C
24 ANACHWREW I	GO AWAY	63A
APOTHN8SKW IAα	DIE	90D
KATHEUDW I	SLEEP	389C
KATAGELAW	RIDICULE	410D
24F KORASION	GIRL	445B
25 EGEIRW 2B	RISE	214A
EISERCHOMAI IAδ	COME	232A
EKBALLW I	DRIVE OUT	236D
KRATEW IB	SEIZE	449C
HOTE IB	WHEN	592D
OCHLOS I	CROWD	605C
26 EXERCHOMAI 2Bα	GO OUT	274C
HO,H8,TO IIIH	THE	553B
PH8M8	REPORT	864A
27 DAUID	DAVID	170B
DUO IA	TWO	208B
EKEITHEN	FROM THERE	238D
ELEEW	HAVE MERCY	249A
KAI I5	AND	394A
KRAZW 2A	CALL	448D
PARAGW 2B	BRING IN	619A

27	HUIOS 2A	SON	842A
27F	TUPHLOS 1B	BLIND	838C
28	AUTOS 3C (OBLIQUE CASE)		123A
	KURIOS 2Cβ	LORD	460D
	NAI 1A	YES	534D
	OIKIA 1A	HOUSE	559D
	PISTEUW 2C	BELIEVE	667D
28A	LEGW III A	ASK	470C
28B	LEGW III B	ANSWER	470C
29	HAPTW 2B	TOUCH	102C
	GINOMAI I3Bβ	TAKE PLACE	158A
	KATA II5Aγ	ACCORDING TO	408B
	LEGW I8A	SAY	470B
	PISTIS 2Bα	FAITH	668D
30	ANOIGW IEβ	OPEN	70D
	GINWSKW 2C	FIND OUT	160B
	EMBRIMAOMAI	SCOLD	254B
	M8DEIS 2A	NO	520A
	HORAW 2B	SEE	582B
31	DIAPH8MIZW	MAKE KNOWN	189C
	HO,H8,TO I3	THE	552A
	HO,H8,TO III H	THE	553B
31F	EXERCHOMAI IAβ	GO OUT	274A
32	DAIMONIZOMAI		168A
	BE POSSESSED BY A DEMON		
	KWPHOS I	MUTE	463A
	PROSPHERW IA	BRING (TO)	727A
33	DAIMONION 2	DEMON	168B
	THAUMAZW IAα	WONDER	352D
	ISRA8L 2	ISRAEL	382B
	KWPHOS I	MUTE	463A
	LALEW 2Aα	SPEAK	464B
	OUDEPOTE	NEVER	596D
	HOUTW 5	THUS	602D
	OCHLOS I	CROWD	605D
	PHAINW 2B	APPEAR	859C
34	ARCHWN 3	AUTHORITIES	113C
	DAIMONION 2	DEMON	168B
	*EKBALLW I	DRIVE OUT	237A
	EN III1B	BY	260B
	LEGW IIBα	SAY	469C
	PHARISAIOS	PHARISEE	861C
35	BASILEIA 3G	KINGDOM	135A
	EUAGGELION IC	GOSPEL	318B
	EUAGGELION 2Bα	GOSPEL	318B
	THERAPEUW 2	HEAL	359D
	KAI I5	AND	394A
	K8RUSSW 2Bβ	ANNOUNCE	432C
	KWM8 I	VILLAGE	462D
	MALAKIA I	SICKNESS	489D
	NOSOS I	DISEASE	545D
	PAS ID α	ALL	637C
	PERIAGW 2	LEAD AROUND	651B
	*POLIS I	CITY	692A
	SUNAGWG8 2A		790C
	PLACE OF ASSEMBLY		
36	ECHW I2Bβ	HAVE	332D
	M8 AII2B	NOT	518B
	OCHLOS I	CROWD	605D
	POIM8N I	SHEPHERD	690C
	PROBATON I	SHEEP	710A
	RIPTW 2	THROW	744A
	SKULLW I	WEARY	765C

36	SPLAGCHNIZOMAI	HAVE PITY	770B
	HWSEI I	AS	907D
37	MEN IAα (PARTICLE)		503D
	OLIGOS IA	FEW	566B
	POLUS IIBα	MANY	694C
37F	ERGAT8S IA	WORKMAN	307C
37F	THERISMOS 2A	HARVEST	360A
38	DEOMAI 4	ASK	174B
	EKBALLW 2	SEND OUT	237A
	KURIOS IAα	LORD	460A
	HOPWS 2B	IN ORDER THAT	580D
	OUN IB	THEREFORE	597B

MATTHEW 10

I	AKATHARTOS 2	IMPURE	28C
	DIDWMI IBβ	GIVE	192B
	EKBALLW I	DRIVE OUT	237A
	EXOUSIA 3	AUTHORITY	278A
	THERAPEUW 2	HEAL	359D
	KAI I5	AND	394A
	MATH8T8S 2Bα	DISCIPLE	486D
	MALAKIA I	SICKNESS	489D
	NOSOS I	DISEASE	545D
	PNEUMA 4C	SPIRIT	682A
	PROSKALEW IA	SUMMON	722C
	HWSTE 2B	THEREFORE	908C
IF	DWDEKA	TWELVE	209B
2	ANDREAS	ANDREW	63B
	APOSTOLOS 3	APOSTLES	99B
	EIMI II6A	TO BE	223C
	ZEBEDAIOS	ZEBEDEE	337D
	IAKWBOS I	JAMES	368B
	IWAN(N)8S 2	JOHN	385C
	LEGW II3	CALL	471B
	HO,H8,TO II7	THE	554C
	ONOMA II	NAME	573D
	PETROS	PETER	660D
	PETROS	PETER	661A
	PRWTOS ICβ	FIRST	733C
3	HALPHAIOS 2	ALPHAEUS	41A
	BARTHOLOMAIOS	BARTHOLOMEW	133B
	THADDAIOS	THADDAEUS	350B
	THWMAS	THOMAS	367D
	IAKWBOS 2	JAMES	368B
	MATTHAIOS	MATTHEW	497A
	TELWN8S	TAX COLLECTOR	820B
	PHILIPPOS 3	PHILIP	868A
4	IOUDAS 6	JUDAS	380D
	ISKARIWTH	ISCARIOT	381D
	KANA	CANA	403C
	KANANAIOS	CANANAEAN	403C
	KANANIT8S	CANANITE	403C
	PARADIDWMI IB	GIVE OVER	620A
	SIMWN 2	SIMON	758C
5	APOSTELLW IC	SEND AWAY	98B
	DWDEKA	TWELVE	209B
	EIS IAα	INTO	227C
	HODOS IA	WAY	556C
	HODOS 2A	WAY	556D
	PARAGGELLW	GIVE ORDERS	618C
	POLIS I	CITY	692A
	SAMARIT8S	SAMARITAN	749A

Ref	Word	Gloss	No.
6	APOLLUMI 2B	BE LOST	95A
	DE 1D	BUT, AND	170C
	ISRA8L 1	ISRAEL	382B
	MALLON 3Aα	RATHER	490C
	OIKOS 3	NATION	563D
	PROBATON 2	SHEEP	710B
7	BASILEIA 3G	KINGDOM	135B
	EGGIZW 5B	APPROACH	212D
	K8RUSSW 2Bβ	ANNOUNCE	432D
	OURANOS 3	HEAVEN	599D
8	ASTHENEW 1A	BE SICK	115A
	DAIMONION 2	DEMON	168B
	DWREAN 1	GRATIS	209D
	EGEIRW 1Aβ	RAISE	213D
	EKBALLW 1	DRIVE OUT	237A
	THERAPEUW 2	HEAL	359C
	KATHARIZW 1Bα	CLEANSE	388A
	LAMBANW 2	RECEIVE	466B
	LEPROS	LEPER	473A
	NEKROS 2A	DEAD	537A
9	ARGUROS 1	SILVER	104C
	EIS 7	TO	229C
	ZWN8	BELT	342A
	KTAOMAI 1	GET	456A
	M8 AIII5A	NOT	518D
	CHALKOS 2	COPPER	883B
	CHRUSOS	GOLD	897A
9F	M8DE 1A	AND NOT	519C
10	AXIOS 2A	WORTHY	77C
	DUO 4	TWO	208C
	EIS 1Aα	INTO	227C
	ERGAT8S 1A	WORKMAN	307C
	HODOS 1B	WAY	556C
	P8RA	KNAPSACK	662B
	RABDOS	ROD	740D
	TROPH8 1	FOOD	835C
	*HUPOD8MA	SANDAL	852B
	CHITWN	SHIRT	890C
11	AN 2A	(PARTICLE)	48A
	AN 3D	(PARTICLE)	48C
	AXIOS 2A	WORTHY	77D
	DE 4B	BUT, AND	170D
	EISERCHOMAI 1Aβ	COME	231D
	EXETAZW 1	SCRUTINIZE	275A
	8 1Aβ	OR	342D
	KAKEI 1	AND THERE	397C
	KWM8 1	VILLAGE	462D
	MENW 1Aα	REMAIN	504D
	MENW 1Aα	REMAIN	504D
	POLIS 1	CITY	692A
12	ASPAZOMAI 1A	GREET	116B
	EIR8N8 2	PEACE	226C
	EISERCHOMAI 1Aβ	COME	231D
	EKEINOS 2Bβ	THAT	239B
12F	OIKIA 3	HOUSEHOLD	560B
13	AXIOS 2A	WORTHY	77D
	EAN 13B	IF	210D
	EIR8N8 2	PEACE	226C
	EPI IIIBγ	ON	288D
	EPISTREPHW 2Aβ	TURN	301B
	ERCHOMAI I2C	COME	311D
	MEN 1Aα	(PARTICLE)	503D
	M8 AII	NOT	517C

Ref	Word	Gloss	No.
14	AKOUW 1Bα	HEAR	31B
	DECHOMAI 1	RECEIVE	176B
	EKTINASSW 1	SHAKE OFF	245B
	EXERCHOMAI 1Aα	GO OUT	274A
	EXW 2B	OUTSIDE	279B
	8 1Aβ	OR	342D
	KONIORTOS	DUST	444A
	LOGOS 1A6	WORD	478D
	M8 AII	NOT	517C
	M8DE 1B	AND NOT	519D
14F	POLIS 1	CITY	692A
15	ANEKTOS	BEARABLE	63D
	G8 4	LAND	156D
	GOMORRA	GOMORRAH	164A
	EKEINOS 2A	THAT	239B
	8 2A	THAN	343B
	H8MERA 3Bβ	DAY	347D
	KRISIS 1Aα	JUDGING	453C
	PL8N 1B	BUT	675B
	SODOMA	SODOM	766B
16	AKERAIOS	PURE	29D
	HAPLOUS	SINCERE	85C
	APOSTELLW 1Bβ	SEND AWAY	98A
	GINOMAI III	BE	159B
	EGW	I	216A
	EN 16	IN	259D
	IDOU 1C	REMEMBER	371D
	LUKOS 1	WOLF	482C
	MESOS 2	THE MIDDLE	509A
	OPHIS 1	SNAKE	604D
	PERISTERA	PIGEON	657D
	PROBATON 1	SHEEP	710A
	PHRONIMOS	THOUGHTFUL	874C
16B	HWS II2	SO	906A
17	ANTHRWPOS 1B	MAN	67D
	MASTIGOW 1	WHIP	496A
	PARADIDWMI 1B	GIVE OVER	620A
	PROSECHW 1B	PAY ATTENTION TO	721D
	SUNAGWG8 2A		790C
		PLACE OF ASSEMBLY	
	SUNEDRION 3	SANHEDRIN	794A
18	AGW 2	LEAD AWAY	14B
	BASILEUS 1	KING	135C
	*DE 4B	BUT, AND	170D
	ETHNOS 2	GENTILES	217C
	EIS 4F	(PURPOSE)	228D
	HENEKA	BECAUSE OF	264B
	EPI IIIAγ	ON	288B
	H8GEMWN 2	GOVERNORS	344A
	HIST8MI IIIB	STAND	383B
	MARTURION 1A	TESTIMONY	494D
19	EN II2	WHILE	259D
	8 IC	NOR	343A
	LALEW 2B	SPEAK	464D
	MERIMNAW 1	HAVE ANXIETY	506A
	HO,H8,TO IIIH	THE	553B
	PARADIDWMI 1B	GIVE OVER	619D
	PWS 2B	HOW	740A
	HWRA 3	TIME OF DAY	905A
19F	GAR 1C	FOR	151B
20	GAR 1B	FOR	151B
	LALEW 2Aγ	SPEAK	464B
	PAT8R 3Cα	FATHER	641C

20	PNEUMA 5A	SPIRIT	682C
21	GONEUS	PARENTS	164B
	EPANIST8MI	RISE UP	282D
	EPI IIIIAɛ	AGAINST	288B
	THANATOS IBα	DEATH	351C
	THANATOW I	PUT TO DEATH	352B
	PARADIDWMI IB	GIVE OVER	620B
	PAT8R IA	FATHER	640C
21A	TEKNON IAα	CHILD	815D
21B	TEKNON IAα	CHILD	816A
22	DIA BIII	BECAUSE OF	180A
	EIS 2Aα	UNTIL	227D
	MISEW 3	HATE	524D
	ONOMA I4Cα	NAME	575C
	HOUTOS IAɛ	THIS	601B
	PAS 2Aɣ	ALL	638B
	SWZW 2B	SAVE	806B
	TELOS IDɣ	END	819D
	HUPOMENW 2	REMAIN	853C
23	DIWKW 2	PERSECUTE	200B
	DIWKW 3	DRIVE AWAY	200B
	ERCHOMAI IIAη	COME	311A
	HETEROS IBɣ	ANOTHER	315B
	HEWS IIB	UNTIL	334D
	ISRA8L 2	ISRAEL	382B
	KAN I	AND IF	403B
	HOTAN IA	WHEN	592A
	TELEW I	FINISH	818C
	HUIOS 2C	SON	843A
	PHEUGW I	FLEE	863C
23A	POLIS I	CITY	692A
23B	POLIS I	CITY	692A
24	OUDE I	AND NOT	595D
24A	HUPER 2	BEYOND	847B
24B	HUPER 2	BEYOND	847B
24F	DIDASKALOS	TEACHER	190D
24F	DOULOS IA	SLAVE	204D
24F	KURIOS IAβ	LORD	460A
24F	MATH8T8S I	PUPIL	486D
25	ARKETOS	SUFFICIENT	106C
	BEEZEBOUL	BEELZEBUB	138C
	GINOMAI III	BE	159B
	EPIKALEW IBα	NAME	294A
	HINA IIIB	IN ORDER THAT	378C
	MALLON 2B	MORE	490C
	OIKIAKOS		560B
	MEMBER OF A HOUSEHOLD		
	OIKODESPOT8S		560C
	MASTER OF THE HOUSE		
	POSOS I	HOW GREAT	701A
26	APOKALUPTW I	REVEAL	91C
	GINWSKW 2A	FIND OUT	160B
	KALUPTW 2B	HIDE	402A
	KRUPTOS I	HIDDEN	455A
	M8 AIII5A	NOT	518D
	OUDEIS 2Bα	NOTHING	596C
	PHOBEW IBα	BE AFRAID	870D
27	DWMA	ROOF	209C
	EPI IIAα	ON	285C
	K8RUSSW 2Bβ	ANNOUNCE	432C
	LEGW IIA	SAY	469B
	HOS,H8,HO I2A	(REL PRON)	587A
	OUS I	EAR	600A

27	SKOTIA I	DARKNESS	764D
	PHWS IA	LIGHT	879D
28	APO V3	WITH	878
	APOKTEINW IB	KILL	93C
	APOLLUMI IAα	RUIN	94C
	GEENNA	HELL	152C
	DE ID	BUT, AND	170C
	KAI I6	AND	394A
	MALLON 3Aα	RATHER	490C
28A	SWMA IB	BODY	806C
28A	PHOBEW IA	BE AFRAID	870D
28A	PSUCH8 IC	SOUL LIFE	902A
28B	M8 AII2A	NOT	518B
28B	SWMA IB	BODY	806D
28B	PHOBEW IBα	BE AFRAID	871A
28B	PSUCH8 IC	SOUL LIFE	902A
29	ANEU I	WITHOUT	65A
	ASSARION	ASSARION	117A
	G8 2	GROUND	156C
	DUO 4	TWO	208C
	HEIS IC	ONE	230A
	EK 4Aα	FROM	235B
	KAI I2G	AND	393C
	OUCHI 3	NOT	603A
	PAT8R 3Cα	FATHER	641C
	PIPTW IA	FALL	665A
	PWLEW	SELL	739A
	STROUTHION	SPARROW	779A
30	ARITHMEW	COUNT	105D
	DE 4A	BUT, AND	170D
	THRIX 2	HAIR	364C
	KAI II2	EVEN	394B
	KEPHAL8 IA	HEAD	431B
31	DIAPHERW 2B	BE SUPERIOR	189C
	M8 AIII3A	NOT	518D
	OUN IB	THEREFORE	597B
	STROUTHION	SPARROW	779A
	*PHOBEW IA	BE AFRAID	870C
32	EN IV5	IN	260D
	HOMOLOGEW 4	CONFESS	571D
	PAS ICɣ	WHOEVER	637C
	PAT8R 3Dα	FATHER	641D
32A	HOMOLOGEW 4	CONFESS	571D
32B	HOMOLOGEW 4	CONFESS	571D
32F	ANTHRWPOS IAβ	MAN	67C
32F	EMPROSTHEN 2B	IN FRONT	256C
32F	KAGW 3B	I	387A
33	ARNEOMAI 3A	DENY	107C
	ARNEOMAI 3C	DENY	107D
	HOSTIS ID	WHOEVER	590D
	HOSTIS IEβ	WHOEVER	591A
	OURANOS 2A	HEAVEN	599B
	PAT8R 3Dα	FATHER	641D
34	BALLW 2B	PUT	131A
	G8 5B	EARTH	156D
	EIR8N8 IB	PEACE	226B
	MACHAIRA 2	SWORD	497C
	NOMIZW 2	THINK	543B
34F	ERCHOMAI IIAη	COME	311A
35	ANTHRWPOS 2Bɣ	MAN	68A
	DICHAZW	SEPARATE	199B
	THUGAT8R I	DAUGHTER	365B
	KATA I2Bα	DOWN	406C

35	NUMPH8 2	DAUGHTER IN LAW 547B
	PENTHERA	MOTHER IN LAW 648B
36	ECHTHROS 2Bβ	THE ENEMY 331D
	OIKIAKOS	560B
	MEMBER OF A HOUSEHOLD	
37	EGW	I 216C
	8 IAβ	OR 342D
	THUGAT8R I	DAUGHTER 365B
	M8T8R I	MOTHER 521D
	HUIOS IAα	SON 841B
37A	HUPER 2	BEYOND 847B
37A	PHILEW IA	LOVE LIKE 866D
37B	HUPER 2	BEYOND 847B
37B	PHILEW IA	LOVE LIKE 866D
37F	AXIOS 2A	WORTHY 77C
38	AKOLOUTHEW 2	ACCOMPANY 30D
	KAI I2E	AND 393C
	LAMBANW IA	TAKE 465C
	OPISW 2Aβ	AFTER 578D
	HOS,H8,HO I2A	(REL PRON) 587A
	OU 5A	NO 595A
	STAUROS 2	THE CROSS 772C
39	APOLLUMI IB	LOSE 94C
	HENEKA	BECAUSE OF 264B
	PSUCH8 ID	SOUL LIFE 902B
39A	PSUCH8 ID	SOUL LIFE 902B
39B	PSUCH8 ID	SOUL LIFE 902B
40	HO,H8,TO II3B	THE 553C
40F	DECHOMAI I	RECEIVE 176B
41	DIKAIOS IB	UPRIGHT 194D
	PROPH8T8S 4	PROPHET 731B
41A	LAMBANW 2	RECEIVE 466B
41A	MISTHOS 2A	REWARD 525B
41A	ONOMA II	TITLE 577A
41B	LAMBANW 2	RECEIVE 466B
41B	ONOMA II	TITLE 577A
41F	EIS 5	FOR 229B
42	APOLLUMI IB	LOSE 94C
	MIKROS IC	SMALL 523A
	MISTHOS 2A	REWARD 525C
	MONOS 2B	ONLY 529D
	ONOMA II	TITLE 577A
	POT8RION I	CUP 702A
	POTIZW I	GIVE TO DRINK 702C
	PSUCHROS IA	COLD 902D
	PSUCHROS IB	COLD 903A

MATTHEW 11

1	AUTOS 3B	(OBLIQUE CASE) 123A
	GINOMAI I3F	TAKE PLACE 158C
	DIATASSW	ORDER 188C
	DIDASKW 2F	TEACH 191B
	DWDEKA	TWELVE 209B
	EKEITHEN	FROM THERE 238D
	K8RUSSW 2Bβ	ANNOUNCE 432D
	MATH8T8S 2Bα	DISCIPLE 486D
	METABAINW IAα	PASS OVER 511D
	HO,H8,TO II4Bζ	THE 554A
	HOTE IB	WHEN 592C
	TELEW I	FINISH 818C
2	AKOUW 3B	LEARN 31D
	DESMWT8RION	PRISON 175B

2	ERGON ICα	DEED 308A
	MATH8T8S 2A	DISCIPLE 486D
	PEMPW I	SEND 647D
	CHRISTOS I	ANOINTED ONE 895C
2F	DIA AIII2A	BY 179C
3	ERCHOMAI IIAη	COME 310D
	HETEROS IBα	ANOTHER 315A
	HO,H8,TO IIIAα	THE 552C
	PROSDOKAW I	EXPECT 719C
	SU IA	YOU 779D
4	AKOUW IBα	HEAR 31B
	APAGGELLW I	REPORT 78C
	APOKRINOMAI I	ANSWER 92D
	BLEPW IA	SEE 142D
	POREUW I	PROCEED 699B
5	AKOUW IA	HEAR 31B
	ANABLEPW 2Aα	GAIN SIGHT 50C
	EGEIRW 2C	RISE 214A
	EUAGGELIZW 2Bβ	PREACH 318A
	KATHARIZW IBα	CLEANSE 388A
	*KWPHOS 2	DEAF 463C
	LEPROS	LEPER 473A
	NEKROS 2A	DEAD 537A
	PERIPATEW IC	GO ABOUT 655A
	PTWCHOS IB	BEGGING POOR 735D
	*TUPHLOS IB	BLIND 838C
	CHWLOS	LAME 897B
6	MAKARIOS IB	BLESSED 487D
	M8 AII	NOT 517C
	SKANDALIZW IB	CAUSE TO FALL 760B
7	ANEMOS IA	WIND 64A
	ARCHW 2Aα	BEGIN 113A
	EXERCHOMAI IAε	GO OUT 274B
	THEAOMAI IA	SEE 353C
	KALAMOS I	REED 399C
	LEGW I4	SAY 469D
	HO,H8,TO II2B	THE 553C
	SALEUW I	SHAKE 747D
	HUPO IAβ	BY 850D
7F	ALLA 3	BUT, YET 38A
8	AMPHIENNUMI	CLOTHE 46D
	ANTHRWPOS 2Bα	MAN 67D
	EN I4B	IN 258B
	EXERCHOMAI IAζ	GO OUT 274B
	IDOU IC	REMEMBER 371D
	OIKOS IAβ	HOUSE 563B
	PHOREW I	WEAR 872D
8A	MALAKOS I	SOFT 489D
8B	MALAKOS I	SOFT 489D
9	KAI II2	EVEN 394B
	NAI IB	YES 534D
	PERISSOTEROS 2	GREATER 657B
	PROPH8T8S 2	PROPHET 731A
	PROPH8T8S 4	PROPHET 731B
10	AGGELOS IB	MESSENGER 7A
	APOSTELLW IBβ	SEND AWAY 98A
	EMPROSTHEN 2E	IN FRONT 256D
	KATASKEUAZW I	MAKE READY 419B
	HODOS IA	WAY 556B
	HOS,H8,HO I8	(REL PRON) 588D
	PRO I	BEFORE 708C
	PROSWPON ICζ	FACE 728D
11	GENN8TOS	BEGOTTEN 155B

11 EGEIRW 2E   APPEAR 214A   20F   DUNAMIS 4   MIRACLE 207B
    MEGAS 2Bα   GREAT 499B   21 AN 1Bβ   (PARTICLE) 47D
    MIKROS IC   SMALL 523B   B8THSAIDA I   BETHSAIDA 139C
11F   BAPTIST8S   BAPTIST 132B   EI IIB   IF 218A
11F   OURANOS 3   HEAVEN 599D   EN I4B   IN 258B
12 APO II2A   FROM 86B   METANOEW   CHANGE ONES MIND 513B
    HARPAZW 2B   SNATCH 1080   OUAI IA   WOE 595C
    ARTI 3   NOW 110A   PALAI I   LONG AGO 610B
    BIAZW 2D   APPLY FORCE 140B   SAKKOS   SACK 747C
    BIAST8S   VIOLENT 140C   SPODOS   ASHES 770D
    HEWS IIIC   UNTIL 335C   CHORAZIN   CHORAZIN 891D
    H8MERA 4B   TIME 348B   21F   SIDWN   SIDON 757C
13 HEWS IIIA   UNTIL 335B   21F   TUROS   TYRE 838C
    NOMOS 4A   LAW 545A   22 ANEKTOS   BEARABLE 63D
    PAS 1Dα   ALL 637C   EN II2   WHILE 259D
    PROPH8TEUW 3   PROPHESY 730C   8   2A   THAN 343B
    PROPH8T8S I   PROPHET 731A   H8MERA 3Bβ   DAY 347D
14 DECHOMAI 3B   ACCEPT 176C   KRISIS IAα   JUDGING 453C
    ERCHOMAI IIAθ   COME 311A   LEGW IIID   ASSURE 470D
    8LIAS   ELIJAH 345D   PL8N IB   BUT 675B
    MELLW ICβ   BE ABOUT TO 502B   23 HAD8S I   HADES 16C
15 AKOUW IA   HEAR 31B   GINOMAI I2A   CREATED 157C
    ECHW I2Cα   HAVE 332D   DUNAMIS 4   MIRACLE 207B
    OUS 2   EAR 600B   HEWS II2A   AS FAR AS 335C
16 AGORA   MARKET PLACE 12B   KATABAINW 2   COME DOWN 409D
    GENEA 2   GENERATION 153B   KATABIBAZW   DRIVE DOWN 410A
    HETAIROS   COMPANION 314D   KAPHARNAOUM   CAPERNAUM 427C
    HETEROS 1Bβ   ANOTHER 315B   MENW ICβ   REMAIN 505C
    KATH8MAI IAα   SIT 390B   MECHRI IB   UNTIL 517A
    HOMOIOS I   LIKE 569D   OURANOS IB   HEAVEN 598B
    HOMOIOW 2   COMPARE 570B   S8MERON   TODAY 756C
    PAIDARION IA   CHILD 608B   HUPSOW I   LIFT UP 858C
    PAIDION 2A   CHILD 609A   23F   SODOMA   SODOM 766B
    PROSPHWNEW I   CALL OUT 727D   24 ANEKTOS   BEARABLE 63D
17 AULEW   PLAY THE FLUTE 120D   G8 4   LAND 156D
    THR8NEW IB   MOURN 363D   8   2A   THAN 343B
    KOPTW 2   BEAT 445A   H8MERA 3Bβ   DAY 347D
    ORCHEOMAI   DANCE 587A   KRISIS IAα   JUDGING 453C
18 DAIMONION 2   DEMON 168B   PL8N IB   BUT 675B
    ERCHOMAI IIAθ   COME 311A   25 APOKALUPTW 2   REVEAL 91C
    ESTHIW IEγ   EAT 313B   APOKRINOMAI 2   CONTINUE 93A
    ECHW I2Eα   HAVE 333A   AUTOS 3A   (OBLIQUE CASE) 122D
    M8TE   AND NOT 521D   EXOMOLOGEW 2C   CONFESS 276D
18F   PINW I   DRINK 664C   KAIROS I   TIME 395D
19 HAMARTWLOS 2   SINNER 43D   KRUPTW 2A   HIDE 455C
    ANTHRWPOS 3Aε   MAN 68C   KURIOS 2A   LORD 460B
    DIKAIOW 2   JUSTIFY 196C   N8PIOS 1Bβ   CHILDLIKE 539D
    ERCHOMAI IIAη   COME 311A   HO,H8,TO IIIH   THE 553B
    ESTHIW IEγ   EAT 313B   OURANOS IAα   HEAVEN 598B
    IDOU 2   THERE IS 371D   PAT8R 3Dα   FATHER 641D
    OINOPOT8S   WINE DRINKER 564D   SOPHOS 2   LEARNED 767D
    SOPHIA 4   WISDOM 767B   SUNETOS   INTELLIGENT 796B
    TEKNON 2Fβ   CHILD 816C   26 EMPROSTHEN 2D   IN FRONT 256D
    TELWN8S   TAX COLLECTOR 820B   EUDOKIA 2   FAVOR 319D
    HUIOS 2C   SON 843A   NAI 3   CERTAINLY 535A
    PHAGOS   GLUTTON 859A   HO,H8,TO IIII   THE 553B
    PHILOS 2Aα   LOVING 869A   HOUTW IB   THUS 602C
20 ARCHW 2Aα   BEGIN 113A   PAT8R 3Dα   FATHER 641D
    METANOEW   CHANGE ONES MIND 513B   27 APOKALUPTW 2   REVEAL 91C
    ONEIDIZW 2   REPROACH 573B   BOULOMAI 2B   DESIRE 146A
    POLIS I   CITY 692A   EI VI8A   IF NOT 219A
    POLUS IIIIA   MANY 696B   EPIGINWSKW 2Aα   KNOW 291A
20F   GINOMAI I2A   CREATED 157C   M8 AII   NOT 517C

27	OUDE I	AND NOT	595D
	OUDEIS 2A	NO ONE	596B
	PARADIDWMI 3	GIVE OVER	620D
	PAS 2Aδ	EVERYTHING	638B
	TIS, TI IAγ	ANY ONE	827D
	HUIOS 2B	SON	842C
27A	PAT8R 3Dα	FATHER	641D
27B	PAT8R 3Dα	FATHER	641D
27C	PAT8R 3Dα	FATHER	641D
28	ANAPAUW I	CAUSE TO REST	58C
	DEUTE 2	COME	175D
	EGW	I	216C
	KAGW I	AND I	386D
	KOPIAW I	BECOME WEARY	444B
	PAS IDβ	ALL	637C
	PHORTIZW	CAUSE TO CARRY	873A
29	AIRW 2	LIFT UP	24A
	ANAPAUSIS 2	REST	58B
	EIMI III	TO BE	222D
	KARDIA IBη	HEART	405B
	MANTHANW I	LEARN	491B
	HOTI 3B	THAT	594A
	PRAUS	HUMBLE	705C
	PRAUS	HUMBLE	705D
	TAPEINOS 2B	LOW	812A
	PSUCH8 IC	SOUL LIFE	902A
	PSUCH8 IF	SOUL LIFE	902C
29F	ZUGOS I	YOKE	340B
30	ELAPHROS I	LIGHT	248A
	PHORTION 2	LOAD	873A
	CHR8STOS IAα	USEFUL	894C

MATTHEW 12

I	ARCHW 2Aα	BEGIN	113A
	ESTHIW ID	EAT	313A
	KAIROS I	TIME	395D
	MATH8T8S 2Bα	DISCIPLE	487A
	HO,H8,TO IIIH	THE	553B
	PEINAW I	HUNGER	645D
	POREUW I	PROCEED	699B
	SABBATON	SABBATH	746B
	SARBATON IBβ	SABBATH	746C
	SPORIMOS	SOWN	770D
	STACHUS I	EAR (OF GRAIN)	773B
	TILLW	PLUCK	824C
2	AUTOS 3B	(OBLIQUE CASE)	123A
	EN II2	WHILE	259D
	EXESTI I	IT IS POSSIBLE	274D
	UU 5A	NO	595A
	POIEW IICγ	DO	688C
	SABBATON IA	SABBATH	746B
	PHARISAIOS	PHARISEE	861C
3	ANAGINWSKW I	READ	51B
	DAUID	DAVID	170B
	HO,H8,TO II5	THE	554B
	PEINAW I	HUNGER	645D
3F	META AIIICα	WITH	510A
4	ARTOS IB	BREAD	110B
	EI VI8B	BUT	219A
	EXESTI 4	IT IS POSSIBLE	275A
	ESTHIW IA	EAT	312C
	M8 AII	NOT	517C

4	MONOS IAβ	ONLY	529C
	MONOS IAγ	ONLY	529C
	OIKOS IAβ	HOUSE	563B
	PROTHESIS I	SETTING FORTH	713A
	PWS 2A	HOW	740A
4F	HIEREUS IBα	PRIEST	372C
5	ANAGINWSKW I	READ	51B
	ANAITIOS	INNOCENT	55A
	BEB8LOW	DESECRATE	138C
8	IDβ	OR	343A
	HIERON 2	TEMPLE	373A
	NOMOS 4A	LAW	545A
	SABBATON IBβ	SABBATH	746C
5B	SABBATON IA	SABBATH	746B
6	HIERON 2	TEMPLE	373A
	MEGAS 2Bα	GREAT	499B
	HWDE 2A	HERE	903D
7	AN IBβ	(PARTICLE)	48A
	ANAITIOS	INNOCENT	55A
	GINWSKW IC	KNOW	160A
	EIMI II3	TO BE	222D
	ELEOS I	MERCY	249C
	THELW 4B	WISH	356A
	THUSIA 2A	SACRIFICE	366D
	KATADIKAZW	CONDEMN	411B
8	KURIOS IAα	LORD	460A
	SABBATON IA	SABBATH	746B
	HUIOS 2C	SON	843A
9	AUTOS 3B	(OBLIQUE CASE)	123A
	EKEITHEN	FROM THERE	238D
	METABAINW IAα	PASS OVER	511D
	SUNAGWG8 2A		790C
		PLACE OF ASSEMBLY	
10	EI VI	IF	218D
	EXESTI I	IT IS POSSIBLE	274D
	EPERWTAW IA	ASK	285A
	THERAPEUW 2	HEAL	359D
	IDOU 2	THERE IS	371D
	KAT8GOREW IA	BRING CHARGES	424B
	X8ROS 2	DRY	551A
	CHEIR I	HAND	888A
10=12	SABBATON IBβ	SABBATH	746C
11	BOTHUNOS	PIT	144B
	EAN IIB	IF	210C
	EGEIRW IAβ	RAISE	213D
	EIMI II	TO BE	222B
	EMPIPTW I	FALL	255D
	KRATEW IB	SEIZE	449C
11F	PROBATON I	SHEEP	710A
12	ANTHRWPOS IAβ	MAN	67C
	DIAPHERW 2B	BE SUPERIOR	189C
	EXESTI I	IT IS POSSIBLE	274D
	KALWS 3	WELL	402B
	OUN ICγ	THEREFORE	597C
	POIEW I2Aα	DO	689A
	POSOS I	HOW GREAT	701A
	SABBATON	SABBATH	746B
	HWSTE IA	THEREFORE	908B
13	ALLOS 3	THE OTHER	39D
	ANTHRWPOS 4A	MAN	68D
	APOKATHIST8MI I	RESTORE	91B
	EKTEINW I	STRETCH OUT	244D
	HUGI8S IA	HEALTHY	840A

14	APOLLUMI IAα	RUIN	94C
	EXERCHOMAI IAβ	GO OUT	274A
	LAMBANW IH	TAKE	466A
	HOPWS 2B	IN ORDER THAT	580D
	SUMBOULION I	PLAN	785D
	PHARISAIOS	PHARISEE	861C
15	AKOLOUTHEW 2	ACCOMPANY	30D
	ANACHWREW 2B	WITHDRAW	63A
	EKEITHEN	FROM THERE	238D
	PAS IEα	ALL	637D
	POLUS I2Aα	MANY	694D
15F	EPIPL8SSW	REBUKE	297D
16	EPITIMAW I	REBUKE	303B
	POIEW IIB:	DO	688B
	PHANEROS I	CLEAR	860B
17	EIPON 4	SAY	225D
	8SAIAS	ISAIAH	349C
	HINA II2	IN ORDER THAT	378D
	HOPWS 2Aα	IN ORDER THAT	580C
	PL8ROW 4A	MAKE FULL	677C
18	AGAP8TOS I	BELOVED	6C
	HAIRETIZW	CHOOSE	23C
	APAGGELLW 2	PROCLAIM	78C
	EPI IIIIBγ	ON	289A
	EUDOKEW 2A	WELL PLEASED	319C
	KRISIS 3	RIGHT	454A
	PAIS IBγ	SERVANT	609D
	PNEUMA 5A	SPIRIT	682C
	TITH8MI IIAβ	PUT	823D
	PSUCH8 IBγ	SOUL LIFE	901D
19	AKOUW IBα	HEAR	31B
	ERIZW	QUARREL	309B
	KRAUGAZW 2A	CRY	450C
	PLATEIA	WIDE ROAD	672C
	TIS, TI IAγ	ANY ONE	827D
	PHWN8 2A	VOICE	879A
20	EKBALLW 3	TAKE OUT	237B
	KALAMOS I	REED	399C
	KATAGNUMI	BREAK	410D
	KRISIS 3	RIGHT	454A
	LINON I	LAMP WICK	476B
	NIKOS I	VICTORY	542A
	SBENNUMI I	EXTINGUISH	752D
	SUNTRIBW IA	SHATTER	801A
	TUPHW	SMOKE	839A
21	ELPIZW 3	HOPE	252A
	ONOMA I4B	NAME	575A
22	BLEPW 2	SEE	143A
	DAIMONIZOMAI		168A
	BE POSSESSED BY A DEMON		
	LALEW 2Aα	SPEAK	464B
	PROSPHERW IA	BRING (TO)	727A
	TOTE 2	AT THAT TIME	831D
	HWSTE 2Aβ	THEREFORE	908C
22A	KWPHOS I	MUTE	463A
22B	KWPHOS I	MUTE	463A
23	DAUID	DAVID	170B
	EXIST8MI 2B	BE AMAZED	276A
	M8TI	PERHAPS	522A
	OCHLOS I	CROWD	605D
	HUIOS 2A	SON	842A
24	ARCHWN 3	AUTHORITIES	113C
	DAIMONION 2	DEMON	168B

24	EI VI8A	IF NOT	219A
	EIPON 2B	SAY	225C
	EKBALLW I	DRIVE OUT	237A
	M8 AII	NOT	517C
	PHARISAIOS	PHARISEE	861C
24FF	BEEZEBOUL	BEELZEBUB	138C
25	HEAUTOU IF	ONESELF	211B
	ENTHUM8SIS	THOUGHT	265D
	ER8MOW	LAY WASTE	309A
	KATA I2Bγ	DOWN	406D
	MERIZW IA	DIVIDE	505D
	OIDA 4	KNOW	559A
	OIKIA 2	HOUSEHOLD	560A
	POLIS 3	CITY	692D
25F	BASILEIA 2	KINGDOM	134C
25F	HIST8MI IIID	STAND	383B
26	EKBALLW I	DRIVE OUT	237A
	EPI IIIIAc	AGAINST	288B
	MERIZW IA	DIVIDE	505D
	OUN ICγ	THEREFORE	597C
	PWS ID	HOW	739C
	SATAN	ADVERSARY	752B
27	DAIMONION 2	DEMON	168B
	DIA BII2	THEREFORE	180B
	EKBALLW I	DRIVE OUT	237A
	KAI I5	AND	394A
	KRIT8S IB	JUDGE	454D
	TIS, TI IBα	WHICH	826D
	HUIOS ICα	SON	841C
28	ARA 3	THEN	103C
	BASILEIA 3B	KINGDOM	134D
	BASILEIA 3G	KINGDOM	135B
	EPI IIIIBγ	ON	288D
	PNEUMA 5A	SPIRIT	682C
	PHTHANW 2	COME	864C
29	HARPAZW I	STEAL	108C
	DEW IB	BIND	176D
	DIARPAZW	PLUNDER	187A
	EAN I3B	IF	210D
	EISERCHOMAI IAβ	COME	231D
	8 ID6	OR	343B
	ISCHUROS IA	STRONG	384A
	M8 AII	NOT	517C
	PRWTOS 2A	FIRST	733D
	PWS ID	HOW	739C
	SKEUOS IA	THING	761C
	TIS, TI IAα	ANY ONE	827C
	TOTE 2	AT THAT TIME	831D
30	EIMI III6A	TO BE	224C
	EIMI III7	TO BE	224D
	KATA I2Bγ	DOWN	406D
	SKORPIZW I	SCATTER	764B
	SUNAGW I	GATHER	790A
30A	META AIIIC6	WITH	510B
30A	M8 AII2A	NOT	518B
30B	META AII2	WITH	510C
30B	M8 AII2A	NOT	518B
31	DIA BII2	THEREFORE	180B
	LEGW IIID	ASSURE	470D
	PAS IAγ	EVERY EACH	637C
	PNEUMA 5Dα	SPIRIT	683A
31A	BLASPH8MIA I	SLANDER	142C
31B	BLASPH8MIA 2B	SLANDER	142C

31F APHI8MI 2	FORGIVE 125C	39 MOICHALIS 2A	ADULTEROUS 528A
32 AIWN 2A	AGE 27A	PON8ROS IBα	WICKED 697C
AIWN 2B	AGE 27B	PROPH8T8S I	PROPHET 730D
EIPON I	SAY 225B	39-41 IWNAS I	JONAH 386A
LOGOS IAɣ	WORD 478C	40 GAR 2	FOR 151C
MELLW 2	IS DESTINED 502C	H8MERA IA	DAY 346C
OUTE	NOT 600D	KARDIA 2	HEART 405B
HOUTOS 2A	THIS 601D	K8TOS	SEA MONSTER 432D
PNEUMA 5Cα	SPIRIT 682C	KOILIA I	BELLY 438B
HUIOS 2C	SON 843A	HOUTW IA	THUS 602B
33 GINWSKW IA	KNOW 159D	TREIS	THREE 833A
DENDRON	TREE 173C	HUIOS 2C	SON 843A
EK 3Gβ	BY 234D	HWSPER I	(JUST) AS 908A
8 IB	OR 342D	40A NUX ID	NIGHT 549A
KALOS 2A	GOOD 401B	40B NUX ID	NIGHT 549A
KARPOS IA	FRUIT 405C	41 ANIST8MI 2C	RISE 69D
33A POIEW IIEβ	DO 688D	EIS 6A	BECAUSE OF 229B
33A SAPROS I	DECAYED 749C	K8RUGMA 2	PROCLAMATION 432A
33B POIEW IIEβ	DO 688D	*METANOEW	CHANGE ONES MIND 513B
33B SAPROS I	DECAYED 749C	NINEUIT8S	MEN OF NINEVEH 542A
34 GENN8MA	CHILD 155A	HO,H8,TO IIIAα	THE 552C
DUNAMAI IA	ABLE 206B	POLUS II2C	MANY 696A
EIMI II8	TO BE 223D	41F GENEA 2	GENERATION 153B
EK 3Gα	BY 234D	41F KATAKRINW	CONDEMN 413B
ECHIDNA	VIPER 332A	41F KRISIS IAα	JUDGING 453D
KARDIA IBc	HEART 405A	41F HWDE 2A	HERE 903D
LALEW 2Ac	SPEAK 464C	42 BASILISSA	QUEEN 136C
PERISSEUMA I	ABUNDANCE 656B	ERCHOMAI IIAc	COME 310D
PON8ROS IBα	WICKED 697C	NOTOS 3	SOUTH 546A
PWS ID	HOW 739C	PERAS I	END 649D
STOMA IA	MOUTH 777C	POLUS II2C	MANY 696A
35 AGATHOS IBα	GOOD 3A	SOPHIA 2	WISDOM 767A
AGATHOS IBβ	GOOD 3B	42A SOLOMWN	SOLOMON 766C
ANTHRWPOS 3B	MAN 68C	42B SOLOMWN	SOLOMON 766C
EKBALLW 3	TAKE OUT 237B	43 AKATHARTOS 2	IMPURE 28C
TH8SAUROS IB	STOREHOUSE 362B	ANAPAUSIS 3	A RESTING PLACE 58B
HO,H8,TO IIIAβ	THE 552C	ANUDROS	WATERLESS 76A
35A PON8ROS IBα	WICKED 697C	DIA AII	THROUGH 178B
35B PON8ROS IBβ	WICKED 697D	DIERCHOMAI IBα	GO THROUGH 193C
35C PON8ROS 2C	WICKED 698A	EXERCHOMAI IA6	GO OUT 274A
36 APODIDWMI I	GIVE AWAY 90A	HEURISKW IA	FIND 325A
ARGOS 3	USELESS 104B	Z8TEW IAβ	SEEK 339B
H8MERA 3Bβ	DAY 347D	KAI I2G	AND 393C
KRISIS IAα	JUDGING 453C	HOTAN IB	WHEN 592A
LALEW 2B	SPEAK 464C	PNEUMA 4C	SPIRIT 682A
LOGOS 2A	ACCOUNT 479D	TOPOS ID	PLACE 830B
R8MA I	WORD 742D	44 EXERCHOMAI IAα	GO OUT 274A
37 DIKAIOW 3A	JUSTIFY 196D	EPISTREPHW IBc	TURN 301A
EK 3I	BY 235A	ERCHOMAI IIAζ	COME 310D
KATADIKAZW	CONDEMN 411B	HEURISKW ICα	FIND 325C
37A LOGOS IA6	WORD 478D	KOSMEW I	PUT IN ORDER 445D
37B LOGOS IA6	WORD 478D	KOSMEW 2Aβ	DECORATE 445D
38 APO V4	FROM 87B	LEGW IIBα	SAY 469C
APOKRINOMAI 2	CONTINUE 93A	HOTHEN I	FROM WHICH 557D
GRAMMATEUS 2	SCRIBES 165A	OIKOS IBβ	HOUSE 563D
DIDASKALOS	TEACHER 190D	SAROW	SWEEP 752A
THELW I	WISH 355C	SCHOLAZW 2	STAND EMPTY 805C
TIS, TI IAα	ANY ONE 827C	45 HEAUTOU IF	ONESELF 211B
PHARISAIOS	PHARISEE 861C	EKEI I	THERE 238C
38F S8MEION 2A	SIGN 755C	HEPTA	SEVEN 306B
39 APOKRINOMAI I	ANSWER 92D	ESCHATOS 3A	LAST 314A
GENEA 2	GENERATION 153B	HETEROS IBβ	ANOTHER 315B
EPIZ8TEW 2B	STRIVE FOR 292D	KAI III	ALSO 394A

45 KATOIKEW 1B   LIVE 425C
   META AIIIB   WITH 509D
   HOUTW 1B   THUS 602B
   PARALAMBANW 1   TAKE 625A
   PNEUMA 4C   SPIRIT 682A
   PON8ROS   SICK 697B
   PRWTOS 1A   FIRST 732D
   CHEIRWN   WORSE 889C
45B PON8ROS 1Bα   WICKED 697C
46 ETI 1Aβ   STILL 315D
   Z8TEW 2Bγ   SEEK 339C
   IDOU 1Bα   BEHOLD 371C
   M8T8R 1   MOTHER 521D
46A LALEW 2A6   SPEAK 464B
46B LALEW 2A6   SPEAK 464B
46F *ADELPHOS 1   BROTHER 15D
46F EXW 1Aα   OUTSIDE 278D
46F HIST8MI II28α   BEING 383B
47 LALEW 2A6   SPEAK 464B
   TIS, TI 1Aα   ANY ONE 827C
48 APOKRINOMAI 1   ANSWER 92D
49 EIPON 2B   SAY 225C
   EKTEINW 1   STRETCH OUT 244D
   EPI IIIIA6   TO 288B
   HO,H8,TO IIID   THE 552D
49F M8T8R 3   MOTHER 521D
50 ADELPH8 1   SISTER 15C
   ADELPHOS 2   BROTHER 15D
   GAR 2   FOR 151C
   THEL8MA 1Cγ   WILL 355A
   HOSTIS 1Eβ   WHOEVER 591A
   OURANOS 2A   HEAVEN 599B
   PAT8R 3Dα   FATHER 641D
   POIEW IICα   DO 688C

                MATTHEW 13

1 EKEINOS 2Bγ   THAT 239B
  EXERCHOMAI 1Aα   GO OUT 274A
  THALASSA 2   LAKE 351A
  KATH8MAI 2   SIT DOWN 390C
  HO,H8,TO IIIH   THE 553B
  PARA IIIIBα   ALONG 616A
2 AIGIALOS   SHORE 21B
  EMBAINW   GO IN 253C
  EPI IIIIAζ   ON 288C
  HIST8MI II28β   BEING 383B
  KATH8MAI 2   SIT DOWN 390C
  PAS ICα   ALL 637B
  PLOION 2   SHIP 679B
  POLUS IIAβ   MANY 694B
  SUNAGW 2   GATHER 790B
  HWSTE 2Aβ   THEREFORE 908C
2A OCHLOS 1   CROWD 605D
2B OCHLOS 1   CROWD 605C
3 EXERCHOMAI 1Aζ   GO OUT 274B
  IDOU 1Bγ   BEHOLD 371C
  LALEW 2B   SPEAK 464D
  LALEW 3   SPEAK 465A
  HO,H8,TO II3A   THE 553C
  HO,H8,TO II4Bζ   THE 554A
  PARABOL8 2   PARABLE 617D
  POLUS I28α   MANY 695A

3A SPEIRW 1Aα   SOW 768C
3B SPEIRW 1Aα   SOW 768C
4 EN II3   WHILE 260A
  ERCHOMAI IICα   COME 311B
  KATESTHIW 1   EAT UP 423B
  HODOS 1A   WAY 556B
  PARA IIIID   ALONG 616A
  PETEINON   BIRD 659D
  PIPTW 1A   FALL 665A
  SPEIRW 1Aα   SOW 768C
4FF MEN 1C   (PARTICLE) 504A
4=8A HOS,H8,HO II2 THIS (ONE) 589B
5 ALLOS 1B   OTHER 39B
  BATHOS 1   DEPTH 129D
  G8 1   EARTH 156C
  EXANATELLW   SPRING UP 272B
  EPI IIIIAβ   ON 288A
  EUTHEWS   IMMEDIATELY 320D
  HOPOU 1Aα   WHERE 579C
  PETRWD8S   ROCKY 661B
  PIPTW 1A   FALL 665A
  POLUS IIBα   MANY 694C
5A ECHW I2G   HAVE 333B
5B ECHW I2G   HAVE 333B
5F DIA BII3   BECAUSE 180B
5F M8 AIIIE   NOT 518A
6 ANATELLW 2   RISE 61C
  ECHW I2Cβ   HAVE 332D
  H8LIOS   THE SUN 346B
  KAUMATIZW   BURN 426C
  KAUMATOW   BE SCORCHED 426C
  X8RAINW 2A   DRY UP 550D
  RIZA 1A   ROOT 743B
7 AKANTHA   THORN PLANT 29A
  ANABAINW 1B   GO UP 50A
  APOPNIGW   CHOKE 97A
  EPI IIIIAγ   ON 288B
  PIPTW 1A   FALL 665A
  PNIGW 1C   CHOKE 686A
7F ALLOS 1B   OTHER 39B
8 G8 1   EARTH 156C
  DIDWMI 4   GIVE 192C
  HEKATON   ONE HUNDRED 236B
  HEX8KONTA   SIXTY 275C
  KALOS 2A   GOOD 401B
  KARPOS 1A   FRUIT 405C
  MEN 1C   (PARTICLE) 504A
  PIPTW 1A   FALL 665A
  TRIAKONTA   THIRTY 833D
8B HOS,H8,HO II2 THIS (ONE) 589B
9 AKOUW 1A   HEAR 31B
  OUS 2   EAR 600B
10 DIA BII2   WHY 180B
   EIPON 3B   SAY 225D
   LALEW 2A6   SPEAK 464B
   LALEW 2Aε   SPEAK 464C
   MATH8T8S 28α   DISCIPLE 487A
   PARABOL8 2   PARABLE 617D
   PROSERCHOMAI 1   APPROACH 720A
11 APOKRINOMAI 1   ANSWER 92D
   BASILEIA 3G   KINGDOM 135A
   GINWSKW 1A   KNOW 159D
   DIDWMI 1Bβ   GIVE 192B

11 EKEINOS IA	THAT 238D
MUST8RION I	MYSTERY 532A
OURANOS 3	HEAVEN 599D
12 GAR ID	FOR 151B
HOS,H8,HO I2Bα	(REL PRON) 587B
PERISSEUW 2A	BE LEFT OVER 657A
12A ECHW I2A	HAVE 332B
12A HOSTIS IA	WHOEVER 590D
12B ECHW I2A	HAVE 332C
12B HOSTIS IA	WHOEVER 590D
13 AKOUW IA	HEAR 31B
AKOUW 7	UNDERSTAND 32B
BLEPW ID	SEE 143A
DIA BII2	THEREFORE 180B
LALEW 2Aϵ	SPEAK 464C
PARABOL8 2	PARABLE 617D
SUNI8MI	UNDERSTAND 797D
13F SUNI8MI	UNDERSTAND 798A
14 AK08 IB	HEARING 30B
AKOUW IA	HEAR 31B
ANAPL8ROW 2	MAKE COMPLETE 59B
BLEPW ID	SEE 143A
8SAIAS	ISAIAH 349C
PROPH8TEIA 3A	PROPHECY 730B
15 AKOUW IA	HEAR 31B
BAREWS	WITH DIFFICULTY 133B
EIDON IA	SEE 219D
EPISTREPHW IBβ	TURN 301B
IAOMAI 2	HEAL 369A
KAI I2E	AND 393C
KAMMUW	CLOSE 403A
M8POTE 28α	(NEG PARTICLE) 521A
PACHUNW 2	MAKE DULL 644A
SUNI8MI	UNDERSTAND 798A
15A KARDIA IBβ	HEART 404D
15A OUS 2	EAR 600B
15B KARDIA IBβ	HEART 404C
15B OUS 2	EAR 600B
15B OPHTHALMOS 2	EYE 604C
16 AKOUW IA	HEAR 31B
MAKARIOS 3A	BLESSED 488A
HOTI 3A	THAT 593D
OUS I	EAR 600B
OPHTHALMOS 2	EYE 604C
16F BLEPW IA	SEE 142D
17 AKOUW IBα	HEAR 31B
DIKAIOS IB	UPRIGHT 194D
EIDON	SEE 219C
EPITHUMEW	DESIRE 293A
KAI I2G	AND 393C
OUS I	EAR 600B
POLUS IIAα	MANY 694A
PROPH8T8S 4	PROPHET 731B
17FF AKOUW IBα	HEAR 31B
18*PARABOL8 2	PARABLE 617D
SPEIRW IAα	SOW 768C
19 HARPAZW 2A	SNATCH 108D
EN IIE	IN 257D
ERCHOMAI IIAζ	COME 310D
LOGOS IBβ	WORD 479C
M8 AII2B	NOT 518B
PARA IIIID	ALONG 616A
PAS IAα	EVERY EACH 636D

19 PON8ROS 2B	WICKED 698A
SUNI8MI	UNDERSTAND 797D
SUNI8MI	UNDERSTAND 798A
19A SPEIRW IBβ	SOW 768D
19B SPEIRW IAγ	SOW 768D
19F EIMI II3	TO BE 223A
20 LAMBANW IE8	RECEIVE 466A
HOUTOS IAϵ	THIS 601B
PETRWD8S	ROCKY 661B
SPEIRW IAγ	SOW 768C
CHARA I	JOY 883C
20F EUTHUS	IMMEDIATELY 321B
20FF AKOUW IBα	HEAR 31B
20=3 LOGOS IBβ	WORD 479C
21 GINOMAI IIBβ	COME ABOUT 157B
DIA BIII	BECAUSE OF 180A
DIWGMOS	PERSECUTION 200A
THLIPSIS I	TRIBULATION 362D
PROSKAIROS	TEMPORARY 722C
RIZA IB	ROOT 743B
SKANDALIZW IA	CAUSE TO FALL 760B
22 AIWN 2A	AGE 27A
AKANTHA	THORN PLANT 29A
AKARPOS 2	UNFRUITFUL 29B
APAT8 I	DECEPTION 81B
GINOMAI III	BE 159B
MERIMNA	ANXIETY 506A
HOUTOS IAϵ	THIS 601B
PLOUTOS I	WEALTH 680B
SPEIRW IAγ	SOW 768C
SUMPNIGW I	CHOKE 787C
22F EIMI II3	TO BE 223A
23 G8 I	EARTH 156C
D8 I	INDEED 177B
HEKATON	ONE HUNDRED 236B
HEX8KONTA	SIXTY 275C
KALOS 2A	GOOD 401B
KARPOPHOREW 2	BEAR FRUIT 406A
MEN IC	(PARTICLE) 504A
HOS,H8,HO II2	THIS (ONE) 589B
SPEIRW IAγ	SOW 768D
*SUNI8MI	UNDERSTAND 797D
SUNI8MI	UNDERSTAND 798A
24 AGROS I	FIELD 13D
ALLOS IB	OTHER 39B
ANTHRWPOS 3Aϵ	MAN 68C
KALOS 2A	GOOD 401B
HOMOIOW I	MAKE LIKE 570B
OURANOS 3	HEAVEN 599D
PARABOL8 2	PARABLE 617D
PARATITH8MI IB	PLACE BESIDE 628B
SPEIRW IAβ	SOW 768C
SPEIRW IAγ	SOW 768C
SPERMA IA	SEED 769A
24FF BASILEIA 3G	KINGDOM 135B
24FF BOTAN8 I	PLANT 145A
25 ANA IA	AMONG 49B
APERCHOMAI IA	GO AWAY 83D
EN II3	WHILE 260A
EPISPEIRW	SOW AFTERWARD 300A
ERCHOMAI IIAζ	COME 310D
ECHTHROS 2Bβ	THE ENEMY 331D
KATHEUDW I	SLEEP 389C

25 MESOS 2	THE MIDDLE	508C
SITOS	WHEAT	759C
25FF ZIZANION	DARNEL	340A
26 BLASTANW 2	SPROUT	141D
KARPOS 1A	FRUIT	405C
HOTE 1B	WHEN	592C
POIEW 118η	DO	688A
TOTE 2	AT THAT TIME	831D
PHAINW 2B	APPEAR	859B
CHORTOS	GRASS	892B
27 AGROS 1	FIELD	13D
EIPON 3B	SAY	225D
KALOS 2A	GOOD	401B
KURIOS 1AB	LORD	460A
OIKODESPOT8S		560C
MASTER OF THE HOUSE		
OUN 1Cα	THEREFORE	597C
POTHEN 2	FROM WHERE	686D
SOS 1	YOURS	766C
SPEIRW 1AB	SOW	768C
SPERMA 1A	SEED	769A
27F DOULOS 1A	SLAVE	204D
28 APERCHOMAI 1A	GO AWAY	83D
ECHTHROS 2A	HOSTILE	331D
THELW 1	WISH	355C
OUN 1Cα	THEREFORE	597B
POIEW 118ε	DO	687D
PH8MI 1Bα	SAY	864A
28=30 SULLEGW	COLLECT	784D
29 HAMA 2	TOGETHER	41B
EKRIZOW 1	UPROOT	244B
M8POTE 2Bα	(NEG PARTICLE)	521A
OU 1	NO	594B
SITOS	WHEAT	759C
PH8MI 1Bα	SAY	864A
29F ZIZANION	DARNEL	340A
30 APOTH8K8	STOREHOUSE	90C
APHI8MI 4	TOLERATE	126A
DESM8	BUNDLE	175A
DEW 1A	BIND	176C
THERIST8S	REAPER	360A
KAIROS 3	TIME	396A
KATAKAIW	CONSUME	412A
MECHRI 1B	UNTIL	517B
PROS III3A	TOWARD	717A
PRWTOS 2A	FIRST	733C
SITOS	WHEAT	759D
SUNAGW 1	GATHER	789D
SUNAUXANW	GROW TOGETHER	793A
30A THERISMOS 1	HARVEST	360A
31 AGROS 1	FIELD	13D
ALLOS 1B	OTHER	39B
AN 3D	(PARTICLE)	48C
ANTHRWPOS 3AB	MAN	68B
KOKKOS 1	SEED	441B
LAMBANW 1A	TAKE	465B
HOMOIOS 1	LIKE	569D
OURANOS 3	HEAVEN	599D
PARABOL8 2	PARABLE	617D
PARATITH8MI 1B	PLACE BESIDE	628B
SINAPI	MUSTARD	759A
SPEIRW 1Aγ	SOW	768C
32 AUXANW 2	GROW	121B
32 DENDRON	TREE	173C
ERCHOMAI 11Cα	COME	311B
KATASK8NOW 2	LIVE	419C
KLADOS	BRANCH	434A
LACHANON	VEGETABLE	468D
MIKROS 2A	SMALL	523B
HOTAN 1B	WHEN	592A
OURANOS 1D	HEAVEN	598D
PETEINON	BIRD	660A
SPERMA 1A	SEED	769A
HWSTE 2AB	THEREFORE	908C
33 ALEURON	WHEAT FLOUR	35A
ALLOS 1B	OTHER	39B
GUN8 1	WOMAN	167B
EGKRUPTW	HIDE	216A
HEWS III8α	UNTIL	335C
ZUM8 1	LEAVEN	340C
ZUMOW	FERMENT	340C
LALEW 2B	SPEAK	464D
LAMBANW 1A	TAKE	465B
HOLOS 2C	WHOLE	567D
HOMOIOS 1	LIKE	569D
HOS,H8,HO III F	(REL PRON)	589A
OURANOS 3	HEAVEN	599D
PARABOL8 2	PARABLE	617C
SATON	MEASURE	752C
34 LALEW 2B	SPEAK	464D
PAS 1EB	ALL	638A
CHWRIS 2BB	APART	899A
34A PARABOL8 2	PARABLE	617D
34B PARABOL8 2	PARABLE	617D
35 ANOIGW 1Eα	OPEN	70D
EIPON 4	SAY	225D
EREUGOMAI	UTTER	308D
8SAIAS	ISAIAH	349C
KATABOL8 1	FOUNDATION	410B
KOSMOS 2	WORLD	446D
KRUPTW 2A	HIDE	455C
HOPWS 2Aα	IN ORDER THAT	580C
PARABOL8 2	PARABLE	617D
PL8ROW 4A	MAKE FULL	677C
STOMA 1A	MOUTH	777B
36 AGROS 1	FIELD	13D
APHI8MI 1Aα	SEND AWAY	125B
DIASAPHEW 1	EXPLAIN	187B
ZIZANION	DARNEL	340A
OIKIA 1A	HOUSE	559D
*PARABOL8 2	PARABLE	617D
PHRAZW	EXPLAIN	873C
36FF BASILEIA 3G	KINGDOM	135B
37 APOKRINOMAI 1	ANSWER	92D
SPEIRW 1AB	SOW	768C
HUIOS 2C	SON	843A
37F KALOS 2A	GOOD	401B
37F SPERMA 1A	SEED	769A
38 AGROS 1	FIELD	13D
BASILEIA 3G	KINGDOM	135B
EIMI II3	TO BE	223A
ZIZANION	DARNEL	340A
KOSMOS 4A	WORLD	447A
HOUTOS 1Aη	THIS	601B
PON8ROS 2B	WICKED	698A
38A HUIOS 1C6	SON	842A

38B	HUIOS ICv	SON 841D
39 DIABOLOS 2	THE SLANDERER	181A
ECHTHROS 2Bα	THE ENEMY	331D
THERISMOS I	HARVEST	360A
THERIST8S	REAPER	360A
SPEIRW IAβ	SOW	768C
39F AIWN 2A	AGE	27B
39F SUNTELEIA	CLOSE	799C
40 EIMI II9B	TO BE	224A
ZIZANION	DARNEL	340A
KATAKAIW	CONSUME	412A
OUN 5	THEREFORE	597D
HOUTW IA	THUS	602B
PUR IA	FIRE	737B
SULLEGW	COLLECT	784D
SUNTELEIA	CLOSE	799C
HWSPER I	(JUST) AS	908A
41 AGGELOS 2A	ANGEL	7D
ANOMIA 2	LAWLESSNESS	71B
APOSTELLW IA	SEND AWAY	98A
BASILEIA 3D	KINGDOM	134D
EK IB	AWAY FROM	233C
POIEW IICv	DO	688C
SKANDALON 3	TRAP	760D
SULLEGW	COLLECT	784D
HUIOS 2C	SON	843A
42 BALLW IB	THROW	130C
BRUGMOS	GNASHING	147B
KAMINOS	FURNACE	402D
KLAUTHMOS	WEEPING	434D
ODOUS	TOOTH	557B
PUR IB	FIRE	737D
43 BASILEIA 3C	KINGDOM	134D
DIKAIOS IB	UPRIGHT	194D
EKLAMPW	SHINE	241C
H8LIOS	THE SUN	346B
OUS 2	EAR	600B
PAT8R 3Cα	FATHER	641C
TOTE IB	AT THAT TIME	831C
HWS II2	SO	905D
44 AGORAZW I	BUY	12C
AGROS I	FIELD	13D
APO V3	WITH	87B
HEURISKW IB	FIND	325B
ECHW I2A	HAVE	332B
TH8SAUROS 2A	TREASURE	362B
HO,H8,TO IIIH	THE	553B
PALIN 3	AGAIN	611D
PWLEW	SELL	738D
HUPAGW 2	GO AWAY	844C
CHARA I	JOY	883C
44A KRUPTW IB	HIDE	455C
44B KRUPTW IA	HIDE	455B
44F BASILEIA 3G	KINGDOM	135A
44F HOMOIOS I	LIKE	569D
44F OURANOS 3	HEAVEN	599D
45 ANTHRWPOS 3Aε	MAN	68C
EMPOROS	MERCHANT	256B
Z8TEW IAβ	SEEK	339B
KALOS 2A	GOOD	401B
MARGARIT8S I	PEARL	492C
PALIN 3	AGAIN	611D
46 AGORAZW I	BUY	12C
46 APERCHOMAI IA	GO AWAY	83D
HEURISKW IA	FIND	325A
ECHW I2A	HAVE	332B
MARGARIT8S I	PEARL	492C
HOSOS 2	HOW GREAT	590B
PAS IEv	ALL	638A
PIPRASKW	SELL	664D
POLUTIMOS	VALUABLE	696D
47 BALLW IB	THROW	130C
GENOS 4	CLASS	155C
EK IB	AWAY FROM	233C
HOMOIOS I	LIKE	569D
OURANOS 3	HEAVEN	599D
PALIN 3	AGAIN	611D
SAG8N8	DRAGNET	746D
SUNAGW I	GATHER	789D
47FF BASILEIA 3G	KINGDOM	135B
48 AGGEION	CONTAINER	6D
AGGOS	CONTAINER	8B
AIGIALOS	SHORE	21B
ANABIBAZW	BRING UP	50B
BALLW IB	THROW	130C
EXW IB	OUTSIDE	279A
KATHIZW 2Aα	SIT DOWN	390D
KALOS 2A	GOOD	401B
KALOS 3C	GOOD	401D
HOTE IB	WHEN	592C
PL8ROW IA	MAKE FULL	676C
SAPROS I	DECAYED	749C
SULLEGW	COLLECT	784D
49 AIWN 2A	AGE	27B
APHORIZW I	SEPARATE	126D
DIKAIOS IB	UPRIGHT	194D
EK IB	AWAY FROM	233C
EXERCHOMAI IAη	GO OUT	274B
MESOS 2	THE MIDDLE	509A
HOUTW IB	THUS	602B
PON8ROS 2A	WICKED	697D
*SUNTELEIA	CLOSE	799C
50 BALLW IB	THROW	130C
BRUGMOS	GNASHING	147B
KAMINOS	FURNACE	402D
KLAUTHMOS	WEEPING	434D
ODOUS	TOOTH	557B
PUR IB	FIRE	737D
51 NAI IA	YES	534D
PAS IEβ	ALL	638A
SUNI8MI	UNDERSTAND	798A
52 ANTHRWPOS 3Aε	MAN	68C
BASILEIA 3G	KINGDOM	135A
GRAMMATEUS 3	SCRIBES	165A
DIA BII2	THEREFORE	180B
EKBALLW 3	TAKE OUT	237B
TH8SAUROS IAβ	STOREHOUSE	362A
KAINOS I	NEW	395A
MATH8TEUW 2	BECOME A DISCIPLE	486D
OIKODESPOT8S		560C
MASTER OF THE HOUSE		
HOMOIOS I	LIKE	569D
OURANOS 3	HEAVEN	599D
PALAIOS I	OLD	610D
53 GINOMAI I3F	TAKE PLACE	158C
EKEITHEN	FROM THERE	238D

53	METAIRW	GO AWAY	512B
	HOTE 1B	WHEN	592C
	PARABOL8 2	PARABLE	617D
	TELEW 1	FINISH	818C
54	ANTIPATRIS	ANTIPATRIS	75A
	DUNAMIS 4	MIRACLE	207B
	EKPL8SSW 2	BE AMAZED	243C
	PATRIS 2	FATHERLAND	642C
	POTHEN 2	FROM WHERE	686D
	SOPHIA 3A	WISDOM	767B
	SUNAGWG8 2A		790C
		PLACE OF ASSEMBLY	
	HWSTE 2A8	THEREFORE	908C
55	ADELPHOS 1	BROTHER	15D
	IAKWBOS 3	JAMES	368C
	IOUDAS 8	JUDAS	381A
	IWS8S 1	JOSES	386B
	IWS8PH 5	JOSEPH	386C
	KAI 11A	AND	392C
	LEGW 113	CALL	471B
	MARIA 1	MARY	492D
	M8T8R 1	MOTHER	521D
	SIMWN 3	SIMON	758C
	TEKTWN	CARPENTER	816D
55F	HOUTOS 1A«	THIS	600D
56	ADELPH8 1	SISTER	15C
	EIMI 1119	TO BE	224D
	OUN 1C«	THEREFORE	597C
	POTHEN 2	FROM WHERE	686D
	PROS 1117	TOWARD	718A
57	ATIMOS 1	DISHONORED	119D
	OIKIA 2	HOUSEHOLD	560B
	PATRIS 2	FATHERLAND	642C
	PROPH8T8S 3	PROPHET	731A
	PROPH8T8S 4	PROPHET	731B
	SKANDALIZW 1B	CAUSE TO FALL	760B
58	APISTIA 2A	UNBELIEF	84D
	DIA 8I11	BECAUSE OF	180A
	DUNAMIS 4	MIRACLE	207B
	POIEW 118P	DO	687C

MATTHEW 14

1	AKO8 2A	REPORT	30C
	H8RWD8S 2	HEROD	349B
	KAIROS 1	TIME	395D
	HO,H8,TO 1111H	THE	553B
	TETRARCH8S	TETRARCH	821D
2	APO IV1A8	FROM	86D
	AUTOS 2	THEY	122D
	BAPTIST8S	BAPTIST	132B
	DIA 8I12	THEREFORE	180B
	DUNAMIS 1	POWER	206D
	EGEIRW 2C	RISE	214A
	EN 15A	IN	258D
	ENERGEW 1A	WORK	264D
	NEKROS 2A	DEAD	537A
	PAIS 1AY	SERVANT	609D
3	APOTITH8MI 2	PUT AWAY	100D
	GUN8 2	WIFE	167C
	DEW 1B	BIND	176D
	H8RWD8S 2	HEROD	349B
	HERODIAS	HERODIAS	349C

3	HERODIAS	HERODIAS	349C
	KRATEW 1A	ARREST	449C
	TITH8MI 111B	PUT	824B
	PHILIPPOS 2	PHILIP	868A
	PHILIPPOS 1	PHILIP	868A
	*PHULAK8 3	GUARD	875D
4	EXESTI 1	IT IS POSSIBLE	274D
	ECHW 128«	HAVE	332C
5	APOKTEINW 1A	KILL	93B
	ECHW 15	CONSIDER	333D
	OCHLOS 2	CROWD	605D
	PROPH8T8S 2	PROPHET	731A
	PHOBEW 18«	BE AFRAID	871A
6	AGW 4	SPEND	14C
	ARESKW 2A	BE PLEASING	105A
	GENESIA	BIRTHDAY CELEBRATION	153D
	H8RWD8S 2	HEROD	349B
	HERODIAS	HERODIAS	349C
	THUGAT8R 1	DAUGHTER	365B
	MESOS 2	THE MIDDLE	508D
	ORCHEOMAI	DANCE	587A
6FF	SALWM8	SALOME	748C
7	DIDWMI 1A	GIVE	191D
	HOTHEN 3	FROM WHICH	558A
	HOMOLOGEW 1	PROMISE	571A
	HORKOS	OATH	585B
8	BAPTIST8S	BAPTIST	132B
	EPI 111A«	ON	286C
	HINA 1112	IN ORDER THAT	379A
	KEPHAL8 1A	HEAD	431A
	M8T8R 1	MOTHER	521D
	PINAX	PLATTER	664B
	PROBIBAZW	BRING FORWARD	710B
	PH8MI 18P	SAY	864A
9	BASILEUS 1	KING	135D
	H8RWD8S 2	HEROD	349B
	KELEUW	COMMAND	428C
	LUPEW 2A	GRIEVE	483A
	HORKOS	OATH	585B
	SUNANAKEIMAI	EAT WITH	792A
9FF	KAI 12B	AND	393A
10	APOKEPHALIZW	BEHEAD	92C
	PEMPW 1	SEND	647C
	PHULAK8 3	GUARD	875C
11	EPI 111A«	ON	286C
	KEPHAL8 1A	HEAD	431A
	KORASION	GIRL	445B
	M8T8R 1	MOTHER	521D
	PINAX	PLATTER	664B
11A	PHERW 4A«	BEAR	863A
11B	PHERW 4A«	BEAR	863A
12	AIRW 3	CARRY	24A
	APAGGELLW 1	REPORT	78C
	ERCHOMAI 11A(	COME	310D
	THAPTW	BURY	352C
	MATH8T8S 2A	DISCIPLE	486D
	*PTWMA	CORPSE	735B
	SWMA 1A	BODY	806D
13	AKOLOUTHEW 2	ACCOMPANY	30D
	AKOUW 3A	LEARN	31D
	ANACHWREW 2B	WITHDRAW	63A
	EKEITHEN	FROM THERE	238D
	ER8MOS 1A	ABANDONED	308D

13	IDIOS 4	PRIVATELY 371A	20	PL8R8S IA8	FULL 675C
	PEZ8	BY LAND 644B		CHORTAZW 2A	FEED 892B
	PEZOS	GOING BY LAND 644B	21	AN8R I	MAN 65D
	POLIS I	CITY 692A		ESTHIW ID	EAT 313A
	TOPOS IC	PLACE 830B		PAIDION 2A	CHILD 609B
14	ARRWSTEW	SICK 109B		PENTAKISCHILIOI	FIVE THOUSAND 648C
	ARRWSTOS	SICK 109B		CHWRIS 2AY	APART 899A
	AUTOS 3F8	(OBLIQUE CASE) 123B		HWSEI 2	AS 907D
	EXERCHOMAI IA8	GO OUT 274A	22	ANAGKAZW 2	INVITE 51D
	EPI IIIBY	ON 287B		APOLUW 2B	SEND AWAY 96B
	OCHLOS I	CROWD 605C		EMBAINW	GO IN 253C
	POLUS IIB«	MANY 694C		HEWS IIIBY	UNTIL 335C
	*SPLAGCHNIZOMAI	HAVE PITY 770B		HOS,H8,HO IIIF	(REL PRON) 589A
15	AGORAZW I	BUY 12C		PERAN I ON THE OTHER SIDE	649C
	APERCHOMAI 2	GO 83D		PLOION 2	SHIP 679B
	APOLUW 2B	SEND AWAY 96B		PROAGW 2B	LEAD 709A
	BRWMA I	FOOD 147C	23	ANABAINW IA«	GO UP 49C
	GINOMAI IIBY	COME ABOUT 157C		GINOMAI IIBY	COME ABOUT 157C
	HEAUTOU I	ONESELF 211A		IDIOS 4	PRIVATELY 371A
	ER8MOS IA	ABANDONED 308D		MONOS IA«	ONLY 529B
	8D8 IB	ALREADY 344D		HO,H8,TO IIIA«	THE 552B
	HINA IIC	IN ORDER THAT 377C		OROS	MOUNTAIN 586B
	KWM8 I	VILLAGE 462D		OPSIOS 2	LATE 606C
	OPSIOS 2	LATE 606C		PROSEUCHOMAI	PRAY 720D
	PARERCHOMAI IA8	GO BY 631B	24	ANEMOS IA	WIND 64A
	TOPOS IC	PLACE 830B		APECHW 2	BE DISTANT 84B
	HWRA I	TIME OF DAY 904B		BASANIZW 3	TORMENT 134B
16	DIDWMI 2	GIVE 192C		ENANTIOS I	OPPOSITE 261C
	ESTHIW ID	EAT 313A		8D8 IB	ALREADY 344D
	ECHW I2I	HAVE 333C		KUMA	WAVE 458B
	SU IC	YOU 779D		MESOS 3B	THE MIDDLE 509A
	CHREIA I	NEED 893B		STADION I	STADE 771C
17	ARTOS IA	BREAD 110A		HUPO IA8	BY 850D
	DUO 4	TWO 208C	24FF	THALASSA 2	LAKE 351A
	ECHW I2D	HAVE 332D	25	EPI IIIIA«	ACROSS 287D
	ICHTHUS	FISH 385A		NUX IA	NIGHT 548C
	LEGW IIIB	ANSWER 470C		PERIPATEW IC	GO ABOUT 654D
	OPSARION	FISH 606B		TETARTOS	FOURTH 821A
	PENTE	FIVE 648D		PHULAK8 4	GUARD 875D
	HWDE 2A	HERE 903D	26	APO V3	WITH 87B
18	EIPON 3A	SAY 225C		EPI IIA«	ON 285C
	PHERW 4A«	BEAR 863A		KRAZW I	CRY OUT 448D
	HWDE I	HERE 903B		PERIPATEW IC	GO ABOUT 654D
19	ANABLEPW I	LOOK UP 50C		TARASSW 2	STIR UP 813A
	ANAKLINW 2	RECLINE 55D		PHANTASMA	APPARITION 861B
	*ARTOS IA	BREAD 110A		PHOBOS 2A«	FEAR 871C
	DIDWMI 2	GIVE 192C	27	EGW	I 216A
	EULOGEW I	SPEAK WELL 322C		EIMI II5	TO BE 223C
	EULOGEW 2B	BLESS 322D		EUTHUS	IMMEDIATELY 321B
	ICHTHUS	FISH 385A		THARSEW	BE CHEERFUL 352C
	KELEUW	COMMAND 428C		LALEW 3	SPEAK 465A
	KLAW	BREAK 434D		M8 AIII3B	NOT 518C
	MATH8T8S 2B«	DISCIPLE 487A		PHOBEW IA	BE AFRAID 870C
	OURANOS 2A	HEAVEN 599B	28	APOKRINOMAI I	ANSWER 92D
	OPSARION	FISH 606B		ERCHOMAI IIA8	COME 310C
	PENTE	FIVE 648D		KELEUW	COMMAND 428C
	CHORTOS	GRASS 892B		KURIOS 2C8	LORD 460D
20	AIRW 3	CARRY 24A		SU 2	YOU 780A
	ESTHIW ID	EAT 313A	28F	EPI IIIIA«	ACROSS 287D
	KLASMA	FRAGMENT 434B	28F	HUDWR I	WATER 840C
	KOPHINOS	BASKET 448C	29	EIPON 2B	SAY 225C
	PAS 2AY	ALL 638B		KATABAINW IA«	COME DOWN 409B
	PERISSEUW IA«	BE LEFT OVER 656C		PERIPATEW IC	GO ABOUT 654D

30 ANEMOS IA WIND 64A
   ARCHW 2Aα BEGIN 113A
   BLEPW 7A SEE 143B
   ISCHUROS 2 STRONG 384A
   KATAPONTIZW BE SUNK 417D
   KRAZW 2A CALL 448D
   KURIOS 2Cβ LORD 460D
   SWZW IA SAVE 805D
   PHOBEW IA BE AFRAID 870B
31 DISTAZW I DOUBT 199A
   EIS 4F (PURPOSE) 228D
   EKTEINW I STRETCH OUT 244D
   EPILAMBANOMAI I GRASP 295A
   EUTHEWS IMMEDIATELY 320D
   OLIGOPISTOS OF LITTLE FAITH 566B
32 ANABAINW IAα GO UP 49D
   ANEMOS IA WIND 64A
   KOPAZW ABATE 444A
   PLOION 2 SHIP 679B
33 AL8THWS I TRULY 36D
   LEGW I8A SAY 470B
   PROSKUNEW 5 DO REVERENCE 724B
   HUIOS 2B SON 842C
34 GENN8SARET GENNESARET 155A
   G8 4 LAND 156C
   DIAPERAW CROSS 186C
35 AN8R 4 MAN 66B
   APOSTELLW IBβ SEND AWAY 98A
   KAKWS I BADLY 399B
   HOLOS 2A WHOLE 567C
   PERICHWROS NEIGHBORING 659B
   PROSPHERW IA BRING (TO) 727A
   TOPOS IA PLACE 830A
36 HAPTW 2B TOUCH 102D
   DIASWZW SAVE 188B
   HINA IIIAγ IN ORDER THAT 378B
   KRASPEDON I EDGE 449B
   MONOS 2A ONLY 529D
   HOSOS 2 HOW GREAT 590C
   PARAKALEW 3 IMPLORE 622D

                MATTHEW 15

 1 GRAMMATEUS 2 SCRIBES 165A
   LEGW IIIA ASK 470C
   PHARISAIOS PHARISEE 861C
 2 AN 3A (PARTICLE) 48B
   ESTHIW IA EAT 312D
   MATH8T8S 2Bα DISCIPLE 487A
   NIPTW 2B WASH 542B
   PARADOSIS 2 TRADITION 621A
   PRESBUTEROS IB OLDER 706C
2F DIA BII2 WHY 180B
 3 DIA BIII BECAUSE OF 180A
   PARABAINW 2A GO ASIDE 616D
   PARADOSIS 2 TRADITION 621A
   SU IC YOU 779D
 4 ENTELLW COMMAND 267D
   THANATOS IBα DEATH 351C
   KAKOLOGEW INSULT 398A
   TELEUTAW DIE 818B
   TIMAW 2 HONOR 824D
4A M8T8R I MOTHER 521D

4B M8T8R I MOTHER 521D
 5 DWRON 2 GIFT 210C
   EK 3Eα BY 234C
   WPHELEW IA HELP 909A
 6 AKUROW MAKE VOID 33D
   LOGOS IBα COMMAND 479A
   M8 D2 NOT 519C
   NOMOS 3 LAW 544C
   PARADOSIS 2 TRADITION 621A
   TIMAW 2 HONOR 824D
 7 8SAIAS ISAIAH 349C
   KALWS 4B WELL 402B
   PROPH8TEUW 3 PROPHESY 730C
   HUPOKRIT8S HYPOCRITE 853A
 8 APECHW 2 BE DISTANT 84C
   EGGIZW I APPROACH 212D
   KARDIA IBα HEART 404C
   LAOS 3A PEOPLE 468A
   HO,H8,TO IIIH THE 553B
   PORRW I FAR AWAY 700C
   TIMAW 2 HONOR 824D
   CHEILOS I LIP 887C
 9 ANTHRWPOS IAβ MAN 67C
   DIDASKALIA 2 TEACHING 190C
   DIDASKW 2B TEACH 191A
   ENTALMA COMMANDMENT 267D
   MAT8N IN VAIN 497A
   SEBW 2A WORSHIP 753C
10 AKOUW IC HEAR 31D
   OCHLOS 2 CROWD 605D
   PROSKALEW IA SUMMON 722C
   SUNI8MI UNDERSTAND 797D
   SUNI8MI UNDERSTAND 798A
11 ANTHRWPOS 3B MAN 68C
   EISERCHOMAI 2B COME 232B
   EKPOREUOMAI 2 GO OUT 244A
   KOINOW IA DEFILE 439B
   KOINWNEW 3 SHARE 439D
   HO,H8,TO IIIAβ THE 552D
11A STOMA IA MOUTH 777B
11B STOMA IA MOUTH 777B
12 LOGOS IAγ WORD 478C
   OIDA IE KNOW 558C
   PROSERCHOMAI I APPROACH 720A
   SKANDALIZW 2 CAUSE TO FALL 760B
   PHARISAIOS PHARISEE 861C
13 EKRIZOW I UPROOT 244B
   OURANIOS HEAVENLY 598A
   PAS IAα EVERY EACH 636C
   PAT8R 3Dα FATHER 641D
   PHUTEIA THE PLANT 878A
   PHUTEUW PLANT 878A
14 AMPHOTEROI I BOTH 47A
   APHI8MI 4 TOLERATE 125D
   BOTHROS PIT 144B
   BOTHUNOS PIT 144B
   EAN IIA IF 210B
   HOD8GEW I LEAD 555D
   HOD8GOS 2 LEADER 556A
   PIPTW IA FALL 665A
   SPHALLW STUMBLE 803D
   TUPHLOS IB BLIND 838C
   TUPHLOS 2Aα BLIND 838C

15	APOKRINOMAI 2	CONTINUE	93A
	PARABOL8 2	PARABLE	617D
	PHRAZW	EXPLAIN	873C
16	AKM8N	STILL	30B
	ASUNETOS 1	FOOLISH	118B
	EIPON 2B	SAY	225C
	SU 1C	YOU	779D
17	APHEDRWN	LATRINE	124B
	EISPOREUOMAI 1	GO	232D
	EKBALLW 3	TAKE OUT	237B
	KOILIA 1	BELLY	436B
	NOEW 1B	UNDERSTAND	542C
	PAS 1Cγ	WHOEVER	637C
	STOMA 1A	MOUTH	777B
	CHWREW 1A	GO	897D
18	ANTHRWPOS 3B	MAN	68C
	EKPOREUOMAI 2	GO OUT	244A
	EXERCHOMAI 2Bβ	GO OUT	274D
	KAKEINOS 2A	AND HE	397C
	KARDIA 1Bα	HEART	404C
	KOINOW 1A	DEFILE	439B
	KOINWNEW 3	SHARE	439D
	STOMA 1A	MOUTH	777B
19	BLASPH8MIA 1	SLANDER	142C
	DIALOGISMOS 1	THOUGHT	185B
	EXERCHOMAI 2Bβ	GO OUT	274D
	KARDIA 1Bβ	HEART	404C
	KLOP8	THEFT	437D
	MOICHEIA	ADULTERY	528A
	PON8ROS 1Bβ	WICKED	697C
	PORNEIA 1	PROSTITUTION	699D
	PHONOS	MURDER	872C
	PSEUDOMARTURIA	FALSE WITNESS	900A
20	ANIPTOS	UNWASHED	69A
	ESTHIW 1D	EAT	313B
	KOINOW 1A	DEFILE	439B
	KOINWNEW 3	SHARE	439D
	HO,H8,TO II4A	THE	553D
21	ANACHWREW 2B	WITHDRAW	63A
	EXERCHOMAI 1Aα	GO OUT	274A
	MEROS 1Bγ	PART	507A
	SIDWN	SIDON	757C
	TUROS	TYRE	838C
22	DAIMONIZOMAI		168A
	BE POSSESSED BY A DEMON		
	DAUID	DAVID	170B
	ELEEW	HAVE MERCY	249A
	THUGAT8R 1	DAUGHTER	365B
	KAKWS 1	BADLY	399B
	KRAZW 2A	CALL	448D
	KURIOS 2Cβ	LORD	460D
	HORION	BOUNDARY	584D
	HORION	BOUNDARY	585A
	HUIOS 2A	SON	842A
	CHANANAIOS	CANAANITE	883C
23	APOKRINOMAI 1	ANSWER	92D
	APOLUW 2B	SEND AWAY	96B
	ERWTAW 2	ASK	312A
	KRAZW 2A	CALL	448D
	LOGOS 1Aα	WORD	478B
	OPISTHEN 2A	FROM BEHIND	578B
24	APOKRINOMAI 1	ANSWER	92D
	APOLLUMI 2B	BE LOST	95A

24	APOSTELLW 1Bα	SEND AWAY	98A
	APOSTELLW 1C	SEND AWAY	98B
	ISRA8L 1	ISRAEL	382B
	OIKOS 3	NATION	563D
	PROBATON 2	SHEEP	710B
25	BO8THEW 2	AID	144A
	KURIOS 2Cβ	LORD	460D
26	ARTOS 1A	BREAD	110A
	BALLW 1B	THROW	130C
	EXESTI 1	IT IS POSSIBLE	274D
	KALOS 3B	GOOD	401C
	KALOS 3C	GOOD	401D
	LAMBANW 1A	TAKE	465B
26F	KUNARION	DOG	458C
27	APO I6	FROM	86B
	APO IV1Aα	FROM	86D
	GAR 1E	FOR	151C
	EIPON 3A	SAY	225C
	ESTHIW 1Bα	EAT	313A
	KURIOS 2Cβ	LORD	460D
	NAI 2	CERTAINLY	534D
	PIPTW 1A	FALL	665A
	TRAPEZA 2	TABLE	832A
	PSICHION	CRUMB	901B
	PSIX	BIT	901B
28	APOKRINOMAI 1	ANSWER	92D
	GINOMAI I3Bβ	TAKE PLACE	158A
	GUN8 1	WOMAN	167C
	THUGAT8R 1	DAUGHTER	365B
	IAOMAI 1	HEAL	369A
	MEGAS 2Aγ	GREAT	499A
	PISTIS 2Bα	FAITH	668D
	W 1	O	903B
	HWRA 3	TIME OF DAY	905A
	HWS 12B	AS	905C
29	ANABAINW 1Aα	GO UP	49C
	GALILAIA	GALILEE	149D
	EIS 1Aα	INTO	227C
	ERCHOMAI I1Aβ	COME	310C
	THALASSA 2	LAKE	351A
	KATH8MAI 2	SIT DOWN	390C
	METABAINW 1Aα	PASS OVER	511D
	OROS	MOUNTAIN	586B
	PARA III1Bβ	ALONG	616A
30	HETEROS 1Bβ	ANOTHER	315B
	ECHW 13	HAVE	333C
	META AII1B	WITH	509D
	OCHLOS 1	CROWD	605D
	PARA III1C	ALONG	616A
	RIPTW 2	THROW	744A
	CHWLOS	LAME	897B
30A	POLUS II1Aβ	MANY	694B
30F	KULLOS	CRIPPLED	458B
30F	KWPHOS 1	MUTE	463A
31	BLEPW 1A	SEE	143A
	BLEPW 2	SEE	143A
	DOXAZW 1	PRAISE	203C
	THAUMAZW 1Aα	WONDER	352D
	THEOS 3C	GOD	358A
	ISRA8L 2	ISRAEL	382B
	LALEW 2Aα	SPEAK	464B
	PERIPATEW 1C	GO ABOUT	655A
	HUGI8S 1A	HEALTHY	840A

31 CHWLOS LAME 897B
   HWSTE 2Aβ THEREFORE 908C
32 APOLUW 2B SEND AWAY 96B
   EIPON 2B SAY 225C
   EKLUW BECOME WEARY 242C
   EPI IIIIBε TOWARD 289A
   ESTHIW IA EAT 312C
   ECHW I2D HAVE 332D
   8D8 IA ALREADY 344C
   H8MERA 2 DAY 346D
   H8MERA 2 DAY 347C
   THELW 2 WISH 355D
   M8POTE 2Bα (NEG PARTICLE) 521A
   N8STIS HUNGRY 540C
   HODOS IB WAY 556C
   PROSMENW IAα REMAIN 724D
   SPLAGCHNIZOMAI HAVE PITY 770B
   TIS, TI IBζ WHICH 827B
33 ER8MIA DESERT 308D
   LEGW IIIB ANSWER 470C
   OCHLOS I CROWD 605C
   POTHEN I FROM WHERE 686C
   TOSOUTOS IB SO GREAT 831B
   CHORTAZW 2A FEED 892B
   HWSTE 2Aβ THEREFORE 908C
33F ARTOS IA BREAD 110A
34 EIPON 3A SAY 225C
   HEPTA SEVEN 306B
   ECHW I2D HAVE 332D
   ICHTHUDION LITTLE FISH 385A
   LEGW IIIA ASK 470C
   OLIGOS IA FEW 566B
   POSOS 2A HOW GREAT 701B
35 ANAPIPTW I RECLINE 59A
   G8 2 GROUND 156C
   EPI IIIIAβ ON 288A
   KELEUW COMMAND 428D
   OCHLOS I CROWD 605C
   PARAGGELLW GIVE ORDERS 618C
36 ARTOS IA BREAD 110A
   DIDWMI 2 GIVE 192C
   EUCHARISTEW 2 GIVE THANKS 328C
   ICHTHUS FISH 385A
   KLAW BREAK 434D
36F HEPTA SEVEN 306B
37 AIRW 3 CARRY 24A
   KLASMA FRAGMENT 434B
   PAS 2Aγ ALL 638B
   PERISSEUW IAα BE LEFT OVER 656C
   PL8R8S IAβ FULL 675C
   SPURIS BASKET 771C
   CHORTAZW 2A FEED 892B
38 AN8R I MAN 65D
   ESTHIW ID EAT 313A
   PAIDION 2A CHILD 609B
   TETRAKISCHILIOI FOUR THOUSAND 821B
   CHWRIS 24γ APART 899A
39 APOLUW 2B SEND AWAY 96B
   EMBAINW GO IN 253C
   MAGADAN MAGADAN 485B
   HORION BOUNDARY 584D
   PLOION 2 SHIP 679B

MATTHEW 16

1 EPERWTAW 2 ASK 285A
  EPIDEIKNUMI I SHOW 291D
  OURANOS 2A HEAVEN 599B
  PEIRAZW 2C TRY 646A
  SADDOUKAIOS SADDUCEE 747A
  S8MEION 2A SIGN 755C
  PHARISAIOS PHARISEE 861C
2 GINOMAI IIBγ COME ABOUT 157C
  EUDIA I FAIR WEATHER 319B
  OURANOS ID HEAVEN 598D
  OPSIOS 2 LATE 606C
2F PURRAZW BE (FIERY) RED 738D
3 DIAKRINW ICβ JUDGE 184B
  DUNAMAI 2 ABLE 206B
  KAIROS 4 TIME 396B
  OURANOS ID HEAVEN 598D
  PROSWPON ID FACE 729A
  PRWI EARLY 732A
  S8MEION I SIGN 755B
  S8MERON TODAY 756B
  STUGNAZW 2B BECOME GLOOMY 779C
  HUPOKRIT8S HYPOCRITE 853A
  CHEIMWN I STORMY WEATHER 888A
4 APERCHOMAI IA GO AWAY 83D
  GENEA 2 GENERATION 153B
  EI VI8A IF NOT 219A
  EPIZ8TEW 2B STRIVE FOR 292D
  IWNAS 2 JONAH 386A
  KATALEIPW IA LEAVE BEHIND 414C
  MOICHALIS 2A ADULTEROUS 528A
  PON8ROS IBα WICKED 697C
  S8MEION 2A SIGN 755C
5 ARTOS IA BREAD 110A
  EPILANTHANOMAI I FORGET 295B
  ERCHOMAI IIAβ COME 310C
  MATH8T8S 2Bα DISCIPLE 487A
  PERAN I ON THE OTHER SIDE 649C
6 ZUM8 2 LEAVEN 340C
  HORAW 2B SEE 582B
  PROSECHW IB PAY ATTENTION TO 721D
  SADDOUKAIOS SADDUCEE 747A
  PHARISAIOS PHARISEE 861C
7 ARTOS IA BREAD 110A
7F DIALOGIZOMAI I CONSIDER 185A
8 GINWSKW 4B PERCEIVE 160B
  OLIGOPISTOS OF LITTLE FAITH 566B
  HOTI IC THAT 593B
8FF ARTOS IA BREAD 110A
9 KOPHINOS BASKET 448C
  MN8MONEUW IB REMEMBER 527A
  NOEW IE UNDERSTAND 542D
  OUDE I AND NOT 595D
  OUPW NOT YET 598A
  PENTAKISCHILIOI FIVE THOUSAND 648C
  PENTE FIVE 648D
  POSOS 2A HOW GREAT 701B
10 HEPTA SEVEN 306B
   KOPHINOS BASKET 448C
   POSOS 2A HOW GREAT 701B
   SPURIS BASKET 771C
   TETRAKISCHILIOI FOUR THOUSAND 821B

11	ZUM8 2	LEAVEN 340C
	NOEW 1B	UNDERSTAND 542C
	PWS 1B	HOW 739C
11F	PROSECHW 1B	721D
	PAY ATTENTION TO	
11F	SADDOUKAIOS	SADDUCEE 747A
11F	PHARISAIOS	PHARISEE 861C
12	DIDACH8 2	TEACHING 191B
	ZUM8 1	LEAVEN 340C
	SUNI8MI	UNDERSTAND 798A
13	ERWTAW 1	ASK 312A
	KAISAREIA 1	CAESAREA 396D
	LEGW 11B8	SAY 469C
	MEROS 1By	PART 507A
	TIS, TI 1Aα	WHICH 826C
	HUIOS 2C	SON 843A
	PHILIPPOS 1	PHILIP 868A
14	BAPTIST8S	BAPTIST 132B
	EIPON 3A	SAY 225C
	HEIS 3A	SOMEONE 230D
	HETEROS 1B6	ANOTHER 315C
	8LIAS	ELIJAH 345D
	MEN 1C	(PARTICLE) 504A
	HO,H8,TO 12	THE 552A
	PROPH8T8S 1	PROPHET 730D
	PROPH8T8S 3	PROPHET 731A
15	EIMI 116C	TO BE 223C
	LEGW 11B8	SAY 469C
	LEGW 111A	ASK 470C
16	APOKRINOMAI 2	BEGIN 93A
	ZAW 1Aε	LIVE 336D
	PETROS	PETER 661A
	SU 1C	YOU 779D
	SWZW 2Aα	SAVE 806A
	HUIOS 2B	SON 842C
	CHRISTOS 1	ANOINTED ONE 895B
17	HAIMA 1A	BLOOD 22A
	APOKALUPTW 2	REVEAL 91C
	BARIWNA	BAR=JONA 133B
	IWNAS 2	JONAH 386A
	MAKARIOS 1B	BLESSED 488A
	OURANOS 2A	HEAVEN 599B
	PAT8R 3Dα	FATHER 641D
	SARX 3	BODY 751B
17FF	PETRA 1B	ROCK 660B
17=19	PETROS	PETER 660D
17=19	PETROS	PETER 661B
18	HAD8S 1	HADES 16C
	DE 4B	BUT, AND 170D
	EKKL8SIA 4D	CHURCH 240C
	EPI 111A8	ON 286C
	KAGW 3B	I 387A
	KATISCHUW 2	425B
	WIN A VICTORY OVER	
	OIKODOMEW 2	BUILD 560D
	HOUTOS 2A	THIS 601D
	PETRA 1B	ROCK 660B
	PETROS	PETER 660C
	PUL8 1	GATE 736C
	SU 1C	YOU 779D
19	BASILEIA 3G	KINGDOM 135A
	G8 5A	EARTH 156D
	DEW 4	BIND 177A

19	DIDWMI 3	GIVE 192C
	KLEIS 1	KEY 435A
	LUW 5	ABOLISH 485C
	OURANOS 3	HEAVEN 599D
20	DIASTELLW	ORDER 187D
	EPITIMAW 1	REBUKE 303B
	HINA 111A6	IN ORDER THAT 378B
	HINA 111A6	IN ORDER THAT 378B
	M8DEIS 2A	NO 520A
	CHRISTOS 1	ANOINTED ONE 895B
21	APO V6	BY 87D
	APOKTEINW 1A	KILL 93B
	ARCHIEREUS 1B	HIGH PRIEST 112B
	ARCHW 2C	BEGIN 113B
	GRAMMATEUS 2	SCRIBES 165A
	DEIKNUMI 2	EXPLAIN 171D
	EGEIRW 2C	RISE 214A
	H8MERA 2	DAY 346D
	HO,H8,TO 1110A	THE 555A
	PASCHW 3B	ENDURE 639D
	POLUS 12Bα	MANY 695A
	PRESBUTEROS 2A8	OLDER 706D
	TOTE 1A	AT THAT TIME 831C
	TRITOS 1	THIRD 834B
22	EIMI 14	TO BE 222C
	EPITIMAW 1	REBUKE 303B
	HILEWS	MERCIFUL 376D
	KURIOS 2C8	LORD 460D
	M8 D2	NOT 519C
	PROSLAMBANW 2A	TAKE 724C
23	THEOS 3Fy	GOD 358B
	HO,H8,TO 117	THE 554D
	OPISW 2Aα	BEHIND 578C
	SATAN	ADVERSARY 752C
	SKANDALON 2	TRAP 760C
	STREPHW 2Aα	TURN 778D
	HUPAGW 1	GO AWAY 844B
	PHRONEW 2	THINK 874B
24	AIRW 2	LIFT UP 24A
	APARNEOMAI	DENY 80B
	HEAUTOU 1	ONESELF 211A
	EI VII	219B
	ERCHOMAI 11	GO 311D
	OPISW 2A8	AFTER 578D
	STAUROS 2	THE CROSS 772C
25	APOLLUMI 1B	LOSE 94C
	HENEKA	BECAUSE OF 264B
	THELW 1	WISH 355C
	SWZW 1A	SAVE 805D
	PSUCH8 1D	SOUL LIFE 902B
25A	PSUCH8 1D	SOUL LIFE 902B
25B	PSUCH8 1D	SOUL LIFE 902B
25=7	GAR 1C	FOR 151B
26	ANTHRWPOS 3Ay	MAN 68B
	ANTALLAGMA	GIVEN IN EXCHANGE 72B
	GAR 1F	WHAT 151C
	DIDWMI 4	GIVE 192D
	Z8MIOW 1	SUFFER DAMAGE 339A
	8 1D6	OR 343B
	KERDAINW 1A	TO GAIN 430C
	KOSMOS 6	WORLD 447C
	HOLOS 2B	WHOLE 567D
	OPHELOS	BENEFIT 604A

26	WPHELEW IA	HELP	909A
26A	PSUCH8 IC	SOUL LIFE	902A
26B	PSUCH8 IC	SOUL LIFE	902A
27	AGGELOS 2A	ANGEL	7D
	APODIDWMI 3	RECOMPENSE	90A
	HEKASTOS 2	EACH	236A
	EN I4B	IN	258B
	ERCHOMAI IIAη	COME	311A
	KATA II5Aβ	ACCORDING TO	408A
	MELLW IC6	IS DESTINED	502C
	META AIIIA	WITH	509D
	PAT8R 3Dα	FATHER	641D
	PRAXIS I	ACTING	704C
	TOTE 2	AT THAT TIME	831D
27F	HUIOS 2C	SON	843A
28	GEUOMAI 2 COME TO KNOW SOMETH		156A
	EIDON IB	SEE	219D
	EIMI II	TO BE	222B
	EN I4Cβ	IN	258C
	ERCHOMAI IIAη	COME	311A
	THANATOS IA	DEATH	351B
	HIST8MI II2Bα	BEING	383C
	M8 DIA	NOT	519B
	HOSTIS 2A	WHOEVER	591A
	HWDE 2A	HERE	903D

MATTHEW 17

I	ANAGW I	LEAD	52D
	ANAPHERW I	BRING	62C
	HEX	SIX	270D
	H8MERA 2	DAY	347B
	IAKWBOS I	JAMES	368B
	IDIOS 4	PRIVATELY	371A
	IWAN(N)8S 2	JOHN	385C
	META BIII	AFTER	511B
	OROS	MOUNTAIN	586B
	PARALAMBANW I	TAKE	624D
	HUPS8LOS I	HIGH	857C
2	EMPROSTHEN 2C	IN FRONT	256C
	H8LIOS	THE SUN	346B
	HIMATION I	GARMENT	377A
	LAMPW IB	SHINE OUT	467B
	LEUKOS I	SHINING	473C
	METAMORPHOW I	TRANSFORM	513A
	PROSWPON IA	FACE	728A
	PHWS IA	LIGHT	879D
3	META AII3B	WITH	510D
	HORAW IA6	SEE	582A
	SULLALEW	TALK	784B
3F	8LIAS	ELIJAH	345D
3F	MWUS8S	MOSES	533D
4	EIMI II9A	TO BE	223D
	HEIS 5B	ONE	231B
	KALOS 3A	GOOD	401C
	KALOS 3C	GOOD	401D
	POIEW IIAα	DO	687A
	SK8N8	TENT	762A
4A	HWDE 2A	HERE	903D
4B	HWDE 2A	HERE	903D
5	AGAP8TOS I	BELOVED	6C
	AKOUW 4	LISTEN	32A
	EKLEGOMAI 4	CHOOSE	242A

5	EPISKIAZW 2	COVER	298D
	ETI IAβ	STILL	315D
	EUDOKEW 2A	WELL PLEASED	319C
	IDOU IBα	BEHOLD	371C
	LALEW 2Aγ	SPEAK	464B
	NEPHEL8	CLOUD	538D
	HOUTOS IAα	THIS	600D
	HUIOS 2B	SON	842C
	PHWN8 2D	VOICE	879B
	PHWS IA	LIGHT	879D
	PHWTEINOS	SHINING	880D
6	EPI IIIIAβ	ON	288A
	PIPTW IBα	FALL	665B
	PROSWPON IA	FACE	728B
	SPHODRA	GREATLY	803D
	PHOBEW IA	BE AFRAID	870B
7	HAPTW 2B	TOUCH	102C
	M8 AIII3B	NOT	518C
	PHOBEW IA	BE AFRAID	870C
8	EPAIRW I	LOOK UP	281C
	MONOS IAγ	ONLY	529C
	OUDEIS 2A	NO ONE	596B
9	ANIST8MI 2A	RISE	69C
	EK 2	AWAY FROM	233D
	ENTELLW	COMMAND	267D
	HEWS IIIBα	UNTIL	335C
	M8DEIS 2A	NO	520A
	NEKROS 2A	DEAD	537A
	HORAMA I	VISION	580D
	HOS,H8,HO IIIF	(REL PRON)	589A
	HUIOS 2C	SON	843A
10	DEI I	IT IS NECESSARY	171A
	EPERWTAW IA	ASK	285A
	ERCHOMAI IIAθ	COME	311A
	OUN ICα	THEREFORE	597B
	PRWTOS 2A	FIRST	733C
10FF	8LIAS	ELIJAH	345D
11	APOKATHIST8MI I	RESTORE	91B
	ERCHOMAI IIAθ	COME	311A
	ERCHOMAI I2C	COME	311D
	PRWTOS 2A	FIRST	733C
12	EN I2	IN	258A
	EPIGINWSKW IC	ACKNOWLEDGE	291A
	ERCHOMAI IIAθ	COME	311A
	8D8 IB	ALREADY	344D
	THELW I	WISH	355D
	MELLW IC6	IS DESTINED	502C
	HOSOS 2	HOW GREAT	590C
	HOUTW IB	THUS	602C
	PASCHW 3Aβ	SUFFER	639C
	PL8N IB	BUT	675B
	POIEW IIDγ	DO	688D
	HUIOS 2C	SON	843A
	HUPO IB	BY	851A
13	BAPTIST8S	BAPTIST	132B
	EIPON I	SAY	225C
	SUNI8MI	UNDERSTAND	798A
14	GONUPETEW	KNEEL DOWN	164B
15	ELEEW	HAVE MERCY	249A
	ENIOTE	SOMETIMES	266B
	*KAKWS I	BADLY	399B
	PASCHW 2	BE BADLY OFF	639C
	PIPTW IBα	FALL	665B

15	POLLAKIS		OFTEN	693B
	PUR IA		FIRE	737B
	SEL8NIAZOMAI	BE MOON STRUCK		754B
	HUDWR I		WATER	840C
16	PROSPHERW IA	BRING (TO)		727A
17	ANECHW IA		ENDURE	65A
	APISTOS 2		FAITHLESS	85A
	*GENEA 2		GENERATION	153B
	DIASTREPHW IB		PERVERT	188A
	EIMI III7		TO BE	224D
	EIPON 2B		SAY	225C
	PHERW 4Bⱷ		BEAR	863C
	HWDE I		HERE	903B
	W I		0	903B
17A	HEWS IIIC		UNTIL	335C
17A	POTE		WHEN	701D
17B	HEWS IIIC		UNTIL	335C
17B	POTE		WHEN	701D
18	DAIMONION 2		DEMON	168B
	EXERCHOMAI IAẟ		GO OUT	274A
	EPITIMAW I		REBUKE	303B
	PAIS IAⱺ		CHILD	609C
	HWRA 3		TIME OF DAY	905A
19	DIA BII2		WHY	180B
	EIPON 3B		SAY	225D
	EKBALLW I		DRIVE OUT	237A
	IDIOS 4		PRIVATELY	371A
20	ADUNATEW	BE POWERLESS		18C
	APISTIA 2B		UNBELIEF	85A
	EKEI 2		THERE	238D
	ENTHEN I		FROM	265C
	ECHW I2Eⱷ		HAVE	333A
	KOKKOS I		SEED	441B
	METABAINW IAⱷ		PASS OVER	511D
	OLIGOPISTIA	POVERTY OF FAITH		566B
	OROS		MOUNTAIN	586C
	OUDEIS 2Bⱺ		NOTHING	596C
	PISTIS 2A		FAITH	668D
	PISTIS 20ς		FAITH	669D
	SINAPI		MUSTARD	759A
	HWS II3B		SO	906A
21	GENOS 4		CLASS	155C
	EKPOREUOMAI IA		GO OUT	243D
	N8STEIA 2B		FASTING	540A
	PROSEUCH8 I		PRAYER	720C
22	ANASTREPHW 2A		LIVE	60D
	MELLW ICẟ		IS DESTINED	502C
	PARADIDWMI IB		GIVE OVER	620A
	SUSTREPHW 2	BRING TOGETHER		803A
	HUIOS 2C		SON	843A
	CHEIR 2B		HAND	888D
23	EGEIRW 2C		RISE	214A
	H8MERA 2		DAY	346D
	LUPEW 2A		GRIEVE	483A
	SPHODRA		GREATLY	803D
	TRITOS I		THIRD	834B
24	DIDASKALOS		TEACHER	190D
	DIDRACHMON	DOUBLE DRACHMA		191C
	EIPON 3B		SAY	225D
	KAPHARNAOUM		CAPERNAUM	427C
	LAMBANW ID		RECEIVE	465D
	OU 4C		NO	594D
	PETROS		PETER	660D

24	TELEW 3		PAY	818D
25	BASILEUS I		KING	135C
	DOKEW 3A		SEEM	201B
	8 IAⱷ		OR	342D
	K8NSOS		POLL TAX	431D
	LAMBANW ID		RECEIVE	465D
	LEGW IIIB		ANSWER	470C
	NAI IA		YES	534D
	OIKIA IA		HOUSE	559D
	PROPHTHANW I	ANTICIPATE		731D
	TELOS 3		TAX	819D
25A	TIS, TI IBⱥ		WHICH	826D
25F	ALLOTRIOS IBⱷ			40B
		THE STRANGER		
25F	APO IV2A		FROM	87A
26	ARA 4		THEN	103C
	ELEUTHEROS 2		FREE	250B
27	AGKISTRON I		FISHHOOK	10C
	AIRW IA		LIFT UP	23D
	ANABAINW IAⱷ		GO UP	50A
	ANOIGW IEⱥ		OPEN	70D
	ANTI 3		FOR	73A
	BALLW IB		THROW	130C
	EIS IB		NEAR	227C
	EKEINOS IB		THAT	239A
	HEURISKW IB		FIND	325B
	HINA IIC	IN ORDER THAT		377C
	ICHTHUS		FISH	385A
	M8 AI2		NOT	517C
	POREUW I		PROCEED	699A
	PRWTOS IB		FIRST	733B
	SKANDALIZW 2	CAUSE TO FALL		760B
	STAT8R		THE STATER	772A
	STOMA IC		MOUTH	777C

MATTHEW 18

I	ARA 2		THEN	103B
	BASILEIA 3G		KINGDOM	135B
	LEGW IIIA		ASK	470C
	MEGAS 2Bⱥ		GREAT	499B
	HO,H8,TO IIIH		THE	553B
	OURANOS 3		HEAVEN	599D
	HWRA 3		TIME OF DAY	905A
2	HIST8MI IIAⱥ		PUT	382D
	MESOS 2		THE MIDDLE	508D
	PAIDION 2A		CHILD	609D
3	BASILEIA 3G		KINGDOM	135A
	GINOMAI III		BE	159B
	EAN I3B		IF	210D
	M8 AII		NOT	517C
	PAIDION 3A		CHILD	609B
	STREPHW 2B		TURN	779A
	HWS II3B		SO	906A
3F	BASILEIA 3G		KINGDOM	135B
3F	OURANOS 3		HEAVEN	599D
4	BASILEIA 3G		KINGDOM	135B
	HEAUTOU I		ONESELF	211A
	MEGAS 2Bⱥ		GREAT	499B
	HOSTIS IC		WHOEVER	590D
	HOUTOS IAⱥ		THIS	601B
	TAPEINOW 2B		LOWER	812C
4F	PAIDION 2A		CHILD	609A

5	DECHOMAI I	RECEIVE 176C		10	HORAW 2B	SEE 582B
	EPI II3	ON 287D			PAT8R 3Dα	FATHER 641D
	ONOMA I4Cε	NAME 576D			PROSWPON IB	FACE 728B
	ONOMA II	TITLE 577A		10A	OURANOS 2C	HEAVEN 599C
	TOIOUTOS 2Aβ	SUCH A KIND 829A		10B	OURANOS 2A	HEAVEN 599B
6	EIS 4Cβ	(GOAL) 228C		11	APOLLUMI 2Aα	PERISH 94D
	HEIS IAβ	ONE 230A			SWZW 2Aα	SAVE 806A
	THALASSA IA	SEA 350D			HUIOS 2C	SON 843A
	HINA IIIβ	IN ORDER THAT 378C		12	ANTHRWPOS 3Aα	MAN 68B
	KATAPONTIZW	BE SUNK 417D			APHI8MI 3A	LEAVE 125D
	KREMANNUMI I	HANG 451A			GINOMAI I3Bγ	TAKE PLACE 158A
	MIKROS IB	SMALL 523A			DOKEW 3A	SEEM 201B
	MULOS 2	MILLSTONE 531B			HEIS IAβ	ONE 230A
	ONIKOS	PERTAINING TO A DONKEY 573D			EK 4Aα	FROM 235B
	PELAGOS I	THE OPEN SEA 647A			HEKATON	ONE HUNDRED 236B
	PERI 2Aβ	ABOUT 650D			Z8TEW IAα	SEEK 339A
	PISTEUW 2Aβ	BELIEVE 667B			OROS	MOUNTAIN 586C
	SKANDALIZW IA	CAUSE TO FALL 760B			POREUW I	PROCEED 699B
	SUMPHERW 2A	BETTER 788A			PROBATON I	SHEEP 710A
	TRACH8LOS	NECK 832D			TIS, TI IBα	WHICH 826D
7	ANAGK8 I	NECESSITY 52A			TIS, TI 2Aα	ANY ONE 828A
	APO VI	BECAUSE OF 87B		12A	PLANAW 2A	DECEIVE 671B
	ERCHOMAI I2B	COME 311C		12B	PLANAW 2A	DECEIVE 671B
	KOSMOS 5A	WORLD 447B		12F	ENEN8KONTA	NINETY 264C
	PL8N IB	BUT 675B		12F	ENNEA	NINE 266C
7A	OUAI IA	WOE 595C		12F	HO,H8,TO II2D	THE 553C
7A	SKANDALON 2	TRAP 760C		13	GINOMAI I3E	TAKE PLACE 158B
7B	OUAI IA	WOE 595C			EPI IIIBγ	ON 287B
7B	SKANDALON 2	TRAP 760C			HEURISKW IA	FIND 325A
7C	SKANDALON 2	TRAP 760C			8 2A	THAN 343B
8	AIWNIOS 3	ETERNAL 28A			MALLON I	MORE 490A
	ASBESTOS I	INEXTINGUISHABLE 114A			PLANAW 2A	DECEIVE 671B
	DUO 4	TWO 208C			CHAIRW I	REJOICE 881B
	EKKOPTW I	CUT OFF 241B		14	EMPROSTHEN 2D	IN FRONT 256D
	8 2Bβ	THAN 343B			THEL8MA IA	WILL 354D
	KULLOS	CRIPPLED 458B			HINA IIICα	IN ORDER THAT 378C
	PUR IB	FIRE 737C			MIKROS IB	SMALL 523A
8A	POUS IA	FOOT 703B			OURANOS 2A	HEAVEN 599B
8A	CHEIR I	HAND 888A			HOUTW IB	THUS 602B
8B	POUS IA	FOOT 703B		15	ADELPHOS 4	NEIGHBOR 16B
8B	CHEIR I	HAND 888A			AKOUW 4	LISTEN 32A
8F	BALLW IB	THROW 130C			HAMARTANW I	SIN 41D
8F	EISERCHOMAI 2A	COME 232B			ELEGCHW 3	EXPOSE 249A
8F	ECHW I2Cα	HAVE 332D			KERDAINW IB	TO GAIN 430C
8F	ZW8 2Bβ	LIFE 341C			METAXU 2B	BETWEEN 514C
8F	KALOS 3C	GOOD 401C			MONOS IAβ	ONLY 529C
8F	KALOS 3A	GOOD 401C			HUPAGW 2	GO AWAY 844C
8F	KALOS 3C	GOOD 401D		15FF	EAN IIB	IF 210B
8F	SKANDALIZW IA	760B		16	AKOUW 4	LISTEN 32A
		CAUSE TO FALL			DUO 2	TWO 208C
9	AUTOS 4B	THE SAME 123B			EPI IIBβ	ON 286B
	*GEENNA	HELL 152C			ETI 2B	STILL 316A
	EXAIREW I	TAKE OUT 271B			HIST8MI IIID	STAND 383B
	8 2Bβ	THAN 343B			KAI IIB	AND 392D
	MONOPHTHALMOS	ONE EYED 530A			MARTUS I	WITNESS 495B
	PUR IB	FIRE 737C			META AII IB	WITH 509D
9B	BALLW IB	THROW 130C			M8 AII	NOT 517C
10	AGGELOS 2A	ANGEL 7D			PARALAMBANW I	TAKE 625A
	BLEPW IA	SEE 142D			R8MA 2	WORD 743A
	DIA AIIIA	THROUGH 178D			SEAUTOU I	YOURSELF 753A
	KATAPHRONEW I	SCORN 421C			STOMA IA	MOUTH 777C
	M8 BIB	NOT 519A		17	DE 4A	BUT, AND 170D
	MIKROS IB	SMALL 523A			EAN I3A	IF 210D

17 ETHNIKOS	GENTILE	217B
EIMI II9B	TO BE	224A
EKKL8SIA 4B	CHURCH	240B
HO,H8,TO IIIAβ	THE	552C
TELWN8S	TAX COLLECTOR	820B
HWSPER 2	(JUST) AS	908B
17A PARAKOUW 3	DISOBEY	624C
17B PARAKOUW 3	DISOBEY	624C
18 DEW 4	BIND	177A
LUW 5	ABOLISH	485C
PALIN 3	AGAIN	611D
CHWLOS	LAME	897C
18A HOSOS 2	HOW GREAT	590C
18B HOSOS 2	HOW GREAT	590C
19 AITEW	ASK	25B
AM8N 2	AMEN	45B
DUO IB	TWO	208B
HOS,H8,HO I4A	(REL PRON)	587D
OURANOS 2A	HEAVEN	599B
PALIN 3	AGAIN	611D
PARA I3B	FROM	614D
PAS IAγ	EVERY EACH	637A
PAT8R 3Dα	FATHER	641D
PERI IA	ABOUT	650B
PRAGMA 4	DEED	703D
SUMPHWNEW 2A	MATCH	788C
20 DUO IC	TWO	208B
EKEI I	THERE	238C
EMOS IAα	MY	255A
MESOS 2	THE MIDDLE	508D
HO,H8,TO IIIE	THE	552D
ONOMA I4Cβ	NAME	575D
HOU IAα	WHERE	594A
SUNAGW 2	GATHER	790B
21 ADELPHOS 4	NEIGHBOR	I6B
HAMARTANW 4B	SIN	42A
APHI8MI 2	FORGIVE	125C
EIPON 3B	SAY	225D
PETROS	PETER	660D
POSAKIS	HOW OFTEN	701A
PROSERCHOMAI I	APPROACH	720A
21F HEPTAKIS	SEVEN TIMES	306B
21F HEWS II4	AS MANY AS	335D
22 HEBDOM8KONTAKIS	SEVENTY TIMES	212A
HEPTA	SEVEN	306B
LEGW IIIB	ANSWER	470C
23 ANTHRWPOS 3Aα	MAN	68C
DIA BII2	THEREFORE	180B
DOULOS 2	SLAVE	205A
LOGOS 2B	SETTLEMENT	479D
META AII3B	WITH	510D
HOMOIOW I	MAKE LIKE	570B
OURANOS 3	HEAVEN	599D
SUNAIRW	SETTLE ACCOUNTS	791B
24 HEIS 3A	SOMEONE	230D
MURIOI	TEN THOUSAND	531C
OPHEILET8S I	DEBTOR	603A
PROSAGW IA	BRING	718B
PROSPHERW IA	BRING (TO)	727A
TALANTON	TALENT	811B
25 GUN8 2	WIFE	167C
DE 4B	BUT, AND	170D
ECHW I2A	HAVE	332B

25 KELEUW	COMMAND	428C
M8 AII2B	NOT	518B
HOSOS 2	HOW GREAT	590B
PAS IEγ	ALL	638A
PIPRASKW	SELL	664D
TEKNON IAα	CHILD	816A
25A ECHW I6A	CAN	333D
25FF APODIDWMI 2	GIVE BACK	90A
26 EPI IIIBγ	ON	287B
MAKROTHUMEW 2	HAVE PATIENCE	489D
PAS 2A6	EVERYTHING	638C
PIPTW IBα	FALL	665B
PROSKUNEW I	DO REVERENCE	724A
26FF DOULOS 2	SLAVE	205A
27 APOLUW I	SET FREE	96A
DAN(E)ION	LOAN	169D
*SPLAGCHNIZOMAI	HAVE PITY	770B
28 D8NARION	DENARIUS	178B
EI VII		219B
HEIS 3A	SOMEONE	230D
HEKATON	ONE HUNDRED	236B
EXERCHOMAI IAβ	GO OUT	274A
HEURISKW IB	FIND	325B
KRATEW IB	SEIZE	449C
PNIGW IA	CHOKE	686A
28A OPHEILW I	OWE	603C
28B OPHEILW I	OWE	603C
28F SUNDOULOS I	FELLOW SLAVE	793C
29 EPI IIIBγ	ON	287B
MAKROTHUMEW 2	HAVE PATIENCE	489D
PARAKALEW 3	IMPLORE	622D
PIPTW IBα	FALL	665B
PIPTW IBα	FALL	665B
PIPTW IBα	FALL	665B
POUS IA	FOOT	703B
30 APERCHOMAI IA	GO AWAY	83D
BALLW IB	THROW	130C
HEWS IIB	UNTIL	334D
THELW 2	WISH	355D
HO,H8,TO II3A	THE	553C
OPHEILW I	OWE	603C
PHULAK8 3	GUARD	875D
31 GINOMAI I3A	TAKE PLACE	157D
DIASAPHEW 2	REPORT	187B
ERCHOMAI IIAζ	COME	310D
LUPEW 2	GRIEVE	483A
PAS IDβ	ALL	637D
SUNDOULOS I	FELLOW SLAVE	793C
SPHODRA	GREATLY	803D
31F KURIOS IAβ	LORD	460A
32 EKEINOS 2A	THAT	239B
EPEI 2	BECAUSE	283D
OPHEIL8 I	DEBT	603B
PARAKALEW 3	IMPLORE	622D
PAS ICα	ALL	637B
PON8ROS IBα	WICKED	697C
PROSKALEW IB	SUMMON	722C
33 DEI 2	IT IS NECESSARY	171B
DEI 6B	IT IS NECESSARY	171C
ELEEW	HAVE MERCY	249A
KAGW 3B	I	387A
SUNDOULOS I	FELLOW SLAVE	793C
34 APODIDWMI 2	GIVE BACK	90A

Verse	Greek	Gloss	Code
34	BASANIST8S	JAILER	134B
	HEWS IIIBα	UNTIL	335C
	HO,H8,TO II3A	THE	553C
	ORGIZW	BE ANGRY	583B
	OPHEILW I	OWE	603C
	PARADIDWMI IB	GIVE OVER	619D
	PAS ICγ	WHOEVER	637C
35	ADELPHOS 4	NEIGHBOR	16B
	APO VI	FROM	88A
	APHI8MI 2	FORGIVE	125C
	HEKASTOS 2	EACH	236B
	EPOURANIOS IAα	HEAVENLY	305D
	KARDIA IBα	HEART	404B
	M8 AII	NOT	517C
	OURANIOS	HEAVENLY	598A
	HOUTW IB	THUS	602C
	PARAPTWMA I	TRANSGRESSION	627B
	PAT8R 3Dα	FATHER	641D
	POIEW I2Aβ	DO	689A

MATTHEW 19

Verse	Greek	Gloss	Code
I	GINOMAI I3F	TAKE PLACE	158C
	IORDAN8S	JORDAN	379C
	IOUDAIA 2	JUDAEA	379D
	METAIRW	GO AWAY	512B
	HORION	BOUNDARY	584D
	HOTE IB	WHEN	592C
	PERAN 2B	ON THE OTHER SIDE	649C
	TELEW I	FINISH	818C
2	OCHLOS I	CROWD	605D
	POLUS IIAβ	MANY	694B
3	AITIA I	CAUSE	25D
	APOLUW 2A	SEND AWAY	96A
	EI VI	IF	218D
	EXESTI I	IT IS POSSIBLE	274D
	KATA II5Aδ	ACCORDING TO	408B
	PAS IAγ	EVERY EACH	637A
	PEIRAZW 2C	TRY	646A
4	ANAGINWSKW I	READ	51B
	APOKRINOMAI I	ANSWER	92D
	ARS8N	MALE	109C
	ARCH8 IC	BEGINNING	111D
	TH8LUS	FEMALE	361B
	KTIZW	CREATE	456C
4A	POIEW IIAβ	DO	687B
4B	POIEW IIAβ	DO	687B
5	ANTHRWPOS 2Bα	MAN	67D
	DUO ID	TWO	208B
	EIMI III2	TO BE	224A
	EIS 8Aβ		229C
	HEIS IB	ONE	230A
	*HENEKA	BECAUSE OF	264B
	KATALEIPW IA	LEAVE BEHIND	414C
	KOLLAW 28α	UNITE	442C
	M8T8R I	MOTHER	521D
	PROSKOLLAW	ADHERE CLOSELY TO	723B
5F	SARX 2	BODY	751A
6	ANTHRWPOS IAβ	MAN	67C
	APOCHWRIZW	SEPARATE	101D
	M8 AIII3A	NOT	518C
	OUKETI I	NO LONGER	596D
	SUZAW	LIVE WITH	783B
6	CHWRIZW I	DIVIDE	898B
	HWSTE IA	THEREFORE	908B
7	APOSTASION		97D
		CERTIFICATE OF DIVORCE	
	BIBLION 2	DOCUMENT	140D
	DIDWMI 2	GIVE	192C
	ENTELLW	COMMAND	268A
	LEGW IIIB	ANSWER	470C
	OUN ICα	THEREFORE	597B
7F	MWUS8S	MOSES	533D
7=9	APOLUW 2A	SEND AWAY	96A
8	ARCH8 IC	BEGINNING	111D
	EPITREPW I	ALLOW	303C
	LEGW IIIB	ANSWER	470C
	PROS III5A	TOWARD	717C
	SKL8ROKARDIA	OBSTINACY	763B
9	GAMEW IA	MARRY	150A
	EPI IIIBγ	ON	287A
	M8 AII	NOT	517C
	MOICHAW 2	COMMIT ADULTERY	528A
	MOICHEUW 2B	COMMIT ADULTERY	528B
	*PAREKTOS 2	OUTSIDE	630C
	PORNEIA I	PROSTITUTION	700A
10	AITIA I	CAUSE	25D
	ANTHRWPOS 2Bβ	MAN	67D
	GAMEW IB	MARRY	150A
	HOUTW 5	THUS	602D
	SUMPHERW 2A	BETTER	788A
11	DIDWMI IBβ	GIVE	192B
	LOGOS IAγ	WORD	478C
	HOS,H8,HO I2Bα	(REL PRON)	587B
	OU 2A	NO	594B
	PAS 2Aγ	ALL	638B
	CHWREW 3Bβ	GRASP	898B
12	GENNAW 2	BEAR	154D
	DUNAMAI IA	ABLE	206B
	HEAUTOU I	ONESELF	211A
	EIMI II	TO BE	222B
	EK 5A	FROM	235C
	KOILIA 2	BELLY	438B
	HO,H8,TO IIII	THE	555B
	OURANOS 3	HEAVEN	599D
12A	EUNOUCHOS 2	EUNUCH	324A
12A	HOSTIS 2A	WHOEVER	591A
12A	CHWREW 3Bβ	GRASP	898B
12B	EUNOUCHOS I	EUNUCH	323D
12B	EUNOUCHIZW	EMASCULATE	323D
12B	HOSTIS 2A	WHOEVER	591A
12B	CHWREW 3Bβ	GRASP	898B
12C	EUNOUCHOS 3	EUNUCH	324A
12C	HOSTIS 2A	WHOEVER	591A
13	EPITITH8MI IAα	PUT UPON	302D
	EPITIMAW I	REBUKE	303B
	HINA IIE	IN ORDER THAT	377C
	PROSPHERW IA	BRING (TO)	727A
13F	PAIDION 2A	CHILD	609A
14	APHI8MI 4	TOLERATE	126A
	BASILEIA 3G	KINGDOM	135B
	EIMI IVI	TO BE	224D
	KWLUW I	HINDER	462C
	OURANOS 3	HEAVEN	599D
	TOIOUTOS 3Aα	SUCH A KIND	829B
15	EPITITH8MI IAα	PUT UPON	302D

15	POREUW I	PROCEED 699A	24	DIERCHOMAI IB«	GO THROUGH 193C
16	AIWNIOS 3	ETERNAL 28A		EISERCHOMAI IA6	COME 232A
	DIDASKALOS	TEACHER 190D		EISERCHOMAI IF	COME 232B
	HEIS 3A	SOMEONE 230D		EISERCHOMAI 2A	COME 232B
	POIEW II8«	DO 687D		EUKOPOS	EASY 322A
	TIS, TI 2	WHICH 827B		8 2A	THAN 343B
16F	ZW8 28β	LIFE 341C		KAM8LOS	CAMEL 402C
17	HEIS 2B	ONE 230B		KAMILOS	ROPE 402D
	EISERCHOMAI 2A	COME 232B		LEGW IIID	ASSURE 470D
	ENTOL8 2Aβ	COMMAND 268C		PALIN 3	AGAIN 611D
	ERWTAW I	ASK 312A		RAPHIS	NEEDLE 742A
	THELW I	WISH 355C		TR8MA	OPENING 833D
	T8REW 5	KEEP 822D		TRUMALIA	HOLE 836A
	TIS, TI 3A	WHICH 827B		TRUP8MA	HOLE 836B
17A	AGATHOS 2A«	GOOD 3B	25	ARA 2	THEN 103B
17B	AGATHOS IB«	GOOD 3A		EKPL8SSW 2	BE AMAZED 243C
18	KLEPTW	STEAL 435C		SPHODRA	GREATLY 803D
	MOICHEUW I	COMMIT ADULTERY 528B		SWZW 2B	SAVE 806B
	HO,H8,TO II8A	THE 554D	26	ADUNATOS 2A	IMPOSSIBLE 18D
	OU 4B	NO 594D		ANTHRWPOS IAβ	MAN 67C
	POIOS 2B«	OF WHAT KIND 691C		DUNATOS 2C	POSSIBLE 208B
	PH8MI IBβ	SAY 864A		EMBLEPW I	LOOK AT 254A
	PHONEUW	MURDER 872C		THEOS 3B	GOD 358A
	PSEUDOMARTUREW	900A	26A	PARA II2C	BESIDE 615D
	BEAR FALSE WITNESS		26B	PARA II2C	BESIDE 615D
19	AGAPAW IA«	LOVE 4B	27	ARA 2	THEN 103B
	M8T8R I	MOTHER 521D		APHI8MI 3A	ABANDON 125D
	PL8SION IB	NEAR 678D		IDOU IB«	BEHOLD 371C
	SEAUTOU 3	YOURSELF 753A		PETROS	PETER 660D
	TIMAW 2	HONOR 824D	27F	AKOLOUTHEW 3	FOLLOW 30D
20	ETI 2A	STILL 316A	28	DOXA IA	GLORY 202D
	LEGW III8	ANSWER 470C		EN II2	WHILE 259D
	NEANISKOS I	YOUTH 536C		EPI IIAβ	ON 285D
	NEOT8S	YOUTH 538B		ISRA8L 2	ISRAEL 382C
	HUSTEREW IC	TO MISS 857A		KATH8MAI IA«	SIT 390B
	PHULASSW IF	WATCH 876C		KRINW 4Bβ	JUDGE 453B
	PHULASSW 2B	WATCH 876D		HO,H8,TO IIID	THE 552D
21	AKOLOUTHEW 3	FOLLOW 30D		PALIGGENESIA IB	REBIRTH 611B
	DEURO I	COME 175C		HUIOS 2C	SON 843A
	ECHW I2A	HAVE 332B		PHUL8 I	TRIBE 876D
	THELW I	WISH 355B	28A	THRONOS IC	THRONE 364D
	TH8SAUROS 2B«	TREASURE 362B	28A	KATHIZW 2A«	SIT DOWN 391A
	PTWCHOS IA	BEGGING POOR 735D	28B	THRONOS ID	THRONE 364D
	PWLEW	SELL 738D	28B	KATHIZW 2B	SIT DOWN 391A
	TELEIOS 2D	PERFECT 817B	29	AGROS I	FIELD 13D
	HUPAGW I	GO AWAY 844B		ADELPH8 I	SISTER 15C
	HUPAGW 2	GO AWAY 844C		AIWNIOS 3	ETERNAL 28A
	HUPARCHW I	BE 845D		APHI8MI 3A	ABANDON 125D
22	EIMI II4F	TO BE 223B		HEKATONTAPLASIWN	236C
	ECHW I2A	HAVE 332B		A HUNDRED FOLD	
	KT8MA I	PROPERTY 456B		HENEKA	BECAUSE OF 264B
	LOGOS IAγ	WORD 478C		ZW8 28β	LIFE 341C
	LUPEW 2B	BE GRIEVED 483A		KL8RONOMEW 2	INHERIT 435D
	NEANISKOS I	YOUTH 536C		M8T8R I	MOTHER 521D
	POLUS IIAβ	MANY 694B		OIKIA IA	HOUSE 559D
23	BASILEIA 3G	KINGDOM 135A		ONOMA I4C6	NAME 576C
	DUSKOLWS	WITH DIFFICULTY 208D		HOSTIS IB	WHOEVER 590D
	OURANOS 3	HEAVEN 599D		PAS ICγ	WHOEVER 637C
	PALIN 3	AGAIN 611D		POLLAPLASIWN	MANIFOLD 693C
23F	BASILEIA 3	KINGDOM 134D		TEKNON IA«	CHILD 816A
23F	BASILEIA 3G	KINGDOM 135B	30	ESCHATOS 2	LAST 314A
23F	PLOUSIOS I	RICH 679C		PRWTOS ICβ	FIRST 733C

MATTHEW 20

1	HAMA 2	TOGETHER 41C
	*EIS 7	TO 229B
	EXERCHOMAI 1A⟨	GO OUT 274B
	MISTHOW	HIRE 525D
	*OIKODESPOT8S	560C
	MASTER OF THE HOUSE	
	HOMOIOS 1	LIKE 569D
	HOSTIS 3	WHOEVER 591B
	OURANOS 3	HEAVEN 599D
	PRWI	EARLY 732B
1F	ERGAT8S 1A	WORKMAN 307C
1FF	AMPELWN	VINEYARD 46B
2	APOSTELLW 1B⌐	SEND AWAY 98A
	D8NARION	DENARIUS 178B
	EK 4B	FROM 235C
	H8MERA 1A	DAY 346D
	META A114	WITH 510D
	SUMPHWNEW 2A	MATCH 788D
3	AGORA	MARKET PLACE 12B
	ALLOS 1B	OTHER 39B
	ARGOS 1	IDLE 104A
	EN 11A	IN 257D
	HIST8MI 112B⌐	BEING 383C
	PALIN 2	AGAIN 611C
	PERI 2B	ABOUT 651A
	TRITOS 1	THIRD 834B
	HWRA 2B	TIME OF DAY 904C
4	DIDWMI 4	GIVE 192C
	DIKAIOS 5	RIGHTEOUS 195B
	KAI 111	ALSO 394B
	HUPAGW 2	GO AWAY 844C
5	HEKTOS	SIXTH 245C
	ENATOS	NINTH 261D
	PALIN 2	AGAIN 611C
	POIEW 12A⍺	DO 689A
	*HWRA 2B	TIME OF DAY 904D
	HWSAUTWS	SIMILARLY 907D
5F	PERI 2B	ABOUT 651A
6	ALLOS 1B	OTHER 39B
	ARGOS 1	IDLE 104A
	HENDEKATOS	ELEVENTH 262B
	HEURISKW 1C⍺	FIND 325C
	H8MERA 1A	DAY 346D
	LEGW 111A	ASK 470C
	HOLOS 2A	WHOLE 567C
	HWDE 2A	HERE 903D
	HWRA 2B	TIME OF DAY 904D
6B	HIST8MI 112B⍺	BEING 383C
7	KAI 111	ALSO 394B
	MISTHOW	HIRE 525D
	HUPAGW 2	GO AWAY 844C
8	APODIDWMI 1	GIVE AWAY 89D
	ARCHW 2C	BEGIN 113B
	ERGAT8S 1A	WORKMAN 307C
	ESCHATOS 3A	LAST 314A
	HEWS 113	AS FAR AS 335D
	KALEW 1C	CALL 400B
	KURIOS 1A⍺	OWNER 459D
	MISTHOS 1	WAGES 525A
	OPSIOS 2	LATE 606C
	PRWTOS 1A	FIRST 732D

9	HENDEKATOS	ELEVENTH 262B
	PERI 2B	ABOUT 651A
	HWRA 2B	TIME OF DAY 904D
9F	ANA 3	EACH 49C
9F	D8NARION	DENARIUS 178B
9F	LAMBANW 2	RECEIVE 466B
10	D8NARION	DENARIUS 178B
	NOMIZW 2	THINK 543B
	POLUS 112C	MANY 696A
	POLUS 112B	MANY 696A
	PRWTOS 1A	FIRST 732D
11	GOGGUZW 1	MURMUR 163C
	KATA 12B⌐	DOWN 406D
	OIKODESPOT8S	560C
	MASTER OF THE HOUSE	
12	BAROS 1	WEIGHT 133C
	BASTAZW 2B⌐	ENDURE 137A
	HEIS 1A⍺	ONE 230A
	ESCHATOS 3A	LAST 314A
	ISOS	EQUAL 381D
	KAUSWN	HEAT 426D
	HOUTOS 2A	THIS 601D
	HWRA 2A⍺	TIME OF DAY 904C
12A	POIEW 12C	DO 689B
12B	POIEW 11B₁	DO 688D
13	ADIKEW 2A	DO WRONG 17B
	D8NARION	DENARIUS 178B
	HETAIROS	COMPANION 314D
	SUMPHWNEW 2A	MATCH 788D
14	AIRW 3	CARRY 24A
	ESCHATOS 3A	LAST 314A
	THELW 2	WISH 355D
	*SOS 2B	YOURS 766D
	HUPAGW 1	GO AWAY 844B
15	AGATHOS 1B⍺	GOOD 3A
	HAPLOUS	SINCERE 85C
	EXESTI 2	IT IS POSSIBLE 274D
	8 1D⌐	OR 343A
	OPHTHALMOS 1	EYE 604B
	PON8ROS 1B⌐	WICKED 697D
15F	EMOS 2	MY 255A
16	EKLEKTOS 1B	CHOSEN 242B
	ESCHATOS 2	LAST 314A
	KL8TOS	CALLED 437A
	OLIGOS 1B	FEW 566C
	HOUTW 1B	THUS 602B
	POLUS 12A⍺	MANY 694D
	PRWTOS 1C⌐	FIRST 733C
17	DWDEKA	TWELVE 209B
	IDIOS 4	PRIVATELY 371A
	HODOS 1B	WAY 556C
	PARALAMBANW 1	TAKE 625A
17F	ANABAINW 1A⍺	GO UP 49D
17F	HIEROSOLUMA 1A	JERUSALEM 373D
18	ARCHIEREUS 1B	HIGH PRIEST 112B
	GRAMMATEUS 2	SCRIBES 165A
	THANATOS 1B⍺	DEATH 351C
	IDOU 1B⍻	BEHOLD 371C
	KATAKRINW	CONDEMN 413A
	PARADIDWMI 1B	GIVE OVER 620A
	HUIOS 2C	SON 843A
19	ANIST8MI 2A	RISE 69C
	EIS 4F	(PURPOSE) 229A

19 EMPAIZW I	RIDICULE	255B
MASTIGOW I	WHIP	496A
PARADIDWMI IB	GIVE OVER	620B
STAUROW I	CRUCIFY	773A
TRITOS I	THIRD	834B
20 AITEW	ASK	25B
ZEBEDAIOS	ZEBEDEE	337D
META AIIIA	WITH	509D
M8T8R I	MOTHER	521D
PARA I3A	FROM	614D
PROSKUNEW 5	DO REVERENCE	724B
TIS, TI IBα	ANY ONE	828A
20F HUIOS IAα	SON	841B
21 DEXIOS 2B	RIGHT	174A
HEIS 5A	ONE	231A
EK 2	AWAY FROM	234A
EUWNUMOS	LEFT	330A
THELW I	WISH	355B
HINA IIIA6	IN ORDER THAT	378B
KATHIZW 2Aα	SIT DOWN	390D
22 AITEW	ASK	25B
BAPTIZW 3C	BAPTIZE	131D
MELLW IC6	IS DESTINED	502C
OIDA IF	KNOW	558D
POT8RION 2	CUP	702B
22B DUNAMAI 2	ABLE	206B
22F BAPTISMA 3	BAPTISM	132B
22F PINW 2Bα	DRINK	664C
23 ALLA IB	BUT, YET	37D
DEXIOS 2B	RIGHT	174A
EK 2	AWAY FROM	234A
EMOS IB	MY	255A
HETOIMAZW 3	PREPARE	316C
EUWNUMOS	LEFT	330A
KATHIZW 2Aα	SIT DOWN	390D
MEN IAα	(PARTICLE)	503D
HO,H8,TO II4A	THE	553D
HOS,H8,HO I2A	(REL PRON)	587A
PAT8R 3Dα	FATHER	641D
POT8RION 2	CUP	702B
24 AGANAKTEW	BE AROUSED	4A
DEKA	TEN	172D
HO,H8,TO II2D	THE	553C
25 ARCHWN I	RULER	113B
ETHNOS I	NATION	217B
KATAKURIEUW 2	RULE	413C
KATEXOUSIAZW		422C
EXERCISE AUTHORITY		
MEGAS 2Bα	GREAT	499B
OIDA IE	KNOW	558C
26 DIAKONOS IA	SERVANT	183C
MEGAS 2Bα	GREAT	499B
HOUTW IB	THUS	602C
27 DOULOS 3	SLAVE	205A
PRWTOS ICβ	FIRST	733C
28 ANAKLINW 2	RECLINE	55D
ANAPIPTW I	RECLINE	59A
ANTI 3	FOR	73B
DEIPNEW	EAT	172B
DEIPNOKL8TWR	HOST	172B
DIAKONEW 2	SERVE	183A
DIDWMI 6	GIVE	192D
ELASSWN	SMALLER	247D

28 EXECHW	STAND OUT	275B
EPERCHOMAI IA	COME	284C
ETI 2B	STILL	316A
*H8SSWN	LESSER	349D
KATW 2	DOWNWARDS	426B
LUTRON	RANSOM	483D
MIKROS 3C	BEING SMALL	523C
PARAKALEW IB	INVITE	622B
POLUS I2Aα	MANY	694D
SUNAGW 6	GATHER	790C
HUIOS 2C	SON	843A
CHR8SIMOS	USEFUL	894B
CHWREW IA	GO	897D
PSUCH8 IAβ	SOUL LIFE	901C
HWSPER 2	(JUST) AS	908A
29 EKPOREUOMAI IB	GO OUT	243D
IERICHW	JERICHO	372D
OCHLOS I	CROWD	605C
POLUS IIBα	MANY	694C
30 DUO IA	TWO	208B
KATH8MAI IAα	SIT	390B
HODOS IA	WAY	556B
PARA IIIIBα	ALONG	616A
PARA IIIID	ALONG	616A
PARAGW 2Aα	BRING IN	619A
TUPHLOS IB	BLIND	838C
30F DAUID	DAVID	170B
30F ELEEW	HAVE MERCY	249A
30F KRAZW 2A	CALL	448D
30F HUIOS 2A	SON	842A
31 EPITIMAW I	REBUKE	303B
HINA IIIA6	IN ORDER THAT	378B
MEGAS 2Aγ	GREAT	498D
SIWPAW 2A	BE SILENT	760A
32 EIPON 3B	SAY	225D
THELW I	WISH	355C
HIST8MI IIIA	STAND	383A
POIEW IIDβ	DO	688D
PHWNEW 2B	CALL	878C
33 ANOIGW IEβ	OPEN	70D
HINA III2	IN ORDER THAT	379A
34 ANABLEPW 2Aα	GAIN SIGHT	50C
HAPTW 2B	TOUCH	102C
OMMA I	EYE	568D
SPLAGCHNIZOMAI	HAVE PITY	770B

MATTHEW 21

1 B8THPHAG8	BETHPHAGE	139D
EGGIZW 2	APPROACH	212D
EIS IB	NEAR	227C
ELAIA I	OLIVE TREE	247B
OROS	MOUNTAIN	586B
HOTE IB	WHEN	592C
TOTE 2	AT THAT TIME	831D
2 AGW IA	LEAD	14A
DEW 2	BIND	177A
HEURISKW ICα	FIND	325C
KATENANTI 2A	OPPOSITE	422B
KWM8 I	VILLAGE	462D
LUW 2A	LOOSE	484D
ONOS	DONKEY	577C
PWLOS	COLT	739A

2F	EUTHUS	IMMEDIATELY	321B
3	APOSTELLW 2	PUT IN	98C
	KURIOS 2Cβ	LORD	460C
	CHREIA I	NEED	893B
3A	TIS, TI IAγ	ANY ONE	827D
4	DE 2	BUT, AND	170D
	HINA IIB	IN ORDER THAT	377C
	HINA II2	IN ORDER THAT	378D
	HOLOS 3	WHOLE	567D
	PL8ROW 4A	MAKE FULL	677C
	PROPH8T8S I	PROPHET	730D
5	BASILEUS 2A	KING	135D
	EPI IIIIAβ	ON	288A
	EPIBAINW I	GO UP	289C
	ERCHOMAI IIA6	COME	310C
	THUGAT8R 2E	DAUGHTER	365C
	KAI I3	AND	393D
	ONOS	DONKEY	577C
	PRAUS	HUMBLE	705D
	PWLOS	COLT	739A
	SIWN 2A	ZION	759D
	HUIOS IAβ	SON	841C
	HUPOZUGION	PACK ANIMAL	852C
6	KATHWS I	JUST AS	392A
	POIEW I2Aα	DO	689A
	POREUW I	PROCEED	699B
	PROSTASSW	COMMAND	725D
	SUNTASSW	ORDER	799C
7	AGW IA	LEAD	14A
	EPANW 2A	ON	283A
	EPIKATHIZW	SIT	293D
	EPITITH8MI IAα	PUT UPON	303A
	ONOS	DONKEY	577C
	PWLOS	COLT	739A
7F	HIMATION I	GARMENT	377A
8	ALLOS IC	OTHER	39B
	HEAUTOU 4	ONESELF	211D
	KLADOS	BRANCH	434A
	KOPTW I	CUT	444D
	OCHLOS I	CROWD	605C
8A	HODOS IA	WAY	556B
8A	STRWNNUW	SPREAD	779B
8B	HODOS IA	WAY	556B
8B	STRWNNUW	SPREAD	779B
9	AKOLOUTHEW I	FOLLOW	30C
	DAUID	DAVID	170B
	ERCHOMAI IIAη	COME	310D
	EULOGEW 2A	BLESS	322D
	KRAZW 2A	CALL	448D
	KURIOS 2A	LORD	460B
	ONOMA I4Cγ	NAME	576C
	*PROAGW 2A	LEAD	709A
	HUIOS 2A	SON	842A
	HUPSISTOS I	HIGHEST	858A
9A	HWSANNA	HOSANNA	907C
9B	HWSANNA	HOSANNA	907C
10	EIMI II6C	TO BE	223C
	EISERCHOMAI IAα	COME	231D
	PAS ICα	ALL	637B
	POLIS 3	CITY	692C
	SEIW 2	SHAKE	754A
11	APO IVIB	FROM	86D
	GALILAIA	GALILEE	149D
11	NAZARA	NAZARETH	534A
	HOUTOS IAα	THIS	600D
	PROPH8T8S 3	PROPHET	731A
12	AGORAZW I	BUY	12D
	EKBALLW I	DRIVE OUT	236D
	HIERON 2	TEMPLE	373A
	KATHEDRA	CHAIR	389B
	KATASTREPHW I	UPSET	420A
	KOLLUBIST8S	MONEY CHANGER	442D
	PAS IDβ	ALL	637C
	PERISTERA	PIGEON	657D
	TRAPEZA 4	TABLE	832B
12A	HIERON 2	TEMPLE	373A
12A	PWLEW	SELL	739A
12B	PWLEW	SELL	738D
13	GRAPHW 2C	WRITE	165D
	KALEW IAβ	CALL	399D
	L8ST8S I	ROBBER	474B
	OIKOS IAβ	HOUSE	563B
	OIKOS IAβ	HOUSE	563B
	POIEW IIB?	DO	688B
	PROSEUCH8 I	PRAYER	720C
	SP8LAION	CAVE	769D
	SU IC	YOU	780A
14	CHWLOS	LAME	897B
15	AGANAKTEW	BE AROUSED	4A
	ARCHIEREUS IB	HIGH PRIEST	112B
	GRAMMATEUS 2	SCRIBES	165A
	DAUID	DAVID	170B
	THAUMASIOS I	WONDERFUL	353B
	KRAZW 2A	CALL	448D
	PAIS IAα	CHILD	609C
	POIEW IIBβ	DO	687C
	HUIOS 2A	SON	842A
	HWSANNA	HOSANNA	907C
16	AINOS	PRAISE	23B
	ANAGINWSKW I	READ	51B
	TH8LAZW 2	SUCK	361A
	KATARTIZW 2B	PREPARE	419A
	LEGW IIA	SAY	469B
	NAI IA	YES	534D
	N8PIOS IA	CHILDREN	539C
	HOTI 2	THAT	593D
	OUDEPOTE	NEVER	596D
	STOMA IA	MOUTH	777B
17	AULIZOMAI I	SPEND THE NIGHT	121A
	B8THANIA I	BETHANY	139B
	EXERCHOMAI IAα	GO OUT	274A
	EXW 2B	OUTSIDE	279B
	KATALEIPW IA	LEAVE BEHIND	414C
17F	POLIS I	CITY	692A
18	EPANAGW 2	RETURN	282C
	PEINAW I	HUNGER	645D
	PRWI	EARLY	732A
	PRWIA	(EARLY) MORNING	732B
19	AIWN IB	TIME	26D
	GINOMAI IIA	BE BORN	157B
	EIS 2B	FOR	228A
	HEIS 3B	SOMEONE	230D
	EPI IIAγ	ON	285D
	ERCHOMAI II	GO	311D
	KARPOS IA	FRUIT	405C
	M8KETI 6A	NO LONGER	520C

```
19 OU  6A              NO 595A        27 POIOS 2Aγ      OF WHAT KIND 691B
   OUDEIS 2Bα     NOTHING 596C           PH8MI IBα             SAY 864A
   PHULLON        FOLIAGE 877A       28 DOKEW 3A               SEEM 201B
19F  X8RAINW 2A    DRY UP 550D           ERGAZOMAI I           WORK 306D
19F  PARACHR8MA  AT ONCE 629B            ECHW I2Bα             HAVE 332C
19=21 SUK8       FIG TREE 783D           PRWTOS IB            FIRST 733A
20 EIDON 1A          SEE 219D            S8MERON             TODAY 756B
   THAUMAZW 1Aα    WONDER 352D           TIS, TI IBα         WHICH 826D
21 AIRW 1A        LIFT UP 23D            HUPAGW 2          GO AWAY 844C
   BALLW 1B         THROW 130C      28A   TEKNON IAβ          CHILD 816A
   GINOMAI I3A   TAKE PLACE 157D    28B   TEKNON IAβ          CHILD 816A
   DIAKRINW 2B      WAVER 184B      28FF  AMPELWN          VINEYARD 46B
   EAN IIC             IF 210C      29 EGW                       I 216B
   EAN I3B             IF 210D         KURIOS IB             LORD 460A
   ECHW I2Eβ         HAVE 333A      30 EIPON 2A                SAY 225C
   KAN 2           EVEN IF 403B        HETEROS IA           OTHER 315A
   MONOS 2C          ONLY 529D         THELW 2               WISH 355D
   HO,H8,TO II7       THE 554C         METAMELOMAI         REPENT 512D
   OROS          MOUNTAIN 586C         HUSTEROS 2A          LATER 857B
   PISTIS 2A         FAITH 668D         HWSAUTWS        SIMILARLY 907D
   PISTIS 2Dζ        FAITH 669D      31 BASILEIA 3B       KINGDOM 134D
22 AITEW              ASK 25C          EK  4Aβ               FROM 235B
   EN  II3          WHILE 259D         THEL8MA ICα           WILL 355A
   HOSOS 2      HOW GREAT 590C         POIEW IICα              DO 688C
   PAS IEγ            ALL 638A         PROAGW 2B             LEAD 709A
   PISTEUW 2C      BELIEVE 667D        PRWTOS I             FIRST 732D
   PROSEUCH8 I     PRAYER 720C         TIS, TI IAα         WHICH 826D
23 ARCHIEREUS IB HIGH PRIEST 112C      HUSTEROS IA     THE LATTER 857B
   EXOUSIA 3     AUTHORITY 278A     31F  PORN8 I       PROSTITUTE 700B
   HIERON 2         TEMPLE 373A     31F  TELWN8S    TAX COLLECTOR 820B
   KAI I2A             AND 393A     32 DIKAIOSUN8 2B RIGHTEOUSNESS 195D
   POIEW IIBα           DO 687D        METAMELOMAI         REPENT 512D
   POIOS 2Aγ   OF WHAT KIND 691B       HO,H8,TO II4Bη         THE 554B
   PRESBUTEROS 2Aβ   OLDER 706D        HODOS 2B               WAY 556D
24 HEIS 2B            ONE 230B         HUSTEROS 2A          LATER 857B
   EXOUSIA 3     AUTHORITY 278A     32A   PISTEUW IB       BELIEVE 666C
   ERWTAW I           ASK 312A      32B   PISTEUW IB       BELIEVE 666C
   KAGW 3B              I 387A      32C   PISTEUW IB       BELIEVE 666C
   LOGOS IAβ          WORD 478B     33 ALLOS IB            OTHER 39B
   POIOS 2Aγ   OF WHAT KIND 691B       ANTHRWPOS 3Aε          MAN 68C
25 ANTHRWPOS IAβ       MAN 67C         APOD8MEW I  GO ON A JOURNEY 89C
   BAPTISMA I      BAPTISM 132A        EKDIDWMI             LEASE 238A
   DIA BII2            WHY 180B         L8NOS          WINE PRESS 474A
  *DIALOGIZOMAI I CONSIDER 185A        OIKODESPOT8S                560C
   EIMI III3         TO BE 224B           MASTER OF THE HOUSE
   EK  3B             FROM 234B         OIKODOMEW IA         BUILD 560C
   8  IAα               OR 342B         OIKODESPOT8S                560C
   OUN ICα        THEREFORE 597B           MASTER OF THE HOUSE
   OURANOS 3        HEAVEN 599D         ORUSSW 2               DIG 586D
   PARA II2E        BESIDE 615D         HOSTIS 3            WHOEVER 591B
   PISTEUW IB      BELIEVE 666C         PARABOL8 2          PARABLE 617D
   POTHEN 2     FROM WHERE 686D         PERITITH8MI I  PLACE AROUND 658B
26 ECHW I5        CONSIDER 333D         PURGOS I             TOWER 738A
   OCHLOS 2          CROWD 605D         PHRAGMOS I           FENCE 873B
   PAS 2Aγ            ALL 638B          PHUTEUW              PLANT 878A
   PROPH8T8S 2     PROPHET 731A     33FF  GEWRGOS 2         FARMER 156B
   PHOBEW IBα    BE AFRAID 871A     34 APOSTELLW IBα    SEND AWAY 98A
   HWS IIIIC            SO 906D         EGGIZW 5B         APPROACH 212D
27 EGW                  I 216A          KAIROS 3              TIME 396A
   EXOUSIA 3     AUTHORITY 278A         KARPOS IA            FRUIT 405C
   LEGW IIBβ          SAY 469C          LAMBANW ID         RECEIVE 465D
   OIDA II            KNOW 558C         HOTE IB               WHEN 592C
   OUDE 2         AND NOT 595D          PALIN 2              AGAIN 611C
```

34FF	DOULOS IA	SLAVE	204D
35	APOKTEINW IA	KILL	93B
	DERW	BEAT	174D
	LAMBANW IC	TAKE	465C
	LITHOBOLEW I	THROW STONES	475B
	MEN IC	(PARTICLE)	504A
	HOS,H8,HO II2	THIS (ONE)	589B
36	PALIN 2	AGAIN	611C
	POIEW I2Aβ	DO	689A
	POLUS IIIA	MANY	695C
	PRWTOS IA	FIRST	732D
	HWSAUTWS	SIMILARLY	907D
37	APOSTELLW IBα	SEND AWAY	98A
	ENTREPW 2B	RESPECT	269B
	HUSTEROS 2B	FINALLY	857B
37A	HUIOS IAα	SON	841B
37B	HUIOS IAα	SON	841B
37F	HUIOS 2B	SON	842C
38	APOKTEINW IA	KILL	93B
	GEWRGOS 2	FARMER	156B
	DEUTE I	COME	175D
	KATECHW IBγ	KEEP	424A
	KL8RONOMIA I	INHERITANCE	436A
	KL8RONOMOS I	HEIR	436B
39	APOKTEINW IA	KILL	93B
	EKBALLW I	DRIVE OUT	236D
	EXW 2B	OUTSIDE	279B
	LAMBANW IC	TAKE	465C
40	AN 3A	(PARTICLE)	48B
	KURIOS IAα	OWNER	459D
	OUN 5	THEREFORE	597D
	POIEW IIDγ	DO	688D
	TIS, TI IBα	WHICH	826D
40F	GEWRGOS 2	FARMER	156B
41	APODIDWMI I	GIVE AWAY	89D
	APOLLUMI IAα	RUIN	94C
	EKDIDWMI	LEASE	238A
	KAIROS 3	TIME	396A
	KAKOS IA	BAD	398C
	KAKWS I	BADLY	399B
	KARPOS IA	FRUIT	405D
	HOSTIS 2A	WHOEVER	591A
42	ANAGINWSKW I	READ	51B
	APODOKIMAZW I	DECLARE USELESS	90B
	GINOMAI I4A	BECOME	158D
	GRAPH8 2Bα	SCRIPTURE	165B
	GWNIA	CORNER	167D
	EIS 8Aα		229C
	EN I3	IN	258A
	THAUMASTOS 2	WONDERFUL	353B
	KEPHAL8 2B	HEAD	431C
	KURIOS 2A	LORD	460C
	LITHOS 2	STONE	475D
	OIKODOMEW IBβ	BUILD	560D
	HOS,H8,HO I4D	(REL PRON)	588A
	OUDEPOTE	NEVER	596D
	OPHTHALMOS 2	EYE	604D
	PARA I2	FROM	614C
43	AIRW 4	TAKE AWAY	24B
	BASILEIA 3B	KINGDOM	134D
	BASILEIA 3G	KINGDOM	135B
	DIA BII2	THEREFORE	180B
	KARPOS 2A	RESULT	405D

43	POIEW IIBη	DO	688A
44	LIKMAW	WINNOW	475D
	LITHOS 2	STONE	475D
	SUNTHLAW	CRUSH	797C
44A	PIPTW IA	FALL	665A
44B	PIPTW IA	FALL	665A
45	GINWSKW 3C	UNDERSTAND	160B
	LEGW I2A	SAY	469C
	PARABOL8 2	PARABLE	617D
46	EIS 8B	TO BE	229C
	EPEI 2	BECAUSE	283D
	*ECHW I5	CONSIDER	333D
	Z8TEW 2Bγ	SEEK	339C
	KRATEW IA	ARREST	449C
	OCHLOS 2	CROWD	605D
	PROPH8T8S 3	PROPHET	731A
	PHOBEW IBα	BE AFRAID	871A

MATTHEW 22

1	APOKRINOMAI 2	CONTINUE	93A
	EIPON 2A	SAY	225C
	LEGW I8A	SAY	470B
	PARABOL8 2	PARABLE	617D
2	ANTHRWPOS 3Aε	MAN	68C
	GAMOS IA	WEDDING	150D
	HOMOIOW I	MAKE LIKE	570B
	OURANOS 3	HEAVEN	599D
2FF	BASILEIA 3G	KINGDOM	135B
3	APOSTELLW IBγ	SEND AWAY	98A
	GAMOS IA	WEDDING	150D
	ERCHOMAI IIAα	COME	310B
	THELW 2	WISH	355D
	KALEW IB	INVITE	400B
3A	KALEW IC	CALL	400B
3B	KALEW IB	INVITE	400B
3F	DOULOS 2	SLAVE	205A
4	ARISTON 2	NOON MEAL	106C
	GAMOS IA	WEDDING	150D
	DEUTE 2	COME	175D
	HETOIMAZW I	PREPARE	316B
	HETOIMOS I	READY	316D
	THUW 2	SACRIFICE	367D
	IDOU IC	REMEMBER	371D
	KALEW IB	INVITE	400B
	PAS 2A6	EVERYTHING	638C
	SITISTOS	FATTENED	759C
	TAUROS	BULL	813D
5	AMELEW	TO NEGLECT	44B
	EMPORIA	BUSINESS	256B
	EPI IIIBη	ON	289B
	IDIOS 2C	ONES OWN	370C
	HOS,H8,HO II2	THIS (ONE)	589B
6	DOULOS 2	SLAVE	205A
	LOIPOS 2Bα	THE OTHERS	481A
	HUBRIZW	MISTREAT	839B
7	APOLLUMI IAα	RUIN	94C
	EMPI(M)PR8MI	BURN	255C
	ORGIZW	BE ANGRY	583B
	PEMPW I	SEND	647C
	POLIS I	CITY	692A
	STRATEUMA	ARMY	778A
	PHONEUS	MURDERER	872B

8 AXIOS 2A WORTHY 77D
   GAMOS IA WEDDING 150D
   DOULOS 2 SLAVE 205A
   KALEW IB INVITE 400B
   MEN IAα (PARTICLE) 503D
9 GAMOS IA WEDDING 150D
   DIEXODOS OUTLET 193B
   EPI IIIIAβ ON 288A
   KALEW IB INVITE 400B
   HOSOS 2 HOW GREAT 590C
   POREUW I PROCEED 699A
10 AGATHOS IBα GOOD 3A
   GAMOS IC WEDDING 150D
   DOULOS 2 SLAVE 205A
   EXERCHOMAI IAε GO OUT 274B
   NUMPHWN I WEDDING HALL 547C
   HODOS IA WAY 556B
   PIMPLĒMI IAα FILL 663D
   PONĒROS 2A WICKED 697D
   SUNAGW 2 GATHER 790A
   TE 3A AND 815B
10F ANAKEIMAI 2 BE AT TABLE 55C
11 ENDUW 2A DRESS 263C
   THEAOMAI IB SEE 353D
   OU 3B NO 594C
11F GAMOS IA WEDDING 150D
11F ENDUMA I GARMENT 263A
12 EISERCHOMAI IH COME 232B
   HETAIROS COMPANION 314D
   ECHW IIB HAVE 332A
   PWS IC HOW 739C
   PHIMOW 2 TIE SHUT 869D
   HWDE I HERE 903B
13 BRUGMOS GNASHING 147B
   DEW IB BIND 176D
   DIAKONOS IA SERVANT 183D
   EKBALLW I DRIVE OUT 236D
   EXWTEROS 2 FARTHEST 279C
   KLAUTHMOS WEEPING 434D
   ODOUS TOOTH 557B
   POUS IA FOOT 703B
   SKOTOS I DARKNESS 765A
   CHEIR I HAND 888A
14 GAR ID FOR 151B
   EKLEKTOS IB CHOSEN 242B
   KLĒTOS CALLED 437A
   OLIGOS IB FEW 566C
15 LAMBANW IH TAKE 466A
   LOGOS IAγ WORD 478C
   HOPWS 2B IN ORDER THAT 580D
   PAGIDEUW SET A SNARE 607A
   POREUW I PROCEED 699B
   SUMBOULION I PLAN 785D
   PHARISAIOS PHARISEE 861C
16 ALĒTHEIA 3 REALITY 35D
   ALĒTHĒS I TRUE 36A
   APOSTELLW IBα SEND AWAY 98A
   BLEPW 5 SEE 143B
   DIDASKALOS TEACHER 190D
   DIDASKW 2B TEACH 191A
   HĒRWDIANOI HERODIANS 349B
  *LEGW I8C SAY 470B
   MATHĒTĒS 2A DISCIPLE 486D

16 MELEI 2 IT IS A CONCERN 501B
   META AII4 WITH 510D
   HODOS 2B WAY 557A
   OIDA IE KNOW 558C
   OU 6A NO 595A
   OUDEIS 2A NO ONE 596B
   PROSWPON ICβ FACE 728D
17 DIDWMI 4 GIVE 192D
   DOKEW 3A SEEM 201B
   EXESTI I IT IS POSSIBLE 274D
   8 IAα OR 342B
   KAISAR EMPEROR 396C
   KĒNSOS POLL TAX 431D
18 GINWSKW 4A PERCEIVE 160B
   PEIRAZW 2C TRY 646A
   PONĒRIA WICKEDNESS 697A
   HUPOKRITĒS HYPOCRITE 853A
19 DĒNARION DENARIUS 178B
   EPIDEIKNUMI I SHOW 291D
   KĒNSOS POLL TAX 431D
   NOMISMA COIN 543D
   PROSPHERW IB BRING (TO) 727A
20 EIKWN IA IMAGE 221B
   EPIGRAPHĒ INSCRIPTION 291C
21 APODIDWMI I GIVE AWAY 89D
   THEOS 3Fγ GOD 358B
   HO,HĒ,TO II7 THE 554C
21A KAISAR EMPEROR 396C
21B KAISAR EMPEROR 396C
22 APHIĒMI 3A LEAVE 125D
   THAUMAZW IAα WONDER 352D
23 ANASTASIS 2B RESURRECTION 60B
   EIMI II TO BE 222B
   EPERWTAW IA ASK 285A
   LEGW IIIE DECLARE 471A
   MĒ AII18α NOT 517D
   SADDOUKAIOS SADDUCEE 747A
24 ANISTĒMI IB RAISE 69B
   APOTHNĒSKW IAα DIE 90D
   DIDASKALOS TEACHER 190D
   EPIGAMBREUW 290C
      MARRY AS NEXT OF KIN
   ECHW I2Bα HAVE 332C
   MWUSĒS MOSES 533D
   SPERMA 2B SEED 769B
   TEKNON IAα CHILD 816A
25 APHIĒMI 3A LEAVE 125D
   GAMEW IB MARRY 150A
   EIMI III8B TO BE 224D
   ECHW I2Bα HAVE 332C
   PARA IIIBβ BESIDE 615C
   PRWTOS IB FIRST 733A
   SPERMA 2B SEED 769B
   TELEUTAW DIE 818B
25F HEPTA SEVEN 306B
26 DEUTEROS I SECOND 176A
   HEWS II3 AS FAR AS 335D
   HOMOIWS LIKEWISE 570D
   TRITOS I THIRD 834C
27 APOTHNĒSKW IAα DIE 90D
   PAS 2Aγ ALL 638B
   HUSTEROS 2B FINALLY 857B
28 ANASTASIS 2B RESURRECTION 60B

28	EN II2	WHILE 259D	40 PROPH8T8S I	PROPHET 731A
	HEPTA	SEVEN 306B	41 SUNAGW 2	GATHER 790A
	TIS, TI IAα	WHICH 826C	PHARISAIOS	PHARISEE 861C
29	GRAPH8 2Bα	SCRIPTURE 165B	42 DAUID	DAVID 170B
	DUNAMIS I	POWER 206C	DOKEW 3A	SEEM 201B
	M8DE IA	AND NOT 519C	PERI IA	ABOUT 650B
	PLANAW 2Cγ	DECEIVE 671C	CHRISTOS I	ANOINTED ONE 895B
30	AGGELOS 2A	ANGEL 7C	42B TIS, TI IAα	WHICH 826C
	GAMEW IB	MARRY 150A	42=5 HUIOS 2A	SON 842A
	GAMIZW 2	GIVE IN MARRIAGE 150C	43 DAUID	DAVID 170B
	EKGAMIZW	MARRY 237C	EN I5D	IN 259C
	OURANOS 2C	HEAVEN 599C	KALEW IAβ	CALL 399D
	OUTE	NOT 600C	OUN ICα	THEREFORE 597C
	HWS II3B	SO 906A	PNEUMA 5Dβ	SPIRIT 683B
30F	ANASTASIS 2B RESURRECTION 60B		PNEUMA 6C	SPIRIT 683D
31	ANAGINWSKW I	READ 51B	PWS IA	HOW 739C
	ANASTASIS 2B RESURRECTION 60A		44 DEXIOS 2B	RIGHT 174A
	EIPON 4	SAY 225D	EK 2	AWAY FROM 234A
	NEKROS 2A	DEAD 537A	ECHTHROS 2Bβ	THE ENEMY 331D
	HO,H8,TO IIII	THE 555B	HEWS IIB	UNTIL 334D
	PERI IH	ABOUT 650D	KATH8MAI 2	SIT DOWN 390C
32	ABRAAM	ABRAHAM 2A	KURIOS 2Cα	LORD 460C
	ALLA IA	BUT, YET 37B	POUS IB	FOOT 703C
	ZAW IAα	LIVE 336C	TITH8MI IIAβ	PUT 823D
	THEOS 3C	GOD 358A	TITH8MI I2Aα	MAKE 824A
	IAKWB I	JACOB 368B	HUPOKATW	UNDER 852C
	ISAAK	ISAAC 381C	HUPOPODION	FOOTSTOOL 854D
	NEKROS 2A	DEAD 536D	45 KALEW IAβ	CALL 399D
33	DIDACH8 3	TEACHING 191C	PWS IA	HOW 739C
	EKPL8SSW 2	BE AMAZED 243D	46 APO II2A	FROM 86B
34	AUTOS 4B	THE SAME 123B	APOKRINOMAI I	ANSWER 92D
	EPI IIIIA[	ON 288C	EKEINOS 2Bγ	THAT 239B
	SADDOUKAIOS	SADDUCEE 747A	EPERWTAW IA	ASK 284D
	SUNAGW 2	GATHER 790B	H8MERA 2	DAY 347A
	PHARISAIOS	PHARISEE 861C	LOGOS IAα	WORD 478B
	PHIMOW 2	TIE SHUT 869D	HO,H8,TO IIIH	THE 553B
35	HEIS IAβ	ONE 230A	OUDE I	AND NOT 595D
	EK 4Aα	FROM 235B	OUKETI I	NO LONGER 597A
	NOMIKOS 2	LAWYER 543C	TOLMAW IA	DARE 829C
	PEIRAZW 2C	TRY 646A		
36	DIDASKALOS	TEACHER 190D	MATTHEW 23	
	ENTOL8 2Aγ	COMMAND 268C		
	MEGAS 2Bβ	GREAT 499C	I LALEW 3	SPEAK 465A
	NOMOS 3	LAW 544C	2 GRAMMATEUS 2	SCRIBES 165A
	POIOS 2Aα	OF WHAT KIND 691B	EPI IIAβ	ON 285D
37	AGAPAW IAβ	LOVE 4C	KATHEDRA	CHAIR 389B
	DIANOIA I	UNDERSTANDING 186A	KATHIZW 2Aα	SIT DOWN 391A
	THEOS 3C	GOD 358A	PHARISAIOS	PHARISEE 861C
	KARDIA IBζ	HEART 405B	3 GAR 2	FOR 151C
	KURIOS 2A	LORD 460B	KATA II58α	ACCORDING TO 408C
	PSUCH8 IBγ	SOUL LIFE 901D	HOSOS 2	HOW GREAT 590C
38	ENTOL8 2Aγ	COMMAND 268C	T8REW 5	KEEP 822D
	MEGAS 2Bβ	GREAT 499C	3B POIEW I2Bα	DO 689B
	PRWTOS ICα	FIRST 733B	3C POIEW I2C	DO 689B
39	AGAPAW IAα	LOVE 4B	4 AUTOS IC	SELF 122C
	DEUTEROS 3	SECOND 176A	BARUS I	HEAVY 133D
	HOMOIOS I	LIKE 569D	DAKTULOS	FINGER 169A
	PL8SION IB	NEAR 678D	DESMEUW 2	TIE UP 174D
	SEAUTOU 3	YOURSELF 753A	DUSBASTAKTOS	HARD TO BEAR 208C
40	EN I5C	IN 259A	EPI IIIIAβ	ON 288A
	ENTOL8 2Aγ	COMMAND 268C	EPITITH8MI IAα	PUT UPON 302D
	KREMANNUMI 2B	HANG 451B	THELW I	WISH 355C
	NOMOS 4A	LAW 545A	KINEW I	MOVE 433C

4	PHORTION 2	LOAD 873A	14	PROPHASIS 2	ACTUAL MOTIVE 730A	
	WMOS	SHOULDER 904B		CH8RA	THE WIDOW 889D	
5	ANTHRWPOS IA6	PEOPLE 67C	15	GEENNA	HELL 152C	
	ERGON IC8	DEED 308A		DIPLOUS	DOUBLE 198D	
	THEAOMAI IC8	SEE 353D		HEIS 2B	ONE 230B	
	KRASPEDON 2	TASSEL 449B		THALASSA IA	SEA 350D	
	MEGALUNW I	MAKE LARGE 498B		X8ROS I	DRY 551A	
	PLATUNW I	ENLARGE 672D		HO,H8,TO II2B	THE 553B	
	PROS III3A	TOWARD 717A		HOTAN IB	WHEN 592A	
	PHULAKT8RION	SAFEGUARD 876A		PERIAGW 2	LEAD AROUND 651B	
6	DEIPNON 2	DINNER 172B		PROS8LUTOS	PROSELYTE 722B	
	PRWTOKLISIA	PLACE OF HONOR 732C		HUIOS IC6	SON 842A	
	PRWTOKATHEDRIA	PLACE OF HONOR 732C		PHARISAIOS	PHARISEE 861C	
	PHILEW IB	LOVE LIKE 867A	15B	POIEW IIB:	DO 688B	
6F	PHILEW IB	LOVE LIKE 867A	16	EN IV5	IN 260D	
7	AGORA	MARKET PLACE 12B		NAOS IA	TEMPLE 535B	
	ASPASMOS I	GREETING 116D		HOD8GOS 2	LEADER 556A	
	KALEW IA8	CALL 399D		OMNUW	TAKE AN OATH 569A	
7F	RABBI	RABBI 740B		OUDEIS 2B8	WORTHLESS 596C	
8	HEIS 2B	ONE 230C		OPHEILW 2Bα	OWE 603D	
	KATH8G8T8S	TEACHER 389D		TUPHLOS 2Aα	BLIND 838C	
	KALEW IA8	CALL 399D	16F	CHRUSOS	GOLD 897A	
	PAS IEα	ALL 637D	17	HAGIAZW I	CONSECRATE 8D	
	CHRISTOS I	ANOINTED ONE 895B		GAR IF	WHAT 151C	
9	HEIS 2B	ONE 230C		MWROS I	FOOLISH 533B	
	EPI IIAα	ON 285C		NAOS IA	TEMPLE 535B	
	KALEW IA8	CALL 399D		TUPHLOS 2B	BLIND 838D	
	OURANIOS	HEAVENLY 598A	18	DWRON 2	GIFT 210C	
9A	PAT8R 2B	FATHER 640D		EPANW 2A	ON 283A	
9B	PAT8R 3Cα	FATHER 641C		OMNUW	TAKE AN OATH 569A	
9B	PAT8R 3Cα	FATHER 641C		OUDEIS 2B8	WORTHLESS 596C	
9F	M8DE IB	AND NOT 519D		OPHEILW 2Bα	OWE 603D	
10	HEIS 2C	ONE 230D	18FF	EN IV5	IN 260D	
	KATH8G8T8S	TEACHER 389D	18=20	THUSIAST8RION IA	ALTAR 367B	
	KALEW IA8	CALL 399D	19	HAGIAZW I	CONSECRATE 8D	
	CHRISTOS I	ANOINTED ONE 895B		GAR IF	WHAT 151C	
11	DIAKONOS IA	SERVANT 183C		DWRON 2	GIFT 210C	
	MEGAS 2Bα	GREAT 499B		MWROS I	FOOLISH 533B	
12	HEAUTOU I	ONESELF 211A		TIS, TI IBγ	WHICH 827A	
12A	HOSTIS IC	WHOEVER 590D		TUPHLOS 2B	BLIND 838C	
12A	TAPEINOW 2A	LOWER 812C	20	EPANW 2A	ON 283A	
12A	HUPSOW 2	LIFT UP 858D		OMNUW	TAKE AN OATH 569A	
12B	HOSTIS IC	WHOEVER 590D	21	KATOIKEW 2	LIVE 425C	
12B	TAPEINOW 2A	LOWER 812B		NAOS IA	TEMPLE 535B	
12B	TAPEINOW 2B	LOWER 812C		OMNUW	TAKE AN OATH 569A	
12B	HUPSOW 2	LIFT UP 858D	22	EPANW 2A	ON 283A	
13	APHI8MI 4	TOLERATE 126A		THRONOS IB	THRONE 364D	
	BASILEIA 3G	KINGDOM 135A		KATH8MAI IAα	SIT 390B	
	DIA BII2	THEREFORE 180B		OMNUW	TAKE AN OATH 568D	
	EISERCHOMAI 2A	COME 232B		OURANOS 2A	HEAVEN 599A	
	EMPROSTHEN 2C	IN FRONT 256C	23	AN8THON	DILL 65C	
	KATESTHIW 2	DESTROY 423B		APODEKATOW I	TITHE 89B	
	KLEIW 2	SHUT 435B		APHI8MI 3B	ABANDON 125D	
	KRIMA 4B	VERDICT 451D		BARUS 2B	IMPORTANT 134A	
	OURANOS 3	HEAVEN 599D		DEI 3	IT IS NECESSARY 171B	
	PERISSOTEROS I	GREATER 657B		DEI 6	IT IS NECESSARY 171B	
	PHARISAIOS	PHARISEE 861C		DEI 6B	IT IS NECESSARY 171C	
13FF	GRAMMATEUS 2	SCRIBES 165A		ELEOS I	MERCY 249C	
13=15	HUPOKRIT8S	HYPOCRITE 853A		H8DUOSMON	MINT 345A	
13=16	OUAI IA	WOE 595C		KAKEINOS IA	AND HE 397C	
14	LAMBANW 2	RECEIVE 466C		KRISIS 3	RIGHT 454A	
	MAKROS I	LONG 489C		KUMINON	CUMIN 458C	
	OIKIA IA	HOUSE 560A		NOMOS 3	LAW 544C	

23	OUAI IA	WOE 595C	30	PAT8R IB	FOREFATHERS 640D
	P8GANON	RUE 661C		PROPH8T8S 4	PROPHET 731B
	PISTIS IA	FAITH 668B	31	HEAUTOU 2	ONESELF 211C
	POIEW IIB«	DO 687D		MARTUREW IA	BEAR WITNESS 493D
	HUPOKRIT8S	HYPOCRITE 853A		HUIOS ICv	SON 841D
24	DIULIZW	FILTER OUT 199B		PHONEUW	MURDER 872C
	KAM8LOS	CAMEL 402D		HWSTE IA	THEREFORE 908B
	KATAPINW IA	SWALLOW 417B	32	KAI I2F	AND 393C
	KWNWPS	GNAT 463A		METRON IA	MEASURE 516D
	HOD8GOS 2	LEADER 556A		PAT8R IB	FOREFATHERS 640D
	TUPHLOS 2A«	BLIND 838C		PL8ROW IA	MAKE FULL 676D
25	AKRA8IA	SELF INDULGENCE 32B	33	GEENNA	HELL 152C
	HARPAG8 2	PLUNDER 108A		GENN8MA	CHILD 155A
	GEMW 2	BE FULL 153A		ECHIDNA	VIPER 332A
	DE IA	BUT, AND 170C		KRISIS IAª	JUDGING 453D
	EK 4Aꜱ	FROM 235C		OPHIS 2	SNAKE 605A
	EXWTHEN IBª	OUTSIDE 279B		PWS IE	HOW 739D
	ESWTHEN 2	INSIDE 314C		PHEUGW 2	FLEE 863C
	HO,H8,TO II6	THE 554B	34	APO III	FROM 868
	OUAI IA	WOE 595C		APOSTELLW IB«	SEND AWAY 98A
	PAROPSIS	DISH 635D		GRAMMATEUS 3	SCRIBES 165A
	HUPOKRIT8S	HYPOCRITE 853A		DIWKW 3	DRIVE AWAY 200B
25F	KATHARIZW IA	CLEANSE 388A		EGW	I 216B
25F	POT8RION I	CUP 702A		EK 4Av	FROM 235B
26	EKTOS I	OUTSIDE 245C		IDOU IB6	BEHOLD 371C
	ENTOS	INSIDE 269A		MASTIGOW I	WHIP 496A
	HINA IIC	IN ORDER THAT 377C		POLIS I	CITY 692B
	KATHARIZW 2B«	CLEANSE 388B		PROPH8T8S 4	PROPHET 731B
	KATHAROS I	CLEAN 388D		SOPHOS 3	LEARNED 767D
	PAROPSIS	DISH 635D		STAUROW I	CRUCIFY 773A
	TUPHLOS 2A«	BLIND 838C		SUNAGWG8 2A	790C
	PHARISAIOS	PHARISEE 861C		PLACE OF ASSEMBLY	
27	AKATHARSIA I	IMPURITY 28B	35	HABEL	ABEL IC
	GEMW I	BE FULL 153A		HAIMA 2A	BLOOD 22B
	KONIAW	WHITEWASH 444A		HAIMA 2A	BLOOD 22C
	NEKROS 2A	DEAD 537B		APO II3B	FROM 86C
	HOMOIAZW	BE LIKE 569C		BARACHIAS	BARACHIAH 132C
	OSTEON	BONE 590D		BARACHIAS	BARACHIAH 132D
	OUAI IA	WOE 595C		DIKAIOS IB	UPRIGHT 194D
	PAROMOIAZW	BE LIKE 634D		DIKAIOS 4	RIGHTEOUS 195A
	PAS IAª	EVERY EACH 636D		EKCHEW I	POUR OUT 246D
	HUPOKRIT8S	HYPOCRITE 853A		EPI IIIIBv	ON 289A
	PHAINW 2D	APPEAR 859D		ERCHOMAI I2C	COME 311D
	HWRAIOS	BEAUTIFUL 905B		ZACHARIAS 2	ZECHARIAH 336B
27F	EXWTHEN IB«	OUTSIDE 279B		THUSIAST8RION IA	ALTAR 367B
27F	ESWTHEN 2	INSIDE 314C		METAXU 2A	BETWEEN 514C
28	ANOMIA I	LAWLESSNESS 71A		NAOS IA	TEMPLE 535B
	DIKAIOS IB	UPRIGHT 194D		HOPWS 2A«	IN ORDER THAT 580C
	MESTOS 2A	FULL 509C		PAS IA«	EVERY EACH 636C
	HUPOKRISIS	HYPOCRISY 852D		PHONEUW	MURDER 872C
	PHAINW 2D	APPEAR 859D	36	GENEA 2	GENERATION 153B
29	DIKAIOS IB	UPRIGHT 194D		H8KW 2	HAVE COME 345C
	KOSMEW 2Aª	DECORATE 446A	37	APOSTELLW IB«	SEND AWAY 98A
	MN8MEION 2	TOMB 526C		HIEROSOLUMA IB	JERUSALEM 373D
	OIKODOMEW IA	BUILD 560C		LITHOBOLEW 2	STONE 475B
	OUAI IA	WOE 595C		NOSSION	YOUNG 545D
	TAPHOS I	GRAVE 814A		ORNIS	COCK 585D
	HUPOKRIT8S	HYPOCRITE 853A		POSAKIS	HOW OFTEN 701A
30	HAIMA 2A	BLOOD 22B		PROPH8T8S 4	PROPHET 731B
	EI IIB	IF 218A		PTERUX	WING 734D
	EIMI I2	TO BE 222B		TEKNON 2F«	CHILD 816C
	H8MERA 4B	TIME 348B		TROPOS I	MANNER 835B
	KOINWNOS IC	COMPANION 440D		HUPO 2A«	UNDER 851A

37A	EPISUNAGW	GATHER	301C
37B	EPISUNAGW	GATHER	301D
38	APHI8MI 3A	ABANDON	125D
	ER8MOS 1A	ABANDONED	308D
	IDOU 1Bε	BEHOLD	371C
	OIKOS 1AΥ	HOUSE	563B
39	ARTI 3	NOW	109D
	ERCHOMAI 11Aη	COME	310D
	EULOGEW 2A	BLESS	322D
	LEGW III D	ASSURE	470D
	ONOMA 14CΥ	NAME	576C

MATTHEW 24

1	APO IVIAβ	FROM	86D
	EXERCHOMAI 1Aα	GO OUT	274A
	EPIDEIKNUMI 1	SHOW	291D
	OIKODOM8 2A	BUILDING	561C
	PROSERCHOMAI 1	APPROACH	720A
1A	HIERON 2	TEMPLE	373A
1B	HIERON 2	TEMPLE	373A
2	APHI8MI 3A	LEAVE	125D
	BLEPW 1A	SEE	142D
	EPI III1Aζ	ON	288C
	KATALUW 1A	THROW DOWN	415B
	LITHOS 1B	STONE	475B
	M8 DIA	NOT	519B
3	AIWN 2A	AGE	27B
	EIMI 14	TO BE	222C
	ELAIA 1	OLIVE TREE	247B
	EPI 11Aα	ON	285C
	IDIOS 4	PRIVATELY	371A
	KATH8MAI 1Aα	SIT	390B
	PAROUSIA 2Bα	COMING	635C
	POTE	WHEN	701D
	S8MEION 1	SIGN	755B
	SUNTELEIA	CLOSE	799C
4	BLEPW 6	SEE	143B
	M8 B1B	NOT	519A
	TIS, TI 1AΥ	ANY ONE	827D
4F	PLANAW 1B	DECEIVE	671B
5	EPI 113	ON	287D
	ERCHOMAI 11Aθ	COME	311B
	ONOMA 14Cε	NAME	576C
	CHRISTOS 1	ANOINTED ONE	895B
5A	POLUS 12Aα	MANY	694D
5B	POLUS 12Aα	MANY	694D
6	AKO8 2A	REPORT	30C
	AKOUW 1Bα	HEAR	31B
	ALLA 2	BUT, YET	37D
	GINOMAI 13A	TAKE PLACE	157D
	DEI 1	IT IS NECESSARY	171A
	THROEW	BE DISTURBED	364C
	HORAW 2B	SEE	582B
	OUPW	NOT YET	597D
	POLEMOS 1A	ARMED CONFLICT	691D
	TELOS 1B	END	819A
7	BASILEIA 2	KINGDOM	134C
	EGEIRW 2D	RISE	214A
	ETHNOS 1	NATION	217B
	EIMI 14	TO BE	222C
	EPI III1Aε	AGAINST	288B
	KATA III A	ALONG	407A

7	LIMOS 2	FAMINE	476B
	LOIMOS 1	PESTILENCE	480D
	SEISMOS	SHAKING	753D
	TOPOS 1D	PLACE	830B
8	ARCH8 1B	BEGINNING	111B
	ODUN8	PAIN	557C
	PAS 1Eβ	ALL	637D
	WDIN 2B	BIRTH PAIN	904A
9	EIMI 114BΥ	TO BE	223A
	EIS 4A	INTO	228B
	THLIPSIS 1	TRIBULATION	363A
	MISEW 3	HATE	524D
	ONOMA 14Cα	NAME	575C
	PARADIDWMI 1B	GIVE OVER	620B
10	ALL8LWN	EACH OTHER	39A
	MISEW 1	HATE	524D
	PARADIDWMI 1B	GIVE OVER	619D
	SKANDALIZW 1A	CAUSE TO FALL	760B
	TOTE 2	AT THAT TIME	831D
11	EGEIRW 2E	APPEAR	214B
	PLANAW 1B	DECEIVE	671B
	POLUS 11Aα	MANY	694D
	PSEUDOPROPH8T8S	FALSE PROPHET	900B
12	AGAP8 11A	LOVE	5B
	ANOMIA 1	LAWLESSNESS	71B
	DIA B1I3	BECAUSE	180C
	PL8THUNW 1B	INCREASE	675A
	POLUS 12Aβ	MANY	695A
	PSUCHW	MAKE COOL	903A
13	EIS 2Aα	UNTIL	227D
	HOUTOS 1Aε	THIS	601B
	SWZW 2B	SAVE	806B
	TELOS 1DΥ	END	819D
	HUPOMENW 2	REMAIN	853C
14	BASILEIA 3G	KINGDOM	135A
	ETHNOS 1	NATION	217B
	EIS 4F	(PURPOSE)	228D
	EUAGGELION 1C	GOSPEL	318B
	EUAGGELION 2Bα	GOSPEL	318B
	H8KW 2	HAVE COME	345C
	K8RUSSW 2Bβ	ANNOUNCE	432C
	MARTURION 1A	TESTIMONY	494D
	OIKOUMEN8 1A	THE WORLD	564A
	TELOS 1B	END	819A
	TOTE 2	AT THAT TIME	831D
15	HAGIOS 1Aα	DEDICATED TO GOD	9C
	ANAGINWSKW 1	READ	51B
	BDELUGMA 3	ABOMINATION	137C
	DANI8L	DANIEL	169D
	EIPON 4	SAY	225D
	ER8MWSIS	DEVASTATION	309B
	HIST8MI 112Bβ	BEING	383C
	NOEW 2	CONSIDER	542D
	OUN 5	THEREFORE	597D
	PROPH8T8S 1	PROPHET	730D
	TOPOS 1B	PLACE	830B
15F	HOTAN 1B	WHEN	592B
16	IOUDAIA 1	JUDAEA	379D
	OROS	MOUNTAIN	586C
	TOTE 2	AT THAT TIME	831D
	*PHEUGW 1	FLEE	863C
17	AIRW 3	CARRY	24A
	DWMA	ROOF	209C

17 EK 6A — FROM 235D
EPI IIAα — ON 285C
KATABAINW IAα — COME DOWN 409B
M8 AIII4 — NOT 518D
18 AGROS I — FIELD 13D
EPISTREPHW IBα — TURN 301A
HIMATION 2 — GARMENT 377A
M8 AIII4 — NOT 518D
OPISW IA — BEHIND 578C
19 GAST8R 2 — WOMB 152A
EKEINOS 2Bβ — THAT 239B
ECHW I2J — HAVE 333C
H8MERA 49 — TIME 348B
TH8LAZW I — GIVE SUCK 361A
OUAI IA — WOE 595C
20 GINOMAI I3A — TAKE PLACE 157D
HINA IIIAγ — IN ORDER THAT 378B
PROSEUCHOMAI — PRAY 721A
SABBATON IA — SABBATH 746B
PHUG8 — FLIGHT 875C
CHEIMWN 2 — WINTER 888A
21 ARCH8 IC — BEGINNING 1110
GINOMAI IIBβ — COME ABOUT 157B
HEWS IIIA — UNTIL 335B
THLIPSIS I — TRIBULATION 362D
THLIPSIS I — TRIBULATION 363A
KOSMOS 2 — WORLD 446D
MEGAS 2Aγ — GREAT 499A
M8 DIA — NOT 519C
NUN 3B — NOW 548B
HOIOS — OF WHAT SORT 565C
OU 6D — NO 595B
22 EI IIA — IF 218A
M8 AII — NOT 517C
PAS IAα — EVERY EACH 636D
SARX 3 — BODY 751B
SWZW IA — SAVE 805D
22A KOLOBOW 2 — SHORTEN 442D
22B KOLOBOW 2 — SHORTEN 442D
23 PISTEUW ID — BELIEVE 666D
TIS, TI IAγ — ANY ONE 827D
CHRISTOS I — ANOINTED ONE 895B
HWDE 2A — HERE 903D
24 DUNATOS 2A — POSSIBLE 208A
EGEIRW 2E — APPEAR 214B
MEGAS 2Aγ — GREAT 499A
PLANAW IB — DECEIVE 671B
PLANAW 2C6 — DECEIVE 671C
S8MEION 2B — SIGN 755D
PSEUDOPROPH8T8S — FALSE PROPHET 900B
PSEUDOCHRISTOS — FALSE MESSIAH 900C
HWSTE 2Aβ — THEREFORE 908C
HWSTE 2Aβ — THEREFORE 908C
25 PROEIPON I — FORETELL 711C
26 EAN IIB — IF 210B
EIMI III4 — TO BE 224B
ER8MOS 2 — DESERT 309A
OUN 5 — THEREFORE 597D
PISTEUW ID — BELIEVE 666D
TAMEION 2 — STOREROOM 811B
TAMIEION — SECRET ROOM 811C
27 ANATOL8 2B — EAST 62A
ASTRAP8 — LIGHTNING 117D

27 DUSM8 — WEST 209A
EIMI II9B — TO BE 224A
EXERCHOMAI 2Bβ — GO OUT 274C
HEWS II2A — AS FAR AS 335C
PAROUSIA 2Bα — COMING 635C
HUIOS 2C — SON 843A
PHAINW 2A — SHINE 859B
HWSPER I — (JUST) AS 908A
28 AETOS — EAGLE 19B
EKEI 2 — THERE 238D
HOPOU IA6 — WHERE 579D
PTWMA — CORPSE 735B
SUNAGW 2 — GATHER 790B
29 AST8R — STAR 117B
DIDWMI IBγ — GIVE 192B
DUNAMIS 5 — RESOURCES 207B
H8LIOS — THE SUN 346B
THLIPSIS I — TRIBULATION 363A
META BII3 — AFTER 511C
PIPTW IA — FALL 665A
SALEUW I — SHAKE 747D
SEL8N8 — MOON 754B
SKOTIZW I — BECOME DARK 764D
PHEGGOS — LIGHT 862C
29A OURANOS IC — HEAVEN 598C
29B OURANOS IC — HEAVEN 598D
30 DOXA IA — GLORY 202D
EPI IIAα — ON 285C
ERCHOMAI IIAη — COME 311A
KOPTW 2 — BEAT 445A
META AIII2 — WITH 511A
NEPHEL8 — CLOUD 538D
HORAW IAα — SEE 581C
OURANOS 2B — HEAVEN 599C
POLUS IIBβ — MANY 694C
S8MEION I — SIGN 755B
HUIOS 2C — SON 843A
PHAINW 2B — APPEAR 859B
PHUL8 2 — NATION 876D
30A TOTE 2 — AT THAT TIME 831D
30B OURANOS ID — HEAVEN 598D
30B TOTE 2 — AT THAT TIME 831D
31 AGGELOS 2A — ANGEL 7D
AKRON — TOP 33C
EPISUNAGW — GATHER 301D
HEWS II2A — AS FAR AS 335C
MEGAS 2Aγ — GREAT 498D
META AIII2 — WITH 511A
SALPIGX 2 — TRUMPET 748B
SALPIGX I — TRUMPET 748B
TESSARES — FOUR 821A
PHWN8 I — SOUND 878C
32 HAPALOS — TENDER 79C
APO IV2B — FROM 87A
GINOMAI I4B — BECOME 158D
GINWSKW 3C — UNDERSTAND 160B
EGGUS 2A — NEAR 213B
EKPHUW — PUT FORTH 246C
THEROS — SUMMER 360B
KLADOS — BRANCH 434A
MANTHANW I — LEARN 491C
PARABOL8 2 — PARABLE 617D
SUK8 — FIG TREE 783D

32	PHULLON	FOLIAGE 877A
32F	HOTAN 1B	WHEN 592A
33	GINWSKW 6C	KNOW 160D
	EGGUS 3	NEAR 213C
	EIMI III5B	TO BE 224C
	EPI IIIA6	AT 286D
	THURA 2A	DOOR 366C
	HOUTW 1B	THUS 602C
34	GENEA 2	GENERATION 153B
	GENEA 1	CLAN 153B
	GINOMAI I3A	TAKE PLACE 157D
	M8 DIA	NOT 519B
	PARERCHOMAI 1Bα	PASS AWAY 631C
35	LOGOS IA6	WORD 478D
	OURANOS IAα	HEAVEN 598B
35A	PARERCHOMAI 1Bα	631C
	PASS AWAY	
35B	PARERCHOMAI 1Bα	631C
	PASS AWAY	
36	AGGELOS 2A	ANGEL 7C
	MONOS IAY	ONLY 529C
	OIDA IH	KNOW 558C
	OUDE 3	NOT EVEN 596A
	OURANOS 2C	HEAVEN 599C
	PAT8R 3Dα	FATHER 641D
	PERI IH	ABOUT 650D
	HWRA I	TIME OF DAY 904B
37	EIMI II9B	TO BE 224A
	NWE	NOAH 549C
	PAROUSIA 28α	COMING 635C
	HUIOS 2C	SON 843A
	HWSPER I	(JUST) AS 908A
38	ACHRI IA	UNTIL 128B
	GAMEW 1B	MARRY 150A
	GAMIZW I	GIVE IN MARRIAGE 150B
	GAMISKW	GIVE IN MARRIAGE 150C
	GAR 2	FOR 151C
	EISERCHOMAI IAβ	COME 231D
	EKGAMIZW	MARRY 237C
	EKEINOS 2Bα	THAT 239B
	H8MERA 4B	TIME 348B
	KIBWTOS I	BOX 433A
	NWE	NOAH 549C
	HOS,H8,HO I5Cα	(REL PRON) 588B
	PINW I	DRINK 664C
	PRO 2	BEFORE 708C
	TRWGW	GNAW 837A
38B	H8MERA 2	DAY 347A
38F	KATAKLUSMOS	FLOOD 412D
39	AIRW 4	TAKE AWAY 24A
	HAPAS 2	ALL 81A
	GINWSKW 3B	UNDERSTAND 160B
	EIMI II9B	TO BE 224A
	HEWS IIA	UNTIL 334D
	PAROUSIA 28α	COMING 635C
	HUIOS 2C	SON 843A
40	AGROS I	FIELD 13D
	PARALAMBANW I	TAKE 625A
40F	HEIS 5A	ONE 231A
41	AL8THW	GRIND 36D
	MULOS I	MILL 531A
	MULWN	MILL HOUSE 531B
	PARALAMBANW I	TAKE 625A

42	GR8GOREW 2	BE AWAKE 166C
	HWRA I	TIME OF DAY 904B
42F	OIDA IF	KNOW 558C
42F	POIOS 2Aβ	OF WHAT KIND 691B
43	GINWSKW 6C	KNOW 160D
	GR8GOREW I	BE AWAKE 166C
	DIORUSSW	DIGS THROUGH 198B
	EAW I	LET 211D
	EI IIB	IF 218A
	EKEINOS ID	THAT 239A
	KLEPT8S	THIEF 435B
	KLEPT8S	THIEF 435C
	HO,H8,TO IIIAβ	THE 552C
	OIKIA IA	HOUSE 559D
	OIKODESPOT8S	560C
	MASTER OF THE HOUSE	
	PHULAK8 4	GUARD 875D
44	DIA BII2	THEREFORE 180B
	DOKEW IF	THINK 201A
	HETOIMOS 2	READY 316D
	HOS,H8,HO I5A	(REL PRON) 588B
	HUIOS 2C	SON 843A
	HWRA I	TIME OF DAY 904B
45	ARA 2	THEN 103B
	EPI IIBα	OVER 286A
	THERAPEIA 2	SERVING 359C
	KATHIST8MI 2A	APPOINT 391B
	KAIROS 2	TIME 395D
	HO,H8,TO II48ζ	THE 554A
	OIKETEIA	559B
	SLAVES IN A HOUSEHOLD	
	PISTOS IAα	TRUSTWORTHY 670B
	TROPH8 I	FOOD 835C
	PHRONIMOS	THOUGHTFUL 874C
45F	DOULOS IA	SLAVE 204D
46	HEURISKW ICα	FIND 325C
	MAKARIOS 1B	BLESSED 488A
	POIEW I2Aα	DO 689A
47	EPI IIIBα	OVER 286D
	KATHIST8MI 2A	APPOINT 391B
	PAS IDβ	ALL 637D
	HUPARCHW I	BE 845D
48	DOULOS IA	SLAVE 204D
	EAN IIB	IF 210C
	KAKOS IA	BAD 398C
	KARDIA IBβ	HEART 404C
	KURIOS IAβ	LORD 460A
	CHRONIZW I	TAKE TIME 896A
	CHRONIZW 2	TAKE TIME 896A
49	ARCHW 2Aα	BEGIN 113A
	ESTHIW IC	EAT 313A
	ESTHIW IEε	EAT 313B
	METHUW I	BE DRUNK 500C
	META AII2	WITH 510C
	PINW I	DRINK 664C
	SUNDOULOS I	FELLOW SLAVE 793B
	TUPTW I	STRIKE 838A
50	GINWSKW 6Aα	KNOW 160C
	DOULOS IA	SLAVE 204D
	EAN IIB	IF 210C
	H8KW IC	HAVE COME 345B
	H8MERA 2	DAY 347A
	PROSDOKAW 3	EXPECT 719C

50	HWRA I	TIME OF DAY 904B
50B	HOS,H8,HO I4A	(REL PRON) 587D
51	BRUGMOS	GNASHING 147B
	DICHOTOMEW	CUT IN TWO 199C
	KLAUTHMOS	WEEPING 434D
	MEROS 2	SHARE 507C
	META AI	WITH 509D
	ODOUS	TOOTH 557B
	TITH8MI II8ε	824A
	MAKE UP (YOUR) MINDS	
	HUPOKRIT8S	HYPOCRITE 853A

MATTHEW 25

I	DEKA	TEN 172D
	HEAUTOU 4	ONESELF 211D
	EIS 4F	(PURPOSE) 228D
	EXERCHOMAI IAε	GO OUT 274B
	LAMBANW IA	TAKE 465B
	LAMPAS 2	LAMP 466D
	NUMPHIOS	BRIDEGROOM 547B
	NUMPH8 I	BRIDE 547B
	HOMOIOW I	MAKE LIKE 570B
	HOSTIS 2A	WHOEVER 591A
	OURANOS 3	HEAVEN 600A
	PARTHENOS I	VIRGIN 632B
	HUPANT8SIS	COMING TO MEET 845C
2	EK 4Aα	FROM 235B
	PHRONIMOS	THOUGHTFUL 874C
2F	MWROS I	FOOLISH 533B
3	HEAUTOU IF	ONESELF 211B
	LAMBANW IA	TAKE 465B
3F	ELAION I	OLIVE OIL 247B
3F	LAMPAS 2	LAMP 466D
4	AGGEION	CONTAINER 6D
	PHRONIMCS	THOUGHTFUL 874C
5	KATHEUDW I	SLEEP 389C
	NUSTAZW I	BECOME DROWSY 549B
	CHRONIZW I	TAKE TIME 896A
5F	NUMPHIOS	BRIDEGROOM 547B
6	APANT8SIS	MEETING 79D
	GINOMAI II8β	COME ABOUT 157B
	ERCHOMAI IIAα	COME 310B
	IDOU 2	THERE IS 371D
	KRAUG8 IB	SHOUT 450C
	MESOS I	MIDNIGHT 508B
	NUX IB	NIGHT 548D
7	EGEIRW 2A	AWAKEN 214A
	KOSMEW I	PUT IN ORDER 445D
	PARTHENOS I	VIRGIN 632B
	PAS IDα	ALL 637C
7F	LAMPAS 2	LAMP 466D
8	DIDWMI IA	GIVE 191D
	EK 4Aε	FROM 235B
	ELAION I	OLIVE OIL 247B
	MWROS I	FOOLISH 533B
	SBENNUMI I	EXTINGUISH 752D
8F	PHRONIMOS	THOUGHTFUL 874C
9	AGORAZW I	BUY 12C
	ARKEW I	BE ENOUGH 106D
	MALLON 3Aβ	RATHER 490C
	M8POTE 4	PERHAPS 521B
	POREUW I	PROCEED 699A
9	PWLEW	SELL 739A
10	AGORAZW I	BUY 12C
	GAMOS IB	WEDDING 150D
	HETOIMOS 2	READY 316D
	THURA IA	DOOR 366B
	KLEIW I	SHUT 435A
	NUMPHIOS	BRIDEGROOM 547B
11	ANOIGW IA	OPEN 70B
	KURIOS IB	LORD 460A
	LOIPOS 2A	OTHER 481A
	PARTHENOS I	VIRGIN 632B
	HUSTEROS 2A	LATER 857B
12	OIDA 2	KNOW 558D
13	GR8GOREW 2	BE AWAKE 166C
	H8MERA 2	DAY 346D
	OIDA IB	KNOW 558B
	OUDE I	AND NOT 595D
	HUIOS 2C	SON 843A
	HWRA I	TIME OF DAY 904B
14	APOD8MEW I	GO ON A JOURNEY 89C
	DOULOS IA	SLAVE 204D
	IDIOS 2C	ONES OWN 370C
	KALEW IC	CALL 400B
	PARADIDWMI IA	GIVE OVER 619D
	HUPARCHW I	BE 845D
	HWSPER I	(JUST) AS 908A
15	APOD8MEW I	GO ON A JOURNEY 89C
	DIDWMI 3	GIVE 192C
	DUNAMIS 2	POWER 207A
	HEIS IAα	ONE 230A
	HEKASTOS 2	EACH 236A
	IDIOS IAβ	ONES OWN 370B
	KATA II5Aγ	ACCORDING TO 408B
	MEN IC	(PARTICLE) 504A
	HOS,H8,HO II2	THIS (ONE) 589B
15=28	TALANTON	TALENT 811B
16	ERGAZOMAI I	WORK 307A
	POIEW II8η	DO 688A
	POREUW I	PROCEED 699B
16F	KERDAINW IA	TO GAIN 430C
17	HO,H8,TO II9A	THE 554D
	HWSAUTWS	SIMILARLY 907D
18	APERCHOMAI IA	GO AWAY 83D
	APOKRUPTW	CONCEAL 93B
	ARGURION 2B	MONEY 104B
	G8 2	GROUND 156C
	KRUPTW IA	HIDE 455B
	ORUSSW I	DIG 586C
	ORUSSW 3	DIG 586D
19	DOULOS IA	SLAVE 204D
	LOGOS 2B	SETTLEMENT 479D
	META AII3B	WITH 510D
	META BIII	AFTER 511B
	POLUS II8α	MANY 694C
	SUNAIRW	SETTLE ACCOUNTS 791B
	CHRONOS	TIME 896A
20	ALLOS 2	MORE 39D
	EPIKERDAINW	GAIN IN ADDITION 294D
	IDE 3	SEE 369D
	KERDAINW IA	TO GAIN 430C
	KURIOS IAβ	LORD 460A
	PARADIDWMI IA	GIVE OVER 619D
	PROSERCHOMAI I	APPROACH 720A

20	PROSPHERW IB	BRING (TO) 727A	27	ARGURION 2B	MONEY 104B
21	AGATHOS IA«	GOOD 2D		BALLW 2B	PUT 131A
	DOULOS IA	SLAVE 204D		EMOS 2	MY 255A
	EISERCHOMAI 2A	COME 232B		KOMIZW 2B	BRING 443D
	EPI IIIIB«	OVER 288D		SUN 4A	WITH 789C
	EU	WELL 317C		TOKOS	INTEREST 829C
	KATHIST8MI 2A	APPOINT 391B		TRAPEZIT8S	BANKER 832C
	OLIGOS IB	FEW 566C	28	DEKA	TEN 172D
	POLUS I2B«	MANY 695A	29	HOS,H8,HO I2B«	(REL PRON) 587B
	CHARA 2B	JOY 884A		PERISSEUW 2A	BE LEFT OVER 657A
	CHARA 2C	JOY 884A	29A	ECHW I2A	HAVE 332C
21A	PISTOS IA«	TRUSTWORTHY 670B	29B	ECHW I2A	HAVE 332C
21B	PISTOS IA«	TRUSTWORTHY 670C	30	ACHREIOS	USELESS 128A
22	EPIKERDAINW	GAIN IN ADDITION 294D		BRUGMOS	GNASHING 147B
	IDE 3	SEE 369D		DOULOS IA	SLAVE 204D
	KERDAINW IA	TO GAIN 430C		EKBALLW I	DRIVE OUT 236D
	KURIOS IAβ	LORD 460A		EXWTEROS 2	FARTHEST 279C
	HO,H8,TO II9A	THE 554D		KLAUTHMOS	WEEPING 434D
	PARADIDWMI IA	GIVE OVER 619D		ODOUS	TOOTH 557B
	PROSERCHOMAI I	APPROACH 720A		SKOTOS I	DARKNESS 765A
23	AGATHOS IA«	GOOD 2D	31	DOXA IA	GLORY 202D
	DOULOS IA	SLAVE 204D		EN I4B	IN 258B
	EISERCHOMAI 2A	COME 232B		EPI IIAβ	ON 285D
	EPI IIIIB«	OVER 288D		ERCHOMAI IIAη	COME 311A
	EU	WELL 317C		THRONOS IC	THRONE 364D
	KATHIST8MI 2A	APPOINT 391B		KATHIZW 2A«	SIT DOWN 391A
	OLIGOS IB	FEW 566C		META AIIIA	WITH 509D
	POLUS I2B«	MANY 695A		HOTAN IB	WHEN 592B
	CHARA 2B	JOY 884A		TOTE 2	AT THAT TIME 831D
	CHARA 2C	JOY 884A		HUIOS 2C	SON 843A
23A	PISTOS IA«	TRUSTWORTHY 670B	32	ALL8LWN	EACH OTHER 38D
23B	PISTOS IA«	TRUSTWORTHY 670C		APHORIZW I	SEPARATE 126D
24	ANTHRWPOS 2B«	MAN 67D		EMPROSTHEN 2B	IN FRONT 256C
	GINWSKW IC	KNOW 160A		ERIPHOS	KID 309D
	DIASKORPIZW	SCATTER 187C		POIM8N I	SHEPHERD 690C
	HEIS IA«	ONE 230A		PROBATON 2	SHEEP 710A
	THERIZW 2A	REAP 360A		SUNAGW 2	GATHER 790A
	KURIOS IAβ	LORD 460A		HWSPER 2	(JUST) AS 908A
	HOTHEN I	FROM WHICH 557D	33	EK 2	AWAY FROM 234A
	HOPOU IA«	WHERE 579C		ERIPHION	KID 309C
	HOTI IB(	THAT 593A		EUWNUMOS	LEFT 330A
	PROSERCHOMAI I	APPROACH 720A		HIST8MI IIA«	PUT 382D
	SKL8ROS 2	HARD 763B	33F	DEXIOS 2B	RIGHT 173D
	SPEIRW IB«	SOW 768D	34*BASILEIA 3G		KINGDOM 135A
	SUNAGW I	GATHER 789D		BASILEUS 2A	KING 135D
25	APERCHOMAI IA	GO AWAY 83D		DEUTE 2	COME 175D
	G8 2	GROUND 156C		HETOIMAZW 3	PREPARE 316C
	ECHW I7B	HAVE 334B		EULOGEW 3	BLESS 322D
	IDE 5	SEE 370A		KATABOL8 I	FOUNDATION 410A
	KRUPTW IB	HIDE 455B		KL8RONOMEW 2	INHERIT 435D
	SOS 2B	YOURS 766D		KOSMOS 2	WORLD 446D
	PHOBEW IA	BE AFRAID 870B		PAT8R 3D«	FATHER 641D
26	DIASKORPIZW	SCATTER 187C	34-45	TOTE 2	AT THAT TIME 831D
	DOULOS IA	SLAVE 204D	35	DIDWMI 2	GIVE 192C
	THERIZW 2A	REAP 360A		DIPSAW I	THIRST 199C
	HOTHEN I	FROM WHICH 557D		ESTHIW ID	EAT 313B
	OIDA	KNOW 558A		XENOS 2A	THE STRANGER 550B
	OKN8ROS I	IDLE 565D		PEINAW I	HUNGER 645D
	HOPOU IA«	WHERE 579C		POTIZW I	GIVE TO DRINK 702C
	PON8ROS IB«	WICKED 697C		SUNAGW 5	GATHER 790B
	SPEIRW IB«	SOW 768D	36	ASTHENEW IA	BE SICK 115A
	SUNAGW I	GATHER 789D		GUMNOS 3	POORLY DRESSED 167A
27	AN IBβ	(PARTICLE) 48A		EPISKEPTOMAI 2	VISIT 298C

36	PERIBALLW 1Bε	THROW AROUND	651D
	PHULAK8 3	GUARD	875C
37	APOKRINOMAI 2	BEGIN	93A
	DIKAIOS 1B	UPRIGHT	195A
	DIPSAW 1	THIRST	199C
	PEINAW 1	HUNGER	645D
	POTIZW 1	GIVE TO DRINK	702C
	TREPHW 1	FEED	833B
37≠9	POTE	WHEN	701D
38	GUMNOS 3	POORLY DRESSED	167A
	XENOS 2A	THE STRANGER	550B
	PERIBALLW 1Bε	THROW AROUND	651D
	SUNAGW 5	GATHER	790B
39	ASTHENEW 1A	BE SICK	115A
	SU 2	YOU	780A
	PHULAK8 3	GUARD	875C
40	ADELPHOS 2	BROTHER	16A
	BASILEUS 2A	KING	135D
	ELACHISTOS 2A	SMALLEST	248B
	EPI III3	ON	289C
	POIEW IID8	DO	688D
41	AGGELOS 2C	ANGEL	8A
	AIWNIOS 3	ETERNAL	28A
	ASBESTOS 1	INEXTINGUISHABLE	114A
	DIABOLOS 2	THE SLANDERER	181A
	HETOIMAZW 3	PREPARE	316C
	EUWNUMOS	LEFT	330A
	KATARAOMAI	CURSE	418B
	HO,H8,TO III F	THE	553A
	HO,H8,TO II5	THE	554B
	POREUW 1	PROCEED	699A
	PUR 1B	FIRE	737C
42	DIDWMI 2	GIVE	192C
	DIPSAW 1	THIRST	199C
	PEINAW 1	HUNGER	645D
	POTIZW 1	GIVE TO DRINK	702C
43	EPISKEPTOMAI 2	VISIT	298C
	PERIBALLW 1Bε	THROW AROUND	651D
	SUNAGW 5	GATHER	790B
43F	ASTHEN8S 1A	SICK	115B
43F	GUMNOS 3	POORLY DRESSED	167A
43F	XENOS 2A	THE STRANGER	550B
43F	PHULAK8 3	GUARD	875C
44	DIAKONEW 4	HELP	183B
	DIPSAW 1	THIRST	199C
	8 1A8	OR	342D
	PEINAW 1	HUNGER	645D
	POTE	WHEN	701D
45	ELACHISTOS 2A	SMALLEST	248B
	EPI III3	ON	289C
	OUDE 2	AND NOT	595D
	POIEW IID8	DO	688D
46*	AIWNIOS 3	ETERNAL	28A
	DIKAIOS 1B	UPRIGHT	195A
	EIS 4A	INTO	228B
	ZW8 2B8	LIFE	341C
	KOLASIS 2	PUNISHMENT	441D

MATTHEW 26

1	GINOMAI 13F	TAKE PLACE	158C
	HOTE 1B	WHEN	592C
	PAS 1Dα	ALL	637C
1	TELEW 1	FINISH	818C
2	GINOMAI 13A	TAKE PLACE	158A
	EIS 4F	(PURPOSE)	229A
	H8MERA 2	DAY	347B
	META BII1	AFTER	511B
	PARADIDWMI 1B	GIVE OVER	620B
	PASCHA 1	THE PASSOVER	639A
	STAUROW 1	CRUCIFY	773A
	HUIOS 2C	SON	843A
3	ARCHIEREUS 1B	HIGH PRIEST	112C
	AUL8 4	COURT	121A
	KAIAPHAS	CAIAPHAS	394D
	LEGW II3	CALL	471B
	PRESBUTEROS 2A8	OLDER	706D
	PRESBUTEROS 2A8	OLDER	706D
	SUNAGW 2	GATHER	790A
4	DOLOS	DECEIT	202B
	HINA III1Aα	IN ORDER THAT	378A
	KRATEW 1A	ARREST	449C
	SUMBOULEUW 2A	ADVISE	785C
5	GINOMAI IIB8	COME ABOUT	157B
	*HEORT8	FESTIVAL	279D
	THORUBOS 3B	NOISE	363C
	LAOS 1Cα	PEOPLE	467D
	M8 AII16	NOT	519A
6	B8THANIA 1	BETHANY	139B
	GINOMAI II4A	BE	159C
	LEPROS	LEPER	473A
	OIKIA 1A	HOUSE	560A
	SIMWN 6	SIMON	758D
7	ALABASTROS	ALABASTER	33D
	ANAKEIMAI 2	BE AT TABLE	55C
	BARUTIMOS	EXPENSIVE	134A
	ECHW II A	HAVE	332A
	KATACHEW	POUR OUT	421D
	KEPHAL8 1A	HEAD	431A
	MURON	OINTMENT	531D
	POLUTIMOS	VALUABLE	696D
8	AGANAKTEW	BE AROUSED	4A
	APWLEIA 1	DESTRUCTION	103A
9	DUNAMAI 1B	ABLE	206B
	PIPRASKW	SELL	664D
	POLUS I2Cα	MANY	695B
	PTWCHOS 1A	BEGGING POOR	735D
10	GINWSKW 4B	PERCEIVE	160B
	ERGAZOMAI 2A	WORK	307A
	ERGON 1C8	DEED	308A
	KALOS 2B	GOOD	401B
	KOPOS 1	TROUBLE	444C
	PARECHW 1C	CAUSE	632A
11	ECHW I3	HAVE	333C
	META AII1B	WITH	509D
	PTWCHOS 1A	BEGGING POOR	735C
11A	PANTOTE	ALWAYS	614A
11B	PANTOTE	ALWAYS	614A
12	BALLW 2B	PUT	130D
	ENTAPHIAZW	PREPARE FOR BURIAL	267D
	MURON	OINTMENT	531D
	PROS III3A	TOWARD	717A
	SWMA 1B	BODY	806D
13	EUAGGELION 1C	GOSPEL	318B
	K8RUSSW 2B8	ANNOUNCE	432C
	KOSMOS 4A	WORLD	447A

13	LALEW 2B	SPEAK 464D	24	GENNAW 2	BEAR 154D
	MN8MOSUNON 2	MEMORY 527B		GRAPHW 2C	WRITE 166A
	HOPOU 1A6	WHERE 579D		KATHWS I	JUST AS 392A
	HOS,H8,HO I2B⍺	(REL PRON) 587B		*KALOS 3C	GOOD 401D
	POIEW IIB∈	DO 687D		OU 5B	NO 595A
14	DWDEKA	TWELVE 209B		*OUAI IA	WOE 595C
	IOUDAS 6	JUDAS 380D		PARADIDWMI IB	GIVE OVER 620A
	ISKARIWTH	ISCARIOT 381D		HUPAGW 3	GO AWAY 844D
	LEGW II3	CALL 471B	24A	HUIOS 2C	SON 843A
	POREUW I	PROCEED 699A	24B	HUIOS 2C	SON 843A
15	ARGURION 2C	SILVER 104C	25	APOKRINOMAI 2	CONTINUE 93A
	DIDWMI 4	GIVE 192C		EIMI II5	TO BE 223C
	EIPON 3B	SAY 225D		EIPON I	SAY 225C
	THELW 2	WISH 355D		IOUDAS 6	JUDAS 380D
	HIST8MI IIBγ	PUT 383A		LEGW IIIE	DECLARE 471A
	PARADIDWMI IB	GIVE OVER 620A		M8TI (INTERROG PARTICLE) 522A	
16	EUKAIRIA	321D		PARADIDWMI IB	GIVE OVER 620A
	FAVORABLE OPPORTUNITY			RABBI	RABBI 740B
	Z8TEW 2A	SEEK 339C	26	ARTOS IC	BREAD IIOB
	PARADIDWMI IB	GIVE OVER 620A		EIMI II3	TO BE 223A
	TOTE IA	AT THAT TIME 831C		ESTHIW ID	EAT 313A
17	AZUMOS IB	UNLEAVENED BREAD 19C		EULOGEW I	SPEAK WELL 322C
	ESTHIW IA	EAT 312D		EULOGEW 2B	BLESS 322D
	HETOIMAZW I	PREPARE 316B		KLAW	BREAK 434D
	THELW I	WISH 355C		HOUTOS IA⍺	THIS 600D
	PASCHA 2	THE PASCHAL LAMB 639A		SWMA IB	BODY 807B
	POU IA	WHERE 702D	26A	LAMBANW IA	TAKE 465B
	PRWTOS IA	FIRST 733A	26B	ESTHIW ID	EAT 313A
18	DEINA	SOMEBODY 172A	26B	LAMBANW IA	TAKE 465B
	DIDASKALOS	TEACHER 190D	26F	DIDWMI 2	GIVE 192C
	EGGUS 2A	NEAR 213B	27	EK IA	AWAY FROM 233C
	EIMI II9A	TO BE 223D		EUCHARISTEW 2	GIVE THANKS 328C
	EIPON 3A	SAY 225C		PAS 2Aγ	ALL 638B
	EIS IA⍺	INTO 227B		PINW I	DRINK 664C
	KAIROS 3	TIME 396A		POT8RION I	CUP 702A
	META AII2	WITH 510C	28	HAIMA 2B	BLOOD 22C
	PASCHA 3	PASSOVER MEAL 639A		HAMARTIA I	SIN 42C
	POIEW IIB⌡	DO 688A		APHESIS 2	PARDON 124C
	POLIS I	CITY 692A		DIATH8K8 2	COVENANT 182B
	HUPAGW 2	GO AWAY 844C		EIS 4F	(PURPOSE) 228D
18B	PROS III7	TOWARD 718A		EKCHEW I	POUR OUT 246D
19	HETOIMAZW I	PREPARE 316B		KAINOS 3B	NEW 395A
	PASCHA 3	PASSOVER MEAL 639A		HOUTOS IA⍺	THIS 600D
	POIEW I2A⍺	DO 689A		PERI IF	ABOUT 650C
	SUNTASSW	ORDER 799C		POLUS I2A⍺	MANY 694D
	HWS I2B	AS 905C	29	AMPELOS I	VINE 46A
20	ANAKEIMAI 2	BE AT TABLE 55C		APARTI	EXACTLY 80C
	GINOMAI IIBγ	COME ABOUT 157C		ARTI 3	NOW 109D
	META AII2	WITH 510B		BASILEIA 3C	KINGDOM 134D
	OPSIOS 2	LATE 606C		BASILEIA 3G	KINGDOM 135B
21	HEIS IA6	ONE 230A		GEN8MA	PRODUCT 154B
	ESTHIW ID	EAT 313A		EK 4A∈	FROM 235B
	PARADIDWMI IB	GIVE OVER 620A		HEWS IIIA	UNTIL 335A
22	ARCHW 2A⍺	BEGIN II3A		KAINOS 3B	NEW 395B
	EIMI II5	TO BE 223C		META AII2	WITH 510C
	HEKASTOS 2	EACH 236A		M8 DIA	NOT 519B
	LUPEW 2B	BE GRIEVED 483A		HOTAN IA	WHEN 592A
	M8TI (INTERROG PARTICLE) 522A			PAT8R 3D⍺	FATHER 641D
	SPHODRA	GREATLY 803D	29A	PINW I	DRINK 664B
23	EMBAPTW	DIP 253C	29B	PINW I	DRINK 664B
	HOUTOS IA∈	THIS 601B	30	ELAIA I	OLIVE TREE 247B
	PARADIDWMI IB	GIVE OVER 620A		EXERCHOMAI IA∈	GO OUT 274B
	TRUBLION	BOWL 836A		OROS	MOUNTAIN 586B

30	HUMNEW 2	SING THE PRAISE OF 844A
31	DIASKORPIZW	SCATTER 187B
	NUX 1C	NIGHT 549A
	PAS 1Eα	ALL 637D
	PATASSW 1C	STRIKE DOWN 640B
	POIM8N 1	SHEPHERD 690C
	POIMN8	FLOCK 691A
	PROBATON 1	SHEEP 710A
	SKANDALIZW 1B	CAUSE TO FALL 760B
32	EGEIRW 2C	RISE 214A
	META BII4A	AFTER 511D
	PROAGW 2B	LEAD 709A
33	EI IIA	IF 218A
	OUDEPOTE	NEVER 596D
	SKANDALIZW 1B	CAUSE TO FALL 760B
34	ALEKTWR	COCK 34D
	NUX 1C	NIGHT 549A
	PRIN 2	BEFORE 708A
	PRIN 1B	BEFORE 708A
	TRIS	THRICE 834A
	PHWNEW 1A	PRODUCE A SOUND 878B
34F	APARNEOMAI	DENY 80B
35	APOTHN8SKW 1Aα	DIE 90D
	DEI 4	IT IS NECESSARY 171B
	EIPON 2A	SAY 225C
	KAN 2	EVEN IF 403B
	M8 D2	NOT 519C
	HOMOIWS	LIKEWISE 570A
	SU 2	YOU 780A
	SUN 2B	WITH 789C
36	AUTOU	HERE 123C
	GETHS8MANI	GETHSEMANE 152D
	EKEI 2	THERE 238D
	HEWS IIIBγ	UNTIL 335C
	KATHIZW 2Aα	SIT DOWN 390D
	LEGW II3	CALL 471B
	PROSEUCHOMAI	PRAY 720D
	CHWRION 1	PLACE 898C
37	AD8MONEW	TROUBLED 16C
	ARCHW 2Aβ	BEGIN 113A
	ZEBEDAIOS	ZEBEDEE 337D
	LUPEW 2B	BE GRIEVED 483A
	PARALAMBANW 1	TAKE 624D
38	GR8GOREW 1	BE AWAKE 166C
	HEWS II4	AS MANY AS 336C
	THANATOS 1A	DEATH 351C
	MENW 1Aα	REMAIN 504D
	META AII2	WITH 510C
	PERILUPOS	VERY SAD 654B
	PSUCH8 1Bγ	SOUL LIFE 901D
	PSUCH8 1F	SOUL LIFE 902C
39	DUNATOS 2A	POSSIBLE 208A
	EPI IIIIAβ	ON 268A
	MIKROS 3D	SHORT 523C
	PARERCHOMAI 1Bγ	PASS AWAY 631C
	PAT8R 3Dα	FATHER 641D
	PIPTW 1Bα	FALL 665B
	PL8N 1B	BUT 675B
	POT8RION 2	CUP 702B
	PROERCHOMAI 1	GO FORWARD 712B
	PROSERCHOMAI 1	APPROACH 720A
	PROSEUCHOMAI	PRAY 721A
	PROSWPON 1A	FACE 728B
39	SU 1A	YOU 779D
39A	HWS I2B	AS 905C
40	GR8GOREW 1	BE AWAKE 166C
	HEURISKW 1Cα	FIND 325C
	ISCHUW 2B	BE STRONG 384C
	KATHEUDW 1	SLEEP 389C
	META AII2	WITH 510C
	HOUTW 1B	THUS 602C
	HWRA 2Aα	TIME OF DAY 904C
41	ASTHEN8S 1B	SICK 115B
	GR8GOREW 2	BE AWAKE 166C
	EISERCHOMAI 2A	COME 232B
	HINA IIIAγ	IN ORDER THAT 378B
	PEIRASMOS 2B	TEST 646C
	PNEUMA 3B	SPIRIT 681C
	PROTHUMOS	READY 713C
	PROSEUCHOMAI	PRAY 721A
	SARX 7	BODY 751D
42	GINOMAI I2A	CREATED 157C
	DEUTEROS 4	SECOND 176B
	EI IIA	IF 218A
	THEL8MA 1A	WILL 354D
	M8 AII	NOT 517C
	PALIN 2	AGAIN 611C
	PALIN 2	AGAIN 611D
	PARERCHOMAI 1Bγ	PASS AWAY 631C
	PAT8R 3Dα	FATHER 641D
	PINW 2Bα	DRINK 664C
	POT8RION 2	CUP 702B
	PROSEUCHOMAI	PRAY 721A
43	BAREW	BURDEN 133A
	HEURISKW 1Cα	FIND 325C
	KATHEUDW 1	SLEEP 389C
	PALIN 1A	BACK 611B
43F	AUTOS 3A	(OBLIQUE CASE) 122D
44	AUTOS 4A	THE SAME 123B
	APHI8MI 3A	LEAVE 125C
	EIPON 1	SAY 225B
	EK 5Bβ	FROM 235D
	LOGOS 1Aβ	WORD 478B
	PALIN 2	AGAIN 611C
	TRITOS 3	THIRD 834C
45	HAMARTWLOS 2	SINNER 43D
	ANAPAUW 2	REST 58C
	EGGIZW 5B	APPROACH 212D
	KATHEUDW 1	SLEEP 389C
	KAI I2C	AND 393B
	LOIPOS 3Aα	THE REST 481B
	PARADIDWMI 1B	GIVE OVER 620A
	HUIOS 2C	SON 843A
	CHEIR 2B	HAND 888D
	HWRA 3	TIME OF DAY 905A
46	AGW 5	GO 14C
	EGGIZW 5A	APPROACH 212D
	EGEIRW 2F	APPEAR 214B
	PARADIDWMI 1B	GIVE OVER 620A
47	ARCHIEREUS 1B	HIGH PRIEST 112C
	ETI 1Aβ	STILL 315D
	IDOU 1Bα	BEHOLD 371C
	IOUDAS 6	JUDAS 380D
	LALEW 2Aγ	SPEAK 464B
	LAOS 3A	PEOPLE 468A
	MACHAIRA 1	SWORD 497B

47	META AIII3	WITH	511B
	XULON 2B	THE POLE	551B
	POLUS II8α	MANY	694C
	PRESBUTEROS 2Aβ	OLDER	706D
48	DIDWMI I8α	GIVE	192A
	KRATEW IA	ARREST	449C
	PARADIDWMI I8	GIVE OVER	620A
	S8MEION I	SIGN	755B
	PHILEW 2	LOVE LIKE	867A
49	KATAPHILEW	KISS	421B
	RABBI	RABBI	740B
	CHAIRW 2A	REJOICE	882A
50	EPI IIIIAβ	ON	288A
	EPI IIII8η	ON	289B
	EPIBALLW I8	LAY ON	289D
	HETAIROS	COMPANION	314D
	KRATEW IA	ARREST	449C
	HOS,H8,HO I2A	(REL PRON)	587B
	HOS,H8,HO I2Bβ	(REL PRON)	587C
	HOS,H8,HO I9B	(REL PRON)	588D
	PAREIMI IA	BE PRESENT	629D
51	APOSPAW I	DRAW	97C
	APHAIREW I	CUT OFF	123D
	DOULOS IA	SLAVE	204D
	EKTEINW I	STRETCH OUT	244D
	MACHAIRA I	SWORD	497B
	META AIIIC α	WITH	510A
	PATASSW I8	STRIKE	640A
	WTION	THE EAR	908D
52	APOLLUMI 2Aα	PERISH	94D
	APOSTREPHW I8	RETURN	100A
	EN IIIIA	BY	260A
	LAMBANW IA	TAKE	465B
	LEGW IIIC	ORDER	470D
	PAS ID8	ALL	637C
	TOPOS IF	PLACE	830C
52A	MACHAIRA I	SWORD	497C
52B	MACHAIRA I	SWORD	497B
53	AGGELOS 2A	ANGEL	7D
	ARTI 2	NOW	109D
	DOKEW ID	THINK	201A
	8 IDα	OR	343A
	LEGIWN	LEGION	469A
	PARAKALEW IC	INVITE	622B
	PARIST8MI IA	PLACE BESIDE	633A
	PAT8R 3Dα	FATHER	641D
	POLUS II2C	MANY	696B
54	GINOMAI I3A	TAKE PLACE	157D
	GRAPH8 2Bα	SCRIPTURE	165B
	DEI I	IT IS NECESSARY	171A
	DEI 6	IT IS NECESSARY	171B
	HOTI I8α	THAT	592D
	OUN ICγ	THEREFORE	597C
	PL8ROW 4A	MAKE FULL	677C
	PwS IE	HOW	739D
55	EXERCHOMAI IAε	GO OUT	274B
	EPI IIIIA6	TO	288B
	H8MERA 2	DAY	347B
	HIERON 2	TEMPLE	373A
	KATHEZOMAI I	SIT	389B
	KATA II2C	EVERY	407C
	KRATEW IA	ARREST	449C
	L8ST8S 2	REVOLUTIONARY	474B
55	MACHAIRA I	SWORD	497B
	META AIII3	WITH	511B
	XULON 2B	THE POLE	551B
	HO,H8,TO IIIH	THE	553B
	SULLAMBANW IAα	SEIZE	784B
	HWRA 3	TIME OF DAY	905A
	HWS II2	SO	905D
56	APHI8MI 3A	ABANDON	125C
	GINOMAI I3A	TAKE PLACE	157D
	GRAPH8 2Bα	SCRIPTURE	165B
	DE 2	BUT, AND	170D
	HINA II2	IN ORDER THAT	378D
	HOLOS 3	WHOLE	567D
	PAS IDα	ALL	637C
	PL8ROW 4A	MAKE FULL	677C
	PHEUGW I	FLEE	863C
57	APAGW 2A	LEAD AWAY	78D
	ARCHIEREUS IB	HIGH PRIEST	112B
	KAIAPHAS	CAIAPHAS	394D
	KRATEW IA	ARREST	449C
	HOPOU IAα	WHERE	579C
	PRESBUTEROS 2Aβ	OLDER	706D
	SUNAGW 2	GATHER	790B
58	AKOLOUTHEW I	FOLLOW	30C
	AUL8 I	COURTYARD	120D
	EISERCHOMAI IH	COME	232B
	ESW I	IN	314B
	HEWS II2A	AS FAR AS	335C
	KATH8MAI 2	SIT DOWN	390C
	MAKROTHEN	FROM FAR AWAY	489A
	TELOS IC	END	819B
	HUP8RET8S	SERVANT	850C
59	ARCHIEREUS IB	HIGH PRIEST	112C
	Z8TEW 2A	SEEK	339C
	THANATOW I	PUT TO DEATH	352B
	KAI IIC	AND	392D
	KATA I2Bβ	DOWN	406D
	HOLOS 2B	WHOLE	567D
	HOPWS 2	IN ORDER THAT	580C
	PRESBUTEROS 2Aβ	OLDER	706D
	SUNEDRION 2	SANHEDRIN	794A
	PSEUDOMARTURIA	FALSE WITNESS	900B
60	DUO IA	TWO	208B
	HEURISKW IA	FIND	325A
	KAI I2G	AND	393C
	HUSTEROS 2B	FINALLY	857B
	PSEUDOMARTUS	A FALSE WITNESS	900B
61	DIA AIII8	DURING	178D
	H8MERA 2	DAY	347A
	KATALUW I8α	DESTROY	415B
	NAOS IA	TEMPLE	535B
	OIKODOMEW IC	BUILD	560D
	PH8MI I8α	SAY	864A
62	ANIST8MI 2A	RISE	69C
	APOKRINOMAI I	ANSWER	92D
	KATAMARTUREW	TESTIFY AGAINST	415D
	OUDEIS 2Bα	NOTHING	596C
62F	ARCHIEREUS IB	HIGH PRIEST	112B
63	APOKRINOMAI 2	BEGIN	93A
	EI V2A	WHETHER	218D
	EXORKIZW	ADJURE	277A
	ZAW IAε	LIVE	336D
	HINA IIIA6	IN ORDER THAT	378B

63	KATA I2A	DOWN 406C
	HORKIZW	ADJURE 585A
	SIWPAW I	BE SILENT 760A
	HUIOS 2B	SON 842C
	CHRISTOS I	ANOINTED ONE 895B
64	APARTI	EXACTLY 80C
	ARTI 3	NOW 109D
	DEXIOS 2B	RIGHT 174A
	DUNAMIS I	POWER 206C
	EIPON I	SAY 225C
	EPI IIAα	ON 285C
	KATH8MAI IAα	SIT 390B
	NEPHEL8	CLOUD 538D
	OURANOS ID	HEAVEN 598D
	PL8N IB	BUT 675B
	HUIOS 2C	SON 843A
65	AKOUW IBα	HEAR 31B
	AKOUW IBγ	HEAR 31C
	ARCHIEREUS IB	HIGH PRIEST II2B
	BLASPH8MEW 2Bα	BLASPHEME 142A
	BLASPH8MIA 2B	SLANDER 142C
	DIA(R)R8GNUMI I	TEAR 187A
	ETI IBβ	STILL 316A
	IDE 4	SEE 369D
	HIMATION 3	GARMENT 377B
	MARTUS I	WITNESS 495B
	NUN IB	NOW 547D
	TOTE 2	AT THAT TIME 831D
	CHREIA I	NEED 893B
66	DOKEW 3A	SEEM 201B
	ENOCHOS 2Bα	SUBJECT TO 267B
	THANATOS IBα	DEATH 351C
67	EMPTUW	SPIT ON 257A
	KOLAPHIZW I	STRIKE 441D
	HO,H8,TO I2	THE 552D
	PROSWPON IA	FACE 728B
	RAPIZW	STRIKE WITH A CLUB 741D
68	PAIW I	STRIKE 610B
	PROPH8TEUW 2	PROPHESY 730C
	TIS, TI IAα	WHICH 826C
69	AUL8 I	COURTYARD 120D
	GALILAIOS	GALILEAN 149D
	HEIS 3B	SOMEONE 230D
	EXW IAα	OUTSIDE 279A
	KATH8MAI IAα	SIT 390B
	META AIIICα	WITH 510A
	NAZWRAIOS	NAZARENE 534B
	HO,H8,TO IIIB	THE 552D
	PAIDISK8	MAID 609B
	PULWN 3	GATE 736D
	SU IC	YOU 779D
70	ARNEOMAI 3A	DENY 107C
	EMPROSTHEN 2B	IN FRONT 256C
	LEGW I2B	SAY 469D
	OIDA 4	KNOW 559A
71	AUTOS 3C	(OBLIQUE CASE) 123A
	EKEI I	THERE 238C
	EXERCHOMAI IAϵ	GO OUT 274B
	META AIIICα	WITH 510A
	NAZWRAIOS	NAZARENE 534B
	HO,H8,TO IIIB	THE 552D
	PULWN 3	GATE 736D
72	ANTHRWPOS 4B	MAN 68D

72	ARNEOMAI 3A	DENY 107C
	OIDA 2	KNOW 558D
	HORKOS	OATH 585B
	PALIN 2	AGAIN 611C
72=5	HOTI 2	THAT 593D
73	AL8THWS I	TRULY 36D
	D8LOS	CLEAR 177B
	EIMI III3	TO BE 224B
	EK 4A6	FROM 235B
	HIST8MI II2Bγ	BEING 383C
	KAI III	ALSO 394B
	LALIA 2A	SPEECH 465A
	META BII3	AFTER 511C
	MIKROS 3E	A LITTLE WHILE 523C
	HOMOIAZW	BE LIKE 569C
	POIEW IIBι	DO 688B
	SU IC	YOU 779D
74	ANTHRWPOS 4B	MAN 68D
	ARCHW 2Aβ	BEGIN 113A
	EUTHUS	IMMEDIATELY 321B
	KATATHEMATIZW	CURSE 411D
	KATANATHEMATIZW	CURSE 415D
	OIDA 2	KNOW 558D
	OMNUW	TAKE AN OATH 569A
74F	ALEKTWR	COCK 34D
74F	PHWNEW IA	PRODUCE A SOUND 878B
75	APARNEOMAI	DENY 80B
	EXERCHOMAI IAβ	GO OUT 274A
	EXW IB	OUTSIDE 279A
	KLAIW I	WEEP 434A
	MIMN8SKOMAI IAα	REMEMBER 524A
	PIKRWS	BITTERLY 663C
	PRIN IB	BEFORE 708A
	PULWN 3	GATE 736D
	R8MA I	WORD 742D
	TRIS	THRICE 834A

MATTHEW 27

1	ARCHIEREUS IB	HIGH PRIEST II2C
	GINOMAI IIBγ	COME ABOUT 157C
	THANATOW I	PUT TO DEATH 352B
	KATA I2Bβ	DOWN 406D
	LAMBANW IH	TAKE 466A
	LAOS 3A	PEOPLE 468A
	PRESBUTEROS 2Aβ	OLDER 706D
	PRWIA	(EARLY) MORNING 732B
	SUMBOULION I	PLAN 785D
	HWSTE 2B	THEREFORE 908C
2	APAGW 2A	LEAD AWAY 78D
	DEW IB	BIND 176D
	H8GEMWN 2	GOVERNORS 344A
	PARADIDWMI IB	GIVE OVER 619D
	PONTIOS	PONTIUS 698C
2FF	PILATOS	PILATE 663C
3	APOSTREPHW IB	RETURN 100A
	ARGURION 2C	SILVER 104C
	ARCHIEREUS IB	HIGH PRIEST II2C
	EIDON 3	NOTICE 220A
	IOUDAS 6	JUDAS 380D
	KATAKRINW	CONDEMN 413A
	METAMELOMAI	REPENT 513A
	PRESBUTEROS 2Aβ	OLDER 706D

3	STREPHW IAγ	TURN 778D
4	ATHWOS	INNOCENT 21B
	HAIMA 2A	BLOOD 22B
	HAMARTANW 2	SIN 41D
	DIKAIOS 4	RIGHTEOUS 195A
	HORAW 2B	SEE 582B
	PROS III5C	TOWARD 717D
5	ANACHWREW I	GO AWAY 63A
	APAGCHW	HANG ONESELF 78D
	NAOS IA	TEMPLE 535B
	RIPTW I	THROW 743D
5F	ARGURION 2C	SILVER 104C
6	HAIMA 2A	BLOOD 22B
	EXESTI I	IT IS POSSIBLE 274D
	EPEI 2	BECAUSE 283D
	KORBANAS	TEMPLE TREASURY 445B
	LAMBANW IB	TAKE 465C
	TIMB I	VALUE 825A
7	AGORAZW I	BUY 12D
	EK 4B	FROM 235C
	KERAMEUS	POTTER 430A
	LAMBANW IH	TAKE 466A
	XENOS 2A	THE STRANGER 550B
	SUMBOULION I	PLAN 785D
	TAPHB 2	BURIAL PLACE 814A
7F	AGROS I	FIELD 13D
8	HAIMA 2A	BLOOD 22B
	DIO	THEREFORE 197D
	HEWS IIIA	UNTIL 335B
	KALEW IAγ	CALL 400A
	S8MERON	TODAY 756C
9	ARGURION 2C	SILVER 104C
	ZACHARIAS 3	ZECHARIAH 336B
	IEREMIAS	JEREMIAH 372C
	ISRA8L I	ISRAEL 382B
	PL8ROW 4A	MAKE FULL 677C
	PROPH8T8S I	PROPHET 730D
	TIMB I	VALUE 825A
	TOTE IA	AT THAT TIME 831C
	HUIOS IB«	SON 841C
9A	TIMAW I	ESTIMATE 824D
9B	TIMAW I	ESTIMATE 824D
10	AGROS I	FIELD 13D
	DIDWMI 4	GIVE 192D
	EIS 4D	FOR 228C
	KATHA	JUST AS 387B
	KERAMEUS	POTTER 430A
	KURIOS 2A	LORD 460B
	SUNTASSW	ORDER 799C
11	BASILEUS 2A	KING 135D
	EMPROSTHEN 2B	IN FRONT 256C
	EPERWTAW IB	ASK 285A
	H8GEMWN 2	GOVERNORS 344A
	IOUDAIOS 2C	JEWISH 380B
	HIST8MI IIIB	STAND 383B
	LEGW IIIE	DECLARE 471A
	SU IC	YOU 779D
	SU IA	YOU 779D
	PH8MI IB«	SAY 864A
12	APOKRINOMAI I	ANSWER 92D
	ARCHIEREUS IB	HIGH PRIEST 112C
	EN II3	WHILE 260A
	KAT8GOREW IA	BRING CHARGES 424C
12	OUDEIS 2B«	NOTHING 596C
	PRESBUTEROS 2Aβ	OLDER 706D
13	KATAMARTUREW	TESTIFY AGAINST 415D
	OU 4C	NO 594D
	POSOS 2B«	HOW GREAT 701B
14	APOKRINOMAI I	ANSWER 93A
	HEIS 2B	ONE 230C
	THAUMAZW IA«	WONDER 352D
	LIAN I	VERY 474C
	OUDE 3	NOT EVEN 596A
	PROS III5A	TOWARD 717C
	R8MA I	WORD 742D
	HWSTE 2Aβ	THEREFORE 908C
14F	H8GEMWN 2	GOVERNORS 344A
15	EIWTHA	ACCUSTOMED 233B
	HEORT8	FESTIVAL 280A
	THELW I	WISH 355C
	KATA II2C	EVERY 407C
15F	DESMIOS	PRISONER 175A
15-26	APOLUW I	SET FREE 96A
16	EPIS8MOS 2	NOTORIOUS 298B
	LEGW II3	CALL 471B
	TOTE IA	AT THAT TIME 831C
16F	BARABBAS I	BARABBAS 132C
17	8 IDγ	OR 343A
	THELW I	WISH 355C
	LEGW II3	CALL 471B
	HO,H8,TO IIIB	THE 552D
	SUNAGW 2	GATHER 790A
	TIS, TI IAγ	WHICH 826D
	CHRISTOS I	ANOINTED ONE 895C
18	DIA BIII	BECAUSE OF 180B
	PARADIDWMI IB	GIVE OVER 619D
	PHTHONOS	ENVY 865C
19	APOSTELLW IB«	SEND AWAY 98A
	B8MA 2	TRIBUNAL 139D
	DIKAIOS 3	RIGHTEOUS 195A
	EPI IIA«	ON 285C
	KATH8MAI IA«	SIT 390B
	LEGW I8C	SAY 470B
	ONAR	DREAM 573A
	PASCHW 3B	ENDURE 639D
	S8MERON	TODAY 756C
20	AITEW	ASK 25B
	APOLLUMI IA«	RUIN 94C
	ARCHIEREUS IB	HIGH PRIEST 112C
	HINA IIIA«	IN ORDER THAT 378B
	PEITHW IB	CONVINCE 645A
	PRESBUTEROS 2Aβ	OLDER 706D
20F	BARABBAS I	BARABBAS 132C
21	APO I6	FROM 86A
	H8GEMWN 2	GOVERNORS 344A
	THELW I	WISH 355C
	TIS, TI IA«	WHICH 826D
21F	PALIN 5	AGAIN 612A
22	HO,H8,TO IIIB	THE 552D
	OUN IC«	THEREFORE 597B
	POIEW IID«	DO 688D
	CHRISTOS I	ANOINTED ONE 895C
22F	STAUROW I	CRUCIFY 773A
23	GAR IF	WHAT 151C
	KAKOS IC	EVIL 398D
	KRAZW 2A	CALL 448D

23	PERISSWS	MORE 657C
	POIEW IIB€	DO 687D
	TIS, TI 2	WHICH 827B
	PH8MI IB«	SAY 864A
24	ATHWOS	INNOCENT 21B
	HAIMA 2A	BLOOD 22B
	APENANTI IA	OPPOSITE 83B
	APO I2	FROM 86A
	APONIZW	WASH OFF 96C
	GINOMAI IIBβ	COME ABOUT 157B
	DIKAIOS 3	RIGHTEOUS 195A
	EIDON 3	NOTICE 220A
	THORUBOS 3B	NOISE 363C
	KATENANTI 2A	OPPOSITE 422B
	MALLON 3A«	RATHER 490C
	HORAW 2B	SEE 582B
	HUDWR I	WATER 840C
	WPHELEW 2A	HELP 909A
	WPHELEW 2B	HELP 909C
25	HAIMA 2A	BLOOD 22C
	EPI IIIIBγ	ON 289A
	LAOS IA	PEOPLE 467D
	PAS IC«	ALL 637B
	TEKNON IB	CHILD 816B
26	BARABBAS I	BARABBAS 132C
	PARADIDWMI IB	GIVE OVER 620B
	STAUROW I	CRUCIFY 773A
	PHRAGELLOW	SCOURGE 873B
27	EPI IIIIAγ	ON 288B
	H8GEMWN 2	GOVERNORS 344A
	PARALAMBANW I	TAKE 625A
	PRAITWRION	THE PRAETORIUM 704B
	SPEIRA	COHORT 768C
	STRATIWT8S I	SOLDIER 778B
	SUNAGW 2	GATHER 790A
28	EKDUW I	STRIP 238C
	ENDUW I	DRESS 263B
	KOKKINOS	SCARLET 441A
	PERITITH8MI I	PLACE AROUND 658C
	CHLAMUS	CLOAK 890C
29	AKANTHA	THORN PLANT 29A
	BASILEUS 2A	KING 135D
	GONUPETEW	KNEEL DOWN 164B
	DEXIOS 2A	RIGHT 173D
	EK 3H	BY 235A
	EMPAIZW I	RIDICULE 255B
	EMPROSTHEN 2A	IN FRONT 256C
	EPITITH8MI IA«	PUT UPON 303A
	IOUDAIOS 2C	JEWISH 380B
	HO,H8,TO IIII	THE 553B
	PLEKW	WEAVE 673A
	STEPHANOS I	WREATH 774D
	CHAIRW 2A	REJOICE 882A
29F	KALAMOS 2	STALK 399C
29F	KEPHAL8 IA	HEAD 431A
30	EIS IC	IN 227C
	LAMBANW IA	TAKE 465B
	TUPTW I	STRIKE 838A
31	APAGW 2C	LEAD AWAY 78D
	EIS 4F	(PURPOSE) 229A
	EKDUW I	STRIP 238C
	EMPAIZW I	RIDICULE 255B
	ENDUW I	DRESS 263B
31	STAUROW I	CRUCIFY 773A
	CHLAMUS	CLOAK 890C
32	AGGAREUW 2	REQUISITION 6D
	AIRW 2	LIFT UP 24A
	ANTHRWPOS 3A€	MAN 68C
	APANT8SIS	MEETING 79D
	HEURISKW IB	FIND 325B
	HINA IIIA€	IN ORDER THAT 378B
	KUR8NAIOS	CYRENIAN 459A
	ONOMA II	NAME 574A
	SIMWN 4	SIMON 758D
	STAUROS I	THE CROSS 772C
33	GOLGOTHA	GOLGOTHA 164A
	KRANION	SKULL 449A
	HOS,H8,HO I7A	(REL PRON) 588C
33A	TOPOS IC	PLACE 830B
33B	LEGW II3	CALL 471B
33B	TOPOS IC	PLACE 830B
34	GEUOMAI I	TASTE 156A
	DIDWMI 2	GIVE 192C
	MEIGNUMI I	MIX 500D
	META AII5	WITH 510D
	OINOS I	WINE 564D
	CHOL8 I	GALL 891D
34A	PINW I	DRINK 664C
34B	PINW I	DRINK 664C
35	BALLW IA	THROW 130B
	DIAMERIZW IB	DIVIDE 185D
	HIMATION I	GARMENT 377A
	KL8ROS I	LOT 436C
	STAUROW I	CRUCIFY 773A
36	KATH8MAI IAγ	SIT 390B
	T8REW I	GUARD 822B
37	AITIA 2A	CHARGE 25D
	BASILEUS 2A	KING 135D
	EPANW 2A	ON 283A
	EPI IIIA«	ON 286C
	EPITITH8MI IA«	PUT UPON 303A
	KEPHAL8 IA	HEAD 431B
38	DEXIOS 2B	RIGHT 174A
	DUO IA	TWO 208B
	HEIS 5A	ONE 231A
	EUWNUMOS	LEFT 330A
	L8ST8S I	ROBBER 474B
	STAUROW I	CRUCIFY 773A
	SUN 2B	WITH 789C
39	BLASPH8MEW 2B6	BLASPHEME 142B
	KEPHAL8 IA	HEAD 431B
	KINEW 2A	MOVE 433C
	PARAPOREUOMAI I	PASS BY 627A
40	EN IIIA	WHILE 259D
	H8MERA 2	DAY 347B
	KATABAINW IA«	COME DOWN 409B
	KATALUW IB«	DESTROY 415B
	NAOS IA	TEMPLE 535B
	OIKODOMEW IC	BUILD 560D
	STAUROS I	THE CROSS 772B
	SWZW IA	SAVE 805D
	HUIOS 2B	SON 842D
41	ARCHIEREUS IB	HIGH PRIEST 112B
	GRAMMATEUS 2	SCRIBES 165A
	EMPAIZW I	RIDICULE 255B
	LEGW I8D	SAY 470C

41	META AII2	WITH	510C
	HOMOIWS	LIKEWISE	570D
	PRESBUTEROS 2Aβ	OLDER	706D
42	ALLOS IA	OTHER	39B
	BASILEUS 2A	KING	135D
	HEAUTOU !	ONESELF	211A
	ISRA8L 2	ISRAEL	382B
	KATABAINW IAα	COME DOWN	409B
	NUN IA6	NOW	547D
	PISTEUW IB	BELIEVE	666C
	PISTEUW 2Aα	BELIEVE	667B
	PISTEUW 2Aγ	BELIEVE	667B
	PISTEUW 2A6	BELIEVE	667B
	STAUROS I	THE CROSS	772B
	SWZW IA	SAVE	805D
43	EPI IIIIBε	TOWARD	289A
	THELW 4B	WISH	356A
	NUN IA6	NOW	547D
	HOTI 2	THAT	593D
*	PEITHW 2A	CONVINCE	645B
	RUOMAI	SAVE	744D
	RUOMAI	SAVE	745A
	HUIOS 2B	SON	842C
44	AUTOS 4B	THE SAME	123B
	L8ST8S I	ROBBER	474B
	ONEIDIZW I	REPROACH	573A
	SUN 2B	WITH	789C
	SUSTAUROW I	CRUCIFY WITH	802C
45	APO II2B	FROM	86C
	G8 4	LAND	156D
	GINOMAI IIBα	COME ABOUT	157D
	HEKTOS	SIXTH	245C
	EPI IIIIAα	ACROSS	287D
	HEWS IIIA	UNTIL	335B
	PAS ICα	ALL	637B
	SKOTOS I	DARKNESS	765A
45A	HWRA 2B	TIME OF DAY	904D
45F	ENATOS	NINTH	261D
45F	HWRA 2B	TIME OF DAY	904D
46	ANABOAW	CRY OUT	50D
	BOAW 3	SHOUT	143D
	EGKATALEIPW 2	FORSAKE	214D
	EIMI II3	TO BE	222D
	ELWI	MY GOD	253A
	8LI	GOD	345C
	HINATI	WHY	379B
	LAMA	WHY	465A
	MEGAS 2Aγ	GREAT	498D
	HOUTOS IBε	THIS	601D
	PERI 2B	ABOUT	651A
	SABACHTHANI	FORSAKE	746A
	PHWN8 2A	VOICE	878D
47	8LIAS	ELIJAH	345D
	HIST8MI II2A	STAND	383B
	PHWNEW 2B	CALL	878C
48	EK 4Aα	FROM	235B
	KALAMOS 2	STALK	399C
	OXOS	WINE VINEGAR	577D
	PERITITH8MI I	PLACE AROUND	658C
	PIMPL8MI IAα	FILL	663D
	POTIZW I	GIVE TO DRINK	702C
	SPOGGOS	SPONGE	770C
	TE IB	AND	815B

48	TRECHW I	RUN	833C
49	APHI8MI 4	TOLERATE	126A
	EI V2A	WHETHER	218D
	ERCHOMAI IIAε	COME	310D
	8LIAS	ELIJAH	345D
	LOGCH8	SPEAR	480C
	LOIPOS 2Bα	THE OTHERS	481A
	NUSSW	STAB	549A
	PLEURA	SIDE	673D
	SWZW IA	SAVE	805D
50	APHI8MI IAβ	GIVE UP	125B
	KRAZW I	CRY OUT	448D
	MEGAS 2Aγ	GREAT	498D
	PALIN 2	AGAIN	611C
	PNEUMA 2	SPIRIT	680D
	PHWN8 2A	VOICE	878D
51	ANWTHEN I	FROM ABOVE	76C
	APO III	FROM	86B
	EIS 4E	SO THAT	228D
	HEWS II2B	AS FAR AS	335D
	KATAPETASMA	CURTAIN	417B
	KATW 2	DOWNWARDS	426B
	NAOS IA	TEMPLE	535B
	PETRA IA	ROCK	660A
	SEIW I	SHAKE	754A
51A	DUO 5	TWO	208C
51A	SCHIZW IB	SPLIT	805A
51B	SCHIZW IB	SPLIT	805A
52	HAGIOS 2Dγ	DEDICATED TO GOD	10B
	ANOIGW IB	OPEN	70C
	EGEIRW 2C	RISE	214A
	KOIMAW 2B	SLEEP	438D
	POLUS IIAα	MANY	694A
	SWMA IA	BODY	806D
52F	MN8MEION 2	TOMB	526C
53	HAGIOS IAα	DEDICATED TO GOD	9B
	EGERSIS	RESURRECTION	214B
	EISERCHOMAI IAβ	COME	231D
	EMPHANIZW IA	MAKE VISIBLE	257A
	EXERCHOMAI IAα	GO OUT	273D
	META BII3	AFTER	511C
	POLIS I	CITY	692B
54	AL8THWS I	TRULY	36D
	GINOMAI I3A	TAKE PLACE	157D
	EIDON 2	FEEL	220A
	HEKATONTARCH8S	CENTURION	236C
	SEISMOS	SHAKING	753D
	SPHODRA	GREATLY	803D
	T8REW I	GUARD	822B
	HUIOS 2B	SON	842C
	PHOBEW IA	BE AFRAID	870B
55	GUN8 I	WOMAN	167B
	DIAKONEW 2	SERVE	183A
	THEWREW I	OBSERVE	360C
	MAKROTHEN	FROM FAR AWAY	489A
	HOSTIS 3	WHOEVER	591B
	POLUS IIAα	MANY	694A
56	EIMI III4	TO BE	224C
	ZEBEDAIOS	ZEBEDEE	337D
	IAKWBOS 3	JAMES	368B
	IWS8S 2	JOSES	386B
	IWS8PH 9	JOSEPH	386D
	MAGDAL8N8	MAGDALENE	485B

56	*MARIA 2	MARY 493A
	MARIA 3	MARY 493A
	SALWM8	SALOME 748C
57	HARIMATHAIA	ARIMATHAEA 106A
	GINOMAI IIBγ	COME ABOUT 157C
	IWS8PH 6	JOSEPH 386C
	MATH8TEUW I BECOME A DISCIPLE 486C	
	MATH8TEUW 2 BECOME A DISCIPLE 486C	
	ONOMA II	NAME 574B
	OPSIOS 2	LATE 606C
	PLOUSIOS I	RICH 679C
58	AITEW	ASK 25B
	APODIDWMI I	GIVE AWAY 89D
	KELEUW	COMMAND 428C
	SWMA IA	BODY 806C
59	ENTULISSW I	WRAP 269D
	IWS8PH 6	JOSEPH 386C
	KATHAROS I	CLEAN 388D
	*SINDWN I	LINEN 759B
	SWMA IA	BODY 806D
60	THURA IB	ENTRANCE 366B
	KAINOS I	NEW 395A
	LATOMEW I	HEW 468C
	LITHOS IE	STONE 475C
	MEGAS IA	LARGE 498C
	PETRA IA	ROCK 660A
	PROSKULIW	ROLL (UP TO) 723D
	TITH8MI IIAβ	PUT 823C
60A	MN8MEION 2	TOMB 526C
60B	MN8MEION 2	TOMB 526C
61	ALLOS 3	THE OTHER 39D
	APENANTI IA	OPPOSITE 83B
	KATH8MAI IAα	SIT 390A
	MAGDAL8N8	MAGDALENE 485B
	MARIA 2	MARY 493A
	MARIA 3	MARY 493A
	TAPHOS I	GRAVE 814A
62	EPAURION	NEXT DAY 283C
	HOSTIS 3	WHOEVER 591B
	PARASKEU8	PREPARATION 627C
	PARASKEU8	PREPARATION 627D
	SUNAGW 2	GATHER 790B
63	ETI IAβ	STILL 315D
	ZAW IAα	LIVE 336B
	H8MERA 2	DAY 347B
	KURIOS IB	LORD 460A
	META BIII	AFTER 511B
	MIMN8SKOMAI IAδ	REMEMBER 524B
	HO,H8,TO IIIH	THE 553B
	PLANOS 2	DECEITFUL 672A
64	EGEIRW 2C	RISE 214A
	ERCHOMAI IIAζ	COME 310D
	ESCHATOS 3A	LAST 314A
	HEWS IIIA	UNTIL 335A
	H8MERA 2	DAY 347A
	KAI I2E	AND 393C
	KELEUW	COMMAND 428C
	KLEPTW	STEAL 435C
	LAOS IB	PEOPLE 467D
	M8POTE 2Bα	(NEG PARTICLE) 521A
	NEKROS 2A	DEAD 537A
	PLAN8	WANDERING 671D
	PRWTOS IA	FIRST 732D

64	TAPHOS I	GRAVE 814A
	TRITOS I	THIRD 834B
	CHEIRWN	WORSE 889C
64FF	ASPHALIZW I	GUARD 118D
65	ECHW I7B	HAVE 334B
	KOUSTWDIA	GUARD 448B
	OIDA 3	KNOW 559A
	HUPAGW 2	GO AWAY 844C
	PHULAX	GUARD 876A
	HWS II	AS 905C
66	KOUSTWDIA	GUARD 448B
	LITHOS IE	STONE 475C
	META AIII2	WITH 511B
	POREUW I	PROCEED 699B
	SPHRAGIZW I	SEAL 803D
	TAPHOS I	GRAVE 814A

MATTHEW 28

I	ALLOS 3	THE OTHER 39D
	HEIS 4	ONE 231A
	EPIPHWSKW	SHINE FORTH 304D
	THEWREW I	OBSERVE 360D
	MAGDAL8N8	MAGDALENE 485B
	*MARIA 2	MARY 493A
	MARIA 3	MARY 493A
	OPSE 3	LATE IN THE DAY 606B
	TAPHOS I	GRAVE 814A
IA	SABBATON IBβ	SABBATH 746C
IB	SABBATON 2B	WEEK 746D
2	AGGELOS 2A	ANGEL 7C
	APOKULIW	ROLL AWAY 93D
	GINOMAI IIBα	COME ABOUT 157B
	EPANW 2A	ON 283A
	KATH8MAI 2	SIT DOWN 390C
	KATABAINW IAγ	COME DOWN 409C
	KURIOS 2A	LORD 460B
	LITHOS IE	STONE 475C
	MEGAS 2Aγ	GREAT 499A
	OURANOS 2C	HEAVEN 599C
	SEISMOS	SHAKING 753D
2FF	AGGELOS 2A	ANGEL 7C
3	AGGELOS 2A	ANGEL 7C
	ASTRAP8	LIGHTNING 117D
	EIDEA	APPEARANCE 219C
	EIMI II9B	TO BE 224A
	ENDUMA I	GARMENT 263A
	LEUKOS 2	WHITE 473D
	CHIWN	SNOW 890C
	HWSEI I	AS 907D
4	GINOMAI III	BE 159B
	NEKROS IAα	DEAD 536C
	SEIW 2	SHAKE 754A
	T8REW I	GUARD 822B
	PHOBOS 2Aα	FEAR 871C
	HWSEI I	AS 907D
5	Z8TEW IAα	SEEK 339A
	STAUROW I	CRUCIFY 773A
	SU ID	YOU 780A
6	DEUTE I	COME 175D
	EGEIRW 2C	RISE 214A
	EIPON 3E	FORETELL 225D
	KATHWS I	JUST AS 392A

6	KEIMAI IA	LIE 427D
	HOPOU IAα	WHERE 579C
	TOPOS IC	PLACE 830B
7	EGEIRW 2C	RISE 214A
	EIPON 2C	SAY 225C
	NEKROS 2A	DEAD 537A
	HORAW IAα	SEE 581B
	POREUW I	PROCEED 699B
	PROAGW 2B	LEAD 709A
	TACHUS 2B	QUICK 814D
8	APAGGELLW I	REPORT 78C
	MEGAS 2AY	GREAT 499A
	META AIIII	WITH 511A
	MN8MEION 2	TOMB 526C
	TACHUS 2A	QUICK 814D
	TRECHW I	RUN 833C
	PHOBOS 2Aα	FEAR 871C
	*CHARA I	JOY 883C
9	APANTAW	MEET 79D
	KRATEW IB	SEIZE 449C
	PROSKUNEW 5	DO REVERENCE 724B
	HUPANTAW	GO TO MEET 845C
	CHAIRW 2A	REJOICE 882A
	HWS IVIB	WHEN 907A
10	ADELPHOS 2	BROTHER 16A
	APAGGELLW 2	PROCLAIM 78D
	APERCHOMAI 2	GO 83D
	HINA IIIAδ	IN ORDER THAT 378B
	KAKEI I	AND THERE 397C
	HORAW IAα	SEE 581B
	HUPAGW I	GO AWAY 844C
11	APAGGELLW I	REPORT 78C
	HAPAS I	WHOLE 81A
	GINOMAI I3A	TAKE PLACE 157D
	IDOU IBα	BEHOLD 371C
	KOUSTWDIA	GUARD 448B
	TIS, TI IAα	ANY ONE 827C
12	ARGURION 2B	MONEY 104B
	DIDWMI 4	GIVE 192C
	HIKANOS IA	SUFFICIENT 375A
	LAMBANW IH	TAKE 466A
	META AII3B	WITH 510D
	PRESBUTEROS 2Aβ	OLDER 706D
	STRATIWT8S I	SOLDIER 778B
	SUMBOULION I	PLAN 785D
	SUNAGW 2	GATHER 790B
	TE IB	AND 815B
13	EIPON 2C	SAY 225C
	ERCHOMAI IIAζ	COME 310D
	KLEPTW	STEAL 435C
	KOIMAW I	SLEEP 438C
	NUX IB	NIGHT 548D
14	AKOUW 3B	LEARN 32A
	AMERIMNOS I	FREE FROM CARE 44D
	EAN IIB	IF 210C
	EPI IIAδ	BEFORE 286A
	H8GEMWN 2	GOVERNORS 344A
	PEITHW ID	CONVINCE 645A
	POIEW IIB:	DO 688B
15	ARGURION 2B	MONEY 104B
	DIAPH8MIZW	MAKE KNOWN 189D
	DIDASKW I	TEACH 191A
	H8MERA 2	DAY 347A

15	LAMBANW 2	RECEIVE 466B
	LOGOS IAβ	WORD 478C
	MECHRI IB	UNTIL 517A
	PARA IIIBY	BESIDE 615C
	*S8MERON	TODAY 756C
	PH8MIZW	SPREAD 864B
	HWS I2B	AS 905C
16	HENDEKA	ELEVEN 262B
	MATH8T8S 2Bα	DISCIPLE 486D
	OROS	MOUNTAIN 586B
	HOU 2	WHERE 594A
	TASSW 2B	PLACE 813D
17	DISTAZW I	DOUBT 199A
	HO,H8,TO I2	THE 552A
	PROSKUNEW 5	DO REVERENCE 724B
18	DIDWMI IBβ	GIVE 192B
	EXOUSIA 3	AUTHORITY 278A
	LALEW 3	SPEAK 465A
	OURANOS IAβ	HEAVEN 598B
	PAS IAβ	EVERY EACH 636D
19	AUTOS 3Fβ	(OBLIQUE CASE) 123B
	BAPTIZW 2Bβ	BAPTIZE 131C
	ETHNOS I	NATION 217B
	MATH8TEUW 3	MAKE A DISCIPLE 486D
	ONOMA I4Cβ	NAME 576A
	PAT8R 3Dα	FATHER 641D
	PNEUMA 5Cα	SPIRIT 682D
	PNEUMA 8	SPIRIT 684B
	HUIOS 2B	SON 842C
	HUIOS 2B	SON 842D
20	AIWN 2A	AGE 27B
	AM8N I	AMEN 45B
	DIDASKW 2E	TEACH 191B
	EGW	I 216B
	ENTELLW	COMMAND 268A
	H8MERA 4B	TIME 348B
	IDOU IBε	BEHOLD 371C
	META AIIICβ	WITH 510A
	HOSOS 2	HOW GREAT 590B
	SUNTELEIA	CLOSE 799C
	T8REW 5	KEEP 822D

MARK 1

1	EUAGGELION IB	GOSPEL 318B
	EUAGGELION 3	GOSPEL 318C
	HUIOS 2B	SON 842C
	CHRISTOS 2	ANOINTED ONE 895C
2	AGGELOS IB	MESSENGER 7A
	APOSTELLW IBβ	SEND AWAY 98A
	GRAPHW 2C	WRITE 166A
	EGW	I 216B
	8SAIAS	ISAIAH 349C
	KATHWS I	JUST AS 392A
	KATASKEUAZW I	MAKE READY 419B
	HODOS IA	WAY 556B
	PRO I	BEFORE 708C
	PROSWPON ICζ	FACE 728D
	PROPH8T8S I	PROPHET 730D
	HWS II4A	SO 906B
3	BOAW 2	SHOUT 143D
	HETOIMAZW I	PREPARE 316B
	EUTHUS I	STRAIGHT 321B

3	KURIOS 2Cα	LORD 460C	9	IWAN(N)8S I	JOHN 385B	
	HODOS IA	WAY 556B		NAZARA	NAZARETH 534A	
	POIEW IIBι	DO 688B		HUPO IAα	BY 850D	
	TRIBOS	BEATEN PATH 834A	.10	ANABAINW IAα	GO UP 49D	
	PHWN8 2E	VOICE 879C		AUTOS 3A	(OBLIQUE CASE) 122D	
4	HAMARTIA I	SIN 42C		EUTHUS	IMMEDIATELY 321B	
	APHESIS 2	PARDON 124C		KATABAINW IB	COME DOWN 409C	
	BAPTIZW 2A	BAPTIZE 131B		OURANOS 2A	HEAVEN 599B	
	BAPTISMA I	BAPTISM 132A		PERISTERA	PIGEON 657D	
	GINOMAI II5	APPEAR 159D		PNEUMA 5Dα	SPIRIT 683A	
	ER8MOS 2	DESERT 309A		SCHIZW IB	SPLIT 805A	
	IWAN(N)8S I	JOHN 385B		HUDWR I	WATER 840C	
	K8RUSSW 2Bβ	ANNOUNCE 432C		HWSEI I	AS 907D	
	METANOIA	REPENTANCE 514A	11	AGAP8TOS I	BELOVED 6C	
5	HAMARTIA I	SIN 42D		GINOMAI 14Cα	COME, GO 159A	
	BAPTIZW 2A	BAPTIZE 131B		EUDOKEW 2A	WELL PLEASED 319C	
	EKPOREUOMAI IC	GO OUT 244A		OURANOS 2A	HEAVEN 599B	
	EXOMOLOGEW 2A	CONFESS 276C		HUIOS 2B	SON 842B	
	HIEROSOLUMIT8S	374A		HUIOS 2B	SON 842C	
	INHABITANT OF JERUSALEM			PHWN8 2D	VOICE 879B	
	IORDAN8S	JORDAN 379C	12	EKBALLW 2	SEND OUT 237A	
	IOUDAIOS I	JEWISH 380A		EUTHUS	IMMEDIATELY 321B	
	PAS IDα	ALL 637C		PNEUMA 5Dα	SPIRIT 683A	
	POTAMOS I	RIVER 701B	12FF	KAI 12B	AND 393A	
	HUPO IAα	BY 850D	13	DIAKONEW 2	SERVE 183A	
	CHWRA IB	COUNTRY 897C		TH8RION IAβ	BEAST 361D	
6	AGRIOS I	WILD 13B		META AI	WITH 509C	
	AKRIS	GRASSHOPPER 32D		PEIRAZW 2D	TRY 646B	
	DERMATINOS	(MADE OF) LEATHER 174C		SATAN	ADVERSARY 752B	
	DERRIS	SKIN 174C		TESSARAKONTA	FORTY 820D	
	ENDUW 2A	DRESS 263C		HUPO IAα	BY 850D	
	ESTHIW IA	EAT 312C	14	AUTOS 2	THEY 122D	
	ZWN8	BELT 342A		EUAGGELION IC	GOSPEL 318B	
	THRIX I	HAIR 364C		EUAGGELION 2Bα	GOSPEL 318B	
	IWAN(N)8S I	JOHN 385B		IWAN(N)8S I	JOHN 385B	
	KAM8LOS	CAMEL 402C		K8RUSSW 2Bβ	ANNOUNCE 432D	
	MELI	HONEY 501C		K8RUSSW 2Bβ	ANNOUNCE 432D	
	OSPHUS I	WAIST 591D		META BII4A	AFTER 511D	
	PERI 2Aβ	ABOUT 650D		PARADIDWMI IB	GIVE OVER 619D	
7	AUTOS 3D	(OBLIQUE CASE) 123B	15	AUTOS 2	THEY 122D	
	ERCHOMAI IIAη	COME 311A		BASILEIA 3B	KINGDOM 134D	
	HIKANOS 2	APPROPRIATE 375B		*BASILEIA 3G	KINGDOM 135B	
	ISCHUROS IA	STRONG 384A		EGGIZW 5B	APPROACH 212D	
	K8RUSSW 2Bβ	ANNOUNCE 432D		EUAGGELION IA	GOSPEL 318A	
	KUPTW	BEND 458D		KAIROS 3	TIME 396B	
	LUW IA	LOOSE 484D		LEGW IIBα	SAY 469C	
	OPISW 2B	AFTER 578D		METANOEW	CHANGE ONES MIND 513B	
	HOS,H8,HO I3A	(REL PRON) 587C		PISTEUW IAε	BELIEVE 666C	
	HUPOD8MA	SANDAL 852C		PISTEUW 2Aε	BELIEVE 667B	
8	AUTOS 2	THEY 122D		PL8ROW 2	MAKE FULL 677A	
	BAPTIZW 3B	BAPTIZE 131D	16	HALIEUS	FISHERMAN 37A	
	PNEUMA 5Cβ	SPIRIT 682D		AMPHIBALLW	CAST 46C	
	PNEUMA 5Cβ	SPIRIT 683A		AMPHIBL8STRON	CASTING NET 46D	
	PNEUMA 5Dα	SPIRIT 683A		ANDREAS	ANDREW 63B	
	HUDWR I	WATER 840D		GALILAIA	GALILEE 149D	
8A	BAPTIZW 2A	BAPTIZE 131B		THALASSA 2	LAKE 351A	
9	BAPTIZW 2A	BAPTIZE 131B		PARA IIIIA	ALONG 616A	
	GALILAIA	GALILEE 149D		PARAGW 2Aα	BRING IN 619A	
	GINOMAI I3F	TAKE PLACE 158C		PETROS	PETER 660C	
	EIS IDγ	IN 227D		SIMWN I	SIMON 758C	
	EKEINOS 2Bα	THAT 239B	17	HALIEUS	FISHERMAN 37A	
	H8MERA 4B	TIME 348B		ANTHRWPOS IAβ	MAN 67C	
	IORDAN8S	JORDAN 379C		GINOMAI 14A	BECOME 158C	

17	DEUTE 2	COME	175D
	OPISW 2Aβ	AFTER	578D
	POIEW IIBθ	DO	688B
18	AKOLOUTHEW 3	FOLLOW	30D
	APHI8MI 3A	LEAVE	125D
	PETROS	PETER	660C
18F	DIKTUON	NET	197D
19	IAKWBOS I	JAMES	368B
	IWAN(N)8S 2	JOHN	385C
	KATARTIZW IA	RESTORE	418D
	OLIGOS 3A	LITTLE	566C
	PROBAINW I	GO ON	709C
19F	ZEBEDAIOS	ZEBEDEE	337D
19F	PLOION 2	SHIP	679B
20	APERCHOMAI 4	GO AFTER	84A
	APHI8MI 3A	LEAVE	125C
	KALEW IE	CALL	400C
	MISTHWTOS	HIRED MAN	525D
	OPISW 2Aβ	AFTER	578D
21	DIDASKW I	TEACH	191A
	EISERCHOMAI IAβ	COME	231D
	EISPOREUOMAI I	GO	232D
	EUTHUS	IMMEDIATELY	321C
	KAPHARNAOUM	CAPERNAUM	427C
	PETROS	PETER	660C
	SABBATON IBβ	SABBATH	746C
	SUNAGWG8 2A		790C
		PLACE OF ASSEMBLY	
22	GAR IA	FOR	151A
	DIDACH8 3	TEACHING	191C
	EIMI II4E	TO BE	223B
	EKPL8SSW 2	BE AMAZED	243D
	EXOUSIA 2	ABILITY	277D
	EPI IIIBγ	ON	287A
23	AKATHARTOS 2	IMPURE	28C
	ANAKRAZW	CRY OUT	55D
	ANTHRWPOS 3Aβ	MAN	68B
	EN I5D	IN	259C
	EUTHUS	IMMEDIATELY	321C
	PNEUMA 4C	SPIRIT	682A
24	HAGIOS 2Cβ	THE HOLY ONE	10A
	APOLLUMI IAα	RUIN	94B
	EA	AH	210A
	EGW	I	216C
	EIMI II6C	TO BE	223C
	NAZAR8NOS	THE NAZARENE	534A
	NAZWRAIOS	NAZARENE	534B
	OIDA IC	KNOW	558B
24A	TIS, TI IBε	WHICH	827B
25	EPITIMAW I	REBUKE	303B
	PHIMOW 2	TIE SHUT	869D
25F	EXERCHOMAI IA6	GO OUT	274A
26	MEGAS 2Aγ	GREAT	498D
	PNEUMA 4C	SPIRIT	682A
	SPARASSW	TEAR	768B
	PHWNEW IB	CRY OUT	878B
	PHWN8 2A	VOICE	878D
26F	AKATHARTOS 2	IMPURE	28C
27	DIDACH8 2	TEACHING	191C
	EIMI II3	TO BE	223D
	EXOUSIA 2	ABILITY	277D
	EPITASSW	COMMAND	302A
	THAMBEW 2	ASTOUND	351B
27	KAI II2	EVEN	394B
	KAINOS 2	NEW	395A
	KATA II5Bβ	ACCORDING TO	408C
	PNEUMA 4C	SPIRIT	682A
	SUZBTEW I	DISCUSS	783B
	TIS, TI IBβ	WHICH	827A
	HUPAKOUW I	LISTEN TO	845B
28	AKO8 2A	REPORT	30C
	GALILAIA	GALILEE	149D
	EXERCHOMAI 2Bα	GO OUT	274C
	PANTACHOU 2	EVERYWHERE	613B
	PERICHWROS	NEIGHBORING	659B
29	ANDREAS	ANDREW	63B
	ERCHOMAI IIAβ	COME	310B
	EUTHUS	IMMEDIATELY	321C
	IAKWBOS I	JAMES	368B
	IWAN(N)8S 2	JOHN	385C
	META AIIIA	WITH	509D
	OIKIA IA	HOUSE	559D
	PETROS	PETER	660C
30	KATAKEIMAI I	LIE DOWN	412B
	LEGW II2	SPEAK	471A
	PENTHERA	MOTHER IN LAW	648B
	PETROS	PETER	660C
	PURESSW	SUFFER WITH A FEVER	738B
31	APHI8MI 3A	LEAVE	125C
	DIAKONEW 2	SERVE	183A
	EGEIRW IAβ	RAISE	213D
	KRATEW IB	SEIZE	449C
	PURETOS	FEVER	738B
32	GINOMAI IIBγ	COME ABOUT	157C
	DAIMONIZOMAI		168A
		BE POSSESSED BY A DEMON	
	DUNW	SET	208B
	H8LIOS	THE SUN	346B
	KAKWS I	BADLY	399B
	HOTE IB	WHEN	592C
	OPSIOS 2	LATE	606C
	PHERW 4Bβ	BEAR	863C
33	EPISUNAGW	GATHER	301D
	THURA IA	DOOR	366B
	HOLOS 2A	WHOLE	567C
	POLIS 3	CITY	692C
	PROS IIIIA	TOWARD	716D
34	APHI8MI 4	TOLERATE	126A
	DAIMONION 2	DEMON	168B
	EKBALLW I	DRIVE OUT	237A
	THERAPEUW 2	HEAL	359C
	KAKWS I	BADLY	399B
	LALEW 2Aβ	SPEAK	464B
	NOSOS I	DISEASE	545D
	OIDA IA	KNOW	558B
	HOTI 3A	THAT	593D
	OU 4A	NO	594D
	POIKILOS I	DIVERSIFIED	690A
	CHRISTOS I	ANOINTED ONE	895B
35	ANIST8MI 2D	RISE	69D
	APERCHOMAI 2	GO	83D
	ENNUCHOS	AT NIGHT	266D
	EXERCHOMAI IAβ	GO OUT	274A
	ER8MOS IA	ABANDONED	308D
	KAKEI I	AND THERE	397C
	LIAN 3	VERY	474C

35	PROSEUCHOMAI	PRAY	720D
	PRWI	EARLY	732A
	TOPOS IC	PLACE	830B
36	META AIIICα	WITH	510A
37	HEURISKW IA	FIND	325A
	Z8TEW IAα	SEEK	339A
	HOTI 2	THAT	593D
	PAS 2Aγ	ALL	638B
38	AGW 5	GO	14C
	ALLACHOU	ELSEWHERE	38D
	EGGUS IC	NEAR	213B
	EIS 4F	(PURPOSE)	228D
	ECHW III2	HOLD FAST	334C
	HINA IIC	IN ORDER THAT	377C
	KAI III	ALSO	394A
	KAKEI 2	THERE ALSO	397C
	K8RUSSW 2Bβ	ANNOUNCE	432D
	KWMOPOLIS	MARKET TOWN	462D
39	DAIMONION 2	DEMON	168B
	EKBALLW I	DRIVE OUT	237A
	K8RUSSW 2Bβ	ANNOUNCE	432C
	SUNAGWG8 2A	PLACE OF ASSEMBLY	790C
40	GONUPETEW	KNEEL DOWN	164B
	EAN IIA	IF	210B
	KATHARIZW IBα	CLEANSE	388A
	LEPROS	LEPER	473A
	PARAKALEW 3	IMPLORE	622D
41	HAPTW 2B	TOUCH	102C
	EKTEINW I	STRETCH OUT	244D
	KATHARIZW IBα	CLEANSE	388A
	ORGIZW	BE ANGRY	583B
	SPLAGCHNIZOMAI	HAVE PITY	770B
42	APERCHOMAI IB	GO AWAY	83D
	KATHARIZW IBα	CLEANSE	388A
	LEPRA	LEPROSY	473A
43	EKBALLW I	DRIVE OUT	237A
	EMBRIMAOMAI	SCOLD	254B
44	DEIKNUMI IA	SHOW	171D
	HIEREUS IBα	PRIEST	372C
	KATHARISMOS I	PURIFICATION	388C
	MARTURION IA	TESTIMONY	494D
	M8DEIS 2Bα	NOTHING	520A
	MWUS8S	MOSES	533D
	HORAW 2B	SEE	582B
	PROSTASSW	COMMAND	725D
	PROSPHERW 2A	BRING (TO)	727B
	SEAUTOU 3	YOURSELF	753A
	HUPAGW 2	GO AWAY	844C
45	DIAPH8MIZW	MAKE KNOWN	189D
	DUNAMAI IB	ABLE	206B
	EIMI I3	TO BE	222B
	EISERCHOMAI IAβ	COME	231D
	EXERCHOMAI IAβ	GO OUT	274A
	EXW IAα	OUTSIDE	278D
	ER8MOS IA	ABANDONED	308D
	K8RUSSW 2A	ANNOUNCE	432B
	LOGOS IAβ	WORD	478C
	M8KETI 2	NO LONGER	520B
	PANTACHOTHEN	FROM EVERY DIRECTION	613B
	PANTOTHEN	FROM ALL DIRECTIONS	613C
	POLIS I	CITY	692A
45	POLUS I2Bβ	MANY	695B
	TOPOS IC	PLACE	830B
	PHANERWS	OPENLY	860D
	HWSTE 2Aβ	THEREFORE	908C

MARK 2

1	AKOUW 3E	LEARN	32A
	DIA AII2	AFTER	179A
	EISERCHOMAI IAα	COME	231D
	H8MERA 2	DAY	347A
	KAPHARNAOUM	CAPERNAUM	427C
	OIKOS IAα	HOUSE	563A
	PALIN IA	BACK	611C
2	THURA IA	DOOR	366B
	LALEW 2B	SPEAK	464D
	LOGOS IBβ	WORD	479C
	M8DE 2	NOT EVEN	519D
	M8KETI 2	NO LONGER	520B
	POLUS I2Aα	MANY	694D
	PROS III7	TOWARD	718A
	SUNAGW 2	GATHER	790A
	CHWREW 3A	HAVE ROOM FOR	898B
	HWSTE 2Aβ	THEREFORE	908C
3	AIRW 2	LIFT UP	24A
	TESSARES	FOUR	821A
	PHERW 4Bβ	BEAR	863C
3-5	PARALUTIKOS	PARALYTIC	625D
4	APO VI	BECAUSE OF	87B
	APOSTEGAZW	UNROOF	98A
	DUNAMAI IB	ABLE	206B
	EIMI II9A	TO BE	223D
	EXORUSSW	TEAR OUT	277A
	KATAKEIMAI I	LIE DOWN	412B
	KRABATTOS	MATTRESS	448C
	OCHLOS I	CROWD	605C
	PROSEGGIZW	APPROACH	719D
	PROSPHERW IA	BRING (TO)	727A
	STEG8	ROOF	773B
	CHALAW	LET DOWN	882C
4A	HOPOU IAα	WHERE	579C
4B	HOPOU IAα	WHERE	579C
5	HAMARTIA I	SIN	42C
	APHI8MI 2	FORGIVE	125C
	PISTIS 2Bα	FAITH	668D
	TEKNON 2A	CHILD	816B
6	DIALOGIZOMAI I	CONSIDER	185A
	KATH8MAI IAβ	SIT	390B
	KARDIA IBβ	HEART	404C
7	HAMARTIA I	SIN	42C
	APHI8MI 2	FORGIVE	125C
	BLASPH8MEW 2Bα	BLASPHEME	142A
	BLASPH8MIA 2B	SLANDER	142C
	DUNAMAI IA	ABLE	206B
	HEIS 2C	ONE	230C
	HOUTW	THUS	602B
	TIS, TI IAα	WHICH	826C
7A	TIS, TI 3A	WHICH	827B
8	ANASTENAZW	SIGH DEEPLY	60D
	*DIALOGIZOMAI I	CONSIDER	185A
	EN I5B	IN	258D
	EPIGINWSKW 2C	KNOW	291B
	KARDIA IBβ	HEART	404C

8	LEGW I3	SAY 469D
	PNEUMA 3B	SPIRIT 681B
	TIS, TI 3A	WHICH 827B
9	AIRW IA	LIFT UP 23D
	APHI8MI 2	FORGIVE 125C
	EGEIRW IB	RAISE UP 214A
	EGEIRW 2F	APPEAR 214B
	EUKOPOS	EASY 322A
	KRABATTOS	MATTRESS 448C
	PARALUTOS	THE PARALYTIC 625D
	PERIPATEW IC	GO ABOUT 655A
	TIS, TI IBv	WHICH 827A
	HUPAGW I	GO AWAY 844B
9F	HAMARTIA I	SIN 42C
9F	PARALUTIKOS	PARALYTIC 625D
10	APHI8MI 2	FORGIVE 125C
	EXOUSIA 3	AUTHORITY 278A
	HINA I6	IN ORDER THAT 378A
	HINA III2	IN ORDER THAT 379A
	HUIOS 2C	SON 843A
11	AIRW IA	LIFT UP 23D
	EGEIRW IB	RAISE UP 214A
	OIKOS IAα	HOUSE 563A
	HUPAGW 2	GO AWAY 844C
11F	KRABATTOS	MATTRESS 448C
12	DOXAZW I	PRAISE 203C
	EIDON	SEE 219C
	EMPROSTHEN 2C	IN FRONT 256C
	ENANTION IA	BEFORE 261B
	EXIST8MI 2B	BE AMAZED 276A
	THEOS 3A	GOD 357D
	LEGW IIBα	SAY 469C
	OUDEPOTE	NEVER 596D
	HOUTW 5	THUS 602D
	HWSTE 2AB	THEREFORE 908C
13	THALASSA 2	LAKE 351A
	OCHLOS I	CROWD 605C
	PALIN 2	AGAIN 611C
	PARA IIIIBθ	ALONG 616A
	PAS ICα	ALL 637B
14	AKOLOUTHEW 3	FOLLOW 30D
	HALPHAIOS I	ALPHAEUS 41A
	ANIST8MI 2D	RISE 69D
	EPI IIIIAζ	ON 288C
	IAKWBOS 2	JAMES 368B
	IAKWBOS 6	JAMES 368C
	KATH8MAI IAα	SIT 390B
	LEUI 4	LEVI 473B
	PARAGW 2Aα	BRING IN 619A
	TELWNION	TAX OFFICE 820B
15	GINOMAI I3F	TAKE PLACE 158B
	KAI I2B	AND 393A
	KATAKEIMAI 3	LIE DOWN 412C
	OIKIA IA	HOUSE 559D
	SUNANAKEIMAI	EAT WITH 792A
	TELWN8S	TAX COLLECTOR 820B
15A	POLUS IIAα	MANY 694A
15F	HAMARTWLOS 2	SINNER 43D
16	GRAMMATEUS 2	SCRIBES 165A
	EIDON ID	SEE 219D
	ESTHIW IC	EAT 313A
	HO TI 4B	WHY 591C
	HOTI IC	THAT 593A
16	HOTI 2	THAT 593D
	PINW I	DRINK 664C
	TIS, TI IBε	WHICH 827B
	PHARISAIOS	PHARISEE 861C
16A	META AII2	WITH 510C
16A	TELWN8S	TAX COLLECTOR 820B
16B	META AII2	WITH 510C
16B	TELWN8S	TAX COLLECTOR 820B
17	HAMARTWLOS 2	SINNER 43C
	DIKAIOS IB	UPRIGHT 194D
	IATROS I	PHYSICIAN 369C
	ISCHUW I	BE STRONG 384C
	KAKWS I	BADLY 399B
	KALEW 2	CALL 400D
	METANOIA	REPENTANCE 514A
	CHREIA I	NEED 893B
17F	LEGW I3	SAY 469D
18	DIA BII2	WHY 180B
	EIMI II4E	TO BE 223B
	ERCHOMAI IIAζ	COME 310D
	IWAN(N)8S I	JOHN 385B
	N8STEUW	TO FAST 540C
	SOS I	YOURS 766C
	PHARISAIOS	PHARISEE 861C
18A	MATH8T8S 2A	DISCIPLE 486D
18B	MATH8T8S 2A	DISCIPLE 486D
18C	MATH8T8S 2A	DISCIPLE 486D
19	DUNAMAI IA	ABLE 206B
	EN IV6B	IN 261A
	ECHW I3	HAVE 333C
	M8 CI	NOT 519A
	NUMPHWN 2	BRIDAL CHAMBER 547C
	HOSOS I	HOW GREAT 590B
	HUIOS IC6	SON 842A
	CHRONOS	TIME 896B
19B	META AIIIB	WITH 509D
19F	N8STEUW	TO FAST 540B
19F	NUMPHIOS	BRIDEGROOM 547B
20	APAIRW	TAKE AWAY 79A
	ERCHOMAI IIBα	COME 311B
	HOTAN IB	WHEN 592B
20A	H8MERA 4B	TIME 348B
20B	H8MERA 4A	TIME 348A
21	AGNAPHOS	UNSHRUNKEN 10D
	AIRW 4	TAKE AWAY 24B
	GINOMAI IIBβ	COME ABOUT 157B
	EPIBL8MA	A PATCH 290B
	EPI(R)RAPTW	SEW 298A
	HIMATION I	GARMENT 377A
	KAINOS I	NEW 395A
	PL8RWMA IB	THAT WHICH FILLS 678A
	RAKOS 2	PATCH 741C
	SCHISMA I	SPLIT 805B
	CHEIRWN	WORSE 889B
21A	PALAIOS I	OLD 610C
21B	PALAIOS I	OLD 610D
21F	EI VI3B	IF NOT 219A
21F	OUDEIS 2A	NO ONE 596B
21FF	DE IA	BUT, AND 170C
22	APOLLUMI 2AB	PASS AWAY 94D
	ASKOS	WINESKIN 116A
	BL8TEOS	MUST BE PUT 143C
	KAINOS I	NEW 394D

22	NEOS IAα	NEW 537D
	OINOS I	WINE 565A
	PALAIOS I	OLD 610C
	R8GNUMI I	TEAR 742C
23	GINOMAI I3E	TAKE PLACE 158B
	DIA AII	THROUGH 178C
	DIAPOREUOMAI	GO THROUGH 186D
	HODOPOIEW	MAKE A WAY 556B
	HODOS IB	WAY 556C
	PARAPOREUOMAI 2	PASS BY 627A
	POIEW IIB6	DO 687D
	SABBATON IBβ	SABBATH 746C
	SPORIMOS	SOWN 770D
	STACHUS I	EAR (OF GRAIN) 773B
	TILLW	PLUCK 824C
24	EXESTI I	IT IS POSSIBLE 274D
	IDE I	SEE 369D
	POIEW IICγ	DO 688C
	SABBATON IBβ	SABBATH 746C
25	ANAGINWSKW I	READ 51B
	AUTOS IC	SELF 122C
	DAUID	DAVID 170B
	META AIIICα	WITH 510A
	OUDEPOTE	NEVER 596D
	PEINAW I	HUNGER 645D
	CHREIA 2	NEED 893B
26	ABIATHAR	ABIATHAR IC
	ARTOS IB	BREAD 110B
	DIDWMI IA	GIVE 191D
	EXESTI 3	IT IS POSSIBLE 274D
	EPI I2	UNDER 286C
	ESTHIW IA	EAT 312C
	HIEREUS IBα	PRIEST 372C
	KAI III	ALSO 394A
	OIKOS IAβ	HOUSE 563B
	PROTHESIS I	SETTING FORTH 713A
	PWS 2A	HOW 740A
	SUN IC	WITH 789B
27	ANTHRWPOS 3B	MAN 68C
	GINOMAI I2A	CREATED 157C
	DIA BIII	BECAUSE OF 180A
27F	SABBATON IA	SABBATH 746B
27F	HUIOS 2C	SON 843C
28	KURIOS IAα	LORD 460A
	HUIOS 2C	SON 843A
	HWSTE IA	THEREFORE 908B

MARK 3

I	ANTHRWPOS 3Aβ	MAN 68B
	EISERCHOMAI IAβ	COME 231D
	X8RAINW 2B	DRY UP 550D
	PALIN 2	AGAIN 611C
	SUNAGWG8 2A	790C
		PLACE OF ASSEMBLY
	CHEIR I	HAND 888A
2	EI V2A	WHETHER 218D
	THERAPEUW 2	HEAL 359C
	HINA IIE	IN ORDER THAT 377C
	KAT8GOREW IA	BRING CHARGES 424B
	PARAT8REW IAα	WATCH 628A
	SABBATON IBβ	SABBATH 746C
3	EGEIRW IB	RAISE UP 214A

3	EIS IAα	INTO 227C
	LEGW IIIC	ORDER 470D
	MESOS 2	THE MIDDLE 508C
	X8RAINW 2B	DRY UP 550D
	X8ROS 2	DRY 551A
	HO,H8,TO II2A	THE 553B
4	AGATHOPOIEW I	DO GOOD 2C
	APOKTEINW IA	KILL 93C
	EXESTI I	IT IS POSSIBLE 274D
	8 IAα	OR 342B
	KAKOPOIEW I	DO WRONG 398B
	POIEW IIBε	DO 687D
	SABBATON IBβ	SABBATH 746C
	SIWPAW I	BE SILENT 760A
	SWZW IA	SAVE 805D
	PSUCH8 2	SOUL LIFE 902C
5	ANTHRWPOS 4A	MAN 68D
	APOKATHIST8MI I	RESTORE 91B
	EKTEINW I	STRETCH OUT 244D
	EPI IIIBγ	ON 287B
	KARDIA IBβ	HEART 404D
	LEGW IIIC	ORDER 470D
	META AIIII	WITH 511A
	NEKRWSIS 2B	DEATH 537D
	ORG8 I	ANGER 582C
	PERIBLEPW I	LOOK AROUND 652A
	P8RWSIS	DISABLING 662C
	PWRWSIS	HARDENING 739B
	SULLUPEW	HURT 784D
	HUGI8S IA	HEALTHY 840A
6	APOLLUMI IAα	RUIN 94C
	DIDWMI 5	GIVE 192D
	H8RWDIANOI	HERODIANS 349B
	KATA I2Bβ	DOWN 406D
	META AII3B	WITH 510D
	HOPWS 2B	IN ORDER THAT
	POIEW IIB6	DO 687D
	SUMBOULION I	PLAN 785D
	PHARISAIOS	PHARISEE 861C
7	ANACHWREW 2B	WITHDRAW 63A
	EIS IB	NEAR 227C
	THALASSA 2	LAKE 351A
	IOUDAIA I	JUDAEA 379D
	META AIIIA	WITH 509D
7F	IOUDAIA I	JUDAEA 379D
7F	PL8THOS 2Bα	QUANTITY 674C
7F	POLUS IIBα	MANY 694C
8	IDOUMAIA	IDUMAEA 372A
	HIEROSOLUMA IA	JERUSALEM
	IORDAN8S	JORDAN 379C
	HOSOS 2	HOW GREAT 590C
	PERAN 2C	ON THE OTHER SIDE 649C
	PERI 2Aγ	ABOUT 650D
	POIEW IIBβ	DO 687C
	SIDWN	SIDON 757C
	TUROS	TYRE 838C
9	THLIBW I	PRESS UPON 362C
	HINA IIIAδ	IN ORDER THAT 378B
	M8 AI2	NOT 517C
	OCHLOS I	CROWD 605C
	PLOIARION	BOAT 679A
	PROSKARTEREW I	ADHERE TO 722D
10	HAPTW 2B	TOUCH 102D

10	EPIPIPTW 1B	FALL UPON 297C
	ECHW I2Eα	HAVE 333A
	THERAPEUW 2	HEAL 359C
	MASTIX 2	TORMENT 496B
	HOSOS 2	HOW GREAT 590C
	POLUS I2Aα	MANY 694D
	HWSTE 2Aβ	THEREFORE 908C
11	AKATHARTOS 2	IMPURE 28C
	EIMI III	TO BE 222D
	THEWREW I	OBSERVE 360D
	KRAZW 2A	CALL 448D
	HOTAN 2C	WHEN 592B
	PNEUMA 4C	SPIRIT 682A
	PROSPIPTW I	FALL DOWN BEFORE 725B
	HUIOS 2B	SON 842C
12	EPITIMAW I	REBUKE 303B
	POIEW IIB:	DO 688B
	POLUS I2Bβ	MANY 695A
	PHANEROS I	CLEAR 860B
13	ANABAINW IAα	GO UP 49C
	APERCHOMAI 2	GO 84A
	EIS IAα	INTO 227C
	THELW 2	WISH 355D
	HO,H8,TO IIIAα	THE 552B
	OROS	MOUNTAIN 586B
	HOS,H8,HO I2A	(REL PRON) 587A
	PROSKALEW IA	SUMMON 722C
14	APOSTELLW IBγ	SEND AWAY 98B
	APOSTELLW IC	SEND AWAY 98B
	APOSTOLOS 3	APOSTLES 99B
	EIMI III7	TO BE 224D
	HINA IIE	IN ORDER THAT 377C
	K8RUSSW 2Bβ	ANNOUNCE 432D
	META AIIICα	WITH 510A
	ONOMAZW I	NAME 577B
15	EKBALLW I	DRIVE OUT 237A
	EXOUSIA 2	ABILITY 277D
16	PETROS	PETER 660D
16F	EPITITH8MI IAβ	GIVE 303A
16F	ONOMA I2A	NAME 574B
17	BOAN8RGES	BOANERGES 143C
	BRONT8	THUNDER 147B
	EIMI II3	TO BE 222D
	ZEBEDAIOS	ZEBEDEE 337D
	IAKWBOS I	JAMES 368B
	IWAN(N)8S 2	JOHN 385C
	HOS,H8,HO I7A	(REL PRON) 588C
	HUIOS IC6	SON 842A
18	HALPHAIOS 2	ALPHAEUS 41A
	ANDREAS	ANDREW 63B
	BARTHOLOMAIOS	BARTHOLOMEW 133B
	THADDAIOS	THADDAEUS 350B
	THWMAS	THOMAS 367D
	IAKWBOS 2	JAMES 368B
	KANANAIOS	CANANAEAN 403C
	KANANIT8S	CANANITE 403C
	MATTHAIOS	MATTHEW 497A
	SIMWN 2	SIMON 758C
	PHILIPPOS 3	PHILIP 868A
19	IOUDAS 6	JUDAS 380D
	ISKARIWTH	ISCARIOT 381D
	HOS,H8,HO I10D	(REL PRON) 588D
	PARADIDWMI IB	GIVE OVER 620A

20	ARTOS 2	FOOD 110B
	ESTHIW IA	EAT 312D
	M8 AI3	NOT 517C
	M8DE 2	NOT EVEN 519D
	OIKOS IAα	HOUSE 563A
	SUNERCHOMAI IA	ASSEMBLE 795D
	HWSTE 2Aβ	THEREFORE 908C
20F	PARA I4Bβ	FROM 615B
21	AKOUW 3A	LEARN 31D
	EXARTAW 2	BE ATTACHED 273A
	EXERCHOMAI IAζ	GO OUT 274B
	EXIST8MI 2A	LOSE ONES MIND 276A
	KRATEW IA	ARREST 449C
	HO,H8,TO II5	THE 554B
	PARA I4Bβ	FROM 615B
21F	LEGW IIBα	SAY 469C
22	ARCHWN 3	AUTHORITIES 113C
	BEEZEBOUL	BEELZEBUB 138C
	EKBALLW I	DRIVE OUT 237A
	ECHW I2Eα	HAVE 333A
	HIEROSOLUMA IA	JERUSALEM 373D
	KATABAINW IAβ	COME DOWN 409B
23	DUNAMAI IA	ABLE 206B
	EKBALLW I	DRIVE OUT 237A
	PARABOL8 2	PARABLE 617D
	PROSKALEW IA	SUMMON 722C
	PWS ID	HOW 739C
	*SATAN	ADVERSARY 752B
24	BASILEIA 2	KINGDOM 134C
	EAN IIB	IF 210B
24F	EKEINOS 2A	THAT 239B
24F	EPI IIIIAε	AGAINST 288B
24F	HIST8MI IIID	STAND 383B
24=6	MERIZW IA	DIVIDE 505D
25	OIKIA 2	HOUSEHOLD 560A
26	ANIST8MI 2C	RISE 69D
	EI IIA	IF 218A
	EPI IIIIAε	AGAINST 288B
	ECHW I2F	HAVE 333B
	HIST8MI IIID	STAND 383B
	SATAN	ADVERSARY 752B
	TELOS IA	END 819A
27	DEW IB	BIND 176D
	EAN I3B	IF 210D
	ISCHUROS IA	STRONG 384A
	M8 AII	NOT 517C
	OUDEIS 2A	NO ONE 596B
	PRWTOS 2A	FIRST 733D
	SKEUOS IA	THING 761C
	TOTE 2	AT THAT TIME 831D
27A	DIARPAZW	PLUNDER 187A
27B	DIARPAZW	PLUNDER 187A
28	HAMART8MA	SIN 42B
	AM8N 2	AMEN 45B
	ANTHRWPOS IA6	PEOPLE 67D
	APHI8MI 2	FORGIVE 125C
	BLASPH8MEW 2Bα	BLASPHEME 142A
	BLASPH8MIA 2B	SLANDER 142C
	LEGW IIID	ASSURE 470D
	HUIOS ICβ	SON 841D
29	AIWN IB	TIME 26D
	AIWNIOS 3	ETERNAL 28A
	HAMART8MA	SIN 42A

```
29  APHESIS 2            PARDON     124C      4  GINOMAI I3F          TAKE PLACE 158C
    BLASPH8MEW 2Bɣ       BLASPHEME  142B         EN   II3             WHILE      260A
    EIS 2B               FOR        228A         ERCHOMAI IICα        COME       311B
    EIS 4Cα              AGAINST    228B         KATESTHIW I          EAT UP     423B
    ENOCHOS 2Bβ          GUILTY     267C         HODOS IA             WAY        556B
    HO,H8,TO IIIF        THE        553A         HOS,H8,HO II2        THIS (ONE) 589B
    PNEUMA 5Cα           SPIRIT     682C         PARA IIIID           ALONG      616A
30  AKATHARTOS 2         IMPURE      28C         PETEINON             BIRD       660A
    ECHW I2Eα            HAVE       333A         PIPTW IA             FALL       665A
    LEGW IIBα            SAY        469C         SPEIRW IAα           SOW        768C
    PNEUMA 4C            SPIRIT     682A      4FF    MEN 2D           (PARTICLE) 504C
31  ADELPHOS I           BROTHER     15D      5  BATHOS I             DEPTH      129D
    APOSTELLW IBα        SEND AWAY   98A         G8 I                 EARTH      156C
    EXW IAα              OUTSIDE    278D         EKBLASTANW           SPROUT UP  237B
    KALEW ID             CALL       400B         EXANATELLW           SPRING UP  272B
    PHWNEW 2B            CALL       878C         HOPOU IAα            WHERE      579C
31F    ADELPHOS I        BROTHER     15D         PETRWD8S             ROCKY      661B
31F    MARIA I           MARY       492D         PIPTW IA             FALL       665A
31≈3  M8T8R I            MOTHER     521D         POLUS IIBα           MANY       694C
32  ADELPH8 I            SISTER      15C      5A     ECHW I2G         HAVE       333B
    EXW IAα              OUTSIDE    278D      5B     ECHW I2G         HAVE       333B
    Z8TEW IB             SEEK       339B      5F     DIA BII3         BECAUSE    180C
    KATH8MAI IAα         SIT        390B      5F     M8 AIIIE         NOT        518A
    PERI 2A6             ABOUT      651A      6  ANATELLW 2           RISE        61C
34  IDE 3                SEE        369D         ECHW I2Cβ            HAVE       332D
    KATH8MAI IAα         SIT        390B         H8LIOS               THE SUN    346B
    KUKLW IA             AROUND     458A         KAUMATIZW            BURN       426C
    PERI 2A6             ABOUT      651A         X8RAINW 2A           DRY UP     550D
    PERIBLEPW I     LOOK AROUND     652A         RIZA IA              ROOT       743B
34F    M8T8R 3           MOTHER     521D      7  AKANTHA              THORN PLANT 29A
35  ADELPH8 I            SISTER      15C         ANABAINW IB          GO UP       50A
    ADELPHOS 2           BROTHER     15D         EIS IAβ              INTO       227C
    THEL8MA ICɣ          WILL       355A         PIPTW IA             FALL       665A
    THEL8MA ICɣ          WILL       355A         SUMPNIGW I           CHOKE      787C
    HOUTOS IAε           THIS       601B      7F     DIDWMI 4         GIVE       192C
    POIEW IICα           DO         688C      7F     KARPOS IA        FRUIT      405C
    POIEW IICα           DO         688C      8  ANABAINW IB          GO UP       50A
                                                  AUXANW 2             GROW       121B
              MARK 4                              G8 I                 EARTH      156C
                                                  EIS 6C               (DISTRIBUTI 229B
1   G8 4                 LAND       156C         HEIS 4               ONE        231A
    EIMI III9            TO BE      224D         HEKATON          ONE HUNDRED    236B
    EMBAINW              GO IN      253C         HEX8KONTA            SIXTY      275C
    KATH8MAI 2           SIT DOWN   390C         KALOS 2A             GOOD       401B
    PALIN 2              AGAIN      611C         PIPTW IA             FALL       665A
    PARA IIIIBα          ALONG      616A         TRIAKONTA            THIRTY     833D
    PAS ICα              ALL        637B         PHERW 2              BEAR       862D
    PLOIARION            BOAT       679A      9  OUS 2                EAR        600B
    PLOION 2             SHIP       679B         *SUNI8MI         UNDERSTAND     797D
    POLUS IIIIBβ         MANY       696B      10  GINOMAI II4B        BE         159D
    SUNAGW 2             GATHER     790B         ERWTAW I             ASK        312A
IA     OCHLOS I          CROWD      605C         KATA IIIC            BY         407B
IB     OCHLOS I          CROWD      605C         MONOS 3              BE ALONE   530A
IB     PROS III7         TOWARD     718A         HO,H8,TO II5         THE        554B
2   DIDASKW 2C           TEACH      191A         HOTE IB              WHEN       592C
    DIDACH8 I            TEACHING   191B         PARABOL8 2           PARABLE    617D
    EN   II3             WHILE      259D         PERI 2A6             ABOUT      651A
    PARABOL8 2           PARABLE    617D      11  BASILEIA 3B         KINGDOM    134D
    POLUS I2Bα           MANY       695A         BASILEIA 3G          KINGDOM    135A
3   AKOUW IC             HEAR        31D         GINOMAI I3Bɣ         TAKE PLACE 158B
    EXERCHOMAI IAʑ       GO OUT     274B         GINWSKW IA           KNOW       159D
3A     SPEIRW IAα        SOW        768C         EKEINOS IA           THAT       238D
3B     SPEIRW IAα        SOW        768C         EXW IAβ              OUTSIDE    279A
```

11	MUST8RION 1	MYSTERY 532A
	PARABOL8 2	PARABLE 617D
	PAS 28β	ALL THINGS 638D
12	EPISTREPHW 18β	TURN 301B
	HINA II2	IN ORDER THAT 378D
	M8 AI2	NOT 517C
	M8POTE 28α	(NEG PARTICLE) 521A
	SUNI8MI	UNDERSTAND 797D
	SUNI8MI	UNDERSTAND 798A
13	GINWSKW 3A	UNDERSTAND 160B
	OIDA 4	KNOW 559A
	PAS 1Dα	ALL 637C
	PWS 1D	HOW 739C
13B	PARABOL8 2	PARABLE 617D
14	SPEIRW 18β	SOW 768D
14=20	LOGOS 18β	WORD 479C
15	AKOUW 18α	HEAR 31B
	ERCHOMAI IIAζ	COME 310D
	HOPOU 1Aα	WHERE 579C
	HOUTOS 1A6	THIS 601A
	PARA IIIID	ALONG 616A
	SATAN	ADVERSARY 752B
15A	SPEIRW 18β	SOW 768D
15B	SPEIRW 18β	SOW 768D
15F	EIMI II3	TO BE 223A
15F	HOTAN 1B	WHEN 592A
16	LAMBANW 1Eβ	RECEIVE 466A
	HOMOIWS	LIKEWISE 570D
	HOUTOS 1A6	THIS 601A
	PETRWD8S	ROCKY 661B
	SPEIRW 1Aγ	SOW 768C
	CHARA !	JOY 883C
17	GINOMAI IIB8	COME ABOUT 157B
	DIWGMOS	PERSECUTION 200A
	EITA 1	THEN 233A
	8 IA8	OR 342D
	THLIPSIS 1	TRIBULATION 362D
	PROSKAIROS	TEMPORARY 722C
	RIZA 1B	ROOT 743B
	SKANDALIZW 1A	CAUSE TO FALL 760B
18	AKANTHA	THORN PLANT 29A
	EIMI II3	TO BE 223A
	HOUTOS 1A6	THIS 601A
	SPEIRW 1Aγ	SOW 768C
	SPEIRW 1Aγ	SOW 768C
19	AIWN 2A	AGE 27A
	AKARPOS 2	UNFRUITFUL 29B
	APAT8 1	DECEPTION 81B
	APAT8 2	PLEASURE 81C
	GINOMAI III	BE 159B
	EISPOREUOMAI 2	GO 232D
	EPITHUMIA 1	DESIRE 293B
	LOIPOS 28β	THE REST 481B
	MERIMNA	ANXIETY 506A
	PERI 2D	ABOUT 651B
	PLOUTOS 1	WEALTH 680B
	SUMPNIGW 1	CHOKE 787C
20	G8 1	EARTH 156C
	EIMI II3	TO BE 223A
	HEIS 4	ONE 231A
	HEKATON	ONE HUNDRED 236B
	HEX8KONTA	SIXTY 275C
	KALOS 2A	GOOD 401B

20	KARPOPHOREW 2	BEAR FRUIT 406A
	HOSTIS 1A	WHOEVER 590D
	PARADECHOMAI 1	ACCEPT 619C
	SPEIRW 1Aγ	SOW 768D
21	HAPTW 1	KINDLE 102B
	ERCHOMAI IIC8	COME 311C
	8 1C	NOR 343A
	HINA IIA	IN ORDER THAT 377C
	KAIW 1A	LIGHT 397A
	KLIN8	COUCH 437B
	LUCHNIA	LAMPSTAND 484B
	LUCHNOS 1	LAMP 484C
	M8TI	(INTERROG PARTICLE) 522A
	MODIOS	A PECK MEASURE 527D
	TITH8MI IIA8	PUT 823D
21A	HUPO 2Aα	UNDER 851A
21B	TITH8MI IIA8	PUT 823D
21B	HUPO 2Aα	UNDER 851A
22	ALLA 1A	BUT, YET 37C
	APOKRUPHOS	HIDDEN 93B
	GAR 1B	FOR 151B
	GAR 1D	FOR 151B
	GINOMAI III	BE 159B
	EAN I3B	IF 210D
	ERCHOMAI I2C	COME 311C
	HINA IIII	IN ORDER THAT 379A
	KRUPTOS 1	HIDDEN 455A
	OUDE 1	AND NOT 595D
	PHANEROS 2	CLEAR 860B
	PHANEROW 1B	REVEAL 860C
23	AKOUW 1A	HEAR 31B
	EI VII	219B
	OUS 2	EAR 600B
24	BLEPW 4C	SEE 143B
	METREW 2	GIVE OUT 516B
	METRON 1A	MEASURE 516C
	HOS,H8,HO I5B	(REL PRON) 588B
	PERICHWROS	NEIGHBORING 659B
	PROSTITH8MI 1A	ADD 726A
	TIS, TI 18ζ	WHICH 827B
25	AIRW 4	TAKE AWAY 24A
	GAR 1D	FOR 151B
	OU 5A	NO 595A
25A	ECHW I2A	HAVE 332B
25B	ECHW I2A	HAVE 332C
26	ANTHRWPOS 3A8	MAN 68B
	BALLW 1A	THROW 130B
	BASILEIA 3B	KINGDOM 134D
	G8 1	EARTH 156C
	EIMI II9B	TO BE 224A
	EPI IIA8	ON 285D
	HOUTW 2	THUS 602C
	SPOROS 2	SEED 770D
	HWS II4C	SO 906B
27	BLASTANW 2	SPROUT 141D
	EGEIRW 2A	AWAKEN 214A
	H8MERA 1A	DAY 346C
	KATHEUDW 1	SLEEP 389C
	M8KUNW	GROW 520C
	NUX 1D	NIGHT 549A
	OIDA II	KNOW 558C
	SPOROS 2	SEED 770D
	HWS II	AS 905C

28 AUTOMATOS   BY ITSELF 122A
    G8 I   EARTH 156C
    EITA 2   THEN 233B
    KARPOPHOREW I   BEAR FRUIT 406A
    PL8R8S 2   FULL 675D
    PRWTOS 2A   FIRST 733D
    SITOS   WHEAT 759D
    CHORTOS   GRASS 892B
28A STACHUS I   EAR (OF GRAIN) 773B
28B STACHUS I   EAR (OF GRAIN) 773B
29 DREPANON   SICKLE 205D
    THERISMOS I   HARVEST 360A
    KARPOS IA   FRUIT 405C
    PARADIDWMI   GIVE OVER 619C
    PARADIDWMI 4   PERMIT 621A
    PARIST8MI 2B9   BE HERE 633D
30 BASILEIA 3B   KINGDOM 134D
    HOMOIOW 2   COMPARE 570B
    HOMOIWMA I   LIKENESS 570C
    PARABALLW IC   COMPARE 616D
    PWS IE   HOW 739D
    TITH8MI IIB«   824A
    MAKE UP (YOUR) MINDS
31 G8 I   EARTH 156C
    EPI IIA9   ON 285D
    KOKKOS I   SEED 441B
    MIKROS 2A   SMALL 523B
    SINAPI   MUSTARD 759A
    SPEIRW IAY   SOW 768C
    SPERMA IA   SEED 769A
31F HOTAN IB   WHEN 592A
31F PAS ID«   ALL 637C
32 ANABAINW IB   GO UP 50A
    KATASK8NOW 2   LIVE 419C
    KLADOS   BRANCH 434A
    LACHANON   VEGETABLE 468D
    MEGAS IA   LARGE 498C
    OURANOS ID   HEAVEN 598D
    PETEINON   BIRD 660A
    POIEW IIBη   DO 688A
    SKIA IA   SHADE 763A
    SPEIRW IA9   SOW 768C
    HUPO 2A9   UNDER 851B
    HWSTE 2A9   THEREFORE 908C
33 AKOUW 7   UNDERSTAND 32B
    AKOUW 5   LISTEN 32B
    DUNAMAI IA   ABLE 206B
    KATHWS 2   AS 392B
    LALEW 2B   SPEAK 464D
    LOGOS IB9   WORD 479C
    PARABOL8 2   PARABLE 617D
    TOIOUTOS 2A9   SUCH A KIND 829A
33FF AUTOS 3A   (OBLIQUE CASE) 122D
34 DE 4B   BUT, AND 170D
    EPILUW I   EXPLAIN 295D
    LALEW 2A«   SPEAK 464C
    PARABOL8 2   PARABLE 617D
    PAS 2A6   EVERYTHING 638C
    CHWRIS 2B9   APART 899A
34A IDIOS 4   PRIVATELY 371A
34B IDIOS 2C   ONES OWN 370C
35 DIERCHOMAI 2   COME 193D
    EKEINOS 2BY   THAT 239B

35 OPSIOS 2   LATE 606C
    PERAN I   ON THE OTHER SIDE 649C
36 APHI8MI IA«   SEND AWAY 125B
    META AIIIC«   WITH 510A
    PARALAMBANW I   TAKE 624D
    PLOIARION   BOAT 679A
    HWS II4B   SO 906B
37 ANEMOS IA   WIND 64A
    GEMIZW 3   FILL 153A
    GINOMAI IIB«   COME ABOUT 157B
    EPIBALLW 2A   BEAT UPON 289D
    8D8 IA   ALREADY 344D
    KUMA   WAVE 458B
    LAILAPS   HURRICANE 463D
    MEGAS 2AY   GREAT 499A
    HWSTE 2A9   THEREFORE 908C
38 APOLLUMI 2A«   PERISH 94D
    DIDASKALOS   TEACHER 190D
    DIEGEIRW   AROUSE 193A
    EIMI II4B9   TO BE 223A
    EPI IIIIAς   ON 288C
    KATHEUDW I   SLEEP 389C
    MELEI 3   IT IS A CONCERN 501B
    OU 4C   NO 595A
    PROSKEPHALAION   PILLOW 723A
    PRUMNA   STERN OF A SHIP 732A
39 ANEMOS IA   WIND 64A
    GAL8N8   CALM 149C
    GINOMAI IIB«   COME ABOUT 157B
    DIEGEIRW   AROUSE 193A
    EPITIMAW I   REBUKE 303B
    KOPAZW   ABATE 444A
    MEGAS 2AY   GREAT 499A
    SIWPAW 2B   BE SILENT 760A
    PHIMOW 2   TIE SHUT 869D
40 DEILOS   COWARDLY 172A
    OUPW   NOT YET 598A
    PISTIS 2B«   FAITH 668D
    PWS IB   HOW 739C
    TIS, TI 3A   WHICH 827B
41 ALL8LWN   EACH OTHER 39A
    ARA 2   THEN 103B
    EIMI II6C   TO BE 223C
    KAI I6   AND 394A
    LEGW I3   SAY 469D
    MEGAS 2AY   GREAT 499A
    HOTI IC   THAT 593B
    HUPAKOUW I   LISTEN TO 845B
    PHOBEW IA   BE AFRAID 870D
    PHOBOS 2A«   FEAR 871C

MARK 5

I GADAR8NOS   GADARENE 148B
    GERAS8NOS   GERASENE 155D
    GERGES8NOS   GERGESENE 155D
    KAI I5   AND 394A
    PERAN 2B   ON THE OTHER SIDE 649C
    POLIS I   CITY 692A
    CHWRA IB   COUNTRY 897C
2 AKATHARTOS 2   IMPURE 28C
    ANTHRWPOS 3A9   MAN 68B
    APANTAW   MEET 79D

2 EXERCHOMAI IAα GO OUT 273D
  MN8MEION 2 TOMB 526C
  PNEUMA 4C SPIRIT 682A
  HUPANTAW GO TO MEET 845C
3 HALUSIS I CHAIN 40D
  DUNAMAI IB ABLE 206B
  KATOIK8SIS DWELLING 425C
  MN8MA TOMB 526C
  OUDE 3 NOT EVEN 596A
  OUDEIS 2A NO ONE 596C
  OUKETI I NO LONGER 597A
  OUTE NOT 600C
3F DEW IB BIND 176D
4 HALUSIS I CHAIN 40D
  DIASPAW TEAR APART 187C
  ISCHUW 2B BE STRONG 384C
  OUDEIS 2A NO ONE 596B
  POLLAKIS OFTEN 693B
  SUNTRIBW IA SHATTER 801A
4A PED8 FETTER 644A
4B PED8 FETTER 644A
5 DIA AIIIA THROUGH 178D
  HEAUTOU I ONESELF 211A
  H8MERA IA DAY 346C
  KATAKOPTW I BEAT 412D
  KRAZW I CRY OUT 448D
  LITHOS IA STONE 475B
  MN8MA TOMB 526C
  NUX IB NIGHT 548D
  OROS MOUNTAIN 586C
6 MAKROTHEN FROM FAR AWAY 489A
  PROSKUNEW 5 DO REVERENCE 724B
  TRECHW I RUN 833C
7 BASANIZW 2A TORMENT 134A
  EGW I 216C
  KRAZW 2A CALL 448D
  LEGW 18D SAY 470C
  MEGAS 2Aγ GREAT 498D
  HORKIZW ADJURE 585A
  HUIOS 2B SON 842C
  HUPSISTOS 2 HIGHEST 858B
  PHWN8 2A VOICE 878D
8 AKATHARTOS 2 IMPURE 28C
  ANTHRWPOS 4A MAN 68D
  EXERCHOMAI IA6 GO OUT 274A
  LEGW IIIC ORDER 470D
  PNEUMA 4C SPIRIT 682A
9 EPERWTAW IA ASK 285A
  LEGIWN LEGION 469A
  HOTI 3A THAT 593D
  POLUS IIAα MANY 694B
9A ONOMA II NAME 574A
9B ONOMA II NAME 574A
10 APOSTELLW IBβ SEND AWAY 98A
  EXW 2B OUTSIDE 279B
  PARAKALEW 3 IMPLORE 622D
  POLUS I2Bβ MANY 695B
  CHWRA IA COUNTRY 897C
11 AGEL8 HERD 8C
  BOSKW 2 FEED 144D
  DE 2 BUT, AND 170C
  EKEI I THERE 238C
  MEGAS IC LARGE 498D

11 OROS MOUNTAIN 586C
  PROS III NEAR 716C
11=13 CHOIROS SWINE 891C
12 DAIMWN DEMON 168D
  PARAKALEW 3 IMPLORE 622D
  PEMPW I SEND 647D
12F EISERCHOMAI IBβ COME 232A
13 AGEL8 HERD 8C
  AKATHARTOS 2 IMPURE 28C
  DISCHILIOI TWO THOUSAND 199A
  EXERCHOMAI IA6 GO OUT 274A
  EPITREPW I ALLOW 303C
  KATA IIA DOWN 406B
  KR8MNOS BANK 451B
  HORMAW RUSH DOWN 585D
  PNEUMA 4C SPIRIT 682A
  PNIGW ID CHOKE 686A
  HWS IV5 WHEN 907C
14 AGROS 3 FARM 13D
  APAGGELLW I REPORT 78C
  BOSKW I FEED 144D
  GINOMAI I3A TAKE PLACE 157D
  EIDON IC SEE 219D
  EIS IDβ IN 227D
 *POLIS I CITY 692A
  PHEUGW I FLEE 863C
15 ECHW I2Eα HAVE 333A
  THEWREW I OBSERVE 360C
  HIMATIZW DRESS 376D
  KATH8MAI IAε SIT 390B
  LEGIWN LEGION 469A
  SWPHRONEW I SOUND MIND 809C
15F DAIMONIZOMAI 168A
        BE POSSESSED BY A DEMON
16 GINOMAI I3Bβ TAKE PLACE 158A
  DI8GEOMAI TELL 194A
  PWS 2A HOW 739D
  CHOIROS SWINE 891C
17 APERCHOMAI IA GO AWAY 83D
  HORION BOUNDARY 584D
  PARAKALEW 3 IMPLORE 622D
18 EIMI III7 TO BE 224D
  EMBAINW GO IN 253C
  HINA IIIAγ IN ORDER THAT 378B
  PARAKALEW 3 IMPLORE 622D
  PLOION 2 SHIP 679B
19 APHI8MI 4 TOLERATE 125D
  DIAGGELLW I 181B
        PROCLAIM FAR AND WIDE
  ELEEW HAVE MERCY 249B
  KURIOS 2A LORD 460B
  OIKOS IAα HOUSE 563A
  SOS 2A YOURS 766D
  HUPAGW 2 GO AWAY 844C
19F HOSOS 2 HOW GREAT 590C
19F POIEW IIDβ DO 688D
20 ARCHW 2Aα BEGIN 113A
  DEKAPOLIS DECAPOLIS 173A
  THAUMAZW IAα WONDER 352D
  K8RUSSW 2A ANNOUNCE 432B
  PAS 2Aγ ALL 638B
21 DIAPERAW CROSS 186C
  EIMI I3 TO BE 222B

```
21 EIMI III8C         TO BE 224D      29 P8G8 I              FOUNTAIN 661C
   EPI IIIIAY            ON 288B         SWMA IB                 BODY 806D
   KAI I5               AND 394A      30 HAPTW 2B             TOUCH 102D
   OCHLOS I           CROWD 605C         EN I4A                   IN 258B
   PALIN IA            BACK 611B         EXERCHOMAI 2BY     GO OUT 274D
   PARA IIIIBα        ALONG 616A         EPIGINWSKW 2C        KNOW 291B
   PERAN I  ON THE OTHER SIDE 649C       EPISTREPHW 2Aα       TURN 301B
   POLUS IIBα          MANY 694C         HIMATION I        GARMENT 377C
   SUNAGW 2          GATHER 790B      30F  LEGW IIIA           ASK 470C
22 ARCHISUNAGWGOS           112D      31 BLEPW IA               SEE 143A
   PRESIDENT OF A SYNAGOGUE             EGW                       I 216C
   EIDON IA             SEE 219D         MATH8T8S 2Bα      DISCIPLE 487A
   IAIROS            JAIRUS 368A         SUNTHLIBW  PRESS TOGETHER 797D
   ONOMA II            NAME 574A      32 PERIBLEPW I    LOOK AROUND 652A
   PIPTW IBα           FALL 665C         POIEW IIBα                DO 687D
   POUS IA             FOOT 703B      33 AL8THEIA 2A          TRUTH 35B
23 HAPTW 2B           TOUCH 102C         GINOMAI I3D     TAKE PLACE 158B
   EPITITH8MI IAα  PUT UPON 302D         ERCHOMAI IIAζ          COME 310D
   ESCHATWS         FINALLY 314B         LATHRA I           SECRETLY 463D
   ECHW III              BE 334B         OIDA                   KNOW 558A
   ZAW IAY             LIVE 336C         OIDA IG                KNOW 558C
   THUGATRION  LITTLE DAUGHTER 365C      PAS ICα                 ALL 637B
   HINA III2   IN ORDER THAT 379A        PROSPIPTW I FALL DOWN BEFORE 725B
   PARAKALEW 3      IMPLORE 622D         TREMW               TREMBLE 833B
   POLUS I2Bβ          MANY 695B         PHOBEW IA        BE AFRAID 870B
   SWZW IC             SAVE 806A      34 EIR8N8 2             PEACE 226C
24 AKOLOUTHEW 2    ACCOMPANY 30D         EIS 9B                   IN 229D
   META AIIIA          WITH 509D         THUGAT8R 2A        DAUGHTER 365B
   OCHLOS I           CROWD 605C         MASTIX 2           TORMENT 496B
   POLUS IIBα          MANY 694C         PISTIS 2Bα           FAITH 668D
   SUNTHLIBW   PRESS TOGETHER 797D       SWZW IC                SAVE 806A
25 HAIMA IA           BLOOD 22A          HUGI8S IA          HEALTHY 840A
   DWDEKA            TWELVE 209B         HUPAGW I           GO AWAY 844B
   EIMI III4           TO BE 224B    35 APOTHN8SKW IAα          DIE 90D
   ETOS                YEAR 317A         DIDASKALOS         TEACHER 190D
   RUSIS               FLOW 745C         ERCHOMAI IIAβ          COME 310B
26 DAPANAW I          SPEND 169D         THUGAT8R I        DAUGHTER 365B
   ERCHOMAI I2C        COME 311C         LALEW 2AY            SPEAK 464B
   IATROS I        PHYSICIAN 369C        LEGW I8A               SAY 470B
   MALLON 3Aα        RATHER 490C         SKULLW 2             WEARY 765C
   M8DEIS 2Bβ       NOTHING 520A    35A  ETI IAβ             STILL 315D
   PARA I4Bα           FROM 615A    35B  ETI IBβ             STILL 316A
   PASCHW 3B         ENDURE 639D    35F  ARCHISUNAGWGOS           112D
   HUPO IB               BY 851A        PRESIDENT OF A SYNAGOGUE
   CHEIRWN            WORSE 889C    36 LOGOS IAY              WORD 478C
   WPHELEW IA          HELP 909A         MONOS 2A               ONLY 529D
26A   POLUS I2Bα       MANY 695A         HO,H8,TO IIIF           THE 553A
27 HAPTW 2B           TOUCH 102D         PARAKOUW I         OVERHEAR 624C
   ERCHOMAI IIAY       COME 310C         PISTEUW 2C          BELIEVE 667D
   HIMATION I        GARMENT 377A        PHOBEW IA        BE AFRAID 870C
   OPISTHEN IA FROM BEHIND 578B    37 IAKWBOS I             JAMES 368B
   PERI II            ABOUT 650D         IWAN(N)8S 2           JOHN 385C
28 HAPTW 2B           TOUCH 102D         META AIIIA            WITH 509D
   HIMATION I        GARMENT 377A        OU 6A                   NO 595A
   KAN 3           AT LEAST 403B         OUDEIS 2A          NO ONE 596B
   LEGW IIBα            SAY 469C         PETROS                PETER 660D
   HOTI 2              THAT 593D         *SUNAKOLOUTHEW      FOLLOW 791C
   SWZW IC             SAVE 806A    38 ARCHISUNAGWGOS            112D
29 HAIMA IA           BLOOD 22A         PRESIDENT OF A SYNAGOGUE
   GINWSKW 4C       PERCEIVE 160C        ERCHOMAI IIAβ          COME 310B
   IAOMAI I            HEAL 369A         THEWREW I           OBSERVE 360D
   MASTIX 2         TORMENT 496B         THORUBOS 3A           NOISE 363C
   X8RAINW 2A        DRY UP 550D         OIKOS IAα             HOUSE 563A
```

38 POLUS I2Bß	MANY	695A
38F KLAIW I	WEEP	434A
39 ALLA IA	BUT, YET	37B
APOTHN8SKW IAα	DIE	90D
THORUBEW 2	BE TROUBLED	363C
KATHEUDW I	SLEEP	389C
39=41 PAIDION 2A	CHILD	609B
40 ANAKEIMAI I	LIE	55B
EIMI II9A	TO BE	223D
EISPOREUOMAI I	GO	232D
KATAGELAW	RIDICULE	410D
KATAKEIMAI I	LIE DOWN	412B
M8T8R I	MOTHER	521D
HOPOU IAα	WHERE	579C
PARALAMBANW I	TAKE	624D
PAT8R IA	FATHER	640C
41 AUTOS 3Fß	(OBLIQUE CASE)	123B
EGEIRW IB	RAISE UP	214A
KORASION	GIRL	445B
KOUM	STAND UP	448B
KRATEW IB	SEIZE	449C
METHERM8NEUW	TRANSLATE	499D
HO,H8,TO IIII	THE	553B
HOS,H8,HC I7A	(REL PRON)	588C
RABITHA	GIRL	740D
TALITHA	GIRL	811B
42 ANIST8MI 2A	RISE	69C
DWDEKA	TWELVE	209B
EIMI IV6	TO BE	225A
EKSTASIS I	DISTRACTION	244C
EXIST8MI 2B	BE AMAZED	276A
ETOS	YEAR	317A
KORASION	GIRL	445B
MEGAS 2Aγ	GREAT	499A
PERIPATEW IC	GO ABOUT	655A
43 GINWSKW 2A	FIND OUT	160A
DIASTELLW	ORDER	187D
DIDWMI 2	GIVE	192C
EIPON 3C	SAY	225D
ESTHIW ID	EAT	313B
HINA IIIA6	IN ORDER THAT	378B
M8DEIS 2A	NO	520A
POLUS I2Bß	MANY	695A

MARK 6

I EXERCHOMAI IAα	GO OUT	274A
MATH8T8S 2Bα	DISCIPLE	487A
PATRIS 2	FATHERLAND	642C
2 GINOMAI I2A	COME ABOUT	157C
GINOMAI I3A	TAKE PLACE	158A
DIA AIIIIA	BY MEANS OF	179A
EKPL8SSW 2	BE AMAZED	243D
POTHEN 2	FROM WHERE	686D
POLUS I2Aß	MANY	694D
SABBATON IA	SABBATH	746B
SOPHIA 3A	WISDOM	767B
SUNAGWG8 2A		790C
PLACE OF ASSEMBLY		
TOIOUTOS 2Aα	SUCH A KIND	829A
CHEIR I	HAND	888C
2F HOUTOS IAα	THIS	600D
3 ADELPH8 I	SISTER	15C

3 EIMI III9	TO BE	224D
IAKWBOS 3	JAMES	368C
IOUDAS 8	JUDAS	381A
IWS8S I	JOSES	386B
MARIA I	MARY	492D
OU 4C	NO	594D
PROS III7	TOWARD	718A
SIMWN 3	SIMON	758C
SKANDALIZW IB	CAUSE TO FALL	760B
TEKTWN	CARPENTER	816D
HUIOS IAα	SON	841B
HWDE 2A	HERE	903D
4 ATIMOS I	DISHONORED	119D
OIKIA 2	HOUSEHOLD	560B
PATRIS 2	FATHERLAND	642C
PROPH8T8S 3	PROPHET	731A
*SUGGEN8S	RELATED	780B
5 ARRWSTOS	SICK	109B
DUNAMIS 4	MIRACLE	207B
EI VI8A	IF NOT	219A
EPITITH8MI IAα	PUT UPON	302D
THERAPEUW 2	HEAL	359D
OLIGOS IA	FEW	566B
OUDEIS I	NO	596B
POIEW IIBß	DO	687C
6 APISTIA 2A	UNBELIEF	84D
THAUMAZW IAß	WONDER	352D
KUKLW IA	AROUND	458A
KWM8 I	VILLAGE	462D
PERIAGW 2	LEAD AROUND	651B
7 AKATHARTOS 2	IMPURE	28C
APOSTELLW IC	SEND AWAY	98B
ARCHW 2Aα	BEGIN	113A
DIDWMI IBß	GIVE	192B
DUO 5	TWO	208C
EXOUSIA 3	AUTHORITY	278A
IB	TWELVE	369D
PNEUMA 4C	SPIRIT	682A
PROSKALEW IA	SUMMON	722C
8 AIRW 2	LIFT UP	24A
ARTOS IA	BREAD	110A
EIS IAα	INTO	227C
EIS 4F	(PURPOSE)	229A
EIS 7	TO	229C
ZWN8	BELT	342A
HINA IIIA6	IN ORDER THAT	378B
M8DEIS 2Bα	NOTHING	520A
HODOS IB	WAY	556C
PARAGGELLW	GIVE ORDERS	618C
P8RA	KNAPSACK	662B
RABDOS	ROD	740D
CHALKOS 2	COPPER	883B
9 ENDUW 2A	DRESS	263C
SANDALION	SANDAL	749B
HUPODEW	TIE	852A
CHITWN	SHIRT	890C
10 EKEI I	THERE	238C
EXERCHOMAI IAα	GO OUT	274A
HEWS IIB	UNTIL	334D
LEGW IIIC	ORDER	470D
MENW IAα	REMAIN	504D
OIKIA IA	HOUSE	559D
HOPOU IA6	WHERE	579D

11 AKOUW 5	LISTEN	32A
ANEKTOS	BEARABLE	63D
GOMORRA	GOMORRAH	164A
DECHOMAI I	RECEIVE	176B
EKPOREUOMAI IB	GO OUT	243D
EKTINASSW I	SHAKE OFF	245B
MARTURION IA	TESTIMONY	494D
M8 AII	NOT	517C
M8DE IB	AND NOT	519D
SODOMA	SODOM	766B
TOPOS IA	PLACE	830A
HUPOKATW	UNDER	852C
CHOUS	SOIL	892C
12 HINA IIIA6	IN ORDER THAT	378B
K8RUSSW 2B?	ANNOUNCE	432C
METANOEW	CHANGE ONES MIND	513B
13 ALEIPHW I	ANOINT	34C
ARRWSTOS	SICK	109B
EKBALLW I	DRIVE OUT	237A
ELAION I	OLIVE OIL	247B
POLUS IIA?	MANY	694A
14 AKOUW 3A	LEARN	31D
BAPTIZW 2A	BAPTIZE	131B
BASILEUS I	KING	135D
GINOMAI I4B	BECOME	158D
DUNAMIS I	POWER	206D
EGEIRW 2C	RISE	214A
EN I5A	IN	258D
ENERGEW IA	WORK	264D
H8RWD8S 2	HEROD	349B
IWAN(N)8S I	JOHN	385B
KAI I2B	AND	393A
NEKROS 2A	DEAD	537A
HO,H8,TO III3A	THE	553C
ONOMA IV	FAME	577B
PHANEROS I	CLEAR	860B
14F LEGW IIB?	SAY	469C
14-22 H8RWD8S 2	HEROD	349B
15 ALLOS IC	OTHER	39B
8LIAS	ELIJAH	345D
HWS II3B	SO	906A
15A PROPH8T8S 3	PROPHET	731A
15B PROPH8T8S I	PROPHET	730D
16 APOKEPHALIZW	BEHEAD	92C
EGEIRW 2C	RISE	214A
HOS,H8,HO I5C?	(REL PRON)	588B
HOUTOS IA?	THIS	601B
16FF IWAN(N)8S I	JOHN	385B
17 APOSTELLW ID	SEND AWAY	98C
GAMEW IA	MARRY	150A
DEW IB	BIND	176D
DIA BIII	BECAUSE OF	180A
*HERODIAS	HERODIAS	349C
KRATEW IA	ARREST	449C
PHILIPPOS I	PHILIP	868A
PHILIPPOS 2	PHILIP	868A
PHULAK8 3	GUARD	875D
18 EXESTI 2	IT IS POSSIBLE	274D
ECHW IIC?	KEEP	332B
ECHW I2B?	HAVE	332C
19 APOKTEINW IA	KILL	93B
DUNAMAI 2	ABLE	206B
ENECHW I	HAVE A GRUDGE	265B
19 HERODIAS	HERODIAS	349C
20 HAGIOS IB?	DEDICATED TO GOD	9C
AN8R 4	MAN	66B
APOREW	UNCERTAIN	97A
DIKAIOS IB	UPRIGHT	194D
H8DEWS	GLADLY	344C
OIDA IC	KNOW	558B
POLUS I2B?	MANY	695A
POLUS I2B?	MANY	695A
SUNT8REW I	PROTECT	800B
PHOBEW IB?	BE AFRAID	870D
21 GENESIA BIRTHDAY	CELEBRATION	153D
GENETHLIOS	BIRTHDAY	153D
GINOMAI IIB?	COME ABOUT	157B
DEIPNON 2	DINNER	172C
EUKAIROS	WELL TIMED	321D
H8MERA 2	DAY	346D
MEGISTAN	GREAT MAN	499D
POIEW IIB?	DO	688A
PRWTOS IC?	FIRST	733C
CHILIARCHOS	TRIBUNE	890A
22 ARESKW 2A	BE PLEASING	105A
HERODIAS	HERODIAS	349C
THELW 2	WISH	355D
THUGAT8R I	DAUGHTER	365B
KAI I2F	AND	393C
KORASION	GIRL	445B
ORCHEOMAI	DANCE	587A
SUNANAKEIMAI	EAT WITH	792A
22F AITEW	ASK	25B
22FF SALWM8	SALOME	748C
23 BASILEIA 2	KINGDOM	134C
HEWS II4	AS MANY AS	335D
H8MISUS 2	HALF	348D
OMNUW	TAKE AN OATH	569B
24 AITEW	ASK	25B
BAPTIZW 2A	BAPTIZE	131B
BAPTIST8S	BAPTIST	132B
M8T8R I	MOTHER	521D
24F KEPHAL8 IA	HEAD	431A
25 AITEW	ASK	25C
BAPTIST8S	BAPTIST	132B
EXAUT8S	AT ONCE	273B
EPI IIIA?	ON	286C
THELW I	WISH	355C
HINA III2	IN ORDER THAT	379A
META AIII	WITH	511A
PINAX	PLATTER	664B
SPOUD8 I	HASTE	771B
26 ATHETEW IB	REJECT	20D
THELW 2	WISH	355D
HORKOS	OATH	585B
PERILUPOS	VERY SAD	654B
SUNANAKEIMAI	EAT WITH	792A
27 APERCHOMAI IA	GO AWAY	83D
APOKEPHALIZW	BEHEAD	92C
EPITASSW	COMMAND	302B
SPEKOULATWR	EXECUTIONER	769A
PHERW 4A?	BEAR	863A
PHULAK8 3	GUARD	875C
27F KEPHAL8 IA	HEAD	431A
28 EPI IIIA?	ON	286C
KORASION	GIRL	445B

28	M8T8R I	MOTHER 521D
	PINAX	PLATTER 664B
	PHERW 4A«	BEAR 863A
29	AIRW 3	CARRY 24A
	ERCHOMAI IIAς	COME 310D
	K8DEUW	BURY 431D
	MATH8T8S 2A	DISCIPLE 486D
	MN8MEION 2	TOMB 526C
	PTWMA	CORPSE 735B
	TITH8MI IIAβ	PUT 823C
30	APAGGELLW I	REPORT 78C
	POIEW IIBβ	DO 687C
	SUNAGW 2	GATHER 790B
30A	HOSOS 2	HOW GREAT 590B
31	ANAPAUW 2	REST 58C
	AUTOS IF	OF HIMSELF 122C
	DEUTE 2	COME 175D
	ERCHOMAI IIA«	COME 310B
	ESTHIW ID	EAT 313B
	EUKAIREW	OPPORTUNITY 321C
	EUKAIRWS	CONVENIENTLY 321D
	OLIGOS 3A	LITTLE 566C
	OUDE 3	NOT EVEN 596A
	POLUS IIA«	MANY 694B
	HUPAGW I	GO AWAY 844C
31F	ER8MOS IA	ABANDONED 308D
31F	IDIOS 4	PRIVATELY 371A
31F	TOPOS IC	PLACE 830B
32	APERCHOMAI 2	GO 84A
33	AUTOU	HERE 123C
	EIDON	SEE 219C
	EKEI 2	THERE 238D
	EPIGINWSKW 2B	KNOW 291A
	OCHLOS I	CROWD 605D
	PAS ID«	ALL 637C
	PEZ8	BY LAND 644B
	POLIS I	CITY 692A
	PROERCHOMAI 3	GO FORWARD 712B
	*SUNERCHOMAI IA	ASSEMBLE 795D
	SUNTRECHW I	RUN TOGETHER 800D
	HUPAGW I	GO AWAY 844B
34	OCHLOS I	CROWD 605C
	PALIN 2	AGAIN 611C
	POIM8N I	SHEPHERD 690C
	PROBATON I	SHEEP 710A
	*SPLAGCHNIZOMAI	HAVE PITY 770B
	HWS II3B	SO 906A
34A	POLUS IIB«	MANY 694C
34B	POLUS I2B«	MANY 695A
35	GINOMAI IIBγ	COME ABOUT 157C
	ER8MOS IA	ABANDONED 308D
	8D8 IB	ALREADY 344D
	LEGW IIB«	SAY 469C
	MATH8T8S 2B«	DISCIPLE 487A
	PROSERCHOMAI I	APPROACH 720A
	TOPOS IC	PLACE 830B
35A	POLUS IIB«	MANY 694C
35A	HWRA I	TIME OF DAY 904C
35B	POLUS IIB«	MANY 694C
35B	HWRA I	TIME OF DAY 904B
36	AGORAZW I	BUY 12C
	AGROS 3	FARM 13D
	APERCHOMAI 2	GO 83D

36	APOLUW 2B	SEND AWAY 96B
	HEAUTOU I	ONESELF 211A
	EGGUS IC	NEAR 213B
	ESTHIW IA	EAT 312C
	KUKLW IB	AROUND 458A
	KWM8 I	VILLAGE 462D
37	AGORAZW I	BUY 12D
	APERCHOMAI IA	GO AWAY 83D
	ARTOS IA	BREAD 110B
	D8NARION	DENARIUS 178B
	DIAKOSIOI	TWO HUNDRED 184A
	DIDWMI	GIVE 191D
	DIDWMI 2	GIVE 192C
	ESTHIW ID	EAT 313B
38	ARTOS IA	BREAD 110A
	GINWSKW IA	KNOW 159D
	EIDON IE	SEE 220A
	ICHTHUS	FISH 385A
	OPSARION	FISH 606B
	POSOS 2A	HOW GREAT 701B
	HUPAGW 2	GO AWAY 844C
39	ANAKLINW IB	LAY 55D
	ANAKLINW 2	RECLINE 55D
	EPI IIIA«	ON 286C
	EPITASSW	COMMAND 302B
	SUMPOSIA	COMMON MEAL 787D
	SUMPOSION	PARTY 787D
	CHLWROS I	YELLOWISH GREEN 891A
	CHORTOS	GRASS 892B
40	ANAPIPTW I	RECLINE 59A
	HEKATON	ONE HUNDRED 236B
	KATA II3A	(DISTRIBUTIVE) 407D
	PENT8KONTA	FIFTY 648D
	PRASIA	GROUP BY GROUP 705A
41	ANABLEPW I	LOOK UP 50C
	ARTOS IA	BREAD 110A
	DIDWMI 2	GIVE 192C
	EIS ID«	TOWARD 227D
	EULOGEW I	SPEAK WELL 322C
	EULOGEW 2B	BLESS 322D
	HINA IIE	IN ORDER THAT 377C
	ICHTHUS	FISH 385A
	KATAKLAW	BREAK IN PIECES 412C
	KATENANTI 2A	OPPOSITE 422B
	MERIZW 2A	DISTRIBUTE 505D
	OURANOS 2A	HEAVEN 599B
	OPSARION	FISH 606B
	PARATITH8MI IA	PLACE BESIDE 628B
42	CHORTAZW 2A	FEED 892B
43	AIRW 3	CARRY 24A
	APO 16	FROM 86B
	ICHTHUS	FISH 385A
	KLASMA	FRAGMENT 434B
	KOPHINOS	BASKET 448C
	PL8R8S IA«	FULL 675C
	PL8RWMA IA	THAT WHICH FILLS 678A
44	AN8R I	MAN 65D
	ARTOS IA	BREAD 110A
	EIMI II7	TO BE 223D
	PENTAKISCHILIOI	FIVE THOUSAND 648C
45	ANAGKAZW 2	INVITE 51D
	APOLUW 2B	SEND AWAY 96B
	B8THSAIDA I	BETHSAIDA 139C

45	EMBAINW	GO IN	253C
	EXEGEIRW I	AWAKEN	273B
	HEWS I2A	UNTIL	335A
	MATH8T8S 2Bα	DISCIPLE	487A
	PERAN I	ON THE OTHER SIDE	649C
	PROAGW 2B	LEAD	709A
45F	AUTOS 3Fβ	(OBLIQUE CASE)	123B
46	APERCHOMAI 2	GO	83D
	APOTASSW I	SAY FAREWELL	100B
	HO,H8,TO IIIAα	THE	552B
	OROS	MOUNTAIN	586B
	PROSEUCHOMAI	PRAY	720D
47	AUTOS IC	SELF	122C
	G8 4	LAND	156C
	GINOMAI IIBγ	COME ABOUT	157C
	EPI IIAα	ON	285C
	MESOS 2	THE MIDDLE	508D
	MONOS IAβ	ONLY	529C
	OPSIOS 2	LATE	606C
	PALAI 2B	LONG AGO	610C
	PALAI 2A	LONG AGO	610C
48	ANEMOS IA	WIND	64A
	BASANIZW 3	TORMENT	134B
	ELAUNW	DRIVE	248A
	EN IIIIB	BY	260B
	ENANTIOS I	OPPOSITE	261C
	NUX IA	NIGHT	548C
	PARERCHOMAI IAα	GO BY	631B
	PERI 2B	ABOUT	651A
	TETARTOS	FOURTH	821A
	PHULAK8 4	GUARD	875D
48F	EPI IIAα	ON	285C
48F	PERIPATEW IC	GO ABOUT	654D
49	ANAKRAZW	CRY OUT	56A
	DOKEW ID	THINK	201A
	PHANTASMA	APPARITION	861B
50	EIMI II5	TO BE	223C
	THARSEW	BE CHEERFUL	352C
	LALEW 2A6	SPEAK	464C
	META AII3B	WITH	510D
	TARASSW 2	STIR UP	813A
51	ANABAINW IAα	GO UP	49D
	ANEMOS IA	WIND	64A
	EK 6C	FROM	235D
	EXIST8MI 2B	BE AMAZED	276A
	KOPAZW	ABATE	444A
	LIAN I	VERY	474C
	PERISSOS 3	EXTRAORDINARY	657B
	PLOION 2	SHIP	679B
52	ARTOS IA	BREAD	110A
	GAR IB	FOR	151B
	EIMI II4A	TO BE	223A
	EPI IIIBγ	ON	287A
	KARDIA IBβ	HEART	404D
	PWROW	HARDEN	739B
	SUNI8MI	UNDERSTAND	798A
53	GENN8SARET	GENNESARET	155A
	DIAPERAW	CROSS	186C
	PROSORMIZW	COME TO ANCHOR	725A
54	EPIGINWSKW 2A	KNOW	291A
	PLOION 2	SHIP	679B
55	EPI IIIAα	ON	286C
	KAKWS I	BADLY	399B

55	KRABATTOS	MATTRESS	448C
	HOLOS 2A	WHOLE	567C
	HOPOU IAα	WHERE	579C
	HOPOU IAα	WHERE	579C
	PERIPHERW I	CARRY ABOUT	659A
	PERITRECHW 2	RUN ABOUT	659A
	PERICHWROS	NEIGHBORING	659B
	CHWRA IA	COUNTRY	897C
56	AGORA	MARKET PLACE	12B
	AGROS 3	FARM	13D
	*AN IA	(PARTICLE)	47D
	*HAPTW 2B	TOUCH	102D
	ASTHENEW IA	BE SICK	115A
	EISPOREUOMAI I	GO	232D
	HINA IIIAγ	IN ORDER THAT	378B
	KAN 3	AT LEAST	403B
	KRASPEDON I	EDGE	449B
	KWM8 I	VILLAGE	462D
	HOPOU IAβ	WHERE	579C
	HOSOS 2	HOW GREAT	590C
	PARAKALEW 3	IMPLORE	622D
	PLATEIA	WIDE ROAD	672C
	POLIS I	CITY	692A
	SWZW IC	SAVE	806A
	TITH8MI IIAβ	PUT	823C

MARK 7

I	GRAMMATEUS 2	SCRIBES	165A
	ERCHOMAI IIAβ	COME	310B
	SUNAGW 2	GATHER	790B
	PHARISAIOS	PHARISEE	861C
IF	TIS, TI IAα	ANY ONE	827C
2	ANIPTOS	UNWASHED	69A
	ARTOS 2	FOOD	110B
	EIMI II3	TO BE	222D
	ESTHIW IA	EAT	312D
	KATAGINWSKW	CONDEMN	410D
	KOINOS 2	COMMON	439B
	MEMPHOMAI	FIND FAULT WITH	503C
	HOUTOS IBε	THIS	601D
3	GAR 2	FOR	151C
	IOUDAIOS 2C	JEWISH	380B
	KRATEW 2Eβ	HOLD	449D
	NIPTW 2B	WASH	542B
	PARADOSIS 2	TRADITION	621A
	PRESBUTEROS IB	OLDER	706C
	PUGM8 I	FIST	736A
	PUKNOS	FREQUENT	736B
3F	ESTHIW ID	EAT	313A
3F	M8 AII	NOT	517C
4	AGORA	MARKET PLACE	12C
	BAPTIZW I	DIP	131A
	BAPTISMOS	WASHING	132B
	KLIN8	COUCH	437B
	KRATEW 2Eβ	HOLD	449D
	XEST8S	PITCHER	550C
	PARALAMBANW 2Bγ	TAKE	625B
	POT8RION I	CUP	702A
	RANTIZW 2A	CLEANSE	741C
	CHALKION	KETTLE	883A
5	ANIPTOS	UNWASHED	69A
	ARTOS 2	FOOD	110B

5	GRAMMATEUS 2	SCRIBES 165A
	EPERWTAW IA	ASK 285A
	ESTHIW IA	EAT 312D
	KATA II5Aα	ACCORDING TO 408A
	KOINOS 2	COMMON 439B
	HO,H8,TO IIIF	THE 553A
	PARADOSIS 2	TRADITION 621A
	PERIPATEW 2Aδ	GO ABOUT 655B
	PRESBUTEROS IB	OLDER 706C
	PHARISAIOS	PHARISEE 861C
6	APECHW 2	BE DISTANT 84C
	GRAPHW 2C	WRITE 165D
	8SAIAS	ISAIAH 349C
	KALWS 4B	WELL 402B
	KALWS 6	WELL 402C
	KARDIA IBα	HEART 404C
	LAOS 3A	PEOPLE 468A
	HO,H8,TO IIIH	THE 553B
	PORRW I	FAR AWAY 700C
	PROPH8TEUW 3	PROPHESY 730C
	TIMAW 2	HONOR 824D
	HUPOKRIT8S	HYPOCRITE 853A
	CHEILOS I	LIP 887C
	HWS II4A	SO 906B
7	ANTHRWPOS IAβ	MAN 67C
	DIDASKALIA 2	TEACHING 190C
	ENTALMA	COMMANDMENT 267D
	MAT8N	IN VAIN 497A
	SEBW 2A	WORSHIP 753C
8	APHI8MI 3B	ABANDON 125D
	BAPTISMOS	WASHING 132B
	KRATEW 2Eβ	HOLD 449D
	PARADOSIS 2	TRADITION 621A
	PAROMOIOS	LIKE 634D
	POT8RION I	CUP 702A
9	ATHETEW IA	SET ASIDE 20C
	HINA IIA	IN ORDER THAT 377C
	KALWS 6	WELL 402C
	PARADOSIS 2	TRADITION 621A
	T8REW 5	KEEP 822D
10	GAR ID	FOR 151B
	THANATOS IBα	DEATH 351C
	KAKOLOGEW	INSULT 398A
	MWUS8S	MOSES 533D
	TELEUTAW	DIE 818B
	TIMAW 2	HONOR 824D
11	ANTHRWPOS 3Aβ	MAN 68B
	DWRON 2	GIFT 210C
	EIMI II3	TO BE 222D
	EK 3Eα	BY 234C
	KORBAN	GIFT 445B
	HOS,H8,HO I7A	(REL PRON) 588C
	WPHELEW IA	HELP 909A
12	APHI8MI 4	TOLERATE 126A
	ENAPHI8MI	PERMIT 261D
	8 IC	NOR 343A
	OUDEIS 2Bα	NOTHING 596C
	OUKETI I	NO LONGER 597A
	POIEW IIDβ	DO 688D
13	AKUROW	MAKE VOID 33D
	LOGOS IBα	COMMAND 479A
	MWROS 2	FOOLISH 533B
	HOS,H8,HO I4A	(REL PRON) 587D
13	PARADIDWMI 3	GIVE OVER 620D
	PARADOSIS 2	TRADITION 621A
	PAROMOIOS	LIKE 634D
14	AKOUW IC	HEAR 3ID
	PROSKALEW IA	SUMMON 722C
	SUNI8MI	UNDERSTAND 798A
15	ANTHRWPOS 3B	MAN 68C
	EISPOREUOMAI I	GO 232D
	EKPOREUOMAI 2	GO OUT 244A
	EXWTHEN 2A	OUTSIDE 279C
	KOINOW IA	DEFILE 439B
	OUDEIS 2Bα	NOTHING 596C
16	ECHW I2Cα	HAVE 332D
	OUS 2	EAR 600B
17	EISERCHOMAI IAβ	COME 231D
	EPERWTAW IA	ASK 285A
	OIKOS IAα	HOUSE 563A
	OCHLOS I	CROWD 605C
	*PARABOL8 2	PARABLE 617D
18	ASUNETOS I	FOOLISH II8B
	EXWTHEN IA	OUTSIDE 279B
	KOINOW IA	DEFILE 439B
	NOEW IB	UNDERSTAND 542C
	OU 4C	NO 595A
	HOUTW IB	THUS 602C
	PAS ICγ	WHOEVER 637C
18F	EISPOREUOMAI I	GO 232D
19	APHEDRWN	LATRINE I24B
	BRWMA I	FOOD I47C
	EKPOREUOMAI IC	GO OUT 243D
	KATHARIZW IA	CLEANSE 388A
	KATHARIZW 2A	CLEANSE 388B
	KOILIA I	BELLY 438B
	OCHETOS	CANAL 605B
	CHWREW IA	GO 897D
20	ANTHRWPOS 3B	MAN 68C
	EKEINOS IB	THAT 239A
	EKPOREUOMAI 2	GO OUT 244A
	KOINOW IA	DEFILE 439B
	LEGW IIBα	SAY 469C
21	DIALOGISMOS I	THOUGHT I85B
	EKPOREUOMAI 2	GO OUT 244A
	ESWTHEN I	FROM INSIDE 314C
	KAKOS IB	BAD 398C
	KARDIA IBβ	HEART 404C
	KLOP8	THEFT 437D
	PORNEIA I	PROSTITUTION 699D
	PHONOS	MURDER 872C
22	HAPLOUS	SINCERE 85C
	ASELGEIA	LICENTIOUSNESS II4C
	APHROSUN8	FOOLISHNESS I27B
	BLASPH8MIA I	SLANDER I42C
	DOLOS	DECEIT 202B
	KLEMMA	THEFT 435B
	MOICHEIA	ADULTERY 528A
	OPHTHALMOS I	EYE 604B
	PLEONEXIA	GREEDINESS 673D
	PON8RIA	WICKEDNESS 697B
	PON8ROS IBβ	WICKED 697D
	HUPER8PHANIA	PRIDE 849C
23	EKPOREUOMAI 2	GO OUT 244A
	ESWTHEN I	FROM INSIDE 314C
	KOINOW IA	DEFILE 439B

23 PONSROS 2C   WICKED 698A
24 ANIST8MI 2D   RISE 69D
   APERCHOMAI 2   GO 83D
   BALLW IB   THROW 130C
   GINWSKW 4B   PERCEIVE 160B
   DE 2   BUT, AND 170C
   THELW I   WISH 355C
   LANTHANW   ESCAPE NOTICE 467C
   METHORION   REGION 500B
   OIKIA IA   HOUSE 559D
   HORION   BOUNDARY 585A
   OUDEIS 2A   NO ONE 596B
   SIDWN   SIDON 757C
   TUROS   TYRE 838C
25 AKATHARTOS 2   IMPURE 28C
   AUTOS 3D   (OBLIQUE CASE) 123B
   ERCHOMAI IIAς   COME 310D
   ECHW I2Eα   HAVE 333A
   THUGATRION   LITTLE DAUGHTER 365C
   HOS,H8,HO I3A   (REL PRON) 587C
   PNEUMA 4C   SPIRIT 682A
   POUS IA   FOOT 703B
   PROSPIPTW I FALL DOWN BEFORE 725B
26 GENOS 3   NATION 155C
   EKBALLW I   DRIVE OUT 237A
   HELL8NIS 2   GENTILE 251C
   ERWTAW 2   ASK 312B
   THUGAT8R I   DAUGHTER 365B
   HINA IIIAY   IN ORDER THAT 378B
   SURA   SYRIAN WOMAN 801C
   SUROPHOINIKISSA   802A
      SYROPHOENICIAN WOMAN
   CHANANAIOS   CANAANITE 883C
27 ARTOS IA   BREAD 110A
   APHI8MI 4   TOLERATE 126A
   KALOS 3B   GOOD 401C
   KALOS 3C   GOOD 401D
   LAMBANW IA   TAKE 465B
   PRWTOS 2A   FIRST 733C
   CHORTAZW 2A   FEED 892B
27F KUNARION   DOG 458C
28 APO I6   FROM 86B
   APOKRINOMAI I   ANSWER 92D
   APOKRINOMAI 2   BEGIN 93A
   ESTHIW IBα   EAT 313A
   KURIOS 2Cβ   LORD 460D
   NAI 2   CERTAINLY 534D
   PAIDION 2A   CHILD 609A
   TRAPEZA 2   TABLE 832A
   HUPOKATW   UNDER 852C
   PSICHION   CRUMB 901B
29 EXERCHOMAI IAδ   GO OUT 274A
   THUGAT8R I   DAUGHTER 365B
   LOGOS IAY   WORD 478C
   HUPAGW I   GO AWAY 844B
29F DAIMONION 2   DEMON 168B
30 APERCHOMAI 2   GO 83D
   BALLW IB   LIE 130C
   EXERCHOMAI IAδ   GO OUT 274A
   KLIN8   COUCH 437B
   OIKOS IAα   HOUSE 563A
   PAIDION 2A   CHILD 609B
31 ANA IA   AMONG 49B

31 GALILAIA   GALILEE 149D
   DEKAPOLIS   DECAPOLIS 173A
   EIS IB   NEAR 227C
   EXERCHOMAI IAα   GO OUT 273D
   ERCHOMAI IIAβ   COME 310C
   THALASSA 2   LAKE 351A
   MESOS 2   THE MIDDLE 508C
   PALIN IA   BACK 611C
   SIDWN   SIDON 757C
   TUROS   TYRE 838C
31A HORION   BOUNDARY 585A
31B HORION   BOUNDARY 585A
32 EPITITH8MI IAα   PUT UPON 302D
   HINA IIIAY   IN ORDER THAT 378B
   KWPHOS 2   DEAF 463C
   MOGGILALOS   527C
      SPEAKING HOARSELY
   MOGILALOS 2   MUTE 527C
   PARAKALEW 3   IMPLORE 622D
   PHERW 4Bβ   BEAR 863C
33 APOLAMBANW 3   TAKE ASIDE 94A
   HAPTW 2B   TOUCH 102C
   BALLW 2B   PUT 130D
   GLWSSA IA   TONGUE 161B
   DAKTULOS   FINGER 169A
   IDIOS 4   PRIVATELY 371A
   MOGILALOS 2   MUTE 527C
   OUS I   EAR 600A
   OCHLOS I   CROWD 605C
   PTUSMA   SALIVA 735A
34 ANABLEPW I   LOOK UP 50C
   EIMI II3   TO BE 222D
   EPHPHATHA   OPENED 331C
   HOS,H8,HO I7A   (REL PRON) 588C
   OURANOS 2A   HEAVEN 599B
   STENAZW   SIGH 773D
34F DIANOIGW IB   OPEN 186B
35 AK08 IC   HEARING 308
   ANOIGW IEY   OPEN 70D
   GLWSSA IA   TONGUE 161B
   DESMOS I   FETTER 175A
   LALEW 2Aα   SPEAK 464B
   LUW IB   LOOSE 484D
   ORTHWS   RIGHTLY 584B
36 HINA IIIAδ   IN ORDER THAT 378B
   K8RUSSW 2A   ANNOUNCE 432B
   LEGW II2   SPEAK 471A
   MALLON I   MORE 490B
   M8DEIS 2A   NO 520A
   HOSOS 3   HOW GREAT 590C
   PERISSOTEROS 3   GREATER 657C
36A DIASTELLW   ORDER 187D
36B DIASTELLW   ORDER 187D
37 AKOUW IA   HEAR 318
   ALALOS   MUTE 34B
   EKPL8SSW 2   BE AMAZED 243D
   KALWS I   WELL 402A
   KWPHOS 2   DEAF 463C
   LALEW 2Aα   SPEAK 464B
   HUPEREKPERISSWS   848C
      BEYOND ALL MEASURE
   HUPERPERISSWS   849D
      BEYOND ALL MEASURE

37B   POIEW IIBT   DO 688B

MARK 8

1	EIMI I6	TO BE 222C
	EKEINOS 2Bα	THAT 239B
	ECHW I2D	HAVE 332D
	MATH8T8S 2Bα	DISCIPLE 487A
	PALIN 2	AGAIN 611C
	PAMPOLUS	VERY GREAT 612B
	POLUS IIBα	MANY 694C
1F	ESTHIW IA	EAT 312C
2	EPI IIIIBε	TOWARD 289A
	8D8 IA	ALREADY 344D
	H8MERA 2	DAY 347C
	POTE	WHEN 701D
	PROSMENW IAα	REMAIN 724D
	SPLAGCHNIZOMAI	HAVE PITY 770B
	TIS, TI IBς	WHICH 827B
	TREIS	THREE 833A
3	APOLUW 2B	SEND AWAY 96B
	EAN IIB	IF 210C
	EKLUW	BECOME WEARY 242C
	H8KW IA	HAVE COME 345B
	MAKROTHEN	FROM FAR AWAY 489A
	N8STIS	HUNGRY 540C
	HODOS IB	WAY 556C
	OIKOS IAα	HOUSE 563A
4	APOKRINOMAI I	ANSWER 93A
	ER8MIA	DESERT 308D
	POTHEN I	FROM WHERE 686D
	TIS, TI IAα	ANY ONE 827C
	CHORTAZW 2A	FEED 892B
	HWDE 2A	HERE 903D
4F	ARTOS IA	BREAD 110A
5	ERWTAW I	ASK 312A
	POSOS 2A	HOW GREAT 701B
5F	HEPTA	SEVEN 306B
6	ANAPIPTW I	RECLINE 59A
	G8 2	GROUND 156C
	DIDWMI 2	GIVE 192C
	EUCHARISTEW 2	GIVE THANKS 328C
	HINA IIE	IN ORDER THAT 377C
	KLAW	BREAK 434D
	PARAGGELLW	GIVE ORDERS 618C
6A	PARATITH8MI IA	628B
	PLACE BESIDE	
6B	PARATITH8MI IA	628B
	PLACE BESIDE	
7	EIPON 3C	SAY 225D
	EULOGEW 2B	BLESS 322D
	ICHTHUDION	LITTLE FISH 385A
	KAI III	ALSO 394A
	OLIGOS IA	FEW 566B
	PARATITH8MI IA	PLACE BESIDE 628B
8	AIRW 3	CARRY 24A
	HEPTA	SEVEN 306B
	KLASMA	FRAGMENT 434B
	PERISSEUMA 2	ABUNDANCE 656B
	SPURI8	BASKET 771C
	CHORTAZW 2A	FEED 892B
9	APOLUW 2B	SEND AWAY 96B
	TETRAKISCHILIOI	FOUR THOUSAND 821B

9	HWS IV5	WHEN 907C
10	DALMANOUTHA	DALMANUTHA 169B
	EMBAINW	GO IN 253C
	MAGADAN	MAGADAN 485B
	MEROS IBγ	PART 507A
	PLOION 2	SHIP 679B
11	APO III	FROM 86B
	EXERCHOMAI IAη	GO OUT 274C
	Z8TEW 2C	SEEK 339D
	OURANOS 2A	HEAVEN 599B
	PARA I3A	FROM 614D
	PEIRAZW 2C	TRY 646A
	S8MEION 2A	SIGN 755C
	SUZ8TEW 2	DISCUSS 783B
	PHARISAIOS	PHARISEE 861C
12	AM8N 2	AMEN 45B
	ANASTENAZW	SIGH DEEPLY 60D
	EI IV	IF 218C
	Z8TEW 2C	SEEK 339C
	PNEUMA 3B	SPIRIT 681B
	S8MEION 2A	SIGN 755C
13	APERCHOMAI 2	GO 84A
	APHI8MI IAα	SEND AWAY 125B
	EMBAINW	GO IN 253C
	PERAN I	ON THE OTHER SIDE 649C
14	ARTOS IA	BREAD 110A
	ARTOS IA	BREAD 110B
	HEIS IC	ONE 230A
	HEIS 2B	ONE 230B
	EPILANTHANOMAI I	FORGET 295B
	META AIIIB	WITH 509D
15	BLEPW 6	SEE 143B
	DIASTELLW	ORDER 187D
	ZUM8 2	LEAVEN 340C
	H8RWD8S 2	HEROD 349B
	H8RWDIANOI	HERODIANS 349B
	HORAW 2B	SEE 582B
	*PHARISAIOS	PHARISEE 861C
16	ALL8LWN	EACH OTHER 39A
	DIALOGIZOMAI 2	ARGUE 185A
	PROS IIIIE	TOWARD 716D
16F	ARTOS IA	BREAD 110A
17	GINWSKW 4B	PERCEIVE 160B
	DIALOGIZOMAI 2	ARGUE 185A
	KARDIA IB⁸	HEART 404D
	NOEW IE	UNDERSTAND 542D
	HOTI IC	THAT 593B
	OUDE I	AND NOT 595D
	OUPW	NOT YET 598A
	P8ROW	DISABLE 662C
	PWROW	HARDEN 739B
	SUNI8MI	UNDERSTAND 797D
	SUNI8MI	UNDERSTAND 798A
18	AKOUW IA	HEAR 31B
	MN8MONEUW IC	REMEMBER 527A
	OUS 2	EAR 600B
	OPHTHALMOS 2	EYE 604C
19	ARTOS IA	BREAD 110A
	KLAW	BREAK 434D
	KOPHINOS	BASKET 448C
	PENTAKISCHILIOI	FIVE THOUSAND 648C
	PL8R8S IAα	FULL 675C
	PL8R8S 2	FULL 675D

19	POSOS 2A	HOW GREAT 701B
19F	AIRW 3	CARRY 24A
19F	EIS 4G	FOR 229A
19F	KLASMA	FRAGMENT 434B
20	HEPTA	SEVEN 306B
	KOPHINOS	BASKET 448C
	PL8RWMA 1A THAT WHICH FILLS	678A
	POSOS 2A	HOW GREAT 701B
	SPURIS	BASKET 771C
	TETRAKISCHILIOI FOUR THOUSAND	821B
21	OUPW	NOT YET 598A
	*PWS 1B	HOW 739C
	SUNI8MI	UNDERSTAND 797D
	SUNI8MI	UNDERSTAND 798A
22	HAPTW 2B	TOUCH 102C
	AUTOS 3A	(OBLIQUE CASE) 123A
	B8THSAIDA 1	BETHSAIDA 139C
	HINA IIIAY	IN ORDER THAT 378B
	PARAKALEW 3	IMPLORE 622D
	PHERW 4B?	BEAR 863C
22F	TUPHLOS 1B	BLIND 838C
23	EIS 1C	IN 227C
	EKPHERW 2	LEAD 246B
	EXAGW 1	LEAD OUT 271B
	EXW 1B	OUTSIDE 279A
	EXW 2B	OUTSIDE 279B
	EPERWTAW 1A	ASK 285A
	EPILAMBANOMAI 1	GRASP 295A
	EPITITH8MI 1A«	PUT UPON 302D
	KWM8 1	VILLAGE 462D
	OMMA 1	EYE 568D
	PTUW	SPIT 735B
	TIS, TI 1B«	ANY ONE 828A
23F	BLEPW 1A	SEE 142D
24	ANABLEPW 1	LOOK UP 50C
	DENDRON	TREE 173C
	LEGW IIIB	ANSWER 470C
	PERIPATEW 1C	GO ABOUT 655A
25	HAPAS 2	ALL 81A
	APOKATHIST8MI 1	RESTORE 91B
	D8LAUGWS SHINING CLEARLY	177B
	DIABLEPW 1 LOOK INTENTLY	180D
	EITA 1	THEN 233A
	EMBLEPW 1	LOOK AT 254A
	EPI IIIIA?	ON 288A
	EPI IIIIA?	ON 288A
	EPITITH8MI 1A«	PUT UPON 302D
	PALIN 2	AGAIN 611C
	T8LAUGWS	CLEARLY 822A
	TITH8MI IIA?	PUT 823D
26	APOSTELLW 1B?	SEND AWAY 98A
	EISERCHOMAI 1A?	COME 231D
	KWM8 1	VILLAGE 462D
	M8DE 2	NOT EVEN 519D
	OIKOS 1A«	HOUSE 563A
27	ANTHRWPOS 1A6	PEOPLE 67C
	EIMI II6C	TO BE 223C
	KAISAREIA 1	CAESAREA 396D
	KWM8 1	VILLAGE 462D
	MATH8T8S 2B«	DISCIPLE 487A
	HO,H8,TO II7	THE 554C
	HODOS 1B	WAY 556C
	PHILIPPOS 1	PHILIP 868A
27FF	PETROS	PETER 660D
28	ALLOS 1C	OTHER 39B
	BAPTIST8S	BAPTIST 132B
	8LIAS	ELIJAH 345D
	IWAN(N)8S 1	JOHN 385B
	PROPH8T8S 3	PROPHET 731A
29	AUTOS 1B	SELF 122B
	EIMI II6C	TO BE 223C
	CHRISTOS 1 ANOINTED ONE	895B
29B	LEGW I8D	SAY 470C
30	EPITIMAW 1	REBUKE 303B
	HINA IIIA6	IN ORDER THAT 378B
	LEGW II2	SPEAK 471A
31	ANIST8MI 2A	RISE 69C
	APODOKIMAZW 2 DECLARE USELESS	90B
	ARCHIEREUS 1B HIGH PRIEST	112B
	ARCHW 2A«	BEGIN 113A
	GRAMMATEUS 2	SCRIBES 165A
	DIDASKW 2E	TEACH 191B
	H8MERA 2	DAY 347B
	META BII1	AFTER 511B
	PASCHW 3B	ENDURE 639D
	PRESBUTEROS 2A?	OLDER 706D
	*HUIOS 2C	SON 843A
32	LALEW 2B	SPEAK 464C
	LOGOS 1A«	MATTER 479A
	LOGOS 1B?	WORD 479C
	PARR8SIA 1	PLAINNESS 635D
	PROSLAMBANW 2A	TAKE 724C
32F	EPITIMAW 1	REBUKE 303B
33	EIDON 1A	SEE 219D
	EPISTREPHW 2A«	TURN 301B
	THEOS 3FY	GOD 358B
	HO,H8,TO II7	THE 554C
	OPISW 2A«	BEHIND 578C
	SATAN	ADVERSARY 752C
	HUPAGW 1	GO AWAY 844B
	PHRONEW 2	THINK 874B
34	AIRW 2	LIFT UP 24A
	AKOLOUTHEW 3	FOLLOW 30D
	AKOLOUTHEW 2	ACCOMPANY 30D
	APARNEOMAI	DENY 80B
	HEAUTOU 1	ONESELF 211A
	ERCHOMAI II	GO 311D
	OPISW 2A?	AFTER 578D
	OPISW 2A?	AFTER 578D
	HOSTIS 1A	WHOEVER 590D
	STAUROS 2	THE CROSS 772C
35	APOLLUMI 1B	LOSE 94C
	GAR 1E	FOR 151C
	HENEKA	BECAUSE OF 264B
	EUAGGELION 1A	GOSPEL 318A
	SWZW 3	SAVE 806C
	PSUCH8 1D	SOUL LIFE 902B
35A	SWZW 1A	SAVE 805D
35A	SWZW 2A?	SAVE 806B
35A	PSUCH8 1D	SOUL LIFE 902B
35B	SWZW 1A	SAVE 805D
35B	SWZW 2A?	SAVE 806B
35B	PSUCH8 1D	SOUL LIFE 902B
35=8	GAR 1C	FOR 151B
36	Z8MIOW 1 SUFFER DAMAGE	339A
	KERDAINW 1A	TO GAIN 430C

36	KOSMOS 6	WORLD 447C
	PSUCH8 IC	SOUL LIFE 902A
	WPHELEW IA	HELP 908D
37	ANTALLAGMA GIVEN IN EXCHANGE 72B	
	DIDWMI	GIVE 191D
	DIDWMI 4	GIVE 192D
	PSUCH8 IC	SOUL LIFE 902A
38	AGGELOS 2A	ANGEL 7C
	HAGIOS 1Bβ	HOLY 9D
	HAMARTWLOS I	SINNER 43C
	AN 3A	(PARTICLE) 48B
	GAR IE	FOR 151C
	GENEA 2	GENERATION 153B
	EN 14A	IN 258B
	EN 14B	IN 258B
	*EPAISCHUNOMAI I	BE ASHAMED 281D
	ERCHOMAI IIAη	COME 311A
	LOGOS 1Bβ	WORD 479B
	META AIIIA	WITH 509D
	MOICHALIS 2A	ADULTEROUS 528A
	HO,H8,TO IIIE	THE 552D
	PAT8R 3Dα	FATHER 641D
	HUIOS 2C	SON 843A

MARK 9

I	AM8N 2	AMEN 45B
	BASILEIA 3G	KINGDOM 135A
	GEUOMAI 2 COME TO KNOW SOMETH 156A	
	DUNAMIS I	POWER 206D
	EIMI II	TO BE 222B
	EN III2	BY 260B
	HEWS IIB	UNTIL 334D
	THANATOS IA	DEATH 351B
	M8 DIA	NOT 519B
	HOSTIS 2A	WHOEVER 591A
	TIS, TI IAα	ANY ONE 827D
	HWDE 2A	HERE 903D
2	ANAPHERW I	BRING 62C
	EMPROSTHEN 2C	IN FRONT 256C
	HEX	SIX 270D
	IAKWBOS I	JAMES 368B
	IDIOS 4	PRIVATELY 371A
	META BIII	AFTER 511B
	METAMORPHOW I	TRANSFORM 513A
	MONOS IAβ	ONLY 529C
	OROS	MOUNTAIN 586B
	PARALAMBANW I	TAKE 624D
	PETROS	PETER 660D
	HUPS8LOS I	HIGH 857C
3	ANATELLW 2	RISE 61C
	GNAPHEUS	BLEACHER 162A
	HIMATION I	GARMENT 377A
	LEUKAINW I	MAKE WHITE 473C
	*LEUKOS 2	WHITE 473D
	LIAN 2B	VERY 474C
	HOIOS	OF WHAT SORT 565C
	STILBW	SHINE 776B
	CHIWN	SNOW 890C
4	EIMI II4E	TO BE 223B
	HORAW IAδ	SEE 582A
	SULLALEW	TALK 784B
4F	8LIAS	ELIJAH 345D

4F	MWUS8S	MOSES 533D
5	APOKRINOMAI 2	BEGIN 93A
	EIMI II9A	TO BE 223D
	KAI I2B	AND 393A
	KALOS 3A	GOOD 401C
	KALOS 3C	GOOD 401D
	LEGW I8D	SAY 470C
	PETROS	PETER 660D
	POIEW IIAα	DO 687A
	RABBI	RABBI 740B
	SK8N8	TENT 762A
	HWDE 2A	HERE 903D
6	APOKRINOMAI I	ANSWER 92D
	GAR IE	FOR 151C
	EKPHOBOS	TERRIFIED 246C
	OIDA IF	KNOW 558C
7	AGAP8TOS I	BELOVED 6C
	EKLEGOMAI 4	CHOOSE 242A
	EPISKIAZW 2	COVER 298D
	NEPHEL8	CLOUD 538D
	HOUTOS IAα	THIS 600D
	HUIOS 2B	SON 842C
	*PHWN8 2D	VOICE 879B
8	ALLA IA	BUT, YET 37B
	EXAPINA	SUDDENLY 272C
	MONOS IAγ	ONLY 529C
	OUDEIS 2A	NO ONE 596B
	OUKETI I	NO LONGER 597A
	PERIBLEPW I	LOOK AROUND 652A
9	DIASTELLW	ORDER 187D
	DI8GEOMAI	TELL 194A
	HINA IIIAδ	IN ORDER THAT 378B
	KATABAINW IAα	COME DOWN 409B
	KATABAINW IAα	COME DOWN 409B
	HUIOS 2C	SON 843A
9F	ANIST8MI 2A	RISE 69C
9F	NEKROS 2A	DEAD 537A
10	ANIST8MI 2A	RISE 69C
	EIMI II3	TO BE 222D
	KRATEW 2E5	HOLD 450A
	LOGOS IAε	MATTER 478D
	HO,H8,TO II4A	THE 553D
	PROS III7	TOWARD 718A
	SUZ8TEW I	DISCUSS 783B
II	DEI I	IT IS NECESSARY 171A
	EPERWTAW IA	ASK 285A
	ERCHOMAI IIAθ	COME 311A
	HO TI 4B	WHY 591C
	HOTI IC	THAT 593B
IIF	PRWTOS 2A	FIRST 733C
IIFF	8LIAS	ELIJAH 345D
12	APOKATHIST8MI I	RESTORE 91B
	EXOUDENEW TREAT WITH CONTEMPT 277B	
	EXOUTHENEW 3	REJECT 277C
	ERCHOMAI IIAθ	COME 311A
	HINA IIIAδ	IN ORDER THAT 378B
	MEN	(PARTICLE) 503C
	MEN IAβ	(PARTICLE) 503D
	PASCHW 3B	ENDURE 639D
	POLUS I2Bα	MANY 695A
	HUIOS 2C	SON 843A
	PH8MI IBα	SAY 864A
12F	GRAPHW 2C	WRITE 166A

```
12F   EPI IIIIBζ            ON 289B      21 GINOMAI I3Bγ      TAKE PLACE 158A
13 ERCHOMAI IIAθ          COME 311A         EIMI II6C             TO BE 223C
   THELW I                WISH 355C         EK 5A                  FROM 235C
   KATHWS I            JUST AS 392A         PAIDIOTHEN   FROM CHILDHOOD 609A
   KAI I6                  AND 394A         PAIDOTHEN    FROM CHILDHOOD 609C
   HOSOS 2          HOW GREAT 590C          PAIS IAα               CHILD 609C
   PL8N IB                BUT 675B          POSOS I            HOW GREAT 701A
   POIEW IIDγ              DO 688D          CHRONOS                 TIME 896B
14 ERCHOMAI IIAβ          COME 310C         HWS IVIB                WHEN 907A
   MATH8T8S 2Bα       DISCIPLE 487A     22 ALLA 6                    NOW 38B
   OCHLOS I             CROWD 605C          BALLW IB              THROW 130C
   PERI 2A6             ABOUT 651A          B08THEW 2               AID 144A
   POLUS IIBα            MANY 694C          DUNAMAI 3              ABLE 206C
  *SUZ8TEW 2          DISCUSS 783B          EPI IIIIBα           TOWARD 289A
15 ASPAZOMAI IA          GREET 116B         KAI I6                  AND 394A
   EKTHAMBEW        BE AMAZED 239D          POLLAKIS              OFTEN 693B
   OCHLOS I             CROWD 605C          PUR IA                 FIRE 737B
   PROSTRECHW     RUN UP (TO) 726D          SPLAGCHNIZOMAI    HAVE PITY 770B
   PROSCHAIRW       BE GLAD 727D            TIS, TI IBα          ANY ONE 828A
16 EPERWTAW IA            ASK 285A          HUDWR I               WATER 840C
   SUZ8TEW 2           DISCUSS 783B     23 DUNATOS 2B          POSSIBLE 208A
17 ALALOS                MUTE 34B           HO,H8,TO II8A           THE 554D
   APOKRINOMAI I       ANSWER 93A       23F  PISTEUW 2C         BELIEVE 667D
   DIDASKALOS         TEACHER 190D      24 APISTIA 2A          UNBELIEF 84D
   EK 4Aα                FROM 235B          B08THEW 2               AID 144A
   ECHW I2Eα             HAVE 333A          DAKRUON                TEAR 169A
   HO,H8,TO IIID         THE 552D           KRAZW 2A               CALL 448D
   PNEUMA 4C            SPIRIT 682A         LEGW I8D                SAY 470C
   HUIOS IAα              SON 841B          META AIIII             WITH 511A
   PHERW 4Bβ             BEAR 863C          PAIDION 2B            CHILD 609B
18 AN 2B            (PARTICLE) 48B      25 AKATHARTOS 2        IMPURE 28C
   APHRIZW   FOAM AT THE MOUTH 127B         ALALOS                 MUTE 34B
   EIPON 3C              SAY 225D           EGW                       I 216A
   EKBALLW I       DRIVE OUT 237A           EIDON ID                SEE 219D
   HINA IIIA6  IN ORDER THAT 378B           EISERCHOMAI I8β        COME 232A
   ISCHUW 2B       BE STRONG 384C           EXERCHOMAI IA6       GO OUT 274A
   KATALAMBANW IB       SEIZE 414A          EPISUNTRECHW  RUN TOGETHER 301D
   X8RAINW 2B          DRY UP 550D          EPITASSW            COMMAND 302A
   ODOUS                TOOTH 557B          EPITIMAW I            REBUKE 303B
   HOPOU IA6            WHERE 579D          KWPHOS 2                DEAF 463C
   RASSW               STRIKE 742A          M8KETI 6A         NO LONGER 520B
   R8SSW           THROW DOWN 743B      25A   PNEUMA 4C          SPIRIT 682A
   TRIZW                GNASH 834A      25B   PNEUMA 4C          SPIRIT 682A
19 ANECHW IA            ENDURE 65B       26 APOTHN8SKW IAα          DIE 90D
   APISTOS 2         FAITHLESS 85A          EXERCHOMAI IA6       GO OUT 274A
   GENEA 2          GENERATION 153B         KRAZW I             CRY OUT 448D
   LEGW I8D               SAY 470C          NEKROS IAα             DEAD 536C
   W I                      O 903B          SPARASSW               TEAR 768B
19A   HEWS IIIC         UNTIL 335C          HWSEI I                  AS 907D
19A   POTE               WHEN 701D          HWSTE 2Aβ         THEREFORE 908C
19A   PROS III7        TOWARD 718A      26A   POLUS I2Bβ          MANY 695B
19B   HEWS IIIC         UNTIL 335C      26B   POLUS I2Aβ          MANY 694D
19B   POTE               WHEN 701D      27 ANIST8MI 2A            RISE 69C
19F   PHERW 4Bβ          BEAR 863C          EGEIRW IAβ            RAISE 213D
20 APHRIZW   FOAM AT THE MOUTH 127B        *KRATEW IB             SEIZE 449C
   G8 2                GROUND 156C      28 EKBALLW I          DRIVE OUT 237A
   EIDON IA               SEE 219D          EPERWTAW IA             ASK 285A
   EPI IIAβ                ON 285D          IDIOS 4            PRIVATELY 371A
   KULIW 2               ROLL 458B          OIKOS IAα             HOUSE 563A
   PIPTW IBα             FALL 665B          HO TI 4B                WHY 591C
   PNEUMA 4C            SPIRIT 682A         HOTI IC                THAT 593B
   SPARASSW              TEAR 768B      29 GENOS 4               CLASS 155C
   SUSPARASSW        CONVULSE 802B          EXERCHOMAI IA6       GO OUT 274A
```

29	N8STEIA 2B	FASTING 540A
	OUDEIS 2Bα	NOTHING 596C
	HOUTOS 2A	THIS 601D
	*PROSEUCH8 I	PRAYER 720C
30	GINWSKW 2C	FIND OUT 160B
	DIA AII	THROUGH 178C
	THELW I	WISH 355C
	HINA IIIAα	IN ORDER THAT 378A
	KAKEITHEN I	AND FROM THERE 397C
	PARAPOREUOMAI 2	PASS BY 627A
	POREUW I	PROCEED 699B
	TIS, TI IAα	ANY ONE 827C
31	ANTHRWPOS IAα	MAN 67C
	ANIST8MI 2A	RISE 69C
	DIDASKW 2A	TEACH 191A
	PARADIDWMI IB	GIVE OVER 620A
	HUIOS 2C	SON 843A
	CHEIR 2B	HAND 888D
32	AGNOEW 3	BE IGNORANT IIC
	EPERWTAW IA	ASK 284D
	R8MA I	WORD 742D
	PHOBEW IA	BE AFRAID 870D
33	GINOMAI II4A	BE 159C
	DIALOGIZOMAI 2	ARGUE 185A
	KAPHARNAOUM	CAPERNAUM 427C
	OIKIA IA	HOUSE 560A
	TIS, TI IBα	WHICH 826D
33F	HODOS IB	WAY 556C
34	DIALEGOMAI I	DISCUSS 184D
	MEGAS 2Bα	GREAT 499B
	PROS IIIIE	TOWARD 716D
	SIWPAW I	BE SILENT 760A
35	DIAKONOS IA	SERVANT 183C
	EI VII	219B
	ESCHATOS 2	LAST 314A
	KATHIZW 2Aα	SIT DOWN 390D
	PRWTOS ICβ	FIRST 733C
	PRWTOS ICβ	FIRST 733C
	PHWNEW 2B	CALL 878C
36	AGKAL8	ARM 10C
	ENAGKALIZOMAI	261A
	TAKE IN ONES ARMS	
	HIST8MI IIAα	PUT 382D
	LAMBANW IA	TAKE 465B
	MESOS 2	THE MIDDLE 508D
36F	PAIDION 2A	CHILD 609A
37	ALLA IB	BUT, YET 37C
	APOSTELLW IC	SEND AWAY 98B
	DECHOMAI I	RECEIVE 176C
	EPI II3	ON 287D
	ONOMA I4Cα	NAME 576D
	ONOMA II	TITLE 577A
	TOIOUTOS 2Aα	SUCH A KIND 829A
38	DIDASKALOS	TEACHER 190D
	EKBALLW I	DRIVE OUT 237A
	ONOMA I4Cγ	NAME 576A
38F	KWLUW I	HINDER 462B
39	EIMI II	TO BE 222B
	EIPON 3A	SAY 225C
	EPI II3	ON 287D
	KAKOLOGEW	INSULT 398A
	M8 AIII3B	NOT 518D
	ONOMA I4Cα	NAME 576C

39	POIEW IIBβ	DO 687C
	TACHUS 2C	QUICK 815A
40	EIMI III6A	TO BE 224C
	EIMI IIIIIA	TO BE 224D
	KATA I2Bγ	DOWN 406D
	HOS,H8,HO I2A	(REL PRON) 587A
	SKORPIZW I	SCATTER 764B
	HUPER IAδ	IN BEHALF OF 846B
41	AM8N 2	AMEN 45B
	APOLLUMI IB	LOSE 94C
	LEGW IIID	ASSURE 470D
	MISTHOS 2A	REWARD 525C
	ONOMA II	TITLE 577A
	POT8RION I	CUP 702A
	POTIZW I	GIVE TO DRINK 702C
	HUDWR I	WATER 840C
	CHRISTOS 2	ANOINTED ONE 895D
42	BALLW IB	THROW 130C
	EI IIB	IF 218B
	EIS 4Cβ	(GOAL) 228C
	HEIS IAβ	ONE 230A
	THALASSA IA	SEA 350B
	KALOS 3C	GOOD 401C
	KALOS 3C	GOOD 401D
	MALLON I	MORE 490B
	MIKROS IC	SMALL 523A
	MULIKOS	MILLSTONE 531A
	MULOS 2	MILLSTONE 531B
	MULWNIKOS	MILLSTONE 531B
	ONIKOS PERTAINING TO A DONKEY 573D	
	PERI 2Aβ	ABOUT 650D
	PERIKEIMAI IA	653C
	BE PLACED AROUND	
	PISTEUW 2Aβ	BELIEVE 667B
	TRACH8LOS	NECK 832D
42F	SKANDALIZW IA	760B
	CAUSE TO FALL	
43	APOKOPTW I	CUT OFF 92C
	ASBESTOS I	INEXTINGUISHABLE 114A
	GEENNA	HELL 152C
	EISERCHOMAI 2A	COME 232B
	ECHW I2Cα	HAVE 332D
	ZW8 2Bβ	LIFE 341C
	8 2Bβ	THAN 343B
	KALOS 3C	GOOD 401C
	KALOS 3C	GOOD 401D
	KULLOS	CRIPPLED 458B
	PUR IB	FIRE 737C
44	SBENNUMI I	EXTINGUISH 752D
	SKWL8X	WORM 765D
	TELEUTAW	DIE 818B
45	APOKOPTW I	CUT OFF 92C
	ASBESTOS I	INEXTINGUISHABLE 114A
	GEENNA	HELL 152C
	EAN IIA	IF 210B
	EISERCHOMAI 2A	COME 232B
	ECHW I2Cα	HAVE 332D
	ZW8 2Bβ	LIFE 341C
	8 2Bβ	THAN 343B
	KALOS 3C	GOOD 401C
	KALOS 3C	GOOD 401D
	PUR IB	FIRE 737C
	SKANDALIZW IA	CAUSE TO FALL 760B

45 CHWLOS	LAME	897C
45A POUS IA	FOOT	703B
45B POUS IA	FOOT	703B
46 SBENNUMI I	EXTINGUISH	752D
SKWL8X	WORM	765D
TELEUTAW	DIE	818B
47 GEENNA	HELL	152C
EAN IIA	IF	210B
EISERCHOMAI 2A	COME	232B
EKBALLW 3	TAKE OUT	237B
ECHW I2C«	HAVE	332D
8 28ß	THAN	343B
KALOS 3C	GOOD	401C
KALOS 3C	GOOD	401D
MONOPHTHALMOS	ONE EYED	530A
OPHTHALMOS I	EYE	604B
PUR IB	FIRE	737C
SKANDALIZW IA	CAUSE TO FALL	760B
48 HOPOU IA«	WHERE	579C
PUR IB	FIRE	737C
SBENNUMI I	EXTINGUISH	752D
SKWL8X	WORM	765D
TELEUTAW	DIE	818B
49 HALIZW	TO SALT	37A
HALS HALOS	SALT	40C
GAR IA	FOR	151A
THUSIA 2A	SACRIFICE	366D
PUR 2	FIRE	737D
50 ALL8LWN	EACH OTHER	39A
ANALOS	WITHOUT SALT	57A
ARTUW	SEASON	110C
GINOMAI III	BE	159B
EIR8NEUW 2B	KEEP IN PEACE	226A
EN IIIIA	BY	260A
KALOS 2A	GOOD	401B
TIS, TI IB«	WHICH	826D
50A HALAS I	SALT	34B
50B HALAS I	SALT	34B
50C HALAS 2	SALT	34C

MARK 10

I ANIST8MI 2D	RISE	69D
EIWTHA	ACCUSTOMED	233B
IORDAN8S	JORDAN	379C
IOUDAIA 2	JUDAEA	379D
HORION	BOUNDARY	584D
OCHLOS I	CROWD	605D
PALIN 2	AGAIN	611C
PERAN 2C	ON THE OTHER SIDE	649C
SUMPOREUOMAI 2	GO WITH	787D
HWS II4B	SO	906B
2 AN8R I	MAN	65D
APOLUW 2A	SEND AWAY	96A
EI VI	IF	218D
EXESTI 2	IT IS POSSIBLE	274D
EPERWTAW IA	ASK	285A
PEIRAZW 2C	TRY	646A
PHARISAIOS	PHARISEE	861C
3 ENTELLW	COMMAND	268A
TIS, TI IB«	WHICH	826D
3F MWUS8S	MOSES	533D
4 APOLUW 2A	SEND AWAY	96A

4 APOSTASION		97D
CERTIFICATE OF DIVORCE		
BIBLION 2	DOCUMENT	140D
GRAPHW 4	WRITE	166B
EPITREPW I	ALLOW	303C
5 GRAPHW 4	WRITE	166B
ENTOL8 2AY	COMMAND	268C
PROS III5A	TOWARD	717C
SKL8ROKARDIA	OBSTINACY	763B
6 ARS8N	MALE	109C
ARCH8 IC	BEGINNING	111D
TH8LUS	FEMALE	361B
KTISIS IBß	CREATION	457A
POIEW IIAß	DO	687B
7 ANTHRWPOS 3Aß	MAN	68B
HENEKA	BECAUSE OF	264B
KATALEIPW IA	LEAVE BEHIND	414C
PROSKOLLAW	ADHERE CLOSELY TO	723B
8 DUO ID	TWO	208B
EIMI III2	TO BE	224A
OUKETI I	NO LONGER	596D
HWSTE IA	THEREFORE	908B
8A SARX 2	BODY	751A
8B SARX 2	BODY	751A
9 ANTHRWPOS IAß	MAN	67C
OUN IB	THEREFORE	597B
SUZAW	LIVE WITH	783B
CHWRIZW I	DIVIDE	898B
10 EIS 9A	IN	229D
EPERWTAW IA	ASK	285A
OIKIA IA	HOUSE	559D
11 APOLUW 2A	SEND AWAY	96A
GAMEW IA	MARRY	150A
EPI IIIIB«	TOWARD	289A
MOICHAW 2	COMMIT ADULTERY	528A
12 AN8R I	MAN	65D
APOLUW 2A	SEND AWAY	96A
GAMEW 3C	MARRY	150B
GAMEW 3A«	MARRY	150B
EAN IIB	IF	210B
EXERCHOMAI IA«	GO OUT	274A
MOICHAW I	COMMIT ADULTERY	528A
13 HAPTW 2B	TOUCH	102C
EPITIMAW I	REBUKE	303B
13A PROSPHERW IA	BRING (TO)	727A
13B PROSPHERW IA	BRING (TO)	727A
13F PAIDION 2A	CHILD	609A
14 AGANAKTEW	BE AROUSED	4A
APHI8MI 4	TOLERATE	126A
EIDON IA	SEE	219D
KWLUW I	HINDER	462D
PAIDION 2A	CHILD	609A
TOIOUTOS 3A«	SUCH A KIND	829B
14F BASILEIA 3G	KINGDOM	135B
15 BASILEIA 3G	KINGDOM	135A
DECHOMAI 3B	ACCEPT	176C
EISERCHOMAI 2A	COME	232B
LEGW IIID	ASSURE	470D
M8 AII	NOT	517C
*PAIDION 2A	CHILD	609A
HWS I2A	AS	905C
16 ENAGKALIZOMAI		261A
TAKE IN ONES ARMS		

16 KATEULOGEW	BLESS	423C
TITH8MI IIAβ	PUT	823D
17 AGATHOS IBα	GOOD	3A
AIWNIOS 3	ETERNAL	28A
GONUPETEW	KNEEL DOWN	164B
DIDASKALOS	TEACHER	190D
EIS IAα	INTO	227C
HEIS 3A	SOMEONE	230D
EKPOREUOMAI IC	GO OUT	243D
ZW8 2Bβ	LIFE	341C
KL8RONOMEW 2	INHERIT	435D
POIEW IIBε	DO	687D
PROSTRECHW	RUN UP (TO)	726D
TIS, TI IBα	WHICH	826D
17F AGATHOS IBα	GOOD	3A
18 LEGW II3	CALL	471A
OUDEIS 2A	NO ONE	596B
18A AGATHOS IBα	GOOD	3A
18B AGATHOS IBα	GOOD	3A
19 APOSTEREW	STEAL	98D
ENTOL8 2Aβ	COMMAND	268C
KLEPTW	STEAL	435C
MOICHEUW I	COMMIT ADULTERY	528B
OIDA IB	KNOW	558B
PORNEUW I	TO PROSTITUTE	700B
TIMAW 2	HONOR	824D
PHONEUW	MURDER	872C
PSEUDOMARTUREW		900A
BEAR FALSE WITNESS		
20 DIDASKALOS	TEACHER	190D
EK 5A	FROM	235C
NEOT8S	YOUTH	538B
PHULASSW 2B	WATCH	876D
21 DEURO I	COME	175C
HEIS 2B	ONE	230C
EMBLEPW I	LOOK AT	254A
ECHW I2A	HAVE	332B
TH8SAUROS 2Bα	TREASURE	362B
HOSOS 2	HOW GREAT	590C
PTWCHOS IA	BEGGING POOR	735D
PWLEW	SELL	738D
STAUROS 2	THE CROSS	772C
HUPAGW 2	GO AWAY	844C
HUSTEREW ID	TO MISS	857A
21B ECHW I2A	HAVE	332B
22 EIMI II4F	TO BE	223B
EPI IIIBγ	ON	287B
ECHW I2A	HAVE	332B
KT8MA I	PROPERTY	456B
LOGOS IAγ	WORD	478C
LUPEW 2B	BE GRIEVED	483A
POLUS IIAβ	MANY	694B
STUGNAZW I	BE SHOCKED	779B
STUGNAZW 2A	BECOME GLOOMY	779C
23 DUSKOLWS	WITH DIFFICULTY	208D
PERIBLEPW I	LOOK AROUND	652A
PWS 3	HOW	740C
CHR8MA I	WEALTH	893D
23FF BASILEIA 3G	KINGDOM	135A
23FF EISERCHOMAI 2A	COME	232B
23=5 BASILEIA 3G	KINGDOM	135B
24 APOKRINOMAI 2	CONTINUE	93A
DUSKOLOS	DIFFICULT	208D

24 EPI IIIBγ	ON	287B
THAMBEW 2	ASTOUND	351B
LEGW I8D	SAY	470C
LOGOS IA6	WORD	478D
MATH8T8S 2Bα	DISCIPLE	487A
PALIN 2	AGAIN	611C
PEITHW 2A	CONVINCE	645B
PWS 3	HOW	740C
TEKNON 2B	CHILD	816B
CHR8MA I	WEALTH	893D
25 DIERCHOMAI IBα	GO THROUGH	193C
EUKOPOS	EASY	322A
8 2A	THAN	343B
KAM8LOS	CAMEL	402C
KAMILOS	ROPE	402D
PLOUSIOS I	RICH	679C
RAPHIS	NEEDLE	742A
TRUMALIA	HOLE	836A
26 HEAUTOU 3	ONESELF	211D
EKPL8SSW 2	BE AMAZED	243C
KAI I2H	AND	393D
PERISSWS	MORE	657C
PROS IIIIE	TOWARD	716D
SWZW 2B	SAVE	806B
27 ADUNATOS 2A	IMPOSSIBLE	18D
DUNATOS 2C	POSSIBLE	208B
EMBLEPW I	LOOK AT	254A
27A PARA II2C	BESIDE	615D
27B PARA II2C	BESIDE	615D
27C PARA II2C	BESIDE	615D
28 IDOU IBε	BEHOLD	371C
PETROS	PETER	660C
28F APHI8MI 3A	ABANDON	125D
29 EIMI II	TO BE	222B
HENEKA	BECAUSE OF	264B
EUAGGELION IA	GOSPEL	318A
8 IAβ	OR	342D
PH8MI IBα	SAY	864A
29F AGROS I	FIELD	13D
29F ADELPH8 I	SISTER	15C
29F OIKIA IA	HOUSE	559D
30 AIWN 2B	AGE	27B
AIWNIOS 3	ETERNAL	28A
DIWGMOS	PERSECUTION	200A
HEKATONTAPLASIWN		236C
A HUNDRED FOLD		
ERCHOMAI IIBβ	COME	311B
ZW8 2Bβ	LIFE	341C
KAIROS 4	TIME	396C
LAMBANW 2	RECEIVE	466B
META AIII2	WITH	511A
M8 AII	NOT	517C
NUN IAγ	NOW	547D
31 ESCHATOS 2	LAST	314A
PRWTOS ICβ	FIRST	733C
32 EIMI II4Bβ	TO BE	223A
EIMI III4	TO BE	224B
THAMBEW 2	ASTOUND	351B
MELLW IC6	IS DESTINED	502C
HODOS IB	WAY	556C
PALIN IA	BACK	611C
PARALAMBANW I	TAKE	625A
PROAGW 2A	LEAD	709A

Ref	Greek	English	Code
32	SUMBAINW	MEET	784D
32F	ANABAINW IAα	GO UP	49D
32F	HIEROSOLUMA IA	JERUSALEM	373D
33	ARCHIEREUS IB	HIGH PRIEST	112B
	GRAMMATEUS 2	SCRIBES	165A
	KATAKRINW	CONDEMN	413A
	HUIOS 2C	SON	843A
33A	PARADIDWMI IB	GIVE OVER	620A
33B	PARADIDWMI IB	GIVE OVER	619D
34	ANIST8MI 2A	RISE	69C
	EMPAIZW I	RIDICULE	255B
	MASTIGOW I	WHIP	496A
	META BIII	AFTER	511B
35	AITEW	ASK	25B
	DIDASKALOS	TEACHER	190D
	ZEBEDAIOS	ZEBEDEE	337D
	THELW I	WISH	355C
	IAKWBOS I	JAMES	368B
	HINA IIIAα	IN ORDER THAT	378A
	PROSPOREUOMAI	APPROACH	725C
35F	POIEW IIDβ	DO	688D
36	THELW I	WISH	355C
37	ARISTEROS	WEAPONS	106B
	DEXIOS 2B	RIGHT	174A
	DIDWMI IBβ	GIVE	192B
	DOXA IA	GLORY	202D
	HINA IIIAζ	IN ORDER THAT	378D
	KATHIZW 2Aα	SIT DOWN	390D
38	AITEW	ASK	25B
	BAPTIZW 3C	BAPTIZE	131D
	OIDA IF	KNOW	558C
	POT8RION 2	CUP	702B
38F	BAPTISMA 3	BAPTISM	132B
38F	PINW 2Bα	DRINK	664C
39	BAPTIZW 3C	BAPTIZE	131D
	DUNAMAI 2	ABLE	206B
	POT8RION 2	CUP	702B
40	DEXIOS 2B	RIGHT	174A
	EIMI II6E	TO BE	223D
	EMOS IB	MY	255A
	HETOIMAZW 3	PREPARE	316C
	EUWNUMOS	LEFT	330A
	8 IAβ	OR	342D
	KATHIZW 2Aα	SIT DOWN	390D
41	AGANAKTEW	BE AROUSED	4A
	DEKA	TEN	172D
	IAKWBOS I	JAMES	368B
	HO,H8,TO II2D	THE	553C
42	ARCHW I	RULE	113A
	DOKEW 2B	SEEM	201B
	ETHNOS I	NATION	217B
	KATAKURIEUW 2	RULE	413C
	KATEXOUSIAZW		422C
		EXERCISE AUTHORITY	
	MEGAS 2Bα	GREAT	499B
	OIDA IE	KNOW	558C
43	DIAKONOS IA	SERVANT	183C
	THELW I	WISH	355C
	MEGAS 2Bα	GREAT	499B
	HOUTW IB	THUS	602C
44	DOULOS 3	SLAVE	205A
	PRWTOS ICβ	FIRST	733C
45	ANTI 3	FOR	73B
45	GAR IB	FOR	151A
	DIAKONEW 2	SERVE	183A
	DIDWMI 6	GIVE	192D
	LUTRON	RANSOM	483D
	POLUS I2Aα	MANY	694D
	POLUS I2Aα	MANY	694D
	HUIOS 2C	SON	843A
	PSUCH8 IAβ	SOUL LIFE	901C
	PSUCH8 IF	SOUL LIFE	902C
46	BARTIMAIOS	BARTIMAEUS	133D
	EKPOREUOMAI IB	GO OUT	243D
	EPAITEW	BEG	282A
	IERICHW	JERICHO	372D
	HIKANOS IA	SUFFICIENT	375A
	KATH8MAI IAα	SIT	390B
	HODOS IA	WAY	556B
	OCHLOS I	CROWD	605C
	PARA IIIIBα	ALONG	616A
	PARA IIIID	ALONG	616A
	PROSAITEW	BEG	718C
	PROSAIT8S	BEGGAR	718C
	TIMAIOS	TIMAEUS	824C
	TUPHLOS IAα	BLIND	838C
47	KRAZW 2A	CALL	448D
	NAZAR8NOS	THE NAZARENE	534A
47F	DAUID	DAVID	170B
47F	ELEEW	HAVE MERCY	249B
47F	HUIOS 2A	SON	842A
48	EPITIMAW I	REBUKE	303C
	HINA IIIAδ	IN ORDER THAT	378B
	KRAZW 2A	CALL	448D
	MALLON I	MORE	490A
	SIWPAW 2A	BE SILENT	760A
48B	POLUS I2Cα	MANY	695B
49	EGEIRW IB	RAISE UP	214A
	THARSEW	BE CHEERFUL	352C
	HIST8MI IIIA	STAND	383A
	TUPHLOS IB	BLIND	838C
49A	PHWNEW 2B	CALL	878C
49B	PHWNEW 2B	CALL	878C
49C	PHWNEW 2B	CALL	878C
50	ANAP8DAW	JUMP UP	59A
51	ANABLEPW 2Aα	GAIN SIGHT	50C
	APOKRINOMAI 2	BEGIN	93A
	THELW I	WISH	355C
	HINA III2	IN ORDER THAT	379A
	POIEW IIDβ	DO	688D
	RABBOUNI	MY LORD	740B
	*RABBI	RABBI	740B
	TUPHLOS IB	BLIND	838C
52	ANABLEPW 2Aα	GAIN SIGHT	50C
	HODOS IB	WAY	556C
	PISTIS 2Bα	FAITH	668D
	SWZW IC	SAVE	806A
	HUPAGW I	GO AWAY	844B

MARK 11

Ref	Greek	English	Code
I	APOSTELLW IA	SEND AWAY	98A
	B8THANIA I	BETHANY	139B
	B8THPHAG8	BETHPHAGE	139D
	EGGIZW 2	APPROACH	212D
	EIS IB	NEAR	227C

1	ELAIA 1	OLIVE TREE 247B
	HOTE 1D	WHEN 592C
2	ANTHRWPOS 3Aζ	MAN 68C
	DEW 2	BIND 177A
	EISPOREUOMAI 1	GO 232D
	HEURISKW 1Cα	FIND 325D
	KATHIZW 2Aα	SIT DOWN 391A
	KATENANTI 2A	OPPOSITE 422B
	KWM8 1	VILLAGE 462D
	LUW 2A	LOOSE 484D
	*OUDEIS 2A	NO ONE 596B
	OUPW	NOT YET 598A
	PWLOS	COLT 739A
	HUPAGW 2	GO AWAY 844C
	PHERW 4Bα	BEAR 863B
3	APOSTELLW 1Bβ	SEND AWAY 98A
	ECHW 12I	HAVE 333C
	KURIOS 2Cβ	LORD 460C
	PALIN 1A	BACK 611B
	POIEW 11Bε	DO 687D
	TIS, TI 3A	WHICH 827B
	TIS, TI 1Aγ	ANY ONE 827D
	CHREIA 1	NEED 893B
	HWDE 1	HERE 903B
4	AMPHODON	STREET 47A
	DEW 2	BIND 177A
	EXW 1Aα	OUTSIDE 278D
	THURA 1A	DOOR 366B
	PROS III7	TOWARD 718A
4F	LUW 2A	LOOSE 484D
4F	PWLOS	COLT 739A
5	HIST8MI II2Bα	BEING 383C
	POIEW 11Bε	DO 688A
6	APHI8MI 4	TOLERATE 125D
7	EPIBALLW 1B	LAY ON 289D
	KATHIZW 2Aα	SIT DOWN 391A
	PWLOS	COLT 739A
	PHERW 4Bα	BEAR 863B
7F	HIMATION 1	GARMENT 377A
8	EIS 1C	IN 227C
	KOPTW 1	CUT 445A
	HODOS 1A	WAY 556B
	POLUS I2Aα	MANY 694D
	STIBAS	LEAVES 776A
	STRWNNUW	SPREAD 779B
9	AKOLOUTHEW 1	FOLLOW 30C
	ERCHOMAI IIAη	COME 310D
	EULOGEW 2A	BLESS 322D
	KRAZW 2A	CALL 448D
	ONOMA I4Cγ	NAME 576C
	PROAGW 2A	LEAD 709A
	HWSANNA	HOSANNA 907C
10	BASILEIA 3E	KINGDOM 135A
	BASILEIA 3G	KINGDOM 135B
	DAUID	DAVID 170B
	EULOGEW 2A	BLESS 322D
	PAT8R 1B	FOREFATHER 640D
	HUPSISTOS 1	HIGHEST 858A
	HWSANNA	HOSANNA 907C
11	EISERCHOMAI 1Aα	COME 231D
	8D8 1A	ALREADY 344D
	HIERON 2	TEMPLE 373A
	META AIII A	WITH 509D
11	OPSE 2	LATE IN THE DAY 606B
	OPSIOS 1	LATE 606C
	PERIBLEPW 1	LOOK AROUND 652A
	HWRA 1	TIME OF DAY 904B
11F	B8THANIA 1	BETHANY 139B
12	EXERCHOMAI 1Aα	GO OUT 274A
	EPAURION	NEXT DAY 283C
	PEINAW 1	HUNGER 645D
13	ARA 2	THEN 103C
	ECHW IIB	HAVE 332B
	KAIROS 3	TIME 396A
	MAKROTHEN	FROM FAR AWAY 489A
	OUDEIS 2Bα	NOTHING 596C
	SUK8	FIG TREE 783D
	SUKON	RIPE FIG 784A
13A	ERCHOMAI II	GO 311D
13A	PHULLON	FOLIAGE 877A
13B	ERCHOMAI IIAβ	COME 310C
13B	PHULLON	FOLIAGE 877A
14	AIWN 1B	TIME 26D
	APOKRINOMAI 2	BEGIN 93A
	EIS 2B	FOR 228A
	ESTHIW 1Bβ	EAT 313A
	KARPOS 1A	FRUIT 405C
	M8DEIS 2A	NO 520A
	M8KETI 6B	NO LONGER 520C
15	AGORAZW 1	BUY 12D
	EKBALLW 1	DRIVE OUT 236D
	KATHEDRA	CHAIR 389B
	KATASTREPHW 1	UPSET 420A
	KOLLUBIST8S	MONEY CHANGER 442D
	PERISTERA	PIGEON 657D
	TRAPEZA 4	TABLE 832C
15A	HIERON 2	TEMPLE 373A
15A	PWLEW	SELL 739A
15B	PWLEW	SELL 738D
15F	HIERON 2	TEMPLE 373A
16	APHI8MI 4	TOLERATE 126A
	DIAPHERW 1A	CARRY THROUGH 189B
	HINA IIIAζ	IN ORDER THAT 378B
	SKEUOS 1A	THING 761C
	TIS, TI 1Aα	ANY ONE 827C
17	GRAPHW 2C	WRITE 165D
	ETHNOS 1	NATION 217B
	KALEW 1Aβ	CALL 399D
	L8ST8S 1	ROBBER 474B
	OIKOS 1Aβ	HOUSE 563B
	OIKOS 1Aβ	HOUSE 563B
	POIEW 11B₁	DO 688B
	PROSEUCH8 1	PRAYER 720C
	SP8LAION	CAVE 769D
18	APOLLUMI 1Aα	RUIN 94C
	ARCHIEREUS 1B	HIGH PRIEST 112B
	GRAMMATEUS 2	SCRIBES 165A
	DIDACH8 3	TEACHING 191C
	EKPL8SSW 2	BE AMAZED 243D
	Z8TEW 1C	INVESTIGATE 339B
	OCHLOS 2	CROWD 605D
	*PWS 2B	HOW 740A
19	GINOMAI IIBγ	COME ABOUT 157C
	EKPOREUOMAI 1B	GO OUT 243D
	EXW 2B	OUTSIDE 279B
	HOTAN 2D	WHEN 592B

19	OPSE 2	LATE IN THE DAY	606B
	POLIS 1	CITY	692A
20	EK 2	AWAY FROM	234A
	PARAPOREUOMAI 1	PASS BY	627A
	PRWI	EARLY	732A
	RIZA 1A	ROOT	743B
20F	X8RAINW 2A	DRY UP	550D
20F	SUK8	FIG TREE	783D
21	ANAMIMN8SKW	REMIND	57C
	IDE 3	SEE	369D
	KATARAOMAI	CURSE	418A
	RABBI	RABBI	740B
22	THEOS 3F?	GOD	358B
	LEGW 18D	SAY	470C
	PISTIS 2A	FAITH	668C
23	AIRW 1A	LIFT UP	23D
	BALLW 1B	THROW	130C
	DIAKRINW 2B	WAVER	184B
	THALASSA 1A	SEA	350B
	KARDIA 13?	HEART	404D
	LALEW 2B	SPEAK	464D
	M8 A11	NOT	517C
	OROS	MOUNTAIN	586C
	HOS,H8,HO I2B«	(REL PRON)	587B
	PISTEUW 1A?	BELIEVE	666A
	PISTEUW 2C	BELIEVE	667D
24	AITEW	ASK	25C
	DIA BII2	THEREFORE	180B
	EIMI I4	TO BE	222C
	LEGW III0	ASSURE	470D
	HOSOS 2	HOW GREAT	590B
	PAS IEy	ALL	638A
	PISTEUW 1A?	BELIEVE	666A
	PROSEUCHOMAI	PRAY	721B
25	APHI8MI 2	FORGIVE	125C
	ECHW I7A	HAVE	334A
	HINA IIC	IN ORDER THAT	377C
	KATA I2By	DOWN	406D
	HOTAN 2B	WHEN	592B
	PARAPTWMA 2B	TRANSGRESSION	627B
	PAT8R 3C«	FATHER	641C
	ST8KW 1	STAND	775C
25F	OURANOS 2A	HEAVEN	599B
26	APHI8MI 2	FORGIVE	125C
	EI IIA	IF	218A
	OU 5B	NO	595A
	PARAPTWMA 2B	TRANSGRESSION	627B
27	ARCHIEREUS 1B	HIGH PRIEST	112B
	GRAMMATEUS 2	SCRIBES	165A
	PALIN 1A	BACK	611B
	PERIPATEW 1A	GO ABOUT	654D
	PRESBUTEROS 2A?	OLDER	706D
28	EXOUSIA 3	AUTHORITY	278A
	8 ID6	OR	343B
	HINA IIE	IN ORDER THAT	377C
	HINA IIIE	IN ORDER THAT	378C
	POIOS 2Ay	OF WHAT KIND	691B
	TIS, TI IA«	WHICH	826C
29	EXOUSIA 3	AUTHORITY	278A
	EPERWTAW 1A	ASK	285A
	LOGOS 1A?	WORD	478B
	POIOS 2Ay	OF WHAT KIND	691B
30	ANTHRWPOS 1A?	MAN	67C
30	BAPTISMA I	BAPTISM	132A
	EIMI III3	TO BE	224B
	EK 3B	FROM	234B
	IWAN(N)8S 1	JOHN	385B
30F	OURANOS 3	HEAVEN	599D
31	DIA BII2	WHY	180B
	DIALOGIZOMAI 1	CONSIDER	185A
	OUN IC«	THEREFORE	597B
	PISTEUW 1B	BELIEVE	666C
32	AL8THWS 1	TRULY	36D
	ECHW I5	CONSIDER	333D
	IWAN(N)8S 1	JOHN	385B
	LAOS IC«	PEOPLE	467D
	ONTWS 1	REALLY	577C
	HOTI IB6	THAT	593A
	PROPH8T8S 2	PROPHET	731A
	PHOBEW 1B«	BE AFRAID	871A
33	EXOUSIA 3	AUTHORITY	278A
	POIOS 2Ay	OF WHAT KIND	691B
33C	LEGW IIB?	SAY	469C

MARK 12

1	APOD8MEW 1	GO ON A JOURNEY	89C
	EKDIDWMI	LEASE	238A
	OIKODOMEW 1A	BUILD	560C
	ORUSSW 2	DIG	586D
	PARABOL8 2	PARABLE	617D
	PERITITH8MI 1	PLACE AROUND	658B
	PURGOS 1	TOWER	738A
	HUPOL8NION	VAT	853D
	PHRAGMOS 1	FENCE	873B
	PHUTEUW	PLANT	878A
IF	GEWRGOS 2	FARMER	156B
IFF	AMPELWN	VINEYARD	46B
2	APO I6	FROM	86B
	APOSTELLW 1By	SEND AWAY	98A
	DOULOS 1A	SLAVE	204D
	HINA I4	IN ORDER THAT	377D
	KAIROS 2	TIME	395D
	KARPOS 1A	FRUIT	405C
	LAMBANW 1D	RECEIVE	465D
	PARA I3B	FROM	614D
3	DERW	BEAT	174D
	KENOS 1	EMPTY	429A
	LAMBANW 1C	TAKE	465C
4	APOSTELLW 1B«	SEND AWAY	98A
	APOSTELLW 1B«	SEND AWAY	98A
	ATIMAZW	DISHONOR	119C
	ATIMOW	DISGRACED	119D
	DOULOS 1A	SLAVE	204D
	KEPHALAIOW	SUM UP	431A
	KEPHALIOW	STRIKE ON THE HEAD	431C
	LITHOBOLEW 1	THROW STONES	475B
4F	KAKEINOS 2B	HE ALSO	397C
5	APOSTELLW 1A	SEND AWAY	98A
	DERW	BEAT	174D
6	AGAP8TOS 1	BELOVED	6C
	APOSTELLW 1B«	SEND AWAY	98A
	HEIS 2B	ONE	230B
	ENTREPW 2B	RESPECT	269B
	ESCHATOS 3A	LAST	314A
	ETI 2A	STILL	316A

6	HUIOS 2B	SON 842C
6A	HUIOS IAα	SON 841B
7	GEWRGOS 2	FARMER 156B
	DEUTE I	COME 175D
	EIMI IVI	TO BE 224D
	EIPON I	SAY 225C
	KL8RONOMIA I	INHERITANCE 436A
	KL8RONOMOS I	HEIR 436B
	PROS IIIIE	TOWARD 716D
8	EKBALLW I	DRIVE OUT 236D
	EXW 2B	OUTSIDE 279B
	LAMBANW IC	TAKE 465C
9	APOLLUMI IAα	RUIN 94C
	GEWRGOS 2	FARMER 156B
	ERCHOMAI IIAζ	COME 310D
	KURIOS IAα	OWNER 459D
10	ANAGINWSKW I	READ 51B
	APODOKIMAZW I	DECLARE USELESS 90B
	GINOMAI I4A	BECOME 158D
	GRAPH8 2A	SCRIPTURE 165B
	GWNIA	CORNER 167D
	KEPHAL8 2B	HEAD 431C
	LITHOS 2	STONE 475D
	OIKODOMEW IBβ	BUILD 560D
	HOS,H8,HO I4D	(REL PRON) 588A
	OUDE 3	NOT EVEN 596A
11	THAUMASTOS 2	WONDERFUL 353B
	KURIOS 2A	LORD 460C
	OPHTHALMOS 2	EYE 604D
	PARA I2	FROM 614C
12	APHI8MI 3A	LEAVE 125C
	GINWSKW 3C	UNDERSTAND 160B
	EIPON I	SAY 225B
	Z8TEW 2Bγ	SEEK 339C
	KAI I2G	AND 393C
	KRATEW IA	ARREST 449C
	OCHLOS 2	CROWD 605D
	PARABOL8 2	PARABLE 617C
	PROS III5A	TOWARD 717C
	PHOBEW IBα	BE AFRAID 871A
13	AGREUW	CATCH 13A
	APOSTELLW IBγ	SEND AWAY 98A
	H8RWDIANOI	HERODIANS 349B
	LOGOS IAγ	WORD 478C
	TIS, TI IAα	ANY ONE 827C
	*PHARISAIOS	PHARISEE 861C
14	AL8THEIA 3	REALITY 35D
	AL8TH8S I	TRUE 36A
	BLEPW 5	SEE 143B
	DIDASKALOS	TEACHER 190D
	DIDWMI 4	GIVE 192D
	DOLOS	DECEIT 202C
	EXESTI I	IT IS POSSIBLE 274D
	EPI IIBβ	ON 286B
	EPIKEPHALAION	POLL TAX 294D
	ERCHOMAI IIAζ	COME 310D
8	IAα	OR 342B
	KAISAR	EMPEROR 396C
	K8NSOS	POLL TAX 431D
	MELEI 2	IT IS A CONCERN 501B
	M8 AI4	NOT 517C
	HODOS 2B	WAY 557A
	OUDEIS 2A	NO ONE 596B

14	PROSWPON ICβ	FACE 728D
15	D8NARION	DENARIUS 178B
	OIDA 4	KNOW 559A
	PEIRAZW 2C	TRY 646A
	HUPOKRISIS	HYPOCRISY 852D
	PHERW 4Aα	BEAR 863A
16	EIKWN IA	IMAGE 221B
	EPIGRAPH8	INSCRIPTION 291C
	KAISAR	EMPEROR 396C
	HOUTOS 2B	THIS 601D
	TIS, TI IAα	WHICH 826C
	PHERW 4Aα	BEAR 863A
17	APODIDWMI I	GIVE AWAY 89D
	EKTHAUMAZW	WONDER GREATLY 239D
	EPI IIIBγ	ON 287B
	THEOS 3Fγ	GOD 358B
	KAISAR	EMPEROR 396C
18	ANASTASIS 2B	RESURRECTION 60B
	EPERWTAW IA	ASK 285A
	LEGW IIIE	DECLARE 471A
	M8 AIIIBα	NOT 517D
	SADDOUKAIOS	SADDUCEE 747A
19	AUTOS 3A	(OBLIQUE CASE) 122D
	GRAPHW 2C	WRITE 166A
	DIDASKALOS	TEACHER 190D
	EXANIST8MI I	RAISE UP 272B
	HINA IIIA6	IN ORDER THAT 378B
	KATALEIPW IB	LEAVE BEHIND 414C
	M8 AII	NOT 517C
	MWUS8S	MOSES 533D
	HOTI 2	THAT 593D
	SPERMA 2B	SEED 769B
19FF	APHI8MI 3A	LEAVE 125D
19=21	LAMBANW IC	TAKE 465C
20	HEPTA	SEVEN 306B
	PRWTOS IB	FIRST 733A
	SPERMA 2B	SEED 769B
21	SPERMA 2B	SEED 769B
	TRITOS 2	THIRD 834C
	HWSAUTWS	SIMILARLY 907D
22	ESCHATOS 3B	LAST 314B
	PAS 2Aγ	ALL 638B
	SPERMA 2B	SEED 769B
22F	HEPTA	SEVEN 306B
23	ANASTASIS 2B	RESURRECTION 60B
	EN II2	WHILE 259D
	TIS, TI IAα	WHICH 826D
24	GRAPH8 2Bα	SCRIPTURE 165B
	DIA BII2	THEREFORE 180B
	M8DE IA	AND NOT 519C
	OU 4C	NO 595A
	PLANAW 2Cγ	DECEIVE 671C
25	AGGELOS 2A	ANGEL 7C
	ANIST8MI 2A	RISE 69C
	GAMEW IB	MARRY 150A
	GAMIZW I	GIVE IN MARRIAGE 150B
	GAMIZW 2	GIVE IN MARRIAGE 150B
	GAMISKW	GIVE IN MARRIAGE 150C
	NEKROS 2A	DEAD 537A
	OURANOS 2C	HEAVEN 599C
	OUTE	NOT 600C
	HWS II3B	SO 906A
26	ABRAAM	ABRAHAM 2A

26 ANAGINWSKW I   READ   51B
   BATOS   THORN BUSH 137B
   BIBLOS I   BOOK 140D
   EGEIRW 2C   RISE 214A
   EGW   I 216B
   EPI IIAY   ON 286A
   THEOS 3C   GOD 358A
   IAKWB I   JACOB 368B
   ISAAK   ISAAC 381C
   PERI IH   ABOUT 650D
   HWS I2D   AS 905D
   HWS IV4   WHEN 907B
27 ALLA IA   BUT, YET   37B
   ZAW IAα   LIVE 336C
   NEKROS 2A   DEAD 536D
   PLANAW 2CY   DECEIVE 671C
   POLUS I2Cβ   MANY 695D
28 APOKRINOMAI I   ANSWER   92D
   ENTOL8 2AY   COMMAND 268C
   KALWS 4B   WELL 402B
   PAS 2AY   ALL 638D
   POIOS 2Aα   OF WHAT KIND 691B
   PRWTOS ICα   FIRST 733B
   SUZ8TEW 2   DISCUSS 783B
28F   PRWTOS ICα   FIRST 733B
29 AKOUW IC   HEAR   31D
   THEOS 3C   GOD 358A
   ISRA8L 2   ISRAEL 382B
   HOTI 2   THAT 593D
   PRWTOS ICα   FIRST 733B
29F   KURIOS 2A   LORD 460B
30 AGAPAW IAβ   LOVE   4C
   DIANOIA I   UNDERSTANDING 186A
   EK 3GY   BY 235A
   ISCHUS   STRENGTH 384B
   KARDIA IBζ   HEART 405B
   PSUCH8 IBY   SOUL LIFE 901D
31 AGAPAW IAα   LOVE   4B
   DEUTEROS 3   SECOND 176A
   ENTOL8 2AY   COMMAND 268C
   HOMOIOS I   LIKE 569D
   PL8SION IB   NEAR 678D
   SEAUTOU 3   YOURSELF 753A
32 AL8THEIA 3   REALITY   35D
   ALLOS IEβ   ANOTHER   39C
   DIDASKALOS   TEACHER 190D
   HEIS 2B   ONE 230B
   EPI IIBβ   ON 286B
   KALWS 4C   WELL 402B
   PL8N 2   BUT 675C
33 AGAPAW IAα   LOVE   4B
   AGAPAW IAβ   LOVE   4C
   THUSIA 2A   SACRIFICE 366D
   ISCHUS   STRENGTH 384B
   KARDIA IBζ   HEART 405B
   HO,H8,TO II4A   THE 553D
   HOLOKAUTWMA I   567B
        WHOLE BURNT OFFERING
   PERISSOTEROS 2   GREATER 657B
   PL8SION IB   NEAR 678D
   SUNESIS I   INTELLIGENCE 796B
   PSUCH8 IBY   SOUL LIFE 901D
34 APOKRINOMAI I   ANSWER   92D

34 EIMI II9A   TO BE 223D
   EPERWTAW IA   ASK 284D
   MAKRAN IAβ   FAR 488D
   NOUNECHWS   WISELY 546B
   HOTI IBζ   THAT 593B
   OUDEIS 2A   NO ONE 596B
   OUKETI I   NO LONGER 597A
   TOLMAW IA   DARE 829C
35 APOKRINOMAI 2   BEGIN   93A
   DAUID   DAVID 170B
   PWS IA   HOW 739C
   CHRISTOS I   ANOINTED ONE 895B
35B   LEGW IIIE   DECLARE 471A
35=7 HUIOS 2A   SON 842A
36 DAUID   DAVID 170B
   DEXIOS 2B   RIGHT 174A
   EN I5D   IN 259C
   ECHTHROS 2Bβ   THE ENEMY 331D
   HEWS IIB   UNTIL 334D
   KATH8MAI 2   SIT DOWN 390C
   KURIOS 2Cα   LORD 460C
   PNEUMA 5Cα   SPIRIT 682D
   PNEUMA 6C   SPIRIT 683D
   POUS IB   FOOT 703C
   TITH8MI IIAβ   PUT 823D
   HUPOKATW   UNDER 852C
   HUPOPODION   FOOTSTOOL 854D
36F   AUTOS IAα   SELF 122B
36F   DAUID   DAVID 170B
37 H8DEWS   GLADLY 344C
   KURIOS 2Cα   LORD 460C
   LEGW II3   CALL 471A
   OCHLOS I   CROWD 605C
   POTHEN 3   FROM WHERE 686D
   POLUS IIBα   MANY 694C
38 AGORA   MARKET PLACE 12B
   ASPASMOS I   GREETING 116D
   BLEPW 6   SEE 143B
   DIDACH8 I   TEACHING 191B
   EN I4B   IN 258B
   EN II3   WHILE 259D
   THELW 4A   WISH 356A
   PERIPATEW IB   GO ABOUT 654D
   STOL8   ROBE 777B
39 DEIPNON 2   DINNER 172B
   PRWTOKATHEDRIA PLACE OF HONOR 732C
   PRWTOKLISIA   PLACE OF HONOR 732C
40 KATESTHIW 2   DESTROY 423B
   KRIMA 4B   VERDICT 451D
   LAMBANW 2   RECEIVE 466C
   MAKROS I   LONG 489C
   OIKIA IA   HOUSE 560A
  *ORPHANOS I   ORPHANED 586D
   HOUTOS IAε   THIS 601B
   PERISSOTEROS I   GREATER 657B
   PROSEUCHOMAI   PRAY 721A
   PROPHASIS 2   ACTUAL MOTIVE 730A
   CH8RA   THE WIDOW 889D
41 APENANTI IA   OPPOSITE   83B
   GAZOPHULAKEION   TREASURY 148D
   THEWREW I   OBSERVE 360C
   KATHIZW 2Aα   SIT DOWN 391A
   KATENANTI 2A   OPPOSITE 422B

```
41  PLOUSIOS I              RICH 679C
    POLUS IIAα              MANY 694A
    PWS 2A                  HOW 739D
    CHALKOS 2               COPPER 883B
41FF BALLW 2B               PUT 130D
42  HEIS 3B                 SOMEONE 230D
    ERCHOMAI IIAʃ           COME 310D
    KODRANT8S               PENNY 438A
    LEPTOS 2   SMALL COPPER COIN 473B
    HOS,H8,HO I7A      (REL PRON) 588C
    PTWCHOS IA     BEGGING POOR 735C
42F CH8RA              THE WIDOW 889D
43  GAZOPHULAKEION     TREASURY 148D
    PAS 2Aγ                 ALL 638B
    POLUS II2C             MANY 696A
    PTWCHOS IA     BEGGING POOR 735C
44  BALLW 2B                PUT 130D
    BIOS 3                 LIFE 141B
    ECHW I2A               HAVE 332B
    HOSOS 2           HOW GREAT 590B
    PERISSEUW IAβ  BE LEFT OVER 656C
    HUSTER8SIS             NEED 857B
44B    PAS IEγ              ALL 638A
45  GENEA 2          GENERATION 153B

            MARK 13

I   DIDASKALOS          TEACHER 190D
    EKPOREUOMAI IB       GO OUT 243D
    IDE I                   SEE 369D
    HIERON 2             TEMPLE 373A
IA     POTAPOS        WHAT SORT 701C
IB     POTAPOS        WHAT SORT 701C
IF     LITHOS IB         STONE 475B
IF     OIKODOM8 2A    BUILDING 561C
2   ANEU 2             WITHOUT 65A
    ANIST8MI 2E            RISE 69D
    APHI8MI 3A           LEAVE 125D
    BLEPW IA                SEE 142D
    KATALUW IA      THROW DOWN 415B
    MEGAS IA              LARGE 498C
    M8  DIA                 NOT 519B
3   ANDREAS             ANDREW 63B
    EIS 9A                   IN 229D
    ELAIA I         OLIVE TREE 247B
    IAKWBOS I             JAMES 368B
    IDIOS 4          PRIVATELY 371A
    HIERON 2             TEMPLE 373A
    KATH8MAI IAα            SIT 390B
    KATENANTI 2A      OPPOSITE 422B
    PETROS                PETER 660D
4   MELLW ICα      BE ABOUT TO 502B
    POTE                   WHEN 701D
    S8MEION I              SIGN 755B
    SUNTELEW I         COMPLETE 799D
    SUNTELEW 2         COMPLETE 800A
5   BLEPW 6                 SEE 143B
    M8  BIB                 NOT 519A
    TIS, TI IAγ         ANY ONE 827D
5F     PLANAW IB         DECEIVE 671B
6   EGW                       I 216B
    EIMI II5              TO BE 223C
    EPI II3                  ON 287D
```

```
6   ERCHOMAI IIAθ          COME 311B
    ONOMA I4Cε             NAME 576C
    HOTI 2                 THAT 593D
7   AK08 2A              REPORT 30C
    DEI I       IT IS NECESSARY 171A
    THORUBEW 2      BE TROUBLED 363C
    THROEW        BE DISTURBED 364C
    OUPW               NOT YET 597D
    POLEMOS IA   ARMED CONFLICT 691D
    TELOS IB               END 819A
8   ARCH8 IB        BEGINNING 111B
    BASILEIA 2        KINGDOM 134C
    EGEIRW 2D            RISE 214A
    ETHNOS I            NATION 217B
    EPI IIIIAε         AGAINST 288B
    KATA IIIA           ALONG 407A
    LIMOS 2            FAMINE 476B
    SEISMOS           SHAKING 753D
    TARACH8 2B    DISTURBANCE 813B
    TOPOS ID            PLACE 830B
    WDIN 2B        BIRTH PAIN 904A
9   BASILEUS I            KING 135C
    BLEPW 6               SEE 143B
    DERW                 BEAT 174D
    EIS 9A                 IN 229D
   *HENEKA        BECAUSE OF 264B
    EPI IIAδ           BEFORE 286A
    H8GEMWN 2        GOVERNORS 344A
    HIST8MI IIIB         STAND 383B
    MARTURION IA     TESTIMONY 494D
    PARADIDWMI IB    GIVE OVER 620A
    SUNAGWG8 2A                790C
         PLACE OF ASSEMBLY
    SUNEDRION 3      SANHEDRIN 794A
10  DEI I       IT IS NECESSARY 171A
    ETHNOS I            NATION 217B
    EIS IDβ                 IN 227D
    EUAGGELION IC       GOSPEL 318B
    K8RUSSW 2Bβ       ANNOUNCE 432C
    PRWTOS 2A            FIRST 733C
11  AGW 2            LEAD AWAY 14B
    LALEW 2B             SPEAK 464D
    MELETAW 3    MEDITATE UPON 501C
    HOTAN IA              WHEN 592A
    PARADIDWMI IB    GIVE OVER 619D
    PNEUMA 5Cα           SPIRIT 682D
    PROMERIMNAW  CONCERN ONESELF 715C
    HWRA 3        TIME OF DAY 905A
12  GONEUS             PARENTS 164B
    EPANIST8MI         RISE UP 282D
    EPI IIIIAε         AGAINST 288B
    THANATOS IBα         DEATH 351C
    THANATOW I     PUT TO DEATH 352B
    PARADIDWMI IB    GIVE OVER 620B
12A    TEKNON IAα        CHILD 815D
12B    TEKNON IAα        CHILD 816A
13  EIMI II4Bγ           TO BE 223A
    EIS 2Aα              UNTIL 227D
    MISEW 3               HATE 524D
    ONOMA I4Cα            NAME 575C
    SWZW 2B               SAVE 806B
    TELOS IDγ              END 819D
    HUPOMENW 2          REMAIN 853C
```

14 ANAGINWSKW 1   READ 51B
   BDELUGMA 3   ABOMINATION 137C
   DANI8L   DANIEL 169D
   EIS 1Aα   INTO 227B
   ER8MWSIS   DEVASTATION 309B
   IOUDAIA 1   JUDAEA 379D
   HIST8MI II2Bα   BEING 383C
   NOEW 2   CONSIDER 542D
   HOPOU 1Aα   WHERE 579C
   OROS   MOUNTAIN 586C
   HOTAN 1B   WHEN 592B
   TOTE 2   AT THAT TIME 831D
   PHEUGW 1   FLEE 863C
15 AIRW 3   CARRY 24A
   DWMA   ROOF 209C
   EISERCHOMAI 1A6   COME 232A
   KATABAINW 1Aα   COME DOWN 409B
   KATABAINW 1A6   COME DOWN 409C
   M8 AIII4   NOT 518D
   M8DE 1B   AND NOT 519D
   TIS, TI 1Bα   ANY ONE 828A
16 AGROS 1   FIELD 13D
   EIS 9A   IN 229D
   EPISTREPHW 1Bα   TURN 301A
   HO,H8,TO II6   THE 554B
   OPISW 1A   BEHIND 578C
17 GAST8R 2   WOMB 152A
   ECHW I2J   HAVE 333C
   TH8LAZW 1   GIVE SUCK 361A
   OUAI 1A   WOE 595C
18 PROSEUCHOMAI   PRAY 721A
   PHUG8   FLIGHT 875C
   CHEIMWN 2   WINTER 888A
19 ARCH8 1C   BEGINNING 111D
   GINOMAI II8β   COME ABOUT 157B
   HEWS III1A   UNTIL 335B
   THEOS 3A   GOD 357D
   THLIPSIS 1   TRIBULATION 363A
   KTIZW   CREATE 456C
   KTISIS 18β   CREATION 457A
   NUN 3B   NOW 548B
   HOIOS   OF WHAT SORT 565C
   HOS,H8,HO I4E   (REL PRON) 588B
   TOIOUTOS 2B   SUCH A KIND 829B
20 EI II1A   IF 218A
   EKLEGOMAI 2A   CHOOSE 241D
   EKLEKTOS 1B   CHOSEN 242B
   KURIOS 2A   LORD 460B
   M8 AII   NOT 517C
   PAS 1Aα   EVERY EACH 636D
   SARX 3   BODY 751B
   SWZW 1A   SAVE 805D
20A KOLOBOW 2   SHORTEN 442D
20B KOLOBOW 2   SHORTEN 442D
21 IDE 3   SEE 369D
   PISTEUW 1D   BELIEVE 660D
   TOTE 2   AT THAT TIME 831D
   CHRISTOS 1   ANOINTED ONE 895B
   HWDE 2A   HERE 903D
22 DUNATOS 2A   POSSIBLE 208A
   EGEIRW 2E   APPEAR 214B
   EKLEKTOS 1B   CHOSEN 242B
   PROS III3A   TOWARD 717A

22 PROS III5E   TOWARD 717D
   S8MEION 2B   SIGN 755D
   PSEUDOPROPH8T8S   FALSE PROPHET 900B
   PSEUDOCHRISTOS   FALSE MESSIAH 900C
23 PROEIPON 1   FORETELL 711C
24 DIDWMI 1Bγ   GIVE 192C
   H8LIOS   THE SUN 346B
   THLIPSIS 1   TRIBULATION 363A
   META BII3   AFTER 511C
   SEL8N8   MOON 754B
   SKOTIZW 1   BECOME DARK 764D
   PHEGGOS   LIGHT 862C
25 AST8R   STAR 117B
   DUNAMIS 5   RESOURCES 207B
   PIPTW 1A   FALL 665A
   SALEUW 1   SHAKE 747D
25A OURANOS 1C   HEAVEN 598C
25B OURANOS 1C   HEAVEN 598D
26 DOXA 1A   GLORY 202D
   ERCHOMAI IIAη   COME 311A
   META AIII2   WITH 511A
   NEPHEL8   CLOUD 538D
   HORAW 1Aα   SEE 581C
   POLUS IIBβ   MANY 694C
   HUIOS 2C   SON 843A
26F TOTE 2   AT THAT TIME 831D
27 AKRON   TOP 33C
   ANEMOS 1B   WIND 64B
   APO III   FROM 86B
   EKLEKTOS 1B   CHOSEN 242B
   EPISUNAGW   GATHER 301D
   HEWS II2A   AS FAR AS 335D
   OURANOS 1Aβ   HEAVEN 598B
   TESSARES   FOUR 821A
28 HAPALOS   TENDER 79C
   APO IV2B   FROM 87A
   GINOMAI I4B   BECOME 158D
   EGGUS 2A   NEAR 213B
   EIMI II9A   TO BE 223D
   EKPHUW   PUT FORTH 246C
   8D8 1B   ALREADY 344D
   THEROS   SUMMER 360B
   KLADOS   BRANCH 434A
   MANTHANW 1   LEARN 491C
   HOTAN 1B   WHEN 592A
   PARABOL8 2   PARABLE 617D
   SUK8   FIG TREE 783D
   PHULLON   FOLIAGE 877A
28F GINWSKW 3C   UNDERSTAND 160B
28F GINWSKW 6C   KNOW 160D
29 EGGUS 3   NEAR 213C
   EIMI III5B   TO BE 224C
   EPI III1A6   AT 286D
   THURA 2A   DOOR 366C
   HOUTW 1B   THUS 602C
30 GENEA 1   CLAN 153B
   GENEA 2   GENERATION 153B
   MECHRI 2   UNTIL 517B
   HOS,H8,HO IIIF   (REL PRON) 589A
   PARERCHOMAI 1Bα   PASS AWAY 631C
31 LOGOS 1A6   WORD 478D
   OURANOS 1Aα   HEAVEN 598B
31A PARERCHOMAI 1Bα   631C
   PASS AWAY

31B	PARERCHOMAI 1Bα		631C
	PASS AWAY		
32	AGGELOS 2A	ANGEL	7C
	OIDA 1H	KNOW	558C
	OUDE 3	NOT EVEN	596A
	OURANOS 2C	HEAVEN	599C
	PAT8R 3Dα	FATHER	641D
	PERI 1H	ABOUT	650D
	HUIOS 2B	SON	842C
	HWRA 1	TIME OF DAY	904B
33	AGRUPNEW 1	BE AWAKE	14A
	BLEPW 4A	SEE	143B
	KAIROS 4	TIME	396B
	OIDA 1F	KNOW	558C
	POTE	WHEN	701D
34	APOD8MOS		89D
	A MAN ON A JOURNEY		
	APHI8MI 3A	ABANDON	125D
	GR8GOREW 1	BE AWAKE	166C
	DOULOS 1A	SLAVE	204D
	ENTELLW	COMMAND	268A
	EXOUSIA 3	AUTHORITY	278A
	ERGON 2	WORK	308B
	THURWROS 1	DOORKEEPER	366D
	HINA III1A6	IN ORDER THAT	378B
	OIKIA 1A	HOUSE	559D
35	ALEXTOROPHWNIA	CROWING	34D
	GR8GOREW 2	BE AWAKE	166C
	8 1Dγ	OR	343A
	KURIOS 1Aα	OWNER	459D
	MESONUKTION	MIDNIGHT	508B
	OIDA 1F	KNOW	558C
	OIKIA 1A	HOUSE	560A
	OUN 1B	THEREFORE	597B
	OPSE 2	LATE IN THE DAY	606B
	POTE	WHEN	701D
	PRWI	EARLY	732A
	PHULAK8 4	GUARD	875D
36	EXAIPHN8S	SUDDENLY	271D
	HEURISKW 1Cα	FIND	325C
	KATHEUDW 1	SLEEP	389C
	M8 B2	NOT	519A
37	GR8GOREW 2	BE AWAKE	166C
	LEGW III1C	ORDER	470D

MARK 14

1	AZUMOS 1B	UNLEAVENED BREAD	19C
	ARCHIEREUS 1B	HIGH PRIEST	112B
	GRAMMATEUS 2	SCRIBES	165A
	DOLOS	DECEIT	202C
	Z8TEW 1C	INVESTIGATE	339B
	KRATEW 1A	ARREST	449C
	META 8III	AFTER	511B
	PASCHA 1	THE PASSOVER	639A
	PWS 2B	HOW	740A
2	EIMI I4	TO BE	222B
	HEORT8	FESTIVAL	279D
	THORUBOS 3B	NOISE	363C
	LAOS 1Cα	PEOPLE	467D
	M8 AIII6	NOT	519A
	M8POTE 2Bγ	(NEG PARTICLE)	521B
3	ALABASTROS	ALABASTER	33D

3	B8THANIA 1	BETHANY	139B
	ECHW II A	HAVE	332A
	ECHW III	BE	334B
	THRAUW 1	BREAK	363D
	KATAKEIMAI 3	LIE DOWN	412B
	KATACHEW	POUR OUT	421D
	KEPHAL8 1A	HEAD	431A
	LEPROS	LEPER	473A
	MURON	OINTMENT	531D
	NARDOS 2	PERFUME OF NARD	536A
	OIKIA 1A	HOUSE	559D
	PISTIKOS 3	FAITHFUL	668A
	POLUTEL8S	COSTLY	696C
	SIMWN 6	SIMON	758D
	SUNTRIBW 1A	SHATTER	801A
4	AGANAKTEW	BE AROUSED	4B
	APWLEIA 1	DESTRUCTION	103A
	DIAPONEOMAI	BE DISTURBED	186D
	EIS 4F	(PURPOSE)	228D
4F	MURON	OINTMENT	531D
5	D8NARION	DENARIUS	178B
	EMBRIMAOMAI	SCOLD	254B
	EPANW 1B	MORE THAN	283A
	PIPRASKW	SELL	664D
	PTWCHOS 1A	BEGGING POOR	735D
	TRIAKOSIOI	THREE HUNDRED	833D
6	APHI8MI 4	TOLERATE	125D
	EN I2	IN	258A
	ERGAZOMAI 2A	WORK	307A
	ERGON 1C8	DEED	308A
	KALOS 2B	GOOD	401B
	KOPOS 1	TROUBLE	444C
	PARECHW 1C	CAUSE	632A
7	EU	WELL	317B
	ECHW I3	HAVE	333C
	META AIII8	WITH	509D
	HOTAN 1A	WHEN	592A
	POIEW I2A8	DO	689A
	PTWCHOS 1A	BEGGING POOR	735C
7A	PANTOTE	ALWAYS	614A
7B	PANTOTE	ALWAYS	614A
8	ENTAPHIASMOS		267D
	PREPARATION FOR BURIAL		
	ECHW I6A	CAN	334A
	MURIZW	ANOINT	531C
	PROLAMBANW 1A	TAKE BEFORE	715A
	SWMA 1B	BODY	806D
9	EIS 1D8	IN	227D
	EIS 4F	(PURPOSE)	228D
	EUAGGELION 1C	GOSPEL	318B
	K8RUSSW 2B8	ANNOUNCE	432C
	KOSMOS 4A	WORLD	447A
	LALEW 2B	SPEAK	464D
	MN8MOSUNON 2	MEMORY	527B
	HOPOU 1A6	WHERE	579D
	POIEW I1B	DO	687D
10	HEIS 1A8	ONE	230A
	ECHW III	BE	334B
	HINA IIE	IN ORDER THAT	377C
	IOUDAS 6	JUDAS	380D
	ISKARIWTH	ISCARIOT	381D
	PARADIDWMI	GIVE OVER	619C
	PARADIDWMI 1B	GIVE OVER	620A

10	PRODIDWMI 2	GIVE IN ADVANCE	711B
11	ARGURION 2B	MONEY	104B
	DIDWMI 4	GIVE	192C
	EPAGGELLOMAI 1A	ANNOUNCE	280C
	EUKAIRWS	CONVENIENTLY	321D
	Z8TEW 1C	INVESTIGATE	339B
	PARADIDWMI	GIVE OVER	619C
	PARADIDWMI 1B	GIVE OVER	620A
	PWS 2B	HOW	740A
	CHAIRW 1	REJOICE	881D
12	AZUMOS 1B	UNLEAVENED BREAD	19C
	ESTHIW 1⌐	EAT	312D
	HETOIMAZW 1	PREPARE	316B
	THELW 1	WISH	355C
	THUW 2	SACRIFICE	367D
	THUW 4	CELEBRATE	367D
	HOTE 1A	WHEN	592B
	PASCHA 1	THE PASSOVER	639A
	POU 1A	WHERE	702D
12A	PASCHA 2	THE PASCHAL LAMB	639A
12B	PASCHA 2	THE PASCHAL LAMB	639A
13	AKOLOUTHEW 1	FOLLOW	30C
	APANTAW	MEET	79D
	BASTAZW 2A	CARRY	136D
	ECHW III	BE	334B
	KERAMION	JAR	430A
	POLIS 1	CITY	692A
	HUDWR 1	WATER	840C
	HUPAGW 2	GO AWAY	844C
14	DIDASKALOS	TEACHER	190D
	EISERCHOMAI 1H	COME	232B
	ESTHIW 1A	EAT	312D
	KATALUMA	GUEST ROOM	415B
	LEGW IIIA	ASK	470C
	META AII2	WITH	510C
	OIKODESPOT8S		560C
	MASTER OF THE HOUSE		
	PASCHA 2	THE PASCHAL LAMB	639A
	POU 1A	WHERE	702D
14A	HOPOU 1A6	WHERE	579D
14B	HOPOU 1Ay	WHERE	579D
15	ANAGAION	ROOM UPSTAIRS	50D
	DEIKNUMI 1A	SHOW	171D
	HETOIMAZW 1	PREPARE	316B
	HETOIMOS 1	READY	316D
	KAKEI 1	AND THERE	397C
	MEGAS 1B	LARGE	498C
	STRWNNUW	SPREAD	779B
16	EIPON 3E	FORETELL	225D
	HETOIMAZW 1	PREPARE	316B
	HEURISKW 1Cy	FIND	325C
	PASCHA 3	PASSOVER MEAL	639A
	POLIS 1	CITY	692A
17	GINOMAI IIBy	COME ABOUT	157C
	META AIIIA	WITH	509D
	OPSIOS 2	LATE	606C
18	ANAKEIMAI 2	BE AT TABLE	55C
	HEIS 1A8	ONE	230A
	ESTHIW 1C	EAT	313A
	META AII2	WITH	510C
	PARADIDWMI 1B	GIVE OVER	620A
18A	ESTHIW 1D	EAT	313A
19	HEIS 5E	ONE	231B
19	KATA II3A	(DISTRIBUTIVE)	407D
	LUPEW 2B	BE GRIEVED	483A
	M8TI	(INTERROG PARTICLE)	522A
20	EMBAPTIZW	DIP	253C
	EMBAPTW	DIP	253C
	TRUBLION	BOWL	836A
21	GENNAW 2	BEAR	154D
	GRAPHW 2C	WRITE	166A
	KATHWS 1	JUST AS	392A
	*KALOS 3C	GOOD	401D
	MEN 1A⍺	(PARTICLE)	503D
	OU 5B	NO	595A
	OUAI 1A	WOE	595C
	PARADIDWMI 1B	GIVE OVER	620A
	HUPAGW 3	GO AWAY	844D
21A	HUIOS 2C	SON	843A
21B	HUIOS 2C	SON	843A
22	ARTOS 1C	BREAD	110B
	EIMI II3	TO BE	223A
	ESTHIW 1D	EAT	313A
	EULOGEW 1	SPEAK WELL	322C
	EULOGEW 2B	BLESS	322D
	KLAW	BREAK	434D
	HOUTOS 1A⍺	THIS	600D
	SWMA 1B	BODY	807B
22A	LAMBANW 1A	TAKE	465B
22B	LAMBANW 1A	TAKE	465B
22F	DIDWMI 2	GIVE	192C
23	EK 1A	AWAY FROM	233C
	EUCHARISTEW 2	GIVE THANKS	328C
	PINW 1	DRINK	664C
	POT8RION 1	CUP	702A
24	HAIMA 2B	BLOOD	22C
	DIATH8K8 2	COVENANT	182B
	EKCHEW 1	POUR OUT	246D
	KAINOS 3B	NEW	395A
	HOUTOS 1A⍺	THIS	600D
	HUPER 1A∊	IN BEHALF OF	846C
25	AMPELOS 1	VINE	46A
	BASILEIA 3G	KINGDOM	135B
	GEN8MA	PRODUCT	154B
	EK 4A∊	FROM	235B
	HEWS IIIA	UNTIL	335A
	KAINOS 3B	NEW	395B
	HOTAN 1A	WHEN	592A
	OUKETI 1	NO LONGER	597A
	PROSTITH8MI 1C	ADD	726C
25A	PINW 1	DRINK	664B
26	ELAIA 1	OLIVE TREE	247B
	EXERCHOMAI 1A∊	GO OUT	274B
	OROS	MOUNTAIN	586B
	HUMNEW 2	SING THE PRAISE OF	844A
27	GRAPHW 2C	WRITE	165D
	DIASKORPIZW	SCATTER	187B
	PATASSW 1C	STRIKE DOWN	640B
	POIM8N 1	SHEPHERD	690C
	PROBATON 1	SHEEP	710A
	SKANDALIZW 1A	CAUSE TO FALL	760B
28	EGEIRW 2C	RISE	214A
	META BII4A	AFTER	511D
	PROAGW 2B	LEAD	709A
29	ALLA 4	BUT, YET	38A
	EI II1A	IF	218⌐

29	SKANDALIZW IA	CAUSE TO FALL	760B
	PH8MI IBα	SAY	864A
30	ALEKTWR	COCK	34D
	DIS	TWICE	198D
	8 2Dα	BEFORE	343C
	NUX IC	NIGHT	548D
	HOUTOS 2B	THIS	602A
	PRIN IB	BEFORE	708A
	S8MERON	TODAY	756C
	SU IC	YOU	779D
	TRIS	THRICE	834A
	PHWNEW IA	PRODUCE A SOUND	878B
30F	APARNEOMAI	DENY	80B
31	DE 4A	BUT, AND	170D
	DEI 4	IT IS NECESSARY	171B
	EKPERISSWS	EXCESSIVELY	243A
	LEGW I5	SAY	469D
	SUNAPOTHN8SKW	DIE WITH	792C
	HWSAUTWS	SIMILARLY	907D
32	GETHS8MANI	GETHSEMANE	152D
	HEWS IIB	UNTIL	334D
	HEWS I2B	UNTIL	335A
	KATHIZW 2Aα	SIT DOWN	390D
	ONOMA II	NAME	574A
	CHWRION I	PLACE	898C
	HWDE 2A	HERE	903D
33	AD8MONEW	TROUBLED	16C
	EKTHAMBEW	BE AMAZED	239D
	IAKWBOS I	JAMES	368B
	META AIIIB	WITH	509D
	PARALAMBANW I	TAKE	625A
	PETROS	PETER	660D
34	GR8GOREW I	BE AWAKE	166C
	HEWS II4	AS MANY AS	336C
	THANATOS IA	DEATH	351C
	MENW IAα	REMAIN	504D
	PERILUPOS	VERY SAD	654B
	PSUCH8 IBγ	SOUL LIFE	901D
	PSUCH8 IF	SOUL LIFE	902C
35	G8 2	GROUND	156C
	DUNATOS 2A	POSSIBLE	208A
	EPI IIAβ	ON	285D
	HINA IIIAγ	IN ORDER THAT	378B
	MIKROS 3D	SHORT	523C
	PARERCHOMAI IBγ	PASS AWAY	631C
	PIPTW IBα	FALL	665B
	PROERCHOMAI I	GO FORWARD	712B
	PROSERCHOMAI I	APPROACH	720A
	HWRA 3	TIME OF DAY	905A
36	ABBA	FATHER	1B
	ALLA IB	BUT, YET	37D
	ALLA 2	BUT, YET	38A
	DUNATOS 2B	POSSIBLE	208A
	THELW I	WISH	355B
	PARAPHERW 2C	TAKE AWAY	628D
	PAT8R 3Dα	FATHER	641D
	PL8N IB	BUT	675B
	POT8RION 2	CUP	702B
	SU IA	YOU	779D
	TIS, TI IBζ	WHICH	827B
37	GR8GOREW I	BE AWAKE	166C
	ERCHOMAI IIAζ	COME	310D
	HEURISKW ICα	FIND	325C

37	ISCHUW 2B	BE STRONG	384C
	KATHEUDW I	SLEEP	389C
	HWRA 2Aα	TIME OF DAY	904C
38	ASTHEN8S IB	SICK	115B
	GR8GOREW 2	BE AWAKE	166C
	ERCHOMAI I2C	COME	311C
	PEIRASMOS 2B	TEST	646C
	PNEUMA 3B	SPIRIT	681C
	PROTHUMOS	READY	713C
	PROSEUCHOMAI	PRAY	721A
	SARX 7	BODY	751D
39	AUTOS 4A	THE SAME	123B
	LOGOS IAβ	WORD	478B
	PALIN IA	BACK	611B
40	APOKRINOMAI I	ANSWER	92D
	BAREW	BURDEN	133A
	HEURISKW ICα	FIND	325C
	KATABARUNW	FELL SHUT	410A
	OIDA IF	KNOW	558C
	HUPOSTREPHW	RETURN	855B
40F	KATHEUDW I	SLEEP	389C
41	HAMARTWLOS 2	SINNER	43D
	ANAPAUW 2	REST	58C
	APECHW I	RECEIVE IN FULL	84B
	IDOU IC	REMEMBER	371D
	LOIPOS 3Aα	THE REST	481B
	PARADIDWMI IB	GIVE OVER	620A
	TRITOS 3	THIRD	834C
	HUIOS 2C	SON	843A
	HWRA 3	TIME OF DAY	905A
41B	ERCHOMAI IIBα	COME	311B
42	AGW 5	GO	14C
	EGGIZW 5A	APPROACH	212D
	EGEIRW 2F	APPEAR	214B
	PARADIDWMI IB	GIVE OVER	620A
43	ARCHIEREUS IB	HIGH PRIEST	112B
	GRAMMATEUS 2	SCRIBES	165A
	ETI IAβ	STILL	315D
	IOUDAS 6	JUDAS	380D
	ISKARIWTH	ISCARIOT	381D
	LALEW 2Aγ	SPEAK	464B
	MACHAIRA I	SWORD	497B
	META AIII3	WITH	511B
	XULON 2B	THE POLE	551B
	PARA II	FROM	614C
	PRESBUTEROS 2Aβ	OLDER	706D
44	APAGW 2B	BRING BEFORE	78D
	ASPHALWS I	SECURELY	118D
	DIDWMI	GIVE	191D
	KRATEW IA	ARREST	449C
	PARADIDWMI IB	GIVE OVER	620A
	SUSS8MON	SIGNAL	802B
	PHILEW 2	LOVE LIKE	867A
45	ERCHOMAI IIAζ	COME	310D
	KATAPHILEW	KISS	421B
	LEGW I8D	SAY	470C
	PROSERCHOMAI I	APPROACH	720A
	RABBI	RABBI	740B
46	EPIBALLW IB	LAY ON	289D
	KRATEW IA	ARREST	449C
47	APHAIREW I	CUT OFF	123D
	DOULOS IA	SLAVE	204D
	HEIS 3C	SOMEONE	231A

47	MACHAIRA I	SWORD	497B
	PAIW I	STRIKE	610B
	PARIST8MI 2Bα	BE PRESENT	633D
	SPAW	DRAW	768B
	WTARION	THE EAR	908C
	WTION	THE EAR	908D
48	EXERCHOMAI IAε	GO OUT	274B
	EPI IIIιA6	TO	288B
	L8ST8S 2	REVOLUTIONARY	474C
	MACHAIRA I	SWORD	497B
	META AIII3	WITH	511B
	XULON 2B	THE POLE	551B
	SULLAMBANW IAα	SEIZE	784B
49	GRAPH8 2Bα	SCRIPTURE	165B
	H8MERA 2	DAY	347B
	HIERON 2	TEMPLE	373A
	HINA IIII	IN ORDER THAT	379A
	KATA II2C	EVERY	407C
	KRATEW IA	ARREST	449C
	PL8ROW 4A	MAKE FULL	677C
	PROS III7	TOWARD	718A
50	APHI8MI 3A	ABANDON	125D
	PHEUGW I	FLEE	863C
51	GUMNOS I	NAKED	166D
	HEIS 3C	SOMEONE	230D
	EPI IIAα	ON	285D
	KRATEW IA	ARREST	449C
	NEANISKOS I	YOUTH	536C
	PERIBALLW IBα	THROW AROUND	651D
	SUNAKOLOUTHEW	FOLLOW	791C
51B	NEANISKOS 2	SERVANT	536C
51F	SINDWN 2	LINEN	759B
52	GUMNOS I	NAKED	166D
	KATALEIPW 2D	LEAVE BEHIND	414D
	PHEUGW I	FLEE	863C
	PHEUGW 2	FLEE	863C
53	APAGW 2A	LEAD AWAY	78D
	ARCHIEREUS IB	HIGH PRIEST	112B
	GRAMMATEUS 2	SCRIBES	165A
	PRESBUTEROS 2Aβ	OLDER	706D
	*SUNERCHOMAI IA	ASSEMBLE	795D
54	AUL8 I	COURTYARD	120D
	ESW I	IN	314B
	HEWS II2B	AS FAR AS	335D
	THERMAINW	WARM ONESELF	360B
	MAKROTHEN	FROM FAR AWAY	489A
	META AI	WITH	509C
	PROS III7	TOWARD	718A
	SUGKATH8MAI	SIT WITH	780D
	HUP8RET8S	SERVANT	850C
	PHWS IBα	LIGHT	879D
55	ARCHIEREUS IB	HIGH PRIEST	112C
	EIS 4F	(PURPOSE)	229A
	HEURISKW IA	FIND	325A
	Z8TEW 2A	SEEK	339C
	THANATOW I	PUT TO DEATH	352B
	KATA I2Bβ	DOWN	406C
	MARTURIA 2A	TESTIMONY	494C
	SUNEDRION 2	SANHEDRIN	794A
56	ISOS	EQUAL	381D
	MARTURIA 2A	TESTIMONY	494C
56F	KATA I2Bβ	DOWN	406D
56F	PSEUDOMARTUREW		900A
	BEAR FALSE WITNESS		
57	ANIST8MI 2A	RISE	69C
	ANIST8MI 2C	RISE	69D
58	AKOUW IC	HEAR	31C
	ANIST8MI IC	RAISE	69B
	ACHEIROPOI8TOS		127D
	NOT MADE BY HAND		
	DIA AIIIB	DURING	178D
	EGW	I	216A
	H8MERA 2	DAY	347A
	KATALUW IBα	DESTROY	415B
	NAOS IA	TEMPLE	535B
	OIKODOMEW IA	BUILD	560C
	CHEIROPOI8TOS		889A
	MADE BY HUMAN HANDS		
59	ISOS	EQUAL	381D
	MARTURIA 2A	TESTIMONY	494C
	HOUTW IB	THUS	602B
60*	ANIST8MI 2A	RISE	69C
	EIS IAα	INTO	227B
	KATAMARTUREW	TESTIFY AGAINST	415D
	MESOS 2	THE MIDDLE	508D
60F	ARCHIEREUS IB	HIGH PRIEST	112B
60F	EPERWTAW IB	ASK	285A
60F	OUDEIS 2Bα	NOTHING	596C
61	APOKRINOMAI I	ANSWER	92D
	EULOG8TOS	BLESSED	323A
	SIGAW IA	BE SILENT	757A
	SIWPAW I	BE SILENT	760A
	CHRISTOS I	ANOINTED ONE	895B
62	DEXIOS 2B	RIGHT	174A
	DUNAMIS I	POWER	206C
	EIMI II5	TO BE	223C
	KATH8MAI IAα	SIT	390B
	NEPHEL8	CLOUD	538D
	HORAW IAα	SEE	581C
	OURANOS ID	HEAVEN	598D
	HUIOS 2C	SON	843A
63	ARCHIEREUS IB	HIGH PRIEST	112B
	DIA(R)R8GNUMI I	TEAR	187A
	ETI IBβ	STILL	316A
	LEGW I8D	SAY	470C
	MARTUS I	WITNESS	495B
	CHITWN	SHIRT	890C
	CHREIA I	NEED	893B
64	AKOUW IBγ	HEAR	31C
	BLASPH8MIA 2B	SLANDER	142C
	ENOCHOS 2Bα	SUBJECT TO	267B
	THANATOS IBα	DEATH	351C
	KATAKRINW	CONDEMN	413B
	PAS 2Bα	IN ALL RESPECTS	638C
	PHAINW 2G	APPEAR	860A
65	KOLAPHIZW I	STRIKE	441D
	LAMBANW IEα	RECEIVE	465D
	PERIKALUPTW	COVER	653C
	PROSWPON IA	FACE	728C
	PROPH8TEUW 2	PROPHESY	730C
	RAPISMA	BLOW WITH A CLUB	741D
	TIS, TI IAα	ANY ONE	827C
	HUP8RET8S	SERVANT	850C
66	AUL8 I	COURTYARD	120D
	KATW I	BELOW	426A

66	PAIDISK8	MAID 609B
67	EMBLEPW 1	LOOK AT 254A
	THERMAINW	WARM ONESELF 360B
	LEGW 18D	SAY 470C
	META AIIICα	WITH 510A
	NAZAR8NOS	THE NAZARENE 534A
68	ARNEOMAI 3A	DENY 107C
	EXERCHOMAI 1Aα	GO OUT 274A
	EXERCHOMAI 1Aε	GO OUT 274B
	EXW 1B	OUTSIDE 279A
	EPISTAMAI 1	UNDERSTAND 300A
	LEGW 12B	SAY 469D
	OUTE	NOT 600C
	PROAULION	FORECOURT 709C
	SU 1D	YOU 780A
	PHWNEW 1A	PRODUCE A SOUND 878B
69	PAIDISK8	MAID 609B
69F	EIMI III3	TO BE 224B
69F	EK 4A6	FROM 235B
69F	PARIST8MI 28α	BE PRESENT 633D
70	AL8THWS 1	TRULY 36D
	ARNEOMAI 3A	DENY 107C
	GALILAIOS	GALILEAN 149D
	META BII3	AFTER 511C
	MIKROS 3E	A LITTLE WHILE 523C
	HOMOIAZW	BE LIKE 569C
71	ANATHEMATIZW 2	CURSE 54A
	ANTHRWPOS 4B	MAN 68D
	LEGW 12B	SAY 469C
	HO,H8,TO IIIH	THE 553B
	OIDA 2	KNOW 558D
	OMNUW	TAKE AN OATH 568D
	OMNUW	TAKE AN OATH 569A
72	ALEKTWR	COCK 34D
	ANAMIMN8SKW	REMIND 57C
	APARNEOMAI	DENY 80B
	DEUTEROS 4	SECOND 176B
	DIS	TWICE 198D
	EPIBALLW 2B	BEAT UPON 289D
	KLAIW 1	WEEP 434A
	PRIN 1B	BEFORE 708A
	R8MA 1	WORD 742D
	TRIS	THRICE 834A
72A	PHWNEW 1A	PRODUCE A SOUND 878B
72B	PHWNEW 1A	PRODUCE A SOUND 878B

MARK 15

1	APOPHERW 1Aβ	TAKE AWAY 101B
	ARCHIEREUS 1B	HIGH PRIEST 112B
	GRAMMATEUS 2	SCRIBES 165A
	DEW 1B	BIND 176D
	HETOIMAZW 1	PREPARE 316B
	HO,H8,TO III0A	THE 555A
	POIEW II B6	DO 687D
	PRESBUTEROS 2Aβ	OLDER 706D
	*PRWI	EARLY 732B
	SUMBOULION 1	PLAN 785D
	SUNEDRION 2	SANHEDRIN 794A
1FF	PILATOS	PILATE 663C
2	BASILEUS 2A	KING 135D
	EPERWTAW 1B	ASK 285A
	IOUDAIOS 2C	JEWISH 380B

2	LEGW IIIE	DECLARE 471A
	SU 1A	YOU 779D
3	KAT8GOREW 1A	BRING CHARGES 424B
	POLUS I2Bβ	MANY 695A
	POLUS I2Bβ	MANY 695B
4	EPERWTAW 1B	ASK 285A
	IDE 4	SEE 370A
	OUDEIS 2Bα	NOTHING 596C
	POSOS 2Bα	HOW GREAT 701B
5	THAUMAZW 1Aα	WONDER 352D
	OUDEIS 2Bα	NOTHING 596C
	OUKETI 1	NO LONGER 597A
	HWSTE 2Aβ	THEREFORE 908C
6	DESMIOS	PRISONER 175A
	HEORT8	FESTIVAL 280A
	KATA II2C	EVERY 407C
	HOS,H8,HO II0E	(REL PRON) 588D
	PARAITEOMAI 1	INTERCEDE 621D
6=15	APOLUW 1	SET FREE 96A
7	BARABBAS 1	BARABBAS 132C
	DEW 1B	BIND 176D
	EN II3	WHILE 259D
	LEGW II3	CALL 471B
	HOSTIS 3	WHOEVER 591B
	POIEW	DO 687A
	POIEW II B6	DO 687D
	STASIAST8S	REBEL 771D
	STASIS 2	UPRISING 772A
	SUSTASIAST8S	802B
	FELLOW INSURRECTIONIST	
	PHONOS	MURDER 872C
8	AEI 3	ALWAYS 19A
	AITEW	ASK 25C
	ANABOAW	CRY OUT 50D
	KATHWS 1	JUST AS 392B
	POIEW I2Aβ	DO 689A
9	BASILEUS 2A	KING 135D
	THELW 1	WISH 355C
10	GINWSKW 4C	PERCEIVE 160C
	PARADIDWMI	GIVE OVER 619C
	PHTHONOS	ENVY 865C
11	ANASEIW	INCITE 59C
	BARABBAS 1	BARABBAS 132C
	MALLON 3Aβ	RATHER 490C
12	BASILEUS 2A	KING 135D
	THELW 1	WISH 355C
	HOS,H8,HO I2A	(REL PRON) 587A
	OUN IC α	THEREFORE 597B
	POIEW II Dα	DO 688D
13	PALIN 5	AGAIN 611D
13FF	STAUROW 1	CRUCIFY 773A
14	GAR 1F	WHAT 151C
	KAKOS IC	EVIL 398C
	KRAZW 2A	CALL 448D
	PERISSOTERWS 1	MORE 657C
	PERISSWS	MORE 657C
	POIEW II Bε	DO 687D
15	BARABBAS 1	BARABBAS 132C
	BOULOMAI 2Aβ	DESIRE 145D
	HIKANOS IC	SUFFICIENT 375B
	OCHLOS 1	CROWD 605D
	PARADIDWMI 1B	GIVE OVER 620B
	PHRAGELLOW	SCOURGE 873B

16 APAGW 2B   BRING BEFORE   78D
   AUL8 4   COURT   121A
   ESW I   IN   314B
   HOS,H8,HO I7A   (REL PRON)   588C
   PRAITWRION   THE PRAETORIUM 704B
   SPEIRA   COHORT   768C
   STRATIWT8S I   SOLDIER   778B
   SUGKALEW I   CALL TOGETHER 780D
17 AKANTHINOS   THORNY   29A
   ENDIDUSKW   DRESS   262C
   PERITITH8MI I   PLACE AROUND   658C
   PLEKW   WEAVE   673A
   PORPHURA   PURPLE   700D
   STEPHANOS I   WREATH   774D
18 ASPAZOMAI IA   GREET   116C
   BASILEUS 2A   KING   135D
   CHAIRW 2A   REJOICE   882A
19 GONU   KNEE   164B
   KALAMOS 2   STALK   399C
   KEPHAL8 IA   HEAD   431A
   PROSKUNEW 5   DO REVERENCE   724B
   TITH8MI IIB8α   PUT   823D
   TUPTW I   STRIKE   838A
20 EKDUW I   STRIP   238C
   EMPAIZW I   RIDICULE   255B
   ENDUW I   DRESS   263C
   EXAGW I   LEAD OUT   271B
   HINA I2   IN ORDER THAT 377C
   PORPHURA   PURPLE   700D
   STAUROW I   CRUCIFY   773A
21 AGGAREUW   REQUISITION   6D
   AGROS 2   THE COUNTRY   13D
   AIRW 2   LIFT UP   24A
   ALEXANDROS I   ALEXANDER   35A
   ERCHOMAI IIA8   COME   310B
   HINA IIIA8   IN ORDER THAT 378B
   KUR8NAIOS   CYRENIAN   459A
   PARAGW 2Aα   BRING IN   619A
   PAT8R IA   FATHER   640C
   ROUPHOS I   RUFUS   744D
   SIMWN 4   SIMON   758D
   STAUROS I   THE CROSS   772C
   TIS, TI 2A8   ANY ONE   828B
22 GOLGOTHA   GOLGOTHA   164A
   KRANION   SKULL   449A
   METHERM8NEUW   TRANSLATE   499D
   HOS,H8,HO I7A   (REL PRON)   588C
   PHERW 48β   BEAR   863C
22A TOPOS IC   PLACE   830B
22B TOPOS IC   PLACE   830B
23 DIDWMI 2   GIVE   192C
   LAMBANW IA   TAKE   465C
   OINOS I   WINE   565A
   HOS,H8,HO III   THIS (ONE)   589A
   PINW I   DRINK   664C
   SMURNIZW   TREAT WITH MYRRH 766B
24 BALLW IA   THROW   130B
   DIAMERIZW IB   DIVIDE   185D
   EPI IIIIB⌐   ON   289B
   HIMATION I   GARMENT   377A
   KL8ROS I   LOT   436C
   TIS, TI IC   WHICH   827B
24F STAUROW I   CRUCIFY   773A

25 EIMI I5   TO BE   222C
   KAI I2C   AND   393B
   TRITOS I   THIRD   834B
   HWRA 2B   TIME OF DAY   904C
26 AITIA 2A   CHARGE   25D
   BASILEUS 2A   KING   135D
   EPIGRAPH8   INSCRIPTION   291C
   EPIGRAPHW I   WRITE ON   291C
27 DEXIOS 2B   RIGHT   174A
   EUWNUMOS   LEFT   330A
   L8ST8S I   ROBBER   474B
   STAUROW I   CRUCIFY   773A
   SUN 2C   WITH   789C
28 ANOMOS 3   LAWLESS   71C
   GRAPH8 2A   SCRIPTURE   165B
   LOGIZOMAI IB   CONSIDER   477B
   META AI   WITH   509C
   PL8ROW 4A   MAKE FULL   677C
29 BLASPH8MEW 2B6   BLASPHEME   142B
   H8MERA 2   DAY   347B
   KATALUW IBα   DESTROY   415B
   KEPHAL8 IA   HEAD   431B
   KINEW 2A   MOVE   433C
   NAOS IA   TEMPLE   535B
   OIKODOMEW IC   BUILD   560D
   OUA   AHA   595B
   PARAPOREUOMAI I PASS BY   627A
30 KATABAINW IAα   COME DOWN   409B
   STAUROS I   THE CROSS   772B
30F SWZW IA   SAVE   805D
31 ALLOS IA   OTHER   39B
   ARCHIEREUS IB   HIGH PRIEST   112B
   GRAMMATEUS 2   SCRIBES   165A
   EMPAIZW I   RIDICULE   255B
   HOMOIWS   LIKEWISE   570D
32 BASILEUS 2A   KING   135D
   ISRA8L 2   ISRAEL   382B
   KATABAINW IAα   COME DOWN   409B
   NUN IA6   NOW   547D
   ONEIDIZW I   REPROACH   573A
   PISTEUW 2B   BELIEVE   667C
   STAUROS I   THE CROSS   772B
   SUSTAUROW I   CRUCIFY WITH   802C
33 G8 4   LAND   156D
   GINOMAI IIB8α   COME ABOUT   157B
   GINOMAI IIB8γ   COME ABOUT   157C
   HEKTOS   SIXTH   245C
   HEWS IIIA   UNTIL   335A
   SKOTOS I   DARKNESS   765A
33A HWRA 2B   TIME OF DAY   904D
33B HWRA 2B   TIME OF DAY   904D
33F ENATOS   NINTH   261D
34 BOAW 3   SHOUT   143D
   EGKATALEIPW 2   FORSAKE   214D
   EIS 4F   (PURPOSE)   228D
   ELWI   MY GOD   253A
   THEOS 3H   GOD   358C
   LAMA   WHY   465A
   MEGAS 2Aγ   GREAT   498D
   METHERM8NEUW   TRANSLATE   499D
   ONEIDIZW I   REPROACH   573B
   SABACHTHANI   FORSAKE   746A
   PHWN8 2A   VOICE   878D

34	HWRA 2B	TIME OF DAY 904D	43	HARIMATHAIA	ARIMATHAEA 106A
35	LEGW 18D	SAY 470C		BASILEIA 3G	KINGDOM 135B
	PARIST8MI 2Bα	BE PRESENT 633D		BOULEUT8S MEMBER OF COUNCIL 145A
	PHWNEW 2B	CALL 878C		EIMI 114E	TO BE 223B
35F	8LIAS	ELIJAH 345D		EISERCHOMAI 1C	COME 232A
36	APHI8MI 4	TOLERATE 126A		EUSCH8MWN 2	PROMINENT 327C
	GEMIZW 1	FILL 152D		IWS8PH 6	JOSEPH 386C
	EI V2A	WHETHER 218D		PROSDECHOMAI 2B	RECEIVE 719B
	EIDON 1C	SEE 219D		SWMA 1A	BODY 806D
	ERCHOMAI 11Aα	COME 310D		TOLMAW 2	DARE 829D
	KATHAIREW 1	LOWER 387B	44	EPERWTAW 1A	ASK 285A
	KALAMOS 2	STALK 399C		8D8 1B	ALREADY 344D
	OXOS	WINE VINEGAR 577D		THAUMAZW 1Aγ	WONDER 353A
	PERITITH8MI 1	PLACE AROUND 658C		THN8SKW 1	DIE 363A
	PIMPL8MI 1Aα	FILL 663D		PALAI 2B	LONG AGO 610C
	POTIZW 1	GIVE TO DRINK 702C	44A	EI II	IF 218C
	SPOGGOS	SPONGE 770C	44B	EI V2A	WHETHER 218D
	TRECHW 1	RUN 833C	44F	KENTURIWN	CENTURION 429D
37	APHI8MI 1Aβ	GIVE UP 125B	45	APO V4	FROM 87B
	EKPNEW	BREATHE OUT 243D		GINWSKW 2D	FIND OUT 160B
	MEGAS 2Aγ	GREAT 498D		DWREOMAI	GIVE 209D
	PHWN8 2C	VOICE 879A		IWS8PH 6	JOSEPH 386C
38	ANWTHEN 1	FROM ABOVE 76C		*PTWMA	CORPSE 735B
	DUO 5	TWO 208C		SWMA 1A	BODY 806D
	EIS 4E	SO THAT 228D	46	AGORAZW 1	BUY 12C
	HEWS 112B	AS FAR AS 335D		ENEILEW	CONFINE 264A
	KATAPETASMA	CURTAIN 417B		THURA 1B	ENTRANCE 366B
	KATW 2	DOWNWARDS 426B		KATHAIREW 1	LOWER 387B
	NAOS 1A	TEMPLE 535B		KATATITH8MI 1	PLACE 420C
	SCHIZW 1B	SPLIT 805A		LATOMEW 1	HEW 468C
39	AL8THWS 1	TRULY 36D		LITHOS 1E	STONE 475C
	EK 2	AWAY FROM 234A		MN8MA	TOMB 526C
	EKPNEW	BREATHE OUT 243D		MN8MEION 2	TOMB 526C
	ENANTIOS 3A	OPPOSED 261C		PETRA 1A	ROCK 660A
	KENTURIWN	CENTURION 429D		PROSKULIW	ROLL (UP TO) 723D
	KRAZW 1	CRY OUT 448D		SINDWN 1	LINEN 759B
	PARIST8MI 2Bα	BE PRESENT 633D		TITH8MI 11Aβ	PUT 823D
	HUIOS 2B	SON 842C	47	THEWREW 1	OBSERVE 360C
40	EIMI 1114	TO BE 224C		IWS8S 2	JOSES 386B
	THEWREW 1	OBSERVE 360C		MAGDAL8N8	MAGDALENE 485B
	IAKWB0S 3	JAMES 368C		MARIA 2	MARY 493A
	IWS8S 2	JOSES 386B		MARIA 3	MARY 493A
	MAGDAL8N8	MAGDALENE 485B		POU 1B	WHERE 702D
	MAKROTHEN	FROM FAR AWAY 489A		TITH8MI 11Aα	PUT 823C
	*MARIA 2	MARY 493A			
	MARIA 3	MARY 493A		**MARK 16**	
	MIKROS 1A	SMALL 523A			
	*SALWM8	SALOME 748C	1	AGORAZW 1	BUY 12C
41	DIAKONEW 2	SERVE 183A		ALEIPHW 1	ANOINT 34C
	HOTE 1A	WHEN 592C		ARWMA	SPICES 113D
	POLUS 11Aα	MANY 694B		DIAGINOMAI	PASS 181B
	SUNANABAINW	GO UP WITH 792A		ERCHOMAI 11Aζ	COME 310D
42	GINOMAI 11Bγ	COME ABOUT 157C		IAKWB0S 3	JAMES 368B
	EIMI 15	TO BE 222C		MAGDAL8N8	MAGDALENE 485B
	EPEI 2	BECAUSE 283D		MARIA 2	MARY 493A
	8D8 1B	ALREADY 344D		MARIA 3	MARY 493A
	HOS,H8,HO 17A	(REL PRON) 588C		SABBATON 1A	SABBATH 746B
	OPSIOS 2	LATE 606C		SALWM8	SALOME 748C
	PARASKEU8	PREPARATION 627C	2	ANATELLW 2	RISE 61C
	PRIN 2	BEFORE 708A		HEIS 4	ONE 231A
	PROSABBATON	FRIDAY 718A		EPI 111Aγ	ON 288A
	SABBATON 1A	SABBATH 746B		H8LIOS	THE SUN 346B
43	AITEW	ASK 25B		LIAN 3	VERY 474C

Verse	Word	Gloss	Ref
2	MN8MA	TOMB	526B
	MN8MEION 2	TOMB	526C
	PRWI	EARLY	732B
	SABBATON 2A	WEEK	746D
	SABBATON 2B	WEEK	746D
3	APOKULIW	ROLL AWAY	93D
	EK IA	AWAY FROM	233C
	THURA IB	ENTRANCE	366B
	LEGW I3	SAY	469D
	MN8MEION 2	TOMB	526C
	PROS IIIIE	TOWARD	716D
	TIS, TI IA∝	WHICH	826C
3F	LITHOS IE	STONE	475C
4	ANABLEPW I	LOOK UP	50C
	ANAKULIW	ROLL AWAY	56B
	APOKULIW	ROLL AWAY	93D
	GENEA 2	GENERATION	153B
	THEWREW I	OBSERVE	360D
	MEGAS IA	LARGE	498C
	SPHODRA	GREATLY	803D
5	DEXIOS 2B	RIGHT	174A
	EISERCHOMAI IAβ	COME	231D
	KATH8MAI IA∝	SIT	390B
	LEUKOS 2	WHITE	473D
	*MN8MEION 2	TOMB	526C
	NEANISKOS I	YOUTH	536C
	PERIBALLW IB∝	THROW AROUND	651D
	STOL8	ROBE	777B
5F	EKTHAMBEW	BE AMAZED	239D
6	IDE 3	SEE	369D
	NAZAR8NOS	THE NAZARENE	534A
	HOPOU IA∝	WHERE	579C
	STAUROW I	CRUCIFY	773A
	TITH8MI IIA∝	PUT	823C
	TOPOS IC	PLACE	830B
	HWDE 2A	HERE	903D
7	KATHWS I	JUST AS	392A
	KAI IIC	AND	392D
	HORAW IA∝	SEE	581C
	PETROS	PETER	661A
	PROAGW 2B	LEAD	709A
	HUPAGW 2	GO AWAY	844C
8	GAR IA	FOR	151A
	EKSTASIS I	DISTRACTION	244C
	ECHW IID	HOLD	332B
	MN8MEION 2	TOMB	526C
	OUDEIS 2A	NO ONE	596C
	TACHUS 2A	QUICK	814D
	TROMOS	TREMBLING	834C
	PHEUGW I	FLEE	863C
	PHOBEW IA	BE AFRAID	870B
	PHOBEW 2A	BE AFRAID	871B
9	ANIST8MI 2A	RISE	69C
	DE 2	BUT, AND	170C
	EKBALLW I	DRIVE OUT	237A
	MAGDAL8N8	MAGDALENE	485B
	*MARIA 2	MARY	493A
	PRWI	EARLY	732A
	PRWTOS IA	FIRST	733A
	PRWTOS 2A	FIRST	733D
	SABBATON 2A	WEEK	746D
	PHAINW 2C	APPEAR	859C
10	APAGGELLW I	REPORT	78C
10	GINOMAI II4A	BE	159C
	KLAIW I	WEEP	434B
	META AIIIA	WITH	509D
	PENTHEW I	BE SAD	648B
	POREUW I	PROCEED	699B
10F	EKEINO6 IB	THAT	238D
11	APISTEW IA	DISBELIEVE	84D
	ZAW IAβ	LIVE	336C
	THEAOMAI IC∝	SEE	353D
	KAKEINOS 2A	AND HE	397C
12	AGROS 2	THE COUNTRY	13D
	DUO 3	TWO	208C
	EIS IA∝	INTO	227C
	EK 4A∝	FROM	235B
	HETEROS 2	ANOTHER	315C
	META BII3	AFTER	511C
	MORPH8	FORM	530B
	PERIPATEW IC	GO ABOUT	655A
	POREUW I	PROCEED	699A
	PHANEROW 2Bβ	REVEAL	860D
13	APAGGELLW I	REPORT	78C
	KAKEINOS 2B	HE ALSO	397C
	LOIPOS 2B∝	THE OTHERS	481A
	OUDE 2	AND NOT	595D
	PISTEUW IB	BELIEVE	666C
14	ANAKEIMAI 2	BE AT TABLE	55C
	HENDEKA	ELEVEN	262B
	THEAOMAI IA	SEE	353D
	ONEIDIZW 2	REPROACH	573B
	PISTEUW IB	BELIEVE	666C
	SKL8ROKARDIA	OBSTINACY	763B
	HUSTEROS 2A	LATER	857B
	PHANEROW 2Bβ	REVEAL	860D
15	EUAGGELION IC	GOSPEL	318B
	K8RUSSW 2Bβ	ANNOUNCE	432C
	KOSMOS 4A	WORLD	447A
	KTISIS IBβ	CREATION	457A
	PAS IC∝	ALL	637B
16	APISTEW IB	DISBELIEVE	84D
	KATAKRINW	CONDEMN	413B
	SWZW 2B	SAVE	806B
16F	PISTEUW 2B	BELIEVE	667C
17	GLWSSA 3	TONGUE	161D
	DAIMONION 2	DEMON	168B
	EKBALLW I	DRIVE OUT	237A
	KAINOS 2	NEW	395A
	ONOMA I4Cγ	NAME	576A
	PARAKOLOUTHEW I	FOLLOW	624B
	S8MEION 2A	SIGN	755C
18	AIRW IA	LIFT UP	23D
	ARRWSTOS	SICK	109D
	BLAPTW	HARM	141D
	EPITITH8MI IA∝	PUT UPON	302D
	ECHW III	BE	334B
	THANASIMOS	DEADLY POISON	351B
	KALWS 3	WELL	402B
	KAN I	AND IF	403B
	OPHIS I	SNAKE	604D
	PINW I	DRINK	664B
19	ANALAMBANW I	TAKE UP	56B
	DEXIOS 2B	RIGHT	174A
	KATHIZW 2A∝	SIT DOWN	390D
	KURIOS 2Cβ	LORD	460D

19	LALEW 2Aδ	SPEAK	464B
	META BII4B	AFTER	511D
	OURANOS 2B	HEAVEN	599C
19F	EKEINOS IA	THAT	238D
19F	OUN 5	THEREFORE	597D
20	AM8N I	AMEN	45B
	BEBAIOW I	ESTABLISH	138A
	EPAKOLOUTHEW 2	FOLLOW	282A
	K8RUSSW 2Bβ	ANNOUNCE	432D
	KURIOS 2Cβ	LORD	460D
	LOGOS IBβ	WORD	479C
	PANTACHOU I	EVERYWHERE	613B
	S8MEION 2A	SIGN	755D
	SUNERGEW	WORK WITH	795A

LUKE I

I	ANATASSOMAI		61B
	REPEAT IN PROPER ORDER		
	DI8G8SIS	NARRATIVE	194A
	EPEID8PER	SINCE	284A
	EPICHEIREW	ATTEMPT	304D
	LOUKAS	LUKE	481C
	PL8ROPHOREW IA	FILL	676A
	POLUS I2Aα	MANY	694D
	PRAGMA I	DEED	703D
2	ARCH8 IB	BEGINNING	IIIC
	AUTOPT8S	EYEWITNESS	122B
	GINOMAI III	BE	159B
	KATHA	JUST AS	387B
	KATHWS I	JUST AS	392A
	LOGOS IBβ	WORD	479C
	PARADIDWMI 3	GIVE OVER	620D
	HUP8RET8S	SERVANT	850C
3	AKRIBWS	ACCURATELY	32D
	ANWTHEN 2A		76C
	FROM THE BEGINNING		
	DOKEW 3B	SEEM	201C
	THEOPHILOS	THEOPHILUS	359B
	KAGW 3A	I ALSO	387A
	KATHEX8S	IN ORDER	389C
	KRATISTOS 2	MOST NOBLE	450A
	LOGOS IAζ	MATTER	479A
	PARAKOLOUTHEW 3	FOLLOW	624C
	PAS 2Aδ	EVERYTHING	638C
4	EPIGINWSKW IA	KNOW	290D
	KAT8CHEW 2A	TEACH	425A
	LOGOS IBβ	WORD	479C
	HOS,H8,HO I5D	(REL PRON)	588B
5	AARWN	AARON	IA
	ABIA 2	ABIJAH	IC
	BASILEUS I	KING	135D
	GINOMAI II5	EXIST	159D
	GUN8 2	WIFE	167C
	ELISABET	ELIZABETH	250D
	EPH8MERIA	CLASS	330D
	ZACHARIAS I	ZECHARIAH	336B
	H8MERA 4B	TIME	348D
	H8RWD8S I	HEROD	349B
	THUGAT8R 2Bα	DAUGHTER	365B
	HIEREUS IBα	PRIEST	372C
	IOUDAIA 2	JUDAEA	379D
	TIS, TI 2Aα	ANY ONE	828A

5A	ONOMA II	NAME	574A
5B	ONOMA II	NAME	574A
6	AMEMPTOS	BLAMELESS	44C
	AMPHOTEROI I	BOTH	47A
	DIKAIOS IB	UPRIGHT	194D
	DIKAIWMA I	REGULATION	197A
	ENANTION IB	BEFORE	261B
	ENWPION 3	BEFORE	270B
	KURIOS 2A	LORD	460B
	HO,H8,TO IIIOA	THE	555A
	PAS IDα	ALL	637C
	POREUW 2C	PROCEED	699C
7	AMPHOTEROI I	BOTH	47A
	ELISABET	ELIZABETH	250D
	H8MERA 4B	DAY	348C
	KATHOTI 2	BECAUSE	392A
	OU 4A	NO	594D
	PROBAINW 2	GO ON	709C
	STEIRA	BARREN	773C
	TEKNON IAα	CHILD	815D
8	GINOMAI I3F	TAKE PLACE	158C
	ENANTI I	BEFORE	261B
	THEOS 3A	GOD	357D
	HIERATEUW		372C
	PERFORM DUTY OF A PRIEST		
	TAXIS I	FIXED ORDER	811C
9	ETHOS 2	CUSTOM	217D
	EISERCHOMAI IAβ	COME	231D
	THUMIAW		365D
	MAKE AN INCENSE OFFERING		
	HIERATEIA	PRIESTLY OFFICE	372B
	KATA II5Aα	ACCORDING TO	408A
	KURIOS 2A	LORD	460B
	LAGCHANW 2	BE APPOINTED	463B
	NAOS IA	TEMPLE	535B
	HO,H8,TO II4Bα	THE	553D
10	EXW IAα	OUTSIDE	279A
	THUMIAMA 2	INCENSE	365D
	LAOS IA	PEOPLE	467D
	PAS ICα	ALL	637B
	PL8THOS 2Bδ	QUANTITY	674D
	PROSEUCHOMAI	PRAY	720D
	HWRA 3	TIME OF DAY	905A
11	AGGELOS 2A	ANGEL	7B
	DEXIOS 2B	RIGHT	174A
	EK 2	AWAY FROM	234A
	THUMIAMA 2	INCENSE	365D
	THUSIAST8RION IBα	ALTAR	367B
	HIST8MI II2Bβ	BEING	383C
	KURIOS 2A	LORD	460B
	HORAW IAδ	SEE	582A
11F	AGGELOS 2A	ANGEL	7C
12	EIDON IA	SEE	219D
	EPI IIIIBγ	ON	289A
	EPIPIPTW 2	FALL UPON	297C
	TARASSW 2	STIR UP	813A
	PHOBOS 2Aα	FEAR	871C
12F	ZACHARIAS I	ZECHARIAH	336B
13	AGGELOS 2A	ANGEL	7C
	GENNAW 2	BEAR	154D
	GUN8 2	WIFE	167C
	DE8SIS	PRAYER	171A
	DIOTI 3	FOR	198C

13	EIPON I	SAY 225C
	EISAKOUW 2B	LISTEN TO 231C
	ELISABET	ELIZABETH 250D
	IWAN(N)8S I	JOHN 385B
	KALEW IAv	CALL 400A
	M8 AIII3B	NOT 518D
	ONOMA I2A	NAME 574B
	HUIOS IA«	SON 841B
	PHOBEW IA	BE AFRAID 870C
14	AGALLIASIS	EXULTATION 3D
	GENESIS I	BIRTH 154A
	GENN8SIS	BIRTH 155A
	EPI IIIBy	ON 287B
	POLUS I2A«	MANY 694D
	CHAIRW I	REJOICE 881B
	CHARA I	JOY 883C
	CHARA I	JOY 883D
15	GAR IA	FOR 151A
	ENWPION 3	BEFORE 270B
	ETI IAv	STILL 315D
	KOILIA 2	BELLY 438B
	KURIOS 2A	LORD 460C
	MEGAS 2B«	GREAT 499B
	M8 DIA	NOT 519B
	OINOS I	WINE 565A
	PIMPL8MI IA8	FILL 663D
	PINW I	DRINK 664B
	PNEUMA 5C8	SPIRIT 682D
	SIKERA	STRONG DRINK 758A
16	EPISTREPHW IA	TURN 301A
	THEOS 3C	GOD 358A
	ISRA8L I	ISRAEL 382B
	KURIOS 2A	LORD 460B
	POLUS I2A«	MANY 694D
	HUIOS IB«	SON 841B
17	APEITH8S 2	DISOBEDIENT 82B
	DIKAIOS IB	UPRIGHT 194D
	EN I4C8	IN 258C
	EN I6	IN 259C
	ENWPION I	BEFORE 270A
	EPI IIIIB6	TOWARD 289A
	EPISTREPHW IA	TURN 301A
	HETOIMAZW 2	PREPARE 316C
	8LIAS	ELIJAH 345D
	KATASKEUAZW I	MAKE READY 419B
	KURIOS 2A	LORD 460B
	LAOS 3B	PEOPLE 468B
	PAT8R IA	FATHER 640C
	PNEUMA 6A	SPIRIT 683D
	PROERCHOMAI 2	GO FORWARD 712B
	TEKNON IA	CHILD 816A
	PHRON8SIS I	WAY OF THINKING 874C
18	AGGELOS 2A	ANGEL 7C
	GINWSKW IA	KNOW 160A
	GUN8 2	WIFE 167C
	ZACHARIAS I	ZECHARIAH 336B
	H8MERA 4B	DAY 348C
	KATA II5A6	ACCORDING TO 408B
	PRESBUT8S	OLD MAN 707C
	PROBAINW 2	GO ON 709C
19	APOKRINOMAI 2	BEGIN 93A
	APOSTELLW IBy	SEND AWAY 98B
	GABRI8L	GABRIEL 148B
19	EIMI III	TO BE 222D
	ENWPION I	BEFORE 270A
	EUAGGELIZW I	317C
		ANNOUNCE GOOD NEWS
	LALEW 2A6	SPEAK 464C
	PARIST8MI 2B«	BE PRESENT 633D
20	ANTI 3	FOR 73B
	ACHRI IA	UNTIL 128B
	EIMI II4By	TO BE 223A
	EIS 2Av	UNTIL 228A
	H8MERA 2	DAY 347A
	IDOU IB8	BEHOLD 371C
	KAIROS 3	TIME 396A
	LALEW 2A«	SPEAK 464B
	LOGOS IA6	WORD 478D
	HOS,H8,HO I5C«	(REL PRON) 588B
	HOS,H8,HO IIIA	(REL PRON) 589A
	PIMPL8MI IB«	FILL 663D
	PISTEUW IA6	BELIEVE 666B
	PL8ROW 4A	MAKE FULL 677C
	SIWPAW 2A	BE SILENT 760A
21	EN IIIIB	BY 260B
	ZACHARIAS I	ZECHARIAH 336B
	THAUMAZW IA8	WONDER 352D
	LAOS IA	PEOPLE 467D
	PROSDECHOMAI 2A	RECEIVE 719B
	PROSDOKAW I	EXPECT 719C
	CHRONIZW 3	TAKE TIME 896A
21F	NAOS IA	TEMPLE 535B
22	AUTOS 3A	(OBLIQUE CASE) 122D
	DIAMENW	REMAIN 185C
	DIANEUW	NOD 186A
	EIMI II4B8	TO BE 223A
	EPIGINWSKW 2C	KNOW 291B
	KWPHOS I	MUTE 463A
	LALEW 2A6	SPEAK 464B
	OPTASIA I	A VISION 580A
	HORAW IA8	SEE 581C
23	APERCHOMAI 2	GO 83D
	GINOMAI I3F	TAKE PLACE 158C
	H8MERA 2	DAY 347C
	LEITOURGIA I	SERVICE 472B
	OIKOS IA«	HOUSE 563A
	PIMPL8MI IB8	FILL 663D
	HWS IVIA	WHEN 906D
24	GUN8 2	WIFE 167C
	ELISABET	ELIZABETH 250D
	H8MERA 2	DAY 347B
	LEGW IIB«	SAY 469C
	M8N I	MONTH 520D
	PERIKRUBW	HIDE 654A
	SULLAMBANW IB	SEIZE 784C
25	APHAIREW I	CUT OFF 123D
	EPEIDON	REPROACH 284A
	ONEIDOS	DISGRACE 573C
	HOTI 2	THAT 593D
	HOUTW 5	THUS 602D
	POIEW I2A8	DO 689A
26	APOSTELLW IB8	SEND AWAY 98A
	APOSTELLW IB6	SEND AWAY 98B
	GABRI8L	GABRIEL 148B
	HEKTOS	SIXTH 245C
	M8N I	MONTH 520D

26	NAZARA	NAZARETH 534A
	ONOMA II	NAME 574A
	POLIS I	CITY 692A
27	DAUID	DAVID 170B
	EK 3B	FROM 234B
	IWS8PH 4	JOSEPH 386C
	MARIA I	MARY 492D
	MNAOMAI	BETROTHED 526A
	MN8STEUW	BECOME ENGAGED 527C
	OIKOS 3	NATION 563D
	PARTHENOS I	VIRGIN 632B
27A	ONOMA II	NAME 574A
27B	ONOMA II	NAME 574A
28	EUAGGELIZW 2AY	PREACH 317D
	EULOGEW 3	BLESS 322D
	KURIOS 2A	LORD 460B
	META AIIIC₿	WITH 510A
	SU 2	YOU 780A
	CHAIRW 2A	REJOICE 882A
	CHARITOW	FAVOR HIGHLY 887B
29	ASPASMOS I	GREETING 116D
	DIALOGIZOMAI I	CONSIDER 185A
	DIATARASSW	CONFUSE 188C
	EIMI II6C	TO BE 223C
	EPI IIIBY	ON 287A
	LOGOS IAY	WORD 478C
	POTAPOS	WHAT SORT 701C
30	HEURISKW 3	FIND 326A
	*MARIA I	MARY 492D
	M8 AIII3B	NOT 518D
	PARA II2B	BESIDE 615D
	PHOBEW IA	BE AFRAID 870C
	CHARIS 2A	FAVOR 885D
31	GAST8R 2	WOMB 152A
	IDOU IB₿	BEHOLD 371C
	KALEW IAY	CALL 400A
	ONOMA I2A	NAME 574B
	SULLAMBANW IB	SEIZE 784C
	TIKTW I	GIVE BIRTH 824C
	HUIOS IA∝	SON 841B
32	THRONOS IA	THRONE 364D
	KALEW IA6	CALL 400B
	KURIOS 2A	LORD 460B
	MEGAS 2B∝	GREAT 499B
	HOUTOS IA₿	THIS 601A
	PAT8R IB	FOREFATHER 640C
	HUIOS 2B	SON 842C
	HUPSISTOS 2	HIGHEST 858B
33	AIWN IB	TIME 26D
	BASILEIA I	KINGDOM 134C
	BASILEUW IB₿	RULE 136C
	EIS 2B	FOR 228A
	EPI IIIIB∝	OVER 288D
	IAKWB I	JACOB 368B
	OIKOS 3	NATION 563D
	TELOS IA	END 819A
34	AN8R I	MAN 65D
	GINWSKW 5	KNOW 160C
	EIMI I4	TO BE 222D
	EIPON I	SAY 225C
	EPEI 2	BECAUSE 283D
	*MARIA I	MARY 492D
	METECHW	SHARE 515C

34	OU 5B	NO 595A
	PWS IA	HOW 739C
35	HAGIOS IBY	HOLY 9D
	GENNAW IA	BEGET 154C
	GENNAW 2	BEAR 154D
	DIO	THEREFORE 197D
	EPERCHOMAI 2C	COME 284D
	EPI IIIIBY	ON 288D
	EPISKIAZW 3	COVER 298D
	KAI II4	ALSO 394C
	KALEW IA6	CALL 400B
	PNEUMA 5C₿	SPIRIT 682D
	SU 2	YOU 780A
	HUIOS 2B	SON 842C
	HUPSISTOS 2	HIGHEST 858B
36	AUTOS 3A	(OBLIQUE CASE) 123A
	G8RAS	OLD AGE 156D
	HEKTOS	SIXTH 245C
	ELISABET	ELIZABETH 250D
	IDOU IB₿	BEHOLD 371C
	KALEW IA6	CALL 400B
	M8N I	MONTH 520D
	HOUTOS 2C	THIS 602A
	STEIRA	BARREN 773C
	SUGGEN8S	RELATED 780B
	SUGGENIS	KINSWOMAN 780C
	SULLAMBANW IB	SEIZE 784C
37	ADUNATEW	BE POWERLESS 18C
	PARA I2	FROM 614C
	PARA II2C	BESIDE 615D
	PAS IA∝	EVERY EACH 636D
	R8MA 2	WORD 743A
38	AGGELOS 2A	ANGEL 7C
	APERCHOMAI IA	GO AWAY 83D
	APHIST8MI 2A	WITHDRAW 126C
	GINOMAI I3B₿	TAKE PLACE 158A
	DOUL8	BONDMAID 204C
	EIPON 3A	SAY 225C
	KATA II5AY	ACCORDING TO 408B
	KURIOS 2A	LORD 460B
	MARIA I	MARY 492D
	R8MA I	WORD 742D
38F	MARIA I	MARY 492D
39	ANIST8MI 2D	RISE 69D
	H8MERA 4B	TIME 348B
	IOUDAS IC	JUDAH 380C
	MARIA I	MARY 492D
	META AIIII	WITH 511A
	OREINOS	HILLY 583C
	POLIS I	CITY 692A
	POREUW I	PROCEED 699A
	SPOUD8 I	HASTE 771B
40	ASPAZOMAI IA	GREET 116B
	EISERCHOMAI IA₿	COME 231D
	ZACHARIAS I	ZECHARIAH 336B
	OIKOS IA∝	HOUSE 563A
40F	ELISABET	ELIZABETH 250D
41	AKOUW IB∝	HEAR 31B
	ASPASMOS I	GREETING 116D
	BREPHOS I	UNBORN CHILD 146D
	GINOMAI I3F	TAKE PLACE 158C
	KOILIA 2	BELLY 438B
	MARIA I	MARY 492D

41 PIMPL8MI IAß   FILL   663D   50 ELEOS 2A   MERCY 249D
    PNEUMA 5Cß   SPIRIT   682D   PHOBEW 2A   BE AFRAID 871A
    SKIRTAW   LEAP   763A   51 BRACHIWN   ARM 146D
    HWS IVIA   WHEN   907A   DIANOIA 2   MIND 186B
42 ANABOAW   CRY OUT   50D   DIASKORPIZW   SCATTER 187B
    ANAPHWNEW   CRY OUT LOUDLY   62D   EN IIIIA   BY 260A
    GUN8 I   WOMAN   167B   KRATOS 2   POWER 450B
    KARPOS IB   FRUIT   405D   HUPER8PHANOS   PROUD 849A
    KOILIA 2   BELLY   438B   52 APO IVIAα   FROM   86D
    KRAUG8 IB   SHOUT   450C   DUNAST8S IB   RULER 207D
    MEGAS 2Aγ   GREAT   498D   THRONOS IA   THRONE 364D
    SU   IC   YOU   779D   KATHAIREW I   LOWER 387B
42A   EULOGEW 3   BLESS   322D   TAPEINOS I   LOW 811D
42B   EULOGEW 3   BLESS   322D   HUPSOW 2   LIFT UP 858D
43 ERCHOMAI IIAß   COME   310C   53 AGATHOS 2Bß   GOOD   3C
    HINA IIIE   IN ORDER THAT   378C   EMPI(M)PL8MI I   FILL 255C
    KAI I2H   AND   393D   EXAPOSTELLW 2   SEND OUT 272D
    HOUTOS IBß   THIS   601C   KENOS I   EMPTY 429A
    POTHEN 3   FROM WHERE   686D   PEINAW I   HUNGER 645D
44 AGALLIASIS   EXULTATION   3D   PLOUTEW I   BE RICH 679D
    ASPASMOS I   GREETING   116D   54 ANTILAMBANW I   HELP   74A
    BREPHOS I   UNBORN CHILD   146D   ELEOS 2A   MERCY 249D
    GAR IB   FOR   151A   ISRA8L 2   ISRAEL 382B
    GINOMAI I4Cα   COME, GO   158D   MIMN8SKOMAI IC   REMEMBER 524B
    IDOU IC   REMEMBER   371D   PAIS IBα   SERVANT 609D
    KOILIA 2   BELLY   438B   55 AIWN IB   TIME   26D
    OUS I   EAR   600B   KATHWS I   JUST AS 392A
    SKIRTAW   LEAP   763A   LALEW 2Aδ   SPEAK 464C
    PHWN8 I   SOUND   878D   PAT8R IB   FOREFATHERS 640D
    HWS IVIA   WHEN   907A   SPERMA 2B   SEED 769B
45 AUTOS 3Fα   (OBLIQUE CASE)   123B   56*MARIA I   MARY 492D
    LALEW 2Aζ   SPEAK   464C   MENW IAα   REMAIN 504D
    MAKARIOS IB   BLESSED   488A   MENW IAα   REMAIN 504D
    PARA I2   FROM   614C   M8N I   MONTH 520D
    PISTEUW IAß   BELIEVE   666A   OIKOS IAα   HOUSE 563A
    TELEIWSIS 2   FULFILMENT   818A   SUN IA   WITH 789A
46 ELISABET   ELIZABETH   250D   TREIS   THREE 833A
    KURIOS 2A   LORD   460B   HUPOSTREPHW   RETURN 855B
   *MARIA I   MARY   492D   HWS IV5   WHEN 907C
    MEGALUNW 2   EXALT   498B   HWSEI 2   AS 907D
    PSUCH8 IBγ   SOUL LIFE   901D   57 GENNAW 2   BEAR 154D
47 AGALLIAW   BE GLAD   3D   ELISABET   ELIZABETH 250D
    EPI IIIBγ   ON   287B   HO,H8,TO II14Bß   THE 553D
    THEOS 3A   GOD   357D   PIMPL8MI IBß   FILL 664A
    PNEUMA 3B   SPIRIT   681B   TIKTW I   GIVE BIRTH 824C
    SWT8R I   SAVIOR   808C   HUIOS IAα   SON 841B
48 GAR IB   FOR   151A   CHRONOS   TIME 896B
    GENEA 3A   AGE   153C   58 ELEOS 2A   MERCY 249D
    DOUL8   BONDMAID   204C   KURIOS 2A   LORD 460B
    EPIBLEPW   LOOK AT   290B   MEGALUNW I   MAKE LARGE 498B
    IDOU IC   REMEMBER   371D   META AIIICγ   WITH 510B
    MAKARIZW   CONSIDER BLESSED   487C   PERIOIKOS   LIVING AROUND 654C
    NUN 3B   NOW   548B   SUGGEN8S   RELATED 780B
    PAS IDα   ALL   637C   SUGCHAIRW I   REJOICE WITH 782C
    TAPEINWSIS 2   HUMILIATION   812D   SUGCHAIRW 2   REJOICE WITH 782D
49 HAGIOS IB6   HOLY   9D   59 GINOMAI I3F   TAKE PLACE 158C
    DUNATOS IAα   POWERFUL   207D   EPI II3   ON 287D
    MEGALEIOS   MAGNIFICENT   497D   ERCHOMAI IIAα   COME 310D
    MEGAS 2Bß   GREAT   499C   ZACHARIAS I   ZECHARIAH 336B
    ONOMA I4A   NAME   574D   H8MERA 2   DAY 347B
    POIEW IIDß   DO   688D   KALEW IAγ   CALL 399D
50*GENEA 3B   AGE   153C   OGDOOS   THE EIGHTH 555B
    EIS 2B   FOR   228A   ONOMA II   NAME 573D

59	ONOMA I2B	NAME	574B
	PAIDION I	INFANT	609A
	PERITEMNW I	CUT AROUND	658A
60	ALLA IA	BUT, YET	37C
	IWAN(N)8S I	JOHN	385B
	KALEW IAY	CALL	400A
	OUCHI 2	NOT	603A
61	EIMI II	TO BE	222B
	EIPON I	SAY	225C
	KALEW IAY	CALL	400A
	ONOMA I2B	NAME	574B
	HOTI 2	THAT	593D
	OUDEIS 2A	NO ONE	596B
	SUGGENEIA	RELATIONSHIP	780A
62	AN 5	(PARTICLE)	48D
	ENNEUW	NOD	266C
	THELW I	WISH	355C
	KALEW IAY	CALL	400A
	HO,H8,TO II8A	THE	554D
63	AITEW	ASK	25B
	GRAPHW 2A	WRITE	165C
	THAUMAZW IA«	WONDER	352D
	IWAN(N)8S I	JOHN	385B
	LEGW I8B	SAY	470B
	LUW IB	LOOSE	484D
	PAS 2AY	ALL	638B
	PINAKIS	LITTLE	664A
	PINAKIDION	LITTLE TABLET	664A
64	ANOIGW IE«	OPEN	70D
	GLWSSA IA	TONGUE	161B
	DIARTHROW		187A
	RENDER CAPABLE OF SPEECH		
	EULOGEW I	SPEAK WELL	322C
	LALEW 2A«	SPEAK	464B
	PARACHR8MA	AT ONCE	629B
	STOMA IA	MOUTH	777B
65	GINOMAI I4CY	COME, GO	159A
	DIALALEW	DISCUSS	184C
	EPI IIIIBY	ON	289A
	OREINOS	HILLY	583C
	PAS ID«	ALL	637C
	PERIOIKEW	LIVE AROUND	654C
	R8MA 2	WORD	743A
	PHOBOS 2A«	FEAR	871C
66	ARA 2	THEN	103B
	EIMI III7	TO BE	224D
	KURIOS 2A	LORD	460B
	LEGW I8A	SAY	470B
	META AIIIC℘	WITH	510A
	PAIDION I	INFANT	609A
	PAS ID℘	ALL	637C
	TITH8MI IIIC	PUT	824B
	CHEIR 2A℘	HAND	888D
67	ZACHARIAS I	ZECHARIAH	336B
	PIMPL8MI IA℘	FILL	663D
	PNEUMA 5C℘	SPIRIT	682D
	PROPH8TEUW 3	PROPHESY	730C
68	EPISKEPTOMAI 3	VISIT	298C
	EULOG8TOS	BLESSED	323A
	THEOS 3C	GOD	358A
	ISRA8L 2	ISRAEL	382B
	KURIOS 2A	LORD	460B
	LAOS 3A	PEOPLE	468A

68	LUTRWSIS I	REDEMPTION	484B
	POIEW IIB∂	DO	687C
69	EGEIRW IA∂	ERECT	213D
	KERAS 3	HORN	430C
	PAIS IB«	SERVANT	609D
	SWT8RIA 2	DELIVERANCE	809A
70	HAGIOS IB«	DEDICATED TO GOD	9C
	AIWN IA	TIME	26C
	KATHWS I	JUST AS	392A
	LALEW 2A€	SPEAK	464C
	PROPH8T8S I	PROPHET	730D
	STOMA IA	MOUTH	777C
71	EK IA	AWAY FROM	233C
	ECHTHROS 2B℘	THE ENEMY	331D
	MISEW I	HATE	524C
	SWT8RIA I	DELIVERANCE	808D
	CHEIR 2B	HAND	888D
72	HAGIOS IA«	DEDICATED TO GOD	9C
	DIATH8K8 2		182B
	LAST WILL AND TESTAMENT		
	ELEOS 2B	MERCY	249D
	META AIIICY	WITH	510B
	MIMN8SKOMAI IC	REMEMBER	524B
	HO,H8,TO IIID	THE	552D
	POIEW IIC℘	DO	688C
73	ABRAAM	ABRAHAM	ID
	OMNUW	TAKE AN OATH	569B
	HORKOS	OATH	585B
	HOS,H8,HO I4D	(REL PRON)	588A
	PAT8R IB	FOREFATHER	640C
	PROS IIIIE	TOWARD	716D
74	APHOBWS I	FEARLESSLY	126C
	EK IA	AWAY FROM	233C
	ECHTHROS 2B«	THE ENEMY	331D
	LATREUW	SERVE	468C
	RUOMAI	SAVE	745A
	CHEIR 2B	HAND	888D
75	DIKAIOSUN8 2B	RIGHTEOUSNESS	195D
	ENWPION 3	BEFORE	270B
	H8MERA 4B	DAY	348C
	HOSIOT8S	DEVOUTNESS	589D
76	ENWPION I	BEFORE	270B
	HETOIMAZW I	PREPARE	316B
	KALEW IA∂	CALL	400B
	HODOS IA	WAY	556B
	PAIDION I	INFANT	609A
	PRO I	BEFORE	708C
	PROPOREUOMAI	GO ON BEFORE	716C
	PROSWPON IC ζ	FACE	729A
	PROPH8T8S 2	PROPHET	731A
	SU IB	YOU	779D
	HUPSISTOS 2	HIGHEST	858B
77	HAMARTIA I	SIN	42C
	APHESIS 2	PARDON	124C
	GNWSIS 2	KNOWLEDGE	163A
	HO,H8,TO II4Bζ	THE	554A
	SWT8RIA 2	DELIVERANCE	809A
78	ANATOL8 3	RISING	62A
	DIA BIII	BECAUSE OF	180B
	ELEOS 2B	MERCY	249D
	EPISKEPTOMAI 3	VISIT	298C
	SPLAGCHNON IB	INWARD PARTS	770C
	HUPSOS IB	HEIGHT	858B

79 EIR8N8 1B .... PEACE 226C
   EPIPHAINW 1B .... APPEAR 304A
   THANATOS 2A .... DEATH 352A
   KATH8MAI 1B .... RESIDE 390C
   KATEUTHUNW .... LEAD 423C
   HO.H8.TO II4B⟨ .... THE 554A
   HODOS 2A .... WAY 556D
   POUS 1B .... FOOT 703C
   SKIA 1A .... SHADE 763A
   SKOTOS 2B .... DARKNESS 765B
80 ANADEIXIS .... COMMISSIONING 53A
   AUXANW 3 .... GROW 121C
   ER8MOS 2 .... DESERT 309A
   HEWS IIIA .... UNTIL 335A
   H8MERA 2 .... DAY 347C
   ISRA8L 2 .... ISRAEL 382B
   KRATAIOW .... STRENGTHEN 449C
   PAIDION 1 .... INFANT 609A
   PNEUMA 3B .... SPIRIT 681C

                    LUKE 2

 1 APOGRAPHW 1 .... REGISTER 89A
   GINOMAI I3F .... TAKE PLACE 158C
   DOGMA 1 .... DECREE 200C
   EKEINOS 2B« .... THAT 239B
   EXERCHOMAI 2B« .... GO OUT 274C
   H8MERA 4B .... TIME 348B
   KAISAR .... EMPEROR 396C
   OIKOUMEN8 1B .... THE WORLD 564A
   PARA II .... FROM 614C
   PAS 1C« .... ALL 637B
 2 APOGRAPH8 .... CENSUS 88D
   GINOMAI III .... BE 159B
   H8GEMONEUW .... BE LEADER 343D
   KUR8NIOS .... QUIRINIUS 459A
   HOUTOS 2C .... THIS 602A
   PRWTOS 1B .... FIRST 733B
   SURIA .... SYRIA 801D
 3 APOGRAPHW 1 .... REGISTER 89A
   HEKASTOS 2 .... EACH 236B
   PATRIS 2 .... FATHERLAND 642C
   POLIS 1 .... CITY 692A
   POREUW 1 .... PROCEED 699B
 4 ANABAINW IA« .... GO UP 49D
   B8THLEEM .... BETHLEHEM 139C
  *DAUID .... DAVID 170B
   DIA BII3 .... BECAUSE 180C
   EK 3B .... FROM 234B
   IOUDAIA 1 .... JUDAEA 379D
   IOUDAS 1C .... JUDAH 380C
   IWS8PH 4 .... JOSEPH 386C
   KALEW IAγ .... CALL 400A
   NAZARA .... NAZARETH 534A
   OIKOS 3 .... NATION 563D
   HOSTIS 3 .... WHOEVER 591B
   PATRIA 1 .... FAMILY 642B
4A   POLIS 1 .... CITY 692B
4B   POLIS 1 .... CITY 692A
 5 APOGRAPHW 1 .... REGISTER 89A
   GUN8 3 .... BRIDE 167C
   EGKUOS .... PREGNANT 216A
   MARIA 1 .... MARY 492D

 5 MN8STEUW .... BECOME ENGAGED 527C
 6 GINOMAI I3F .... TAKE PLACE 158C
   HO.H8.TO II4Bβ .... THE 553D
   PIMPL8MI 1Bβ .... FILL 664A
   TELEW I .... FINISH 818C
   TIKTW I .... GIVE BIRTH 824C
 7 ANAKLINW IA .... LAY 55D
   DIOTI I .... BECAUSE 198C
   KATALUMA .... INN 415B
   PRWTOTOKOS I .... FIRSTBORN 734A
   SPARGANOW WRAP (UP) IN CLOTHS 768B
   TIKTW I .... GIVE BIRTH 824C
   TOPOS IE .... PLACE 830C
   HUIOS IA« .... SON 841B
   PHATN8 .... MANGER 862B
 8 AGRAULEW   LIVE OUT OF DOORS 13A
   EPI IIIIB« .... OVER 288D
   NUX IB .... NIGHT 548D
   POIM8N I .... SHEPHERD 690C
   POIMN8 .... FLOCK 691A
   PHULAK8 I .... GUARD 875C
   PHULASSW IA .... WATCH 876B
   CHWRA IA .... COUNTRY 897C
 9 AGGELOS 2A .... ANGEL 7B
   AGGELOS 2A .... ANGEL 7C
   DOXA IA .... BRIGHTNESS 202C
   EPHIST8MI IA .... STAND BY 331A
   MEGAS 2Aγ .... GREAT 499A
   PERILAMPW .... SHINE AROUND 654A
   PHOBEW IA .... BE AFRAID 870D
   PHOBOS 2A« .... FEAR 871C
9A   KURIOS 2A .... LORD 460B
9B   KURIOS 2A .... LORD 460B
10 AGGELOS 2A .... ANGEL 7C
   GAR IB .... FOR 151A
   EIMI I4 .... TO BE 222C
   EUAGGELIZW I 317C
         ANNOUNCE GOOD NEWS
   IDOU IC .... REMEMBER 371D
   LAOS 3A .... PEOPLE 468A
   MEGAS 2Aγ .... GREAT 499A
   M8 AIII3B .... NOT 518C
   PAS IC« .... ALL 637B
   PHOBEW IA .... BE AFRAID 870C
   CHARA 2A .... JOY 884A
11 DAUID .... DAVID 170B
   KURIOS 2Cγ .... LORD 461A
   POLIS I .... CITY 692A
   S8MERON .... TODAY 756C
   SWT8R 2 .... SAVIOR 808C
   TIKTW I .... GIVE BIRTH 824C
12 BREPHOS 2 .... INFANT 147A
   HEURISKW IC« .... FIND 325C
   KEIMAI IA .... LIE 427D
   HOUTOS IAη .... THIS 601B
   S8MEION I .... SIGN 755B
   SPARGANOW WRAP (UP) IN CLOTHS 768B
   PHATN8 .... MANGER 862B
13 AGGELOS 2A .... ANGEL 7C
   AINEW .... TO PRAISE 23A
   GINOMAI I4C⟨ .... COME, GO 159A
   EXAIPHN8S .... SUDDENLY 271D
   THEOS 3A .... GOD 357D

```
13 OURANIOS          HEAVENLY  598A
   PL8THOS 2B«       QUANTITY  674C
   STRATIA I             ARMY  778B
   SUN ID               WITH   789B
14 ANTHRWPOS 2A        MAN      67D
   G8  5A              EARTH   156D
   DOXA 3              FAME    203B
   EIR8N8 3            PEACE   227A
   EN  IV4A              IN    260D
   EUDOKIA I        GOOD WILL  319D
   THEOS 3B             GOD    357D
   HUPSISTOS I       HIGHEST   858A
15*AGGELOS 2A          ANGEL     7C
   APERCHOMAI IA      GO AWAY   83D
   B8THLEEM          BETHLEHEM 139C
   GINOMAI I3A      TAKE PLACE 157D
   GINOMAI I3F      TAKE PLACE 158B
   GNWRIZW I        MAKE KNOWN 162C
   D8  2                NOW    177B
   DIERCHOMAI 2        COME    193D
   EIS IA«             INTO    227B
   KURIOS 2A           LORD    460B
   OURANOS 2C         HEAVEN   599C
   POIM8N I         SHEPHERD   690C
   R8MA 2              WORD    743A
   HWS IVIA            WHEN    907A
16 ANEURISKW           LOOK     65A
   BREPHOS 2          INFANT   147A
   IWS8PH 4           JOSEPH   386C
   KEIMAI IA            LIE    427D
   MARIA I             MARY    492D
   SPEUDW IA          HURRY    769D
   TE  3A               AND    815C
   PHATN8            MANGER    862B
17 GNWRIZW I        MAKE KNOWN 162C
   DIAGNWRIZW                  181C
       GIVE AN EXACT REPORT
   EIDON IA             SEE    219D
   PAIDION I          INFANT   609A
   R8MA I              WORD    742D
18 THAUMAZW IA        WONDER   353A
   POIM8N I         SHEPHERD   690C
   HUPO IA«             BY     850D
19 KARDIA IB          HEART    404C
  *MARIA I             MARY    492D
   HOUTOS 2B           THIS    602A
   PAS ID«              ALL    637C
   R8MA 2              WORD    743A
   SUMBALLW IA      CONVERSE   785A
   SUNT8REW 3         PROTECT   800B
20 AINEW            TO PRAISE   23A
   DOXAZW I           PRAISE   203C
   EPI IIIB             ON     287B
   HOS,H8,HO I4A   (REL PRON)  587D
   POIM8N I         SHEPHERD   690C
   HUPOSTREPHW        RETURN    855B
21 AGGELOS 2A          ANGEL     7C
   H8MERA 2             DAY    347C
   KAI I2D              AND    393B
   KALEW IAய           CALL    400A
   KOILIA 2            BELLY   438B
   HO,H8,TO II4B        THE    554A
   OKTW               EIGHT    565D
```

```
21 ONOMA I2A           NAME    574B
   ONOMAZW I           NAME    577B
   HOTE IB             WHEN    592C
   PAIDION I          INFANT   609A
   PERITEMNW I      CUT AROUND 658A
   PIMPL8MI IB          FILL   664A
   PRO 2              BEFORE   708D
   SULLAMBANW IB       SEIZE   784C
   SUNTELEW I        COMPLETE  799D
22 ANAGW I             LEAD     52D
   AUTOS 3B     (OBLIQUE CASE) 123A
   H8MERA 2             DAY    347C
   KATHARISMOS I   PURIFICATION 388C
   KATA II5A«      ACCORDING TO 408A
   KURIOS 2A           LORD    460B
   NOMOS 3             LAW     544C
   PARIST8MI IB«      PRESENT  633A
   PIMPL8MI IB          FILL   664A
23 HAGIOS IB«  DEDICATED TO GOD  9D
   ARS8N              MALE    109C
   DIANOIGW IA         OPEN    186B
   KATHWS I         JUST AS    392A
   KALEW IA            CALL    400B
   M8TRA              WOMB     522B
   NOMOS 4A            LAW     545A
   HOTI 2              THAT    593D
   PAS IA«        EVERY EACH   636C
23F  KURIOS 2A          LORD    460B
24 DIDWMI IA          GIVE    191D
   EIPON 4              SAY    225D
   ZEUGOS 2           PAIR    337D
   8  IA«               OR     342B
   THUSIA 2A        SACRIFICE  366D
   KATA II5A«      ACCORDING TO 408A
   NOSSOS           THE YOUNG  545D
   HO,H8,TO II4B        THE    554A
   PERISTERA          PIGEON   657D
   TRUGWN        TURTLE DOVE   836A
25 ANTHRWPOS 3A        MAN     68B
   DIKAIOS IB        UPRIGHT   194D
   EIMI III5C         TO BE    224C
   EPI IIIB             ON     289A
   EULAB8S            DEVOUT   322B
   IDOU IB           BEHOLD   371C
   HIEROSOLUMA IA   JERUSALEM  373D
   HO,H8,TO IIIH        THE    553B
   ONOMA II            NAME    574A
   PARAKL8SIS 3      COMFORT   623C
   PNEUMA 5C          SPIRIT   682D
   PROSDECHOMAI 2B    RECEIVE  719B
   SUMEWN 3           SYMEON   786A
26 AN  3D          (PARTICLE)   48D
   EIDON 5              SEE    220A
   8   2D             BEFORE   343C
   THANATOS IA         DEATH   351B
   THEWREW 2C        OBSERVE   360D
   KURIOS 2A           LORD    460B
   M8  AIIIB«           NOT    517D
   PNEUMA 5C«         SPIRIT   682D
   PRIN IA            BEFORE   707D
   CHR8MATIZW IB«             894A
       IMPART A WARNING
```

Verse	Greek	Gloss	Ref
26	CHR8MATIZW I8ß		894A
		IMPART A WARNING	
	CHRISTOS I	ANOINTED ONE	895B
27	GONEUS	PARENTS	I64B
	ETHIZW	THE LAW	2I7A
	EISAGW	BRING	23IC
	EN I5D	IN	259C
	ERCHOMAI IIAß	COME	3I0C
	HIERON 2	TEMPLE	373A
	KATA II5Aα	ACCORDING TO	408A
	NOMOS 3	LAW	544C
	HO,H8,TO II48ς	THE	554A
	PAIDION I	INFANT	609A
	PNEUMA 5Dα	SPIRIT	683A
	POIEW I28α	DO	689B
28	AGKAL8	ARM	I0C
	DECHOMAI I	TAKE	I76B
	EIS IAγ	INTO	227C
	EULOGEW I	SPEAK WELL	322C
29	APOLUW 2B	SEND AWAY	96B
	DESPOT8S	MASTER	I75C
	*DOULOS 4	SLAVE	205B
	EIR8N8 3	PEACE	227A
	KATA II5Aγ	ACCORDING TO	408B
	NUN IB	NOW	547D
	R8MA I	WORD	742D
30	OPHTHALMOS I	EYE	604B
	SWT8RIOS 2	SAVING	809C
31	HETOIMAZW 3	PREPARE	3I6C
	KATA IIIB	TO	407B
	LAOS 2	PEOPLE	468A
	PROSWPON IC6	FACE	728D
32	APOKALUPSIS I	REVELATION	9ID
	EIS 4D	FOR	228C
	ISRA8L 2	ISRAEL	382B
	LAOS 3A	PEOPLE	468A
	HO,H8,TO IIID	THE	552D
	PHWS 2	LIGHT	880B
33	THAUMAZW IAß	WONDER	353A
	IWS8PH 4	JOSEPH	386C
34	ANASTASIS I	RISE	59D
	ANTILEGW 2	OPPOSE	74B
	EULOGEW 2A	BLESS	322D
	IDOU IBα	BEHOLD	37IC
	ISRA8L 2	ISRAEL	382B
	KEIMAI 2A	SET	428A
	MARIA I	MARY	492D
	PTWSIS	COLLAPSE	735B
	S8MEION I	SIGN	755B
	SUMEWN 3	SYMEON	786A
35	AN 4	(PARTICLE)	48D
	APOKALUPTW I	REVEAL	9IC
	DIALOGISMOS I	THOUGHT	I85A
	DIERCHOMAI IA	GO THROUGH	I93C
	KARDIA I8ß	HEART	404C
	HOPWS 2Aß	IN ORDER THAT	580D
	ROMPHAIA	SWORD	744C
	SU 2	YOU	780A
	PSUCH8 I8γ	SOUL LIFE	90ID
36	AN8R I	MAN	65D
	HANNA	ANNA	69D
	APO II2A	FROM	86B
	AS8R	ASHER	II4C
36	EK 3B	FROM	234B
	ETOS	YEAR	3I7A
	ZAW 3A	LIVE	337C
	H8MERA 4B	DAY	348C
	THUGAT8R I	DAUGHTER	365B
	META AIIIA	WITH	509D
	PARTHENIA	VIRGINITY	632B
	PROBAINW 2	GO ON	709C
	PROPH8TIS	PROPHETESS	73ID
	PHANOU8L	PHANUEL	86IA
37	APHIST8MI 2A	WITHDRAW	I26B
	DE8SIS	PRAYER	I7IA
	ETOS	YEAR	3I7B
	HEWS IIIA	UNTIL	335B
	H8MERA IA	DAY	346C
	HIERON 2	TEMPLE	373A
	LATREUW	SERVE	468D
	N8STEIA 2B	FASTING	540A
	NUX ID	NIGHT	549A
	OGDO8KONTA	EIGHTY	555B
	TESSARES	FOUR	82IA
	CH8RA	THE WIDOW	889D
38	ANTHMOLOGEOMAI	PRAISE	66D
	AUTOS IH	EVEN	I22D
	EPHIST8MI IA	STAND BY	33IA
	HIEROSOLUMA IB	JERUSALEM	373D
	LALEW 2A6	SPEAK	464C
	LUTRWSIS I	REDEMPTION	484B
	PROSDECHOMAI 2B	RECEIVE	7I9B
	HWRA 2B	TIME OF DAY	904D
39	HAPAS 2	ALL	8IA
	HEAUTOU 4	ONESELF	2IID
	EPISTREPHW I8α	TURN	30IA
	KATA II5Aα	ACCORDING TO	408A
	KURIOS 2A	LORD	460B
	NAZARA	NAZARETH	534A
	NOMOS 3	LAW	544C
	HO,H8,TO II5	THE	554B
	POLIS I	CITY	692A
	POLIS I	CITY	692B
	TELEW I	FINISH	8I8C
	HWS IVIA	WHEN	907A
40	AUXANW 3	GROW	I2IC
	EIMI III5C	TO BE	224C
	EPI IIIIBγ	ON	288D
	KRATAIOW	STRENGTHEN	449C
	PAIDION I	INFANT	609A
	*PL8ROW IB	MAKE FULL	677A
	PNEUMA 3B	SPIRIT	68IC
	SOPHIA 3A	WISDOM	767B
	CHARIS 2A	FAVOR	885C
41	GONEUS	PARENTS	I64B
	HEORT8	FESTIVAL	279D
	ETOS	YEAR	3I7B
	HIEROSOLUMA IA	JERUSALEM	373D
	KATA II2C	EVERY	407C
	PASCHA I	THE PASSOVER	639A
42	AZUMOS IB	UNLEAVENED BREAD	I9C
	GINOMAI II2B	BE	I59C
	DWDEKA	TWELVE	209B
	ETHOS 2	CUSTOM	2I7D
	HEORT8	FESTIVAL	279D
	HEORT8	FESTIVAL	280A

42	ETOS	YEAR 317A	51	HOUTOS 2B	THIS 602A
	ECHW I3	HAVE 333C		PAS IDα	ALL 637C
	KATA II5Aα	ACCORDING TO 408A		R8MA 2	WORD 743A
	HOTE IB	WHEN 592C		HUPOTASSW IBβ	SUBJECT 855D
43	APOMENW	REMAIN BEHIND 96B	52	H8LIKIA IB	AGE 345D
	GINWSKW 6F	KNOW 160D		H8LIKIA 2	BODILY STATURE 346A
	GONEUS	PARENTS 164B		THEOS 3B	GOD 358A
	PAIS IAα	CHILD 609C		PARA II2B	BESIDE 615D
	TELEIOW I	COMPLETE 817C		PROKOPTW 2	GO FORWARD 714D
	HUPOMENW I	REMAIN 853C		SOPHIA 3A	WISDOM 767B
	HUPOSTREPHW	RETURN 855B		CHARIS 2B	FAVOR 885D
44	ANAZ8TEW	LOOK 53C			
	GNWSTOS IB	ACQUAINTANCE 163C			LUKE 3
	ERCHOMAI II	GO 311D			
	H8MERA IA	DAY 346D	I	ABIL8N8	ABILENE ID
	NOMIZW 2	THINK 543B		EPITROPEUW	BE PROCURATOR 303C
	HODOS IB	WAY 556C		ETOS	YEAR 317B
	*SUGGEN8S	RELATED 780B		H8GEMONEUW	BE LEADER 343D
	SUNODIA	CARAVAN 798D		H8GEMONIA I	CHIEF COMMAND 343D
45	ANAZ8TEW	LOOK 53C		H8RWD8S 2	HEROD 349B
	HEURISKW IA	FIND 325A		IOUDAIA I	JUDAEA 379D
	HUPOSTREPHW	RETURN 855B		ITOURAIOS	ITURAEA 385A
46	AKOUW IC	HEAR 31D		KAISAR	EMPEROR 396C
	GINOMAI I3F	TAKE PLACE 158C		LUSANIAS	LYSANIAS 483C
	DIDASKALOS	TEACHER 190D		PENTEKAIDEKATOS	FIFTEENTH 648D
	EPERWTAW IA	ASK 284D		PILATOS	PILATE 663C
	KATHEZOMAI I	SIT 389B		PONTIOS	PONTIUS 698C
	MESOS 2	THE MIDDLE 508D		TETRARCHEW	BE TETRARCH 821C
	META BII1	AFTER 511B		TIBERIOS	TIBERIUS 823B
47	AKOUW 1C	HEAR 31D		TRACHWNITIS	TRACHONITIS 833A
	APOKRISIS	ANSWER 93A		PHILIPPOS I	PHILIP 867D
	EXIST8MI 2B	BE AMAZED 276B		CHWRA IB	COUNTRY 897C
	EPI IIIBγ	ON 287A	2	ANADEIXIS	COMMISSIONING 53A
	KAI IID	AND 392D		HANNAS	ANNAS 69D
	PAS IDβ	ALL 637C		GINOMAI I4Cγ	COME, GO 159A
	SUNESIS I	INTELLIGENCE 796A		EPI I2	UNDER 286C
48	EIDON IA	SEE 219D		EPI IIIBγ	ON 288D
	EKPL8SSW 2	BE AMAZED 243D		ER8MOS 2	DESERT 309A
	IDOU IC	REMEMBER 371D		ZACHARIAS I	ZECHARIAH 336B
	KAGW I	AND I 386D		IWAN(N)8S I	JOHN 385B
	ODUNAW 2	CAUSE PAIN 557C		KAIAPHAS	CAIAPHAS 394D
	HOUTW 5	THUS 602D		R8MA I	WORD 742D
	POIEW I2Aβ	DO 689A		HUIOS IAα	SON 841B
	TEKNON IAβ	CHILD 816A	3	HAMARTIA I	SIN 42C
	TIS, TI 3A	WHICH 827B		APHESIS 2	PARDON 124C
48F	Z8TEW IAα	SEEK 339A		BAPTISMA I	BAPTISM 132A
49	DEI 2	IT IS NECESSARY 171B		EIS 4F	(PURPOSE) 228D
	EIMI III4	TO BE 224B		IORDAN8S	JORDAN 379C
	EN IIA	IN 257C		K8RUSSW 2Bβ	ANNOUNCE 432C
	HO,H8,TO II7	THE 554C		METANOIA	REPENTANCE 514A
	OIDA IE	KNOW 558C		OUN 2A	THEREFORE 597C
	HOTI IC	THAT 593A		PERICHWROS	NEIGHBORING 659B
	PAT8R 3Dα	FATHER 641D	4	BIBLOS I	BOOK 140D
	TIS, TI IBε	WHICH 827B		BOAW 2	SHOUT 143D
50	LALEW 2B	SPEAK 464D		HETOIMAZW I	PREPARE 316B
	R8MA I	WORD 742D		EUTHUS I	STRAIGHT 321B
	SUNI8MI	UNDERSTAND 798A		8SAIAS	ISAIAH 349C
51	DIAT8REW	KEEP 188D		KURIOS 2Cα	LORD 460C
	EIMI II4F	TO BE 223B		LOGOS IAζ	MATTER 479A
	KARDIA IBβ	HEART 404C		HODOS IA	WAY 556B
	KATABAINW IAβ	COME DOWN 409B		POIEW IIBι	DO 688B
	META AIIIA	WITH 509D		PROPH8T8S I	PROPHET 730D
	NAZARA	NAZARETH 534A		TRIBOS	BEATEN PATH 834A

4	PHWN8 2E	VOICE 879C	11	POIEW I2A«	DO 689A
	HWS II4A	SO 906B		CHITWN	SHIRT 890C
5	BOUNOS	HILL 146A	12	BAPTIZW 2A	BAPTIZE 131B
	EIMI III2	TO BE 224A		DIDASKALOS	TEACHER 190D
	EIS 8Aß	229C		ERCHOMAI IIA«	COME 310D
	EUTHUS I	STRAIGHT 321B		TELWN8S	TAX COLLECTOR 820B
	LEIOS	SMOOTH 471C	13	DIATASSW	ORDER 188C
	HODOS IA	WAY 556B		PARA III3	IN COMPARISON 616B
	OROS	MOUNTAIN 586A		POLUS II	MANY 695C
	PAS IA«	EVERY EACH 636C		POLUS IIC	MANY 696A
	PL8ROW IA	MAKE FULL 676C	14	ARKEW 2	BE SATISFIED 106D
	SKOLIOS I	CROOKED 763C		DIASEIW	EXTORT 187B
	TAPEINOW I	LOWER 812B		KAI I2E	AND 393B
	TRACHUS	ROUGH 832D		M8DE IB	AND NOT 519D
	PHARAGX	RAVINE 861B		M8DEIS 2A	NO 520A
6	HORAW IB	SEE 582A		OPSWNION IA	WAGES 607A
	PAS IA«	EVERY EACH 636C		STRATEUW I	778A
	SARX 3	BODY 751A			DO MILITARY SERVICE
	SWT8RIOS 2	SAVING 809C		SUKOPHANTEW I	SLANDER 784A
7	BAPTIZW 2A	BAPTIZE 131B	15	DIALOGIZOMAI I	CONSIDER 185A
	GENN8MA	CHILD 155A		KARDIA IBß	HEART 404C
	EKPOREUOMAI IA	GO OUT 243D		LAOS IA	PEOPLE 467D
	ENWPION 2A	BEFORE 270B		M8POTE 3B«	WHETHER PERHAPS 521B
	ENWPION 5C	BEFORE 270C		PERI IB	ABOUT 650B
	ECHIDNA	VIPER 332A		PROSDOKAW 3	EXPECT 719C
	LEGW I3	SAY 469D		CHRISTOS I	ANOINTED ONE 895B
	ORG8 2B	ANGER 583A	15F	IWAN(N)8S I	JOHN 385B
	OUN 2A	THEREFORE 597C	16	DIANO8MA	THOUGHT 186A
	OCHLOS I	CROWD 605D		ERCHOMAI IIAη	COME 310D
	TIS, TI IA«	WHICH 826C		HIKANOS 2	APPROPRIATE 375B
	HUPODEIKNUMI 2	SHOW 852A		ISCHUROS IA	STRONG 384A
	PHEUGW 2	FLEE 863C		LUW IA	LOOSE 484D
8	ABRAAM	ABRAHAM 1D		HOS,H8,HO I3A	(REL PRON) 587C
	AXIOS IB	WORTHY 77B		PNEUMA 5Cß	SPIRIT 683A
	ARCHW 2A«	BEGIN 113A		PUR IB	FIRE 737D
	EGEIRW IA«	RAISE UP 213D		HUDWR I	WATER 840D
	EK 3A	FROM 234A		HUPOD8MA	SANDAL 852B
	KARPOS 2A	RESULT 405D	16A	BAPTIZW 2A	BAPTIZE 131B
	LEGW I6	SAY 470A	16B	BAPTIZW 3B	BAPTIZE 131D
	LITHOS IA	STONE 475B	17	HALWN 2	WHAT WAS THRESHED 41A
	METANOIA	REPENTANCE 514A		APOTH8K8	STOREHOUSE 90C
	POIEW IIBη	DO 688A		ASBESTOS I	INEXTINGUISHABLE 114A
	TEKNON 2D	CHILD 816C		AUTOS 3D	(OBLIQUE CASE) 123A
9	AXIN8	AX 77A		ACHURON	CHAFF 128D
	BALLW IB	THROW 130C		DIAKATHAIRW	CLEAN OUT 182D
	EKKOPTW I	CUT DOWN 241B		DIAKATHARIZW	CLEAN OUT 183A
	8D8 2A	ALREADY 344D		KATAKAIW	CONSUME 412A
	KALOS 2A	GOOD 401B		HOS,H8,HO I3A	(REL PRON) 587C
	KARPOS IA	FRUIT 405C		PTUON	WINNOWING SHOVEL 735A
	KEIMAI IB	LIE 428A		PUR IB	FIRE 737C
	OUN IA	THEREFORE 597C		SITOS	WHEAT 759D
	PAS IA«	EVERY EACH 636C		SUNAGW	WITH 789D
	POIEW IIBη	DO 688A		SUNAGW I	GATHER 789D
	PUR IB	FIRE 737D		CHEIR I	HAND 888B
	RIZA IA	ROOT 743B	18	HETEROS IBß	ANOTHER 315B
10	EPERWTAW IA	ASK 285A		EUAGGELIZW 2Aγ	PREACH 317D
	OUN IC«	THEREFORE 597B		KAI I4	AND 394A
	OCHLOS I	CROWD 605D		LAOS IA	PEOPLE 467D
11	APOKRINOMAI I	ANSWER 92D		MEN 2E	(PARTICLE) 504C
	BRWMA I	FOOD 147C		PARAINEW	ADVISE 621D
	LEGW I8D	SAY 470C		PARAKALEW 2	APPEAL TO 622C
	METADIDWMI	SHARE 512B		POLUS I2B«	MANY 695A
	HOMOIWS	LIKEWISE 570D	18F	OUN 5	THEREFORE 597D

```
19 ELEGCHW 3            EXPOSE 249A        23FF  OZIAS              UZZIAH 557D
   H8RWD8S 2           HEROD 349B          23FF  OCHOZIAS          AHAZIAH 606A
   HERODIAS          HERODIAS 349C         23FF  ROBOAM          REHOBOAM 744A
   HOS,H8,HO 14A    (REL PRON) 587D        23FF  SADWK              ZADOK 747A
   HOS,H8,HO 15Cα   (REL PRON) 588B        24 IANNAI              JANNAI 368D
   PON8ROS 2C          WICKED 698A            IWS8PH 3           JOSEPH 386C
   TETRARCH8S        TETRARCH 821D            LEVI 2               LEVI 473B
   PHILIPPOS 1         PHILIP 868A            MATTHAT 1          MATTHAT 497A
20 EGKLEIW            ENCLOSE 215B            MELCHI 1            MELCHI 503A
   EPI III8β               TO 286D         25 AMWS 1               AMOS 47C
   IWAN(N)8S 1            JOHN 385B            HESLI                ESLI 313B
   KATAKLEIW          SHUT UP 412C            MATTATHIAS 1     MATTATHIAS 497B
   PHULAK8 3            GUARD 875D            NAGGAI              NAGGAI 534A
21 ANOIGW 1B             OPEN 70C             NAOUM               NAHUM 535D
   HAPAS 1               WHOLE 81A         26 IWDA                  JODA 385D
   GINOMAI I3E      TAKE PLACE 158B           IWS8CH             JOSECH 386D
   DE 2                BUT, AND 170C          MAATH                MAATH 485B
   LAOS 1A              PEOPLE 467D           MATTATHIAS 2     MATTATHIAS 497B
   OURANOS 2A          HEAVEN 599B            SEMEIN             SEMEIN 754B
22 AGAP8TOS 1         BELOVED 6C           27 ZOROBABEL       ZERUBBABEL 340A
   GENNAW 1B            BEGET 154D            IWANAN             JOANAN 385B
   GINOMAI I4Cα      COME, GO 159A            N8RI                 NERI 540A
   EIDOS 1               FORM 220B            R8SA                RHESA 743A
   EPI III8γ               ON 288D           SALATHI8L       SHEALTIEL 747D
   EUDOKEW 2A     WELL PLEASED 319C       28 ADDI                  ADDI 15C
   KATABAINW IB    COME DOWN 409C            ELMADAM           ELMADAM 251D
   OURANOS 2A          HEAVEN 599B            8R                    ER 349A
   PERISTERA           PIGEON 657D           KWSAM               COSAM 463A
   PNEUMA 5Cα          SPIRIT 682D           MELCHI 2           MELCHI 503A
   S8MERON              TODAY 756B        29 ELIEZER           ELIEZER 250D
   SWMATIKOS 1         BODILY 807D            I8SOUS 2            JESUS 374C
   HUIOS 2B               SON 842B            IWRIM               JORIM 386B
   HUIOS 2B               SON 842C            LEVI 3               LEVI 473B
   PHWN8 2D              VOICE 879B           MATTHAT 2         MATTHAT 497A
23 ARCHW 2B             BEGIN 113B        30 ELIAKIM          ELIAKIM 250C
   EIMI IV6              TO BE 225A           IOUDAS 2            JUDAS 380C
   ETOS                   YEAR 317A           IWNAM               JONAM 386A
   8LI                    HELI 345C           IWS8PH 2          JOSEPH 386C
   IAKWB 2               JACOB 368B           SUMEWN 2          SYMEON 766A
   IWS8PH 4            JOSEPH 386C         31 DAUID               DAVID 170B
   L                    THIRTY 463A           MATTATHA        MATTATHA 497B
   NOMIZW 2             THINK 543B            MELEA               MELEA 501B
   TRIAKONTA           THIRTY 833D            MENNA               MENNA 504C
   HWS II4B                SO 906B            NATHAM             NATHAN 534C
   HWSEI 2                 AS 907D        32 BOOS                  BOAZ 144B
23FF ABIOUD            ABIUD 1D              IESSAI              JESSE 374B
23FF AZWR              AZOR 19C              IWB8D                OBED 385D
23FF AMASIAS          AMAZIAH 43D            NAASSWN           NAHSHON 534A
23FF AMWS 2            AMOS 47C              SALA 1              SHELAH 747C
23FF ASALEUTOS 2   IMMOVABLE 113D           SALMWN             SALMON 746B
23FF ACHAZ            AHAZ 127C           33 ADMIN               ADMIN 18B
23FF HEZEKIAS      HEZEKIAH 217A            AMINADAB         AMMINADAB 45D
23FF ELEAZAR        ELEAZAR 248C            ARAM                 ARAM 103C
23FF ELIAKIM        ELIAKIM 250C            ARNI                 ARNI 107B
23FF ELIOUD          ELIUD 250D             HESRWM             HEZRON 313D
23FF IWATHAM         JOTHAM 385B            IOUDAS 1A           JUDAH 380C
23FF IWAKIM       JEHOIAKIM 385B            PHARES              PEREZ 861B
23FF IWAS            JOASH 385D          34 ABRAAM            ABRAHAM 1D
23FF IWRAM           JORAM 386A             THARA               TERAH 352C
23FF IWSAPHAT  JEHOSHAPHAT 386B            IAKWB 1             JACOB 368A
23FF IWSIAS         JOSIAH 386D             ISAAK               ISAAC 381C
23FF MANASS8S 2   MANASSEH 491B             NACHWR             NAHOR 536B
23FF MATTHAN       MATTHAN 497A         35 EBER                  EBER 212B
```

35 RAGAU — REU 741A
   SALA 2 — SHELAH 747C
   SEROUCH — SERUG 755A
   PHALEK — PELEG 860A
36 ARPHAXAD — ARPHAXAD 110D
   KAINAM 1 — CAINAN 394D
   LAMECH — LAMECH 466D
   NWE — NOAH 549C
   S8M — SHEM 755A
37 ENWCH — ENOCH 270D
   IARET — JARED 369A
   KAINAM 2 — CAINAN 394D
   MATHOUSALA — METHUSELAH 487B
   MALELE8L — MALELEEL 490A
38 ADAM — ADAM 15B
   ENWS — ENOS 270C
   S8TH — SETH 755A

               LUKE 4

1 AGW 3 — LEAD 14B
   DE 3 — BUT, AND 170D
   IORDAN8S — JORDAN 379C
   PL8R8S 1B — FULL 675D
   PNEUMA 5C8 — SPIRIT 682D
   HUPOSTREPHW — RETURN 855B
1A   PNEUMA 5D« — SPIRIT 683B
1B   PNEUMA 5D« — SPIRIT 683A
2 EKEINOS 2B« — THAT 239B
   ESTHIW 1A — EAT 312D
   ESTHIW 1Ey — EAT 313B
   OU 6A — NO 595A
   OUDEIS 2B« — NOTHING 596C
   PEINAW 1 — HUNGER 645D
   PEIRAZW 2D — TRY 646B
   SUNTELEW 1 — COMPLETE 799D
   TESSARAKONTA — FORTY 820D
   HUSTEROS 2A — LATER 857B
2B   H8MERA 4B — TIME 348B
2F   DIABOLOS 2 — THE SLANDERER 181A
3 ARTOS 1A — BREAD 110A
   EIPON 3C — SAY 225D
   HINA III1A6 — IN ORDER THAT 378B
   LITHOS 1A — STONE 475B
   HUIOS 2B — SON 842C
4 APOKRINOMAI 1 — ANSWER 92D
   ARTOS 1A — BREAD 110A
   EPI III8y — ON 287A
   ZAW 1C — LIVE 336D
   PAS 1Ay — EVERY EACH 637A
5 ANAGW 1 — LEAD 52D
   DEIKNUMI 1A — SHOW 171D
   OIKOUMEN8 1A — THE WORLD 564A
   STIGM8 — POINT 776B
   HUPS8LOS 1 — HIGH 857C
   CHRONOS — TIME 896B
6 HAPAS 1 — WHOLE 81A
   DIABOLOS 2 — THE SLANDERER 181A
   DOXA 2 — MAGNIFICENCE 203A
   EXOUSIA 4B — AUTHORITY 278B
   PARADIDWMI — GIVE OVER 619D
   PARADIDWMI 1A — GIVE OVER 619D
7 EAN II1B — IF 210C

7 EGW — I 216C
   ENWPION 1 — BEFORE 270A
   PROSKUNEW 3 — DO REVERENCE 724B
8 GRAPHW 2C — WRITE 165D
   THEOS 3C — GOD 358A
   LATREUW — SERVE 468C
   MONOS 1A8 — ONLY 529C
   OPISW 2A« — BEHIND 578C
   PROSKUNEW — DO REVERENCE 723D
   PROSKUNEW 2A — DO REVERENCE 724A
   HUPAGW 1 — GO AWAY 844B
9 AGW 3 — LEAD 14B
   BALLW 1B — LIE 130D
   ENTEUTHEN 1 — FROM HERE 268A
   HIERON 2 — TEMPLE 373B
   HIST8MI II1A« — PUT 382D
   KATW 2 — DOWNWARDS 426B
   PTERUGION — END EDGE 734D
   HUIOS 2B — SON 842C
10 AGGELOS 2A — ANGEL 7D
   DIAPHULASSW — GUARD 190A
   «ENTELLW — COMMAND 268A
   HO,H8,TO II14B« — THE 554A
11 AIRW 2 — LIFT UP 24A
   EPI II1A« — ON 285D
   LITHOS 1A — STONE 475B
   M8POTE 2B« — (NEG PARTICLE) 521A
   PROSKOPTW 1A — STRIKE AGAINST 723C
   CHEIR 1 — HAND 888B
   CHEIR 1 — HAND 888C
12 EKPEIRAZW — PUT TO THE TEST 243A
   OU 4B — NO 594D
13 APHIST8MI 2B — KEEP AWAY 126C
   ACHRI 1A — UNTIL 128B
   DIABOLOS 2 — THE SLANDERER 181A
   KAIROS 1 — TIME 395C
   PAS 1A« — EVERY EACH 636C
   PEIRASMOS 2A — TEST 646C
   SUNTELEW 1 — COMPLETE 799D
14 DUNAMIS 1 — POWER 206D
   EXERCHOMAI 2B« — GO OUT 274C
   KATA II C — DOWN 406C
   PERICHWROS — NEIGHBORING 659B
   PNEUMA 5D« — SPIRIT 683A
   HUPOSTREPHW — RETURN 855B
   PH8M8 — REPORT 864A
15 AUTOS 2 — THEY 122D
   SUNAGWG8 2A — 790C
       PLACE OF ASSEMBLY
16 ANAGINWSKW 2 — READ 51C
   ANATREPHW 3 — BRING UP 62C
   ANIST8MI 2A — RISE 69C
   EISERCHOMAI 1A8 — COME 231D
   EIWTHA — ACCUSTOMED 233B
   H8MERA 2 — DAY 347C
   NAZARA — NAZARETH 534A
   HOU 1A8 — WHERE 594A
   SABBATON 1B8 — SABBATH 746C
   SUNAGWG8 2A — 790C
       PLACE OF ASSEMBLY
   TREPHW 2 — FEED 833C
17 ANAPTUSSW — UNROLL 59C
   ANOIGW 1C — OPEN 70C

17	BIBLION 1	BOOK	140D
	EPIDIDWMI 1	GIVE	292B
	HEURISKW 1B	FIND	325B
	8SAIAS	ISAIAH	349C
	HOU 1A8	WHERE	594A
	TOPOS 2A	PLACE	830D
17A	HO,H8,TO IIIA«	THE	552B
17B	HO,H8,TO IIIA«	THE	552B
18	AICHMALWTOS	CAPTIVE	26C
	ANABLEPHIS	RECOVERY OF SIGHT	50C
	HEINEKEN	ON ACCOUNT OF	225A
	HENEKA	BECAUSE OF	264B
	EUAGGELIZW 2AY	PREACH	317D
	THRAUMATIZW	BREAK	363D
	THRAUW 2B	BREAK	363D
	IAOMAI 2	HEAL	369A
	K8RUSSW 2B8	ANNOUNCE	432C
	KURIOS 2A	LORD	460B
	PNEUMA 5A	SPIRIT	682C
	PTWCHOS 1B	BEGGING POOR	735D
	SUNTRIBW 2	SHATTER	801B
	CHRIW 1	ANOINT	895D
18A	APOSTELLW 1BY	SEND AWAY	98B
18A	APHESIS 1	RELEASE	124C
18B	APOSTELLW 1D	SEND AWAY	98C
18B	APHESIS 1	RELEASE	124C
19	DEKTOS	ACCEPTABLE	173B
	ENIAUTOS 2	YEAR	266A
	K8RUSSW 2B8	ANNOUNCE	432C
20	APODIDWMI 2	GIVE BACK	90A
	ATENIZW	LOOK INTENTLY AT	119C
	BIBLION 1	BOOK	140D
	KATHIZW 2A«	SIT DOWN	390D
	HO,H8,TO IIIA«	THE	552B
	OPHTHALMOS 1	EYE	604B
	PTUSSW	FOLD UP	735B
	HUP8RET8S	SERVANT	850C
21	ARCHW 2A8	BEGIN	113A
	GRAPH8 2A	SCRIPTURE	165B
	EN 13	IN	258A
	LEGW 13	SAY	469D
	OUS 1	EAR	600B
	PL8ROW 4A	MAKE FULL	677C
	S8MERON	TODAY	756B
22	EKPOREUOMAI 2	GO OUT	244A
	THAUMAZW 1A8	WONDER	353A
	IWS8PH 4	JOSEPH	386C
	LOGOS 1B8	WORD	479C
	MARTUREW 1C		494A
	TESTIFY FAVORABLY		
	STOMA 1A«	MOUTH	777B
	HUIOS 1A«	SON	841B
	CHARIS 1	GRACIOUSNESS	885B
23	EIS 9A	IN	229D
	THERAPEUW 2	HEAL	359C
	IATROS 1	PHYSICIAN	369C
	KAPHARNAOUM	CAPERNAUM	427C
	PANTWS 1	BY ALL MEANS	614B
	PANTWS 3	OF COURSE	614B
	PARABOL8 2	PARABLE	617C
	PATRIS 2	FATHERLAND	642C
	HWDE 2A	HERE	903D
24	AM8N 2	AMEN	45B

24	DEKTOS	ACCEPTABLE	173B
	LEGW IIID	ASSURE	470D
	OUDEIS 1	NO	596B
	PATRIS 2	FATHERLAND	642C
	PROPH8T8S 3	PROPHET	731A
25	AL8THEIA 3	REALITY	35D
	G8 4	LAND	156D
	GINOMAI 11B8	COME ABOUT	157B
	HEX	SIX	270D
	EPI 11B8	ON	286B
	EPI 1112B	ON	289B
	ETOS	YEAR	317B
	H8MERA 4B	TIME	348B
	ISRA8L 2	ISRAEL	382B
	KLEIW 2	SHUT	435B
	LEGW IIID	ASSURE	470D
	LIMOS 2	FAMINE	476B
	MEGAS 2AY	GREAT	499A
	*M8N 1	MONTH	520D
	OURANOS 1B	HEAVEN	598C
	PAS 1C«	ALL	637B
	POLUS IIA«	MANY	694A
	CH8RA	THE WIDOW	889D
	HWS IVIA	WHEN	907A
25F	8LIAS	ELIJAH	345D
26	GUN8 2	WIFE	167C
	PEMPW 1	SEND	647D
	SAREPTA	ZAREPHATH	750A
	SIDWN	SIDON	757C
	SIDWNIOS 1	SIDONIAN	757D
27	ELISAIOS	ELISHA	250D
	EPI 12	UNDER	286B
	ISRA8L 2	ISRAEL	382B
	LEPROS	LEPER	473A
	NAIMAN	NAAMAN	535B
	POLUS IIA«	MANY	694A
	PROPH8T8S 1	PROPHET	730D
	SUROS	SYRIAN	801D
28	THUMOS 2	ANGER	366A
	PIMPL8MI 1A8	FILL	663D
29	ANIST8MI 2D	RISE	69D
	EKBALLW 1	DRIVE OUT	236D
	EXW 2B	OUTSIDE	279B
	HEWS 112A	AS FAR AS	335C
	KATAKR8MNIZW	THROW DOWN	413A
	OIKODOMEW 1A	BUILD	560D
	OPHRUS	EYEBROW	605B
	HWSTE 2B	THEREFORE	906C
29A	POLIS 1	CITY	692A
29B	POLIS 1	CITY	692A
30	DIERCHOMAI 1B«	GO THROUGH	193C
	MESOS 2	THE MIDDLE	508C
31	DIDASKW 2A	TEACH	191A
	EIMI 114E	TO BE	223B
	ZABOULWN	ZEBULUN	336A
	KATERCHOMAI 1	COME DOWN	423A
	KAPHARNAOUM	CAPERNAUM	427C
	NEPHTHALIM	NAPHTALI	538D
	PARATHALASSIOS	BY THE SEA	621B
	POLIS 1	CITY	692A
	SABBATON 1B8	SABBATH	746C
32	DIDACH8 3	TEACHING	191C
	EKPL8SSW 2	BE AMAZED	243D

32	EXOUSIA 2	ABILITY	277D
	EPI IIIBɣ	ON	287A
	LOGOS IAβ	WORD	478C
33	AKATHARTOS 2	IMPURE	28C
	ANAKRAZW	CRY OUT	56A
	ANTHRWPOS 3Aβ	MAN	68B
	ECHW I2Eα	HAVE	333A
	MEGAS 2Aɣ	GREAT	498D
	PNEUMA 4C	SPIRIT	682A
	SUNAGWG8 2A		790C
	PLACE OF ASSEMBLY		
	PHWN8 2A	VOICE	878D
34	HAGIOS 2Cβ	THE HOLY ONE	10A
	APOLLUMI IAα	RUIN	94B
*EA		AH	210A
	EAW 2	LET	212A
	EGW	I	216C
	EIMI II6C	TO BE	223C
	NAZAR8NOS	THE NAZARENE	534A
	NAZWRAIOS	NAZARENE	534B
	OIDA IC	KNOW	558B
34A	TIS, TI IBε	WHICH	827B
35	ANAKRAUGAZW	CRY OUT	56A
	BLAPTW	HARM	141D
	EXERCHOMAI IA6	GO OUT	274A
	EPITIMAW I	REBUKE	303B
	MESOS 2	THE MIDDLE	508C
	M8DEIS 2Bβ	NOTHING	520A
	RIPTW I	THROW	744A
	PHIMOW 2	TIE SHUT	869D
36	AKATHARTOS 2	IMPURE	28C
	GINOMAI I4Cɣ	COME, GO	159A
	EXERCHOMAI IA6	GO OUT	274A
	EXOUSIA 2	ABILITY	277D
	EPI IIIBɣ	ON	289A
	EPITASSW	COMMAND	302A
	THAMBOS	ASTONISHMENT	351B
	LOGOS IAβ	WORD	478B
	HOTI IC	THAT	593B
	PNEUMA 4C	SPIRIT	682A
	SULLALEW	TALK	784B
37	EKPOREUOMAI 2	GO OUT	244A
	8CHOS 2	REPORT	350C
	PAS IAα	EVERY EACH	636C
	PERICHWROS	NEIGHBORING	659B
	TOPOS IA	PLACE	830A
38	ANIST8MI 2A	RISE	69C
	ERWTAW 2	ASK	312A
	KATECHW IDβ	BE BOUND	424B
	MEGAS 2Aɣ	GREAT	499A
	OIKIA IA	HOUSE	559D
	PENTHERA	MOTHER IN LAW	648B
	PURETOS	FEVER	738B
	SIMWN I	SIMON	758C
	SUNECHW 5	DISTRESS	797A
39	ANIST8MI 2D	RISE	69D
	APHI8MI 3A	LEAVE	125C
	EPANW 2A	ON	283A
	EPITIMAW I	REBUKE	303B
	EPHIST8MI IA	STAND BY	331A
	PARACHR8MA	AT ONCE	629B
	PURETOS	FEVER	738B
40	AGW IA	LEAD	14A
40	ASTHENEW IA	BE SICK	115A
	DUNW	SET	208B
	HEKASTOS 2	EACH	236A
	EPITITH8MI IAα	PUT UPON	302D
	ECHW I2Bβ	HAVE	332C
	H8LIOS	THE SUN	346B
	THERAPEUW 2	HEAL	359C
	NOSOS I	DISEASE	545D
	HOSOS 2	HOW GREAT	590B
	PAS IEɣ	ALL	638A
	POIKILOS I	DIVERSIFIED	690A
41	AUTOS 3A	(OBLIQUE CASE)	122D
	DAIMONION 2	DEMON	168B
	EAW I	LET	211D
	EXERCHOMAI IA6	GO OUT	274A
	EPITIMAW I	REBUKE	303B
	KRAZW 2A	CALL	448D
	KRAUGAZW 2A	CRY	450C
	LALEW 2Aβ	SPEAK	464B
	LEGW IIBα	SAY	469C
	OIDA ID	KNOW	558B
	HUIOS 2B	SON	842C
	CHRISTOS I	ANOINTED ONE	895B
41A	HOTI 2	THAT	593D
41B	HOTI 3A	THAT	593D
42	GINOMAI IIBɣ	COME ABOUT	157B
	EXERCHOMAI IAβ	GO OUT	274A
	EPECHW I	HOLD FAST	285B
	EPIZ8TEW IA	SEEK AFTER	292D
	ER8MOS IA	ABANDONED	308D
	ERCHOMAI IIAɣ	COME	310C
	HEWS II2A	AS FAR AS	335D
	H8MERA IA	DAY	346C
	KATECHW IAα	HOLD BACK	423D
	M8 AIIIDα	NOT	518A
	HO,H8,TO II4B6	THE	554A
	OCHLOS I	CROWD	605D
	TOPOS IC	PLACE	830B
42A	POREUW I	PROCEED	699A
42B	POREUW I	PROCEED	699A
43	APOSTELLW IBɣ	SEND AWAY	98B
	BASILEIA 3B	KINGDOM	134D
	DEI I	IT IS NECESSARY	171A
	EPI IIIB𝜂	ON	289B
	HETEROS IBβ	ANOTHER	315B
	EUAGGELIZW 2Aα	PREACH	317D
	HOTI 2	THAT	593D
	POLIS 3	CITY	692C
44	IOUDAIA 2	JUDAEA	379D
	K8RUSSW 2Bβ	ANNOUNCE	432C

LUKE 5

I	GENN8SARET	GENNESARET	155A
	GINOMAI I3F	TAKE PLACE	158B
	EIMI II4A	TO BE	223A
	EPIKEIMAI 2B	BE URGENT	294C
	KAI I2B	AND	393A
	LIMN8 I	LAKE	476A
	LOGOS IBβ	WORD	479B
	OCHLOS I	CROWD	605C
	PARA IIIIBα	ALONG	616A
IF	HIST8MI II2Bβ	BEING	383C

2	HALIEUS	FISHERMAN	37A
	APOBAINW I	GO AWAY	88A
	APOPLUNW	WASH OFF	96D
	DIKTUON	NET	197D
	EIDON	SEE	219C
	LIMN8 I	LAKE	476A
	PARA IIIB«	ALONG	616A
	PLOIARION	BOAT	679A
	PLOION 2	SHIP	679B
	PLUNW I	WASH	680C
3	G8 4	LAND	156C
	EK 2	AWAY FROM	234A
	EMBAINW	GO IN	253C
	EPANAGW I	PUT OUT	282C
	ERWTAW 2	ASK	312B
	KATHIZW 2A«	SIT DOWN	390D
	OLIGOS 3A	LITTLE	566C
	HOSOS I	HOW GREAT	590B
	OCHLOS I	CROWD	605D
4	AGRA I	CATCHING	13A
	BATHOS I	DEPTH	129D
	EIS 4F	(PURPOSE)	228D
	ENWPION 3	BEFORE	270B
	EPANAGW I	PUT OUT	282C
	LALEW 2Av	SPEAK	464B
	PAUW 2	STOP	643C
	HWS IVIA	WHEN	907A
4F	CHALAW	LET DOWN	882C
4FF	DIKTUON	NET	197D
5	DIA AIIIA	THROUGH	178D
	EPI IIIBv	ON	287A
	EPISTAT8S	MASTER	300B
	KOPIAW 2	BECOME WEARY	444B
	LAMBANW IC	TAKE	465D
	NUX IB	NIGHT	548D
	HOLOS I	WHOLE	567C
	R8MA I	WORD	742D
6	DIA(R)R8GNUMI I	BREAK	187A
	ICHTHUS	FISH	385A
	HOUTOS IB«	THIS	601C
	PL8THOS 2A	QUANTITY	674B
	POIEW IIB«	DO	687D
	POLUS IIB«	MANY	694C
	R8GNUMI I	TEAR	742C
	SUGKLEIW I	ENCLOSE	781C
7	AMPHOTEROI I	BOTH	47A
	BUTHIZW I	SINK	148A
	HETEROS IA	OTHER	315A
	KATANEUW	SIGNAL	416A
	METOCHOS 2	PARTNER	516A
	HO,H8,TO II4B«	THE	554A
	PARA III4	ALMOST	616C
	PIMPL8MI IA«	FILL	663D
	PLOION 2	SHIP	679B
	SULLAMBANW 2B	SEIZE	784D
	HWSTE 2A9	THEREFORE	908C
8	HAMARTWLOS I	SINNER	43C
	AN8R 4	MAN	66B
	GONU	KNEE	164B
	EXERCHOMAI IA«	GO OUT	274A
	KURIOS 2C9	LORD	460D
	LEGW I8A	SAY	470B
	PETROS	PETER	661A
8	PROSPIPTW I	FALL DOWN BEFORE	725B
9	AGRA I	CATCHING	13A
	EPI IIIBv	ON	287B
	THAMBOS	ASTONISHMENT	351B
	ICHTHUS	FISH	385A
	HOS,H8,HO I4A	(REL PRON)	587D
	PAS IDv	ALL	637D
	PERIECHW IB	SEIZE	652D
	SULLAMBANW IA9	SEIZE	784C
	SUN IC	WITH	789B
10	ANTHRWPOS IA9	MAN	67C
	EIMI II4Bv	TO BE	223A
	ZEBEDAIOS	ZEBEDEE	337D
	ZWGREW	CAPTURE ALIVE	340C
	IAKWBOS I	JAMES	368B
	IWAN(N)8S 2	JOHN	385C
	KOINWNOS IA«	COMPANION	440C
	NUN 3B	NOW	548B
	HOMOIWS	LIKEWISE	570D
	PHOBEW IA	BE AFRAID	870C
11	AKOLOUTHEW 3	FOLLOW	30D
	APHI8MI 3A	ABANDON	125D
	G8 4	LAND	156C
	KATAGW	LEAD	411A
	KATALEIPW 2A	LEAVE BEHIND	414D
	PLOION 2	SHIP	679B
12	AN8R 4	MAN	66B
	GINOMAI I3F	TAKE PLACE	158B
	DEOMAI 3	ASK	174B
	EAN IIA	IF	210B
	HEIS 3A	SOMEONE	230D
	EPI IIIIA9	ON	288A
	IDOU 2	THERE IS	371D
	KATHARIZW IB«	CLEANSE	388A
	KAI I2B	AND	393A
	KURIOS 2C9	LORD	460D
	PIPTW IB«	FALL	665B
	PL8R8S IB	FULL	675C
	POLIS I	CITY	692A
	PROSWPON IA	FACE	728B
12F	LEPRA	LEPROSY	473A
13	APERCHOMAI IB	GO AWAY	83D
	HAPTW 2B	TOUCH	102C
	EKTEINW I	STRETCH OUT	244D
	KATHARIZW IB«	CLEANSE	388A
14	APERCHOMAI IA	GO AWAY	83D
	DEIKNUMI IA	SHOW	171D
	HIEREUS IB«	PRIEST	372C
	KATHARISMOS I	PURIFICATION	388C
	MARTURION IA	TESTIMONY	494D
	M8DEIS 2A	NO	520A
	MWUS8S	MOSES	533D
	PARAGGELLW	GIVE ORDERS	618C
	PETRA IA	ROCK	660A
	PROSTASSW	COMMAND	725D
	PROSPHERW 2A	BRING (TO)	727B
	SEAUTOU 3	YOURSELF	753A
15	ASTHENEIA IA	WEAKNESS	114D
	DIERCHOMAI 3	GO ABOUT	193D
	THERAPEUW 2	HEAL	359C
	LOGOS IA9	WORD	478C
	MALLON I	MORE	490B
	OCHLOS I	CROWD	605D

15 POLUS IIAᵱ	MANY 694B	22 EPIGINWSKW 2C	KNOW 291A
SUNERCHOMAI IA	ASSEMBLE 795D	KARDIA 18ᵱ	HEART 404C
16 ER8MOS 2	DESERT 309A	23 APHI8MI 2	FORGIVE 125C
PROSEUCHOMAI	PRAY 721A	EUKOPOS	EASY 322A
HUPOCHWREW I	RETREAT 856B	PERIPATEW IC	GO ABOUT 655A
16F AUTOS IB	SELF 122B	TIS, TI I8γ	WHICH 827A
17 GALILAIA	GALILEE 149D	23F EGEIRW IB	RAISE UP 214A
GINOMAI I3F	TAKE PLACE 158B	24 AIRW IA	LIFT UP 23D
EIMI II4A	TO BE 223A	APHI8MI 2	FORGIVE 125C
EIMI II49ᵱ	TO BE 223A	EXOUSIA 3	AUTHORITY 278A
HEIS 3A	SOMEONE 230D	KLINIDION	STRETCHER 437C
ERCHOMAI IIAᵱ	COME 310B	LEGW I3	SAY 469D
H8MERA 2	DAY 347A	OIKOS IAα	HOUSE 563A
IAOMAI I	HEAL 369A	PARALUTIKOS	PARALYTIC 625D
IOUDAIA I	JUDAEA 379D	PARALUW	WEAKEN 625D
KATH8MAI IAγ	SIT 390B	HUIOS 2C	SON 843A
KAI I2B	AND 393A	25 ENWPION 2A	BEFORE 270B
KWM8 I	VILLAGE 462D	EPI IIIIA⟨	ON 288C
NOMODIDASKALOS	543D	KATAKEIMAI I	LIE DOWN 412B
TEACHER OF THE LAW		OIKOS IAα	HOUSE 563A
HO,H8,TO IIIOA	THE 555A	HOS,H8,HO I28ᵱ	(REL PRON) 587B
18 AN8R 6	MAN 66B	PARACHR8MA	AT ONCE 629B
ANTHRWPOS 3Aᵱ	MAN 68B	25F DOXAZW I	PRAISE 203C
EISPHERW I	BRING IN 233A	26 HAPAS 2	ALL 81A
ENWPION I	BEFORE 270A	EKSTASIS I	DISTRACTION 244C
Z8TEW 2Bγ	SEEK 339D	LAMBANW IC	TAKE 465D
IDOU 2	THERE IS 371D	HOTI 2	THAT 593D
KLIN8	COUCH 437C	PARADOXOS	WONDERFUL 621A
PARALUW	WEAKEN 625D	PIMPL8MI IAᵱ	FILL 663D
TITH8MI IIAᵱ	PUT 823C	PHOBOS 2Aα	FEAR 871C
PHERW 4Bᵱ	BEAR 863C	27 HALPHAIOS I	ALPHAᴣUS 41A
19 ANABAINW IAα	GO UP 49D	EXERCHOMAI IAᵱ	GO OUT 274A
DIA AI2	THROUGH 178C	KATH8MAI IAα	SIT 390B
DIA BIII	BECAUSE OF 180A	LEUI 4	LEVI 473B
DWMA	ROOF 209C	META BII3	AFTER 511C
EISPHERW I	BRING IN 233A	ONOMA II	NAME 574A
EMPROSTHEN 2A	IN FRONT 256C	TELWN8S	TAX COLLECTOR 820B
EPI IIIIAᵱ	ON 288A	TELWNION	TAX OFFICE 820B
HEURISKW 2	FIND 325D	27F AKOLOUTHEW 3	FOLLOW 30D
KATHI8MI	LET DOWN 391A	28 ANIST8MI 2D	RISE 69D
KERAMOS 2	TILE 430A	KATALEIPW 2D	LEAVE BEHIND 414D
KLINIDION	STRETCHER 437C	29 DOCH8	BANQUET 205C
MESOS 2	THE MIDDLE 508C	KATAKEIMAI 3	LIE DOWN 412B
POIOS 2Bᵱ	OF WHAT KIND 691C	LEUI 4	LEVI 473B
SUN 4A	WITH 789C	MEGAS IC	LARGE 498D
20 ANTHRWPOS IAγ	MAN 67C	OIKIA IA	HOUSE 559D
APHI8MI 2	FORGIVE 125C	OCHLOS 3	CROWD 605D
PISTIS 28α	FAITH 668D	POIEW II8⟨	DO 688A
20FF HAMARTIA I	SIN 42C	POLUS IIBα	MANY 694C
21 ARCHW 2Aᵱ	BEGIN II3A	TELWN8S	TAX COLLECTOR 820B
APHI8MI 2	FORGIVE 125C	30 HAMARTWLOS 2	SINNER 43D
BLASPH8MIA 2B	SLANDER 142C	GOGGUZW I	MURMUR 163D
DIALOGIZOMAI I	CONSIDER 185A	DIA BII2	WHY 180B
HEIS 2C	ONE 230C	ESTHIW IC	EAT 313A
LALEW 2B	SPEAK 464C	ESTHIW I8ᵱ	EAT 313B
MONOS IAγ	ONLY 529C	META AII2	WITH 510C
HOUTOS IAα	THIS 600D	PINW I	DRINK 664C
HOUTOS IAδ	THIS 601A	TELWN8S	TAX COLLECTOR 820B
PHARISAIOS	PHARISEE 861C	PHARISAIOS	PHARISEE 861C
21A TIS, TI IAᵱ	WHICH 826D	31 IATROS I	PHYSICIAN 369C
21B TIS, TI IAα	WHICH 826C	KAKWS I	BADLY 399B
22 DIALOGIZOMAI I	CONSIDER 185A	HUGIAINW I	BE HEALTHY 839D
DIALOGISMOS I	THOUGHT 185A	CHREIA I	NEED 893B

32	ALLA 1B	BUT, YET	37C
	HAMARTWLOS 2	SINNER	43C
	DIKAIOS 1B	UPRIGHT	194D
	8　2BY	THAN	343C
	*KALEW 2	CALL	400D
	METANOIA	REPENTANCE	514A
33	DE8SIS	PRAYER	171A
	ESTHIW 1EY	EAT	313B
	MATH8T8S 2A	DISCIPLE	486D
	N8STEUW	TO FAST	540C
	HOMOIWS	LIKEWISE	570D
	PINW 1	DRINK	664C
	POIEW III	DO	689C
	PUKNOS	FREQUENT	736B
34	EN　IV6B	IN	261A
	M8　CI	NOT	519A
	NUMPHWN 2	BRIDAL CHAMBER	547C
	POIEW II8θ	DO	688B
	HUIOS 1C6	SON	842A
34F	N8STEUW	TO FAST	540B
34F	NUMPHIOS	BRIDEGROOM	547B
35	APAIRW	TAKE AWAY	79A
	ERCHOMAI IIB«	COME	311B
	HOTAN 1B	WHEN	592B
	TOTE 2	AT THAT TIME	831D
35A	H8MERA 4B	TIME	348B
35B	H8MERA 4B	TIME	348B
36	GE　3BP	OTHERWISE	152B
	EPIBALLW 1B	LAY ON	289D
	EPIBL8MA	A PATCH	290B
	HIMATION 1	GARMENT	377A
	KAI 16	AND	394A
	*KAINOS 1	NEW	395A
	LEGW IIA	SAY	469B
	PARABOL8 2	PARABLE	617C
	SUMPHWNEW 1A	MATCH	788C
36A	PALAIOS 1	OLD	610C
36A	SCHIZW 1A	SPLIT	805A
36B	SCHIZW 1A	SPLIT	805A
36F	DE 1A	BUT, AND	170C
36F	OUDEIS 2A	NO ONE	596B
37	APOLLUMI 2AP	PASS AWAY	94D
	EKCHEW 1	POUR OUT	246D
	PALAIOS 1	OLD	610C
	R8GNUMI 1	TEAR	742C
37F	ASKOS	WINESKIN	116A
37F	BALLW 2B	PUT	130D
37F	NEOS 1A«	NEW	537D
37F	OINOS 1	WINE	565A
38	AMPHOTEROI 1	BOTH	47A
	BL8TEOS	MUST BE PUT	143C
	KAINOS 1	NEW	395A
	SUNT8REW 1	PROTECT	800B
39	THELW 1	WISH	355B
	LEGW IIB«	SAY	469C
	NEOS 1A«	NEW	537D
	OUDEIS 2A	NO ONE	596B
	PINW 1	DRINK	664B
	CHR8STOS 1A«	USEFUL	894C
39A	PALAIOS 1	OLD	610C
39B	PALAIOS 1	OLD	610C

LUKE 6

1	GINOMAI I3E	TAKE PLACE	158B
	DEUTEROPRWTOS	FIRST BUT ONE	176A
	DIA AII	THROUGH	178C
	DIAPOREUOMAI	GO THROUGH	186D
	SABBATON 1A	SABBATH	746B
	SPORIMOS	SOWN	770D
	STACHUS 1	EAR (OF GRAIN)	773B
	TILLW	PLUCK	824C
	CHEIR 1	HAND	888B
	PSWCHW	RUB	903C
2	EXESTI 1	IT IS POSSIBLE	274D
	OU　5A	NO	595A
	SABBATON 1BP	SABBATH	746C
	TIS, TI 1A«	ANY ONE	827C
3	ANAGINWSKW 1	READ	51B
	APOKRINOMAI 1	ANSWER	92D
	DAUID	DAVID	170B
	HOPOTE	WHEN	579C
	OUDE 3	NOT EVEN	596A
	PEINAW 1	HUNGER	645D
	PETRA 1A	ROCK	660A
3F	META AIIIC«	WITH	510A
4	ARTOS 1B	BREAD	110B
	DIDWMI 1A	GIVE	191D
	EXESTI 3	IT IS POSSIBLE	274D
	ESTHIW 1A	EAT	312C
	HIEREUS 1B«	PRIEST	372C
	MONOS 1AY	ONLY	529C
	OIKOS 1AP	HOUSE	563B
	PROTHESIS 1	SETTING FORTH	713A
	HWS IV4	WHEN	907B
5	EPIKATARATOS	CURSED	294C
	KURIOS 1A«	LORD	460A
	PARABAT8S	TRANSGRESSOR	617A
	SABBATON 1A	SABBATH	746B
	HUIOS 2C	SON	843A
6	GINOMAI I3E	TAKE PLACE	158B
	DEXIOS 1	RIGHT	173C
	EISERCHOMAI 1AP	COME	231D
	HETEROS 1B«	ANOTHER	315A
	KAI I2B	AND	393A
	X8ROS 2	DRY	551A
	SABBATON 1A	SABBATH	746B
	SUNAGWG8 2A		790C

PLACE OF ASSEMBLY

	CHEIR 1	HAND	888A
7	EI　V2A	WHETHER	218D
	HEURISKW 2	FIND	325D
	THERAPEUW 2	HEAL	359D
	HINA IIE	IN ORDER THAT	377C
	KAT8GOREW 1A	BRING CHARGES	424B
	KAT8GORIA	ACCUSATION	424C
	PARAT8REW 1A«	WATCH	628A
	PARAT8REW 1AP	WATCH	628A
	SABBATON 1A	SABBATH	746B
	PHARISAIOS	PHARISEE	861C
8	ANIST8MI 2D	RISE	69D
	EGEIRW 1B	RAISE UP	214A
	EIS 1A«	INTO	227C
	HIST8MI IIIB	STAND	383B
	MESOS 2	THE MIDDLE	508C

8	X8ROS 2	DRY	551A
	OIDA 4	KNOW	559A
	CHEIR 1	HAND	888A
8B	HIST8MI IIIB	STAND	383B
9	AGATHOPOIEW 1	DO GOOD	2C
	APOKTEINW 1A	KILL	93C
	EXESTI 1	IT IS POSSIBLE	274D
	EPERWTAW 1A	ASK	285A
	IAOMAI 1	HEAL	369A
	KAKOPOIEW 1	DO WRONG	398C
	SABBATON 1A	SABBATH	746B
	SWZW 1A	SAVE	805D
	PSUCH8 2	SOUL LIFE	902C
10	APOKATHIST8MI 1	RESTORE	91B
	EKTEINW 1	STRETCH OUT	244D
	PERIBLEPW 1	LOOK AROUND	652A
	HUGI8S 1A	HEALTHY	840A
11	AN 5	(PARTICLE)	48D
	ANOIA	FOLLY	70A
	AUTOS 1C	SELF	122C
	DIALALEW	DISCUSS	184C
	IAOMAI 1	HEAL	369A
	PIMPL8MI 1A8	FILL	663D
	POIEW 11Dy	DO	688D
12	GINOMAI 13F	TAKE PLACE	158C
	DIANUKTEREUW		186C
	SPEND THE WHOLE NIGHT		
	H8MERA 48	TIME	348B
	THEOS 3F8	GOD	358B
	KAI 12B	AND	393A
	HO,H8,TO IIIA«	THE	552B
	OROS	MOUNTAIN	586B
	PROSEUCH8 1	PRAYER	720C
13	APOSTOLOS 3	APOSTLES	99B
	GINOMAI 11By	COME ABOUT	157B
	EKLEGOMAI 1	CHOOSE	241D
	H8MERA 1A	DAY	346C
	ONOMAZW 1	NAME	577B
	PROSPHWNEW 2	CALL OUT	727D
13F	HOS,H8,HO 11OD	(REL PRON)	588D
14	ANDREAS	ANDREW	63B
	BARTHOLOMAIOS	BARTHOLOMEW	133B
	IAKWBOS 1	JAMES	368B
	IWAN(N)8S 2	JOHN	385C
	ONOMAZW 1	NAME	577B
	PETROS	PETER	660D
	PHILIPPOS 3	PHILIP	868A
15	HALPHAIOS 2	ALPHAEUS	41A
	Z8LWT8S 2	THE ZEALOT	338D
	THWMAS	THOMAS	367D
	IAKWBOS 2	JAMES	368B
	KALEW 1Ay	CALL	400A
	MATTHAIOS	MATTHEW	497A
	SIMWN 2	SIMON	758C
16	GINOMAI 14A	BECOME	158C
	IOUDAS 5	JUDAS	380D
	IOUDAS 6	JUDAS	380D
	ISKARIWTH	ISCARIOT	381D
	PRODOT8S	TRAITOR	711C
16A	IAKWBOS 5	JAMES	368C
17	HIST8MI IIIA	STAND	383A
	KATABAINW 1A«	COME DOWN	409B
	LAOS 1A	PEOPLE	467D
17	MATH8T8S 2B8	DISCIPLE	487A
	META AIIIA	WITH	509D
	OCHLOS 3	CROWD	605D
	PARALIOS	BY THE SEA	625C
	PEDINOS	FLAT	644A
	PERAN 2C	ON THE OTHER SIDE	649C
	PL8THOS 2B«	QUANTITY	674C
	SIDWN	SIDON	757C
	TOPOS 1C	PLACE	830B
	TUROS	TYRE	838C
17A	POLUS IIB«	MANY	694C
17B	POLUS IIB«	MANY	694C
17F	HOS,H8,HO I3B8	(REL PRON)	587C
18	AKATHARTOS 2	IMPURE	28C
	ENOCHLEW	TROUBLE	267B
	THERAPEUW 2	HEAL	359C
	IAOMAI 1	HEAL	369A
	OCHLEW	TROUBLE	605B
	PNEUMA 4C	SPIRIT	682A
19	HAPTW 2B	TOUCH	102D
	Z8TEW 2By	SEEK	339C
	IAOMAI 1	HEAL	369A
	PARA 11	FROM	614C
20	BASILEIA 3B	KINGDOM	134D
	EIMI 116E	TO BE	223D
	EIS 1D«	TOWARD	227D
	EPAIRW 1	LOOK UP	281C
	LEGW 18D	SAY	470C
	PTWCHOS 1A	BEGGING POOR	735C
	HUMETEROS 1	YOUR	843D
20FF	MAKARIOS 1B	BLESSED	488A
20FF	HOTI 3A	THAT	593D
21	GELAW	LAUGH	152D
	KLAIW 1	WEEP	434B
	PEINAW 1	HUNGER	645D
	CHORTAZW 2A	FEED	892B
22	ANTHRWPOS 1B	MAN	67D
	APHORIZW 1	SEPARATE	126D
	EKBALLW 1	DRIVE OUT	236D
	*HENEKA	BECAUSE OF	264B
	MISEW 1	HATE	524C
	ONEIDIZW 1	REPROACH	573A
	HOTAN 1B	WHEN	592A
	PON8ROS 18B	WICKED	697D
	HUIOS 2C	SON	843A
23	GAR 1B	FOR	151A
	EKEINOS 2B8	THAT	239B
	H8MERA 3B8	DAY	348A
	IDOU 1B«	BEHOLD	371C
	KATA II5B«	ACCORDING TO	408C
	MISTHOS 2A	REWARD	525B
	OURANOS 2D	HEAVEN	599D
	PAT8R 1B	FOREFATHERS	640D
	POIEW 12B8	DO	689B
	POLUS IIB«	MANY	694C
	PROPH8T8S 1	PROPHET	730D
	SKIRTAW	LEAP	763A
	CHAIRW 1	REJOICE	881B
24	APECHW 1	RECEIVE IN FULL	84B
	PARAKL8SIS 3	COMFORT	623C
	PL8N 1B	BUT	675B
	PLOUSIOS 1	RICH	679C
	PTWCHOS 1A	BEGGING POOR	735C

24F	OUAI 1A	WOE 595C
25 GELAW		LAUGH 152D
EMPI(M)PL8MI 2		FILL 255C
*KLAIW 1		WEEP 434B
HO,H8,TO II3B		THE 553D
PEINAW 1		HUNGER 645D
PENTHEW 1		BE SAD 648B
25A	OUAI 1A	WOE 595C
25B	OUAI 1B	WOE 595C
26 ANTHRWPOS 1B		MAN 67D
EIPON 1		SAY 225B
KALWS 3		WELL 402B
KATA II58«	ACCORDING TO	408C
HOTAN 1B		WHEN 592A
OUAI 1A		WOE 595C
PAS 1D«		ALL 637C
PAT8R 1B	FOREFATHERS	640D
POIEW I28ß		DO 689B
PSEUDOPROPH8T8S	FALSE PROPHET	900B
27 AGAPAW 1A«		LOVE 4C
AKOUW 1C		HEAR 31D
ECHTHROS 28ß	THE ENEMY	331D
KALWS 3		WELL 402B
LEGW III1C		ORDER 470D
MISEW 1		HATE 524C
HO,H8,TO II1D		THE 552D
POIEW I24ß		DO 689A
28 EP8REAZW		MISTREAT 285C
EULOGEW 2A		BLESS 322C
*KATARAOMAI		CURSE 418A
PERI 1		ABOUT 650C
PROSEUCHOMAI		PRAY 721A
29 AIRW 4		TAKE AWAY 24A
ALLOS 3		THE OTHER 39D
EPI III1Aß		ON 288A
HIMATION 2		GARMENT 377A
KWLUW 3		HINDER 462D
HO,H8,TO II3B		THE 553C
PARECHW 1A		PRESENT 631D
SIAGWN		CHEEK 757A
TUPTW 1		STRIKE 838A
CHITWN		SHIRT 890C
30 AIRW 4		TAKE AWAY 24A
AITEW		ASK 25B
APAITEW 1		DEMAND 79B
M8 AII13A		NOT 518C
SOS 2B		YOURS 766D
31*THELW 1		WISH 355D
HINA III1A«	IN ORDER THAT	378A
KATHWS 1		JUST AS 392A
KAI II3		ALSO 394B
HOMOIWS		LIKEWISE 570D
31B	POIEW I2Aß	DO 689A
32 AGAPAW 1A«		LOVE 4C
HAMARTWLOS 2		SINNER 43D
POIOS 1Aß	OF WHAT KIND	691B
32F	GAR 1ß	FOR 151A
32FF	HAMARTWLOS 2	SINNER 43D
32-4	CHARIS 2B	FAVOR 885D
33 AGATHOPOIEW 1		DO GOOD 2C
AUTOS 4B		THE SAME 123B
EAN II1A		IF 210B
POIOS 1Aß	OF WHAT KIND	691B
34 APELPIZW		DESPAIR 83B
APOLAMBANW 2		RECOVER 94A
ELPIZW 2		HOPE 252A
HINA II1A	IN ORDER THAT	377C
ISOS		EQUAL 381D
KAN 1		AND IF 403B
HOS,H8,HO I28Y	(REL PRON)	587C
PARA I3B		FROM 614D
POIOS 1Aß	OF WHAT KIND	691B
34A	DAN(E)IZW 1	LEND 169D
34B	DAN(E)IZW 1	LEND 169D
35 AGATHOPOIEW 1		DO GOOD 2C
AGAPAW 1A«		LOVE 4C
APELPIZW		DESPAIR 83B
ACHARISTOS	UNGRATEFULLY	127D
DAN(E)IZW 1		LEND 169D
EPI III1B«		TOWARD 289A
ECHTHROS 28ß	THE ENEMY	331D
M8DEIS 28«		NOTHING 520A
MISTHOS 2A		REWARD 525B
PL8N 1B		BUT 675B
POLUS II8«		MANY 694C
HUIOS 1CY		SON 841D
HUPSISTOS 2		HIGHEST 858B
CHR8STOS 1Bß		USEFUL 894C
36 GINOMAI II1		BE 159B
OIKTIRMWN		MERCIFUL 564C
PAT8R 3C«		FATHER 641C
37 APOLUW 1		SET FREE 96A
DIKAZW		JUDGE 194C
37A	KATADIKAZW	CONDEMN 411B
37A	KRINW 6A	JUDGE 453B
37A	M8 DIA	NOT 519B
37B	KATADIKAZW	CONDEMN 411B
37B	KRINW 4B«	JUDGE 452D
37B	M8 DIA	NOT 519B
38 ANTIMETREW	MEASURE IN RETURN	74C
KALOS 2Cß		GOOD 401C
KOLPOS 2		FOLD 443B
*METREW 2		GIVE OUT 516B
PIEZW		PRESS 663A
SALEUW 1		SHAKE 748A
HUPEREKCHUN(N)W		OVERFLOW 848C
38A	METRON 1A	MEASURE 516C
38B	METRON 1A	MEASURE 516C
39 AMPHOTEROI 1		BOTH 47A
BOTHUNOS		PIT 144B
EMPIPTW 1		FALL 255D
M8TI	(INTERROG PARTICLE)	522A
HOD8GEW 1		LEAD 555D
OUCHI 3		NOT 603A
PARABOL8 2		PARABLE 617C
TUPHLOS 1B		BLIND 838C
40 DIDASKALOS		TEACHER 190D
EIMI II9B		TO BE 224A
EIMI III11B		TO BE 224D
KATARTIZW 1B		RESTORE 418D
MATH8T8S 1		PUPIL 486D
HUPER 2		BEYOND 847B
41 IDIOS 2B		ONES OWN 370C
KATANOEW 1		NOTICE 416A
41F	ADELPHOS 4	NEIGHBOR 16B
41F	BLEPW 1A	SEE 142D

41F	DOKOS	BEAM	202A
41F	KARPHOS	SPECK	406B
41F	OPHTHALMOS I	EYE	604B
42 APHI8MI 4		TOLERATE	126A
DIABLEPW 2		SEE CLEARLY	180D
DUNAMAI IA		ABLE	206B
EKBALLW 3		TAKE OUT	237B
IAOMAI I		HEAL	369A
OU 3B		NO	594C
PRWTOS 2A		FIRST	733D
PWS IC		HOW	739C
TOTE 2		AT THAT TIME	831D
HUPOKEIMAI IB		LIE BELOW	852D
HUPOKRIT8S		HYPOCRITE	853A
43 GAR IB		FOR	151B
KALOS 2A		GOOD	401B
KARPOS IA		FRUIT	405C
PALIN 4		AGAIN	611D
43A POIEW IIBη		DO	688A
43A SAPROS I		DECAYED	749C
43B POIEW IIBη		DO	688A
43B SAPROS I		DECAYED	749C
43F GAR IE		FOR	151C
43F DENDRON		TREE	173C
43F OUDE I		AND NOT	595D
44 AKANTHA		THORN PLANT	29A
BATOS		THORN BUSH	137B
GINWSKW IA		KNOW	159D
EK 3Gβ		BY	234D
HEKASTOS 2		EACH	236A
EKLEGOMAI 5		CHOOSE	242A
EPIGINWSKW 2A		KNOW	291A
IDIOS IB		ONES OWN	370B
KARPOS IA		FRUIT	405C
STAPHUL8	BUNCH OF GRAPES	773A
SUKON		RIPE FIG	784A
SULLEGW		COLLECT	784D
TRUGAW	PICK (GRAPES)	836A
45 AGATHOS IBβ		GOOD	3B
TH8SAUROS IB		STOREHOUSE	362B
LALEW 2Aɛ		SPEAK	464C
PERISSEUMA I		ABUNDANCE	656B
45A PON8ROS IBα		WICKED	697C
45A PROPHERW		PRODUCE	730A
45B PON8ROS IBβ		WICKED	697D
45B PROPHERW		PRODUCE	730A
45C PON8ROS 2C		WICKED	698A
46 KALEW IAβ		CALL	399D
KURIOS 2Cβ		LORD	460D
LEGW IIIC		ORDER	470D
POIEW IICα		DO	688C
TIS, TI 3A		WHICH	827B
47 AKOUW IBɣ		HEAR	31C
LOGOS IAδ		WORD	478D
PAS ICɣ		WHOEVER	637B
HUPODEIKNUMI 2		SHOW	852A
47=9 HOMOIOS I		LIKE	569D
48 BATHUNW		MAKE DEEP	130A
GINOMAI IIBα		COME ABOUT	157B
DIA BII3		BECAUSE	180C
THEMELIOS IB		FOUNDATION	356B
THEMELIOW I			356C
LAY THE FOUNDATION OF			

48 ISCHUW 2B		BE STRONG	384C
KAI IIE		AND	393A
KALWS I		WELL	402A
PL8MMURA		FLOOD	675B
PROSR8SSW 2		BURST UPON	725C
SALEUW I		SHAKE	747D
SKAPTW I		DIG	761A
TITH8MI IIAβ		PUT	823D
48A OIKODOMEW IA		BUILD	560C
48A PETRA IA		ROCK	660A
48B PETRA IA		ROCK	660A
48F ANTHRWPOS 3Aβ		MAN	68B
48F EKEINOS 2A		THAT	239B
48F OIKIA IA		HOUSE	559D
48F POTAMOS I		RIVER	701B
49 G8 2		GROUND	156D
GINOMAI IIBβ		COME ABOUT	157B
EUTHUS		IMMEDIATELY	321C
THEMELIOS IB		FOUNDATION	356B
OIKODOMEW IA		BUILD	560D
PIPTW IBβ		FALL	665C
PROSR8SSW 2		BURST UPON	725C
R8GMA		WRECK	742C
SUMPIPTW I	FALL TOGETHER	787B
SURR8GNUMI	DASH (TOGETHER)	802A
CHWRIS 2Bβ		APART	899A

LUKE 7

1 AKO8 IC		HEARING	30B
EISERCHOMAI IAα		COME	231D
EPEI I		WHEN	283D
EPEID8 I		WHEN	284A
KAPHARNAOUM		CAPERNAUM	427C
LAOS IA		PEOPLE	467D
R8MA I		WORD	742D
TELEW I		FINISH	818C
2 HEKATONTARCH8S		CENTURION	236C
ENTIMOS 2		HONORED	268C
KAKWS I		BADLY	399B
MELLW ICα		BE ABOUT TO	502A
TELEUTAW		DIE	818B
TIS, TI 2Aα		ANY ONE	828A
2F DOULOS IA		SLAVE	204D
3 AKOUW 3C		LEARN	32A
DIASWZW		SAVE	188B
ERWTAW 2		ASK	312B
HOPWS 2B		IN ORDER THAT	580D
PRESBUTEROS 2Aα		OLDER	706C
4 AXIOS 2A		WORTHY	77D
HOS,H8,HO I8		(REL PRON)	588D
PARAGINOMAI I		COME	618D
PARAKALEW 3		IMPLORE	622D
PARECHW 2B		GRANT	632B
SPOUDAIWS 2		DILIGENTLY	771B
5 AGAPAW IAα		LOVE	4C
AUTOS IE		OF HIMSELF	122C
OIKODOMEW IA		BUILD	560C
SUNAGWG8 2A			790C
PLACE OF ASSEMBLY			
6 APECHW 2		BE DISTANT	84B
EISERCHOMAI IG		COME	232B
HEKATONTARCH8S		CENTURION	236C

6	8D8 IA	ALREADY 344D
	HIKANOS 2	APPROPRIATE 375B
	HINA IIICβ	IN ORDER THAT 378C
	MAKRAN 2	FAR 488D
	MAKRAN IA«	FAR 488D
	M8 AIII3B	NOT 518D
	PEMPW I	SEND 647C
	POREUW I	PROCEED 699A
	SKULLW 3	WEARY 765C
	STEG8	ROOF 773B
	SUN IB	WITH 789B
	HUPO 2A«	UNDER 851A
	PHILOS 2A«	LOVING 868D
7	AXIOW IA	CONSIDER WORTHY 77D
	DIO	THEREFORE 197D
	EIPON 2A	SAY 225C
	EMAUTOU 2	MYSELF 253B
	IAOMAI I	HEAL 369A
	KAI I2F	AND 393C
	LOGOS IA«	WORD 478B
	PAIS IAy	SERVANT 609D
8	GAR IB	FOR 151A
	DOULOS IA	SLAVE 204D
	EMAUTOU 3	MYSELF 253B
	EXOUSIA 4A	AUTHORITY 278A
	ERCHOMAI IIA«	COME 310B
	ECHW I2Bβ	HAVE 332D
	LEGW IIIC	ORDER 470D
	STRATIWT8S I	SOLDIER 778B
	TASSW IB	PLACE 813C
8A	HUPO 2B	UNDER 851B
8B	HUPO 2B	UNDER 851B
9	AKOLOUTHEW 2	ACCOMPANY 30D
	HEURISKW IB	FIND 325B
	THAUMAZW IBβ	WONDER 353A
	LEGW IIID	ASSURE 470D
	OUDE 3	NOT EVEN 596A
	PISTIS 2Bα	FAITH 668D
	STREPHW 2A«	TURN 778D
	TOSOUTOS IAβ	SO GREAT 831B
10	ASTHENEW IA	BE SICK 115A
	DOULOS IA	SLAVE 204D
	HEURISKW IC«	FIND 325C
	OIKOS IA«	HOUSE 563A
	PEMPW I	SEND 648A
	HUGIAINW I	BE HEALTHY 839D
11	EN IIIB	WHILE 259D
	HEX8S 2	NEXT 275C
	KALEW IAy	CALL 400A
	MATH8T8S 2Bβ	DISCIPLE 487A
	NAIN	NAIN 535B
	POLIS I	CITY 692B
	SUMPOREUOMAI I	GO WITH 787C
12	EGGIZW I	APPROACH 212C
	EKKOMIZW	CARRY OUT 241B
	THN8SKW I	DIE 363B
	HIKANOS IA	SUFFICIENT 375A
	KAI I2D	AND 393C
	MONOGEN8S	ONLY 529A
	OCHLOS I	CROWD 605C
	PUL8 I	GATE 736C
	SUN IC	WITH 789B
	HUIOS IA«	SON 841B

12	CH8RA	THE WIDOW 889D
	HWS IVIA	WHEN 907A
12A	POLIS I	CITY 692A
12B	POLIS I	CITY 692A
13	EPI IIIBy	ON 287B
	KLAIW I	WEEP 434A
	KURIOS 2Cβ	LORD 460D
	M8 AIII3B	NOT 518D
	*SPLAGCHNIZOMAI	HAVE PITY 770B
14	HAPTW 2B	TOUCH 102C
	BASTAZW 2A	CARRY 136D
	EGEIRW 2B	RISE 214A
	HIST8MI IIIA	STAND 383A
	NEANISKOS I	YOUTH 536C
	SOROS	COFFIN 766C
15	ANAKATHIZW	SIT UP 55A
	ARCHW 2Aβ	BEGIN 113A
16	AGATHOS 2Aβ	GOOD 3B
	HAPAS 2	ALL 81A
	DOXAZW I	PRAISE 203C
	EGEIRW 2E	APPEAR 214A
	EPISKEPTOMAI 3	VISIT 298C
	LAMBANW IC	TAKE 465D
	LAOS 3A	PEOPLE 468A
	MEGAS 2Bα	GREAT 499B
	PROPH8T8S 3	PROPHET 731A
	PHOBOS 2A«	FEAR 871C
17	EN I6	IN 259C
	EXERCHOMAI 2B«	GO OUT 274C
	IOUDAIA 2	JUDAEA 379D
	PERICHWROS	NEIGHBORING 659B
18	APAGGELLW I	REPORT 78C
	MATH8T8S 2A	DISCIPLE 486D
	PAS IEβ	ALL 637D
	PROSKALEW IA	SUMMON 722C
	TIS, TI 2Bα	ANY ONE 828B
19	LEGW I8C	SAY 470B
	HO,H8,TO IIIA«	THE 552C
	PEMPW I	SEND 647C
19F	ERCHOMAI IIAη	COME 310D
19F	PROSDOKAW I	EXPECT 719C
20	BAPTIST8S	BAPTIST 132B
	LEGW I8C	SAY 470B
	PARAGINOMAI I	COME 618D
21	BLEPW 2	SEE 143A
	THERAPEUW 2	HEAL 359C
	MASTIX 2	TORMENT 496B
	NOSOS I	DISEASE 545D
	PNEUMA 4C	SPIRIT 682A
	PON8ROS IB«	WICKED 697C
	CHARIZOMAI I	GIVE FREELY 884D
	HWRA 3	TIME OF DAY 905A
21B	POLUS IIA«	MANY 694A
21F	TUPHLOS IB	BLIND 838C
22	AKOUW IB«	HEAR 31B
	AKOUW IA	HEAR 31B
	ANABLEPW 2A«	GAIN SIGHT 50C
	APAGGELLW I	REPORT 78C
	APOKRINOMAI I	ANSWER 92D
	EIDON	SEE 219C
	EIDON IA	SEE 219C
	EUAGGELIZW 2Bβ	PREACH 318A
	KATHARIZW IB«	CLEANSE 388A

22*KWPHOS 2   DEAF 463C   32 PAIDION 2A   CHILD 609A
   LEPROS   LEPER 473A   PROSPHWNEW I   CALL OUT 727D
   NEKROS 2A   DEAD 537A   33 ARTOS 2   FOOD 110C
   PERIPATEW IC   GO ABOUT 655A   BAPTIST8S   BAPTIST 132B
   POREUW I   PROCEED 699B   DAIMONION 2   DEMON 168B
   PTWCHOS IB   BEGGING POOR 735D   ERCHOMAI IIAθ   COME 311A
   TUPHLOS IB   BLIND 838C   ESTHIW IA   EAT 312D
   CHWLOS   LAME 897B   ESTHIW IEγ   EAT 313B
23 MAKARIOS IB   BLESSED 487D   ECHW I2Eα   HAVE 333A
   SKANDALIZW IB CAUSE TO FALL 760B   M8TE   AND NOT 521C
24 AGGELOS IA   MESSENGER 7A   OINOS I   WINE 565A
   ANEMOS IA   WIND 64A   34 HAMARTWLOS 2   SINNER 43D
   ARCHW 2Aß   BEGIN 113A   ANTHRWPOS 3Aα   MAN 68C
   THEAOMAI IA   SEE 353C   ERCHOMAI IIAη   COME 311A
   KALAMOS I   REED 399C   ESTHIW IEγ   EAT 313B
   LEGW I4   SAY 469D   IDOU 2   THERE IS 371D
   SALEUW I   SHAKE 747D   OINOPOT8S   WINE DRINKER 564D
   HUPO IAß   BY 850D   TELWN8S   TAX COLLECTOR 820B
25 AMPHIENNUMI   CLOTHE 46D   HUIOS 2C   SON 843A
   ANTHRWPOS 2Bα   MAN 67D   PHAGOS   GLUTTON 859A
   BASILEIOS   ROYAL 135C   PHILOS 2Aα   LOVING 869A
   DIAGW   SPEND ONES LIFE 181C   35 DIKAIOW 2   JUSTIFY 196C
   IDOU IC   REMEMBER 371D   SOPHIA 4   WISDOM 767B
   HIMATION I   GARMENT 377A   TEKNON 2Fß   CHILD 816C
   HIMATISMOS   CLOTHING 377B   36 ANAKLINW 2   RECLINE 55D
   MALAKOS I   SOFT 489D   ERWTAW 2   ASK 312B
   TRUPH8 2   SPLENDOR 836C   ESTHIW IC   EAT 313A
   HUPARCHW 2   BE 846A   HINA IIIAγ   IN ORDER THAT 378B
25F   EXERCHOMAI IAζ GO OUT 274B   KATAKLINW RECLINE AT TABLE 412D
26 NAI IB   YES 534D   META AII2   WITH 510C
   PERISSOTEROS 2 GREATER 657B   OIKOS IAα   HOUSE 563A
   PROPH8T8S 2   PROPHET 731A   TIS, TI IAα   ANY ONE 827C
27 AGGELOS IB   MESSENGER 7A   36B PHARISAIOS   PHARISEE 861C
   EMPROSTHEN 2E IN FRONT 256D   37 ALABASTROS   ALABASTER 33D
   KATHARIZW IBα   CLEANSE 388A   HAMARTWLOS 2   SINNER 43D
   KATASKEUAZW I MAKE READY 419B   EN IIA   IN 257C
   HODOS IA   WAY 556B   EPIGINWSKW 2B   KNOW 291A
   PRO I   BEFORE 708C   IDOU 2   THERE IS 371D
   PROSWPON ICζ   FACE 728D   KATAKEIMAI 3   LIE DOWN 412C
28 BASILEIA 3B   KINGDOM 134D   KOMIZW I   BRING 443C
   GENN8TOS   BEGOTTEN 155B   MARIA 2   MARY 493A
   LEGW IIID   ASSURE 470D   MURON   OINTMENT 531D
   MEGAS 2Bα   GREAT 499B   OIKIA IA   HOUSE 559D
   MIKROS IC   SMALL 523B   PHARISAIOS   PHARISEE 861C
29 BAPTIZW 2A   BAPTIZE 131B   38 ALEIPHW I   ANOINT 34C
   BAPTISMA I   BAPTISM 132A   ARCHW 2Aß   BEGIN 113A
   DIKAIOW 2   JUSTIFY 196D   BRECHW I   WET 147A
   LAOS ICß   PEOPLE 467D   DAKRUON   TEAR 169A
   TELWN8S   TAX COLLECTOR 820B   EKMASSW   WIPE 242D
30 ATHETEW IA   SET ASIDE 20C   THRIX 2   HAIR 364C
   BOUL8 2B   WILL 145B   HIST8MI IIIB   STAND 383B
   NOMIKOS 2   LAWYER 543C   KATAPHILEW   KISS 421B
31 GENEA 2   GENERATION 153B   KEPHAL8 IA   HEAD 431B
   HOMOIOW 2   COMPARE 570B   KLAIW I   WEEP 434A
   OUN ICγ   THEREFORE 597C   MURON   OINTMENT 531D
31F   HOMOIOS I   LIKE 569D   OPISW IB   BEHIND 578C
32 AGORA   MARKET PLACE 12B   PARA IIIIC   ALONG 616A
   AULEW   PLAY THE FLUTE 120D   38C POUS IA   FOOT 703C
   THR8NEW IB   MOURN 363D   39 HAMARTWLOS 2   SINNER 43D
   KATH8MAI IAα   SIT 390B   AN IBα   (PARTICLE) 47D
   KLAIW I   WEEP 434A   HAPTW 2B   TOUCH 102D
   HO,H8,TO II3B   THE 553C   GINWSKW 6D   KNOW 160D
   ORCHEOMAI   DANCE 587A   EIPON 5   SAY 225D

39 EN I5B	IN	258D
KALEW IB	INVITE	400B
LEGW I6	SAY	470A
MARIA 2	MARY	493A
HOSTIS 3	WHOEVER	591B
HOUTOS IA«	THIS	600D
POTAPOS	WHAT SORT	701C
PROPH8T8S 3	PROPHET	731A
PROPH8T8S 3	PROPHET	731B
PHARISAIOS	PHARISEE	861C
40 DIDASKALOS	TEACHER	190D
EIPON I	SAY	225B
ECHW I6B	MUST	334A
SIMWN 7	SIMON	758D
TIS, TI IB«	ANY ONE	828A
PH8MI IB/3	SAY	864A
41 DAN(E)IST8S	MONEY LENDER	169D
D8NARION	DENARIUS	178B
HEIS 5D	ONE	231B
HETEROS IA	OTHER	315A
OPHEILW I	OWE	603C
PENT8KONTA	FIFTY	648D
PENTAKOSIOI	FIVE HUNDRED	648D
TIS, TI 2A«	ANY ONE	828A
CHREOPHEILET8S	DEBTOR	893C
42 AGAPAW IA«	LOVE	4C
AMPHOTEROI I	BOTH	47A
APODIDWMI 2	GIVE BACK	90A
ECHW I6A	CAN	333D
OUN IC«	THEREFORE	597B
POLUS II2C	MANY	696A
42F CHARIZOMAI I	GIVE FREELY	885A
43 KRINW 2	JUDGE	452C
ORTHWS	RIGHTLY	584C
HOS,H8,HO I2B«	(REL PRON)	587B
POLUS II2C	MANY	696A
HUPOLAMBANW 4	TAKE UP	853A
43F SIMWN 7	SIMON	758D
44 BLEPW IA	SEE	142D
BRECHW I	WET	147A
DAKRUON	TEAR	169A
EKMASSW	WIPE	242D
THRIX 2	HAIR	364C
OIKIA IA	HOUSE	559D
HOUTOS 2A	THIS	601D
STREPHW 2A«	TURN	779A
HUDWR I	WATER	840C
PH8MI IB«	SAY	864A
44A POUS IA	FOOT	703C
44FF HOUTOS IA«	THIS	600D
45 APO II2C	SINCE	86C
DIALEIPW	STOP	184D
DIDWMI IB«	GIVE	192A
HOS,H8,HO IIIF	(REL PRON)	589A
POUS IA	FOOT	703C
PHIL8MA	A KISS	867B
46 ALEIPHW I	ANOINT	34C
ELAION 2	OLIVE OIL	247B
KEPHAL8 IA	HEAD	431A
MURON	OINTMENT	531D
POUS IA	FOOT	703C
47 AGAPAW IA«	LOVE	4C
HOS,H8,HO IIIE	(REL PRON)	589A

47 CHARIN 2	FOR THE SAKE OF	885B
47A OLIGOS 2A	LITTLE	566C
47A POLUS IIA«	MANY	694A
47B APHI8MI 2	FORGIVE	125C
47B OLIGOS 3A	LITTLE	566D
47B POLUS I2C/3	MANY	695C
47F APHI8MI 2	FORGIVE	125C
48 SU 3	YOU	780A
49 ARCHW 2A/3	BEGIN	II3A
APHI8MI 2	FORGIVE	125C
EN I5B	IN	258D
LEGW I6	SAY	470A
HOS,H8,HO IIOD	(REL PRON)	588D
HOUTOS IA«	THIS	600D
SUNANAKEIMAI	EAT WITH	792A
50 EIR8N8 2	PEACE	226C
EIS 9B	IN	229D
PISTIS 2B«	FAITH	668D
POREUW I	PROCEED	699B
SWZW 2AY	SAVE	806B

LUKE 8

I	BASILEIA 3B	KINGDOM	134D
	BASILEIA 3G	KINGDOM	135A
	GINOMAI I3F	TAKE PLACE	158B
	DIODEUW 2	GO	198A
	EUAGGELIZW 2A/3	PREACH	317D
	KATHEX8S	IN ORDER	389C
	KATA IIID	(DISTRIBUTIVE)	407C
	K8RUSSW 2B/3	ANNOUNCE	432C
	KWM8 I	VILLAGE	462D
	POLIS I	CITY	692A
	POLIS I	CITY	692B
2	ASTHENEIA IA	WEAKNESS	II4D
	DAIMONION 2	DEMON	168B
	HEPTA	SEVEN	306B
	THERAPEUW 2	HEAL	359C
	KALEW IAY	CALL	400A
	MAGDAL8N8	MAGDALENE	485B
	*MARIA 2	MARY	493A
	PNEUMA 4C	SPIRIT	682A
	PON8ROS IB«	WICKED	697C
	TIS, TI 2D	ANY ONE	828B
3	DIAKONEW 4	HELP	183B
	EK 3F	BY	234D
	EPITROPOS I	MANAGER	303D
	HETEROS IB/3	ANOTHER	315B
	H8RWD8S 2	HEROD	349B
	IWAN(N)A	JOANNA	385B
	SOUSANNA	SUSANNA	766D
	HUPARCHW I	BE	845D
	CHOUZAS	CHUZA	892C
4	DIA AIIIB	BY MEANS OF	179B
	EIPON 2A	SAY	225C
	EPIPOREUOMAI	JOURNEY	298A
	KATA IIID	(DISTRIBUTIVE)	407C
	OCHLOS I	CROWD	605C
	PARABOL8 2	PARABLE	617D
	POLIS I	CITY	692B
	POLUS IIB«	MANY	694C
	SUNEIMI II	COME TOGETHER	794D
5	EXERCHOMAI IA{	GO OUT	274B

5	KATAPATEW IAⱥ	TRAMPLE 416D
	KATESTHIW I	EAT UP 423B
	HO,H8,TO II3A	THE 553C
	HO,H8,TO II4Bʒ	THE 554A
	HODOS IA	WAY 556B
	HOS,H8,HO II2	THIS (ONE) 589B
	OURANOS ID	HEAVEN 598D
	PARA IIIID	ALONG 616A
	PETEINON	BIRD 660A
	PIPTW IA	FALL 665A
	SPOROS 2	SEED 770D
5A	SPEIRW IAⱥ	SOW 768C
5B	SPEIRW IAβ	SOW 768C
5C	SPEIRW IAⱥ	SOW 768C
5FF	MEN 2D	(PARTICLE) 504C
6	HETEROS IBδ	ANOTHER 315B
	IKMAS	MOISTURE 375D
	KATAPIPTW	FALL 417C
	M8 AIIIE	NOT 518A
	X8RAINW 2A	DRY UP 550D
	PETRA IA	ROCK 660A
	PHUW	GROW 878B
7	AKANTHA	THORN PLANT 29A
	APOPNIGW	CHOKE 97A
	EN I6	IN 259D
	HETEROS IBδ	ANOTHER 315B
	MESOS 2	THE MIDDLE 509A
	PIPTW IA	FALL 665A
	SUMPHUW	GROW UP WITH 788C
8	AGATHOS IAβ	GOOD 2D
	HEKATONTAPLASIWN	
		A HUNDRED FOLD 236B
	HETEROS IBδ	ANOTHER 315B
	ECHW I2Cⱥ	HAVE 332D
	KARPOS IA	FRUIT 405C
	OUS 2	EAR 600B
	HOUTOS IBⱥ	THIS 601C
	PIPTW IA	FALL 665A
	POIEW II8η	DO 688A
	PHUW	GROW 878B
	PHWNEW IB	CRY OUT 878B
9	EPERWTAW IA	ASK 285A
	MATH8T8S 2Bⱥ	DISCIPLE 487A
	PARABOL8 2	PARABLE 617D
10	BLEPW ID	SEE 143A
	GINWSKW IA	KNOW 159D
	DIDWMI IBβ	GIVE 192B
	HINA II2	IN ORDER THAT 378D
	LOIPOS 2Bⱥ	THE OTHERS 481A
	M8 AI2	NOT 517C
	MUST8RION I	MYSTERY 532A
	PARABOL8 2	PARABLE 617D
	SUNI8MI	UNDERSTAND 797D
	SUNI8MI	UNDERSTAND 798A
11	LOGOS IBβ	WORD 479B
	HOUTOS IAη	THIS 601B
	PARABOL8 2	PARABLE 617D
	SPOROS 2	SEED 770D
11FF	EIMI II3	TO BE 223A
12	DIABOLOS 2	THE SLANDERER 181A
	EITA I	THEN 233A
	ERCHOMAI IIAʒ	COME 310D
	M8 AI2	NOT 517C

12	PARA IIIID	ALONG 616A
	SWZW 2B	SAVE 806B
12F	LOGOS IBβ	WORD 479C
12F	PISTEUW 2B	BELIEVE 667C
13	APHIST8MI 2A	FALL AWAY 126C
	DECHOMAI 3B	ACCEPT 176C
	KAIROS I	TIME 395C
	PEIRASMOS 2B	TEST 646D
	PETRA IA	ROCK 660A
	PROS III2B	TOWARD 717A
	RIZA IB	ROOT 743B
	CHARA I	JOY 883C
13B	KAIROS 3	TIME 396A
14	AKANTHA	THORN PLANT 29A
	BIOS I	LIFE 141B
	H8DON8 I	PLEASURE 345A
	MERIMNA	ANXIETY 506A
	PIPTW IA	FALL 665A
	PLOUTOS I	WEALTH 680B
	POREUW 2D	PROCEED 699C
	SUMPNIGW I	CHOKE 787C
	TELESPHOREW	818B
	BEAR FRUIT TO MATURITY	
	HUPO IAβ	BY 850D
14F	HOUTOS IAη	THIS 601B
15	AGATHOS IBβ	GOOD 3B
	KALOS 2A	GOOD 401B
	KALOS 2B	GOOD 401C
	KARPOPHOREW 2	BEAR FRUIT 406A
	KATECHW IBβ	HOLD FAST 424A
	LOGOS IBβ	WORD 479C
	HOUTOS IAδ	THIS 601A
	TELESPHOREW	818B
	BEAR FRUIT TO MATURITY	
	HUPOMON8 I	PATIENCE 854B
16	HAPTW I	KINDLE 102B
	BLEPW IA	SEE 142D
	EISPOREUOMAI I	GO 232D
	EPI IIAβ	ON 285D
	EPITITH8MI IAⱥ	PUT UPON 303A
	HINA IIA	IN ORDER THAT 377C
	KALUPTW I	COVER 402A
	KLIN8	COUCH 437B
	LUCHNIA	LAMPSTAND 484B
	LUCHNOS I	LAMP 484C
	SKEUOS IB	THING 761D
	HUPOKATW	UNDER 852C
	PHWS IA	LIGHT 879D
16A	TITH8MI IIAβ	PUT 823D
16B	TITH8MI IIAβ	PUT 823D
17	APOKRUPHOS	HIDDEN 93B
	GINWSKW 2A	FIND OUT 160B
	ERCHOMAI I2C	COME 311C
	KRUPTOS 2A	HIDDEN 455A
17A	PHANEROS I	CLEAR 860B
17B	PHANEROS 2	CLEAR 860B
18	BLEPW 4C	SEE 143B
	DOKEW IA	THINK 200D
	M8 AII	NOT 517C
	OUN IB	THEREFORE 597B
18A	ECHW I2A	HAVE 332B
18B	ECHW I2A	HAVE 332C
19	DIA BIII	BECAUSE OF 180A

19	DUNAMAI 1B	ABLE	206B
	PARAGINOMAI 1	COME	618D
	SUNTUGCHANW	MEET	801B
20	EIDON 6	VISIT	220A
	EXW 1Aα	OUTSIDE	278D
	THELW 1	WISH	355C
	HISTEMI II2Bα	BEING	383B
21	LOGOS 1Bβ	WORD	479B
	HOUTOS 1AΔ	THIS	601A
22	ANAGW 3	PUT TO SEA	53A
	GINOMAI I3F	TAKE PLACE	158B
	DIERCHOMAI 2	COME	193D
	EMBAINW	GO IN	253C
	HEMERA 2	DAY	347A
	PERAN 2B	ON THE OTHER SIDE	649C
	PLOION 2	SHIP	679B
22F	LIMNE 1	LAKE	476A
23	ANEMOS 1A	WIND	64A
	APHUPNOW	FALL ASLEEP	127C
	KATABAINW 1B	COME DOWN	409D
	KINDUNEUW	RUN A RISK	433B
	LAILAPS	HURRICANE	463D
	PLEW	SAIL	674A
	SUMPLEROW 1	FILL COMPLETELY	787B
24	APOLLUMI 2Aα	PERISH	94D
	GALENE	CALM	149C
	GINOMAI IIBα	COME ABOUT	157B
	DIEGEIRW	AROUSE	193A
	EPISTATES	MASTER	300B
	EPITIMAW 1	REBUKE	303B
	KLUDWN	ROUGH WATER	437D
	PAUW 2	STOP	643D
	HUDWR 1	WATER	840C
25	ANEMOS 1A	WIND	64A
	ARA 2	THEN	103B
	EPITASSW	COMMAND	302A
	THAUMAZW 1Aα	WONDER	352D
	LEGW I3	SAY	469D
	PISTIS 2Bα	FAITH	668D
	POU 1A	WHERE	702D
	HUPAKOUW 1	LISTEN TO	845B
26	ANTIPERA	OPPOSITE	75A
	GADARENOS	GADARENE	148B
	GERGESENOS	GERGESENE	155D
	GERASENOS	GERASENE	155D
	EIMI II9A	TO BE	223D
	KAI I5	AND	394A
	POLIS 1	CITY	692A
	CHWRA 1B	COUNTRY	897C
27	ANER 6	MAN	66B
	DAIMONION 2	DEMON	168B
	ENDIDUSKW	DRESS	262C
	ENDUW 2A	DRESS	263C
	EXERCHOMAI 1Aα	GO OUT	274B
	EPI III1Aβ	ON	288A
	ECHW I2Eα	HAVE	333A
	HIKANOS 1B	SUFFICIENT	375A
	HIMATION 1	GARMENT	377A
	MENW 1Aα	REMAIN	504D
	MNEMA	TOMB	526C
	OIKIA 1A	HOUSE	560A
	POLIS 1	CITY	692A
	HUPANTAW	GO TO MEET	845C

27	CHRONOS	TIME	896B
	CHRONOS	TIME	896C
28	ANAKRAZW	CRY OUT	56A
	BASANIZW 2A	TORMENT	134A
	DEOMAI 3	ASK	174B
	EGW	I	216C
	MEGAS 2Aγ	GREAT	498D
	PROSPIPTW 1	FALL DOWN BEFORE	725B
	HUIOS 2B	SON	842C
	HUPSISTOS 2	HIGHEST	858B
	PHWNE 2A	VOICE	878D
29	AKATHARTOS 2	IMPURE	28C
	HALUSIS 1	CHAIN	40D
	GAR 1C	FOR	151B
	DAIMONION 2	DEMON	168B
	DAIMWN	DEMON	168D
	DESMEUW 1	BIND	174D
	DESMOS 1	FETTER	175A
	DIA(R)REGNUMI 1	BREAK	187A
	ELAUNW	DRIVE	248A
	EXERCHOMAI 1AΔ	GO OUT	274A
	EREMOS 2	DESERT	309A
	PARAGGELLW	GIVE ORDERS	618C
	PEDE	FETTER	644A
	PNEUMA 4C	SPIRIT	682A
	POLUS IIAβ	MANY	694B
	SUNARPAZW	SEIZE	792D
	PHULASSW 1B	WATCH	876B
	CHRONOS	TIME	896C
30	DAIMONION 2	DEMON	168B
	EISERCHOMAI 1Bβ	COME	232A
	LEGIWN	LEGION	469A
	ONOMA II	NAME	574A
	HOTI 3A	THAT	593D
31	ABUSSOS 2	ABYSS	2B
	EIS 1Aα	INTO	227B
	EPITASSW	COMMAND	302B
31F	PARAKALEW 3	IMPLORE	622D
32	BOSKW 2	FEED	144D
	HIKANOS 1A	SUFFICIENT	375A
	HINA I1Aγ	IN ORDER THAT	378B
	OROS	MOUNTAIN	586C
32A	EPITREPW 1	ALLOW	303C
32B	EPITREPW 1	ALLOW	303C
32F	AGELE	HERD	8C
32F	EISERCHOMAI 1Bβ	COME	232A
32F	CHOIROS	SWINE	891C
33	APOPNIGW	CHOKE	97A
	DAIMONION 2	DEMON	168B
	EXERCHOMAI 1AΔ	GO OUT	274A
	KATA II1A	DOWN	406B
	KREMNOS	BANK	451B
	LIMNE 1	LAKE	476A
	HORMAW	RUSH DOWN	585C
34	AGROS 3	FARM	13D
	APAGGELLW 1	REPORT	78C
	BOSKW 1	FEED	144D
	GINOMAI I3A	TAKE PLACE	157D
	EIS 1Dβ	IN	227D
	POLIS 1	CITY	692A
	PHEUGW 1	FLEE	863C
35	DAIMONIZOMAI		168A
		BE POSSESSED BY A DEMON	

35 DAIMONION 2	DEMON	168B
EXERCHOMAI IAδ	GO OUT	274A
EXERCHOMAI IAζ	GO OUT	274B
HEURISKW ICα	FIND	325C
HIMATIZW	DRESS	376D
KATH8MAI IAε	SIT	390B
PARA IIIIC	ALONG	616A
POUS IA	FOOT	703B
SWPHRONEW I	SOUND MIND	809C
36 APAGGELLW I	REPORT	78C
PWS 2A	HOW	739D
SWZW IC	SAVE	806A
37 HAPAS I	WHOLE	81A
APERCHOMAI IA	GO AWAY	83D
GADAR8NOS	GADARENE	148B
GERGES8NOS	GERGESENE	155D
GERAS8NOS	GERASENE	155D
EMBAINW	GO IN	253C
ERWTAW 2	ASK	312B
MEGAS 2Aγ	GREAT	499A
PERICHWROS	NEIGHBORING	659B
PL8THOS 2Bγ	QUANTITY	674D
PLOION 2	SHIP	679B
SUNECHW 5	DISTRESS	797A
HUPOSTREPHW	RETURN	855B
PHOBOS 2Aα	FEAR	871C
38 APOLUW 2B	SEND AWAY	96B
DAIMONION 2	DEMON	168B
DEOMAI I	ASK	174A
EIMI IIIIO	TO BE	224D
EXERCHOMAI IAδ	GO OUT	274A
LEGW I8A	SAY	470B
SUN IC	WITH	789B
39 DI8GEOMAI	TELL	194A
KATA IIIA	ALONG	407A
K8RUSSW 2A	ANNOUNCE	432B
OIKOS IAα	HOUSE	563A
POLIS I	CITY	692B
39A HOSOS 2	HOW GREAT	590C
39A POIEW IIDβ	DO	688D
39B HOSOS 2	HOW GREAT	590C
39B POIEW IIDβ	DO	688D
40 APODECHOMAI I	WELCOME	89C
PROSDOKAW I	EXPECT	719C
HUPOSTREPHW	RETURN	855B
41 ARCHWN 2A	AUTHORITIES	113C
EISERCHOMAI IAβ	COME	231D
IAIROS	JAIRUS	368A
OIKOS IAα	HOUSE	563A
ONOMA II	NAME	574A
PARA IIIIC	ALONG	616A
PARAKALEW IB	INVITE	622B
PIPTW IBα	FALL	665C
POUS IA	FOOT	703B
HUPARCHW 2	BE	846A
42 APOTHN8SKW IAα	DIE	900D
ETOS	YEAR	317A
THUGAT8R I	DAUGHTER	365B
MONOGEN8S	ONLY	529A
OCHLOS I	CROWD	605D
SUMPNIGW 2	CHOKE	787C
HUPAGW 2	GO AWAY	844C
HWS IV5	WHEN	907C

43 APO II2A	FROM	86B
BIOS 3	LIFE	141B
EIMI III4	TO BE	224B
ETOS	YEAR	317B
THERAPEUW 2	HEAL	359C
IATROS I	PHYSICIAN	369C
ISCHUW 2B	BE STRONG	384C
HOLOS 2A	WHOLE	567C
HOSTIS 3	WHOEVER	591B
OUDEIS 2A	NO ONE	596B
PROSANALISKW	SPEND LAVISHLY	718D
43B APO V6	BY	87D
43F HAIMA IA	BLOOD	22A
43F RUSIS	FLOW	745C
44 HAPTW 2B	TOUCH	102D
HIMATION 2	GARMENT	377A
HIST8MI IIIA	STAND	383A
KRASPEDON I	EDGE	449B
OPISTHEN IA	FROM BEHIND	578B
PARACHR8MA	AT ONCE	629B
45 APOTHLIBW	PRESS UPON	90D
ARNEOMAI 2	DENY	107C
EPISTAT8S	MASTER	300B
OCHLOS I	CROWD	605D
SUN IC	WITH	789B
SUNECHW 3	CROWD	796D
45FF HAPTW 2B	TOUCH	102D
46 GINWSKW 4A	PERCEIVE	160B
EPIGINWSKW 2C	KNOW	291B
TIS, TI IAα	ANY ONE	827C
47 AITIA I	CAUSE	25D
APAGGELLW I	REPORT	78C
APAGGELLW 2	PROCLAIM	78D
ENTROMOS	TREMBLING	269B
ENWPION 2A	BEFORE	270B
ERCHOMAI IIAζ	COME	310D
IAOMAI I	HEAL	369A
LANTHANW	ESCAPE NOTICE	467C
LAOS IA	PEOPLE	467D
PARACHR8MA	AT ONCE	629B
PROSPIPTW I	FALL DOWN BEFORE	725B
TREMW	TREMBLE	833B
HWS I2D	AS	905D
48 EIR8N8 2	PEACE	226C
EIS 9B	IN	229D
THUGAT8R 2A	DAUGHTER	365B
PISTIS 2Bα	FAITH	668D
POREUW I	PROCEED	699B
SWZW IC	SAVE	806A
49 ARCHISUNAGWGOS		112D
PRESIDENT OF A SYNAGOGUE		
ERCHOMAI IIAβ	COME	310C
ETI IAβ	STILL	315D
THN8SKW I	DIE	363A
THUGAT8R I	DAUGHTER	365B
LALEW 2Aγ	SPEAK	464B
M8 AIII3B	NOT	518D
M8KETI 6A	NO LONGER	520B
PARA II	FROM	614C
SKULLW 2	WEARY	765C
50 MONOS 2A	ONLY	529D
PISTEUW 2C	BELIEVE	667D
SWZW IC	SAVE	806A

50	PHOBEW IA	BE AFRAID 870C
51	APHI8MI 4	TOLERATE 126A
	IAKWBOS I	JAMES 368B
	IWAN(N)8S 2	JOHN 385C
	OIKIA IA	HOUSE 559D
	PAIS 2	SERVANT 610A
	SUN IB	WITH 789B
52	APOTHN8SKW IA«	DIE 90D
	KATHEUDW I	SLEEP 389C
	*KLAIW I	WEEP 434A
	KOPTW 2	BEAT 445A
52B	KLAIW I	WEEP 434A
53	KATAGELAW	RIDICULE 410D
	OIDA IE	KNOW 558C
54	EGEIRW IB	RAISE UP 214A
	EGEIRW 2F	APPEAR 214B
	KRATEW IB	SEIZE 449C
	HO,H8,TO IIII	THE 553B
	PAIS 2	SERVANT 610A
	PHWNEW IB	CRY OUT 878B
55	ANIST8MI 2A	RISE 69C
	DIATASSW	ORDER 188C
	EPISTREPHW IB«	TURN 301A
	ESTHIW ID	EAT 313B
	PARACHR8MA	AT ONCE 629B
	PNEUMA 2	SPIRIT 680D
56	GONEUS	PARENTS 164B
	EXIST8MI 2B	BE AMAZED 276A
	PARAGGELLW	GIVE ORDERS 618C

LUKE 9

1	DUNAMIS I	POWER 206D
	EXOUSIA 3	AUTHORITY 278A
	EPI IIIIB«	OVER 288D
	THERAPEUW 2	HEAL 359D
	NOSOS I	DISEASE 545D
	SUGKALEW 2	CALL TOGETHER 780D
2	APOSTELLW IBy	SEND AWAY 98B
	APOSTELLW IC	SEND AWAY 98B
	ASTHENEW IA	BE SICK 115A
	BASILEIA 3G	KINGDOM 135A
	K8RUSSW 2B?	ANNOUNCE 432C
3	AIRW 2	LIFT UP 24A
	ANA 3	EACH 49C
	ARGURION 2B	MONEY 104B
	ARTOS IA	BREAD 110A
	DUO 5	TWO 208C
	M8DEIS 2B«	NOTHING 520A
	M8TE	AND NOT 521D
	HODOS IB	WAY 556C
	P8RA	KNAPSACK 662B
	RABDOS	ROD 740D
	CHITWN	SHIRT 890C
4	EXERCHOMAI IA«	GO OUT 274A
	MENW IA«	REMAIN 504D
5	APOTINASSW	SHAKE OFF 100D
	DECHOMAI I	RECEIVE 176B
	EKTINASSW I	SHAKE OFF 245B
	EXERCHOMAI IA«	GO OUT 274A
	EPI IIIIB«	TOWARD 289A
	KONIORTOS	DUST 444A
	MARTURION IA	TESTIMONY 494D

5	M8 AII	NOT 517C
	HOSOS 2	HOW GREAT 590C
	POLIS I	CITY 692A
6	DIERCHOMAI 3	GO ABOUT 193D
	EUAGGELIZW 2A6	PREACH 318A
	THERAPEUW 2	HEAL 359D
	KATA IIIA	ALONG 407A
	KWM8 I	VILLAGE 462D
	PANTACHOU I	EVERYWHERE 613B
7	GINOMAI I2A	COME ABOUT 157C
	DIA BII3	BECAUSE 180C
	DIAPOREW	BE PERPLEXED 186D
	EGEIRW 2C	RISE 214A
	H8RWD8S 2	HEROD 349B
	NEKROS 2A	DEAD 537A
	HO,H8,TO II3A	THE 553C
	PAS ID?	ALL 637D
	TETRARCH8S	TETRARCH 821D
7F	TIS, TI IA«	ANY ONE 828A
8	ARCHAIOS 2	ANCIENT IIIA
	8LIAS	ELIJAH 345D
	PHAINW 2C	APPEAR 859C
9	AKOUW 3C	LEARN 32A
	APOKEPHALIZW	BEHEAD 92C
	EIDON 6	VISIT 220B
	Z8TEW 2By	SEEK 339C
	H8RWD8S 2	HEROD 349B
	HOS,H8,HO II	(REL PRON) 587A
	TIS, TI IA«	WHICH 826C
	TOIOUTOS 3B	SUCH A KIND 829B
10	APOSTOLOS 3	APOSTLES 99B
	B8THSAIDA I	BETHSAIDA 139C
	DI8GEOMAI	TELL 194A
	IDIOS 4	PRIVATELY 371A
	KALEW IAy	CALL 400A
	PARALAMBANW I	TAKE 625A
	POIEW IIB?	DO 687C
	POLIS I	CITY 692B
	HUPOCHWREW I	RETREAT 856B
11	AKOLOUTHEW 2	ACCOMPANY 30D
	APODECHOMAI I	WELCOME 89C
	BASILEIA 3G	KINGDOM 135A
	DECHOMAI I	RECEIVE 176B
	THERAPEIA IA	SERVING 359C
	LALEW 2A6	SPEAK 464C
	CHREIA I	NEED 893B
12	AGROS 3	FARM 13D
	EPISITISMOS	PROVISIONS 298B
	ER8MOS IA	ABANDONED 308D
	H8MERA IA	DAY 346C
	KATALUW 2	HALT 415C
	KLINW 2	DECLINE 437C
	KUKLW IB	AROUND 458A
	KWM8 I	VILLAGE 462D
	HOTI 3B	THAT 594A
	PROSERCHOMAI I	APPROACH 720A
	TOPOS IC	PLACE 830B
13	AGORAZW I	BUY 12C
	ARTOS IA	BREAD 110A
	BRWMA I	FOOD 147C
	EI VI9	UNLESS INDEED 219A
	EIS 4G	FOR 229A
	ESTHIW ID	EAT 313B

13 8	2A		THAN	343B
	ICHTHUS		FISH	385A
	LAOS IA		PEOPLE	467D
	HO,H8,TO IIIAα		THE	552B
	OPSARION		FISH	606B
	PAS ICα		ALL	637B
	POLUS II2C		MANY	696B
	POREUW I		PROCEED	699B
14	ANA 3		EACH	49C
	AN8R I		MAN	65D
	GAR 2		FOR	151C
	KATAKLINW	CAUSE TO LIE DOWN		412C
	KLISIA		GROUP	437D
	PENTAKISCHILIOI	FIVE THOUSAND		648C
	PENT8KONTA		FIFTY	648D
14A	HWSEI 2		AS	907D
14B	HWSEI 2		AS	907D
15	ANAKLINW IB		LAY	55D
	HAPAS 2		ALL	81A
	KATAKLINW	CAUSE TO LIE DOWN		412C
	POIEW I2Aα		DO	689A
16	ANABLEPW I		LOOK UP	50C
	ARTOS IA		BREAD	110A
	EIS IDα		TOWARD	227D
	EULOGEW I		SPEAK WELL	322C
	EULOGEW 2B		BLESS	322D
	ICHTHUS		FISH	385A
	KATAKLAW	BREAK IN PIECES		412C
	MATH8T8S 2Bα		DISCIPLE	487A
	HO,H8,TO IIIAα		THE	552B
	OURANOS 2A		HEAVEN	599B
	OPSARION		FISH	606B
	PARATITH8MI IA	PLACE BESIDE		628B
17	AIRW 3		CARRY	24A
	KLASMA		FRAGMENT	434B
	KOPHINOS		BASKET	448C
	PERISSEUW IAα	BE LEFT OVER		656C
	CHORTAZW 2A		FEED	892B
18	KATA IIIC		BY	407B
	MONOS 3		BE ALONE	530A
	PROPH8T8S 3		PROPHET	731A
	SUNANTAW I		MEET	792B
	SUNEIMI I		BE WITH	794D
	TIS, TI IAα		WHICH	826C
19	ALLOS IC		OTHER	39B
	ARCHAIOS 2		ANCIENT	111A
	BAPTIST8S		BAPTIST	132B
	8LIAS		ELIJAH	345D
	PROPH8T8S 3		PROPHET	731A
20	LEGW IIBβ		SAY	469C
	CHRISTOS I	ANOINTED ONE		895B
21	EPITIMAW I		REBUKE	303B
	LEGW IIA		SAY	469B
	PARAGGELLW	GIVE ORDERS		618C
22	APO V6		BY	87D
	APODOKIMAZW 2	DECLARE USELESS		90B
	ARCHIEREUS IB	HIGH PRIEST		112B
	H8MERA 2		DAY	346D
	*PASCHW 3β		ENDURE	639D
	POLUS I28α		MANY	695A
	PRESBUTEROS 2Aβ		OLDER	706D
	TRITOS I		THIRD	834B
	HUIOS 2C		SON	843A
23	AIRW 2		LIFT UP	24A
	APARNEOMAI		DENY	80B
	ARNEOMAI 4		DENY	107D
	EI VII			219B
	ERCHOMAI II		GO	311D
	LEGW I3		SAY	469D
	OPISW 2Aβ		AFTER	578D
	STAUROS 2		THE CROSS	772C
24	APOLLUMI IB		LOSE	94C
	GAR IE		FOR	151C
	HENEKA	BECAUSE OF		264B
	SWZW 3		SAVE	806C
	PSUCH8 ID		SOUL LIFE	902B
24A	SWZW IA		SAVE	805D
24A	SWZW 2Aβ		SAVE	806B
24A	PSUCH8 ID		SOUL LIFE	902B
24B	HOUTOS IAα		THIS	601B
24B	SWZW IA		SAVE	805D
24B	SWZW 2Aβ		SAVE	806B
24B	PSUCH8 ID		SOUL LIFE	902B
24-6	GAR IC		FOR	151B
25	APOLLUMI IB		LOSE	94C
	Z8MIOW I	SUFFER DAMAGE		339A
	KERDAINW IA	TO GAIN		430C
	KOSMOS 6		WORLD	447C
	HOLOS 2B		WHOLE	567D
	WPHELEW IA		HELP	909A
26	AGGELOS 2A		ANGEL	7C
	HAGIOS IBβ		HOLY	9D
	DOXA IA		GLORY	202D
	*EPAISCHUNOMAI I	BE ASHAMED		281D
	ERCHOMAI IIAη		COME	311A
	HO,H8,TO IIIE		THE	552B
	HOUTOS IAα		THIS	601B
	HUIOS 2C		SON	843A
27	AL8THWS I		TRULY	36D
	AN 3D		(PARTICLE)	48C
	AUTOU		HERE	123C
	BASILEIA 3G		KINGDOM	135A
	GEUOMAI 2	COME TO KNOW SOMETH		156A
	EIMI II		TO BE	222B
	THANATOS IA		DEATH	351B
	HIST8MI II2Bα		BEING	383C
	LEGW IIID		ASSURE	470D
28	ANABAINW IAα		GO UP	49C
	H8MERA 2		DAY	347D
	IAKWBOS I		JAMES	368B
	HO,H8,TO IIIAα		THE	552C
	OKTW		EIGHT	565D
	OROS		MOUNTAIN	586B
	PARALAMBANW I		TAKE	624D
	HWSEI 2		AS	907D
29	ALLOIOW		CHANGE	39A
	EIDOS I		FORM	220B
	EXASTRAPTW		FLASH	273B
	HETEROS 2		ANOTHER	315C
	*HIMATISMOS		CLOTHING	377B
	LEUKOS I		SHINING	473C
	PROSWPON IA		FACE	728A
30	8LIAS		ELIJAH	345D
	IDOU IBβ		BEHOLD	371C
	MWUS8S		MOSES	533D
	SULLALEW		TALK	784B

31	DOXA IA	BRIGHTNESS 202C	38	MONOGEN8S	ONLY 529A
	EN I4B	IN 258B		OCHLOS I	CROWD 605C
	EXODOS 2	GOING OUT 276B	39	APOCHWREW	LEAVE 101D
	LEGW II2	SPEAK 471A		APHROS	FOAM 127B
	MELLW IC6	IS DESTINED 502C		EXAIPHN8S	SUDDENLY 271D
	HORAW IA6	SEE 582A		KRAZW I	CRY OUT 448D
	PL8ROW 4A	MAKE FULL 677C		LAMBANW IC	TAKE 465C
32	BAREW	BURDEN 133A		MOGIS	WITH DIFFICULTY 527C
	BLEPW 2	SEE 143A		MOLIS I	WITH DIFFICULTY 528C
	DIAGR8GOREW	KEEP AWAKE 181C		PNEUMA 4C	SPIRIT 682A
	DOXA IA	BRIGHTNESS 202C		SPARASSW	TEAR 768B
	SUN IC	WITH 789B		SUNTRIBW IB	SHATTER 801A
	SUNIST8MI III	UNITE 798C	40	APPALLASSW I	RELEASE 79B
	HUPNOS	SLEEP 850D		DEOMAI 4	ASK 174B
33	DIACHWRIZW	SEPARATE 190B		DUNAMAI 2	ABLE 206B
	EIMI II9A	TO BE 223D		EKBALLW I	DRIVE OUT 237A
	EPISTAT8S	MASTER 300B		HINA IIIAγ	IN ORDER THAT 378B
	8LIAS	ELIJAH 345D	41	ANECHW IA	ENDURE 65B
	KALOS 3A	GOOD 401C		APISTOS 2	FAITHLESS 85A
	KALOS 3C	GOOD 401D	*GENEA 2	GENERATION 153B
	LEGW IIA	SAY 469B		DIASTREPHW IB	PERVERT 188A
	MWUS8S	MOSES 533D		HEWS IIIC	UNTIL 335C
	POIEW II4α	DO 687A		POTE	WHEN 701D
	SK8N8	TENT 762A		PROS III7	TOWARD 718A
	HWDE 2A	HERE 903D		PROSAGW IA	BRING 718B
34	GINOMAI II8α	COME ABOUT 157B		HWDE I	HERE 903B
	EISERCHOMAI IAβ	COME 231D		W I	O 903B
	EN II3	WHILE 260A	42	AKATHARTOS 2	IMPURE 28C
	EPISKIAZW 2	COVER 298D		APODIDWMI 2	GIVE BACK 90A
	LEGW IIA	SAY 469B		APHI8MI 3A	LEAVE 125C
34F	NEPHEL8	CLOUD 538D		EPITIMAW I	REBUKE 303B
35	AGAP8TOS I	BELOVED 6C		ETI IAβ	STILL 315D
	AKOUW 4	LISTEN 32A		PAIS IAα	CHILD 609C
	GINOMAI I4Cα	COME, GO 159A		PNEUMA 4C	SPIRIT 682A
	EKLEGOMAI	CHOOSE 241C		PROSERCHOMAI I	APPROACH 720A
	EKLEGOMAI 4	CHOOSE 242A		R8SSW	THROW DOWN 743B
	PON8ROS 2A	WICKED 698A		SUNTARASSW	DISTURB 799C
	HUIOS 2B	SON 842C		SUSPARASSW	CONVULSE 802B
35F	PHWN8 2D	VOICE 879B	43	EKPL8SSW 2	BE AMAZED 243D
36	GINOMAI I4Cα	COME, GO 159A		THAUMAZW IAβ	WONDER 353A
	EKEINOS 2Bα	THAT 239D		MEGALEIOT8S	GRANDEUR 498A
	EN II3	WHILE 260A		HOS,H8,HO I4A	(REL PRON) 587D
	HEURISKW IСα	FIND 325C	44	MELLW IC6	IS DESTINED 502C
	MONOS IAα	ONLY 529B		OUS 2	EAR 600B
	HORAW IAβ	SEE 581C		PARADIDWMI IB	GIVE OVER 620A
	HOS,H8,HO I4A	(REL PRON) 587D		TITH8MI IIIC	PUT 824B
	OUDEIS 2A	NO ONE 596C		HUIOS 2C	SON 843A
	SIGAW IC	BE SILENT 757B		CHEIR 2B	HAND 888D
36B	OUDEIS 2Bα	NOTHING 596C	45	AGNOEW 3	BE IGNORANT IIC
37	DIA AII9	DURING 178D		AISTHANOMAI 2	UNDERSTAND 24B
	HEX8S 2	NEXT 275C		ERWTAW I	ASK 312A
	H8MERA 2	DAY 347A		HINA II2	IN ORDER THAT 378D
	KATERCHOMAI I	COME DOWN 423A		PARAKALUPTW	HIDE 623A
	SUNANTAW I	MEET 792B		PHOBEW IA	BE AFRAID 870D
38	ANABOAW	CRY OUT 50D	45A	R8MA I	WORD 742D
	AN8R 6	MAN 66B	45B	R8MA I	WORD 742D
	APO I6	FROM 86A	46	AN 5	(PARTICLE) 48D
	APO IVIB	FROM 86D		DIALOGISMOS 2	DOUBT 185B
	BOAW 3	SHOUT 143D		EISERCHOMAI IBβ	COME 232A
	DEOMAI I	ASK 174A		EISERCHOMAI 2B	COME 232C
	DIDASKALOS	TEACHER 190D		EN I6	IN 259C
	EPIBLEPW	LOOK AT 290B		MEGAS 2Bα	GREAT 499B
	IDOU IBβ	BEHOLD 371C		HO,H8,TO II8A	THE 554D

47	DIALOGISMOS I	THOUGHT 185A
	EIDON 3	NOTICE 220A
	EPILAMBANOMAI I	GRASP 295A
	HIST8MI IIAα	PUT 382D
	KARDIA IBβ	HEART 404C
	PARA IIIAβ	BESIDE 615B
47F	PAIDION 2A	CHILD 609A
48	APOSTELLW IC	SEND AWAY 98B
	DECHOMAI I	RECEIVE 176C
	EPI II3	ON 287D
	MEGAS 2Bα	GREAT 499B
	MIKROS IC	SMALL 523B
	ONOMA I4Cε	NAME 576D
	ONOMA II	TITLE 577A
	HOUTOS IAε	THIS 601B
	PAS IEα	ALL 637D
	HUPARCHW 2	BE 846A
49	AKOLOUTHEW 2	ACCOMPANY 30D
	DAIMONION 2	DEMON 168B
	EKBALLW I	DRIVE OUT 237A
	EPI II3	ON 287D
	EPISTAT8S	MASTER 300B
	KWLUW I	HINDER 462C
	META AIIIA	WITH 509D
	ONOMA I4Cγ	NAME 576A
	ONOMA I4Cε	NAME 576C
	TIS, TI IAβ	ANY ONE 827D
50	EIMI III6A	TO BE 224C
	EIMI IIIIIA	TO BE 224D
	KWLUW I	HINDER 462B
	M8 AIII3B	NOT 518D
	SKORPIZW I	SCATTER 764B
	HUPER IAδ	IN BEHALF OF 846B
51	AUTOS IB	SELF 122B
	HO,H8,TO II4Bε	THE 554A
	PROSWPON IB	FACE 728C
	ST8RIZW I	ESTABLISH 775D
	SUMPL8ROW 2	FILL COMPLETELY 787B
52	AGGELOS IA	MESSENGER 7A
	APOSTELLW IBβ	SEND AWAY 98A
	EISERCHOMAI IAβ	COME 231D
	HETOIMAZW I	PREPARE 316B
	KWM8 I	VILLAGE 462D
	POLIS I	CITY 692A
	PRO I	BEFORE 708C
	PROSWPON ICζ	FACE 729A
	SAMARIT8S	SAMARITAN 749A
	HWSTE 2B	THEREFORE 908C
53	DECHOMAI I	RECEIVE 176B
	PROSWPON IB	FACE 728C
54	ANALISKW	CONSUME 56D
	8LIAS	ELIJAH 345D
	THELW I	WISH 355C
	IAKWB0S I	JAMES 368B
	KATABAINW IB	COME DOWN 409D
	KURIOS 2Cβ	LORD 460D
	OURANOS IB	HEAVEN 598C
	PUR IB	FIRE 737C
	HWS II4A	SO 906B
55	EPITIMAW I	REBUKE 303B
	HOIOS	OF WHAT SORT 565C
	PNEUMA 7	SPIRIT 684B
	POIOS IAγ	OF WHAT KIND 691B
55	STREPHW 2Aα	TURN 778D
56	HETEROS IBα	ANOTHER 315A
	KWM8 I	VILLAGE 462D
	POREUW I	PROCEED 699A
	SWZW 3	SAVE 806C
	HUIOS 2C	SON 843A
	PSUCH8 2	SOUL LIFE 902C
57	HOPOU IBβ	WHERE 579D
	POREUW I	PROCEED 699B
	TIS, TI IAα	ANY ONE 827C
58	ALWP8X I	FOX 41B
	KATASK8NWSIS 2	NEST 419D
	KEPHAL8 IA	HEAD 431B
	KLINW IB	LAY DOWN 437C
	OURANOS ID	HEAVEN 598D
	PETEINON	BIRD 660A
	POU IB	WHERE 703A
	HUIOS 2C	SON 843A
	PHWLEOS	DEN 878B
59	EPITREPW I	ALLOW 303C
	HETEROS IBα	ANOTHER 315A
	PRWTOS 2A	FIRST 733C
59F	THAPTW	BURY 352C
60	APHI8MI 4	TOLERATE 126A
	BASILEIA 3G	KINGDOM 135A
	DIAGGELLW I	181B
	PROCLAIM FAR AND WIDE	
	HEAUTOU 4	ONESELF 211D
	NEKROS 2B	DEAD 537B
	SU IC	YOU 780A
61	APOTASSW I	SAY FAREWELL 100B
	EIS 9A	IN 229D
	EPITREPW I	ALLOW 303C
	HETEROS IBα	ANOTHER 315A
	KURIOS 2Cβ	LORD 460D
	OIKOS IAα	HOUSE 563A
	PRWTOS 2A	FIRST 733C
62	AROTRON	A PLOW 108A
	BASILEIA 3G	KINGDOM 135A
	BLEPW 3	SEE 143B
	EPIBALLW IB	LAY ON 289D
	EUTHETOS	SUITABLE 320C
	OPISW IA	BEHIND 578C

LUKE 10

1	*ANA 3	EACH 49C
	ANADEIKNUMI 2	APPOINT 53A
	APOSTELLW IBβ	SEND AWAY 98A
	APOSTELLW IBβ	SEND AWAY 98A
	DUO 5	TWO 208C
	*HEBDOM8KONTA	SEVENTY 212A
	HETEROS IBβ	ANOTHER 315B
	KURIOS 2Cβ	LORD 460D
	MELLW ICγ	INTEND 502B
	META BII3	AFTER 511C
	HOU 2	WHERE 594A
	*POLIS I	CITY 692A
	PRO I	BEFORE 708C
	PROSWPON ICζ	FACE 729A
	TOPOS IA	PLACE 830A
2	DEOMAI 4	ASK 174B
	EKBALLW 2	SEND OUT 237A

2	ERGAT8S IA	WORKMAN 307C
	THERISMOS 2A	HARVEST 360A
	KURIOS IA«	LORD 460A
	OLIGOS IA	FEW 566B
	HOPWS 2B	IN ORDER THAT 580D
	OUN IB	THEREFORE 597B
	POLUS IIB«	MANY 694C
3	APOSTELLW IB∅	SEND AWAY 98A
	AR8N	LAMB 105D
	EN I6	IN 259D
	LUKOS I	WOLF 482C
	MESOS 2	THE MIDDLE 509A
	HUPAGW 2	GO AWAY 844C
3F	BLEPW IA	SEE 142D
4	ASPAZOMAI IA	GREET 116B
	BALLANTION	PURSE 130B
	BASTAZW 2A	CARRY 137A
	KATA III A	ALONG 407A
	M8 AIII3A	NOT 518C
	M8DEIS 2A	NO 520A
	HODOS IB	WAY 556C
	P8RA	KNAPSACK 662B
	*HUPOD8MA	SANDAL 852B
5	EIR8N8 2	PEACE 226C
	OIKOS 2	HOUSEHOLD 563C
6	ANAKAMPTW IB	RETURN 55B
	GE 3B«	OTHERWISE 152B
	DE IA	BUT, AND 170C
	EAN IIA	IF 210B
	EIR8N8 2	PEACE 226C
	EPANAPAUOMAI I	REST 282C
	EPI IIIIBy	ON 288D
	EPISTREPHW IB«	TURN 301B
	HUIOS IC6	SON 842A
7	AXIOS 2A	WORTHY 77C
	AUTOS IH	EVEN 122D
	ERGAT8S IA	WORKMAN 307C
	ESTHIW IA	EAT 312D
	METABAINW IB	MOVE 511D
	M8 AIII3A	NOT 518C
	MISTHOS I	WAGES 525A
	HO,H8,TO IIIA∅	THE 552C
	HO,H8,TO IIID	THE 552D
	HO,H8,TO II5	THE 554B
	PARA I4B«	FROM 615C
	PINW I	DRINK 664B
8	DECHOMAI I	RECEIVE 176B
	EISERCHOMAI IA∅	COME 231D
	ESTHIW IA	EAT 312D
	PARATITH8MI IA	PLACE BESIDE 628B
	POLIS I	CITY 692A
9	ASTHEN8S IA	SICK 115B
	BASILEIA 3G	KINGDOM 135B
	EGGIZW 3	APPROACH 212D
	EGGIZW 5B	APPROACH 212D
	EPI IIIIBy	ON 288D
	THERAPEUW 2	HEAL 359C
10	DECHOMAI I	RECEIVE 176B
	PLATEIA	WIDE ROAD 672C
	POLIS I	CITY 692A
11	APOMASSW	WIPE OFF 96B
	BASILEIA 3G	KINGDOM 135B
	GINWSKW 6C	KNOW 160D

11	EGGIZW 5B	APPROACH 212D
	KOLLAW 2A«	UNITE 442B
	KONIORTOS	DUST 444A
	HOUTOS IB∅	THIS 601C
	PL8N IB	BUT 675B
12	ANEKTOS	BEARABLE 63D
	EIMI II9B	TO BE 224A
	8 2A	THAN 343B
	H8MERA 3B∅	DAY 348A
	POLIS I	CITY 692A
	SODOMA	SODOM 766B
13	B8THSAIDA I	BETHSAIDA 139C
	GINOMAI I2A	CREATED 157C
	DUNAMIS 4	MIRACLE 207B
	EN I4B	IN 258B
	KATH8MAI IA«	SIT 390B
	METANOEW	CHANGE ONES MIND 513B
	HOTI 3A	THAT 593D
	OUAI IA	WOE 595C
	PALAI I	LONG AGO 610B
	SAKKOS	SACK 747C
	SPODOS	ASHES 770D
	CHORAZIN	CHORAZIN 891D
13F	SIDWN	SIDON 757C
13F	TUROS	TYRE 838C
14	ANEKTOS	BEARABLE 63D
	EIMI II9B	TO BE 224A
	KRISIS IA«	JUDGING 453D
	PL8N IB	BUT 675B
15	HAD8S I	HADES 16C
	HEWS II2A	AS FAR AS 335C
	KATABAINW 2	COME DOWN 409D
	KATABIBAZW	DRIVE DOWN 410A
	KAPHARNAOUM	CAPERNAUM 427C
	OURANOS IB	HEAVEN 598B
	HUPSOW I	LIFT UP 858C
16	ATHETEW IB	REJECT 20C
	EGW	I 216B
17*	HEBDOM8KONTA	SEVENTY 212A
	KAI II2	EVEN 394B
	KURIOS 2C∅	LORD 460D
	ONOMA I4Cy	NAME 576A
	HUPOTASSW IB∅	SUBJECT 855D
	CHARA I	JOY 883C
18	ASTRAP8	LIGHTNING 117D
	HEIS 2C	ONE 230D
	THEWREW I	OBSERVE 360C
	OURANOS IB	HEAVEN 598C
	OURANOS ID	HEAVEN 598D
	PIPTW IA	FALL 665A
	SATAN	ADVERSARY 752C
19	ADIKEW 2B	INJURE 17B
	DIDWMI IB∅	GIVE 192B
	EXOUSIA 2	ABILITY 277D
	EPANW 2A	ON 283A
	EPI IIIIB«	OVER 288D
	ECHTHROS 2B«	THE ENEMY 331D
	HO,H8,TO II4B∅	THE 553D
	OU 6D	NO 595B
	OUDEIS 2B«	NOTHING 596C
	OPHIS I	SNAKE 604D
	SKORPIOS I	THE SCORPION 764C
20	DE ID	BUT, AND 170C

Ref	Greek	Gloss	Ref	Greek	Gloss
20	EGGRAPHW I	RECORD 213A	27	ISCHUS	STRENGTH 384B
	ONOMA I2A	NAME 574B		KARDIA IB(	HEART 405B
	OURANOS 2D	HEAVEN 599D		PL8SION IB	NEAR 678D
	HOUTOS IB8	THIS 601C		SEAUTOU 3	YOURSELF 753A
	PL8N IB	BUT 675B		PSUCH8 IBγ	SOUL LIFE 901D
	PNEUMA 4C	SPIRIT 682A		PSUCH8 IBγ	SOUL LIFE 901D
	HUPOTASSW IB8	SUBJECT 855D	28	ZAW 2B«	LIVE 337A
20A	CHAIRW I	REJOICE 881D		KAI I2F	AND 393C
20B	CHAIRW I	REJOICE 881D		ORTHWS	RIGHTLY 584C
21	AGALLIAW	BE GLAD 4A	29	DIKAIOW 2	JUSTIFY 196C
	APOKALUPTW 2	REVEAL 91C		KAI I2H	AND 393D
	APOKRUPTW	CONCEAL 93B		PL8SION IB	NEAR 678D
	AUTOS IH	EVEN 122D	30	ANTHRWPOS 3A«	MAN 68B
	EMPROSTHEN 2D	IN FRONT 256D		APHI8MI 3A	LEAVE 125D
	EXOMOLOGEW 2C	CONFESS 276D		EKDUW I	STRIP 238C
	EUDOKIA 2	FAVOR 319D		EPITITH8MI IA8	303A
	KURIOS 2A	LORD 460B			INFLICT BLOWS
	NAI 3	CERTAINLY 535A		H8MITHAN8S	HALF DEAD 348C
	N8PIOS IB8	CHILDLIKE 539D		IERICHW	JERICHO 372D
	OURANOS IA«	HEAVEN 598B		HIEROSOLUMA IA	JERUSALEM 373D
	PNEUMA 3B	SPIRIT 681B		KAI II6	394C
	PNEUMA 5C«	SPIRIT 682D		KATABAINW IA8	COME DOWN 409B
	SOPHOS 2	LEARNED 767D		L8ST8S I	ROBBER 474B
	SUNETOS	INTELLIGENT 796C		PERIPIPTW I	FALL IN WITH 655C
	HWRA 3	TIME OF DAY 905A		PL8G8 I	BLOW 674A
21A	PAT8R 3D«	FATHER 641D		TUGCHANW 2A	HAPPEN 837A
21B	PAT8R 3D«	FATHER 641D		HUPOLAMBANW 3	TAKE UP 853A
22	APO V6	BY 87D	31	DE 4B	BUT, AND 170D
	APOKALUPTW 2	REVEAL 91C		HIEREUS IB«	PRIEST 372C
	BOULOMAI 2B	DESIRE 146A		HIEREUS IB«	PRIEST 372C
	GINWSKW 6D	KNOW 160D		KATA II5B8	ACCORDING TO 408C
	EPIGINWSKW 2A	KNOW 291A		KATABAINW IA8	COME DOWN 409B
	OUDEIS 2A	NO ONE 596B		HODOS IA	WAY 556B
	PARADIDWMI 3	GIVE OVER 620D		SUGKURIA	COINCIDENCE 782C
	PAS 2A6	EVERYTHING 638B		TIC, TI 2A«	ANY ONE 828A
	STREPHW 2A«	TURN 779A	31F	ANTIPARERCHOMAI	PASS BY 75A
	HUIOS 2B	SON 842C	32	GINOMAI I4C6	COME, GO 159A
22A	PAT8R 3D«	FATHER 641D		HIEREUS IB«	PRIEST 372C
22B	PAT8R 3D«	FATHER 641D		KATA II1B	TO 407A
22C	PAT8R 3D«	FATHER 641D		LEUIT8S	A LEVITE 473B
23	IDIOS 4	PRIVATELY 371A		HOMOIWS	LIKEWISE 570D
	MAKARIOS 3A	BLESSED 488A		TOPOS IC	PLACE 830B
	OPHTHALMOS I	EYE 604B	33	ERCHOMAI IIA8	COME 310C
	STREPHW 2A«	TURN 779A		HODEUW	GO 555D
24	BASILEUS I	KING 135C		SAMARIT8S	SAMARITAN 748D
	EIDON	SEE 219D		SPLAGCHNIZOMAI	HAVE PITY 770B
	POLUS IIA«	MANY 694A	34	ELAION I	OLIVE OIL 247B
	PROPH8T8S 4	PROPHET 731B		EPIBIBAZW	CAUSE TO MOUNT 290B
25	AIWNIOS 3	ETERNAL 28A		EPICHEW I	POUR OVER 304D
	ANIST8MI 2C	RISE 69D		IDIOS 2C	ONES OWN 370C
	EKPEIRAZW	PUT TO THE TEST 243A		KATADEW	BANDAGE 411B
	ZW8 2B8	LIFE 341C		KT8NOS	ANIMAL 456B
	IDOU IB8	BEHOLD 371C		OINOS I	WINE 565A
	KL8RONOMEW 2	INHERIT 435D		PANDOCHEION	INN 612C
	NOMIKOS 2	LAWYER 543C		TRAUMA	A WOUND 832C
26	ANAGINWSKW I	READ 51B	34F	EPIMELEOMAI	CARE FOR 296C
	NOMOS 4B	LAW 545A	35	APODIDWMI 2	GIVE BACK 90A
	PWS IA	HOW 739C		AURION 2	TOMORROW 121D
	TIS, TI IB«	WHICH 826D		D8NARION	DENARIUS 178B
27	AGAPAW IA8	LOVE 4C		EKBALLW 3	TAKE OUT 237B
	DIANOIA I	UNDERSTANDING 186A		EPANERCHOMAI	RETURN 282D
	EK 3Gγ	BY 235A		EPI III2A	ON 289B
	THEOS 3C	GOD 358A		HOSTIS IE8	WHOEVER 591A

35 PANDOCHEUS	INN KEEPER	612C
PROSDAPANAW	SPEND IN ADDITION	719A
36 DOKEW 2A	SEEM	201A
EIS IAß	INTO	227C
EMPIPTW 2	FALL	255D
L8ST8S I	ROBBER	474B
PL8SION IB	NEAR	678D
TIS, TI IAα	WHICH	826C
37 ELEOS I	MERCY	249C
META AIIICγ	WITH	510B
HOMOIWS	LIKEWISE	570D
POREUW I	PROCEED	699B
37A POIEW IICß	DO	688C
37B POIEW I2Aα	DO	689A
38 AUTOS IB	SELF	122B
KWM8 I	VILLAGE	462D
MARTHA	MARTHA	492C
OIKIA IA	HOUSE	559D
ONOMA II	NAME	574A
POREUW I	PROCEED	699B
HUPODECHOMAI	RECEIVE	852A
39 KALEW IAγ	CALL	400A
KURIOS 2Cß	LORD	460D
LOGOS IAß	WORD	478C
MARIA 5	MARY	493A
MARIA 5	MARY	493B
HODE 2	THIS	555C
PARA IIIIC	ALONG	616A
PARAKATHIZW	SIT DOWN BESIDE	622A
PARAKATHEZOMAI	SIT BESIDE	622A
POUS IA	FOOT	703B
39F ADELPH8 I	SISTER	15C
40 DIAKONEW I	WAIT ON SOMEONE	183A
DIAKONIA 2	SERVICE	183B
EPHIST8MI IA	STAND BY	331A
HINA IIIA6	IN ORDER THAT	378B
KATALEIPW ID	LEAVE BEHIND	414D
KURIOS 2Cß	LORD	460D
MELEI 3	IT IS A CONCERN	501B
MONOS IAα	ONLY	529B
OUN IB	THEREFORE	597B
PERISPAW 2	BE DISTRACTED	656B
POLUS IIBß	MANY	694C
SUNANTILAMBANOMAI	HELP	792B
40F MARTHA	MARTHA	492C
40F PERI 2C	ABOUT	651A
41 THORUBAZW	CAUSE TROUBLE	363B
KURIOS 2Cß	LORD	460D
MERIMNAW I	HAVE ANXIETY	506A
TURBAZW	TROUBLE	838B
41F MERIMNAW I	HAVE ANXIETY	506B
42 AGATHOS IBß	GOOD	3B
APHAIREW 2	BE TAKEN AWAY	124A
HEIS 2B	ONE	230C
EKLEGOMAI 2B	CHOOSE	241D
MARIA 5	MARY	493A
*MARIA 5	MARY	493B
MERIS 2	SHARE	506C
HO.H8.TO IIIF	THE	553A
OLIGOS IB	FEW	566C
CHREIA I	NEED	893A

LUKE 11

I DIDASKW 2E	TEACH	191B
KATHWS I	JUST AS	392A
KURIOS 2Cß	LORD	460D
MATH8T8S 2A	DISCIPLE	486D
PAUW 2	STOP	643D
2 HAGIAZW 3	TO REVERENCE	9A
BASILEIA 3G	KINGDOM	135B
BATTALOGEW	BABBLE	137B
GINOMAI I2A	CREATED	157C
ERCHOMAI I2B	COME	311C
*ERCHOMAI I2C	COME	311D
THEL8MA IA	WILL	354D
KATHARIZW 2Bα	CLEANSE	388B
ONOMA I4B	NAME	574D
HOTAN 2B	WHEN	592B
OURANOS IAß	HEAVEN	598B
OURANOS 2A	HEAVEN	599B
PAT8R 3Cα	FATHER	641C
POLULOGIA	WORDINESS	693D
3 ARTOS 2	FOOD	110C
EPIOUSIOS	CONTINUAL	296D
H8MERA 2	DAY	347B
KATA II2C	EVERY	407C
HO.H8.TO II6	THE	554C
4 APHI8MI 2	FORGIVE	125C
GAR IB	FOR	151A
EISPHERW 2	BRING IN	233A
OPHEIL8MA 2	DEBT	603C
OPHEILW 2Bß	OWE	603D
PAS IAα	EVERY EACH	636D
PEIRASMOS 2B	TEST	646C
PETRA IA	ROCK	660A
PON8ROS 2B	WICKED	698A
RUOMAI	SAVE	744D
HWS IIIIB	SO	906C
5 ARTOS IA	BREAD	110A
EK 4Aß	FROM	235B
ECHW I2Bß	HAVE	332C
KICHR8MI	LEND	433D
MESONUKTION	MIDNIGHT	508B
POREUW I	PROCEED	699A
TIS, TI IAα	WHICH	826D
5A PHILOS 2Aα	LOVING	868D
5B PHILOS 2Aα	LOVING	868D
6 AGROS 2	THE COUNTRY	13D
EK IA	AWAY FROM	233C
EPEID8 2	SINCE	284A
ECHW I2D	HAVE	332D
HODOS IB	WAY	556C
PARAGINOMAI I	COME	618D
PARATITH8MI IA	PLACE BESIDE	628B
PAREIMI IA	BE PRESENT	629D
PHILOS 2Aα	LOVING	868D
7 ANIST8MI 2A	RISE	69C
DUNAMAI IA	ABLE	206B
EIMI III2	TO BE	224A
EIS 9A	IN	229D
ESTHIW IB α	EAT	313A
ESWTHEN I	FROM INSIDE	314C
THURA IA	DOOR	366B
KAKEINOS IA	AND HE	397C

7	KLEIW I	SHUT 435A
	KOIT8 IA	BED 440D
	KOPOS I	TROUBLE 444C
	PAIDION 2B	CHILD 609B
	PARECHW IC	CAUSE 632A
7F	DIDWMI 2	GIVE 192C
8	ANAIDEIA	PERSISTENCE 54B
	ANIST8MI 2A	RISE 69C
	GE I (EMPHASIZING PARTICLE) 152A
	EGEIRW 2B	RISE 214A
	EI IIA	IF 218A
	EI VI4	EVEN IF 219A
	OU 5B	NO 595A
	PHILOS 2A«	LOVING 868D
	*CHR8ZW	NEED 893D
9	KAGW 3B	I 387A
9F	AITEW	ASK 25C
9F	ANOIGW IA	OPEN 70B
9F	HEURISKW IA	FIND 325A
9F	Z8TEW IA8	SEEK 339B
9F	KROUW	STRIKE 454D
10	LAMBANW 2	RECEIVE 466B
	PAS ICy	WHOEVER 637B
11	AITEW	ASK 25B
	ANTI I	OPPOSITE 73A
	ARTOS IA	BREAD 110A
	ICHTHUS IA	FISH 385A
	LITHOS IA	STONE 475B
	M8 CI	NOT 519A
	OPHIS I	SNAKE 604D
	HUIOS IA«	SON 841B
12	AITEW	ASK 25B
	EPIDIDWMI I	GIVE 292B
	8 IA8	OR 342D
	SKORPIOS I	THE SCORPION 764C
	WON	EGG 904B
13	AGATHOS IA8	GOOD 2D
	AGATHOS IB8	GOOD 3A
	AITEW	ASK 25B
	DOMA	GIFT 202C
	EI III	IF 218C
	EK 6A	FROM 235D
	MALLON 2B	MORE 490C
	OIDA 3	KNOW 558D
	OURANOS 2A	HEAVEN 599B
	PAT8R 3C«	FATHER 641C
	PNEUMA 5C8	SPIRIT 682D
	PON8ROS IB«	WICKED 697C
	POSOS I	HOW GREAT 701A
14	EIMI II4B8	TO BE 223A
	EKBALLW I	DRIVE OUT 237A
	THAUMAZW IA«	WONDER 352D
	LALEW 2A«	SPEAK 464B
14A	KWPHOS I	MUTE 463A
14B	KWPHOS I	MUTE 463A
14F	DAIMONION 2	DEMON 168B
15	ARCHWN 3	AUTHORITIES 113C
	BEEZEBOUL	BEELZEBUB 138C
	DAIMONION 2	DEMON 168B
	EK 4A8	FROM 235B
	EKBALLW I	DRIVE OUT 237A
	TIS, TI IA«	ANY ONE 827D
16	HETEROS IB6	ANOTHER 315C
16	Z8TEW 2C	SEEK 339D
	OURANOS 2A	HEAVEN 599B
	PARA I3A	FROM 614D
	PEIRAZW 2C	TRY 646A
	S8MEION 2A	SIGN 755D
17	DIANO8MA	THOUGHT 186A
	ER8MOW	LAY WASTE 309A
	OIDA 4	KNOW 559A
	OIKOS IA«	HOUSE 562D
	PIPTW IB8	FALL 665C
17F	BASILEIA 2	KINGDOM 134C
17F	DIAMERIZW 2	DIVIDE 185D
17F	EPI IIIIA«	AGAINST 288B
18	DE 4A	BUT, AND 170D
	EI VI2	BUT IF 218D
	HIST8MI IIID	STAND 383B
	LEGW IIB8	SAY 469C
	PWS ID	HOW 739C
	SATAN	ADVERSARY 752B
18F	BEEZEBOUL	BEELZEBUB 138C
18F	DAIMONION 2	DEMON 168B
18F	EKBALLW I	DRIVE OUT 237A
18FF	DAIMONION 2	DEMON 168B
19	DIA BII2	THEREFORE 180B
	EKBALLW I	DRIVE OUT 237A
	KRIT8S IB	JUDGE 454D
	TIS, TI IB«	WHICH 826D
	HUIOS IC«	SON 841C
20	ARA 3	THEN 103C
	BASILEIA 3G	KINGDOM 135A
	BASILEIA 3G	KINGDOM 135B
	DAKTULOS	FINGER 169A
	EKBALLW I	DRIVE OUT 237A
	EN IIIIA	BY 260A
	EPI IIIBy	ON 288D
	PHTHANW 2	COME 864C
21	AUL8 2	FARM 121A
	HEAUTOU 4	ONESELF 211D
	EIMI III4	TO BE 224B
	EIR8N8 IA	PEACE 226B
	*ISCHUROS IA	STRONG 384A
	KATHOPLIZW I	EQUIP 391D
	HUPARCHW I	BE 845D
	PHULASSW IC	WATCH 876B
22	AIRW 4	TAKE AWAY 24A
	DIADIDWMI	DISTRIBUTE 181D
	EPAN	WHEN 282B
	EPERCHOMAI 2B	COME 284D
	EPI IIIBy	ON 287A
	ISCHUROS IA	STRONG 384A
	NIKAW 2A	CONQUER 541B
	PANOPLIA I	FULL ARMOR 612D
	PEITHW	CONVINCE 644D
	PEITHW 2A	CONVINCE 645B
	SKULON	SPOILS 765C
23	EIMI III7	TO BE 224D
	KATA I2By	DOWN 406D
	SKORPIZW I	SCATTER 764B
	SUNAGW I	GATHER 790A
23A	META AIIIC6	WITH 510B
23A	M8 AII2A	NOT 518B
23B	META AII2	WITH 510C
23B	M8 AII2A	NOT 518B

24 AKATHARTOS 2	IMPURE 28C	31B SOLOMWN	SOLOMON 766C
ANAPAUSIS 3	A RESTING PLACE 58B	31F KATAKRINW	CONDEMN 413B
ANUDROS	WATERLESS 76A	31F KRISIS IA«	JUDGING 453D
DIA AII	THROUGH 178B	31F POLUS II2C	MANY 696A
DIERCHOMAI IB«	GO THROUGH 193C	31F HWDE 2A	HERE 903D
EXERCHOMAI IA6	GO OUT 274A	32 ANIST8MI 2C	RISE 69D
HEURISKW IA	FIND 325A	EIS 6A	BECAUSE OF 229B
Z8TEW IAß	SEEK 339B	IWNAS I	JONAH 386A
M8 AII2B	NOT 518B	K8RUGMA 2	PROCLAMATION 432A
HOTHEN I	FROM WHICH 557D	«METANOEW	CHANGE ONES MIND 513B
OIKOS IBß	HOUSE 563C	NINEUIT8S	MEN OF NINEVEH 542A
PNEUMA 4C	SPIRIT 682A	NINEU8	NINEVEH 542A
TOPOS ID	PLACE 830B	33 HAPTW I	KINDLE 102B
24B EXERCHOMAI IA«	GO OUT 274A	BLEPW IA	SEE 142D
25 HEURISKW IC«	FIND 325C	EISPOREUOMAI I	GO 232D
KOSMEW I	PUT IN ORDER 445D	EPI IIIIAß	ON 288A
KOSMEW 2Aß	DECORATE 445D	KRUPT8 DARK AND HIDDEN PLACE 455A	
SAROW	SWEEP 752A	KRUPTOS 2B	HIDDEN 455B
SCHOLAZW 2	STAND EMPTY 805C	LUCHNIA	LAMPSTAND 484B
26 HEPTA	SEVEN 306B	LUCHNOS I	LAMP 484C
ESCHATOS 3A	LAST 314A	MODIOS	A PECK MEASURE 527D
HETEROS IBß	ANOTHER 315B	TITH8MI IIAß	PUT 823C
KATOIKEW IB	LIVE 425C	HUPO 2A«	UNDER 851A
PARALAMBANW I	TAKE 624D	PHEGGOS	LIGHT 862C
PNEUMA 4C	SPIRIT 682A	PHWS IA	LIGHT 879D
PON8ROS	SICK 697B	34 HAPLOUS	SINCERE 85C
PRWTOS IA	FIRST 732D	EPAN	WHEN 282B
TOTE 2	AT THAT TIME 831D	LUCHNOS 2	LAMP 484C
CHEIRWN	WORSE 889C	OPHTHALMOS I	EYE 604B
27 BASTAZW 2A	CARRY 137A	PON8ROS IA«	SICK 697B
EPAIRW I	RAISE UP 281C	SKOTEINOS	DARK 764C
TH8LAZW 2	SUCK 361A	PHWTEINOS	SHINING 880D
KOILIA 2	BELLY 438B	34A SWMA IB	BODY 806D
MAKARIOS 3A	BLESSED 488A	34B SWMA IB	BODY 806D
MASTOS 2	BREAST 496B	34C SWMA IB	BODY 806D
HOUTOS IB«	THIS 601C	35 M8 C2	NOT 519B
OCHLOS I	CROWD 605C	OUN IA	THEREFORE 597B
PHWN8 2A	VOICE 878D	SKOPEW	NOTICE 764A
28 GE 3E	OF COURSE 152B	SKOTOS 2B	DARKNESS 765B
LOGOS IBß	WORD 479B	PHWS IB«	LIGHT 880A
MAKARIOS IB	BLESSED 488A	36 ASTRAP8	LIGHTNING 117D
MENOUNGE	RATHER 504C	EI VIIO	IF 219A
PHULASSW IF	WATCH 876C	LUCHNOS I	LAMP 484C
29 GENEA 2	GENERATION 153B	MEROS IA	PART 507A
EPATHROIZW	COLLECT BESIDES 281A	SKOTEINOS	DARK 764C
PON8ROS IB«	WICKED 697C	TIS, TI 2Aγ	ANY ONE 828B
S8MEION I	SIGN 755B	PHWTIZW 2A	SHINE 881A
S8MEION 2A	SIGN 755D	36A HOLOS 2B	WHOLE 567D
29F IWNAS I	JONAH 386A	36A PHWTEINOS	SHINING 880D
29=32 GENEA 2	GENERATION 153B	36B HOLOS 2C	WHOLE 567D
30 EIMI II9B	TO BE 224A	36B PHWTEINOS	SHINING 880D
KATHWS I	JUST AS 392A	37 ANAPIPTW I	RECLINE 59A
NINEUIT8S	MEN OF NINEVEH 542A	ARISTAW 2	DINE 106B
HOUTW IA	THUS 602B	DEOMAI 4	ASK 174B
S8MEION I	SIGN 755B	ERWTAW 2	ASK 312B
HUIOS 2C	SON 843A	HOPWS 2B	IN ORDER THAT 580D
31 BASILISSA	QUEEN 136C	PARA II1B«	BESIDE 615B
IDOU 2	THERE IS 371D	37F PHARISAIOS	PHARISEE 861C
NOTOS 3	SOUTH 546A	38 ARISTON 2	NOON MEAL 106C
HOUTOS 2B	THIS 601D	BAPTIZW I	DIP 131A
PERAS I	END 649D	DIAKRINW 2B	WAVER 184B
SOPHIA 2	WISDOM 767A	THAUMAZW IAγ	WONDER 353A
31A SOLOMWN	SOLOMON 766C	PRO 2	BEFORE 708C

38 PRWTOS 2A	FIRST	733D
39 HARPAG8 3	GREEDINESS	108A
GEMW 1	BE FULL	153A
ESWTHEN 2	INSIDE	314C
KATHARIZW 1A	CLEANSE	388A
KURIOS 2C₽	LORD	460D
HO,H8,TO IIII	THE	553B
PINAX	PLATTER	664B
PON8RIA	WICKEDNESS	697A
POT8RION 1	CUP	702A
SU 1B	YOU	779D
HUPOKRIT8S	HYPOCRITE	853A
39F EXWTHEN 18₽	OUTSIDE	279B
40 APHRWN	FOOLISH	127B
ESWTHEN 2	INSIDE	314C
OU 4C	NO	595A
POIEW IIA₽	DO	687B
41 ELE8MOSUN8	CHARITABLE GIVING	249B
ENEIMI	. BE IN	264A
KATHAROS 4	CLEAN	389A
PL8N 1B	BUT	675B
42 AGAP8 IIBy	LOVE	5D
APODEKATOW 1	TITHE	89B
DEI 3	IT IS NECESSARY	171B
H8DUOSMON	MINT	345A
THEOS 3F₽	GOD	358B
KAKEINOS 1A	AND HE	397C
KL8SIS 1	CALL	436D
KRISIS 3	RIGHT	454A
LACHANON	VEGETABLE	468D
PARERCHOMAI 18₽	PASS AWAY	631C
PARI8MI 1	LEAVE UNDONE	632D
P8GANON	RUE	661C
42FF HOTI 3A	THAT	593D
42-4 OUAI 1A	WOE	595C
43 AGAPAW 2	LOVE	5A
AGORA	MARKET PLACE	12B
ASPASMOS 1	GREETING	116D
DEIPNON 2	DINNER	172B
PRWTOKATHEDRIA	PLACE OF HONOR	732C
44 EIMI II9B	TO BE	224A
EPANW 1A	ABOVE	283A
KAI I2B	AND	393A
MN8MEION 2	TOMB	526C
OIDA II	KNOW	558C
PERIPATEW 1C	GO ABOUT	654D
45 LEGW I8D	SAY	470C
TIS, TI 1A≈	ANY ONE	827C
HUBRIZW	MISTREAT	839B
45B LEGW IIA	SAY	469B
45F NOMIKOS 2	LAWYER	543C
46 AUTOS 1C	SELF	122C
DAKTULOS	FINGER	169A
DUSBASTAKTOS	HARD TO BEAR	208C
HEIS 1C	ONE	230A
OUAI 1A	WOE	595C
PROSPSAUW	TOUCH	727D
PHORTIZW	CAUSE TO CARRY	873A
46A PHORTION 2	LOAD	873A
46B PHORTION 2	LOAD	873A
47 APOKTEINW 1A	KILL	93B
MN8MEION 1	MEMORIAL	526C
OIKODOMEW 1A	BUILD	560C
47 OUAI 1A	WOE	595C
47F PAT8R 1B	FOREFATHERS	640D
48 ARA 4	THEN	103C
ERGON 1C₽	DEED	308A
MARTUS 2B	WITNESS	495C
MEN 1B	(PARTICLE)	504A
OIKODOMEW 18≈	BUILD	560D
SUNEUDOKEW	AGREE WITH	796C
49 APOSTELLW 18≈	SEND AWAY	98A
APOSTOLOS 2	MESSENGER	99A
DIWKW 2	PERSECUTE	200B
EK 4Av	FROM	235B
EKDIWKW	PERSECUTE SEVERELY	238B
KAI II4	ALSO	394C
*PROPH8T8S 4	PROPHET	731B
PROPH8T8S 5	PROPHET	731B
SOPHIA 4	WISDOM	767B
50 HAIMA 2A	BLOOD	22B
HAIMA 2A	BLOOD	22C
EKCHEW 1	POUR OUT	246D
HINA II2	IN ORDER THAT	378D
KATABOL8 1	FOUNDATION	410A
KOSMOS 2	WORLD	446D
50F GENEA 2	GENERATION	153B
50F EKZ8TEW 4	CHARGE WITH	239D
51 HABEL	ABEL	1C
HAIMA 2A	BLOOD	22B
APO IV2A	FROM	87A
BARACHIAS	BARACHIAH	132C
ZACHARIAS 2	ZECHARIAH	336B
THUSIAST8RION 1A	ALTAR	367B
METAXU 2A	BETWEEN	514C
NAI 3	CERTAINLY	535A
OIKOS 1A₽	HOUSE	563B
52 AUTOS 1C	SELF	122C
GNWSIS 1	KNOWLEDGE	162D
EISERCHOMAI 2A	COME	232B
KLEIS 2	KEY	435A
KRUPTW 1A	HIDE	455B
KWLUW 1	HINDER	462C
NOMIKOS 2	LAWYER	543C
OUAI 1A	WOE	595C
53 APOSTOMATIZW	QUESTION CLOSELY	99D
DEINWS	TERRIBLY	172B
ENECHW 1	HAVE A GRUDGE	265B
ENWPION 2A	BEFORE	270B
KAKEITHEN 1	AND FROM THERE	397C
LEGW IIA	SAY	469B
NOMIKOS 2	LAWYER	543C
POLUS II2B	MANY	696A
SUMBALLW 1B	CONVERSE	785B
PHARISAIOS	PHARISEE	861C
54 APOSTOMATIZW	QUESTION CLOSELY	99D
APHORM8	PRETEXT	127A
ENEDREUW	LIE IN WAIT	264C
HEURISKW 2	FIND	325D
TH8REUW	HUNT	361B
KAT8GOREW 1A	BRING CHARGES	424B
STOMA 1A	MOUTH	777B
TIS, TI 1B≈	ANY ONE	828A

LUKE 12

1	EPISUNAGW	GATHER	301D
	ZUMB 2	LEAVEN	340C
	KATAPATEW IB	TRAMPLE	416D
	LEGW 13	SAY	469D
	MURIAS 2	MYRIADS	531C
	HOS,H8,HO IIIC	(REL PRON)	589A
	OCHLOS I	CROWD	605C
	PRWTOS 2A	FIRST	733C
	SUMPERIECHW	SURROUND	787A
	SUMPNIGW 2	CHOKE	787C
	HUPOKRISIS	HYPOCRISY	852D
	HWSTE 2AB	THEREFORE	908C
2	APOKALUPTW I	REVEAL	91C
	GINWSKW 2A	FIND OUT	160B
	DE 2	BUT, AND	170C
	KRUPTOS I	HIDDEN	455A
	SUGKALUPTW	COVER	781A
3	ANTI 3	FOR	73B
	DWMA	ROOF	209C
	EIPON I	SAY	225B
	KBRUSSW 2BB	ANNOUNCE	432C
	LALEW 2B	SPEAK	465A
	OPTASIA I	A VISION	580A
	HOS,H8,HO I2Bα	(REL PRON)	587B
	HOS,H8,HO IIIA	(REL PRON)	589A
	OUS I	EAR	600A
	SKOTIA I	DARKNESS	764D
	TAMEION 2	STOREROOM	811B
	PHWS IA	LIGHT	879D
4	APO V3	WITH	87B
	ECHW I6A	CAN	333D
	PERISSOTEROS 2	GREATER	657B
	PTOEW	FRIGHTEN	734D
	SWMA IB	BODY	806D
	PHILOS 2Aα	LOVING	868D
	PHOBEW IA	BE AFRAID	870D
5	GEENNA	HELL	152C
	EMBALLW	THROW	253C
	*EXOUSIA 2	ABILITY	277D
	META BII4B	AFTER	511D
	NAI 3	CERTAINLY	535A
	HUPODEIKNUMI 2	SHOW	852A
5A	PHOBEW IBα	BE AFRAID	871A
5B	PHOBEW IBα	BE AFRAID	871A
5C	PHOBEW IBα	BE AFRAID	871A
6	ASSARION	ASSARION	117A
	DUO 2	TWO	208C
	HEIS IC	ONE	230A
	ENWPION 5A	BEFORE	270C
	EPILANTHANOMAI 2	NEGLECT	295C
	OUCHI 3	NOT	603A
	PWLEW	SELL	739A
6F	STROUTHION	SPARROW	779A
7	ALLA 3	BUT, YET	38A
	ARITHMEW	COUNT	105D
	DIAPHERW 2B	BE SUPERIOR	189C
	THRIX 2	HAIR	364C
	KEPHAL8 IA	HEAD	431B
	PHOBEW IA	BE AFRAID	870C
8	EMPROSTHEN 2B	IN FRONT	256C
	EN IV5	IN	260D
8	PAS ICγ	WHOEVER	637C
	HUIOS 2C	SON	843A
8A	HOMOLOGEW 4	CONFESS	571C
8B	HOMOLOGEW 4	CONFESS	571D
8F	AGGELOS 2A	ANGEL	7C
9	APARNEOMAI	DENY	80B
	ARNEOMAI 3A	DENY	107C
	ENWPION 2B	BEFORE	270B
9F	DE IA	BUT, AND	170C
10	APHI8MI 2	FORGIVE	125C
	BLASPH8MEW 2Bγ	BLASPHEME	142B
	EIPON I	SAY	225B
	EIS 4Cα	AGAINST	228B
	LOGOS IAγ	WORD	478C
	HO,H8,TO IIIF	THE	553A
	PAS ICγ	WHOEVER	637C
	PNEUMA 5Cα	SPIRIT	682C
	PNEUMA 5Cα	SPIRIT	682D
	HUIOS 2C	SON	843A
11	APOLOGEOMAI	DEFEND ONESELF	95B
	ARCH8 3	RULER	112A
	DE 2	BUT, AND	170C
	EIPON I	SAY	225B
	EISPHERW I	BRING IN	233A
	EXOUSIA 4Cα	AUTHORITY	278B
	EPI IIIIAγ	ON	288B
	MERIMNAW I	HAVE ANXIETY	506A
	HOTAN IA	WHEN	592A
	PROSPHERW IA	BRING (TO)	727A
	PWS 2B	HOW	740A
	SUNAGWG8 2A		790C
		PLACE OF ASSEMBLY	
12	AUTOS IH	EVEN	122D
	DEI 5	IT IS NECESSARY	171B
	PNEUMA 5Cα	SPIRIT	682D
	HWRA 3	TIME OF DAY	905A
13	DE 2	BUT, AND	170C
	KL8RONOMIA I	INHERITANCE	436A
	MERIZW IB	SHARE	505D
	OCHLOS I	CROWD	605C
14	ANTHRWPOS IAγ	MAN	67C
	DIKAST8S	JUDGE	197C
	EPI IIIIBα	OVER	288D
	KATHIST8MI 2B	APPOINT	391B
	KRIT8S IAα	JUDGE	454C
	MERIST8S	ARBITRATOR	506D
15	EK 3F	BY	234D
	ZW8 IA	LIFE	340D
	HORAW 2B	SEE	582B
	PERISSEUW IAB	BE LEFT OVER	656C
	PLEONEXIA	GREEDINESS	673D
	PRWTOS 2A	FIRST	733C
	HUPARCHW I	BE	845D
	PHULASSW 2A	WATCH	876D
15F	DE 2	BUT, AND	170C
16	ANTHRWPOS 3Aα	MAN	68B
	EIPON I	SAY	225B
	EUPHOREW	BE FRUITFUL	327D
	LEGW I8A	SAY	470B
	PARABOL8 2	PARABLE	617C
	PLOUSIOS I	RICH	679C
	CHWRA 4	COUNTRY	897D
17	DIALOGIZOMAI I	CONSIDER	185A

17 EN I5B IN 258D
   ECHW I2D HAVE 332D
   KARPOS IA FRUIT 405C
   POU IB WHERE 703A
   SUNAGW I GATHER 789D
18 APOTH8K8 STOREHOUSE 90C
   GEN8MA PRODUCT I54B
   KATHAIREW 2A« DESTROY 387C
   OIKODOMEW IA BUILD 560C
   SITOS WHEAT 759D
   SUNAGW I GATHER 789D
I8F AGATHOS 2BP GOOD 3C
19 ANAPAUW 2 REST 58C
   EIS 2B FOR 228A
   ESTHIW ID EAT 3I3A
   ESTHIW IE« EAT 3I3B
   ETOS YEAR 3I7B
   EUPHRAINW 2 GLADDEN 328A
   ECHW I2A HAVE 332B
   KEIMAI IB LIE 428A
   PINW I DRINK 664D
   PSUCH8 IB« SOUL LIFE 90ID
   PSUCH8 IF SOUL LIFE 902C
19B POLUS IIA« MANY 694A
20 APAITEW I DEMAND 79B
   APO IV2A FROM 87A
   APHRWN FOOLISH I27B
   HETOIMAZW I PREPARE 3I6B
   NUX IC NIGHT 548D
   HOS,H8,HO I2B« (REL PRON) 587B
   PSUCH8 IA« SOUL LIFE 90IC
21 TH8SAURIZW I STORE UP 362A
   HOUTW IB THUS 602B
   PLOUTEW 2 BE RICH 679D
22 ENDUW 2A DRESS 263C
   ESTHIW IA EAT 3I2C
   MERIMNAW I HAVE ANXIETY 506A
   M8 AIII3A NOT 5I8C
   M8DE IA AND NOT 5I9C
22F SWMA IB BODY 806D
22F PSUCH8 IAP SOUL LIFE 90IC
23 ENDUMA I GARMENT 263A
   POLUS II2C MANY 696A
   TROPH8 I FOOD 835C
24 APOTH8K8 STOREHOUSE 90C
   DIAPHERW 2B BE SUPERIOR I89C
   THERIZW I REAP 359D
   KATANOEW 2 NOTICE 4I6A
   MALLON I MORE 490B
   OUTE NOT 600C
   PETEINON BIRD 660A
   POSOS I HOW GREAT 70IA
   SPEIRW IA« SOW 768C
   TAMEION I STOREROOM 8IIB
   TREPHW I FEED 833B
25 EK 4AP FROM 235B
   EPI IIIIBP TO 288D
   H8LIKIA IA AGE 345D
   H8LIKIA 2 BODILY STATURE 346A
   MERIMNAW I HAVE ANXIETY 506A
   P8CHUS FOREARM 662D
   PROSTITH8MI IA ADD 726B
26 APOLOGEOMAI DEFEND ONESELF 95B

26 DUNAMAI 3 ABLE 206C
   EI VIIO IF 2I9A
   ELACHISTOS 2A SMALLEST 248B
   LOIPOS 2BP THE REST 48IA
   MERIMNAW I HAVE ANXIETY 506A
   OUDE 3 NOT EVEN 596A
   OUTE NOT 600C
27 AUXANW 3 GROW I2IC
   DOXA 2 MAGNIFICENCE 203A
   HEIS IAP ONE 230A
   KATANOEW 2 NOTICE 4I6A
   KOPIAW 2 BECOME WEARY 444B
   KRINON LILY 452A
   N8THW SPIN 539B
   OUTE NOT 600C
   PERIBALLW IB« THROW AROUND 65ID
   PWS 2A HOW 739D
   SOLOMWN SOLOMON 766C
   HUFHAINW WEAVE 857C
   HWS II2 SO 906A
28 AMPHIAZW CLOTHE 46C
   AMPHIENNUMI CLOTHE 46D
   AURION 2 SOON I2ID
   BALLW IB THROW I30C
   EI III IF 2I8C
   KLIBANOS OVEN 437B
   MALLON 2B MORE 490C
   OLIGOPISTOS OF LITTLE FAITH 566B
   POSOS I HOW GREAT 70IA
   S8MERON TODAY 756C
   CHORTOS GRASS 892B
29 HEIS 2C ONE 230D
   Z8TEW IC INVESTIGATE 339B
   METEWRIZOMAI 5I5D
   DO NOT BE ANXIOUS ABOUT
   PINW I DRINK 664B
29-3I PL8N IB BUT 675B
30 ETHNOS I NATION 2I7B
   ETHNOS 2 GENTILES 2I7C
   EPIZ8TEW 2A STRIVE FOR 292D
   PAS IEP ALL 638A
   PAT8R 3C« FATHER 64IC
   CHR8ZW NEED 893D
31 BASILEIA 3G KINGDOM I35A
   Z8TEW 2A SEEK 339C
   PROSTITH8MI 2 ADD 726C
32 BASILEIA 3G KINGDOM I35A
   EUDOKEW I WELL PLEASED 3I9C
   MIKROS 2B SMALL 523B
   PAT8R 3C« FATHER 64IC
   POIMNION 2B FLOCK 69IA
33 ANEKLEIPTOS UNFAILING 63D
   BALLANTION PURSE I30B
   DIAPHTHEIRW I SPOIL I89D
   EGGIZW 5A APPROACH 2I2D
   ELE8MOSUN8 CHARITABLE GIVING 249B
   TH8SAUROS 2B« TREASURE 362B
   KLEPT8S THIEF 435B
   HOPOU IA« WHERE 579C
   OURANOS 2D HEAVEN 599D
   PALAIOW 2 MAKE OLD 6I0D
   POIEW IIE« DO 688D
   PWLEW SELL 738D

33	S8S	MOTH	756D
	HUPARCHW I	BE	845D
34	EKEI I	THERE	238C
	TH8SAUROS 2	TREASURE	362B
	KARDIA IB«	HEART	405A
	HOPOU IA«	WHERE	579C
35	KAIW IA	LIGHT	397A
	LUCHNOS I	LAMP	484C
	OSPHUS I	WAIST	591D
	PERIZWNNUMI I	GIRD ABOUT	653A
36	ANALUW 2	DEPART	57A
	ANTHRWPOS 2B∂	MAN	68A
	GAMOS IB	WEDDING	150D
	HEAUTOU 4	ONESELF	211D
	KROUW	STRIKE	454D
	KURIOS IAβ	LORD	460A
	HOMOIOS I	LIKE	569D
	POTE	WHEN	701D
	PROSDECHOMAI 2A	RECEIVE	719B
37	AM8N 2	AMEN	45B
	ANAKLINW IB	LAY	55D
	GR8GOREW I	BE AWAKE	166C
	DIAKONEW I	WAIT ON SOMEONE	183A
	DOULOS IA	SLAVE	204D
	HEURISKW IC«	FIND	325C
	KURIOS IAβ	LORD	460A
	MAKARIOS IB	BLESSED	488A
	PARERCHOMAI 3	COME	631D
	PERIZWNNUMI 2A	GIRD ABOUT	653A
38	DEUTEROS 2	SECOND	176A
	HESPERINOS		313D
		IN THE EVENING	
	KAN I	AND IF	403B
	MAKARIOS IB	BLESSED	488A
	TRITOS I	THIRD	834B
	PHULAK8 4	GUARD	875D
39	APHI8MI 4	TOLERATE	126A
	GINWSKW 6C	KNOW	160D
	GR8GOREW I	BE AWAKE	166C
	DIORUSSW	DIGS THROUGH	198B
	KLEPT8S	THIEF	435B
	KLEPT8S	THIEF	435C
	OIDA IF	KNOW	558C
	OIKODESPOT8S		560C
		MASTER OF THE HOUSE	
	OIKOS IA«	HOUSE	562D
	HOUTOS IBβ	THIS	601C
	POIOS 2Aβ	OF WHAT KIND	691B
	HWRA I	TIME OF DAY	904B
40	DOKEW IF	THINK	201A
	HETOIMOS 2	READY	316D
	HOS,H8,HO I5A	(REL PRON)	588B
	HUIOS 2C	SON	843A
	HWRA I	TIME OF DAY	904B
41	ATOPOS 2	IMPROPER	120B
	8　IAβ	OR	342D
	KURIOS 2Cβ	LORD	460D
	LEGW I2A	SAY	469C
	PARABOL8 2	PARABLE	617C
	PETROS	PETER	660D
	PROS III5A	TOWARD	717C
42	ARA 2	THEN	103B
	EPI IIB«	OVER	286A

42	THERAPEIA 2	SERVING	359C
	KATHIST8MI 2A	APPOINT	391B
	KAIROS 2	TIME	395D
	OIKONOMOS IA	MANAGER	562C
	PISTOS IA«	TRUSTWORTHY	670B
	SITOMETRION	RATION	759C
	PHRONIMOS	THOUGHTFUL	874C
42A	KURIOS 2Cβ	LORD	460D
42B	KURIOS IAβ	LORD	460A
43	DOULOS IA	SLAVE	204D
	HEURISKW IC«	FIND	325C
	MAKARIOS IB	BLESSED	488A
	POIEW I2A«	DO	689A
44	AL8THWS I	TRULY	36D
	EPI IIIB«	OVER	286D
	KATHIST8MI 2A	APPOINT	391B
	LEGW I5	SAY	470A
	PAS IDβ	ALL	637D
	HUPARCHW I	BE	845D
45	EIPON 5	SAY	225D
	ESTHIW IE«	EAT	313B
	KARDIA IBβ	HEART	404C
	METHUSKW	GET DRUNK	500B
	PAIDISK8	MAID	609B
	PAIS IAγ	SERVANT	609D
	PINW I	DRINK	664C
	TE 3A	AND	815C
	TUPTW I	STRIKE	838A
	CHRONIZW 2	TAKE TIME	896A
45F	DOULOS IA	SLAVE	204D
46	APISTOS 2	FAITHLESS	85A
	GINWSKW 6A«	KNOW	160C
	DICHOTOMEW	CUT IN TWO	199C
	H8KW IC	HAVE COME	345B
	KURIOS IAβ	LORD	460A
	MEROS 2	SHARE	507C
	META AI	WITH	509D
	PROSDOKAW 3	EXPECT	719C
	TITH8MI IIB«		824A
		MAKE UP (YOUR) MINDS	
	HWRA I	TIME OF DAY	904B
47	HETOIMAZW I	PREPARE	316B
	THEL8MA IC«	WILL	354D
	POIEW I2B«	DO	689B
	PROS III5D	TOWARD	717D
47F	GINWSKW IA	KNOW	159D
47F	DERW	BEAT	174D
48	AXIOS 2B	WORTHY	77D
	DIDWMI 3	GIVE	192C
	Z8TEW 2C	SEEK	339D
	OLIGOS IB	FEW	566C
	HOS,H8,HO I4D	(REL PRON)	588A
	PARA I3A	FROM	614D
	PARATITH8MI 2B«		628C
		PLACE BESIDE	
	PAS ICγ	WHOEVER	637C
	PERISSOTEROS 2	GREATER	657B
	POLUS I2C«	MANY	695B
49	ANAPTW	KINDLE	59C
	G8 5B	EARTH	156D
	8D8 IB	ALREADY	344D
	THELW I	WISH	355C
	PUR 2	FIRE	737D

49 TIS, TI 3B	WHICH	827C
50 BAPTIZW 3C	BAPTIZE	131D
BAPTISMA 3	BAPTISM	132B
DE 2	BUT, AND	170C
ECHW I6B	MUST	334A
PWS 3	HOW	740C
SUNECHW 5	DISTRESS	797A
TELEW 2	PERFORM	818D
51 ALLA 1A	BUT, YET	37C
G8 5B	EARTH	156D
DIAMERISMOS	DISSENSION	186A
DOKEW 1D	THINK	201A
EIR8N8 1B	PEACE	226B
OUCHI 2	NOT	603A
PARAGINOMAI 2	COME	619A
51=3 PUR 2	FIRE	737D
52 GAR 1D	FOR	151B
HEIS 2A	ONE	230A
NUN 3B	NOW	548B
52F DIAMERIZW 2	DIVIDE	185D
52F EPI IIIAγ	AGAINST	286D
53 DIAMERIZW 2	DIVIDE	185D
THUGAT8R 1	DAUGHTER	365B
NUMPH8 2	DAUGHTER IN LAW	547B
PENTHERA	MOTHER IN LAW	648B
54 ANATELLW 2	RISE	61C
DUSM8	WEST	209A
ERCHOMAI I2C	COME	311D
NEPHEL8	CLOUD	538C
OMBROS	RAIN STORM	568B
55 EIMI I5	TO BE	222C
KAUSWN	HEAT	426D
NOTOS 1	SOUTHWEST WIND	546A
PNEW 1A	BLOW	686A
56 DOKIMAZW 1	EXAMINE	201C
KAIROS 4	TIME	396C
OURANOS 1Aβ	HEAVEN	598B
PROSWPON 1D	FACE	729A
PWS 1B	HOW	739C
HUPOKRIT8S	HYPOCRITE	853A
56A OIDA 3	KNOW	558D
57 APO V5	OF	87D
DIKAIOS 5	RIGHTEOUS	195B
HEAUTOU 1A	ONESELF	211B
KRINW 4Aα	JUDGE	452D
58 ANTIDIKOS	OPPONENT	73C
APPALLASSW 2A	RELEASE	79C
ARCHWN 2A	AUTHORITIES	113C
DIDWMI Z	GIVE	193A
EPI IIIAγ	ON	288B
ERGASIA 5	TRADE	307C
KAI I2E	AND	393C
KATASURW	DRAG	420C
KRINW 4Aα	JUDGE	452D
KRIT8S 1Aα	JUDGE	454C
M8POTE 2Bβ	(NEG PARTICLE)	521B
HODOS 1B	WAY	556C
PARADIDWMI 1B	GIVE OVER	619D
PRAKTWR	BAILIFF	704C
HUPAGW 2	GO AWAY	844C
PHULAK8 3	GUARD	875D
HWS IV1B	WHEN	907A
59 APODIDWMI 2	GIVE BACK	90A

59 EXERCHOMAI 1Aη	GO OUT	274B
ESCHATOS 3B	LAST	314A
KODRANT8S	PENNY	438A
LEPTOS 2	SMALL COPPER COIN	473B

LUKE 13

1 APAGGELLW 1	REPORT	78C
AUTOS 1H	EVEN	122D
DE 2	BUT, AND	170C
THUSIA 2A	SACRIFICE	366D
KAIROS 1	TIME	395D
MEIGNUMI 1	MIX	500D
META AII5	WITH	510D
PAREIMI 1A	BE PRESENT	629D
PILATOS	PILATE	663C
TIS, TI 1Aα	ANY ONE	827C
1F GALILAIOS	GALILEAN	149D
2 HAMARTWLOS 2	SINNER	43C
DOKEW 1D	THINK	201A
OPHEILET8S 2Cβ	DEBTOR	603B
PARA III3	IN COMPARISON	616B
PASCHW 3B	ENDURE	639D
2B HOTI 3A	THAT	593D
3 ALLA 1A	BUT, YET	37C
EAN I3B	IF	210D
METANOEW	CHANGE ONES MIND	513B
M8 AII	NOT	517C
HOMOIWS	LIKEWISE	570D
OUCHI 2	NOT	603A
HWSAUTWS	SIMILARLY	907D
4 APOKTEINW 1A	KILL	93C
DEKAOKTW	EIGHTEEN	172D
DOKEW 1D	THINK	201A
EN IIC	IN	257D
ENOIKEW	LIVE	266D
EPI IIIAβ	ON	288A
8 ID β	OR	343A
KATOIKEW 2	LIVE	425C
OPHEILET8S 2Cβ	DEBTOR	603B
OPHEILET8S 2Cβ	DEBTOR	603B
PARA III3	IN COMPARISON	616B
PIPTW 1Bβ	FALL	665C
PURGOS 1	TOWER	738A
SILWAM	SILOAM	758B
5 ALLA 1A	BUT, YET	37C
METANOEW	CHANGE ONES MIND	513B
M8 AII	NOT	517C
OUCHI 2	NOT	603A
HWSAUTWS	SIMILARLY	907D
6 AMPELWN	VINEYARD	46B
DE 2	BUT, AND	170C
ERCHOMAI IIAε	COME	310D
LEGW IIA	SAY	469B
PARABOL8 2	PARABLE	617C
TIS, TI 1Aα	ANY ONE	827C
PHUTEUW	PLANT	878A
6F HEURISKW 1A	FIND	325A
6F Z8TEW 1Aβ	SEEK	339B
6F KARPOS 1A	FRUIT	405C
6F SUK8	FIG TREE	783D
7 AMPELOURGOS	VINE DRESSER	46B
AXIN8	AX	77A

Ref	Word	Gloss	No.
7	APO II2C	SINCE	86C
	G8 I	EARTH	156C
	EKKOPTW I	CUT DOWN	241B
	IDOU IBε	BEHOLD	371C
	HINATI	WHY	379B
	KAI I2G	AND	393C
	KAI II5	STILL	394C
	KATARGEW IA	MAKE INEFFECTIVE	418B
	PHERW 4Aα	BEAR	863A
7F	ETOS	YEAR	317A
8	APHI8MI 4	TOLERATE	125D
	BALLW 2A	PUT	130D
	HEWS III6β	UNTIL	335C
	KOPRON	MANURE	444D
	KOPROS	MANURE	444D
	KOPRION	MANURE	444D
	KOPHINOS	BASKET	448C
	KURIOS IAβ	LORD	460A
	LEGW I8D	SAY	470C
	PERI 2Aα	ABOUT	650D
	SKAPTW I	DIG	761A
9	GE 3Bα	OTHERWISE	152B
	DE IA	BUT, AND	170C
	EIS 2Aγ	UNTIL	228A
	EKKOPTW I	CUT DOWN	241B
	KAN I	AND IF	403B
	KARPOS IA	FRUIT	405C
	MELLW 2	IS DESTINED	502D
	MEN IAα	(PARTICLE)	503D
	POIEW II8η	DO	688A
10	DE 2	BUT, AND	170C
	SABBATON IBβ	SABBATH	746C
11	ANAKUPTW I	STAND ERECT	56B
	ASTHENEIA IA	WEAKNESS	114D
	GUN8 I	WOMAN	167B
	DUNAMAI IB	ABLE	206B
	EIMI II4E	TO BE	223B
	EIS 3	COMPLETELY	228B
	ETOS	YEAR	317A
	ECHW I2Eα	HAVE	333A
	IDOU 2	THERE IS	371D
	PANTEL8S I	COMPLETE	613B
	PANTEL8S 2	COMPLETE	613B
	PNEUMA 4C	SPIRIT	682A
	SUGKUPTW	WAS BENT DOUBLE	782C
12	APOLUW I	SET FREE	96A
	ASTHENEIA IA	WEAKNESS	114D
	PROSPHWNEW 2	CALL OUT	727D
13	ANORTHOW	REBUILD	71D
	DOXAZW I	PRAISE	203C
	EPITITH8MI IAα	PUT UPON	302D
	PARACHR8MA	AT ONCE	629B
14	AGANAKTEW	BE AROUSED	4B
	APOKRINOMAI 2	BEGIN	93A
	ARCHISUNAGWGOS	PRESIDENT OF A SYNAGOGUE	112D
	DEI 3	IT IS NECESSARY	171B
	HEX	SIX	270D
	ERGAZOMAI I	WORK	307A
	ERCHOMAI IIAζ	COME	310D
	H8MERA 2	DAY	346D
	THERAPEUW 2	HEAL	359D
14A	SABBATON IA	SABBATH	746B
14B	H8MERA 2	DAY	347C
14B	SABBATON IA	SABBATH	746B
15	APAGW I	LEAD AWAY	78D
	BOUS	OX	146A
	HEKASTOS 2	EACH	236A
	KURIOS 2Cβ	LORD	460D
	LUW 2A	LOOSE	484D
	ONOS	DONKEY	577C
	POTIZW 2	GIVE TO DRINK	702C
	SABBATON IA	SABBATH	746B
	HUPOKRIT8S	HYPOCRITE	853A
	PHATN8	MANGER	862B
16	DEI 6	IT IS NECESSARY	171B
	DESMOS I	FETTER	175A
	DEW IB	BIND	176D
	ETOS	YEAR	317A
	H8MERA 2	DAY	347C
	THUGAT8R 2Bα	DAUGHTER	365B
	IDOU IBε	BEHOLD	371C
	KAI IIB	AND	392C
	LUW 2B	RELEASE	485A
	SABBATON IA	SABBATH	746B
	SATAN	ADVERSARY	752B
17	ANTIKEIMAI	BE OPPOSED	73D
	GINOMAI I2A	COME ABOUT	157C
	ENDOXOS 2	GLORIOUS	262D
	EPI IIIBγ	ON	287B
	KATAISCHUNW 2	BE HUMILIATED	411D
	LEGW IIA	SAY	469B
	OCHLOS I	CROWD	605C
	PAS IDβ	ALL	637C
	HUPO IB	BY	851A
	CHAIRW I	REJOICE	881B
18	HOMOIOW 2	COMPARE	570B
	PALIN 3	AGAIN	611D
18A	TIS, TI IBα	WHICH	826D
18B	TIS, TI IBα	WHICH	826D
18F	HOMOIOS I	LIKE	569D
19	ANTHRWPOS 3Aβ	MAN	68B
	AUXANW 3	GROW	121C
	BALLW 2	THROW	130B
	GINOMAI I4A	BECOME	158D
	DENDRON	TREE	173C
	EIS 8Aα		229C
	KATASK8NOW 2	LIVE	419C
	K8POS	GARDEN	431D
	KLADOS	BRANCH	434A
	KOKKOS I	SEED	441B
	LAMBANW IA	TAKE	465B
	MEGAS IA	LARGE	498C
	PETEINON	BIRD	660A
	SINAPI	MUSTARD	759A
20	HOMOIOW 2	COMPARE	570B
	PALIN 3	AGAIN	611D
	TIS, TI IBα	WHICH	826D
21	ALEURON	WHEAT FLOUR	35A
	EGKRUPTW	HIDE	216A
	HEWS IIIBα	UNTIL	335C
	ZUM8 I	LEAVEN	340C
	ZUMOW	FERMENT	340C
	KRUPTW ID	HIDE	455C
	LAMBANW IA	TAKE	465B
	HOLOS 2C	WHOLE	567D

21 HOMOIOS I   LIKE 569D
    HOS,H8,HC IIIF   (REL PRON) 589A
    SATON   MEASURE 752C
22 DIAPOREUOMAI   GO THROUGH 186D
    KATA IIIA   ALONG 407A
    KWM8 I   VILLAGE 462D
    POIEW III   DO 689C
    POLIS I   CITY 692A
    POLIS I   CITY 692B
    POREIA I   GOING 698D
23 EI VI   IF 218D
    OLIGOS IB   FEW 566C
    SWZW 2B   SAVE 806C
    TIS, TI IAα   ANY ONE 827C
24 AGWNIZOMAI 2B   STRUGGLE 15A
    EISERCHOMAI IF   COME 232B
    THURA 2B   DOOR 366C
    ISCHUW 2B   BE STRONG 384C
    LEGW 19   SAY 470C
    PUL8 2   GATE 736C
    STENOS   NARROW 773D
25 AN 3D   (PARTICLE) 48C
    ANOIGW IA   OPEN 70B
    APO II2C   SINCE 86C
    APOKLEIW   CLOSE 92C
    EGEIRW 2B   RISE 214A
    EXW IAα   OUTSIDE 278D
    HIST8MI II2Bα   BEING 383B
    KROUW   STRIKE 455A
    OIDA IC   KNOW 558B
    OIKODESPOT8S   560C
    MASTER OF THE HOUSE
    HOS,H8,HO IIIF   (REL PRON) 589A
    HO TI 6   WHOEVER 591C
    POTHEN I   FROM WHERE 686C
25A THURA IA   DOOR 366B
25B THURA IA   DOOR 366B
26 ENWPION 2A   BEFORE 270B
    ESTHIW IC   EAT 313A
    PLATEIA   WIDE ROAD 672C
27 ADIKIA 2   UNRIGHTEOUSNESS 17D
    APHIST8MI 2A   WITHDRAW 126C
    ERGAT8S 2   A DOER 307D
    POTHEN I   FROM WHERE 686C
28 ABRAAM   ABRAHAM 2A
    BRUGMOS   GNASHING 147B
    EKBALLW I   DRIVE OUT 236D
    EXW IB   OUTSIDE 279A
    IAKWB I   JACOB 368B
    ISAAK   ISAAC 381C
    KLAUTHMOS   WEEPING 434D
    ODOUS   TOOTH 557B
    HORAW   SEE 581B
    HOTAN 2A   WHEN 592B
    PROPH8T8S I   PROPHET 730D
28F BASILEIA 3G   KINGDOM 135B
29 ANAKLINW 2   RECLINE 55D
    ANATOL8 2B   EAST 62A
    BORRAS   NORTH 144D
    DUSM8   WEST 209A
    H8KW IA   HAVE COME 345B
    NOTOS 2   SOUTH 546A
30 IDOU IBα   BEHOLD 371D

30 PRWTOS ICβ   FIRST 733C
31 ENTEUTHEN I   FROM HERE 268A
    H8RWD8S 2   HEROD 349B
    HOTI 3B   THAT 594A
    POREUW I   PROCEED 699A
    HWRA 3   TIME OF DAY 905A
32 APOTELEW 2   PERFORM 100C
    DAIMONION 2   DEMON 168B
    EKBALLW I   DRIVE OUT 237A
    IASIS I   HEALING 369B
    POREUW I   PROCEED 699B
    TELEIOW I   COMPLETE 817C
    TELEIOW 2D   PERFECTION 817D
    TRITOS I   THIRD 834C
32F AURION 2   SOON 121D
32F S8MERON   TODAY 756C
33 ENDECHOMAI   IT IS POSSIBLE 262B
    EXW 2A   OUTSIDE 279B
    ECHW III3   HOLD FAST 334C
    PL8N IB   BUT 675B
    POREUW I   PROCEED 699B
    PROPH8T8S 3   PROPHET 731A
33F PROPH8T8S 4   PROPHET 731B
34 EPISUNAGW   GATHER 301C
    HIEROSOLUMA IB   JERUSALEM 373D
    LITHOBOLEW 2   STONE 475B
    NOSSIA 2   BROOD 545D
    ORNIX   COCK 585D
    ORNIS   COCK 585D
    POSAKIS   HOW OFTEN 701A
    PROPH8T8S 4   PROPHET 731B
    PTERUX   WING 734D
    TEKNON 2Fα   CHILD 816C
    TROPOS I   MANNER 835B
    HUPO 2Aα   UNDER 851A
35 APHI8MI 3A   ABANDON 125D
    ERCHOMAI IIAη   COME 310D
    EULOGEW 2A   BLESS 322D
    HEWS IID   UNTIL 335A
    H8KW 2   HAVE COME 345C
    M8 DIA   NOT 519B
    OIKOS IAγ   HOUSE 563B
    ONOMA I4Cγ   NAME 576C
    HOTE 2B   WHEN 592C

LUKE 14

1 ARTOS 2   FOOD 110B
    ARCHWN 2A   AUTHORITIES 113C
    GINOMAI I3F   TAKE PLACE 158B
    ESTHIW IA   EAT 312D
    KAI I2B   AND 393A
    OIKOS IAα   HOUSE 563A
    PARAT8REW IAβ   WATCH 628A
    SABBATON IA   SABBATH 746B
2 ANTHRWPOS 3Aα   MAN 68B
    EIMI II9A   TO BE 223D
    EMPROSTHEN 2A   IN FRONT 256C
    HUDRWPIKOS   840C
    SUFFERING FROM DROPSY
3 APOKRINOMAI 2   BEGIN 93A
    EXESTI I   IT IS POSSIBLE 274D
    THERAPEUW 2   HEAL 359D

3	*NOMIKOS 2	LAWYER	543C
	SABBATON 1A	SABBATH	746B
4	APOLUW 2B	SEND AWAY	96B
	EPILAMBANOMAI 1	GRASP	295A
	H8SUCHAZW 2	REST	349D
	IAOMAI 1	HEAL	369A
5	ANASPAW	DRAW	59D
	BOUS	OX	146A
	ONOS	DONKEY	577C
	PIPTW 1A	FALL	665A
	*SABBATON 1A	SABBATH	746B
	TIS, TI 1Aα	WHICH	826C
	PHREAR	A WELL	873C
6	ANTAPOKRINOMAI	ANSWER IN TURN	72C
	ISCHUW 2B	BE STRONG	384C
	PROS III5A	TOWARD	717C
7	EKLEGOMAI 2B	CHOOSE	241D
	EPECHW 2A	AIM AT	285B
	KALEW 1B	INVITE	400B
	LEGW IIA	SAY	469B
	PARABOL8 2	PARABLE	617C
	PWS 2A	HOW	739D
7F	PRWTOKLISIA	PLACE OF HONOR	732C
8	GAMOS 1B	WEDDING	150D
	ENTIMOS 1A	HONORED	268B
	KALEW 1B	INVITE	400B
	M8POTE 2Bβ	(NEG PARTICLE)	521B
9	APHESIS 1	RELEASE	124C
	DIDWMI 1Bα	GIVE	192A
	ESCHATOS 2	LAST	314A
	KALEW 1B	INVITE	400B
	KATECHW 1C	OCCUPY	424A
	META AIIII	WITH	511A
9A	TOPOS 1E	PLACE	830C
9B	TOPOS 1E	PLACE	830C
9F	ESCHATOS 1	LAST	313D
10	ANAPIPTW 1	RECLINE	59A
	ANWTEROS 1	HIGHER	76D
	EIMI II9A	TO BE	223D
	EIS 1C	IN	227C
	ENWPION 5A	BEFORE	270C
	ESCHATOS 2	LAST	314A
	HINA I2	IN ORDER THAT	377C
	POREUW 1	PROCEED	699B
	PROSANABAINW	GO UP	718C
	SUNANAKEIMAI	EAT WITH	792A
	TOPOS 1E	PLACE	830C
	PHILOS 2Aα	LOVING	868D
11	PAS 1Cγ	WHOEVER	637B
11A	TAPEINOW 2A	LOWER	812C
11A	HUPSOW 2	LIFT UP	858D
11B	TAPEINOW 2A	LOWER	812B
11B	TAPEINOW 2B	LOWER	812C
11B	HUPSOW 2	LIFT UP	858D
12	ANTAPODOMA	REPAYMENT	72C
	ANTIKALEW	INVITE IN RETURN	73D
	ARISTON 1	BREAKFAST	106C
	GEITWN	NEIGHBOR	152D
	GINOMAI I3Bγ	TAKE PLACE	158B
	DEIPNON 1	DINNER	172B
	DEIPNON 2	DINNER	172C
	8 1Aβ	OR	342D
	M8DE 1A	AND NOT	519C

12	M8POTE 2Bα	(NEG PARTICLE)	521A
	PLOUSIOS 1	RICH	679C
	*POIEW IIBζ	DO	688A
	SUGGEN8S	RELATED	780B
	PHILOS 2Aα	LOVING	868D
	PHWNEW 2C	CALL	878C
12F	KALEW 1B	INVITE	400B
12F	HOTAN 1A	WHEN	592A
13	ANAP8ROS	CRIPPLED	59A
	DOCH8	BANQUET	205C
	POIEW IIBζ	DO	688A
	PTWCHOS 1A	BEGGING POOR	735C
	CHWLOS	LAME	897B
14	ANASTASIS 2B	RESURRECTION	60B
	ANTAPODIDWMI 1	REPAY	72B
	DIKAIOS 1B	UPRIGHT	195A
	EN II2	WHILE	259D
	ECHW I6A	CAN	333D
	MAKARIOS 1B	BLESSED	488A
15	ARISTON 2	NOON MEAL	106C
	ARTOS 2	FOOD	110C
	AUTOS 1C	SELF	122C
	ESTHIW 1A	EAT	312D
	MAKARIOS 1B	BLESSED	487D
	SUNANAKEIMAI	EAT WITH	792A
15FF	BASILEIA 3G	KINGDOM	135B
16	ANTHRWPOS 3Aα	MAN	68B
	DEIPNON 1	DINNER	172C
	DEIPNON 2	DINNER	172C
	MEGAS 1C	LARGE	498D
	POIEW IIBζ	DO	688A
17	APOSTELLW 1Bγ	SEND AWAY	98B
	DEIPNON 1	DINNER	172B
	DEIPNON 2	DINNER	172B
	HETOIMOS 1	READY	316D
	KALEW 1B	INVITE	400B
	HWRA 3	TIME OF DAY	905A
18	AGORAZW 1	BUY	12C
	AGROS 1	FIELD	13D
	ANAGK8 1	NECESSITY	52A
	APO VI	FROM	88A
	EIDON 1A	SEE	219D
	ECHW I2I	HAVE	333C
	PRWTOS 1B	FIRST	733A
18A	PARAITEOMAI 1	EXCUSE	621D
18B	ECHW I5	CONSIDER	333D
18B	PARAITEOMAI 1	EXCUSE	621D
18F	ERWTAW 2	ASK	312A
19	AGORAZW 1	BUY	12C
	BOUS	OX	146A
	DOKIMAZW 1	EXAMINE	201C
	ECHW I5	CONSIDER	333D
	ZEUGOS 1	YOKE	337D
	PARAITEOMAI 1	EXCUSE	621D
	POREUW 1	PROCEED	699B
19F	HETEROS 1Bδ	ANOTHER	315B
20	GAMEW 1A	MARRY	150A
	DUNAMAI 1B	ABLE	206B
21	ANAP8ROS	CRIPPLED	59A
	EISAGW	BRING	231C
	OIKODESPOT8S MASTER OF THE HOUSE		560C
	ORGIZW	BE ANGRY	583B

21 PARAGINOMAI I	COME	618D
PLATEIA	WIDE ROAD	672D
PTWCHOS IA	BEGGING POOR	735C
RUM8	LANE	744D
TACHEWS IA	QUICKLY	814B
TOTE 2	AT THAT TIME	831D
CHWLOS	LAME	897B
HWDE I	HERE	903B
22 GINOMAI I2A	CREATED	157C
EPITASSW	COMMAND	302B
KURIOS IAβ	LORD	460A
TOPOS IE	PLACE	830C
HWS I2B	AS	905C
23 ANAGKAZW 2	INVITE	51D
GEMIZW 3	FILL	153A
EIS IAα	INTO	227C
EIS IB	NEAR	227C
KURIOS IAβ	LORD	460A
HO,H8,TO IIIOA	THE	555A
HODOS IA	WAY	556B
OIKOS IAα	HOUSE	562D
PHRAGMOS I	FENCE	873B
24 GEUOMAI I	TASTE	156A
DEIPNON 2	DINNER	172B
KALEW IB	INVITE	400B
OUDEIS 2A	NO ONE	596B
25 OCHLOS I	CROWD	605D
POLUS IIAβ	MANY	694B
STREPHW 2Aα	TURN	778D
SUMPOREUOMAI I	GO WITH	787C
26 ADELPH8 I	SISTER	15C
DE 4A	BUT, AND	170D
EI VII		219B
ETI 2B	STILL	316A
MISEW I	HATE	524C
MISEW 2	HATE	524D
TEKNON IAα	CHILD	816A
PSUCH8 IAβ	SOUL LIFE	901C
PSUCH8 IF	SOUL LIFE	902C
27 BASTAZW 2Bα	CARRY	137A
ERCHOMAI II	GO	311D
OPISW 2Aβ	AFTER	578D
HOSTIS IA	WHOEVER	590D
STAUROS 2	THE CROSS	772C
28 APARTISMOS	COMPLETION	80C
DAPAN8	COST	170A
EK 4Aβ	FROM	235B
ECHW I2A	HAVE	332C
KATHIZW 2Aα	SIT DOWN	390D
OIKODOMEW IA	BUILD	560C
PROS III5B	TOWARD	717D
PRWTOS 2A	FIRST	733D
PURGOS 2	TOWER	738A
PURGOS I	TOWER	738A
TIS, TI IAα	WHICH	826D
PS8PHIZW	COUNT	901A
29 EMPAIZW I	RIDICULE	255B
THEMELIOS IB	FOUNDATION	356B
THEWREW I	OBSERVE	360C
M8POTE 2Bα	(NEG PARTICLE)	521A
TITH8MI IIAα	PUT	823C
29F EKTELEW	FINISH	244D
29F ISCHUW 2B	BE STRONG	384C
30 HO,H8,TO IIIH	THE	553B
OIKODOMEW IBα	BUILD	560D
HOUTOS 2A	THIS	601D
31 APANTAW	MEET	79D
BOULEUW I	DELIBERATE	145A
DUNATOS IAβ	POWERFUL	208A
EI V2A	WHETHER	218D
EIKOSI	TWENTY	221A
EN I4Cα	IN	258C
EPI IIIIAє	AGAINST	288B
ERCHOMAI IIAβ	COME	310C
HETEROS IA	OTHER	315A
8 ID6	OR	343B
KATHIZW 2Aα	SIT DOWN	390D
META AIIIA	WITH	509D
POLEMOS IA	ARMED CONFLICT	691D
POREUW I	PROCEED	699B
PRWTOS 2A	FIRST	733D
SUMBALLW IB	CONVERSE	785A
TIS, TI 2	WHICH	827B
HUPANTAW	GO TO MEET	845C
31A CHILIAS	THOUSAND	890B
31B CHILIAS	THOUSAND	890B
32 EIMI II9A	TO BE	223D
EIR8N8 IA	PEACE	226B
ERWTAW 2	ASK	312A
ETI IAα	STILL	315D
PORRW I	FAR AWAY	700C
PRESBEIA	AMBASSADOR	706A
PROS III5B	TOWARD	717D
33 APOTASSW 2	RENOUNCE	100B
PAS ICγ	WHOEVER	637C
HUPARCHW I	BE	845D
34 HALAS I	SALT	34B
ARTUW	SEASON	110C
EAN IIB	IF	210C
EN IIIIA	BY	260A
KALOS 2A	GOOD	401B
MWRAINW 2	BECOME TASTELESS	533A
TIS, TI I8α	WHICH	826D
35 BALLW IB	THROW	130C
EIS 5	FOR	229A
EXW IB	OUTSIDE	279A
EPIGINWSKW 2A	KNOW	291A
EUTHETOS	SUITABLE	320C
KOPRIA	DUNG HEAP	444D
OUS 2	EAR	600B
OUTE	NOT	600C

LUKE 15

1 AKOUW IC	HEAR	31D
HAMARTWLOS 2	SINNER	43D
DE 2	BUT, AND	170C
EGGIZW I	APPROACH	212C
TELWN8S	TAX COLLECTOR	820B
2 HAMARTWLOS 2	SINNER	43C
DIAGOGGUZW	COMPLAIN	181C
PROSDECHOMAI IA	RECEIVE	719B
SUNESTHIW	EAT WITH	796A
PHARISAIOS	PHARISEE	861C
3 PARABOL8 2	PARABLE	617C
4 ANTHRWPOS 3Aζ	MAN	68C

Verse	Word	Gloss	Ref
4	APOLLUMI 2B	BE LOST	95A
	HEKATON	ONE HUNDRED	,236B
	ENEN8KONTA	NINETY	264C
	ENNEA	NINE	266C
	EPI IIIIA6	TO	288B
	ER8MOS 2	DESERT	309A
	ECHW I2A	HAVE	332B
	HEWS IIB	UNTIL	334D
	KATALEIPW 2A	LEAVE BEHIND	414D
	HO,H8,TO II2D	THE	553C
	POREUW I	PROCEED	699A
	PROBATON I	SHEEP	710A
	TIS, TI 2	WHICH	827B
5	EPI IIIIAß	ON	288A
	EPITITH8MI IAα	PUT UPON	302D
	CHAIRW I	REJOICE	881B
	WMOS	SHOULDER	904B
6	APOLLUMI 2B	BE LOST	95A
	GEITWN	NEIGHBOR	152D
	OIKOS IAα	HOUSE	563A
	PROBATON I	SHEEP	710A
	SUGKALEW 2	CALL TOGETHER	780D
	SUGKALEW I	CALL TOGETHER	780D
	SUGCHAIRW I	REJOICE WITH	782C
	PHILOS 2Aα	LOVING	868D
7	HAMARTWLOS 2	SINNER	43C
	DIKAIOS IB	UPRIGHT	194D
	ENEN8KONTA	NINETY	264C
	ENNEA	NINE	266C
	EPI IIIBγ	ON	287B
8	2Bα	THAN	343B
	METANOEW	CHANGE ONES MIND	513B
	METANOIA	REPENTANCE	514A
	HOUTW IB	THUS	602B
	CHARA I	JOY	883D
	CHREIA I	NEED	893B
8	HAPTW I	KINDLE	102B
	DEKA	TEN	172D
	EAN IIB	IF	210B
	EPIMELWS	CAREFULLY	296A
	ECHW I2A	HAVE	332B
	HEWS IIIBß	UNTIL	335C
	HEWS IIIBα	UNTIL	335C
	Z8TEW IAα	SEEK	339A
	LUCHNOS I	LAMP	484C
	OIKIA IA	HOUSE	559D
	OUCHI 3	NOT	603A
	SAROW	SWEEP	752A
	TIS, TI 2	WHICH	827B
6F	APOLLUMI IB	LOSE	94C
8F	DRACHM8	DRACHMA	205D
9	GEITWN	NEIGHBOR	152D
	LEGW I8A	SAY	470B
	SUGKALEW 2	CALL TOGETHER	780D
	SUGKALEW I	CALL TOGETHER	780D
	SUGCHAIRW I	REJOICE WITH	782C
	PHILOS 2B	LOVING	869A
10	AGGELOS 2A	ANGEL	7C
	AGGELOS 2A	ANGEL	7D
	HAMARTWLOS 2	SINNER	43C
	ENWPION 5A	BEFORE	270C
	EPI IIIBγ	ON	287B
	METANOEW	CHANGE ONES MIND	513B
10	HOUTW IB	THUS	602B
	CHARA I	JOY	883D
11	ANTHRWPOS 3Aα	MAN	68B
	DE 2	BUT, AND	170C
	ECHW I2Bα	HAVE	332C
	HUIOS IAα	SON	841B
12	BIOS 3	LIFE	141B
	DIAIRE	DISTRIBUTE	182D
	DIDWMI 2	GIVE	192C
	EPIBALLW 2C	BELONG TO	290A
	MEROS IA	PART	506D
	NEOS IBß	YOUNG	538A
12F	OUSIA	PROPERTY	600C
13	HAPAS 2	ALL	81A
	APOD8MEW I	GO ON A JOURNEY	89C
	ASWTWS	DISSOLUTELY	119A
	DIASKORPIZW	SCATTER	187C
	ZAW 3A	LIVE	337B
	MAKROS 2	DISTANT	489C
	META BIII	AFTER	511B
	NEOS IBß	YOUNG	538A
	POLUS IIAα	MANY	694B
	SUNAGW I	GATHER	789D
	CHWRA IA	COUNTRY	897C
14	ARCHW 2Aα	BEGIN	113A
	GINOMAI IIBß	COME ABOUT	157B
	DAPANAW I	SPEND	170A
	ISCHUROS 2	STRONG	384A
	KATA IIIA	ALONG	407A
	LIMOS 2	FAMINE	476B
	HUSTEREW 2	TO MISS	857A
14F	CHWRA IA	COUNTRY	897C
15	AGROS 3	FARM	13D
	BOSKW I	FEED	144D
	KOLLAW 2Bα	UNITE	442C
	PEMPW I	SEND	647C
	PEMPW I	SEND	647D
	POLIT8S I	CITIZEN	693B
15F	CHOIROS	SWINE	891C
16	APO V2	WITH	87B
	GEMIZW 2	FILL	152D
	EK 4Aζ	FROM	235C
	EPITHUMEW	DESIRE	293A
	ESTHIW IA	EAT	312D
	KERATION	CAROB	430C
	KOILIA I	BELLY	438B
	HOS,H8,HO I4A	(REL PRON)	587D
	CHORTAZW 2A	FEED	892B
17	APOLLUMI 2Aα	PERISH	94D
	ARTOS 2	FOOD	110B
	HEAUTOU ID	ONESELF	211B
	ERCHOMAI I2C	COME	311C
	LIMOS I	HUNGER	476B
	MISTHIOS	HIRED MAN	525A
	PERISSEUW IBα	BE LEFT OVER	656D
	PERISSEUW 2B	BE LEFT OVER	657A
	POSOS 2A	HOW GREAT	701B
	HWDE 2A	HERE	903D
18	HAMARTANW 4B	SIN	42A
	HAMARTANW 4C	SIN	42A
	ANIST8MI 2D	RISE	69D
	EIS 4Cα	AGAINST	228B
	ENWPION 5B	BEFORE	270C

18 OURANOS 3   HEAVEN 599D   26 PUNTHANOMAI 1   INQUIRE 737A
   POREUW 1   PROCEED 699A   TIS, TI 186   WHICH 827A
19 AXIOS 2A   WORTHY 77C   27 APOLAMBANW 2   RECOVER 94A
   HEIS 3A   SOMEONE 230D   H8KW 1C   HAVE COME 345B
   KALEW 1A6   CALL 400B   THUW 2   SACRIFICE 367D
   MISTHIOS   HIRED MAN 525A   MOSCHOS   CALF 530C
   OUKETI 1   NO LONGER 596D   SITEUTOS   FATTENED 759C
   POIEW 11B1   DO 688B   HUGIAINW 1   BE HEALTHY 839D
   HUIOS 1Aα   SON 841B   27A HOTI 2   THAT 593D
   HWS 113B   SO 906A   27B HOTI 3A   THAT 593D
20 ANIST8MI 2D   RISE 69D   28 THELW 2   WISH 355D
   APECHW 2   BE DISTANT 84B   ORGIZW   BE ANGRY 583B
   EPIPIPTW 1B   FALL UPON 297C   PARAKALEW 1B   INVITE 622B
   ERCHOMAI 11   GO 311D   PARAKALEW 5   IMPLORE 623A
   ETI 1Aβ   STILL 315D   29 AIX   GOAT 23B
   KATAPHILEW   KISS 421B   ARISTAW 2   DINE 106B
   MAKRAN 1Aα   FAR 488D   DOULEUW 2A   SERVE 204B
   SPLAGCHNIZOMAI   HAVE PITY 770B   ENTOL8 1B   COMMAND 268C
   TRACH8LOS   NECK 832D   ERIPHION   KID 309C
   TRECHW 1   RUN 833C   ERIPHOS   KID 309D
21 HAMARTANW 4B   SIN 42A   ETOS   YEAR 317A
   HAMARTANW 4C   SIN 42A   EUPHRAINW 2   GLADDEN 328A
   AXIOS 2A   WORTHY 77C   IDOU 1Bα   BEHOLD 371C
   EIS 4Cα   AGAINST 228B   META A112   WITH 510C
   ENWPION 5B   BEFORE 270C   PARERCHOMAI 18β   PASS AWAY 631C
   KALEW 1A6   CALL 400B   TOSOUTOS 1B   SO GREAT 831B
   MISTHIOS   HIRED MAN 525A   PHILOS 2Aα   LOVING 868D
   OUKETI 1   NO LONGER 596D 29A OUDEPOTE   NEVER 596D
   OURANOS 3   HEAVEN 599D   29B OUDEPOTE   NEVER 596D
   POIEW 11B1   DO 688B   30 BIOS 3   LIFE 141B
22 DAKTULIOS   RING 169A   THUW 2   SACRIFICE 367D
   DIDWMI 2   GIVE 192C   KATESTHIW 2   DESTROY 423B
   EIS 1C   IN 227D   MOSCHOS   CALF 530C
   EKPHERW 1   CARRY 246B   HO,H8,TO III H   THE 553B
   ENDUW 1   DRESS 263B   HOTE 1B   WHEN 592C
   PRWTOS 1Cα   FIRST 733B   HOUTOS 2A   THIS 601D
   STOL8   ROBE 777A   PORN8 1   PROSTITUTE 700B
   TACHEWS 1A   QUICKLY 814B   SITEUTOS   FATTENED 759C
   TACHUS 2B   QUICK 814D   31 EMOS 2   MY 255D
   HUPOD8MA   SANDAL 852B   PANTOTE   ALWAYS 614A
23 THUW 2   SACRIFICE 367D   TEKNON 1Aβ   CHILD 816A
   MOSCHOS   CALF 530C   32 ANAZAW 2   COME TO LIFE AGAIN 53B
   SITEUTOS   FATTENED 759C   DEI 2   IT IS NECESSARY 171B
   PHERW 4Bα   BEAR 863B   DEI 6A   IT IS NECESSARY 171C
23F EUPHRAINW 2   GLADDEN 328A   EUPHRAINW 2   GLADDEN 328A
24 ANAZAW 2   COME TO LIFE AGAIN 53B   ZAW 1Aα   LIVE 336C
   APOLLUMI 2B   BE LOST 95A   NEKROS 1Bα   DEAD 536D
   ZAW 1Aα   LIVE 336C   CHAIRW 1   REJOICE 881B
   NEKROS 1Bα   DEAD 536D
   HO,H8,TO III H   THE 553B
25 AGROS 1   FIELD 13D   LUKE 16
   AKOUW 1By   HEAR 31C
   EGGIZW 1   APPROACH 212C 1 ANTHRWPOS 3Aα   MAN 68B
   EIMI 1114   TO BE 224B   DIABALLW   180D
   PRESBUTEROS 1A   OLDER 706B   BRING CHARGES HOSTILELY
   SUMPHWNIA   MUSIC 788D   DIASKORPIZW   SCATTER 187C
   CHOROS 1   DANCE 892A   EIMI 11   TO BE 222B
   HWS IV1A   WHEN 907A   ECHW 12Bβ   HAVE 332D
26 EIMI 113   TO BE 222D   LEGW 13   SAY 469D
   HEIS 3A   SOMEONE 230D   OIKONOMOS 1A   MANAGER 562D
   THELW 3   WISH 356A   HOUTOS 1Aβ   THIS 601A
   PAIS 1Ay   SERVANT 609D   PLOUSIOS 1   RICH 679C
   PROSKALEW 1A   SUMMON 722C   HUPARCHW 1   BE 845D
                                            HWS III1C   SO 906D

2	AKOUW 3C	LEARN	32A	9	SK8N8	TENT	762B
	APODIDWMI I	GIVE AWAY	90A		PHILOS 2Aα	LOVING	868D
	ETI IBB	STILL	316A	10	ADIKOS I	UNJUST	18A
	LOGOS 2A	ACCOUNT	479D		ELACHISTOS 2A	SMALLEST	248B
	OIKONOMEW I	BE MANAGER	562A		PISTOS IAα	TRUSTWORTHY	670C
	PHWNEW 2B	CALL	878C	10A	POLUS I2Cα	MANY	695B
2=4	OIKONOMIA IA	MANAGEMENT	562B	10B	POLUS I2Cα	MANY	695B
3	AISCHUNW I	BE ASHAMED	25A	11	ADIKIA 2	UNRIGHTEOUSNESS	17D
	APHAIREW 3	TAKE AWAY	124A		ADIKOS 2	UNJUST	18A
	EIPON 5	SAY	225D		AL8THINOS 3	GENUINE	36D
	EPAITEW	BEG	282A		MAMWNAS	WEALTH	491A
	ISCHUW 2B	BE STRONG	384C		PISTEUW 3	BELIEVE	667D
	OIKONOMOS IA	MANAGER	562D		PISTOS IAα	TRUSTWORTHY	670C
	HOTI IC	THAT	593B	11F	EI IIA	IF	218A
	SKAPTW I	DIG	761A	12	ALLOTRIOS IBα	TO ANOTHER	40B
4	DECHOMAI I	RECEIVE	176B		H8METEROS	OUR	348C
	HINA IID	IN ORDER THAT	377C		OU 5B	NO	595A
	METHIST8MI I	BE REMOVED	500A		PISTOS IAα	TRUSTWORTHY	670C
5	HEKASTOS 2	EACH	236A		HUMETEROS I	YOUR	844A
	OPHEILW I	OWE	603C	13	AGAPAW IAα	LOVE	4C
	POSOS 2BB	HOW GREAT	701B		ANTECHW I	CLING TO	72D
	PRWTOS IB	FIRST	733A		DOULEUW 2B	SERVE	204B
	CHREOPHEILET8S	DEBTOR	893C		DOULEUW 2A	SERVE	204B
6	BATOS	BATH	137B		DUNAMAI IA	ABLE	206B
	ELAION I	OLIVE OIL	247B		DUO 3	TWO	208C
	KABOS	MEASURE	386B		HEIS 5D	ONE	231B
	KADOS	JAR	387A		HETEROS IA	OTHER	315A
	KATHIZW 2Aα	SIT DOWN	390D	8	IB	OR	342D
	HO,H8,TO IIID	THE	552D		KATAPHRONEW I	SCORN	421C
	PENT8KONTA	FIFTY	648D		MAMWNAS	MAMMON	491A
	TACHEWS IA	QUICKLY	814B		MISEW I	HATE	524C
6F	GRAMMA 2B	NOTE	164C		OIKET8S	HOUSE SLAVE	559C
6F	DECHOMAI 2	GRASP	176C		OUDEIS I	NO	596B
6F	HEKATON	ONE HUNDRED	236B	14	EKMUKT8RIZW	RIDICULE	242D
7	EPEITA I	THEN	284B		HUPARCHW 2	BE	846A
	HETEROS IB6	ANOTHER	315B		PHILARGUROS	FOND OF MONEY	866D
	KOROS	MEASURE	445D	15	BDELUGMA I	ABOMINATION	137C
	OGDO8KONTA	EIGHTY	555B		GINWSKW 6Aα	KNOW	160C
	OPHEILW I	OWE	603C		DIKAIOW 2	JUSTIFY	196C
	POSOS 2BB	HOW GREAT	701B		ENWPION 2B	BEFORE	270B
	SITOS	WHEAT	759C		ENWPION 3	BEFORE	270B
8	ADIKIA 2	UNRIGHTEOUSNESS	17D		KARDIA IBα	HEART	404B
	AIWN 2A	AGE	27A		HUPS8LOS 2	HIGH	857C
	GENEA I	CLAN	153B	16	BASILEIA 3G	KINGDOM	135A
	EPAINEW	PRAISE	281A		BIAZW 2D	APPLY FORCE	140B
	POIEW I2Aα	DO	689A		EUAGGELIZW 2Bα	PREACH	318A
	HUPER 2	BEYOND	847B		MECHRI IB	UNTIL	517B
	PHRONIMOS	THOUGHTFUL	874D		NOMOS 4A	LAW	545A
	PHRONIMWS	WISELY	874D		PAS 2Aα	EVERYONE	638A
	PHWS 3A	LIGHT	880B		PROPH8T8S I	PROPHET	731A
8A	HUIOS IC6	SON	842A		TOTE IA	AT THAT TIME	831C
8B	HUIOS IC6	SON	842A	17	EUKOPOS	EASY	322A
8B	HUIOS IC6	SON	842A		KERAIA	HOOK	429D
9	ADIKIA 2	UNRIGHTEOUSNESS	17D		NOMOS 3	LAW	544D
	ADIKOS 2	UNJUST	18A		NOMOS 4B	LAW	545A
	AIWNIOS 3	ETERNAL	28A		OURANOS IAα	HEAVEN	598B
	DECHOMAI I	RECEIVE	176B		PARERCHOMAI IBα	PASS AWAY	631C
	EK 3F	BY	234D		PIPTW 2B6	FALL	665D
	EKLEIPW	FAIL	242A	18	APO I2	FROM	85D
	KAGW 3B	I	387A		APOLUW 2A	SEND AWAY	96A
	MAMWNAS	WEALTH	491A		HETEROS IBα	ANOTHER	315A
	POIEW IIEα	DO	688D		PAS ICγ	WHOEVER	637B
	SK8N8	TENT	762B	18A	GAMEW IA	MARRY	150A

18A   MOICHEUW 2A   528B
         COMMIT ADULTERY
18B   GAMEW 1A   MARRY   150A
18B   MOICHEUW 2A   528B
         COMMIT ADULTERY
19 ANTHRWPOS 3Aα   MAN   68B
   BUSSOS   LINEN   148C
   EIMI 11   TO BE   222B
   ENDIDUSKW   DRESS   262C
   EUPHRAINW 2   GLADDEN   328A
   H8MERA 2   DAY   347B
   KATA 112C   EVERY   407C
   LAMPRWS   SUMPTUOUSLY   467B
   PLOUSIOS 1   RICH   679C
   PORPHURA   PURPLE   700D
20 BALLW 1B   LIE   130D
   HELKOW   CAUSE SORES   251A
   LAZAROS 2   LAZARUS   463B
   ONOMA 11   NAME   574A
   PTWCHOS 1A   BEGGING POOR   735C
   PULWN 1   GATE   736D
21 ALLA 3   BUT, YET   38A
   APO 16   FROM   86B
   APOLEICHW   LICK   94B
   HELKOS   SORE   251A
   EPITHUMEW   DESIRE   293A
   EPILEICHW   LICK   295C
   ERCHOMAI 11Aζ   COME   310D
   KUWN 1   DOG   462B
   LEICHW   LICK   472D
   PERILEICHW   LICK OFF   654B
   PIPTW 1A   FALL   665A
   TRAPEZA 2   TABLE   832A
   CHORTAZW 2A   FEED   892B
   PSIX   BIT   901B
   PSICHION   CRUMB   901B
21F   PLOUSIOS 1   RICH   679C
22 AGGELOS 2A   ANGEL   7D
   APOPHERW 1Aα   TAKE AWAY   101B
   GINOMAI 13E   TAKE PLACE   158B
   DE 4A   BUT, AND   170D
   THAPTW   BURY   352C
   KOLPOS 1   BOSOM   443A
   PTWCHOS 1A   BEGGING POOR   735C
22FF ABRAAM   ABRAHAM   2A
23 HAD8S 1   HADES   16C
   ANAKEIMAI 2   BE AT TABLE   55C
   ANAPAUW 2   REST   58C
   BASANOS 1   TORMENT   134B
   EN 14D   IN   258C
   EPAIRW 1   LOOK UP   281C
   KOLPOS 1   BOSOM   443A
   MAKROTHEN   FROM FAR AWAY   489A
   HORAW 1Aα   SEE   581C
   HUPARCHW 2   BE   846A
23FF LAZAROS 2   LAZARUS   463B
24 AKRON   TOP   33B
   BAPTW 1   DIP   132B
   GLWSSA 1A   TONGUE   161B
   DAKTULOS   FINGER   169A
   EKPHWNEW   CRY OUT   246C
   ELEEW   HAVE MERCY   249B
   KATAPSUCHW   REFRESH   422A

24 ODUNAW 1   CAUSE PAIN   557C
   HOTI 3B   THAT   594A
   PAT8R 1B   FOREFATHER   640C
   PEMPW 1   SEND   647D
   PHLOX   FLAME   870A
   PHWNEW 1B   CRY OUT   878B
25 AGATHOS 2Bα   GOOD   3C
   APOLAMBANW 1   RECEIVE   93D
   ZW8 1A   LIFE   340D
   KAKOS 2   EVIL   398D
   MIMN8SKOMAI 1Aδ   REMEMBER   524B
   NUN 1Aα   NOW   547C
   HO,H8,TO 112A   THE   553B
   HODE 3   THIS   555D
   ODUNAW 1   CAUSE PAIN   557C
   PARAKALEW 4   IMPLORE   623A
   TEKNON 1B   CHILD   816B
26 DIABAINW   COME OVER   180D
   DIAPERAW   CROSS   186C
   DUNAMAI 2   ABLE   206B
   EKEITHEN   FROM THERE   238D
   ENTHEN 1   FROM   265C
   EPI 111Bθ   TO   286D
   MEGAS 1B   LARGE   498D
   METAXU 2A   BETWEEN   514C
   M8 A12   NOT   517C
   M8DE 1B   AND NOT   519D
   HOPWS 2Aα   IN ORDER THAT   580C
   PAS 2Aδ   IN ALL RESPECTS   638C
   ST8RIZW 1   ESTABLISH   775D
   CHASMA   CHASM   887C
27 ERWTAW 2   ASK   312C
   HINA 111Aγ   IN ORDER THAT   378B
   PEMPW 1   SEND   647C
27F   HOPWS 2Aα   IN ORDER THAT   580C
28 BASANOS 1   TORMENT   134C
   DIAMARTUROMAI 1   CHARGE   185C
   ECHW 12Bα   HAVE   332C
   M8 A12   NOT   517C
   TOPOS 1G   PLACE   830D
29 AKOUW 4   LISTEN   32A
   ECHW 12D   HAVE   333A
   MWUS8S   MOSES   533D
   PROPH8T8S 1   PROPHET   731A
30 ALLA 1A   BUT, YET   37C
   METANOEW   CHANGE ONES MIND   531B
   NEKROS 2A   DEAD   537A
   OUCHI 2   NOT   603A
   POREUW 1   PROCEED   699A
   TIS, TI 1Aγ   ANY ONE   827D
31 AKOUW 4   LISTEN   32A
   EI 11A   IF   218A
   MWUS8S   MOSES   533D
   NEKROS 2A   DEAD   537A
   OUDE 2   AND NOT   595D
   PEITHW 3A   BELIEVE   645B
   PROPH8T8S 1   PROPHET   731A

LUKE 17

1 ANENDEKTOS   IMPOSSIBLE   64B
   ERCHOMAI 12B   COME   311C
   M8 A111Dα   NOT   518A

1	OUAI 1A	WOE 595C	9	ECHW I2Eβ	HAVE 333B
	PL8N 1B	BUT 675B		M8 C1	NOT 519A
	SKANDALON 2	TRAP 760C		CHARIS 5	FAVOR 886C
2	EI II1β	IF 218B	10	AN 3A	(PARTICLE) 48B
	HEIS 1Aβ	ONE 230A		ACHREIOS	USELESS 128A
	8 2Bα	THAN 343B		DIATASSW	ORDER 188C
	THALASSA 1A	SEA 350B		LEGW I1Bα	SAY 469C
	HINA IIIβ	IN ORDER THAT 378C		HOUTW 1B	THUS 602C
	LITHOS 1D	STONE 475C		OPHEILW 2Aβ	OWE 603D
	LUSITELEW	IT IS BETTER 483C		PAS 1Dβ	ALL 637D
	MIKROS 1C	SMALL 523A		SU 1C	YOU 779D
	MULIKOS	MILLSTONE 531A	11	GALILAIA	GALILEE 149D
	ONIKOS PERTAINING TO A DONKEY 573D			DIA 8I	THROUGH 180A
	PERI 2Aβ	ABOUT 650D		DIERCHOMAI 1Bα	GO THROUGH 193C
	PERIKEIMAI 1A	653C		KAI I2B	AND 393A
	BE PLACED AROUND			MESOS 2	THE MIDDLE 508C
	RIPTW 1	THROW 743D		SAMAREIA	SAMARIA 748D
	SKANDALIZW 1A	CAUSE TO FALL 760B	12	APANTAW	MEET 79D
	TRACH8LOS	NECK 832D		DEKA	TEN 172D
3	ADELPHOS 4	NEIGHBOR 16B		EISERCHOMAI 1Aβ	COME 231D
	HAMARTANW 1	SIN 41D		HIST8MI IIIA	STAND 383A
	EAN II8	IF 210B		KWM8 1	VILLAGE 462D
	EPITIMAW 1	REBUKE 303B		LEPROS	LEPROUS 473A
	PROSECHW 1B	PAY ATTENTION TO 721D		PORRWTHEN	FROM A DISTANCE 700C
3F	APHI8MI 2	FORGIVE 125C		TIS, TI 2Aα	ANY ONE 828A
3F	METANOEW	CHANGE ONES MIND 513C		HUPANTAW	GO TO MEET 845C
4	HAMARTANW 4B	SIN 42A	13	AIRW 1B	LIFT UP 23D
	EPISTREPHW 1Bα	TURN 301B		ELEEW	HAVE MERCY 249B
	H8MERA 2	DAY 347A		EPISTAT8S	MASTER 300B
4A	HEPTAKIS	SEVEN TIMES 306B		PHWN8 2A	VOICE 878D
4B	HEPTAKIS	SEVEN TIMES 306B	14	EPIDEIKNUMI 1	SHOW 291D
5	APOSTOLOS 3	APOSTLES 99B		HIEREUS 1Bα	PRIEST 372C
	PISTIS 2D ζ	FAITH 669D		KATHARIZW 1Bα	CLEANSE 388A
	PROSTITH8MI 2	ADD 726C		HUPAGW 2	GO AWAY 844D
5F	KURIOS 2Cβ	LORD 460D	15	DOXAZW 1	PRAISE 203C
6	AN 1Bα	(PARTICLE) 47D		IAOMAI 1	HEAL 369A
	EKRIZOW 1	UPROOT 244B		MEGAS 2Aγ	GREAT 498D
	THALASSA 1A	SEA 350B		META AIII2	WITH 511A
	KOKKOS 1	SEED 441B		PHWN8 2A	VOICE 878D
	METAPHUTEUW	BE TRANSPLANTED 515C	16	AUTOS 2	THEY 122D
	PISTIS 2D ζ	FAITH 669D		EPI IIIIAβ	ON 288A
	SINAPI	MUSTARD 759A		EUCHARISTEW 2	GIVE THANKS 328C
	SUKAMINOS	MULBERRY TREE 783D		PARA IIIIC	ALONG 616A
	HUPAKOUW 1	LISTEN TO 845B		PIPTW 1Bα	FALL 665B
	PHUTEUW	PLANT 878A		PIPTW 1Bα	FALL 665C
	HWS II3B	SO 906A		POUS 1A	FOOT 703B
7	AGROS 1	FIELD 13D		PROSWPON 1A	FACE 728B
	ANAPIPTW 1	RECLINE 59A		SAMARIT8S	SAMARITAN 748D
	EISERCHOMAI 1E	COME 232A	17	DEKA	TEN 172D
	ECHW I2Bβ	HAVE 332D		ENNEA	NINE 266C
	PARERCHOMAI 3	COME 631D		ERCHOMAI IIAα	COME 310B
	POIMAINW 1	TEND 690B		KATHARIZW 1Bα	CLEANSE 388A
8	DEIPNEW	EAT 172B		HO,H8,TO II2D	THE 553C
	DIAKONEW 1	WAIT ON SOMEONE 183A		OUCHI 3	NOT 603A
	ESTHIW IE8	EAT 313B		POU 1A	WHERE 702D
	HETOIMAZW 1	PREPARE 316B	18	ALLOGEN8S	FOREIGN 39A
	HEWS I2B	UNTIL 335A		DIDWMI 1A	GIVE 191D
	OUCHI 3	NOT 603A		DOXA 3	FAME 203B
	PERIZWNNUMI 2A	GIRD ABOUT 653A		HEURISKW 2	FIND 326A
	SU 1A	YOU 779D		HUPOSTREPHW	RETURN 855B
	TIS, TI 1Bζ	WHICH 827B	19	PISTIS 2Bα	FAITH 668D
9	DIATASSW	ORDER 188C		SWZW 1C	SAVE 806A
	DOKEW IE	THINK 201A	20	BASILEIA 3G	KINGDOM 135B

20	EPERWTAW IA	ASK 285A
	ERCHOMAI I2B	COME 311C
	META AIII2	WITH 511A
	PARAT8R8SIS I	OBSERVATION 628B
	POTE	WHEN 701D
20F	BASILEIA 3G	KINGDOM 135B
21	GAR IB	FOR 151A
	EIMI II9A	TO BE 223D
	ENTOS	INSIDE 269A
	HWDE 2A	HERE 903D
21A	IDOU 2	THERE IS 371D
22	EIDON 5	SEE 220A
	HEIS IAβ	ONE 230A
	EPITHUMEW	DESIRE 293A
	ERCHOMAI IIBα	COME 311B
	H8MERA 4B	TIME 348B
	HORAW IB	SEE 582A
	HOTE 2Aα	WHEN 592C
	HUIOS 2C	SON 843A
23	APERCHOMAI 2	GO 84A
	DIWKW 4A	PURSUE 200B
	M8DE IB	AND NOT 519D
	HWDE 2A	HERE 903D
24	ASTRAP8	LIGHTNING 117D
	ASTRAPTW	LIGHTNING FLASHING 117D
	H8MERA 3Bβ	DAY 347D
	LAMPW IA	SHINE 467B
	OURANOS IB	HEAVEN 598C
	HOUTW IA	THUS 602B
	HUIOS 2C	SON 843A
	HWSPER I	(JUST) AS 908A
24A	HUPO 2Aβ	UNDER 851B
24B	HUPO 2Aβ	UNDER 851B
25	APO V6	BY 87D
	APODOKIMAZW 2	DECLARE USELESS 90B
	GENEA 2	GENERATION 153B
	PASCHW 3B	ENDURE 639D
	POLUS I2Bα	MANY 695A
26	GINOMAI III	BE 159B
	EIMI II9B	TO BE 224A
	KATHWS I	JUST AS 392A
	NWE	NOAH 549C
	HOUTW IA	THUS 602B
	HUIOS 2C	SON 843A
26A	H8MERA 4B	TIME 348B
26B	H8MERA 4B	TIME 348B
27	APOLLUMI IAα	RUIN 94C
	ACHRI IA	UNTIL 128B
	GAMEW IB	MARRY 150A
	GAMIZW 2	GIVE IN MARRIAGE 150C
	EISERCHOMAI IAβ	COME 231D
	EKGAMIZW	MARRY 237C
	ERCHOMAI IICα	COME 311B
	H8MERA 2	DAY 347A
	KATAKLUSMOS	FLOOD 412D
	KIBWTOS I	BOX 433A
	NWE	NOAH 549C
	HOS,H8,HO I5Cα	(REL PRON) 588B
27F	ESTHIW IE6	EAT 313B
28	AGORAZW I	BUY 12D
	GINOMAI III	BE 159B
	OIKODOMEW IBβ	BUILD 560D
	HOMOIWS	LIKEWISE 570D
28	PWLEW	SELL 739A
	PHUTEUW	PLANT 878A
28F	LWT	LOT 485C
29	APOLLUMI IAα	RUIN 94C
	BRECHW 2A	SEND RAIN 147A
	EXERCHOMAI IAα	GO OUT 274A
	H8MERA 2	DAY 346D
	THEION	SULPHUR 354B
	HOS,H8,HO I5A	(REL PRON) 588B
	OURANOS IB	HEAVEN 598C
	PUR IB	FIRE 737C
	SODOMA	SODOM 766B
30	APOKALUPTW 4	REVEAL 91D
	H8MERA 2	DAY 346D
	H8MERA 3Bβ	DAY 347D
	KATA II5Bα	ACCORDING TO 408C
	HOS,H8,HO I5A	(REL PRON) 588B
	HUIOS 2C	SON 843A
31	AGROS I	FIELD 13D
	DWMA	ROOF 209C
	EIMI III5A	TO BE 224C
	EKEINOS 2Bβ	THAT 239B
	EPI IIAα	ON 285C
	EPISTREPHW IBα	TURN 301A
	KATABAINW IAα	COME DOWN 409B
	OPISW IA	BEHIND 578C
	SKEUOS IA	THING 761C
31A	M8 AIII4	NOT 518D
31B	M8 AIII4	NOT 518D
32	LWT	LOT 485C
	MN8MONEUW IA	REMEMBER 526D
33	APOLLUMI IB	LOSE 94C
	Z8TEW 2Bγ	SEEK 339C
	ZWOGONEW 2	PRESERVE ALIVE 342A
	PERIPOIEW I	SAVE 655D
	SWZW IA	SAVE 805D
	*PSUCH8 ID	SOUL LIFE 902B
34	EPI IIAα	ON 285C
	KLIN8	COUCH 437B
	NUX IC	NIGHT 548D
34F	HEIS 5D	ONE 231B
34F	HETEROS IA	OTHER 315A
34F	PARALAMBANW I	TAKE 625A
35	AL8THW	GRIND 36D
	AUTOS 4B	THE SAME 123B
	EPI IIIIAζ	ON 288C
36	AGROS I	FIELD 13D
37	AETOS	EAGLE 19B
	EPISUNAGW	GATHER 301D
	HOPOU IAα	WHERE 579C
	POU IA	WHERE 702D
	SUNAGW 2	GATHER 790B
	SWMA IA	BODY 806D

LUKE 18

1	DEI 2	IT IS NECESSARY 171B
	EGKAKEW I	BECOME WEARY 214C
	EKKAKEW	LOSE HEART 240A
	LEGW IIA	SAY 469B
	PANTOTE	ALWAYS 614A
	PARABOL8 2	PARABLE 617C
	PROS III5A	TOWARD 717C

2	ENTREPW 2B	RESPECT 269B
	KRIT8S 1Aα	JUDGE 454C
	POLIS 1	CITY 692A
	TIS, TI 2Aα	ANY ONE 828A
	PHOBEW 2A	BE AFRAID 871A
3	*ANTIDIKOS	OPPONENT 73C
	EKDIKEW 1	AVENGE SOMEONE 238A
	LEGW 18A	SAY 470B
	POLIS 1	CITY 692A
	CH8RA	THE WIDOW 889D
4	EI 11A	IF 218A
	EI VI4	EVEN IF 219A
	EIPON 5	SAY 225D
	ENTREPW 2B	RESPECT 269B
	EPI III2B	ON 289B
	THELW 2	WISH 355D
	OU 5B	NO 595A
	PHOBEW 2A	BE AFRAID 871A
	CHRONOS	TIME 896B
5	GE 1	(EMPHASIZING PARTICLE) 152A
	EIS 2AY	UNTIL 228A
	ERCHOMAI 11Aζ	COME 3100
	HINA 11D	IN ORDER THAT 377C
	KOPOS 1	TROUBLE 444C
	PARECHW !C	CAUSE 632A
	TELOS 1DY	END 819D
	HUPWPIAZW 1	856C
	STRIKE UNDER THE EYE	
	CH8RA	THE WIDOW 889D
6	ADIKIA 2	UNRIGHTEOUSNESS 17D
	KRIT8S 1Aα	JUDGE 454C
	KURIOS 2Cβ	LORD 460D
	LEGW 11A	SAY 469B
7	BOAW 4	SHOUT 143D
	EKLEKTOS 1B	CHOSEN 242B
	EPI III8Y	ON 287B
	H8MERA 1A	DAY 346C
	MAKROTHUMEW 3	HAVE PATIENCE 489B
	M8 DIA	NOT 519D
	NUX 1B	NIGHT 548D
7F	EKDIK8SIS	VENGEANCE 238B
7F	POIEW 11B6	DO 687C
8	ARA	(PARTICLE) 103C
	G8 5B	EARTH 156D
	EN III2	BY 260C
	PISTIS 2Dα	FAITH 669A
	PL8N 1B	BUT 675B
	TACHOS	SPEED 814D
	HUIOS 2C	SON 843A
9	EPI III8Y	ON 287A
	LOIPOS 2Bα	THE OTHERS 481A
	HO,H8,TO 113B	THE 553D
	PARABOL8 2	PARABLE 617C
	PEITHW 2A	CONVINCE 645B
	TIS, TI 1A6	ANY ONE 828A
10	ANABAINW 1Aα	GO UP 49D
	ANTHRWPOS 3Aζ	MAN 68C
	HEIS 5D	ONE 231B
	HETEROS 1A	OTHER 315A
10F	TELWN8S	TAX COLLECTOR 820B
10F	PHARISAIOS	PHARISEE 861C
11	ADIKOS 1	UNJUST 18A
	HARPAX 2	SWINDLER 108D
11	HEAUTOU 11	ONESELF 211C
	EIMI 119B	TO BE 224A
	EUCHARISTEW 1	BE THANKFUL 328B
	EUCHARISTEW 2	GIVE THANKS 328D
	8 1Aβ	OR 342D
	THEOS 3H	GOD 358C
	HIST8MI III1B	STAND 383B
	LOIPOS 2Bα	THE OTHERS 481A
	MOICHOS 1	ADULTERER 528C
	HO,H8,TO III1H	THE 553B
	HO,H8,TO III1	THE 553B
	HOUTOS 2A	THIS 601D
	PROS III7	TOWARD 718A
	PROSEUCHOMAI	PRAY 721A
	HWSPER 2	(JUST) AS 908A
12	APODEKATEUW	TITHE 89B
	DIS	TWICE 198D
	KTAOMAI 1	GET 456A
	N8STEUW	TO FAST 540C
	HOSOS 2	HOW GREAT 590B
	PAS 1EY	ALL 638A
	SABBATON 2A	WEEK 746D
	PHARISAIOS	PHARISEE 861C
13	HAMARTWLOS 2	SINNER 43C
	EPAIRW 1	LOOK UP 281C
	HILASKOMAI 1	PROPITIATE 376A
	HIST8MI II2Bα	BEING 383B
	MAKROTHEN	FROM FAR AWAY 489A
	HO,H8,TO III1	THE 553B
	OUDE 3	NOT EVEN 596A
	ST8THOS	CHEST 775B
	TELWN8S	TAX COLLECTOR 820B
	TUPTW 1	STRIKE 838A
14	DIKAIOW 1	JUSTIFY 196C
	DIKAIOW 2	JUSTIFY 196D
	EKEINOS 1A	THAT 238D
	8 2BY	THAN 343C
	KATABAINW 1A6	COME DOWN 409C
	OIKOS 1Aα	HOUSE 563A
	HOUTOS	THIS 600D
	PARA III3	IN COMPARISON 616B
	PAS 1CY	WHOEVER 637B
14A	TAPEINOW 2A	LOWER 812C
14A	HUPSOW 2	LIFT UP 858D
14B	TAPEINOW 2A	LOWER 812B
14B	TAPEINOW 2B	LOWER 812C
14B	HUPSOW 2	LIFT UP 858D
15	HAPTW 2B	TOUCH 102C
	AUTOS 3B	(OBLIQUE CASE) 123A
	BREPHOS 2	INFANT 147A
	EPITIMAW 1	REBUKE 303B
	HINA 11E	IN ORDER THAT 377C
	PROSPHERW 1A	BRING (TO) 727A
16	APHI8MI 4	TOLERATE 126A
	EIMI IV1	TO BE 224D
	KWLUW 1	HINDER 462C
	PAIDION 2A	CHILD 609A
	TOIOUTOS 3Aα	SUCH A KIND 829B
16F	BASILEIA 3G	KINGDOM 135B
17	AM8N 2	AMEN 45B
	DECHOMAI 3B	ACCEPT 176C
	EISERCHOMAI 2A	COME 232B
	LEGW III D	ASSURE 470D

17 M8   AI I   NOT 517C   28 PETROS   PETER 660D
   PAIDION 2A   CHILD 609A   28F APHI8MI 3A   ABANDON 125D
18 AGATHOS IBα   GOOD   3A   29 BASILEIA 3G   KINGDOM 135B
   AGATHOS IBα   GOOD   3A   GONEUS   PARENTS 164B
   AIWNIOS 3   ETERNAL 28A   EIMI II   TO BE 222B
   ARCHWN 2A   AUTHORITIES 113C   HENEKA   BECAUSE OF 264B
   ZW8 2Bβ   LIFE 341C   8   IAβ   OR 342D
   KL8RONOMEW 2   INHERIT 435D   LEGW IIID   ASSURE 470D
19 HEIS 2C   ONE 230D   OIKIA IA   HOUSE 559D
   LEGW II3   CALL 471A   30 AIWN 2B   AGE 27B
   OUDEIS 2A   NO ONE 596B   AIWNIOS 3   ETERNAL 28A
19A   AGATHOS IBα   GOOD   3A   APOLAMBANW I   RECEIVE 93D
19B   AGATHOS IBα   GOOD   3A   HEKATONTAPLASIWN   236C
20 ENTOL8 2Aβ   COMMAND 268C   A HUNDRED FOLD
   KLEPTW   STEAL 435C   HEPTAPLASIWN   SEVENFOLD 306C
   MOICHEUW I   COMMIT ADULTERY 528B   ERCHOMAI IIBβ   COME 311B
   OIDA IB   KNOW 558B   ZW8 2Bβ   LIFE 341C
   TIMAW 2   HONOR 824D   KAIROS 4   TIME 396C
   PHONEUW   MURDER 872C   M8 DIA   NOT 519B
   PSEUDOMARTUREW   900A   OUCHI I   NOT 602D
         BEAR FALSE WITNESS   POLLAPLASIWN   MANIFOLD 693C
21 EK 5A   FROM 235C   31 ANABAINW IAα   GO UP 49D
   NEOT8S   YOUTH 538B   GRAPHW 2C   WRITE 166A
   PHULASSW IF   WATCH 876C   DIA AIII2A   BY 179C
   PHULASSW 2B   WATCH 876D   HIEROSOLUMA IA   JERUSALEM 373D
22 DEURO I   COME 175C   PARALAMBANW I   TAKE 625A
   DIADIDWMI   DISTRIBUTE 181D   PAS IDβ   ALL 637D
   HEIS 2B   ONE 230C   TELEW 2   PERFORM 818D
   ETI 2A   STILL 316A   HUIOS 2C   SON 843A
   TH8SAUROS 2Bα   TREASURE 362B   32 EMPAIZW I   RIDICULE 255B
   LEIPW 2   LACK 471D   EMPTUW   SPIT ON 257A
   HOSOS 2   HOW GREAT 590B   PARADIDWMI IB   GIVE OVER 620A
   PAS IEY   ALL 638A   HUBRIZW   MISTREAT 839B
   PTWCHOS IA   BEGGING POOR 735D   32FF KAI I2B   AND 393A
   PWLEW   SELL 739A   33 ANIST8MI 2A   RISE 69C
23 PERILUPOS   VERY SAD 654B   MASTIGOW I   WHIP 496A
   PLOUSIOS I   RICH 679C   TRITOS I   THIRD 834B
   SPHODRA   GREATLY 803D   34 GINWSKW 3A   UNDERSTAND 160B
24 DUSKOLWS   WITH DIFFICULTY 208D   KRUPTW 2A   HIDE 455C
   EISPOREUOMAI I   GO 232D   LEGW IIO   SAY 470C
   PWS 3   HOW 740C   OUDEIS 2Bα   NOTHING 596C
   CHR8MA I   WEALTH 893D   R8MA I   WORD 742D
24F   BASILEIA 3G   KINGDOM 135B   SUNI8MI   UNDERSTAND 798A
25 BELON8   NEEDLE 138D   35 EGGIZW 2   APPROACH 212D
   DIERCHOMAI IBα   GO THROUGH 193C   EIS IB   NEAR 227C
   EISERCHOMAI 2A   COME 232B   EPAITEW   BEG 282A
   EUKOPOS   EASY 322A   IERICHW   JERICHO 372D
   KAM8LOS   CAMEL 402C   KATH8MAI IAα   SIT 390B
   KAMILOS   ROPE 402D   HODOS IA   WAY 556B
   PLOUSIOS I   RICH 679C   PARA IIIBα   ALONG 616A
   RAPHIS   NEEDLE 742A   PARA IIID   ALONG 616A
   TR8MA   OPENING 833D   PROSAITEW   BEG 718C
   TRUMALIA   HOLE 836A   36 DIAPOREUOMAI   GO THROUGH 186D
25A   EISERCHOMAI IAδ   COME 232A   EIMI II3   TO BE 222D
25A   EISERCHOMAI IF   COME 232B   PUNTHANOMAI I   INQUIRE 737A
26 SWZW 2B   SAVE 806B   37 APAGGELLW I   REPORT 78C
27 ADUNATOS 2A   IMPOSSIBLE 18D   NAZWRAIOS   NAZARENE 534B
   ANTHRWPOS IAβ   MAN 67C   PARERCHOMAI IAα   GO BY 631B
   DUNATOS 2C   POSSIBLE 208B   PARERCHOMAI IAα   GO BY 631B
   HO,H8,TO II2A   THE 553B   38 BOAW 3   SHOUT 143D
27A   PARA II2C   BESIDE 615D   38F   DAUID   DAVID 170B
27B   PARA II2C   BESIDE 615D   38F   ELEEW   HAVE MERCY 249B
28 IDIOS 3B   ONES OWN 370D   38F   HUIOS 2A   SON 842A

```
39 HINA IIIA6      IN ORDER THAT 378B
   KRAZW 2A                  CALL 448D
   MALLON I                  MORE 490A
   POLUS I2Cα                MANY 695C
   PROAGW 2A                 LEAD 709A
   SIGAW IB             BE SILENT 757A
   SIWPAW 2A           BE SILENT 760A
40 AGW IA                    LEAD  14A
   EGGIZW 5A             APPROACH 212D
   HIST8MI IIIA            STAND 383A
   KELEUW               COMMAND 428C
41 THELW I                   WISH 355C
41FF ANABLEPW 2Aα      GAIN SIGHT  50C
42 PISTIS 2Bα             FAITH 668D
   SWZW IC                   SAVE 806A
43 AINOS                   PRAISE  23B
   DOXAZW I               PRAISE 203C
   LAOS IA                 PEOPLE 467D
   PARACHR8MA            AT ONCE 629B
```

LUKE 19

```
I  DIERCHOMAI IA     GO THROUGH 193C
   EISERCHOMAI IA6         COME 232A
   IERICHW             JERICHO 372D
2  AN8R 6                  MAN  66B
   ARCHITELWN8S                 112D
      CHIEF TAX COLLECTOR
   ZAKCHAIOS         ZACCHAEUS 336A
   IDOU 2              THERE IS 371D
   KALEW IAγ              CALL 400A
   ONOMA I2B              NAME 574B
   PLOUSIOS I             RICH 679C
3  APO VI          BECAUSE OF  87B
   DUNAMAI 2              ABLE 206B
   EIDON IC               SEE 219D
   H8LIKIA 2   BODILY STATURE 346A
   MIKROS IA             SMALL 523A
   OCHLOS I              CROWD 605C
   TIS, TI IAβ           WHICH 826D
4  ANABAINW IAβ          GO UP  50A
   DIERCHOMAI ID    GO THROUGH 193D
   EKEINOS 3             THAT 239C
   EMPROSTHEN IA        AHEAD 256B
   HINA IIE      IN ORDER THAT 377C
   MELLW ICα       BE ABOUT TO 502A
   HO,H8,TO II6           THE 554B
   PROTRECHW         RUN AHEAD 729D
   SUKAMINOS      MULBERRY TREE 783D
   SUKOMOREA      SYCAMORE FIG 784A
5  ANABLEPW I          LOOK UP  50C
   DEI 5        IT IS NECESSARY 171B
   ERCHOMAI IIAβ          COME 310C
   ZAKCHAIOS         ZACCHAEUS 336A
   MENW IAα             REMAIN 504D
  *SPEUDW IA             HURRY 769D
   TOPOS IC              PLACE 830B
   HWS IVIA              WHEN 907A
5F   KATABAINW IAα  COME DOWN 409B
6  SPEUDW IA            HURRY 769D
   HUPODECHOMAI        RECEIVE 852A
   CHAIRW I            REJOICE 881B
7  HAMARTWLOS I        SINNER  43C
```

```
7  AN8R 4                  MAN  66B
   DIAGOGGUZW         COMPLAIN 181C
   KATALUW 2              HALT 415C
   PARA IIIBα           BESIDE 615B
8  APODIDWMI 2       GIVE BACK  90A
   ZAKCHAIOS         ZACCHAEUS 336A
   H8MISUS I              HALF 348D
   IDOU IBε             BEHOLD 371C
   HIST8MI IIIB          STAND 383B
   KURIOS 2Cβ             LORD 460D
   PTWCHOS IA     BEGGING POOR 735D
   SUKOPHANTEW 2       SLANDER 784A
   TETRAPLOUS         FOURFOLD 821C
   HUPARCHW I              BE 845D
9  AUTOS 3B    (OBLIQUE CASE) 123A
   GINOMAI I3Bγ     TAKE PLACE 158B
   KATHOTI 2           BECAUSE 392A
   OIKOS 2           HOUSEHOLD 563C
   SWT8RIA 2       DELIVERANCE 809B
   HUIOS IBα              SON 841C
10 APOLLUMI 2Aα         PERISH  94D
   ERCHOMAI IIAη          COME 311A
   Z8TEW IAα              SEEK 339A
   SWZW 2Aα               SAVE 806A
   HUIOS 2C               SON 843A
11 ANAPHAINW          LIGHT UP  62C
   BASILEIA 3G         KINGDOM 135B
   EGGUS IA               NEAR 213B
   EIPON I                SAY 225B
   PARABOL8 2          PARABLE 617C
   PARACHR8MA          AT ONCE 629B
   PROSTITH8MI IC          ADD 726C
12 ANTHRWPOS 3Aα          MAN  68B
   BASILEIA I          KINGDOM 134C
   EUGEN8S I          WELL BORN 319B
   LAMBANW IC             TAKE 465C
   MAKROS 2            DISTANT 489C
   OUN 2A            THEREFORE 597C
   CHWRA IA            COUNTRY 897C
13 DIDWMI 3               GIVE 192C
   ERCHOMAI I2C           COME 311D
   KALEW IC               CALL 400B
   MNA                    MINA 526A
   PRAGMATEUOMAI       CONDUCT 704A
14 APOSTELLW IBβ     SEND AWAY  98A
   BASILEUW IA            RULE 136B
   EMPEMPW                SEND 255B
   EPI IIIIBα             OVER 288D
   THELW I                WISH 355C
   LEGW I8C               SAY 470B
   MISEW I               HATE 524C
   OPISW 2Aβ             AFTER 578C
   POLIT8S 2           CITIZEN 693B
   PRESBEIA        AMBASSADOR 706A
15 ARGURION 2B           MONEY 104B
   BASILEIA I          KINGDOM 134C
   GINWSKW IC             KNOW 160A
   DIAPRAGMATEUOMAI            186D
      GAIN BY TRADING
   DIDWMI                 GIVE 191D
   DIDWMI 3               GIVE 192C
   EN II3                WHILE 260A
   EPANERCHOMAI         RETURN 282D
```

15 HINA IIE   IN ORDER THAT 377C
   TIS, TI IC   WHICH 827B
   PHWNEW 2B   CALL 878C
16 KURIOS IAβ   LORD 460A
   MNA   MINA 526A
   PARAGINOMAI I   COME 618D
   PROSERGAZOMAI   MAKE MORE 720A
   PRWTOS IB   FIRST 733A
17 AGATHOS IAα   GOOD 2D
   EIMI II4F   TO BE 223B
   ELACHISTOS 2A   SMALLEST 248B
   EXOUSIA 4A   AUTHORITY 278A
   EU   WELL 317C
   EUGE   EXCELLENT 319B
   HOTI 3A   THAT 593D
   PISTOS IAα   TRUSTWORTHY 670C
   POLIS I   CITY 692A
18 DEUTEROS 3   SECOND 176A
   KURIOS IAβ   LORD 460A
   LEGW I8A   SAY 470B
   MNA   MINA 526A
   POIEW IIBη   DO 688A
19 POLIS I   CITY 692A
   SU IC   YOU 779D
20 APOKEIMAI I   BE PUT AWAY 92B
   HETEROS IBδ   ANOTHER 315C
   ECHW IICα   KEEP 332B
   IDOU 2   THERE IS 371D
   KURIOS IAβ   LORD 460A
   MNA   MINA 526A
   SOUDARION   FACE CLOTH 766D
21 TITH8MI IIBγ   DEPOSIT 823D
21F   AIRW 4   TAKE AWAY 24A
21F   ANTHRWPOS 2Bα MAN 67D
21F   AUST8ROS   SEVERE 121D
21F   THERIZW 2A   REAP 360A
21F   SPEIRW IBα   SOW 768D
22 EK   3I   BY 235A
   KRINW 4Aα   JUDGE 452D
   OIDA   KNOW 558A
   PON8ROS IBα   WICKED 697C
   STOMA IA   MOUTH 777C
   TITH8MI IIBγ   DEPOSIT 823D
23 AN   IBβ   (PARTICLE) 48A
   ANAPRASSW   DEMAND 59C
   ARGURION 2B   MONEY I04B
   DIA 8II2   WHY 180B
   DIDWMI 5   GIVE 192D
   PRASSW IB   DO 705C
   TOKOS   INTEREST 829C
   TRAPEZA 4   TABLE 832C
24 APOPHERW IB   TAKE I01B
   PARIST8MI 2Bα   BE PRESENT 633D
24F   MNA   MINA 526A
25 KURIOS IAβ   LORD 460A
26 PAS ICγ   WHOEVER 637B
26A   ECHW I2A   HAVE 332C
26B   ECHW I2A   HAVE 332C
27 AGW IA   LEAD 14A
   BASILEUW IA   RULE 136B
   EMPROSTHEN 2C   IN FRONT 256C
   EPI IIIIBα   OVER 288D
   ECHTHROS 2Bβ   THE ENEMY 331D

27 THELW I   WISH 355C
   KATASPHAZW   SLAUGHTER 420C
   PL8N IB   BUT 675B
   HWDE I   HERE 903B
28 ANABAINW IAα   GO UP 490
   HIEROSOLUMA IA   JERUSALEM 373D
29 88THANIA I   BETHANY 139B
   88THPHAG8   BETHPHAGE 139D
   EGGIZW 2   APPROACH 212D
   EIS IB   NEAR 227C
   ELAIWN   OLIVE GROVE 247C
   KALEW IAγ   CALL 400A
   OROS   MOUNTAIN 586B
30 ANTHRWPOS 3Aζ   MAN 68C
   DEW 2   BIND 177A
   EISPOREUOMAI I   GO 232D
   HEURISKW ICα   FIND 325C
   KATHIZW 2Aα   SIT DOWN 391A
   KATENANTI I   OPPOSITE 422B
   KWM8 I   VILLAGE 462D
   PWLOS   COLT 739A
   PWPOTE   EVER 739B
   HUPAGW 2   GO AWAY 844C
30F   LUW 2A   LOOSE 484D
31 DIA 8II2   WHY 180B
   ERWTAW I   ASK 312A
   ECHW I2I   HAVE 333C
   HOUTW 2   THUS 602C
   CHREIA I   NEED 893B
32 HEURISKW ICγ   FIND 325C
33 KURIOS IAα   OWNER 459D
   TIS, TI 3A   WHICH 827B
33A   LUW 2A   LOOSE 484D
33A   PWLOS   COLT 739A
33B   LUW 2A   LOOSE 484D
33B   PWLOS   COLT 739A
34 ECHW I2I   HAVE 333C
   CHREIA I   NEED 893B
35 AGW IA   LEAD 14A
   EPIBIBAZW   CAUSE TO MOUNT 290B
   HIMATION I   GARMENT 377A
   PWLOS   COLT 739A
36 HIMATION I   GARMENT 377A
   HODOS IA   WAY 556B
   HUPOSTRWNNUW   855B
              SPREAD UNDERNEATH
37 AINEW   TO PRAISE 23A
   HAPAS I   WHOLE 81A
   DUNAMIS 4   MIRACLE 207B
   EGGIZW 2   APPROACH 212D
   ELAIA I   OLIVE TREE 247D
   KATABASIS   DESCENT 410A
   MATH8T8S 2Bβ   DISCIPLE 487A
   MEGAS 2Aγ   GREAT 498D
   OROS   MOUNTAIN 586B
   HOS,H8,HO I5Cα   (REL PRON) 588B
   PERI IB   ABOUT 650B
   PL8THOS 2B6   QUANTITY 674D
   PROS III   NEAR 716C
   PHWN8 2A   VOICE 878D
   CHAIRW I   REJOICE 881B
38 DOXA 3   FAME 203B
   EIR8N8 3   PEACE 227A

38	ERCHOMAI IIAη	COME	310D
	EULOGEW 2A	BLESS	322D
	ONOMA I4Cγ	NAME	576C
	OURANOS 2D	HEAVEN	599D
	HUPSISTOS I	HIGHEST	858A
39	APO I6	FROM	86A
	EPITIMAW I	REBUKE	303B
	OCHLOS I	CROWD	605C
40	EAN I2A	IF	210D
	KRAZW 2Bβ	CALL	449A
	LITHOS IA	STONE	475B
	SIGAW IA	BE SILENT	757A
	SIWPAW 2A	BE SILENT	760A
41	EGGIZW 5A	APPROACH	212D
	*KLAIW I	WEEP	434A
42	GE 3C	AT LEAST	152B
	GINWSKW IA	KNOW	159D
	EI IV	IF	218C
	EIR8N8 IB	PEACE	226C
	KRUPTW 2A	HIDE	455C
	NUN 2	NOW	548A
	OPHTHALMOS 2	EYE	604C
	PROS III5B	TOWARD	717D
43	EPI IIIIBγ	ON	289A
	H8KW 2	HAVE COME	345C
	H8MERA 4B	TIME	348B
	KAI I2C	AND	393B
	PANTOTHEN	FROM ALL DIRECTIONS	613C
	PAREMBALLW I	THROW UP	630C
	PERIBALLW IA	THROW AROUND	651C
	PERIKUKLOW	SURROUND	654A
	SUNECHW 3	CROWD	796D
	CHARAX 2	PALISADE	884C
44	ANTI 3	FOR	73B
	EDAPHIZW	RAZE	216D
	EPISKOP8 I	A VISITATION	299A
	KAIROS 3	TIME	396A
	LITHOS IB	STONE	475B
	HOS,H8,HO IIIA	(REL PRON)	589A
	TEKNON 2Fα	CHILD	816C
45	AGORAZW I	BUY	12D
	EKBALLW I	DRIVE OUT	236D
	HIERON 2	TEMPLE	373A
	PWLEW	SELL	739A
46	GRAPHW 2C	WRITE	165D
	L8ST8S I	ROBBER	474B
	OIKOS IAβ	HOUSE	563B
	OIKOS IAβ	HOUSE	563B
	POIEW IIBι	DO	688B
	PROSEUCH8 I	PRAYER	720C
	SP8LAION	CAVE	769D
47	APOLLUMI IAα	RUIN	94C
	EIMI II4E	TO BE	223B
	H8MERA 2	DAY	347B
	HIERON 2	TEMPLE	373A
	KATA II2C	EVERY	407C
	LAOS 3A	PEOPLE	468A
	PRWTOS ICβ	FIRST	733C
48	AKOUW IC	HEAR	31D
	HAPAS I	WHOLE	81A
	EKKREMANNUMI 2	HANG	241C
	HEURISKW 2	FIND	325D
	LAOS IA	PEOPLE	467D

48	LAOS ICα	PEOPLE	467D
	HO,H8,TO II8A	THE	554D

LUKE 20

1	EUAGGELIZW 2A6	PREACH	318A
	EPHIST8MI IA	STAND BY	331A
	H8MERA 2	DAY	347A
	HIEREUS I8α	PRIEST	372C
	LAOS IA	PEOPLE	467D
	PRESBUTEROS 2Aβ	OLDER	706D
	SUN 4B	WITH	789D
2	EXOUSIA 3	AUTHORITY	278A
	8 ID6	OR	343B
	LEGW I8A	SAY	470B
	POIOS 2Aγ	OF WHAT KIND	691B
3	ERWTAW I	ASK	312A
	LOGOS IAβ	WORD	478B
4	BAPTISMA I	BAPTISM	132A
	EIMI III3	TO BE	224B
4F	OURANOS 3	HEAVEN	599D
5	DIA 8II2	WHY	180B
	PISTEUW IB	BELIEVE	666C
	SULLOGIZOMAI	REASON	784D
6	KATALITHAZW	STONE TO DEATH	415A
	LAOS ICα	PEOPLE	467D
	PEITHW 4	OBEY	645C
	PROPH8T8S 2	PROPHET	731A
7	APOKRINOMAI I	ANSWER	93A
	M8 ΔIIIBα	NOT	517D
	POTHEN 2	FROM WHERE	686D
8	EXOUSIA 3	AUTHORITY	278A
	LEGW IIBβ	SAY	469C
	POIOS 2Aγ	OF WHAT KIND	691B
9	APOD8MEW I	GO ON A JOURNEY	89C
	EKDIDWMI	LEASE	238A
	HIKANOS IB	SUFFICIENT	375A
	LEGW IIA	SAY	469B
	PARABOL8 2	PARABLE	617C
	PHUTEUW	PLANT	878A
	CHRONOS 2	TIME	896C
9F	GEWRGOS 2	FARMER	156B
9FF	AMPELWN	VINEYARD	46B
10	APOSTELLW IBγ	SEND AWAY	98A
	DIDWMI 4	GIVE	192D
	HINA I2	IN ORDER THAT	377C
	KAIROS 2	TIME	395D
	KARPOS IA	FRUIT	405C
10F	DERW	BEAT	174D
10F	EXAPOSTELLW 2	SEND OUT	272D
10F	KENOS I	EMPTY	429A
11	ATIMAZW	DISHONOR	119C
	HETEROS I86	ANOTHER	315C
	KAKEINOS 2B	HE ALSO	397C
	PEMPW I	SEND	647B
11F	PROSTITH8MI IC	ADD	726C
12	EKBALLW I	DRIVE OUT	236D
	PEMPW I	SEND	647B
	TRAUMATIZW	TO WOUND	832C
	TRITOS I	THIRD	834C
13	AGAP8TOS I	BELOVED	6C
	ENTREPW 28	RESPECT	269B
	ISWS	PERHAPS	384D

13	KURIOS 1Aα	OWNER 459D	
	TUGCHANW 2C	HAPPEN 837B	
14	GEWRGOS 2	FARMER 156B	
	GINOMAI II2A	BE 159B	
	DEUTE 1	COME 175D	
	DIALOGIZOMAI 2	ARGUE 185A	
	HINA IIC	IN ORDER THAT 377C	
	KL8RONOMIA 1	INHERITANCE 436A	
	KL8RONOMOS 1	HEIR 436B	
	PROS III'E	TOWARD 716D	
15	EKBALLW 1	DRIVE OUT 236D	
	EXW 2B	OUTSIDE 279B	
	KURIOS 1Aα	OWNER 459D	
	OUN ICα	THEREFORE 597B	
	POIEW IIOγ	DO 688D	
16	APOLLUMI 1Aα	RUIN 94C	
	GEWRGOS 2	FARMER 156B	
	GINOMAI I3A	TAKE PLACE 157D	
	M8 AIII2	NOT 518C	
17	APODOKIMAZW 1	DECLARE USELESS 90B	
	GINOMAI I4A	BECOME 158D	
	GWNIA	CORNER 167D	
	EIMI II3	TO BE 222D	
	EMBLEPW 1	LOOK AT 254A	
	KEPHAL8 2B	HEAD 431C	
	LEGW I8A	SAY 470B	
	LITHOS 2	STONE 475D	
	OIKODOMEW IB8	BUILD 560D	
	HOS,H8,HO 14D	(REL PRON) 588A	
	OUN ICα	THEREFORE 597B	
18	LITHOS 2	STONE 475D	
	LIKMAW	WINNOW 475D	
	SUNTHLAW	CRUSH 797C	
18A	PIPTW 1A	FALL 665A	
18B	PIPTW 1A	FALL 665A	
19	ARCHIEREUS 1B	HIGH PRIEST 112B	
	EIPON 1	SAY 225B	
	EPIBALLW 1B	LAY ON 289D	
	LAOS ICα	PEOPLE 467D	
	PARABOL8 2	PARABLE 617C	
	PROS III5A	TOWARD 717C	
	PHOBEW 1B8	BE AFRAID 871A	
	HWRA 3	TIME OF DAY 905A	
20	APOCHWREW	LEAVE 101D	
	ARCH8 3	RULER 112A	
	DIKAIOS iB	UPRIGHT 194D	
	EGKATHETOS	SPIES 214B	
	EXOUSIA 4A	AUTHORITY 278A	
	EPILAMBANOMAI 2A	GRASP 295A	
	H8GEMWN 2	GOVERNORS 344A	
	LOGOS IA8	WORD 478B	
	PARADIDWMI IB	GIVE OVER 620A	
	PARAT8REW IB	WATCH 628A	
	HUPOKRINOMAI	PRETEND 852D	
	HWSTE 2B	THEREFORE 908C	
21	AL8THEIA 3	REALITY 35D	
	EPI IIB8	ON 286B	
	LAMBANW IE8	RECEIVE 466A	
	HODOS 2B	WAY 557A	
	OIDA IE	KNOW 558D	
	ORTHWS	RIGHTLY 584C	
	PROSWPON IB	FACE 728C	
22	DIDWMI 4	GIVE 192D	
22	EXESTI 3	IT IS POSSIBLE 274D	
	KAISAR	EMPEROR 396C	
	PHOROS	TAX 872D	
23	KATANOEW 3	NOTICE 416A	
	PANOURGIA	CUNNING 613A	
	PEIRAZW 2C	TRY 646A	
24	D8NARION	DENARIUS 178B	
	EIKWN IA	IMAGE 221B	
	EPIGRAPH8	INSCRIPTION 291C	
	KAISAR	EMPEROR 396C	
25	APODIDWMI 1	GIVE AWAY 89D	
	THEOS 3Fγ	GOD 358B	
	KAISAR	EMPEROR 396C	
	TOINUN	HENCE 828D	
26	APOKRISIS	ANSWER 93A	
	ENANTION IA	BEFORE 261B	
	EPILAMBANOMAI 2A	GRASP 295A	
	THAUMAZW IA8	WONDER 353A	
	ISCHUW 2B	BE STRONG 384C	
	LAOS ICα	PEOPLE 467D	
	R8MA I	WORD 742D	
	SIGAW IA	BE SILENT 757A	
27	ANASTASIS 2B	RESURRECTION 60B	
	ANTILEGW I	CONTRADICT 74B	
	M8 AIIIA	NOT 517D	
	M8 AIIIBα	NOT 517D	
	SADDOUKAIOS	SADDUCEE 747A	
28	EXANIST8MI I	RAISE UP 272B	
	HINA IIIA6	IN ORDER THAT 378B	
	MWUS8S	MOSES 533D	
	SPERMA 2B	SEED 769B	
28F	ATEKNOS	CHILDLESS 119C	
28=31	LAMBANW IC	TAKE 465C	
29	HEPTA	SEVEN 306B	
	PRWTOS IB	FIRST 733A	
31	HEPTA	SEVEN 306B	
	KATALEIPW IB	LEAVE BEHIND 414C	
	TRITOS I	THIRD 834C	
	HWSAUTWS	SIMILARLY 907D	
32*	HUSTEROS 2B	FINALLY 857B	
33	ANASTASIS 2B	RESURRECTION 60B	
	GINOMAI II2A	BE 159B	
	EN II2	WHILE 259D	
	HEPTA	SEVEN 306B	
34	AIWN 2A	AGE 27A	
	GAMISKW	GIVE IN MARRIAGE 150C	
	HUIOS IC6	SON 842A	
34F	GAMEW IB	MARRY 150A	
35	AIWN 2B	AGE 27B	
	ANASTASIS 2B	RESURRECTION 60A	
	GAMISKW	GIVE IN MARRIAGE 150C	
	GAMIZW 2	GIVE IN MARRIAGE 150C	
	EK IB	AWAY FROM 233C	
	EKGAMIZW	MARRY 237C	
	EKEINOS 28β	THAT 239B	
	KATAXIOW I	CONSIDER WORTHY 416C	
	NEKROS 2A	DEAD 537A	
	OUTE	NOT 600C	
	TUGCHANW I	MEET 837B	
35F	ANASTASIS 2B	RESURRECTION 60B	
36	ANASTASIS 2B	RESURRECTION 60B	
	GAR IB	FOR 151B	
	EIMI II8	TO BE 223D	

36 ETI 1Bβ	STILL	316A
ISAGGELOS	LIKE AN ANGEL	381C
OUTE	NOT	600C
HUIOS 1Cγ	SON	841D
36B HUIOS 1C6	SON	842A
37 ABRAAM	ABRAHAM	2A
BATOS	THORN BUSH	137B
D8LOW	REVEAL	177C
EPI 11Aγ	ON	286A
THEOS 3C	GOD	358A
IAKWB 1	JACOB	368B
ISAAK	ISAAC	381C
MWUS8S	MOSES	533D
NEKROS 2A	DEAD	537A
38 ALLA 1A	BUT, YET	37B
THEOS 3B	GOD	357D
NEKROS 2A	DEAD	536D
38A ZAW 1Aα	LIVE	336C
38B ZAW 3B	LIVE	337C
39 KALWS 4B	WELL	402B
40 EPERWTAW 1A	ASK	285A
OUDEIS 2Bα	NOTHING	596C
OUKETI 1	NO LONGER	597A
TOLMAW 1A	DARE	829C
41 DAUID	DAVID	170B
LEGW 111E	DECLARE	471A
PWS 1A	HOW	739C
CHRISTOS 1	ANOINTED ONE	895B
41-4 HUIOS 2A	SON	842A
42 AUTOS 1Aα	SELF	122B
BIBLOS 1	BOOK	140D
DAUID	DAVID	170B
DEXIOS 2B	RIGHT	174A
KATH8MAI 2	SIT DOWN	390C
KURIOS 2Cα	LORD	460C
LEGW 17	SAY	470A
PSALMOS 1	PSALM	899B
43 ECHTHROS 2Bβ	THE ENEMY	331D
HEWS 11B	UNTIL	334D
POUS 1B	FOOT	703C
TITH8MI 12Aα	MAKE	824A
HUPOPODIUN	FOOTSTOOL	854D
44 DAUID	DAVID	170B
KALEW 1Aβ	CALL	399D
KURIOS 2Cα	LORD	460C
PWS 1A	HOW	739C
46 AGORA	MARKET PLACE	12B
ASPASMOS 1	GREETING	116D
DEIPNON 2	DINNER	172B
THELW 4A	WISH	356A
PERIPATEW 1B	GO ABOUT	654D
PROSECHW 1B	PAY ATTENTION TO	721D
PRWTOKLISIA	PLACE OF HONOR	732C
PRWTOKATHEDRIA	PLACE OF HONOR	732C
STOL8	ROBE	778B
PHILEW 1B	LOVE LIKE	867A
47 KATESTHIW 2	DESTROY	423B
KRIMA 4B	VERDICT	451D
LAMBANW 2	RECEIVE	466C
MAKROS 1	LONG	489C
OIKIA 1A	HOUSE	560A
PERISSOTEROS 1	GREATER	657B
PROSEUCHOMAI	PRAY	721A

47 PROPHASIS 2	ACTUAL MOTIVE	730A
CH8RA	THE WIDOW	889D

LUKE 21

1 ANABLEPW 1	LOOK UP	50C
BALLW 2B	PUT	130D
GAZOPHULAKEION	TREASURY	148D
PLOUSIOS 1	RICH	679C
2 EKEI 2	THERE	238D
LEPTOS 2	SMALL COPPER COIN	473B
PENICHROS	POOR	648C
2F CH8RA	THE WIDOW	889D
3 AL8THWS 1	TRULY	36D
LEGW 15	SAY	470A
HOUTOS 2B	THIS	602A
POLUS 112C	MANY	696A
PTWCHOS 1A	BEGGING POOR	735C
3F BALLW 2B	PUT	130D
4 HAPAS 1	WHOLE	81A
HAPAS 2	ALL	81A
BALLW 2B	PUT	130D
BIOS 3	LIFE	141B
GAR 1A	FOR	151A
DWRON 2	GIFT	210C
ECHW 12A	HAVE	332B
PERISSEUW 1Aβ	BE LEFT OVER	656C
HUSTER8MA 1	NEED	857A
5 ANATHEMA 1	VOTIVE OFFERING	53D
ANATH8MA	VOTIVE OFFERING	54B
HIERON 2	TEMPLE	373A
KALOS 1	BEAUTIFUL	401B
KOSMEW 2Aβ	DECORATE	446A
LEGW 14	SAY	469D
LITHOS 1B	STONE	475B
TIS, TI 1A6	ANY ONE	828A
6 APHI8MI 3A	LEAVE	125D
ERCHOMAI 11Bα	COME	311B
H8MERA 4B	TIME	348B
THEWREW 1	OBSERVE	360C
KATALUW 1A	THROW DOWN	415B
LITHOS 1B	STONE	475B
7 ELEUSIS	COMING	250C
MELLW 1Cα	BE ABOUT TO	502B
OUN 1Cα	THEREFORE	597C
POTE	WHEN	701D
S8MEION 1	SIGN	755B
8 BLEPW 6	SEE	143B
EGGIZW 5B	APPROACH	212D
EGW	I	216B
EPI 113	ON	287D
ERCHOMAI 11Aθ	COME	311B
KAIROS 4	TIME	396B
M8 B1B	NOT	519A
ONOMA 14Cε	NAME	576C
OPISW 2Aβ	AFTER	578D
PLANAW 2C6	DECEIVE	671C
POREUW 1	PROCEED	699D
9 AKATASTASIA 2	DISTURBANCE	29C
ALLA 2	BUT, YET	37D
DEI 1	IT IS NECESSARY	171A
POLEMOS 1A	ARMED CONFLICT	691D
PTOEW	FRIGHTEN	734D

9 TELOS IB	END 819A	20 HOTAN IB	WHEN 592B
10 BASILEIA 2	KINGDOM 134C	STRATOPEDON	CAMP 778C
EGEIRW 2D	RISE 214A	TOTE 2	AT THAT TIME 831D
ETHNOS I	NATION 217B	21 MESOS 2	THE MIDDLE 508D
TOTE 2	AT THAT TIME 831D	OROS	MOUNTAIN 586C
11 KATA III A	ALONG 407A	PHEUGW I	FLEE 863C
LIMOS 2	FAMINE 476B	CHWRA 4	COUNTRY 897D
LOIMOS I	PESTILENCE 480D	22 EKDIK8SIS	VENGEANCE 238B
OURANOS 2A	HEAVEN 599B	H8MERA 4B	TIME 348B
SEISMOS	SHAKING 753D	PIMPL8MI IBα	FILL 663D
S8MEION 2C	SIGN 755D	PL8ROW 4A	MAKE FULL 677C
TOPOS ID	PLACE 830B	23 ANAGK8 2	DISTRESS 52B
PHOB8TRON	HORROR 871B	GAST8R 2	WOMB 152A
11A MEGAS 2AY	GREAT 499A	ECHW I2J	HAVE 333C
11B MEGAS 2AY	GREAT 499A	TH8LAZW I	GIVE SUCK 361A
11B TE 3A	AND 815B	LAOS 3A	PEOPLE 468A
12 BASILEUS I	KING 135C	MEGAS 2AY	GREAT 499A
DIWKW 2	PERSECUTE 200B	ORG8 2B	ANGER 583A
HENEKA	BECAUSE OF 264B	OUAI IA	WOE 595C
EPI IIIIAβ	ON 288A	24 AICHMALWTIZW I	CAPTURE 26B
EPI IIIIAY	ON 288B	ACHRI 2A	UNTIL 128C
EPIBALLW IB	LAY ON 289D	EIMI II4BY	TO BE 223A
H8GEMWN 2	GOVERNORS 344A	KAIROS 3	TIME 396A
ONOMA I4C6	NAME 576C	MACHAIRA I	SWORD 497C
PARADIDWMI IB	GIVE OVER 620B	PATEW IAY	TRAMPLE 640C
PRO 2	BEFORE 708C	PIPTW IBα	FALL 665B
SUNAGWG8 2A	790C	PL8ROW 5	MAKE FULL 677D
PLACE OF ASSEMBLY		ROMPHAIA	SWORD 744C
PHULAK8 3	GUARD 875C	STOMA 2	MOUTH 777D
PHULAK8 3	GUARD 875D	25 APORIA	PERPLEXITY 97A
13 APOBAINW 2	TURN OUT 88A	ASTRON	STAR 118A
MARTURION IA	TESTIMONY 494D	G8 5A	EARTH 156D
14 APOLOGEOMAI	DEFEND ONESELF 95B	H8LIOS	THE SUN 346B
KARDIA IBY	HEART 404D	8CHOS	SOUND 350C
PROMELETAW	PREPARE 715C	8CHEW	SOUND 350C
TITH8MI II8ε	823D	SALOS	ROLLING 748B
MAKE UP (YOUR) MINDS		SEL8N8	MOON 754A
TITH8MI IIIC	PUT 824B	S8MEION 2C	SIGN 755D
15 ANTHIST8MI 2	SET AGAINST 66C	SUNOCH8 2	DISTRESS 799C
ANTEIPON	SAY AGAINST 72D	26 APO V3	WITH 87B
ANTIKEIMAI	BE OPPOSED 73D	APOPSUCHW	FAINT 101D
KAI IID	AND 392D	DUNAMIS 5	RESOURCES 207B
SOPHIA 2	WISDOM 767A	EPERCHOMAI IBβ	COME 284D
STOMA IA	MOUTH 777C	OIKOUMEN8 IA	THE WORLD 564A
16 GONEUS	PARENTS 164B	OURANOS IC	HEAVEN 598D
EK 4AY	FROM 235B	PROSDOKIA	EXPECTATION 719D
THANATOW I	PUT TO DEATH 352B	SALEUW I	SHAKE 747D
PARADIDWMI IB	GIVE OVER 619D	PHOBOS 2Aα	FEAR 871C
SUGGEN8S	RELATED 780B	27 DOXA IA	GLORY 202D
PHILOS 2Aα	LOVING 868D	ERCHOMAI IIAη	COME 311A
17 EIMI II4BY	TO BE 223A	META AIII2	WITH 511A
MISEW 3	HATE 524D	NEPHEL8	CLOUD 538D
ONOMA I4Cα	NAME 575C	HORAW IAα	SEE 581C
18 APOLLUMI 2B	BE LOST 95A	TOTE 2	AT THAT TIME 831D
EK 2	AWAY FROM 233D	HUIOS 2C	SON 843A
THRIX 2	HAIR 364C	28 ANAKUPTW 2	STAND ERECT 56B
KEPHAL8 IA	HEAD 431B	APOLUTRWSIS 2A	REDEMPTION 95D
19 KTAOMAI I	GET 456A	ARCHW 2Aα	BEGIN 113A
HUPOMON8 I	PATIENCE 854A	DIOTI I	BECAUSE 198C
PSUCH8 IC	SOUL LIFE 902B	EGGIZW 5B	APPROACH 212D
20 EGGIZW 5B	APPROACH 212D	EPAIRW I	LIFT UP 281C
ER8MWSIS	DEVASTATION 309B	KEPHAL8 IA	HEAD 431B
KUKLOW I	SURROUND 457D	29 PARABOL8 2	PARABLE 617C

29 SUK8	FIG TREE	783D
30 APO V5	OF	87D
HEAUTOU 1A	ONESELF	211B
EGGUS 2A	NEAR	213B
8D8 1A	ALREADY	344D
THEROS	SUMMER	360B
PROBALLW 2	PUT OUT	709D
30F GINWSKW 3C	UNDERSTAND	160B
31 BASILEIA 3G	KINGDOM	135B
GINWSKW 6C	KNOW	160D
EGGUS 2A	NEAR	213B
KAI 1I1	ALSO	394B
32 GENEA 2	GENERATION	153B
GENEA 1	CLAN	153B
HEWS 11B	UNTIL	334D
PARERCHOMAI 1Bα	PASS AWAY	631C
33 LOGOS 1A6	WORD	478D
M8 D2	NOT	519C
OURANOS 1Aα	HEAVEN	598B
33A PARERCHOMAI 1Bα		631C
PASS AWAY		
33B PARERCHOMAI 1Bα		631C
PASS AWAY		
34 AIPHNIDIOS	SUDDEN	26A
BAREW	BURDEN	133A
BIWTIKOS	BELONGING TO LIFE	141C
EPI 1111Bγ	ON	289A
EPHIST8MI 1B	STAND BY	331A
H8MERA 33β	DAY	348A
KAI 12E	AND	393C
KARDIA 1B6	HEART	405A
KRAIPAL8	CAROUSING	449A
METH8	DRUNKENNESS	500A
MERIMNA	ANXIETY	506A
M8POTE 2Aα	(NEG PARTICLE)	521A
PROSECHW 1B	PAY ATTENTION TO	721D
35 G8 5B	EARTH	156D
EPEISERCHOMAI		284B
RUSH IN SUDDENLY		
EPI 1111Bγ	ON	289A
KATH8MAI 1B	RESIDE	390C
PAGIS 1	TRAP	607A
PROSWPON 1E	FACE	729A
HWS 112	SO	906A
35B EPI 1111Aζ	ON	288C
36 AGRUPNEW 1	BE AWAKE	14A
DEOMAI 4	ASK	174B
EKPHEUGW 2Bβ	RUN AWAY	246B
EMPROSTHEN 2B	IN FRONT	256C
HINA 1Dγ	IN ORDER THAT	378B
HIST8MI 111B	STAND	383B
KAIROS 1	TIME	395C
KATAXIOW 1	CONSIDER WORTHY	416C
KATISCHUW 1	BE STRONG	425B
PAS 1Aα	EVERY EACH	636C
PAS 1Dβ	ALL	637D
HUIOS 2C	SON	843A
37 AULIZOMAI 1	SPEND THE NIGHT	121A
ELAIWN	OLIVE GROVE	247C
H8MERA 1A	DAY	346D
HIERON 2	TEMPLE	373A
KALEW 1Aγ	CALL	400A
NUX 1D	NIGHT	549A

37 OROS	MOUNTAIN	586B
38 AKOUW 1C	HEAR	31D
LAOS 1A	PEOPLE	467D
ORTHRIZW	GET UP VERY EARLY	584B

LUKE 22

1 AZUMOS 1B	UNLEAVENED BREAD	19C
EGGIZW 5B	APPROACH	212D
HEORT8	FESTIVAL	279D
*PASCHA 1	THE PASSOVER	639A
2 ANAIREW 1A	DO AWAY WITH	54C
ARCHIEREUS 1B	HIGH PRIEST	112C
Z8TEW 1C	INVESTIGATE	339B
HO,H8,TO 118A	THE	554D
PWS 2B	HOW	740C
PHOBEW 1Bα	BE AFRAID	871A
3 ARITHMOS 1	NUMBER	105D
EIMI 1113	TO BE	224B
EISERCHOMAI 1Bβ	COME	232A
IOUDAS 6	JUDAS	380D
ISKARIWTH	ISCARIOT	381D
KALEW 1Aγ	CALL	400A
*SATAN	ADVERSARY	752B
4 HO,H8,TO 118A	THE	554D
PARADIDWMI 1B	GIVE OVER	620A
PWS 2B	HOW	740C
STRAT8GOS 2	CHIEF MAGISTRATE	778B
SULLALEW	TALK	784B
5 ARGURION 2B	MONEY	104B
DIDWMI 4	GIVE	192C
SUNTITH8MI 2Aα	AGREE	800C
CHAIRW 1	REJOICE	882A
6 ATER	WITHOUT	119C
EXOMOLOGEW 1	PROMISE	276C
Z8TEW 2A	SEEK	339C
HO,H8,TO 114Bβ	THE	553D
OCHLOS 1	CROWD	605C
PARADIDWMI 1B	GIVE OVER	620A
7 AZUMOS 1B	UNLEAVENED BREAD	19C
DEI 3	IT IS NECESSARY	171B
DEI 6A	IT IS NECESSARY	171C
ERCHOMAI 11Bα	COME	311B
H8MERA 2	DAY	347C
THUW 2	SACRIFICE	367D
THUW 4	CELEBRATE	367D
LOGOS 1Aζ	MATTER	479A
PASCHA 2	THE PASCHAL LAMB	639A
8 ESTHIW 1A	EAT	312D
HETOIMAZW 1	PREPARE	316B
PASCHA 3	PASSOVER MEAL	639A
9 HETOIMAZW 1	PREPARE	316B
THELW 1	WISH	355C
POU 1A	WHERE	702D
9F LOGOS 1Aζ	MATTER	479A
10 AKOLOUTHEW 1	FOLLOW	30C
BASTAZW 2A	CARRY	136D
EISERCHOMAI 1Aβ	COME	231D
EISPOREUOMAI 1	GO	232D
IDOU 1A	BEHOLD	371C
KERAMION	JAR	430A
OIKIA 1A	HOUSE	559D
SUNANTAW 1	MEET	792B

10	HUDWR I	WATER	840C
	11 DIDASKALOS	TEACHER	190D
	ESTHIW IA	EAT	312D
	KATALUMA	GUEST ROOM	415B
	OIKIA IA	HOUSE	560C
	OIKODESPOT8S		560C
	MASTER OF THE HOUSE		
	HOPOU IAY	WHERE	579D
	PASCHA 2	THE PASCHAL LAMB	639A
	POU IA	WHERE	702D
12	ANAGAION	ROOM UPSTAIRS	50D
	DEIKNUMI IA	SHOW	171D
	HETOIMAZW I	PREPARE	316B
	KAKEINOS IA	AND HE	397C
	MEGAS IB	LARGE	498C
	STRWNNUW	SPREAD	779B
13	EIPON 3E	FORETELL	225D
	HETOIMAZW I	PREPARE	316B
	HEURISKW ICY	FIND	325C
	PASCHA 3	PASSOVER MEAL	639A
14	ANAPIPTW I	RECLINE	59A
	APOSTOLOS 3	APOSTLES	99B
	GINOMAI IIBY	COME ABOUT	157C
	HWRA 3	TIME OF DAY	905A
15	EPITHUMEW	DESIRE	293B
	EPITHUMIA 2	DESIRE	293B
	ESTHIW IA	EAT	312D
	PASCHA 2	THE PASCHAL LAMB	639A
	PASCHA I	THE PASSOVER	639A
	PASCHW 3Aα	SUFFER	639C
	PRO 2	BEFORE	708D
16	BASILEIA 3G	KINGDOM	135B
	HEWS IIIBβ	UNTIL	335C
	M8 DIA	NOT	519B
	OUKETI I	NO LONGER	597A
	PL8ROW 4A	MAKE FULL	677C
17	DECHOMAI 2	GRASP	176C
	DIAMERIZW IB	DIVIDE	185D
	EUCHARISTEW 2	GIVE THANKS	328C
	POT8RION I	CUP	702A
18	AMPELOS I	VINE	46A
	APO I6	FROM	86B
	BASILEIA 3G	KINGDOM	135B
	GEN8MA	PRODUCT	154B
	ERCHOMAI I2B	COME	311C
	HEWS IIIBβ	UNTIL	335C
	HEWS IIIBα	UNTIL	335C
	PINW I	DRINK	664B
18F	LOGOS IAζ	MATTER	479A
19	ANAMN8SIS	REMINDER	57C
	ARTOS IC	BREAD	110B
	DIDWMI 2	GIVE	192C
	DIDWMI 6	GIVE	192D
	EIMI II3	TO BE	223A
	EIS 4F	(PURPOSE)	228D
	EMOS IAβ	MY	255A
	EUCHARISTEW 2	GIVE THANKS	328C
	KLAW	BREAK	434D
	HOUTOS IAα	THIS	600D
	SWMA IB	BODY	807B
19F	HUPER IAε	IN BEHALF OF	846C
20	HAIMA 2B	BLOOD	22C
	DEIPNEW	EAT	172B
20	DIATH8K8 2	COVENANT	182B
	EKCHEW I	POUR OUT	246D
	KAINOS 3B	NEW	395B
	HWSAUTWS	SIMILARLY	907D
20A	POT8RION I	CUP	702A
20B	POT8RION I	CUP	702A
21	PARADIDWMI IB	GIVE OVER	620A
	PL8N IB	BUT	675B
	TRAPEZA 2	TABLE	832A
22	KATA II5Aα	ACCORDING TO	408A
	MEN IAY	(PARTICLE)	504A
	HORIZW IAα	DETERMINE	584D
	OUAI IA	WOE	595C
	PARADIDWMI IB	GIVE OVER	620A
	PL8N IA	BUT	675B
	POREUW 2A	PROCEED	699B
	HUIOS 2C	SON	843A
23	ARA 2	THEN	103B
	AUTOS 2	THEY	122D
	MELLW ICβ	BE ABOUT TO	502B
	PRASSW IA	DO	705A
	SUZ8TEW 2	DISCUSS	783B
23F	HO,H8,TO II8A	THE	554D
24	GINOMAI IIBβ	COME ABOUT	157B
	MEGAS 2Bα	GREAT	499B
	PHILON(E)IKIA 2	DISPUTE	868C
25	BASILEUS I	KING	135C
	ETHNOS I	NATION	217B
	EXOUSIAZW	ONE IN AUTHORITY	278C
	EUERGET8S	BENEFACTOR	320B
	KALEW IAβ	CALL	399D
	KURIEUW I	RULE	459C
26	GINOMAI III	BE	159B
	H8GEOMAI I	LEAD	344A
	H8GEOMAI I	LEAD	344B
	MEGAS 2Bα	GREAT	499B
	NEOS 2Bβ	NOVICE	538B
	HOUTW IB	THUS	602C
26A	HWS II3B	SO	906A
26B	HWS II3B	SO	906A
26F	DIAKONEW I WAIT ON SOMEONE		183A
26F	MEGAS 2Bα	GREAT	499B
27	ANAKEIMAI 2	BE AT TABLE	55C
	EIMI II9B	TO BE	224A
	MESOS 2	THE MIDDLE	509A
	TIS, TI IAY	WHICH	826D
28	DIAMENW	REMAIN	185D
	PEIRASMOS 2B	TEST	646D
29	BASILEIA I	KINGDOM	134C
	DIATITH8MI 2	ASSIGN	189A
	KAGW 3B	I	387A
	PAT8R 3Dα	FATHER	641D
30	BASILEIA 3G	KINGDOM	135B
	EPI IIAY	ON	285D
	ESTHIW IC	EAT	313A
	THRONOS ID	THRONE	365A
	ISRA8L 2	ISRAEL	382C
	KRINW 4Bβ	JUDGE	453B
	TRAPEZA 2	TABLE	832A
	PHUL8 I	TRIBE	876D
31	EXAITEW I	ASK FOR	271C
	HO,H8,TO II4Bζ	THE	554A
	SATAN	ADVERSARY	752B

31	SINIAZW	SIFT 759B	41	HWSEI 2	AS 908A
	SITOS	WHEAT 759D	42	BOULOMAI 2B	DESIRE 146A
	HWS II2	SO 906A		GINOMAI I2A	CREATED 157C
32	DEOMAI 4	ASK 174B		EI IV	IF 218C
	EKLEIPW	FAIL 242A		THEL8MA IA	WILL 354D
	EPISTREPHW IBβ	TURN 301B		PARAPHERW 2C	TAKE AWAY 628D
	HINA IIIAγ	IN ORDER THAT 378B		PAT8R 3Dα	FATHER 641D
	PISTIS 2Dα	FAITH 669A		PL8N IB	BUT 675B
	POTE I	ONCE 701D		POT8RION 2	CUP 702B
	ST8RIZW 2	ESTABLISH 775D	43	AGGELOS 2A	ANGEL 7C
33	EIS 4A	INTO 228B		ENISCHUW 2	STRENGTHEN 266B
	HETOIMOS 2	READY 316D		HORAW IAδ	SEE 582A
	THANATOS IA	DEATH 351C		OURANOS 2C	HEAVEN 599C
	POREUW I	PROCEED 699A	44	AGWNIA	AGONY 15A
	POREUW 2A	PROCEED 699B		HAIMA IA	BLOOD 22A
	PHULAK8 3	GUARD 875C		G8 2	GROUND 156C
34	ALEKTWR	COCK 34D		GINOMAI III	BE 159B
	APARNEOMAI	DENY 80B		GINOMAI II4A	BE 159C
	HEWS IIB	UNTIL 334D		EKTENWS	FERVENTLY 245A
	M8 ΔIIIA	NOT 517D		THROMBOS	DROP 364D
	PRIN IA	BEFORE 708A		HIDRWS	SWEAT 372A
	S8MERON	TODAY 756C		KATABAINW IB	COME DOWN 409D
	TRIS	THRICE 834A		HWSEI I	AS 907D
	PHWNEW IA	PRODUCE A SOUND 878B	45	ANIST8MI 2A	RISE 69C
35	ATER	WITHOUT 119C		APO V3	WITH 87B
	M8 CI	NOT 519A		KOIMAW I	SLEEP 438C
	P8RA	KNAPSACK 662B		LUP8	GRIEF 483B
	HUPOD8MA	SANDAL 852B		PROSEUCH8 I	PRAYER 720C
	HUSTEREW IB	TO MISS 856D	46	EISERCHOMAI 2A	COME 232B
35F	BALLANTION	PURSE 130B		HINA IIIAγ	IN ORDER THAT 378B
36	AGORAZW I	BUY 12C		KATHEUDW I	SLEEP 389C
	AIRW 2	LIFT UP 24A		PEIRASMOS 2B	TEST 646C
	ALLA 2	BUT, YET 37D	47	EGGIZW I	APPROACH 212C
	HIMATION 2	GARMENT 377A		HEIS 3A	SOMEONE 230D
	MACHAIRA I	SWORD 497B		IDOU 2	THERE IS 371D
	NUN IC	NOW 547D		ISKARIWTH	ISCARIOT 381D
	P8RA	KNAPSACK 662B		LALEW 2Aγ	SPEAK 464B
	PWLEW	SELL 739A		LEGW II3	CALL 471B
37	ANOMOS 3	LAWLESS 71C		PROERCHOMAI 2	GO FORWARD 712B
	GAR IB	FOR 151A		PHILEW 2	LOVE LIKE 867A
	ECHW I2F	HAVE 333B	47F	IOUDAS 6	JUDAS 380D
	LOGIZOMAI IB	CONSIDER 477B	48	PARADIDWMI IB	GIVE OVER 620A
	META AI	WITH 509C		HUIOS 2C	SON 843A
	HO,H8,TO II8A	THE 554D		PHIL8MA	A KISS 867B
	TELEW 2	PERFORM 818D	49	EI VI	IF 218D
	TELOS IA	END 819A		EIMI I4	TO BE 222C
38	IDOU 2	THERE IS 371D		EN IIIIA	BY 260A
	HIKANOS IC	SUFFICIENT 375A		MACHAIRA I	SWORD 497C
	MACHAIRA I	SWORD 497B		HO,H8,TO II5	THE 554B
39	ETHOS I	HABIT 217C		PATASSW IB	STRIKE 640A
	ELAIA I	OLIVE TREE 247B		PERI 2A6	ABOUT 651A
	OROS	MOUNTAIN 586B	50	APHAIREW I	CUT OFF 123D
40	GINOMAI I4Cγ	COME, GO 159A		DEXIOS I	RIGHT 173C
	EISERCHOMAI 2A	COME 232B		HEIS 3C	SOMEONE 231A
	EPI IIAβ	ON 285D		OUS I	EAR 600A
	PEIRASMOS 2B	TEST 646C		PATASSW IB	STRIKE 640A
	TOPOS IC	PLACE 830B	51	APOKATHIST8MI I	RESTORE 91B
41	APOSPAW 3	WITHDRAW 97C		HAPTW 2B	TOUCH 102C
	BOL8	THROW 144B		EAW 2	LET 212A
	GONU	KNEE 164B		HEWS II4	AS MANY AS 336A
	LITHOS IA	STONE 475B		IAOMAI I	HEAL 369A
	PROSEUCHOMAI	PRAY 721A		WTION	THE EAR 908D
	TITH8MI II8α	PUT 823D	52	EPI IIIIA6	TO 288B

52	HIERON 2	TEMPLE	373A
	L8ST8S 2	REVOLUTIONARY	474C
	META AIII3	WITH	511B
	XULON 2B	THE POLE	551B
	*PARAGINOMAI 1	COME	618D
	PRESBUTEROS 2AB	OLDER	706D
	STRAT8GOS 2	CHIEF MAGISTRATE	778B
53	EKTEINW 1	STRETCH OUT	244D
	EXOUSIA 4B	AUTHORITY	278B
	EPI IIIIA6	TO	288B
	H8MERA 2	DAY	347B
	HIERON 2	TEMPLE	373A
	KATA II2C	EVERY	407C
	HOUTOS 1Aη	THIS	601B
	SKOTOS 2B	DARKNESS	765B
	HWRA 3	TIME OF DAY	905A
54	AGW 2	LEAD AWAY	148
	EISAGW	BRING	231C
	MAKROTHEN	FROM FAR AWAY	489A
	OIKIA 1A	HOUSE	559D
	SULLAMBANW 1Aα	SEIZE	784B
55	HAPTW 1	KINDLE	102B
	AUL8 1	COURTYARD	120D
	KATH8MAI 2	SIT DOWN	390C
	MESOS 1	AMONG	508C
	PERIAPTW	KINDLE	651C
	PERIKATHIZW	SIT AROUND	653C
	PUR 1A	FIRE	737B
	PURA	A FIRE	738A
	SUGKATHIZW 2		780D
		CAUSE TO SIT DOWN WITH	
55A	MESOS 2	THE MIDDLE	508D
56	ATENIZW	LOOK INTENTLY AT	119C
	EIMI IIII0	TO BE	224D
	KATH8MAI 1Aα	SIT	390B
	PAIDISK8	MAID	609B
	PROS III7	TOWARD	718A
	SUN 1C	WITH	789D
	PHWS 1Bα	LIGHT	879D
57	ARNEOMAI 3A	DENY	107C
	GUN8 1	WOMAN	167C
	OIDA 2	KNOW	558D
58	ANTHRWPOS 1AY	MAN	67C
	BRACHUS 2	SHORT	146D
	EIMI III3	TO BE	224B
	EK 4A6	FROM	235B
	HETEROS 1B6	ANOTHER	315B
	META BII3	AFTER	511C
	SU 1C	YOU	779D
59	AL8THEIA 3	REALITY	35D
	ALLOS 1D	OTHER	39C
	GALILAIOS	GALILEAN	149D
	DIIST8MI 1	GO AWAY	194B
	DIISCHURIZOMAI	INSIST	194C
	META AIIICα	WITH	510A
	HWRA 2Aα	TIME OF DAY	904C
	HWSEI 2	AS	907D
60	ANTHRWPOS 1AY	MAN	67C
	LALEW 2AY	SPEAK	464B
	LEGW I2B	SAY	469D
	OIDA 4	KNOW	559A
	PARACHR8MA	AT ONCE	629B
60F	ALEKTWR	COCK	34D

60F	PHWNEW 1A	PRODUCE A SOUND	878B
61	APARNEOMAI	DENY	80B
	EMBLEPW 1	LOOK AT	254A
	PRIN 1B	BEFORE	708A
	R8MA 1	WORD	742D
	STREPHW 2Aα	TURN	778D
	TRIS	THRICE	834A
	HUPOMIMN8SKW 2	REMIND	854A
	HWS IV4	WHEN	907B
62	EXERCHOMAI 1AB	GO OUT	274A
	EXW 1B	OUTSIDE	279A
	KLAIW 1	WEEP	434A
	PIKRWS	BITTERLY	663C
63	AN8R 1	MAN	66A
	DERW	BEAT	174D
	EMPAIZW 1	RIDICULE	255B
	SUNECHW 4	HOLD IN CUSTODY	796D
64	PAIW 1	STRIKE	610B
	PERIKALUPTW	COVER	653C
	PROPH8TEUW 2	PROPHESY	730C
	TUPTW 1	STRIKE	838A
65	BLASPH8MEW 2B6	BLASPHEME	142B
	EIS 4Cα	AGAINST	228B
	HETEROS 1BB	ANOTHER	315B
	LEGW I4	SAY	469D
	POLUS IIAα	MANY	694B
66	ARCHIEREUS 1B	HIGH PRIEST	112C
	GINOMAI IIBγ	COME ABOUT	157B
	H8MERA 1A	DAY	346C
	LAOS 3A	PEOPLE	468A
	PRESBUTERION 1		706B
		COUNCIL OF ELDERS	
	SUNAGW 2	GATHER	790A
	*SUNEDRION 2	SANHEDRIN	794A
	TE 3A	AND	815B
	HWS IV1A	WHEN	907A
67	EAN 11B	IF	210B
	EIPON 1	SAY	225C
	PISTEUW 1D	BELIEVE	666D
	CHRISTOS 1	ANOINTED ONE	895B
68	EAN 11B	IF	210B
	ERWTAW 1	ASK	311D
69	DEXIOS 2B	RIGHT	174A
	KATH8MAI 1Aα	SIT	390B
	NUN 3B	NOW	548B
	HUIOS 2C	SON	843A
70	EIMI II5	TO BE	223C
	LEGW II8B	SAY	469C
	LEGW II1E	DECLARE	471A
	OUN 1Cα	THEREFORE	597B
	PH8MI 1Bα	SAY	864A
71	AKOUW 1BB	HEAR	31C
	APO V4	FROM	87C
	ETI 1BB	STILL	316A
	MARTURIA 2A	TESTIMONY	494C
	STOMA 1A	MOUTH	777B
	CHREIA 1	NEED	893B

LUKE 23

1	HAPAS 1	WHOLE	81A
	EPI IIIIAγ	ON	288B
	PL8THOS 2B8	QUANTITY	674C

1FF PILATOS	PILATE	663C
2 APOSTREPHW 1AB	TURN AWAY	99D
DIASTREPHW 2	MISLEAD	188A
HEURISKW 2	FIND	325D
KAISAR	EMPEROR	396C
KATALUW 1C	ANNUL	415C
KAT8GOREW 1A	BRING CHARGES	424B
KWLUW 2	HINDER	462C
PHOROS	TAX	872D
CHRISTOS 1	ANOINTED ONE	895B
2B LEGW 11BB	SAY	469C
2B LEGW 11IE	DECLARE	471A
3 APOKRINOMAI 2	BEGIN	93A
BASILEUS 2A	KING	135D
LEGW 111E	DECLARE	471A
SU 1A	YOU	779D
PH8MI 1Ba	SAY	864A
4 AITIOS 2	GUILT	26A
HEURISKW 1Ca	FIND	325C
HO,H8,TO 111H	THE	553B
5 ANASEIW	INCITE	59C
ARCHW 2C	BEGIN	113B
EPISCHUW	GROW STRONG	302A
HEWS 112B	AS FAR AS	335D
IOUDAIA 2	JUDAEA	379D
KATA 11C	DOWN	406C
HWDE 1	HERE	903C
6 ANTHRWPOS 4B	MAN	68D
GALILAICS	GALILEAN	149D
EPERWTAW 1A	ASK	285A
7 ANAPEMPW 1B	SEND	58D
EIMI 1113	TO BE	224B
EK 3B	FROM	234B
EXOUSIA 4B	AUTHORITY	278B
EPIGINWSKW 2B	KNOW	291A
PROS 111IB	TOWARD	716D
7-15 H8RWD8S 2	HEROD	349B
8 GINOMAI 12A	COME ABOUT	157C
EIDON 6	VISIT	220B
EIMI 114E	TO BE	223B
EK 5A	FROM	235C
ELPIZW 2	HOPE	252A
THELW 1	WISH	355C
HIKANOS 1B	SUFFICIENT	375A
HIKANOS 1C	SUFFICIENT	375B
LIAN 1	VERY	474C
S8MEION 2A	SIGN	755D
HUPO 1B	BY	851A
CHAIRW 1	REJOICE	881D
CHRONOS	TIME	896C
9 APOKRINOMAI 1	ANSWER	92D
HIKANOS 1A	SUFFICIENT	375A
LOGOS 1A6	WORD	478D
10 ARCHIEREUS 1B	HIGH PRIEST	112C
EUTONWS	POWERFULLY	327C
HIST8MI 112A	STAND	383B
KAT8GOREW 1A	BRING CHARGES	424B
11 ANAPEMPW 2	SEND	58D
EMPA1ZW 1	RIDICULE	255B
EXOUTHENEW 3	REJECT	277C
ESTH8S	CLOTHING	312B
LAMPROS 3	BRIGHT	467A
PERIBALLW 18d	THROW AROUND	651D
11 STRATEUMA	ARMY	778A
SUN 4B	WITH	789D
12 A8DIA	ENMITY	19D
AUTOS 1H	EVEN	122D
GINOMAI 14A	BECOME	158C
EIMI 1114	TO BE	224B
ECHTHRA	ENMITY	331C
META A113B	WITH	510D
PROS 1114A	TOWARD	717C
PROUPARCHW	EXIST BEFORE	729D
TE 3A	AND	815C
PHILOS 2Aa	LOVING	868D
13 ARCHIEREUS 1B	HIGH PRIEST	112B
ARCHWN 2A	AUTHORITIES	113C
LAOS 1Ca	PEOPLE	467D
PALIN 2	AGAIN	611C
SUGKALEW 2	CALL TOGETHER	780D
14 AITIOS 2	GUILT	26A
ANAKRINW 1B	QUESTION	56A
ANTHRWPOS 4B	MAN	68D
APOSTREPHW 1AB	TURN AWAY	99D
ENWPION 2A	BEFORE	270B
KATA 12BB	DOWN	406D
KAT8GOREW 1A	BRING CHARGES	424C
HO,H8,TO 111H	THE	553B
HOS,H8,HO 14A	(REL PRON)	587D
PROSPHERW 1A	BRING (TO)	727A
HWS 1112	SO	906D
15 ALLA 3	BUT, YET	38A
ANAPEMPW 2	SEND	58D
AXIOS 1B	WORTHY	77C
THANATOS 1Ba	DEATH	351C
OUDE 2	AND NOT	596A
PRASSW 1A	DO	705B
PROS 1111B	TOWARD	716D
16 PAIDEUW 2BY	WHIP	609A
16-25 APOLUW 1	SET FREE	96A
17 ANAGK8 1	NECESSITY	52A
HEORT8	FESTIVAL	280A
18 AIRW 4	TAKE AWAY	24A
ANAKRAZW	CRY OUT	56A
BARABBAS 1	BARABBAS	132C
PAMPL8THEI	ALL TOGETHER	612A
19 GINOMAI 11BB	COME ABOUT	157B
EIMI 114C	TO BE	223B
HOSTIS 3	WHOEVER	591B
STASIS 2	UPRISING	772A
PHONOS	MURDER	872C
PHULAK8 3	GUARD	875D
20 PALIN 2	AGAIN	611C
*PROSPHWNEW 1	CALL OUT	727D
21 EPIPHWNEW	CRY OUT	304C
STAUROW 1	CRUCIFY	773A
22 AITIOS 2	GUILT	26A
GAR 1F	WHAT	151C
HEURISKW 1Ca	FIND	325C
THANATOS 1Ba	DEATH	351C
KAKOS 1C	EVIL	398D
PAIDEUW 2BY	WHIP	609A
POIEW 11B6	DO	687D
TRITOS 3	THIRD	834C
23 AITEW	ASK	25C
EPIKEIMAI 2B	BE URGENT	294C

23	KATISCHUW I	BE STRONG	425B
	MEGAS 2AY	GREAT	498D
	STAUROW I	CRUCIFY	773A
23A	PHWN8 2C	VOICE	879A
23B	PHWN8 2C	VOICE	879A
24	AIT8MA	REQUEST	25C
	GINOMAI I2A	CREATED	157C
	EPIKRINW	DECIDE	295A
25	DIA BIII	BECAUSE OF	180A
	THEL8MA 2A	WILL	355A
	PARADIDWMI IB	GIVE OVER	620A
	STASIS 2	UPRISING	772A
	PHONOS	MURDER	872C
	PHULAK8 3	GUARD	875D
26	AGROS 2	THE COUNTRY	13D
	APAGW 2C	LEAD AWAY	78D
	EPILAMBANOMAI I	GRASP	295A
	EPITITH8MI IAα	PUT UPON	302D
	KUR8NAIOS	CYRENIAN	459A
	OPISTHEN 2A	FROM BEHIND	578B
	SIMWN 4	SIMON	758D
	STAUROS I	THE CROSS	772C
	TIS, TI 2Aβ	ANY ONE	828B
	PHERW IA	BEAR	862D
	HWS IVIA	WHEN	907A
27	THR8NEW 2	MOURN	363D
	*KOPTW 2	BEAT	445A
	LAOS IA	PEOPLE	467D
	PL8THOS 2Bα	QUANTITY	674C
	POLUS IIBα	MANY	694D
28	THUGAT8R 2D	DAUGHTER	365C
	M8 AIII3B	NOT	518D
	PL8N IB	BUT	675B
	STREPHW 2Aα	TURN	779A
28A	*KLAIW I	WEEP	434A
28B	KLAIW I	WEEP	434A
29	GENNAW 2	BEAR	154D
	ERCHOMAI IIBα	COME	311B
	H8MERA 4B	TIME	348B
	KOILIA 2	BELLY	438B
	MAKARIOS IA	BLESSED	487C
	MASTOS 2	BREAST	496B
	STEIRA	BARREN	773C
	TREPHW I	FEED	833B
30	BOUNOS	HILL	146A
	EPI IIIIAβ	ON	288A
	KALUPTW I	COVER	402A
	OROS	MOUNTAIN	586A
	PIPTW IA	FALL	665A
31	GINOMAI I2B	BECOME	157D
	EN IB	IN	258A
	X8ROS I	ORY	550D
	XULON 3	TREE	551C
	POIEW IIDγ	DO	688D
	HUGROS	MOIST	840B
32	AGW 2	LEAD AWAY	14B
	ANAIREW IA	DO AWAY WITH	54C
	HETEROS IBβ	ANOTHER	315B
	SUN 2B	WITH	789C
32F	KAKOURGOS	CRIMINAL	399B
33	ARISTEROS	WEAPONS	106B
	DEXIOS 2B	RIGHT	174A
	KALEW IAγ	CALL	400A
33	KRANION	SKULL	449A
	MEN IC	(PARTICLE)	504A
	HOS,H8,HO II2	THIS (ONE)	589B
	STAUROW I	CRUCIFY	773A
	TOPOS IC	PLACE	830B
34	APHI8MI 2	FORGIVE	125C
	BALLW IA	THROW	130B
	DIAMERIZW IB	DIVIDE	185D
	KL8ROS I	LOT	436C
	PAT8R 3Dα	FATHER	641D
35	ALLOS IA	OTHER	39B
	ARCHWN 2A	AUTHORITIES	113C
	EKLEKTOS IA	CHOSEN	242A
	EKMUKT8RIZW	RIDICULE	242D
	THEWREW I	OBSERVE	360C
	HIST8MI II2A	STAND	383B
	MUKT8RIZW	TREAT WITH CONTEMPT	531A
	CHRISTOS I	ANOINTED ONE	895B
35A	SWZW IA	SAVE	805D
35B	SWZW IA	SAVE	805D
36	EMPAIZW I	RIDICULE	255B
	OXOS	WINE VINEGAR	577D
	PROSPHERW IB	BRING (TO)	727A
37	SWZW IA	SAVE	805D
37F	BASILEUS 2A	KING	135D
38	GRAMMA I	LETTER	164C
	HEBRAIKOS	HEBREW	212B
	HELL8NIKOS	GREEK	251C
	EPI IIIAα	ON	286C
	EPIGRAPH8	INSCRIPTION	291C
	RWMAIKOS	ROMAN	745C
39	BLASPH8MEW 2B6	BLASPHEME	142B
	HEIS IAβ	ONE	230A
	KAKOURGOS	CRIMINAL	399B
	KREMANNUMI I	HANG	451A
	SWZW IA	SAVE	805D
	CHRISTOS I	ANOINTED ONE	895B
40	AUTOS 4A	THE SAME	123B
	EIMI III4	TO BE	224B
	EPITIMAW I	REBUKE	303B
	HETEROS IA	OTHER	315A
	KRIMA 4B	VERDICT	451D
	OUDE 3	NOT EVEN	596A
	PH8MI IBα	SAY	864A
	PHOBEW IBα	BE AFRAID	871A
41	AXIOS IB	WORTHY	77C
	APOLAMBANW I	RECEIVE	93D
	DIKAIWS 2	JUSTLY	197C
	HOS,H8,HO I4A	(REL PRON)	587D
41B	PRASSW IA	DO	705B
42	BASILEIA I	KINGDOM	134C
	ELEUSIS	COMING	250C
	ERCHOMAI IIAη	COME	311A
	MIMN8SKOMAI IC	REMEMBER	524B
43	THARSEW	BE CHEERFUL	352C
	LEGW IIID	ASSURE	470D
	PARADEISOS 2	PARADISE	619B
	S8MERON	TODAY	756B
44	GINOMAI IIBα	COME ABOUT	157B
	EIMI I5	TO BE	222C
	HEKTOS	SIXTH	245C
	ENATOS	NINTH	261D
	EPI IIIIAα	ACROSS	287D

44	HEWS IIIA	UNTIL	335A
	KAI I2C	AND	393B
	SKOTOS I	DARKNESS	765A
	HWSEI 2	AS	907D
44A	HWRA 2B	TIME OF DAY	904D
44B	HWRA 2B	TIME OF DAY	904D
45	EKLEIPW	FAIL	242A
	*H8LIOS	THE SUN	346B
	KATAPETASMA	CURTAIN	417B
	MESOS I	IN TWO	508C
	NAOS IA	TEMPLE	535B
	SKOTIZW I	BECOME DARK	764D
	SCHIZW IB	SPLIT	805A
46	EKPNEW	BREATHE OUT	243D
	MEGAS 2AɣY	GREAT	498D
	PARATITH8MI 2Bβ		628C
	PLACE BESIDE		
	PAT8R 3Dα	FATHER	641D
	PNEUMA 2	SPIRIT	680D
	*PHWNEW IB	CRY OUT	878B
	CHEIR 2Aβ	HAND	888D
47	DIKAIOS 4	RIGHTEOUS	195A
	DIKAIOS 3	RIGHTEOUS	195A
	DOXAZW I	PRAISE	203C
	HEKATONTARCH8S	CENTURION	236C
	HO,H8,TO IIIH	THE	553B
	ONTWS I	REALLY	577C
48	EPI IIIIBη	ON	289B
	THEWREW I	OBSERVE	360C
	THEWRIA	SPECTACLE	360D
	METWPON	FOREHEAD	516D
	ST8THOS	CHEST	775B
	SUMPARAGINOMAI I		786D
	COME TOGETHER		
	TUPTW I	STRIKE	838A
49	GNWSTOS IB	ACQUAINTANCE	163C
	HIST8MI II2Bα	BEING	383C
	MAKROTHEN	FROM FAR AWAY	489A
	HORAW IAβ	SEE	581C
	SUNAKOLOUTHEW	FOLLOW	791C
50	AGATHOS IAα	GOOD	2D
	AN8R 4	MAN	66B
	BOULEUT8S	MEMBER OF COUNCIL	145A
	DIKAIOS IB	UPRIGHT	194D
	IDOU 2	THERE IS	371D
	IWS8PH 6	JOSEPH	386C
	ONOMA II	NAME	574A
	HUPARCHW 2	BE	846A
51	HARIMATHAIA	ARIMATHAEA	106A
	AUTOS 3B	(OBLIQUE CASE)	123A
	BOUL8 2A	DECISION	145B
	IOUDAIOS 2C	JEWISH	380B
	POLIS I	CITY	692A
	PRAXIS 4B	ACTING	704D
	PROSDECHOMAI 2B	RECEIVE	719B
	SUGKATATITH8MI	AGREE WITH	781B
52	AITEW	ASK	25B
	PROSERCHOMAI I	APPROACH	720A
	SWMA IA	BODY	806D
53	EIKOSI	TWENTY	221A
	ENTULISSW I	WRAP	269D
	EPITITH8MI IAα	PUT UPON	303A
	KATHAIREW I	LOWER	387B

53	KEIMAI IA	LIE	427D
	KULIW I	ROLL	458B
	LAXEUTOS	A TOMB	467C
	LATOMEW I	HEW	468C
	MN8MA	TOMB	526C
	MOGIS	WITH DIFFICULTY	527C
	HOU IAβ	WHERE	594A
	OU 6A	NO	595A
	OUDEIS 2A	NO ONE	596B
	OUDEPW	NOT YET	596D
	OUPW	NOT YET	598A
	PROSKULIW	ROLL (UP TO)	723D
	SINDWN I	LINEN	759B
	TITH8MI IIAβ	PUT	823C
54	EPIPHWSKW	SHINE FORTH	304D
	PARASKEU8	PREPARATION	627C
	*SABBATON IA	SABBATH	746B
55	THEAOMAI IA	SEE	353D
	KATAKOLOUTHEW	FOLLOW	412D
	MN8MEION 2	TOMB	526C
	SUNERCHOMAI 2	ASSEMBLE	796A
	SWMA IA	BODY	806D
	TITH8MI IIAα	PUT	823C
	HWS I2D	AS	905D
56	ARWMA	SPICES	113D
	ENTOL8 2Aα	COMMAND	268C
	HETOIMAZW I	PREPARE	316B
	H8SUCHAZW I	REST	349D
	MURON	OINTMENT	531D
	SABBATON IA	SABBATH	746B

LUKE 24

I	ARWMA	SPICES	113D
	BATHUS 2	DEEP	130A
	HEIS 4	ONE	231A
	EPI IIIIAɣY	ON	288A
	HETOIMAZW I	PREPARE	316B
	LOGIZOMAI 2	CONSIDER	477B
	MN8MA	TOMB	526B
	ORTHROS	DAWN	584B
	HOS,H8,HO I5A	(REL PRON)	588B
	SABBATON 2B	WEEK	746D
	PHERW ID	BEAR	862D
2	APOKULIW	ROLL AWAY	93D
	LITHOS IE	STONE	475C
	MN8MEION 2	TOMB	526C
3	AUTOS ID	IN PERSON	122C
	HEURISKW IA	FIND	325A
	SWMA IA	BODY	806D
4	AGGELOS 2A	ANGEL	7C
	APOREW	UNCERTAIN	97A
	ASTRAPTW	LIGHTNING FLASHING	117D
	DIAPOREW	BE PERPLEXED	186D
	*ESTH8S	CLOTHING	312B
	EPHIST8MI IA	STAND BY	331A
5	G8 2	GROUND	156C
	EIS IB	NEAR	227C
	EMPHOBOS	AFRAID	257B
	ZAW IAβ	LIVE	336C
	KLINW IA	INCLINE	437C
	META AI	WITH	509D
	NEKROS 2A	DEAD	537A

5	PROSWPON 1B	FACE	728B
6	ETI 1AβB	STILL	315D
	LALEW 2Aδ	SPEAK	464B
	MIMN8SKOMAI 1Aδ	REMEMBER	524B
	HWS IV4	WHEN	907B
7	HAMARTWLOS I	SINNER	43C
	ANIST8MI 2A	RISE	69C
	H8MERA 2	DAY	346D
	PARADIDWMI 1B	GIVE OVER	620A
	STAUROW I	CRUCIFY	773A
	TRITOS I	THIRD	834B
	HUIOS 2C	SON	843A
	CHEIR 2B	HAND	888D
8	MIMN8SKOMAI 1Aα	REMEMBER	524B
9	HENDEKA	ELEVEN	262B
	LOIPOS 2Bα	THE OTHERS	481A
	MN8MEION 2	TOMB	526C
	HUPOSTREPHW	RETURN	855B
10	IAKWBOS 3	JAMES	368C
	IWAN(N)A	JOANNA	385B
	LEGW IIA	SAY	469B
	LOIPOS 2Bα	THE OTHERS	481A
	MAGDAL8N8	MAGDALENE	485B
	MARIA 3	MARY	493A
	MARIA 2	MARY	493A
	HO,H8,TO II7	THE	554C
	SUN IC	WITH	789B
11	APISTEW 1A	DISBELIEVE	84D
	ENWPION 4	BEFORE	270C
	L8ROS	NONSENSE	474B
	PHAINW 2D	APPEAR	859D
	HWSEI I	AS	907D
12	APERCHOMAI 2	GO	84A
	BLEPW 1A	SEE	143A
	HEAUTOU II	ONESELF	211C
	THAUMAZW 1Bα	WONDER	353A
	MN8MEION 2	TOMB	526C
	MONOS 1Aβ	ONLY	529C
	OTHONION	LINEN CLOTH	558A
	PARAKUPTW I	LOOK INTO	624D
	PROS III7	TOWARD	718A
	TRECHW I	RUN	833C
13	APECHW 2	BE DISTANT	84C
	AUTOS IH	EVEN	122D
	DUO IB	TWO	208B
	EK 4Aα	FROM	235B
	HEKATON	ONE HUNDRED	236B
	EMMAOUS	EMMAUS	254C
	HEX8KONTA	SIXTY	275C
	KWM8 I	VILLAGE	462D
	ONOMA II	NAME	574A
	STADION I	STADE	771C
14	HOMILEW	SPEAK	568C
	PAS 1Dβ	ALL	637D
	SUMBAINW	MEET	785A
15	EGGIZW 5A	APPROACH	212D
	HOMILEW	SPEAK	568C
	SUZ8TEW I	DISCUSS	783B
	SUMPOREUOMAI I	GO WITH	787C
16	EPIGINWSKW 1B	KNOW	291A
	KRATEW 2D	HOLD	449D
	M8 AIIIDα	NOT	518A
	HO,H8,TO II4Bδ	THE	554A

17	ANTIBALLW	PLACE AGAINST	73B
	HIST8MI IIIA	STAND	383A
	LOGOS 1Aδ	WORD	478D
	PERIPATEW IC	GO ABOUT	655A
	SKUTHRWPOS	SULLEN LOOK	765C
18	GINWSKW 2A	FIND OUT	160A
	HEIS 3A	SOMEONE	230D
	KLEOPAS	CLEOPAS	435B
	MONOS 1Aβ	ONLY	529C
	*ONOMA II	NAME	574A
	PAROIKEW 1B		634B
	INHABIT AS A STRANGER		
	PAROIKEW 2	INHABIT	634B
	PAROIKEW 1A		634B
	INHABIT AS A STRANGER		
	SU IC	YOU	779D
19	AN8R 4	MAN	66B
	DUNATOS 1Aβ	POWERFUL	208A
	ENANTION 1B	BEFORE	261B
	ERGON 1A	DEED	307D
	LOGOS 1Aα	WORD	478A
	NAZAR8NOS	THE NAZARENE	534A
	NAZWRAIOS	NAZARENE	534B
	HO,H8,TO II5	THE	554B
	PERI II	ABOUT	650D
	POIOS 2Bα	OF WHAT KIND	691C
	PROPH8T8S 3	PROPHET	731A
20	ARCHIEREUS 1B	HIGH PRIEST	112B
	ARCHWN 2A	AUTHORITIES	113C
	EIS 4A	INTO	228B
	THANATOS 1Bα	DEATH	351C
	KRIMA 4B	VERDICT	451D
	HOPWS I	HOW	580B
	PARADIDWMI 1B	GIVE OVER	620B
	STAUROW I	CRUCIFY	773A
21	AGW 4	SPEND	14C
	ALLA 3	BUT, YET	38A
	APO II2C	SINCE	86C
	ELPIZW 2	HOPE	252A
	LUTROW 2	REDEEM	484A
	MELLW 1Cβ	BE ABOUT TO	502B
	HOS,H8,HO IIIF	(REL PRON)	589A
	HOUTOS 2C	THIS	602A
	SUN 5	WITH	789D
	TRITOS I	THIRD	834C
22	ALLA 3	BUT, YET	38A
	GINOMAI I4Cγ	COME, GO	159A
	EXIST8MI I	CHANGE	276A
	EPI IIIIAγ	ON	288A
	MN8MEION 2	TOMB	526C
	ORTHRINOS		584B
	EARLY IN THE MORNING		
	ORTHRIOS EARLY IN THE MORNING		584B
23	ZAW 1Aβ	LIVE	336C
	OPTASIA I	A VISION	580A
	HORAW 1Aβ	SEE	581C
	SWMA 1A	BODY	806D
23A	LEGW II8β	SAY	469C
23B	LEGW II8β	SAY	469C
24	APERCHOMAI 2	GO	83D
	EPI IIIIAγ	ON	288A
	KATHWS I	JUST AS	392A
	MN8MEION 2	TOMB	526C

24	HOUTW 2	THUS 602C
25	ANO8TOS I	UNINTELLIGENT 70A
	BRADUS	SLOW 146C
	EPI IIIBγ	ON 287A
	KARDIA IBβ	HEART 404D
	HOS,H8,HO I4A	(REL PRON) 587D
	PISTEUW IAε	BELIEVE 666C
	PROPH8T8S I	PROPHET 731A
	W I	O 903B
26	DEI 6A	IT IS NECESSARY 171C
	DOXA IBα	GLORY 203A
	EISERCHOMAI 2A	COME 232B
	HOUTOS I9α	THIS 601C
	OUCHI 3	NOT 603A
	PASCHW 3β	ENDURE 639D
	CHRISTOS I	ANOINTED ONE 895B
27	APO II3A	FROM 86C
	ARCHW 2C	BEGIN II3B
	GRAPH8 23α	SCRIPTURE 165B
	DIERM8NEUW 2	EXPLAIN 193C
	HEAUTOU IH	ONESELF 211C
	HERM8NEUW I	EXPLAIN 309D
	MWUS8S	MOSES 533D
	HO,H8,TO II5	THE 554B
	PERI II	ABOUT 650D
	PROPH8T8S I	PROPHET 731A
28	EGGIZW 2	APPROACH 212D
	KWM8 I	VILLAGE 462D
	HOU 2	WHERE 594A
	PORRW 2	FAR AWAY 700C
	PROSPOIEW I	PRETEND 725C
28A	POREUW I	PROCEED 699B
29	EIMI III9	TO BE 224D
	HESPERA	EVENING 313C
	H8MERA IA	DAY 346C
	KLINW 2	DECLINE 437C
	HO,H8,TO II4Bζ	THE 554A
	PARABIAZOMAI	USE FORCE 617B
	PROS III2A	TOWARD 717A
	SUN IA	WITH 789A
29A	MENW IAα	REMAIN 504D
29B	MENW IAα	REMAIN 504D
30	ARTOS IA	BREAD II0A
	*EPIDIDWMI I	GIVE 292B
	EULOGEW I	SPEAK WELL 322C
	KATAKLINW	RECLINE AT TABLE 412D
	KLAW	BREAK 434D
	META AII2	WITH 510B
	PROSDIDWMI	GIVE OVER 719C
31	ANOIGW IEβ	OPEN 70D
	APHANTOS	VANISH 124B
	GINOMAI I4B	BECOME 158D
	DIANOIGW IB	OPEN 186B
	EPIGINWSKW IB	KNOW 291A
32	GRAPH8 28α	SCRIPTURE 165B
	DIANOIGW 2	EXPLAIN 186C
	KAIW IB	LIGHT 397A
	KALUPTW 2C	VEIL 402A
	KARDIA IBε	HEART 405A
	LALEW 2Aδ	SPEAK 464B
	HODOS IB	WAY 556C
	PROS IIIIE	TOWARD 716D
	HWS IVIB	WHEN 907A

33	ATHROIZW	COLLECT 21A
	HENDEKA	ELEVEN 262B
	SUN IC	WITH 789B
	SUNATHROIZW I	GATHER 791A
	HWRA 2B	TIME OF DAY 904D
34	ONTWS I	REALLY 577C
	HORAW IA6	SEE 582A
	PETROS	PETER 661A
35	GINWSKW IB	KNOW 160A
	EN I2	IN 258A
	EX8GEOMAI	EXPLAIN 275B
	KLASIS I	BREAKING 434B
	HODOS IB	WAY 556C
	HWS I2D	AS 905D
36	AUTOS IB	SELF 122B
	AUTOS ID	IN PERSON 122C
	EIR8N8 2	PEACE 226C
	HIST8MI IIIB	STAND 383B
	LALEW 2B	SPEAK 464D
	MESOS 2	THE MIDDLE 508D
37	DOKEW IA	THINK 200D
	EMPHOBOS	AFRAID 257B
	THEWREW I	OBSERVE 360C
	THROEW	BE DISTURBED 364C
	PNEUMA 4B	SPIRIT 682A
	PTOEW	FRIGHTEN 735A
	PHANTASMA	APPARITION 861B
38	ANABAINW 2	GO UP 50B
	DIA BII2	WHY 180B
	DIALOGISMOS 2	DOUBT 185B
	KARDIA IBβ	HEART 404C
	TARASSW 2	STIR UP 813A
38A	TIS, TI 3A	WHICH 827B
39	AUTOS ID	IN PERSON 122C
	EGW	I 216A
	ECHW I2Cα	HAVE 332D
	THEWREW I	OBSERVE 360C
	OSTEON	BONE 590C
	OSTEON	BONE 590D
	PNEUMA 4B	SPIRIT 682A
	*SARX I	FLESH 750D
	CHEIR I	HAND 888A
	PS8LAPHAW	TOUCH 900D
39F	POUS IA	FOOT 703B
40	HOUTOS IBα	THIS 601C
41	APISTEW IA	DISBELIEVE 84D
	APO V3	WITH 87B
	BRWSIMOS	EATABLE 147C
	ENTHADE 2	HERE 265C
	ETI IAβ	STILL 315D
	THAUMAZW IAα	WONDER 352D
	CHARA I	JOY 883C
42	EPIDIDWMI I	GIVE 292B
	ICHTHUS	FISH 385A
	K8RION	HONEY COMB 431D
	MELISSIOS	HONEYCOMB 501D
	MEROS IBε	PIECE 507A
	OPTOS	BROILED 580B
43	ENWPION 2A	BEFORE 270B
	EPILOIPOS	REMAINING 295D
	EPIPL8SSW	REBUKE 297D
	ESTHIW IC	EAT 313A
44	EIMI IIII0	TO BE 224D

44 EN IID	IN	257D
EN IV6B	IN	261A
ETI IAβ	STILL	315D
LALEW 2B	SPEAK	464D
NOMOS 4A	LAW	545A
HO,H8,TO III0A	THE	555A
PL8ROW 4A	MAKE FULL	677C
PROPH8T8S I	PROPHET	731A
SUN IC	WITH	789B
PSALMOS !	PSALM	899B
45 GRAPH8 2Bα	SCRIPTURE	165B
DIANOIGW IB	OPEN	186B
NOUS I	THE UNDERSTANDING	546C
SUNI8MI	UNDERSTAND	797D
SUNI8MI	UNDERSTAND	798A
TOTE 2	AT THAT TIME	831D
46 ANIST8MI 2A	RISE	69C
H8MERA 2	DAY	346D
PASCHW 3Aα	SUFFER	639C
TRITOS I	THIRD	834B
CHRISTOS I	ANOINTED ONE	895B
47 HAMARTIA I	SIN	42C
APO III	FROM	86B
APHESIS 2	PARDON	124C
EIS IDβ	IN	227D
EPI II3	ON	287D
K8RUSSW 2Bβ	ANNOUNCE	432C
METANOIA	REPENTANCE	514A
ONOMA 14Cε	NAME	576C
48 MARTUS 2C	WITNESS	495C
49 EGW	I	216B
ENDUW 2B	DRESS	263C
ENDUW 2B	DRESS	263D
EXAPOSTELLW IB	SEND OUT	272D
EPAGGELIA 2B	PROMISE	280B
EPI IIIIBγ	ON	288D
HEWS IIIBα	UNTIL	335D
KATHIZW 2Aβ	STAY	391A
PAT8R 3Dα	FATHER	641D
HUPSOS IB	HEIGHT	858B
50 B8THANIA I	BETHANY	139B
*EXAGW I	LEAD OUT	271B
EXW IB	OUTSIDE	279A
EPAIRW I	LIFT UP	281C
HEWS II2C	AS FAR AS	335D
50F EULOGEW 2A	BLESS	322C
51 ANAPHERW I	BRING	62C
APHIST8MI 2A	WITHDRAW	126C
DIIST8MI I	GO AWAY	194B
OURANOS 2B	HEAVEN	599C
52 MEGAS 2Aγ	GREAT	499A
PROSKUNEW 5	DO REVERENCE	724B
*CHARA I	JOY	883C
53*AINEW	TO PRAISE	23A
AM8N I	AMEN	45B
DIA AIIIA	THROUGH	178D
EULOGEW I	SPEAK WELL	322C
HIERON 2	TEMPLE	373A

JOHN I

I EIMI II	TO BE	222A
HO,H8,TO IIIAα	THE	552B

IA THEOS 2	GOD	357C
IA LOGOS 3	THE LOGOS	480A
IB THEOS 2	GOD	357C
IB LOGOS 3	THE LOGOS	480A
IC LOGOS 3	THE LOGOS	480A
IF ARCH8 IC	BEGINNING	111D
IF PROS III7	TOWARD	718A
2 THEOS 3A	GOD	357D
HOUTOS IAβ	THIS	601A
3 DIA AIII2A	BY	179D
HEIS 2B	ONE	230C
OUDE 3	NOT EVEN	596A
PAS 2A6	EVERYTHING	638B
CHWRIS 2Aβ	APART	899A
3A GINOMAI I2A	CREATED	157C
4 PHWS 2	LIGHT	880B
4A ZW8 2Aβ	LIFE	341A
4B ZW8 2Aβ	LIFE	341A
5 AKOUW 3D	LEARN	32A
KAI I2G	AND	393C
KATALAMBANW IA	SEIZE	414A
PHAINW I	SHINE	859B
PHWS 2	LIGHT	880B
5A SKOTIA 2	DARKNESS	764D
5B SKOTIA 2	DARKNESS	764D
6 APOSTELLW IB6	SEND AWAY	98B
APOSTELLW IC	SEND AWAY	98B
GINOMAI II5	APPEAR	159D
IWAN(N)8S I	JOHN	385B
ONOMA II	NAME	574A
PARA I2	FROM	614D
7 ERCHOMAI IIAθ	COME	311A
MARTURIA I	TESTIMONY	494C
PISTEUW 2B	BELIEVE	667C
7F MARTUREW IA	BEAR WITNESS	493D
7-9 PHWS 2	LIGHT	880A
8 ALLA IB	BUT, YET	37D
HINA IIII	IN ORDER THAT	379A
9 AL8THINOS 3	GENUINE	36C
EIMI II4B6	TO BE	223A
EIS IAα	INTO	227B
KOSMOS 4C	WORLD	447B
PAS IAα	EVERY EACH	636C
PHWTIZW 2B	SHINE	881A
10 AUTOS 3Fβ	(OBLIQUE CASE)	123B
GINWSKW 7	ACKNOWLEDGE	160D
DIA AIII2A	BY	179D
KAI I2G	AND	393C
10C KOSMOS 7	WORLD	447D
11 PARALAMBANW 3A	TAKE	625B
IIA IDIOS 3B	ONES OWN	370D
IIB IDIOS 3A	ONES OWN	370D
12 GINOMAI I4A	BECOME	158C
EXOUSIA 2	ABILITY	277D
LAMBANW IEα	RECEIVE	465D
ONOMA I4Cβ	NAME	576A
HOSOS 2	HOW GREAT	590B
PISTEUW 2Aβ	BELIEVE	667B
TEKNON 2E	CHILD	816C
13 HAIMA IA	BLOOD	22A
AN8R I	MAN	65D
GENNAW IA	BEGET	154C
GENNAW IB	BEGET	154D

13	EK 3A	FROM 234A
	EK 3A	FROM 234B
	THEL8MA 2A	WILL 355A
	MONOGEN8S	ONLY 529A
	OUDE 1	AND NOT 595D
	SARX 8	BODY 752A
13A	HAIMA 1A	BLOOD 22A
14	AL8THEIA 2B	TRUTH 35C
	GINOMAI 14A	BECOME 158C
	DOXA 1A	GLORY 202D
	THEAOMAI 2	SEE 353D
	LOGOS 3	THE LOGOS 480A
	MONOGEN8S	ONLY 529B
	HO,H8,TO IIIA«	THE 552B
	PL8R8S 1B	FULL 675D
	PL8R8S 2	FULL 675D
	SARX 3	BODY 751A
	SK8NOW	LIVE 762D
	CHARIS 3B	FAVOR 886A
	HWS IIIIA	SO 906C
15	GINOMAI 14C1	COME, GO 159B
	EIPON 1	SAY 225B
	EMPROSTHEN 2F	IN FRONT 256D
	ERCHOMAI IIAη	COME 311A
	IWAN(N)8S 1	JOHN 385B
	KRAZW 2A	CALL 448D
	MARTUREW 1A	BEAR WITNESS 493D
	OPISW 2B	AFTER 578D
	HOUTOS 1A«	THIS 600D
	PRWTOS 1	FIRST 732D
	PRWTOS 1A	FIRST 733A
16	EK 4A€	FROM 235B
	KAI 13	AND 393D
	LAMBANW 2	RECEIVE 466D
	PAS 1E«	ALL 637D
	PL8RWMA 3B	THAT WHICH FILLS 678B
	CHARIS 3B	FAVOR 886A
16F	HOTI 3B	THAT 594A
17*	AL8THEIA 2B	TRUTH 35C
	DIA AIII2A	BY 179C
	MWUS8S	MOSES 533D
	NOMOS 3	LAW 544C
	CHARIS 3B	FAVOR 886B
	CHRISTOS 2	ANOINTED ONE 895C
18	EIMI III2	TO BE 224A
	EIS 9A	IN 229D
	*EX8GEOMAI	EXPLAIN 275B
	KOLPOS 1	BOSOM 443B
	HORAW 1A«	SEE 581C
	OUDEIS 2A	NO ONE 596B
	PWPOTE	EVER 739B
18A	THEOS 3B	GOD 357D
18B	THEOS 2	GOD 357C
19	APOSTELLW 1B«	SEND AWAY 98A
	APOSTELLW 1Bγ	SEND AWAY 98A
	EIMI II6A	TO BE 223C
	EIMI II6C	TO BE 223C
	ERWTAW 1	ASK 312A
	HIEREUS 1B«	PRIEST 372C
*	HIEROSOLUMA 1A	JERUSALEM 373D
	IOUDAIOS 2E	JEWISH 380B
	IWAN(N)8S 1	JOHN 385B
	KAI 15	AND 394A
19	LEUIT8S	A LEVITE 473B
	MARTURIA 2D«	TESTIMONY 494C
	HOTE 1B	WHEN 592C
	HOUTOS 1Aη	THIS 601B
	TIS, TI 1Aβ	WHICH 826D
20	ARNEOMAI 2	DENY 107C
	HOMOLOGEW 3A	CONFESS 571B
	HOTI 2	THAT 593D
	CHRISTOS 1	ANOINTED ONE 895B
21	APOKRINOMAI 1	ANSWER 92D
	APOKRINOMAI 1	ANSWER 93A
	ERWTAW 1	ASK 312A
	8LIAS	ELIJAH 345D
	LEGW IIIB	ANSWER 470C
	HO,H8,TO IIIA«	THE 552B
	OU 1	NO 594B
	OUN 1Cβ	THEREFORE 597C
	PROPH8T8S 3	PROPHET 731A
	PROPH8T8S 3	PROPHET 731B
	TIS, TI 1B€	WHICH 827A
22	APOKRISIS	ANSWER 93A
	LEGW 14	SAY 469D
	OUN 2B	THEREFORE 597C
	PEMPW 1	SEND 647B
	SEAUTOU 1	YOURSELF 753A
22B	TIS, TI 1B«	WHICH 826D
23	BOAW 2	SHOUT 143D
	EUTHUNW 1	STRAIGHTEN 321A
	8SAIAS	ISAIAH 349C
	KATHWS 1	JUST AS 392A
	KURIOS 2C«	LORD 460C
	HODOS 1A	WAY 556B
	PROPH8T8S 1	PROPHET 730D
	PHWN8 2E	VOICE 879C
25	BAPTIZW 2A	BAPTIZE 131B
	ERWTAW 1	ASK 312A
	8LIAS	ELIJAH 345D
	HO,H8,TO IIIA«	THE 552C
	OU 5B	NO 595A
	OUDE 1	AND NOT 595D
	OUN 1C«	THEREFORE 597B
	OUTE	NOT 600C
	PROPH8T8S 3	PROPHET 731A
	CHRISTOS 1	ANOINTED ONE 895B
26	APOKRINOMAI 1	ANSWER 92D
	BAPTIZW 2A	BAPTIZE 131B
	IWAN(N)8S 1	JOHN 385B
	MESOS 1	AMONG 508C
	OIDA 1A	KNOW 558B
	ST8KW 1	STAND 775C
	HUDWR 1	WATER 840D
27	AXIOS 2A	WORTHY 77C
	ERCHOMAI IIAη	COME 311A
	HINA IIICβ	IN ORDER THAT 378C
	LUW 1A	LOOSE 484D
	OPISW 2B	AFTER 578D
	HUPOD8MA	SANDAL 852B
28	BAPTIZW 2A	BAPTIZE 131B
	B8THABARA	BETHABARA 139B
	B8THANIA 2	BETHANY 139B
	IORDAN8S	JORDAN 379C
	IWAN(N)8S 1	JOHN 385B
	HOROU 1A«	WHERE 579C

28 PERAN 2B　　ON THE OTHER SIDE 649C
29 AIRW 4　　　TAKE AWAY 248
   HAMARTIA I　SIN 42C
   AMNOS　　　　LAMB 45D
   BLEPW IA　　SEE 142D
   EPAURION　　NEXT DAY 283C
   ERCHOMAI IIAβ　COME 310C
   IDE 3　　　　SEE 369D
   KOSMOS 5A　　WORLD 447B
   LEGW IIBα　　SAY 469C
   PALIN 2　　　AGAIN 611C
30 ANβR 6　　　MAN 66B
   GINOMAI I4Cι　COME, GO 159B
   EMPROSTHEN 2F　IN FRONT 256D
   ERCHOMAI IIAη　COME 311A
   OPISW 2B　　AFTER 578D
   HOTI 3A　　　THAT 593D
   HOUTOS IAα　THIS 600D
   PRWTOS IA　　FIRST 733A
   HUPER IF　　IN BEHALF OF 847A
31 ALLA IB　　　BUT, YET 37D
   BAPTIZW 2A　BAPTIZE 131B
   DIA BII2　　FOR THIS REASON 180B
   ERCHOMAI IIAθ　COME 311A
   HINA I5　　　IN ORDER THAT 378A
   KAGW I　　　AND I 387A
   OIDA IA　　　KNOW 558B
   HUDWR I　　　WATER 840D
   PHANEROW 2Bα　REVEAL 860D
32 THEAOMAI 2　SEE 353D
   IWAN(N)8S I　JOHN 385B
   MARTUREW IA　BEAR WITNESS 493D
   HOTI 2　　　THAT 593D
   OURANOS 2A　HEAVEN 599B
   PERISTERA　　PIGEON 657D
   PNEUMA 5Dα　SPIRIT 683A
32F EPI IIIIBγ　ON 289A
32F KATABAINW IB　COME DOWN 409C
32F MENW IAα　REMAIN 504D
33 BAPTIZW 2A　BAPTIZE 131B
   BAPTIZW 3B　BAPTIZE 131D
   EKEINOS IB　THAT 239A
   EPI IIIIAβ　ON 288A
   EPI IIIIBγ　ON 288D
   KAGW I　　　AND I 387A
   OIDA IA　　　KNOW 558B
   *PEMPW I　　SEND 647D
   HUDWR I　　　WATER 840D
33A PNEUMA 5Dα　SPIRIT 683A
33B PNEUMA 5Cβ　SPIRIT 683A
34 EKLEKTOS IA　CHOSEN 242A
   KAGW I　　　AND I 387A
   MARTUREW IA　BEAR WITNESS 493D
   HUIOS 2B　　SON 842B
   HUIOS 2B　　SON 842C
35 ANDREAS　　ANDREW 63B
   DUO IB　　　TWO 208B
   EK 4Aα　　　FROM 235B
   EPAURION　　NEXT DAY 283C
   HIST8MI II2Bγ　BEING 383C
   IWAN(N)8S I　JOHN 385B
   MATH8T8S 2A　DISCIPLE 486D
   PALIN 2　　　AGAIN 611C

36 AMNOS　　　　LAMB 45D
   EMBLEPW I　　LOOK AT 254A
   IDE 3　　　　SEE 369D
   LEGW IIBα　　SAY 469C
   LEGW I8D　　SAY 470C
   PERIPATEW IC　GO ABOUT 655A
37 MATH8T8S 2A　DISCIPLE 486D
38 DIDASKALOS　TEACHER 190D
   HERM8NEUW 2　TRANSLATE 310A
   Z8TEW 2Bβ　　SEEK 339C
   THEAOMAI IA　SEE 353D
   LEGW II3　　CALL 471B
   METHERM8NEUW　TRANSLATE 499D
   MENW IAα　　REMAIN 504D
   HOS,H8,HO I7A　(REL PRON) 588C
   POU IA　　　WHERE 702D
   RABBI　　　　RABBI 740B
   STREPHW 2Aα　TURN 778D
39 DEKATOS I　　TENTH 173A
   EIDON IE　　SEE 220A
   EIMI I5　　　TO BE 222C
   EKEINOS 2Bγ　THAT 239B
   ERCHOMAI IIAζ　COME 310D
   H8MERA IA　　DAY 346D
   LEGW I3　　　SAY 469D
   MENW IAα　　REMAIN 504D
   PARA IIIBα　BESIDE 615B
   POU IB　　　WHERE 702D
   HWRA 2B　　　TIME OF DAY 904D
   HWS IV5　　　WHEN 907C
39B　MENW IAα　REMAIN 504D
39B　MENW IAα　REMAIN 504D
40 AKOUW 3D　　LEARN 32A
   ANDREAS　　ANDREW 63B
   HEIS IAβ　　ONE 230A
   PARA I3C　　FROM 615A
   PETROS　　　PETER 661A
41 ADELPHOS I　BROTHER 15C
   IDIOS 2C　　ONES OWN 370C
   LEGW I3　　　SAY 469D
   METHERM8NEUW　TRANSLATE 499D
   MESSIAS　　THE MESSIAH 509B
   HOUTOS IAβ　THIS 601A
   CHRISTOS I　ANOINTED ONE 895B
41A　HEURISKW IB　FIND 325B
41F　HOS,H8,HO I7A　(REL PRON) 588C
42 BARIWNA　　BAR=JONA 133B
   EMBLEPW I　　LOOK AT 254A
   HERM8NEUW 2　TRANSLATE 310A
   IWAN(N)8S 4　JOHN 385D
   IWNAS 2　　　JONAH 386A
   KALEW IAγ　　CALL 400A
   K8PHAS　　　CEPHAS 432D
   PETROS　　　PETER 660C
43 EXERCHOMAI IAε　GO OUT 274B
   EPAURION　　NEXT DAY 283C
   HEURISKW IB　FIND 325B
   LEGW I3　　　SAY 469D
43=6 PHILIPPOS 3　PHILIP 868A
44 ANDREAS　　ANDREW 63B
   B8THSAIDA I　BETHSAIDA 139C
   EIMI IIII　　TO BE 224A
   EK 3B　　　　FROM 234B

44	PETROS	PETER	660C
	POLIS I	CITY	692A
45	GRAPHW 2C	WRITE	166A
	EN IID	IN	257D
	HEURISKW IB	FIND	325B
	IWS8PH 4	JOSEPH	386C
	NOMOS 4A	LAW	545A
	HOS,H8,HO I2A	(REL PRON)	587A
	PROPH8T8S I	PROPHET	730D
45F	NAZARA	NAZARETH	534A
45=9	NATHANA8L	NATHANAEL	534C
46	EIDON IE	SEE	220A
	EIMI III3	TO BE	224B
	EK 3B	FROM	234B
	ERCHOMAI IIAζ	COME	310D
47	AL8THWS 2	TRULY	37A
	DOLOS	DECEIT	202B
	ERCHOMAI IIAβ	COME	310C
	IDE 3	SEE	369D
	ISRA8LIT8S	ISRAELITE	382C
	LEGW I2A	SAY	469C
	HOS,H8,HO II	(REL PRON)	587A
48	APOKRINOMAI I	ANSWER	92D
	GINWSKW 6Aβ	KNOW	160C
	EIMI III12	TO BE	224D
	POTHEN 3	FROM WHERE	686D
	PRO 2	BEFORE	708D
	SUK8	FIG TREE	783D
	HUPO 2Aβ	UNDER	851B
	PHILIPPOS 3	PHILIP	868A
	PHWNEW 2B	CALL	878C
49	BASILEUS 2A	KING	135D
	EIMI III	TO BE	222D
	ISRA8L 2	ISRAEL	382B
	RABBI	RABBI	740B
	HUIOS 2B	SON	842D
50	MEGAS 2AY	GREAT	499A
	HORAW IB	SEE	582A
	PISTEUW 2B	BELIEVE	667C
	SUK8	FIG TREE	783D
	HUPOKATW	UNDER	852C
50A	HOTI 3A	THAT	593D
51	AGGELOS 2A	ANGEL	7C
	AM8N 2	AMEN	45B
	ANABAINW IAβ	GO UP	50A
	ANOIGW 2	OPEN	70D
	ARTI 3	NOW	109D
	KATABAINW IAY	COME DOWN	409C
	LEGW IIID	ASSURE	470D
	HORAW IAβ	SEE	581C
	OURANOS 2C	HEAVEN	599C
	HUIOS 2C	SON	843B

JOHN 2

I	GALILAIA	GALILEE	149D
	GINOMAI I3A	TAKE PLACE	158A
	KANA	CANA	403C
	TRITOS I	THIRD	834B
IF	GAMOS IA	WEDDING	150D
2	DE 4A	BUT AND	170D
	KALEW IB	INVITE	400B
	MATH8T8S 2Bα	DISCIPLE	487A

3	LEGW I3	SAY	469D
	OINOS I	WINE	564D
	SUNTELEW 3	COMPLETE	800A
	HUSTEREW ID	TO MISS	857A
4	GUN8 I	WOMAN	167C
	EGW	I	216C
	H8KW 2	HAVE COME	345C
	OUPW	NOT YET	597D
	HWRA 3	TIME OF DAY	905A
5	DIAKONOS IA	SERVANT	183D
	HOSTIS IEα	WHOEVER	591A
	POIEW IICα	DO	688C
5B	LEGW IIIC	ORDER	470D
6	ANA 3	EACH	49C
	DUO IC	TWO	208B
	DUO 5	TWO	208C
	HEX	SIX	270D
	8 IAβ	OR	342D
	IOUDAIOS 2C	JEWISH	380B
	KATHARISMOS I	PURIFICATION	388C
	KATA II4	FOR (PURPOSE)	407D
	KEIMAI IB	LIE	428A
	LITHINOS I	STONE	475A
	METR8T8S	MEASURE	516C
	HUDRIA	WATER JAR	840B
	CHWREW 3A	HAVE ROOM FOR	898A
7	AKOUW 3D	LEARN	32A
	ANW I	ABOVE	76B
	GEMIZW I	FILL	152D
	HUDRIA	WATER JAR	840B
7F	LEGW IIIC	ORDER	470D
8	ANTLEW I	DRAW	75D
	NUN IA6	NOW	547D
8A	PHERW 4Aα	BEAR	863A
8B	PHERW 4Aα	BEAR	863A
8F	ARCHITRIKLINOS	HEAD WAITER	112D
9	ANTLEW I	DRAW	75D
	GEUOMAI I	TASTE	156A
	DIAKONOS IA	SERVANT	183D
	NUMPHIOS	BRIDEGROOM	547B
	POTHEN 2	FROM WHERE	686D
	HUDWR 2	WATER	840D
	PHWNEW 2B	CALL	878C
	HWS IVIA	WHEN	907A
9A	OIDA IF	KNOW	558C
9B	OIDA II	KNOW	558C
9F	OINOS I	WINE	564D
10	ANTHRWPOS 3Aζ	MAN	68C
	ARTI 3	NOW	110A
	ELASSWN	SMALLER	247C
	HEWS IIIC	UNTIL	335C
	METHUSKW	GET DRUNK	500B
	PAS IAα	EVERY EACH	636C
	PRWTOS 2A	FIRST	733D
	SU IA	YOU	779D
	T8REW 2A	KEEP	822C
	TITH8MI IIBβ	PUT	823D
	TOTE 2	AT THAT TIME	831D
10A	KALOS 2A	GOOD	401B
10B	KALOS 2A	GOOD	401B
11	ARCH8 IB	BEGINNING	111B
	GALILAIA	GALILEE	149D
	DO%A IA	GLORY	202D

11	DOXA IA	GLORY 202D
	KANA	CANA 403C
	HOUTOS 2C	THIS 602A
	PISTEUW 2Aβ	BELIEVE 667B
	POIEW IIB1	DO 688B
	*S8MEION 2A	SIGN 755D
	PHANEROW IA	REVEAL 860C
12	*ADELPHOS I	BROTHER 150
	AUTOS IC	SELF 122C
	H8MERA 2	DAY 347A
	KATABAINW IAβ	COME DOWN 409B
	KAPHARNAOUM	CAPERNAUM 427C
	MENW IAα	REMAIN 504D
	META BII3	AFTER 511C
	OU 2B	NO 594C
	POLUS IIAα	MANY 694B
13	ANABAINW IAα	GO UP 49D
	EGGUS 2A	NEAR 213B
	HIEROSOLUMA IA	JERUSALEM 373D
	IOUDAIOS 2C	JEWISH 380B
	KAI I2C	AND 393B
	PASCHA I	THE PASSOVER 639A
14	HEURISKW IB	FIND 325B
	KATH8MAI IAγ	SIT 390B
	KERMATIST8S	MONEY CHANGER 430D
	PERISTERA	PIGEON 657D
	PWLEW	SELL 739A
14F	BOUS	OX 146A
14F	HIERON 2	TEMPLE 373A
14F	PROBATON I	SHEEP 710A
15	ANASTREPHW I	UPSET 60D
	ANATREPW I	OVERTURN 62B
	EK 3H	BY 235A
	EKBALLW I	DRIVE OUT 236D
	EKCHEW I	POUR OUT 246D
	KATASTREPHW I	UPSET 420B
	KERMA	COIN 430D
	KOLLUBIST8S	MONEY CHANGER 442D
	POIEW IIAα	DO 687B
	SCHOINION	ROPE 805B
	TE 3A	AND 815C
	TRAPEZA 4	TABLE 832C
	PHRAGELLION	WHIP 873B
16	AIRW 3	CARRY 24A
	EMPORION	MARKET 256B
	ENTEUTHEN I	FROM HERE 268A
	M8 AIII3B	NOT 518D
	PAT8R 3Dα	FATHER 641D
	PERISTERA	PIGEON 657D
	POIEW IIB1	DO 688B
	PWLEW	SELL 739A
16A	OIKOS IAβ	HOUSE 563B
16B	OIKOS IAβ	HOUSE 563B
17	GAR IB	FOR 151B
	GRAPHW 2C	WRITE 165D
	Z8LOS I	ZEAL 338B
	KATESTHIW 2	DESTROY 423B
	MIMN8SKOMAI IAδ	REMEMBER 524B
18	APOKRINOMAI I	ANSWER 92D
	DEIKNUMI IA	SHOW 171D
	IOUDAIOS 2E	JEWISH 380B
	HOTI IC	THAT 593B
	OUN 2B	THEREFORE 597C
18	S8MEION 2A	SIGN 755D
	TIS, TI 2	WHICH 827B
19	APOKRINOMAI 2	BEGIN 93A
	LUW 3	DESTROY 485A
	NAOS 2	TEMPLE 535C
	TREIS	THREE 833A
19F	EGEIRW IAδ	ERECT 213D
19F	EN IIIA	WHILE 259D
19F	H8MERA 2	DAY 347B
20	HEX	SIX 270D
	ETOS	YEAR 317A
	IOUDAIOS 2E	JEWISH 380B
	KAI IIB	AND 392C
	*NAOS IA	TEMPLE 535B
	OIKODOMEW	BUILD 560C
	OIKODOMEW IA	BUILD 560C
	OUN 2B	THEREFORE 597C
	TESSARAKONTA	FORTY 820D
20F	EKEINOS IA	THAT 238D
21	LEGW I2A	SAY 469C
	NAOS 2	TEMPLE 535C
	SWMA IB	BODY 806D
22	GRAPH8 2Bβ	SCRIPTURE 165B
	EGEIRW 2C	RISE 214A
	LEGW IIA	SAY 469D
	LOGOS IAβ	WORD 478B
	MIMN8SKOMAI IAδ	REMEMBER 524B
	NEKROS 2A	DEAD 537A
	HOS,H8,HO I4E	(REL PRON) 588B
	HOTE IB	WHEN 592C
	OUN 5	THEREFORE 597D
	PISTEUW IAδ	BELIEVE 666B
23	AUTOS 3A	(OBLIQUE CASE) 123A
	EIMI III4	TO BE 224C
	HEORT8	FESTIVAL 279D
	THEWREW I	OBSERVE 360C
	HIEROSOLUMA	JERUSALEM 373D
	ONOMA I4Cβ	NAME 576A
	PASCHA I	THE PASSOVER 639A
	PISTEUW 2Aβ	BELIEVE 667B
	POIEW IIBβ	DO 687C
	POLUS I2Aα	MANY 694D
	S8MEION 2A	SIGN 755D
	HWS IVIB	WHEN 907A
24	AKOUW 3D	LEARN 32A
	GINWSKW 6Aβ	KNOW 160C
	PISTEUW 3	BELIEVE 667D
25	ANTHRWPOS 3B	MAN 68C
	AUTOS IE	OF HIMSELF 122C
	GAR IA	FOR 151A
	GINWSKW 6D	KNOW 160D
	HINA IIICα	IN ORDER THAT 378C
	MARTUREW IA	BEAR WITNESS 493D
	HO,H8,TO IIIAβ	THE 552C
	HOTI 3A	THAT 593D
	TIS, TI IAα	ANY ONE 827C
	CHREIA I	NEED 893B

JOHN 3

1	ARCHWN 2A	AUTHORITIES 113C
	EIMI II	TO BE 222B
	IOUDAIOS 2C	JEWISH 380B

Verse	Greek	Gloss
1	NIKOD8MOS	NICODEMUS 541C
	ONOMA II	NAME 574A
2	APO IVIAβ	FROM 86D
	EIMI III7	TO BE 224D
	META AIIICβ	WITH 510A
	NUX IB	NIGHT 548D
	OIDA IE	KNOW 558C
	OUDEIS 2A	NO ONE 596B
	HOUTOS IAβ	THIS 601A
	POIEW IIBβ	DO 687C
	RABBI	RABBI 740B
	S8MEION 2A	SIGN 755D
	SU IA	YOU 779D
2A	THEOS 3B	GOD 357D
2B	ERCHOMAI IIAβ	COME 310B
2B	THEOS 3A	GOD 357D
2F	EAN I3B	IF 210D
2F	M8 AII	NOT 517C
3	AM8N 2	AMEN 45B
	ANWTHEN 3	AGAIN 76D
	BASILEIA 3B	KINGDOM 134D
	BASILEIA 3G	KINGDOM 135A
	*GENNAW IB	BEGET 154D
	EIDON 5	SEE 220A
	LEGW IIID	ASSURE 470D
	TIS, TI IAγ	ANY ONE 827D
4	ANTHRWPOS 3Aβ	MAN 68B
	GENNAW 2	BEAR 154D
	GERWN	OLD MAN 156A
	DEUTEROS 4	SECOND 176B
	EIMI II8	TO BE 223D
	KOILIA 2	BELLY 438B
	LEGW I3	SAY 469D
	M8 CI	NOT 519A
	NIKOD8MOS	NICODEMUS 541C
	HO,H8,TO IIII	THE 555B
	PWS IA	HOW 739C
5	AM8N 2	AMEN 45B
	APOKRINOMAI I	ANSWER 92D
	BASILEIA 3B	KINGDOM 134D
	BASILEIA 3G	KINGDOM 135A
	EAN I3B	IF 210D
	EISERCHOMAI 2A	COME 232B
	LEGW IIID	ASSURE 470D
	M8 AII	NOT 517C
	OURANOS 3	HEAVEN 600A
	PNEUMA 5Dβ	SPIRIT 683B
	TIS, TI IAγ	ANY ONE 827D
	HUDWR I	WATER 840D
6	GENNAW IA	BEGET 154C
	EK 3A	FROM 234A
	EK 3A	FROM 234B
	PNEUMA 5Gα	SPIRIT 683C
	SARX 7	BODY 751D
6A	PNEUMA 5Dα	SPIRIT 683A
7	ANWTHEN 3	AGAIN 76D
	THAUMAZW IAγ	WONDER 353A
	M8 AIII5B	NOT 518D
8	AKOUW IBα	HEAR 31B
	ERCHOMAI IIAγ	COME 310C
	*OIDA IF	KNOW 558C
	HOPOU IAα	WHERE 579C
	HOUTW IB	THUS 602B
8	PAS ICγ	WHOEVER 637B
	PNEUMA 5A	SPIRIT 682C
	PNEW IA	BLOW 686A
	POTHEN I	FROM WHERE 686C
	POU 2B	WHERE 703A
	HUDWR I	WATER 840D
	HUPAGW 2	GO AWAY 844C
	PHWN8 I	SOUND 878C
8A	PNEUMA IA	WIND 680C
8B	PNEUMA 5Dα	SPIRIT 683A
9	APOKRINOMAI I	ANSWER 92D
	NIKOD8MOS	NICODEMUS 541C
	PWS IA	HOW 739C
10	GINWSKW 3A	UNDERSTAND 160B
	DIDASKALOS	TEACHER 190D
	ISRA8L 2	ISRAEL 382B
	HO,H8,TO IIIAα	THE 552C
11	AM8N 2	AMEN 45B
	KAI I2G	AND 393C
	LAMBANW ID	RECEIVE 465D
	LEGW IIID	ASSURE 470D
	MARTUREW IB	BEAR WITNESS 494A
	MARTURIA 2Dβ	TESTIMONY 494D
	HORAW IAβ	SEE 581D
12	EPIGEIOS 2A	EARTHLY 290D
	PWS ID	HOW 739C
12A	PISTEUW ID	BELIEVE 666D
12B	PISTEUW ID	BELIEVE 666D
13	ANABAINW IAβ	GO UP 50A
	EI VI8A	IF NOT 219A
	KATABAINW IAγ	COME DOWN 409C
	HUIOS 2C	SON 843B
13B	OURANOS 2B	HEAVEN 599B
14	DEI I	IT IS NECESSARY 171A
	KATHWS I	JUST AS 392A
	MWUS8S	MOSES 533D
	HOUTW IA	THUS 602B
	HUIOS 2C	SON 843B
14A	HUPSOW I	LIFT UP 858C
14B	HUPSOW I	LIFT UP 858C
15	EN I2	IN 258A
	HINA IIA	IN ORDER THAT 377C
	PISTEUW 2Aβ	BELIEVE 667B
	PISTEUW 2Aε	BELIEVE 667B
	PISTEUW 2Aγ	BELIEVE 667B
	PISTEUW 2Aδ	BELIEVE 667B
	PISTEUW 2B	BELIEVE 667C
15F	AIWNIOS 3	ETERNAL 28A
15F	ZW8 2Bα	LIFE 341B
15F	ZW8 2Bα	LIFE 341C
15F	PAS ICγ	WHOEVER 637B
16	APOLLUMI 2Aα	PERISH 94D
	GAR 2	FOR 151C
	KOSMOS 5B	WORLD 447C
	MONOGEN8S	ONLY 529A
	HOUTW 2	THUS 602C
	PISTEUW 2Aβ	BELIEVE 667B
	HWSTE 2Aα	THEREFORE 908B
16=18	HUIOS 2B	SON 842D
17	APOSTELLW IBγ	SEND AWAY 98A
	APOSTELLW IBβ	SEND AWAY 98A
	APOSTELLW IC	SEND AWAY 98B
	KRIMA 7	JUDGMENT 452A

17 KRINW 4Bα   JUDGE 453A   24 OUPW   NOT YET 598A
    PEMPW I   SEND 647D   PHULAK8 3   GUARD 875D
    SWZW 2B   SAVE 806B   25 GINOMAI IIBβ   COME ABOUT 157B
17A   KOSMOS 4C   WORLD 447B   EK 3C   FROM 234C
17B   KOSMOS 5A   WORLD 447B   Z8T8SIS 3   DISCUSSION 339D
17C   KOSMOS 5B   WORLD 447C   IOUDAIOS 2A   JEWISH 380B
18 8D8 2   ALREADY 344D   KATHARISMOS I   PURIFICATION 388C
    M8 AI6   NOT 517D   MATH8T8S 2A   DISCIPLE 486D
    M8 AII2A   NOT 518B   META AII3A   WITH 510C
    MONOGEN8S   ONLY 529B   OUN 2B   THEREFORE 597C
    ONOMA I4Cβ   NAME 576A   26 BAPTIZW 2Bα   BAPTIZE 131C
    HOTI 3A   THAT 593D   EIMI III7   TO BE 224D
18A   KRINW 4Bα   JUDGE 453A   IDE 2   SEE 369D
18A   PISTEUW 2Aβ   BELIEVE 667B   IORDAN8S   JORDAN 379C
18B   KRINW 4Bα   JUDGE 453A   MARTUREW IC   494A
18B   PISTEUW 2B   BELIEVE 667C   TESTIFY FAVORABLY
18C   PISTEUW 2Aβ   BELIEVE 667B   META AIIICα   WITH 510A
19 AGAPAW 2   LOVE 5A   HOUTOS IAδ   THIS 601B
    AUTOS 3A   (OBLIQUE CASE) 123A   PERAN 2B   ON THE OTHER SIDE 649C
    EIMI II6A   TO BE 223C   RABBI   RABBI 740B
    ERGON ICβ   DEED 308B   27 ANTHRWPOS 3Aβ   MAN 68B
    8   2A   THAN 343B   ANWTHEN I   FROM ABOVE 76C
    KOSMOS 4C   WORLD 447B   EAN I3B   IF 210D
    KRISIS IAβ   JUDGING 453D   LAMBANW IC   TAKE 465C
    MALLON 3C   RATHER 490D   M8 AII   NOT 517C
    HOTI IA   THAT 592D   OUDEIS 2Bα   NOTHING 596C
    HOUTOS IAδ   THIS 601A   28 ALLA IB   BUT, YET 37D
    PON8ROS IBβ   WICKED 697D   APOSTELLW IBβ   SEND AWAY 98A
    SKOTOS 2B   DARKNESS 765B   AUTOS IAβ   SELF 122B
19A   PHWS 2   LIGHT 880B   EMPROSTHEN 2E   IN FRONT 256D
19B   PHWS 2   LIGHT 880B   MARTUREW IA   BEAR WITNESS 493D
19F   GAR IC   FOR 151B   CHRISTOS I   ANOINTED ONE 895B
19*21 AUXANW 3   GROW 121C   29 AKOUW IC   HEAR 31D
20 ELEGCHW I   EXPOSE 248D   EMOS IAα   MY 255A
    M8 AI2   NOT 517C   HIST8MI II2Bγ   BEING 383C
    MISEW 2   HATE 524D   NUMPH8 I   BRIDE 547B
    PAS ICγ   WHOEVER 637B   PL8ROW 3   MAKE FULL 677B
    PRASSW IA   DO 705B   PHILOS 2Aβ   LOVING 869A
    PHAULOS I   WORTHLESS 862B   PHWN8 2A   VOICE 879A
    PHWS IA   LIGHT 879D   CHAIRW I   REJOICE 881B
20F   ERGON ICβ   DEED 308A   29A NUMPHIOS   BRIDEGROOM 547B
21 AL8THEIA 2B   TRUTH 35D   29A CHARA I   JOY 883D
    AUTOS 3A   (OBLIQUE CASE) 123A   29B NUMPHIOS   BRIDEGROOM 547B
    EN I3   IN 258A   29B CHARA I   JOY 883D
    EN I5D   IN 259A   29C NUMPHIOS   BRIDEGROOM 547B
    ERGAZOMAI 2A   WORK 307A   30 AUXANW 3   GROW 121C
    POIEW IICβ   DO 688C   DEI I   IT IS NECESSARY 171A
    PHANEROW IB   REVEAL 860C   EKEINOS IA   THAT 238D
    PHWS 2   LIGHT 880B   ELATTOW 2B   INFERIOR 247D
22 BAPTIZW 2Bα   BAPTIZE 131C   31 ANWTHEN I   FROM ABOVE 76C
    G8 4   LAND 156C   EIMI II9A   TO BE 223D
    DIATRIBW   STAY 189A   EIMI III3   TO BE 224B
    IOUDAIOS I   JEWISH 380A   EK 3B   FROM 234B
    MATH8T8S 2Bα   DISCIPLE 487A   EPANW 2B   ABOVE ALL 283A
    META AIIIA   WITH 509D   ERCHOMAI IIAγ   COME 310C
23 AINWN   AENON 23B   LALEW 2Aε   SPEAK 464C
    DE 4A   BUT, AND 170D   OURANOS 2B   HEAVEN 599B
    EGGUS IA   NEAR 213B   31B ERCHOMAI IIAβ   COME 310B
    PARAGINOMAI I   COME 618D   32 KAI I2G   AND 393C
    POLUS IIAβ   MANY 694B   MARTUREW IB   BEAR WITNESS 494A
    SALIM   SALIM 748A   HORAW IAβ   SEE 581D
    HUDWR I   WATER 840C   32F LAMBANW ID   RECEIVE 465D
23B   BAPTIZW 2A   BAPTIZE 131B   32F MARTURIA 2Dβ   TESTIMONY 494D

```
33  AL8TH8S I            TRUE      36A      6   OUN 2A               THEREFORE 597C
    AUTOS 3A        (OBLIQUE CASE) 123A         HOUTW 4                  THUS 602D
    SPHRAGIZW 2C         SEAL     804B          HWRA 2B           TIME OF DAY 904D
34  APOSTELLW IC        SEND AWAY  98B          HWS IV5                  WHEN 907C
    EK  6C               FROM     235D          HWSEI 2                    AS 907D
    LALEW 2B             SPEAK    464C      6A    P8G8 I            FOUNTAIN 661C
    METRON 2B           MEASURE   516D      6B    P8G8 I            FOUNTAIN 661C
    HOS,H8,HO I2Bα     (REL PRON) 587B      7   ANTLEW I                DRAW  75D
    OU  2B                 NO     594C          DIDWMI 2                GIVE 192C
    PNEUMA 50α          SPIRIT    683A          PINW I                 DRINK 664C
    R8MA I               WORD     743A          SAMAREIA             SAMARIA 748D
35  AGAPAW IBβ           LOVE       4D          HUDWR I                WATER 840C
    DIDWMI 3             GIVE     192C      8   AGORAZW I                BUY  12C
    PAS 2A6           EVERYTHING  638B          HINA IIE         IN ORDER THAT 377C
    CHEIR 2A6           HAND      888D          POLIS I                 CITY 692A
35F   HUIOS 2B           SON      842D          TROPH8 I                FOOD 835C
36  AIWNIOS 3          ETERNAL    28A      8F   GAR 2                    FOR 151C
    APEITHEW I         DISOBEY    82A      9   AITEW                    ASK  25B
    ZW8 2Bα             LIFE     341C          AITEW                    ASK  25C
    MENW IAβ            REMAIN    505B          EIMI II8               TO BE 223D
    HORAW IB            SEE       582A          IOUDAIOS 2A           JEWISH 380B
    PISTEUW 2Aβ        BELIEVE    667B          OUN 2C              THEREFORE 597C
36A   ZW8 2Bα           LIFE     341B          PARA I3A                FROM 614D
36B   ZW8 2Bα           LIFE     341B          PINW I                 DRINK 664C
                                                PWS IB                   HOW 739C
         JOHN 4                                 SAMARIT8S           SAMARITAN 749A
                                                SU IC                    YOU 779D
I   BAPTIZW 2Bα        BAPTIZE   131C          SUGCHRAOMAI 2                783A
    GINWSKW 2B         FIND OUT  160B               HAVE DEALINGS WITH
    8  2A                THAN     343B      9A    SAMARITIS         SAMARITAN 749A
    KURIOS 2Cβ           LORD     460D      9B    SAMARITIS         SAMARITAN 749A
    OUN 5             THEREFORE  597D      10   AITEW                    ASK  25B
    POIEW IIEα            DO      688D          DWREA                   GIFT 209C
    POLUS IIIA           MANY     695C          PINW I                 DRINK 664C
    HWS IVIA             WHEN     907A      IOF   ZAW 4A                LIVE 337C
2   AUTOS ID          IN PERSON  122C      IOF   HUDWR 2               WATER 840D
    BAPTIZW 2Bα        BAPTIZE   131C      II   ANTL8MA               BUCKET  75D
    GE  3D            OF COURSE  152B          BATHUS I                DEEP 130A
    KAITOIGE          AND YET    397A          KAI I2E                  AND 393B
3   APERCHOMAI 2          GO      83D          KURIOS 2Cβ              LORD 460D
    APHI8MI 3A          ABANDON  125D          OUN ICα             THEREFORE 597C
    IOUDAIA I           JUDAEA   379D          OUTE                     NOT 600D
    PALIN IA             BACK     611B          POTHEN I          FROM WHERE 686D
4   DEI 4        IT IS NECESSARY 171B          PHREAR                A WELL 873D
    DEI 6A       IT IS NECESSARY 171C      IIA   ECHW I2D              HAVE 332D
    DIERCHOMAI IB α   GO THROUGH 193C      IIF   P8G8 I            FOUNTAIN 661C
    SAMAREIA            SAMARIA   748D      I2   EK IA            AWAY FROM 233C
5   EIS IB               NEAR     227C          THREMMA               ANIMAL 363D
    IWS8PH I            JOSEPH    386C          IAKWB I                JACOB 368A
    LEGW II3             CALL     471B          MEGAS 2Bα              GREAT 499B
    HOS,H8,HO I4E      (REL PRON) 588B          M8 CI                    NOT 519A
    POLIS I              CITY     692A          PAT8R IB          FOREFATHER 640C
    SAMAREIA           SAMARIA    748D          PINW I                 DRINK 664C
    SUCHAR              SYCHAR    803B          PHREAR                A WELL 873D
    CHWRION I            PLACE    898C      13   DIPSAW I              THIRST 199C
5F    IAKWB I           JACOB     368A          HOUTOS 2B               THIS 601D
6   EIMI I5             TO BE     222C          PALIN IB               AGAIN 611C
    EK  3Eβ               BY      234C          PAS ICγ             WHOEVER 637B
    HEKTOS              SIXTH     245C      13F   EK 4Aε                FROM 235B
    EPI IIIA6             AT      286D      13F   PINW I                DRINK 664B
    KATHEZOMAI 2          SIT     389C      14   AIWNIOS 3           ETERNAL  28A
    KOPIAW I      BECOME WEARY   444B          HALLOMAI 2               LEAP  39A
    HODOIPORIA         JOURNEY    556A          GINOMAI I4A           BECOME 158C
```

```
14 DIPSAW 2             THIRST 199C
   ZW8 2Bα             LIFE 341C
   M8  D2              NOT 519C
   HOS,H8,HO 14A       (REL PRON) 587D
   *P8G8 2             FOUNTAIN 661D
   PINW 2Bβ            DRINK 664C
   HUDWR 2             WATER 841A
14A  HUDWR 2           WATER 840D
14B  HUDWR 2           WATER 840D
14C  HUDWR 2           WATER 840D
15 ANTLEW 1            DRAW 75D
   DIERCHOMAI 2        COME 193D
   DIPSAW 1            THIRST 199C
   ENTHADE 1           HERE 265C
   HINA IIC            IN ORDER THAT 377C
   KURIOS 2Cβ          LORD 460D
   M8DE 1B             AND NOT 519D
   HOUTOS 2A           THIS 601D
   P8G8 2              FOUNTAIN 661D
16 ENTHADE 1           HERE 265C
   ERCHOMAI IIAγ       COME 310C
   HUPAGW 2            GO AWAY 844C
   PHWNEW 2B           CALL 878C
16FF AN8R 1            MAN 65D
17 KALWS 4B            WELL 402B
   HOTI 2              THAT 593D
17F ECHW I2Bα          HAVE 332C
18 AL8TH8S 2           TRUE 36A
   EIPON 1             SAY 225B
   NUN IAα             NOW 547C
   HOS,H8,HO I2Bα      (REL PRON) 587B
   HOUTOS 2C           THIS 602A
19 THEWREW 2A          OBSERVE 360D
   KURIOS 2Cβ          LORD 460D
   PROPH8T8S 3         PROPHET 731A
20 DEI 3               IT IS NECESSARY 171B
   HOPOU IAα           WHERE 579C
   HOUTOS 2B           THIS 602A
   PAT8R 1B            FOREFATHERS 640D
   TOPOS 1C            PLACE 830B
20A  PROSKUNEW 2A      DO REVERENCE 724A
20B  PROSKUNEW 2A      DO REVERENCE 724A
20F  EN IIB            IN 257D
20F  OROS              MOUNTAIN 586B
21 ERCHOMAI IIBα       COME 311B
   HOTE 2Aα            WHEN 592C
   OUTE                NOT 600C
   HOUTOS 2B           THIS 601D
   PAT8R 3Dα           FATHER 641D
   PISTEUW 1C          BELIEVE 666D
   PROSKUNEW 2A        DO REVERENCE 724A
   HWRA 3              TIME OF DAY 905A
22 EK 3C               FROM 234B
   IOUDAIOS 2C         JEWISH 380B
   SU 1A               YOU 779D
   SWT8RIA 2           DELIVERANCE 809B
22A  PROSKUNEW         DO REVERENCE 723D
22B  PROSKUNEW         DO REVERENCE 723D
23 AL8THINOS 3         GENUINE 36C
   ALLA 2              BUT, YET 37D
   GAR 1B              FOR 151A
   ERCHOMAI IIBα       COME 311B
   Z8TEW 2C            SEEK 339C

23 HOTE 2Aα            WHEN 592C
   PNEUMA 3B           SPIRIT 681C
   PROSKUN8T8S         WORSHIPER 724B
   TOIOUTOS 2B         SUCH A KIND 829A
   HWRA 3              TIME OF DAY 905A
23A  PAT8R 3Dα         FATHER 641D
23A  PROSKUNEW 2A      DO REVERENCE 724A
23B  PAT8R 3Dα         FATHER 641D
23B  PROSKUNEW         DO REVERENCE 723D
23B  PROSKUNEW 2A      DO REVERENCE 724A
23F  AL8THEIA 2B       TRUTH 35C
24 DEI 3           IT IS NECESSARY 171B
24A  PNEUMA 4A         SPIRIT 681D
24A  PROSKUNEW         DO REVERENCE 723D
24A  PROSKUNEW 2A      DO REVERENCE 724A
24B  PNEUMA 3B         SPIRIT 681C
24B  PROSKUNEW 2A      DO REVERENCE 724A
25 AN 3A               (PARTICLE) 48B
   ANAGGELLW 2         DISCLOSE 51A
   ERCHOMAI IIAη       COME 310D
   LEGW II3            CALL 471B
   MESSIAS             THE MESSIAH 509B
   OIDA IE             KNOW 558C
   CHRISTOS 1          ANOINTED ONE 895B
26 EIMI II5            TO BE 223C
   LALEW 2A6           SPEAK 464B
27 EPI II2             AT 287D
   ERCHOMAI IIAα       COME 310B
   Z8TEW 2Bβ           SEEK 339C
   THAUMAZW IAγ        WONDER 353A
   LALEW 2A6           SPEAK 464C
   MENTOI 2            THOUGH 504C
27A  META AII3B        WITH 510D
27B  META AII3B        WITH 510D
28 APHI8MI 3A          LEAVE 125D
   EIS 1B              NEAR 227C
   OUN 2A              THEREFORE 597C
   POLIS 1             CITY 692A
   HUDRIA             WATER JAR 840B
29 ANTHRWPOS 3A6       MAN 68C
   DEUTE 1             COME 175D
   M8TI                PERHAPS 522A
   CHRISTOS 1          ANOINTED ONE 895B
30 EXERCHOMAI IAα      GO OUT 273D
   POLIS 1             CITY 692A
31 EN IIB              WHILE 259D
   ERWTAW 2            ASK 312A
   MATH8T8S 2Bα        DISCIPLE 487A
   METAXU IBα          BETWEEN 514B
   RABBI               RABBI 740B
32 BRWSIS 3B           FOOD 147D
   ESTHIW ID           EAT 313B
   OIDA IB             KNOW 558B
33 ESTHIW ID           EAT 313B
   M8 CI               NOT 519A
   OUN 2B              THEREFORE 597C
   PHERW 4Aα           BEAR 863B
34 BRWMA 2             FOOD 147C
   ERGON 2             WORK 308B
   THEL8MA ICγ         WILL 355A
   HINA IIICα          IN ORDER THAT 378C
   PEMPW 1             SEND 647D
   POIEW IICα          DO 688C
```

34	TELEIOW 1	COMPLETE 817B
35	HARPAGMOS 2	ROBBERY 108B
	ERCHOMAI IIBβ	COME 311B
	ETI IC	STILL 316A
	THEAOMAI IA	SEE 353D
	IDOU IA	BEHOLD 371C
	KAI I2C	AND 393B
	LEUKOS 2	WHITE 473D
	OU 4C	NO 595A
	PROS III3B	TOWARD 717B
	TETRAM8NOS	FOUR MONTHS MORE 821C
	CHWRA 4	COUNTRY 897D
35A	THERISMOS 1	HARVEST 360A
35B	THERISMOS 2A	HARVEST 360A
36	AIWNIOS 3	ETERNAL 28A
	ZW8 2Bα	LIFE 341C
	8D8 IA	ALREADY 344D
	THERIZW 1	REAP 359D
	HINA II2	IN ORDER THAT 378D
	KARPOS IA	FRUIT 405C
	LAMBANW 2	RECEIVE 466B
	MISTHOS 1	WAGES 525A
	HOMOU 2	TOGETHER 572C
	SPEIRW IBβ	SOW 768D
	SUNAGW I	GATHER 790A
	CHAIRW I	REJOICE 882A
37	AL8THINOS 2	TRUE 36B
	ALLOS IEγ	ANOTHER 39C
	THERIZW 2A	REAP 359D
	LOGOS IAβ	WORD 478C
	SPEIRW IBα	SOW 768D
38	APOSTELLW IBγ	SEND AWAY 98B
	APOSTELLW IC	SEND AWAY 98B
	EISERCHOMAI 2A	COME 232B
	KOPOS 2	WORK 444C
38A	KOPIAW 2	BECOME WEARY 444B
38B	KOPIAW 2	BECOME WEARY 444B
39	LOGOS IAγ	WORD 478C
	MARTUREW IA	BEAR WITNESS 493D
	PISTEUW 2Aβ	BELIEVE 667B
	POLIS I	CITY 692A
	POLUS I2Aα	MANY 694D
39F	SAMARIT8S	SAMARITAN 748D
40	ERWTAW 2	ASK 312B
	H8MERA 2	DAY 347A
	HO,H8,TO IIIAα	THE 552B
	OUN 5	THEREFORE 597D
	PARA IIIBβ	BESIDE 615C
	HWS IVIA	WHEN 907A
40A	MENW IAα	REMAIN 504D
40B	MENW IAα	REMAIN 504D
41	LOGOS IAβ	WORD 478C
	POLUS I2Cα	MANY 695C
	POLUS II2Aβ	MANY 695D
41F	PISTEUW 2B	BELIEVE 667C
42	AL8THWS I	TRULY 36D
	AUTOS IE	OF HIMSELF 122C
	KOSMOS 5A	WORLD 447B
	LALIA I	SPEECH 465A
	HO,H8,TO IIIE	THE 553A
	OUKETI I	NO LONGER 596D
	SOS I	YOURS 766C
	SWT8R 2	SAVIOR 808D
42	TE IA	AND 815A
	CHRISTOS I	ANOINTED ONE 895B
43	EXERCHOMAI IAα	GO OUT 274A
	H8MERA 2	DAY 347B
	HO,H8,TO IIIAα	THE 552B
44	IDIOS 2C	ONES OWN 370C
	MARTUREW IA	BEAR WITNESS 493D
	PATRIS I	FATHERLAND 642B
	PATRIS 2	FATHERLAND 642C
	PROPH8T8S 3	PROPHET 731A
	TIM8 2B	HONOR 825B
45	GALILAIOS	GALILEAN 149D
	GAR IB	FOR 151A
	DECHOMAI I	RECEIVE 176B
	*HEORT8	FESTIVAL 279D
	HEORT8	FESTIVAL 280A
	HORAW IAβ	SEE 581C
	OUN 5	THEREFORE 597D
45B	ERCHOMAI IIAβ	COME 310C
46	ASTHENEW IA	BE SICK 115A
	BASILIKOS	ROYAL 136C
	BASILISKOS	KING 136C
	GALILAIA	GALILEE 149D
	KANA	CANA 403C
	KAPHARNAOUM	CAPERNAUM 427C
	OINOS I	WINE 564D
	HOPOU IAα	WHERE 579C
	OUN 2B	THEREFORE 597C
	PALIN IA	BACK 611B
	POIEW IIB:	DO 688B
	TIS, TI 2Aα	ANY ONE 828A
47	AUTOS 3A	(OBLIQUE CASE) 123A
	GALILAIA	GALILEE 149D
	ERWTAW 2	ASK 312B
	H8KW IB	HAVE COME 345B
	H8KW IA	HAVE COME 345B
	IAOMAI I	HEAL 369A
	HINA IIIAγ	IN ORDER THAT 378B
	IOUDAIA I	JUDAEA 379D
	KATABAINW IAβ	COME DOWN 409B
	MELLW ICα	BE ABOUT TO 502A
48	EAN I3B	IF 210D
	OUN 2C	THEREFORE 597C
	PISTEUW 2B	BELIEVE 667C
	S8MEION 2A	SIGN 755D
49	BASILIKOS	ROYAL 136C
	BASILISKOS	KING 136C
	KATABAINW IAβ	COME DOWN 409B
	KURIOS 2Cβ	LORD 460D
	PAIDION 2B	CHILD 609B
	PRIN IB	BEFORE 708A
50	ANTHRWPOS 4A	MAN 68D
	ZAW IAγ	LIVE 336C
	LOGOS IAγ	WORD 478C
	PISTEUW IA6	BELIEVE 666B
51	AGGELLW	ANNOUNCE 7A
	APAGGELLW I	REPORT 78C
	APANTAW	MEET 79D
	ZAW IAγ	LIVE 336C
	KATABAINW IAβ	COME DOWN 409B
	PAIS IAβ	CHILD 609C
	HUPANTAW	GO TO MEET 845C
52	AUTOS IC	SELF 122C

```
52  HEBDOMOS              SEVENTH 212A
    ECHTHES               YESTERDAY 331C
    ECHW III              BE 334B
    KOMPSOTERON           IMPROVE 443D
    PARA I3C              FROM 615A
    PUNTHANOMAI I         INQUIRE 737A
    PURETOS               FEVER 738B
52A   HWRA 2B             TIME OF DAY 904D
52B   HWRA 2B             TIME OF DAY 904D
53  GINWSKW 3C            UNDERSTAND 160B
    ZAW IAY               LIVE 336C
    OIKIA 2               HOUSEHOLD 560A
    HOLOS 2B              WHOLE 567D
    PAT8R IA              FATHER 640C
    PISTEUW 2B            BELIEVE 667C
    HWRA 2B               TIME OF DAY 904D
54  GALILAIA             GALILEE 149D
    DEUTEROS I            SECOND 176A
    ERCHOMAI IIAß         COME 310C
    IOUDAIA I             JUDAEA 379D
    HOUTOS 2              THIS 602A
    POIEW IIB:            DO 688B
    S8MEION 2A            SIGN 755D
```

JOHN 5

```
1   ANABAINW IAα          GO UP 49D
    EIMI I5               TO BE 222C
    HEORT8                FESTIVAL 279D
    HIEROSOLUMA IA        JERUSALEM 373D
    IOUDAIOS 2C           JEWISH 380B
    SK8NOP8GIA   BUILDING OF TENTS 762C
2   B8THESDA             BETHESDA 139B
    B8THZATHA            BETHZATHA 139C
    B8THSAIDA 2          BETHSAIDA 139D
    HEBRAISTI            IN HEBREW 212C
    EPI IIIAδ            AT 286D
    EPILEGW I            CALL 295C
    HIEROSOLUMA         JERUSALEM 373D
    KOLUMB8THRA          POOL 443C
    STOA                 PORTICO 776B
3   ASTHENEW IA          BE SICK 115A
    EKDECHOMAI           WAIT 237D
    KATAKEIMAI I         LIE DOWN 412B
    KIN8SIS              MOTION 433D
    X8ROS 2              DRY 551A
    PARALUTIKOS          PARALYTIC 625D
    PL8THOS 2Bα          QUANTITY 674C
    TUPHLOS IB           BLIND 838C
    CHWLOS               LAME 897B
3F    HUDWR I            WATER 840C
4   D8POTE              AT ANY TIME 178B
    EMBAINW              GO IN 253C
    EN I6                IN 259C
    KAIROS I             TIME 395C
    KATABAINW IAδ        COME DOWN 409C
    KATECHW IDⱳ          BE BOUND 424B
    KOLUMB8THRA          POOL 443C
    NOS8MA               DISEASE 545C
    HOIOS               OF WHAT SORT 565C
    HOS,H8,HO IIOC       (REL PRON) 588D
    PRWTOS IA            FIRST 732D
    TARASSW I            STIR UP 812D
```

```
4    TARACH8 I            DISTURBANCE 813A
     HUGI8S IA            HEALTHY 840A
5    ANTHRWPOS 3Aα        MAN 68B
     ASTHENEIA IA         WEAKNESS 114D
     ETOS                 YEAR 317A
6    GINWSKW 2B           FIND OUT 160B
     ECHW I2F             HAVE 333B
     KATAKEIMAI I         LIE DOWN 412B
     POLUS IIBα           MANY 694C
     HUGI8S IA            HEALTHY 840A
     CHRONOS              TIME 896A
     CHRONOS              TIME 896B
7    ANTHRWPOS 3Aß        MAN 68B
     ASTHENEW IA          BE SICK 115A
     BALLW 2B             PUT 130D
     EN IV6B              IN 261A
     ERCHOMAI IIAα        COME 310B
     ECHW I2D             HAVE 333A
     IASIS I              HEALING 369B
     KATABAINW IAα        COME DOWN 409B
     KOLUMB8THRA          POOL 443C
     KURIOS 2Cß           LORD 460D
     PRO 2                BEFORE 708D
     TARASSW I            STIR UP 812D
     HUDWR I              WATER 840C
8    EGEIRW IB            RAISE UP 214A
8F     PERIPATEW IC       GO ABOUT 655A
8=11   KRABATTOS          MATTRESS 448C
8=12   AIRW IA            LIFT UP 23D
9    H8MERA 2             DAY 347B
     HUGI8S IA            HEALTHY 840A
9F     SABBATON IA        SABBATH 746B
10   EIMI I5              TO BE 222C
     EXESTI 2             IT IS POSSIBLE 274D
     IOUDAIOS 2E          JEWISH 380B
     OUN 2B               THEREFORE 597C
11   EKEINOS IB           THAT 239A
     HOS,H8,HO III        THIS (ONE) 589A
     POIEW IIB:           DO 688B
     HUGI8S IA            HEALTHY 840A
11F    PERIPATEW IC       GO ABOUT 655A
12   ANTHRWPOS 4B         MAN 68D
     ERWTAW I             ASK 312A
13   ASTHENEW IA          BE SICK 115A
     EKNEUW               TURN 242D
     IAOMAI I             HEAL 369A
     OIDA IF              KNOW 558C
     OCHLOS I             CROWD 605C
     TOPOS IC             PLACE 830B
14   HAMARTANW I          SIN 41D
     GINOMAI I3Bγ         TAKE PLACE 158A
     HEURISKW IB          FIND 325B
     IDE I                SEE 369D
     HIERON 2             TEMPLE 373A
     HINA IIC             IN ORDER THAT 377C
     M8KETI 6A            NO LONGER 520B
     HUGI8S IA            HEALTHY 840A
     CHEIRWN              WORSE 889B
15   ANAGGELLW 2          DISCLOSE 51A
     POIEW IIB:           DO 688B
     HUGI8S IA            HEALTHY 840A
15F    IOUDAIOS 2E        JEWISH 380B
16   DIA BII2             THEREFORE 180B
```

Ref	Greek	Gloss
16	DIWKW 2	PERSECUTE 200B
	HOUTOS 1Bβ	THIS 601C
	SABBATON 1A	SABBATH 746B
17	ARTI 3	NOW 110A
	ERGAZOMAI 1	WORK 307A
	HEWS IIIC	UNTIL 335C
	KAGW 3A	I ALSO 387A
	PAT8R 3Dα	FATHER 641D
18	DIA BII2	THEREFORE 180B
	Z8TEW 2Bγ	SEEK 339C
	IDIOS 1Aβ	ONES OWN 370B
	ISOS	EQUAL 381D
	LEGW II3	CALL 471A
	LUW 4	ABOLISH 485C
	MALLON 1	MORE 490B
	MONOS 2C	ONLY 529D
	HOUTOS 1Bβ	THIS 601C
	POIEW IIB₁	DO 688B
	SABBATON 1A	SABBATH 746B
19	AM8N 2	AMEN 45B
	AN 2B	(PARTICLE) 48A
	APO V5	OF 87D
	APOKRINOMAI 2	BEGIN 93A
	BLEPW 1A	SEE 143A
	HEAUTOU 1A	ONESELF 211B
	LEGW IIID	ASSURE 470D
	HOMOIWS	LIKEWISE 571A
	OUDEIS 2Bα	NOTHING 596C
	OUN 2B	THEREFORE 597C
19A	AN	IF 49A
19=23	PAT8R 3Dα	FATHER 641D
19=26	HUIOS 2B	SON 842D
20	DEIKNUMI 1A	SHOW 171D
	ERGON ICα	DEED 308A
	THAUMAZW 1Aα	WONDER 352D
	HINA IID	IN ORDER THAT 377C
	HINA I3	IN ORDER THAT 377D
	MEGAS 2Aγ	GREAT 499A
	PHILEW 1A	LOVE LIKE 867A
21	EGEIRW 1Aβ	RAISE 213D
	THELW 2	WISH 355D
	NEKROS 2A	DEAD 537A
	HOS,H8,HO I2A	(REL PRON) 587A
	HOUTW 1A	THUS 602B
	HWSPER 1	(JUST) AS 908A
21A	ZWOPOIEW 1	MAKE ALIVE 342C
21B	ZWOPOIEW 1	MAKE ALIVE 342C
21F	GAR IC	FOR 151B
22	GAR 1B	FOR 151B
	KRINW 4Bα	JUDGE 452D
	KRISIS 1Aα	JUDGING 453C
	OUDE 1	AND NOT 595D
	OUDEIS 2A	NO ONE 596C
	PAS ICα	ALL 637B
23	HINA IIB	IN ORDER THAT 377C
	KATHWS 1	JUST AS 392A
23A	TIMAW 2	HONOR 824D
23B	TIMAW 2	HONOR 824D
23C	TIMAW 2	HONOR 824D
23D	TIMAW 2	HONOR 824D
23F	PEMPW 1	SEND 647D
24	AKOUW 1Bα	HEAR 31B
	EK IC	AWAY FROM 233D
24	ERCHOMAI I2C	COME 311C
	ZW8 2Bα	LIFE 341C
	ZW8 2Bα	LIFE 341C
	THANATOS 2A	DEATH 352A
	KRISIS 1Aβ	JUDGING 453D
	LOGOS 1Bβ	WORD 479B
	METABAINW 2A	PASS 512A
	PISTEUW 1B	BELIEVE 666C
24A	ZW8 2Bα	LIFE 341B
24F	AM8N 2	AMEN 45B
24F	LEGW IIID	ASSURE 470D
25	AKOUW 1Bγ	HEAR 31C
	ERCHOMAI IIBα	COME 311B
	ZAW 2A	LIVE 337A
	HOTE 2Aα	WHEN 592C
	PHWN8 2A	VOICE 878D
	HWRA 3	TIME OF DAY 905A
25B	AKOUW 4	LISTEN 32A
26	DIDWMI 1Bβ	GIVE 192B
	HEAUTOU IC	ONESELF 211B
	ECHW I2J	HAVE 333C
	HOUTW 1A	THUS 602B
	PAT8R 3Dα	FATHER 641D
	HWSPER 1	(JUST) AS 908A
26A	ZW8 2Aα	LIFE 340D
26B	ZW8 2Aβ	LIFE 341A
27	EXOUSIA 3	AUTHORITY 278A
	KRISIS 1Aα	JUDGING 453C
	HOTI 3A	THAT 593D
	POIEW IIB6	DO 687C
	HUIOS 2C	SON 843B
28	AKOUW 1Bγ	HEAR 31C
	ERCHOMAI IIBα	COME 311B
	THAUMAZW 1Bα	WONDER 353A
	MN8MEION 2	TOMB 526C
	PAS 1Dγ	ALL 637D
	PHWN8 2A	VOICE 878D
	HWRA 3	TIME OF DAY 905A
29	AGATHOS 2B6	GOOD 3C
	ANASTASIS 2B	RESURRECTION 60A
	EKPOREUOMAI IC	GO OUT 243D
	ZW8 2Bα	LIFE 341C
	KRISIS 1Aβ	JUDGING 453D
	POIEW IIBε	DO 687D
	PRASSW 1A	DO 705B
	PHAULOS 1	WORTHLESS 862B
30	AKOUW 1Bα	HEAR 31B
	ALLA 1B	BUT, YET 37D
	APO V5	OF 87D
	DIKAIOS 4	RIGHTEOUS 195B
	EMAUTOU 3	MYSELF 253B
	Z8TEW 2Bα	SEEK 339C
	KRINW 4Bα	JUDGE 452D
	KRISIS 1Aα	JUDGING 453C
	HO,H8,TO IIIE	THE 553A
	OUDEIS 2Bα	NOTHING 596C
	PEMPW 1	SEND 647D
30A	THEL8MA 1B	WILL 354D
30B	THEL8MA ICγ	WILL 355A
31	EAN IIA	IF 210B
	MARTUREW 1A	BEAR WITNESS 493D
	MARTURIA 2Dβ	TESTIMONY 494D
31F	AL8TH8S 2	TRUE 36B

32	ALLOS 1A	OTHER 39B
	MARTURIA 2DP	TESTIMONY 494D
32A	MARTUREW 1A	BEAR WITNESS 493D
32B	MARTUREW 1B	BEAR WITNESS 494A
33	AL8THEIA 2B	TRUTH 35D
	MARTUREW 1A	BEAR WITNESS 493D
34	HINA 11A	IN ORDER THAT 377C
	LAMBANW 1D	RECEIVE 465D
	MARTURIA 2DX	TESTIMONY 494C
	HOUTOS 1BX	THIS 601C
	PARA 13B	FROM 614D
	SWZW 2B	SAVE 806B
35	AGALLIAW	BE GLAD 4A
	KAIROS 1	TIME 395C
	KAIW 1A	LIGHT 397A
	LUCHNOS 1	LAMP 484C
	PROS 1112B	TOWARD 717A
	PHAINW 1	SHINE 859B
	PHWS 1A	LIGHT 879D
	HWRA 2AP	TIME OF DAY 904C
36	APOSTELLW 1C	SEND AWAY 98B
	AUTOS 1H	EVEN 122C
	ERGON 1CX	DEED 308A
	HINA 11B	IN ORDER THAT 377C
	MARTURIA 2DP	TESTIMONY 494D
	MEGAS 2BP	GREAT 499C
	HO,H8,TO 111AX	THE 552C
	TELEIOW 1	COMPLETE 817B
36A	PAT8R 3DX	FATHER 641D
36B	PAT8R 3DX	FATHER 641D
36F	MARTUREW 1A	BEAR WITNESS 493D
37	EIDOS 1	FORM 220B
	EKEINOS 1B	THAT 238D
	OUTE	NOT 600C
	PAT8R 3DX	FATHER 641D
	PEMPW 1	SEND 647D
	PWPOTE	EVER 739B
	PHWN8 2A	VOICE 879A
38	APOSTELLW 1C	SEND AWAY 98B
	EN 15A	IN 258D
	LOGOS 1BX	COMMAND 479A
	MENW 1AP	REMAIN 505B
	PISTEUW 1B	BELIEVE 666C
39	GRAPH8 2BX	SCRIPTURE 165B
	DOKEW 1A	THINK 200D
	ERAUNAW	SEARCH 306C
	ZW8 2BX	LIFE 341C
	MARTUREW 1A	BEAR WITNESS 493D
40	ERCHOMAI 12C	COME 311D
	ZW8 2BX	LIFE 341B
	THELW 2	WISH 355D
	KAI 12G	AND 393C
41	DOXA 3	FAME 203A
	PARA 13B	FROM 614D
42	AGAP8 11BY	LOVE 5D
	HEAUTOU 1C	ONESELF 211B
	ECHW 12EP	HAVE 333A
	THEOS 3FP	GOD 358B
	OU 5B	NO 595A
43	EKEINOS 1B	THAT 239A
	ERCHOMAI 11An	COME 311A
	IDIOS 1AP	ONES OWN 370B
	PAT8R 3DX	FATHER 641D

43A	LAMBANW 1EX	RECEIVE 465D
43A	ONOMA 14CY	NAME 576B
43B	LAMBANW 1EX	RECEIVE 465D
43B	ONOMA 14CY	NAME 576C
44	ALL8LWN	EACH OTHER 38D
	*DOXA 3	FAME 203A
	Z8TEW 2A	SEEK 339C
	THEOS 3I	GOD 358C
	LAMBANW 1D	RECEIVE 465D
	MONOS 1A6	ONLY 529C
	PARA 13B	FROM 614D
	PISTEUW 2B	BELIEVE 667C
	PWS 1D	HOW 739B
45	DOKEW 1D	THINK 201A
	ELPIZW 3	HOPE 252A
	PAT8R 3DX	FATHER 641D
45A	KAT8GOREW 1B	424C
		BRING CHARGES
45B	KAT8GOREW 1B	424C
		BRING CHARGES
46	AN 1BX	(PARTICLE) 47D
	GAR 1C	FOR 151B
	GRAPHW 2C	WRITE 166A
46A	PISTEUW 1B	BELIEVE 666C
46B	PISTEUW 1B	BELIEVE 666C
47	GRAMMA 2C	WRITING 164C
	EI 11A	IF 218A
	HO,H8,TO 111E	THE 553A
	PWS 1D	HOW 739C
	R8MA 1	WORD 742D
47A	PISTEUW 1A6	BELIEVE 666B
47B	PISTEUW 1A6	BELIEVE 666B

JOHN 6

1	GALILAIA	GALILEE 149D
	THALASSA 2	LAKE 351A
	MEROS 1BY	PART 507A
	PERAN 2A	ON THE OTHER SIDE 649C
	TIBERIAS	TIBERIAS 823A
2	AKOLOUTHEW 2	ACCOMPANY 30D
	ASTHENEW 1A	BE SICK 115A
	EPI 11BY	ON 286B
	HORAW	SEE 581B
	HORAW 1AP	SEE 581C
	OCHLOS 1	CROWD 605C
	POLUS 11BX	MANY 694C
	S8MEION 2A	SIGN 755D
3	ANERCHOMAI	GO UP 64C
	KATHEZOMAI 2	SIT 389D
	KATH8MAI 2	SIT DOWN 390C
	OROS	MOUNTAIN 586B
4	EGGUS 2A	NEAR 213B
	HEORT8	FESTIVAL 279D
	IOUDAIOS 2C	JEWISH 380B
	PASCHA 1	THE PASSOVER 639A
5	AGORAZW 1	BUY 12C
	ARTOS 1A	BREAD 110A
	THEAOMAI 1A	SEE 353D
	POTHEN 3	FROM WHERE 686D
	POLUS 11BX	MANY 694C
	PHILIPPOS 3	PHILIP 868A
6	AUTOS 1E	OF HIMSELF 122C

6	MELLW ICα	BE ABOUT TO 502A	15	AUTOS IC	SELF 122C
	OIDA IF	KNOW 558C		BASILEUS I	KING 135C
	HOUTOS IBα	THIS 601C		GINWSKW 4C	PERCEIVE 160C
	PEIRAZW 2B	TRY 646A		ERCHOMAI IIAζ	COME 310D
7	ARKEW I	BE ENOUGH 106D		MELLW ICγ	INTEND 502B
	ARTOS IA	BREAD 110B		MONOS IAβ	ONLY 529C
	BRACHUS 3	LITTLE 146D		PALIN IA	BACK 611B
	D8NARION	DENARIUS 178B		POIEW IIBι	DO 688B
	DIAKOSIOI	TWO HUNDRED 184A		PHEUGW I	FLEE 863C
	HEKASTOS 2	EACH 236A	16	GINOMAI IIBγ	COME ABOUT 157C
	LAMBANW 2	RECEIVE 466B		EPI IIIAγ	ON 288B
	PHILIPPOS 3	PHILIP 868A		KATABAINW IAδ	COME DOWN 409C
8	ANDREAS	ANDREW 63B		OPSIOS 2	LATE 606C
	HEIS IAβ	ONE 230A		HWS IVIA	WHEN 907A
	PETROS	PETER 661A	17	GINOMAI IIBα	COME ABOUT 157D
9	ARTOS IA	BREAD 110B		EIS IAα	INTO 227B
	HEIS 3B	SOMEONE 230D		EMBAINW	GO IN 253C
	KRITHINOS	MADE OF BARLEY 451C		KATALAMBANW IB	SEIZE 414B
	HOS,H8,HO I3Bγ	(REL PRON) 587D		KAPHARNAOUM	CAPERNAUM 427C
	OPSARION	FISH 606B		OUPW	NOT YET 597D
	PAIDARION IB	CHILD 608B		PERAN 2A ON THE OTHER SIDE	649C
	TIS, TI I8δ	WHICH 827A		SKOTIA I	DARKNESS 764D
	TOSOUTOS 2Aα	SO GREAT 831B	18	ANEMOS IA	WIND 64A
	HWDE 2A	HERE 903D		DIEGEIRW	AROUSE 193D
10	ANAPIPTW I	RECLINE 59A		MEGAS 2Aγ	GREAT 499A
	ARITHMOS I	NUMBER 105D		PNEW IA	BLOW 686A
	PENTAKISCHILIO:	FIVE THOUSAND 648C		TE IA	AND 815A
	POIEW IIBτ	DO 688B	19	GINOMAI I4Cη	COME, GO 159A
	POLUS IIBα	MANY 694C		EGGUS ID	NEAR 213B
	TOPOS IC	PLACE 830B		EIKOSI	TWENTY 221A
	CHORTOS	GRASS 892B		ELAUNW	DRIVE 248A
	HWS IV5	WHEN 907C		EPI IIAα	ON 285C
	HWSEI 2	AS 907D		THEWREW I	OBSERVE 360C
11	ANAKEIMAI 2	BE AT TABLE 55C		PERIPATEW IC	GO ABOUT 654D
	ARTOS IA	BREAD 110A		PLOION 2	SHIP 679B
	DIADIDWMI	DISTRIBUTE 181D		STADION I	STADE 771C
	EK 4Aε	FROM 235B		HWS IV5	WHEN 907C
	EUCHARISTEW 2	GIVE THANKS 328C	20	EGW	I 216A
	KAI II3	ALSO 394B		EIMI II5	TO BE 223C
	HOMOIWS	LIKEWISE 571A	21	G8 4	LAND 156C
	HOSOS 2	HOW GREAT 590B		GINOMAI I4Cγ	COME, GO 159A
	OPSARION	FISH 606B		EPI IIAβ	ON 285D
12	APOLLUMI 2B	BE LOST 95A		THELW 2	WISH 355D
	EMPI(M)PL6MI 2	FILL 255C		LAMBANW IEα	RECEIVE 465D
	PERISSEUW IAα	BE LEFT OVER 656C		HUPAGW 2	GO AWAY 844C
	HWS IVIA	WHEN 907A	21A	PLOION 2	SHIP 679B
12F	KLASMA	FRAGMENT 434B	21B	PLOION 2	SHIP 679B
12F	SUNAGW I	GATHER 789D	22	ALLOS IEβ	ANOTHER 39C
13	ARTOS IA	BREAD 110B		APERCHOMAI IA	GO AWAY 83D
	GEMIZW I	FILL 152D		EPAURION	NEXT DAY 283C
	KOPHINOS	BASKET 448C		HIST8MI II2Bβ	BEING 383C
	KRITHINOS	MADE OF BARLEY 451C		MONOS IAβ	ONLY 529C
	OUN IA	THEREFORE 597B		OCHLOS I	CROWD 605C
	PERISSEUW IAα	BE LEFT OVER 656C		PERAN 2B ON THE OTHER SIDE	649C
14	AL8THWS I	TRULY 36D		PLOIARION	BOAT 679A
	ERCHOMAI IIAη	COME 310D		PLOION 2	SHIP 679B
	KOSMOS 4C	WORLD 447B		SUNEISERCHOMAI	ENTER WITH 794D
	LEGW IIBα	SAY 469C	23	ARTOS IA	BREAD 110A
	HOS,H8,HO I5A	(REL PRON) 588D		EGGUS IA	NEAR 213B
	PROPH8T8S 3	PROPHET 731A		EUCHARISTEW 2	GIVE THANKS 328C
	S8MEION 2A	SIGN 755D		KURIOS 2Cβ	LORD 460D
15	ANACHWREW 2B	WITHDRAW 63A		PLOIARION	BOAT 679A
	HARPAZW 2A	SNATCH 108C		TIBERIAS	TIBERIAS 823A

Verse	Word	Gloss	Ref
23	TOPOS 1C	PLACE	830B
24	AUTOS 2	THEY	122D
	EIDON 1D	SEE	219D
	EMBAINW	GO IN	253C
	Z8TEW 1Aα	SEEK	339A
	KAPHARNAOUM	CAPERNAUM	427C
	OUDE 1	AND NOT	5950
	OUN 5	THEREFORE	597D
	PLOIARION	BOAT	679A
25	GINOMAI 14Cθ	COME, GO	159B
	HEURISKW 1A	FIND	325A
	PERAN 2B	ON THE OTHER SIDE	649C
	POTE	WHEN	701D
	RABBI	RABBI	740B
	HWDE 1	HERE	903B
26	ARTOS 1A	BREAD	110A
	EIDON	SEE	219C
	EK 4Aε	FROM	235B
	ESTHIW 18β	EAT	313A
	Z8TEW 1Aα	SEEK	339A
	LEGW III0	ASSURE	470D
	HOTI 3A	THAT	593D
	*S8MEION 2A	SIGN	755D
	CHORTAZW 2A	FEED	892B
27	APOLLUMI 2Aβ	PASS AWAY	94D
	BRWSIS 3B	FOOD	147D
	EIS 6E	WITH	229B
	ERGAZOMAI 2E	WORK	307D
	ZW8 2Bα	LIFE	341C
	MENW 1Cβ	REMAIN	505C
	PAT8R 3Dα	FATHER	641D
	SPHRAGIZW 2B	SEAL	804D
	HUIOS 2C	SON	843B
28	ERGAZOMAI 2A	WORK	307A
	ERGAZOMAI 2E	WORK	307B
	ERGON 1Cβ	DEED	308A
29	APOSTELLW 1C	SEND AWAY	98B
	EIMI II6A	TO BE	223C
	ERGON 1Cβ	DEED	308A
	HINA III1E	IN ORDER THAT	378C
	HOS,H8,HO I2A	(REL PRON)	587B
	HOUTOS 1A6	THIS	601A
	HOUTOS 1Bβ	THIS	601C
	PISTEUW 2Aα	BELIEVE	667A
	PISTEUW 2Aβ	BELIEVE	667B
30	ERGAZOMAI 2A	WORK	307B
	HINA II1A	IN ORDER THAT	377C
	PISTEUW 1B	BELIEVE	666C
	PISTEUW 2Aα	BELIEVE	667A
	POIEW II8β	DO	687C
	S8MEION 2A	SIGN	755D
30B	OUN 1Cα	THEREFORE	597B
31	GRAPHW 2C	WRITE	165D
	DIDWMI 2	GIVE	192C
	ESTHIW 1A	EAT	312C
	MANNA 1	MANNA	492A
	PAT8R 1B	FOREFATHERS	640D
31FF	ARTOS 2	FOOD	110C
32	AL8THINOS 3	GENUINE	36C
	LEGW III0	ASSURE	470D
	MWUS8S	MOSES	533D
33	ZW8 2Aβ	LIFE	341A
	KATABAINW 1Aγ	COME DOWN	409C
33	KOSMOS 5B	WORLD	447C
34	KURIOS 2Cβ	LORD	460D
	PANTOTE	ALWAYS	614A
35	ARTOS 2	FOOD	110C
	DIPSAW 2	THIRST	199C
	ERCHOMAI I2C	COME	311D
	ZW8 2Aβ	LIFE	341A
	PEINAW 2	HUNGER	645D
	PISTEUW 2Aβ	BELIEVE	667B
	PWPOTE	EVER	739B
35B	M8 D2	NOT	519C
36	ALLA 2	BUT, YET	37D
	KAI I6	AND	394A
	PISTEUW 2B	BELIEVE	667C
37	DIDWMI 3	GIVE	192C
	EKBALLW 1	DRIVE OUT	236D
	EXW 1B	OUTSIDE	279A
	ERCHOMAI I2C	COME	311D
	H8KW 1Dβ	HAVE COME	345C
	PAS 1Cγ	WHOEVER	637C
	PAT8R 3Dα	FATHER	641D
38	ALLA 1B	BUT, YET	37D
	THEL8MA 1B	WILL	354D
	HINA 11B	IN ORDER THAT	377C
	KATABAINW 1Aγ	COME DOWN	409C
	OURANOS 2B	HEAVEN	599B
	POIEW IICα	DO	688C
38B	THEL8MA 1Cγ	WILL	355A
38F	PEMPW 1	SEND	647D
39	APOLLUMI 1B	LOSE	94C
	AUTOS 3D	(OBLIQUE CASE)	123B
	DIDWMI 3	GIVE	192C
	HINA III1E	IN ORDER THAT	378C
	HOUTOS 1Bβ	THIS	601C
	PAS 1Cγ	WHOEVER	637C
39F	ANIST8MI 1A	RAISE	69B
39F	EIMI II6A	TO BE	223C
39F	ESCHATOS 3B	LAST	314B
39F	H8MERA 3Bβ	DAY	347D
39F	THEL8MA 1A	WILL	354D
39F	HOUTOS 1A6	THIS	601A
40	ZW8 2Bα	LIFE	341B
	ZW8 2Bα	LIFE	341C
	THEWREW 1	OBSERVE	360C
	HINA III1Cα	IN ORDER THAT	378C
	PAS 1Cγ	WHOEVER	637B
	PAT8R 3Dα	FATHER	641D
	PISTEUW 2Aβ	BELIEVE	667B
	HUIOS 2B	SON	842D
41	ARTOS 2	FOOD	110C
	GOGGUZW 1	MURMUR	163C
	IOUDAIOS 2E	JEWISH	380B
41F	KATABAINW 1Aγ	COME DOWN	409C
42	IWS8PH 4	JOSEPH	386C
	OIDA 1A	KNOW	558B
	HOTI 2	THAT	593D
	OURANOS 2B	HEAVEN	599B
	HOUTOS 1Aα	THIS	600D
	POTHEN 2	FROM WHERE	686D
	PWS 1C	HOW	739C
43	ALL8LWN	EACH OTHER	38D
	GOGGUZW 1	MURMUR	163C
	META AI	WITH	509D

43	M8 AIII3B	
44	ANIST8MI IA	RAISE 69B
	EAN I3B	IF 210D
	HELKW IB	DRAG 251B
	EN II2	WHILE 259D
	ESCHATOS 3B	LAST 314B
	H8MERA 39β	DAY 347D
	OUDEIS 2A	NO ONE 596B
	PEMPW I	SEND 647D
44F	ERCHOMAI I2C	COME 311D
45	AKOUW 3D	LEARN 32A
	GRAPHW 2J	WRITE 165D
	DIDAKTOS I	TAUGHT 190C
	MANTHANW I	LEARN 491C
	PARA I3C	FROM 615A
	PAT8R 3Dx	FATHER 641D
	PROPH8T8S I	PROPHET 731A
46	EIMI IIIβA	TO BE 224D
	HOTI IC	THAT 593A
	HOUTOS IAε	THIS 601B
	PARA II	FROM 614C
	TIS, TI IAα	ANY ONE 827C
46A	HORAW IAα	SEE 581C
46A	PAT8R 3Dα	FATHER 641D
46B	HORAW IAα	SEE 581C
47	ZW8 2Bα	LIFE 341B
	ZW8 2Bα	LIFE 341C
	PISTEUW 2Aβ	BELIEVE 667B
	PISTEUW 2B	BELIEVE 667C
48	ARTOS 2	FOOD 110C
	ZW8 2Aβ	LIFE 341A
49	ESTHIW IA	EAT 312C
	MANNA I	MANNA 492A
50	APOTHN8SKW IBα	DIE 91A
	HINA IIIE	IN ORDER THAT 378C
	OURANOS 2B	HEAVEN 599B
50F	EK 4Aε	FROM 235B
50F	ESTHIW IBβ	EAT 313A
50F	KATABAINW IAY	COME DOWN 409C
51	AIWN IB	TIME 26D
	ARTOS 2	FOOD 110C
*DE	4B	BUT, AND 170D
	ZAW 2Bβ	LIVE 337A
	KOSMOS 5B	WORLD 447C
	TIS, TI IAY	ANY ONE 827D
	HUPER IB	IN BEHALF OF 846D
51A	ZAW 4B	LIVE 337C
51=6	SARX I	FLESH 750D
52	DUNAMAI IA	ABLE 206B
	ESTHIW ID	EAT 313B
	IOUDAIOS 2E	JEWISH 380B
	MACHOMAI 2	DISPUTE 497D
	HOUTOS IAα	THIS 600D
	PWS ID	HOW 739C
53	HEAUTOU IC	ONESELF 211B
	ESTHIW IA	EAT 312D
	KAI I2E	AND 393C
	OSM8 2	ODOR 590A
	OUN 2C	THEREFORE 597C
	HUIOS 2C	SON 843B
53F	ZW8 29α	LIFE 341B
53F	PINW I	DRINK 664B
53=5	HAIMA 2B	BLOOD 22C
54	ANIST8MI IA	RAISE 69B
	ESCHATOS 3B	LAST 314B
	ZW8 2Bα	LIFE 341C
	H8MERA 3Bβ	DAY 347D
55	AL8TH8S 3	REAL 36B
	BRWSIS 3B	FOOD 147D
	POSIS 2	DRINKING 701A
56	EN I5A	IN 258D
	KAGW I	AND I 387A
	MENW IAβ	REMAIN 505A
	PINW I	DRINK 664B
57	APOSTELLW IC	SEND AWAY 98B
	DIA BII4B	BY 180C
	ZAW IAε	LIVE 336D
	KAGW I	AND I 386D
	KAI II3	ALSO 394B
57C	ZAW 2A	LIVE 337A
58	AIWN IB	TIME 26D
	APOTHN8SKW IBα	DIE 91A
	ARTOS 2	FOOD 110C
	ZAW 2Bβ	LIVE 337A
	KATHWS I	JUST AS 392B
	KATABAINW IAY	COME DOWN 409C
59	KAPHARNAOUM	CAPERNAUM 427C
	SABBATON IA	SABBATH 746B
	SUNAGWG8 2A	790C
		PLACE OF ASSEMBLY
60	AKOUW IBα	HEAR 31B
	DUNAMAI IA	ABLE 206B
	EK 4Aα	FROM 235B
	LOGOS IAY	WORD 478C
	OUN 2B	THEREFORE 597C
	HOUTOS 2B	THIS 602A
	POLUS I2Aα	MANY 694D
	SKL8ROS IB	HARD 763B
60B	AKOUW 5	LISTEN 32A
61	GOGGUZW I	MURMUR 163D
	EN I5B	IN 258D
	OIDA 2	KNOW 559A
	HOUTOS IBα	THIS 601C
	SKANDALIZW 2	CAUSE TO FALL 760B
62	ANABAINW IAβ	GO UP 50A
	THEWREW I	OBSERVE 360C
	HO,H8,TO II6	THE 554C
	HOPOU IAα	WHERE 579C
	OUN 5	THEREFORE 597D
	PROTEROS IBβ	EARLIER 729C
	HUIOS 2C	SON 843B
63	ZW8 2Bα	LIFE 341B
	ZW8 2Bα	LIFE 341B
	ZWOPOIEW I	MAKE ALIVE 342C
	LALEW 2B	SPEAK 464D
	OU 6A	NO 595A
	OUDEIS 2By	IN NO RESPECT 596C
	R8MA I	WORD 742D
	SARX 2	BODY 751A
	WPHELEW 2B	HELP 909A
63A	PNEUMA 5Gβ	SPIRIT 683C
63B	PNEUMA 6A	SPIRIT 683D
64	ALLA 2	BUT, YET 37D
	ARCH8 IB	BEGINNING 111C
	EIMI II	TO BE 222B
	EK 4Aβ	FROM 235B

```
64  EK      5A            FROM 235C        4  KOSMOS 5A           WORLD 447C
    OU      5A            NO 595A             KRUPTOS 2B          HIDDEN 455B
    PARADIDWMI IB         GIVE OVER 620A      PARR8SIA 2          PUBLICLY 636A
    TIS, TI IAα           ANY ONE 827D        PHANEROW 2A         REVEAL 860D
64A   PISTEUW 2B          BELIEVE 667C     5  *ADELPHOS I         BROTHER 15D
64B   PISTEUW 2B          BELIEVE 667C        GAR IB              FOR 151B
65  ERCHOMAI I2C          COME 311D           PISTEUW 2Aβ         BELIEVE 667B
    OUDEIS 2A             NO ONE 596B      6  EMOS IAα            MY 255A
    PAT8R 3Dα             FATHER 641D         HETOIMOS I          READY 316D
66  APERCHOMAI 4          GO AFTER 84A        KAIROS 2            TIME 395D
    EK    3F              BY 234D             HO,H8,TO IIIE       THE 553A
    MATH8T8S 2Bβ          DISCIPLE 487A       OUPW                NOT YET 597D
    META AIIIA            WITH 509D           PANTOTE             ALWAYS 614A
    OPISW IA              BEHIND 578C         PAREIMI IB          BE PRESENT 629D
    OUKETI I              NO LONGER 596D      HUMETEROS I         YOUR 843D
    PERIPATEW IC          GO ABOUT 654D    7  ERGON ICβ           DEED 308A
    POLUS I2Aα            MANY 694D           ERGON ICβ           DEED 308B
67  THELW 2               WISH 355D           KOSMOS 7            WORLD 447D
    M8  CI                NOT 519A            MARTUREW IA         BEAR WITNESS 493D
    OUN 2B                THEREFORE 597C      PON8ROS IBβ         WICKED 697D
    HUPAGW I              GO AWAY 844B     7A    MISEW I          HATE 524C
68  ZW8 2Bα               LIFE 341B        7B    MISEW I          HATE 524C
    ZW8 2Bα               LIFE 341C        8  EMOS IAα            MY 255A
    KURIOS 2Cβ            LORD 460D           *HEORT8             FESTIVAL 279D
    PETROS                PETER 661A          KAIROS 2            TIME 395D
    R8MA I                WORD 743A           PL8ROW 2            MAKE FULL 677A
69  HAGIOS 2Cβ    THE HOLY ONE 10A          8A    OUPW           NOT YET 597D
    GINWSKW IC            KNOW 160A        8B    OUPW             NOT YET 597D
    PISTEUW 2B            BELIEVE 667C     9  MENW IAα            REMAIN 504D
    CHRISTOS I     ANOINTED ONE 895D          HOUTOS IBα          THIS 601C
70  DIABOLOS 2     THE SLANDERER 181B     10  HEORT8             FESTIVAL 279D
    EKLEGOMAI 2A          CHOOSE 241D         KRUPTOS 2B          HIDDEN 455B
    KAI I2G               AND 393C            TOTE 2              AT THAT TIME 831D
    OU  4C                NO 595A             PHANERWS            OPENLY 860D
71  IOUDAS 6              JUDAS 380D          HWS IVIA            WHEN 907A
    *ISKARIWTH            ISCARIOT 381D    IOF   HEORT8           FESTIVAL 279D
    LEGW I2B              SAY 469C         II  EKEINOS IC         THAT 239A
    MELLW ICγ             INTEND 502B         HEORT8             FESTIVAL 279D
    HOUTOS IAβ            THIS 601A           IOUDAIOS 2E         JEWISH 380B
    PARADIDWMI IB         GIVE OVER 620A      POU IA              WHERE 702D
    SIMWN 5               SIMON 758D       12  AGATHOS IBα        GOOD 3A
                                              ALLA IA            BUT, YET 37C
            JOHN 7                            ALLOS IC            OTHER 39B
                                              GOGGUSMOS 2        SECRET TALK 163D
I   Z8TEW 2Bγ             SEEK 339C           EIMI I4             TO BE 222B
    THELW 2               WISH 355D           LEGW IIBα           SAY 469C
    IOUDAIA I             JUDAEA 379D         HO,H8,TO I2         THE 552A
    IOUDAIOS 2E           JEWISH 380B         OU  I               NO 594B
IA    PERIPATEW IA        GO ABOUT 654D       PLANAW IB           DECEIVE 671B
IB    PERIPATEW IA        GO ABOUT 654D       POLUS IIBβ          MANY 694C
2   EGGUS 2A              NEAR 213B        12A   OCHLOS I         CROWD 605D
    HEORT8                FESTIVAL 279D    13  DIA BIII           BECAUSE OF 180D
    IOUDAIOS 2C           JEWISH 380B         IOUDAIOS 2E         JEWISH 380B
    SK8NOP8GIA  BUILDING OF TENTS 762C        LALEW 2Aα           SPEAK 464C
3   *ADELPHOS I           BROTHER 15D         MENTOI 2            THOUGH 504C
    ENTEUTHEN I           FROM HERE 268A      PARR8SIA I          PLAINNESS 635D
    ERGON ICα             DEED 308A           PHOBOS 2Aα          FEAR 871C
    THEWREW I             OBSERVE 360C     14  ANABAINW IAα       GO UP 49D
    HINA I2        IN ORDER THAT 377C          DIDASKW I          TEACH 191A
    IOUDAIA I             JUDAEA 379D         HEORT8             FESTIVAL 279D
    METABAINW IAα         PASS OVER 511D      HEORT8             FESTIVAL 280A
    HUPAGW 2              GO AWAY 844C        HIERON 2            TEMPLE 373A
4   EN III2               BY 260C             MESAZW    BE IN THE MIDDLE 507D
```

14 MESOW	BE IN THE MIDDLE 509B	24A KRINW 6A	JUDGE 453B
15 GRAMMA 3 ELEMENTARY KNOWLEDGE 164D		24B KRINW 6A	JUDGE 453B
THAUMAZW IAα	WONDER 352D	25 EK 4Aβ	FROM 235B
MANTHANW I	LEARN 491B	HIEROSOLUMIT8S	374A
M8 AII2B	NOT 518B	INHABITANT OF JERUSALEM	
HOUTOS IAα	THIS 600D	OU 4C	NO 595A
PWS IB	HOW 739C	OUN 2B	THEREFORE 597C
16 ALLA IB	BUT, YET 37D	TIS, TI IAα	ANY ONE 827D
EMOS IB	MY 255A	26 AL8THWS I	TRULY 36D
HO,H8,TO IIIE	THE 553A	ARCHWN 2A	AUTHORITIES 113C
PEMPW I	SEND 647D	GINWSKW IC	KNOW 160A
16F DIDACH8 2	TEACHING 191B	IDE 2	SEE 369D
17 EK 3C	FROM 234B	LALEW 2Aε	SPEAK 464C
EMAUTOU 3	MYSELF 253B	LEGW IIA	SAY 469B
8 IDγ	OR 343A	M8POTE 3A	WHETHER PERHAPS 521B
THEL8MA ICγ	WILL 355A	PARR8SIA 2	PUBLICLY 636A
THELW 2	WISH 355D	26F CHRISTOS I	ANOINTED ONE 895B
PERI IA	ABOUT 650B	27 ERCHOMAI IIAη	COME 310D
POIEW IICα	DO 688C	OIDA IC	KNOW 558B
POTEROS	WHETHER 702A	HOTAN 2B	WHEN 592B
17F APO V5	OF 87D	27A POTHEN 2	FROM WHERE 686D
18 ADIKIA 2	UNRIGHTEOUSNESS 17C	27B POTHEN 2	FROM WHERE 686D
AL8TH8S I	TRUE 36A	28 AL8THINOS 3	GENUINE 36C
DOXA 3	FAME 203A	APO V5	OF 87D
HEAUTOU IA	ONESELF 211B	EMAUTOU 3	MYSELF 253B
EIMI III4	TO BE 224C	ERCHOMAI IIAη	COME 311A
Z8TEW 2A	SEEK 339C	HIERON 2	TEMPLE 373A
IDIOS IAβ	ONES OWN 370B	KAGW I	AND I 386D
PEMPW I	SEND 647D	KAI I2G	AND 393C
19 EK 4Aα	FROM 235B	KAI I6	AND 394A
MWUS8S	MOSES 533D	KRAZW 2A	CALL 448D
OUDEIS 2A	NO ONE 596B	OUN 2B	THEREFORE 597C
POIEW IICα	DO 688C	PEMPW I	SEND 647D
TIS, TI 3A	WHICH 827B	28A OIDA IA	KNOW 558B
19B NOMOS 3	LAW 544D	28B OIDA IF	KNOW 558C
20 DAIMONION 2	DEMON 168B	28B OIDA 2	KNOW 558D
ECHW I2Eα	HAVE 333A	29 APOSTELLW IC	SEND AWAY 98B
21 ERGON ICα	DEED 308A	EIMI III8A	TO BE 224D
THAUMAZW IAα	WONDER 352D	KAKEINOS 2A	AND HE 397C
POIEW IIBα	DO 687C	PARA II	FROM 614C
22 EK 3C	FROM 234B	30 EPIBALLW IB	LAY ON 289D
HOTI IC	THAT 593A	ERCHOMAI IIBα	COME 311B
PERITEMNW I	CUT AROUND 658A	OUPW	NOT YET 597C
PERITOM8 I	CIRCUMCISION 658C	PIAZW 2A	GRASP 662D
22F MWUS8S	MOSES 533D	HWRA 3	TIME OF DAY 905A
22F SABBATON IA	SABBATH 746B	31 EK 4Aα	FROM 235B
23 EI III	IF 218C	ERCHOMAI IIAη	COME 310D
EN II2	WHILE 259D	HOS,H8,HO I4A	(REL PRON) 587D
LAMBANW 2	RECEIVE 466C	PISTEUW 2Aβ	BELIEVE 667B
LUW 4	ABOLISH 485C	POIEW IIBβ	DO 687C
M8 AI2	NOT 517C	POLUS I2Aα	MANY 694D
NOMOS 3	LAW 544C	POLUS IIIA	MANY 695C
HOLOS I	WHOLE 567C	S8MEION 2A	SIGN 755D
PERITOM8 2	CIRCUMCISION 658D	CHRISTOS I	ANOINTED ONE 895B
POIEW IIB₁	DO 688B	32 APOSTELLW IBγ	SEND AWAY 98A
HUGI8S IA	HEALTHY 840A	GOGGUZW 2	WHISPER 163D
CHOLAW	BE ANGRY 891C	HINA IIE	IN ORDER THAT 377C
24 DIKAIOS 4	RIGHTEOUS 195B	PIAZW 2A	GRASP 662D
KATA II5Aβ	ACCORDING TO 408A	HUP8RET8S	SERVANT 850C
KRISIS IBα	JUDGING 454A	33 ETI IC	STILL 316A
KRISIS 3	RIGHT 454B	KAI I2C	AND 393B
HO,H8,TO IIIF	THE 553A	MIKROS 2D	SHORT 523B
OPSIS 2	APPEARANCE 606D	OUN 2B	THEREFORE 597C

33	HUPAGW 3	GO AWAY 844D	42	EIPON 2C	SAY 225C
	CHRONOS	TIME 896B		EK 3B	FROM 234B
34	EIMI II9A	TO BE 223D		KWM8 I	VILLAGE 462D
	HEURISKW IA	FIND 325A		HOPOU IA∝	WHERE 579C
	Z8TEW IA∝	SEEK 339A		SPERMA IB	SEED 769A
	HOPOU IA∝	WHERE 579C		SPERMA 2B	SEED 769B
	SU IA	YOU 779D		CHRISTOS I	ANOINTED ONE 895B
35	DIASPORA I	DISPERSION 187D	43	SCHISMA 2	SPLIT 805B
	DIDASKW 2A	TEACH 191A	44	EK 4Aβ	FROM 235B
	HELL8N 2A	GENTILE 251C		EPIBALLW IB	LAY ON 289D
	MELLW ICɤ	INTEND 502B		THELW 2	WISH 355D
	M8 CI	NOT 519A		PIAZW 2A	GRASP 662D
	HOTI IDɤ	THAT 593C		TIS, TI IA∝	ANY ONE 827D
	OUN 2B	THEREFORE 597C	45	AGW 2	LEAD AWAY 14B
	POU 2A	WHERE 703A		DIA 8II2	WHY 180B
	PROS IIIIE	TOWARD 716D	45F	HUP8RET8S	SERVANT 850C
35A	POREUW I	PROCEED 699B	46	ANTHRWPOS 3Aβ	MAN 68B
35B	POREUW I	PROCEED 699A		OUDEPOTE	NEVER 596D
36	EIMI II9A	TO BE 223D		HOUTW 2	THUS 602C
	HEURISKW IA	FIND 325A		HWS III	SO 905D
	Z8TEW IA∝	SEEK 339A	47	KAI III	ALSO 394B
	LOGOS IAɤ	WORD 478C		PLANAW 2C6	DECEIVE 671C
	HOPOU IA∝	WHERE 579C	48	ARCHWN 2A	AUTHORITIES 113C
	HOUTOS 2B	THIS 602A		EK 4Aβ	FROM 235B
	SU IA	YOU 779D		PISTEUW 2Aβ	BELIEVE 667B
37	DIPSAW 2	THIRST 199C	49	ALLA 3	BUT, YET 38A
	EGW	I 216C		GINWSKW 3A	UNDERSTAND 160B
	EN II2	WHILE 259D		EPARATOS	ACCURSED 283B
	HEORT8	FESTIVAL 279D		NOMOS 4B	LAW 545A
	ESCHATOS 3B	LAST 314A		OCHLOS 2	CROWD 605D
	HIST8MI II2A	STAND 383B	50	EK 4A6	FROM 235B
	KOILIA 3	BELLY 438C		NIKOD8MOS	NICODEMUS 541C
	KRAZW 2A	CALL 448D		PROTEROS IB∝	EARLIER 729B
	MEGAS 28β	GREAT 499C	51	AKOUW 2	HEAR 31D
	PINW 2Bβ	DRINK 664C		ANTHRWPOS 3B	MAN 68D
38	GRAPH8 2Bβ	SCRIPTURE 165B		GINWSKW IC	KNOW 160A
	ZAW 4A	LIVE 337C		EAN I3B	IF 210D
	KOILIA 3	BELLY 438C		KRINW 4A∝	JUDGE 452D
	POTAMOS 2	RIVER 701C		NOMOS 3	LAW 545A
	REW I	FLOW 742B		PARA I3C	FROM 615A
	HUDWR 2	WATER 840D		PROTEROS IB∝	EARLIER 729B
38F	PISTEUW 2Aβ	BELIEVE 667B		PRWTOS 2A	FIRST 733D
39	DOXAZW 2	GLORIFY 203D	51F	M8 CI	NOT 519A
	EIMI I6	TO BE 222C	52	GALILAIOS	GALILEAN 149D
	EIPON I	SAY 225B		EGEIRW 2E	APPEAR 214A
	LAMBANW 2	RECEIVE 466B		ERAUNAW	SEARCH 306D
	MELLW IC6	IS DESTINED 502C		PROPH8T8S 3	PROPHET 731A
	OUDEPW	NOT YET 596D			
39A	OUPW	NOT YET 597D			
39A	PNEUMA 5D∝	SPIRIT 683A			JOHN 8
39B	OUPW	NOT YET 597D			
39B	PNEUMA 5Dβ	SPIRIT 683B	I	ELAIA I	OLIVE TREE 247B
40	AL8THWS I	TRULY 36D		OROS	MOUNTAIN 586B
	HO,H8,TO IIIA∝	THE 552C	2	KATHIZW 2A∝	SIT DOWN 390D
	OUN 2B	THEREFORE 597C		LAOS IA	PEOPLE 467D
	PROPH8T8S 3	PROPHET 731A		ORTHROS	DAWN 584B
41	GAR IF	WHAT 151C		PALIN IA	BACK 611C
	M8 CI	NOT 519B		PARAGINOMAI I	COME 618D
41A	CHRISTOS I	ANOINTED ONE 895B	3	AGW IA	LEAD 14A
41B	CHRISTOS I	ANOINTED ONE 895B		HIST8MI IIA∝	PUT 382D
42	B8THLEEM	BETHLEHEM 139C		KATALAMBANW IC	CATCH 414B
	GRAPH8 2Bβ	SCRIPTURE 165B		MESOS 2	THE MIDDLE 508D
	DAUID	DAVID 170B		MOICHEIA	ADULTERY 528B
				PHARISAIOS	PHARISEE 861C

3F	GUN8 3	BRIDE	167C
4	AUTOPHWROS	IN THE ACT	123O
	MOICHEUW 2B	COMMIT ADULTERY	528B
5	DIAKELEUW	ORDER	183A
	ENTELLW	COMMAND	268A
	LITHAZW	STONE	475A
	LITHOBOLEW 2	STONE	475B
	MWUS8S	MOSES	533D
	NOMOS 4A	LAW	545A
	SU IA	YOU	779D
6	G8 2	GROUND	156C
	GRAPHW I	WRITE	165C
	DAKTULOS	FINGER	169A
	ECHW 16A	CAN	333D
	KATAGRAPHW	WRITE	411A
	KAT8GOREW IA	BRING CHARGES	424B
	KATW 2	DOWNWARDS	426B
	KUPTW	BEND	458D
	HOUTOS 1Bα	THIS	601C
	PEIRAZW 2C	TRY	646A
	PROSPOIEW 2	PRETEND	725C
7	ANAMART8TOS	WITHOUT SIN	57B
	BALLW 1B	THROW	130C
	EPI IIIAβ	ON	286O
	EPIMENW 2	CONTINUE	296B
	ERWTAW I	ASK	312A
	LITHOS IA	STONE	475B
	HWS IVIB	WHEN	907A
8	G8 2	GROUND	156C
	GRAPHW I	WRITE	165C
	DAKTULOS	FINGER	169A
	KATAGRAPHW	WRITE	411A
	KATAKUPTW	BEND DOWN	413B
	KATW 2	DOWNWARDS	426B
	KUPTW	BEND	458D
	PALIN 2	AGAIN	611C
9	ARCHW 2C	BEGIN	113B
	HEIS 5E	ONE	231B
	ELEGCHW 2	EXPOSE	248D
	ESCHATOS 3A	LAST	314A
	HEWS II3	AS FAR AS	335D
	KATA II3A	(DISTRIBUTIVE)	407D
	KATALEIPW IA	LEAVE BEHIND	414C
	MESOS 2	THE MIDDLE	508D
	MONOS IAα	ONLY	529C
	PRESBUTEROS IA	OLDER	706B
	SUNEID8SIS 2	CONSCIOUSNESS	794B
10	PL8N 2	BUT	675C
	POU IA	WHERE	702D
IOF	KATAKRINW	CONDEMN	413A
11	M8KETI 6A	NO LONGER	520B
12	ZW8 2Aβ	LIFE	341A
	KOSMOS 5A	WORLD	447B
	LALEW 3	SPEAK	465A
	PERIPATEW ID	GO ABOUT	655A
	SKOTIA 2	DARKNESS	764D
12A	PHWS 2	LIGHT	880B
12B	PHWS 3A	LIGHT	880B
13	MARTURIA 2Dβ	TESTIMONY	494D
	OUN 2B	THEREFORE	597C
	SEAUTOU I	YOURSELF	753A
13F	AL8TH8S 2	TRUE	36B
13F	MARTUREW IA	BEAR WITNESS	493D
14	EMAUTOU 3	MYSELF	253B
	ERCHOMAI IIAγ	COME	310C
	8 IC	NOR	343A
	KAN 2	EVEN IF	403B
	MARTURIA 2Dβ	TESTIMONY	494D
	OIDA IF	KNOW	558C
14A	POTHEN I	FROM WHERE	686D
14A	POU 2B	WHERE	703A
14A	HUPAGW 3	GO AWAY	844D
14B	POTHEN I	FROM WHERE	686D
14B	POU 2B	WHERE	703A
14B	HUPAGW 3	GO AWAY	844D
15	KATA II5Aβ	ACCORDING TO	408A
	KRINW 6A	JUDGE	453B
	OUDEIS 2A	NO ONE	596B
	SARX 6	BODY	751C
	SU IA	YOU	779D
15B	KRINW 4Bα	JUDGE	452D
16	DE 4B	BUT, AND	170D
	EAN IIA	IF	210B
	KRINW 4Bα	JUDGE	452D
	KRISIS 1Bα	JUDGING	454A
	MONOS IAα	ONLY	529B
16F	DE 4B	BUT, AND	170D
17	AL8TH8S 2	TRUE	36B
	DE 4B	BUT, AND	170D
	DUO 2	TWO	208C
	MARTURIA 2A	TESTIMONY	494C
	NOMOS 4A	LAW	545A
	HUMETEROS I	YOUR	843D
18	EMAUTOU 3	MYSELF	253B
18A	MARTUREW IA	BEAR WITNESS	493D
18B	MARTUREW IA	BEAR WITNESS	493D
19	AN 1Bα	(PARTICLE)	47D
	OIDA 2	KNOW	558D
	OUTE	NOT	600C
	POU IA	WHERE	702D
20	GAZOPHULAKEION	TREASURY	148D
	EN IIC	IN	257D
	ERCHOMAI IIBα	COME	311B
	LALEW 2B	SPEAK	464C
	OUPW	NOT YET	597D
	PIAZW 2A	GRASP	662D
	R8MA I	WORD	742D
	HWRA 3	TIME OF DAY	905A
21	HAMARTIA 2	SIN	42D
	APOTHN8SKW 1Bα	DIE	91A
	OUN 2B	THEREFORE	597C
21A	HUPAGW 3	GO AWAY	844D
21B	HUPAGW 3	GO AWAY	844D
21F	HOPOU 1Bα	WHERE	579D
22	APOKTEINW IA	KILL	93C
	M8TI	(INTERROG PARTICLE)	522A
	HOTI IC	THAT	593B
	OUN 2B	THEREFORE	597C
	HUPAGW 3	GO AWAY	844D
22F	SU IA	YOU	779D
23	ANW I	ABOVE	76B
	EK 3B	FROM	234B
	KATW I	BELOW	426B
	KOSMOS 7	WORLD	447D
	*HO,H8,TO II6	THE	554B
24	HAMARTIA 2	SIN	42D

Verse / Greek	Gloss	Ref
24 APOTHN8SKW IBα	DIE	91A
EGW	I	216B
EIMI II5	TO BE	223C
PISTEUW IAβ	BELIEVE	666A
25 ARCH8 IB	BEGINNING	IIIC
EIMI II6C	TO BE	223C
HO TI 5	WHY	591C
OUN 2B	THEREFORE	597C
TIS, TI IAβ	WHICH	826D
26 AKOUW IBβ	HEAR	31C
AL8TH8S I	TRUE	36A
EIS IDβ	IN	227D
KAGW I	AND I	386D
KRINW 4Bα	JUDGE	452D
LALEW 2Aδ	SPEAK	464C
HOUTOS IA∊	THIS	601B
PARA I3C	FROM	615A
PERI IB	ABOUT	650B
27F GINWSKW 3C	UNDERSTAND	160B
28 APO V5	OF	87D
EGW	I	216B
EIMI II5	TO BE	223C
EMAUTOU 3	MYSELF	253B
KATHWS I	JUST AS	392A
LALEW 2B	SPEAK	464D
HOTAN IB	WHEN	592B
HOUTOS IA∊	THIS	601B
TOTE 2	AT THAT TIME	831D
HUIOS 2C	SON	843B
HUPSOW I	LIFT UP	858C
29 ARESTOS	PLEASING	105B
EIMI III7	TO BE	224D
META AIIICβ	WITH	510A
MONOS IB	ALONE	529D
POIEW IIB∊	DO	687D
30 LALEW 2B	SPEAK	464D
PISTEUW 2Aβ	BELIEVE	667B
POLUS I2Aα	MANY	694D
31 AL8THWS 2	TRULY	37A
EAN IIB	IF	210B
LOGOS IBβ	WORD	479B
MENW IAβ	REMAIN	505A
OUN 2B	THEREFORE	597C
PISTEUW 2Aα	BELIEVE	667A
32*AL8THEIA 2B	TRUTH	35D
GINWSKW IA	KNOW	159D
ELEUTHEROW 2	SET FREE	250C
33 ABRAAM	ABRAHAM	ID
DOULEUW IA	BE A SLAVE	204B
ELEUTHEROS I	FREE	250A
LEGW IIBα	SAY	469C
PWPOTE	EVER	739B
PWS IC	HOW	739C
SPERMA 2B	SEED	769B
34 DOULOS 3	SLAVE	205A
PAS ICγ	WHOEVER	637B
POIEW IICγ	DO	688C
35 DOULOS IC	SLAVE	204D
EIS 2B	FOR	228A
OIKIA IA	HOUSE	560A
35A AIWN IB	TIME	26D
35A MENW IAα	REMAIN	504D
35B AIWN IB	TIME	26D
35B MENW IAα	REMAIN	504D
35F HUIOS 2B	SON	842D
36 ELEUTHEROS 3	FREE	250B
ELEUTHEROW 2	SET FREE	250C
ONTWS I	REALLY	577C
37 ABRAAM	ABRAHAM	ID
ALLA 2	BUT, YET	37D
LOGOS IBβ	WORD	479B
SPERMA 2B	SEED	769B
CHWREW 2	GO	898A
38 HORAW IAβ	SEE	581D
38A PARA IIIBγ	BESIDE	615C
39 ABRAAM	ABRAHAM	ID
ERGON ICβ	DEED	308B
PAT8R IB	FOREFATHER	640C
POIEW IIBα	DO	687B
TEKNON 2D	CHILD	816C
40 AKOUW IBβ	HEAR	31C
AL8THEIA 2B	TRUTH	35D
ANTHRWPOS 3Aδ	MAN	68C
THEOS 3A	GOD	357D
LALEW 2B	SPEAK	464D
NUN 2	NOW	548A
PARA I3C	FROM	615A
41 GENNAW IA	BEGET	154C
EK 3A	FROM	234A
ERGON ICβ	DEED	308B
ECHW I2Bα	HAVE	332C
POIEW IIBα	DO	687B
PORNEIA I	PROSTITUTION	700A
41B PAT8R 3Cγ	FATHER	641D
42 AGAPAW IAβ	LOVE	4C
AN IBα	(PARTICLE)	47D
APO V5	OF	87D
APOSTELLW IC	SEND AWAY	98B
GAR IC	FOR	151B
GAR IB	FOR	151B
EMAUTOU 3	MYSELF	253B
EXERCHOMAI IAγ	GO OUT	274A
ERCHOMAI IIAη	COME	311A
H8KW IC	HAVE COME	345B
H8KW IDα	HAVE COME	345C
OUDE I	AND NOT	595D
PAT8R 3Cγ	FATHER	641D
42B THEOS 3A	GOD	357D
43 GINWSKW 3A	UNDERSTAND	160B
DIA BII2	WHY	180B
LALIA 2B	SPEECH	465A
LOGOS IBβ	WORD	479B
44 AL8THEIA 2B	TRUTH	35D
AN 3A	(PARTICLE)	48B
ANTHRWPOKTONOS	MURDERER	67B
ARCH8 IC	BEGINNING	IIID
AUTOS 3B	(OBLIQUE CASE)	123A
DIABOLOS 2	THE SLANDERER	181B
EIMI III3	TO BE	224B
EIMI III4	TO BE	224C
EK 3A	FROM	234B
EK 3Gα	BY	234D
EKEINOS IB	THAT	238D
EPITHUMIA 3	DESIRE	293C
EPITHUMIA 3	DESIRE	293D
THELW 2	WISH	355D

44 IDIOS 3B	ONES OWN 370D	55 KAN I	AND IF 403B
HIST8MI II2Cβ	STAND 383C	LOGOS IBα	COMMAND 479A
LALEW 2Aε	SPEAK 464C	HOMOIOS I	LIKE 569D
POIEW IICα	DO 688C	HOMOIOS 2	LIKE 570A
ST8KW	STAND 775C	T8REW 5	KEEP 822D
TEKNON 2E	CHILD 816C	PSEUST8S	LIAR 900D
HUIOS ICγ	SON 841D	56 ABRAAM	ABRAHAM 1D
PSEUDOS	LIE 900C	AGALLIAW	BE GLAD 4A
PSEUST8S	LIAR 900D	EIDON 5	SEE 220A
44A PAT8R 5A	FATHER 642A	EMOS IAα	MY 255A
44A PAT8R 5B	FATHER 642A	H8MERA 4A	TIME 348B
44B PAT8R 5A	FATHER 642A	HINA IIIAα	IN ORDER THAT 378A
44C PAT8R 5B	FATHER 642A	PAT8R IB	FOREFATHER 640C
45 PISTEUW IB	BELIEVE 666C	CHAIRW I	REJOICE 882A
45F AL8THEIA 2B	TRUTH 35D	57 ETOS	YEAR 317A
45F LEGW IIA	SAY 469B	ECHW I2F	HAVE 333B
46 HAMARTIA I	SIN 42D	HORAW IAα	SEE 581C
DIA BII2	WHY 180B	OUN 2B	THEREFORE 597C
ELEGCHW 2	EXPOSE 248D	OUPW	NOT YET 597D
PISTEUW IB	BELIEVE 666C	PENT8KONTA	FIFTY 648D
47 AKOUW IBα	HEAR 31B	58 GINOMAI IIA	BE BORN 157A
AKOUW IB	LISTEN 32A	EIMI II	TO BE 222A
DIA BII2	THEREFORE 180B	PRIN IB	BEFORE 708A
EK 3A	FROM 234B	PRIN 2	BEFORE 708A
THEOS 3A	GOD 357D	59 AIRW IA	LIFT UP 23D
HOTI 3A	THAT 593D	BALLW IB	THROW 130C
HOUTOS IBβ	THIS 601C	DIERCHOMAI IBα	GO THROUGH 193C
R8MA I	WORD 743A	KAI IIE	AND 393A
48 KALWS 4B	WELL 402B	KRUPTW IC	HIDE 455C
LEGW I5	SAY 469D	LITHOS IA	STONE 475B
SAMARIT8S	SAMARITAN 749A	MESOS 2	THE MIDDLE 508C
48F DAIMONION 2	DEMON 168B	HOUTW 4	THUS 602D
48F ECHW I2Eα	HAVE 333A	PARAGW 2B	BRING IN 619A
49 ATIMAZW	DISHONOR 119C		
TIMAW 2	HONOR 824D		
50 DOXA 3	FAME 203A		JOHN 9
KRINW 4βα	JUDGE 452D	I ANTHRWPOS 3Aε	MAN 68C
50A Z8TEW 2A	SEEK 339C	EK 5A	FROM 235C
50B Z8TEW IC	INVESTIGATE 339B	PARAGW 2Aα	BRING IN 619A
51 THANATOS 2A	DEATH 352A	TUPHLOS IAα	BLIND 838C
THEWREW 2C	OBSERVE 360D	2 GENNAW 2	BEAR 154D
51F LOGOS IBβ	WORD 479B	ERWTAW I	ASK 312A
51F T8REW 5	KEEP 822D	HINA II2	IN ORDER THAT 378D
52 GEUOMAI 2 COME TO KNOW SOMETH	KNOW SOMETH 156A	RABBI	RABBI 740B
GINWSKW IC	KNOW 160A	TIS, TI IAγ	WHICH 826D
DAIMONION 2	DEMON 168B	2F HAMARTANW I	SIN 41D
ECHW I2Eα	HAVE 333A	2F GONEUS	PARENTS 164B
THANATOS IA	DEATH 351B	3 ALLA IB	BUT, YET 37D
M8 DIA	NOT 519B	ERGON ICα	DEED 308A
NUN IAβ	NOW 547C	HINA IIII	IN ORDER THAT 379A
52F PROPH8T8S I	PROPHET 730D	OUTE	NOT 600C
53 ABRAAM	ABRAHAM 1D	PHANEROW IB	REVEAL 860C
MEGAS 2Bα	GREAT 499B	4 DEI I	IT IS NECESSARY 171A
HOSTIS 2B	WHOEVER 591A	ERGAZOMAI 2A	WORK 307A
PAT8R IB	FOREFATHER 640C	ERGON ICβ	DEED 308B
POIEW IIB:	DO 688B	ERCHOMAI IIBα	COME 311B
TIS, TI IAβ	WHICH 826D	HEWS I2A	UNTIL 335A
54 DOXA 3	FAME 203A	H8MERA IB	DAY 346D
DOXAZW 2	GLORIFY 203D	NUX 2	NIGHT 549A
EMAUTOU 2	MYSELF 253B	HOTE 2Aβ	WHEN 592C
HOTI IBζ	THAT 593A	4B ERGAZOMAI I	WORK 307A
OUDEIS 2Bβ	WORTHLESS 596C	5 KOSMOS 5A	WORLD 447B
55 EIPON 2C	SAY 225C	PHWS 2	LIGHT 880B

5A	KOSMOS 4C	WORLD	447B
6	EK 3H	BY	235A
	EPI IIIIAβ	ON	288A
	EPITITH8MI IAα	PUT UPON	302D
	EPICHRIW I	SPREAD	305B
	OPHTHALMOS I	EYE	604B
	POIEW IIAα	DO	687B
	PTUSMA	SALIVA	735A
	PTUW	SPIT	735B
	CHAMAI 2	TO THE GROUND	883B
6A	P8LOS 2	CLAY	662B
6B	P8LOS 2	CLAY	662B
7	APOSTELLW IC	SEND AWAY	98B
	BLEPW 2	SEE	143A
	EIS IDγ	IN	227D
	HERM8NEUW 2	TRANSLATE	310A
	ERCHOMAI IIAα	COME	310B
	SILWAM	SILOAM	758B
	HUPAGW 2	GO AWAY	844C
7A	NIPTW 2A	WASH	542B
7B	NIPTW 2A	WASH	542B
7F	OUN 2B	THEREFORE	597C
8	GEITWN	NEIGHBOR	152D
	THEWREW I	OBSERVE	360C
	KATH8MAI IAγ	SIT	390B
	HOTI IBζ	THAT	593A
	PROSAITEW	BEG	718C
	PROSAIT8S	BEGGAR	718C
	PROTEROS IBβ	EARLIER	729C
9	ALLOS IC	OTHER	39B
	EGW	I	216A
	EKEINOS IA	THAT	238D
	HOMOIOS I	LIKE	569C
	HOUTOS IAβ	THIS	601A
	OUCHI 2	NOT	603A
10	ANOIGW IEβ	OPEN	70D
	OUN 2B	THEREFORE	597C
	PWS IA	HOW	739C
11	ANABLEPW 2Aβ	GAIN SIGHT	50C
	EPICHRIW 2	ANOINT	305B
	LEGW II3	CALL	471B
	P8LOS 2	CLAY	662B
	POIEW IIAα	DO	687A
	SILWAM	SILOAM	758B
	HUPAGW 2	GO AWAY	844C
11A	NIPTW 2A	WASH	542B
11B	NIPTW 2A	WASH	542B
12	EKEINOS IC	THAT	239A
	POU IA	WHERE	702D
13	AGW IIAα	LEAD	14A
	POTE I	ONCE	701D
14	ANOIGW IEβ	OPEN	70D
	P8LOS 2	CLAY	662B
	POIEW IIAα	DO	687A
	SABBATON IA	SABBATH	746B
15	ANABLEPW 2Aβ	GAIN SIGHT	50C
	BLEPW 2	SEE	143A
	EPI IIIIAβ	ON	288A
	EPITITH8MI IAα	PUT UPON	302D
	ERWTAW I	ASK	312A
	NIPTW 2A	WASH	542B
	P8LOS 2	CLAY	662B
	PWS 2A	HOW	739D
16	ALLOS IC	OTHER	39B
	HAMARTWLOS I	SINNER	43C
	ANTHRWPOS 3Aε	MAN	68C
	EIMI I4	TO BE	222B
	EK 4Aβ	FROM	235B
	HOTI 3A	THAT	593D
	OUN 2B	THEREFORE	597C
	PARA II	FROM	614C
	POIEW IIBβ	DO	687C
	PWS ID	HOW	739C
	SABBATON IA	SABBATH	746B
	S8MEION 2A	SIGN	755D
	SCHISMA 2	SPLIT	805B
	T8REW 5	KEEP	822D
	TIS, TI IAα	ANY ONE	827D
	TOIOUTOS 2Aβ	SUCH A KIND	829A
17	ANOIGW IEβ	OPEN	70D
	HOTI IC	THAT	593B
	PROPH8T8S 3	PROPHET	731A
17B	LEGW I4	SAY	469D
18	ANABLEPW 2Aβ	GAIN SIGHT	50C
	GONEUS	PARENTS	164B
	HEWS IIIBβ	UNTIL	335C
	IOUDAIOS 2E	JEWISH	380B
	OUN 4	THEREFORE	597D
	PISTEUW IAβ	BELIEVE	666A
	TUPHLOS IAβ	BLIND	838C
	PHWNEW 2B	CALL	878C
19	ARTI 3	NOW	109D
	ERWTAW I	ASK	312A
	OUN ICα	THEREFORE	597C
	PWS IA	HOW	739C
19F	GENNAW 2	BEAR	154D
19F	HUIOS IAα	SON	841B
20	GONEUS	PARENTS	164B
21	ANOIGW IEβ	OPEN	70D
	AUTOS IC	SELF	122C
	ERWTAW I	ASK	312A
	ECHW I2F	HAVE	333B
	8 ID6	OR	343B
	H8LIKIA ICβ	AGE	346A
	NUN IAα	NOW	547C
	PWS 2A	HOW	739D
21A	OIDA IF	KNOW	558C
21B	OIDA IF	KNOW	558C
22	APOSUNAGWGOS	EXCOMMUNICATED	100B
	HINA IIIAα	IN ORDER THAT	378A
	IOUDAIOS 2E	JEWISH	380B
	HOMOLOGEW 4	CONFESS	571C
	HOTI 3A	THAT	593D
	SUNTITH8MI 2Aβ	AGREE	800C
	PHOBEW IBα	BE AFRAID	870D
	CHRISTOS I	ANOINTED ONE	895B
22F	GONEUS	PARENTS	164B
23	EPERWTAW IB	ASK	285A
	ECHW I2F	HAVE	333B
	H8LIKIA ICβ	AGE	346A
24	HAMARTWLOS 2	SINNER	43C
	DEUTEROS 4	SECOND	176B
	DIDWMI IA	GIVE	191D
	DOXA 3	FAME	203B
	HO,H8,TO IIIH	THE	553B
	HOUTOS 2B	THIS	602A

24 TUPHLOS IAβ	BLIND 838C	40F	TUPHLOS 2Aβ	BLIND 838C
PHWNEW 2B	CALL 878C	41*HAMARTIA 2		SIN 420
25 HAMARTWLOS 2	SINNER 43C	AN IBα		(PARTICLE) 470
ARTI 3	NOW 109D	ECHW I2Eβ		HAVE 333A
BLEPW 2	SEE 143A	MENW ICβ		REMAIN 505C
HEIS 2B	ONE 230C	NUN 2		NOW 548A
OIDA IF	KNOW 558C			
25B OIDA IE	KNOW 558C		JOHN 10	
26 ANOIGW IEβ	OPEN 70D			
POIEW IIDα	DO 688D	1 ALLACHOTHEN		38D
PWS IA	HOW 739C	FROM ANOTHER PLACE		
27 EIPON I	SAY 225C	ANABAINW IAα		GO UP 490
27A AKOUW 4	LISTEN 32A	AUL8 I		COURTYARD 120D
27A THELW I	WISH 355B	EISERCHOMAI IAβ		COME 231D
28 EKEINOS IC	THAT 239A	EISERCHOMAI IF		COME 232B
LOIDOREW	REVILE 480C	EKEINOS IB		THAT 239A
28B MATH8T8S 2A	DISCIPLE 486D	KLEPT8S		THIEF 435C
29 LALEW 2A6	SPEAK 464B	L8ST8S I		ROBBER 474B
MWUS8S	MOSES 533D	IF DIA AII		THROUGH 178C
29B OIDA IC	KNOW 558B	IF THURA IA		DOOR 366B
29F POTHEN I	FROM WHERE 686D	I=16 PROBATON 2		SHEEP 710A
30 ANOIGW IEβ	OPEN 70D	2 EISERCHOMAI IF		COME 232B
THAUMASTOS 2	WONDERFUL 353C	POIM8N I		SHEPHERD 690C
OIDA IF	KNOW 558C	3 EXAGW I		LEAD OUT 271A
HOUTOS IBβ	THIS 601C	THURWROS I		DOORKEEPER 366D
31 AKOUW 5	LISTEN 32A	KATA II3B		(DISTRIBUTIVE) 407D
HAMARTWLOS 2	SINNER 43C	ONOMA I3		NAME 574C
THEL8MA ICγ	WILL 355A	PHWNEW 2B		CALL 878C
THEOSEB8S	DEVOUT 359A	PHWN8 2A		VOICE 878D
OIDA IE	KNOW 558C	3F IDIOS IB		ONES OWN 370B
HOUTOS IAε	THIS 601B	4 EKBALLW 2		SEND OUT 237A
POIEW IICα	DO 688C	EMPROSTHEN 2E		IN FRONT 256D
32 AIWN IA	TIME 26D	POREUW I		PROCEED 699B
AKOUW 3E	LEARN 32A	4F AKOLOUTHEW I		FOLLOW 30C
ANOIGW IEβ	OPEN 70D	4F PHWN8 2B		VOICE 879A
GENNAW 2	BEAR 154D	5 M8 D2		NOT 519C
EK 5A	FROM 235C	PHEUGW I		FLEE 863C
33 EI IIB	IF 218B	5A ALLOTRIOS IBβ		40B
M8 AII	NOT 517C	THE STRANGER		
OUDEIS 2Bα	NOTHING 596C	5B ALLOTRIOS IBβ		40B
PARA II	FROM 614C	THE STRANGER		
34 HAMARTIA 2	SIN 420	6 GINWSKW 3D		UNDERSTAND 160B
GENNAW IA	BEGET 154C	EKEINOS IB		THAT 238D
HOLOS 3	WHOLE 567D	LALEW 2B		SPEAK 464D
34F EKBALLW I	DRIVE OUT 236D	PAROIMIA 2		FIGURE 634C
34F EKBALLW I	DRIVE OUT 237A	7 THURA 2D		DOOR 366C
34F EXW IB	OUTSIDE 279A	7=14 EGW		I 216B
35 HEURISKW IB	FIND 325B	8 AKOUW 4		LISTEN 32A
HUIOS 2C	SON 843B	ERCHOMAI IIAθ		COME 311B
35F PISTEUW 2Aβ	BELIEVE 667B	*KLEPT8S		THIEF 435C
36 KAI I2H	AND 393D	L8ST8S I		ROBBER 474B
37 EKEINOS IB	THAT 239A	HOSOS 2		HOW GREAT 590B
KAI I6	AND 394A	PAS IEγ		ALL 638A
LALEW 2A6	SPEAK 464C	PRO 2		BEFORE 708D
HORAW IAα	SEE 581C	9 DIA AII		THROUGH 178C
38 PISTEUW 2B	BELIEVE 667C	EISERCHOMAI IF		COME 232B
PROSKUNEW 5	DO REVERENCE 724B	EXERCHOMAI IAη		GO OUT 274C
PH8MI IBα	SAY 864A	HEURISKW IA		FIND 325A
39 BLEPW 2	SEE 143A	THURA 2D		DOOR 366C
ERCHOMAI IIAη	COME 311A	NOM8 I		PASTURE 543A
KOSMOS 4C	WORLD 447B	SWZW 2B		SAVE 806B
KRIMA 7	JUDGMENT 452A	10 APOLLUMI IAβ		RUIN 94C
40 META AIIICα	WITH 510A	ERCHOMAI IIAε		COME 310D

```
10  ZW8 2Bα                    LIFE 341B
    THUW 3                     KILL 367D
    KLEPT8S                    THIEF 435C
    KLEPTW                     STEAL 435C
    PERISSOS 2A   EXTRAORDINARY 657A
10B ERCHOMAI IIAη              COME 311A
11  TITH8MI IIB6           LAY DOWN 823D
    HUPER IAϵ        IN BEHALF OF 846C
    PSUCH8 IAβ           SOUL LIFE 901C
11A KALOS 2Cα                  GOOD 401C
11A POIM8N I               SHEPHERD 690C
11B KALOS 2Cα                  GOOD 401C
11B HO,H8,TO IIIAβ              THE 552C
11B POIM8N I               SHEPHERD 690C
12  HARPAZW I                 STEAL 108C
    APHI8MI 3A              ABANDON 125D
    THEWREW I               OBSERVE 360C
    HO,H8,TO IIIAβ              THE 552C
    OU 3B                       NO 594D
    POIM8N I               SHEPHERD 690C
    SKORPIZW I              SCATTER 764B
    PHEUGW I                   FLEE 863C
12A LUKOS I                    WOLF 482C
12B LUKOS I                    WOLF 482C
12F MISTHWTOS            HIRED MAN 525D
13  MELEI 2       IT IS A CONCERN 501B
    PHEUGW I                   FLEE 863C
14  KALOS 2Cα                  GOOD 401C
14F GINWSKW 6Aβ                KNOW 160C
15  KAGW I                    AND I 387A
    TITH8MI IIB6           LAY DOWN 823D
    HUPER IAϵ        IN BEHALF OF 846C
    PSUCH8 IAβ           SOUL LIFE 901C
16  AGW IA                     LEAD 14A
    AUL8 I                COURTYARD 120D
    DEI I       IT IS NECESSARY 171A
    ECHW I2A                   HAVE 332B
    POIM8N I               SHEPHERD 690C
    PHWN8 2A                  VOICE 879A
17  AGAPAW I9β                 LOVE   4D
    DIA BII2              THEREFORE 180B
    HOTI 3A                    THAT 593D
    TITH8MI IIB6           LAY DOWN 823D
    TITH8MI IIB6           LAY DOWN 823D
    PSUCH8 IAβ           SOUL LIFE 901C
17F PALIN IA                   BACK 611C
18  AIRW 4                TAKE AWAY 24A
    APO V5                       OF 87D
    EMAUTOU 3                MYSELF 253B
    ENTOL8 2C              COMMAND 268D
    EXOUSIA I                 RIGHT 277C
    PARA I3B                   FROM 614D
    TITH8MI IIB6           LAY DOWN 823D
    PSUCH8 IAβ           SOUL LIFE 901C
18A LAMBANW IC                 TAKE 465C
18A TITH8MI IIB6           LAY DOWN 823D
18B LAMBANW 2               RECEIVE 466C
18B TITH8MI IIB6           LAY DOWN 823D
19  SCHISMA 2                 SPLIT 805B
20  DAIMONION 2               DEMON 168B
    ECHW I2Eα                  HAVE 333A
    MAINOMAI  BE OUT OF ONES MIND 487B
    POLUS I2Aα                 MANY 694D

21  ANOIGW IEβ                 OPEN 70D
    DAIMONIZOMAI                    168A
       BE POSSESSED BY A DEMON
    DAIMONION 2               DEMON 168C
    TUPHLOS IB                BLIND 838C
22  GINOMAI I3A          TAKE PLACE 158A
    EIMI I5                   TO BE 222C
    HIEROSOLUMA          JERUSALEM 373D
    CHEIMWN 2                WINTER 888A
23  HIERON 2                 TEMPLE 373A
    PERIPATEW IA          GO ABOUT 654D
    SOLOMWN                SOLOMON 766C
    STOA                   PORTICO 776B
24  AIRW IB                 LIFT UP 23D
    HEWS IIIC                 UNTIL 335C
    IOUDAIOS 2E             JEWISH 380B
    KUKLEUW               SURROUND 457D
    KUKLOW I              SURROUND 457D
    PARR8SIA I           PLAINNESS 635D
    POTE                      WHEN 701D
    CHRISTOS I       ANOINTED ONE 895B
    PSUCH8 IBγ          SOUL LIFE 901D
    PSUCH8 IF           SOUL LIFE 902C
25  ERGON ICα                 DEED 308A
    MARTUREW IA      BEAR WITNESS 493D
    ONOMA I4Cγ                NAME 576A
    ONOMA I4Cγ                NAME 576B
    HOUTOS IAϵ                THIS 601B
25F PISTEUW ID             BELIEVE 666D
26  EK 4A6                    FROM 235B
    PISTEUW 2B              BELIEVE 667C
26F PROBATON 2               SHEEP 710A
27  GINWSKW 6Aβ               KNOW 160C
    EMOS IAα                    MY 255A
    PHWN8 2A                  VOICE 879A
28  APOLLUMI 2Aα             PERISH 94D
    ZW8 2Bα                   LIFE 341B
    ZW8 2Bα                   LIFE 341C
    KAGW I                    AND I 386D
    M8 DIA                     NOT 519B
    TIS, TI IAγ             ANY ONE 827D
    CHEIR 2A6                 HAND 888D
28F HARPAZW 2A              SNATCH 108D
28F EK IA               AWAY FROM 233C
29  CHEIR 2Aβ                 HAND 888D
30  EIMI II7                 TO BE 223D
    HEIS IB                    ONE 230A
31  BASTAZW I              TAKE UP 136D
    IOUDAIOS 2E             JEWISH 380B
    LITHOS IA                STONE 475B
31FF LITHAZW                 STONE 475A
32  EK 3C                     FROM 234B
    ERGON ICβ                 DEED 308A
    POIOS 2Aα        OF WHAT KIND 691B
    POLUS IIAα                MANY 694A
32F KALOS 2B                  GOOD 401B
33  ANTHRWPOS IAβ              MAN 67C
    BLASPH8MIA 2B           SLANDER 142C
    ERGON ICβ                 DEED 308A
    IOUDAIOS 2E             JEWISH 380B
    PERI IB                  ABOUT 650B
    POIEW IIBι                  DO 688B
34  GRAPHW 2C                WRITE 165D
```

34	EGW	I	216B
	NOMOS 4B	LAW	545A
	HOTI 2	THAT	593D
34F	THEOS 4A	GOD	358C
35	GINOMAI 14Cε	COME, GO	159A
	GRAPH8 2Bβ	SCRIPTURE	165C
	EI III	IF	218C
	EIPON 3D	CALL	225D
	LOGOS 1Bα	COMMAND	479A
	LUW 4	ABOLISH	485C
36	HAGIAZW 2	CONSECRATE	9A
	BLASPH8MEW 2Bα	BLASPHEME	142A
	KOSMOS 4C	WORLD	447B
	HOTI 2	THAT	593D
	HUIOS 2B	SON	842D
37	EI IIA	IF	218A
	OU 5B	NO	595A
	PISTEUW 1B	BELIEVE	666C
	POIEW I1Bα	DO	687B
37F	ERGON ICα	DEED	308A
38	EN 15D	IN	259A
	HINA IIC	IN ORDER THAT	377C
	KAGW 1	AND I	387A
	KAN 2	EVEN IF,	403B
38A	PISTEUW 1B	BELIEVE	666C
38B	PISTEUW 1A6	BELIEVE	666B
39	EK 1A	AWAY FROM	233C
	EXERCHOMAI 1Bγ	GO OUT	274C
	PIAZW 2A	GRASP	662D
	CHEIR 2B	HAND	888D
40	BAPTIZW 2A	BAPTIZE	131B
	IORDAN8S	JORDAN	379C
	MENW 1Aα	REMAIN	504D
	HO,H8,TO II6	THE	554D
	PERAN 2A ON THE OTHER SIDE		649C
	PRWTOS 2A	FIRST	733D
	TOPOS IC	PLACE	830B
41	AL8TH8S 2	TRUE	36A
	EIPON 1	SAY	225B
	OUDEIS 1	NO	596B
	PAS 1Eγ	ALL	638A
	POIEW I1Bβ	DO	687C
42	PISTEUW 2Aβ	BELIEVE	667B

JOHN 11

1	ADELPH8 1	SISTER	15C
	ASTHENEW 1A	BE SICK	115A
	B8THANIA 1	BETHANY	139B
	KWM8 1	VILLAGE	462D
	MARTHA	MARTHA	492C
	MARIA 5	MARY	493B
	TIS, TI 1Aβ	ANY ONE	827D
1F	LAZAROS 1	LAZARUS	463B
1F	MARIA 5	MARY	493A
2	ALEIPHW 1	ANOINT	34C
	ASTHENEW 1A	BE SICK	115A
	EKMASSW	WIPE	242D
	THRIX 2	HAIR	364C
	KURIOS 2Cβ	LORD	460D
*MARIA 5		MARY	493B
	MURON	OINTMENT	531D
	POUS 1A	FOOT	703C

3	ADELPH8 1	SISTER	15C
	APOSTELLW 1D	SEND AWAY	98C
	ASTHENEW 1A	BE SICK	115A
	IDE 2	SEE	369D
	LEGW 18C	SAY	470B
	PHILEW 1A	LOVE LIKE	867A
4	DOXAZW 2	GLORIFY	203D
	THANATOS 1A	DEATH	351B
	PROS III3B	TOWARD	717B
	HUIOS 2B	SON	842D
	HUPER 1B	IN BEHALF OF	846D
5	AGAPAW 1Bα	LOVE	4D
	ADELPH8 1	SISTER	15C
	LAZARUS 1	LAZARUS	463B
	MARTHA	MARTHA	492C
6	ASTHENEW 1A	BE SICK	115A
	H8MERA 2	DAY	347A
	MENW 1Aα	REMAIN	504D
	HOS,H8,HO 15B	(REL PRON)	588B
	OUN 5	THEREFORE	597D
	TOTE 2	AT THAT TIME	831D
	HWS IV1A	WHEN	907A
6F	MEN 2B	(PARTICLE)	504B
7	AGW 5	GO	14C
	EPEITA 1	THEN	284B
	IOUDAIA 1	JUDAEA	379D
	META BII3	AFTER	511C
	PALIN 1A	BACK	611B
7F	MATH8T8S 2Bα	DISCIPLE	487A
8	EKEI 2	THERE	238D
	IOUDAIOS 2E	JEWISH	380B
	LITHAZW	STONE	475A
	NUN 1B	NOW	547D
	RABBI	RABBI	740B
	HUPAGW 2	GO AWAY	844C
9	EN II2	WHILE	259D
	KOSMOS 4A	WORLD	447A
	OUCHI 3	NOT	603A
	PROSKOPTW 1B	STRIKE AGAINST	723C
	PHWS 1Bα	LIGHT	880A
	HWRA 2Aα	TIME OF DAY	904C
9A	H8MERA 1A	DAY	346D
9B	H8MERA 1A	DAY	346D
9B	H8MERA 2	DAY	347A
9F	PERIPATEW 1C	GO ABOUT	655A
10	EN II2	WHILE	259D
	NUX 1C	NIGHT	549A
	PROSKOPTW 1B	STRIKE AGAINST	723C
	PHWS 1A	LIGHT	879D
11	ALLA 2	BUT, YET	37D
	EXUPNIZW	WAKE UP	278D
	KOIMAW 2A	SLEEP	438D
	LAZAROS 1	LAZARUS	463B
	META BII3	AFTER	511C
	POREUW 1	PROCEED	699B
	PHILOS 2Aα	LOVING	868D
12	KOIMAW 1	SLEEP	438C
	SWZW 1A	SAVE	805D
13	DOKEW 1D	THINK	201A
	EIPON 1	SAY	225B
	THANATOS 1A	DEATH	351B
	KOIM8SIS 1	SLEEP	438D
	LEGW 12A	SAY	469C

13 HUPNOS	SLEEP 850D	27 CHRISTOS I	ANOINTED ONE 895B
14 LAZAROS I	LAZARUS 463B	28 ADELPH8 I	SISTER 15C
OUN 5	THEREFORE 597D	DIDASKALOS	TEACHER 190D
PARR8SIA I	PLAINNESS 635D	LATHRA I	SECRETLY 463D
TOTE 2	AT THAT TIME 831D	MARIA 5	MARY 493A
15 AGW 5	GO 14C	*MARIA 5	MARY 493B
ALLA 2	BUT, YET 37D	PAREIMI IA	BE PRESENT 629C
PISTEUW 2B	BELIEVE 667C	SIWP8	QUIETLY 760A
CHAIRW I	REJOICE 881B	28A PHWNEW 2B	CALL 878C
CHAIRW I	REJOICE 881D	28B PHWNEW 2B	CALL 878C
16 AGW 5	GO 14C	29 EGEIRW 2B	RISE 214A
DIDUMOS	TWIN 191C	EKEINOS IB	THAT 238D
THWMAS	THOMAS 367D	TACHUS 2B	QUICK 814D
HINA IIC	IN ORDER THAT 377C	HWS IVIA	WHEN 907A
LEGW II3	CALL 471B	30 ERCHOMAI IIAβ	COME 310B
SUMMATH8T8S	FELLOW PUPIL 786A	ETI IAβ	STILL 315D
17 ECHW I2F	HAVE 333B	KWM8 I	VILLAGE 462D
MN8MEION 2	TOMB 526C	MARTHA	MARTHA 492C
TESSARES	FOUR 821A	OUPW	NOT YET 597D
18 APO III	AWAY FROM 86D	TOPOS IC	PLACE 830B
B8THANIA I	BETHANY 139B	HUPANTAW	GO TO MEET 845C
DEKAPENTE	FIFTEEN 173A	31 AKOLOUTHEW I	FOLLOW 30C
EGGUS IA	NEAR 213B	DOKEW ID	THINK 201A
EIMI II9A	TO BE 223D	EIDON ID	SEE 219D
HIEROSOLUMA	JERUSALEM 373D	EIS IB	NEAR 227C
STADION I	STADE 771C	EXERCHOMAI IAβ	GO OUT 274A
19 EK 4Aα	FROM 235B	KLAIW I	WEEP 434A
*MARIA 5	MARY 493B	*MARIA 5	MARY 493B
PARAMUTHEOMAI	ENCOURAGE 626B	MN8MEION 2	TOMB 526C
PERI 2A6	ABOUT 651A	OIKIA IA	HOUSE 560A
POLUS I2Aα	MANY 694D	PARAMUTHEOMAI	ENCOURAGE 626B
19F MARIA 5	MARY 493B	TACHEWS IA	QUICKLY 814B
19FF MARTHA	MARTHA 492C	HUPAGW 2	GO AWAY 844C
20 KATHEZOMAI I	SIT 389B	31F MARIA 5	MARY 493A
*MARIA 5	MARY 493B	32*MARIA 5	MARY 493B
OIKOS IAα	HOUSE 563A	HOPOU IAα	WHERE 579C
HUPANTAW	GO TO MEET 845C	PIPTW IBα	FALL 665B
HWS IVIA	WHEN 907A	PIPTW IBα	FALL 665C
21 AN IBβ	(PARTICLE) 48A	POUS IA	FOOT 703B
THN8SKW	DIE 363A	32F HWS IVIA	WHEN 907A
22 AITEW	ASK 25B	33 EMBRIMAOMAI	SCOLD 254B
*NUN IC	NOW 547D	KLAIW I	WEEP 434A
HOSOS 2	HOW GREAT 590C	PNEUMA 3B	SPIRIT 681B
23F ANIST8MI 2A	RISE 69C	SUNERCHOMAI 2	ASSEMBLE 796A
24 ANASTASIS 2B	RESURRECTION 60A	TARASSW 2	STIR UP 813A
*EN II2	WHILE 259D	34 EIDON IE	SEE 220A
ESCHATOS 3B	LAST 314B	ERCHOMAI IIAζ	COME 310D
H8MERA 3Bβ	DAY 347D	POU IA	WHERE 702D
MARTHA	MARTHA 492C	TITH8MI IIAα	PUT 823C
25 ANASTASIS 2B	RESURRECTION 60A	35 DAKRUW	WEEP 169A
ZAW 2Bα	LIVE 337A	36 IDE I	SEE 369D
ZW8 2Aβ	LIFE 341A	PWS 3	HOW 740C
KAN 2	EVEN IF 403B	PHILEW IA	LOVE LIKE 867A
PISTEUW 2Aβ	BELIEVE 667B	37 EK 4Aβ	FROM 235B
26 APOTHN8SKW IBα	DIE 91A	HINA IIIAε	IN ORDER THAT 378B
M8 DIA	NOT 519B	HOUTOS IA6	THIS 601A
26A PISTEUW 2Aβ	BELIEVE 667B	POIEW IIBθ	DO 688B
26B PISTEUW IAα	BELIEVE 666A	TIS, TI IAα	ANY ONE 827D
27 ERCHOMAI IIAη	COME 310D	TUPHLOS IB	BLIND 838C
KOSMOS 4C	WORLD 447B	38 EIS IB	NEAR 227C
NAI IA	YES 534D	EMBRIMAOMAI	SCOLD 254B
PISTEUW IAβ	BELIEVE 666A	EN I5B	IN 258D
HUIOS 2B	SON 842D	EPI IIIAα	ON 286C

38	EPIKEIMAI I	LIE UPON	294C	49	KAIAPHAS	CAIAPHAS	394D
	ERCHOMAI IIAβ	COME	310C		OU 6A	NO	595A
	MN8MEION 2	TOMB	526C		OUDEIS 2Bα	NOTHING	596C
	SP8LAION	CAVE	769D	50	ANTHRWPOS 3Aβ	MAN	68B
38F	LITHOS IE	STONE	475C		ANTHRWPOS 3Aζ	MAN	68C
39	ADELPH8 I	SISTER	15C		APOLLUMI 2Aα	PERISH	94D
	AIRW 3	CARRY	24A		HINA IIIB	IN ORDER THAT	378C
	8D8 IA	ALREADY	344D		LOGIZOMAI 2	CONSIDER	477B
	MARTHA	MARTHA	492C		SUMPHERW 2A	BETTER	788A
	OZW	SMELL	557D	50F	APOTHN8SKW IAα	DIE	90D
	TELEUTAW	DIE	818B	50ç2	HUPER IAε	IN BEHALF OF	846C
	TETARTAIОS	FOUR DAYS	821A	51	APO V5	OF	87D
40	HORAW IAγ	SEE	581D		ARCHIEREUS IB	HIGH PRIEST	112C
41	AIRW IB	LIFT UP	23D		HEAUTOU IA	ONESELF	211B
	ANW 2	UPWARDS	76B		ENIAUTOS I	YEAR	265D
	EUCHARISTEW 2	GIVE THANKS	328D		MELLW IC6	IS DESTINED	502C
	LITHOS IE	STONE	475C		PROPH8TEUW 3	PROPHESY	730C
41F	AKOUW 5	LISTEN	32A	52	DIASKORPIZW	SCATTER	187B
42	APOSTELLW IC	SEND AWAY	98B		HEIS 2A	ONE	230B
	PERIIST8MI IB	STAND AROUND	653B		HINA IIII	IN ORDER THAT	379A
	PISTEUW IAβ	BELIEVE	666A		MONOS 2C	ONLY	529D
43	DEURO I	COME	175D		SUNAGW 2	GATHER	790A
	EXW IB	OUTSIDE	279A		TEKNON 2E	CHILD	816C
	KRAUGAZW 2B	CRY	450C	53	APO II2A	FROM	86B
	LAZAROS I	LAZARUS	463B		BOULEUW 2	DECIDE	145A
	MEGAS 2Aγ	GREAT	498D		H8MERA 2	DAY	347A
	PHWN8 2A	VOICE	878D		HINA IIIAα	IN ORDER THAT	378A
44	APHI8MI 4	TOLERATE	126A		SUMBOULEUW 2A	ADVISE	785C
	DEW IA	BIND	176C	54	DIATRIB8W	STAY	189A
	EXERCHOMAI IAβ	GO OUT	274A		EGGUS IA	NEAR	213B
	THN8SKW I	DIE	363B		ER8MOS 2	DESERT	309A
	KEIRIA	GRAVE CLOTHES	428B		EPHRAIM 2	EPHRAIM	331B
	LUW 2A	LOOSE	484D		KAKEI I	AND THERE	397C
	OPSIS 3	APPEARANCE	606D		LEGW II3	CALL	471B
	PERIDEW	WRAP AROUND	652B		MENW IAα	REMAIN	504D
	POUS IA	FOOT	703B		META AIIIA	WITH	509D
	SOUDARION	FACE CLOTH	766D		OUKETI I	NO LONGER	596D
	HUPAGW I	GO AWAY	844C		PARR8SIA 2	PUBLICLY	636A
	CHEIR I	HAND	888A		PERIPATEW IA	GO ABOUT	654D
45	EK 4Aα	FROM	235B		POLIS I	CITY	692B
	THEAOMAI IA	SEE	353D		SAMPHOUREIN	SAMPHOUREIN	749B
	MARIA 5	MARY	493A		CHWRA IA	COUNTRY	897C
	*MARIA 5	MARY	493B	55	HAGNIZW IA	PURIFY	11A
	PISTEUW 2Aβ	BELIEVE	667B		ANABAINW IAα	GO UP	49D
	POLUS I2Aα	MANY	694D		EGGUS 2A	NEAR	213B
46	EK 4Aβ	FROM	235B		HIEROSOLUMA IA	JERUSALEM	373D
	TIS, TI IAα	ANY ONE	827D		PRO 2	BEFORE	708C
47	HOTI IC	THAT	593B		CHWRA 2	COUNTRY	897D
	SUNAGW 2	GATHER	790A	55A	PASCHA I	THE PASSOVER	639A
	SUNEDRION 2	SANHEDRIN	794A	55B	PASCHA I	THE PASSOVER	639A
47B	POIEW IIB8β	DO	687C	56	ALL8LWN	EACH OTHER	38D
48	AIRW 4	TAKE AWAY	24A		DOKEW 3A	SEEM	201B
	APHI8MI 4	TOLERATE	126A		HEORT8	FESTIVAL	279D
	ERCHOMAI IIAζ	COME	310D		HEORT8	FESTIVAL	280A
	HOUTW IB	THUS	602C		ERCHOMAI IIAβ	COME	310C
	PISTEUW 2Aβ	BELIEVE	667B		HIST8MI II2Bβ	BEING	383C
	RWMAIOS	ROMAN	745C		LEGW I3	SAY	469D
	TOPOS IA	PLACE	830A		M8 DIA	NOT	519B
	TOPOS IB	PLACE	830B	57	GINWSKW 6D	KNOW	160D
49	ARCHIEREUS IB	HIGH PRIEST	112C		DIDWMI	GIVE	191D
	HEIS 3C	SOMEONE	231A		DIDWMI IBα	GIVE	192A
	EK 4Aα	FROM	235B		ENTOL8 IA	COMMAND	268C
	ENIAUTOS I	YEAR	265D		HINA IIIСα	IN ORDER THAT	378C

57	M8NUW	REVEAL 521A
	HOPWS 2Aα	IN ORDER THAT 580C
	HOPWS 2Aα	IN ORDER THAT 580C
	PIAZW 2A	GRASP 662D
	POU 1B	WHERE 702D

JOHN 12

1	B8THANIA 1	BETHANY 139B
	EGEIRW 1Aβ	RAISE 213D
	EK 1B	AWAY FROM 233C
	HEX	SIX 270D
	H8MERA 2	DAY 347B
	NEKROS 2A	DEAD 537A
	PASCHA 1	THE PASSOVER 639A
	PRO 2	BEFORE 708C
1F	LAZAROS 1	LAZARUS 463B
2	ANAKEIMAI 2	BE AT TABLE 55C
	DEIPNON 2	DINNER 172C
	DIAKONEW 1	WAIT ON SOMEONE 183A
	EIMI II7	TO BE 223D
	MARTHA	MARTHA 492C
	POIEW IIBζ	DO 688A
	SUN 1A	WITH 789A
	SUNANAKEIMAI	EAT WITH 792A
3	ALEIPHW 1	ANOINT 34C
	EK 4Aζ	FROM 235C
	EKMASSW	WIPE 242D
	THRIX 2	HAIR 364C
	LAMBANW 1A	TAKE 465D
	LITRA	POUND 476D
	MARIA 5	MARY 493A
	*MARIA 5	MARY 493B
	NARDOS 2	PERFUME OF NARD 536A
	OIKIA 1A	HOUSE 559D
	OSM8 1A	ODOR 590A
	PIMPL8MI 1Aα	FILL 663D
	PISTIKOS	FAITHFUL 668A
	PL8ROW 1A	MAKE FULL 676C
	POLUTIMOS	VALUABLE 696D
3A	MURON	OINTMENT 531D
3A	POUS 1A	FOOT 703C
3B	MURON	OINTMENT 531D
4	_IOUDAS 6	JUDAS 380D
	*ISKARIWTH	ISCARIOT 381D
	MELLW 1Cγ	INTEND 502B
	PARADIDWMI 1B	GIVE OVER 620A
	SIMWN 5	SIMON 758D
5	D8NARION	DENARIUS 178B
	DIA BII2	WHY 180B
	MURON	OINTMENT 531D
	HO,H8,TO IIIAα	THE 552B
	PIPRASKW	SELL 664D
	PTWCHOS 1A	BEGGING POOR 735D
	TRIAKOSIOI	THREE HUNDRED 833D
6	BALLW 2B	PUT 130D
	BASTAZW 3B	REMOVE 137A
	GLWSSOKOMON	MONEY BOX 161D
	ECHW I2H	HAVE 333C
	KLEPT8S	THIEF 435C
	MELEI 2	IT IS A CONCERN 501B
	HO,H8,TO IIIAα	THE 552B
	HOTI 3A	THAT 593D

6	PTWCHOS 1A	BEGGING POOR 735C
7	APHI8MI 4	TOLERATE 126A
	ENTAPHIASMOS	267D
	PREPARATION FOR BURIAL	
	H8MERA 2	DAY 347A
	H8MERA 2	DAY 347C
	T8REW 2A	KEEP 822C
8	ECHW 13	HAVE 333C
	META AIIIB	WITH 509D
	PTWCHOS 1A	BEGGING POOR 735C
9	GINWSKW 2B	FIND OUT 160B
	EGEIRW 1Aβ	RAISE 213D
	EK 1B	AWAY FROM 233C
	HINA IIE	IN ORDER THAT 377C
	MONOS 2C	ONLY 529D
	NEKROS 2A	DEAD 537A
	OCHLOS 1	CROWD 605C
9A	ERCHOMAI IIAε	COME 310D
9B	ERCHOMAI IIAε	COME 310D
9F	LAZAROS 1	LAZARUS 463B
10	BOULEUW 2	DECIDE 145A
	HINA IIIAα	IN ORDER THAT 378A
11	PISTEUW 2Aβ	BELIEVE 667B
	POLUS I2Aα	MANY 694D
	HUPAGW 2	GO AWAY 844D
12	HEORT8	FESTIVAL 279D
	HEORT8	FESTIVAL 280A
	EPAURION	NEXT DAY 283C
	HO,H8,TO II3B	THE 553D
	OCHLOS 1	CROWD 605C
13	BAION	PALM BRANCH 130A
	BASILEUS 2A	KING 135D
	EIS 4F	(PURPOSE) 228D
	EXERCHOMAI 1Aε	GO OUT 274B
	ERCHOMAI IIAη	COME 310D
	EULOGEW 2A	BLESS 322D
	ISRA8L 2	ISRAEL 382B
	KRAUGAZW 2B	CRY 450C
	ONOMA I4Cγ	NAME 576C
	SUNANT8SIS	MEETING 792B
	HUPANT8SIS	COMING TO MEET 845C
	PHOINIX I1	PALM TREE 872A
	HWSANNA	HOSANNA 907C
14	GRAPHW 2C	WRITE 165D
	HEURISKW 1B	FIND 325B
	KATHIZW 2Aα	SIT DOWN 391A
	ONARION	DONKEY 573A
15	EPI IIIIAζ	ON 288C
	THUGAT8R 2E	DAUGHTER 365C
	KATH8MAI 1Aα	SIT 390B
	ONOS	DONKEY 577C
	PWLOS	COLT 739A
	SIWN 2A	ZION 759D
16	GINWSKW 3A	UNDERSTAND 160D
	GRAPHW 2C	WRITE 166A
	DOXAZW 2	GLORIFY 203D
	EPI IIIB6	ON 287C
	MIMN8SKOMAI 1A6	REMEMBER 524B
	HO,H8,TO II6	THE 554C
	HOTE 1B	WHEN 592C
	POIEW IID α	DO 688D
	PRWTOS 2A	FIRST 733D
	TOTE 2	AT THAT TIME 831D

17 EGEIRW IAβ	RAISE 213D	26 EIMI II9A	TO BE 223D
EIMI III7	TO BE 224D	HOPOU IAα	WHERE 579C
EK IB	AWAY FROM 233C	TIMAW 2	HONOR 825A
LAZAROS I	LAZARUS 463B	27 EIPON I	SAY 225B
MARTUREW IA	BEAR WITNESS 493C	EK IC	AWAY FROM 233D
MARTUREW IA	BEAR WITNESS 493D	ERCHOMAI I2C	COME 311C
META AIIICα	WITH 510A	NUN IAβ	NOW 547C
MN8MEION 2	TOMB 526C	SWZW IB	SAVE 805D
NEKROS 2A	DEAD 537A	TARASSW 2	STIR UP 813A
PHWNEW 2B	CALL 878C	PSUCH8 IBγ	SOUL LIFE 901D
18 DIA BII2	THEREFORE 180B	PSUCH8 IF	SOUL LIFE 902C
KAI II4	ALSO 394C	27A HWRA 3	TIME OF DAY 905A
HUPANTAW	GO TO MEET 845C	27B HWRA 3	TIME OF DAY 905A
19 APERCHOMAI 4	GO AFTER 84A	28*DOXAZW 2	GLORIFY 203D
HEAUTOU 3	ONESELF 211D	ERCHOMAI IICα	COME 311C
THEWREW 2A	OBSERVE 360D	KAI I6	AND 394A
IDE 2	SEE 369D	OURANOS 2A	HEAVEN 599B
KOSMOS 5A	WORLD 447C	PHWN8 2D	VOICE 879B
OPISW 2Aβ	AFTER 578D	29 AGGELOS 2A	ANGEL 7C
OU 6A	NO 595A	ALLOS IC	OTHER 39B
WPHELEW 2A	HELP 909A	BRONT8	THUNDER 147A
20*HEORT8	FESTIVAL 279D	GINOMAI IIBα	COME ABOUT 157B
PROSKUNEW 2A	DO REVERENCE 724A	HIST8MI II2A	STAND 383B
21 B8THSAIDA I	BETHSAIDA 139C	LALEW I	SOUND 464B
B8THSAIDA I	BETHSAIDA 139D	LALEW 2Aδ	SPEAK 464B
GALILAIA	GALILEE 149D	29A LEGW IIBβ	SAY 469C
EIDON 6	VISIT 220B	30 PHWN8 2D	VOICE 879B
ERWTAW 2	ASK 312A	31 ARCHWN 3	AUTHORITIES 113C
THELW I	WISH 355C	EKBALLW I	DRIVE OUT 236D
KURIOS IB	LORD 460A	EXW IB	OUTSIDE 279A
HOUTOS IAβ	THIS 601A	KATW 2	DOWNWARDS 426B
PROSERCHOMAI I	APPROACH 720A	KRISIS IAβ	JUDGING 453D
21F PHILIPPOS 3	PHILIP 868A	KRISIS 3	RIGHT 454B
22 ANDREAS	ANDREW 63B	31A KOSMOS 7	WORLD 447D
ERCHOMAI IIAζ	COME 310D	31A NUN IB	NOW 547D
PALIN 4	AGAIN 611D	31B KOSMOS 7	WORLD 447D
23 DOXAZW 2	GLORIFY 203D	31B NUN IB	NOW 547D
ERCHOMAI IIBα	COME 311B	32 AN	IF 49A
HINA IIID	IN ORDER THAT 378C	EAN IID	IF 210D
HUIOS 2C	SON 843B	HELKW IB	DRAG 251B
HWRA 3	TIME OF DAY 905A	EMAUTOU 3	MYSELF 253B
24 APOTHN8SKW IAβ	DIE 91A	KAGW 2	BUT I 387A
G8 I	EARTH 156C	PROS IIIID	TOWARD 716D
KARPOS IA	FRUIT 405C	32=34 HUPSOW I	LIFT UP 858C
KOKKOS I	SEED 441B	33 APOTHN8SKW IAα	DIE 90D
MENW IB	REMAIN 505B	THANATOS ID	DEATH 351D
MONOS IC	ALONE 529D	MELLW IC6	IS DESTINED 502C
PIPTW IA	FALL 665A	HOUTOS IBα	THIS 601C
POLUS IIBα	MANY 694C	POIOS IAγ	OF WHAT KIND 691B
SITOS	WHEAT 759C	S8MAINW 2	MAKE KNOWN 755B
PHERW 2	BEAR 862D	34 AIWN 2	TIME 26D
25 APOLLUMI IB	LOSE 94C	AKOUW 3D	LEARN 32A
ZW8 2Bα	LIFE 341C	EK 3Gβ	BY 234D
KOSMOS 4B	WORLD 447B	MENW ICα	REMAIN 505B
KOSMOS 7	WORLD 447D	NOMOS 4B	LAW 545A
MISEW 2	HATE 524D	PWS IA	HOW 739C
PHILEW IB	LOVE LIKE 867A	HUIOS 2C	SON 843B
PHULASSW IC	WATCH 876B	CHRISTOS I	ANOINTED ONE 895B
PSUCH8 ID	SOUL LIFE 902B	35 ETI IC	STILL 316A
25A PSUCH8 ID	SOUL LIFE 902B	KATALAMBANW IB	SEIZE 414B
25B PSUCH8 ID	SOUL LIFE 902B	MIKROS 2D	SHORT 523B
26 DIAKONEW 2	SERVE 183A	OIDA IF	KNOW 558C
DIAKONOS IA	SERVANT 183D	POU 2B	WHERE 703A

35	HUPAGW 2	GO AWAY	844C
	CHRONOS	TIME	896B
35A	PERIPATEW 1D	GO ABOUT	655A
35A	SKOTIA 2	DARKNESS	764D
35A	PHWS 2	LIGHT	880A
35B	PERIPATEW 1D	GO ABOUT	655A
35B	SKOTIA 1	DARKNESS	764D
35B	SKOTIA 2	DARKNESS	764D
35B	PHWS 2	LIGHT	880A
35F	HEWS 12A	UNTIL	335A
35F	HWS IV1B	WHEN	907A
36	GINOMAI 14A	BECOME	158C
	KRUPTW 1C	HIDE	455C
	LALEW 2B	SPEAK	464C
	PISTEUW 2AB	BELIEVE	667B
	HUIOS 1C6	SON	842A
36A	PHWS 2	LIGHT	880A
36B	PHWS 2	LIGHT	880A
36C	PHWS 3A	LIGHT	880B
37	EMPROSTHEN 2C	IN FRONT	256C
	PISTEUW 2AB	BELIEVE	667B
	TOSOUTOS 1B	SO GREAT	831B
38	AKO8 2B	REPORT	30C
	APOKALUPTW 1	REVEAL	91C
	BRACHIWN	ARM	146D
	HINA II2	IN ORDER THAT	378D
	LOGOS 1A5	MATTER	479A
	PISTEUW 1A6	BELIEVE	666B
	PL8ROW 4A	MAKE FULL	677C
	PROPH8T8S !	PROPHET	730D
38F	8SAIAS	ISAIAH	349C
39	DIA BII2	THEREFORE	180B
	HOTI 3A	THAT	593D
	PALIN 3	AGAIN	611D
	PISTEUW 2B	BELIEVE	667C
40	AUTOS 3A	(OBLIQUE CASE)	123A
	EIDON 1A	SEE	219D
	EPISTREPHW 2B	TURN	301C
	IAOMAI 2	HEAL	369A
	HINA IIB	IN ORDER THAT	377C
	HINA II2	IN ORDER THAT	378D
	KAI I2E	AND	393C
	NOEW 1E	UNDERSTAND	542D
	P8ROW	DISABLE	662C
	PWROW	HARDEN	739B
	STREPHW 2B	TURN	779A
	TUPHLOW	TO BLIND	838D
40A	KARDIA 1BB	HEART	404D
40B	KARDIA 1BB	HEART	404C
40B	OPHTHALMOS 2	EYE	604C
41	8SAIAS	ISAIAH	349C
	LALEW 2A6	SPEAK	464C
42	APOSUNAGWGOS	EXCOMMUNICATED	100B
	ARCHWN 2A	AUTHORITIES	113C
	GINOMAI 14B	BECOME	158D
	MENTOI 2	THOUGH	504C
	HOMOLOGEW 4	CONFESS	571C
	HOMWS	ALL THE SAME	572D
	PISTEUW 2AB	BELIEVE	667B
	POLUS I2Aα	MANY	694D
43	AGAPAW 2	LOVE	5A
	DOXA 3	FAME	203B
	8 2EB	THAN	343C

43	MALLON 3C	RATHER	490D
	HUPER 2	BEYOND	847B
44	KRAZW 2A	CALL	448D
44A	PISTEUW 2AB	BELIEVE	667B
44B	PISTEUW 2AB	BELIEVE	667B
45	THEWREW 1	OBSERVE	360C
46	ERCHOMAI IIAη	COME	311A
	HINA IIB	IN ORDER THAT	377C
	KOSMOS 4C	WORLD	447B
	MENW 1AB	REMAIN	505A
	PISTEUW 2AB	BELIEVE	667B
	SKOTIA 2	DARKNESS	764D
	PHWS 2	LIGHT	880B
47	AKOUW 1Bγ	HEAR	31C
	KOSMOS 5B	WORLD	447C
	PISTEUW 1D	BELIEVE	666D
	SWZW 2Aα	SAVE	806A
	PHULASSW 1F	WATCH	876C
47A	KRINW 4Bα	JUDGE	453A
47B	KRINW 4Bα	JUDGE	453A
47F	R8MA 1	WORD	742D
48	ATHETEW 1B	REJECT	20C
	EKEINOS 1B	THAT	238D
	ESCHATOS 3B	LAST	314B
	H8MERA 3Bβ	DAY	347D
	LALEW 2B	SPEAK	464C
	LAMBANW 1EB	RECEIVE	466A
	LOGOS 1Bβ	WORD	479B
48A	KRINW 4Bα	JUDGE	453A
48B	KRINW 4Bα	JUDGE	453A
49	DIDWMI 1Bα	GIVE	192A
	EK 3Eα	BY	234C
	EMAUTOU 3	MYSELF	253B
	LALEW 2B	SPEAK	464D
50	ZW8 2Aα	LIFE	341A
	ZW8 2Bα	LIFE	341C
	LALEW 2B	SPEAK	464D
	HOUTW 1A	THUS	602B

JOHN 13

1	AGAPAW 1C	LOVE	4D
	AGAP8 II	LOVE FEAST	6B
	EIS 3	COMPLETELY	228A
	HEORT8	FESTIVAL	279D
	ERCHOMAI IIBα	COME	311B
	IDIOS 3A	ONES OWN	370D
	HINA IIID	IN ORDER THAT	378C
	KOSMOS 4C	WORLD	447B
	KOSMOS 7	WORLD	447D
	METABAINW 1Aα	PASS OVER	511D
	PASCHA 1	THE PASSOVER	639A
	PRO 2	BEFORE	708C
	HWRA 3	TIME OF DAY	905A
2	BALLW 2B	PUT	130D
	DEIPNON 2	DINNER	172C
	DIABOLOS 2	THE SLANDERER	181A
	DIABOLOS 2	THE SLANDERER	181B
	HINA I4	IN ORDER THAT	378A
	IOUDAS 6	JUDAS	380D
	*ISKARIWTH	ISCARIOT	381D
	KARDIA 1Bγ	HEART	404D
	PARADIDWMI	GIVE OVER	619C

2	SIMWN 5	SIMON	758D
3	APO IVIAβ	FROM	86D
	DIDWMI 3	GIVE	192C
	EXERCHOMAI IAY	GO OUT	274A
	HUPAGW 3	GO AWAY	844D
	CHEIR 2Aδ	HAND	888D
4	DEIPNON I	DINNER	172B
	DIAZWNNUMI	TIE AROUND	182A
	EGEIRW 2B	RISE	214A
	HIMATION 3	GARMENT	377B
	TITH8MI IIB6	TAKE OFF	823D
4F	LENTION	TOWEL	472D
5	ARCHW 2Aα	BEGIN	113A
	BALLW 2B	PUT	130D
	DIAZWNNUMI	TIE AROUND	182A
	EITA I	THEN	233A
	EKMASSW	WIPE	242D
	NIPT8R	BASIN	542A
	HO,H8,TO IIIAα	THE	552B
	HUDWR I	WATER	840C
5F	NIPTW I	WASH	542A
5F	POUS IA	FOOT	703C
6	PETROS	PETER	661A
	SU IC	YOU	779D
7	ARTI 3	NOW	109D
	HOS,H8,HO I9A	(REL PRON)	588D
	POIEW IIBε	DO	687D
	SU IA	YOU	779D
8	MEROS 2	SHARE	507C
	M8 DIA	NOT	519B
8A	NIPTW I	WASH	542A
8B	NIPTW I	WASH	542B
8=10	POUS IA	FOOT	703C
9	KEPHAL8 IA	HEAD	431A
	MONOS 2C	ONLY	529D
	PETROS	PETER	661A
10	ECHW I2I	HAVE	333C
	LOUW 2Aβ	BATHE	482B
	NIPTW 2A	WASH	542B
	NIPTW 2B	WASH	542B
	HOLOS 2C	WHOLE	567D
	OUCHI I	NOT	602D
	PAS 2AY	ALL	638B
	CHREIA I	NEED	893B
10A	KATHAROS I	CLEAN	388D
10B	KATHAROS 3A	CLEAN	389A
11	KATHAROS 3A	CLEAN	389A
	OUCHI I	NOT	602D
	PARADIDWMI IB	GIVE OVER	620A
12	ANAPIPTW I	RECLINE	59A
	GINWSKW 3D	UNDERSTAND	160B
	HIMATION 3	GARMENT	377B
	LAMBANW IA	TAKE	465C
	NIPTW I	WASH	542A
	OUN 5	THEREFORE	597D
	POIEW IIDα	DO	688D
	POUS IA	FOOT	703C
13	KALWS 4B	WELL	402B
	LEGW I5	SAY	469D
	PHWNEW 2A	CALL	878C
13F	DIDASKALOS	TEACHER	190D
13F	KURIOS 2CY	LORD	461A
14	EI III	IF	218C

14	EI VIIO	IF	219A
	OPHEILW 2Aβ	OWE	603D
	POSOS I	HOW GREAT	701A
	POUS IA	FOOT	703C
14A	NIPTW I	WASH	542B
14B	NIPTW I	WASH	542B
15	DIDWMI IBα	GIVE	192A
	KAI II3	ALSO	394B
	SU IA	YOU	779D
	HUPODEIGMA I	EXAMPLE	851D
15A	POIEW IIDβ	DO	688D
15B	POIEW I2Aα	DO	689A
16	APOSTOLOS I	MESSENGER	99A
	KURIOS IAβ	LORD	460A
	PEMPW I	SEND	647B
16A	MEGAS 2Bα	GREAT	499B
16B	MEGAS 2Bα	GREAT	499B
17	EI III	IF	218C
	MAKARIOS IB	BLESSED	487D
	POIEW IIBε	DO	687D
18	ARTOS 2	FOOD	110C
	GRAPH8 2A	SCRIPTURE	165B
	EKLEGOMAI 2A	CHOOSE	241D
	EPAIRW I	RAISE UP	281C
	EPI IIIIAε	AGAINST	288B
	HINA IIII	IN ORDER THAT	379A
	LEGW I2A	SAY	469C
	META AII2	WITH	510C
	OIDA IF	KNOW	558C
	PL8ROW 4A	MAKE FULL	677C
	PTERNA	HEEL	734C
	TRWGW	GNAW	836D
19	ARTI 3	NOW	109D
	EIMI II5	TO BE	223C
	PISTEUW IAβ	BELIEVE	666A
	PRO 2	BEFORE	708D
20	AN	IF	49A
20A	LAMBANW IEα	RECEIVE	465D
20B	LAMBANW IEα	RECEIVE	465D
20C	LAMBANW IEα	RECEIVE	465D
20D	LAMBANW IEα	RECEIVE	465D
21	MARTUREW IA	BEAR WITNESS	493D
	PNEUMA 3B	SPIRIT	681B
	TARASSW 2	STIR UP	813A
22	ALL8LWN	EACH OTHER	39A
	APOREW	UNCERTAIN	97A
	BLEPW 3	SEE	143B
	LEGW I2A	SAY	469C
23	AGAPAW IBα	LOVE	4D
	ANAKEIMAI 2	BE AT TABLE	55C
	KOLPOS I	BOSOM	443A
	MATH8T8S 2Bα	DISCIPLE	487A
	PETROS	PETER	660D
24	NEUW	NOD	538C
	PETROS	PETER	661A
	PUNTHANOMAI I	INQUIRE	737A
25	ANAPIPTW 2	RECLINE	59A
	EPI IIIIAY	ON	288B
	EPIPIPTW IB	FALL UPON	297C
	HOUTW 4	THUS	602D
	ST8THOS	CHEST	775B
26	BAPTW I	DIP	132B
	EKEINOS ID	THAT	239A

26 IOUDAS 6	JUDAS	380D
ISKARIWTH	ISCARIOT	381D
SIMWN 5	SIMON	758D
26A PSWMION	BIT OF BREAD	903C
26B PSWMION	BIT OF BREAD	903C
27 DIABOLOS 2	THE SLANDERER	181B
EISERCHOMAI 18β	COME	232A
META BII3	AFTER	511C
SATAN	ADVERSARY	752B
TACHEWS 2B	QUICKLY	814C
TOTE 2	AT THAT TIME	831D
PSWMION	BIT OF BREAD	903C
27A POIEW IIBε	DO	687D
28 ANAKEIMAI 2	BE AT TABLE	55C
GINWSKW 3D	UNDERSTAND	160B
OUDEIS 2A	NO ONE	596B
PROS III5A	TOWARD	717C
TIS, TI I8α	WHICH	827A
29 AGORAZW I	BUY	12C
GLWSSOKOMON	MONEY BOX	161D
EIS 4G	FOR	229A
HEORT8	FESTIVAL	279D
EPEI 2	BECAUSE	283D
ECHW I2H	HAVE	333C
ECHW I2I	HAVE	333C
HINA IV	IN ORDER THAT	379B
IOUDAS 6	JUDAS	380D
HOS,H8,HO I2Bβ	(REL PRON)	587B
PTWCHOS IA	BEGGING POOR	735D
TIS, TI I8α	ANY ONE	828A
CHREIA I	NEED	893B
29A TIS, TI IAα	ANY ONE	827C
30 EIMI I5	TO BE	222C
EUTHUS	IMMEDIATELY	321C
LAMBANW 2	RECEIVE	466B
NUX IA	NIGHT	548C
PSWMION	BIT OF BREAD	903C
30F EXERCHOMAI IAβ	GO OUT	274A
31*DOXAZW 2	GLORIFY	203D
NUN IAγ	NOW	547C
OUN 5	THEREFORE	597D
HUIOS 2C	SON	843B
31F DOXAZW 2	GLORIFY	203D
32 DOXAZW 2	GLORIFY	203D
EI III	IF	218C
EUTHUS	IMMEDIATELY	321C
33 ARTI 3	NOW	109D
ETI IC	STILL	316A
IOUDAIOS 2E	JEWISH	380B
META AIIICα	WITH	510A
HOPOU I8α	WHERE	579D
TEKNION	CHILD	815D
HUPAGW 3	GO AWAY	844D
34 AGAPAW IAα	LOVE	4B
AGAPAW IC	LOVE	4D
AGAP8 II	LOVE FEAST	6B
ALL8LWN	EACH OTHER	39A
DIDWMI I8α	GIVE	192A
ENTOL8 2D	COMMAND	268D
HINA IIICα	IN ORDER THAT	378C
KAINOS 2	NEW	395A
35 AGAP8 IIBβ	LOVE	5D
ALL8LWN	EACH OTHER	39A
35 GINWSKW IC	KNOW	160A
EN I2	IN	258A
ECHW I2Eβ	HAVE	333A
HOUTOS I8β	THIS	601C
36 NUN IAγ	NOW	547D
HOPOU I8α	WHERE	579D
PETROS	PETER	661A
POU 2A	WHERE	703A
SUNAKOLOUTHEW	FOLLOW	791C
HUSTEROS 2A	LATER	857B
36A HUPAGW 3	GO AWAY	844D
36B HUPAGW 3	GO AWAY	844D
37 ARTI 2	NOW	109D
DIA BII2	WHY	180B
37F TITH8MI II86	LAY DOWN	823D
37F HUPER IAε	IN BEHALF OF	846C
37F PSUCH8 IAβ	SOUL LIFE	901C
38 ALEKTWR	COCK	34D
ARNEOMAI 3A	DENY	107C
HEWS IIIB8α	UNTIL	335C
TRIS	THRICE	834A
PHWNEW IA	PRODUCE A SOUND	878B

JOHN 14

1 KARDIA I8ε	HEART	405A
TARASSW 2	STIR UP	813A
1A PISTEUW 2Aβ	BELIEVE	667B
1B PISTEUW 2Aβ	BELIEVE	667B
2 EI VI3A	IF NOT	218D
HETOIMAZW I	PREPARE	316B
MON8 2	ABODE	529A
OIKIA I8	HOUSE	560A
POLUS IIAα	MANY	694B
POREUW I	PROCEED	699B
2F TOPOS IE	PLACE	830C
3 EAN IID	IF	210D
EIMI II9A	TO BE	223D
EMAUTOU 3	MYSELF	253B
ERCHOMAI I2A	COME	311C
ERCHOMAI I2C	COME	311D
HETOIMAZW I	PREPARE	316B
HINA IID	IN ORDER THAT	377C
HOPOU IAα	WHERE	579C
PARALAMBANW I	TAKE	625A
4 HOPOU I8α	WHERE	579D
HUPAGW 3	GO AWAY	844D
5 THWMAS	THOMAS	367D
OIDA IF	KNOW	558C
POU 2B	WHERE	703A
PWS ID	HOW	739C
HUPAGW 3	GO AWAY	844D
6 AL8THEIA 2B	TRUTH	35C
ERCHOMAI I2C	COME	311D
ZW8 2Aβ	LIFE	341A
HODOS 2A	WAY	556D
OUDEIS 2A	NO ONE	596B
7 ARTI 3	NOW	109D
*GINWSKW IB	KNOW	160A
8 ARKEW I	BE ENOUGH	106D
8F DEIKNUMI IA	SHOW	171D
8F PHILIPPOS 3	PHILIP	868A
9 META AIIICα	WITH	510A

9	HORAW IAα	SEE 581C
	PWS IC	HOW 739C
	TOSOUTOS IAα	SO GREAT 831A
	CHRONOS	TIME 896B
10	APO V5	OF 87D
	EMAUTOU 3	MYSELF 253B
	ERGON ICα	DEED 308A
	MENW IAβ	REMAIN 505A
	PISTEUW IAβ	BELIEVE 666A
	R8MA I	WORD 742D
10F	EN I5D	IN 259A
11	EI VI3A	IF NOT 218D
	ERGON ICα	DEED 308A
11A	PISTEUW IC	BELIEVE 666D
12	ERGON ICα	DEED 308A
	KAI II2	EVEN 394B
	KAKEINOS 2B	HE ALSO 397C
	MEGAS 2Aγ	GREAT 499A
	PISTEUW 2Aβ	BELIEVE 667B
	POREUW I	PROCEED 699A
12A	POIEW IIBα	DO 687C
12B	POIEW IIBα	DO 687C
12C	POIEW IIBα	DO 687C
13*DOXAZW 2		GLORIFY 203D
	HINA IID	IN ORDER THAT 377C
	ONOMA I4Cγ	NAME 576B
	HOSTIS IEβ	WHOEVER 591A
	POIEW IIBε	DO 687D
	HUIOS 2B	SON 842D
13F	AITEW	ASK 25C
14	ONOMA I4Cγ	NAME 576B
	POIEW IIBε	DO 687D
15	AGAPAW IAβ	LOVE 4C
	ENTOL8 2D	COMMAND 268D
	T8REW 5	KEEP 822D
16	AIWN IB	TIME 26D
	ERWTAW 2	ASK 312A
	HINA IID	IN ORDER THAT 377C
	KAI I2F	AND 393C
*PARAKL8TOS		HELPER 624A
17	AL8THEIA 2B	TRUTH 35C
	EIMI II14	TO BE 224C
	THEWREW 2B	OBSERVE 360D
	KOSMOS 7	WORLD 447D
	MENW IAβ	REMAIN 505B
	PARA IIIBγ	BESIDE 615C
	PNEUMA 5E	SPIRIT 683B
18	APHI8MI 3A	LEAVE 125D
	ERCHOMAI I2A	COME 311C
	ORPHANOS 2	ORPHANED 586D
19	ETI IC	STILL 316A
	ZAW 2Bα	LIVE 337A
	MIKROS 3E	A LITTLE WHILE 523C
	OUKETI I	NO LONGER 596D
19A	THEWREW I	OBSERVE 360C
19B	THEWREW 2B	OBSERVE 360D
20	GINWSKW IC	KNOW 160A
	EN I5D	IN 259A
	H8MERA 4A	TIME 348A
	KAGW I	AND I 387A
21	AGAPAW IAβ	LOVE 4C
	AGAPAW IBα	LOVE 4D
	EKEINOS IB	THAT 238D

21	EMAUTOU 2	MYSELF 253B
	EMPHANIZW IB	MAKE VISIBLE 257A
	ENTOL8 2D	COMMAND 268D
	ECHW I2I	HAVE 333C
	T8REW 5	KEEP 822D
	HUPO IAα	BY 850D
22	GINOMAI I3A	TAKE PLACE 157D
	EMPHANIZW IA	MAKE VISIBLE 257A
	IOUDAS 5	JUDAS 380D
*ISKARIWTH		ISCARIOT 381D
	KAI I2H	AND 393D
	KOSMOS 5A	WORLD 447C
	MELLW ICγ	INTEND 502B
	HOTI IDγ	THAT 593C
	OUCHI I	NOT 602D
	TIS, TI IBε	WHICH 827B
23	ERCHOMAI I2A	COME 311C
	MON8 I	STAY 529A
	PARA IIIBγ	BESIDE 615C
	POIEW III	DO 689C
	T8REW 5	KEEP 823A
23F	AGAPAW IAβ	LOVE 4C
23F	LOGOS IBβ	WORD 479B
24	EMOS IB	MY 255D
	T8REW 5	KEEP 823A
24A	LOGOS IAδ	WORD 478D
25	LALEW 2B	SPEAK 464D
	MENW IAα	REMAIN 504D
	PARA IIIBγ	BESIDE 615C
26	DIDASKW 2C	TEACH 191A
	EKEINOS IB	THAT 238D
	HO,H8,TO IIIF	THE 553A
	ONOMA I4Cγ	NAME 576B
	PARAKL8TOS	HELPER 624A
	PEMPW I	SEND 647D
	PNEUMA 5Cα	SPIRIT 682D
	HUPOMIMN8SKW IA	REMIND 853D
27	APHI8MI 3A	LEAVE 125D
	DEILIAW	BE COWARDLY 172A
	EIR8N8 3	PEACE 226D
	KARDIA IBε	HEART 405A
	KOSMOS 7	WORLD 448A
	M8DE IB	AND NOT 519D
	TARASSW 2	STIR UP 813A
28	AKOUW IC	HEAR 31D
	AN IBβ	(PARTICLE) 48A
	EIPON 3E	FORETELL 225D
	ERCHOMAI I2A	COME 311C
	MEGAS 2Bα	GREAT 499B
	POREUW I	PROCEED 699A
	HUPAGW 3	GO AWAY 844D
	CHAIRW I	REJOICE 881D
29	HINA IIB	IN ORDER THAT 377C
	PISTEUW ID	BELIEVE 666D
	PRIN IB	BEFORE 708A
30	ARCHWN 3	AUTHORITIES 113C
	EN I2	IN 258A
	ECHW I7A	HAVE 334A
	KOSMOS 7	WORLD 447D
	LALEW 2Aδ	SPEAK 464C
31	AGAPAW IBβ	LOVE 4D
	AGW 5	GO 14C
	GINWSKW IC	KNOW 160A

```
31 EGEIRW 2F        APPEAR 214B
   ENTELLW          COMMAND 267D
   ENTEUTHEN I      FROM HERE 268A
   HOUTW IA         THUS 602B
   POIEW I2Aα       DO 689A

         JOHN 15

1  AL8THINOS 3      GENUINE 36C
   AMPELOS 2        VINE 46B
   GEWRGOS 2        FARMER 156B
2  AIRW 4           TAKE AWAY 24B
   AUTOS 3C         (OBLIQUE CASE) 123A
   KATHAIRW I       MAKE CLEAN 387C
   KARPOS IA        FRUIT 405C
   KARPOPHOROS      FRUITBEARING 406B
   KL8MA            BRANCH 435C
   POLUS IIIB       MANY 695D
2A     PHERW 2      BEAR 862D
2B     PHERW 2      BEAR 862D
2C     PHERW 2      BEAR 862D
3  KATHAROS 3A      CLEAN 389A
   LALEW 2B         SPEAK 464D
   LOGOS IB8β       WORD 479B
4  APO V5           OF 87D
   HEAUTOU IA       ONESELF 211B
   EN I5C           IN 258D
   KAGW I           AND I 387A
   KARPOS IA        FRUIT 405C
   OUDE 2           AND NOT 595D
   HOUTW IA         THUS 602B
4A     MENW IAβ     REMAIN 505A
4A     MENW IAβ     REMAIN 505A
4B     MENW IAα     REMAIN 505A
4C     MENW IAβ     REMAIN 505A
4F     AMPELOS 2    VINE 46B
4F     EN I5D       IN 259A
4F     PHERW 2      BEAR 862D
4-6    KL8MA        BRANCH 435C
5  KARPOS 2A        RESULT 405D
   MENW IAβ         REMAIN 505A
   OU 6A            NO 595A
   HOUTW IAε        THIS 601B
   POLUS IIBα       MANY 694C
   SU IA            YOU 779D
   CHWRIS 2Aα       APART 898D
5-7    MENW IAβ     REMAIN 505A
6  *BALLW IB        THROW 130C
   EXW IB           OUTSIDE 279A
   KAIW 2           BURN 397B
   X8RAINW 2A       DRY UP 550D
   PUR IB           FIRE 737D
   SUNAGW I         GATHER 789D
   TIS, TI IAγ      ANY ONE 827D
   HWS II2          SO 906A
7  GINOMAI I3Bγ     TAKE PLACE 158B
   THELW I          WISH 355B
   R8MA I           WORD 742D
7B     MENW IAβ     REMAIN 505B
8  GINOMAI III      BE 159B
   *DOXAZW 2        GLORIFY 203D
   HINA IIIE        IN ORDER THAT 378C
   KARPOS 2A        RESULT 405D

8  HOUTOS IBβ       THIS 601C
   POLUS IIBα       MANY 694C
   PHERW 2          BEAR 862D
9  AGAPAW IBα       LOVE 4D
   AGAP8 I2A        LOVE 6A
   KAGW 3A          I ALSO 387C
   KATHWS I         JUST AS 392A
9F     MENW IAβ     REMAIN 505A
10 EAN IIB          IF 210C
   EGW              I 216C
10A    AGAP8 I2A    LOVE 6A
10A    ENTOL8 2D    COMMAND 268D
10A    T8REW 5      KEEP 822D
10B    AGAP8 I2B    LOVE 6A
10B    T8REW 5      KEEP 822D
11 EMOS IAα         MY 255A
   LALEW 2B         SPEAK 464D
   HOUTOS IBα       THIS 601C
   PL8ROW 3         MAKE FULL 677B
11B    CHARA I      JOY 883C
11B    CHARA I      JOY 883D
12 AGAPAW IAα       LOVE 4B
   EIMI II6A        TO BE 223C
   ENTOL8 2D        COMMAND 268D
   HINA IIICα       IN ORDER THAT 378C
   HOUTOS IAδ       THIS 601A
13 AGAP8 I2A        LOVE 6A
   ECHW I2Eβ        HAVE 333A
   HINA IIIE        IN ORDER THAT 378C
   MEGAS 2Aγ        GREAT 499A
   TITH8MI IIB6     LAY DOWN 823D
   HUPER IAε        IN BEHALF OF 846C
   PHILOS 2Aα       LOVING 868D
   PSUCH8 IAβ       SOUL LIFE 901C
13F    PHILOS 2Aα   LOVING 868D
14 EAN IIA          IF 210B
   ENTELLW          COMMAND 268A
15 AKOUW IBβ        HEAR 31C
   GNWRIZW I        MAKE KNOWN 162C
   DOULOS 4         SLAVE 205B
   EIPON 3D         CALL 225D
   KURIOS IAβ       LORD 460A
   LEGW II3         CALL 471B
   OIDA IF          KNOW 558C
   OUKETI I         NO LONGER 596D
   PARA I3C         FROM 615A
   PHILOS 2Aα       LOVING 868D
16 AITEW            ASK 25B
   AITEW            ASK 25C
   DIDWMI           GIVE 191D
   EKLEGOMAI 2A     CHOOSE 241D
   HINA IIIAε       IN ORDER THAT 378B
   KARPOS 2A        RESULT 405D
   MENW ICβ         REMAIN 505C
   ONOMA I4Cγ       NAME 576B
   HOSTIS IEβ       WHOEVER 591A
   TITH8MI I2B      MAKE 824A
   HUPAGW 2         GO AWAY 844C
   PHERW 2          BEAR 862D
17 AGAPAW IAα       LOVE 4B
   ENTELLW          COMMAND 268A
   HINA IIIAδ       IN ORDER THAT 378B
18 GINWSKW 6C       KNOW 160D
```

18*KOSMOS 7	WORLD 447D		
PRWTOS 1A	FIRST 733A		
PRWTOS 2A	FIRST 733D		
18F MISEW 1	HATE 524C		
19 AN 1Bα	(PARTICLE) 47D		
DIA 8II2	THEREFORE 180B		
EIMI III3	TO BE 224B		
EK 1B	AWAY FROM 233C		
EK 3B	FROM 234B		
EKLEGOMAI 1	CHOOSE 241D		
IDIOS 3B	ONES OWN 370D		
HOTI 3A	THAT 593D		
PHILEW 1A	LOVE LIKE 866D		
19A KOSMOS 7	WORLD 447D		
19B KOSMOS 7	WORLD 448A		
19C KOSMOS 7	WORLD 448A		
19D KOSMOS 7	WORLD 447D		
20 DIWKW 2	PERSECUTE 200B		
MN8MONEUW 1A	REMEMBER 527A		
HOS,H8,HO I4A	(REL PRON) 587D		
HUMETEROS 1	YOUR 843D		
20A LOGOS 1Aγ	WORD 478C		
20A T8REW 5	KEEP 823A		
20B T8REW 5	KEEP 823A		
21 ONOMA I4Cα	NAME 575C		
POIEW IIDγ	DO 688D		
22 EI IIB	IF 218B		
LALEW 2Aδ	SPEAK 464B		
M8 AII	NOT 517C		
NUN 2	NOW 548A		
PROPHASIS 1	ACTUAL MOTIVE 730A		
22A ECHW I2Eβ	HAVE 333A		
23 HO,H8,TO II3B	THE 553C		
23F MISEW 1	HATE 524C		
24 ALLOS ID	OTHER 39C		
HAMARTIA 2	SIN 42D		
EI IIB	IF 218B		
ERGON ICα	DEED 308A		
KAI I6	AND 394A		
M8 AII	NOT 517C		
NUN 2	NOW 548A		
OUDEIS 1	NO 596B		
25 DWREAN 2	GRATIS 209D		
LOGOS IAζ	MATTER 479A		
MISEW 1	HATE 524D		
NOMOS 4B	LAW 545A		
PL8ROW 4A	MAKE FULL 677C		
26 AL8THEIA 2B	TRUTH 35C		
EKPOREUOMAI 1B	GO OUT 243D		
ERCHOMAI I2A	COME 311C		
MARTUREW 1A	BEAR WITNESS 493D		
PARAKL8TOS	HELPER 624A		
PEMPW 1	SEND 647D		
PNEUMA 5E	SPIRIT 683B		
26A PARA II	FROM 614C		
26B PARA II	FROM 614C		
27 ARCH8 1B	BEGINNING 111C		
DE 4B	BUT, AND 170D		
MARTUREW 1A	BEAR WITNESS 493C		
META AIIICα	WITH 510A		

JOHN 16

1	HINA IIB	IN ORDER THAT 377C	
	LALEW 2B	SPEAK 464D	
	SKANDALIZW IA	CAUSE TO FALL 760B	
2	APOKTEINW IA	KILL 93B	
	APOSUNAGWGOS	EXCOMMUNICATED 100B	
	DOKEW IA	THINK 200D	
	ERCHOMAI IIBα	COME 311B	
	HINA IIID	IN ORDER THAT 378C	
	LATREIA	SERVICE 468C	
	POIEW IIBι	DO 688B	
	PROSPHERW 2B	BRING (TO) 727B	
	HWRA 3	TIME OF DAY 905A	
4	ARCH8 1B	BEGINNING 111C	
	EIPON 3E	FORETELL 225D	
	ERCHOMAI IIBα	COME 311B	
	HINA IIB	IN ORDER THAT 377C	
	LALEW 2B	SPEAK 464D	
	META AIIICα	WITH 510A	
	MN8MONEUW IA	REMEMBER 527A	
	HWRA 3	TIME OF DAY 905A	
5	EK 4Aα	FROM 235B	
	ERWTAW 1	ASK 312A	
	NUN IC	NOW 547D	
	NUN IB	NOW 547D	
	OUDEIS 2A	NO ONE 596B	
	POU 2A	WHERE 703A	
5A	HUPAGW 3	GO AWAY 844D	
5B	HUPAGW 3	GO AWAY 844D	
6	KARDIA 1Bε	HEART 405A	
	LALEW 2B	SPEAK 464D	
	LUP8	GRIEF 483A	
	PL8ROW IA	MAKE FULL 676D	
7	AL8THEIA 2B	TRUTH 35D	
	APERCHOMAI 2	GO 84A	
	ERCHOMAI I2A	COME 311C	
	LEGW IIA	SAY 469B	
	PARAKL8TOS	HELPER 624A	
	PEMPW 1	SEND 647D	
	SUMPHERW 2A	BETTER 788A	
8	DIKAIOSUN8 2B	RIGHTEOUSNESS 196A	
	ELEGCHW 2	EXPOSE 248D	
	ERCHOMAI IIAζ	COME 310D	
	KRISIS IAβ	JUDGING 453D	
	KRISIS 3	RIGHT 454B	
9	PISTEUW 2Aβ	BELIEVE 667B	
9=11	HOTI IC	THAT 593B	
10	DIKAIOSUN8 2B	RIGHTEOUSNESS 196A	
	THEWREW 1	OBSERVE 360C	
	OUKETI 1	NO LONGER 596D	
	HUPAGW 3	GO AWAY 844D	
11	ARCHWN 3	AUTHORITIES 113C	
	*KOSMOS 7	WORLD 447D	
	KRINW 4Bα	JUDGE 453A	
	KRISIS IAβ	JUDGING 453D	
	KRISIS 3	RIGHT 454B	
12	ARTI 3	NOW 109D	
	BASTAZW 2Bβ	ENDURE 137A	
	ETI 2A	STILL 316A	
13*AL8THEIA 2B		TRUTH 35C	
	AN 3A	(PARTICLE) 48B	
	ANAGGELLW 2	DISCLOSE 51A	

13 APO V5	OF 87D	23 EKEINOS 2Bβ	THAT 239B
HEAUTOU IA	ONESELF 211B	ERWTAW I	ASK 312A
ERCHOMAI IIBβ	COME 311B	H8MERA 4A	TIME 348B
ERCHOMAI I2A	COME 311C	ONOMA I4Cγ	NAME 576B
HO,H8,TO III3A	THE 553C	24*AITEW	ASK 25C
HODBGEW 2	LEAD 555D	ARTI 3	NOW 110A
PAS ICα	ALL 637B	HEWS IIIC	UNTIL 335C
PNEUMA 5E	SPIRIT 683B	LAMBANW 2	RECEIVE 466B
14 DOXAZW 2	GLORIFY 203D	ONOMA I4Cγ	NAME 576B
EKEINOS IB	THAT 238D	PL8ROW 3	MAKE FULL 677B
14F ANAGGELLW 2	DISCLOSE 51A	CHARA I	JOY 883D
14F EMOS 2	MY 255A	25 APAGGELLW I	REPORT 78C
15 EIPON 2C	SAY 225C	ERCHOMAI IIBα	COME 311B
EMOS IB	MY 255A	HOTE 2Aα	WHEN 592C
16 HORAW IAα	SEE 581C	PARR8SIA I	PLAINNESS 635D
OUKETI I	NO LONGER 596D	HWRA 3	TIME OF DAY 905A
16F THEWREW I	OBSERVE 360C	25A LALEW 2B	SPEAK 464D
16=19 MIKROS 3E	A LITTLE WHILE 523C	25A PAROIMIA 2	FIGURE 634C
17 EIMI II3	TO BE 222D	25B PAROIMIA 2	FIGURE 634C
EK 4Aγ	FROM 235B	26 AITEW	ASK 25C
HOTI 2	THAT 593D	EKEINOS 2Bβ	THAT 239B
PROS IIIIE	TOWARD 716D	ERWTAW 2	ASK 312A
HUPAGW 3	GO AWAY 844D	H8MERA 4A	TIME 348B
18 OIDA 4	KNOW 559A	ONOMA I4Cγ	NAME 576B
19 ALLBLWN	EACH OTHER 38D	27 AUTOS IE	OF HIMSELF 122C
GINWSKW 4C	PERCEIVE 160C	EXERCHOMAI IAγ	GO OUT 274A
EPERWTAW IA	ASK 285A	PARA II	FROM 614C
ERWTAW I	ASK 312A	PISTEUW IAβ	BELIEVE 666A
Z8TEW IC	INVESTIGATE 339B	27A PHILEW IA	LOVE LIKE 867A
THEWREW I	OBSERVE 360C	27B PHILEW IA	LOVE LIKE 866D
META AII3A	WITH 510C	28 EXERCHOMAI IAγ	GO OUT 274A
HORAW IAα	SEE 581C	ERCHOMAI IIAη	COME 310D
HOTI IA	THAT 592D	POREUW I	PROCEED 699A
HOUTOS IBβ	THIS 601C	28A KOSMOS 4C	WORLD 447B
20 ALLA 2	BUT, YET 37D	28B KOSMOS 4C	WORLD 447B
GINOMAI I4A	BECOME 158D	29 EN III2	BY 260C
EIS 8Aα	229C	IDE I	SEE 369D
THR8NEW IA	MOURN 363D	LALEW 2Aε	SPEAK 464C
*KLAIW I	WEEP 434B	LEGW IIA	SAY 469B
KOSMOS 7	WORLD 447D	NUN IAα	NOW 547C
LUPEW 2A	GRIEVE 483A	OUDEIS I	NO 596B
LUP8	GRIEF 483B	PAROIMIA 2	FIGURE 634C
CHAIRW I	REJOICE 881B	*PARR8SIA I	PLAINNESS 636A
20F CHARA I	JOY 883C	30 APO IVIAβ	FROM 86D
21 ANTHRWPOS IAα	MAN 67C	EN III3A	BECAUSE OF 260C
*GENNAW 2	BEAR 154D	EXERCHOMAI IAγ	GO OUT 274A
THLIPSIS I	TRIBULATION 363A	ERWTAW I	ASK 312A
KOSMOS 4B	WORLD 447A	THEOS 3B	GOD 357D
LUP8	GRIEF 483B	HINA IIICα	IN ORDER THAT 378C
MN8MONEUW IA	REMEMBER 527A	HOUTOS IBα	THIS 601C
PAIDION I	INFANT 609A	PISTEUW IAβ	BELIEVE 666A
TIKTW I	GIVE BIRTH 824C	CHREIA I	NEED 893D
CHARA I	JOY 883D	31 ARTI 3	NOW 109D
HWRA 3	TIME OF DAY 905A	PISTEUW ID	BELIEVE 666D
21F ECHW I2Eβ	HAVE 333A	32 HEKASTOS I	EACH 236B
22 KARDIA IBε	HEART 405A	ERCHOMAI IIBα	COME 311B
LUP8	GRIEF 483B	ERCHOMAI IIBα	COME 311B
NUN IC	NOW 547D	IDIOS 3B	ONES OWN 370D
HORAW IAα	SEE 581C	HINA IIID	IN ORDER THAT 378C
CHAIRW I	REJOICE 881B	META AIIICβ	WITH 510A
CHARA I	JOY 883C	NUN IAβ	NOW 547C
23 AITEW	ASK 25B	SKORPIZW I	SCATTER 764B
AN	IF 49A	HWRA 3	TIME OF DAY 905A

32A	MONOS 1B	ALONE	529D
32B	MONOS 1B	ALONE	529D
33	EIR8N8 3	PEACE	226D
	THARSEW	BE CHEERFUL	352C
	THLIPSIS 1	TRIBULATION	363A
	NIKAW 2A	CONQUER	541B
33A	KOSMOS 7	WORLD	448A
33B	ECHW I2Eα	HAVE	333A
33B	KOSMOS 7	WORLD	448A

JOHN 17

1	*DOXAZW 2	GLORIFY	203D
	EPAIRW 1	LOOK UP	281C
	ERCHOMAI IIBα	COME	311B
	LALEW 2B	SPEAK	464D
	OURANOS 2A	HEAVEN	599B
	HUIOS 2B	SON	842D
	HWRA 3	TIME OF DAY	905A
2	DIDWMI	GIVE	191D
	DIDWMI 1Bβ	GIVE	192B
	EXOUSIA 3	AUTHORITY	278A
	ZW8 2Bα	LIFE	341B
	HINA I2	IN ORDER THAT	377C
	KATHWS 3	AS	392B
	SARX 3	BODY	751A
2B	PAS ICγ	WHOEVER	637C
2F	ZW8 2Bα	LIFE	341C
3	AL8THINOS 3	GENUINE	36C
	APOSTELLW IC	SEND AWAY	98B
	*GINWSKW IB	KNOW	160A
	EIMI II6A	TO BE	223C
	THEOS 3I	GOD	358C
	HINA I3	IN ORDER THAT	377D
	HINA IIIE	IN ORDER THAT	378C
	MONOS IA6	ONLY	529C
	HOUTOS IA6	THIS	601A
	CHRISTOS 2	ANOINTED ONE	895C
4	G8 5B	EARTH	156D
	DOXAZW 2	GLORIFY	203D
	ERGON 2	WORK	308B
	HINA IIB	IN ORDER THAT	377C
	TELEIOW I	COMPLETE	817B
5	DOXA IBα	GLORY	203A
	DOXAZW 2	GLORIFY	203D
	EIMI II	TO BE	222A
	KOSMOS 2	WORLD	446D
	NUN IC	NOW	547D
	HOS,H8,HO I4A	(REL PRON)	587D
	PARA IIIBγ	BESIDE	615C
	PRO 2	BEFORE	708D
	SEAUTOU 2	YOURSELF	753A
6	DIDWMI 3	GIVE	192C
	KOSMOS 5A	WORLD	447B
	LOGOS IBβ	WORD	479B
	ONOMA I4B	NAME	575B
	T8REW 5	KEEP	823A
	PHANEROW IA	REVEAL	860C
7	NUN IAβ	NOW	547C
	PARA II	FROM	614C
7F	GINWSKW IC	KNOW	160A
8	AL8THWS I	TRULY	36D
	APOSTELLW IC	SEND AWAY	98B

8	DIDWMI 3	GIVE	192C
	EXERCHOMAI IAγ	GO OUT	274A
	LAMBANW IEβ	RECEIVE	466A
	PARA II	FROM	614C
	PISTEUW IAβ	BELIEVE	666A
	R8MA I	WORD	742D
	SU IC	YOU	779D
9	DIDWMI 3	GIVE	192C
	ERWTAW 2	ASK	312A
	KOSMOS 7	WORLD	448A
	HOS,H8,HO I4A	(REL PRON)	587D
10	*DOXAZW 2	GLORIFY	203D
	EMOS 2	MY	255A
10B	SOS 2B	YOURS	766D
11	HAGIOS IB6	HOLY	9D
	EIMI II7	TO BE	223D
	HEIS IB	ONE	230A
	OUKETI I	NO LONGER	596D
11B	KOSMOS 7	WORLD	448A
11F	ONOMA I4Cγ	NAME	576B
11F	T8REW 2B	KEEP	822C
12	APOLLUMI 2Aα	PERISH	94D
	APWLEIA 2	DESTRUCTION	103B
	GRAPH8 2Bβ	SCRIPTURE	165B
	DIDWMI 3	GIVE	192C
	HINA II2	IN ORDER THAT	378D
	META AIIICα	WITH	510A
	OUDEIS 2A	NO ONE	596B
	PL8ROW 4A	MAKE FULL	677C
	HUIOS IC6	SON	842A
	PHULASSW IC	WATCH	876B
13	HEAUTOU IC	ONESELF	211B
	NUN IC	NOW	547D
	PL8ROW 3	MAKE FULL	677B
	CHARA I	JOY	883D
	CHARA 2C	JOY	884A
14	DIDWMI 3	GIVE	192C
	EIMI III3	TO BE	224B
	EK 3B	FROM	234B
	LOGOS IBβ	WORD	479B
	MISEW I	HATE	524C
14A	KOSMOS 7	WORLD	447D
14B	KOSMOS 7	WORLD	448A
14C	KOSMOS 7	WORLD	448A
15	AIRW 3	CARRY	24A
	EK IA	AWAY FROM	233C
	EK ID	AWAY FROM	233D
	ERWTAW 2	ASK	312B
	HINA IIIAγ	IN ORDER THAT	378B
	KOSMOS 7	WORLD	448A
	PON8ROS 2B	WICKED	698A
	T8REW 4	KEEP	822D
16	EIMI III3	TO BE	224B
16A	KOSMOS 7	WORLD	448A
16B	KOSMOS 7	WORLD	448A
17	HAGIAZW 2	CONSECRATE	9A
	AL8THEIA 2B	TRUTH	35C
	LOGOS IBβ	WORD	479B
	HO,H8,TO IIIE	THE	553A
18	APOSTELLW IC	SEND AWAY	98B
	KAGW 3A	I ALSO	387A
	KATHWS I	JUST AS	392A
18B	KOSMOS 7	WORLD	448A

19	ALΘTHEIA 3	REALITY	35D
	EMAUTOU 2	MYSELF	253B
19A	HAGIAZW 2	CONSECRATE	9A
19B	HAGIAZW 2	CONSECRATE	8D
20	ERWTAW 2	ASK	312A
	LOGOS 1Aβ	WORD	478C
	MONOS 2C	ONLY	529D
	PISTEUW 2Aβ	BELIEVE	667B
21	APOSTELLW 1C	SEND AWAY	98B
	PISTEUW 1Aβ	BELIEVE	666A
21FF	EIMI II7	TO BE	223D
21=3	HEIS 1B	ONE	230A
22	DOXA 1Bα	GLORY	203A
	KAGW 1	AND I	386D
23	APOSTELLW 1C	SEND AWAY	98B
	TELEIOW 2Eα	MAKE PERFECT	817D
24	AGAPAW 1Bβ	LOVE	4D
	DIDWMI 3	GIVE	192C
	DOXA 1Bα	GLORY	203A
	EIMI II9A	TO BE	223D
	THELW 1	WISH	355C
	THEWREW 2B	OBSERVE	360D
	HINA III1Aα	IN ORDER THAT	378A
	KAKEINOS 2B	HE ALSO	397C
	KATABOLΘ 1	FOUNDATION	410A
	KOSMOS 2	WORLD	446D
	META AIIICα	WITH	510A
	HOPOU 1Aα	WHERE	579C
	PRO 2	BEFORE	708C
25	APOSTELLW 1C	SEND AWAY	98B
	GINWSKW 1B	KNOW	160A
	GINWSKW 1C	KNOW	160A
	DIKAIOS 2	RIGHTEOUS	195A
	KAI I6	AND	394A
	KOSMOS 7	WORLD	448A
26	AGAPAW 1Bβ	LOVE	4D
	AGAPAW 2	LOVE	5A
	AGAPΘ I2B	LOVE	6A
	GNWRIZW 1	MAKE KNOWN	162C
	ONOMA I4B	NAME	575B

JOHN 18

1	AUTOS 1C	SELF	122C
	EISERCHOMAI 1Aβ	COME	231D
	EXERCHOMAI 1Aβ	GO OUT	274A
	KEDRWN	THE KIDRON VALLEY	427D
	KEDROS	CEDAR TREE	427D
	KΘPOS	GARDEN	431D
	HOPOU 1Aα	WHERE	579C
	PERAN 2A	ON THE OTHER SIDE	649C
	SUN 1B	WITH	789B
	CHEIMARROS	RAVINE	887D
2	DE 4A	BUT, AND	170D
	EKEI 2	THERE	238D
	META AII3B	WITH	510D
	PARADIDWMI 1B	GIVE OVER	620A
	POLLAKIS	OFTEN	693B
	SUNAGW 2	GATHER	790B
2F	IOUDAS 6	JUDAS	380D
3	EKEI 2	THERE	238D
	ERCHOMAI II1Aγ	COME	310C
	LAMBANW 1A	TAKE	465B

3	LAMPAS 1	TORCH	466D
	META AIII3	WITH	511B
	HOPLON 2A	WEAPON	579A
	SPEIRA	COHORT	768C
	HUPΘRET8S	SERVANT	850C
	PHANOS	LAMP	861A
4	EXERCHOMAI 1Aβ	GO OUT	274A
	EPI III1Bγ	ON	289A
	ERCHOMAI I2C	COME	311D
	ZΘTEW 1Aβ	SEEK	339B
	PAS 1Dβ	ALL	637D
	TIS, TI 1Aα	WHICH	826C
5	DE 4A	BUT, AND	170D
	IOUDAS 6	JUDAS	380D
	HISTΘMI II2A	STAND	383B
	META AI	WITH	509D
	NAZARΘNOS	THE NAZARENE	534A
	NAZWRAIOS	NAZARENE	534B
	PARADIDWMI 1B	GIVE OVER	620A
5F	EIMI II5	TO BE	223C
6	APERCHOMAI 4	GO AFTER	84A
	OPISW 1A	BEHIND	578C
	OUN 5	THEREFORE	597D
	PIPTW 1Bα	FALL	665B
	CHAMAI 2	TO THE GROUND	883B
	HWS IV1A	WHEN	907A
7	NAZWRAIOS	NAZARENE	534B
	TIS, TI 1Aα	WHICH	826C
7F	ZΘTEW 1Aβ	SEEK	339B
8	APHIΘMI 4	TOLERATE	126A
	EI VII0	IF	219A
	HUPAGW 1	GO AWAY	844B
9	LOGOS 1Aγ	WORD	478C
	OUDEIS 2A	NO ONE	596B
	PLΘROW 4A	MAKE FULL	677C
10	APOKOPTW 1	CUT OFF	92C
	DEXIOS 1	RIGHT	173C
	HELKW 1A	DRAG	251A
	ECHW IIB	HAVE	332B
	MALCHOS	MALCHUS	491A
	MACHAIRA 1	SWORD	497B
	ONOMA I1	NAME	574A
	PAIW 1	STRIKE	610B
	PETROS	PETER	661A
	WTARION	THE EAR	908C
	WTION	THE EAR	908D
11	AUTOS 3C	(OBLIQUE CASE)	123A
	BALLW 2B	PUT	130D
	MACHAIRA 1	SWORD	497C
	MΘ DIA	NOT	519B
	PINW 2Bα	DRINK	664C
	POTΘRION 2	CUP	702B
12	DEW 1B	BIND	176D
	SPEIRA	COHORT	768C
	SULLAMBANW 1Aα	SEIZE	784B
	HUPΘRET8S	SERVANT	850C
	CHILIARCHOS	TRIBUNE	890A
13	HANNAS	ANNAS	69D
	ARCHIEREUS 1B	HIGH PRIEST	112C
	ENIAUTOS 1	YEAR	265D
	KAIAPHAS	CAIAPHAS	394D
	PENTHEROS	FATHER IN LAW	648B
	PRWTOS 2A	FIRST	733D

13F	KAIAPHAS	CAIAPHAS 394D
14	ANTHRWPOS 3Aβ	MAN 68B
	IOUDAIOS 2E	JEWISH 380B
	SUMBOULEUW 1	ADVISE 785C
	SUMPHERW 2A	BETTER 788A
	HUPER 1Aє	IN BEHALF OF 846C
15	AUL8 1	COURTYARD 120D
	EKEINOS 2A	THAT 239B
	PETROS	PETER 661A
	SUNEISERCHOMAI	ENTER WITH 794D
15F	GNWSTOS 1B	ACQUAINTANCE 163C
16	ALLOS 3	THE OTHER 39D
	GNWRIMOS	ACQUAINTED WITH 162D
	EISAGW	BRING 231C
	EXW 1Aα	OUTSIDE 278D
	THURA 1A	DOOR 366B
	HIST8MI II2A	STAND 383B
	PROS III	NEAR 716C
16F	THURWROS 2	DOORKEEPER 366D
17	PAIDISK8	MAID 609B
17B	LEGW IIIB	ANSWER 470C
18	ANTHRAKIA	A CHARCOAL FIRE 66D
	EIMI I5	TO BE 222C
	POIEW IIAα	DO 687A
	HUP8RET8S	SERVANT 850C
	PSUCHOS	COLD 902D
18A	THERMAINW	WARM ONESELF 360B
18A	HIST8MI II2A	STAND 383B
18B	THERMAINW	WARM ONESELF 360B
18B	HIST8MI II2A	STAND 383B
19	ARCHIEREUS 1B	HIGH PRIEST 112B
	DIDACH8 2	TEACHING 191B
	ERWTAW 1	ASK 312A
20	KOSMOS 5A	WORLD 447C
	KRUPTOS 2B	HIDDEN 455B
	HO,H8,TO IIIAα	THE 552B
	PARR8SIA 2	PUBLICLY 636A
	PAS 1Dα	ALL 637C
	SUNAGWG8 2A	790C
	PLACE OF ASSEMBLY	
	SUNERCHOMAI 1A	ASSEMBLE 795D
21	IDE 1	SEE 369D
	HOS,H8,HO I9A	(REL PRON) 588D
22	ARCHIEREUS 1B	HIGH PRIEST 112B
	DIDWMI 1Bα	GIVE 192A
	HOUTW 1B	THUS 602B
	HOUTW 1B	THUS 602C
	PARIST8MI 2Bα	BE PRESENT 633D
	RAPISMA	BLOW WITH A CLUB 741D
	HUP8RET8S	SERVANT 850C
23	DERW	BEAT 174D
	KAKOS 1C	EVIL 398D
	KAKWS 2	BADLY 399B
	KALWS 4B	WELL 402B
	LALEW 2Aє	SPEAK 464C
	MARTUREW 1A	BEAR WITNESS 493D
	TIS, TI 3A	WHICH 827B
24	HANNAS	ANNAS 69D
	ARCHIEREUS 1B	HIGH PRIEST 112B
	DEW 1B	BIND 176D
	KAIAPHAS	CAIAPHAS 394D
25	ARNEOMAI 3A	DENY 107C
	THERMAINW	WARM ONESELF 360B

25	HIST8MI II2A	STAND 383B
	PETROS	PETER 661A
26	APOKOPTW 1	CUT OFF 92C
	K8POS	GARDEN 431D
	HOS,H8,HO I2A	(REL PRON) 587A
	SUGGEN8S	RELATED 780B
	WTION	THE EAR 908D
27	ALEKTWR	COCK 34D
	ARNEOMAI 3A	DENY 107C
	PHWNEW 1A	PRODUCE A SOUND 878B
28	AGW 2	LEAD AWAY 14B
	EIMI I5	TO BE 222C
	EISERCHOMAI 1Aβ	COME 231D
	ESTHIW 1A	EAT 312D
	KAIAPHAS	CAIAPHAS 394D
	MIAINW 1	DEFILE 522C
	PASCHA 2	THE PASCHAL LAMB 639A
	PRWI	EARLY 732B
	PRWIA	(EARLY) MORNING 732B
28A	PRAITWRION	THE PRAETORIUM 704B
28B	PRAITWRION	THE PRAETORIUM 704B
29	EXERCHOMAI 1Aє	GO OUT 274B
	EXW 1B	OUTSIDE 279A
	KAT8GORIA	ACCUSATION 424C
	TIS, TI 2	WHICH 827B
	PHERW 4Aβ	BEAR 863B
	PH8MI 1Bα	SAY 864A
29FF	PILATOS	PILATE 663C
30	EIMI II4C	TO BE 223B
	KAKOPOIOS	CRIMINAL 398C
	KAKOS 1C	EVIL 398D
	M8 AII	NOT 517C
	PARADIDWMI 1B	GIVE OVER 620A
31	EXESTI 2	IT IS POSSIBLE 274D
	KATA II5Aα	ACCORDING TO 408A
	KRINW 4Aα	JUDGE 452D
	NOMOS 3	LAW 544C
	OUDEIS 2A	NO ONE 596B
	SUNEDRION 2	SANHEDRIN 793D
32	APOTHN8SKW 1Aα	DIE 90D
	THANATOS 1D	DEATH 351D
	LOGOS 2A	WORD 478B
	MELLW 1C6	IS DESTINED 502C
	PL8ROW 4A	MAKE FULL 677C
	POIOS 1Aγ	OF WHAT KIND 691B
	S8MAINW 2	MAKE KNOWN 755B
33	BASILEUS 2A	KING 135D
	PRAITWRION	THE PRAETORIUM 704B
	PHWNEW 2B	CALL 878C
34	APO V5	OF 87D
	HEAUTOU 1A	ONESELF 211B
	HEAUTOU 2	ONESELF 211C
	EIPON 1	SAY 225C
	8 IDγ	OR 343A
	LEGW I4	SAY 469D
35	IOUDAIOS 2A	JEWISH 380B
	M8TI	(INTERROG PARTICLE) 522A
	PARADIDWMI 1B	GIVE OVER 620A
	POIEW IIB6	DO 687D
	SOS 1	YOURS 766C
36	AGWNIZOMAI 2A	STRUGGLE 15A
	ENTEUTHEN 1	FROM HERE 268A
	KOSMOS 7	WORLD 447D

36	NUN 2	NOW 548A
	PARADIDWMI 1B	GIVE OVER 620A
	HUP8RET8S	SERVANT 850C
36A	KOSMOS 4C	WORLD 447B
36B	KOSMOS 4C	WORLD 447B
37*	AL8THEIA 2B	TRUTH 35D
	BASILEUS 2A	KING 135D
	GENNAW 2	BEAR 154D
	EIMI III3	TO BE 224B
	EIS 4F	(PURPOSE) 228D
	ERCHOMAI IIAη	COME 311A
	HINA I5	IN ORDER THAT 378A
	KOSMOS 4C	WORLD 447B
	LEGW IIIF	DECLARE 471A
	MARTUREW IA	BEAR WITNESS 493D
	OUKOUN 2	THEN 597A
	HOUTOS 1Bβ	THIS 601C
	PAS ICγ	WHOEVER 637B
	PHWN8 2A	VOICE 879A
38	AITIA 2A	CHARGE 25D
	AL8THEIA 2B	TRUTH 35D
	EXERCHOMAI IAε	GO OUT 274B
	HEURISKW 2	FIND 325D
	OUDEIS I	NO 596B
	HOUTOS 1Bα	THIS 601C
	TIS, TI 1Bα	WHICH 826D
39	APOLUW I	SET FREE 96A
	BOULOMAI 2Aε	DESIRE 145D
	HINA IIICα	IN ORDER THAT 378C
	OUN ICα	THEREFORE 597B
	PASCHA I	THE PASSOVER 639A
	SUN8THEIA 2B	HABIT 797B
40	ARCHIL8ST8S	ROBBER CHIEFTAIN 112C
	BARABBAS I	BARABBAS 132C
	KRAUGAZW 2A	CRY 450C
	L8ST8S 2	REVOLUTIONARY 474B
	M8 AIII6	NOT 519A
	PALIN 5	AGAIN 612A

JOHN 19

I	LAMBANW IA	TAKE 465B
	MASTIGOW I	WHIP 496A
	OUN 5	THEREFORE 597D
	TOTE 2	AT THAT TIME 831D
IFF	PILATOS	PILATE 663C
2	AKANTHA	THORN PLANT 29A
	EK 3H	BY 235A
	EPITITH8MI IAα	PUT UPON 302D
	HIMATION 2	GARMENT 377A
	HIMATION 2	GARMENT 377B
	KEPHAL8 IA	HEAD 431A
	PERIBALLW 1Bδ	THROW AROUND 651D
	PLEKW	WEAVE 673A
	PORPHUROUS	A PURPLE CLOAK 700D
	STEPHANOS I	WREATH 774D
	STRATIWT8S I	SOLDIER 778B
3	DIDWMI	GIVE 191D
	DIDWMI 1Bα	GIVE 192A
	HO,H8,TO IIII	THE 553B
	RAPISMA	BLOW WITH A CLUB 742A
	CHAIRW 2A	REJOICE 882A
4	AGW IA	LEAD 14A

4	AITIA 2A	CHARGE 25D
	GINWSKW IC	KNOW 160A
	EXW IB	OUTSIDE 279A
	*HEURISKW 2	FIND 325D
	IDE I	SEE 369D
4F	EXERCHOMAI IAβ	GO OUT 274A
5	AKANTHINOS	THORNY 29A
	ANTHRWPOS 4B	MAN 68D
	EXW IB	OUTSIDE 279A
	IDOU 2	THERE IS 371D
	HO,H8,TO IIIAα	THE 552B
	PORPHUROUS	A PURPLE CLOAK 700D
	STEPHANOS I	WREATH 774D
	PHOREW I	WEAR 872D
6	AITIA 2A	CHARGE 25D
	HEURISKW 2	FIND 325D
	KRAUGAZW 2A	CRY 450C
	OUN 5	THEREFORE 597D
	HUP8RET8S	SERVANT 850C
6A	STAUROW I	CRUCIFY 773A
6B	STAUROW I	CRUCIFY 773A
6C	STAUROW I	CRUCIFY 773A
7	APOTHN8SKW IAα	DIE 90D
	ECHW I2I	HAVE 333C
	KATA II5Aα	ACCORDING TO 408A
	OPHEILW 2Aβ	OWE 603D
	POIEW IIB1	DO 688B
	HUIOS 2B	SON 842D
7B	NOMOS 3	LAW 544C
8	LOGOS IAγ	WORD 478C
	MALLON I	MORE 490B
	OUN 5	THEREFORE 597D
9	APOKRISIS	ANSWER 93A
	EISERCHOMAI IAβ	COME 231D
	POTHEN I	FROM WHERE 686D
	PRAITWRION	THE PRAETORIUM 704B
10	APOLUW I	SET FREE 96A
	EXOUSIA 3	AUTHORITY 278A
	STAUROW I	CRUCIFY 773A
IOF	EXOUSIA 4A	AUTHORITY 278A
II	HAMARTIA 2	SIN 42D
	ANWTHEN I	FROM ABOVE 76C
	DIDWMI 1Bβ	GIVE 192B
	EI IIB	IF 218B
	EXOUSIA 3	AUTHORITY 278A
	KATA I2Bγ	DOWN 406D
	MEGAS 2Bβ	GREAT 499C
	M8 AII	NOT 517C
	PARADIDWMI 1B	GIVE OVER 620A
12	ANTILEGW 2	OPPOSE 74B
	APOLUW I	SET FREE 96A
	EAN IIB	IF 210B
	EK 3F	BY 234D
	KRAUGAZW 2A	CRY 450C
	POIEW IIB1	DO 688B
12A	KAISAR	EMPEROR 396C
12B	KAISAR	EMPEROR 396C
13	AGW IA	LEAD 14A
	B8MA 2	TRIBUNAL 139D
	GABBATHA	GABBATHA 148B
	HEBRAISTI	IN HEBREW 212C
	EXW IB	OUTSIDE 279A
	EPI IIAβ	ON 285D

13	KATHIZW 1A	SET 390D	23	HUPHANTOS	WOVEN 857C
	KATHIZW 2Aα	SIT DOWN 391A	23A	CHITWN	SHIRT 890C
	LEGW II3	CALL 471B	23B	CHITWN	SHIRT 890C
	LITHOSTRWTOS	PAVEMENT 475D	24	HARPAGMOS 2	ROBBERY 108B
	TOPOS 1C	PLACE 830B		BALLW 1A	THROW 130B
14	EIMI I5	TO BE 222C		GRAPH8 2A	SCRIPTURE 165B
	HEKTOS	SIXTH 245C		DIAMERIZW 1B	DIVIDE 185D
	IDE 3	SEE 369D		HEAUTOU I	ONESELF 211B
	PARASKEU8	PREPARATION 627C		EPI IIIIBζ	ON 289B
	PASCHA I	THE PASSOVER 639A		HIMATISMOS	CLOTHING 377B
	HWRA 2B	TIME OF DAY 904D		HINA II2	IN ORDER THAT 378D
	HWS IV5	WHEN 907C		KL8ROS I	LOT 436C
	HWSEI 2	AS 907D		LAGCHANW 3	CAST LOTS 463B
15	AIRW 4	TAKE AWAY 24A		MEN 1Aα	(PARTICLE) 503D
	ECHW I28β	HAVE 332D		M8 AIIII	NOT 518C
	KAISAR	EMPEROR 396C		PL8ROW 4A	MAKE FULL 677C
	KRAUGAZW 2A	CRY 450C		PROS IIIIE	TOWARD 716D
15F	STAUROW I	CRUCIFY 773A		SCHIZW 1A	SPLIT 805A
16	APAGW 2C	LEAD AWAY 78D	24F	OUN 5	THEREFORE 597D
	OUN 5	THEREFORE 597D	25	ADELPH8 I	SISTER 15C
	TOTE 2	AT THAT TIME 831D		HIST8MI II2A	STAND 383B
16A	PARALAMBANW 2A	TAKE 625A		KLWPAS	CLOPAS 437D
16B	PARALAMBANW 2A	TAKE 625A		MAGDAL8N8	MAGDALENE 485B
17	BASTAZW 2A	CARRY 136D		MARIA 2	MARY 493A
	GOLGOTHA	GOLGOTHA 164A		MARIA 4	MARY 493A
	HEBRAISTI	IN HEBREW 212C		MARIA 2	MARY 493A
	EXERCHOMAI 1Aε	GO OUT 274B		PARA IIIAα	BESIDE 615B
	KRANION	SKULL 449A		STAUROS I	THE CROSS 772B
	HOS,H8,HC 17A	(REL PRON) 588C	26	AGAPAW 1Bα	LOVE 4D
	STAUROS I	THE CROSS 772B		GUN8 I	WOMAN 167C
	TOPOS 1C	PLACE 830B		PARIST8MI 2Bα	BE PRESENT 633D
17B	LEGW II3	CALL 471B		HUIOS 1Bβ	SON 841C
18	ALLOS 2	MORE 39D	26F	IDE 3	SEE 369D
	ENTEUTHEN I	FROM HERE 268A	27	EITA I	THEN 233A
	MESOS I	BETWEEN 508C		IDIOS 3B	ONES OWN 370D
	STAUROW I	CRUCIFY 773A		LAMBANW 1Eα	RECEIVE 465D
19	GRAPHW 4	WRITE 166B		M8T8R 3	MOTHER 521D
	EPI IIAβ	ON 285D		HWRA 3	TIME OF DAY 905A
	NAZWRAIOS	NAZARENE 534B	28	GRAPH8 2Bβ	SCRIPTURE 165B
	STAUROS I	THE CROSS 772C		DIPSAW I	THIRST 199C
	TITH8MI IIAβ	PUT 823D		HINA II2	IN ORDER THAT 378D
19F	TITLOS	INSCRIPTION 828C		META BII3	AFTER 511C
20	ANAGINWSKW I	READ 51B		TELEIOW I	COMPLETE 817C
	HEBRAISTI	IN HEBREW 212C		TELEIOW 2C	FULFILL 817D
	EGGUS IA	NEAR 213B		TELEW I	FINISH 818C
	EIMI II9A	TO BE 223D	29	KEIMAI 1B	LIE 428A
	HELL8NISTI	THE GREEK LANGUAGE 251D		PERITITH8MI I	PLACE AROUND 658C
	RWMAISTI	IN LATIN 745D		PIMPL8MI 1Aα	FILL 663D
	STAUROW I	CRUCIFY 773A		PROSPHERW IB	BRING (TO) 727A
	TOPOS 1C	PLACE 830B		SKEUOS 1B	THING 761D
21	GRAPHW 2A	WRITE 165C		SPOGGOS	SPONGE 770C
	M8 AIII3B	NOT 518D		STOMA 1A	MOUTH 777B
22	GRAPHW 2A	WRITE 165D		HUSSWPOS	HYSSOP 856C
23	ANWTHEN I	FROM ABOVE 76C	29A	MESTOS I	FULL 509B
	ARAPHOS	SEAMLESS 104A	29B	MESTOS I	FULL 509B
	DIA AI2	THROUGH 178C	29F	OXOS	WINE VINEGAR 577D
	HEKASTOS I	EACH 236A	30	KLINW 1A	INCLINE 437C
	LAMBANW 1A	TAKE 465C		LAMBANW 1A	TAKE 465C
	MEROS 1A	PART 507A		OUN 5	THEREFORE 597D
	HOLOS 4	WHOLE 567D		PARADIDWMI 1A	GIVE OVER 619D
	POIEW IIAα	DO 687A		TELEW I	FINISH 818C
	STAUROW I	CRUCIFY 773A	31	EPEI 2	BECAUSE 283D
	TESSARES	FOUR 821A		ERWTAW 2	ASK 312B

31	H8MERA 2	DAY	347C
	KATAGNUMI	BREAK	410D
	MEGAS 2B8	GREAT	499C
	MENW IA∝	REMAIN	505A
	PARASKEU8	PREPARATION	627C
	STAUROS I	THE CROSS	772B
	SWMA IA	BODY	806D
31A	SABBATON IA	SABBATH	746B
31B	SABBATON IA	SABBATH	746C
31=3	SKELOS	BREAK THE LEGS	761B
32	ALLOS 3	THE OTHER	39D
	KATAGNUMI	BREAK	410D
	MEN IA∝	(PARTICLE)	503D
	PRWTOS IB	FIRST	733A
	SUSTAUROW I	CRUCIFY WITH	802C
33	EPI IIIIAY	ON	288B
	ERCHOMAI IIA8	COME	310C
	THN8SKW I	DIE	363A
	KATAGNUMI	BREAK	410D
	HWS IVIA	WHEN	907A
34	HAIMA IA	BLOOD	22A
	HEIS IA8	ONE	230A
	EXERCHOMAI 2A	GO OUT	274C
	EUTHUS	IMMEDIATELY	321C
	LOGCH8	SPEAR	480C
	NUSSW	STAB	549A
	PLEURA	SIDE	673D
	HUDWR I	WATER	840D
35	AL8TH8S 2	TRUE	36A
	AL8THINOS 2	TRUE	36B
	EKEINOS IB	THAT	238D
	EKEINOS IC	THAT	239A
	EKEINOS IE	THAT	239B
	KAKEINOS 2A	AND HE	397C
	LEGW IIA	SAY	469B
	MARTUREW'IB	BEAR WITNESS	494A
	MARTURIA 2B	TESTIMONY	494C
	HORAW IA8	SEE	581D
	PISTEUW ID	BELIEVE	666D
36	HINA II2	IN ORDER THAT	378D
	PL8ROW 4A	MAKE FULL	677C
	SKELOS	BREAK THE LEGS	761B
	SUNTRIBW IA	SHATTER	801A
36F	GRAPH8 2A	SCRIPTURE	165B
37	EKKENTEW	PIERCE	240A
	HETEROS IB∝	ANOTHER	315A
	HORAW 2A	SEE	582B
	PALIN 3	AGAIN	611D
38	AIRW 3	CARRY	24A
	HARIMATHAIA	ARIMATHAEA	106A
	EPITREPW I	ALLOW	303C
	ERCHOMAI IIA5	COME	310D
	ERWTAW 2	ASK	312B
	IWS8PH 6	JOSEPH	386C
	KRUPTW 2A	HIDE	455C
	PHOBOS 2A∝	FEAR	871C
38A	SWMA IA	BODY	806D
38B	SWMA IA	BODY	806D
39	ALO8	ALOES	40C
	HEKATON	ONE HUNDRED	236B
	HELIGMA	PACKAGE	250C
	LITRA	POUND	476D
	MIGMA	COMPOUND	523A

39	NIKOD8MOS	NICODEMUS	541C
	NUX IB	NIGHT	548D
	HO,H8,TO II6	THE	554C
	PRWTOS 2A	FIRST	733D
	SM8GMA	OINTMENT	766A
	SMURNA	MYRRH	766A
	PHERW ID	BEAR	862D
	HWS IV5	WHEN	907C
40	ARWMA	SPICES	113D
	DEW IA	BIND	176D
	ETHOS I	HABIT	217C
	ENTAPHIAZW	PREPARE FOR BURIAL	267D
	OTHONION	LINEN CLOTH	558A
	SWMA IA	BODY	806D
41	KAINOS I	NEW	395A
	K8POS	GARDEN	431D
	MN8MEION 2	TOMB	526C
	HO,H8,TO IIIA∝	THE	552B
	OUDEIS 2A	NO ONE	596B
	OUDEPW	NOT YET	596D
	STAUROW I	CRUCIFY	773A
	TITH8MI IIA8	PUT	823D
	TOPOS IC	PLACE	830D
42	EGGUS IC	NEAR	213B
	MN8MEION 2	TOMB	526C
	PARASKEU8	PREPARATION	627C
	TITH8MI IIA∝	PUT	823C

JOHN 20

1	AIRW 3	CARRY	24A
	BLEPW IA	SEE	143A
	EIS IB	NEAR	227C
	HEIS 4	ONE	231A
	EK IA	AWAY FROM	233C
	ETI IA8	STILL	315D
	LITHOS IE	STONE	475C
	MAGDAL8N8	MAGDALENE	485B
	*MARIA 2	MARY	493A
	HO,H8,TO IIIA∝	THE	552B
	PRWI	EARLY	732B
	SABBATON 2B	WEEK	746D
	SKOTIA I	DARKNESS	764D
1=4	MN8MEION 2	TOMB	526C
2	AIRW 3	CARRY	24A
	KURIOS 2C8	LORD	460D
	OIDA IF	KNOW	558C
	PETROS	PETER	661A
	POU IB	WHERE	702D
	TITH8MI IIA∝	PUT	823C
	TRECHW I	RUN	833C
	PHILEW IA	LOVE LIKE	867C
3	ERCHOMAI IIA8	COME	310C
3F	EIS IB	NEAR	227C
4	HOMOU 2	TOGETHER	572C
	PROTRECHW	RUN AHEAD	729D
	PRWTOS IA	FIRST	732D
	TACHEWS 2A	QUICKLY	814C
	TRECHW I	RUN	833C
5	BLEPW IA	SEE	143A
	KEIMAI IB	LIE	428A
	MENTOI 2	THOUGH	504C
	PARAKUPTW I	LOOK INTO	624D

5FF	OTHONION	LINEN CLOTH 558A	15 AUTOS 3B	(OBLIQUE CASE) 123A
6	EIS 1B	NEAR 227C	BASTAZW 3A	REMOVE 137A
	EISERCHOMAI 1Aβ	COME 231D	GUN8 1	WOMAN 167C
	THEWREW 1	OBSERVE 360D	K8POUROS	GARDENER 431D
	KEIMAI 1B	LIE 428A	KLAIW 1	WEEP 434A
	*MN8MEION 2	TOMB 526C	KURIOS 1B	LORD 460A
	PETROS	PETER 661A	POU 1B	WHERE 702D
7	EIMI III5A	TO BE 224C	SU 1C	YOU 779D
	EIS 7	TO 229C	TITH8MI IIAα	PUT 823C
	HEIS 2A	ONE 230B	16 DIDASKALOS	TEACHER 190D
	ENTULISSW 2	FOLD 269D	HEBRAISTI	IN HEBREW 212C
	EPI IIAα	ON 285D	LEGW II3	CALL 471B
	KEIMAI 1B	LIE 428A	MARIA 2	MARY 493A
	KEPHAL8 1A	HEAD 431A	PROSTRECHW	RUN UP (TO) 726C
	SOUDARION	FACE CLOTH 766D	RABBOUNI	MY LORD 740B
	CHWRIS 1	APART 898D	STREPHW 2Aα	TURN 778D
8	MN8MEION 2	TOMB 526C	17 ADELPHOS 2	BROTHER 16A
	OUN 5	THEREFORE 597D	M8 AIII3B	NOT 518D
	PISTEUW 1D	BELIEVE 666D	HO,H8,TO II10B	THE 555A
	PRWTOS 1A	FIRST 732D	OUPW	NOT YET 597D
	TOTE 2	AT THAT TIME 831D	17C PAT8R 3Cα	FATHER 641C
9	ANIST8MI 2A	RISE 69C	18 AGGELLW	ANNOUNCE 7A
	GRAPH8 2Pβ	SCRIPTURE 165B	KURIOS 2Cβ	LORD 460D
	DEI 1	IT IS NECESSARY 171A	MAGDAL8N8	MAGDALENE 485B
	NEKROS 2A	DEAD 537A	*MARIA 2	MARY 493A
	OUDEPW	NOT YET 596D	HORAW 1Aα	SEE 581C
10	APERCHOMAI 2	GO 84A	19 EIR8N8 2	PEACE 226C
	HEAUTOU 11	ONESELF 211C	EIS 1Aα	INTO 227B
11	EXW 1Aα	OUTSIDE 279A	HEIS 4	ONE 231A
	HIST8MI II2Bβ	BEING 383C	ERCHOMAI IIAζ	COME 310D
	KLAIW 1	WEEP 434A	THURA 1A	DOOR 366B
	*MARIA 2	MARY 493A	HIST8MI III8	STAND 383B
	OUN 5	THEREFORE 597D	KLEIW 1	SHUT 435A
	PARAKUPTW 1	LOOK INTO 624D	MESOS 2	THE MIDDLE 508C
	PROS III	NEAR 716C	HOPOU 1Aα	WHERE 579C
	HWS IVIB	WHEN 907A	OPSIOS 2	LATE 606C
11A	MN8MEION 2	TOMB 526C	SABBATON 2B	WEEK 746D
11B	MN8MEION 2	TOMB 526C	SUNAGW 2	GATHER 790B
12	*AGGELOS 2A	ANGEL 7C	PHOBOS 2Aα	FEAR 871C
	HEIS 5A	ONE 231A	20 DEIKNUMI 1A	SHOW 171D
	EN I4B	IN 258B	KURIOS 2Cβ	LORD 460D
	THEWREW 1	OBSERVE 360C	PLEURA	SIDE 673D
	HIMATION 1	GARMENT 377A	CHAIRW 1	REJOICE 881D
	KATHEZOMAI 1	SIT 389B	21 APOSTELLW 1C	SEND AWAY 98B
	KEIMAI 1A	LIE 427D	EIR8N8 2	PEACE 226C
	KEPHAL8 1A	HEAD 431B	KAGW 3A	I ALSO 387A
	LEUKOS 2	WHITE 473D	KATHWS 1	JUST AS 392A
	HOPOU 1Aα	WHERE 579C	21B PEMPW 1	SEND 647B
	POUS 1A	FOOT 703B	22 EMPHUSAW	BREATHE ON 257B
	PROS III	NEAR 716C	PNEUMA 5A	SPIRIT 682C
	SWMA 1A	BODY 806D	PNEUMA 5Cβ	SPIRIT 682D
13	AIRW 3	CARRY 24A	22F DEW 4	BIND 177A
	GUN8 1	WOMAN 167C	23 AN	IF 49A
	KLAIW 1	WEEP 434A	APHI8MI 2	FORGIVE 125C
	KURIOS 2Cβ	LORD 460D	KRATEW 2Eε	HOLD 450A
	OIDA 1F	KNOW 558C	23B APHI8MI 2	FORGIVE 125C
	POU 1B	WHERE 702D	24 DIDUMOS	TWIN 191C
	TITH8MI IIAα	PUT 823C	THWMAS	THOMAS 367D
14	THEWREW 1	OBSERVE 360C	LEGW II3	CALL 471B
	HIST8MI II2Bγ	BEING 383C	META AIIICα	WITH 510A
	OPISW 1	BEHIND 578C	25 ALLOS 1C	OTHER 39B
	STREPHW 2Aα	TURN 779A	BALLW 2B	PUT 130D
15	AIRW 3	CARRY 24A	DAKTULOS	FINGER 169A

25	KURIOS 2Cβ	LORD	460D
	HORAW 1Aα	SEE	581C
	PISTEUW 1D	BELIEVE	666D
	PLEURA	SIDE	673D
	TOPOS 1F	PLACE	830C
25A	H8LOS	NAIL	346C
25A	TUPOS 1	MARK	837C
25B	H8LOS	NAIL	346C
25B	TUPOS 1	MARK	837C
25B	CHEIR 1	HAND	888A
26	EIMI 119A	TO BE	223D
	EIR8N8 2	PEACE	226C
	EIS 1Aα	INTO	227B
	ERCHOMAI 11Aζ	COME	310D
	ESW 2	IN	314C
	H8MERA 2	DAY	347B
	THURA 1A	DOOR	366B
	HIST8MI 111B	STAND	383B
	KLEIW 1	SHUT	435A
	MESOS 2	THE MIDDLE	508C
	META A111Cα	WITH	510A
	OKTW	EIGHT	565D
	PALIN 2	AGAIN	611C
26=8	THWMAS	THOMAS	367D
27	APISTOS 2	FAITHLESS	85A
	BALLW 2B	PUT	130D
	DAKTULOS	FINGER	169A
	EITA 1	THEN	233A
	M8 A1113B	NOT	518D
	PISTOS 2	TRUSTWORTHY	670D
	PLEURA	SIDE	673D
	HWDE 1	HERE	903B
27A	PHERW 4Aγ	BEAR	863B
27B	PHERW 4Aγ	BEAR	863B
28	THEOS 2	GOD	357C
	KURIOS 2Cβ	LORD	460D
	KURIOS 2Cγ	LORD	461B
29	EIDON 1A	SEE	219D
	EIDOS 3	SIGHT	220B
	MAKARIOS 1B	BLESSED	488A
	M8 A112A	NOT	518B
	HORAW 1Aα	SEE	581C
	HOTI 3A	THAT	593D
29A	PISTEUW 1D	BELIEVE	666D
29B	PISTEUW 1D	BELIEVE	666D
30	BIBLION 1	BOOK	140D
	GRAPHW 2B	WRITE	165D
	ENWPION 2A	BEFORE	270B
	KAI 14	AND	394A
	MEN 1Aα	(PARTICLE)	503D
	OUN 3	THEREFORE	597D
	POIEW 11Bβ	DO	687C
	POLUS 11Aα	MANY	694B
31	ZW8 2Bα	LIFE	341B
	ONOMA 14Cγ	NAME	576B
	HUIOS 2B	SON	842D
	CHRISTOS 1	ANOINTED ONE	895B
31A	PISTEUW 1Aβ	BELIEVE	666A
31B	PISTEUW 2B	BELIEVE	667C

JOHN 21

1	EPI 11Aγ	ON	285D

1	THALASSA 2	LAKE	351A
	HOUTW 2	THUS	602C
	TIBERIAS	TIBERIAS	823A
1A	PHANEROW 2A	REVEAL	860D
1B	PHANEROW 2A	REVEAL	860D
2	GALILAIA	GALILEE	149D
	DIDUMOS	TWIN	191C
	DUO 1B	TWO	208B
	EIMI 119A	TO BE	223D
	EK 4Aα	FROM	235B
	ZEBEDAIOS	ZEBEDEE	337D
	THWMAS	THOMAS	367D
	KANA	CANA	403C
	LEGW 113	CALL	471B
	*NATHANA8L	NATHANAEL	534C
	HOMOU 1	TOGETHER	572C
2F	PETROS	PETER	661A
3	HALIEUW	TO FISH	37A
	EMBAINW	GO IN	253C
	ERCHOMAI II	GO	311D
	NUX 1C	NIGHT	549A
	PIAZW 2B	GRASP	662D
	PLOION 2	SHIP	679B
	SUN 1B	WITH	789B
	HUPAGW 2	GO AWAY	844C
4	AIGIALOS	SHORE	21B
	ARISTAW 1	EAT BREAKFAST	106B
	GINOMAI 11Bγ	COME ABOUT	157C
	HIST8MI 111B	STAND	383B
	MENTOI 2	THOUGH	504C
	PRWIA	(EARLY) MORNING	732B
5	M8 C1	NOT	519A
	M8TI	(INTERROG PARTICLE)	522A
	OU 1	NO	594B
	PAIDION 3C	CHILD	609B
	PROSPHAGION	A RELISH	726D
6	APO V1	BECAUSE OF	87B
	BALLW 1B	THROW	130C
	DEXIOS 1	RIGHT	173D
	DIKTUON	NET	197D
	HELKW 1A	DRAG	251A
	ISCHUW 2B	BE STRONG	384C
	ICHTHUS	FISH	385A
	MEROS 1Bδ	SIDE	507A
	PL8THOS 2A	QUANTITY	674B
7	AGAPAW 1Bα	LOVE	4D
	BALLW 1B	THROW	130C
	GUMNOS 2		167A
		WITHOUT AN OUTER GARMENT	
	DIAZWNNUMI	TIE AROUND	182A
	EPENDUT8S	OUTER GARMENT	284C
7A	KURIOS 2Cβ	LORD	460D
7B	KURIOS 2Cβ	LORD	460D
7B	PETROS	PETER	661A
8	ALLOS 1C	OTHER	39B
	APO III	AWAY FROM	86D
	DIAKOSIOI	TWO HUNDRED	184A
	DIKTUON	NET	197D
	EIMI 119A	TO BE	223D
	ICHTHUS	FISH	385A
	MAKRAN 1Aα	FAR	488D
	P8CHUS	FOREARM	662D
	PLOIARION	BOAT	679A

8	SURW	DRAG	802A
	HWS IV5	WHEN	907C
8F	G8 4	LAND	156C
9	ANTHRAKIA	A CHARCOAL FIRE	66D
	APOBAINW I	GO AWAY	88A
	ARTOS IA	BREAD	110A
	BLEPW IA	SEE	143A
	EPIKEIMAI I	LIE UPON	294C
	KEIMAI IB	LIE	428A
	OUN 5	THEREFORE	597D
	HWS IVIA	WHEN	907A
9F	OPSARION	FISH	606B
10	APO 16	FROM	86B
	NUN IB	NOW	547D
	HOS,H8,HO I4A	(REL PRON)	587D
	PIAZW 2B	GRASP	662D
11	G8 4	LAND	156C
	EIMI II6A	TO BE	223C
	HEKATON	ONE HUNDRED	236B
	HELKW IA	DRAG	251A
	ICHTHUS	FISH	385A
	MEGAS IA	LARGE	498C
	MESTOS I	FULL	509B
	PENT8KONTA	FIFTY	648D
	PETROS	PETER	661A
	SCHIZW IB	SPLIT	805A
	TOSOUTOS IB	SO GREAT	831B
12	ARISTAW I	EAT BREAKFAST	106B
	DEUTE I	COME	175D
	EIMI II6C	TO BE	223C
	EXETAZW 2	SCRUTINIZE	275A
	KURIOS 2C8	LORD	460D
	TIS, TI IA8	WHICH	826D
	TOLMAW IA	DARE	829C
13	ARTOS IA	BREAD	110A
	DIDWMI 2	GIVE	192C
	ERCHOMAI IIA?	COME	310D
	HOMOIWS	LIKEWISE	571A
	OPSARION	FISH	606B
14	EGEIRW 2C	RISE	214A
	NEKROS 2A	DEAD	537A
	HOUTOS 2B	THIS	602A
	TRITOS 3	THIRD	834C
	PHANEROW 2B8	REVEAL	860D
15	ARISTAW I	EAT BREAKFAST	106B
	ARNION	SHEEP	107D
	BOSKW I	FEED	144D
	OUN 5	THEREFORE	597D
	PETROS	PETER	661A
	POLUS II	MANY	695C
	POLUS II2C	MANY	696A
15F	AGAPAW IA8	LOVE	4C
15F	NAI IA	YES	534D
15F	OIDA	KNOW	558A
15®17	IWAN(N)8S 4	JOHN	385D
15®17	IWNAS 2	JONAH	386A
15®17	PHILEW IA	LOVE LIKE	866D
16	DEUTEROS 4	SECOND	176B
	PALIN 2	AGAIN	611D
	POIMAINW 2A«	TEND	690B
	PROBATON 2	SHEEP	710A
16F	PROBATION	SHEEP	709D
17	BOSKW I	FEED	144D
17	GINWSKW 6C	KNOW	160D
	LUPEW 2A	GRIEVE	483A
	PAS 2A6	EVERYTHING	638B
	PROBATON 2	SHEEP	710A
17A	TRITOS 3	THIRD	834C
17B	TRITOS 3	THIRD	834C
18	APOPHERW IA8	TAKE AWAY	101B
	G8RASKW	GROW OLD	157A
	EKTEINW I	STRETCH OUT	244D
	THELW I	WISH	355C
	NEOS IB8	YOUNG	538A
	HOPOU IB«	WHERE	579D
	HOTE IA	WHEN	592C
	PERIPATEW IC	GO ABOUT	655A
	PHERW	BEAR	862D
	PHERW 4B8	BEAR	863C
18A	ZWNNUMI	GIRD	342A
18B	ZWNNUMI	GIRD	342A
19	DOXAZW 2	GLORIFY	203D
	THANATOS ID	DEATH	351D
	POIOS IAy	OF WHAT KIND	691B
	S8MAINW 2	MAKE KNOWN	755B
20	AGAPAW IB«	LOVE	4D
	AKOLOUTHEW I	FOLLOW	30C
	ANAPIPTW 2	RECLINE	59A
	BLEPW IA	SEE	143A
	DEIPNON I	DINNER	172B
	EPI IIIIAy	ON	288B
	EPISTREPHW 2A«	TURN	301B
	ST8THOS	CHEST	775B
21	EIDON IA	SEE	219D
	TIS, TI IB6	WHICH	827A
21A	HOUTOS IA8	THIS	601A
22F	ERCHOMAI I2C	COME	311D
22F	HEWS IIC	UNTIL	334D
22F	THELW I	WISH	355C
22F	MENW IC«	REMAIN	505C
22F	PROS III5C	TOWARD	717D
23	EXERCHOMAI 2B«	GO OUT	274C
	LOGOS IA8	WORD	478C
	HOUTOS 2B	THIS	602A
24	AL8TH8S 2	TRUE	36B
	EIMI II6A	TO BE	223C
	MARTUREW IA	BEAR WITNESS	493D
	MARTURIA 2B	TESTIMONY	494C
	HOUTOS IB«	THIS	601C
25	AM8N I	AMEN	45B
	BIBLION I	BOOK	140D
	HEIS 5E	ONE	231B
	KOSMOS 2	WORLD	446D
	OIOMAI	THINK	565B
	OUDE 3	NOT EVEN	596A
	POLUS IIA«	MANY	694B
	CHWREW 3A	HAVE ROOM FOR	898A
25B	GRAPHW 4	WRITE	166B

ACTS I

I	ARCHW 2A8	BEGIN	113A
	THEOPHILOS	THEOPHILUS	359B
	LOGOS IAζ	MATTER	479A
	MEN 2C	(PARTICLE)	504B
	HOS,H8,HO I4A	(REL PRON)	587D

1	PRWTOS 1B	FIRST 733A	7	TITH8MI IIIA	ESTABLISH 824B
	TE 3A	AND 815B		CHRONOS	TIME 896C
	W 2	O 903B	8	G8 5B	EARTH 156D
1A	POIEW III	DO 689C		DUNAMIS I	POWER 206C
2	ANALAMBANW I	TAKE UP 56B		DUNAMIS I	POWER 206D
	APOSTOLOS 3	APOSTLES 99B		EPERCHOMAI 2C	COME 284D
	ACHRI IA	UNTIL 128B		EPI IIIIBγ	ON 288D
	EKLEGOMAI 2A	CHOOSE 241D		ESCHATOS I	LAST 313D
	ENTELLW	COMMAND 267D		HEWS II2A	AS FAR AS 335C
	EUAGGELION IC	GOSPEL 318B		IOUDAIA I	JUDAEA 379D
	H8MERA 2	DAY 347A		MARTUS 2C	WITNESS 495C
	K8RUSSW 28β	ANNOUNCE 432C		HO,H8,TO IIIF	THE 553A
	HOS,H8,HO 15Cα	(REL PRON) 588B		HO,H8,TO IIIOA	THE 555A
	PNEUMA 5Cβ	SPIRIT 682D		PNEUMA 5Cα	SPIRIT 682D
3	BASILEIA 3B	KINGDOM 134D		SAMAREIA	SAMARIA 748D
	DIA AII1A	THROUGH 178D		TE 3A	AND 815C
	ZAW 1Aβ	LIVE 336C	9	APAIRW	TAKE AWAY 79A
	H8MERA 2	DAY 346D		BLEPW 1B	SEE 143A
	H8MERA 2	DAY 347A		EPAIRW 2A	RAISE UP 281C
	KAI II6	394C		NEPHEL8	CLOUD 538D
	LEGW II2	SPEAK 471A		OPHTHALMOS I	EYE 604C
	META BII4A	AFTER 511D		HUPOLAMBANW I	TAKE UP 853A
	OPTANOMAI	APPEAR 580A	10	ATENIZW	LOOK INTENTLY AT 119C
	PARIST8MI 1Bα	PRESENT 633B		ESTH8S	CLOTHING 312B
	PASCHW 3Aα	SUFFER 639C		KAI I2D	AND 393B
	PERI II	ABOUT 650D		LEUKOS 2	WHITE 473D
	POLUS IIAα	MANY 694A		PARIST8MI 2Bα	BE PRESENT 633C
	TEKM8RION	PROOF 815D		HWS IVIB	WHEN 907A
	TESSARAKONTA	FORTY 820D	10F	OURANOS 2B	HEAVEN 599C
4	AKOUW 1Bβ	HEAR 31C	11	ANALAMBANW I	TAKE UP 56B
	EPAGGELIA 2B	PROMISE 280B		BLEPW 3	SEE 143B
	M8 AIII8β	NOT 517D		GALILAIOS	GALILEAN 149D
	PARAGGELLW	GIVE ORDERS 618C		*EMBLEPW I	LOOK AT 254A
	PERIMENW	WAIT FOR 654B		ERCHOMAI IIAη	COME 311A
	STOMA 1A	MOUTH 777B		THEAOMAI IA	SEE 353D
	SUNALIZW	STAY WITH 791C		HIST8MI II2A	STAND 383B
	CHWRIZW 2B	DIVIDE 898C		KAI II6	394C
5	H8MERA 2	DAY 347B		OURANOS 2B	HEAVEN 599C
	IWAN(N)8S I	JOHN 385B		HOUTOS 2A	THIS 601D
	META BIII	AFTER 511B		HOUTW 2	THUS 602C
	OU 2B	NO 594C		POREUW I	PROCEED 699A
	HOUTOS 2C	THIS 602A		TIS, TI 3A	WHICH 827B
	PNEUMA 5Cβ	SPIRIT 683A		TROPOS I	MANNER 835B
	POLUS IIAα	MANY 694B	12	EGGUS IA	NEAR 213B
	HUDWR I	WATER 840D		ELAIWN	OLIVE GROVE 247C
5A	BAPTIZW 2A	BAPTIZE 131B		ECHW I7B	HAVE 334B
5B	BAPTIZW 3B	BAPTIZE 131D		KALEW IAγ	CALL 400A
6	APOKATHIST8MI I	RESTORE 91B		HODOS 1B	WAY 556C
	BASILEIA I	KINGDOM 134C		OROS	MOUNTAIN 586B
	EI VI	IF 218D		SABBATON IA	SABBATH 746C
	MEN 2E	(PARTICLE) 504C		TOTE 2	AT THAT TIME 831D
	HO,H8,TO I3	THE 552A		HUPOSTREPHW	RETURN 855B
	OUN 5	THEREFORE 597D	13	HALPHAIOS 2	ALPHAEUS 41A
	SUNERCHOMAI IA	ASSEMBLE 795D		ANABAINW IAα	GO UP 49C
	CHRONOS	TIME 896B		ANDREAS	ANDREW 63B
	CHRONOS	TIME 896C		BARTHOLOMAIOS	BARTHOLOMEW 133B
7	GINWSKW IA	KNOW 159D		EISERCHOMAI IA6	COME 232A
	EIMI IV3	TO BE 225A		Z8LWT8S 2	THE ZEALOT 338D
	EXOUSIA 2	ABILITY 277D		THWMAS	THOMAS 367D
	8 IC	NOR 343A		IOUDAS 5	JUDAS 380D
	IDIOS 2C	ONES OWN 370C		IWAN(N)8S 2	JOHN 385C
	KAIROS 4	TIME 396B		KATAMENW	STAY 415D
	OU 4A	NO 594D		MATTHAIOS	MATTHEW 497A

13 HOTE 1B	WHEN	592C
HOU 1AB	WHERE	594A
PETROS	PETER	660D
SIMWN 2	SIMON	758C
TE 3A	AND	815C
HUPERWON	UPPER STORY	850A
PHILIPPOS 3	PHILIP	868A
13A IAKWBOS 1	JAMES	368B
13B IAKWBOS 2	JAMES	368B
13C IAKWBOS 5	JAMES	368C
14*ADELPHOS 1	BROTHER	15D
DE8SIS	PRAYER	171A
KAI IIC	AND	392D
*MARIA 1	MARY	492D
HO,H8,TO IIIB	THE	552D
HOMOTHUMADON	WITH ONE MIND	569C
PAS IEB	ALL	637D
PROSEUCH8 1	PRAYER	720B
PROSEUCH8 1	PRAYER	720C
PROSKARTEREW 2A	ADHERE TO	722D
15 AUTOS 4B	THE SAME	123B
EIKOSI	TWENTY	221A
EIMI III5C	TO BE	224C
HEKATON	ONE HUNDRED	236B
EPI IIIIAζ	ON	288C
H8MERA 4B	TIME	348B
MESOS 2	THE MIDDLE	508D
ONOMA III	PEOPLE	577A
OCHLOS 3	CROWD	605D
TE 1A	AND	815A
HWSEI 2	AS	907D
16 ADELPHOS 2	BROTHER	16A
GINOMAI III	BE	159B
GRAPH8 2A	SCRIPTURE	165B
DAUID	DAVID	170B
DEI 1	IT IS NECESSARY	171A
DEI 6A	IT IS NECESSARY	171C
DIA AIIIIA	BY MEANS OF	179A
IOUDAS 6	JUDAS	380D
HO,H8,TO IIIF	THE	553A
HOD8GOS 1	LEADER	556A
PL8ROW 4A	MAKE FULL	677C
PNEUMA 5Cα	SPIRIT	682D
PNEUMA 6C	SPIRIT	683D
PROEIPON 1	FORETELL	711C
STOMA 1A	MOUTH	777C
SULLAMBANW 1Aα	SEIZE	784B
17 DIAKONIA 3	SERVICE	183B
KATARITHMEW 2	COUNT AMONG	418C
KL8ROS 2	LOT	436C
LAGCHANW 1	RECEIVE	463B
18 ADIKIA 2	UNRIGHTEOUSNESS	17D
EK 4B	FROM	235C
EKCHEW 1	POUR OUT	246D
KTAOMAI 1	GET	456A
LAKAW	BURST OPEN	464A
LASKW	CRASH	468B
MEN 2E	(PARTICLE)	504C
MESOS 1	IN TWO	508C
MISTHOS 1	WAGES	525A
OUN 5	THEREFORE	597D
PAS 1Dα	ALL	637C
PR8N8S	HEAD FIRST	707C

18 SPLAGCHNON 1A	INWARD PARTS	770B
18F CHWRION 1	PLACE	898C
19 HAIMA 2A	BLOOD	22B
AKELDAMACH	FIELD OF BLOOD	29D
GINOMAI I4B	BECOME	158D
GNWSTOS 1A	KNOWN	163C
DIALEKTOS	LANGUAGE	184D
EIMI II3	TO BE	222D
EKEINOS 2A	THAT	239B
IDIOS 2C	ONES OWN	370C
KALEW 1Aγ	CALL	400A
KATOIKEW 2	LIVE	425C
HOUTOS 1Bε	THIS	601D
PAS 1DB	ALL	637C
HWSTE 2AB	THEREFORE	908C
20 BIBLOS 1	BOOK	140D
GRAPHW 2C	WRITE	166A
EPAULIS	RESIDENCE	283C
EPISKOP8 3		299B
OFFICE AS AN OVERSEER		
ER8MOS 1A	ABANDONED	308D
HETEROS 1Bα	ANOTHER	315B
KATOIKEW 1A	LIVE	425B
LAMBANW 2	RECEIVE	466B
PSALMOS 1	PSALM	899B
21 EISERCHOMAI 1D	COME	232A
EXERCHOMAI 1Aη	GO OUT	274C
EPI IIIIAζ	ON	288C
KURIOS 2Cγ	LORD	461A
HOS,H8,HO I6	(REL PRON)	588C
OUN 1A	THEREFORE	597B
SUNERCHOMAI 2	ASSEMBLE	796A
CHRONOS	TIME	896B
21F HOUTOS 1Aε	THIS	601B
22 ANALAMBANW 1	TAKE UP	56B
ANASTASIS 2A	RESURRECTION	59D
ARCHW 2C	BEGIN	113B
ACHRI 1A	UNTIL	128B
BAPTISMA 1	BAPTISM	132A
HEWS IIIA	UNTIL	335B
H8MERA 2	DAY	347A
IWAN(N)8S 1	JOHN	385B
MARTUS 2C	WITNESS	495C
HOS,H8,HO I4B	(REL PRON)	588A
23 BARSABBAS 1	BARSABBAS	133D
EPIKALEW 1Bα	NAME	294A
IOUSTOS 1	JUSTUS	381B
HIST8MI IIAB	PUT	382C
IWS8PH 8	JOSEPH	386D
KALEW 1Aγ	CALL	400A
MATTHIAS	MATTHIAS	497B
24 ANADEIKNUMI 1	SHOW FORTH	53A
EK 1B	AWAY FROM	233C
EKLEGOMAI 1	CHOOSE	241D
KARDIOGNWST8S		405C
KNOWER OF HEARTS		
PROSEUCHOMAI	PRAY	721A
SU 1B	YOU	779D
25 APOSTOL8	APOSTLESHIP	98D
DIAKONIA 3	SERVICE	183C
IDIOS 1B	ONES OWN	370B
IOUDAS 6	JUDAS	380D
KL8ROS 2	LOT	436C

25 PARABAINW I   GO ASIDE 616D   5 PAS IAβ   EVERY EACH 636D
   POREUW I   PROCEED 699A   HUPO 2Aβ   UNDER 851B
25A   TOPOS 2B   PLACE 830D   6 AKOUW IC   HEAR 31C
25B   TOPOS IG   PLACE 830D   GINOMAI IIBβ   COME ABOUT 157B
26 APOSTOLOS 3   APOSTLES 99B   DIALEKTOS   LANGUAGE 184D
   HENDEKA   ELEVEN 262B   HEKASTOS 2   EACH 236A
   IB   TWELVE 369D   IDIOS IAβ   ONES OWN 370B
   KATAPS8PHIZOMAI   BE ENROLLED 422A   PL8THOS 2Bγ   QUANTITY 674C
   MATTHIAS   MATTHIAS 497B   SUGCHEW   CONFUSE 782D
   META AIIIB   WITH 510A   SUNERCHOMAI IA   ASSEMBLE 795D
   PIPTW 2Bβ   FALL 665D   PHWN8 I   SOUND 878C
   SUGKATAPS8PHIZOMAI BE ADDED 781B   7 HAPAS 2   ALL 81A
   SUMPS8PHIZW   COUNT UP 789A   GALILAIOS   GALILEAN 149D
26A   KL8ROS I   LOT 436C   EXIST8MI 2B   BE AMAZED 276A
26B   KL8ROS I   LOT 436C   THAUMAZW IAα   WONDER 352D
                                                      IDOU IB6   BEHOLD 371C
                ACTS 2   PAS IEβ   ALL 637D
                                                    8 GENNAW 2   BEAR 155A
I AUTOS 4B   THE SAME 123C   DIALEKTOS   LANGUAGE 184D
   EIMI III5C   TO BE 224C   HEKASTOS 2   EACH 236A
   EPI IIIIAζ   ON 288C   IDIOS IAβ   ONES OWN 370B
   H8MERA 2   DAY 347C   PWS IB   HOW 739C
   HOMOTHUMADON   WITH ONE MIND 569C   9 ASIA   ASIA 115C
   HOMOU I   TOGETHER 572C   ELAMIT8S   ELAMITE 247C
   PENT8KOST8   FIFTIETH 649A   IDOUMAIA   IDUMAEA 372A
   SUMPL8ROW 2   FILL COMPLETELY 787B   IOUDAIA 2   JUDAEA 379D
2 APHNW   SUDDENLY 126C   KAPPADOKIA   CAPPADOCIA 404A
   BIAIOS 2   VIOLENT 140C   KATOIKEW 2   LIVE 425C
   GINOMAI IIBβ   COME ABOUT 157B   MESOPOTAMIA   MESOPOTAMIA 508B
   8CHOS I   SOUND 350A   M8DOS 2   A MEDE 520B
   8CHOS 2   REPORT 350C   PARTHOI   PARTHIANS 632D
   KATH8MAI IAβ   SIT 390B   PONTOS   PONTUS 698C
   OIKOS IAα   HOUSE 563A   10 AIGUPTOS   EGYPT 21C
   HOU IAβ   WHERE 594A   EPID8MEW I   STAY 292A
   PL8ROW IA   MAKE FULL 676C   KATA IIIA   ALONG 407A
   PNO8 I   WIND 686C   KUR8N8   CYRENE 459A
   PHERW 3C   BEAR 863A   LIBU8   LIBYA 475A
   HWSPER 2   (JUST) AS 908A   MEROS IBγ   PART 507A
2=4   OURANOS 2A   HEAVEN 599B   PAMPHULIA   PAMPHYLIA 612B
2=4   TE 3B   AND 815C   RWMAIOS   ROMAN 745C
3 GLWSSA IB   TONGUE 161C   PHRUGIA   PHRYGIA 875B
   DIAMERIZW IA   DIVIDE 185D   11 AKOUW IC   HEAR 31C
   HEKASTOS 2   EACH 236A   ARAPS   ARAB 104A
   EPI IIIIAβ   ON 288A   H8METEROS   OUR 348C
   KATHIZW 2Aα   SIT DOWN 391A   IOUDAIOS 2C   JEWISH 380B
   HORAW IA6   SEE 581D   LALEW 2B   SPEAK 464C
   PUR IA   FIRE 737B   MEGALEIOS   MAGNIFICENT 497D
   HWSEI I   AS 907D   PROS8LUTOS   PROSELYTE 722A
4 ARCHW 2Aα   BEGIN 113A   12 ALLOS IC   OTHER 39C
   GLWSSA 3   TONGUE 161D   DIAPOREW   BE PERPLEXED 186D
   HETEROS 2   ANOTHER 315C   EXIST8MI 2B   BE AMAZED 276A
   KATHWS 2   AS 392B   THELW 3   WISH 356A
   PIMPL8MI IAβ   FILL 663D   LEGW I3   SAY 469D
   PNEUMA 5A   SPIRIT 682C   13 GLEUKOS   SWEET NEW WINE 161A
   PNEUMA 6E   SPIRIT 684A   DIACHLEUAZW   DERIDE 190A
4A   PNEUMA 5Cβ   SPIRIT 682D   HETEROS IBβ   ANOTHER 315B
4A   PNEUMA 5Dα   SPIRIT 683A   LEGW IIB8α   SAY 469C
4B   PNEUMA 5Dα   SPIRIT 683A   MESTOW   FILL 509D
5 APO IVIB   FROM 86D   CHLEUAZW I   MOCK 890D
   EIS 9A   IN 229D   14 AN8R 3   MAN 66A
   EULAB8S   DEVOUT 322B   APOPHTHEGGOMAI   DECLARE 101C
   *KATOIKEW IA   LIVE 425B   GNWSTOS IA   KNOWN 163B
   OURANOS IB   HEAVEN 598C   DEKA   TEN 172D

14	HENDEKA	ELEVEN 262B
	ENWTIZOMAI	GIVE EAR 270D
	EPAIRW 1	RAISE UP 281C
	HIST8MI III1B	STAND 383B
	KATOIKEW 2	LIVE 425C
	PAS 1DB	ALL 637D
	R8MA 1	WORD 742D
	SUN 4B	WITH 789D
	PHWN8 2A	VOICE 878D
15	GAR 1C	FOR 151B
	METHUW 1	BE DRUNK 500C
	HOUTOS 1Aα	THIS 600D
	TRITOS 1	THIRD 834B
	HUPOLAMBANW 4	TAKE UP 853A
	HWRA 2B	TIME OF DAY 904C
16	EIPON 4	SAY 225D
	IW8L	JOEL 386A
	PROPH8T8S 1	PROPHET 730D
17	EIMI 14	TO BE 222C
	ENUPNION	A DREAM 270A
	ENUPNAZOMAI	TO DREAM 270A
	ESCHATOS 3B	LAST 314B
	H8MERA 4B	TIME 348B
	THUGAT8R 1	DAUGHTER 365B
	NEANISKOS 1	YOUTH 536C
	HORASIS 3	APPEARANCE 581B
	HORAW 1AB	SEE 581C
	PRESBUTEROS 1A	OLDER 706B
	SARX 3	BODY 751A
17F	APO 16	FROM 86A
17F	EKCHEW 2	POUR OUT 246D
17F	EPI III1By	ON 288D
17F	PNEUMA 5A	SPIRIT 682C
17F	PROPH8TEUW 1	PROPHESY 730B
18	GE 3C	AT LEAST 152B
	DOUL8	BONDMAID 204C
	EKEINOS 2BB	THAT 239B
19	HAIMA 3	BLOOD 22D
	ANW 1	ABOVE 76B
	ATMIS	MIST 120A
	DIDWMI 1By	GIVE 192B
	EN II A	IN 257D
	KAPNOS	SMOKE 404A
	KATW 1	BELOW 426A
	OURANOS 1B	HEAVEN 598C
	PUR 1B	FIRE 737C
	S8MEION 2C	SIGN 755D
20	HAIMA 3	BLOOD 22D
	EIS 4B	TO 228B
	EPIPHAN8S	GLORIOUS 304B
	H8LIOS	THE SUN 346B
	H8MERA 3BB	DAY 347D
	KURIOS 2A	LORD 460B
	MEGAS 2BB	GREAT 499C
	METASTREPHW	CHANGE 514D
	PRIN 1B	BEFORE 708A
	SEL8N8	MOON 754B
	SKOTOS 1	DARKNESS 765A
21	EPIKALEW 2B	CALL UPON 294B
	KURIOS 2A	LORD 460B
	ONOMA 14B	NAME 575A
	PAS 1Cy	WHOEVER 637C
	SWZW 2B	SAVE 806B

22	AKOUW 1Bα	HEAR 31B
	AN8R 3	MAN 66A
	APO V6	BY 87D
	APODEIKNUMI 2	SHOW FORTH 89B
	DIA AIII2A	BY 179C
	DOKIMAZW 2B	APPROVE 201D
	DUNAMIS 4	MIRACLE 207B
	ISRA8LIT8S	ISRAELITE 382C
	LOGOS 1A6	WORD 478D
	MESOS 2	THE MIDDLE 508D
	NAZWRAIOS	NAZARENE 534B
	OIDA II	KNOW 558D
	HOS,H8,HO I4A	(REL PRON) 587D
	S8MEION 2A	SIGN 755D
22B	THEOS 3A	GOD 357D
23	ANAIREW 1A	DO AWAY WITH 54C
	ANOMOS 2B	LAWLESS 71C
	BOUL8 2B	WILL 145B
	EKDOTOS	GIVEN UP 238C
	HORIZW 1Aα	DETERMINE 584C
	HOUTOS 1Aε	THIS 601B
	PROGNWSIS	FOREKNOWLEDGE 710D
	PROSP8GNUMI	FASTEN TO 725A
	CHEIR 1	HAND 888C
24	ANIST8MI 1A	RAISE 69B
	DUNATOS 2A	POSSIBLE 208A
	THANATOS 1BB	DEATH 351D
	KATHOTI 2	BECAUSE 392A
	KRATEW 2Eα	HOLD 449D
	LUW 4	DESTROY 485A
	WDIN 2A	BIRTH PAIN 904A
25	GAR 1A	FOR 151A
	DAUID	DAVID 170B
	DEXIOS 2B	RIGHT 174A
	DIA AIIIA	THROUGH 178D
	EIS 5	FOR 229B
	EK 2	AWAY FROM 234A
	ENWPION 2B	BEFORE 270B
	HINA IIA	IN ORDER THAT 377C
	LEGW I2A	SAY 469C
	M8 AI2	NOT 517C
	PROORAW 3	SEE PREVIOUSLY 716A
	SALEUW 2	SHAKE 748A
26	AGALLIAW	BE GLAD 3D
	GLWSSA 1A	TONGUE 161C
	DE 4A	BUT, AND 170D
	ELPIS 2A	HOPE 252C
	EPI III1By	ON 287D
	EUPHRAINW 2	GLADDEN 328A
	KARDIA 1Bε	HEART 405A
	KATASK8NOW 2	LIVE 419C
	SARX 2	BODY 750D
27	HAD8S 1	HADES 16C
	DIAPHTHORA	DESTRUCTION 189D
	DIDWMI 1BB	GIVE 192B
	EGKATALEIPW 3	LEAVE 215A
	EIDON 5	SEE 220A
	HOSIOS 2B	PIOUS 589D
	OUDE 1	AND NOT 595D
	PSUCH8 1Aα	SOUL LIFE 901C
28	GNWRIZW 1	MAKE KNOWN 162C
	EUPHROSUN8	JOY 328B
	ZW8 1A	LIFE 340D

28	META AIIICⱽ	WITH 510B
	HODOS 2A	WAY 556D
	PL8ROW 1B	MAKE FULL 676D
	PROSWPON 1Cᴇ	FACE 728D
29	ADELPHOS 3	FELLOW COUNTRYMAN 16A
	ACHRI 1A	UNTIL 128B
	DAUID	DAVID 170B
	EXESTI 4	IT IS POSSIBLE 275A
	H8MERA 2	DAY 347A
	THAPTW	BURY 352C
	META AIIII	WITH 511A
	MN8MA	TOMB 526B
	PARR8SIA 1	PLAINLY 636A
	PARR8SIA 3A	COURAGE 636A
	TELEUTAW	DIE 818B
30	EK 3A	FROM 234A
	THRONOS 1A	THRONE 364D
	KATHIZW 1A	SET 390D
	KARPOS 1B	FRUIT 405D
	KOILIA 3	BELLY 438B
	OIDA 1E	KNOW 558C
	OMNUW	TAKE AN OATH 569B
	HORKOS	OATH 585B
	OSPHUS 2	LOINS 591D
	PROPH8T8S 1	PROPHET 730D
	HUPARCHW 2	BE 846A
	CHRISTOS 1	ANOINTED ONE 895B
31	HAD8S 1	HADES 16C
	HAD8S 1	HADES 16D
	ANASTASIS 2A	RESURRECTION 59D
	DIAPHTHORA	DESTRUCTION 189D
	EIDON 5	SEE 220A
	LALEW 2A∆	SPEAK 464C
	OUTE	NOT 600C
	PROORAW 2	SEE PREVIOUSLY 716A
	PROOIDA	KNOW BEFOREHAND 716A
	SARX 2	BODY 750D
	CHRISTOS 1	ANOINTED ONE 895B
	PSUCH8 1Aᵅ	SOUL LIFE 901C
32	ANIST8MI 1A	RAISE 69B
	HOS,H8,HO I7B	(REL PRON) 588C
	PAS 1Eᵅ	ALL 637D
33	BLEPW 1A	SEE 142D
	DEXIOS 2A	RIGHT 173D
	EKCHEW 2	POUR OUT 246D
	EPAGGELIA 2B	PROMISE 280B
	LAMBANW 2	RECEIVE 466C
	PARA I3B	FROM 614D
	PNEUMA 5Cᵅ	SPIRIT 682D
	TE 1B	AND 815B
	HUPSOW 1	LIFT UP 858C
34	ANABAINW 1Aᵝ	GO UP 50A
	GAR 1B	FOR 151B
	DEXIOS 2B	RIGHT 174A
	EK 2	AWAY FROM 234A
	KATH8MAI 2	SIT DOWN 390C
	KURIOS 2Cᵅ	LORD 460C
	OURANOS 2B	HEAVEN 599C
35	ECHTHROS 2Bᵝ	THE ENEMY 331D
	HEWS 11B	UNTIL 334D
	POUS 1B	FOOT 703C
	TITH8MI 12Aᵅ	MAKE 824A
	HUPOPODION	FOOTSTOOL 854D

36	ASPHALWS 2	SECURELY 118D
	ISRA8L 1	ISRAEL 382B
	KURIOS 2Cⱽ	LORD 461A
	OIKOS 3	NATION 563D
	OUN 1B	THEREFORE 597B
	PAS 1Aᴇ	ALL 637A
	POIEW 11B₁	DO 688B
	STAUROW 1	CRUCIFY 773A
	CHRISTOS 1	ANOINTED ONE 895B
37	AKOUW 1Bᵅ	HEAR 31B
	KARDIA 1Bᴇ	HEART 405A
	KATANUSSOMAI	STABBED 416C
	LOIPOS 2A	OTHER 481A
	SUNERCHOMAI 1A	ASSEMBLE 795D
	TE 1A	AND 815A
38	HAMARTIA 1	SIN 42C
	APHESIS 2	PARDON 124C
	BAPTIZW 2Bⱽ	BAPTIZE 131C
	BAPTIZW 2Bβ	BAPTIZE 131C
	BAPTIZW 2Bβ	BAPTIZE 131C
	DWREA	GIFT 209C
	EIS 4F	(PURPOSE) 228D
	HEKASTOS 2	EACH 236A
	EPI I13	ON 287D
	LAMBANW 2	RECEIVE 466B
	METANOEW	CHANGE ONES MIND 513C
	ONOMA 14Cⱽ	NAME 576A
	ONOMA 14Cᴇ	NAME 576D
	PNEUMA 5Cᵅ	SPIRIT 682D
	PH8MI 1Bβ	SAY 864A
	CHRISTOS 2	ANOINTED ONE 895C
39	AN 2B	(PARTICLE) 48B
	EPAGGELIA 2A	PROMISE 280A
	THEOS 3C	GOD 358A
	MAKRAN 1B	FAR 488D
	HOSOS 2	HOW GREAT 590C
	PAS 1Dⱽ	ALL 637D
	PROSKALEW 2A	SUMMON 722C
	TEKNON 1B	CHILD 816B
40	GENEA 2	GENERATION 153B
	DIAMARTUROMAI 2	TESTIFY 185C
	HETEROS 1Bβ	ANOTHER 315B
	LOGOS 1A∆	WORD 478D
	HOUTOS 2B	THIS 602A
	PARAKALEW 2	APPEAL TO 622C
	POLUS III1A	MANY 695C
	SKOLIOS 2	CROOKED 763D
	SWZW 2B	SAVE 806B
	TE 1A	AND 815A
41	APODECHOMAI 1	WELCOME 89C
	ASMENWS	GLADLY 116A
	BAPTIZW 2Bᵅ	BAPTIZE 131C
	LOGOS 1Aᵝ	WORD 478C
	MEN 2E	(PARTICLE) 504C
	OUN 5	THEREFORE 597D
	PROSTITH8MI 1B	ADD 726B
	TRISCHILIOI	THREE THOUSAND 834B
	PSUCH8 2	SOUL LIFE 902C
	HWSEI 2	AS 907D
42	ARTOS 1C	BREAD 110B
	DIDACH8 2	TEACHING 191B
	KLASIS 1	BREAKING 434B
	KOINWNIA 1	ASSOCIATION 440A

42	PROSEUCH8 1	PRAYER 720C	2	LEGW II3	CALL 471B	
	PROSKARTEREW 2B	ADHERE TO 722D		HO,H8,TO II4B⟨	THE 554A	
42F	APOSTOLOS 3	APOSTLES 99B		PARA I3A	FROM 614D	
43	GINOMAI I2A	COME ABOUT 157C		TITH8MI IIAβ	PUT 823D	
	GINOMAI I3By	TAKE PLACE 158A		TIS, TI 2Aα	ANY ONE 828A	
	PAS IAα	EVERY EACH 636C		HUPARCHW 2	BE 846A	
	POLUS IIAα	MANY 694A		CHWLOS	LAME 897B	
	S8MEION 2A	SIGN 755D		HWRAIOS	BEAUTIFUL 905B	
	PHOBOS 2Aα	FEAR 871C	2A	HIERON 2	TEMPLE 373A	
	PSUCH8 IBy	SOUL LIFE 901D	3	EISEIMI	GO IN 231C	
	PSUCH8 2	SOUL LIFE 902C		ELE8MOSUN8	CHARITABLE GIVING 249B	
44	HAPAS 2	ALL 81A		ERWTAW 2	ASK 312B	
	EIMI III5C	TO BE 224C		LAMBANW 2	RECEIVE 466B	
	EPI IIIIAζ	ON 288C		MELLW ICα	BE ABOUT TO 502A	
	ECHW I2A	HAVE 332B	3F	IWAN(N)8S 2	JOHN 385C	
	KOINOS IA	COMMON 439A	4	ATENIZW	LOOK INTENTLY AT 119C	
	PAS ID8	ALL 637C		BLEPW 3	SEE 143B	
	*PISTEUW 2B	BELIEVE 667C	5	SUN 4B	WITH 789D	
45	AN IA	(PARTICLE) 47D	5	ATENIZW	LOOK INTENTLY AT 119C	
	DIAMERIZW IB	DIVIDE 185D		EPECHW 2A	AIM AT 285B	
	KATHOTI 1	AS 392A		LAMBANW 2	RECEIVE 466C	
	KT8MA 1	PROPERTY 456B		PARA I3B	FROM 614D	
	PIPRASKW	SELL 664D		PROSDOKAW 4	EXPECT 719D	
	HUPARXIS 2	PROPERTY 845D	6	ARGURION 2A	SILVER 104B	
	CHREIA 2	NEED 893B		NAZWRAIOS	NAZARENE 534B	
46	AGALLIASIS	EXULTATION 3D		ONOMA I4Cy	NAME 576A	
	ARTOS IC	BREAD 110B		HOUTOS IAε	THIS 601B	
	APHELOT8S	SIMPLICITY 124C		PERIPATEW IC	GO ABOUT 655A	
	KLAW	BREAK 434D		HUPARCHW 1	BE 845D	
	METALAMBANW 1	RECEIVE 512D		CHRISTOS 2	ANOINTED ONE 895C	
	HOMOTHUMADON	WITH ONE MIND 569C		CHRUSION	GOLD 896D	
	PROSKARTEREW 3	ADHERE TO 722D	7	BASIS	FOOT 136C	
	TE 2	AND 815B		DEXIOS 1	RIGHT 173C	
	TROPH8 1	FOOD 835C		EGEIRW IAβ	RAISE 213D	
46B	KATA III D	(DISTRIBUTIVE) 407B		PARACHR8MA	AT ONCE 629B	
46F	H8MERA 2	DAY 347B		PIAZW 1	GRASP 662D	
46F	KATA II2C	EVERY 407C		STEREOW 1	MAKE FIRM 774B	
47	AINEW	TO PRAISE 23A		SPHURON 2	HEEL 804D	
	EPI IIIIAζ	ON 288C		SPHUDRON	ANKLE 804D	
	KOSMOS 5A	WORLD 447C	8	HALLOMAI 1	LEAP 39A	
	LAOS ICα	PEOPLE 467D		HIST8MI IIIE	STAND 383B	
	PROSTITH8MI	ADD 726A		SUN IB	WITH 789B	
	PROSTITH8MI IB	ADD 726B		CHAIRW 1	REJOICE 882A	
	SWZW 2B	SAVE 806C	8A	PERIPATEW IC	GO ABOUT 655A	
	CHARIS 2B	FAVOR 885C	8B	PERIPATEW IC	GO ABOUT 655A	
			8F	AINEW	TO PRAISE 23A	
	ACTS 3		9	LAOS IA	PEOPLE 467D	
				PAS ICα	ALL 637B	
1	ANABAINW IAα	GO UP 49D		PERIPATEW IC	GO ABOUT 655A	
	DEILINOS	TOWARD EVENING 172A	10	GINOMAI I3By	TAKE PLACE 158A	
	ENATOS	NINTH 261D		EKSTASIS 1	DISTRACTION 244C	
	EPI III2A	ON 289B		ELE8MOSUN8	CHARITABLE GIVING 249B	
	IWAN(N)8S 2	JOHN 385C		EPI IIIAδ	AT 286D	
	PROSEUCH8 1	PRAYER 720C		EPI IIIBy	ON 287B	
	HWRA 2B	TIME OF DAY 904D		EPIGINWSKW IB	KNOW 291A	
2	AITEW	ASK 25B		THAMBOS	ASTONISHMENT 351B	
	BASTAZW 2A	CARRY 136D		KATHEZOMAI 1	SIT 389B	
	EISPOREUOMAI 1	GO 232D		KATH8MAI IAα	SIT 390B	
	ELE8MOSUN8	CHARITABLE GIVING 249B		HOTI IBζ	THAT 593A	
	H8MERA 2	DAY 347B		PIMPL8MI IAβ	FILL 663D	
	THURA IA	DOOR 366B		PROS III3A	TOWARD 717A	
	KATA II2C	EVERY 407C		PUL8 1	GATE 736C	
	KOILIA 2	BELLY 438B		SUMBAINW	MEET 785A	

10	HWRAIOS	BEAUTIFUL	905B
11	EKTHAMBOS UTTERLY	ASTONISHED	239D
	EKPOREUOMAI IA	GO OUT	243D
	EPI IIIA«	ON	286C
	THAMBEW 2	ASTOUND	351B
	IWAN(N)8S 2	JOHN	385C
	KALEW IAY	CALL	400A
	KRATEW 2A	HOLD	449D
	LAOS IA	PEOPLE	467D
	PAS IC«	ALL	637B
	SOLOMWN	SOLOMON	766C
	STOA	PORTICO	776B
	SUNEKPOREUOMAI	GO OUT WITH	794D
	SUNTRECHW I	RUN TOGETHER	800D
12	APOKRINOMAI I	ANSWER	92D
	ATENIZW LOOK	INTENTLY AT	119C
	DUNAMIS I	POWER	206C
	EIDON IA	SEE	219D
	EUSEBEIA	GODLINESS	326B
	THAUMAZW IAB	WONDER	353A
	IDIOS IAB	ONES OWN	370B
	ISRA8LIT8S	ISRAELITE	382C
	LAOS IA	PEOPLE	467D
	HO,H8,TO II4Bη	THE	554B
	PERIPATEW IC	GO ABOUT	655A
	POIEW IIBθ	DO	688B
	HWS III2	SO	906D
13	ABRAAM	ABRAHAM	2A
	APOLUW I	SET FREE	96A
	ARNEOMAI 3A	DENY	107C
	DOXAZW 2	GLORIFY	203D
	THEOS 3C	GOD	358A
	IAKWB I	JACOB	368B
	ISAAK	ISAAC	381C
	KATA IIIB	TO	407B
	KRINW 3	DECIDE	452C
	PAIS IBY	SERVANT	610A
	PARADIDWMI IB	GIVE OVER	619D
	PARADIDWMI IB	GIVE OVER	620A
	PAT8R IB	FOREFATHERS	640D
	PILATOS	PILATE	663C
	PROSWPON IC6	FACE	728D
14	HAGIOS 2CB	THE HOLY ONE	10A
	AITEW	ASK	25C
	ARNEOMAI 3A	DENY	107C
	BARUNW	BURDEN	133D
	DIKAIOS 3	RIGHTEOUS	195A
	PHONEUS	MURDERER	872B
	CHARIZOMAI I	GIVE FREELY	884D
15	ARCH8GOS I	RULER	112A
	EGEIRW IAB	RAISE	213D
	EK IB	AWAY FROM	233C
	ZW8 2AB	LIFE	341A
	MARTUS 2C	WITNESS	495C
	NEKROS 2A	DEAD	537A
	HOS,H8,HO I7B	(REL PRON)	588C
16	APENANTI IA	OPPOSITE	83B
	EPI IIIBY	ON	287A
	THEWREW I	OBSERVE	360C
	OIDA IA	KNOW	558B
	HOLOKL8RIA	WHOLENESS	567B
	STEREOW I	MAKE FIRM	774B
16A	PISTIS 2C	FAITH	669A

16B	PISTIS 2BB	FAITH	669A
17	AGNOIA I	IGNORANCE	11C
	ADELPHOS 3 FELLOW	COUNTRYMAN	16A
	ARCHWN 2A	AUTHORITIES	113C
	KATA II5BB	ACCORDING TO	408C
	OIDA IE	KNOW	558C
	PRASSW 2A	DO	705C
	HWSPER 2	(JUST) AS	908A
18	DIA AIIIIA	BY MEANS OF	179A
	PAS ID«	ALL	637C
	PASCHW 3A«	SUFFER	639C
	PL8ROW 4A	MAKE FULL	677C
	PROKATAGGELLW	FORETELL	714B
	STOMA IA	MOUTH	777C
	CHRISTOS I	ANOINTED ONE	895B
19	HAMARTIA I	SIN	42C
	EXALEIPHW 2	REMOVE	272A
	EPISTREPHW 18B	TURN	301B
	METANOEW CHANGE	ONES MIND	513C
	OUN IB	THEREFORE	597B
	PROS III5E	TOWARD	717D
20	AN 4	(PARTICLE)	48D
	ANAPSUXIS	RELAXATION	63A
	APOSTELLW IC	SEND AWAY	98B
	ERCHOMAI IIB«	COME	311D
	KAIROS 4	TIME	396B
	HOPWS 2AB IN	ORDER THAT	580D
	PROK8RUSSW PROCLAIM	PUBLICLY	714D
	PROSWPON IC«	FACE	728C
	PROCHEIRIZW	SELECT	732A
21	HAGIOS IB« DEDICATED	TO GOD	9C
	AIWN IA	TIME	26C
	APOKATASTASIS	RESTORATION	92B
	DEI I IT	IS NECESSARY	171A
	DECHOMAI I	RECEIVE	176C
	DIA AIIIIA	BY MEANS OF	179A
	PROPH8T8S I	PROPHET	730D
	STOMA IA	MOUTH	777C
	CHRONOS	TIME	896C
22	ADELPHOS 3 FELLOW	COUNTRYMAN	16A
	AKOUW 4	LISTEN	32A
	ANIST8MI IB	RAISE	69B
	EK IB	AWAY FROM	233C
	LALEW 2B	SPEAK	464D
	HOSOS 2	HOW GREAT	590C
	HWS II3B	SO	906A
22F	PROPH8T8S 3	PROPHET	731A
23	EIMI I4	TO BE	222C
	EK IB	AWAY FROM	233C
	EKEINOS 2A	THAT	239B
	EXOLETHREUW DESTROY	UTTERLY	276C
	LAOS 3A	PEOPLE	468A
	M8 AII	NOT	517C
	HOSTIS IEB	WHOEVER	591A
	PAS IA« EVERY	EACH	636C
	PSUCH8 2	SOUL LIFE	902C
24	DE 4B	BUT, AND	170D
	KATHEX8S	IN ORDER	389C
	KATAGGELLW I	PROCLAIM	410C
	HO,H8,TO II6	THE	554B
	HOSOS 2	HOW GREAT	590B
	PROKATAGGELLW	FORETELL	714B
	PROPH8T8S I	PROPHET	730D

24	SAMOU8L	SAMUEL 749B
25	ABRAAM	ABRAHAM ID
	DIATH8K8 2	182B
	LAST WILL AND TESTAMENT	
	DIATITH8MI I	DECREE 189A
	ENEULOGEW 3	BLESS 265B
	EULOGEW 3	BLESS 322D
	HOS,H8,HO I4A	(REL PRON) 587D
	PAT8R IB	FOREFATHERS 640D
	PATRIA 2	PEOPLE 642B
	PROS IIIIE	TOWARD 716D
	HUIOS IC6	SON 842A
26	ANIST8MI IA	RAISE 69B
	APOSTREPHW 2	TURN AWAY 100A
	EN IIIIB	BY 260B
	EULOGEW 3	BLESS 322D
	PAIS IBy	SERVANT 610A
	PON8RIA	WICKEDNESS 697B
	PRWTOS 2C	FIRST 734A

ACTS 4

1	EPHIST8MI IA	STAND BY 331A
	HIEREUS IBα	PRIEST 372C
	HIERON 2	TEMPLE 373A
	LALEW 2A6	SPEAK 464C
	SADDOUKAIOS	SADDUCEE 747A
	STRAT8GOS 2	CHIEF MAGISTRATE 778B
IF	LAOS IA	PEOPLE 467D
2	ANASTASIS 2A	RESURRECTION 60A
	DIAPONEOMAI	BE DISTURBED 186D
	KATAGGELLW I	PROCLAIM 410C
	KATAPONEW	SUBDUE 417D
	KATOIKEW IA	LIVE 425B
	NEKROS 2A	DEAD 537A
3	AURION I	TOMORROW 121D
	EIMI I5	TO BE 222C
	EPAURION	NEXT DAY 283C
	EPIBALLW IB	LAY ON 289D
	HESPERA	EVENING 313C
	T8R8SIS 2	PRISON 823A
	TITH8MI IIIB	PUT 824B
4	AN8R I	MAN 65D
	ARITHMOS I	NUMBER 105D
	LOGOS IAβ	WORD 478C
	PISTEUW ID	BELIEVE 666D
	PISTEUW 2B	BELIEVE 667C
	POLUS I2Aα	MANY 694D
	CHILIAS	THOUSAND 890B
	HWS IV5	WHEN 907C
5	ARCHWN 2A	AUTHORITIES 113C
	AURION I	TOMORROW 121D
	AUTOS 3B	(OBLIQUE CASE) 123A
	GINOMAI I3E	TAKE PLACE 158B
	DE 2	BUT, AND 170C
	EPI III2A	ON 289B
	PRESBUTEROS 2Aβ	OLDER 706D
	SUNAGW 2	GATHER 790A
	SUNAGW 2	GATHER 790B
6	ALEXANDROS 2	ALEXANDER 35A
	HANNAS	ANNAS 69D
	ARCHIERATIKOS	HIGHPRIESTLY 112B
	GENOS I	DESCENDANTS 155B

6	EK 3B	FROM 234B
	IWAN(N)8S 5	JOHN 385D
	IWNATHAS	JONATHAS 386A
	KAIAPHAS	CAIAPHAS 394D
	HOSOS 2	HOW GREAT 590C
7	DUNAMIS I	POWER 206D
	MESOS 2	THE MIDDLE 508D
	ONOMA I4Cy	NAME 576A
	POIOS 2Ay	OF WHAT KIND 691B
	PUNTHANOMAI I	INQUIRE 737A
8	ARCHWN 2A	AUTHORITIES 113C
	LAOS 3A	PEOPLE 468A
	PIMPL8MI IAβ	FILL 663D
	PNEUMA 5Cβ	SPIRIT 682D
	PRESBUTEROS 2Aβ	OLDER 706D
	TOTE 2	AT THAT TIME 831D
9	ANAKRINW IB	QUESTION 56A
	ASTHEN8S IA	SICK 115B
	EI III	IF 218C
	EPI IIIBy	ON 287A
	EUERGESIA 2	KINDNESS 320A
	S8MERON	TODAY 756B
	SWZW	SAVE 805C
	SWZW IC	SAVE 806A
	TIS, TI IBα	WHICH 827A
10	GNWSTOS IA	KNOWN 163C
	EGEIRW IAβ	RAISE 213D
	EK IB	AWAY FROM 233C
	ENWPION I	BEFORE 270A
	ISRA8L 2	ISRAEL 382B
	LAOS 3A	PEOPLE 468A
	NAZWRAIOS	NAZARENE 534B
	NEKROS 2A	DEAD 537A
	ONOMA I4Cy	NAME 576A
	HOUTOS IAα	THIS 600D
	HOUTOS IAβ	THIS 601A
	HOUTOS IAε	THIS 601B
	PARIST8MI 2Bα	BE PRESENT 633D
	STAUROW I	CRUCIFY 773A
	HUGI8S IA	HEALTHY 840A
	CHRISTOS 2	ANOINTED ONE 895C
10A	PAS IEα	ALL 637D
11	GINOMAI I4A	BECOME 158D
	GWNIA	CORNER 167D
	EXOUTHENEW 2	REJECT 277B
	KEPHAL8 2B	HEAD 431C
	LITHOS 2	STONE 475D
	OIKODOMEW IBβ	BUILD 560D
	OIKODOMOS	BUILDER 562A
	HOUTOS IAy	THIS 601A
	HUPO IAα	BY 850D
12	DEI I	IT IS NECESSARY 171A
	EIMI III4	TO BE 224C
	EN IV4A	IN 260D
	HO,H8,TO III3B	THE 553C
	ONOMA I4Cy	NAME 576A
	OUDE I	AND NOT 595D
	OUDEIS 2A	NO ONE 596B
	OURANOS IB	HEAVEN 598C
	OUTE	NOT 600C
	SWZW 2B	SAVE 806B
	SWT8RIA 2	DELIVERANCE 809B
	HUPO 2Aβ	UNDER 851B

Verse	Greek	Gloss	Ref
13	AGRAMMATOS	ILLITERAT	13A
	EIMI IIIIO	TO BE	224D
	EPIGINWSKW IB	KNOW	291A
	THAUMAZW IA«	WONDER	352D
	THEWREW 2A	OBSERVE	360D
	IDIWT8S I	LAYMAN	371B
	IWAN(N)8S 2	JOHN	385C
	KATALAMBANW 2	GRASP	414B
	HOTI IB(	THAT	593A
	PARR8SIA 3A	COURAGE	636A
	SUN IC	WITH	789B
	TE IA	AND	815A
14	ANTEIPON	SAY AGAINST	72D
	BLEPW IA	SEE	143A
	ECHW I6A	CAN	333D
	HIST8MI II2B9	BEING	383C
	SUN IA	WITH	789A
15	APERCHOMAI IA	GO AWAY	83D
	EXW 2B	OUTSIDE	279B
	KELEUW	COMMAND	428C
	SUMBALLW IA«	CONVERSE	785A
	SUNEDRION 2	SANHEDRIN	794A
16	ARNEOMAI 2	DENY	107C
	GAR IB	FOR	151B
	GINOMAI I2A	COME ABOUT	157C
	GNWSTOS IA	KNOWN	163B
	KATOIKEW 2	LIVE	425C
	MEN IA9	(PARTICLE)	503D
	PAS ID9	ALL	637D
	POIEW IID«	DO	688D
	S8MEION 2A	SIGN	755D
	PHANEROS I	CLEAR	860A
17	ALLA 6	NOW	38B
	ANTHRWPOS 3A(	MAN	68C
	APEIL8	THREAT	82B
	APEILEW	THREATEN	82B
	DIANEMW	DISTRIBUTE	186A
	EIS IA9	INTO	227C
	EPI II3	ON	287D
	EPI IIIIA«	ACROSS	287D
	LAOS IC«	PEOPLE	467D
	M8 AI2	NOT	517C
	M8DEIS 2A	NO	520A
	M8KETI 4	NO LONGER	520B
	ONOMA I4C«	NAME	576C
	POLUS II2C	MANY	696A
18	GNWM8 2	JUDGMENT	162B
	EPI II3	ON	287D
	KATHOLOU	ENTIRELY	391D
	KALEW IE	CALL	400C
	M8 AIIIB9	NOT	517D
	M8DE IB	AND NOT	519D
	ONOMA I4C«	NAME	576C
	PARAGGELLW	GIVE ORDERS	618C
	SUGKATATITH8MI	AGREE WITH	781B
	PHTHEGGOMAI	SPEAK	864D
	PHWNEW 2B	CALL	878C
19	AKOUW 4	LISTEN	32A
	DIKAIOS 5	RIGHTEOUS	195B
	EIMI II9A	TO BE	223D
	ENWPION 3	BEFORE	270B
	8 2A	THAN	343B
	IWAN(N)8S 2	JOHN	385C
19	KRINW 2	JUDGE	452C
	MALLON 3C	RATHER	490D
20	GAR IE	FOR	151C
	DUNAMAI IA	ABLE	206B
	EIDON	SEE	219C
	M8 AIIIA	NOT	517D
	OU 6B	NO	595A
21	DOXAZW I	PRAISE	203C
	EPI IIIBy	ON	287B
	HEURISKW 2	FIND	325D
	KOLAZW	PUNISH	441C
	LAOS IC«	PEOPLE	467D
	M8DEIS 2B9	NOTHING	520A
	HO,H8,TO II8A	THE	554D
	PROSAPEILEW	THREATEN FURTHER	718D
	PWS 2B	HOW	740C
22	GINOMAI I2A	COME ABOUT	157C
	EIMI IV6	TO BE	225A
	EPI IIIIB(	ON	289B
	ETOS	YEAR	317A
	IASIS I	HEALING	369B
	POLUS IIIA	MANY	695D
	S8MEION 2A	SIGN	755D
23	APAGGELLW I	REPORT	78C
	APOLUW 2B	SEND AWAY	96B
	ARCHIEREUS IB	HIGH PRIEST	112C
	IDIOS 3A	ONES OWN	370D
	PRESBUTEROS 2A9	OLDER	706D
24	AIRW IB	LIFT UP	23D
	DESPOT8S	MASTER	175C
	ENERGEIA I	WORKING	264C
	THALASSA IA	SEA	350D
	HOMOTHUMADON	WITH ONE MIND	569C
	OURANOS IA«	HEAVEN	598B
	PAS IDy	ALL	637D
	POIEW IIA9	DO	687B
	PHWN8 2A	VOICE	878D
25	DAUID	DAVID	170B
	DIA AIIIIA	BY MEANS OF	179A
	HINATI	WHY	379B
	ISRA8L 2	ISRAEL	382B
	KENOS 2A9	EMPTY	429A
	LAOS 3A	PEOPLE	468B
	MELETAW 3	MEDITATE UPON	501C
	PAIS IB«	SERVANT	609D
	PAIS IBy	SERVANT	610A
	PNEUMA 5C9	SPIRIT	682D
	PNEUMA 6C	SPIRIT	683D
	PHRUASSW	BE ARROGANT	875B
26	ARCHWN I	RULER	113B
	BASILEUS I	KING	135C
	EPI IIIIA(	ON	288C
	KURIOS 2A	LORD	460B
	PARIST8MI 2A9	APPROACH	633C
	SUNAGW 2	GATHER	790B
	CHRISTOS I	ANOINTED ONE	895B
27	HAGIOS IBy	HOLY	9D
	AL8THEIA 3	REALITY	35D
	EPI IIB9	ON	286B
	EPI IIIIA«	AGAINST	288B
	H8RWD8S 2	HEROD	349B
	ISRA8L 2	ISRAEL	382B
	LAOS 3A	PEOPLE	468B

27 PAIS IBγ	SERVANT 610A
PILATOS	PILATE 663C
POLIS I	CITY 692A
PONTIOS	PONTIUS 698C
SUNAGW 2	GATHER 790B
TE 3A	AND 815B
CHRIW I	ANOINT 895D
28 BOUL8 2B	WILL 145B
PROORIZW	716A
DECIDE UPON BEFOREHAND	
CHEIR 2Aβ	HAND 888D
29 APEIL8	THREAT 82B
DIDWMI IBβ	GIVE 192B
DOULOS 4	SLAVE 205A
DOULOS 4	SLAVE 205B
EPEIDON	LOOK AT 284A
LALEW 2B	SPEAK 464C
LOGOS IBβ	WORD 479B
META AIIII	WITH 511A
NUN 3C	NOW 548B
PARR8SIA 3A	COURAGE 636B
PAS IA6	ALL 637A
30 HAGIOS IBγ	HOLY 9D
GINOMAI I2A	COME ABOUT 157C
EKTEINW I	STRETCH OUT 244D
EN IIII8	BY 260B
IASIS I	HEALING 369B
ONOMA I4Cα	NAME 575C
PAIS IBγ	SERVANT 610A
S8MEION 2A	SIGN 755D
CHEIR 2Aβ	HAND 888D
31 HAPAS 2	ALL 81A
DEOMAI 4	ASK 174B
LALEW 2B	SPEAK 464C
LOGOS IBβ	WORD 479B
META AIIII	WITH 511A
PARR8SIA 3A	COURAGE 636B
PIMPL8MI IAβ	FILL 663D
PNEUMA 5Cα	SPIRIT 682D
SALEUW I	SHAKE 747D
SUNAGW 2	GATHER 790B
TOPOS IB	PLACE 830A
32 HAPAS 2	ALL 81A
DIAKRISIS 2	QUARREL 184C
EIMI II7	TO BE 223D
HEIS 2A	ONE 230B
HEIS 2B	ONE 230C
IDIOS IAα	ONES OWN 370A
KARDIA IBη	HEART 405B
KOINOS IA	COMMON 439A
LEGW IIBβ	SAY 469C
OUDE 3	NOT EVEN 596A
PISTEUW 2B	BELIEVE 667C
PL8THOS 2B6	QUANTITY 674D
TIS, TI IBα	ANY ONE 828A
HUPARCHW I	BE 845D
CHWRISMOS	DIVISION 899C
PSUCH8 IBγ	SOUL LIFE 901D
33 ANASTASIS 2A	RESURRECTION 59D
APODIDWMI I	GIVE AWAY 90A
APOSTOLOS 3	APOSTLES 99B
DUNAMIS I	POWER 206D
EIMI III5C	TO BE 224C

33 KURIOS 2Cγ	LORD 461A
MARTURION IB	TESTIMONY 495A
MEGAS 2Aγ	GREAT 498D
PAS IEα	ALL 637D
TE IA	AND 815A
CHARIS 2B	FAVOR 885D
34 ENDE8S	POOR 261D
8 IAβ	OR 342D
KT8TWR	OWNER 456C
OIKIA IA	HOUSE 559D
HOSOS 2	HOW GREAT 590C
OUDE I	AND NOT 595D
PIPRASKW	SELL 664D
PWLEW	SELL 739A
TIM8 I	VALUE 825A
HUPARCHW I	BE 845D
PHERW 4Aα	BEAR 863A
CHWRION I	PLACE 898C
35 AN IA	(PARTICLE) 47D
APOSTOLOS 3	APOSTLES 99B
DIADIDWMI	DISTRIBUTE 181D
HEKASTOS 2	EACH 236A
KATHOTI I	AS 392A
PARA IIIIC	ALONG 616A
POUS IA	FOOT 703B
TITH8MI IIAβ	PUT 823D
CHREIA 2	NEED 893B
36 APO V6	BY 87D
*BARNABAS	BARNABAS 133C
GENOS 3	NATION 155C
EPIKALEW IBα	NAME 294A
IWS8S 3	JOSES 386B
IWS8PH 7	JOSEPH 386D
KUPRIOS	CYPRIAN 458D
LEUIT8S	A LEVITE 473B
METHERM8NEUW	TRANSLATE 499D
HOS,H8,HO I7A	(REL PRON) 588C
PARAKL8SIS 3	COMFORT 623C
HUIOS IC6	SON 842A
37 AGROS I	FIELD 13D
APOSTOLOS 3	APOSTLES 99B
PARA IIIIC	ALONG 616A
POUS IA	FOOT 703B
PWLEW	SELL 739A
TITH8MI IIAβ	PUT 823D
TITH8MI IIAβ	PUT 823D
HUPARCHW I	BE 845D
PHERW 4Aα	BEAR 863A
CHR8MA 2B	WEALTH 893D
CHWRION I	PLACE 898C

ACTS 5

I HANANIAS 2	ANANIAS 58A
KT8MA 2	PROPERTY 456B
ONOMA II	NAME 574A
PWLEW	SELL 739A
SAPPHIRA	SAPPHIRA 749D
SUN 2A	WITH 789C
2 APOSTOLOS 3	APOSTLES 99B
MEROS IA	PART 507A
PARA IIIIC	ALONG 616A
POUS IA	FOOT 703B

2	SUNOIDA I	SHARE KNOWLEDGE	799A
	TITH8MI IIAβ	PUT	823D
	TIM8 I	VALUE	825A
	PHERW 4A«	BEAR	863A
2F	NOSPHIZW	MISAPPROPRIATE	546A
3	HANANIAS 2	ANANIAS	58A
	DIA BII2	WHY	180B
	KARDIA IBγ	HEART	404D
	P8ROW	DISABLE	662C
	PL8ROW IA	MAKE FULL	676D
	PNEUMA 5C«	SPIRIT	682D
	SATAN	ADVERSARY	752B
	TIM8 I	VALUE	825A
	CHWRION I	PLACE	898C
	PSEUDOMAI 2	LIE	900A
4	EXOUSIA I	RIGHT	277C
	KARDIA IBγ	HEART	404D
	MENW IB	REMAIN	505B
	HOTI IC	THAT	593A
	PIPRASKW	SELL	664D
	PON8ROS 2C	WICKED	698A
	PRAGMA I	DEED	703D
	SOS I	YOURS	766C
	TITH8MI IIIC	PUT	824B
	TIS, TI IB«	WHICH	827B
	HUPARCHW 2	BE	846A
	PSEUDOMAI I	LIE	900A
5	HANANIAS 2	ANANIAS	58A
	GINOMAI 14θγ	COME, GO	159A
	EKPSUCHW	DIE	247A
	MEGAS 2Aγ	GREAT	499A
	PAS IDβ	ALL	637D
	PIPTW IB«	FALL	665B
	PHOBOS 2A«	FEAR	871C
6	EKPHERW I	CARRY	246B
	THAPTW	BURY	352C
	NEOS 28β	NOVICE	538A
	SUSTELLW 2	LIMIT	802D
7	DIAST8MA	INTERVAL	187D
	EISERCHOMAI IA6	COME	232A
	KAI I2C	AND	393B
	OIDA	KNOW	558A
	HWRA 2A«	TIME OF DAY	904C
	HWS IV5	WHEN	907C
8	APODIDWMI 4A	SELL	90A
	APOKRINOMAI 2	BEGIN	93A
	ARA 2	THEN	103C
	EPERWTAW IA	ASK	285A
	NAI IA	YES	534D
	CHWRION I	PLACE	898C
8A	TOSOUTOS 2B«	SO GREAT	831B
8B	TOSOUTOS 2B«	SO GREAT	831B
9	EPI IIIA6	AT	286D
	THAPTW	BURY	352C
	THURA IA	DOOR	366B
	THURA 2A	DOOR	366C
	HOTI IC	THAT	593A
	PEIRAZW 2E	TRY	646C
	PNEUMA 5A	SPIRIT	682C
	POUS IB	FOOT	703C
	SUMPHWNEW 2A	MATCH	788D
	TIS, TI IB«	WHICH	827B
9F	AN8R I	MAN	65D

9F	EKPHERW I	CARRY	246B
10	EISERCHOMAI IA6	COME	232A
	EKPSUCHW	DIE	247A
	HEURISKW ICβ	FIND	325C
	THAPTW	BURY	352C
	NEANISKOS 2	SERVANT	536C
	NEKROS IA«	DEAD	536C
	PARACHR8MA	AT ONCE	629B
	PIPTW IB«	FALL	665B
	POUS IA	FOOT	703B
	SUSTELLW 2	LIMIT	802D
11	EKKL8SIA 4B	CHURCH	240B
	MEGAS 2Aγ	GREAT	499A
	PAS IDβ	ALL	637D
	PHOBOS 2A«	FEAR	871C
12	HAPAS 2	ALL	81A
	APOSTOLOS 3	APOSTLES	99B
	DIA AIIIA	BY MEANS OF	179A
	HOMOTHUMADON	WITH ONE MIND	569C
	S8MEION 2A	SIGN	755D
	SOLOMWN	SOLOMON	766C
	STOA	PORTICO	776B
	CHEIR I	HAND	888C
13	KOLLAW 2B«	UNITE	442C
	LOIPOS 2B«	THE OTHERS	481A
	MEGALUNW 2	EXALT	498B
	OUDEIS 2A	NO ONE	596B
	TOLMAW IA	DARE	829C
14	GUN8 I	WOMAN	167C
	KURIOS 2Cγ	LORD	460D
	MALLON I	MORE	490B
	PISTEUW 2A«	BELIEVE	667A
	PL8THOS 28«	QUANTITY	674C
	PROSTITH8MI IB	ADD	726B
15	APPALLASSW 2A	RELEASE	79C
	ASTHENEIA IA	WEAKNESS	114D
	EKPHERW I	CARRY	246B
	EPI IIAβ	ON	285D
	EPISKIAZW I	CAST A SHADOW	298D
	HINA I2	IN ORDER THAT	377C
	KAN 3	AT LEAST	403B
	KLINARION	BED	437B
	KRABATTOS	MATTRESS	448C
	PLATEIA	WIDE ROAD	672C
	RUOMAI	SAVE	745A
	SKIA IA	SHADE	763A
	TITH8MI IIAβ	PUT	823D
	TIS, TI IA«	ANY ONE	827C
	HWSTE 2Aβ	THEREFORE	908C
15F	ASTHEN8S IA	SICK	115B
16	AKATHARTOS 2	IMPURE	28C
	HAPAS 2	ALL	81A
	IAOMAI I	HEAL	369A
	OCHLEW	TROUBLE	605B
	PERIX	AROUND	654C
	PL8THOS 2Bγ	QUANTITY	674D
	PNEUMA 4C	SPIRIT	682A
	POLIS I	CITY	692B
	*SUNERCHOMAI IA	ASSEMBLE	795D
	PHERW 4Bβ	BEAR	863B
17	HAIRESIS IA	SECT	23B
	Z8LOS 2	JEALOUSY	338B
	PAS IDγ	ALL	637D

17	PIMPL8MI IAβ	FILL	663D
	SADDOUKAIOS	SADDUCEE	747A
	SUN IC	WITH	789B
18	APOSTOLOS 3	APOSTLES	99B
	D8MOSIOS I	PUBLIC	178A
	EPI IIIIAβ	ON	288A
	EPIBALLW IB	LAY ON	289D
	IDIOS 3B	ONES OWN	370D
	T8R8SIS 2	PRISON	823A
	TITH8MI IIIB	PUT	824B
19	AGGELOS 2A	ANGEL	7B
	ANOIGW IA	OPEN	70B
	DIA AIIIB	DURING	178D
	EXAGW I	LEAD OUT	271A
	THURA IA	DOOR	366B
	KURIOS 2A	LORD	460B
	NUX IB	NIGHT	548D
	TE IA	AND	815A
	PHULAK8 3	GUARD	875C
20	ZW8 2Bα	LIFE	341B
	HIST8MI IIIB	STAND	383B
	R8MA I	WORD	743A
21	APOSTELLW IBγ	SEND AWAY	98B
	GEROUSIA	COUNCIL OF ELDERS	155D
	DESMWT8RION	PRISON	175B
	ISRA8L I	ISRAEL	382B
	KAI I2A	AND	393A
	ORTHROS	DAWN	584B
	PAS ICα	ALL	637B
	PRWI	EARLY	732B
	SUGKALEW I	CALL TOGETHER	780D
	SUGKALEW 2	CALL TOGETHER	780D
	SUNEDRION 2	SANHEDRIN	794A
	HUIOS IBα	SON	841C
	HUPO 2C	UNDER	851C
	PHULAK8 3	GUARD	875C
21F	PARAGINOMAI I	COME	618D
22	ANASTREPHW 3B	RETURN	61A
	APAGGELLW I	REPORT	78C
	ESW 2	IN	314B
	HEURISKW IA	FIND	325A
	HUP8RET8S	SERVANT	850C
	PHULAK8 3	GUARD	875C
23	ASPHALEIA IA	FIRMNESS	118B
	DESMWT8RION	PRISON	175B
	EN III2	BY	260C
	EPI IIAγ	ON	285D
	ESW 2	IN	314B
	HEURISKW ICα	FIND	325C
	THURA IA	DOOR	366B
	HIST8MI II2Bβ	BEING	383C
	KLEIW I	SHUT	435B
	HOTI 2	THAT	593D
	PAS IAδ	ALL	637A
	PRO I	BEFORE	708B
	PHULAX	GUARD	876A
24	AN 5	(PARTICLE)	48D
	HIERON 2	TEMPLE	373A
	STRAT8GOS 2	CHIEF MAGISTRATE	778B
	TE 3A	AND	815C
	HWS IVIA	WHEN	907A
25	HIST8MI II2A	STAND	383B
	PARAGINOMAI I	COME	618D

25	TITH8MI IIIB	PUT	824B
	TIS, TI IAα	ANY ONE	827C
	PHULAK8 3	GUARD	875D
26	AGW 2	LEAD AWAY	14B
	BIA 2	FORCE	140A
	LAOS ICα	PEOPLE	467D
	LITHAZW	STONE	475A
	STRAT8GOS 2	CHIEF MAGISTRATE	778B
	SUN IB	WITH	789B
	HUP8RET8S	SERVANT	850C
	PHOBEW IBα	BE AFRAID	871A
27	EPERWTAW IB	ASK	285A
	HIEREUS IBβ	PRIEST	372D
	HIST8MI IIAα	PUT	382D
	PERIX	AROUND	654C
	SUNEDRION 2	SANHEDRIN	794A
28	HAIMA 2A	BLOOD	22C
	BOULOMAI 2Aβ	DESIRE	145D
	DIDACH8 2	TEACHING	191B
	EPAGW	BRING ON	280D
	EPI II3	ON	287D
	EPI IIIIBγ	ON	289A
	HIEROSOLUMA	JERUSALEM	373D
	M8 AIIIBβ	NOT	517D
	ONOMA I4Cα	NAME	576C
	PARAGGELIA	ORDER	618B
	PARAGGELLW	GIVE ORDERS	618C
	PL8ROW IA	MAKE FULL	676D
29	APOSTOLOS 3	APOSTLES	99B
	DEI 2	IT IS NECESSARY	171B
	DEI 6	IT IS NECESSARY	171B
	8 2A	THAN	343B
	KAI IIC	AND	392D
	MALLON 3C	RATHER	490D
	PEITHARCHEW	OBEY	644B
30	DIACHEIRIZW	KILL	190A
	EGEIRW IAβ	RAISE	213D
	EPI IIAβ	ON	285D
	KREMANNUMI I	HANG	451A
	XULON 2C	CROSS	551C
31	HAMARTIA I	SIN	42C
	ARCH8GOS I	RULER	112A
	APHESIS 2	PARDON	124C
	DEXIOS 2A	RIGHT	173D
	METANOIA	REPENTANCE	514A
	SWT8R 2	SAVIOR	808C
	HUPSOW 2	LIFT UP	858D
32	MARTUS 2C	WITNESS	495C
	PNEUMA 5Cα	SPIRIT	682D
	R8MA 2	WORD	743A
33	ANAIREW IA	DO AWAY WITH	54C
	BOULEUW 2	DECIDE	145A
	BOULOMAI 2Aβ	DESIRE	145D
	DIAPRIW	INFURIATE	187A
34	BRACHUS 2	SHORT	146D
	GAMALI8L	GAMALIEL	150A
	EXW IB	OUTSIDE	279A
	KELEUW	COMMAND	428C
	NOMODIDASKALOS		543D
		TEACHER OF THE LAW	
	ONOMA II	NAME	574A
	POIEW IIEγ	DO	689A
	SUNEDRION 2	SANHEDRIN	794A

34 SUNEDRIOS MEMBER OF A COUNCIL 794A
    TIMIOS 2   VALUABLE 825D
    PHARISAIOS   PHARISEE 861C
35 AN8R 3   MAN 66A
    EPI III8δ   ON 287C
    ISRA8LIT8S   ISRAELITE 382C
    MELLW ICα   BE ABOUT TO 502A
    PRASSW IA   DO 705A
    PROSECHW IB PAY ATTENTION TO 721D
    SUNEDRIOS MEMBER OF A COUNCIL 794A
    TE IA   AND 815A
36 ANAIREW IA   DO AWAY WITH 54C
    ARITHMOS I   NUMBER 105D
    GINOMAI I4A   BECOME 158D
    DIALUW 2   BREAK UP 185B
    EIMI II68   TO BE 223C
    EIS 8Aα   229C
    H8MERA 4B   TIME 348B
    THEUDAS   THEUDAS 360C
    PRO 2   BEFORE 708C
    PROSKLINW   JOIN SOMEONE 723A
    PROSKOLLAW ADHERE CLOSELY TO 723B
    TETRAKOSIOI   FOUR HUNDRED 821B
    TIS, TI IAς   ANY ONE 828A
    HWS IV5   WHEN 907C
36F   HOSOS 2   HOW GREAT 590B
36F   PEITHW 3C   OBEY 645C
37 APOGRAPH8   CENSUS 88D
    APOLLUMI 2Aα   PERISH 94D
    APHIST8MI I   MISLEAD 126B
    GALILAIOS   GALILEAN 149D
    DIASKORPIZW   SCATTER 187B
    H8MERA 4B   TIME 348B
    IOUDAS 3   JUDAS 380D
    LAOS IA   PEOPLE 467C
    OPISW 2Aβ   AFTER 578D
38 APHI8MI 4   TOLERATE 125D
    APHIST8MI 2B   KEEP AWAY 126C
    BOUL8 2A   DECISION 145B
    EAW 2   LET 212A
    ERGON 4   THING 308C
    KATALUW IC   ANNUL 415C
    MIAINW 2   DEFILE 522C
    MOLUNW 2   DEFILE 528D
    NUN 3C   NOW 548B
39 APECHW 3   KEEP AWAY 84C
    EI IIA   IF 217D
    HEURISKW 2   FIND 326A
    THEOMACHOS   357A
         FIGHTING AGAINST GOD
    THEOS 3B   GOD 357D
    KAI II2   EVEN 394B
    KATALUW IC   ANNUL 415C
    M8POTE 2Bα (NEG PARTICLE) 521A
    PEITHW 3C   OBEY 645C
    TURANNOS   TYRANT 838B
40 APOLUW I   SET FREE 96A
    APOSTOLOS 3   APOSTLES 99B
    DERW   BEAT 174D
    EPI II3   ON 287D
    M8 AIII8β   NOT 517D
    ONOMA I4Cε   NAME 576C
    PARAGGELLW   GIVE ORDERS 618C

40 PROSKALEW IB   SUMMON 722C
41 ATIMAZW   DISHONOR 119C
    KATAXIOW I CONSIDER WORTHY 416C
    MEN 2E   (PARTICLE) 504C
    HO,H8,TO I3   THE 552A
    ONOMA I4D   NAME 576D
    ONOMA I4Cθ   NAME 576D
    OUN IA   THEREFORE 597B
    OUN 5   THEREFORE 597D
    PROSWPON ICα   FACE 728C
    SUNEDRION 2   SANHEDRIN 794A
    HUPER ID   IN BEHALF OF 846D
    CHAIRW I   REJOICE 881B
42 EN IIA   IN 257C
    EUAGGELIZW 2Aβ   PREACH 317D
    H8MERA IA   DAY 346D
    KATA IIID   (DISTRIBUTIVE) 407B
    PAS IAα   EVERY EACH 636C
    PAUW 2   STOP 643C
    CHRISTOS I   ANOINTED ONE 895C

                    ACTS 6

I   GINOMAI II8β   COME ABOUT 157B
    GOGGUSMOS I   COMPLAINT 163D
    DE 2   BUT, AND 170C
    DIAKONIA 4   SUPPORT 183C
    HEBRAIOS 2   HEBREW 212C
    HELL8NIST8S   HELLENIST 251C
    KATH8MERINOS   DAILY 390C
    PARATHEWREW   OVERLOOK 621C
    PL8THUNW 2   INCREASE 675A
    PROS III4A   TOWARD 717C
    CHARIS 3B   FAVOR 886B
    CH8RA   THE WIDOW 889D
IF   MATH8T8S 2Bγ   DISCIPLE 487A
2   DIAKONEW 3   CARE FOR 183B
    KATALEIPW 2C LEAVE BEHIND 414D
    LOGOS I8β   WORD 479B
    PL8THOS 28δ   QUANTITY 674D
    PROSKALEW IA   SUMMON 722C
    TRAPEZA 3   TABLE 832B
3   ADELPHOS 2   BROTHER 16A
    D8 2   NOW 177B
    EPI II8α   OVER 286A
    EPISKEPTOMAI I   LOOK AT 298C
    HEPTA   SEVEN 306B
    KATHIST8MI 2A   APPOINT 391B
    MARTUREW 2B   BE APPROVED 494B
    PL8R8S 2   FULL 675D
    PL8R8S IB   FULL 675D
    PNEUMA 6A   SPIRIT 683D
    SOPHIA 2   WISDOM 767A
    CHREIA 4   NEED 893C
4   DIAKONIA I   SERVICE 183B
    LOGOS I8β   WORD 479C
    PROSEUCH8 I   PRAYER 720C
    PROSKARTEREW 2A   ADHERE TO 722D
5   AN8R 4   MAN 66B
    ANTIOCHEUS A MAN FROM ANTIOCH 75A
    ARESKW 2B   BE PLEASING 105B
    EKLEGOMAI 2A   CHOOSE 241D
    ENWPION 4   BEFORE 270B

5 LOGOS IAγ   WORD 478C
   NIKANWR   NICANOR 541A
   NIKOLAOS   NICOLAUS 541D
   PARMENAS   PARMENAS 633D
   PISTIS 2Dα   FAITH 669A
   PL8THOS 2Bδ   QUANTITY 674D
   PL8R8S 2   FULL 675D
   PL8R8S 1B   FULL 675D
   PNEUMA 6A   SPIRIT 683D
   PROCHOROS   PROCHORUS 732A
   STEPHANOS   STEPHEN 774C
   TIMWN   TIMON 826B
   PHILIPPOS 4   PHILIP 868A
6 APOSTOLOS 3   APOSTLES 99B
   ENWPION I   BEFORE 270A
   EPITITH8MI IAα   PUT UPON 302D
   HIST8MI IIAα   PUT 382D
   PROSEUCHOMAI   PRAY 721A
7 ARITHMOS 2   NUMBER 106A
   AUXANW 3   GROW 121C
   HIEREUS IBα   PRIEST 372C
   LOGOS IBβ   WORD 479B
   MATH8T8S 2Bγ   DISCIPLE 487A
   OCHLOS 3   CROWD 605D
   PISTIS 2Dα   FAITH 669A
   PL8THUNW IB   INCREASE 675A
   POLUS II3α   MANY 694C
   SPHODRA   GREATLY 803D
   TE IA   AND 815A
   HUPAKOUW I   LISTEN TO 845B
8 DE 2   BUT, AND 170C
   DUNAMIS I   POWER 206D
   LAOS IB   PEOPLE 467D
   MEGAS 2Aγ   GREAT 499A
   PISTIS 2Dα   FAITH 669A
   PL8R8S IB   FULL 675D
   POIEW II3β   DO 687C
   S8MEION 2A   SIGN 755D
   CHARIS 4   FAVOR 886C
8F   STEPHANOS   STEPHEN 774C
9 ALEXANDREUS   ALEXANDRIAN 34D
   ALEXANDRINOS   ALEXANDRIAN 35A
   ANIST8MI 2C   RISE 69D
   APO IVIB   FROM 86D
   ASIA   ASIA 115C
   EK 3D   FROM 234C
   KILIKIA   CILICIA 433B
   KUR8NAIOS   CYRENIAN 459A
   LEGW II3   CALL 471B
   SUZ8TEW 2   DISCUSS 783B
   SUNAGWG8 3 PLACE OF ASSEMBLY 790D
10 ANTHIST8MI 2   SET AGAINST 66C
   ANTOPHTHALMEW   75D
         LOOK DIRECTLY AT
   ELEGCHW 2   EXPOSE 248D
   ISCHUW 2β   BE STRONG 384C
   PARR8SIA 3A   COURAGE 636B
   PNEUMA 6A   SPIRIT 683D
   SOPHIA 2   WISDOM 767A
11 AN8R 6   MAN 668B
   BLASPH8MOS   SLANDEROUS 142C
   BLASPH8MIA 2B   SLANDER 142C
   EIS 4Cα   AGAINST 228C

11 LALEW 2B   SPEAK 464C
   R8MA I   WORD 742D
   TOTE 2   AT THAT TIME 831D
   HUPOBALLW   INSTIGATE 851C
12 AGW 2   LEAD AWAY 14B
   EPHIST8MI IA   STAND BY 331A
   LAOS ICα   PEOPLE 467D
   PRESBUTEROS 2Aβ   OLDER 706D
   SUGKINEW   AROUSE SOMEONE 781C
   SUNARPAZW   SEIZE 792D
   SUNEDRION 2   SANHEDRIN 794A
12F   TE IA   AND 815A
13 HAGIOS IAα   DEDICATED TO GOD 9C
   BLASPH8MOS   SLANDEROUS 142C
   HIST8MI IIAβ   PUT 382D
   KATA I2Bβ   DOWN 406D
   MARTUS I   WITNESS 495B
   NOMOS 3   LAW 544C
   HOUTOS 2B   THIS 601D
   PAUW 2   STOP 643C
   R8MA I   WORD 742D
   TOPOS IB   PLACE 830B
   PSEUD8S I   FALSE 899D
14 ALLASSW I   CHANGE 38C
   ETHOS 2   CUSTOM 217D
   KATALUW IBα   DESTROY 415B
   NAZWRAIOS   NAZARENE 534B
   PARADIDWMI 3   GIVE OVER 620D
15 AGGELOS 2A   ANGEL 7C
   ATENIZW   LOOK INTENTLY AT 119C
   KATHEZOMAI I   SIT 389B
   MESOS 2   THE MIDDLE 508D
   PAS IDβ   ALL 637D
   SUNEDRION 2   SANHEDRIN 794A
   HWSEI I   AS 907D
15A   PROSWPON IA   FACE 728A
15B   PROSWPON IA   FACE 728A

                ACTS 7

1 ARA 2   THEN 103B
   EI VI   IF 218D
   ECHW II2   BE 334C
   STEPHANOS   STEPHEN 774C
2 ABRAAM   ABRAHAM 1D
   ADELPHOS 3 FELLOW COUNTRYMAN 16A
   AKOUW IC   HEAR 31D
   AN8R I   MAN 66A
   DOXA IA   BRIGHTNESS 202C
8   2Dα   BEFORE 343C
   KATOIKEW IA   LIVE 425B
   MESOPOTAMIA   MESOPOTAMIA 508B
   HORAW IAδ   SEE 582A
   PRIN IB   BEFORE 708A
   PH8MI IBα   SAY 864A
   CHARRAN   HARAN 887B
2A   PAT8R 2B   FATHER 640D
2B   PAT8R IB   FOREFATHER 640C
3 DEURO I   COME 175C
   SUGGENEIA   RELATIONSHIP 780A
3F   G8 4   LAND 156C
4 G8 4   LAND 156C
   EIS 9A   IN 229D

4	EXERCHOMAI IA∝	GO OUT 273D
	KAKEITHEN I	AND FROM THERE 397C
	META BII4A	AFTER 511D
	METOIKIZW	RESETTLE 515D
	NUN IA∝	NOW 547C
	PRO 2	BEFORE 708D
	CHALDAIOS	CHALDAEAN 882C
	CHARRAN	HARAN 887B
4A	KATOIKEW IA	LIVE 425B
4B	KATOIKEW IA	LIVE 425B
5	B8MA I	STEP 139D
	EPAGGELLOMAI IB	ANNOUNCE 280C
	KATASCHESIS I	POSSESSION 420C
	KL8RONOMIA 2	INHERITANCE 436A
	OU 3B	NO 594C
	OUDE 3	NOT EVEN 596A
	SPERMA 2B	SEED 769B
	TEKNON IA∝	CHILD 815D
6	ALLOTRIOS IA	TO ANOTHER 40A
	G8 4	LAND 156C
	DOULOW I	ENSLAVE 205B
	ETOS	YEAR 317A
	KAKOW I	HARM 399B
	*HOUTW 2	THUS 602C
	PAROIKOS I	STRANGER 634C
	SPERMA 2B	SEED 769B
	TETRAKOSIOI	FOUR HUNDRED 821B
7	DOULEUW IA	BE A SLAVE 204B
	KRINW 4B∝	JUDGE 453A
	LATREUW	SERVE 468C
8	GENNAW IA	BEGET 154C
	DIATH8K8 2	182B
	LAST WILL AND TESTAMENT	
	IAKW8 I	JACOB 368A
	OGDOOS	THE EIGHTH 555B
	HOUTW IB	THUS 602C
	PERITEMNW I	CUT AROUND 658A
	PERITOM8 I	CIRCUMCISION 658C
8A	ISAAK	ISAAC 381C
8F	PATRIARCH8S	PATRIARCH 642B
9	APODIDWMI 4A	SELL 90A
	EIS 7	TO 229C
	Z8LOW 2	338C
	BE FILLED WITH JEALOUSY	
	IWS8PH I	JOSEPH 386C
	META AIIIC8	WITH 510A
9FF	AIGUPTOS	EGYPT 21C
10	BASILEUS I	KING 135D
	EK IC	AWAY FROM 233D
	ENANTION IB	BEFORE 261B
	ENANTI 2	BEFORE 261B
	EXAIREW 2A	DELIVER 271C
	EPI IIII8∝	OVER 288D
	H8GEOMAI I	LEAD 344B
	THLIPSIS I	TRIBULATION 363A
	KATHIST8MI 2B	APPOINT 391B
	OIKOS 4	PROPERTY 563D
	SOPHIA 2	WISDOM 767A
	PHARAW	PHARAOH 861B
	CHARIS 2B	FAVOR 885D
11	EPI IIIIA∝	ACROSS 287D
	ERCHOMAI IIC∝	COME 311B
	HEURISKW IA	FIND 325A
11	THLIPSIS I	TRIBULATION 362D
	LIMOS 2	FAMINE 476B
	MEGAS 2A⊻	GREAT 499A
	CHANAAN	CANAAN 883B
	CHORTASMA	FOOD 892B
12	AKOUW 3F	LEARN 32A
	EIMI I6	TO BE 222C
	EXAPOSTELLW IB	SEND OUT 272D
	IAKW8 I	JACOB 368A
	PRWTOS 2A	FIRST 733D
	SITION	FOOD 759C
13	GENOS 2	FAMILY 155B
	GNWRIZW I	MAKE KNOWN 162D
	DEUTEROS 4	SECOND 176B
	EN II2	WHILE 259D
	PHANEROS I	CLEAR 860B
	PHARAW	PHARAOH 861B
13F	IWS8PH I	JOSEPH 386C
14	APOSTELLW ID	SEND AWAY 98C
	HEBDOM8KONTA	SEVENTY 212A
	EN IV2	IN 260D
	METAKALEW	SUMMON 512C
	PAT8R IA	FATHER 640C
	SUGGENEIA	RELATIONSHIP 780A
	PSUCH8 2	SOUL LIFE 902C
14F	IAKW8 I	JACOB 368A
15	KATABAINW IA8	COME DOWN 409B
	TELEUTAW	DIE 818B
16	ARGURION 2A	SILVER 104B
	HEMMWR	HAMOR 254D
	METAGW I	GUIDE 512A
	MN8MA	TOMB 526C
	PARA I3B	FROM 615A
	SUCHEM 2	SHECHEM 803C
	TITH8MI IIA8	PUT 823C
	TIM8 I	VALUE 825A
	WNEOMAI	BUY 904B
16A	SUCHEM I	SHECHEM 803B
16B	SUCHEM I	SHECHEM 803B
17	ABRAAM	ABRAHAM ID
	AUXANW 3	GROW 121C
	EGGIZW 5B	APPROACH 212D
	EPAGGELIA 2C	PROMISE 280B
	EPAGGELLOMAI IB	ANNOUNCE 280C
	KATHWS 4	WHEN 392B
	LAOS 3A	PEOPLE 468A
	OMNUW	TAKE AN OATH 569B
	HOMOLOGEW I	PROMISE 571A
	PL8THUNW IB	INCREASE 675A
	CHRONOS	TIME 896B
18	ANIST8MI 2C	RISE 69C
	ACHRI 2A	UNTIL 128C
	IWS8PH I	JOSEPH 386C
	OIDA IA	KNOW 558B
	HOS,H8,HO IIIF	(REL PRON) 589A
19	ARS8N	MALE 109B
	BREPHOS 2	INFANT 147A
	GENOS 3	NATION 155C
	EKTHETOS	EXPOSED 239D
	ZWOGONEW 2	PRESERVE ALIVE 342A
	KAKOW I	HARM 399B
	KATASOPHIZOMAI	419D
	GET THE BETTER OF	

19	M8 AIIIE	NOT	518A
	HO,H8,TO II48η	THE	554B
	HOUTOS IAY	THIS	601A
	POIEW II8ι	DO	688B
20	ANATREPHW I	BRING UP	628
	ASTEIOS 2	ACCEPTABLE	1178
	THEOS 3G8	GOD	358C
	KAIROS I	TIME	395D
	M8N I	MONTH	520D
	OIKOS IA«	HOUSE	563A
20FF	MWUS8S	MOSES	533D
21	ANAIREW 2	TAKE UP	540
	ANATREPHW 2	BRING UP	628
	EIS 8B	TO BE	229C
	EKTITH8MI I	EXPOSE	2458
	THUGAT8R I	DAUGHTER	3658
	HUIOS I88	SON	841C
	PHARAW	PHARAOH	8618
22	AIGUPTIOS	EGYPTIAN	218
	DUNATOS IA8	POWERFUL	208A
	ERGON IA	DEED	307D
	LOGOS IA8	WORD	478D
	PAIDEUW I	INSTRUCT	608D
	PAS IA8	EVERY EACH	636D
	SOPHIA I	WISDOM	766D
23	ADELPHOS 3 FELLOW COUNTRYMAN		16A
	EPISKEPTOMAI 2	VISIT	298C
	ISRA8L I	ISRAEL	3828
	KARDIA I88	HEART	404C
	PL8ROW 2	MAKE FULL	6778
	TESSARAKONTAET8S	FORTY YEARS	820D
	HUIOS I8«	SON	841C
	CHRONOS	TIME	896D
	HWS IVIB	WHEN	907A
24	ADIKEW 2A	DO WRONG	178
	AIGUPTIOS	EGYPTIAN	218
	AMMOS	SAND	45D
	AMUNOMAI	RETALIATE	46C
	EKDIK8SIS	VENGEANCE	2388
	KATAPONEW	SUBDUE	417D
	KRUPTW I8	HIDE	455C
	PATASSW IC	STRIKE DOWN	640B
	POIEW II86	DO	687C
25	NOMIZW 2	THINK	543B
	SWT8RIA I	DELIVERANCE	808D
	CHEIR I	HAND	888C
25A	SUNI8MI	UNDERSTAND	797D
25A	SUNI8MI	UNDERSTAND	798A
25B	SUNI8MI	UNDERSTAND	798A
25F	ADELPHOS 3		16A
	FELLOW COUNTRYMAN		
26	ADIKEW 2A	DO WRONG	178
	EIR8N8 I9	PEACE	2268
	EPEIMI	THE NEXT	284A
	HINATI	WHY	3798
	MACHOMAI I	FIGHT	497D
	HORAW IA8	SEE	5810
	SUNALLASSW	RECONCILE	7910
	SUNELAUNW	FORCE	795A
27	ADIKEW 2A	DO WRONG	178
	APWTHEW I	PUSH ASIDE	102D
	ARCHWN I	RULER	1138
	DIKAST8S	JUDGE	197C
27	KATHIST8MI 28	APPOINT	3918
	PL8SION I8	NEAR	678C
28	AIGUPTIOS	EGYPTIAN	218
	ANAIREW IA	DO AWAY WITH	54C
	ECHTHES	YESTERDAY	331C
	M8 CI	NOT	519A
	SU ID	YOU	780A
	TROPOS I	MANNER	835B
29	GENNAW IA	BEGET	154C
	G8 4	LAND	156C
	EN III3A	BECAUSE OF	260C
	LOGOS IAY	WORD	478C
	MADIAM	MIDIAN	486B
	HOU IA8	WHERE	594A
	PAROIKOS I	STRANGER	634C
	HUIOS IA«	SON	8418
	PHEUGW I	FLEE	863C
	PHUGADEUW 2	BANISH	875C
	PHUGADEUW I	BANISH	875C
30	AGGELOS 2A	ANGEL	7C
	BATOS	THORN BUSH	1378
	ER8MOS 2	DESERT	309A
	ETOS	YEAR	317A
	HORAW IA8	SEE	582A
	OROS	MOUNTAIN	586B
	PL8ROW 2	MAKE FULL	6778
	PUR I8	FIRE	7378
	SINA	SINAI	759A
	PHLOX	FLAME	870A
31	GINOMAI I4C«	COME, GO	159A
	THAUMAZW I8«	WONDER	353A
	KURIOS 2A	LORD	460B
	HORAMA I	VISION	580D
	PROSERCHOMAI I	APPROACH	720A
	PHWN8 2D	VOICE	879B
31F	KATANOEW 2	NOTICE	416A
32	ABRAAM	ABRAHAM	2A
	ENTROMOS	TREMBLING	269B
	THEOS 3C	GOD	358A
	IAKWB I	JACOB	368B
	ISAAK	ISAAC	381C
	TOLMAW IA	DARE	829C
33	HAGIOS IA« DEDICATED TO GOD		9C
	HIST8MI II2B8	BEING	383C
	KURIOS 2A	LORD	460B
	LUW 2A	LOOSE	484D
	TOPOS IC	PLACE	830B
	HUPOD8MA	SANDAL	852B
34	AIGUPTOS	EGYPT	2IC
	DEURO I	COME	175C
	EIDON IA	SEE	219D
	EXAIREW 2A	DELIVER	271C
	KAKWSIS	MISTREATMENT	399C
	KATABAINW IAY	COME DOWN	409C
	LAOS 3A	PEOPLE	468A
	STENAGMOS	SIGH	773D
35	APOSTELLW I8Y	SEND AWAY	98B
	ARNEOMAI 3	DENY	107C
	ARCHWN I	RULER	1138
	BATOS	THORN BUSH	1378
	DIKAST8S	JUDGE	197C
	KATHIST8MI 28	APPOINT	3918
	LUTRWT8S	REDEEMER	484B

35	HORAW 1A∂	SEE 582A
	HOUTOS 1A∈	THIS 601B
	CHEIR 2A∂	HAND 888D
36	AIGUPTOS	EGYPT 21C
	G8 4	LAND 156C
	EXAGW 1	LEAD OUT 271A
	ER8MOS 2	DESERT 309A
	ERUTHROS	RED 310B
	ETOS	YEAR 317A
	THALASSA 1B∝	SEA 350D
	POIEW 113β	DO 687C
	S8MEION 2A	SIGN 755D
37	ISRA8L 1	ISRAEL 382B
	PROPH8T8S 3	PROPHET 731A
	HUIOS 1B∝	SON 841C
	HWS 113B	SO 906A
38	AGGELOS 2A	ANGEL 7D
	GINOMAI 114A	BE 159C
	DECHOMAI 1	TAKE 176B
	DIDWMI 3	GIVE 192C
	EKKL8SIA 3	ASSEMBLY 240B
	ER8MOS 2	DESERT 309A
	ZAW 4B	LIVE 337C
	LOGION	A SAYING 477D
	META AIIIA	WITH 509D
	OROS	MOUNTAIN 586B
39	AIGUPTOS	EGYPT 21C
	APOSTREPHW 3B	TURN AWAY 100A
	APWTHEW 2	REJECT 102D
	THELW 2	WISH 355D
	KARDIA 1B∈	HEART 405A
	STREPHW 2Aβ	TURN 779A
	HUP8KOOS	OBEDIENT 850B
40	AARWN	AARON 1A
	AIGUPTOS	EGYPT 21C
	G8 4	LAND 156C
	GINOMAI 13Bγ	TAKE PLACE 158A
	EXAGW 1	LEAD OUT 271A
	THEOS 1	GOD 357B
	POIEW 11A∝	DO 687A
	PROPOREUOMAI	GO ON BEFORE 716C
41	ANAGW 2	BRING 52D
	EIDWLON 1	IDOL 220D
	ERGON 3	WORK 308C
	EUPHRAINW 2	GLADDEN 328A
	THUSIA 2A	SACRIFICE 366D
	MOSCHOPOIEW	MAKE A CALF 530C
42	BIBLOS 1	BOOK 140D
	ER8MOS 2	DESERT 309A
	ETOS	YEAR 317A
	THUSIA 2A	SACRIFICE 366D
	ISRA8L 1	ISRAEL 382B
	LATREUW	SERVE 468D
	M8 C1	NOT 519A
	OIKOS 3	NATION 563D
	OURANOS 1C	HEAVEN 598D
	PARADIDWMI 1B	GIVE OVER 620C
	PROSPHERW 2A	BRING (TO) 727A
	STRATIA 1	ARMY 788B
	STREPHW 1A∝	TURN 778D
	STREPHW 1B	TURN 778D
	SPHAGION	OFFERING 803C
43	ANALAMBANW 2	TAKE UP 56C

43	ASTRON	STAR 118A
	BABULWN	BABYLON 129B
	EPEKEINA	BEYOND 284C
	THEOS 1	GOD 357B
	MEROS 1Bγ	PART 507A
	METOIKIZW	RESETTLE 516A
	MOLOCH	MOLOCH 528C
	PROSKUNEW 2B	DO REVERENCE 724B
	ROMPHA	REPHAN 744B
	SK8N8	TENT 762B
	TUPOS 3	MARK 837D
44	DIATASSW	ORDER 188D
	ER8MOS 2	DESERT 309A
	MARTURION 2	TESTIMONY 495A
	POIEW 11A∝	DO 687A
	POIEW 11A∝	DO 687A
	SK8N8	TENT 762A
	TUPOS 5A	MARK 837D
45	DIADECHOMAI	IN TURN 181D
	EISAGW	BRING 231C
	EXWTHEW	PUSH OUT 279C
	H8MERA 4B	TIME 348B
	I8SOUS 1	JOSHUA 374C
	KAI 116	394C
	KATASCHESIS 1	POSSESSION 420C
	PROSWPON 1C∝	FACE 728C
46	AITEW	ASK 25C
	ENHPION 5A	BEFORE 270C
	IAKWB 1	JACOB 368A
	IAKWB 1	JACOB 368B
	OIKOS 3	NATION 563D
	SK8NWMA 1	DWELLING 762D
	CHARIS 2B	FAVOR 885D
46A	HEURISKW 3	FIND 326A
46B	HEURISKW 3	FIND 326A
47	OIKODOMEW 1A	BUILD 560C
	OIKOS 1Aβ	HOUSE 563B
	SOLOMWN	SOLOMON 766C
48	KATOIKEW 1A	LIVE 425B
	NAOS 1A	TEMPLE 535B
	PROPH8T8S 1	PROPHET 730D
	HUPSISTOS 2	HIGHEST 858B
	*CHEIROPOI8TOS	889A
	MADE BY HUMAN HANDS	
49	THRONOS 1B	THRONE 364D
	KATAPAUSIS 1	REST 416D
	KURIOS 2A	LORD 460B
	OIKODOMEW 1A	BUILD 560C
	OIKOS 1Aβ	HOUSE 563B
	OURANOS 1Aβ	HEAVEN 598B
	POIOS 1A∝	OF WHAT KIND 691B
	POUS 1B	FOOT 703C
	TOPOS 1C	PLACE 830B
	HUPOPODION	FOOTSTOOL 854D
50	PAS 1Eβ	ALL 638A
	POIEW 11Aβ	DO 687B
	CHEIR 2A∝	HAND 888C
51	AEI 3	ALWAYS 19A
	ANTIPIPTW	RESIST 75B
	APERITM8TOS 2	UNCIRCUMCISED 83C
	KAI 113	ALSO 394B
	KARDIA 1B∂	HEART 405A
	OUS 2	EAR 600B

51	PNEUMA 5Cα	SPIRIT 682D
	SKL8ROTRACH8LOS	STIFF NECKED 763C
	HWS III	SO 905D
52	DIKAIOS 3	RIGHTEOUS 195A
	DIWKW 2	PERSECUTE 200B
	ELEUSIS	COMING 250C
	NUN 1B	NOW 547D
	PRODOT8S	TRAITOR 711B
	PROKATAGGELLW	FORETELL 714B
	PROPH8T8S 1	PROPHET 730D
	PROPH8T8S 4	PROPHET 731B
	TIS, TI 1Aα	WHICH 826C
	PHONEUS	MURDERER 872B
53	AGGELOS 2A	ANGEL 7C
	AGGELOS 2A	ANGEL 7D
	DIATAG8	ORDINANCE 188B
	EIS 9B	IN 229D
	NOMOS 3	LAW 544C
	HOSTIS 2B	WHOEVER 591A
	PHULASSW 1F	WATCH 876C
54	BRUCHW	GNASH 147B
	DIAPRIW	INFURIATE 187A
	EPI III13α	TOWARD 289A
	KARDIA 13α	HEART 405A
	ODOUS	TOOTH 557B
55	ATENIZW	LOOK INTENTLY AT 119C
	DOXA 1A	BRIGHTNESS 202C
	OURANOS 2A	HEAVEN 599B
	PL8R8S 19	FULL 675D
	PNEUMA 5Cβ	SPIRIT 682D
	HUPARCHW 2	BE 846A
55F	DEXIOS 2B	RIGHT 174A
55F	EK 2	AWAY FROM 234A
55F	HIST8MI II2Bβ	BEING 383C
55F	OURANOS 2A	HEAVEN 599A
55F	OURANOS 2B	HEAVEN 599C
56	DIANOIGW 1A	OPEN 186B
	THEWREW 1	OBSERVE 360D
	HUIOS 2C	SON 843B
57	EPI III1Aα	AGAINST 288B
	KRAZW 1	CRY OUT 448D
	MEGAS 2Aγ	GREAT 498D
	HOMOTHUMADON	WITH ONE MIND 569C
	HORMAW	RUSH DOWN 585C
	OUS 1	EAR 600B
	SUNECHW 2	SHUT 796D
	PHWN8 2A	VOICE 878D
58	APOTITH8MI 1A	TAKE OFF 100C
	EKBALLW 1	DRIVE OUT 236D
	EXW 2B	OUTSIDE 279B
	HIMATION 2	GARMENT 377B
	KALEW 1Aγ	CALL 400A
	MARTUS 1	WITNESS 495B
	NEANIAS	YOUTH 536B
	PARA III1C	ALONG 616A
	SAULOS	SAUL 752D
58F	LITHOBOLEW 2	STONE 475B
59	DECHOMAI 1	TAKE 176B
	EPIKALEW 2B	CALL UPON 294B
	PNEUMA 2	SPIRIT 680D
	STEPHANOS	STEPHEN 774C
60	HAMARTIA 1	SIN 42C
	GONU	KNEE 164B

60	HIST8MI II8Bγ	PUT 383A
	KOIMAW 2A	SLEEP 438D
	KRAZW 2A	CALL 448D
	MEGAS 2Aγ	GREAT 498D
	TITH8MI IIB8α	PUT 823D
	PHWN8 2A	VOICE 878D

ACTS 8

1	ANAIRESIS	MURDER 54B
	APOSTOLOS 3	APOSTLES 99B
	DIASPEIRW	SCATTER 187C
	DIWGMOS	PERSECUTION 200A
	EKKL8SIA 4B	CHURCH 240C
	THLIPSIS 1	TRIBULATION 362D
	IOUDAIA 1	JUDAEA 379D
	KATA III1A	ALONG 407A
	MEGAS 2Aγ	GREAT 499A
	HO.H8.TO III10A	THE 555A
	PL8N 2	BUT 675C
	SAMAREIA	SAMARIA 748D
	SAULOS	SAUL 752D
	SUNEUDOKEW	AGREE WITH 796C
	CHWRA 2	COUNTRY 897D
2	AN8R 4	MAN 66B
	EPI III1Bγ	ON 287B
	EULAB8S	DEVOUT 322B
	KOPETOS	MOURNING 444A
	MEGAS 2Aγ	GREAT 498D
	POIEW II B6	DO 687C
	POIEW III	DO 689C
	STEPHANOS	STEPHEN 774C
	SUGKOMIZW 2	BURY 782A
3	AN8R 1	MAN 65D
	GUN8 1	WOMAN 167C
	EISPOREUOMAI 1	GO 232D
	EKKL8SIA 4B	CHURCH 240B
	KATA III1D	(DISTRIBUTIVE) 407B
	LUMAINW	DESTROY 482D
	OIKOS 1Aα	HOUSE 563A
	PARADIDWMI	GIVE OVER 619C
	PARADIDWMI 1B	GIVE OVER 620B
	SAULOS	SAUL 752D
	SURW	DRAG 802A
	PHULAK8 3	GUARD 875D
4	DIASPEIRW	SCATTER 187C
	DIERCHOMAI 3	GO ABOUT 193D
	EUAGGELIZW 2Aβ	PREACH 317D
	LOGOS 1Bβ	WORD 479C
	MEN 1Aα	(PARTICLE) 503D
4F	OUN 5	THEREFORE 597D
5	AUTOS 3B	(OBLIQUE CASE) 123A
	KATERCHOMAI 1	COME DOWN 423A
	K8RUSSW 2Bβ	ANNOUNCE 432C
	POLIS 1	CITY 692A
	SAMAREIA	SAMARIA 748D
	CHRISTOS 1	ANOINTED ONE 895C
5=13	PHILIPPOS 4	PHILIP 868A
6	BLEPW 1A	SEE 142D
	EN III3A	BECAUSE OF 260C
	LEGW II0	SAY 470C
	HOMOTHUMADON	WITH ONE MIND 569C
	OCHLOS 1	CROWD 605D

```
6   PROSECHW IAβ                        721C
       PAY ATTENTION TO
    S8MEION 2A 2             SIGN        755D
7   AKATHARTOS 2            IMPURE        28C
    BOAW 3                  SHOUT        143D
    EXERCHOMAI IA6          GO OUT       274A
    ECHW I2Eα              HAVE          333A
    MEGAS 2AY              GREAT         498D
    PARALUW               WEAKEN         625D
    PNEUMA 4C             SPIRIT         682A
    PHWN8 2A              VOICE          878D
    CHWLOS                LAME           897C
7A      POLUS I2Aα        MANY           694D
7B      POLUS IIAα        MANY           694A
8   EKEINOS 2A            THAT           239B
    POLIS I               CITY           692A
    POLUS IIBβ            MANY           694D
    CHARA I               JOY            883C
    CHARA I               JOY            883D
9   ETHNOS I              NATION         217B
    EXIST8MI I            CHANGE         276A
    LEGW IIBβ             SAY            469C
    MAGEUW          PRACTISE MAGIC       485D
    MEGAS 2Bα             GREAT          499B
    ONOMA II              NAME           574A
    POLIS I               CITY           692A
    PROUPARCHW       EXIST BEFORE        729D
    SAMAREIA              SAMARIA         748D
    SIMWN 9               SIMON          758D
9A      TIS, TI 2Aα      ANY ONE         828A
9B      TIS, TI 2AY      ANY ONE         828B
10  APO II3B              FROM            86C
    DUNAMIS 6             POWER           207B
    HEWS II3             AS FAR AS        335D
    KALEW IAY             CALL            400A
    LEGW I8A              SAY             470B
    MEGAS 2Aα             GREAT           498D
    MIKROS 19             SMALL           523A
10B     MEGAS 2Bα        GREAT           499B
10F     PROSECHW IAα                     721C
       PAY ATTENTION TO
11  EXIST8MI I            CHANGE          276A
    HIKANOS IB           SUFFICIENT       375A
    MAGEIA                MAGIC           485D
    SIMWN 9               SIMON           758D
    CHRONOS               TIME            896B
12  AN8R I                MAN             65D
    BASILEIA 3B           KINGDOM         134D
    EUAGGELIZW 2Aβ        PREACH          317D
    ONOMA I4Cζ            NAME            576D
    PISTEUW IB            BELIEVE         666C
    TE 3A                 AND             815B
    CHRISTOS 2        ANOINTED ONE        895C
12F     BAPTIZW 2Bα      BAPTIZE         131C
13  GINOMAI I2A           CREATED         157C
    EXIST8MI 2B           BE AMAZED       276A
    THEWREW I             OBSERVE         360D
    MEGAS 2AY             GREAT           499A
    PISTEUW 2B            BELIEVE         667C
    PROSKARTEREW I        ADHERE TO       722D
    S8MEION 2A            SIGN            755D
    SIMWN 9               SIMON           758D
14  APOSTOLOS 3           APOSTLES        99B

14  DECHOMAI 3B           ACCEPT          176C
    IWAN(N)8S 2           JOHN            385C
    LOGOS IBβ             WORD            479B
    SAMAREIA              SAMARIA         748D
15  KATABAINW IAβ         COME DOWN       409B
    HOPWS 2B          IN ORDER THAT       580D
    HOSTIS 3              WHOEVER         591B
    PNEUMA 5Cβ            SPIRIT          682D
    PROSEUCHOMAI          PRAY            721A
16  BAPTIZW 2Bβ           BAPTIZE         131C
    EPI IIIAβ             ON              286D
    EPIPIPTW 2            FALL UPON       297D
    KURIOS 2CY            LORD            461A
    MONOS 2C              ONLY            529D
    ONOMA I4Cβ            NAME            576A
    OUDEIS 2A             NO ONE          596B
    OUDEPW                NOT YET         596D
    OUPW                  NOT YET         598A
    HUPARCHW 2            BE              846A
17  EPITITH8MI IAα        PUT UPON        302D
    PNEUMA 5Cβ            SPIRIT          682D
18  APOSTOLOS 3           APOSTLES        99B
    EPITHESIS             LAYING ON       293A
    PNEUMA 5Cα            SPIRIT          682D
    PROSPHERW IB          BRING (TO)      727A
    SIMWN 9               SIMON           758D
    CHR8MA 2A             WEALTH          893D
19  EXOUSIA 2             ABILITY         277D
    EPITITH8MI IAα        PUT UPON        302D
    HINA IIICα        IN ORDER THAT       378C
    KAGW 3A               I ALSO          387A
    LEGW I8A              SAY             470B
    PNEUMA 5Cβ            SPIRIT          682D
20  APWLEIA 2             DESTRUCTION     103A
    ARGURION 2B           MONEY           104B
    DIA AIIIIA        BY MEANS OF         179A
    DWREA                 GIFT            209C
    KTAOMAI I             GET             456A
    NOMIZW 2              THINK           543B
    SUN 2B                WITH            789C
    CHR8MA 2A             WEALTH          893D
21  EIMI II9A             TO BE           223D
    ENANTI 2              BEFORE          261B
    EUTHUS 2B             STRAIGHT        321B
    KL8ROS 2              LOT             436C
    LOGOS IAε             MATTER          478D
    MERIS 2               SHARE           506C
21F     KARDIA IB6        HEART           405A
22  APO I5                FROM            86A
    ARA 2                 THEN            103C
    DEOMAI 4              ASK             174B
    EPINOIA               THOUGHT         296C
    KAKIA IA              BADNESS         397D
    METANOEW         CHANGE ONES MIND     513C
    OUN IB                THEREFORE       597B
23  ADIKIA 2          UNRIGHTEOUSNESS     17D
    EIMI III2             TO BE           224A
    HORAW ICα             SEE             582A
    PIKRIA I              BITTERNESS      663B
    SUNDESMOS 2           BOND            793B
    SUNDESMOS 3           BOND            793B
24  DEOMAI 4              ASK             174B
    DIALIMPANW            STOP            185A
```

24	EPERCHOMAI 2A	COME	284D
	KAKOS 2	EVIL	398D
	KLAIW I	WEEP	434A
	KURIOS 2A	LORD	460B
	M8OEIS 23α	NOTHING	520A
	HOPWS 2B	IN ORDER THAT	580D
	HOS,H8,HO I4Δ	(REL PRON)	587D
	POLUS I23β	MANY	695B
	PROS IIIIF	TOWARD	717A
	SIMWN 9	SIMON	758D
25	OIAMARTUROMAI 2	TESTIFY	185C
	EUAGGELIZW 2Aγ	PREACH	317D
	KWM8 2	VILLAGE	462D
	LALEW 2B	SPEAK	464C
	LOGOS I8β	WORD	479B
	MEN 2E	(PARTICLE)	504C
	OUN 2A	THEREFORE	597C
	OUN 5	THEREFORE	597D
	SAMARIT8S	SAMARITAN	749A
	HUPOSTREPHW	RETURN	855B
26	ANIST8MI 2D	RISE	69D
	GAZA	GAZA	148D
	EPI IIIIAβ	ON	288A
	ER8MOS IA	ABANDONED	308D
	HIEROSOLUMA IA	JERUSALEM	373D
	KATA III8	TO	407A
	KATA II23	TOWARD	407C
	KATABAINW IB	COME DOWN	409D
	KURIOS 2A	LORD	460B
	LALEW 2Aδ	SPEAK	464C
	LALEW 3	SPEAK	465A
	MES8MBRIA 2	THE SOUTH	507D
	MES8MBRIA I	MIDDAY	507D
	HODOS IA	WAY	556D
	POREUW I	PROCEED	699A
26=39	PHILIPPOS 4	PHILIP	868A
27	AITHIOPS	ETHIOPIAN	21D
	AN8R 7	MAN	66A
	ANIST8MI 2D	RISE	69D
	BASILISSA	QUEEN	136C
	GAZA	TREASURY	148D
	DUNAST8S 2	RULER	207D
	EPI IIB α	OVER	286A
	ERCHOMAI IIAε	COME	310D
	EUNOUCHOS I	EUNUCH	324A
	IDOU 2	THERE IS	371D
	KANDAK8	CANDACE	403D
	PROSKUNEW 2A	DO REVERENCE	724A
28	ANAGINWSKW I	READ	51B
	EPI IIAα	ON	285C
	8SAIAS	ISAIAH	349C
	KATH8MAI IAα	SIT	390B
	PROPH8T8S I	PROPHET	730D
	HUPOSTREPHW	RETURN	855B
28F	HARMA	CARRIAGE	107A
29	KOLLAW 23α	UNITE	442B
	PNEUMA 5Dα	SPIRIT	683A
	PROSERCHOMAI I	APPROACH	720A
30	AKOUW I8α	HEAR	31B
	*ANAGINWSKW I	READ	51B
	ARA	(PARTICLE)	103C
	GINWSKW 3A	UNDERSTAND	160B
	8SAIAS	ISAIAH	349C
30	PROSTRECHW	RUN UP (TO)	726D
	PROPH8T8S I	PROPHET	730D
31	AN 5	(PARTICLE)	48D
	GAR IF	WHAT	151C
	EAN I2A	IF	210D
	KATHIZW 2Aα	SIT DOWN	391A
	HOD8GEW 2	LEAD	556A
	PARAKALEW IB	INVITE	622B
	PWS ID	HOW	739D
	SUN ID	WITH	789C
	TIS, TI IAγ	ANY ONE	827D
32	AGW IA	LEAD	14A
	AMNOS	LAMB	45D
	ANAGINWSKW I	READ	51B
	ANOIGW IEα	OPEN	70D
	APHWNOS I	SILENT	127C
	GRAPH8 2Bβ	SCRIPTURE	165B
	ENANTION IA	BEFORE	261B
	EPI IIIIB η	ON	289B
	KEIRW	SHEAR	428B
	HOS,H8,HO I4E	(REL PRON)	588B
	HOUTW IA	THUS	602B
	PERIOCH8 2		654C
		PORTION OF SCRIPTURE	
	STOMA IA	MOUTH	777C
	SPHAG8	SLAUGHTER	803C
	HWS III	SO	905D
33	GENEA 4	FAMILY	153C
	G8 5B	EARTH	156D
	DI8GEOMAI	TELL	194A
	ZW8 IA	LIFE	340D
	KRISIS IAβ	JUDGING	453D
	KRISIS 3	RIGHT	454B
	TAPEINWSIS I	HUMILIATION	812D
	TIS, TI IAα	WHICH	826C
33B	AIRW 4	TAKE AWAY	24A
34	DEOMAI 3	ASK	174B
	HETEROS IBα	ANOTHER	315B
	EUNOUCHOS I	EUNUCH	324A
	8 IDγ	OR	343A
	LEGW I4	SAY	469D
	TIS, TI 2Aγ	ANY ONE	828B
35	ANOIGW IEα	OPEN	70D
	ARCHW 2C	BEGIN	113B
	GRAPH8 2A	SCRIPTURE	165B
	EUAGGELIZW 2Aα	PREACH	317D
	STOMA IA	MOUTH	777B
36	BAPTIZW 28α	BAPTIZE	131C
	EPI IIIIAY	ON	288A
	EUNOUCHOS I	EUNUCH	324A
	IDOU 2	THERE IS	371D
	KWLUW I	HINDER	462C
	HODOS IA	WAY	556B
	POREUW I	PROCEED	699B
	TIS, TI IBα	WHICH	826D
	TIS, TI 2Aα	ANY ONE	828A
	PH8MI IBα	SAY	864A
	HWS IVIB	WHEN	907A
36A	HUDWR I	WATER	840C
37	EXESTI I	IT IS POSSIBLE	274D
	KARDIA IBα	HEART	404C
37A	PISTEUW 2B	BELIEVE	667C
38	AMPHOTEROI I	BOTH	47A

38	HARMA	CARRIAGE 107A
	BAPTIZW 2Bα	BAPTIZE 131C
	HIST8MI III A	STAND 383A
	KATABAINW IA6	COME DOWN 409C
	KELEUW	COMMAND 428C
	TE 3A	AND 815C
38F	EUNOUCHOS I	EUNUCH 324A
38F	HUDWR I	WATER 840C
39	ANABAINW IAα	GO UP 49D
	HARPAZW 2B	SNATCH 108D
	EPIPIPTW 2	FALL UPON 297D
	KURIOS 2A	LORD 460B
	HODOS IB	WAY 556C
	HOTE IB	WHEN 592C
	OU 6A	NO 595A
	OUKETI I	NO LONGER 596D
	PNEUMA 5A	SPIRIT 682D
	POREUW I	PROCEED 699B
	CHAIRW I	REJOICE 881B
40	AZWTOS	AZOTUS 19C
	DIERCHOMAI ID	GO THROUGH 193D
	EIS 9A	IN 229D
	EUAGGELIZW 2AY	PREACH 317D
	HEURISKW IB	FIND 325B
	HEWS IIIA	UNTIL 335B
	HEWS II2A	AS FAR AS 335D
	KAISAREIA 2	CAESAREA 396D
	PAS IDα	ALL 637C
	POLIS I	CITY 692A

ACTS 9

1	APEIL8	THREAT 82B
	EMPNEW I	BREATHE 256A
	ETI IAβ	STILL 315D
	MATH8T8S 2BY	DISCIPLE 487A
	PROSERCHOMAI I	APPROACH 720A
	SAULOS	SAUL 752D
	PHONOS	MURDER 872C
2	AGW 2	LEAD AWAY 14B
	AITEW	ASK 25B
	AN	IF 49A
	DEW IB	BIND 176D
	EIMI IV2	TO BE 225A
	EPISTOL8	LETTER 300D
	EPISTOL8	LETTER 301A
	HEURISKW ICα	FIND 325C
	HODOS 2C	WAY 557B
	HOPWS 2Aα	IN ORDER THAT 580C
	PARA I3A	FROM 614D
	SUNAGWG8 3	PLACE OF ASSEMBLY 790D
	TE 3A	AND 815B
2FF	DAMASKOS	DAMASCUS 169C
3	GINOMAI I3E	TAKE PLACE 158B
	EGGIZW I	APPROACH 212C
	ENWTIZOMAI	GIVE EAR 270D
	EXAIPHN8S	SUDDENLY 271D
	OURANOS 2B	HEAVEN 599C
	PERIASTRAPTW I	SHINE AROUND 651C
	POREUW I	PROCEED 699B
	PHWS IA	LIGHT 879D
4	G8 2	GROUND 156C
	EPI IIIIAβ	ON 288A

4	PIPTW IBα	FALL 665B
	SAOUL 2	SAUL 749C
	PHWN8 2D	VOICE 879C
4F	DIWKW 2	PERSECUTE 200B
5	KENTRON 2	A GOAD 429C
	LAKTIZW	KICK 464A
	SKL8ROS 3B	HARD 763B
6	ALLA 2	BUT, YET 37D
	ANIST8MI 2D	RISE 69D
	DEI 5	IT IS NECESSARY 171B
	EISERCHOMAI IAβ	COME 231D
	THAMBEW I	BE ASTOUNDED 351A
	HO TI 4A	WHY 591B
	TREMW	TREMBLE 833B
7	AKOUW IBY	HEAR 31C
	ENEOS	SPEECHLESS 264C
	THEWREW I	OBSERVE 360D
	HIST8MI II2BY	BEING 383C
	M8DEIS 2A	NO 520A
	SUNODEUW I	GO WITH 798D
	PHWN8 2D	VOICE 879C
8	ANOIGW IEβ	OPEN 70D
	G8 2	GROUND 156C
	EGEIRW 2B	RISE 214A
	EIS 8AY	229C
	EISAGW	BRING 231C
	EMBLEPW I	LOOK AT 254A
	SAULOS	SAUL 752D
	CHEIRAGWGEW	LEAD BY THE HAND 889A
8F	BLEPW IA	SEE 142D
9	BLEPW 2	SEE 143A
	ESTHIW IEY	EAT 313B
10	HANANIAS 3	ANANIAS 58A
	DE 2	BUT, AND 170C
	EGW	I 216B
	IDOU 2	THERE IS 371D
10F	KURIOS 2CY	LORD 460D
10=12	ONOMA II	NAME 574A
11	ANIST8MI 2D	RISE 69D
	GAR IB	FOR 151A
	EPI IIIIAβ	ON 288B
	EUTHUS I	STRAIGHT 321B
	Z8TEW IB	SEEK 339B
	IDOU IC	REMEMBER 371D
	IOUDAS 4	JUDAS 380D
	KALEW IAY	CALL 400A
	HO,H8,TO IIIAα	THE 552B
	OIKIA IA	HOUSE 560A
	POREUW I	PROCEED 699A
	RUM8	LANE 744D
	SAULOS	SAUL 752D
	TARSEUS	FROM TARSUS 813B
12	ANABLEPW 2Aα	GAIN SIGHT 50C
	EIDON IA	SEE 219D
	EPITITH8MI IAα	PUT UPON 302D
	HOPWS 2Aα	IN ORDER THAT 580C
12F	HANANIAS 3	ANANIAS 58A
13	HAGIOS 2Dβ	SAINTS 10A
	HAGIOS 2Dβ SAINTS	O GOD 10A
	AKOUW 3D	LEARN 32A
	APO V4	FROM 87C
	KAKOS 3	EVIL 399A
	HOSOS 2	HOW GREAT 590B

13 POIEW IIDy	DO	688D
14 ARCHIEREUS IB	HIGH PRIEST	112C
DEW IB	BIND	176D
EXOUSIA 3	AUTHORITY	278A
EPIKALEW 2B	CALL UPON	294B
ONOMA I49	NAME	575A
PARA I3B	FROM	614D
PAS IDB	ALL	637D
HWDE 2A	HERE	903D
15 BASTAZW 2C	CARRY	137A
ETHNOS I	NATION	217B
EKLOG8 I	SELECTION	242C
ENWPION 2B	BEFORE	270B
ONOMA I48	NAME	575B
SKEUOS 2	THING	761D
TE 3A	AND	815C
HUIOS IBα	SON	841C
16 ONOMA I4Cθ	NAME	576D
PASCHW 3B	ENDURE	640A
HUPER ID	IN BEHALF OF	846D
HUPODEIKNUMI 2	SHOW	852A
17 HANANIAS 3	ANANIAS	58A
APOSTELLW IBy	SEND AWAY	98A
EPITITH8MI IAα	PUT UPON	302D
HO,H8,TO IIIAα	THE	552B
HODOS IA	WAY	556B
HOPWS 2Aα	IN ORDER THAT	580C
HORAW IA6	SEE	582A
PIMPL8MI IAB	FILL	663D
PNEUMA 5CB	SPIRIT	682D
SAOUL 2	SAUL	749C
17F ANABLEPW 2Aα	GAIN SIGHT	50C
18 APOPIPTW I	FALL	96D
LEPIS 2	SCALE	472D
HWSEI I	AS	907D
19 GINOMAI II4A	BE	159C
ENISCHUW I	GROW STRONG	266B
H8MERA 2	DAY	347A
LAMBANW IA	TAKE	465C
MATH8T8S 2By	DISCIPLE	487A
META AIIIA	WITH	509D
TIS, TI 2D	ANY ONE	828B
TROPH8 I	FOOD	835C
20 K8RUSSW 2BB	ANNOUNCE	432D
HOTI IB	THAT	593A
HOUTOS IAB	THIS	601A
SUNAGWG8 2A		790C
PLACE OF ASSEMBLY		
HUIOS 2B	SON	842D
CHRISTOS I	ANOINTED ONE	895C
21 AKOUW IBα	HEAR	31B
DEW IB	BIND	176D
EIS 4F	(PURPOSE)	228D
EXIST8MI 2B	BE AMAZED	276A
EPI IIIIAy	ON	288B
EPIKALEW 2B	CALL UPON	294B
ERCHOMAI IIAy	COME	310C
ERCHOMAI IIAε	COME	310D
ONOMA I4B	NAME	575A
OU 4C	NO	595A
HOUTOS IAα	THIS	600D
HOUTOS IBB	THIS	601C
PORTHEW	PILLAGE	699D
21 HWDE I	HERE	903B
22 ENDUNAMOW 2A	BECOME STRONG	263B
KATOIKEW IA	LIVE	425B
MALLON I	MORE	490B
SAULOS	SAUL	752D
SUGCHEW	CONFUSE	782D
SUMBIBAZW 3	UNITE	785C
CHRISTOS I	ANOINTED ONE	895B
23 HIKANOS IB	SUFFICIENT	375A
PL8ROW 2	MAKE FULL	677A
SUMBOULEUW 2A	ADVISE	785C
HWS IVIB	WHEN	907A
23F ANAIREW IA	DO AWAY WITH	54C
24 GINWSKW 2A	FIND OUT	160B
EPIBOUL8	A PLOT	290C
H8MERA IA	DAY	346C
NUX IB	NIGHT	548D
HOPWS 2Aα	IN ORDER THAT	580C
PARAT8REW 2A	WATCH	628A
PARAT8REW 2B	WATCH	628A
PUL8 I	GATE	736C
SAULOS	SAUL	752D
25 DIA AI2	THROUGH	178C
KATHI8MI	LET DOWN	391A
LAMBANW IA	TAKE	465B
NUX IB	NIGHT	548D
SPURIS	BASKET	771C
TEICHOS	WALL	815C
CHALAW	LET DOWN	882C
26 KOLLAW 2Bα	UNITE	442C
PARAGINOMAI I	COME	618D
PEIRAW I	TRY	646D
PISTEUW IAB	BELIEVE	666A
27 AGW IA	LEAD	14A
APOSTOLOS 3	APOSTLES	99B
BARNABAS	BARNABAS	133C
DI8GEOMAI	TELL	194A
EPILAMBANOMAI I	GRASP	295A
LALEW 2A6	SPEAK	464B
HODOS IB	WAY	556C
PARR8SIAZOMAI I	SPEAK FREELY	636B
27F ONOMA I4Cy	NAME	576A
28 EISPOREUOMAI I	GO	232D
EKPOREUOMAI IA	GO OUT	243D
PARR8SIAZOMAI I	SPEAK FREELY	636B
29 ANAIREW IA	DO AWAY WITH	54C
HELL8N 2A	GENTILE	251C
HELL8NIST8S	HELLENIST	251C
EPICHEIREW	ATTEMPT	304D
SUZ8TEW 2	DISCUSS	783B
30 ADELPHOS 2	BROTHER	16A
EXAPOSTELLW IA	SEND OUT	272D
EPIGINWSKW 2C	KNOW	291A
KAISAREIA 2	CAESAREA	396D
KATAGW	LEAD	411A
TARSOS	TARSUS	813B
31*GALILAIA	GALILEE	149D
EIR8N8 IB	PEACE	226B
EKKL8SIA 4D	CHURCH	240C
*IOUDAIA I	JUDAEA	379D
KATA IIC	DOWN	406C
KURIOS 2D	LORD	461B
MEN 2E	(PARTICLE)	504C

31	OIKODOMEW 3	BUILD 561A
	PARAKL8SIS 3	COMFORT 623C
	PL8THUNW 1B	INCREASE 675A
	PNEUMA 5Cα	SPIRIT 682D
	POREUW 2C	PROCEED 699C
	SAMAREIA	SAMARIA 748D
	PHOBOS 2Bα	FEAR 871D
32	HAGIOS 2Dβ	SAINTS 10A
	GINOMAI 13E	TAKE PLACE 158B
	DIA AII	THROUGH 178B
	DIERCHOMAI 1Bα	GO THROUGH 193C
	KATERCHOMAI 1	COME DOWN 423A
	KATOIKEW 2	LIVE 425C
	LUDDA	LYDDA 482B
33	EK 5A	FROM 235C
	ETOS	YEAR 317B
	KATAKEIMAI 1	LIE DOWN 412B
	KRABATTOS	MATTRESS 448C
	OKTW	EIGHT 565D
	ONOMA II	NAME 574A
	PARALUW	WEAKEN 625D
34	ANIST8MI 2D	RISE 69D
	IAOMAI 1	HEAL 369A
	SEAUTOU 2	YOURSELF 753A
	STRWNNUW	SPREAD 779B
	CHRISTOS 1	ANOINTED ONE 895C
	CHRISTOS 2	ANOINTED ONE 895C
35	EPI III1B6	TOWARD 289A
	EPISTREPHW 1Bβ	TURN 301B
	KATOIKEW 2	LIVE 425C
	LUDDA	LYDDA 482B
	SARWN	SHARON 752B
36	AGATHOS 1Bβ	GOOD 3B
	DIERM8NEUW 1	TRANSLATE 193C
	DORKAS	DORCAS 203D
	ELE8MOSUN8	CHARITABLE GIVING 249B
	ERGON 1Cβ	DEED 308A
	IOPP8	JOPPA 379C
	LEGW II3	CALL 471B
	MATH8TRIA	DISCIPLE 487B
	ONOMA II	NAME 574A
	PL8R8S 1B	FULL 675D
	POIEW IICβ	DO 688C
	TABITHA	TABITHA 810B
37	ASTHENEW 1A	BE SICK 115A
	GINOMAI 13E	TAKE PLACE 158B
	LOUW 1	BATHE 482A
	TITH8MI IIAβ	PUT 823C
	HUPERWON	UPPER STORY 850A
38	DIERCHOMAI 2	COME 193D
	EGGUS 1B	NEAR 213B
	EIMI II9A	TO BE 223D
	HEWS II2A	AS FAR AS 335D
	IOPP8	JOPPA 379C
	LUDDA	LYDDA 482B
	OKNEW	HESITATE 565D
	PARAKALEW 1B	INVITE 622B
39	ANAGW 1	LEAD 52D
	DORKAS	DORCAS 203D
	EPIDEIKNUMI 1	SHOW 291D
	HIMATION 2	GARMENT 377A
	KLAIW 1	WEEP 434A
	HOSOS 2	HOW GREAT 590B

39	PARAGINOMAI 1	COME 618D
	PARIST8MI 2Aα	APPROACH 633C
	POIEW IIAα	DO 687A
	SUNERCHOMAI 2	ASSEMBLE 796A
	HUPERWON	UPPER STORY 850A
	CH8RA	THE WIDOW 889D
	CHITWN	SHIRT 890C
40	ANAKATHIZW	SIT UP 55A
	ANOIGW 1Eβ	OPEN 70D
	GONU	KNEE 164B
	EKBALLW 1	DRIVE OUT 236D
	EXW 1B	OUTSIDE 279A
	EPISTREPHW 1Bα	TURN 301B
	SWMA 1A	BODY 806D
	TABITHA	TABITHA 810B
	TITH8MI II1Bα	PUT 823D
41	ANIST8MI 1A	RAISE 69B
	DIDWMI 2	GIVE 192C
	ZAW 1Aβ	LIVE 336C
	PARIST8MI 1Bα	PRESENT 633B
	PHWNEW 2B	CALL 878C
	CH8RA	THE WIDOW 889D
42	GINOMAI 14B	BECOME 158D
	GNWSTOS 1A	KNOWN 163C
	EPI III1Bc	TOWARD 289A
	KATA IIC	DOWN 406C
	KURIOS 2Cγ	LORD 460D
	PISTEUW 2A6	BELIEVE 667B
	POLUS I2Aα	MANY 694D
42F	IOPP8	JOPPA 379C
43	BURSEUS	TANNER 148A
	GINOMAI 13E	TAKE PLACE 158B
	HIKANOS 1B	SUFFICIENT 375A
	MENW 1Aα	REMAIN 504D
	PARA II1Bα	BESIDE 615B
	SIMWN 8	SIMON 758D

ACTS 10

1	AN8R 6	MAN 66B
	HEKATONTARCH8S	CENTURION 236C
	ITALIKOS	ITALIAN 384D
	KAISAREIA 2	CAESAREA 396D
	KALEW 1Aγ	CALL 400A
	KORN8LIOS	CORNELIUS 445D
	ONOMA II	NAME 574A
	SPEIRA	COHORT 768C
2	DEOMAI 4	ASK 174B
	DIA AIIIA	THROUGH 178D
	ELE8MOSUN8	CHARITABLE GIVING 249B
	OIKOS 2	HOUSEHOLD 563C
	POIEW IICβ	DO 688C
	SUN 4B	WITH 789D
	PHOBEW 2A	BE AFRAID 871B
3	EIDON 1A	SEE 219D
	EISERCHOMAI 1C	COME 232A
	ENATOS	NINTH 261D
	KORN8LIOS	CORNELIUS 445D
	HORAMA 2	VISION 581A
	PERI 2B	ABOUT 651A
	PHANERWS	OPENLY 860D
	HWRA 2B	TIME OF DAY 904D
	HWSEI 2	AS 907D

```
4   ANABAINW 1B              GO UP          50A
    ATENIZW      LOOK INTENTLY AT          119C
    EIS 4E                  SO THAT        228D
    ELE8MOSUN8   CHARITABLE GIVING         249B
    EMPROSTHEN 2C           IN FRONT       256D
    EMPHOBOS                AFRAID         257B
    KURIOS 2Eα              LORD           461B
    MN8MOSUNON 3                           527B
         MEMORIAL OFFERING
    PROSEUCH8 1             PRAYER         720B
5   EPIKALEW 1Bα            NAME           294A
    IOPP8                   JOPPA          379C
    METAPEMPW               SUMMON         514D
    NUN 2                   NOW            548A
    PEMPW 1                 SEND           647C
    PETROS                  PETER          661A
5F     TIS, TI 2Aβ          ANY ONE        828B
6   BURSEUS                 TANNER         148A
    EIMI III8C              TO BE          224D
    EIMI III8B              TO BE          224D
    THALASSA 1Bβ            SEA            350D
    XENIZW 1    RECEIVE AS A GUEST         550A
    OIKIA 1A                HOUSE          559D
    PARA III·Bα             BESIDE         615B
    PARA III1Bα             ALONG          616A
    SIMWN 8                 SIMON          758D
7   APERCHOMAI 1A           GO AWAY        83D
    EUSEB8S                 DEVOUT         326C
    OIKET8S             HOUSE SLAVE        559D
    PROSKARTEREW 1         ADHERE TO       722D
    STRATIWT8S 1            SOLDIER        778B
    PHWNEW 2B               CALL           878C
    HWS IV1A                WHEN           907A
8   EX8GEOMAI 1A            EXPLAIN        275B
    IOPP8                   JOPPA          379C
9   ANABAINW 1Aα            GO UP          49D
    DWMA                    ROOF           209C
    EGGIZW 1                APPROACH       212C
    HEKTOS                  SIXTH          245C
    EPAURION               NEXT DAY        283C
    HODOIPOREW              TRAVEL         556A
    PERI 2B                 ABOUT          651A
    HWRA 2B             TIME OF DAY        904D
10  GEUOMAI 1               TASTE          156A
    EPI III1Bγ              ON             288D
    EPIPIPTW 2             FALL UPON       297D
    PARASKEUAZW 1           PREPARE        627C
    PROSPEINOS              HUNGRY         725A
11  ANOIGW 1B               OPEN           70C
    ARCH8 1A                CORNERS        111B
    DEW 2                   BIND           177A
    EPI IIAβ                ON             285D
    THEWREW 1               OBSERVE        360D
    KATHI8MI                LET DOWN       391A
    KATABAINW 1B           COME DOWN       409C
    OTHON8              LINEN CLOTH        558A
    SKEUOS 1A               THING          761C
    TESSARES                FOUR           821A
    TIS, TI 2Aα             ANY ONE        828B
    HWS II3B                SO             906A
12  G8  5B                  EARTH          156D
    HERPETON                REPTILE        310A
    OURANOS 1D              HEAVEN         598D

12  PAS 1Dα                 ALL            637C
   *PETEINON                BIRD           660A
    TETRAPOUS            QUADRUPEDS        821C
    HUPARCHW 1              BE             845D
13  GINOMAI 14Cε           COME, GO        159A
    THUW 2               SACRIFICE         367D
    PHWN8 2D                VOICE          879B
14  AKATHARTOS 1            IMPURE         28C
    ESTHIW 1A               EAT            312D
    KOINOS 2                COMMON         439B
    M8DAMWS            BY NO MEANS         519C
    OUDEPOTE                NEVER          596D
    PAS 1Aα            EVERY EACH          636D
15  DEUTEROS 4              SECOND         176B
    KATHARIZW 2A            CLEANSE        388A
    KOINOW 2        DECLARE UNCLEAN        439C
    M8 AIII3B               NOT            518D
    PALIN 2                 AGAIN          611D
    PHWN8 2D                VOICE          879B
16  ANALAMBANW 1            TAKE UP        56C
    EPI III3                ON             289C
    EUTHUS              IMMEDIATELY        321C
    SKEUOS 1A               THING          761C
    TRIS                    THRICE         834B
17  AN  5                  (PARTICLE)      49A
    DIAPOREW          BE PERPLEXED         186D
    DIERWTAW       FIND BY INQUIRY         193D
    HEAUTOU 1C              ONESELF        211B
    EIDON 1A                SEE            219D
    EN 15B                  IN             258D
    EPHIST8MI 1A           STAND BY        331A
    KORN8LIOS             CORNELIUS        445D
    HORAMA 1                VISION         580D
    PULWN 2                 GATE           736D
    SIMWN 8                 SIMON          758D
    HWS IV1B                WHEN           907A
18  ENTHADE 2               HERE           265C
    EPIKALEW 1Bα            NAME           294A
    XENIZW 1   RECEIVE AS A GUEST          550A
    PETROS                  PETER          661A
    PUNTHANOMAI 1           INQUIRE        737A
    PHWNEW 2B               CALL           878C
19  DIENTHUMEOMAI           PONDER         193A
    ENTHUMEOMAI             CONSIDER       265D
    Z8TEW 1Aβ               SEEK           339B
    HORAMA 1                VISION         580D
    PNEUMA 5Dα              SPIRIT         683A
20  ALLA 6                  NOW            38B
    ANIST8MI 2D             RISE           69D
    DIAKRINW 2B             WAVER          184B
    DIOTI 3                 FOR            198C
    KATABAINW 1Aβ         COME DOWN        409B
    M8DEIS 2Bβ              NOTHING        520A
    POREUW 1                PROCEED        699A
    SUN 1B                  WITH           789B
21  AITIA 1                 CAUSE          25D
    APOSTELLW 1Bδ         SEND AWAY        98B
    Z8TEW 1Aβ               SEEK           339B
    KATABAINW 1Aδ         COME DOWN        409C
    PAREIMI 1A           BE PRESENT        629D
22  AGGELOS 2A              ANGEL          7C
    HAGIOS 1Bβ              HOLY           9D
    AKOUW 1Bβ               HEAR           31C
```

22	DIKAIOS IB	UPRIGHT 194D
	HEKATONTARCH8S	CENTURION 236C
	IOUDAIOS 2C	JEWISH 380B
	KORN8LIOS	CORNELIUS 445D
	MARTUREW 2B	BE APPROVED 494B
	METAPEMPW	SUMMON 514D
	PARA I3C	FROM 615A
	R8MA I	WORD 742D
	TE IB	AND 815B
	PHOBEW 2A	BE AFRAID 871B
	CHR8MATIZW IB∝	894A
	IMPART A WARNING	
23	ADELPHOS 2	BROTHER 16A
	APO IVIB	FROM 86D
	EISKALEOMAI	INVITE IN 232C
	IOPP8	JOPPA 379C
	SUN IB	WITH 789B
	SUNERCHOMAI 2	ASSEMBLE 796A
	TIS, TI IA∝	ANY ONE 827C
23F	EPAURION	NEXT DAY 283C
24	ANAGKAIOS 2	NECESSARY 52A
	EISERCHOMAI IA∝	COME 231D
	KAISAREIA 2	CAESAREA 396D
	PROSDECHOMAI 2A	RECEIVE 719B
	PROSDOKAW I	EXPECT 719C
	SUGGEN8S	RELATED 780B
	PHILOS 2A∝	LOVING 868D
24F	KORN8LIOS	CORNELIUS 445D
25	DIASAPHEW 2	REPORT 187B
	EISERCHOMAI IA6	COME 232A
	EKP8DAW 2	RUSH OUT 243B
	EPI IIIIAγ	ON 288B
	HO,H8,TO II48η	THE 554B
	PIPTW IB∝	FALL 665B
	*POUS IA	FOOT 703B
	PROSEGGIZW	APPROACH 719D
	PROSKUNEW I	DO REVERENCE 724A
	PROTRECHW	RUN AHEAD 729D
	SUNANTAW I	MEET 792B
	HWS IVIA	WHEN 907A
26	ANTHRWPOS IAβ	MAN 67C
	EGEIRW IA∝	RAISE 213D
27	HEURISKW IC∝	FIND 325C
	SUNERCHOMAI IA	ASSEMBLE 795D
	SUNOMILEW	TALK 799B
28	ATHEMITOS	UNLAWFUL 20B
	AKATHARTOS I	IMPURE 28C
	ALLOPHULOS	FOREIGN 40B
	BELTIWN	BETTER 139A
	DEIKNUMI 2	EXPLAIN 171D
	EPISTAMAI 2	KNOW 300A
	IOUDAIOS I	JEWISH 380A
	KAGW 2	BUT I 387A
	KOINOS 2	COMMON 439B
	KOLLAW 2B∝	UNITE 442C
	LEGW II3	CALL 471B
	PH8MI IB∝	SAY 864A
	HWS IV4	WHEN 907B
29	ANANTIRR8TWS	58A
	NOT RAISING OBJECTION	
	DIO	THEREFORE 197D
	ERCHOMAI IIA∝	COME 310B
	KAI II4	ALSO 394C

29	LOGOS 2D	REASON 479D
	PUNTHANOMAI I	INQUIRE 737A
	TIS, TI 2	WHICH 827B
29A	METAPEMPW	SUMMON 514D
29B	METAPEMPW	SUMMON 514D
30	APO II2B	FROM 86C
	EGW	I 216C
	EN I4B	IN 258B
	ENATOS	NINTH 261D
	ENWPION I	BEFORE 270A
	ESTH8S	CLOTHING 312B
	H8MERA 2	DAY 347A
	HIST8MI IIIB	STAND 383B
	LAMPROS 3	BRIGHT 467A
	MECHRI IB	UNTIL 517B
	OIKOS IA∝	HOUSE 563A
	TETARTOS	FOURTH 821A
	PH8MI IB∝	SAY 864A
	HWRA 2B	TIME OF DAY 904D
30F	KORN8LIOS	CORNELIUS 445D
31	EISAKOUW 2B	LISTEN TO 231C
	ELE8MOSUN8	CHARITABLE GIVING 249B
	ENWPION 5A	BEFORE 270C
	MIMN8SKOMAI 2B	524C
	BE CALLED TO REMEMBRANCE	
	MIMN8SKOMAI 2A	BE MENTIONED 524C
	PROSEUCH8 I	PRAYER 720C
32	BURSEUS	TANNER 148A
	EPIKALEW IB∝	NAME 294A
	THALASSA IBβ	SEA 350D
	IOPP8	JOPPA 379C
	METAKALEW	SUMMON 512C
	XENIZW I	RECEIVE AS A GUEST 550A
	OIKIA IA	HOUSE 560A
	PARA IIIIB∝	ALONG 616A
	PEMPW I	SEND 647C
	PETROS	PETER 661A
32B	SIMWN 8	SIMON 758D
33	ENWPION 2B	BEFORE 270B
	EXAUT8S	AT ONCE 273B
	KALWS 4A	WELL 402B
	PARAGINOMAI I	COME 618D
	PAREIMI IA	BE PRESENT 629C
	PEMPW I	SEND 647C
	POIEW I2Aγ	DO 689B
	PROSTASSW	COMMAND 725D
	TACHOS	SPEED 814D
33A	PAS IE∝	ALL 637D
33B	OUN 5	THEREFORE 597D
33B	PAS IDβ	ALL 637D
34	AL8THEIA 3	REALITY 35D
	ANOIGW IE∝	OPEN 70D
	KATALAMBANW 2	GRASP 414B
	PROSWPOL8MPT8S	728A
	ONE WHO SHOWS PARTIALITY	
	STOMA IA	MOUTH 777B
35	DEKTOS	ACCEPTABLE 173B
	DIKAIOSUN8 2B	RIGHTEOUSNESS 195C
	ERGAZOMAI 2A	WORK 307A
	PHOBEW 2A	BE AFRAID 871A
36	APOSTELLW 2	PUT IN 98C
	DIA AIII2A	BY 179C
	EIR8N8 3	PEACE 226D

36	EUAGGELIZW 2Aβ	PREACH 317D	43B	PAS ICγ	WHOEVER 637B
	KURIOS 2Cγ	LORD 461B	44	EPI IIIIBγ	ON 288D
	LOGOS IBβ	WORD 479C		EPIPIPTW 2	FALL UPON 297D
	HUIOS IBα	SON 841C		ETI IAβ	STILL 315D
37	ARCHW 2C	BEGIN 113B		LOGOS IAβ	WORD 478C
	BAPTISMA I	BAPTISM 132A		PNEUMA 5Cα	SPIRIT 682D
	GALILAIA	GALILEE 149D		R8MA I	WORD 742D
	GINOMAI 14C6	COME, GO 159A	45	DWREA	GIFT 209C
	IOUDAIA 2	JUDAEA 379D		EKCHEW 2	POUR OUT 246D
	IWAN(N)8S I	JOHN 385B		EXIST8MI 2B	BE AMAZED 276A
	KATA IIC	DOWN 406C		EPI IIIIBγ	ON 288D
	K8RUSSW 2Bβ	ANNOUNCE 432C		HOSOS 2	HOW GREAT 590B
	META BIJ3	AFTER 511C		PERITOM8 4A	CIRCUMCISION 658D
	R8MA 2	WORD 743A		PISTOS 2	TRUSTWORTHY 671A
38	DIERCHOMAI ID	GO THROUGH 193D		PNEUMA 5Cα	SPIRIT 682D
	DUNAMIS 7	POWER 207C		SUNERCHOMAI 2	ASSEMBLE 796A
	EIMI III7	TO BE 224D	46	GLWSSA 3	TONGUE 161C
	IAOMAI I	HEAL 369A		MEGALUNW 2	EXALT 498B
	KATADUNASTEUW	OPPRESS 411C	47	KWLUW 3	HINDER 462C
	META AIIICβ	WITH 510A		M8 AIIIDα	NOT 518A
	NAZARA	NAZARETH 534A		M8TI (INTERROG PARTICLE) 522A
	PNEUMA 5Cβ	SPIRIT 682D		HO,H8,TO II4B6	THE 554A
	PNEUMA 6A	SPIRIT 683D		HOSTIS 2B	WHOEVER 591A
	CHRIW I	ANOINT 895D		PNEUMA 5Cα	SPIRIT 682D
	HWS I2D	AS 905D		HUDWR I	WATER 840D
39	ANAIREW IA	DO AWAY WITH 54C	48	BAPTIZW 2Bβ	BAPTIZE 131C
	EPI IIAβ	ON 285D		DIAMENW	REMAIN 185D
	IOUDAIOS 2C	JEWISH 380B		EPIMENW I	REMAIN 296A
	KAI II6	394C		ERWTAW 2	ASK 312B
	KREMANNUMI I	HANG 451A		H8MERA 2	DAY 347A
	MARTUS 2C	WITNESS 495C		ONOMA 14Cγ	NAME 576A
	XULON 2C	CROSS 551C		PROS III7	TOWARD 718A
	POIEW IIBβ	DO 687C		PROSTASSW	COMMAND 725D
	CHWRA IB	COUNTRY 897C		TIS, TI 2D	ANY ONE 828B
40	DIDWMI IBβ	GIVE 192B			
	EGEIRW IAβ	RAISE 213D			
	EMPHAN8S	VISIBLE 257A		**ACTS 11**	
	TRITOS I	THIRD 834B	I	AKOUSTOS	AUDIBLE 31A
41	EK IB	AWAY FROM 233C		APOSTOLOS 3	APOSTLES 99B
	M	FORTY 485B		DECHOMAI 3B	ACCEPT 176C
	MARTUS 2C	WITNESS 495C		ETHNOS 2	GENTILES 217C
	META BII4A	AFTER 511D		EIMI III6B	TO BE 224D
	NEKROS 2A	DEAD 537A		IOUDAIA 2	JUDAEA 379D
	PROCHEIROTONEW	CHOOSE 732A		KATA IIIA	ALONG 407A
	SUMPINW	DRINK WITH 787A		LOGOS IBβ	WORD 479B
	SUNANASTREPHOMAI	ASSOCIATE 792A	2	ANABAINW IAα	GO UP 49D
	SUNESTHIW	EAT WITH 796A		DIA AII2	AFTER 179A
	SUSTREPHW 2	BRING TOGETHER 803A		DIAKRINW 2A	TAKE ISSUE 184B
42	DIAMARTUROMAI 2	TESTIFY 185C		EK 3D	FROM 234C
	ZAW IAα	LIVE 336C		EPIST8RIZW	STRENGTHEN 300C
	K8RUSSW 2Bβ	ANNOUNCE 432D		HIEROSOLUMA IA	JERUSALEM 373D
	KRIT8S IAβ	JUDGE 454C		LOGOS IAγ	WORD 478C
	NEKROS 2A	DEAD 536D		PERITOM8 4A	CIRCUMCISION 658D
	HORIZW IB	DETERMINE 584D		POIEW III	DO 689C
	PARAGGELLW	GIVE ORDERS 618C		PROSPHWNEW 2	CALL OUT 727D
43	HAMARTIA I	SIN 42C		CHARIS 2A	FAVOR 885C
	APHESIS 2	PARDON 124C		CHWRA 2	COUNTRY 897D
	LAMBANW 2	RECEIVE 466B	3	AKROBUSTIA I	UNCIRCUMCISED 33A
	MARTUREW IA	BEAR WITNESS 493D		EISERCHOMAI IC	COME 232A
	ONOMA 14Cα	NAME 575C		ECHW I2Cα	HAVE 332D
	PISTEUW 2Aβ	BELIEVE 667B		LEGW IIBα	SAY 469C
	PROPH8T8S I	PROPHET 730D		SUNESTHIW	EAT WITH 796A
43A	PAS IDα	ALL 637C	4	ARCHW 2B	BEGIN 113B

4	EKTITH8MI 2	EXPLAIN 245B
	KATHEX8S	IN ORDER 389C
5	ARCH8 IA	CORNERS 111B
	ACHRI IB	AS FAR AS 128C
	EIDON IA	SEE 219D
	EN I4D	IN 258C
	ERCHOMAI IIAʏ	COME 310C
	IOPP8	JOPPA 379C
	KATHI8MI	LET DOWN 391A
	KATABAINW IB	COME DOWN 409C
	OTHON8	LINEN CLOTH 558A
	HORAMA I	VISION 580D
	OURANOS 2A	HEAVEN 599B
	POLIS I	CITY 692B
	SKEUOS IA	THING 761C
	HWS II3B	SO 906A
6	ATENIZW	LOOK INTENTLY AT 119C
	G8 5B	EARTH 156D
	HERPETON	REPTILE 310A
	TH8RION IAβ	BEAST 361D
	KATANOEW 2	NOTICE 416A
	OURANOS ID	HEAVEN 598D
	*PETEINON	BIRD 660A
	TETRAPOUS	QUADRUPEDS 821C
7	THUW 2	SACRIFICE 367D
	PHWN8 2D	VOICE 879C
8	AKATHARTOS I	IMPURE 28C
	EISERCHOMAI 2B	COME 232B
	KOINOS 2	COMMON 439B
	M8DAMWS	BY NO MEANS 519C
	OUDEPOTE	NEVER 596D
	STOMA IA	MOUTH 777B
9	DEUTEROS 4	SECOND 176B
	KATHARIZW 2A	CLEANSE 388A
	KOINOW 2	DECLARE UNCLEAN 439C
	OURANOS 2A	HEAVEN 599B
	PHWN8 2D	VOICE 879B
10	ANASPAW	DRAW 59D
	EPI III3	ON 289C
	OURANOS 2A	HEAVEN 599B
	PALIN IA	BACK 611C
	TRIS	THRICE 834B
11	APOSTELLW IB6	SEND AWAY 98B
	EGW	I 216C
	EXAUT8S	AT ONCE 273B
	EPHIST8MI IA	STAND BY 331A
	KAISAREIA 2	CAESAREA 396D
12	DIAKRINW IB	DIFFERENTIATE 184B
	EISERCHOMAI IAβ	COME 231D
	M8DEIS 2Bβ	NOTHING 520A
	OIKOS IAα	HOUSE 563B
	PNEUMA 5Dα	SPIRIT 683A
	SUN IB	WITH 789B
	SUNERCHOMAI 2	ASSEMBLE 796A
13	APAGGELLW I	REPORT 78C
	EPIKALEW IBα	NAME 294A
	IOPP8	JOPPA 379C
	HIST8MI III B	STAND 383B
	METAPEMPW	SUMMON 514D
	OIKOS IAα	HOUSE 563A
	PETROS	PETER 661A
	PWS 2A	HOW 740A
14	LALEW 2B	SPEAK 464D

14	OIKOS 2	HOUSEHOLD 563C
	R8MA I	WORD 743A
	SWZW 2B	SAVE 806B
15	ARCH8 IB	BEGINNING 111C
	ARCHW 2Aα	BEGIN 113A
	EPIPIPTW 2	FALL UPON 297D
	PNEUMA 5Cα	SPIRIT 682D
	HWSPER 2	(JUST) AS 908A
16	IWAN(N)8S I	JOHN 385B
	MIMN8SKOMAI IA6	REMEMBER 524B
	PNEUMA 5Cβ	SPIRIT 683A
	R8MA I	WORD 742D
	HUDWR I	WATER 840D
16A	BAPTIZW 2A	BAPTIZE 131B
16B	BAPTIZW 3B	BAPTIZE 131D
17	DE IE	BUT, AND 170C
	DUNATOS IAβ	POWERFUL 208A
	DWREA	GIFT 209C
	EI III	IF 218C
	EIMI II6C	TO BE 223C
	EPI IIIIBϵ	TOWARD 289A
	ISOS	EQUAL 381D
	KAI II3	ALSO 394B
	KURIOS 2Cʏ	LORD 461A
	*KWLUW I	HINDER 462C
	PISTEUW 2Aʏ	BELIEVE 667B
	PISTEUW 2A6	BELIEVE 667B
	TIS, TI IAβ	WHICH 826D
18	DOXAZW I	PRAISE 203C
	ETHNOS 2	GENTILES 217C
	ZW8 2Bα	LIFE 341B
	H8SUCHAZW 2	REST 349D
	METANOIA	REPENTANCE 514A
19	APO VI	BECAUSE OF 87B
	GINOMAI IIBβ	COME ABOUT 157B
	DIASPEIRW	SCATTER 187C
	DIERCHOMAI 2	COME 193D
	EPI IIIAʏ	AGAINST 286D
	HEWS II2A	AS FAR AS 335C
	THLIPSIS I	TRIBULATION 362D
	KUPROS	CYPRUS 458D
	LALEW 2B	SPEAK 464D
	LOGOS IBβ	WORD 479C
	MEN 2E	(PARTICLE) 504C
	M8DEIS 2A	NO 520A
	STEPHANOS	STEPHEN 774C
	PHOINIK8	PHOENICIA 872A
19F	OUN 5	THEREFORE 597D
19=26	ANTIOCHEIA I	ANTIOCH 74D
20	AN8R 3	MAN 66A
	EIMI II	TO BE 222B
	HELL8N 2A	GENTILE 251C
	HELL8NIST8S	HELLENIST 251C
	EUAGGELIZW 2Aβ	PREACH 317D
	KUPRIOS	CYPRIAN 458D
	KUR8NAIOS	CYRENIAN 459A
	KURIOS 2Cʏ	LORD 461A
	LALEW 2A6	SPEAK 464C
	HOSTIS 3	WHOEVER 591B
21	ARITHMOS 2	NUMBER 106A
	EPI IIIIB6	TOWARD 289A
	EPISTREPHW IBβ	TURN 301B
	META AIIICβ	WITH 510A

21	PISTEUW 2B	BELIEVE	667C
	POLUS IIBα	MANY	694B
	CHEIR 2Aβ	HAND	888D
22	AKOUW IBα	HEAR	31B
	BARNABAS	BARNABAS	133C
	DIERCHOMAI 2	COME	193D
	EKKL8SIA 4B	CHURCH	240C
	EXAPOSTELLW IB	SEND OUT	272D
	LOGOS IAβ	WORD	478C
	OUS I	EAR	600B
23	KARDIA IBγ	HEART	404D
	PARAGINOMAI I	COME	618D
	PARAKALEW 2	APPEAL TO	622C
	PROTHESIS 2A	SETTING FORTH	713A
	PROSMENW IAβ	REMAIN	724D
	PROSMENW IB	REMAIN	724D
	CHAIRW I	REJOICE	881D
	CHARIS 3B	FAVOR	886B
23F	KURIOS 2Cγ	LORD	460D
24	AGATHOS IAα	GOOD	2D
	*AN8R 4	MAN	66B
	HIKANOS IA	SUFFICIENT	375A
	OCHLOS I	CROWD	605C
	PISTIS 2Dα	FAITH	669A
	PL8R8S IB	FULL	675D
	PNEUMA 5Cβ	SPIRIT	682D
	PROSTITH8MI IB	ADD	726B
25	ANAZ8TEW	LOOK	53C
	SAULOS	SAUL	752D
	TARSOS	TARSUS	813B
26	AGW IB	BRING	14B
	GINOMAI I3E	TAKE PLACE	158B
	ENIAUTOS I	YEAR	266A
	HEURISKW IA	FIND	325A
	HIKANOS IA	SUFFICIENT	375A
	MATH8T8S 2Bγ	DISCIPLE	487A
	HOLOS I	WHOLE	567C
	OCHLOS I	CROWD	605C
	PRWTOS 2A	FIRST	733D
	PRWTWS	FOR THE FIRST TIME	734B
	SUNAGW 2	GATHER	790B
	SUNTUGCHANW	MEET	801B
	TE IB	AND	815B
	CHR8MATIZW 2	IMPART A WARNING	894A
	CHRISTIANOS	THE CHRISTIAN	895A
27	HIEROSOLUMA IA	JERUSALEM	373D
	KATERCHOMAI I	COME DOWN	423A
27F	PROPH8T8S 5	PROPHET	731C
28	HAGABOS	AGABUS	2B
	AGALLIASIS	EXULTATION	3D
	GINOMAI IIBβ	COME ABOUT	157B
	DIA AIII2B8	BY	179D
	HEIS IAβ	ONE	230A
	EPI I2	UNDER	286C
	EPI IIIIAα	ACROSS	287D
	KLAUDIOS I	CLAUDIUS	434C
	LIMOS 2	FAMINE	476B
	MEGAS 2Aγ	GREAT	499A
	MELLW IA	WILL BE	502A
	OIKOUMEN8 IA	THE WORLD	564A
	ONOMA II	NAME	574A
	HOSTIS 3	WHOEVER	591B
	PNEUMA 5Dα	SPIRIT	683A

28	PNEUMA 6C	SPIRIT	684A
	S8MAINW 2	MAKE KNOWN	755A
	SUSTREPHW 2	BRING TOGETHER	803A
29	DIAKONIA 4	SUPPORT	183C
	HEKASTOS 2	EACH	236B
	EUPOREW	BE WELL OFF	324C
	IOUDAIA 2	JUDAEA	379D
	KATHWS 2	AS	392B
	KATOIKEW IA	LIVE	425B
	MATH8T8S 2Bγ	DISCIPLE	487A
	HORIZW IAβ	DETERMINE	584D
	PEMPW 2	SEND	648A
30	BARNABAS	BARNABAS	133C
	DIA AIIIIA	BY MEANS OF	179A
	KAI II6		394C
	HOS,H8,HO I7Bα	(REL PRON)	588C
	PRESBUTEROS 2Bα	OLDER	707A
	SAULOS	SAUL	752D
	CHEIR I	HAND	888C

ACTS 12

I	APO IVIB	FROM	87A
	BASILEUS I	KING	135D
	EKEINOS 2Bγ	THAT	239B
	EPIBALLW IB	LAY ON	289D
	H8RWD8S 3	HEROD	349B
	KAIROS I	TIME	395D
	KAKOW I	HARM	399B
	KATA II2A	DURING	407C
	TIS, TI IAα	ANY ONE	827C
IFF	AGRIPPAS I	AGRIPPA	13C
2	ANAIREW IA	DO AWAY WITH	54C
	IAKWBOS I	JAMES	368B
	IWAN(N)8S 2	JOHN	385C
	MACHAIRA I	SWORD	497C
3	AZUMOS IB	UNLEAVENED BREAD	19C
	ARESTOS	PLEASING	105B
	EIDON 3	NOTICE	220A
	EPICHEIR8SIS	ATTEMPT	304D
	H8MERA 2	DAY	347C
	PISTOS 2	TRUSTWORTHY	671A
	PROSTITH8MI IC	ADD	726C
	SULLAMBANW IAα	SEIZE	784B
4	ANAGW I	LEAD	52D
	BOULOMAI 2Aβ	DESIRE	145D
	KAI II6		394C
	LAOS ICα	PEOPLE	467D
	META BII2	AFTER	511C
	PARADIDWMI IB	GIVE OVER	620A
	PASCHA I	THE PASSOVER	639A
	PIAZW 2A	GRASP	662D
	TETRADION	FOUR SOLDIERS	821B
	TITH8MI IIIB	PUT	824B
	PHULAK8 3	GUARD	875D
	PHULASSW IB	WATCH	876B
5	EKTENEIA	PERSEVERANCE	245A
	EKTEN8S	EARNEST	245A
	EKTENWS	FERVENTLY	245A
	MEN IAα	(PARTICLE)	503D
	OUN 2A	THEREFORE	597C
	PERI IF	ABOUT	650C
	PROSEUCH8 I	PRAYER	720C

5   T8REW I   GUARD 822B
   PHULAK8 3   GUARD 875D
6   DEW IB   BIND 176D
   DUO 2   TWO 208C
   DUO 3   TWO 208C
   H8RWD8S 3   HEROD 349B
   THURA IA   DOOR 366B
   KOIMAW I   SLEEP 438C
   MELLW IB«   BE ABOUT TO 502A
   METAXU 2A   BETWEEN 514C
   NUX IC   NIGHT 548D
   HOTE IA   WHEN 592B
   PRO I   BEFORE 708B
   PROAGW I   LEAD 708D
   PROSAGW IA   BRING 718B
   T8REW I   GUARD 822B
   PHULAK8 3   GUARD 875C
   PHULAX   GUARD 876A
6F   HALU6IS I   CHAIN 40D
7   AGGELOS 2A   ANGEL 7B
   EGEIRW IA«   WAKE 213C
   EK 2   AWAY FROM 234A
   EKPIPTW I   FALL OFF 243B
   EPILAMPW I   SHINE FORTH 295B
   *EPHIST8MI IA   STAND BY 331A
   IDOU IBP   BEHOLD 371C
   KURIOS 2A   LORD 460B
   LAMPW IB   SHINE OUT 467B
   LEGW I8A   SAY 470B
   NUSSW   NUDGE 549B
   OIK8MA 2   ROOM 559C
   PATASSW IA   STRIKE 640A
   PLEURA   SIDE 673D
   TACHOS   SPEED 814D
   PHWS IA   LIGHT 879D
   CHEIR I   HAND 888A
8   ZWNNUMI   GIRD 342A
   HIMATION 2   GARMENT 377B
   PERIBALLW IB«   THROW AROUND 651D
   PERIZWNNUMI 2A   GIRD ABOUT 653A
   POIEW I2A«   DO 689A
   SANDALION   SANDAL 749B
   HUPODEW   TIE 852A
9   AL8TH8S 3   REAL 36B
   BLEPW IA   SEE 142D
   GINOMAI I2A   COME ABOUT 157C
   DE ID   BUT, AND 170C
   HORAMA I   VISION 580D
   OU 7B   NO 595B
9F   EXERCHOMAI IAP   GO OUT 274A
10 ANOIGW IA   OPEN 70B
   AUTOMATOS   BY ITSELF 122A
   APHIST8MI 2A   WITHDRAW 126C
   DE 2   BUT, AND 170C
   DEUTEROS 4   SECOND 176B
   DIERCHOMAI IA   GO THROUGH 193C
   EPI IIIIAY   ON 288B
   ERCHOMAI IIAP   COME 310C
   HO,H8,TO IIIF   THE 553A
   HOSTIS 3   WHOEVER 591B
   POLIS I   CITY 692A
   PROERCHOMAI I   GO FORWARD 712B
   PRWTOS IB   FIRST 733A

10 PUL8 I   GATE 736C
   RUM8   LANE 744D
   SID8ROUS   IRON 757C
   PHERW 4C   BEAR 863C
   PHULAK8 2   GUARD 875D
11 AL8THWS I   TRULY 36D
   GINOMAI II4A   BE 159C
   HEAUTOU IC   ONESELF 211B
   EK IA   AWAY FROM 233C
   EN I5D   IN 259C
   EXAIREW 2A   DELIVER 271C
   EXAPOSTELLW IB   SEND OUT 272D
   H8RWD8S 3   HEROD 349B
   IOUDAIOS 2C   JEWISH 380B
   NUN IAP   NOW 547C
   PROSDOKIA   EXPECTATION 719D
   CHEIR 2B   HAND 888D
12 EPIKALEW IB«   NAME 294A
   HIKANOS IC   SUFFICIENT 375A
   IWAN(N)8S 6   JOHN 385D
   MARIA 6   MARY 493B
   MARKOS   MARK 493C
   HOU IAP   WHERE 594A
   SUNATHROIZW I   GATHER 791A
   SUNORAW   PERCEIVE 799B
13 THURA IA   DOOR 366B
   KROUW   STRIKE 455A
   ONOMA II   NAME 574A
   PAIDISK8   MAID 609B
   PROSERCHOMAI I   APPROACH 720A
   PULWN 2   GATE 736D
   ROD8 I   RHODA 744A
   HUPAKOUW 3   LISTEN TO 845B
14 ANOIGW IA   OPEN 70B
   APAGGELLW I   REPORT 78C
   APO V3   WITH 87B
   DE ID   BUT, AND 170C
   EISTRECHW   RUN IN 232D
   EPIGINWSKW IB   KNOW 291A
   HIST8MI II2BP   BEING 383C
   OU 7B   NO 595B
   PHWN8 2B   VOICE 879A
   CHARA I   JOY 883C
14A   PULWN 2   GATE 736D
14B   PULWN 2   GATE 736D
15 AGGELOS 2A   ANGEL 7D
   DIISCHURIZOMAI   INSIST 194C
   ECHW II2   BE 334C
   MAINOMAI   BE OUT OF ONES MIND 487C
   TUGCHANW 2C   HAPPEN 837B
16 EXANOIGW   TO OPEN 272B
   EXIST8MI 2B   BE AMAZED 276A
   EPIMENW 2   CONTINUE 296B
   KROUW   STRIKE 454D
17 DE 2   BUT, AND 170C
   DI8GEOMAI   TELL 194A
   EXAGW I   LEAD OUT 271A
   EXERCHOMAI IAP   GO OUT 274A
   IAKWBOS 3   JAMES 368C
   POREUW I   PROCEED 699A
   PWS 2A   HOW 739D
   *SIGAW IA   BE SILENT 757A
   TOPOS IA   PLACE 830A

17	PHULAK8 3	GUARD 875C
18	ARA 2	THEN 103B
	GINOMAI IIBγ	COME ABOUT 157B
	H8MERA IA	DAY 346C
	OLIGOS 2B	LITTLE 566C
	TARACHOS I	MENTAL AGITATION 813B
	TIS, TI IB6	WHICH 827A
19	ANAKRINW IB	QUESTION 56A
	APAGW 2C	LEAD AWAY 79A
	DIATRIBW	STAY 189A
	EPIZ8TEW IA	SEEK AFTER 292D
	H8RWD8S 3	HEROD 349B
	IOUDAIA I	JUDAEA 379D
	KAISAREIA 2	CAESAREA 396D
	KATERCHOMAI I	COME DOWN 423A
	KELEUW	COMMAND 428C
	PHULAX	GUARD 876A
20	AITEW	ASK 25B
	BASILIKOS	ROYAL 136C
	BLASTOS	BLASTUS 142A
	DE 2	BUT, AND 170C
	EIR8N8 IA	PEACE 226B
	EPI IIB«	OVER 286B
	THUMOMACHEW	BE VERY ANGRY 365D
	KOITWN	BEDROOM 441A
	HOMOTHUMADON	WITH ONE MIND 569C
	PAREIMI IA	BE PRESENT 629D
	PEITHW IC	CONVINCE 645A
	PROS III7	TOWARD 718A
	SIDWNIOS 2	SIDONIAN 757D
	TREPHW I	FEED 833C
	TURIOS	TYRIAN 838B
	CHWRA IB	COUNTRY 897C
21	AUTOS 3B	(OBLIQUE CASE) 123A
	BASILIKOS	ROYAL 136B
	88MA 2	TRIBUNAL 139D
	D8M8GOREW	177D
	DELIVER A PUBLIC ADDRESS	
	ENDUW 2A	DRESS 263C
	ESTH8S	CLOTHING 312B
	H8MERA 3A	DAY 347D
	H8RWD8S 3	HEROD 349B
	KATHIZW 2A«	SIT DOWN 391A
	PROS IIIIE	TOWARD 716D
	TAKTOS	FIXED 810D
22	ANTHRWPOS IAβ	MAN 67C
	D8MOS	CROWD 178A
	EPIPHWNEW	CRY OUT 304C
	THEOS I	GOD 357B
	KATALLASSW 2B	RECONCILE 415A
	TURIOS	TYRIAN 838B
	PHWN8 2C	VOICE 879A
23	AGGELOS 2A	ANGEL 7B
	ANTI 3	FOR 73B
	GINOMAI I4B	BECOME 158D
	DIDWMI IA	GIVE 191D
	DOXA 3	FAME 203B
	EKPSUCHW	DIE 247A
	KURIOS 2A	LORD 460B
	HOS,H8,HO IIIA	(REL PRON) 589A
	PARACHR8MA	AT ONCE 629B
	PATASSW 2	STRIKE 640B
	SKWL8KOBRWTOS	EATEN BY WORMS 765D

24	AUXANW 3	GROW 121C
	LOGOS IBβ	WORD 479B
	LOGOS IBβ	WORD 479B
	PL8THUNW IB	INCREASE 675A
25	BARNABAS	BARNABAS 133C
	DIAKONIA 4	SUPPORT 183C
	EI VI8A	IF NOT 219A
	EPIKALEW IB«	NAME 294A
	IWAN(N)8S 6	JOHN 385D
	MARKOS	MARK 493C
	PL8ROW 5	MAKE FULL 677D
	SAULOS	SAUL 752D
	SUMPARALAMBANW	TAKE ALONG 786D
	HUPOSTREPHW	RETURN 855B

ACTS 13

1	ANTIOCHEIA I	ANTIOCH 74D
	DIDASKALOS	TEACHER 190D
	EIMI III6B	TO BE 224D
	EIMI V	TO BE 225A
	EKKL8SIA 4B	CHURCH 240C
	H8RWD8S 2	HEROD 349B
	KALEW IAγ	CALL 400A
	KATA III A	ALONG 407A
	KUR8NAIOS	CYRENIAN 459A
	LOUKAS	LUKE 481D
	MANA8N	MANAEN 491B
	NIGER	NIGER 541A
	PROPH8T8S 5	PROPHET 731C
	SUMEWN 4	SYMEON 786A
	SUNTROPHOS	FAMILIAR 801B
	TETRARCH8S	TETRARCH 821D
IF	SAULOS	SAUL 752D
2	APHORIZW 2	SET APART 127A
	D8 2	NOW 177B
	EIS 4D	FOR 228C
	ERGON 2	WORK 308B
	LEITOURGEW 2	472A
	PERFORM A PUBLIC SERVICE	
	N8STEUW	TO FAST 540C
	HOS,H8,HO I6	(REL PRON) 588C
	PNEUMA 5C«	SPIRIT 682D
	PROSKALEW 2B	SUMMON 722D
3	EPITITH8MI IA«	PUT UPON 302D
	N8STEUW	TO FAST 540C
4	APOPLEW	SAIL AWAY 96D
	EKPEMPW	SEND OUT 243A
	KATERCHOMAI I	COME DOWN 423A
	KUPROS	CYPRUS 458D
	MEN 2E	(PARTICLE) 504C
	PNEUMA 5C«	SPIRIT 682D
	SELEUKEIA	SELEUCIA 754A
5	GINOMAI II4A	BE 159C
	ECHW I2Bβ	HAVE 332D
	IWAN(N)8S 6	JOHN 385D
	KATAGGELLW I	PROCLAIM 410C
	LOGOS IBβ	WORD 479B
	SALAMIS	SALAMIS 747D
	SUNAGWG8 2A	790C
	PLACE OF ASSEMBLY	
	HUP8RET8S	SERVANT 850B
6	ACHRI IB	AS FAR AS 128C

6	BARI8SOUS	BAR-JESUS 133B
	DIERCHOMAI IA	GO THROUGH 193C
	ELUMAS	ELYMAS 253A
	HEURISKW IB	FIND 325B
	IOUDAIOS I	JEWISH 380A
	MAGOS 2	MAGICIAN 486B
	N8SOS	ISLAND 540A
	ONOMA II	NAME 574A
	HOS,H8,HO II	(REL PRON) 587A
	PAPHOS	PAPHOS 643D
	PERIERCHOMAI	GO AROUND 652C
	PSEUDOPROPH8T8S	FALSE PROPHET 900B
7	AN8R 4	MAN 668
	ANTHUPATOS	PROCONSUL 68D
	EIMI IIII0	TO BE 224D
	EPIZ8TEW 2A	STRIVE FOR 292D
	Z8TEW 2Bγ	SEEK 339C
	LOGOS IBβ	WORD 479B
	SAULOS	SAUL 752D
	SERGIOS	SERGIUS 754D
	SUN IC	WITH 789B
	SUNETOS	INTELLIGENT 796B
8	ANTHIST8MI I	SET AGAINST 66C
	ANTHUPATOS	PROCONSUL 68D
	DIASTREPHW 2	MISLEAD 188A
	*ELUMAS	ELYMAS 253A
	EPEID8 2	SINCE 284A
	H8DEWS	GLADLY 344C
	MAGOS 2	MAGICIAN 486B
	METHERM8NEUW	TRANSLATE 499D
	PISTIS 20α	FAITH 669A
9	ATENIZW	LOOK INTENTLY AT 119C
	KAI II8	ALSO 394C
	HO,H8,TO II9B	THE 554D
	PIMPL8MI IAβ	FILL 663D
	PNEUMA 5Cβ	SPIRIT 682D
	SAULOS	SAUL 752D
10	DIABOLOS 2	THE SLANDERER 181B
	DIASTREPHW IB	PERVERT 188A
	DIKAIOSUN8 2B	RIGHTEOUSNESS 195D
	DOLOS	DECEIT 202B
	EUTHUS 2A	STRAIGHT 321B
	ECHTHROS 2Bγ	THE ENEMY 332A
	OU 4C	NO 595A
	PAUW 2	STOP 643C
	PL8R8S IB	FULL 675D
	RADIOURGIA	FRIVOLITY 741A
	HUIOS ICγ	SON 841D
	W I	O 903B
10A	PAS IAβ	EVERY EACH 636D
10B	PAS IAβ	EVERY EACH 636D
11	ACHLUS I	MISTINESS 128A
	ACHRI IA	UNTIL 128B
	EPI IIIIBγ	ON 289A
	H8LIOS	THE SUN 346B
	IDOU IB8	BEHOLD 371C
	KAIROS I	TIME 395C
	M8 AII2D	NOT 518C
	PARACHR8MA	AT ONCE 629B
	PERIAGW 2	LEAD AROUND 651B
	PIPTW 2Bγ	FALL 665D
	SKOTOS I	DARKNESS 765A
	TUPHLOS IAβ	BLIND 838C
11	CHEIR 2Aγ	HAND 888D
	CHEIRAGWGOS	LEADER 889A
12	ANTHUPATOS	PROCONSUL 68D
	DIDACH8 2	TEACHING 191B
	EKPL8SSW 2	BE AMAZED 243D
	EPI IIIBγ	ON 287A
	THAUMAZW IAα	WONDER 352D
	PISTEUW 2Aα	BELIEVE 667A
	PISTEUW 2B	BELIEVE 667C
13	ANAGW 3	PUT TO SEA 52D
	APOCHWREW	LEAVE 101C
	IWAN(N)8S 6	JOHN 385D
	PAMPHULIA	PAMPHYLIA 612B
	PAPHOS	PAPHOS 643D
	PERG8	PERGA 650A
	PERI 2A8	ABOUT 651A
	HUPOSTREPHW	RETURN 855B
14	ANTIOCHEIA 2	ANTIOCH 74D
	DIERCHOMAI 3	GO ABOUT 193D
	H8MERA 2	DAY 347C
	KATHIZW 2Aα	SIT DOWN 390D
	PARAGINOMAI I	COME 618D
	PERG8	PERGA 650A
	PISIDIOS	PISIDIAN 665D
	PISIDIA	PISIDIA 665D
	SABBATON IBβ	SABBATH 746C
	SUNAGWG8 2A	790C

PLACE OF ASSEMBLY

15	ANAGNWSIS I	READING 52C
	ARCHISUNAGWGOS	112D

PRESIDENT OF A SYNAGOGUE

	LAOS IA	PEOPLE 467D
	LOGOS IAβ	WORD 478B
	META BII3	AFTER 511C
	NOMOS 4A	LAW 545A
	PARAKL8SIS I	ENCOURAGEMENT 623C
	PROPH8T8S I	PROPHET 731A
16	AKOUW IC	HEAR 31D
	AN8R 3	MAN 66A
	ISRA8LIT8S	ISRAELITE 382C
	PHOBEW 2A	BE AFRAID 871B
17	AIGUPTOS	EGYPT 21C
	BRACHIWN	ARM 146D
	G8 4	LAND 156C
	EKLEGOMAI 2A	CHOOSE 241D
	EXAGW I	LEAD OUT 271A
	THEOS 3C	GOD 358A
	META AIII2	WITH 511A
	PAROIKIA IA	SOJOURN 634B
	HUPS8LOS I	HIGH 857C
	HUPSOW 2	LIFT UP 858D
18	TESSARAKONTAET8S	FORTY YEARS 820D
	TROPOPHOREW	PUT UP WITH 835B
	TROPHOPHOREW	CARE FOR 835D
	CHRONOS	TIME 896B
	HWS IV5	WHEN 907C
19	ALLOPHULOS	FOREIGN 40B
	G8 4	LAND 156C
	ETHNOS I	NATION 217B
	KATHAIREW 2Aβ	DESTROY 387C
	KATAKL8RONOMEW I	412C

GIVE AS AN INHERITANCE

Ref	Greek	English	No.
19	KATAKL8RODOTEW		412C
	PARCEL OUT BY LOT		
	CHANAAN	CANAAN	883C
20	DIDWMI 5	GIVE	192D
	ETOS	YEAR	317A
	HEWS III!A	UNTIL	335B
	KAI IIB	AND	392C
	KRIT8S 2	JUDGE	454D
	PENT8KONTA	FIFTY	648D
	PROPH8T8S I	PROPHET	730D
	SAMOU8L	SAMUEL	749A
	TETRAKOSIOI	FOUR HUNDRED	821B
	HWS IV5	WHEN	907C
21	AITEW	ASK	25B
	BENIAMIN	BENJAMIN	139A
	EK 38	FROM	234B
	KAKEITHEN 2	AND THEN	397C
	KIS	KISH	433D
	SAOUL I	SAUL	749B
	HUIOS IAα	SON	841B
	PHUL8 I	TRIBE	876D
22	BASILEUS I	KING	135D
	EGEIRW iAε	RAISE UP	213D
	EIS 8B	TO BE	229C
	THEL8MA ICγ	WILL	355A
	IESSAI	JESSE	374B
	KAI II6		394C
	KARDIA I8ε	HEART	405A
	KATA II5Aγ	ACCORDING TO	408B
	MARTUREW IC		494A
	TESTIFY FAVORABLY		
	METHIST8MI I	BE REMOVED	500A
	POIEW IICα	DO	688C
23	AGW IA	LEAD	14B
	EGEIRW IAε	RAISE UP	213D
	SPERMA 2B	SEED	769B
	SWT8R 2	SAVIOR	808C
24	BAPTISMA I	BAPTISM	132A
	EISODOS I	ENTRANCE	232C
	METANOIA	REPENTANCE	514A
	PRO I	BEFORE	708C
	PROK8RUSSW	PROCLAIM PUBLICLY	714D
	PROSWPON ICζ	FACE	729A
24F	IWAN(N)8S I	JOHN	385B
25	AXIOS 2A	WORTHY	77C
	DROMOS 2	COURSE	206A
	LUW 2A	LOOSE	484D
	HOS,H8,HO I2Bα	(REL PRON)	587B
	PL8ROW 5	MAKE FULL	677D
	TIS, TI IAδ	WHICH	826D
	TIS, TI IBζ	WHICH	827B
	HUPOD8MA	SANDAL	852B
	HWS IVIB	WHEN	907A
26	APOSTELLW 2	PUT IN	98C
	GENOS I	DESCENDANTS	155B
	EXAPOSTELLW IB	SEND OUT	272D
	LOGOS I8β	WORD	479C
	SWT8RIA 2	DELIVERANCE	809A
	HUIOS ICβ	SON	841C
	PHOBEW 2A	BE AFRAID	871B
27	AGNOEW 2	NOT TO KNOW	11B
	ANAGINWSKW 2	READ	51C
	ARCHWN 2A	AUTHORITIES	113C
27	KATA II2C	EVERY	407C
	KATOIKEW IA	LIVE	425B
	KRINW 4Aα	JUDGE	452D
	PL8ROW 4A	MAKE FULL	677C
	SABBATON IA	SABBATH	746B
	SUNI8MI	UNDERSTAND	798A
	PHWN8 2C	VOICE	879A
28	AITEW	ASK	25B
	AITIA 2A	CHARGE	25D
	ANAIRESIS	MURDER	54B
	*ANAIREW IA	DO AWAY WITH	54C
	HEURISKW 2	FIND	325D
	THANATOS I8α	DEATH	351C
	M8DEIS I	NO	519D
	PILATOS	PILATE	663C
29	GRAPHW 2C	WRITE	166A
	EPITUGCHANW	OBTAIN	304A
	KATHAIREW I	LOWER	387B
	MN8MEION 2	TOMB	526C
	XULON 2C	CROSS	551C
	PILATOS	PILATE	663C
	STAUROW I	CRUCIFY	773A
	TELEW 2	PERFORM	818D
	TITH8MI IIAβ	PUT	823D
	HWS IVIA	WHEN	907A
30	EGEIRW IAβ	RAISE	213D
	EK I8	AWAY FROM	233C
	NEKROS 2A	DEAD	537A
31	GALILAIA	GALILEE	149D
	EPI III2B	ON	289B
	H8MERA 2	DAY	347B
	MARTUS 2C	WITNESS	495C
	HORAW IA6	SEE	582A
	POLUS IIIA	MANY	695C
	SUNANABAINW	GO UP WITH	792A
32	GINOMAI I4Cε	COME, GO	159A
	EPAGGELIA 2A	PROMISE	280B
	EUAGGELIZW 2Aα	PREACH	317D
33	AITEW	ASK	25B
	EKPL8ROW	FULFILL	243C
	KATASCHESIS I	POSSESSION	420C
	KL8RONOMIA 2	INHERITANCE	436A
	PERAS I	END	649D
	PRWTOS IB	FIRST	733A
	TEKNON IB	CHILD	816B
	HUIOS 2B	SON	842B
	PSALMOS I	PSALM	899B
	HWS II4A	SO	906B
33F	ANIST8MI IA	RAISE	69B
34	ANIST8MI IA	RAISE	69B
	DIAPHTHORA	DESTRUCTION	189D
	MELLW ICβ	BE ABOUT TO	502B
	M8KETI 3	NO LONGER	520B
	NEKROS 2A	DEAD	537A
	HOSIOS 2A	PIOUS	589C
	*HOUTW 2	THUS	602C
	PISTOS IB	TRUSTWORTHY	670D
	HUPOSTREPHW	RETURN	855B
35	DIDWMI I8β	GIVE	192B
	DIOTI 2	THEREFORE	189D
	HETEROS I8ζ	ANOTHER	315C
	HOSIOS 2B	PIOUS	589D
35FF	DIAPHTHORA	DESTRUCTION	189D

36	BOUL8 2B	WILL 145B	45	BLASPH8MEW 1	DEFAME 142A
	GAR 1B	FOR 151B		ENANTIOOMAI	OPPOSE 261C
	GAR 1E	FOR 151C		Z8LOS 2	JEALOUSY 338B
	GENEA 2	GENERATION 153B		LALEW 2Aζ	SPEAK 464C
	KOIMAW 2A	SLEEP 438D		OCHLOS 1	CROWD 605D
	MEN 1B	(PARTICLE) 504A		PIMPL8MI 1AB	FILL 663D
	PROSTITH8MI 1B	ADD 726C	46	AIWNIOS 3	ETERNAL 28A
	HUP8RETEW	SERVE 850B		ANAGKAIOS 1	NECESSARY 51D
37	EGEIRW 1AB	RAISE 213D		AXIOS 2A	WORTHY 77C
38	HAMARTIA 1	SIN 42C		APWTHEW 2	REJECT 102D
	APHESIS 2	PARDON 124C		ZW8 2Bα	LIFE 341B
	GNWSTOS 1A	KNOWN 163C		KRINW 2	JUDGE 452B
	DIKAIOW 3C	MAKE FREE 197A		LOGOS 1BB	WORD 479B
	KATAGGELLW 1	PROCLAIM 410C		PARR8SIAZOMAI 1	SPEAK FREELY 636B
	NOMOS 3	LAW 544C		STREPHW 2AB	TURN 779A
	HOS,H8,HO 16	(REL PRON) 588C	47	EIS 8B	TO BE 229C
39	DIKAIOW 3A	JUSTIFY 196D		ENTELLW	COMMAND 267D
	DIKAIOW 3C	MAKE FREE 197A		ESCHATOS 1	LAST 313D
	PAS 1Cγ	WHOEVER 637B		HOUTW	THUS 602B
	PISTEUW 2B	BELIEVE 667C		HOUTW 2	THUS 602C
40	BLEPW 6	SEE 143B		SWT8RIA 2	DELIVERANCE 809B
	EIPON 4	SAY 225D		TITH8MI 12B	MAKE 824A
	EN 11D	IN 257D		PHWS 3B	LIGHT 880C
	EPERCHOMAI 2A	COME 284D	48	AIWNIOS 3	ETERNAL 28A
	M8 B1B	NOT 519A		DECHOMAI 3B	ACCEPT 176C
41	APHANIZW	RENDER INVISIBLE 124B		ZW8 2Bα	LIFE 341B
	EKDI8GEOMAI	TELL 238A		HOSOS 2	HOW GREAT 590C
	ERGAZOMAI 2A	WORK 307A		PISTEUW 2B	BELIEVE 667C
	ERGON 1Cα	DEED 308A		TASSW 1B	PLACE 813D
	H8MERA 4B	TIME 348B		CHAIRW 1	REJOICE 881D
	THAUMAZW 1Aα	WONDER 352D	48F	LOGOS 1BB	WORD 479B
	KATAPHRON8T8S	DESPISER 421C	49	DIA A12	THROUGH 178C
	M8 DIA	NOT 519B		DIAPHERW 1B	SPREAD 189B
	PISTEUW 1Aα	BELIEVE 666A		CHWRA 1A	COUNTRY 897C
	SIGAW 1B	BE SILENT 757A	50	DIWGMOS	PERSECUTION 200A
	TIS, TI 1Aγ	ANY ONE 827D		EKBALLW 1	DRIVE OUT 236D
42	AXIOW 2B	ASK 78A		EPEGEIRW	ROUSE UP 283D
	EIS 2AB	FOR 228A		EPI IIIIAε	AGAINST 288B
	METAXU 1BB	AFTERWARD 514B		EUSCH8MWN 2	PROMINENT 327C
	PARAKALEW 3	IMPLORE 622D		THLIPSIS 1	TRIBULATION 362D
	R8MA 2	WORD 743A		HORION	BOUNDARY 584D
	SABBATON 1A	SABBATH 746B		PAROTRUNW	AROUSE 635A
43	IOUDAIOS 2C	JEWISH 380B		PRWTOS 1Cβ	FIRST 733C
	LUW 3	DESTROY 485A		SEBW 2A	WORSHIP 753C
	HOSTIS 3	WHOEVER 591B	51	EKTINASSW 1	SHAKE OFF 245B
	PEITHW 1B	CONVINCE 644D		IKONION	ICONIUM 375D
	POLUS 12Aα	MANY 694D		KATANTAW 1	ARRIVE 416B
	PROS8LUTOS	PROSELYTE 722B		KONIORTOS	DUST 444A
	PROSLALEW	SPEAK TO 724B	52	MATH8T8S 2Bγ	DISCIPLE 487A
	PROSMENW 1B	REMAIN 724D		PL8ROW 1B	MAKE FULL 677A
	SEBW 2A	WORSHIP 753C		PNEUMA 6A	SPIRIT 683D
	SUNAGWG8 5	PLACE OF ASSEMBLY 790D		CHARA 1	JOY 883D
	PH8MIZW	SPREAD 864B			
	CHARIS 3B	FAVOR 886B			ACTS 14
44	ECHW III3	HOLD FAST 334C			
	LOGOS 1BB	WORD 479B	1	AUTOS 4B	THE SAME 123C
	LOGOS 1BB	WORD 479B		GINOMAI I3E	TAKE PLACE 158B
	POLIS 3	CITY 692C		EISERCHOMAI 1AB	COME 231D
	SABBATON 1A	SABBATH 746B		HELL8N 2A	GENTILE 251C
	SUNAGW 2	GATHER 790A		IKONION	ICONIUM 375D
	SUNAGW 2	GATHER 790B		KATA II5Bα	ACCORDING TO 408C
	SCHEDON	NEARLY 804D		HOUTW 2	THUS 602C
45	ANTILEGW 1	CONTRADICT 74A		PISTEUW 2B	BELIEVE 667C

1	PL8THOS 2Bα	QUANTITY 674C	8	ADUNATOS 1A	POWERLESS 18C
	POLUS 11Bα	MANY 694C		KOILIA 2	BELLY 438B
	HWSTE 2Aβ	THEREFORE 908C		LUSTRA	LYSTRA 483D
1A	IOUDAIOS 2C	JEWISH 380B		OUDEPOTE	NEVER 596D
1B	IOUDAIOS 2C	JEWISH 380B		PERIPATEW	GO ABOUT 654C
2	APEITHEW 3	DISOBEY 82A		PERIPATEW 1C	GO ABOUT 655A
	APEITHEW 2	DISOBEY 82A		TIS, TI 2Aα	ANY ONE 828A
	ARCHISUNAGWGOS	112D		CHWLOS	LAME 897B
	PRESIDENT OF A SYNAGOGUE		9	ATENIZW	LOOK INTENTLY AT 119C
	ARCHWN 2A	AUTHORITIES 113C		ECHW I2Eβ	HAVE 333A
	DIKAIOS 1B	UPRIGHT 194D		PISTIS 2Bα	FAITH 668D
	EIR8N8 1B	PEACE 226B		SWZW 1C	SAVE 806A
	EPAGW	BRING ON 281A		HUPARCHW 2	BE 846A
	EPEGEIRW	ROUSE UP 283D	10	HALLOMAI 1	LEAP 39A
	KAKOW 2	EMBITTER 399B		ANALLOMAI	JUMP UP 56D
	KATA I2Bα	DOWN 406C		MEGAS 2Aγ	GREAT 498D
	PNEUMA 6C	SPIRIT 683D		MEGAS 2Aγ	GREAT 498D
	TACHUS 2B	QUICK 814D		HO,H8,TO IIIF	THE 553A
	PSUCH8 1Bγ	SOUL LIFE 901D		ONOMA I4Cγ	NAME 576A
3	GINOMAI I2A	COME ABOUT !57C		ORTHOS 1A	UPRIGHT 583D
	DIA AIIIIA	BY MEANS OF 179A		PARACHR8MA	AT ONCE 629B
	DIATRIBW	SPEND 189A		PERIPATEW 1C	GO ABOUT 655A
	EPI IIIBγ	ON 287A		PHWN8 2A	VOICE 878D
	HIKANOS 1B	SUFFICIENT 375A	11	ANTHRWPOS 1Aβ	MAN 67C
	LOGOS 1Bβ	WORD 479C		EPAIRW 1	RAISE UP 281C
	MARTUREW 1C	494A		THEOS 1	GOD 357B
	TESTIFY FAVORABLY			KATABAINW 1Aδ	COME DOWN 409C
	MEN 2E	(PARTICLE) 504C		LEGW 15	SAY 469D
	PARR8SIAZOMAI 1	SPEAK FREELY 636B		LUKAONISTI	LYCAONIAN LANGUAGE 482C
	S8MEION 2A	SIGN 755D		HOMOIOW 1	MAKE LIKE 570B
	CHARIS 3B	FAVOR 886B		OCHLOS 1	CROWD 605D
	CHEIR 1	HAND 888C		POIEW 11Bβ	DO 687C
*	CHRONOS	TIME 896B		PHWN8 2A	VOICE 878D
4	EIMI IIII0	TO BE 224D	12	HERM8S 1	HERMES 310A
	MEN 1C	(PARTICLE) 504A		ZEUS	ZEUS 338A
	HO,H8,TO I2	THE 552A		H8GEOMAI 1	LEAD 344B
	PL8THOS 2Bγ	QUANTITY 674D		KALEW 1Aβ	CALL 399D
	POLIS 1	CITY 692A		LOGOS 1Aβ	WORD 478B
	SUN 1C	WITH 789B	13	EPITHUW	OFFER A SACRIFICE 293D
	SCHIZW 2B	SPLIT 805B		ZEUS	ZEUS 338A
5	ARCHWN 2A	AUTHORITIES 113C		THELW 2	WISH 355D
	GINOMAI 11Bβ	COME ABOUT 157B		THUW 1	SACRIFICE 367D
	ETHNOS 2	GENTILES 217C		HIEREUS 1A	PRIEST 372C
	IOUDAIOS 2C	JEWISH 380B		OCHLOS 1	CROWD 605D
	LITHOBOLEW 1	THROW STONES 475B		POLIS 1	CITY 692B
	HORM8	IMPULSE 585C		PRO 1	BEFORE 708B
	SUN 4B	WITH 789D		PULWN 1	GATE 736D
	HUBRIZW	MISTREAT 839B		STEMMA	GARLAND OF FLOWERS 773D
	HWS IVIA	WHEN 907A		TAUROS	BULL 813D
6	DERB8	DERBE 174C		PHERW 4Bα	BEAR 863B
	KATAPHEUGW 1	FLEE 421A	14	APOSTOLOS 3	APOSTLES 99B
	LUKAONIA	LYCAONIA 482C		DIA(R)R8GNUMI 1	TEAR 187A
	LUSTRA	LYSTRA 483D		EKP8DAW 1	RUSH OUT 243A
	PERICHWROS	NEIGHBORING 659B		HIMATION 2	GARMENT 377B
	POLIS 1	CITY 692A		OCHLOS 1	CROWD 605C
	SUNORAW	PERCEIVE 799B	14F	KRAZW 2A	CALL 448D
7	DIATRIBW	STAY 189A	15	AN8R 1	MAN 66A
	EUAGGELIZW 2Aδ	PREACH 318A		ANTHRWPOS 1Aβ	MAN 67C
	KAKEI 1	AND THERE 397C		EPI IIIBδ	TOWARD 289A
	KINEW 2B	MOVE 433C		EPISTREPHW 1Bβ	TURN 301B
	PL8THOS 2Bγ	QUANTITY 674D		EUAGGELIZW 2Aβ	PREACH 317D
	POLUPL8THEIA	LARGE CROWD 693D		ZAW 1Aε	LIVE 336D
7-21	LUSTRA	LYSTRA 483D		THALASSA 1A	SEA 350D

15 MATAIOS | IDLE 496D
  HOMOIOPATH8S | 569C
  WITH THE SAME NATURE
  OURANOS IA« | HEAVEN 598B
  PAS IDγ | ALL 637D
  TIS, TI 3A | WHICH 827B
15A POIEW IIB« | DO 687D
15B POIEW IIAβ | DO 687B
16 GENEA 3B | AGE 153C
  EAW I | LET 211D
  HODOS 2B | WAY 557A
  PAROICHOMAI | PASS BY 634D
  PAS ID« | ALL 637C
  POREUW 2C | PROCEED 699C
17 AGATHOERGEW | DO GOOD 2B
  AMARTUROS | WITHOUT WITNESS 43C
  APHI8MI 4 | TOLERATE 126A
  DIDWMI IBγ | GIVE 192B
  EMPI(M)PL8MI I | FILL 255C
  EMPI(M)PL8MI 2 | FILL 255C
  EUPHROSUN8 | JOY 328B
  KAI IID | AND 392D
  KAIROS I | TIME 395C
  KAITOI | AND YET 396D
  KAITOIGE | AND YET 397A
  KARDIA IA | HEART 404B
  KARPOPHOROS | FRUITBEARING 406B
  OURANOTHEN | FROM HEAVEN 598A
  TROPH8 I | FOOD 835C
  HUETOS | RAIN 841A
18 THUW I | SACRIFICE 367D
  IDIOS 3B | ONES OWN 370D
  KATAPAUW IB« | BRING TO REST 417A
  M8 AIIID« | NOT 518A
  MOGIS | WITH DIFFICULTY 527C
  MOLIS I | WITH DIFFICULTY 528C
  HO,H8,TO II486 | THE 554A
18F OCHLOS I | CROWD 605D
19 AL8TH8S 2 | TRUE 368
  ANTIOCHEIA 2 | ANTIOCH 74D
  DIATRIBW | STAY 189A
  EXW 2B | OUTSIDE 279B
  EPERCHOMAI IA | COME 284D
  EPISEIW 2 | INCITE 298B
  THN8SKW I | DIE 363A
  IKONION | ICONIUM 375D
  LITHAZW | STONE 475A
  NOMIZW 2 | THINK 543B
  PARR8SIA 2 | PUBLICLY 636A
  PEITHW IC | CONVINCE 645A
  SURW | DRAG 802B
  PSEUDOMAI I | LIE 900A
20 DERB8 | DERBE 174C
  EISERCHOMAI IAβ | COME 231D
  EPAURION | NEXT DAY 283C
  KUKLOW I | SURROUND 457D
  SUN IB | WITH 789B
21 ANTIOCHEIA 2 | ANTIOCH 74D
  EKEINOS 2A | THAT 239B
  EUAGGELIZW 2Aγ | PREACH 317D
  HIKANOS IC | SUFFICIENT 375D
  IKONION | ICONIUM 375D
  LUSTRA | LYSTRA 483D

21 MATH8TEUW 3 | MAKE A DISCIPLE 486D
  POLIS 3 | CITY 692C
22 BASILEIA 3B | KINGDOM 134D
  BASILEIA 3G | KINGDOM 135A
  DEI 4 | IT IS NECESSARY 171B
  EMMENW 2 | PERSEVERE IN 254D
  EPIST8RIZW | STRENGTHEN 300C
  THLIPSIS I | TRIBULATION 363A
  HOTI ID« | THAT 593B
  PARAKALEW 2 | APPEAL TO 622C
  PISTIS 2D« | FAITH 669A
  POLUS IIA« | MANY 694A
  PSUCH8 IBγ | SOUL LIFE 901D
23 EKKL8SIA 4B | CHURCH 240C
  META AIII2 | WITH 511A
  N8STEIA 2B | FASTING 540B
  PARATITH8MI 2Bβ | 628C
  PLACE BESIDE
  PISTEUW | BELIEVE 665D
  PISTEUW 2Aβ | BELIEVE 667B
  PRESBUTEROS 2B« | OLDER 707A
  CHEIROTONEW | CHOOSE 889B
24 DIERCHOMAI IA | GO THROUGH 193C
  PAMPHULIA | PAMPHYLIA 612B
25 ATTALEIA | ATTALIA 120B
  KATABAINW IAβ | COME DOWN 409B
  LALEW 2B | SPEAK 464C
  LOGOS IBβ | WORD 479C
  PERG8 | PERGA 650A
26 ANTIOCHEIA I | ANTIOCH 74D
  APOPLEW | SAIL AWAY 96D
  ERGON 2 | WORK 308B
  KAKEITHEN I | AND FROM THERE 397C
  HOTHEN I | FROM WHICH 557D
  PARADIDWMI | GIVE OVER 619D
  PARADIDWMI 2 | GIVE OVER 620D
  PL8ROW 5 | MAKE FULL 677D
  CHARIS 2A | FAVOR 885C
27 ANAGGELLW I | TO REPORT 50D
  ANOIGW IA | OPEN 70C
  ETHNOS 2 | GENTILES 217C
  THURA 2C | DOOR 366C
  META AIIICγ | WITH 510B
  HOSOS 2 | HOW GREAT 590C
  PARAGINOMAI I | COME 618D
  PISTIS 2D« | FAITH 669B
  POIEW IIDβ | DO 688D
  SUNAGW 2 | GATHER 790A
28 DIATRIBW | SPEND 189A
  HOTHEN I | FROM WHICH 557D
  OLIGOS 2C | LITTLE 566C
  SUN IA | WITH 789A
  CHRONOS | TIME 896B

ACTS 15

1 DIDASKW 2E | TEACH 191B
  ETHOS 2 | CUSTOM 217D
  IOUDAIA I | JUDAEA 379D
  KATERCHOMAI I | COME DOWN 423A
  HOTI 2 | THAT 593D
  PERIPATEW 2Aβ | GO ABOUT 655B
  PERITEMNW I | CUT AROUND 658A

1	SWZW 2B	SAVE 806B
	TIS, TI IAα	ANY ONE 827C
2	ANABAINW IAα	GO UP 49D
	GINOMAI IIBβ	COME ABOUT 157B
	DIISCHURIZOMAI	INSIST 194C
	Z8T8SIS 3	DISCUSSION 339D
	Z8T8MA	ISSUE 339D
	OLIGOS 2B	LITTLE 566C
	PERI IE	ABOUT 650B
	PRESBUTEROS 2Bα	OLDER 707A
	STASIS 3	UPRISING 772A
	SUZ8T8SIS	DISPUTE 783C
	TASSW 2A	PLACE 813D
	TIS, TI 2D	ANY ONE 828B
	TIS, TI 2Aγ	ANY ONE 828B
3	DIERCHOMAI IA	GO THROUGH 193C
	ETHNOS 2	GENTILES 217C
	EKDI8GEOMAI	TELL 238A
	EPISTROPH8 2	CONVERSION 301C
	MEN 2E	(PARTICLE) 504C
	HO,H8,TO I3	THE 552A
	POIEW IIBγ	DO 687C
	PROPEMPW 2	ACCOMPANY 716B
	SAMAREIA	SAMARIA 748D
	PHOINIK8	PHOENICIA 872A
	CHARA I	JOY 883C
	CHARA I	JOY 883D
4	ANAGGELLW I	TO REPORT 50D
	MEGALWS	HEARTILY 498B
	META AIIICγ	WITH 510B
	PARADECHOMAI 2	ACCEPT 619C
	POIEW IIDβ	DO 688D
	PRESBUTEROS 2Bα	OLDER 707A
5	HAIRESIS IA	SECT 23B
	APO IVIB	FROM 87A
	DEI 3	IT IS NECESSARY 171B
	EXANIST8MI 2A	RAISE UP 272B
	NOMOS 3	LAW 544C
	PARAGGELLW	GIVE ORDERS 618C
	PERITEMNW I	CUT AROUND 658A
	PISTEUW 2B	BELIEVE 667C
	T8REW 5	KEEP 822D
6	EIDON 4	CONSIDER 220A
	LOGOS IAε	MATTER 478D
	PRESBUTEROS 2Bα	OLDER 707A
	SUNAGW 2	GATHER 790B
7	ADELPHOS 2	BROTHER 16A
	AN8R I	MAN 66A
	ARCHAIOS 2	ANCIENT 111A
	GINOMAI IIBβ	COME ABOUT 157B
	ETHNOS 2	GENTILES 217C
	EKLEGOMAI 3C	CHOOSE 241D
	EPISTAMAI 2	KNOW 300A
	EUAGGELION IB	GOSPEL 318A
	Z8T8SIS 3	DISCUSSION 339D
	H8MERA 4B	TIME 348B
	LOGOS IBβ	WORD 479C
	PETROS	PETER 661A
	PISTEUW 2B	BELIEVE 667C
	POLUS IIBβ	MANY 694C
	STOMA IA	MOUTH 777B
	SUZ8T8SIS	DISPUTE 783C
8	KATHWS I	JUST AS 392A

8	KARDIOGNWST8S	405C
	KNOWER OF HEARTS	
	MARTUREW IA	BEAR WITNESS 493D
	PEIRAZW 2E	TRY 646C
	PNEUMA 5Cα	SPIRIT 682D
9	DIAKRINW IB	DIFFERENTIATE 184B
	KATHARIZW 2Bα	CLEANSE 388C
	KARDIA IBδ	HEART 404D
	METAXU 2B	BETWEEN 514C
	OUDEIS 2Bγ	IN NO RESPECT 596C
	PISTIS 2Dα	FAITH 669A
10	BASTAZW 2Bα	CARRY 137A
	EPI IIIAβ	ON 288A
	EPITITH8MI IAα	PUT UPON 302D
	ZUGOS I	YOKE 340B
	ISCHUW 2B	BE STRONG 384C
	MATH8T8S 2Bγ	DISCIPLE 487A
	NUN 2	NOW 548A
	OUN 5	THEREFORE 597D
	OUTE	NOT 600C
	PEIRAZW 2E	TRY 646C
	TRACH8LOS	NECK 832D
11	KAKEINOS IB	AND HE 397C
	KATA II5Bα	ACCORDING TO 408C
	KURIOS 2Cγ	LORD 461A
	HOS,H8,HO I5B	(REL PRON) 588B
	PISTEUW IAγ	BELIEVE 666B
	SWZW 2B	SAVE 806B
	TROPOS I	MANNER 835A
	CHARIS 2A	FAVOR 885C
12	DIA AIII2A	BY 179C
	EX8GEOMAI	EXPLAIN 275B
	PAS ICα	ALL 637B
	PL8THOS 2Bδ	QUANTITY 674D
	S8MEION 2A	SIGN 755D
	SIGAW IA	BE SILENT 757A
	SUGKATATITH8MI	AGREE WITH 781B
13	ADELPHOS 2	BROTHER 16A
	AN8R I	MAN 66A
	IAKWBOS 3	JAMES 368C
	META BII4A	AFTER 511D
	SIGAW IB	BE SILENT 757A
14	EX8GEOMAI	EXPLAIN 275B
	EPISKEPTOMAI 3	VISIT 298C
	KATHWS 5	HOW 392C
	LAOS 3B	PEOPLE 468B
	PETROS	PETER 661A
	SUMEWN 5	SYMEON 786A
15	GRAPHW 2C	WRITE 165D
	KATHWS I	JUST AS 392A
	LOGOS IAζ	MATTER 479A
	SUMPHWNEW IA	MATCH 788C
16	ANASTREPHW 3B	RETURN 61A
	ANORTHOW	REBUILD 71D
	DAUID	DAVID 170B
	EPISTREPHW IBβ	TURN 301B
	KATASKAPTW	TEAR DOWN 419B
	KATASTREPHW 2	DESTROY 420B
	PIPTW IBβ	FALL 665C
	SK8N8	TENT 762B
16A	ANOIKODOMEW	BUILD UP AGAIN 71A
16B	ANOIKODOMEW	BUILD UP AGAIN 71A
17	AN 4	(PARTICLE) 48D

17	AUTOS 3D	(OBLIQUE CASE)	123B
	EKZ8TEW 1	SEEK OUT	239C
	EPI IIIIAζ	ON	288C
	EPIKALEW 1Bβ	NAME	294A
	KATALOIPOS	LEFT	415B
	ONOMA 14B	NAME	575A
	HOPWS 2Aβ	IN ORDER THAT	580D
	HOS,H8,HO 13A	(REL PRON)	587C
	HOS,H8,HO 13Bγ	(REL PRON)	587D
17F	GNWSTOS 1A	KNOWN	163C
18	AIWN 1A	TIME	26C
19	DIO	THEREFORE	197D
	EPISTREPHW 1Bβ	TURN	301B
	THEOS 3A	GOD	357D
	KRINW 2	JUDGE	452C
	PARENOCHLEW	TROUBLE	631A
20	HAIMA 1B	BLOOD	22B
	ALISG8MA	POLLUTION	37B
	*APECHW 3	KEEP AWAY	84C
	EIDWLON 2	IDOL	220D
	EPISTELLW	WRITE	300C
	HO,H8,TO 114Bε	THE	554A
	PNIKTOS	STRANGLED	686B
	PORNEIA 1	PROSTITUTION	700A
21	ANAGINWSKW 2	READ	51C
	ARCHAIOS 2	ANCIENT	111A
	GENEA 3B	AGE	153C
	EK 5A	FROM	235C
	KATA III0	(DISTRIBUTIVE)	407B
	K8RUSSW 28β	ANNOUNCE	432C
	POLIS 1	CITY	692B
	SABBATON 1A	SABBATH	746B
21B	KATA II2C	EVERY	407C
22	BARABBAS 2	BARABBAS	132C
	BARSABBAS 2	BARSABBAS	133D
	DOKEW 3B	SEEM	201C
	EK 1B	AWAY FROM	233C
	EKKL8SIA 4B	CHURCH	240C
	EKLEGOMAI 1	CHOOSE	241D
	H8GEOMAI 1	LEAD	344B
	IOUDAS 7	JUDAS	381A
	KALEW 1Aγ	CALL	400A
	PEMPW 1	SEND	647C
	SILAS	SILAS	758A
22F	PRESBUTEROS 2Bα	OLDER	707A
22FF	ANTIOCHEIA 1	ANTIOCH	74D
23	GRAPHW 2D	WRITE	166B
	DIA AIIIIA	BY MEANS OF	179A
	EPISTOL8	LETTER	300D
	KATA IIIA	ALONG	407A
	KILIKIA	CILICIA	433B
	HODE 3	THIS	555D
	PERIECHW 2A	SEIZE	652D
	SURIA	SYRIA	801C
	CHAIRW 2B	REJOICE	882B
	CHEIR 1	HAND	888C
24	ANASKEUAZW	TEAR DOWN	59D
	DIASTELLW	ORDER	187D
	EKTARASSW	AGITATE	244C
	LOGOS 1Aδ	WORD	478D
	PERITEMNW 1	CUT AROUND	658A
	TARASSW 2	STIR UP	813A
	TIS, TI 1Aα	ANY ONE	827D

24	PSUCH8 1Bγ	SOUL LIFE	901D
25	AGAP8TOS 2	BELOVED	6C
	GINOMAI 14Cθ	COME, GO	159B
	DOKEW 3B	SEEM	201C
	EKLEGOMAI 1	CHOOSE	241D
	HOMOTHUMADON	WITH ONE MIND	569C
	PEMPW 1	SEND	647C
26	KURIOS 2Cγ	LORD	461B
	ONOMA 14Cθ	NAME	576D
	PARADIDWMI	GIVE OVER	619C
	PARADIDWMI 1A	GIVE OVER	619D
	PEIRASMOS 2B	TEST	646D
	PSUCH8 1Aβ	SOUL LIFE	901C
27	AUTOS 4B	THE SAME	123B
	DIA AIIIIB	BY MEANS OF	179A
	IOUDAS 7	JUDAS	381A
	LOGOS 1Aα	WORD	478B
	SILAS	SILAS	758A
28	BAROS 1	WEIGHT	133C
	DOKEW 3B	SEEM	201C
	EPANAGKES	NECESSARILY	282B
	EPITITH8MI 1Aβ	INFLICT BLOWS	303A
	PL8N 2	BUT	675C
	PNEUMA 5Cα	SPIRIT	682D
	POLUS II	MANY	695C
	POLUS II2C	MANY	696A
29	HAIMA 1B	BLOOD	22B
	APECHW 3	KEEP AWAY	84C
	DIAT8REW	KEEP	188D
	EIDWLOTHUTOS	MEAT OFFERED TO AN IDOL	220C
	EK 1D	AWAY FROM	233D
	EU	WELL	317B
	M8 AI5	NOT	517D
	OU 5A	NO	595A
	PNIKTOS	STRANGLED	686B
	PRASSW 2A	DO	705C
	PRASSW 2B	DO	705C
	RWNNUMI	BE STRONG	745D
	PHERW 3B	BEAR	863A
30	APOLUW 2B	SEND AWAY	96B
	EPIDIDWMI 1	GIVE	292B
	EPISTOL8	LETTER	300D
	KATERCHOMAI 1	COME DOWN	423A
	MEN 2E	(PARTICLE)	504C
	HO,H8,TO I3	THE	552A
	OLIGOS 1A	FEW	566B
	PL8THOS 2B6	QUANTITY	674D
	SUNAGW 2	GATHER	790A
31	ANAGINWSKW 1	READ	51B
	PARAKL8SIS 3	COMFORT	623C
	CHAIRW 1	REJOICE	881B
32	DIA AIIIIB	BY MEANS OF	179B
	EPIST8RIZW	STRENGTHEN	300C
	IOUDAS 7	JUDAS	381A
	LOGOS 1Aβ	WORD	478C
	PARAKALEW 2	APPEAL TO	622C
	POLUS IIBα	MANY	694C
	PROPH8T8S 5	PROPHET	731B
	SILAS	SILAS	758A
33	APO I2	FROM	85D
	APOLUW 2B	SEND AWAY	96B

33 EIR8N8 2	PEACE	226C
META AIII	WITH	511A
POIEW IIE6	DO	689A
CHRONOS	TIME	896B
34 AUTOU	THERE	123C
IOUDAS 7	JUDAS	381A
MONOS IA«	ONLY	529C
SILAS	SILAS	758A
35 DIATRIBW	STAY	189A
DIDASKW 2B	TEACH	191A
DIDASKW 2F	TEACH	191B
HETEROS 1B8	ANOTHER	315B
EUAGGELIZW 2A8	PREACH	317D
LOGOS 1B8	WORD	479B
POLUS IIA«	MANY	694B
36 D8 2	NOW	177B
EPISKEPTOMAI 2	VISIT	298C
EPISTREPHW 1B«	TURN	301A
ECHW III	BE	334B
H8MERA 2	DAY	347B
KATA IIID	(DISTRIBUTIVE)	407C
KATAGGELLW I	PROCLAIM	410C
LOGOS 1B8	WORD	479B
META 8III	AFTER	511B
HOS,H8,HO I3B8	(REL PRON)	587D
POLIS I	CITY	692B
PWS 2A	HOW	739D
TIS, TI 2D	ANY ONE	828B
36=40 BARNABAS	BARNABAS	133C
37 BOULEUW 2	DECIDE	145A
BOULOMAI 2A8	DESIRE	145D
IWAN(N)8S 6	JOHN	385D
KALEW IAϒ	CALL	400A
MARKOS	MARK	493C
37F SUMPARALAMBANW	TAKE ALONG	786D
38 AXIOW 2A CONSIDER SUITABLE		78A
APO IVIA8	FROM	86D
APHIST8MI 2A	WITHDRAW	126C
ERGON 2	WORK	308B
M8 AIII8ß	NOT	518A
HOUTOS IA«	THIS	601B
PAMPHULIA	PAMPHYLIA	612B
SUNERCHOMAI 2	ASSEMBLE	796A
39 ALL8LWN	EACH OTHER	38D
APOCHWRIZW	SEPARATE	101D
GINOMAI IIB8	COME ABOUT	157B
EKPLEW	SAIL AWAY	243C
KUPROS	CYPRUS	458D
MARKOS	MARK	493C
PARALAMBANW I	TAKE	624D
PAROXUSMOS 2		635A
A SHARP DISAGREEMENT		
HWSTE 2A8	THEREFORE	908C
40 EPIDECHOMAI I	RECEIVE	292A
EPILEGW 2	CHOOSE	295C
PARADIDWMI 2	GIVE OVER	620C
CHARIS 2A	FAVOR	885C
41 DIERCHOMAI IA	GO THROUGH	193C
EKKL8SIA 4B	CHURCH	240C
EPIST8RIZW	STRENGTHEN	300C
KILIKIA	CILICIA	433B
SURIA	SYRIA	801D

ACTS 16

I	DERB8	DERBE	174C
	HELL8N 2A	GENTILE	251C
	IDOU 1B8	BEHOLD	371C
	IOUDAIOS I	JEWISH	380A
	KATANTAW I	ARRIVE	416B
	ONOMA II	NAME	574A
	PISTOS 2	TRUSTWORTHY	671A
	HUIOS IA«	SON	841B
IF	LUSTRA	LYSTRA	483D
IFF	TIMOTHEOS	TIMOTHY	826A
2	IKONION	ICONIUM	375D
	MARTUREW 2B	BE APPROVED	494B
3	HAPAS 2	ALL	81A
	DIA BIII	BECAUSE OF	180A
	EKEINOS 2A	THAT	239B
	HELL8N 2A	GENTILE	251C
	EXERCHOMAI IA8	GO OUT	274A
	THELW I	WISH	355C
	LAMBANW IA	TAKE	465B
	OIDA IC	KNOW	558B
	PERITEMNW I	CUT AROUND	658A
	TOPOS IA	PLACE	830A
	HUPARCHW 2	BE	846A
4	HAMA IA	TOGETHER	41B
	DIAPOREUOMAI	GO THROUGH	186D
	DOGMA I	DECREE	200C
	KRINW 3	DECIDE	452C
	*PARADIDWMI	GIVE OVER	619C
	PARADIDWMI 3	GIVE OVER	620D
	PARR8SIA 3A	COURAGE	636B
	POLIS I	CITY	692A
	PRESBUTEROS 2B«	OLDER	707A
	PHULASSW IF	WATCH	876C
	HWS IV1B	WHEN	907A
5	ARITHMOS 2	NUMBER	106A
	EKKL8SIA 4B	CHURCH	240C
	H8MERA 2	DAY	347B
	KATA II2C	EVERY	407C
	MEN 2E	(PARTICLE)	504C
	PERISSEUW IA6	BE LEFT OVER	656D
	PISTIS 2D«	FAITH	669A
	STEREOW 2	MAKE FIRM	774B
6	ASIA	ASIA	115C
	GALATIKOS	GALATIAN	149C
	DIERCHOMAI IA	GO THROUGH	193C
	KWLUW I	HINDER	462C
	LALEW 2B	SPEAK	464C
	LOGOS 1B8	WORD	479C
	PAMPHULIA	PAMPHYLIA	612B
	PNEUMA 5C«	SPIRIT	682D
	PNEUMA 6F	SPIRIT	684B
	PHRUGIA	PHRYGIA	875B
	CHWRA 1B	COUNTRY	897C
7	BITHUNIA	BITHYNIA	141A
	EAW I	LET	211D
	ERCHOMAI IIA8	COME	310C
	KATA IIIB	TO	407A
	OU 2D	NO	594C
	PNEUMA 5B	SPIRIT	682C
	PNEUMA 6F	SPIRIT	684B
7F	MUSIA	MYSIA	531D

8 KATABAINW IAβ   COME DOWN   409B
   PARERCHOMAI 2   PASS THROUGH   631D
   TRWAS   TROAS   836D
9 AN8R 3   MAN   66A
   BO8THEW 2   AID   144A
   DIA AIIIB   DURING   178D
   DIABAINW   COME OVER   180D
   HIST8MI II2A   STAND   383B
   MAKEDWN   MACEDONIAN   488B
   NUX IB   NIGHT   548D
   HORAW IA6   SEE   581D
   PARAKALEW IB   INVITE   622B
   PROSWPON IC6   FACE   728D
   HWSEI I   AS   907D
9F   MAKEDONIA   MACEDONIA   488B
9F   HORAMA I   VISION   580D
9F   PNEUMA 6F   SPIRIT   684B
10 DIEGEIRW   AROUSE   193A
   DI8GEOMAI   TELL   194A
   EIDON IA   SEE   219D
   EXERCHOMAI IAε   GO OUT   274B
   EUAGGELIZW 2Aγ   PREACH   317D
   NOEW IB   UNDERSTAND   542C
   PROSKALEW 2B   SUMMON   722D
   SUMBIBAZW 2   UNITE   785C
   HWS IVIA   WHEN   907A
11 ANAGW 3   PUT TO SEA   52D
   EPEIMI   THE NEXT   284A
   EUTHUDROMEW   321A
      RUN A STRAIGHT COURSE
   HO,H8,TO II2B   THE   553C
   SAMOTHRAK8   SAMOTHRACE   749A
   TRWAS   TROAS   836D
12 DIATRIBW   SPEND   189A
   H8MERA 2   DAY   347A
   KAKEITHEN I   AND FROM THERE   397C
   KEPHAL8 2B   HEAD   431C
   KOLWNIA   COLONY   443C
   MAKEDONIA   MACEDONIA   488B
   MERIS I   DISTRICT   506B
   HOSTIS 3   WHOEVER   591B
   PRWTOS IB   FIRST   733A
   PHILIPPOI   PHILIPPI   867C
13 EXERCHOMAI IAα   GO OUT   274A
   EXW 2B   OUTSIDE   279B
   KATHIZW 2Aα   SIT DOWN   390D
   NOMIZW I   BE THE CUSTOM   543B
   NOMIZW 2   THINK   543B
   HOU IAβ   WHERE   594A
   PARA IIIIBβ   ALONG   616A
   POTAMOS I   RIVER   701B
   PROSEUCH8 2   CHAPEL   720C
   PROSEUCH8 2   CHAPEL   720D
   PUL8 I   GATE   736C
   SABBATON IBβ   SABBATH   746C
   SUNERCHOMAI IA   ASSEMBLE   795D
14 DIANOIGW IB   OPEN   186B
   THUATIRA   THYATIRA   365B
   KARDIA IBβ   HEART   404D
   LALEW 2Aς   SPEAK   464C
   LUDIA   LYDIA   482C
   ONOMA II   NAME   574A
   POLIS I   CITY   692B

14 PORPHUROPWLIS   700D
      DEALER IN PURPLE CLOTH
   PROSECHW IAβ   721C
      PAY ATTENTION TO
   SEBW 2A   WORSHIP   753C
15 EISERCHOMAI IAβ   COME   231D
   KRINW 2   JUDGE   452B
   PARABIAZOMAI   USE FORCE   617B
   PARAKALEW IB   INVITE   622B
   PISTOS 2   TRUSTWORTHY   671A
   HWS IVIA   WHEN   907A
15B OIKOS IAα   HOUSE   563A
16*APANTAW   MEET   79D
   GINOMAI I3E   TAKE PLACE   158B
   ERGASIA 4   TRADE   307C
   KURIOS IAα   OWNER   460A
   KURIOS IAβ   LORD   460A
   MANTEUOMAI I   PROPHESY   492A
   PAIDISK8   MAID   609B
   PARECHW IC   CAUSE   632A
   PNEUMA 4C   SPIRIT   682A
   POLUS IIBα   MANY   694C
   PROSEUCH8 2   CHAPEL   720C
   PROSEUCH8 2   CHAPEL   720D
   PUTHWN   THE PYTHON   736B
   HUPANTAW   GO TO MEET   845C
17 DOULOS 4   SLAVE   205A
   KATAGGELLW I   PROCLAIM   410C
   KATAKOLOUTHEW   FOLLOW   412D
   HODOS 2A   WAY   556D
   SWT8RIA 2   DELIVERANCE   809A
   HUPSISTOS 2   HIGHEST   858B
18 DIAPONEOMAI   BE DISTURBED   186D
   EXERCHOMAI IA6   GO OUT   274A
   EPI III2B   ON   289B
   EPISTREPHW IBα   TURN   301A
   H8MERA 2   DAY   347B
   ONOMA I4Cγ   NAME   576A
   PARAGGELLW   GIVE ORDERS   618C
   PNEUMA 4C   SPIRIT   682A
   HWRA 2B   TIME OF DAY   904D
19 AGORA   MARKET PLACE   12B
   APOSTEREW   STEAL   98D
   AREIOSPAGO   AREOPAGUS   104D
   ARCHWN 2B   AUTHORITIES   113C
   HELKW IA   DRAG   251A
   ELPIS I   HOPE   252B
   EXERCHOMAI 2Bγ   GO OUT   274D
   EPI IIIAγ   ON   288B
   EPILAMBANOMAI I   GRASP   295A
   KURIOS IAα   OWNER   460A
   KURIOS IAβ   LORD   460A
   PAIDISK8   MAID   609B
20 EKTARASSW   AGITATE   244C
   POLIS 3   CITY   692C
   PROSAGW IA   BRING   718B
   STRAT8GOS I CHIEF MAGISTRATE   778B
21 ETHOS 2   CUSTOM   217D
   EIMI II8   TO BE   223D
   EXESTI 2   IT IS POSSIBLE   274D
   8THOS   CUSTOM   345B
   KATAGGELLW I   PROCLAIM   410C
   PARADECHOMAI I   ACCEPT   619C

21	RWMAIOS	ROMAN	745C
22	HIMATION 2	GARMENT	377B
	KELEUW	COMMAND	428C
	PERI(R)R8GNUMI	TEAR OFF	656A
	RABDIZW	BEAT WITH A ROD	740C
	STRAT8GOS I	CHIEF MAGISTRATE	778B
	SUNEPHIST8MI	JOIN IN ATTACK	796D
23	ASPHALWS I	SECURELY	118D
	DESMOPHULAX	JAILER	175B
	EPITITH8MI IAβ		303A
	INFLICT BLOWS		
	PARAGGELLW	GIVE ORDERS	618C
	PL8G8 I	BLOW	674A
	T8REW I	GUARD	822B
23F	PHULAK8 3	GUARD	875D
24	ASPHALIZW I	GUARD	118D
	ESWTEROS	INNER	314C
	XULON 2A	WOOD	551B
	PARAGGELIA	ORDER	618B
	TOIOUTOS 2Aβ	SUCH A KIND	829A
25	DESMIOS	PRISONER	175A
	EPAKROAOMAI	LISTEN TO	282B
	KATA II2B	TOWARD	407C
	MESONUKTION	MIDNIGHT	508B
	MESOS 2	THE MIDDLE	509A
	NUX IA	NIGHT	548C
	HUMNEW I	SING THE PRAISE OF	844A
26	ANALUW I	LOOSE	57A
	ANI8MI I	LOOSEN	69A
	APHNW	SUDDENLY	126C
	GINOMAI II8α	COME ABOUT	157B
	DESMOS I	FETTER	175A
	DESMWT8RION	PRISON	175B
	MEGAS 2Aγ	GREAT	499A
	PARACHR8MA	AT ONCE	629B
	SALEUW I	SHAKE	747D
	SEISMOS	SHAKING	753D
	TE 3B	AND	815C
26A	PAS IDα	ALL	637C
26F	ANOIGW IA	OPEN	70B
26F	THURA IA	DOOR	366B
27	ANAIREW IA	DO AWAY WITH	54C
	GINOMAI I4B	BECOME	158D
	DESMIOS	PRISONER	175A
	DESMOPHULAX	JAILER	175B
	EKPHEUGW 2A	RUN AWAY	246B
	EXUPNOS	AWAKEN	278D
	MACHAIRA I	SWORD	497B
	MELLW ICα	BE ABOUT TO	502A
	NOMIZW 2	THINK	543B
	SPAW	DRAW	768B
	PHULAK8 3	GUARD	875C
28	HAPAS 2	ALL	81A
	EIMI II9A	TO BE	223D
	ENTHADE 2	HERE	265C
	KAKOS 2	EVIL	398D
	MEGAS 2Aγ	GREAT	498D
	PRASSW IA	DO	705B
	SEAUTOU 2	YOURSELF	753A
*PHWNEW IB		CRY OUT	878B
29	AITEW	ASK	25B
	EISP8DAW	LEAP IN	232D
	ENTROMOS	TREMBLING	269B
29	POUS IA	FOOT	703B
	PROSPIPTW I	FALL DOWN BEFORE	725B
	PHWS IBα	LIGHT	879D
30	ASPHALIZW I	GUARD	118D
	DEI 6	IT IS NECESSARY	171C
	EXW IB	OUTSIDE	279A
	HINA IIA	IN ORDER THAT	377C
	KURIOS IB	LORD	460B
	LOIPOS 2Bα	THE OTHERS	481A
	PROAGW I	LEAD	708D
30F	SWZW 2B	SAVE	806B
31	EPI IIIIBε	TOWARD	289A
	KURIOS 2Cγ	LORD	461A
	OIKOS 2	HOUSEHOLD	563C
	PISTEUW 2A6	BELIEVE	667B
32	LALEW 2B	SPEAK	464C
	LOGOS IBβ	WORD	479B
	OIKIA IA	HOUSE	560A
	PAS IDγ	ALL	637D
33	BAPTIZW 2Bα	BAPTIZE	131C
	LOUW I	BATHE	482A
	NUX IA	NIGHT	548C
	HO,H8,TO II7	THE	554C
	PARALAMBANW I	TAKE	624D
	PARACHR8MA	AT ONCE	629B
	PL8G8 2	BLOW	674A
	HWRA 3	TIME OF DAY	905A
34	AGALLIAW	BE GLAD	4A
	ANAGW I	LEAD	52D
	OIKOS IAα	HOUSE	563A
	PANOIKEI		612D
	WITH WHOLE HOUSEHOLD		
	PARATITH8MI IA	PLACE BESIDE	628B
	PISTEUW 2Aα	BELIEVE	667A
	PISTEUW 2A6	BELIEVE	667B
	TRAPEZA 3	TABLE	832B
35	AGORA	MARKET PLACE	12B
	ANAMIMN8SKW	REMIND	57C
	GINOMAI IIBγ	COME ABOUT	157B
	ECHTHES	YESTERDAY	331C
	H8MERA IA	DAY	346C
	PARALAMBANW I	TAKE	625A
	RABDOUCHOS	POLICEMAN	740D
	SEISMOS	SHAKING	753D
35F	APOLUW I	SET FREE	96A
35F	STRAT8GOS I		778B
	CHIEF MAGISTRATE		
36	APAGGELLW I	REPORT	78C
	EIR8N8 2	PEACE	226C
	HINA IIIA6	IN ORDER THAT	378B
	NUN IC	NOW	547D
	NUN 2	NOW	548A
	OUN IB	THEREFORE	597B
	POREUW I	PROCEED	699B
37	AKATAKRITOS	UNCONDEMNED	29B
	ALLA IA	BUT, YET	37C
	ANAITIOS	INNOCENT	55A
	ANTHRWPOS 3Aε	MAN	68C
	GAR 3	CERTAINLY	151D
	DERW	BEAT	174D
	D8MOSIOS 2	PUBLIC	178B
	EKBALLW 2	SEND OUT	237A
	EXAGW I	LEAD OUT	271A

37	ERCHOMAI IIA⟨	COME	310D
	LATHRA I	SECRETLY	463D
	NUN IC	NOW	547D
	PH8MI IB⍺	SAY	864A
	PHULAK8 3	GUARD	875D
37F	RWMAIOS	ROMAN	745C
38	APAGGELLW I	REPORT	78C
	RABDOUCHOS	POLICEMAN	740D
	STRAT8GOS I	CHIEF MAGISTRATE	778B
	PHOBEW IA	BE AFRAID	870B
39	EXAGW I	LEAD OUT	271A
	EPIKRAZW	SHOUT THREATS	294D
	ERCHOMAI IIA⟨	COME	310D
	ERWTAW 2	ASK	312B
	M8POTE 2B⍺	(NEG PARTICLE)	521A
	PARAKALEW 5	IMPLORE	623A
	SUSTREPHW 2	BRING TOGETHER	803A
	PHILOS 2A⍺	LOVING	868D
	PHULAK8 3	GUARD	875C
40	DI8GEOMAI	TELL	194A
	EIDON 6	VISIT	220A
	EISERCHOMAI IC	COME	232A
	EXERCHOMAI IA⍺	GO OUT	274A
	LUDIA	LYDIA	482C
	PARAKALEW 2	APPEAL TO	622B
	PHULAK8 3	GUARD	875C

ACTS 17

I	AMPHIPOLIS	AMPHIPOLIS	46D
	APOLLWNIA	APOLLONIA	95A
	DIODEUW I	GO	197D
	THESSALONIK8	THESSALONICA	360C
	HOPOU IA⍺	WHERE	579C
	PROSEUCH8 2	CHAPEL	720D
	SUNAGWG8 2A		790D
	PLACE OF ASSEMBLY		
2	GRAPH8 2B⍺	SCRIPTURE	165B
	DIALEGOMAI I	DISCUSS	184C
	EIWTHA	ACCUSTOMED	233B
	EPI III2B	ON	289B
	KATA II5A⍺	ACCORDING TO	408A
	SABBATON IB⍺	SABBATH	746C
3	ANIST8MI 2A	RISE	69C
	DEI 6A	IT IS NECESSARY	171C
	DIANOIGW 2	EXPLAIN	186C
	EK IB	AWAY FROM	233C
	KATAGGELLW 2	PROCLAIM	410C
	NEKROS 2A	DEAD	537A
	HOS,H8,HO II	(REL PRON)	587A
	PARATITH8MI 2C	PLACE BESIDE	628C
	PASCHW 3A⍺	SUFFER	639C
	CHRISTOS I	ANOINTED ONE	895B
4	HELL8N 2B	GENTILE	251C
	OLIGOS IB	FEW	566C
	OU 2B	NO	594C
	PEITHW 3A	BELIEVE	645B
	PL8THOS 2B⍺	QUANTITY	674C
	POLUS II8⍺	MANY	694C
	PROSKL8ROW	ALLOT	723A
	SEBW 2A	WORSHIP	753C
	TE 2	AND	815B
5	AGORAIOS I	MARKET PEOPLE	13A

5	AN8R 4	MAN	66B
	D8MOS	CROWD	178A
	EPHIST8MI IA	STAND BY	331A
	Z8LOW 2		338C
	BE FILLED WITH JEALOUSY		
	THORUBEW I		363C
	THROW INTO DISORDER		
	OCHLOPOIEW	FORM A MOB	605B
	PON8ROS IB⍺	WICKED	697C
	PROAGW I	LEAD	708D
	PROSLAMBANW 2C	TAKE	724C
	SUSTREPHW I	BRING TOGETHER	803A
5F	TIS, TI 2D	ANY ONE	828B
5⊷7	IASWN I	JASON	369C
6	ANASTATOW	DISTURB	60C
	AREIOSPAGO	AREOPAGUS	104D
	BOAW 2	SHOUT	143D
	DE 4B	BUT, AND	170D
	ENTHADE 2	HERE	265C
	OIKOUMEN8 2B	THE WORLD	564B
	PAREIMI IA	BE PRESENT	629D
	POLITARCH8S	CIVIC MAGISTRATE	692C
	SURW	DRAG	802A
7	APENANTI 2	AGAINST	83C
	DOGMA I	DECREE	200C
	KAISAR	EMPEROR	396C
	LEGW II8β	SAY	469C
	PAS IE8	ALL	637D
	PRASSW	DO	705A
	PRASSW 2A	DO	705C
	HUPODECHOMAI	RECEIVE	852A
8	POLITARCH8S	CIVIC MAGISTRATE	692C
	TARASSW 2	STIR UP	813A
9	IASWN I	JASON	369C
	HIKANOS IC	SUFFICIENT	375B
	LAMBANW 2	RECEIVE	466C
	LOIPOS 2B⍺	THE OTHERS	481A
	PARA I3B	FROM	614D
10	APEIMI II	GO AWAY	82D
	BEROIA	BEROEA	139A
	DIA AIIIB	DURING	178D
	EIS IA⍺	INTO	227B
	EKPEMPW	SEND OUT	243A
	NUX IB	NIGHT	548D
	HOSTIS 3	WHOEVER	591B
	PARAGINOMAI I	COME	618D
	PROSEUCH8 2	CHAPEL	720D
	SUNAGWG8 2A		790C
	PLACE OF ASSEMBLY		
	TE 3A	AND	815C
11	ANAKRINW IA	QUESTION	56A
	GRAPH8 2B⍺	SCRIPTURE	165B
	EI V2C	WHETHER	218D
	EUGEN8S 2	NOBLE MINDED	319B
	ECHW II2	BE	334C
	H8MERA 2	DAY	347B
	THESSALONIK8	THESSALONICA	360C
	KATA II2C	EVERY	407C
	LOGOS IB⍺	WORD	479C
	HOSTIS 2B	WHOEVER	591A
	PAS IA⍺	ALL	637A
	PROTHUMIA	WILLINGNESS	713C
12	HELL8NIS IB	GENTILE	251C

12 EUSCH8MWN 2	PROMINENT	327C
MEN 2E	(PARTICLE)	504C
OLIGOS 1B	FEW	566C
OU 2B	NO	594C
PISTEUW 2B	BELIEVE	667C
POLUS I2Aα	MANY	694D
13 APO IVIB	FROM	86D
BEROIA	BEROEA	139A
DIALIMPANW	STOP	185A
THESSALONIK8	THESSALONICA	360C
KAKEI 2	THERE ALSO	397C
KATAGGELLW I	PROCLAIM	410C
LOGOS IBβ	WORD	479B
OCHLOS I	CROWD	605D
TARASSW 2	STIR UP	813A
HWS IVIA	WHEN	907A
14 EXAPOSTELLW IA	SEND OUT	272D
THALASSA IBβ	SEA	350D
POREUW I	PROCEED	699A
TOTE 2	AT THAT TIME	831D
HUPOMENW I	REMAIN	853C
HWS IV3C	WHEN	907B
14F TIMOTHEOS	TIMOTHY	826A
15 AGW IB	BRING	14B
ATH8NAI	ATHENS	20D
ENTOL8 IB	COMMAND	268C
THESSALIA	THESSALY	360B
HINA IIICα	IN ORDER THAT	378C
KATHIST8MI I	BRING	391B
KWLUW I	HINDER	462C
PARERCHOMAI 2	PASS THROUGH	631D
TACHEWS 3	QUICKLY	814C
TACHOS	SPEED	814D
HWS IV7	WHEN	907C
15F ATH8NAI	ATHENS	20D
16 EKDECHOMAI	WAIT	237D
THEWREW I	OBSERVE	360D
KATEIDWLOS	FULL OF IDOLS	422B
PAROXUNW	IRRITATE	634D
PNEUMA 3B	SPIRIT	681B
17 AGORA	MARKET PLACE	12B
DIALEGOMAI I	DISCUSS	184C
H8MERA 2	DAY	347D
KATA II2C	EVERY	407C
MEN 2E	(PARTICLE)	504C
PARATUGCHANW		628C
HAPPENED TO BE THERE		
PAS IAα	EVERY EACH	636C
PROSEUCH8 2	CHAPEL	720D
SEBW 2A	WORSHIP	753C
SUNAGWG8 2A		790C
PLACE OF ASSEMBLY		
18 AN 5	(PARTICLE)	48D
ANASTASIS 2A	RESURRECTION	60A
ANASTASIS 2B	RESURRECTION	60B
DAIMONION I	DEITY	168B
DOKEW 2A	SEEM	201A
EPIKOUREIOS	EPICUREAN	294D
EUAGGELIZW 2Aβ	PREACH	317D
EUAGGELIZW 2Aβ	PREACH	317D
THELW 2	WISH	355D
KATAGGELEUS	PREACHER	410B
XENOS IA	STRANGE	550B

18 HO,H8,TO I2	THE	552A
SPERMOLOGOS	PICKING UP SEEDS	769D
STOIKOS	STOIC	776B
SUMBALLW IAα	CONVERSE	785A
PHILOSOPHOS	PHILOSOPHER	869B
18A TIS, TI IAα	ANY ONE	827C
19 AGW IB	BRING	14B
AREIOSPAGO	AREOPAGUS	104D
DIDACH8 2	TEACHING	191C
EPILAMBANOMAI I	GRASP	295A
KAINOS 2	NEW	395A
LALEW 2B	SPEAK	464D
PUNTHANOMAI I	INQUIRE	737A
20 AK08 IC	HEARING	30B
BOULOMAI 2Aβ	DESIRE	145D
EIMI II3	TO BE	222D
EISPHERW 2	BRING IN	233A
THELW 3	WISH	356A
XENIZW 2	SURPRISE	550A
21 ATH8NAIOS	ATHENIAN	20D
ANAKAMPTW IA	RETURN	55B
EIS 5	FOR	229B
EPID8MEW I	STAY	292A
HETEROS IBζ	ANOTHER	315C
EUKAIREW	OPPORTUNITY	321C
8 2C	THAN	343C
KAINOS 2	NEW	395A
LEGW IIA	SAY	469B
XENOS 2A	THE STRANGER	550C
22 ATH8NAIOS	ATHENIAN	20D
AREIOSPAGO	AREOPAGUS	104D
*DEISIDAIMWN	SUPERSTITIOUS	172D
THEWREW 2A	OBSERVE	360D
HIST8MI IIIB	STAND	383B
KATA II6	WITH RESPECT TO	408D
MESOS 2	THE MIDDLE	508D
23 AGNOEW 2	NOT TO KNOW	11B
AGNWSTOS	UNKNOWN	12B
ANATHEWREW I	EXAMINE	54A
BWMOS	ALTAR	148C
DIERCHOMAI ID	GO THROUGH	193D
DIISTOREW	EXAMINE	194C
EPIGRAPHW I	WRITE ON	291C
HEURISKW IB	FIND	325B
EUSEBEW I	BE REVERENT	326C
HISTOREW	VISIT	383D
KATAGGELLW I	PROCLAIM	410C
SEBASMA	OBJECT OF WORSHIP	753A
24 KATOIKEW IA	LIVE	425B
KOSMOS 2	WORLD	446D
KURIOS 2A	LORD	460B
NAOS IC	TEMPLE	535C
OURANOS IAα	HEAVEN	598B
PAS IDγ	ALL	637D
POIEW IIAβ	DO	687B
HUPARCHW 2	BE	846A
CHEIROPOI8TOS		889A
MADE BY HUMAN HANDS		
25 ANTHRWPINOS 3	HUMAN	67B
THERAPEUW I	SERVE	359C
PN08 2	BREATH	686C
PROSDEOMAI	NEED IN ADDITION	719A
TIS, TI IAα	ANY ONE	827C

25 CHEIR 1   HAND 888C
25B   PAS 2Bβ   ALL THINGS 638D
26 HAIMA 1A   BLOOD 22B
   G8   5B   EARTH 156D
   ETHNOS 1   NATION 217B
   HEIS 2A   ONE 230B
   KAIROS 3   TIME 396B
   KATOIKEW 1A   LIVE 425C
   KATOIKIA   HABITATION 425D
   HORIZW 1Aα   DETERMINE 584C
   HOROTHESIA   FIXED BOUNDARY 585D
   POIEW 11Bθ   DO 688B
   PROSTASSW   COMMAND 725D
   PROSWPON 1E   FACE 729A
   PROTASSW   DETERMINE 729B
26A   PAS 1Aα   EVERY EACH 636C
26B   PAS 1Aε   ALL 637A
27 ARA 2   THEN 103C
   GE   3C   AT LEAST 152B
   EI   V2C   WHETHER 218D
   HEKASTOS 2   EACH 236A
   HEURISKW 2   FIND 325D
   Z8TEW 1Aβ   SEEK 339B
   THEIOS 1B   DIVINE 354C
   MAKRAN 1Aα   FAR 488D
   HUPARCHW 1   BE 845D
   PS8LAPHAW   TOUCH 900D
28 GENOS 1   DESCENDANTS 155B
   EIMI III4   TO BE 224C
   ZAW 1B   LIVE 336D
   KATA II7β   (POSSESSIVE) 409A
   KINEW 3   MOVE 433C
   HO,H8,TO 11   THE 552A
   POI8T8S 1   MAKER 689D
   TIS, TI 1Aα   ANY ONE 827C
   HWS II4A   SO 906B
29 ARGUROS 2   SILVER 104C
   GENOS 1   DESCENDANTS 155B
   ENTHUM8SIS   THOUGHT 265D
   THEIOS 1β   DIVINE 354C
   LITHOS 1F   STONE 475C
   NOMIZW 2   THINK 543B
   HOMOIOS 1   LIKE 569C
   OPHEILW 2Aβ   OWE 603D
   TECHN8   TRADE 821D
   CHARAGMA 2   A MARK 884B
   CHRUSOS   GOLD 897A
30 AGNOIA 2   IGNORANCE 110
   MEN 2E   (PARTICLE) 504C
   METANOEW   CHANGE ONES MIND 513B
   NUN 3C   NOW 548B
   PANTACHOU 1   EVERYWHERE 613B
   PARAGGELLW   GIVE ORDERS 618C
   PARORAW   OVERLOOK 635A
   HUPERORAW 2   DISREGARD 849C
   CHRONOS   TIME 896C
31 ANIST8MI 1A   RAISE 69B
   DIKAIOSUN8 1   RIGHTEOUSNESS 195C
   DIOTI 1   BECAUSE 198C
   EK 1B   AWAY FROM 233C
   EN III1β   BY 260B
   EN III2   BY 260B
   H8MERA 3A   DAY 347D

31 HIST8MI 11Bγ   PUT 383A
   KATHOTI 2   BECAUSE 392A
   KRINW 4Bα   JUDGE 453A
   MELLW 1Cγ   INTEND 502B
   NEKROS 2A   DEAD 537A
   OIKOUMEN8 1B   THE WORLD 564A
   HORIZW 1B   DETERMINE 584D
   PARECHW 1B   GRANT 632A
   PISTIS 1C   FAITH 668B
32 AKOUW 1C   HEAR 31D
   ANASTASIS 2A   RESURRECTION 60A
   MEN 1C   (PARTICLE) 504A
   NEKROS 2A   DEAD 537A
   HO,H8,TO I2   THE 552A
   PALIN 2   AGAIN 611C
33 EK 1B   AWAY FROM 233C
   MESOS 2   THE MIDDLE 509A
34 AREOPAGIT8S   AREOPAGITE 105A
   DAMARIS   DAMARIS 169B
   DIONUSIOS   DIONYSIUS 198A
   EUSCH8MWN 2   PROMINENT 327C
   KOLLAW 2Bα   UNITE 442C
   ONOMA 11   NAME 574A
   PISTEUW 2B   BELIEVE 667C
   TIMIOS 2   VALUABLE 825D

ACTS 18

1   ATH8NAI   ATHENS 20D
   ANACHWREW 2B   WITHDRAW 63A
   KORINTHOS   CORINTH 445C
   CHWRIZW 2B   DIVIDE 898C
2   AKULAS   AQUILA 33C
   ACHAIA   ACHAIA 127C
   GENOS 3   NATION 155C
   DIATASSW   ORDER 188C
   ERCHOMAI IIAβ   COME 310B
   HEURISKW 1B   FIND 325B
   IOUDAIOS 2A   JEWISH 380B
   ITALIA   ITALY 384D
   KLAUDIOS 1   CLAUDIUS 434C
   ONOMA 11   NAME 574A
   PONTIKOS   FROM PONTUS 698B
   PRISKA   PRISCILLA 708B
   PROSERCHOMAI 1   APPROACH 720A
   PROSPHATWS   RECENTLY 726D
   RWM8   ROME 745D
   TASSW 2A   PLACE 813D
   CHWRIZW 2B   DIVIDE 898C
3   ERGAZOMAI 1   WORK 307A
   MENW 1Aα   REMAIN 504D
   MENW 1Aα   REMAIN 504D
   HOMOTECHNOS   572B
     PRACTISING SAME TRADE
   PARA II1Bα   BESIDE 615B
   PROS III7   TOWARD 718A
   SK8NOPOIOS   TENT MAKER 762C
   TECHN8   TRADE 821D
4   DIALEGOMAI 1   DISCUSS 184C
   DIALEGOMAI 2   SPEAK 184D
   EISPOREUOMAI 1   GO 232D
   HELL8N 2A   GENTILE 251C
   IOUDAIOS 2C   JEWISH 380B

4	KATA II2C	EVERY	407C
	PAS IAα	EVERY EACH	636C
	PEITHW IA	CONVINCE	644D
	SABBATON IA	SABBATH	746B
	SUNAGWG8 2A		790C
	PLACE OF ASSEMBLY		
5	DIAMARTUROMAI 2	TESTIFY	185C
	KATERCHOMAI I	COME DOWN	423A
	LOGOS I8β	WORD	479C
	MAKEDONIA	MACEDONIA	488B
	SUNECHW 7	INCLUDE	797A
	SUNECHW 6	ABSORBED	797A
	TIMOTHEOS	TIMOTHY	826A
	CHRISTOS I	ANOINTED ONE	895B
	HWS IVIA	WHEN	907A
6	HAIMA 2A	BLOOD	22C
	ANTITASSW	OPPOSE	75B
	BLASPH8MEW I	DEFAME	142A
	DIERM8NEUW 2	EXPLAIN	193C
	EKTINASSW 2	SHAKE OFF	245B
	HIMATION 3	GARMENT	377B
	KATHAROS 3A	CLEAN	389A
	KEPHAL8 IA	HEAD	431B
	NUN 3B	NOW	548B
	POREUW I	PROCEED	699A
7	IOUSTOS 2	JUSTUS	381B
	METABAINW IAα	PASS OVER	511D
	OIKIA IA	HOUSE	559D
	ONOMA II	NAME	574A
	SEBW 2A	WORSHIP	753C
	SUNOMOREW	BORDER ON	799B
	TIS, TI IAβ	ANY ONE	827D
	TITIOS	TITIUS	828B
	TITOS I	TITUS	828C
8	ARCHISUNAGWGOS		112D
	PRESIDENT OF A SYNAGOGUE		
	KORINTHIOS	CORINTHIAN	445C
	KRISPOS	CRISPUS	454B
	OIKOS 2	HOUSEHOLD	563C
	PISTEUW 2Aβ	BELIEVE	667B
	POLUS I2Aα	MANY	694D
	SUN 2A	WITH	789C
8A	PISTEUW 2Aα	BELIEVE	667A
8B	PISTEUW 2B	BELIEVE	667C
9	DIA AIIIIB	BY MEANS OF	179B
	LALEW 2Aβ	SPEAK	464B
	NUX IC	NIGHT	549A
	HORAMA 2	VISION	581A
	SIWPAW I	BE SILENT	760A
10	DIOTI 3	FOR	198C
	EPITITH8MI 2B	ATTACK	303A
	KAKOW I	HARM	399B
	LAOS 3B	PEOPLE	468B
	META AIIICβ	WITH	510A
	POLIS I	CITY	692A
	POLUS I18α	MANY	694C
11	DIDASKW 2B	TEACH	191A
	ENIAUTOS I	YEAR	265D
	KATHIZW 2Aβ	STAY	391A
	LOGOS I8β	WORD	479B
	M8N I	MONTH	520D
12	AGW 2	LEAD AWAY	14B
	ANTHUPATEUW	BE PROCONSUL	68D

12	ANTHUPATOS	PROCONSUL	68D
	ACHAIA	ACHAIA	127C
	B8MA 2	TRIBUNAL	139D
	GALLIWN	GALLIO	149D
	EPI IIIIAγ	ON	288B
	KATEPHISTAMAI	RISE UP	423C
	HOMOTHUMADON	WITH ONE MIND	569C
	SULLALEW	TALK	784B
13	ANAPEITHW	PERSUADE	58D
	KATABOAW	CRY OUT	410A
	NOMOS 3	LAW	544C
	PARA III6	AGAINST	616C
	SEBW 2A	WORSHIP	753C
14	ADIK8MA	A WRONG	17C
	ANECHW 2	ENDURE	65B
	ANOIGW IEα	OPEN	70D
	GALLIWN	GALLIO	149D
	KATA II5Aα	ACCORDING TO	408A
	KATA II5Bβ	ACCORDING TO	408C
	LOGOS 2D	REASON	479D
	MELLW ICα	BE ABOUT TO	502A
	MEN IB	(PARTICLE)	504A
	PON8ROS I8β	WICKED	697D
	RADIOURG8MA	PRANK	741A
	STOMA IA	MOUTH	777B
	W 2	O	903B
15	AKRIBWS	ACCURATELY	32D
	AUTOS IC	SELF	122C
	BOULOMAI 2Aγ	DESIRE	145D
	Z8T8MA	ISSUE	339C
	KATA II7B	(POSSESSIVE)	409A
	KRIT8S IAα	JUDGE	454C
	NOMOS 3	LAW	544C
	ONOMA III	PEOPLE	577A
	HORAW 2B	SEE	582B
16	APELAUNW	DRIVE AWAY	83A
16F	B8MA 2	TRIBUNAL	139D
17	ARCHISUNAGWGOS		112D
	PRESIDENT OF A SYNAGOGUE		
	GALLIWN	GALLIO	149D
	EMPROSTHEN 2A	IN FRONT	256C
	EPILAMBANOMAI I	GRASP	295A
	MELEI 5	IT IS A CONCERN	501B
	OUDEIS 2Bα	NOTHING	596C
	OUDEIS 2Bγ	IN NO RESPECT	596D
	SWSTHEN8S I	SOSTHENES	808A
	TUPTW I	STRIKE	838A
18	AKULAS	AQUILA	33C
	APOTASSW I	SAY FAREWELL	100B
	EKPLEW	SAIL AWAY	243C
	EUCH8 2	OATH	329C
	HIKANOS IB	SUFFICIENT	375A
	KEGCHREAI	CENCHREAE	427D
	KEIRW	CUT	428B
	KEPHAL8 IA	HEAD	431B
	PRISKA	PRISCILLA	708B
	PROSMENW 2	REMAIN	724D
	SURIA	SYRIA	801C
19	AUTOU	THERE	123C
	DIALEGOMAI I	DISCUSS	184C
	EISERCHOMAI IAβ	COME	231D
	EPEIMI	THE NEXT	284A
	EPHESOS	EPHESUS	330B

19 KAKEINOS IA   AND HE 397C
   KATALEIPW IA   LEAVE BEHIND 414C
   KATANTAW I   ARRIVE 416B
   SUNAGWG8 2A   790C
        PLACE OF ASSEMBLY
20 AKRIBWS   ACCURATELY 32D
   EPI III2B   ON 289B
   EPINEUW   GIVE CONSENT 296C
   ERWTAW 2   ASK 312B
   POLUS IIIB   MANY 695D
   CHRONOS   TIME 896B
21 AKULAS   AQUILA 33C
   ANAGW 3   PUT TO SEA 52D
   DEI 3   IT IS NECESSARY 171B
   HEORT8   FESTIVAL 280A
   ERCHOMAI IIB&   COME 311B
   EPHESOS   EPHESUS 330B
   THELW 2   WISH 355D
   PALIN IA   BACK 611C
  *PANTWS I   BY ALL MEANS 614B
   POIEW IIB5   DO 688A
22 ANABAINW IA«   GO UP 49D
   ANTIOCHEIA I   ANTIOCH 74D
   ASPAZOMAI IB   GREET 116C
   KAISAREIA 2   CAESAREA 396D
   KATABAINW IA&   COME DOWN 409B
   KATERCHOMAI I   COME DOWN 423A
23 AKRIBWS   ACCURATELY 32D
   GALATIKOS   GALATIAN 149C
   DIERCHOMAI IA   GO THROUGH 193C
   EPIST8RIZW   STRENGTHEN 300C
   KATHEX8S   IN ORDER 389C
   POIEW IIE6   DO 689A
   ST8RIZW 2   ESTABLISH 775D
   TIS, TI 2C   ANY ONE 828B
   PHRUGIA   PHRYGIA 875B
   CHRONOS   TIME 896B
   CHWRA IB   COUNTRY 897C
24 ALEXANDREUS   ALEXANDRIAN 34D
   AN8R 4   MAN 66B
   APELL8S   APELLES 83B
   APOLLWNIOS   APOLLONIUS 95A
  *APOLLWS   APOLLOS 95A
   GENOS 3   NATION 155C
   GRAPH8 29«   SCRIPTURE 165B
   DUNATOS IA&   POWERFUL 208A
   EPHESOS   EPHESUS 330B
   IOUDAIOS 2A   JEWISH 380B
   KATANTAW I   ARRIVE 416B
   LOGIOS 2   LEARNED 477D
   ONOMA II   NAME 574A
24«19 APOLLWS   APOLLOS 95B
25 AKRIBWS   ACCURATELY 32D
   APOLALEW   SPEAK OUT FREELY 93D
   BAPTISMA I   BAPTISM 132A
   DIDASKW 2B   TEACH 191A
   EPISTAMAI 2   KNOW 300A
   ZEW   BOIL 338A
   IWAN(N)8S I   JOHN 385B
   KAT8CHEW 2A   TEACH 425A
   MONOS 2B   ONLY 529D
   PATRIS 2   FATHERLAND 642C
   PERI II   ABOUT 650D

25 PNEUMA 3B   SPIRIT 681B
26 AKRIBWS   ACCURATELY 32D
   AKULAS   AQUILA 33C
   EKTITH8MI 2   EXPLAIN 245B
   PARR8SIAZOMAI I SPEAK FREELY 636B
   PRISKA   PRISCILLA 708B
   PROSLAMBANW 2A   TAKE 724C
27 APODECHOMAI I   WELCOME 89C
   ACHAIA   ACHAIA 127D
   BOULOMAI 2A&   DESIRE 145D
   GRAPHW 2D   WRITE 166B
   DIERCHOMAI 2   COME 193D
   EPID8MEW I   STAY 292A
   EPHESIOS   EPHESIAN 330B
   EPHESOS   EPHESUS 330B
   KORINTHIOS   CORINTHIAN 445C
   KORINTHOS   CORINTH 445C
   PARAGINOMAI I   COME 618D
   PATRIS 2   FATHERLAND 642C
   PISTEUW 2B   BELIEVE 667C
   POLUS I2C&   MANY 695C
   PROTREPW   ENCOURAGE 729D
   SUGKATANEUW   AGREE 781A
   SUMBALLW 2   CONVERSE 785B
   CHARIS 3B   FAVOR 886B
28 GRAPH8 2B«   SCRIPTURE 165B
   D8MOSIOS 2   PUBLIC 178B
   DIAKATELEGCHOMAI   REFUTE 183A
   EPIDEIKNUMI 2B   SHOW 291D
   EUTONWS   POWERFULLY 327C
   CHRISTOS I   ANOINTED ONE 895B

                ACTS 19

 1 ANATOLIKOS   EASTERN 62A
   ANWTERIKOS   THE UPPER 76D
   APELL8S   APELLES 83B
   APOLLWS   APOLLOS 95A
   ASIA   ASIA 115C
   BOUL8 2B   WILL 145B
   GINOMAI I3E   TAKE PLACE 158B
   DIERCHOMAI IA   GO THROUGH 193C
   HEURISKW IB   FIND 325B
   EPHESOS   EPHESUS 330B
   KATERCHOMAI I   COME DOWN 423A
   KORINTHOS   CORINTH 445C
   MEROS IBƴ   PART 507A
   PNEUMA 5D«   SPIRIT 683A
 2 ALLA 3   BUT, YET 38A
   EI VI   IF 218D
   OUDE 3   NOT EVEN 596A
   PISTEUW 2B   BELIEVE 667C
2A   PNEUMA 5C&   SPIRIT 682D
2B   PNEUMA 5C&   SPIRIT 682D
 3 APEITHEW 3   DISOBEY 82A
   BAPTIZW 2A   BAPTIZE 131B
   BAPTISMA I   BAPTISM 132A
3F   IWAN(N)8S I   JOHN 385B
 4 BAPTIZW 2A   BAPTIZE 131B
   BAPTISMA I   BAPTISM 132A
   EIMI II3   TO BE 222D
   HINA IV   IN ORDER THAT 379B
   LEGW IIIC   ORDER 470D

4	METANOIA	REPENTANCE	514A
	HOUTOS 13c	THIS	601D
	PISTEUW 2Aβ	BELIEVE	667B
	CHRISTOS 1	ANOINTED ONE	895C
5	BAPTIZW 2A	BAPTIZE	131B
	BAPTIZW 2Bβ	BAPTIZE	131C
	KURIOS 2Cγ	LORD	461A
	ONOMA 14Cβ	NAME	576A
	PROSERCHOMAI 1	APPROACH	720A
6	GLWSSA 3	TONGUE	161C
	EPIPIPTW 2	FALL UPON	297D
	EPITITH8MI 1Aα	PUT UPON	302D
	ERCHOMAI I2C	COME	311D
	PNEUMA 5Cα	SPIRIT	682D
	PROPH8TEUW 1	PROPHESY	730B
7	DEKADUO	TWELVE	172D
	EIMI II7	TO BE	223D
	PAS 1Fβ	ALL	638A
	HWSEI 2	AS	907D
8	BASILEIA 3B	KINGDOM	134D
	EPI III23	ON	289B
	MEGAS 2Aγ	GREAT	498D
	M8N 1	MONTH	520D
	PARR8SIAZOMAI 1	SPEAK FREELY	636B
	PEITHW 1A	CONVINCE	644D
	PERI II	ABOUT	650D
	SUNAGWG8 2A		790C
	PLACE OF ASSEMBLY		
8F	DIALEGOMAI 1	DISCUSS	184C
9	APEITHEW 2	DISOBEY	82A
	APHIST8MI 2A	WITHDRAW	126C
	APHORIZW 1	SEPARATE	126D
	DEKATOS 1	TENTH	173A
	E	FIFTH	210A
	ENWPION 2A	BEFORE	270B
	H8MERA 2	DAY	347B
	KAKOLOGEW	INSULT	398A
	KATA II2C	EVERY	407C
	HODOS 2C	WAY	557B
	PL8THOS 2B6	QUANTITY	674D
	SKL8RUNW 2	HARDEN	763C
	SCHOL8	SCHOOL	805C
	TURANNOS	TYRANNUS	838B
	HWRA 2B	TIME OF DAY	904D
	HWS IV1B	WHEN	907A
10	ASIA	ASIA	115C
	HELL8N 2A	GENTILE	251C
	EPI III23	ON	289B
	ETOS	YEAR	317B
	HEWS IIA	UNTIL	334D
	IOUDAIOS 2C	JEWISH	380B
	KATOIKEW 2	LIVE	425C
	LOGOS 1Bβ	WORD	479B
11	DIA AIII1A	BY MEANS OF	179A
	OU 3A	NO	594C
	POIEW I19β	DO	687C
	TUGCHANW 2D	HAPPEN	837B
	CHEIR 1	HAND	888C
12	APPALLASSW 2B	LEAVE	79C
	APOPHERW 1B	TAKE	101B
	ASTHENEW 1A	BE SICK	115A
	EKPOREUOMAI 1A	GO OUT	243D
	EPIPHERW 2A	BRING OVER	304C
12	NOSOS 1	DISEASE	545D
	SIMIKINTHION	APRON	758C
	SOUDARION	FACE CLOTH	766D
	CHRWS	SKIN	897B
12F	PNEUMA 4C	SPIRIT	682A
12F	PON8ROS 1Bα	WICKED	697C
13	EXORKIZW	ADJURE	277A
	EXORKIST8S	EXORCIST	277A
	EPI IIIIA⟨	ON	288C
	EPICHEIREW	ATTEMPT	304D
	ECHW I2Eα	HAVE	333A
	IOUDAIOS 1	JEWISH	380A
	K8RUSSW 2Bβ	ANNOUNCE	432C
	KURIOS 2Cγ	LORD	461A
	ONOMAZW 2	NAME	577C
	HORKIZW	ADJURE	585A
	PERIERCHOMAI	GO AROUND	652C
14	DAIMONIZOMAI		168A
	BE POSSESSED BY A DEMON		
	ETHOS 1	HABIT	217C
	EN IV5	IN	260D
	IOUDAIOS 1	JEWISH	380A
	SKEUAS	SCEVA	761B
15	GINWSKW 6Aβ	KNOW	160C
	EPISTAMAI 2	KNOW	300A
	TIS, TI 1Aα	WHICH	826C
15F	PNEUMA 4C	SPIRIT	682A
15F	PON8ROS 1Bα	WICKED	697C
16	AMPHOTEROI 2	ALL	47A
	ANTHRWPOS 3A6	MAN	68C
	GUMNOS 1	NAKED	166D
	EKPHEUGW 1	RUN AWAY	246B
	ENALLOMAI	LEAP UPON	261B
	EPHALLOMAI	LEAP UPON	330B
	ISCHUW 3	BE STRONG	384D
	KATA I2Bα	DOWN	406C
	KATAKURIEUW 1	SUBDUE	413C
	KURIEUW 1	RULE	459C
	OIKOS 1Aα	HOUSE	563A
	TRAUMATIZW	TO WOUND	832C
	HWSTE 2Aβ	THEREFORE	908C
17	GINOMAI I4B	BECOME	158D
	GNWSTOS 1A	KNOWN	163C
	HELL8N 2A	GENTILE	251C
	EPI IIIIBγ	ON	289A
	EPIPIPTW 2	FALL UPON	297C
	EPHESOS	EPHESUS	330B
	KATOIKEW 2	LIVE	425C
	KURIOS 2Cγ	LORD	461A
	MEGALUNW 2	EXALT	498B
	HOUTOS 1Bα	THIS	601C
	PHOBOS 2Aα	FEAR	871C
	PHOBOS 2Aα	FEAR	871C
17B	PAS 1Eα	ALL	637D
18	ANAGGELLW 2	DISCLOSE	51A
	EXOMOLOGEW 2A	CONFESS	276D
	PISTEUW 2B	BELIEVE	667C
	POLUS I2Aα	MANY	694D
	PRAXIS 4B	ACTING	704D
19	ARGURION 2C	SILVER	104C
	BIBLOS 1	BOOK	141A
	ENWPION 2A	BEFORE	270B
	HEURISKW 2	FIND	325D

19	HIKANOS IC	SUFFICIENT	375A
	KATAKAIW	CONSUME	412A
	MURIAS I	MYRIAD	531C
	PERIERGOS 2	MEDDLESOME	652C
	PRASSW IA	DO	705B
	SUMPHERW I	BRING TOGETHER	787D
	SUMPS8PHIZW	COUNT UP	789A
	TIM8 I	VALUE	825A
20	AUXANW 3	GROW	121C
	ISCHUW 3	BE STRONG	384C
	KATA II5B?	ACCORDING TO	408C
	KRATOS I	POWER	450B
	PISTIS 2A	FAITH	668C
	PL8THUNW 2	INCREASE	675A
21	ACHAIA	ACHAIA	127D
	GINOMAI II4B	BE	159D
	DIERCHOMAI IA	GO THROUGH	193C
	META BII4A	AFTER	511D
	HOS,H8,HO I2B?	(REL PRON)	587B
	PL8ROW 5	MAKE FULL	677D
	PNEUMA 3B	SPIRIT	681C
	POREUW I	PROCEED	699A
	RWM8	ROME	745D
	TITH8MI IIIC	PUT	824B
	HWS IVIA	WHEN	907A
21F	MAKEDONIA	MACEDONIA	488B
22	ASIA	ASIA	115C
	DIAKONEW 2	SERVE	183A
	EPECHW 2B	STOP	285B
	ERASTOS 2	ERASTUS	306C
	TIMOTHEOS	TIMOTHY	826A
	CHRONOS	TIME	896B
23	GINOMAI IIB?	COME ABOUT	157B
	EKEINOS 2BY	THAT	239B
	KAIROS I	TIME	395D
	KATA II2A	DURING	407C
	HODOS 2C	WAY	557B
	OLIGOS 2B	LITTLE	566C
	TARACHOS 2	MENTAL AGITATION	813B
23F	OU 2B	NO	594C
24	ARGUROUS	(MADE OF) SILVER	104C
	ARGUROKOPOS	SILVERSMITH	104C
	ARTEMIS	ARTEMIS	109C
	D8M8TRIOS 2	DEMETRIUS	177D
	ERGASIA 4	TRADE	307C
	KIBWRION	VESSEL	432D
	NAOS IC	TEMPLE	535C
	OLIGOS 2A	LITTLE	566C
	ONOMA II	NAME	574A
	PARECHW 2C	GET FOR ONESELF	632B
	POIEW IIA?	DO	687A
	TECHNIT8S	CRAFTSMAN	821D
25	AN8R I	MAN	66A
	EK 3F	BY	234D
	EPISTAMAI 2	KNOW	300A
	ERGAT8S IA	WORKMAN	307C
	ERGASIA 3	TRADE	307C
	EUPORIA	PROSPERITY	324C
	PERI 2C	ABOUT	651A
	SUNATHROIZW I	GATHER	791A
	SUNTECHNIT8S	FELLOW CRAFTSMEN	800B
	TECHNIT8S	CRAFTSMAN	821D
	TOIOUTOS 3A?	SUCH A KIND	829B
25A	EPHESIOS	EPHESIAN	330B
26	GINOMAI I2A	CREATED	157C
	EPHESOS	EPHESUS	330B
	THEOS I	GOD	357B
	THEWREW I	OBSERVE	3600
	HIKANOS IA	SUFFICIENT	375A
	METHIST8MI 2	MISLEAD	500A
	MONOS 2C	ONLY	529D
	OCHLOS I	CROWD	605C
	PEITHW IA	CONVINCE	644D
	SCHEDON	NEARLY	804D
	CHEIR I	HAND	888C
26F	ASIA	ASIA	115C
27	APELEGMOS	REFUTATION	83A
	EIS 8AY		229C
	ERCHOMAI I2C	COME	311C
	THEA	GODDESS	353C
	HIERON I	TEMPLE	373A
	KATHAIREW 2B	DESTROY	387C
	KINDUNEUW	RUN A RISK	433B
	LOGIZOMAI IB	CONSIDER	477A
	MEGALEIOT8S	GRANDEUR	498A
	MEROS IBη	BRANCH	507B
	MONOS 2C	ONLY	529D
	NAOS IC	TEMPLE	535C
	OIKOUMEN8 IB	THE WORLD	564A
	OUDEIS 2B?	WORTHLESS	596C
	SEBW 2A	WORSHIP	753C
27F	ARTEMIS	ARTEMIS	109C
27F	MEGAS 2B?	GREAT	499B
28	AMPHODON	STREET	47A
	EPHESIOS	EPHESIAN	330B
	THUMOS 2	ANGER	366A
	PL8R8S 2	FULL	675D
	PL8R8S IB	FULL	675D
	TRECHW I	RUN	833C
29	ARISTARCHOS	ARISTARCHUS	106B
	GAIOS 2	GAIUS	149A
	THEATRON I	THEATER	354A
	HOMOTHUMADON	WITH ONE MIND	569C
	HORMAW	RUSH DOWN	585C
	PIMPL8MI IA?	FILL	663D
	SUGCHEW	CONFUSE	782D
	SUGCHUSIS	CONFUSION	783A
	SUNARPAZW	SEIZE	792D
	SUNEKD8MOS		794D
		TRAVELING COMPANION	
30	BOULOMAI 2A?	DESIRE	145D
	D8MOS	ASSEMBLY	178A
	EAW I	LET	211D
	EISERCHOMAI IB?	COME	232A
	KWLUW I	HINDER	462B
	OU 2D	NO	594C
31	ASIARCH8S	ASIARCH	115D
	DIDWMI 6	GIVE	192D
	THEATRON I	THEATER	354A
	PARAKALEW 3	IMPLORE	622D
	*PEMPW I	SEND	647D
	PHILOS I	LOVING	868D
32	ALLOS IC	OTHER	39C
	EKKL8SIA 2	ASSEMBLY	240B
	HENEKA	BECAUSE OF	264B
	KRAZW 2A	CALL	448D

32	MEN 2E	(PARTICLE) 504C
	POLUS II2Aα	MANY 695D
	POLUS III2A	MANY 696B
	SUGCHEW	CONFUSE 782D
	SUNERCHOMAI IA	ASSEMBLE 795D
33	ALEXANDROS 3	ALEXANDER 35A
	APOLOGEOMAI	DEFEND ONESELF 95B
	D8MOS	ASSEMBLY 178A
	EK IB	AWAY FROM 233C
	KATABIBAZW	DRIVE DOWN 410A
	KATASEIW I	SHAKE 419A
	PROBALLW I	PUT BEFORE 709D
	PROBIBAZW	BRING FORWARD 710B
	SUMBIBAZW 4	UNITE 785C
34	GINOMAI IIBβ	COME ABOUT 157B
	EPI III2B	ON 289B
	EPIGINWSKW 2A	KNOW 291A
	EPHESIOS	EPHESIAN 330B
	IOUDAIOS 2A	JEWISH 380B
	KRAZW 2A	CALL 448D
	PHWN8 2C	VOICE 879A
	HWRA 2Aα	TIME OF DAY 904C
34F	ARTEMIS	ARTEMIS 109C
34F	MEGAS 2Bα	GREAT 499B
35	ANTHRWPOS 3Aζ	MAN 68C
	GINWSKW 6Aα	KNOW 160C
	GRAMMATEUS I	CLERK 164D
	DIOPET8S	FALLEN FROM HEAVEN 198A
	H8METEROS	OUR 348C
	KATASTELLW	RESTRAIN 420A
	NEWKOROS	TEMPLE KEEPER 539B
	POLIS I	CITY 692A
36	ANANTIRR8TOS	UNDENIABLE 58A
	DEI 6	IT IS NECESSARY 171B
	EIMI II4D	TO BE 223B
	KATASTELLW	RESTRAIN 420A
	PRASSW IA	DO 705B
	PROPET8S	RECKLESS 716B
	HUPARCHW 2	BE 846A
37	BLASPH8MEW 2A	BLASPHEME 142A
	THEA	GODDESS 353C
	THEOS I	GOD 357B
	OUTE	NOT 600C
38	AGORAIOS 2	COURT DAYS 13A
	AGW 4	SPEND 14C
	ALL8LWN	EACH OTHER 38D
	ANTHUPATOS	PROCONSUL 68D
	D8M8TRIOS 2	DEMETRIUS 177D
	EGKALEW	ACCUSE 214C
	EI VI6	IF 219A
	ECHW I7A	HAVE 334B
	LOGOS IAε	MATTER 478D
	SUN IC	WITH 789B
	TECHNIT8S	CRAFTSMAN 821D
38F	MEN IAα	(PARTICLE) 503D
39	EKKL8SIA I	ASSEMBLY 240B
	EPIZ8TEW IB	INQUIRE 292D
	EPILUW 2	DECIDE 295D
	PERAITERW	FURTHER 649B
40	AITIOS 2	GUILT 26A
	APODIDWMI I	GIVE AWAY 90A
	APOLUW 2B	SEND AWAY 96B
	GAR IB	FOR 151A

40	EGKALEW	ACCUSE 214C
	EKKL8SIA 2	ASSEMBLY 240B
	KINDUNEUW	RUN A RISK 433B
	LOGOS 2A	ACCOUNT 479D
	S8MERON	TODAY 756C
	STASIS 2	UPRISING 772A
	SUSTROPH8 I	COMMOTION 803B
	HUPARCHW I	BE 845D

ACTS 20

1	APASPAZOMAI	TAKE LEAVE 81A
	ASPAZOMAI IA	GREET 116B
	EXERCHOMAI IAζ	GO OUT 274B
	THORUBOS 3B	NOISE 363C
	MAKEDONIA	MACEDONIA 488B
	META BII4A	AFTER 511D
	METAPEMPW	SUMMON 514D
	PARAKALEW 2	APPEAL TO 622B
	PAUW 2	STOP 643D
	POLUS I2Bβ	MANY 695B
	POREUW I	PROCEED 699A
2	AUTOS 3B	(OBLIQUE CASE) 123A
	DIERCHOMAI IA	GO THROUGH 193C
	HELLAS	GREECE 251B
	LOGOS IAβ	WORD 478C
	MEROS I8γ	PART 507A
	PARAKALEW 2	APPEAL TO 622C
	POLUS IIBα	MANY 694C
3	ANAGW 3	PUT TO SEA 52D
	GINOMAI II2A	BE 159B
	GNWM8 4	DECISION 162C
	DIA AII	THROUGH 178C
	EPIBOUL8	A PLOT 290C
	MAKEDONIA	MACEDONIA 488B
	MELLW ICγ	INTEND 502B
	M8N I	MONTH 520D
	HO,H8,TO II4Bε	THE 554A
	PNEUMA 5Dα	SPIRIT 683A
	POIEW IIEδ	DO 689A
	SURIA	SYRIA 801C
	HUPO IB	BY 851A
	HUPOSTREPHW	RETURN 855B
4	ARISTARCHOS	ARISTARCHUS 106B
	ASIANOS	A MAN FROM ASIA 115C
	ASIA	ASIA 115C
	ACHRI IB	AS FAR AS 128C
	BEROIAIOS	BEROEAN 139A
	GAIOS I	GAIUS 149A
	EXEIMI	GO OUT 273C
	EPHESIOS	EPHESIAN 330B
	THESSALONIKEUS	THESSALONIAN 360B
	MECHRI IA	UNTIL 517A
	PURROS	PYRRHUS 738D
	SEKOUNDOS	SECUNDUS 754A
	SUNEPOMAI	ACCOMPANY 795A
	SWPATROS	SOPATER 807D
	TIMOTHEOS	TIMOTHY 826A
	TROPHIMOS	TROPHIMUS 835C
	TUCHIKOS	TYCHICUS 839C
5	MENW 2A	WAIT FOR 505C
	PROERCHOMAI 3	GO FORWARD 712B
5F	TRWAS	TROAS 836D

6	AZUMOS 13	UNLEAVENED BREAD	19C
	ACHRI 1A	UNTIL	128B
	DIATRIBW	SPEND	189A
	EKPLEW	SAIL AWAY	243C
	H8MERA 2	DAY	347C
	PEMPTAIOS	ON THE FIFTH DAY	647B
	PHILIPPOI	PHILIPPI	867C
6B	H8MERA 2	DAY	347A
6C	H8MERA 2	DAY	347A
7	ARTOS 1C	BREAD	110B
	DIALEGOMAI 1	DISCUSS	184C
	HEIS 4	ONE	231A
	EPAURION	NEXT DAY	283C
	KLAW	BREAK	434D
	MELLW 1Cy	INTEND	502B
	MESONUKTION	MIDNIGHT	508B
	MECHRI 1B	UNTIL	517A
	PARATEINW	PROLONG	627D
	SABBATON 2B	WEEK	746D
	SUNAGW 2	GATHER	790B
8	HIKANOS 1A	SUFFICIENT	375A
	LAMPAS 2	LAMP	466D
	SUNAGW 2	GATHER	790B
	HUPERWON	UPPER STORY	850A
	HUPOLAMPAS	WINDOW	853B
9	AIRW 1A	LIFT UP	23D
	APO V6	BY	87D
	BATHUS 2	DEEP	130A
	BARUS 1	HEAVY	133D
	DIALEGOMAI 1	DISCUSS	184C
	EPI III2B	ON	289C
	EUTUCHOS	EUTYCHUS	327D
	THURIS	WINDOW	366D
	KATHEZOMAI 1	SIT	389B
	KATW 2	DOWNWARDS	426B
	NEANIAS	YOUTH	536B
	NEKROS 1Aα	DEAD	536C
	ONOMA 11	NAME	574A
	PIPTW 1A	FALL	665A
	POLUS 112C	MANY	696A
	TRISTEGON	THIRD STORY	834B
9A	KATAPHERW 3	BRING DOWN	421A
9A	HUPNOS	SLEEP	850D
9B	KATAPHERW 3	BRING DOWN	421A
9B	HUPNOS	SLEEP	850D
10	EPIPIPTW 1B	FALL UPON	297C
	THORUBEW 2	BE TROUBLED	363C
	KATABAINW 1Aα	COME DOWN	409B
	M8 AIII3B	NOT	518D
	SUMPERILAMBANW	EMBRACE	787A
	PSUCH8 1Aα	SOUL LIFE	901C
11	ANABAINW 1Aα	GO UP	49D
	ARTOS 1A	BREAD	110A
	AUG8	DAWN	120B
	ACHRI 1A	UNTIL	128B
	GEUOMAI 1	TASTE	156A
	HIKANOS 1C	SUFFICIENT	375B
	KLAW	BREAK	434D
	HOMILEW	SPEAK	568C
	HOUTW 1B	THUS	602C
	TE 1B	AND	815B
12	AGW 1A	LEAD	14A
	ASPAZOMAI 1A	GREET	116B
12	ZAW 1Aβ	LIVE	336C
	METRIWS	MODERATELY	516C
	NEANISKOS 1	YOUTH	536C
	OU 2B	NO	594C
	PAIS 1Aα	CHILD	609C
	PARAKALEW 4	IMPLORE	623A
13	ANAGW 3	PUT TO SEA	52D
	DIATASSW	ORDER	188D
	EPI III1Aβ	ON	288A
	EPI III1A6	TO	288B
	PEZEUW	TRAVEL BY LAND	644B
	PLOION 1	SHIP	679B
	PROERCHOMAI 3	GO FORWARD	712B
13A	MELLW 1Cy	INTEND	502B
13B	MELLW 1Cy	INTEND	502B
13F	ANALAMBANW 4	TAKE ALONG	56C
13F	ASSOS	ASSOS	117A
14	MITUL8N8	MITYLENE	526A
	SUMBALLW 1B	CONVERSE	785A
15	ANTIKRUS	OPPOSITE	73D
	APOPLEW	SAIL AWAY	96D
	EPEIMI	THE NEXT	284A
	HESPERA	EVENING	313C
	HETEROS 1Bζ	ANOTHER	315C
	ECHW III3	HOLD FAST	334C
	KAKEITHEN 1	AND FROM THERE	397C
	KATANTAW 1	ARRIVE	416B
	MENW 1Aα	REMAIN	504D
	MIL8TOS	MILETUS	523C
	PARABALLW 2	APPROACH	617A
	SAMOS	SAMOS	749A
	TRWGULLION	TROGYLLIUM	836D
	CHIOS	CHIOS	890B
16	ASIA	ASIA	115C
	GINOMAI 13Bα	TAKE PLACE	158A
	GINOMAI 14Cα	COME, GO	158D
	DUNATOS 2B	POSSIBLE	208A
	EI 13	IF	218B
	H8MERA 2	DAY	347A
	H8MERA 2	DAY	347C
	KATASCHESIS 2	RESTRAINING	420C
	KRINW 3	DECIDE	452C
	M8 AI2	NOT	517C
	HOPWS 2Aα	IN ORDER THAT	580C
	PARAPLEW	SAIL PAST	626D
	PENT8KOST8	FIFTIETH	649A
	SPEUDW 1A	HURRY	769D
	CHRONOTRIBEW	SPEND TIME	896D
16F	EPHESOS	EPHESUS	330B
17	METAKALEW	SUMMON	512C
	MIL8TOS	MILETUS	523C
	PEMPW 1	SEND	647C
	PRESBUTEROS 2Bα	OLDER	707A
18	ASIA	ASIA	115C
	GINOMAI 114A	BE	159C
	EPIBAINW 2	GO UP	289D
	EPISTAMAI 2	KNOW	300A
	H8MERA 2	DAY	347A
	META AIIIA	WITH	509D
	HOMOTHUMADON	WITH ONE MIND	569C
	HOMOSE	TOGETHER	572B
	PARAGINOMAI 1	COME	618D
	PAS 1Fα	WHOLE	638A

18 POLUS II2C	MANY	696A
POTAPWS	HOW	701D
PRWTOS IA	FIRST	732D
PWS 2A	HOW	739D
TRIETIA	THREE YEARS	834A
CHRONOS	TIME	896B
18B HWS IV4	WHEN	907B
19 DAKRUON	TEAR	169A
DOULEUW 2B	SERVE	204C
EPIBOUL8	A PLOT	290C
META AIIII	WITH	511A
PEIRASMOS 2B	TEST	646D
SUMBAINW	MEET	784D
TAPEINOPHROSUN8	HUMILITY	812A
20 ANAGGELLW 2	DISCLOSE	51A
D8MOSIOS 2	PUBLIC	178B
HO,H8,TO II4B6	THE	554A
OIKOS IA∝	HOUSE	563A
SUMPHERW 2B∝	PROFITABLE	788A
HUPOSTELLW 2C	WITHDRAW	855A
HWS I2D	AS	905D
21 DIAMARTUROMAI 2	TESTIFY	185C
EIS 4Cβ	(GOAL)	228C
HELL8N 2A	GENTILE	251C
IOUDAIOS 2C	JEWISH	380B
KURIOS 2Cγ	LORD	461B
METANOIA	REPENTANCE	514A
PISTIS 2Bβ	FAITH	669A
PISTIS 2Bβ	FAITH	669A
22 DEW IB	BIND	176D
IDOU IB6	BEHOLD	371C
PNEUMA 5D∝	SPIRIT	683A
POREUW I	PROCEED	699A
SUNANTAW 2	MEET	792B
23 DESMOS I	FETTER	175A
DIAMARTUROMAI 2	TESTIFY	185C
THLIPSIS I	TRIBULATION	362D
KATA IIID	(DISTRIBUTIVE)	407B
KATA IIID	(DISTRIBUTIVE)	407C
LEGW IIBβ	SAY	469C
MENW 2B	AWAIT	505C
PL8N ID	BUT	675C
PNEUMA 5C∝	SPIRIT	682D
POLIS I	CITY	692B
24 DIAKONIA 3	SERVICE	183C
DIAMARTUROMAI 2	TESTIFY	185C
DROMOS 2	COURSE	206A
EUAGGELION 2B∝	GOSPEL	318B
KURIOS 2Cγ	LORD	461A
LAMBANW 2	RECEIVE	466C
LOGOS IA∝	WORD	478B
PARA I3B	FROM	614D
POIEW III	DO	689C
TELEIOW I	COMPLETE	817C
TIMIOS ID	VALUABLE	825D
CHARIS 3B	FAVOR	886B
PSUCH8 IAβ	SOUL LIFE	901C
HWS IV3A	WHEN	907B
HWS IV3B	WHEN	907B
25 DIERCHOMAI IBβ	GO THROUGH	193D
IDOU IB6	BEHOLD	371C
K8RUSSW 2Bβ	ANNOUNCE	432C
HORAW IAγ	SEE	581D

25 OUKETI I	NO LONGER	596D
PAS IE∝	ALL	637D
PROSWPON IB	FACE	728C
26 HAIMA 2A	BLOOD	22C
APO I2	FROM	86A
DIOTI 2	THEREFORE	198C
KATHAROS 3A	CLEAN	389A
MARTUROMAI I	TESTIFY	495B
HOTI IB∝	THAT	592D
S8MERON	TODAY	756C
27 ANAGGELLW 2	DISCLOSE	51A
BOUL8 2B	WILL	145B
HO,H8,TO II4B6	THE	554A
HUPOSTELLW 2B	WITHDRAW	855A
28 HAIMA 2B	BLOOD	22C
DIA AIIIIA	BY MEANS OF	179A
EKKL8SIA 4E∝	CHURCH	240D
EPISKOPOS 2	OVERSEER	299C
IDIOS IB	ONES OWN	370B
PERIPOIEW 2	SAVE	655D
PNEUMA 5C∝	SPIRIT	682D
POIMAINW 2Aβ	TEND	690B
PROSECHW IB	PAY ATTENTION TO	721C
TITH8MI II2B	MAKE	824B
28F POIMNION 2B	FLOCK	691A
29 APHIXIS	DEPARTURE	126B
BARUS 2D	CRUEL	134A
EISERCHOMAI IB∝	COME	232A
LUKOS 2	WOLF	482D
META BII2	AFTER	511C
PHEIDOMAI I	SPARE	862C
30 APOSPAW 2	DRAW	97C
APOSTREPHW IAβ	TURN AWAY	99D
DIASTREPHW IB	PERVERT	188A
HO,H8,TO II4B(	THE	554A
OPISW 2Aβ	AFTER	578D
31 GR8GOREW 2	BE AWAKE	166C
DAKRUON	TEAR	169A
DIO	THEREFORE	197D
HEKASTOS 2	EACH	236A
H8MERA IA	DAY	346C
MN8MONEUW IC	REMEMBER	527A
NOUTHETEW	ADMONISH	546B
NUX ID	NIGHT	549A
PAUW 2	STOP	643C
TRIETIA	THREE YEARS	834A
32 HAGIAZW 2	CONSECRATE	8D
EPOIKODOMEW 2	BUILD ON TO	305C
KL8RONOMIA 3	INHERITANCE	436B
LOGOS IBβ	WORD	479C
NUN 3C	NOW	548B
OIKODOMEW 3	BUILD	561A
PARATITH8MI 2Bβ PLACE BESIDE		628C
PAS IDβ	ALL	637D
CHARIS 3B	FAVOR	886B
33 ARGURION 2A	SILVER	104B
EPITHUMEW	DESIRE	293A
HIMATISMOS	CLOTHING	377B
CHRUSION	GOLD	896D
34 AUTOS IE	OF HIMSELF	122C
GINWSKW 6C	KNOW	160D
HUP8RETEW	SERVE	850B

34	CHEIR 1	HAND 888A
	CHREIA 2	NEED 893B
35	ANTILAMBANW 1	HELP 74A
	ASTHENEW 3	BE IN NEED 115A
	DIDWMI 1A	GIVE 192A
	KOPIAW 2	BECOME WEARY 444B
	KURIOS 2Cγ	LORD 461A
	LAMBANW 2	RECEIVE 466B
	LOGOS 1A6	WORD 478D
	MAKARIOS 3C	BLESSED 488B
	MALLON 1	MORE 490B
	MALLON 3C	RATHER 490D
	HUPODEIKNUMI 2	SHOW 852A
36	GONU	KNEE 164B
	PAS 1Eα	ALL 637D
	SUN 2A	WITH 789C
	TITH8MI 11Bα	PUT 823D
37	GINOMAI 11Bβ	COME ABOUT 157B
	EPIPIPTW 1B	FALL UPON 297C
	HIKANOS 1A	SUFFICIENT 375A
	KATAPHILEW	KISS 421B
	KLAUTHMOS	WEEPING 434D
	TRACH8LOS	NECK 832D
38	EPI 111Bγ	ON 287B
	THEWREW 1	OBSERVE 360D
	MALISTA 1	ABOVE ALL 490A
	MELLW 1C6	IS DESTINED 502C
	ODUNAW 2	CAUSE PAIN 557C
	OUKETI 1	NO LONGER 596D
	PLOION 1	SHIP 679B
	PROPEMPW 1	ACCOMPANY 716B
	PROSWPON 1B	FACE 728C

ACTS 21

	GINOMAI 13E	TAKE PLACE 158B
	HEX8S 2	NEXT 275C
	EPIBAINW 1	GO UP 289C
	KAKEITHEN 1	AND FROM THERE 397C
	KWS	COS 463A
	MURA	MYRA 531B
	PATARA	PATARA 640A
	RODOS	RHODES 744B
	HWS IV1A	WHEN 907A
1F	ANAGW 3	PUT TO SEA 53A
2	DIAPERAW	CROSS 186C
	EPIBAINW 1	GO UP 289C
	PHOINIK8	PHOENICIA 872A
2F	PLOION 1	SHIP 679B
3	ANAPHAINW	LIGHT UP 62C
	APOPHORTIZOMAI	UNLOAD 101C
	GOMOS	CARGO 164A
	EKEISE 2	THERE 239C
	EUWNUMOS	LEFT 330A
	KATAGW	LEAD 411A
	KATALEIPW 2E	LEAVE BEHIND 414D
	KATERCHOMAI 1	COME DOWN 423A
	KUPROS	CYPRUS 458D
	SURIA	SYRIA 801C
	TUROS	TYRE 838C
4	ANEURISKW	LOOK 65A
	AUTOU	THERE 123C
	DIA AIII2B6	BY 179D

4	EPIBAINW 1	GO UP 289C
	EPIMENW 1	REMAIN 296A
	H8MERA 2	DAY 347A
	M8 AIII8β	NOT 517D
	HOSTIS 3	WHOEVER 591B
	PNEUMA 5Dα	SPIRIT 683A
5	AIGIALOS	SHORE 21B
	GINOMAI 13E	TAKE PLACE 158B
	GONU	KNEE 164B
	GUN8 1	WOMAN 167C
	EXARTIZW 1	FINISH 273A
	EXW 2B	OUTSIDE 279B
	HEWS 112C	AS FAR AS 335D
	PROPEMPW 1	ACCOMPANY 716B
	TITH8MI 11Bα	PUT 823D
6	APASPAZOMAI	TAKE LEAVE 81A
	ASPAZOMAI 1A	GREET 116B
	EMBAINW	GO IN 253C
	IDIOS 3B	ONES OWN 370D
	PLOION 1	SHIP 679B
	HUPOSTREPHW	RETURN 855B
7	ASPAZOMAI 1B	GREET 116C
	DIANUW 1	COMPLETE 186C
	HEIS 1Aα	ONE 230A
	H8MERA 2	DAY 347A
	KATANTAW 1	ARRIVE 416B
	MENW 1Aα	REMAIN 504D
	MENW 1Aα	REMAIN 504D
	PARA 111Bγ	BESIDE 615C
	PLOOS	VOYAGE 679C
	PTOLEMAIS	PTOLEMAIS 735A
	TUROS	TYRE 838C
8	EISERCHOMAI 1Aβ	COME 231D
	EK 4A6	FROM 235B
	EPAURION	NEXT DAY 283C
	HEPTA	SEVEN 306B
	EUAGGELIST8S	EVANGELIST 318C
	KAISAREIA 2	CAESAREA 396D
	MENW 1Aα	REMAIN 504D
	PARA 111Bα	BESIDE 615B
	PERI 2A6	ABOUT 651A
	PHILIPPOS 4	PHILIP 868A
8F	PHILIPPOS 4	PHILIP 868A
9	THUGAT8R 1	DAUGHTER 365B
	PARTHENOS 1	VIRGIN 632C
	PROPH8TEUW 1	PROPHESY 730B
10	HAGABOS	AGABUS 2B
	EPIMENW 1	REMAIN 296A
	H8MERA 2	DAY 347A
	IOUDAIA 1	JUDAEA 379D
	KATERCHOMAI 1	COME DOWN 423A
	ONOMA 11	NAME 574A
	POLUS 111A	MANY 695C
	PROPH8T8S 5	PROPHET 731C
11	AIRW 3	CARRY 24A
	*DEW 1B	BIND 176D
	LEGW III C	ORDER 470D
	HODE 1	THIS 555C
	PARADIDWMI 1B	GIVE OVER 620D
	PNEUMA 5Cα	SPIRIT 682D
	PNEUMA 6C	SPIRIT 684A
11A	ZWN8	BELT 342A
11A	CHEIR 1	HAND 888A

11B	ZWN8	BELT	342A
11B	CHEIR 2B	HAND	888D
12	ANABAINW IAα	GO UP	49D
	ENTOPIOS	LOCAL	268D
	HIEROSOLUMA IA	JERUSALEM	373D
	HO,H8,TO II48є	THE	554A
	PARAKALEW 3	IMPLORE	622D
	HWS IVIA	WHEN	907A
13	ALLA IA	BUT, YET	37B
	APOTHN8SKW IAα	DIE	90D
	GAR IE	FOR	151C
	DEW IB	BIND	176D
	EIS 9A	IN	229D
	HETOIMWS	BE READY	317A
	ECHW III	BE	334B
	THORUBEW I		363C

THROW INTO DISORDER

	KARDIA I8є	HEART	405A
	KLAIW I	WEEP	434A
	KURIOS 2Cγ	LORD	461A
	ONOMA I4Cθ	NAME	576D
	POIEW II8є	DO	688A
	SUNTHRUPTW	BREAK IN PIECES	797C
	HUPER ID	IN BEHALF OF	846D
14	H8SUCHAZW 2	REST	349D
	THEL8MA IA	WILL	354D
	PEITHW 3A	BELIEVE	645B
15	ANABAINW IAα	GO UP	49D
	APOSKEUAZW	LAY ASIDE	97C
	EPISKEUAZOMAI		298C

MAKE PREPARATIONS

	HIEROSOLUMA IA	JERUSALEM	373D
16	AGW IB	BRING	14B
	ARCHAIOS I	ANCIENT	110D
	IASWN 3	JASON	369C
	KAISAREIA 2	CAESAREA	396D
	KUPRIOS 2	CYPRIAN	458D
	KWM8 I	VILLAGE	462D
	MNASWN	MNASON	526A
	XENIZW I RECEIVE AS A GUEST		550A
	HOS,H8,HO I5D	(REL PRON)	588C
	PARA III8α	BESIDE	615B
	SUN IB	WITH	789B
	SUNERCHOMAI 2	ASSEMBLE	796A
	TIS, TI 2Aβ	ANY ONE	828B
17	APODECHOMAI I	WELCOME	89C
	ASMENWS	GLADLY	116A
	GINOMAI I4Cα	COME, GO	158D
	DECHOMAI I	RECEIVE	176C
18	EISEIMI	GO IN	231D
	EPEIMI	THE NEXT	284A
	IAKWBOS 3	JAMES	368C
	PARAGINOMAI I	COME	618D
	PRESBUTEROS 2B	OLDER	707A
	SUNAGW 2	GATHER	790B
19	ASPAZOMAI IA	GREET	116B
	DIAKONIA 3	SERVICE	183C
	HEIS 5E	ONE	231B
	HEKASTOS 2	EACH	236A
	EX8GEOMAI	EXPLAIN	275B
	KATA II3A	(DISTRIBUTIVE)	407D
	HOS,H8,HO I4A	(REL PRON)	587D
20	DOXAZW I	PRAISE	203C

20	Z8LWT8S IAβ	ZEALOT	338D
	THEWREW 2A	OBSERVE	360D
	IOUDAIOS 2D	JEWISH	380B
	MURIAS 2	MYRIADS	531C
	NOMOS 3	LAW	544C
	PISTEUW 2B	BELIEVE	667C
	POSOS 2A	HOW GREAT	701B
	HUPARCHW 2	BE	846A
21	DIDASKW 2C	TEACH	191A
	ETHNOS 2	GENTILES	217C
	ETHOS 2	CUSTOM	217D
	IOUDAIOS 2C	JEWISH	380B
	KATA IIIA	ALONG	407A
	KAT8CHEW I		425A

MAKE ONE SELF UNDERSTOOD

	M8DE IB	AND NOT	519D
	PAS IFβ	ALL	638A
	PERIPATEW 2Aβ	GO ABOUT	655B
	PERITEMNW I	CUT AROUND	658A
22	OUN IСβ	THEREFORE	597C
	PANTWS I	BY ALL MEANS	614B
	PANTWS 3	OF COURSE	614B
	PL8THOS 2B6	QUANTITY	674D
	SUNERCHOMAI IA	ASSEMBLE	795D
23	EPI IIAα	ON	285D
	EUCH8 2	OATH	329C
	LEGW IIIC	ORDER	470D
24	HAGNIZW 2A	PURIFY	11A
	DAPANAW I	SPEND	170A
	EPI IIIBγ	ON	287A
	HINA I2	IN ORDER THAT	377D
	KAT8CHEW I		425A

MAKE ONE SELF UNDERSTOOD

	KEPHAL8 IA	HEAD	431B
	NOMOS 3	LAW	544D
	XURAW HAVE ONESELF SHAVED		551D
	HOS,H8,HO I4A	(REL PRON)	587D
	OUDEIS 2Bβ	WORTHLESS	596C
	HOUTOS IAβ	THIS	601A
	PARALAMBANW I	TAKE	624D
	STOICHEW BE IN LINE WITH		777A
	SUN 2A	WITH	789C
	PHULASSW IF	WATCH	876C
25	HAIMA IB	BLOOD	22B
	EIDWLOTHUTOS		220C

MEAT OFFERED TO AN IDOL

	EPISTELLW	WRITE	300C
	KRINW 3	DECIDE	452C
	PISTEUW 2B	BELIEVE	667C
	PNIKTOS	STRANGLED	686B
	T8REW 5	KEEP	822D
	TOIOUTOS	SUCH A KIND	828D
	PHULASSW 2A	WATCH	876C
26	HAGNIZW 2A	PURIFY	11A
	HAGNISMOS I	PURIFICATION	11A
	DIAGGELLW 2	GIVE NOTICE OF	181B
	EISEIMI	GO IN	231C
	HEKASTOS 2	EACH	236A
	EKPL8RWSIS	COMPLETION	243C
	ECHW III3	HOLD FAST	334C
	HEWS IIIBα	UNTIL	335C
	H8MERA 2	DAY	347C
	PARALAMBANW I	TAKE	624D

26 PROSPHERW 2A   BRING (TO) 727B
   PROSPHORA 2   PRESENTING 727D
   HUPER IAY   IN BEHALF OF 846B
27 ASIA   ASIA 115C
   HEBDOMOS   SEVENTH 212A
   EPIBALLW IB   LAY ON 289D
   THEAOMAI IA   SEE 353C
   MELLW ICα   BE ABOUT TO 502A
   OCHLOS I   CROWD 605C
   SUGCHEW   CONFUSE 782D
   SUNTELEW I   COMPLETE 799D
   HWS IVIB   WHEN 907A
28 HAGIOS IAα   DEDICATED TO GOD 9C
   AN8R 3   MAN 66A
   BO8THEW I   AID 144A
   HELL8N 2A   GENTILE 251C
   ETI 2B   STILL 316A
   ISRA8LIT8S   ISRAELITE 382C
   KATA I2Bβ   DOWN 406D
   KOINOW IB   DEFILE 439B
   KRAZW 2A   CALL 448D
   NOMOS 3   LAW 544D
   PANTACH8   EVERYWHERE 613A
28B TOPOS IB   PLACE 830B
28F EISAGW   BRING 231C
29 EPHESIOS   EPHESIAN 330B
   NOMIZW 2   THINK 543D
   PROORAW I   SEE PREVIOUSLY 716A
   TROPHIMOS   TROPHIMUS 835C
30 GINOMAI IIBβ   COME ABOUT 157B
   HELKW IA   DRAG 251A
   EXW 2B   OUTSIDE 279B
   EPILAMBANOMAI I   GRASP 295A
   THURA IA   DOOR 366B
   KINEW 2B   MOVE 433D
   KLEIW I   SHUT 435A
   LAOS IA   PEOPLE 467D
   HOLOS 2B   WHOLE 567D
   POLIS 3   CITY 692C
   SUNDROM8   RUNNING TOGETHER 793C
   TE 3B   AND 815C
31 ANABAINW 2   GO UP 50A
   HIEROSOLUMA IB   JERUSALEM 373D
   KLAUDIOS 2   CLAUDIUS 434C
   HOLOS I   WHOLE 567C
   HOTI IBα   THAT 592D
   SPEIRA   COHORT 768C
   SUGCHEW   CONFUSE 782D
   PHASIS   INFORMATION 862A
31•3 CHILIARCHOS   TRIBUNE 890A
32 HEKATONTARCH8S   CENTURION 236C
   EXAUT8S   AT ONCE 273B
   KATATRECHW   RUN DOWN 420D
   PARALAMBANW I   TAKE 624D
   PAUW 2   STOP 643C
   TUPTW I   STRIKE 838A
33 HALUSIS I   CHAIN 40D
   DEW IB   BIND 176D
   DUO 3   TWO 208C
   EGGIZW 5A   APPROACH 212D
   EPILAMBANOMAI I   GRASP 295A
   KELEUW   COMMAND 428C
   PUNTHANOMAI I   INQUIRE 737A

34 AGW 2   LEAD AWAY 14B
   ALLOS IC   OTHER 39C
   GINWSKW 2A   FIND OUT 160A
   DIA BIII   BECAUSE OF 180A
   EPIPHWNEW   CRY OUT 304C
   THORUBOS I   NOISE 363C
   KELEUW   COMMAND 428C
   PAREMBOL8 2   A CAMP 630D
34F OCHLOS I   CROWD 605C
35 ANABATHMOS   STEP 49C
   BASTAZW 2A   CARRY 136D
   BIA IB   FORCE 140A
   GINOMAI I4Cγ   COME, GO 159A
   SUMBAINW   MEET 785A
36 AIRW 4   TAKE AWAY 24A
   AKOLOUTHEW I   FOLLOW 30C
   KRAZW 2A   CALL 448D
   LAOS IA   PEOPLE 467D
   PL8THOS 2Bα   QUANTITY 674C
37 GINWSKW 6E   KNOW 160D
   EI VI   IF 218D
   EISAGW   BRING 231C
   HELL8NISTI THE GREEK LANGUAGE 251D
   EXESTI 2   IT IS POSSIBLE 274D
   PAREMBOL8 2   A CAMP 630D
   CHILIARCHOS   TRIBUNE 890A
38 AIGUPTIOS   EGYPTIAN 21C
   ANASTATOW   DISTURB 60C
   ARA 2   THEN 103C
   EXAGW I   LEAD OUT 271B
   ER8MOS 2   DESERT 309A
   H8MERA 4B   TIME 348B
   PRO 2   BEFORE 708C
   SIKARIOS   ASSASSIN 757D
   TETRAKOSIOI   FOUR HUNDRED 821B
   TETRAKISCHILIOI FOUR THOUSAND 821B
39 ANTHRWPOS 3Aα   MAN 68C
   AS8MOS 2   INSIGNIFICANT 114C
   DEOMAI 3   ASK 174B
   EPITREPW I   ALLOW 303C
   IOUDAIOS I   JEWISH 380A
   KILIKIA   CILICIA 433B
   OU 2B   NO 594C
   POLIS I   CITY 692A
   POLIT8S I   CITIZEN 693B
   SUGCHWREW 2   CONFUSION 783A
   TARSEUS   FROM TARSUS 813B
   TARSOS   TARSUS 813B
40 ANABATHMOS   STEP 49C
   GINOMAI IIBβ   COME ABOUT 157B
   DIALEKTOS   LANGUAGE 184D
   HEBRAIS   HEBREW LANGUAGE 212C
   EPI IIAα   ON 285D
   EPITREPW I   ALLOW 303C
   H8SUCHIA 2   SILENCE 350A
   HIST8MI II2Bβ   BEING 383C
   POLUS IIBβ   MANY 694D
   SIG8   SILENCE 757B

ACTS 22

1 APOLOGIA I   DEFENSE 95B
  NUNI   NOW 548B

1	NUNI ID	NOW 548C
	PAT8R 2B	FATHER 640D
2	AKOUW IC	HEAR 31D
	DIALEKTOS	LANGUAGE 184D
	HEBRAIS	HEBREW LANGUAGE 212C
	H8SUCHAZW 2	REST 349D
	H8SUCHIA 2	SILENCE 350A
	MALLON I	MORE 490B
	PARECHW 1B	GRANT 632A
	PROSPHWNEW I	CALL OUT 727D
3	AKRIBEIA	EXACTNESS 32C
	ANATREPHW 2	BRING UP 62B
	GAMALI8L	GAMALIEL 150A
	EIMI 119B	TO BE 224A
	Z8LWT8S IAα	ZEALOT 338C
	IOUDAIOS I	JEWISH 380A
	KATA II5Aα	ACCORDING TO 408A
	KILIKIA	CILICIA 433B
	NOMOS 3	LAW 544C
	PAIDEUW I	INSTRUCT 608D
	PARA IIIIC	ALONG 616A
	PAS IEα	ALL 637D
	PATRWOS	PATERNAL 642D
	POLIS I	CITY 692A
	POUS IA	FOOT 703B
	TARSEUS	FROM TARSUS 813B
	TARSOS	TARSUS 813B
	HUPARCHW 2	BE 846A
4	ACHRI IC	AS FAR AS 128C
	DESMEUW I	BIND 174D
	DIWKW 2	PERSECUTE 200B
	THANATOS IA	DEATH 351C
	HODOS 2C	WAY 557B
	PARADIDWMI 1B	GIVE OVER 620B
	TE 3A	AND 815B
	PHULAK8 3	GUARD 875C
5	AGW 2	LEAD AWAY 14B
	HANANIAS 4	ANANIAS 58A
	DECHOMAI I	TAKE 176B
	DEW 1B	BIND 176D
	EKEISE 2	THERE 239C
	EPISTOL8	LETTER 301A
	MARTUREW IA	BEAR WITNESS 493D
	PARA I3B	FROM 614D
	POREUW I	PROCEED 699A
	PRESBUTERION I	706B
	COUNCIL OF ELDERS	
	TIMWREW	PUNISH 826B
	HWS II4A	SO 906B
5F	DAMASKOS	DAMASCUS 169C
6	GINOMAI I3E	TAKE PLACE 158B
	EGGIZW I	APPROACH 212C
	EXAIPHN8S	SUDDENLY 271D
	HIKANOS IA	SUFFICIENT 375A
	OURANOS 2B	HEAVEN 599C
	PERIASTRAPTW 2	SHINE AROUND 651C
	PERIASTRAPTW I	SHINE AROUND 651C
	POREUW I	PROCEED 699B
	PHWS IA	LIGHT 879D
6A	PERI 2B	ABOUT 651A
6B	PERI 2Aα	ABOUT 650D
7	EDAPHOS	GROUND 216D
	PIPTW 1Bα	FALL 665B
7	SAOUL 2	SAUL 749C
	SAULOS	SAUL 752D
	PHWN8 2D	VOICE 879C
7F	DIWKW 2	PERSECUTE 200B
8	NAZWRAIOS	NAZARENE 534B
9	AKOUW 1Bα	HEAR 31B
	EIMI IIIIO	TO BE 224D
	EMPHOBOS	AFRAID 257B
	THEAOMAI IA	SEE 353C
	SUN IC	WITH 789B
	PHWN8 2D	VOICE 879C
	PHWS IA	LIGHT 879D
10	KAKEI I	AND THERE 397C
	LALEW 2A6	SPEAK 464C
	HOS,H8,HO I4A	(REL PRON) 587D
	POREUW I	PROCEED 699A
	TASSW 2A	PLACE 813D
10B	KURIOS 2Cγ	LORD 460D
10F	DAMASKOS	DAMASCUS 169C
11	APO VI	BECAUSE OF 87B
	DOXA IA	BRIGHTNESS 202C
	EMBLEPW I	LOOK AT 254A
	SUNEIMI I	BE WITH 794D
	PHWS IA	LIGHT 879D
	CHEIRAGWGEW	LEAD BY THE HAND 889A
	HWS IVIB	WHEN 907A
12	HANANIAS 3	ANANIAS 58A
	AN8R 4	MAN 66B
	EULAB8S	DEVOUT 322B
	KATOIKEW IA	LIVE 425C
	MARTUREW 2B	BE APPROVED 494B
	NOMOS 3	LAW 544C
	TIS, TI 2Aβ	ANY ONE 828B
13	EIS IDα	TOWARD 227D
	EPHIST8MI IA	STAND BY 331A
	SAOUL 2	SAUL 749C
	HWRA 2B	TIME OF DAY 904D
13A	ANABLEPW I	LOOK UP 50C
13B	ANABLEPW I	LOOK UP 50C
14	EIDON IA	SEE 219C
	EK 3C	FROM 234B
	THEL8MA ICγ	WILL 355A
	PROCHEIRIZW	SELECT 731D
	STOMA IA	MOUTH 777B
	PHWN8 2C	VOICE 879A
15	ANTHRWPOS 3Aζ	MAN 68C
	MARTUS 2C	WITNESS 495C
	HORAW IAβ	SEE 581C
	HOS,H8,HO I4A	(REL PRON) 587D
	PAS IB	ALL 637A
16	HAMARTIA I	SIN 42C
	APOLOUW	WASH ONESELF 95C
	BAPTIZW 2Bα	BAPTIZE 131C
	EPIKALEW 2B	CALL UPON 294B
	MELLW 3	DELAY 502D
	NUN 2	NOW 548A
	ONOMA I4B	NAME 575A
17	GINOMAI I3E	TAKE PLACE 158B
	GINOMAI II4A	BE 159C
18	DIOTI 3	FOR 198C
	EXERCHOMAI IAα	GO OUT 273D
	MARTURIA 2Dα	TESTIMONY 494C
	PARADECHOMAI I	ACCEPT 619C

18 SPEUDW IA   HURRY 769D   26 HORAW 2B   SEE 582B
   TACHOS   SPEED 814D   26=9 CHILIARCHOS   TRIBUNE 890A
19 AUTOS 2   THEY 122D   27 NAI IA   YES 534D
   DERW   BEAT 174D   28 GENNAW 2   BEAR 155A
   EPI III1Bα   TOWARD 289A   DE 4A   BUT, AND 170D
   EPISTAMAI 2   KNOW 300A   KAI II2   EVEN 394B
   KAGW 2   BUT I 387A   KEPHALAION 2 SUM OF MONEY 431A
   KATA III0   (DISTRIBUTIVE) 407B   KTAOMAI I   GET 456A
   PISTEUW 2Aδ   BELIEVE 667B   POLITEIA I   CITIZENSHIP 692D
   SUNAGWG8 2A   790C   POLUS IIBα   MANY 694C
        PLACE OF ASSEMBLY   POSOS I   HOW GREAT 701A
   PHULAKIZW   IMPRISON 876A   29 ANETAZW   GIVE A HEARING 64D
20 HAIMA 2A   BLOOD 22B   APHIST8MI 2B   KEEP AWAY 126C
   ANAIREW IA   DO AWAY WITH 54C   DE 4B   BUT, AND 170D
   EKCHEW I   POUR OUT 246D   DEW IB   BIND 176D
   EPHIST8MI 2A   STAND BY 331A   EPIGINWSKW 2B   KNOW 291A
   HIMATION 2   GARMENT 377B   LUW 2A   LOOSE 484D
   MARTUS 3   WITNESS 495C   PARACHR8MA   AT ONCE 629B
   HOTE IA   WHEN 592C   RWMAIOS   ROMAN 745C
   PRWTOMARTUS FIRST MARTYR 732C   30 ARCHIEREUS IB HIGH PRIEST 112C
   STEPHANOS   STEPHEN 774C   BOULOMAI 2Aβ   DESIRE 145D
   SUNEUDOKEW   AGREE WITH 796C   GINWSKW 2A   FIND OUT 160A
   PHULASSW IC   WATCH 876B   DESMOS I   FETTER 175A
21 EXAPOSTELLW IB   SEND OUT 272D   EPAURION   NEXT DAY 283C
   MAKRAN IAα   FAR 488D   HIST8MI IIAα   PUT 382D
22 AIRW 4   TAKE AWAY 24A   KATAGW   LEAD 411A
   ACHRI IB   AS FAR AS 128C   KAT8GOREW IA BRING CHARGES 424C
   G8 5B   EARTH 156D   KELEUW   COMMAND 428C
   EPAIRW I   RAISE UP 281C   LUW 2A   LOOSE 484D
   KATH8KW   TO BE PROPER 389D   HO,H8,TO II8A   THE 554D
   TOIOUTOS 3Aα SUCH A KIND 829B   SUNEDRION 2   SANHEDRIN 794A
   PHWN8 2A   VOICE 878D   SUNERCHOMAI IA   ASSEMBLE 795D
23 A8R   AIR 19D
   BALLW IB   THROW 130C   ACTS 23
   HIMATION 2   GARMENT 377B
   KONIORTOS   DUST 444A   1 AGATHOS IBβ   GOOD   3B
   KRAUGAZW 2A   CRY 450C   AN8R I   MAN 66A
   RIPTW I   THROW 743D   ATENIZW LOOK INTENTLY AT 119C
24 AITIA I   CAUSE 25D   ACHRI IA   UNTIL 128B
   ANETAZW   GIVE A HEARING 64D   PAS IAδ   ALL 637A
   EISAGW   BRING 231C   POLITEUOMAI 3   LIVE 693B
   EPIGINWSKW 2B   KNOW 291A   SUNEDRION 2   SANHEDRIN 794A
   EPIPHWNEW   CRY OUT 304C   SUNEID8SIS 2 CONSCIOUSNESS 794B
   KELEUW   COMMAND 428C   2 HANANIAS 4   ANANIAS 58A
   MASTIX I   WHIP 496B   EPITASSW   COMMAND 302A
   PAREMBOL8 2   A CAMP 630D   PARIST8MI 2Bα   BE PRESENT 633D
   CHILIARCHOS   TRIBUNE 890A   PARIST8MI 2Bα   BE PRESENT 633D
25 AKATAKRITOS UNCONDEMNED 29B   PARIST8MI 2Bα   BE PRESENT 633D
   ANTHRWPOS 3Aα   MAN 68C   STOMA IA   MOUTH 777B
   EI VI   IF 218D   TUPTW I   STRIKE 838A
   HEKATONTARCH8S CENTURION 236C   2B ANATHEMATIZW I   54A
   EXESTI 2   IT IS POSSIBLE 274D   BIND WITH AN OATH
   HIMAS   STRAP 376D   3 KATH8MAI IAδ   SIT 390B
   HIST8MI II2Bγ   BEING 383C   KAI 16   AND 394A
   KAI I3   AND 394A   KELEUW   COMMAND 428C
   MASTIZW   SCOURGE 496B   KONIAW   WHITEWASH 444A
   PROTEINW   STRETCH OUT 729B   KRINW 4Aα   JUDGE 452D
   HWS IVIA   WHEN 907A   NOMOS 3   LAW 544C
25=7 RWMAIOS   ROMAN 745C   PARANOMEW   BREAK THE LAW 626C
26 APAGGELLW I   REPORT 78C   TOICHOS   WALL 829B
   GAR IE   FOR 151C   3A TUPTW 2   STRIKE 838B
   HEKATONTARCH8S CENTURION 236C   3B TUPTW I   STRIKE 838A
   MELLW IСα   BE ABOUT TO 502A   4 LOIDOREW   REVILE 480C

4	PARIST8MI 2Bα	BE PRESENT 633D	10 CHILIARCHOS	TRIBUNE 890A
5	ARCHWN 2A	AUTHORITIES 113C	11 DIAMARTUROMAI 2	TESTIFY 185C
	EIPON 1	SAY 225C	EIS 1Dβ	IN 227D
	KAKWS 2	BADLY 399B	EPEIMI	THE NEXT 284A
	OU 4B	NO 594D	EPHIST8MI 1A	STAND BY 331A
6	ANASTASIS 2B	RESURRECTION 60A	THARSEW	BE CHEERFUL 352C
	AN8R 1	MAN 66A	MARTUREW 1B	BEAR WITNESS 494A
	GINWSKW 4C	PERCEIVE 160C	HOUTW	THUS 602B
	EIMI IV2	TO BE 225A	HOUTW 1A	THUS 602B
	ELPIS 2A	HOPE 252C	PERI II	ABOUT 650D
	HETEROS 1A	OTHER 315A	RWM8	ROME 745D
	KAI IID	AND 392D	HWS III	SO 905D
	KRAZW 2A	CALL 448D	12 ANATHEMATIZW 1	54A
	KRINW 4Aα	JUDGE 452D	BIND WITH AN OATH	
	MEROS 1Bζ	PARTY 507B	GINOMAI IIBγ	COME ABOUT 157B
	NEKROS 2A	DEAD 537A	ESTHIW 1Eγ	EAT 313B
	HO,H8,TO III1	THE 555B	HEWS IIIBα	UNTIL 335C
	SUNEDRION 2	SANHEDRIN 794A	M8TE	AND NOT 521D
	HUIOS 1Aα	SON 841B	POIEW IIB6	DO 687D
6B	*PHARISAIOS	PHARISEE 861C	SUSTROPH8 1	COMMOTION 803B
6F	SADDOUKAIOS	SADDUCEE 747A	13 EIMI II7	TO BE 223D
6=8	PHARISAIOS	PHARISEE 861C	POIEW IIB6	DO 687D
7	GINOMAI IIBβ	COME ABOUT 157B	POIEW II1	DO 689C
	EPIPIPTW 2	FALL UPON 297D	POLUS IIIA	MANY 695D
	PL8THOS 2Bβ	QUANTITY 674C	SUNWMOSIA	PLOT 801C
	STASIS 3	UPRISING 772A	14 ANATHEMA 2B	ACCURSED 54A
	SCHIZW 2B	SPLIT 805B	ANATHEMATIZW 1	54A
8	AMPHOTEROI 2	ALL 47A	BIND WITH AN OATH	
	GAR 1B	FOR 151B	ARCHIEREUS 1B	HIGH PRIEST 112C
	EIMI I1	TO BE 222B	GEUOMAI 1	TASTE 156A
	MEN	(PARTICLE) 503C	HEWS IIIBα	UNTIL 335C
	M8 AIIIBα	NOT 517D	HOSTIS 3	WHOEVER 591B
	M8TE	AND NOT 521D	PRESBUTEROS 2Aβ	OLDER 706D
	HOMOLOGEW 4	CONFESS 571B	15 ANAIREW 1A	DO AWAY WITH 54C
	SADDOUKAIOS	SADDUCEE 747A	AURION 1	TOMORROW 121D
8F	PNEUMA 4B	SPIRIT 681D	DIAGINWSKW	DECIDE 181C
9	GINOMAI IIBβ	COME ABOUT 157B	EGGIZW 5A	APPROACH 212D
	GRAMMATEUS 2	SCRIBES 165A	EMPHANIZW 2	MAKE VISIBLE 257B
	DIAMACHOMAI	CONTEND SHARPLY 185C	HETOIMOS 2	READY 316D
	HEURISKW 2	FIND 325D	KATAGW	LEAD 411A
	THEOMACHEW	OPPOSE GOD 357A	MELLW 1Cγ	INTEND 502B
	KAKOS 1C	EVIL 398D	NUN 1C	NOW 547D
	KRAUG8 1A	SHOUT 450C	NUN 2	NOW 548A
	MEGAS 2Aγ	GREAT 498D	HOPWS 2Aα	IN ORDER THAT 580C
	MEROS 1Bζ	PARTY 507B	OUN 5	THEREFORE 597D
	PHARISAIOS	PHARISEE 861C	PERI II	ABOUT 650D
10	AGW 2	LEAD AWAY 14B	PRO 2	BEFORE 708D
	HARPAZW 2A	SNATCH 108D	SUN 4B	WITH 789D
	GINOMAI IIBβ	COME ABOUT 157B	SUNEDRION 2	SANHEDRIN 794A
	DE 2	BUT, AND 170D	CHILIARCHOS	TRIBUNE 890A
	DIASPAW	TEAR APART 187C	HWS III2	SO 906D
	EK 1B	AWAY FROM 233C	16 ADELPH8 1	SISTER 15C
	EULABEOMAI 1	BE AFRAID 322B	AKOUW 3B	LEARN 31D
	KATABAINW 1Aα	COME DOWN 409B	APAGGELLW 1	REPORT 78C
	KELEUW	COMMAND 428C	EISERCHOMAI 1Aβ	COME 231D
	MESOS 2	THE MIDDLE 509A	ENEDRON	AMBUSH 264A
	M8 B1B	NOT 519A	ENEDRA	AMBUSH 264A
	PAREMBOL8 2	A CAMP 630D	PARAGINOMAI 1	COME 618D
	POLUS IIBβ	MANY 694D	PAREMBOL8 2	A CAMP 630D
	STASIS 3	UPRISING 772A	HUIOS 1Aα	SON 841B
	STRATEUMA	ARMY 778A	17 APAGW 2A	LEAD AWAY 78D
	TE 1B	AND 815B	HEKATONTARCH8S	CENTURION 236C
	PHOBEW 1A	BE AFRAID 870D	ECHW I6B	MUST 334A

17	NEANIAS	YOUTH 536B		24	DIASWZW	SAVE 188B
17F	PROSKALEW 1A	SUMMON 722C			EGKL8MA 2	REPROACH 215B
17=19	CHILIARCHOS	TRIBUNE 890A			EPIBIBAZW	CAUSE TO MOUNT 290B
18	AGW 1A	LEAD 14A			H8GEMWN 2	GOVERNORS 344A
	DESMIOS	PRISONER 175A			KT8NOS	ANIMAL 456B
	ECHW 16B	MUST 334A			PARIST8MI 1A	PLACE BESIDE 633A
	MEN 2E	(PARTICLE) 504C			PH8LIX	FELIX 863D
	NEANIAS	YOUTH 536B		25	GRAPHW 4	WRITE 166B
	NEANISKOS 1	YOUTH 536C			EPISTOL8	LETTER 300D
	HO,H8,TO I3	THE 552A			PERIECHW 2A	SEIZE 652D
19	ANACHWREW 2B	WITHDRAW 63A			TUPOS 4	MARK 837D
	APAGGELLW 1	REPORT 78C		26	H8GEMWN 2	GOVERNORS 344A
	EPILAMBANOMAI 1	GRASP 295A			KLAUDIOS 2	CLAUDIUS 434C
	ECHW 16B	MUST 334A			KRATISTOS 1	MOST NOBLE 450A
	IDIOS 4	PRIVATELY 371A			LUSIAS	LYSIAS 483C
	PUNTHANOMAI 1	INQUIRE 737A			PH8LIX	FELIX 863D
20	AURION 1	TOMORROW 121D			CHAIRW 2B	REJOICE 882B
	ERWTAW 2	ASK 312B		27	ANAIREW 1A	DO AWAY WITH 54C
	KATAGW	LEAD 411A			EXAIREW 2A	DELIVER 271C
	HO,H8,TO II4B«	THE 554A			EPHIST8MI 1A	STAND BY 331A
	HOPWS 2B	IN ORDER THAT 580D			MANTHANW 3	FIND OUT 491C
	PUNTHANOMAI 1	INQUIRE 737A			MELLW 1C«	BE ABOUT TO 502A
	SUNEDRION 2	SANHEDRIN 794A			RWMAIOS	ROMAN 745C
	SUNTITH8MI 2Aβ	AGREE 800C			STRATEUMA	ARMY 778A
	HWS III2	SO 906D			SULLAMBANW 1A«	SEIZE 784B
21	ANATHEMATIZW 1	54A		28	AITIA 2A	CHARGE 25D
	BIND WITH AN OATH				BOULOMAI 2Aβ	DESIRE 145D
	ANAIREW 1A	DO AWAY WITH 54C			EGKALEW	ACCUSE 214C
	APO V4	FROM 87C			EPIGINWSKW 2B	KNOW 291A
	ENEDREUW	LIE IN WAIT 264A			KATAGW	LEAD 411A
	EPAGGELIA 1	PROMISE 280A			SUNEDRION 2	SANHEDRIN 794A
	ESTHIW 1Eγ	EAT 313B		29	DESMOS 1	FETTER 175A
	HETOIMOS 2	READY 316D			EGKALEW	ACCUSE 214C
	HEWS III8«	UNTIL 335C			EGKL8MA 1	ACCUSATION 215B
	M8TE	AND NOT 521D			HEURISKW 2	FIND 325D
	NUN 1C	NOW 547D			ECHW 12I	HAVE 333C
	HOSTIS 3	WHOEVER 591B			Z8T8MA	ISSUE 339D
	OUN 4	THEREFORE 597D			THANATOS 1B«	DEATH 351C
	PEITHW 3C	OBEY 645C			MOLIS 1	WITH DIFFICULTY 528C
	POLUS III A	MANY 695D			NOMOS 3	LAW 544C
	PROSDECHOMAI 2B	RECEIVE 719B		30	EIMI III2	TO BE 224A
22	EKLALEW	TELL 241C			EIS 4C«	AGAINST 228C
	EMPHANIZW 2	MAKE VISIBLE 257B			EXAUT8S	AT ONCE 273B
	MEN 2E	(PARTICLE) 504C			EPI I1A6	BEFORE 286A
	NEANIAS	YOUTH 536B			EPIBOUL8	A PLOT 290C
	NEANISKOS 1	YOUTH 536C			KAT8GOROS	ACCUSER 424D
	PARAGGELLW	GIVE ORDERS 618C			LEGW 14	SAY 469D
	CHILIARCHOS	TRIBUNE 890A			M8NUW	REVEAL 521A
23	APO II2A	FROM 86B			*PARAGGELLW	GIVE ORDERS 618C
	DEXIOLABOS	BOWMAN 173C			PEMPW !	SEND 647C
	HEBDOM8KONTA	SEVENTY 212A			PEMPW 1	SEND 647D
	HEKATONTARCH8S	CENTURION 236C			PEMPW 1	SEND 648A
	HETOIMAZW 2	PREPARE 316B			RWNNUMI	BE STRONG 745D
	HIPPEUS	HORSEMAN 381B			HUPO 1B	BY 851A
	KAISAREIA 2	CAESAREA 396D		31	AGW 2	LEAD AWAY 14B
	NUX 1A	NIGHT 548C			ANALAMBANW 4	TAKE ALONG 56C
	HOPWS 2A«	IN ORDER THAT 580C			ANTIPATRIS	ANTIPATRIS 75A
	POREUW 1	PROCEED 699A			DIA AIIIA	THROUGH 178D
	PROSKALEW 1A	SUMMON 722C			DIATASSW	ORDER 188C
	TIS, TI 2B«	ANY ONE 828B			MEN 2E	(PARTICLE) 504C
	TRITOS 1	THIRD 834B			NUX 1B	NIGHT 548D
	HWRA 2B	TIME OF DAY 904C		32	EAW 1	LET 211D
24	HARPAZW 2A	SNATCH 108D			EPAURION	NEXT DAY 283C

32	HIPPEUS	HORSEMAN 381B
	PAREMBOL8 2	A CAMP 630D
33	EISERCHOMAI IAα	COME 231D
	EPISTOL8	LETTER 300D
	H8GEMWN 2	GOVERNORS 344A
	KAISAREIA 2	CAESAREA 396D
	HOSTIS 3	WHOEVER 591B
	PARIST8MI IBα	PRESENT 633A
34	ANAGINWSKW I	READ 51C
	EK 3B	FROM 234B
	EPARCHEIA	PROVINCE 283B
	EPERWTAW IA	ASK 285A
	KILIX	CILICIAN 433B
	KILIKIA	CILICIA 433B
	POIOS 2Aβ	OF WHAT KIND 691B
	PUNTHANOMAI 2	INQUIRE 737A
35	AN 3A	(PARTICLE) 48B
	DIAKOUW	GIVE A HEARING 184A
	H8RWD8S I	HEROD 349B
	KAT8GOROS	ACCUSER 424D
	KELEUW	COMMAND 428C
	PARAGINOMAI I	COME 618D
	PRAITWRION	THE PRAETORIUM 704B
	PH8MI IBβ	SAY 864A
	PHULASSW IB	WATCH 876B

ACTS 24

I	HANANIAS 4	ANANIAS 58A
	EMPHANIZW 2	MAKE VISIBLE 257B
	H8GEMWN 2	GOVERNORS 344A
	H8MERA 2	DAY 347B
	KATA I2Bβ	DOWN 406D
	KATABAINW IAβ	COME DOWN 409B
	META AIIIA	WITH 509D
	HOSTIS 3	WHOEVER 591B
	PRESBUTEROS 2Aβ	OLDER 706D
	R8TWR	PUBLIC SPEAKER 743B
IF	TERTULLOS	TERTULLUS 820C
2	GINOMAI I2A	COME ABOUT 157C
	DIORTHWMA	REFORM 198A
	EIR8N8 IA	PEACE 226B
	KALEW IE	CALL 400C
	KAT8GOREW IA	BRING CHARGES 424C
	KATORTHWMA	SUCCESS 426A
	POLUS IIBβ	MANY 694C
	PRONOIA 2	FORESIGHT 715D
	SOS I	YOURS 766C
	TUGCHANW I	MEET 837A
3	APODECHOMAI 2	RECOGNIZE 89C
	EUCHARISTIA I	THANKFULNESS 328D
	KRATISTOS I	MOST NOBLE 450A
	META AIIII	WITH 511A
	PANTACHOU I	EVERYWHERE 613B
	PANT8	ALTOGETHER 613C
	PAS IAδ	ALL 637A
	TE 3A	AND 815B
	PH8LIX	FELIX 863D
4	AKOUW IC	HEAR 31D
	EGKOPTW	HINDER 215C
	EPI III2B	ON 289C
	EPIEIKEIA	CLEMENCY 292C
	M8 AI2	NOT 517C

4	PARAKALEW 3	IMPLORE 622D
	POLUS II2C	MANY 696A
	SOS I	YOURS 766C
	SUNTOMWS 2	BRIEFLY 800D
5	HAIRESIS IA	SECT 23B
	KINEW 4A	MOVE 433D
	LOIMOS II	DISEASED 480D
	NAZWRAIOS	NAZARENE 534B
	OIKOUMEN8 2A	THE WORLD 564A
	PRWTOSTAT8S	LEADER 734A
	STASIS 3	UPRISING 772A
6	BEB8LOW	DESECRATE 138C
	H8METEROS	OUR 348C
	HIERON 2	TEMPLE 373A
	KRATEW IA	ARREST 449C
	KRINW 4Aα	JUDGE 452D
	NOMOS 3	LAW 544C
7	BIA 2	FORCE 140A
	LUSIAS	LYSIAS 483C
	PARERCHOMAI 3	COME 631D
	POLUS IIBβ	MANY 694C
	CHEIR 2B	HAND 888D
	CHILIARCHOS	TRIBUNE 890A
8	ANAKRINW IB	QUESTION 56A
	EPIGINWSKW 2B	KNOW 291A
	ERCHOMAI IIAβ	COME 310C
	KAT8GOREW IA	BRING CHARGES 424B
	KAT8GOROS	ACCUSER 424D
	PARA I3C	FROM 615A
	PAS IEβ	ALL 637D
9	ECHW II2	BE 334C
	SUNEPITITH8MI	JOIN IN ATTACK 795A
	SUNTITH8MI 2B	AGREE 800C
	PHASKW	SAY 862B
10	APOLOGEOMAI	DEFEND ONESELF 95B
	EK 5A	FROM 235C
	EMAUTOU 3	MYSELF 253B
	EPISTAMAI 2	KNOW 300B
	ETOS	YEAR 317B
	EUTHUMWS	CHEERFULLY 321A
	H8GEMWN 2	GOVERNORS 344A
	KRIT8S IAα	JUDGE 454C
	NEUW	NOD 538C
	HO,H8,TO II5	THE 554B
	PERI II	ABOUT 650D
	POLUS IIAα	MANY 694A
11	ANABAINW IAα	GO UP 49D
	APO II2C	SINCE 86C
	GINWSKW 2B	FIND OUT 160B
	DEKADUO	TWELVE 172D
	EPIGINWSKW 2B	KNOW 291A
	HOS,H8,HO IIIF	(REL PRON) 589A
	POLUS IIIA	MANY 695D
	PROSKUNEW 2A	DO REVERENCE 724A
12	DIALEGOMAI I	DISCUSS 184C
	EPISTASIS	PRESSURE 300B
	EPISUSTASIS	UPRISING 301D
	KATA IIIA	ALONG 407A
	OCHLOS I	CROWD 605C
	OCHLOS 2	CROWD 605D
	PISTEUW IAδ	BELIEVE 666B
	POIEW IIBγ	DO 687C
	POLIS I	CITY 692B

12F	OUTE	NOT 600C
13	KAT8GOREW IA	BRING CHARGES 424C
	NUNI IA	NOW 548B
	NUNI	NOW 548B
	HOS,H8,HO I2B@	(REL PRON) 587B
	PARIST8MI IF	PROVE 633C
14	HAIRESIS IA	SECT 23B
	LATREUW	SERVE 468C
	NOMOS 4A	LAW 545A
	HODOS 2C	WAY 557B
	HOMOLOGEW 3A	CONFESS 571B
	HOUTOS IB@	THIS 601C
	PATRWOS	PATERNAL 642D
	PROPH8T8S I	PROPHET 731A
14B	KATA IIIA	ALONG 407A
15	ADIKOS I	UNJUST 17D
	ANASTASIS 2B	RESURRECTION 60A
	AUTOS IA@	SELF 122B
	DIKAIOS IB	UPRIGHT 194D
	EIS 4C@	(GOAL) 228C
	*ELPIS 2B	HOPE 252D
	ECHW I2E@	HAVE 333A
	THEOS 3A	GOD 357D
	MELLW IA	WILL BE 502A
	PROSDECHOMAI IB	RECEIVE 719B
16	APROSKOPOS I	BLAMELESS 102A
	DIA AIIIA	THROUGH 178D
	EN III3A	BECAUSE OF 260C
	ECHW I2E@	HAVE 333B
	THEOS 3A	GOD 357D
	HOUTOS IB«	THIS 601C
	PROS III5A	TOWARD 717D
	SUNEID8SIS 2	CONSCIOUSNESS 794B
17	DE 2	BUT, AND 170D
	DIA AII2	AFTER 179A
	EIS 4G	FOR 229A
	ELE8MOSUN8	CHARITABLE GIVING 249B
	ETOS	YEAR 317B
	PARAGINOMAI I	COME 618D
	POIEW IIC@	DO 688C
	POLUS IIIA	MANY 695C
	PROSPHORA I	PRESENTING 727C
18	HAGNIZW 2A	PURIFY 11A
	THORUBOS 3B	NOISE 363C
	META AIII2	WITH 511A
	HOS,H8,HO IIIC	(REL PRON) 589A
	OCHLOS I	CROWD 605C
19	ASIA	ASIA 115C
	DEI 6B	IT IS NECESSARY 171C
	EI 13	IF 218B
	ECHW I7A	HAVE 334A
	KAT8GOREW IA	BRING CHARGES 424C
	PAREIMI IA	BE PRESENT 629C
	PROS III4A	TOWARD 717B
20	ADIK8MA	A WRONG 17C
	EPI IIA6	BEFORE 286A
	HEURISKW 2	FIND 325D
	HIST8MI II2B@	BEING 383C
	SUNEDRION 2	SANHEDRIN 794A
21	ANASTASIS 2B	RESURRECTION 60A
	8 2C	THAN 343C
	HIST8MI II2B@	BEING 383C
	KRAZW 2A	CALL 448D
21	KRINW 4A«	JUDGE 452D
	NEKROS 2A	DEAD 537A
	HOUTOS 2C	THIS 602A
	PHWN8 2C	VOICE 879A
22	ANABALLW	POSTPONE 50B
	DIAGINWSKW	DECIDE 181C
	KATA II6	WITH RESPECT TO 408D
	KATABAINW IA@	COME DOWN 409B
	LUSIAS	LYSIAS 483C
	HODOS 2C	WAY 557B
	PERI II	ABOUT 650D
	PH8LIX	FELIX 863D
	CHILIARCHOS	TRIBUNE 890A
23	ANESIS I	RELAXING 64D
	DIATASSW	ORDER 188C
	HEKATONTARCH8S	CENTURION 236C
	IDIOS 3A	ONES OWN 370D
	KWLUW I	HINDER 462C
	TE IB	AND 815B
	T8REW I	GUARD 822B
	HUP8RETEW	SERVE 850B
24	AKOUW IC	HEAR 31D
	DROUSILLA	DRUSILLA 206A
	EIS 4C@	(GOAL) 228C
	IDIOS 2C	ONES OWN 370C
	IOUDAIOS 2B	JEWISH 380B
	META BIII	AFTER 511B
	METAPEMPW	SUMMON 514D
	PARAGINOMAI I	COME 618D
	PISTIS 2B@	FAITH 669A
	CHRISTOS 2	ANOINTED ONE 895D
24F	PH8LIX	FELIX 863D
25	DIALEGOMAI I	DISCUSS 184C
	DIKAIOSUN8 2B	RIGHTEOUSNESS 195C
	EGKRATEIA	SELF CONTROL 215C
	EMPHOBOS	AFRAID 257B
	EPIT8DEIOS	PROPER 302C
	ECHW II2	BE 334C
	KAIROS 2	TIME 395D
	KRIMA 3	JUDGING 451D
	MELLW 2	IS DESTINED 502C
	METAKALEW	SUMMON 512C
	METALAMBANW 2	RECEIVE 512D
	NUN 3C	NOW 548B
26	HAMA IA	TOGETHER 41B
	DIO	THEREFORE 197D
	ELPIZW 2	HOPE 252A
	LUW 2A	LOOSE 484D
	METAPEMPW	SUMMON 514D
	HOMILEW	SPEAK 568B
	PUKNOS	FREQUENT 736C
	CHR8MA 2A	WEALTH 893D
27	DEW IB	BIND 176D
	DIADOCHOS	SUCCESSOR 181D
	DIETIA	TWO YEARS 194A
	DROUSILLA	DRUSILLA 206A
	KATALEIPW IA	LEAVE BEHIND 414C
	KATATITH8MI 2	GRANT A FAVOR 420D
	LAMBANW 2	RECEIVE 466B
	PL8ROW 2	MAKE FULL 677B
	PORKIOS	PORCIUS 699D
	PH8LIX	FELIX 863D
	PH8STOS	FESTUS 864B

27 CHARIS 3A   FAVOR 886A   8 HAMARTANW 4B   SIN 42A
                                                 APOLOGEOMAI   DEFEND ONESELF 95B
            ACTS 25   HIERON 2   TEMPLE 373A
                                                 KAISAR   EMPEROR 396B
1 ANABAINW 1Aα   GO UP   49D   NOMOS 3   LAW 544C
   EPARCHEIA   PROVINCE 283B   OUTE   NOT 600C
   EPARCHEIOS   PROVINCE 283B   TIS, TI 1Bβ   ANY ONE 828A
   EPIBAINW 2   GO UP 289D   9 ANABAINW 1Aα   GO UP 49D
   HIEROSOLUMA 1A   JERUSALEM 373D   KRINW 4Aα   JUDGE 452D
   KAISAREIA 2   CAESAREA 396D   PH8STOS   FESTUS 864C
   OUN 2B   THEREFORE 597C   CHARIS 3A   FAVOR 886A
   PH8STOS   FESTUS 864B   9A   THELW 2   WISH 355D
2 EMPHANIZW 2   MAKE VISIBLE 257B   9B   THELW 1   WISH 355D
   KATA 12Bβ   DOWN 406D   10 ADIKEW 2A   DO WRONG 17B
   PARAKALEW 3   IMPLORE 622D   B8MA 2   TRIBUNAL 139D
   PRWTOS 1Cβ   FIRST 733C   DEI 3   IT IS NECESSARY 171B
3 AITEW   ASK 25C   EPI 11A6   BEFORE 286A
   ANAIREW 1A   DO AWAY WITH 54C   EPIGINWSKW 2D   KNOW 291B
   ENEDRA   AMBUSH 264A   HIST8MI 112Bβ   BEING 383C
   KATA 12Bβ   DOWN 406D   KALWS 7   WELL 402C
   KATA 111A   ALONG 407A   KRINW 4Aα   JUDGE 452D
   METAPEMPW   SUMMON 514D   OUDEIS 2Bγ   IN NO RESPECT 596C
   HODOS 1B   WAY 556C   HWS 114A   SO 906B
   HOPWS 2B   IN ORDER THAT 580D   10=12 KAISAR   EMPEROR 396C
   POIEW 119δ   DO 687C   11 ADIKEW 1B   DO WRONG 17B
   CHARIS 3A   FAVOR 886A   AXIOS 1B   WORTHY 77C
4 APOKRINOMAI 1   ANSWER 92D   APOTHN8SKW 1Aα   DIE 90D
   APOKRINOMAI 1   ANSWER 93A   EI VI5   FOR IF 219A
   EKPOREUOMAI 1A   GO OUT 243D   THANATOS 1Bα   DEATH 351C
   KAISAREIA 2   CAESAREA 396D   KAT8GOREW 1A   BRING CHARGES 424B
   MEN 2E   (PARTICLE) 504C   MEN 1Aα   (PARTICLE) 503D
   OUN 4   THEREFORE 597D   HOS,H8,HO 14A   (REL PRON) 587D
   TACHOS   SPEED 814D   OUDEIS 28β   WORTHLESS 596C
   T8REW 1   GUARD 822B   PARAITEOMAI 2B   ESCAPE 622A
   PH8STOS   FESTUS 864C   PRASSW 1A   DO 705B
5 ATOPOS 2   IMPROPER 120B   CHARIZOMAI 1   GIVE FREELY 884D
   DUNATOS 1Aα   POWERFUL 207D   11F EPIKALEW 2Aβ   CALL UPON 294A
   KAT8GOREW 1A   BRING CHARGES 424B   12 EPI 1111Aγ   ON 288B
   SUGKATABAINW   GO DOWN WITH 781A   META A113β   WITH 510D
   SUNERCHOMAI 2   ASSEMBLE 796A   POREUW 1   PROCEED 699A
   PH8MI 1Bβ   SAY 864A   SULLALEW   TALK 784B
6 AGW 2   LEAD AWAY 14B   SUMBOULION 3   PLAN 785D
   B8MA 2   TRIBUNAL 139D   12=14 PH8STOS   FESTUS 864C
   DIATRIBW   SPEND 189A   13 ASPAZOMAI 1B   GREET 116C
   EPAURION   NEXT DAY 283C   BASILEUS 1   KING 135D
   KATHIZW 2Aα   SIT DOWN 391A   BERNIK8   BERNICE 139A
   KAISAREIA 2   CAESAREA 396D   DIAGINOMAI   PASS 181B
   KATABAINW 1Aβ   COME DOWN 409B   KAISAREIA 2   CAESAREA 396D
   KELEUW   COMMAND 428C   KATANTAW 1   ARRIVE 416B
   OKTW   EIGHT 565D   13FF AGRIPPAS 2   AGRIPPA 13C
   POLUS 111A   MANY 695D   14 ANATITH8MI 2   DECLARE 61D
7 AITIWMA   CHARGE 26A   DESMIOS   PRISONER 175A
   APODEIKNUMI 3   PROVE 89B   DIATRIBW   SPEND 189A
   BARUS 2B   IMPORTANT 134A   DIATRIBW   STAY 189A
   HIEROSOLUMA 1A   JERUSALEM 373D   KATA 116   WITH RESPECT TO 408D
   ISCHUW 2B   BE STRONG 384C   KATALEIPW 1A   LEAVE BEHIND 414C
   KAI 14   AND 394A   POLUS 111A   MANY 695C
   KATABAINW 1Aβ   COME DOWN 409B   PH8LIX   FELIX 863D
   KATAPHERW 2   BRING DOWN 421A   HWS IV1B   WHEN 907A
   PARAGINOMAI 1   COME 618D   15 AITEW   ASK 25C
   PERIIST8MI 1A   STAND AROUND 653B   ARCHIEREUS 1B   HIGH PRIEST 112C
   POLUS 11Aα   MANY 694B   GINOMAI 14Cα   COME, GO 158D
   PHERW 4Aβ   BEAR 863B   DIK8 1   PENALTY 197C

15 EMPHANIZW 2	MAKE VISIBLE	257B
KATA I2Bβ	DOWN	406D
KATADIK8	CONDEMNATION	411C
PRESBUTEROS 2Aβ	OLDER	706D
16 APOKRINOMAI I	ANSWER	92D
APOKRINOMAI I	ANSWER	93A
APOLOGIA 2A	DEFENSE	95C
APWLEIA 2	DESTRUCTION	103A
EGKL8MA I	ACCUSATION	215B
ETHOS I	HABIT	217C
ECHW I7A	HAVE	334A
8 2DY	BEFORE	343C
KATA IIIB	TO	407B
KAT8GOREW IA	BRING CHARGES	424C
KAT8GOROS	ACCUSER	424D
LAMBANW 2	RECEIVE	466B
PRIN IA	BEFORE	708A
PROSWPON IC6	FACE	728D
RWMAIOS	ROMAN	745C
TOPOS 2C	PLACE	830D
CHARIZOMAI I	GIVE FREELY	884D
17 AGW 2	LEAD AWAY	14B
ANABOL8	DELAY	50D
B8MA 2	TRIBUNAL	139D
ENTHADE I	HERE	265C
HEX8S 2	NEXT	275C
KATHIZW 2Aα	SIT DOWN	391A
KELEUW	COMMAND	428C
M8DEIS I	NO	520A
POIEW III	DO	689C
SUNERCHOMAI 2	ASSEMBLE	796A
18 AITIA 2B	CHARGE	25D
EPIPHERW 3	BRING	304C
KAT8GOROS	ACCUSER	424D
HOS,H8,HO I5Cα	(REL PRON)	588B
OUDEIS I	NO	596B
PERI IB	ABOUT	650B
PHERW 4Aβ	BEAR	863B
19 DEISIDAIMONIA 3	RELIGION	172C
ECHW I7A	HAVE	334A
Z8T8MA	ISSUE	339D
THN8SKW I	DIE	363A
IDIOS 2C	ONES OWN	370C
PHASKW	SAY	862B
19B TIS, TI 2Aβ	ANY ONE	828B
20 APOREW	UNCERTAIN	97A
BOULOMAI 2AY	DESIRE	145D
EI V2C	WHETHER	218D
Z8T8SIS I	INVESTIGATION	339D
KAKEI I	AND THERE	397C
KRINW 4Aα	JUDGE	452D
21 ANAPEMPW IB	SEND	58D
DIAGNWSIS	DECISION	181C
EPIKALEW 2Aβ	CALL UPON	294B
HEWS IIIBα	UNTIL	335C
KAISAR	EMPEROR	396C
KELEUW	COMMAND	428C
PROS IIIIB	TOWARD	716D
SEBASTOS	REVERED	753B
21A T8REW 2A	KEEP	822C
21B T8REW I	GUARD	822B
22 AKOUW 2	HEAR	31D
AURION I	TOMORROW	121D
22 BOULOMAI I	DESIRE	145C
PH8MI IBβ	SAY	864A
22=4 AGRIPPAS 2	AGRIPPA	13C
22=4 PH8STOS	FESTUS	864C
23 AGW 2	LEAD AWAY	14B
AKROAT8RION	AUDIENCE ROOM	33A
BERNIK8	BERNICE	139A
EISERCHOMAI IAβ	COME	231D
EXOCH8	PROMINENCE	278D
EPAURION	NEXT DAY	283C
KELEUW	COMMAND	428C
META AIII2	WITH	511A
POLUS IIBβ	MANY	694D
PHANTASIA	POMP	861A
CHILIARCHOS	TRIBUNE	890A
24 HAPAS I	WHOLE	81A
BASILEUS I	KING	135D
BOAW 2	SHOUT	143D
DEI 6	IT IS NECESSARY	171B
ENTHADE 2	HERE	265C
ENTUGCHANW I	MEET	269C
EPIBOAW	CRY OUT LOUDLY	290C
ZAW IA6	LIVE	336D
THEWREW I	OBSERVE	360C
M8 AIIIBβ	NOT	518A
M8KETI 4	NO LONGER	520B
PL8THOS 2BY	QUANTITY	674D
SUMPAREIMI	BE PRESENT	786D
25 AXIOS IB	WORTHY	77C
EPIKALEW 2Aβ	CALL UPON	294A
THANATOS IBα	DEATH	351C
KATALAMBANW 2	GRASP	414B
KRINW 3	DECIDE	452C
HOUTOS IA ζ	THIS	601B
PEMPW I	SEND	647D
PRASSW IA	DO	705B
SEBASTOS	REVERED	753B
26 AGRIPPAS 2	AGRIPPA	13C
ANAKRISIS	INVESTIGATION	56B
ASPHAL8S IB	CERTAIN	118C
BASILEUS I	KING	135D
GRAPHW 2D	WRITE	166A
DIO	THEREFORE	197D
KURIOS 2B	LORD	460C
MALISTA I	ABOVE ALL	490A
HOPWS 2Aα	IN ORDER THAT	580C
PROAGW I	LEAD	708D
TIS, TI 2AY	ANY ONE	828B
26A ECHW I6A	CAN	333D
26B ECHW I6A	CAN	333D
27 AITIA 2B	CHARGE	26A
ALOGOS 2	WITHOUT REASON	40C
DESMIOS	PRISONER	175A
KATA I2Bβ	DOWN	406D
M8 AIIIC	NOT	518A
PEMPW I	SEND	647D
S8MAINW I	MAKE KNOWN	755A

ACTS 26

I APOLOGEOMAI	DEFEND ONESELF	95B
EKTEINW I	STRETCH OUT	244D
EPITREPW I	ALLOW	303C

1	LEGW 14	SAY 469D
	HUPER 1A6	IN BEHALF OF 846C
	PH8MI 1Bα	SAY 864A
1F	AGRIPPAS 2	AGRIPPA 13C
2	EGKALEW	ACCUSE 214C
	EMAUTOU 2	MYSELF 253B
	H8GEOMAI 2	CONSIDER 344B
	MAKARIOS 1A	BLESSED 487C
	MELLW 1Cγ	INTEND 502B
3	AKOUW 1C	HEAR 31D
	GNWST8S	EXPERT 163B
	DEOMAI 1	ASK 174A
	DIO	THEREFORE 197D
	ETHOS 2	CUSTOM 217D
	Z8T8MA	ISSUE 339D
	8THOS	CUSTOM 345B
	KATA II7C	(GENITIVE) 409A
	MAKROTHUMWS	PATIENTLY 489C
	MALISTA 1	ABOVE ALL 490A
	TE 3A	AND 815B
4	ARCH8 1B	BEGINNING 111C
	BIWSIS	MANNER OF LIFE 141C
	GINOMAI IIBγ	COME ABOUT 157C
	MEN 2E	(PARTICLE) 504C
	NEOT8S	YOUTH 538B
	OIDA	KNOW 558A
5	HAIRESIS 1A	SECT 23B
	AKRIB8S	EXACT 32C
	ANWTHEN 2B	FOR A LONG TIME 76C
	ZAW 3A	LIVE 337B
	H8METEROS	OUR 348C
	THR8SKEIA	RELIGION 364A
	MARTUREW 1A	BEAR WITNESS 493C
	HO,H8,TO IIIE	THE 553A
	PROGINWSKW	KNOWS BEFOREHAND 710C
*	PHARISAIOS	PHARISEE 861C
6	ELPIS 2A	HOPE 252A
	ELPIS 2B	HOPE 252C
	EPAGGELIA 2A	PROMISE 280B
	EPI III8γ	ON 287A
	HIST8MI II2Bγ	BEING 383C
	KRINW 4Aα	JUDGE 452D
	NUN 1C	NOW 547D
	HUPO 1B	BY 851A
7	AGRIPPAS 2	AGRIPPA 13C
	DWDEKAPHULON	209B
	THE TWELVE TRIBES	
	EGKALEW	ACCUSE 214C
	EKTENEIA	PERSEVERANCE 245A
	ELPIZW 2	HOPE 252A
	ELPIS 2B	HOPE 252C
	EN III2	BY 260C
	H8MERA 1A	DAY 346C
	KATANTAW 2A	ARRIVE 416B
	LATREUW	SERVE 468D
	NUX 1D	NIGHT 549A
8	APISTOS 1	UNBELIEVABLE 85A
	EGEIRW 1Aβ	RAISE 213D
	KRINW 2	JUDGE 452B
	NEKROS 2A	DEAD 537A
	PARA II2B	BESIDE 615C
	TIS, TI 3A	WHICH 827B
9	DOKEW 2A	SEEM 201A
9	EMAUTOU 2	MYSELF 253B
	ENANTIOS 2	OPPOSED 261C
	MEN 2E	(PARTICLE) 504C
	NAZWRAIOS	NAZARENE 534B
	ONOMA I4C η	NAME 576D
	PRASSW 1A	DO 705B
9F	HOS,H8,HO I7B	(REL PRON) 588C
10	ANAIREW 1A	DO AWAY WITH 54C
	EXOUSIA 3	AUTHORITY 278A
	KATAKLEIW	SHUT UP 412C
	KATAPHERW 2	BRING DOWN 421A
	PARA I3B	FROM 614D
	TE 2	AND 815B
	PHULAK8 3	GUARD 875C
	PHULAK8 3	GUARD 875D
	PS8PHOS 1	CAST A VOTE AGAINST 901A
10F	TE 3A	AND 815C
11	ANAGKAZW 1	COMPEL 51C
	BLASPH8MEW 2Bα	BLASPHEME 142A
	DIWKW 2	PERSECUTE 200B
	EMMAINOMAI	BE ENRAGED 254B
	EXW 1Aγ	OUTSIDE 279A
	HEWS II2C	AS FAR AS 335D
	PERISSWS	MORE 657C
	POLIS 1	CITY 692B
	POLLAKIS	OFTEN 693B
	SUNAGWG8 2A	790C
	PLACE OF ASSEMBLY	
	TIMWREW	PUNISH 826B
12	DAMASKOS	DAMASCUS 169C
	EXOUSIA 3	AUTHORITY 277D
	EPITROP8	PERMISSION 303D
	META AIII2	WITH 511A
	HOS,H8,HO IIIC	(REL PRON) 589A
	PARA I4A	FROM 615A
13	H8LIOS	THE SUN 346B
	H8MERA 1A	DAY 346C
	KATA IIIA	ALONG 407A
	LAMPROT8S 1	BRILLIANCE 467B
	MESOS 1	MIDDAY 508B
	HODOS 1B	WAY 556C
	OURANOTHEN	FROM HEAVEN 598A
	PERILAMPW	SHINE AROUND 654A
	POREUW 1	PROCEED 699A
	HUPER 2	BEYOND 847B
	PHWS 1A	LIGHT 879D
14	DIALEKTOS	LANGUAGE 184D
	HEBRAIS	HEBREW LANGUAGE 212C
	KATAPIPTW	FALL 417C
	KENTRON 2	A GOAD 429C
	MONOS 1Aβ	ONLY 529C
	PAS 1Eα	ALL 637D
	SAOUL 2	SAUL 749C
	SAULOS	SAUL 752D
	SKL8ROS 3B	HARD 763B
	PHOBOS 2Aα	FEAR 871C
	PHWN8 2D	VOICE 879C
14F	DIWKW 2	PERSECUTE 200B
16	ALLA 6	NOW 38B
	EIS 4F	(PURPOSE) 228D
	HIST8MI IIIE	STAND 383B
	MARTUS 2C	WITNESS 495C
	HOS,H8,HO I4A	(REL PRON) 587D

16	PROCHEIRIZW	SELECT	732A
	TE 2	AND	815B
	HUP8RET8S	SERVANT	850C
16A	HORAW 1A6	SEE	582A
16B	HORAW 1Aβ	SEE	581C
17	APOSTELLW 1Bα	SEND AWAY	98A
	ETHNOS 2	GENTILES	217C
	EXAIREW 2B	SELECT	271C
	LAOS 3A	PEOPLE	468A
	HOS,H8,HO I3Bγ	(REL PRON)	587D
18	HAGIAZW 2	CONSECRATE	8D
	HAMARTIA 1	SIN	42C
	ANOIGW 1Eβ	OPEN	70D
	APHESIS 2	PARDON	124C
	EIS 4Cβ	(GOAL)	228C
	EXOUSIA 2	ABILITY	277D
	EPISTREPHW 1Bβ	TURN	301B
	THEOS 3A	GOD	357D
	KL8ROS 2	LOT	436C
	HO,H8,TO II4Bζ	THE	554B
	PISTIS 2Bβ	FAITH	669A
	SATAN	ADVERSARY	752C
	SKOTOS 2B	DARKNESS	765B
	PHWS 3A	LIGHT	880B
19	AGRIPPAS 2	AGRIPPA	13C
	APEITH8S 1	DISOBEDIENT	82B
	GINOMAI 14B	BECOME	158D
	HOTHEN 3	FROM WHICH	558A
	OPTASIA 1	A VISION	580A
	OURANIOS	HEAVENLY	598A
20	AXIOS 1B	WORTHY	77B
	APAGGELLW 2	PROCLAIM	78D
	DAMASKOS	DAMASCUS	169C
	EPI III1B6	TOWARD	289A
	EPISTREPHW 1Bβ	TURN	301B
	ERGON 1Cβ	DEED	308A
	THEOS 3A	GOD	357D
	IOUDAIA 2	JUDAEA	379D
	METANOEW	CHANGE ONES MIND	513B
	METANOEW	CHANGE ONES MIND	513C
	METANOIA	REPENTANCE	514A
	PRASSW 1A	DO	705A
	PRWTOS 2A	FIRST	733D
	TE 3A	AND	815C
	CHWRA 1B	COUNTRY	897C
21	DIACHEIRIZW	KILL	190A
	*HENEKA	BECAUSE OF	264B
	PEIRAW 1	TRY	646D
	SULLAMBANW 2A	SEIZE	784C
22	ACHRI 1A	UNTIL	128B
	EKTOS 2B	OUTSIDE	245C
	EPIKOURIA	HELP	294D
	MARTUROMAI 1	TESTIFY	495B
	MEGAS 2Aα	GREAT	498D
	MELLW 1C6	IS DESTINED	502C
	MIKROS 1B	SMALL	523A
	MWUS8S	MOSES	533D
	OUDEIS 2Bα	NOTHING	596C
	PARA 14A	FROM	615A
	TUGCHANW 1	MEET	837A
22A	TE 3A	AND	815C
23	ANASTASIS 2B	RESURRECTION	60A
	EI II	IF	218C
23	KATAGGELLW 1	PROCLAIM	410C
	LAOS 3A	PEOPLE	468A
	NEKROS 2A	DEAD	537A
	PATH8TOS	SUBJECT TO SUFFERING	607D
	PRWTOS 1A	FIRST	732D
	PHWS 3A	LIGHT	880B
	CHRISTOS 1	ANOINTED ONE	895B
24	APOLOGEOMAI	DEFEND ONESELF	95B
	MAINOMAI	BE OUT OF ONES MIND	487C
	MANIA	MADNESS	491D
	MEGAS 2Aγ	GREAT	498D
	HO,H8,TO IIIF	THE	553A
	PERITOM8 4B	CIRCUMCISION	659A
	POLUS IIAβ	MANY	694B
	PHWN8 2A	VOICE	878D
24F	PH8STOS	FESTUS	864C
25	AL8THEIA 2A	TRUTH	35B
	APOPHTHEGGOMAI	DECLARE	101C
	KRATISTOS 1	MOST NOBLE	450A
	MAINOMAI	BE OUT OF ONES MIND	487B
	SWPHROSUN8 1	REASONABLENESS	810A
	PH8MI 1Bβ	SAY	864A
26	GWNIA	CORNER	167D
	EPISTAMAI 2	KNOW	300A
	LANTHANW	ESCAPE NOTICE	467C
	PARR8SIAZOMAI 1	SPEAK FREELY	636B
	PEITHW 3A	BELIEVE	645C
	PRASSW 1A	DO	705A
27	PISTEUW 1B	BELIEVE	666C
27B	PISTEUW 1D	BELIEVE	666D
27F	AGRIPPAS 2	AGRIPPA	13C
28	OLIGOS 3B	LITTLE	566D
	PEITHW 1B	CONVINCE	644D
	PEITHW 2A	BELIEVE	645B
	CHRISTIANOS	THE CHRISTIAN	895A
29	ALLA 1A	BUT, YET	37C
	AN 5	(PARTICLE)	48D
	GINOMAI 14A	BECOME	158C
	DESMOS 1	FETTER	175A
	EIMI II6D	TO BE	223C
	*EUCHOMAI 1	PRAY	329C
	KAGW 3C	I	387A
	KAI 16	AND	394A
	MONOS 2C	ONLY	529D
	OLIGOS 3B	LITTLE	566D
	HOPOIOS	WHAT SORT	579B
	PAREKTOS 2	OUTSIDE	630C
	TOIOUTOS 1	SUCH A KIND	829A
30	ANIST8MI 2A	RISE	69C
	BERNIK8	BERNICE	139A
	HO,H8,TO III0C	THE	555A
	SUGKATH8MAI	SIT WITH	780D
31	ANACHWREW 2B	WITHDRAW	63A
	AXIOS 1B	WORTHY	77C
	DESMOS 1	FETTER	175A
	LALEW 2A6	SPEAK	464C
	PRASSW 1A	DO	705B
32	AGRIPPAS 2	AGRIPPA	13C
	APOLUW 1	SET FREE	96A
	DUNAMAI 1C	ABLE	206B
	EPIKALEW 2Aβ	CALL UPON	294A
	KAISAR	EMPEROR	396C
	M8 AI1	NOT	517C

32	PH8MI 1B«	SAY 864A
	PH8STOS	FESTUS 864C

ACTS 27

1	ANAPEMPW 1B	SEND 58D
	APOPLEW	SAIL AWAY 96D
	DESMWT8S	PRISONER 175B
	HEKATONTARCH8S	CENTURION 236C
	HETEROS 1B&	ANOTHER 315B
	IOULIOS	JULIUS 381A
	ITALIA	ITALY 384D
	KRINW 3	DECIDE 452C
	HO,H8,TO II4B«	THE 554A
	ONOMA II	NAME 574A
	PARADIDWMI	GIVE OVER 619C
	PARADIDWMI 1B	GIVE OVER 620A
	SEBASTOS	REVERED 753B
	SPEIRA	COHORT 768C
	TE 3A	AND 815C
	HWS IVIA	WHEN 907A
2	ADRAMUTT8NOS	ADRAMYTTIUM 18C
	ANAGW 3	PUT TO SEA 53A
	ARISTARCHOS	ARISTARCHUS 106B
	ASIA	ASIA 115C
	EPIBAINW 1	GO UP 289C
	THESSALONIKEUS	THESSALONIAN 360B
	KATA II7C	(GENITIVE) 409A
	TOPOS 1A	PLACE 830A
	TOPOS 1D	PLACE 830B
2=44	PLOION 1	SHIP 679B
3	EPIMELEIA	CARE 296A
	EPITREPW 1	ALLOW 303C
	HETEROS 1B(	ANOTHER 315C
	IOULIOS	JULIUS 381A
	KATAGW	LEAD 411A
	POREUW 1	PROCEED 699A
	SIDWN	SIDON 757C
	TUGCHANW 1	MEET 837A
	PHILANTHRWPWS	BENEVOLENTLY 866C
	PHILOS 2A«	LOVING 868D
	CHRAOMAI 2	USE 893A
4	ANAGW 3	PUT TO SEA 52D
	ANEMOS 1A	WIND 64A
	ENANTIOS 1	OPPOSITE 261C
	KAKEITHEN 1	AND FROM THERE 397C
	KUPROS	CYPRUS 458D
	HUPOPLEW	SAIL UNDER 854C
5	DEKAPENTE	FIFTEEN 173A
	DIAPLEW	SAIL THROUGH 186D
	KATA III A	ALONG 407A
	KATERCHOMAI 1	COME DOWN 423A
	KILIKIA	CILICIA 433B
	LUKIA	LYCIA 482C
	LUSTRA	LYSTRA 483D
	MURA	MYRA 531B
	PAMPHULIA	PAMPHYLIA 612B
	PELAGOS 2	THE OPEN SEA 647B
6	ALEXANDRINOS	ALEXANDRIAN 35A
	HEKATONTARCH8S	CENTURION 236C
	EMBIBAZW	PUT IN 253D
	HEURISKW 1C«	FIND 325C
	ITALIA	ITALY 384D

6	KAKEI 1	AND THERE 397C
7	BRADUPLOEW	SAIL SLOWLY 146C
	GINOMAI 14C6	COME, GO 159A
	HIKANOS 1B	SUFFICIENT 375A
	KATA III B	TO 407A
	KNIDOS	CNIDUS 438A
	KR8T8	CRETE 451C
	PROSEAW PERMIT TO GO FARTHER	719D
	SALMWN8	SALMONE 748B
	HUPOPLEW	SAIL UNDER 854C
7F	MOLIS 1 WITH DIFFICULTY	528C
8	EGGUS 1B	NEAR 213B
	EIMI II9A	TO BE 223D
	KALEW 1AV	CALL 400A
	KALOI LIMENES	FAIR HAVENS 401A
	LASAIA	LASAEA 468B
	LIM8N	HARBOR 476A
	PARALEGOMAI	SAIL PAST 625B
	POLIS 1	CITY 692B
	TIS, TI 2A«	ANY ONE 828A
	TOPOS 1C	PLACE 830B
9	DIAGINOMAI	PASS 181B
	EPISPHAL8S	UNSAFE 301D
	HIKANOS 1B	SUFFICIENT 375A
	N8STEIA 2A	FASTING 540A
	PARAINEW	ADVISE 621D
	PARERCHOMAI 1A&	GO BY 631B
	CHRONOS	TIME 896B
9F	PLOOS	VOYAGE 679C
10	ALLA 1A	BUT, YET 37C
	AN8R 1	MAN 66A
	Z8MIA	LOSS 338D
	THEWREW 2A	OBSERVE 360D
	MELLW 1A	WILL BE 502A
	META AIII2	WITH 511A
	MONOS 2C	ONLY 529D
	POLUS II B&	MANY 694C
	HUBRIS 3	SHAME 839D
	PHORTION 1	LOAD 873A
	PHORTOS	BURDEN 873A
	PSUCH8 1A&	SOUL LIFE 901C
11	HEKATONTARCH8S	CENTURION 236C
	KUBERN8T8S 1	STEERSMAN 457C
	MALLON 3C	RATHER 490D
	NAUKL8ROS	SHIP OWNER 536B
	PEITHW 3C	OBEY 645C
12	ANAGW 3	PUT TO SEA 52D
	ANEUTHETOS	POOR 65A
	BLEPW 8	SEE 143C
	BOUL8 2A	DECISION 145B
	EI VII2A	IF 219B
	KATA III B	TO 407A
	KATANTAW 1	ARRIVE 416B
	PARACHEIMAZW SPEND THE WINTER	629A
	PARACHEIMASIA	WINTERING 629A
	POLUS II2A«	MANY 695D
	PROS III3C	TOWARD 717B
	TITH8MI II2A	MAKE 824B
	PHOINIX III	PHOENIX 872B
	CHWROS	NORTHWEST 899C
12A	LIM8N	HARBOR 476A
12B	LIM8N	HARBOR 476A
12F	KR8T8	CRETE 451C

13 AIRW IA	LIFT UP	23D
ASSON	CLOSE	117A
DOKEW IA	THINK	200D
KRATEW IC	ATTAIN	449C
NOTOS I	SOUTHWEST WIND	546A
PARALEGOMAI	SAIL PAST	625B
PROTHESIS 2A	SETTING FORTH	713A
HUPOPNEW	BLOW GENTLY	854C
14 ANEMOS IA	WIND	64A
BALLW 3	RUSH	131A
EURAKULWN THE NORTHEAST WIND		325A
EUROKLUDWN THE SOUTHEAST WIND		326A
KALEW IAY	CALL	400A
KATA I2BY	DOWN	406D
META 8II3	AFTER	511C
OU 2B	NO	594C
POLUS I2Cα	MANY	695B
TUPHWNIKOS	HURRICANE	839A
15 ANTOPHTHALMEW		75D
LOOK DIRECTLY AT		
EPIDIDWMI 2	GIVE	292B
PNEW IA	BLOW	686A
SUNARPAZW	SEIZE	793A
SUSTELLW I	LIMIT	802D
PHERW 3A	BEAR	863A
16 HISTION	SAIL	383D
ISCHUW 2B	BE STRONG	384C
KALEW IAY	CALL	400A
KLAUDA	CLAUDA	434C
MOLIS I	WITH DIFFICULTY	528C
N8SION	LITTLE ISLAND	540A
PERIKRAT8S	HAVING POWER	654A
SKAPH8	BOAT	761A
HUPOTRECHW	SAIL UNDER	856A
17 AIRW IA	LIFT UP	23D
BO8THEIA	HELP	144A
EKPIPTW 2	FALL OFF	243B
M8 BIB	NOT	519A
HOUTW IB	THUS	602C
SKEUOS IA	THING	761C
SURTIS	SYRTIS	802A
HUPOZWNNUMI	UNDERGIRD	852C
PHERW 3A	BEAR	863A
PHOBEW IA	BE AFRAID	870D
CHALAW	LET DOWN	882C
CHRAOMAI IA	USE	892C
18 EKBOL8	JETTISONING	237C
HEX8S 2	NEXT	275C
POIEW III	DO	689C
SPHODRWS	VIOLENTLY	803D
CHEIMAZW	TOSS IN A STORM	887D
19 AUTOCHEIR	ONES OWN HAND	123D
RIPTW I	THROW	743D
SKEU8	EQUIPMENT	761C
TRITOS I	THIRD	834C
20 ASTRON	STAR	118A
EPI III2B	ON	289B
EPIKEIMAI 2B	BE URGENT	294C
EPIPHAINW IB	APPEAR	304A
H8LIOS	THE SUN	346B
H8MERA 2	DAY	347B
LOIPOS 3Aα	THE REST	481B
M8TE	AND NOT	521D
20 HO,H8,TO II4Bβ	THE	553D
OLIGOS 2B	LITTLE	566C
OU 2B	NO	594C
PERIAIREW 2	TAKE AWAY	651C
POLUS IIIA	MANY	695C
SWZW IA	SAVE	805D
CHEIMWN I	STORMY WEATHER	888A
21 ANAGW 3	PUT TO SEA	52D
AN8R I	MAN	66A
DEI 4	IT IS NECESSARY	171B
DEI 6B	IT IS NECESSARY	171C
Z8MIA	LOSS	338D
KERDAINW 2	TO GAIN	430D
KR8T8	CRETE	451C
MESOS 2	THE MIDDLE	508D
M8 AIIIC	NOT	518A
PEITHARCHEW	OBEY	644B
POLUS IIBβ	MANY	694C
TOTE 2	AT THAT TIME	831D
HUPARCHW I	BE	845D
W 2	O	903B
21B TE IB	AND	815B
22 APOBOL8 2	LOSS	88C
EUTHUMEW	BE CHEERFUL	321A
NUN 3C	NOW	548B
OUDEIS I	NO	596B
PARAINEW	ADVISE	621C
PL8N 2	BUT	675C
PSUCH8 IAβ	SOUL LIFE	901C
23 EIMI IVI	TO BE	225A
LATREUW	SERVE	468C
NUX IC	NIGHT	548D
PARIST8MI 2Aα	APPROACH	633C
23F LEGW I8A	SAY	470B
24 IDOU IBβ	BEHOLD	371C
KAISAR	EMPEROR	396C
PARIST8MI 2Aα	APPROACH	633C
PLEW	SAIL	674A
CHARIZOMAI I	GIVE FREELY	884D
25 AN8R I	MAN	66A
DIO	THEREFORE	197D
EUTHUMEW	BE CHEERFUL	321A
KATA II5Bα	ACCORDING TO	408C
HOUTW 2	THUS	602C
PISTEUW IC	BELIEVE	666D
TROPOS I	MANNER	835A
26 EKPIPTW 2	FALL OFF	243B
N8SOS	ISLAND	540A
27 ADRIAS	ADRIATIC SEA	18C
GINOMAI IIBY	COME ABOUT	157C
DIAPHERW IC	DRIVE	189C
EPIGINOMAI	COME UP	290D
KATA II2B	TOWARD	407C
MESOS 2	THE MIDDLE	509A
NAUT8S	SAILOR	536B
HO,H8,TO IIIC	THE	552D
PROSAGW 2A	BRING	718C
PROSANECHW	RISE UP	718D
PROSACHEW	RESOUND	719A
PROSEGGIZW	APPROACH	719D
TESSARESKAIDEKATOS	FOURTEENTH	821A
CHWRA 3	COUNTRY	897D
HWS IVIA	WHEN	907A

27A	NUX 1A	NIGHT	548C
27B	NUX 1A	NIGHT	548C
28	BOLIZW	TAKE SOUNDINGS	144B
	BRACHUS 1	SHORT	146D
	DEKAPENTE	FIFTEEN	173A
	DIIST8MI 2	GO AWAY	194B
	EIKOSI	TWENTY	221A
	HEURISKW 2	FIND	325D
28A	ORGUIA	FATHOM	583C
28B	ORGUIA	FATHOM	583C
29	AGKURA 1	ANCHOR	10C
	GINOMAI 11Bγ	COME ABOUT	157B
	EK 2	AWAY FROM	234A
	EKPIPTW 2	FALL OFF	243B
	EUCHOMAI 2	WISH	329D
	H8MERA 1A	DAY	346C
	M8POU	LEST	521B
	M8PWS 1B	LEST SOMEHOW	521C
	PRUMNA	STERN OF A SHIP	732A
	RIPTW 1	THROW	743D
	TOPOS 1C	PLACE	830B
	TRACHUS	ROUGH	832D
	PHOBEW 1A	BE AFRAID	870D
30	AGKURA 1	ANCHOR	10C
	EKTEINW 1	STRETCH OUT	244D
	THALASSA 1Bβ	SEA	350D
	MELLW 1Cγ	INTEND	502B
	NAUT8S	SAILOR	536B
	PROPHASIS 2	ACTUAL MOTIVE	730A
	PRWRA	PROW OF A SHIP	732C
	SKAPH8	BOAT	761A
	PHEUGW 1	FLEE	863C
	CHALAW	LET DOWN	882C
	HWS 1112	SO	906D
31	HEKATONTARCH8S	CENTURION	236C
	MENW 1Aα	REMAIN	504D
	SWZW 1A	SAVE	805D
32	APOKOPTW 1	CUT OFF	92C
	EAW 1	LET	211D
	EKPIPTW 2	FALL OFF	243B
	EKPIPTW 1	FALL OFF	243B
	SKAPH8	BOAT	761A
	SCHOINION	ROPE	805B
33	HAPAS 2	ALL	81A
	ASITOS	WITHOUT EATING	115D
	ACHRI 2A	UNTIL	128C
	GINOMAI 11Bγ	COME ABOUT	157B
	DIATELEW	CONTINUE	188D
	H8MERA 2	DAY	347A
	PROSDOKAW 3	EXPECT	719C
	PROSLAMBANW 2D	TAKE	724C
	TESSARESKAIDEKATOS	FOURTEENTH	821A
33F	METALAMBANW 1	RECEIVE	512D
33F	PARAKALEW 2	APPEAL TO	622C
33F	TROPH8 1	FOOD	835C
34	APOLLUMI 2B	BE LOST	95A
	DIO	THEREFORE	197D
	THRIX 2	HAIR	364C
	KEPHAL8 1A	HEAD	431B
	OUDEIS 2A	NO ONE	596B
	PIPTW 1A	FALL	665A
	PROS 1	ADVANTAGEOUS FOR	716C
	PROSLAMBANW 1A	TAKE	724C

34	SWT8RIA 1	DELIVERANCE	808D
	HUMETEROS 1	YOUR	843D
	HUPARCHW 2	BE	846A
35	ARTOS 1A	BREAD	110A
	ARCHW 2Aα	BEGIN	113A
	ENWPION 2A	BEFORE	270B
	EPIDIDWMI 1	GIVE	292B
	ESTHIW 1D	EAT	313A
	EUCHARISTEW 2	GIVE THANKS	328C
	KLAW	BREAK	434D
	LAMBANW 1A	TAKE	465B
36	EUTHUMOS	CHEERFUL	321A
	PROSLAMBANW 2D	TAKE	724C
	TROPH8 1	FOOD	835C
37	HEBDOM8KONTA	SEVENTY	212A
	PAS 1Fβ	ALL	638A
	PSUCH8 2	SOUL LIFE	902C
38	EKBALLW 1	DRIVE OUT	236D
	THALASSA 1Bβ	SEA	350D
	KORENNUMI 1	SATIATE	445B
	KOUPHIZW	LIGHTEN	448B
	HO,H8,TO 111Aα	THE	552B
	SITOS	WHEAT	759D
	TROPH8 1	FOOD	835C
39	AIGIALOS	SHORE	21B
	BOULEUW 2	DECIDE	145A
	G8 4	LAND	156C
	GINOMAI 11Bγ	COME ABOUT	157B
	DUNAMAI 2	ABLE	206B
	EKSWZW	BRING SAFELY	244C
	EXWTHEW	RUN ASHORE	279C
	EPIGINWSKW 2A	KNOW	291A
	H8MERA 1A	DAY	346C
	KATANOEW 1	NOTICE	416A
	KOLPOS 3	BAY	443B
40	AGKURA 1	ANCHOR	10C
	AIGIALOS	SHORE	21B
	HAMA 1A	TOGETHER	41B
	ANI8MI 1	LOOSEN	69A
	ARTEMWN	SAIL	109D
	EAW 3	LET	212A
	EPAIRW 1	LIFT UP	281C
	ZEUKT8RIA	BANDS	337D
	THALASSA 1Bβ	SEA	350D
	KATECHW 2	STEER TOWARD	424B
	PERIAIREW 1	TAKE AWAY	651C
	P8DALION	RUDDER	662A
	PNEW 1A	BLOW	686A
41	ASALEUTOS 1	IMMOVABLE	113D
	BIA 1A	FORCE	140A
	DIALUW 1	BREAK UP	185B
	DITHALASSOS	SANDBANK	194B
	EPIKELLW	RUN AGROUND	294D
	EPOKELLW	RUN AGROUND	305C
	EREIDW	JAM FAST	308D
	KUMA	WAVE	458C
	LUW 3	DESTROY	485A
	MENW 1B	REMAIN	505B
	NAUS	SHIP	536B
	PERIPIPTW 1	FALL IN WITH	655C
	PRUMNA	STERN OF A SHIP	732A
	PRWRA	PROW OF A SHIP	732C
	TOPOS 1C	PLACE	830B

41	HUPO IAβ	BY	850D
42	BOUL8 2A	DECISION	145B
	DESMWT8S	PRISONER	175B
	DIAPHEUGW	ESCAPE	189C
	EKKOLUMBAW	SWIM AWAY	241A
	HINA IIICα	IN ORDER THAT	378C
	M8 B2	NOT	519A
	TIS, TI IAγ	ANY ONE	827D
43	APO(R)RIPTW 2		97B
	THROW ONESELF DOWN		
	BOUL8MA	INTENTION	145B
	BOULOMAI 2Aβ	DESIRE	145D
	DIASWZW	SAVE	188B
	HEKATONTARCH8S	CENTURION	236C
	EXEIMI	GO OUT	273C
	EPI IIIIAβ	ON	288A
	KELEUW	COMMAND	428C
	KOLUMBAW 2	SWIM	443B
	KWLUW I	HINDER	462C
43F	G8 4	LAND	156C
44	APO I6	FROM	86A
	GINOMAI I3E	TAKE PLACE	158B
	DIASWZW	SAVE	188B
	EPI IIIAα	ON	286C
	EPI IIIIAβ	ON	288A
	LOIPOS 2Bα	THE OTHERS	481A
	MEN IC	(PARTICLE)	504A
	HO,H8,TO II5	THE	554B
	HOS,H8,HO II2	THIS (ONE)	589B
	SANIS	BOARD	749B

ACTS 28

1	DIASWZW	SAVE	188B
	EPIGINWSKW 2B	KNOW	291A
	KALEW IAγ	CALL	400A
	MELIT8	MALTA	501D
	N8SOS	ISLAND	540A
	TOTE 2	AT THAT TIME	831D
2	ANAPTW	KINDLE	59C
	HAPTW I	KINDLE	102B
	BARBAROS 2B	FOREIGN	133A
	DIA BIII	BECAUSE OF	180A
	EPHIST8MI 2A	STAND BY	331A
	OU 3A	NO	594C
	PARECHW IB	GRANT	632A
	PAS IEα	ALL	637D
	PROSANALAMBANW	WELCOME	718D
	PROSLAMBANW 2B	TAKE	724C
	PURA	A FIRE	738A
	TUGCHANW 2D	HAPPEN	837B
	HUETOS	RAIN	841A
	PHILANTHRWPIA		866C
	LOVE FOR MANKIND		
	PSUCHOS	COLD	902D
3	DIEXERCHOMAI	COME OUT	193B
	EXERCHOMAI IC	GO OUT	274C
	EPITITH8MI IAα	PUT UPON	302D
	ECHIDNA	VIPER	332A
	THERM8	HEAT	360B
	KATHAPTW	SEIZE	387D
	PL8THOS 2A	QUANTITY	674C
	PURA	A FIRE	738A

3	SUSTREPHW I	BRING TOGETHER	803A
	PHRUGANON 2	DRY WOOD	875B
4	BARBAROS 2B	FOREIGN	133A
	DIASWZW	SAVE	188B
	DIK8 2	JUSTICE	197C
	EAW I	LET	211D
	EIDON IB	SEE	219D
	EK IA	AWAY FROM	233C
	ZAW IAδ	LIVE	336D
	KREMANNUMI 2A	HANG	451A
	LEGW I3	SAY	469D
	PANTWS I	BY ALL MEANS	614B
	PANTWS 3	OF COURSE	614B
	PHONEUS	MURDERER	872B
	HWS IVIA	WHEN	907A
4F	TH8RION IAβ	BEAST	361D
5	APOTINASSW	SHAKE OFF	100D
	KAKOS 2	EVIL	398D
	MEN 2E	(PARTICLE)	504C
	HO,H8,TO I3	THE	552A
	OUN 4	THEREFORE	597D
	PASCHW 3B	ENDURE	639D
	PUR IA	FIRE	737B
6	ATOPOS I	UNUSUAL	120A
	APHNW	SUDDENLY	126C
	GINOMAI I3D	TAKE PLACE	158B
	DE 4B	BUT, AND	170D
	EMPI(M)PR8MI	BURN	255D
	EPI III2B	ON	289C
	THEOS I	GOD	357B
	THEWREW 2A	OBSERVE	360D
	KATAPIPTW	FALL	417C
	MELLW ICβ	BE ABOUT TO	502B
	METABALLW 2	CHANGE ONES MIND	512A
	NEKROS IAα	DEAD	536C
	PIMPR8MI 2	SWELL UP	664A
	POLUS I2Cα	MANY	695B
6A	PROSDOKAW 4	EXPECT	719D
6B	PROSDOKAW 3	EXPECT	719E
7	ANADECHOMAI 2	RECEIVE	53C
	N8SOS	ISLAND	540A
	XENIZW I	RECEIVE AS A GUEST	550A
	ONOMA II	NAME	574A
	PERI 2Aγ	ABOUT	650D
	PRWTOS ICβ	FIRST	733C
	HUPARCHW I	BE	845D
	PHILOPHRONWS	HOSPITABLY	869C
	CHWRION I	PLACE	898C
7F	POPLIOS	PUBLIUS	698C
8	GINOMAI I3E	TAKE PLACE	158B
	DUSENTERION	DYSENTERY	208D
	EPITITH8MI IAα	PUT UPON	302D
	IAOMAI I	HEAL	369A
	KATAKEIMAI I	LIE DOWN	412B
	PURETOS	FEVER	738B
	SUNECHW 5	DISTRESS	797A
9	ASTHENEIA IA	WEAKNESS	114D
	GINOMAI I3A	TAKE PLACE	157D
	ECHW I2Eα	HAVE	333A
	LOIPOS 2Bα	THE OTHERS	481A
	N8SOS	ISLAND	540A
10	EPITITH8MI 2A	GIVE	303A
	KAI II6		394C

10	PROS III5B	TOWARD 7|7D
	TIMAW 2	HONOR 824D
	TIM8 2A	HONOR 825B
	CHREIA 2	NEED 893B
11	ALEXANDRINOS	ALEXANDRIAN 35A
	ANAGW 3	PUT TO SEA 52D
	META BIII	AFTER 511C
	M8N I	MONTH 520D
	N8SOS	ISLAND 540A
	PARAS8MOS 2	DISTINGUISHED 627C
	PARACHEIMAZW	SPEND THE WINTER 629A
	PLOION I	SHIP 679B
12	EPIMENW I	REMAIN 296A
	KATAGW	LEAD 411A
	SURAKOUSAI	SYRACUSE 801C
13	DEUTERAIOS	ON THE SECOND DAY 175D
	HEIS IA∝	ONE 230A
	EPIGINOMAI	COME UP 290D
	H8MERA 2	DAY 347B
	KATANTAW I	ARRIVE 416B
	NOTOS I	SOUTHWEST WIND 546A
	PERIAIREW I	TAKE AWAY 651C
	PERIERCHOMAI	GO AROUND 652C
	POTIOLOI	PUTEOLI 702D
	R8GION	RHEGIUM 742B
14	AN8R I	MAN 66A
	EPI III A6	AT 286D
	EPIMENW I	REMAIN 296A
	EPIMENW I	REMAIN 296B
	HEURISKW IB	FIND 325B
	PARA IIIBy	BESIDE 615C
	PARAKALEW 3	IMPLORE 622D
	RWM8	ROME 745D
15	APANT8SIS	MEETING 79D
	APPIOU PHORON	APPII FORUM 101D
	ACHRI IB	AS FAR AS 128C
	EUCHARISTEW 2	GIVE THANKS 328C
	THARSOS	COURAGE 352C
	KAKEITHEN I	AND FROM THERE 397C
	PERI II	ABOUT 650D
	TABERNAI	TAVERN 810B
16	DESMIOS	PRISONER 175A
	HEAUTOU IF	ONESELF 211B
	HEKATONTARCH8S	CENTURION 236C
	EXW 2A	OUTSIDE 279B
	EPITREPW I	ALLOW 303C
	KATA IIIC	BY 407B
	MENW IA∝	REMAIN 504D
	PARADIDWMI IB	GIVE OVER 620A
	PAREMBOL8 2	A CAMP 630D
	RWM8	ROME 745D
	STRATOPEDARCH8S	778C
	MILITARY COMMANDER	
	PHULASSW IB	WATCH 876B
17	DESMIOS	PRISONER 175A
	ETHOS 2	CUSTOM 217D
	ENANTIOS 2	OPPOSED 261C
	LAOS 3A	PEOPLE 468A
	PARADIDWMI IB	GIVE OVER 620A
	PATRWOS	PATERNAL 642D
	PRWTOS IC8	FIRST 733C
	RWMAIOS	ROMAN 745C
	SUNERCHOMAI IA	ASSEMBLE 795D

17	CHEIR 2B	HAND 888D
18	AITIA 2A	CHARGE 25D
	ANAKRINW IB	QUESTION 56A
	APOLUW I	SET FREE 96A
	BOULOMAI 2A8	DESIRE 145D
	THANATOS IB∝	DEATH 351C
	M8DEIS I	NO 519D
	HOSTIS 3	WHOEVER 591B
	POLUS I2B8	MANY 695A
	HUPARCHW I	BE 845D
19	ANAGKAZW I	COMPEL 51D
	ANTILEGW I	CONTRADICT 74A
	EPIKALEW 2A8	CALL UPON 294A
	EPIKRAZW	SHOUT THREATS 294D
	KAISAR	EMPEROR 396C
	KAT8GOREW IA	BRING CHARGES 424B
	LUTROW 2	REDEEM 484A
	OU 3B	NO 594C
	PSUCH8 IA8	SOUL LIFE 901C
	HWS III IB	SO 906C
20	AITIA I	CAUSE 25D
	HALUSIS I	CHAIN 40D
	EIDON 6	VISIT 220B
	HEINEKEN	ON ACCOUNT OF 225A
	ELPIS 2A	HOPE 252C
	HENEKA	BECAUSE OF 264B
	ISRA8L 2	ISRAEL 382C
	PARAKALEW IA	SUMMON 622B
	PARAKALEW 3	IMPLORE 622D
	PERIKEIMAI 2A	653D
	BE PLACED AROUND	
	PROSLALEW	SPEAK TO 724C
21	APAGGELLW I	REPORT 78C
	GRAMMA 2A	LETTER 164C
	DECHOMAI I	TAKE 176B
	IOUDAIA I	JUDAEA 379D
	LALEW 2B	SPEAK 464D
	OUTE	NOT 600C
	PARAGINOMAI I	COME 618D
	PON8ROS 2C	WICKED 698A
	TIS, TI IAY	ANY ONE 827D
22	HAIRESIS IA	SECT 23B
	AKOUW IB8	HEAR 31C
	ANTILEGW I	CONTRADICT 74A
	AXIOW 2A	CONSIDER SUITABLE 78A
	GAR IB	FOR 151B
	GNWSTOS IA	KNOWN 163C
	PANTACHOU I	EVERYWHERE 613B
	PARA I3C	FROM 615A
	PHRONEW I	THINK 874A
23	BASILEIA 3B	KINGDOM 134D
	BASILEIA 3G	KINGDOM 135A
	DIAMARTUROMAI 2	TESTIFY 185C
	EKTITH8MI 2	EXPLAIN 245B
	HESPERA	EVENING 313C
	HEWS III A	UNTIL 335B
	H8KW IB	HAVE COME 345B
	H8MERA 3A	DAY 347D
	NOMOS 4A	LAW 545A
	XENIA	GUEST ROOM 549D
	PARATITH8MI 2C	PLACE BESIDE 628C
	PEITHW IA	CONVINCE 644D
	POLUS II2A8	MANY 695D

23	PROPH8T8S I	PROPHET 731A
	PRWI	EARLY 732B
	TASSW 2B	PLACE 813D
23A	TE IB	AND 815B
24	APISTEW IA	DISBELIEVE 84D
	HO,H8,TO I2	THE 552A
	PEITHW 3A	BELIEVE 645B
25	APOLUW 3	GO AWAY 96B
	ASUMPHWNOS	BEING AT VARIANCE 118A
	8SAIAS	ISAIAH 349C
	KALWS 4B	WELL 402B
	LALEW 2A€	SPEAK 464C
	PNEUMA 5C«	SPIRIT 682D
	PNEUMA 6C	SPIRIT 683D
	PROS III4A	TOWARD 717C
	PROPH8T8S I	PROPHET 730D
	R8MA I	WORD 742D
26	AKO8 IB	HEARING 30B
	AKOUW IA	HEAR 31B
	SUNI8MI	UNDERSTAND 798A
27	BAREWS	WITH DIFFICULTY 133B
	BARUNW	BURDEN 133D
	EIDON IA	SEE 219D
	EPISTREPHW IB9	TURN 301B
	IAOMAI 2	HEAL 369A
	KAI I2E	AND 393C
	KAMMUW	CLOSE 403A
	PACHUNW 2	MAKE DULL 644A
	SUNI8MI	UNDERSTAND 798A
27A	KARDIA IB9	HEART 404D
27A	OUS 2	EAR 600B
27B	KARDIA IB9	HEART 404C
27B	OUS 2	EAR 600B
27B	OPHTHALMOS 2	EYE 604C
28	AKOUW 4	LISTEN 32A
	APOSTELLW IB«	SEND AWAY 98A
	APOSTELLW 2	PUT IN 98C
	GNWSTOS IA	KNOWN 163C
	SWT8RIOS 2	SAVING 809C
29	APERCHOMAI IA	GO AWAY 83D
	SUZ8T8SIS	DISPUTE 783C
30	APODECHOMAI I	WELCOME 89C
	DIETIA	TWO YEARS 194A
	EISPOREUOMAI I	GO 232D
	EMMENW IA	STAY 254C
	IDIOS IA9	ONES OWN 370B
	MISTHWMA	RENT 525D
	XENIA	GUEST ROOM 549D
	HOLOS I	WHOLE 567C
	PAS ID9	ALL 637D
31	AKWLUTWS	WITHOUT HINDRANCE 33D
	AM8N I	AMEN 45B
	BASILEIA 3B	KINGDOM 134D
	BASILEIA 3G	KINGDOM 135A
	K8RUSSW 2B9	ANNOUNCE 432C
	KURIOS 2Cγ	LORD 461A
	META AIII	WITH 511A
	PARR8SIA 2	OPENLY 636A
	PERI II	ABOUT 650D

ROMANS I

I	APOSTOLOS 3	APOSTLES 99B

I	APHORIZW 2	SET APART 127A
	DOULOS 4	SLAVE 205B
	EIS 4D	FOR 228C
	EUAGGELION 2B«	GOSPEL 318B
	EUAGGELION 2B9	GOSPEL 318B
	KL8TOS	CALLED 437B
	PAULOS	PAUL 643A
2	HAGIOS IA«	DEDICATED TO GOD 9C
	GRAPH8 2B«	SCRIPTURE 165B
	PROEPAGGELLW	PROMISE BEFORE 712A
	PROPH8T8S I	PROPHET 730D
3	GINOMAI IIA	BE BORN 157B
	DAUID	DAVID 170B
	EK 3B	FROM 234B
	KATA II6	WITH RESPECT TO 408D
	SARX 4	BODY 751B
	SPERMA IB	SEED 769A
	SPERMA 2B	SEED 769B
	HUIOS 2B	SON 842D
3F	PNEUMA 2	SPIRIT 681B
4	HAGIWSUN8	HOLINESS 10C
	ANASTASIS 2A	RESURRECTION 60A
	DUNAMIS I	POWER 206D
	EN III2	BY 260B
	KATA II6	WITH RESPECT TO 408D
	KURIOS 2Cγ	LORD 461B
	NEKROS 2A	DEAD 537A
	HORIZW IB	DETERMINE 584D
	HUIOS 2B	SON 842D
	CHRISTOS 2	ANOINTED ONE 895C
5	APOSTOL8	APOSTLESHIP 98D
	DIA AIII2Bγ	BY 179D
	KAI I3	AND 393D
	LAMBANW 2	RECEIVE 466B
	ONOMA I4Cθ	NAME 576D
	PAS ID«	ALL 637C
	PISTIS 2D«	FAITH 669A
	PISTIS 2D«	FAITH 669C
	PISTIS 3	FAITH 669D
	HUPAKO8 IB	OBEDIENCE 845A
	HUPER IB	IN BEHALF OF 846D
	CHARIS 4	FAVOR 886C
6	EIMI III4	TO BE 224C
	KL8TOS	CALLED 437A
	CHRISTOS 2	ANOINTED ONE 895C
7	AGAP8TOS 2	BELOVED 6C
	HAGIOS 2D9	SAINTS 10A
	APO V4	FROM 87C
	EIR8N8 2	PEACE 226D
	KL8TOS	CALLED 437A
	KURIOS 2Cγ	LORD 461A
	PAS ID9	ALL 637D
	PAT8R 3C9	FATHER 641C
	RWM8	ROME 745D
	CHARIS 2C	FAVOR 885D
7B	THEOS 3D	GOD 358A
8	DIA AIII2A	BY 179D
	EUCHARISTEW 2	GIVE THANKS 328C
	THEOS 3C	GOD 358A
	KATAGGELLW I	PROCLAIM 410C
	KOSMOS 4A	WORLD 447A
	MEN 2C	(PARTICLE) 504B
	HOLOS 2A	WHOLE 567D

8	PAS IEα	ALL 637D
	PISTIS 2Dα	FAITH 669A
	PRWTOS 2B	FIRST 733D
	SU 3	YOU 780A
	CHRISTOS 2	ANOINTED ONE 895C
9	ADIALEIPTWS	CONSTANTLY 17A
	GAR IA	FOR 151A
	EUAGGELION 2Bα	GOSPEL 318B
	LATREUW	SERVE 468D
	MARTUS 2A	WITNESS 495B
	MNEIA 2	MENTION 526B
	PNEUMA 3B	SPIRIT 681C
	POIEW III	DO 689C
	HUIOS 2B	SON 842D
	HWS IV4	WHEN 907B
10	DEOMAI 4	ASK 174B
	EI VII2B	IF 219B
	EPI 12	UNDER 286C
	EUODOW	PROSPER 324A
	8D8 IC	ALREADY 344D
	THEL8MA 2B	WILL 355A
	PANTOTE	ALWAYS 614A
	POTE I	ONCE 701D
	PROSEUCH8 I	PRAYER 720C
11	EIDON 6	VISIT 220B
	EPIPOTHEW	DESIRE 297D
	HINA IIA	IN ORDER THAT 377C
	METADIDWMI	SHARE 512B
	PNEUMATIKOS 2Aβ	SPIRITUAL 685B
	ST8RIZW 2	ESTABLISH 775D
	TIS, TI 2C	ANY ONE 828B
	CHARISMA I	A GIFT 887A
12	DIA AIIIID	THROUGH 179C
	EGW	I 216C
	EN I4A	IN 258B
	HOUTOS IBα	THIS 601D
	PISTIS 2Dα	FAITH 669A
	SUMPARAKALEW	ENCOURAGE TOGETHER 786D
	TE 3A	AND 815B
13	AGNOEW I	BE IGNORANT 11B
	ADELPHOS 2	BROTHER 16A
	ACHRI IA	UNTIL 128B
	DEURO 2	UNTIL NOW 175D
	THELW I	WISH 355C
	KATHWS I	JUST AS 392A
	KAI I2I	AND 393D
	KAI II3	ALSO 394B
	KARPOS 2B	GAIN 406A
	KWLUW I	HINDER 462C
	LOIPOS 2A	OTHER 481A
	POLLAKIS	OFTEN 693B
	POLUS I2Bβ	MANY 695B
	PROTITH8MI 2B	PLAN 729C
	TIS, TI 2C	ANY ONE 828B
14	ANO8TOS I	UNINTELLIGENT 70A
	BARBAROS 2B	FOREIGN 133A
	HELL8N I	A GREEK 251B
	OPHEILET8S 2B	DEBTOR 603A
	SOPHOS 2	LEARNED 767D
	TE 3A	AND 815C
15	EUAGGELIZW 2Aγ	PREACH 317D
	KATA II7B	(POSSESSIVE) 409A
15	HOUTW	THUS 602B
	HOUTW IB	THUS 602C
	PROTHUMOS	READY 713C
	RWM8	ROME 745D
16	GAR IB	FOR 151B
	DUNAMIS I	POWER 206C
	EIS 4E	SO THAT 228D
	HELL8N 2A	GENTILE 251C
	EPAISCHUNOMAI I	BE ASHAMED 281D
	EUAGGELION IA	GOSPEL 318A
	IOUDAIOS 2A	JEWISH 380B
	OU 4A	NO 594D
	PISTEUW 2B	BELIEVE 667C
	PRWTOS 2C	FIRST 734A
	SWT8RIA 2	DELIVERANCE 809B
16=18	GAR IC	FOR 151B
17	APOKALUPTW I	REVEAL 91C
	GRAPHW 2C	WRITE 165D
	DIKAIOS IB	UPRIGHT 195A
	*DIKAIOSUN8 3	RIGHTEOUSNESS 196A
	EK 6D	FROM 236A
	ZAW 2Bβ	LIVE 337B
	KATHWS I	JUST AS 392A
17A	PISTIS 2Dα	FAITH 669A
17B	PISTIS 2Dα	FAITH 669A
18	ADIKIA 2	UNRIGHTEOUSNESS 17C
	AL8THEIA 2B	TRUTH 35C
	APOKALUPTW I	REVEAL 91C
	ASEBEIA	GODLESSNESS 114A
	GAR 4	INDEED 151D
	KATECHW IAβ	HOLD BACK 423D
	ORG8 2A	ANGER 582D
	OURANOS 2A	HEAVEN 599B
	PAS IAβ	EVERY EACH 636D
19	EN IV4A	IN 260D
	HO,H8,TO II2A	THE 553B
	PHANEROS I	CLEAR 860A
	PHANEROW IA	REVEAL 860C
19=21	DIOTI 3	FOR 198C
20	AIDIOS	ETERNAL 21C
	ANAPOLOG8TOS	WITHOUT EXCUSE 59C
	AORATOS	UNSEEN 78B
	APO II2A	FROM 86B
	DUNAMIS I	POWER 206C
	EIS 4E	SO THAT 228D
	THEIOT8S	DIVINITY 354C
	KATHORAW	PERCEIVE 392A
	KOSMOS 2	WORLD 446D
	KTISIS IA	CREATION 456D
	NOEW IA	UNDERSTAND 542C
	HO,H8,TO II2A	THE 553B
	POI8MA	WORK 689D
21	ASUNETOS 2	FOOLISH 118B
	GINWSKW IB	KNOW 160A
	DIALOGISMOS I	THOUGHT 185A
	DOXAZW I	PRAISE 203C
	EUCHARISTEW 2	GIVE THANKS 328C
	8 IC	NOR 343A
	KARDIA IBβ	HEART 404C
	MATAIOW	RENDER FUTILE 496D
	SKOTIZW 2	BECOME DARK 764D
	HWS IIIIA	SO 906C
22	MWRAINW I	SHOW TO BE FOOLISH 533A

22	SOPHOS 2	LEARNED 767D
	PHASKW	SAY 862B
23	ALLASSW 2	EXCHANGE 38C
	APHTHARTOS	IMPERISHABLE 125A
	DOXA 1A	GLORY 202D
	EIKWN 2	FORM 221C
	EN IV5	IN 261A
	HERPETON	REPTILE 310A
	HOMOIWMA 2	LIKENESS 570C
	PETEINON	BIRD 660A
	TETRAPOUS	QUADRUPEDS 821C
	PHTHARTOS	PERISHABLE 864D
24	AKATHARSIA 2	IMPURITY 28B
	DIO	THEREFORE 197D
	EN III3A	BECAUSE OF 260C
	EPITHUMIA 3	DESIRE 293C
	KARDIA 1Bε	HEART 405A
	HO,H8,TO II4Bγ	THE 554A
	PARADIDWMI 1B	GIVE OVER 620C
	SWMA 1B	BODY 806D
25	AIWN 1B	TIME 26D
	AL8THEIA 2B	TRUTH 35C
	AM8N 1	AMEN 45A
	EN IV5	IN 261A
	EULOG8TOS	BLESSED 323A
	KTIZW	CREATE 456C
	KTISIS 1Bβ	CREATION 457A
	LATREUW	SERVE 468D
	METALLASSW	EXCHANGE 512D
	HOSTIS 2B	WHOEVER 591A
	PARA III3	IN COMPARISON 616B
	SEBAZOMAI	WORSHIP 753A
	PSEUDOS	LIE 900C
26	ATIMIA	DISHONOR 119D
	GAR 1B	FOR 151B
	EIS 4B	TO 228B
	METALLASSW	EXCHANGE 512D
	PATHOS 2	PASSION 608A
	PARADIDWMI 1B	GIVE OVER 620C
	PHUSIS 3	NATURE 877D
	CHR8SIS 3	FUNCTION 894B
26F	PHUSIKOS 1	NATURAL 877A
27	ANTIMISTHIA	PENALTY 74C
	APOLAMBANW 1	RECEIVE 93D
	ARSENOKOIT8S	109B
	A MALE HOMOSEXUAL	
	ASCH8MOSUN8 1	SHAMELESS DEED 119A
	APHI8MI 3B	ABANDON 125D
	DEI 1	IT IS NECESSARY 171A
	EKKAIW	BE INFLAMED 240A
	KATERGAZOMAI 1	ACHIEVE 422D
	HOMOIWS	LIKEWISE 570D
	OREXIS	DESIRE 583D
	PLAN8	WANDERING 671D
	CHR8SIS 3	FUNCTION 894B
27A	ARS8N	MALE 109C
27B	ARS8N	MALE 109C
27C	ARS8N	MALE 109C
28	ADOKIMOS	UNQUALIFIED 18B
	DOKIMAZW 2B	APPROVE 201D
	EPIGNWSIS	KNOWLEDGE 291C
	ECHW 17A	HAVE 334A
	KATH8KW	TO BE PROPER 390A
28	KATHWS 3	AS 392B
	M8 AII2D	NOT 518C
	NOUS 3A	THE MIND 546D
	PARADIDWMI 1B	GIVE OVER 620C
	POIEW IICγ	DO 688C
29	ADIKIA 2	UNRIGHTEOUSNESS 17D
	DOLOS	DECEIT 202B
	ERIS	STRIFE 309C
	KAKIA 1B	MALICE 397D
	KAKO8THEIA	MALICE 398A
	MESTOS 2A	FULL 509C
	PAS 1Aβ	EVERY EACH 636D
	PLEONEXIA	GREEDINESS 673D
	PL8ROW 1B	MAKE FULL 677A
	PON8RIA	WICKEDNESS 697A
	PORNEIA 1	PROSTITUTION 699D
	PHTHONOS	ENVY 865C
	PHONOS	MURDER 872C
	PSITHURIST8S	WHISPERER 901B
30	ALAZWN	BOASTER 34A
	APEITH8S 1	DISOBEDIENT 82B
	GONEUS	PARENTS 164B
	EPHEURET8S	CONTRIVER 330C
	THEOSTUG8S	HATING GOD 359A
	KAKOS IC	EVIL 398D
	KATALALOS	SLANDERER 413D
	HUBRIST8S	INSOLENT MAN 839D
	HUPER8PHANOS	PROUD 849A
31	ANELE8MWN	UNMERCIFUL 63D
	ASPONDOS	IRRECONCILABLE 116D
	ASTORGOS	UNLOVING 117C
	ASUNTHETOS	FAITHLESS 118B
	ASUNETOS 1	FOOLISH 118B
32	ALLA 1A	BUT, YET 37C
	AXIOS 2B	WORTHY 77D
	DIKAIWMA 1	REGULATION 197A
	EPIGINWSKW 1A	KNOW 290D
	THANATOS 2B	DEATH 352A
	MONOS 2C	ONLY 529D
	HOSTIS 2B	WHOEVER 591A
	POIEW IIBε	DO 687D
	PRASSW 1A	DO 705A
	SUNEUDOKEW	AGREE WITH 796C
	TOIOUTOS 3Aβ	SUCH A KIND 829B
32A	PRASSW 1A	DO 705A
32B	PRASSW 1A	DO 705A

ROMANS 2

1	ANAPOLOG8TOS	WITHOUT EXCUSE 59C
	ANTHRWPOS 1Aγ	MAN 67C
	AUTOS 4B	THE SAME 123B
	DIO	THEREFORE 197D
	EN IV6A	IN 261A
	HETEROS 1Bε	ANOTHER 315C
	KATAKRINW	CONDEMN 413A
	KRIMA 6	JUDGMENT 452A
	HO,H8,TO II3B	THE 553D
	PAS ICγ	WHOEVER 637B
	W 1	O 903B
1A	KRINW 6B	JUDGE 453B
1B	KRINW 6B	JUDGE 453B
1C	KRINW 6B	JUDGE 453B

1-3	PRASSW IA	DO 705A
2	AL8THEIA 3	REALITY 35D
	EPI IIIIBγ	ON 289A
	KATA II5Aβ	ACCORDING TO 408B
	OIDA IE	KNOW 558C
2F	KRIMA 4B	VERDICT 451D
2F	TOIOUTOS 3Aβ	SUCH A KIND 829B
3	ANTHRWPOS IAγ	MAN 67C
	EKPHEUGW 2Bβ	RUN AWAY 246B
	KRINW 6B	JUDGE 453B
	LOGIZOMAI 3	THINK 477B
	HOUTOS IBβ	THIS 601C
	POIEW IIBε	DO 687D
	PRASSW IA	DO 705A
	SU IA	YOU 779D
	W I	O 903B
4	AGNOEW I	BE IGNORANT IIB
	AGW IC	LEAD I4B
	ANOCH 2	FORBEARANCE 72A
	EIS 4A	INTO 228B
	8 IDβ	OR 343A
	KATAPHRONEW I	SCORN 421C
	MAKROTHUMIA 2Bα	PATIENCE 489B
	METANOIA	REPENTANCE 514A
	HO,H8,TO II2C	THE 553C
	PLOUTOS 2	WEALTH 680B
	CHR8STOS 2	USEFUL 894C
	CHR8STOT8S 2B	GOODNESS 894D
5	AMETANO8TOS	UNREPENTANT 45A
	ANTAPODOSIS	REPAYING 72C
	APOKALUPSIS 3	REVELATION 92A
	DIKAIOKRISIA	194C
	RIGHTEOUS JUDGMENT	
	H8MERA 3Bβ	DAY 348A
	TH8SAURIZW 2B	STORE UP 362A
	KARDIA IB6	HEART 404D
	KATA II5A6	ACCORDING TO 408B
	SEAUTOU 2	YOURSELF 753A
	SKL8ROT8S	HARDNESS 763C
5A	ORG8 2B	ANGER 583A
5B	ORG8 2B	ANGER 583A
6	APODIDWMI 3	RECOMPENSE 90A
	HEKASTOS 2	EACH 236A
	ERGON ICβ	DEED 308A
	KATA II5Aβ	ACCORDING TO 408A
	KATARGEW IB	MAKE INEFFECTIVE 418B
7	AGATHOS IBβ	GOOD 3B
	AIWNIOS 3	ETERNAL 28A
	APHTHARSIA	INCORRUPTIBILITY 124D
	DOXA IA	GLORY 202D
	ERGON ICβ	DEED 308A
	Z8TEW 2A	SEEK 339C
	ZW8 2Bβ	LIFE 341C
	KATA II5A6	ACCORDING TO 408B
	TIM8 2B	HONOR 825C
	HUPOMON8 I	PATIENCE 854B
8	ADIKIA 2	UNRIGHTEOUSNESS I7C
	AL8THEIA 2B	TRUTH 35C
	APEITHEW 3	DISOBEY 82A
	APEITHEW I	DISOBEY 82A
	EK 3D	FROM 234C
	ERITHEIA	SELFISHNESS 309C
	HO,H8,TO II5	THE 554B

8	ORG8 2B	ANGER 583A
	PEITHW 3B	OBEY 645C
9	ANTHRWPOS IAα	MAN 67C
	EPI IIIIBγ	ON 289A
	THLIPSIS I	TRIBULATION 362D
	KAKOS IC	EVIL 398D
	KATERGAZOMAI I	ACHIEVE 422D
	PAS IAα	EVERY EACH 636C
	STENOCHWRIA	DISTRESS 774A
	PSUCH8 IBγ	SOUL LIFE 901D
	PSUCH8 2	SOUL LIFE 902C
9F	HELL8N 2A	GENTILE 251C
9F	IOUDAIOS 2A	JEWISH 380B
9F	PRWTOS 2C	FIRST 734A
10	AGATHOS 2Aα	GOOD 3B
	DOXA IA	GLORY 202D
	EIR8N8 3	PEACE 227A
	ERGAZOMAI 2A	WORK 307A
	PAS ICγ	WHOEVER 637B
	TIM8 2B	HONOR 825C
11	GAR IB	FOR 151B
	EIMI IIIBB	TO BE 224D
	PARA II2D	BESIDE 615D
	PROSWPOL8MPSIA	PARTIALITY 728A
12	HAMARTANW 3	SIN 41D
	ANOMWS	WITHOUT THE LAW 71D
	APOLLUMI 2Aα	PERISH 94D
	ENNOMWS	SUBJECT TO 266D
	KRINW 4Bα	JUDGE 453A
12A	NOMOS 3	LAW 544C
12A	HOSOS 2	HOW GREAT 590C
12B	NOMOS 3	LAW 544C
12B	HOSOS 2	HOW GREAT 590C
13	AKROAT8S	A HEARER 33A
	GAR IB	FOR 151B
	DIKAIOS IB	UPRIGHT 194D
	DIKAIOW 3A	JUSTIFY 196D
	THEOS 3A	GOD 357D
	PARA II2B	BESIDE 615C
	POI8T8S 2	MAKER 689D
13A	NOMOS 3	LAW 544C
13B	NOMOS 3	LAW 544C
14	M8 AII2B	NOT 518B
	HO,H8,TO II7	THE 554C
	HOUTOS IAε	THIS 601B
	POIEW IICα	DO 688C
	PHUSIS 3	NATURE 877D
14B	NOMOS 3	LAW 544D
15	ALL8LWN	EACH OTHER 38D
	APOLOGEOMAI	DEFEND ONESELF 95B
	GRAPTOS	WRITTEN 165A
	ENDEIKNUMI I	DEMONSTRATE 262A
	ERGON IB	MANIFESTATION 307D
	8 IAβ	OR 342D
	KARDIA IBγ	HEART 404D
	KAT8GOREW 2	ACCUSE 424C
	LOGISMOS I	THOUGHT 478A
	METAXU 2B	BETWEEN 514C
	NOMOS 3	LAW 544C
	HOSTIS 2B	WHOEVER 591A
	SUMMARTUREW	TESTIFY 786A
	*SUNEID8SIS 2	CONSCIOUSNESS 794B
16	DIA AIII2A	BY 179D

16	EUAGGELION 2Bβ	GOSPEL	318C
	H8MERA 3Bβ	DAY	348A
	KATA II5Aα	ACCORDING TO	408A
	KRINW 4Bα	JUDGE	453A
	KRUPTOS 2A	HIDDEN	455A
	HOTE 2Aα	WHEN	592C
17	EI IIA	IF	217D
	EPANAPAUOMAI 2	REST	282C
	EPONOMAZW	CALL	305C
	IOUDAIOS 2A	JEWISH	380B
	KAUCHAOMAI I	BOAST	426D
	NOMOS 3	LAW	544C
18	GINWSKW 6Aα	KNOW	160C
	DIAPHERW 2B	BE SUPERIOR	189C
	DOKIMAZW I	EXAMINE	201C
	DOKIMAZW 2B	APPROVE	201D
	EK 3Gβ	BY	234D
	THEL8MA IA	WILL	354D
	THEL8MA ICγ	WILL	355A
	KAT8CHEW 2A	TEACH	425A
	NOMOS 3	LAW	544C
19	HOD8GOS 2	LEADER	556A
	PEITHW 2B	CONVINCE	645B
	SKOTOS 2B	DARKNESS	765B
	TE IA	AND	815A
	TUPHLOS 2B	BLIND	838C
	PHWS 3B	LIGHT	880C
19F	DIDASKALOS	TEACHER	190D
20	AL8THEIA 2A	TRUTH	35B
	APHRWN	FOOLISH	127B
	GNWSIS I	KNOWLEDGE	162D
	MORPHWSIS I	EMBODIMENT	530B
	N8PIOS I8α	CHILDREN	539C
	PAIDEUT8S	INSTRUCTOR	608D
21	HETEROS I8ε	ANOTHER	315C
	K8RUSSW 2Bβ	ANNOUNCE	432C
	KLEPTW	STEAL	435C
	M8 AIIIBβ	NOT	517D
	SEAUTOU 3	YOURSELF	753A
22	BDELUSSOMAI	ABHORE	137D
	EIDWLON 2	IDOL	220D
	HIEROSULEW	ROB TEMPLES	374A
	LEGW IIIC	ORDER	470C
	M8 AIIIBβ	NOT	517D
	MOICHEUW 2A	COMMIT ADULTERY	528B
23	ATIMAZW	DISHONOR	119C
	KAUCHAOMAI I	BOAST	427A
	NOMOS 3	LAW	544C
	PARABASIS	OVERSTEPPING	617A
23B	NOMOS 3	LAW	544C
24	BLASPH8MEW 2Bβ	BLASPHEME	142A
	GRAPHW 2C	WRITE	165D
	DIA BIII	BECAUSE OF	180A
	KATHWS I	JUST AS	392A
	ONOMA I4B	NAME	575A
25	GAR IB	FOR	151B
	GAR IE	FOR	151C
	GAR 4	INDEED	151D
	GINOMAI I4A	BECOME	158C
	EAN IIA	IF	210B
	MEN IAα	(PARTICLE)	503D
	PARABAT8S	TRANSGRESSOR	617A
	PRASSW IA	DO	705B

25	WPHELEW 2B	HELP	909A
25A	NOMOS 3	LAW	544C
25A	NOMOS 3	LAW	544D
25A	PERITOM8 2	CIRCUMCISION	658D
25B	NOMOS 3	LAW	544D
25B	PERITOM8 2	CIRCUMCISION	658D
25FF	AKROBUSTIA 2	UNCIRCUMCISED	33A
26	AUTOS 3B	(OBLIQUE CASE)	123A
	DIKAIWMA I	REGULATION	197A
	EIS 8Aγ		229C
	LOGIZOMAI IB	CONSIDER	477A
	NOMOS 3	LAW	544C
	NOMOS 3	LAW	544D
	PERITOM8 2	CIRCUMCISION	658D
	PHULASSW IF	WATCH	876C
27	GRAMMA 2C	WRITING	164D
	DIA AIIIC	THROUGH	179B
	KRINW 4Bβ	JUDGE	453B
	NOMOS 3	LAW	544D
	PARABAT8S	TRANSGRESSOR	617A
	PERITOM8 2	CIRCUMCISION	658D
	TELEW 2	PERFORM	818D
	PHUSIS I	NATURE	877C
28	GAR IB	FOR	151B
	OUDE I	AND NOT	595D
	PERITOM8 2	CIRCUMCISION	658D
	SARX I	FLESH	750D
28A	PHANEROS 2	CLEAR	860B
28B	PHANEROS 2	CLEAR	860B
28F	IOUDAIOS 2A	JEWISH	380B
29	GRAMMA 2C	WRITING	164D
	EK 3C	FROM	234B
	EPAINOS IAα	PRAISE	281B
	EPAINOS IAβ	PRAISE	281B
	KARDIA I8δ	HEART	405A
	KRUPTOS 2B	HIDDEN	455B
	HOS,H8,HO II	(REL PRON)	587A
	PERITOM8 3	CIRCUMCISION	658D
	PNEUMA 5Gγ	SPIRIT	683C

ROMANS 3

I	8 ID∂	OR	343B
	IOUDAIOS 2A	JEWISH	380B
	PERISSOS I	EXTRAORDINARY	657A
	PERITOM8 2	CIRCUMCISION	658D
	WPHELEIA	USE	908D
2	KATA II5Bα	ACCORDING TO	408C
	LOGION	A SAYING	477D
	MEN 2C	(PARTICLE)	504B
	PISTEUW 3	BELIEVE	667D
	POLUS I2Cα	MANY	695B
	PRWTOS 2B	FIRST	733D
	TROPOS I	MANNER	835A
3	APISTEW 2	BE UNFAITHFUL	84D
	APISTIA I	UNFAITHFULNESS	84D
	GAR IF	WHAT	151C
	KATARGEW IB	MAKE INEFFECTIVE	418B
	M8 CI	NOT	519A
	PISTIS IA	FAITH	668B
	TIS, TI I8ε	WHICH	827A
4	AL8TH8S I	TRUE	36A
	AN 4	(PARTICLE)	48D

4	GINOMAI I3A	TAKE PLACE 157D	10 HEIS 2B	ONE 230C

4   GINOMAI I3A   TAKE PLACE 157D   10 HEIS 2B   ONE 230C
    GRAPHW 2C   WRITE 165D   KATHWS I   JUST AS 392A
    DE ID   BUT, AND 170C   *OUDE 3   NOT EVEN 596A
    DIKAIOW 3D   MAKE FREE 197A   11 EKZ8TEW I   SEEK OUT 239C
    KATHAPER   JUST AS 387D   SUNI8MI   UNDERSTAND 797D
    KRINW 6B   JUDGE 453C   SUNI8MI   UNDERSTAND 798A
    LOGOS IBα   COMMAND 479A   12 HAMA IB   TOGETHER 41B
    M8 AIII2   NOT 518C   ACHREIOW 2   BECOME DEPRAVED 128A
    NIKAW IB   BE VICTOR 541B   HEIS 2B   ONE 230C
    HOPWS 2Aβ   IN ORDER THAT 580D   EKKLINW   TURN AWAY 241A
    PAS IAα   EVERY EACH 636C   HEWS II4   AS MANY AS 336A
    PSEUST8S   LIAR 900D   POIEW IICβ   DO 688C
5   ADIKIA 2   UNRIGHTEOUSNESS 17D   CHR8STOT8S I   GOODNESS 894D
    ADIKOS I   UNJUST 18A   13 ANOIGW IB   OPEN 70C
    ANTHRWPOS IC   HUMAN 67D   ASPIS   ASP 116D
    DIKAIOSUN8 3   RIGHTEOUSNESS 196B   GLWSSA IA   TONGUE 161B
    EIPON I   SAY 225B   DOLIOW   DECEIVE 202B
    EPIPHERW 4   INFLICT 304C   IOS IA   POISON 379C
    LEGW I5   SAY 470A   LARUGX   THROAT 468B
    M8 CI   NOT 519A   TAPHOS 2   GRAVE 814B
    ORG8 2B   ANGER 583A   HUPO 2Aβ   · UNDER 851B
    SUNIST8MI   UNITE 798B   CHEILOS I   LIP 887C
    SUNIST8MI IIC   UNITE 798C   14 ARA   CURSE 103B
6   GINOMAI I3A   TAKE PLACE 157D   GEMW I   BE FULL 153A
    EPEI 2   BECAUSE 283D   PIKRIA 2   BITTERNESS 663B
    KOSMOS 5A   WORLD 447B   15 HAIMA 2A   BLOOD 22B
    PWS ID   HOW 739D   EKCHEW I   POUR OUT 246D
6F   KRINW 4Bα   JUDGE 453A   OXUS 2   QUICK 578A
7   AL8THEIA I   TRUTHFULNESS 35A   POUS IB   FOOT 703C
    ETI 2C   STILL 316B   16 HODOS 2B   WAY 557A
    KAGW 4   I 387A   SUNTRIMMA   RUIN 801B
    HO,H8,TO IIIE   THE 553A   TALAIPWRIA   DISTRESS 810D
    PERISSEUW IAγ   BE LEFT OVER 656D   17 EIR8N8 IB   PEACE 226B
    PSEUSMA   LIE 900D   HODOS 2A   WAY 556D
    HWS IIIIA   SO 906B   18 APENANTI IB   BEFORE 83B
8   AGATHOS 2Bγ   GOOD 3C   EIMI II9A   TO BE 223D
    BLASPH8MEW I   DEFAME 142A   THEOS 3Fβ   GOD 358D
    ENDIKOS   DESERVED 262C   PHOBOS 2Bα   FEAR 871D
    ERCHOMAI I2B   COME 311C   19 EN I5D   IN 259C
    KAKOS IC   EVIL 398D   HINA IIA   IN ORDER THAT 377C
    KRIMA 4B   VERDICT 451D   HINA II2   IN ORDER THAT 378D
    M8 AIII6   NOT 519A   KOSMOS 5A   WORLD 447B
    HOTI 2   THAT 593D   NOMOS 3   LAW 545A
    POIEW IIBε   DO 687D   NOMOS 4B   LAW 545A
    TIS, TI IAβ   ANY ONE 827D   OIDA IE   KNOW 558C
    PH8MI   SAY 864A   STOMA IA   MOUTH 777C
    PH8MI 2   SAY 864B   HUPODIKOS   ACCOUNTABLE 852B
9   AITIAOMAI   BLAME 26A   PHRASSW IB   SHUT 873C
    EIMI IIII2   TO BE 224D   19B PAS ICα   ALL 637B
    HELL8N 2A   GENTILE 251C   20 HAMARTIA I   SIN 42D
    OU 2A   NO 594B   DIA AIIIID   THROUGH 179B
    OUN ICβ   THEREFORE 597C   DIKAIOW 3A   JUSTIFY 196D
    PANTWS 5A   NOT AT ALL 614B   DIOTI 3   FOR 198C
    PROAITIAOMAI   709B   EK 3F   BY 234D
        ACCUSE BEFOREHAND   ENWPION 3   BEFORE 270B
    PROECHW 3   EXCEL 712C   EPIGNWSIS   KNOWLEDGE 291B
    PROECHW 2   EXCEL 712C   ERGON ICβ   DEED 308B
    PROKATECHW OCCUPY PREVIOUSLY 714B   PAS IAα   EVERY EACH 636D
    TIS, TI IBε   WHICH 827A   SARX 3   BODY 751B
    HUPO 2B   UNDER 851B   20A NOMOS 3   LAW 544D
10 GRAPHW 2C   WRITE 165D   20B NOMOS 3   LAW 544C
    DIKAIOS IB   UPRIGHT 194D   21 DIKAIOSUN8 3   RIGHTEOUSNESS 196A
    EIMI II   TO BE 222B   MARTUREW 2A   BE WITNESSED 494B

21 NUNI 1B	NOW	548C
PROPH8T8S 1	PROPHET	731A
HUPO 1AP	BY	850D
PHANEROW 1B	REVEAL	860C
CHWRIS 2B6	APART	899C
21A NOMOS 3	LAW	544D
21B NOMOS 4A	LAW	545A
21F DIKAIOSUN8 3	RIGHTEOUSNESS	196A
22 DE 2	BUT, AND	170D
DIA AIIIID	THROUGH	179C
DIASTOL8	DIFFERENCE	188A
DIKAIOSUN8 3	RIGHTEOUSNESS	196A
*PISTEUW 2B	BELIEVE	667C
PISTIS 2BP	FAITH	668D
CHRISTOS 2	ANOINTED ONE	895C
23 HAMARTANW 1	SIN	41D
DOXA 1A	BRIGHTNESS	202D
DOXA 3	FAME	203A
HUSTEREW 2	TO MISS	857A
24 APOLUTRWSIS 2A	REDEMPTION	95D
DIKAIOW 3A	JUSTIFY	196D
DWREAN 1	GRATIS	209D
EN IIIIP	BY	260B
CHARIS 2A	FAVOR	885C
CHRISTOS 2	ANOINTED ONE	895D
25 HAIMA 2B	BLOOD	22C
HAMART8MA	SIN	42A
DIA AIIIID	THROUGH	179C
DIA BIII	BECAUSE OF	180A
DIKAIOSUN8 3	RIGHTEOUSNESS	196B
ENDEIXIS 2	PROOF	262A
HILAST8RION		376B
THAT WHICH PROPITIATES		
PARESIS	PASSING OVER	631D
PISTIS 2BP	FAITH	669A
PROGINOMAI	FORMER TIMES	710C
PROTITH8MI 2A		729C
DISPLAY PUBLICLY		
26 ANOCH 2	FORBEARANCE	72A
DIKAIOS 2	RIGHTEOUS	195A
*DIKAIOSUN8 3	RIGHTEOUSNESS	196A
DIKAIOW 3B	JUSTIFY	196D
EIS 4E	SO THAT	228D
EK 3D	FROM	234C
EN 14D	IN	258C
ENDEIXIS 2	PROOF	262A
KAIROS 1	TIME	395C
NUN 3A	NOW	548A
PISTIS 2BP	FAITH	668D
PROS III3A	TOWARD	717A
27 ALLA 1A	BUT, YET	37C
DIA AIIIID	THROUGH	179B
EKKLEIW 2	EXCLUDE	240B
KAUCH8SIS 1	BOASTING	427B
NOMOS 1	LAW	544B
OUN 1C«	THEREFORE	597C
OUCHI 2	NOT	603A
POIOS 1AP	OF WHAT KIND	691B
POU 1A	WHERE	702D
27B NOMOS 5	LAW	545B
27F PISTIS 2D«	FAITH	669B
28 ANTHRWPOS 3AY	MAN	68B
DIKAIOW 3A	JUSTIFY	196D
28 ERGON 1CP	DEED	308B
LOGIZOMAI 3	THINK	477B
NOMOS 3	LAW	544D
CHWRIS 2B6	APART	899C
29 ETHNOS 2	GENTILES	217C
8 1D«	OR	343A
MONOS 2B	ONLY	529D
NAI 1B	YES	534D
OUCHI 3	NOT	603A
30 AKROBUSTIA 3	HEATHENISM	33B
DIKAIOW 3B	JUSTIFY	196D
EI VIII	IF	219B
HEIS 2A	ONE	230B
EK 3F	BY	234D
EPEIPER	SINCE INDEED	284B
PERITOM8 4A	CIRCUMCISION	658D
30F DIA AIIIID	THROUGH	179C
30F PISTIS 2D«	FAITH	669B
31 ALLA 1A	BUT, YET	37C
GINOMAI I3A	TAKE PLACE	157D
HIST8MI 11B«	PUT	383A
KATARGEW 1B	MAKE INEFFECTIVE	418B
M8 AIII2	NOT	518C
OUN 1C«	THEREFORE	597B
31A NOMOS 3	LAW	544C
31B NOMOS 3	LAW	544C

ROMANS 4

1 ABRAAM	ABRAHAM	1D
EIPON 2D	SAY	225C
KATA 116	WITH RESPECT TO	408D
PROPATWR	FOREFATHER	716B
SARX 4	BODY	751B
2 DIKAIOW 3A	JUSTIFY	196D
EK 3F	BY	234D
ERGON 1CP	DEED	308B
KAUCH8MA 1	BOAST	427B
3 *ABRAAM	ABRAHAM	1D
GAR 4	INDEED	151D
GRAPH8 2BP	SCRIPTURE	165B
DIKAIOSUN8 3	RIGHTEOUSNESS	196A
EIS 8AY		229C
LEGW 17	SAY	470A
LOGIZOMAI 1A	RECKON	477A
PISTEUW 1B	BELIEVE	666C
3FF DIKAIOSUN8 3	RIGHTEOUSNESS	196A
4 ERGAZOMAI 1	WORK	307A
LOGIZOMAI 1A	RECKON	477A
MISTHOS 2A	REWARD	525C
OPHEIL8MA 1	DEBT	603B
CHARIS 2A	FAVOR	885C
5 ASEB8S 1	GODLESS	114B
DIKAIOW 3B	JUSTIFY	196D
ERGAZOMAI 1	WORK	307A
LOGIZOMAI 1A	RECKON	477A
PISTEUW 2A6	BELIEVE	667B
PISTIS 2A	FAITH	668C
5F DIKAIOSUN8 3	RIGHTEOUSNESS	196A
5=20 PISTIS 2D«	FAITH	669B
6 DAUID	DAVID	170B
ERGON 1CP	DEED	308B
KATHAPER	JUST AS	387D

6	KAI II3	ALSO 394B
	LOGIZOMAI IA	RECKON 477A
	MAKARISMOS	BLESSING 488B
	CHWRIS 2B6	APART 899C
7	ANOMIA 2	LAWLESSNESS 71B
	APHI8MI 2	FORGIVE 125C
	EPIKALUPTW	COVER 294B
	HOS,H8,HO I2Bα	(REL PRON) 587B
7F	MAKARIOS IB	BLESSED 487D
8	HAMARTIA I	SIN 42C
	AN8R 6	MAN 66B
	LOGIZOMAI IA	RECKON 477A
	M8 DIA	NOT 519B
9	ABRAAM	ABRAHAM ID
	AKROBUSTIA 3	HEATHENISM 33B
	GAR 4	INDEED 151D
	DIKAIOSUN8 3	RIGHTEOUSNESS 196A
	EPI IIIIB(	ON 289D
	8 IAβ	OR 342D
	LOGIZOMAI IA	RECKON 477A
	MAKARISMOS	BLESSING 488B
	PERITOM8 4A	CIRCUMCISION 658D
	PISTIS 2A	FAITH 668C
10	8 IDγ	OR 343A
	LOGIZOMAI IA	RECKON 477A
	OUN ICα	THEREFORE 597C
	PWS IA	HOW 739C
10A	PERITOM8 2	CIRCUMCISION 658D
10B	PERITOM8 2	CIRCUMCISION 658D
10=12	AKROBUSTIA 2	UNCIRCUMCISED 33A
11	AKROBUSTIA 2	UNCIRCUMCISED 33A
	DIA AIIIC	THROUGH 179B
	DIKAIOSUN8 3	RIGHTEOUSNESS 196A
	LOGIZOMAI IA	RECKON 477A
	PAS IDβ	ALL 637D
	PAT8R 2F	FATHERS 641A
	PISTEUW 2B	BELIEVE 667C
	S8MEION I	SIGN 755C
	SPHRAGIS 2A	SEAL 804C
11=13	PISTIS 2A	FAITH 668C
12	ABRAAM	ABRAHAM ID
	ALLA IA	BUT, YET 37C
	EK 3D	FROM 234C
	ICHNOS	FOOTPRINT 385A
	MONOS 2C	ONLY 529D
	STOICHEW	BE IN LINE WITH 777A
12A	PAT8R 2F	FATHERS 641A
12A	PERITOM8 4A	CIRCUMCISION 658D
12B	PAT8R 2E	FATHERS 641A
12B	PERITOM8 4A	CIRCUMCISION 658D
13	ABRAAM	ABRAHAM ID
	GAR IB	FOR 151B
	DIA AIIID	THROUGH 179B
	DIKAIOSUN8 3	RIGHTEOUSNESS 196A
	KOSMOS 4A	WORLD 447A
	NOMOS 3	LAW 544C
	SPERMA 2B	SEED 769B
13F	EPAGGELIA 2A	PROMISE 280A
13F	KL8RONOMOS 2B	HEIR 436B
13=15	GAR IC	FOR 151B
14	EK 3D	FROM 234C
	KATARGEW IB	MAKE INEFFECTIVE 418B
	KENOW 2	MAKE EMPTY 429C
14	NOMOS 3	LAW 544C
	HO,H8,TO II5	THE 554B
15	KATERGAZOMAI 2	ACHIEVE 422D
	ORG8 2B	ANGER 583A
	HOU IB	WHERE 594A
	OUDE 2	AND NOT 595D
	PARABASIS	OVERSTEPPING 617A
15A	NOMOS 3	LAW 544C
16	ABRAAM	ABRAHAM ID
	ALLA IA	BUT, YET 37C
	BEBAIOS 2	FIRM 137D
	*EK 3D	FROM 234C
	EPAGGELIA 2A	PROMISE 280A
	HINA III3	IN ORDER THAT 379A
	MONOS 2C	ONLY 529D
	HO,H8,TO II5	THE 554B
	PAS ICα	ALL 637B
	PAT8R 2F	FATHERS 641A
	PISTIS 2A	FAITH 668C
	SPERMA 2B	SEED 769B
	CHARIS 2A	FAVOR 885C
16B	PAS IEα	ALL 637D
17	GRAPHW 2C	WRITE 165D
	EIMI II	TO BE 222A
	ZWOPOIEW I	MAKE ALIVE 342C
	KATHWS I	JUST AS 392B
	KALEW 2	CALL 400D
	KATENANTI 2B	IN THE SIGHT OF 422B
	M8 AII2D	NOT 518B
	NEKROS 2A	DEAD 537A
	HOS,H8,HO I4B	(REL PRON) 588A
	PAT8R 2F	FATHERS 641A
	PISTEUW IB	BELIEVE 666C
	TITH8MI I2Aα	MAKE 824A
17F	POLUS IIAα	MANY 694A
18	AMMON	SAND 45D
	GINOMAI I4A	BECOME 158C
	EIPON 4	SAY 225D
	EIS 4E	SO THAT 228D
	ELPIS I	HOPE 252B
	ELPIS 2A	HOPE 252C
	EPI IIIBγ	ON 287A
	KATA II5Aα	ACCORDING TO 408A
	HOUTW 5	THUS 602D
	PARA III6	AGAINST 616C
	PISTEUW IAε	BELIEVE 666B
	SPERMA 2B	SEED 769B
19	ASTHENEW 2	WEAK II5A
	HEKATONTAET8S	236B
	A HUNDRED YEARS OLD	
	KATANOEW 2	NOTICE 416A
	M8 AII2D	NOT 518C
	M8TRA	WOMB 522B
	NEKROW	PUT TO DEATH 537C
	NEKRWSIS 2A	DEATH 537C
	HO,H8,TO IIID	THE 552D
	POU 2	SOMEWHERE 703A
	SARRA	SARAH 752B
	SWMA IB	BODY 806D
	HUPARCHW 2	BE 846A
19F	PISTIS 2A	FAITH 668C
20	APISTIA 2B	UNBELIEF 85A
	DIAKRINW 2B	WAVER 184B

20	DOXA 3	FAME 203B
	EIS 6A	BECAUSE OF 229B
	ENDUNAMOW 2B	BECOME STRONG 263B
	EPAGGELIA 2A	PROMISE 280B
21	DUNATOS 1Aβ	POWERFUL 208A
	EPAGGELLOMAI 1B	ANNOUNCE 280C
	*PL8ROPHOREW 2	FILL 676B
22	DIKAIOSUN8 3	RIGHTEOUSNESS 196A
	DIO	THEREFORE 197D
	KAI II4	ALSO 394C
	LOGIZOMAI 1A	RECKON 477A
23	GRAPHW 2C	WRITE 166A
23F	LOGIZOMAI 1A	RECKON 477A
24	EGEIRW 1Aβ	RAISE 213D
	EPI IIIIBε	TOWARD 289A
	MELLW 1Cδ	IS DESTINED 502C
	PISTEUW 2Aδ	BELIEVE 667B
25	DIA BIII	BECAUSE OF 180A
	DIKAIWSIS	JUSTIFICATION 197C
	PARADIDWMI 1B	GIVE OVER 620B
	PARAPTWMA 2B	TRANSGRESSION 627B
	PISTIS 3	FAITH 670A

ROMANS 5

1	DIKAIOW 3A	JUSTIFY 196D
	EIR8N8 3	PEACE 226D
	ECHW I2G	HAVE 333B
	KURIOS 2Cγ	LORD 461B
	OUN IA	THEREFORE 597B
	PROS III4B	TOWARD 717C
1F	PISTIS 2Dα	FAITH 669B
2	DOXA 1A	BRIGHTNESS 202D
	DOXA 3	FAME 203A
	ELPIS 2B	HOPE 252C
	EPI IIIBγ	ON 287B
	HIST8MI II2Cβ	STAND 383C
	KAUCHAOMAI 1	BOAST 427A
	PROSAGWG8	APPROACH 718C
	CHARIS 3B	FAVOR 886B
3	ALLA 1A	BUT, YET 37C
	KATERGAZOMAI 2	ACHIEVE 422D
	KAUCHAOMAI 1	BOAST 427A
	MONOS 2C	ONLY 530A
3A	THLIPSIS 1	TRIBULATION 362D
3B	THLIPSIS 1	TRIBULATION 362D
3F	HUPOMON8 1	PATIENCE 854A
4	DOKIM8 1	CHARACTER 201D
4F	ELPIS 2B	HOPE 252C
5	AGAP8 I2A	LOVE 5D
	DIA AIII2Bδ	BY 179D
	EKCHEW 2	POUR OUT 246D
	KARDIA 1B8	HEART 405B
	KATAISCHUNW 3A	DISAPPOINT 411D
	PNEUMA 5Cβ	SPIRIT 682D
6	ASEB8S 1	GODLESS 114B
	ASTHEN8S 2B	WEAK 115B
	ETI IAβ	STILL 315D
	KAIROS 1	TIME 395D
	KAIROS 2	TIME 396A
	KATA II2A	DURING 407C
	HUPER IAε	IN BEHALF OF 846C
	CHRISTOS 2	ANOINTED ONE 895D

6FF	APOTHN8SKW IAα	DIE 90D
7	AGATHOS IBα	GOOD 3A
	GAR 4	INDEED 151D
	DIKAIOS IA	UPRIGHT 194D
	MOGIS	WITH DIFFICULTY 527C
	MOLIS 2	NOT READILY 528C
	TACHA	PERHAPS 814B
	TOLMAW IA	DARE 829C
7A	TIS, TI IAε	ANY ONE 827C
7A	HUPER IAε	IN BEHALF OF 846C
7B	TIS, TI IAε	ANY ONE 827C
7B	HUPER IAε	IN BEHALF OF 846C
8	AGAP8 I2A	LOVE 5D
	HAMARTWLOS 2	SINNER 43D
	APOTHN8SKW IAα	DIE 90D
	DE 3	BUT, AND 170D
	EIS 4Cβ	(GOAL) 228C
	ETI IAβ	STILL 315D
	HOTI IC	THAT 593B
	SUNIST8MI	UNITE 798B
	SUNIST8MI IIC	UNITE 798C
	HUPER IAε	IN BEHALF OF 846C
	CHRISTOS 2	ANOINTED ONE 895D
9	HAIMA 2B	BLOOD 22C
	DIA AIII2Bγ	BY 179D
	DIKAIOW 3A	JUSTIFY 196D
	EN IIIIA	BY 260B
	MALLON 2B	MORE 490C
	NUN IAγ	NOW 547D
	ORG8 2B	ANGER 583A
	SWZW 2B	SAVE 806B
9F	POLUS I2Cα	MANY 695C
10	DIA AIIIIA	BY MEANS OF 179A
	EIMI II8	TO BE 223D
	EN I4D	IN 258C
	ECHTHROS 2Bα	THE ENEMY 331D
	ZW8 IA	LIFE 340D
	THANATOS IBβ	DEATH 351C
	MALLON 2B	MORE 490C
	SWZW 2B	SAVE 806B
	HUIOS 2B	SON 842D
10A	KATALLASSW 2A	RECONCILE 415A
10B	KATALLASSW 2A	RECONCILE 415A
11	ALLA 1A	BUT, YET 37C
	THEOS 3A	GOD 357D
	KATALLAG8	RECONCILIATION 415A
	KAUCHAOMAI 1	BOAST 426D
	KURIOS 2Cγ	LORD 461B
	LAMBANW 2	RECEIVE 466C
	MONOS 2C	ONLY 530A
	NUN IAγ	NOW 547C
12	HAMARTANW 1	SIN 41D
	HAMARTIA 3	SIN 42D
	HAMARTIA 3	SIN 43A
	ANTHRWPOS 1B	MAN 67D
	DIERCHOMAI 2	COME 193D
	HEIS IAε	ONE 230A
	EISERCHOMAI IAγ	COME 231D
	EPI IIIBγ	ON 287C
	KOSMOS 5A	WORLD 447B
	HOS,H8,HO IIID	(REL PRON) 589A
	HOUTW IA	THUS 602B
	PAS 2Aγ	ALL 638B

12 HWSPER I	(JUST) AS 908A
12A THANATOS IBY	DEATH 351D
12A PAS IB	ALL 637A
12B THANATOS IBY	DEATH 351D
13 HAMARTIA I	SIN 42D
ACHRI IA	UNTIL 128C
ELLOGEW	251D
CHARGE TO ONES ACCOUNT	
KOSMOS 5A	WORLD 447B
M8 AII2B	NOT 518B
NOMOS 3	LAW 544C
13A NOMOS 3	LAW 544D
14*ADAM	ADAM 15B
ALLA 2	BUT, YET 37D
APO II2B	FROM 86C
BASILEUW IC	RULE 136B
EPI IIIBY	ON 287A
EPI IIIBα	OVER 288D
THANATOS IF	DEATH 352A
MELLW 2	IS DESTINED 502D
MECHRI IB	UNTIL 517B
HOMOIWMA I	LIKENESS 570C
PARABASIS	OVERSTEPPING 617A
TUPOS 6	MARK 838A
15 ALLA 2	BUT, YET 38A
ANTHRWPOS 2D	MAN 68A
DWREA	GIFT 209C
EN IV4B	IN 260D
KAI II3	ALSO 394B
MALLON 2B	MORE 490C
HOUTW IA	THUS 602B
PERISSEUW IAβ	BE LEFT OVER 656C
CHRISTOS 2	ANOINTED ONE 895C
HWS III	SO 905D
15A PARAPTWMA 2Aα	627B
TRANSGRESSION	
15A POLUS I2Aβ	MANY 694D
15A CHARIS 2A	FAVOR 885C
15B PARAPTWMA 2Aα	627B
TRANSGRESSION	
15B POLUS I2Cα	MANY 695C
15B CHARIS 2A	FAVOR 885C
15C POLUS I2Aβ	MANY 694D
15F CHARISMA I	A GIFT 887A
16 HAMART8MA	SIN 42A
DIKAIWMA 3	RIGHTEOUS DEED 197B
DWR8MA	GIFT 210A
KRIMA 4A	VERDICT 451D
PARAPTWMA 2B	TRANSGRESSION 627B
17 DIKAIOSUN8 3	RIGHTEOUSNESS 196A
*DWREA	GIFT 209C
THANATOS IF	DEATH 352A
LAMBANW 2	RECEIVE 466B
MALLON 2B	MORE 490C
PERISSEIA	SURPLUS 656B
POLUS I2Cα	MANY 695C
CHARIS 3B	FAVOR 886B
17A BASILEUW IC	RULE 136B
17B BASILEUW IBδ	RULE 136B
17F DIA AIII2BY	179D
BY	
17F ZW8 2Bβ	LIFE 341C

17F PARAPTWMA 2Aα	627B
TRANSGRESSION	
18 ARA 4	THEN 103C
GINOMAI I4A	BECOME 158D
DIKAIWMA 2	RIGHTEOUS DEED 197B
DIKAIWSIS	JUSTIFICATION 197C
KAI II3	ALSO 394B
KATAKRIMA	DOOM 413A
HOUTW IA	THUS 602B
HWS III	SO 905D
18A PAS IB	ALL 637A
18B PAS IB	ALL 637A
18F ANTHRWPOS IB	MAN 67D
19 HAMARTWLOS 2	SINNER 43D
DIKAIOS IB	UPRIGHT 195A
KATHIST8MI 3	CAUSE 391C
KAI II3	ALSO 394B
HOUTW IA	THUS 602B
PARAKO8	DISOBEDIENCE 624B
HUPAKO8 IB	OBEDIENCE 844D
HWSPER I	(JUST) AS 908A
19A POLUS I2Aβ	MANY 694D
19B POLUS I2Aβ	MANY 694D
20 HINA II2	IN ORDER THAT 378D
NOMOS 3	LAW 544C
HOU IB	WHERE 594A
PARAPTWMA 2Aβ	TRANSGRESSION 627B
PAREISERCHOMAI I	SLIP IN 630B
HUPERPERISSEUW I	BE ABUNDANT 849D
20A PLEONAZW IA	INCREASE 673B
20F CHARIS 2A	FAVOR 885C
21 AIWNIOS 3	ETERNAL 28A
DIA AIII2BY	BY 179D
DIKAIOSUN8 3	RIGHTEOUSNESS 196A
ZW8 2Bβ	LIFE 341C
KURIOS 2CY	LORD 461B
HOUTW IA	THUS 602B
HWSPER I	(JUST) AS 908A
21A BASILEUW IC	RULE 136B
21B BASILEUW IC	RULE 136B

ROMANS 6

I EIPON I	SAY 225B
EPIMENW 2	CONTINUE 296B
OUN ICβ	THEREFORE 597C
PLEONAZW IA	INCREASE 673B
TIS, TI IBα	WHICH 827A
CHARIS 2A	FAVOR 885C
2 APOTHN8SKW IBY	DIE 91A
GINOMAI I3A	TAKE PLACE 157D
ETI IBβ	STILL 316A
ZAW 3A	LIVE 337B
M8 AIII2	NOT 518C
HOSTIS 2B	WHOEVER 591A
PWS ID	HOW 739D
3 AGNOEW I	BE IGNORANT 11B
8 IDα	OR 343A
HOSOS 2	HOW GREAT 590C
CHRISTOS 2	ANOINTED ONE 895D
3A BAPTIZW 2Bβ	BAPTIZE 131C
3B BAPTIZW 2Bβ	BAPTIZE 131C
3FF THANATOS IBβ	DEATH 351C

4	BAPTISMA 2	BAPTISM	132B
	DOXA 1A	GLORY	202D
	EGEIRW 2C	RISE	214A
	ZW8 2Bα	LIFE	341A
	KAINOT8S	NEWNESS	395B
	NEKROS 2A	DEAD	537A
	HOMOIWMA 1	LIKENESS	570C
	OUN 1A	THEREFORE	597B
	HOUTW 1A	THUS	602B
	PERIPATEW 2A6	GO ABOUT	655B
	SUNTHAPTW	BURY WITH	797C
	CHRISTOS 2	ANOINTED ONE	895D
5	ALLA 4	BUT, YET	38B
	ANASTASIS 2A	RESURRECTION	59D
	HOMOIWMA 1	LIKENESS	570C
	SUMPHUTOS	GROWN TOGETHER	788B
6	*HAMARTIA 3	SIN	43A
	ANTHRWPOS 2Cβ	MAN	68A
	DOULEUW 2C	SERVE	204C
	KATARGEW 2	ABOLISH	418C
	M8KETI 4	NO LONGER	520B
	HO,H8,TO II1D	THE	552D
	HO,H8,TO II4Bζ	THE	554A
	HOUTOS 1Bβ	THIS	601C
	PALAIOS 2	OLD	610D
	SUSTAUROW 2	CRUCIFY WITH	802C
	SWMA 1B	BODY	807B
7	DIKAIOW	JUSTIFY	196C
	DIKAIOW 3C	MAKE FREE	197A
8	APOTHN8SKW 1Bβ	DIE	91A
	EI III	IF	218C
	PISTEUW 1Aβ	BELIEVE	666A
	SUZAW	LIVE WITH	783B
	SUN 2B	WITH	789C
9	EGEIRW 2C	RISE	214A
	THANATOS 1F	DEATH	352A
	KURIEUW 2	RULE	459D
	CHRISTOS 2	ANOINTED ONE	895D
9A	OUKETI 1	NO LONGER	596D
9B	OUKETI 1	NO LONGER	596D
10	APOTHN8SKW 1Aα	DIE	90D
	EPHAPAX 2	ONCE FOR ALL	330B
	ZAW 3B	LIVE	337C
10A	HOS,H8,HO I7C	(REL PRON)	588D
10B	HOS,H8,HO I7C	(REL PRON)	588D
10F	THEOS 3Gα	GOD	358C
11	EN I5D	IN	259A
	ZAW 2A	LIVE	337A
	ZAW 3B	LIVE	337C
	KAI II3	ALSO	394B
	LOGIZOMAI 1B	CONSIDER	477B
	MEN 1Aα	(PARTICLE)	503D
	NEKROS 1Bα	DEAD	536D
	HOUTW 1B	THUS	602C
	CHRISTOS 2	ANOINTED ONE	895D
12	BASILEUW 1C	RULE	136B
	EIS 4E	SO THAT	228D
	EPITHUMIA 3	DESIRE	293C
	EPITHUMIA 3	DESIRE	293D
	THN8TOS	MORTAL	363B
	OUN 1B	THEREFORE	597B
	HUPAKOUW 1	LISTEN TO	845B
12F	M8DE 1B	AND NOT	519D
13	ADIKIA 2	UNRIGHTEOUSNESS	17D
	DIKAIOSUN8 2B	RIGHTEOUSNESS	195D
	DIKAIOSUN8 3	RIGHTEOUSNESS	196A
	EK IC	AWAY FROM	233D
	ZAW 2A	LIVE	337A
	HWSEI I	AS	907D
13A	MELOS 1	MEMBER	502D
13A	HOPLON 1	TOOL	579A
13A	PARIST8MI 1A	PLACE BESIDE	633A
13B	MELOS 1	MEMBER	502D
13B	HOPLON 1	TOOL	579A
13B	PARIST8MI 1A	PLACE BESIDE	633A
14	GAR 1C	FOR	151B
	KURIEUW 2	RULE	459D
	HUPO 2B	UNDER	851B
14F	EIMI III12	TO BE	224D
14F	NOMOS 3	LAW	544D
14F	CHARIS 3B	FAVOR	886B
15	GINOMAI I3A	TAKE PLACE	157D
	M8 ΔIII2	NOT	518C
	HOTI 3A	THAT	593D
	OUN 1Cβ	THEREFORE	597C
	TIS, TI 1Bε	WHICH	827A
	HUPO 2B	UNDER	851B
16	DIKAIOSUN8 3	RIGHTEOUSNESS	196A
	DOULOS 3	SLAVE	205A
	EIS 4E	SO THAT	228D
	8 1B	OR	343A
	THANATOS 2B	DEATH	352A
	OIDA 1E	KNOW	558C
	HOS,H8,HO I2A	(REL PRON)	587B
	PARIST8MI 1A	PLACE BESIDE	633A
	HUPAKOUW 1	LISTEN TO	845A
16A	HUPAKO8 1A	OBEDIENCE	844D
16B	HUPAKO8 1B	OBEDIENCE	844D
17	HAMARTIA 3	SIN	43A
	DIDACH8 2	TEACHING	191C
	DOULOS 3	SLAVE	205A
	EK 3Gγ	BY	234D
	KARDIA 1Bα	HEART	404B
	HOS,H8,HO I5Cβ	(REL PRON)	588B
	PARADIDWMI 1B	GIVE OVER	620C
	TUPOS 4	MARK	837D
	HUPAKOUW 1	LISTEN TO	845D
	CHARIS 5	FAVOR	886D
18	DOULOW 2	ENSLAVE	205B
	ELEUTHEROW 2	SET FREE	250C
18FF	DIKAIOSUN8 3	RIGHTEOUSNESS	196A
19	HAGIASMOS	HOLINESS	9A
	AKATHARSIA 2	IMPURITY	28B
	ANTHRWPINOS 1	HUMAN	67A
	ASTHENEIA 2	TIMIDITY	114D
	DOULOS	SLAVISH	204C
	HOUTW	THUS	602B
	SARX 7	BODY	751D
	SU 3	YOU	780A
19A	ANOMIA 1	LAWLESSNESS	71A
19A	MELOS 1	MEMBER	502D
19A	PARIST8MI 1A	PLACE BESIDE	633A
19B	ANOMIA 2	LAWLESSNESS	71B
19B	MELOS 1	MEMBER	502D
19B	PARIST8MI 1A	PLACE BESIDE	633A
20	HAMARTIA 3	SIN	43A

20	DOULOS 3	SLAVE	205A
	ELEUTHEROS 2	FREE	250B
	HOTE 1A	WHEN	592C
21	EPAISCHUNOMAI 2	BE ASHAMED	281D
	EPI III8γ	ON	287A
	THANATOS 2B	DEATH	352A
	HOS,H8,HO I2Bβ	(REL PRON)	587B
21F	KARPOS 2A	RESULT	406A
21F	TELOS 1C	END	819C
22	HAGIASMOS	HOLINESS	9A
	HAMARTIA 3	SIN	43A
	DOULOW 2	ENSLAVE	205B
	ELEUTHEROW 2	SET FREE	250C
	NUNI 1C	NOW	548C
22F	ZW8 2Bβ	LIFE	341C
23	HAMARTIA 3	SIN	43A
	EN I5D	IN	259A
	THANATOS 2B	DEATH	352A
	KURIOS 2Cγ	LORD	461B
	OPSWNION 1B	WAGES	607C
	OPSWNION 2	WAGES	607C
	CHARISMA 1	A GIFT	887A

ROMANS 7

1	AGNOEW 1	BE IGNORANT	11B
	ANTHRWPOS 3B	MAN	68D
	GINWSKW 3A	UNDERSTAND	160B
	EPI III2B	ON	289B
	ZAW 1Aα	LIVE	336B
	8 1Dα	OR	343A
	KURIEUW 2	RULE	459D
	LALEW 2Aδ	SPEAK	464B
	HOSOS 1	HOW GREAT	590B
	CHRONOS	TIME	896B
1A	NOMOS 3	LAW	544C
1B	NOMOS 3	LAW	544C
1F	NOMOS 1	LAW	544B
2	APOTHN8SKW 1Aα	DIE	90D
	GAR 1D	FOR	151B
	GAR 2	FOR	151C
	DEW 3	BIND	177A
	ZAW 1Aα	LIVE	336B
	KATARGEW 3	BE RELEASED	418C
	HUPANDROS	SUBJECT TO	845C
2A	NOMOS 3	LAW	545A
2B	NOMOS 3	LAW	545A
2F	AN8R 1	MAN	65D
3	ARA 4	THEN	103C
	ELEUTHEROS 2	FREE	250B
	HETEROS 18α	ANOTHER	315B
	ZAW 1Aα	LIVE	336B
	M8 AIIIDβ	NOT	518A
	HO,H8,TO II4Bη	THE	554B
	CHR8MATIZW 2	IMPART A WARNING	894A
3A	MOICHALIS 1	ADULTERESS	527D
3B	MOICHALIS 1	ADULTERESS	527D
3F	GINOMAI II3	BELONG TO	159C
4	DIA AIIIIA	BY MEANS OF	179A
	EIS 4E	SO THAT	228D
	THANATOW 2B	PUT TO DEATH	352B
	HINA IIE	IN ORDER THAT	377C

4	KARPOPHOREW 2	BEAR FRUIT	406A
	NEKROS 2A	DEAD	537A
	SWMA 1B	BODY	807B
	HWSTE 1A	THEREFORE	908B
4=7	NOMOS 3	LAW	544C
5	DIA AIIIID	THROUGH	179B
	EIMI III4	TO BE	224B
	ENERGEW 1A	WORK	264D
	ENERGEW 1B	WORK	264D
	THANATOS 2B	DEATH	352A
	KARPOPHOREW 2	BEAR FRUIT	406A
	MELOS 1	MEMBER	502D
	HOTE 1A	WHEN	592C
	PATH8MA 2	PASSION	607D
	SARX 7	BODY	752A
6	APOTHN8SKW 1Bγ	DIE	91A
	GRAMMA 2C	WRITING	164D
	DOULEUW 1B	BE A SLAVE	204B
	KAINOT8S	NEWNESS	395B
	KATARGEW 3	BE RELEASED	418C
	KATECHW 1Dα	BE BOUND	424B
	NUNI 1C	NOW	548C
	PALAIOT8S	AGE	610D
	PNEUMA 5Gγ	SPIRIT	683C
	HWSTE 2Aβ	THEREFORE	908C
7	ALLA 1A	BUT, YET	37C
	HAMARTIA 1	SIN	42D
	GAR 1B	FOR	151B
	GINOMAI I3A	TAKE PLACE	157D
	GINWSKW 1A	KNOW	159D
	EI VI8A	IF NOT	219A
	EIPON 1	SAY	225B
	EPITHUMEW	DESIRE	293A
	M8 AII	NOT	517C
	M8 AIII2	NOT	518C
	OIDA 1B	KNOW	558B
	OU 4B	NO	594D
	OUN 1Cβ	THEREFORE	597C
	TIS, TI 1Bε	WHICH	827A
7B	NOMOS 3	LAW	544C
7F	EPITHUMIA 3	DESIRE	293C
8	HAMARTIA 3	SIN	43A
	APHORM8	PRETEXT	127A
	DIA AIIIID	THROUGH	179B
	EN I5A	IN	258D
	KATERGAZOMAI 2	ACHIEVE	422D
	LAMBANW 1A	TAKE	465C
	NEKROS 18β	DEAD	536D
	PAS 1Aβ	EVERY EACH	636D
	CHWRIS 2Bγ	APART	899C
8F	NOMOS 3	LAW	544D
8FF	ENTOL8 2Aα	COMMAND	268C
9	HAMARTIA 3	SIN	43A
	ANAZAW 1B	COME TO LIFE AGAIN	53B
	ANOMWS	WITHOUT THE LAW	71D
	APOTHN8SKW 18α	DIE	91A
	ERCHOMAI IICβ	COME	311C
	ZAW 2A	LIVE	337A
	POTE 1	ONCE	701D
	CHWRIS 2Bγ	APART	899C
10	APOTHN8SKW 18α	DIE	91A
	HEURISKW 2	FIND	325D
	ZW8 2Bα	LIFE	341B

10 THANATOS 2A	DEATH	352A
HO,H8,TO IIIG	THE	553A
HOUTOS IAε	THIS	601B
11 APOKTEINW IB	KILL	93C
APHORM8	PRETEXT	127A
DIA AIIIID	THROUGH	179B
EXAPATAW	DECEIVE	272C
LAMBANW IA	TAKE	465C
12 AGATHOS IBβ	GOOD	3A
HAGIOS IAβ	WORTHY OF GOD	9C
DIKAIOS 4	RIGHTEOUS	195B
KAI IIA	AND	392C
MEN 2B	(PARTICLE)	504B
NOMOS 3	LAW	544C
HWSTE IA	THEREFORE	908B
13 AGATHOS 2Aα	GOOD	3B
ALLA IA	BUT, YET	37C
HAMARTWLOS I	SINNER	43C
GINOMAI I3A	TAKE PLACE	157D
GINOMAI III	BE	159B
DIA AIIIID	THROUGH	179B
HINA II2	IN ORDER THAT	378D
KATA II5Bβ	ACCORDING TO	408D
KATERGAZOMAI 2	ACHIEVE	422D
M8 AIII2	NOT	518C
HUPERBOL8	EXCESS	848B
PHAINW 2E	APPEAR	859D
13A THANATOS 2A	DEATH	352A
13B THANATOS 2A	DEATH	352A
13FF MEN 2B	(PARTICLE)	504B
14 HAMARTIA 3	SIN	43A
NOMOS 3	LAW	544C
OIDA IE	KNOW	558C
PIPRASKW	SELL	664D
PNEUMATIKOS 2Aβ	SPIRITUAL	685B
SARKIKOS 3	FLESHLY	750B
SARKINOS 2	FLESHY	750C
SARX 8	BODY	752A
HUPO 2B	UNDER	851B
15 GINWSKW 6Aα	KNOW	160C
THELW 2	WISH	355D
KATERGAZOMAI I	ACHIEVE	422C
MISEW 2	HATE	524D
15F THELW 2	WISH	355D
15F HOUTOS IAε	THIS	601B
15F POIEW IIBε	DO	687D
16 KALOS 2B	GOOD	401C
NOMOS 3	LAW	544C
SUMPH8MI	AGREE	788A
17 HAMARTIA 3	SIN	43A
ENOIKEW	LIVE	267A
NUNI 2A	NOW	548C
OUKETI 2	NO LONGER	597A
17F EN I5A	IN	258D
17F KATERGAZOMAI I	ACHIEVE	422C
18 EIMI II3	TO BE	222D
THELW 2	WISH	355D
KALOS 2B	GOOD	401B
HO,H8,TO II4A	THE	553D
OIKEW I	DWELL	559C
HOUTOS IBε	THIS	601D
SARX 7	BODY	751D
19 THELW 2	WISH	355D
19 KAKOS IC	EVIL	398D
HOS,H8,HO I5A	(REL PRON)	588B
PRASSW IA	DO	705B
19F THELW 2	WISH	355D
19F HOUTOS IAε	THIS	601B
20 HAMARTIA 3	SIN	43A
KATERGAZOMAI I	ACHIEVE	422C
OIKEW I	DWELL	559C
OUKETI 2	NO-LONGER	597A
POIEW IIBε	DO	687D
21 ARA I	THEN	103B
HEURISKW 2	FIND	325D
THELW 2	WISH	355D
KAKOS IC	EVIL	398D
KALOS 2B	GOOD	401B
NOMOS 2	A RULE	544B
POIEW IIBε	DO	687D
22 ANTHRWPOS 2Cα	MAN	68A
ESW 2	IN	314C
KATA II6	WITH RESPECT TO	408D
NOMOS 3	LAW	544D
SUN8DOMAI	AGREE WITH	797B
23 AICHMALWTIZW 2	CAPTURE	26B
HAMARTIA 3	SIN	43A
ANTISTRATEUOMAI	BE AT WAR	75B
BLEPW 7B	SEE	143B
HETEROS 2	ANOTHER	315C
NOUS 2	THE MIND	546D
23A MELOS I	MEMBER	502D
23A NOMOS 2	A RULE	544B
23B MELOS I	MEMBER	502D
23B NOMOS 2	A RULE	544B
23C NOMOS 2	A RULE	544B
24 THANATOS 2A	DEATH	352A
RUOMAI	SAVE	745A
SWMA IB	BODY	807B
TALAIPWROS	MISERABLE	811A
TIS, TI IAα	WHICH	826C
25 HAMARTIA 3	SIN	43A
ARA	(PARTICLE)	103C
ARA 4	THEN	103C
AUTOS IF	OF HIMSELF	122C
DIA AIII2A	BY	179D
DOULEUW 2C	SERVE	204C
KURIOS 2Cγ	LORD	461B
MEN	(PARTICLE)	503C
NOUS 2	THE MIND	546D
SARX 7	BODY	751D
CHARIS 5	FAVOR	886D
25A NOMOS 3	LAW	544D

ROMANS 8

1 ARA I	THEN	103B
EN I5D	IN	259B
KATAKRIMA	DOOM	413A
NUN IC	NOW	547D
HO,H8,TO II5	THE	554B
IF CHRISTOS 2	ANOINTED ONE	895D
2 *HAMARTIA 3	SIN	43A
ELEUTHEROW 2	SET FREE	250C
ZW8 2Bα	LIFE	341B
PNEUMA 5E	SPIRIT	683C

Ref	Word	Gloss	No.
2A	NOMOS 5	LAW	545B
2B	NOMOS 2	A RULE	544B
2F	GAR IC	FOR	151B
3	ADUNATOS 2B	IMPOSSIBLE	18D
	HAMARTIA 3	SIN	43A
	ASTHENEW IB	WEAK	115A
	DIA AIV	BECAUSE OF	180A
	EN I4D	IN	258C
	EN IV6D	IN	261A
	KATAKRINW	CONDEMN	413B
	HO,H8,TO II2A	THE	553B
	HOMOIWMA 4	LIKENESS	570D
	PEMPW I	SEND	647D
	PERI IG	ABOUT	650C
	HUIOS 2B	SON	842D
3A	SARX 7	BODY	751D
3B	SARX 7	BODY	751D
3C	SARX 4	BODY	751B
3F	NOMOS 3	LAW	544C
4	DIKAIWMA I	REGULATION	197A
	KATA II5AY	ACCORDING TO	408B
	NOMOS 3	LAW	544D
	PERIPATEW 2A6	GO ABOUT	655B
	PL8ROW 48	MAKE FULL	677D
	SARX 7	BODY	751D
	SARX 7	BODY	752A
4F	PNEUMA 5D8	SPIRIT	683B
4=6	PNEUMA 5G4	SPIRIT	683C
4=9	SARX 7	BODY	751D
5	EIMI III68	TO BE	224C
	HO,H8,TO II7	THE	554C
	SARX 7	BODY	751D
	PHRONEW 2	THINK	874B
5A	SARX 7	BODY	752A
5B	SARX 7	BODY	751D
6	EIR8N8 3	PEACE	227A
	ZW8 2B8	LIFE	341B
	ZW8 2B4	LIFE	341B
	THANATOS 2A	DEATH	352A
	SARX 7	BODY	751D
6A	PHRON8MA	AIM	874C
6B	PHRON8MA	AIM	874C
7	GAR IB	FOR	151B
	DIOTI 3	FOR	198C
	DUNAMAI 2	ABLE	206B
	EIS 4C4	AGAINST	228C
	ECHTHRA	ENMITY	331C
	NOMOS 3	LAW	544D
	OUDE I	AND NOT	595D
	HUPOTASSW IB8	SUBJECT	855D
	PHRON8MA	AIM	874C
8	ARESKW 2A	BE PLEASING	105A
	EIMI III4	TO BE	224B
	THEOS 3B	GOD	357D
8F	SARX 7	BODY	752A
9	EI IIA	IF	218A
	EI VIII	IF	219B
	EIMI IV2	TO BE	225A
	EN I5A	IN	258D
	EN I5D	IN	259C
	HO,H8,TO IIII	THE	555A
	OIKEW I	DWELL	559C
	HOUTOS IAc	THIS	601B
9	SARX 7	BODY	751D
9A	PNEUMA 5G4	SPIRIT	683C
9B	OU 5B	NO	595A
9B	PNEUMA 5A	SPIRIT	682D
9C	PNEUMA 5B	SPIRIT	682C
10	DIKAIOSUN8 3	RIGHTEOUSNESS	196B
	EI IIA	IF	218A
	EN I5A	IN	258D
	ZW8 2B4	LIFE	341B
	NEKROS IB8	DEAD	536D
	PNEUMA 5G8	SPIRIT	683C
	SWMA IB	BODY	806D
	CHRISTOS 2	ANOINTED ONE	895D
11	EGEIRW IA8	RAISE	213D
	EN I5A	IN	258D
	ENOIKEW	LIVE	267A
	ZWOPOIEW I	MAKE ALIVE	342C
	THN8TOS	MORTAL	363B
	OIKEW I	DWELL	559C
	PNEUMA 5A	SPIRIT	682D
	PNEUMA 8	SPIRIT	685A
	SARX 8	BODY	752A
	SWMA IB	BODY	807B
	CHRISTOS 2	ANOINTED ONE	895D
11A	NEKROS 2A	DEAD	537A
11B	NEKROS 2A	DEAD	537A
12	ARA 4	THEN	103C
	HO,H8,TO II48Y	THE	554A
	OPHEILET8S 2B	DEBTOR	603A
	OPHEILET8S 2B	DEBTOR	603B
12B	SARX 7	BODY	752A
12F	ZAW 3A	LIVE	337B
12F	KATA II58B8	ACCORDING TO	408C
12F	SARX 7	BODY	751D
13	APOTHN8SKW IB4	DIE	91A
	THANATOW 2C	PUT TO DEATH	352B
	MELLW IC6	IS DESTINED	502C
	PNEUMA 5G4	SPIRIT	683C
	PRAXIS 4B	ACTING	704D
	SARX 7	BODY	751D
	SARX 7	BODY	752A
	SWMA IB	BODY	806D
	SWMA IB	BODY	807B
13B	ZAW 2B4	LIVE	337A
14	AGW 3	LEAD	14B
	HOSOS 2	HOW GREAT	590B
	HOUTOS IAc	THIS	601B
	PNEUMA 5A	SPIRIT	682C
	HUIOS ICY	SON	841D
15	ABBA	FATHER	IB
	GAR IE	FOR	151C
	DOULEIA 2	SLAVERY	204A
	EIS 4E	SO THAT	228D
	KRAZW 2B4	CALL	449A
	PALIN IB	AGAIN	611C
	PAT8R 3C8	FATHER	641C
	HUIOTHESIA 2	ADOPTION	841B
	PHOBOS 2A8	FEAR	871D
15B	PNEUMA 5E	SPIRIT	683C
16	PNEUMA 3B	SPIRIT	681C
	SUMMARTUREW	TESTIFY	786A
16F	TEKNON 2E	CHILD	816C
17	EI IIA	IF	218A

17	EI VIII	IF	219B
	HINA II2	IN ORDER THAT	378D
	KL8RONOMOS 2B	HEIR	436B
	SUGKL8RONOMOS		781D
	INHERITING TOGETHER		
	SUMPASCHW	SUFFER WITH	787A
	SUNDOXAZW 2	SHARE IN GLORY	793B
18	AXIOS IA	WORTHY	77B
	APOKALUPTW 4	REVEAL	91D
	GAR IE	FOR	151C
	DOXA IBβ	GLORY	203A
	KAIROS I	TIME	395C
	LOGIZOMAI 3	THINK	477B
	MELLW IBα	BE ABOUT TO	502A
	NUN 3A	NOW	548A
	PATH8MA I	SUFFERING	607B
	PROS III5D	TOWARD	717D
19	APEKDECHOMAI	AWAIT	82D
	APOKALUPSIS 3	REVELATION	92A
	APOKARADOKIA		92A
	EAGER EXPECTATION		
	HUIOS ICγ	SON	841D
19-22	KTISIS IBβ	CREATION	457A
20	DIA BII4B	BY	180C
	HEKWN	WILLING	247A
	ELPIS I	HOPE	252B
	ELPIS 2A	HOPE	252C
	*ELPIS 2B	HOPE	252D
	EPI IIIBγ	ON	287A
	MATAIOT8S	FUTILITY	496D
20A	HUPOTASSW IBα	SUBJECT	855D
20B	HUPOTASSW IA	SUBJECT	855C
21	AUTOS IG	EVEN	122C
	DIOTI I	BECAUSE	198C
	DIOTI 4	THAT	198C
	DOXA IBβ	GLORY	203A
	DOULEIA 2	SLAVERY	204B
	EIS 7	TO	229B
	ELEUTHERIA	FREEDOM	250A
	ELEUTHEROW 2	SET FREE	250C
	TEKNON 2E	CHILD	816C
	PHTHORA I	RUIN	865D
22	ACHRI IA	UNTIL	128B
	NUN 3B	NOW	548B
	OIDA IE	KNOW	558C
	PAS ICα	ALL	637B
	SUNWDINW		801C
	SUFFER AGONY TOGETHER		
	SUSTENAZW	LAMENT	802D
23	ALLA IA	BUT, YET	37C
	APARCH8 2B	FIRST FRUITS	81A
	APEKDECHOMAI	AWAIT	82D
	APOLUTRWSIS 2A	REDEMPTION	95D
	HEAUTOU 2	ONESELF	211C
	MONOS 2C	ONLY	530A
	PNEUMA 5Dα	SPIRIT	683A
	STENAZW	SIGH	773D
	HUIOTHESIA 2	ADOPTION	841B
24	ELPIZW 2	HOPE	252A
	ELPIS I	HOPE	252B
	ELPIS 4	HOPE	252D
	KAI II5	STILL	394C
	SWZW 2B	SAVE	806C
24F	BLEPW IA	SEE	142D
25	APEKDECHOMAI	AWAIT	82D
	DIA AIIIIC	THROUGH	179B
	ELPIZW 2	HOPE	252A
	HUPOMON8 I	PATIENCE	854B
26	ALAL8TOS	UNEXPRESSED	34B
	ASTHENEIA 2	TIMIDITY	114D
	DEI 6	IT IS NECESSARY	171B
	KATHO I	AS	391C
	HO,H8,TO II8A	THE	554D
	PROSEUCHOMAI	PRAY	721B
	STENAGMOS	SIGH	773D
	SUNANTILAMBANOMAI	HELP	792B
	HUPERENTUGCHANW	PLEAD	848C
	HWSAUTWS	SIMILARLY	907D
26A	PNEUMA 5Dα	SPIRIT	683A
26B	PNEUMA 6E	SPIRIT	684A
27	HAGIOS 2Dβ	SAINTS	10A
	ENTUGCHANW I	MEET	269C
	ERAUNAW	SEARCH	306C
	THEOS 3B	GOD	358A
	KARDIA IBα	HEART	404B
	KATA II5Aα	ACCORDING TO	408A
	OIDA IF	KNOW	558C
	PNEUMA 5Dα	SPIRIT	683A
	PHRON8MA	AIM	874C
28	AGATHOS 2Aβ	GOOD	3B
	AGAPAW IAβ	LOVE	4C
	DE 2	BUT, AND	170D
	EIS 5	FOR	229B
	KATA II5Aδ	ACCORDING TO	408B
	KL8TOS	CALLED	437A
	OIDA IE	KNOW	558C
	PAS 2A6	EVERYTHING	638C
	PROTHESIS 2B	SETTING FORTH	713B
	SUNERGEW	WORK WITH	795B
29	ADELPHOS 2	BROTHER	16A
	EIKWN 2	FORM	221C
	MONOGEN8S	ONLY	529A
	POLUS IIAα	MANY	694A
	PROGINWSKW	KNOWS BEFOREHAND	710C
	PROORIZW		716A
	DECIDE UPON BEFOREHAND		
	PRWTOTOKOS 2A	FIRSTBORN	734A
	SUMMORPHOS	SAME FORM	786B
	HUIOS 2B	SON	842D
30	DIKAIOW 3B	JUSTIFY	196D
	DOXAZW 2	GLORIFY	203D
	KALEW 2	CALL	400C
	HOUTOS IAε	THIS	601B
	PROORIZW		716A
	DECIDE UPON BEFOREHAND		
31	EIPON I	SAY	225B
	KATA I2Bγ	DOWN	406D
	OUN ICβ	THEREFORE	597C
	HUPER IA6	IN BEHALF OF	846B
32	GE 2 (EMPHASIZING PARTICLE)		152A
	IDIOS IB	ONES OWN	370B
	HOS,H8,HO IIOB	(REL PRON)	588D
	OUCHI 3	NOT	603A
	PARADIDWMI IB	GIVE OVER	620B
	PWS ID	HOW	739D
	SUN 4A	WITH	789C

32	HUIOS 2B	SON	842D
	HUPER IAɛ	IN BEHALF OF	846C
	PHEIDOMAI I	SPARE	862C
	CHARIZOMAI I	GIVE FREELY	884D
32A	PAS IEα	ALL	637D
32B	PAS 2Bβ	ALL THINGS	638D
33	DIKAIOW 3B	JUSTIFY	196D
	EGKALEW	ACCUSE	214C
	EKLEKTOS IB	CHOSEN	242B
	KATA I2Bβ	DOWN	406C
33B	THEOS 3B	GOD	357D
33=5	TIS, TI IAα	WHICH	826C
34	DEXIOS 2A	RIGHT	173D
	EGEIRW 2C	RISE	214A
	EIMI III4	TO BE	224B
	ENTUGCHANW I	MEET	269C
	KATAKRINW	CONDEMN	413B
	MALLON 3D	RATHER	490D
	NEKROS 2A	DEAD	537A
35	AGAP8 I2A	LOVE	6A
	GUMNOT8S 2	DESTITUTION	167B
	DIWGMOS	PERSECUTION	200A
	8 IAβ	OR	342D
	THLIPSIS I	TRIBULATION	362D
	KINDUNOS	DANGER	433B
	LIMOS I	HUNGER	476B
	MACHAIRA 2	SWORD	497C
	STENOCHWRIA	DISTRESS	774A
	CHWRIZW I	DIVIDE	898C
36	GRAPHW 2C	WRITE	165D
	HENEKA	BECAUSE OF	264B
	H8MERA 2	DAY	347A
	THANATOW I	PUT TO DEATH	352B
	KATHWS I	JUST AS	392B
	LOGIZOMAI IB	CONSIDER	477B
	HOLOS 2A	WHOLE	567C
	HOTI 2	THAT	593D
	PROBATON I	SHEEP	710A
	SPHAG8	SLAUGHTER	803C
37	AGAPAW IBα	LOVE	4D
	ALLA 3	BUT, YET	38A
	DIA AIII2Bγ	BY	179D
	PAS IEβ	ALL	638A
	HUPERNIKAW	WIN GLORIOUS VICTORY	849B
38	AGGELOS 2B	ANGEL	8A
	ARCH8 3	RULER	112A
	DUNAMIS 6	POWER	207B
	ENIST8MI I	BE PRESENT	266B
	ZW8 IA	LIFE	340D
	THANATOS IA	DEATH	351B
	MELLW 2	IS DESTINED	502D
	PEITHW 4	OBEY	645C
38F	OUTE	NOT	600C
39	BATHOS I	DEPTH	129D
	EN I5D	IN	259A
	HETEROS IBα	ANOTHER	315B
	KTISIS IBα	CREATION	456D
	KURIOS 2Cγ	LORD	461B
	HUPSWMA I	HEIGHT	858D
	CHWRIZW I	DIVIDE	898C

ROMANS 9

I	AL8THEIA 2A	TRUTH	35B
	EN I5D	IN	259B
	LEGW IIA	SAY	469B
	M8DE IB	AND NOT	519D
	PNEUMA 5Cβ	SPIRIT	683A
	SUMMARTUREW	TESTIFY	786A
	*SUNEID8SIS 2	CONSCIOUSNESS	794B
	PSEUDOMAI I	LIE	900A
2	ADIALEIPTOS	UNCEASING	17A
	KARDIA IBɛ	HEART	405A
	LUP8	GRIEF	483B
	MEGAS 2Aγ	GREAT	499A
	ODUN8	PAIN	557C
3	ADELPHOS 3	FELLOW COUNTRYMAN	16A
	ANATHEMA 2A	ACCURSED	53D
	APO I5	FROM	86A
	AUTOS IF	OF HIMSELF	122C
	EUCHOMAI 2	WISH	329D
	KATA II6	WITH RESPECT TO	408D
	SARX 4	BODY	751B
	SUGGEN8S	RELATED	780B
	HUPER IC	IN BEHALF OF	846D
	CHRISTOS I	ANOINTED ONE	895C
4	DIATH8K8 2		182C
	LAST WILL AND TESTAMENT		
	DOXA 3	FAME	203A
	EPAGGELIA 2A	PROMISE	280A
	ISRA8LIT8S	ISRAELITE	382C
	KATARGEW IB	MAKE INEFFECTIVE	418B
	LATREIA	SERVICE	468C
	NOMOTHESIA	LAW	543D
	HUIOTHESIA I	ADOPTION	841A
5	AIWN IB	TIME	26D
	AM8N I	AMEN	45A
	EIMI II	TO BE	222A
	EIMI III5A	TO BE	224C
	EPI IIBα	OVER	286B
	EULOG8TOS	BLESSED	323A
	THEOS 2	GOD	357C
	KATA II6	WITH RESPECT TO	408D
	HO,H8,TO II6	THE	554B
	PAS 2A6	EVERYTHING	638D
	SARX 4	BODY	751B
	CHRISTOS I	ANOINTED ONE	895C
6	EK 3D	FROM	234C
	EKPIPTW 3B	FAIL	243B
	ISRA8L 3	ISRAEL	382C
	LOGOS IBα	COMMAND	479A
	HOIOS	OF WHAT SORT	565C
	HOTI IC	THAT	593A
	OU 2A	NO	594B
	HOUTOS IAɛ	THIS	601B
	PAS IDγ	ALL	637D
6A	ISRA8L I	ISRAEL	382B
7	ABRAAM	ABRAHAM	ID
	EN III3A	BECAUSE OF	260C
	ISAAK	ISAAC	381C
	KALEW IA6	CALL	400B
	TEKNON 2D	CHILD	816C
7A	SPERMA 2B	SEED	769B
7B	SPERMA 2B	SEED	769B

8	EIMI II3	TO BE 222D
	EPAGGELIA 2A	PROMISE 280B
	LOGIZOMAI 1B	CONSIDER 477A
	HOUTOS 1Aɛ	THIS 601B
	HOUTOS 1Bɛ	THIS 601D
	SARX 4	BODY 751B
	SPERMA 2B	SEED 769B
8A	TEKNON 1B	CHILD 816B
8B	TEKNON 2E	CHILD 816C
9	EPAGGELIA 2A	PROMISE 280A
	ERCHOMAI IIAα	COME 310B
	KAIROS 1	TIME 395D
	KATA II2A	DURING 407C
	LOGOS 1Bα	COMMAND 479A
	SARRA	SARAH 752B
	HUIOS 1Aα	SON 841B
10	ALLA 1A	BUT, YET 37C
	HEIS 2A	ONE 230B
	EK 3A	FROM 234A
	*ISAAK	ISAAC 381C
	KOIT8 2B	BED 441A
	MONOS 2C	ONLY 530A
	PAT8R 1B	FOREFATHER 640C
	REBEKKA	REBECCA 742B
11	EKLOG8 1	SELECTION 242C
	KATA II7C	(GENITIVE) 409A
	MENW 1Cβ	REMAIN 505C
	M8PW	NOT YET 521C
	HO,H8,TO IIIG	THE 553A
	PRASSW 1A	DO 705A
	PROTHESIS 2B	SETTING FORTH 713B
	TIS, TI 2Aᵧ	ANY ONE 828B
	PHAULOS 1	WORTHLESS 862B
12	DOULEUW 1A	BE A SLAVE 204B
	EIPON 4	SAY 225D
	EK 3I	BY 235A
	ELASSWN	SMALLER 247C
	ERGON 1Cβ	DEED 308B
	KALEW 2	CALL 400C
	MEGAS 2Aα	GREAT 498D
13	AGAPAW 1Bα	LOVE 4D
	GRAPHW 2C	WRITE 165D
	8SAU	ESAU 349C
	IAKWB 1	JACOB 368A
	KATHAPER	JUST AS 387D
	MISEW 1	HATE 524D
14	ADIKIA 2	UNRIGHTEOUSNESS 17C
	GINOMAI I13A	TAKE PLACE 157D
	EIMI III8B	TO BE 224D
	EIPON 1	SAY 225B
	THEOS 3A	GOD 357D
	M8 AIII2	NOT 518C
	M8 C1	NOT 519A
	OUN 1Cβ	THEREFORE 597C
	PARA II2D	BESIDE 615D
	TIS, TI 1Bɛ	WHICH 827A
15	ELEEW	HAVE MERCY 249B
	OIKTIRW	HAVE COMPASSION 564D
16	*ARA 4	THEN 103C
	ELEAW	HAVE MERCY ON 248C
	EUDOKEW 2A	WELL PLEASED 319C
	THELW 2	WISH 355D
	TRECHW 2A	RUN 833C
17	AUTOS 1H	EVEN 122D
	GRAPH8 2Bβ	SCRIPTURE 165B
	DIAGGELLW 1	181B
		PROCLAIM FAR AND WIDE
	DUNAMIS 1	POWER 206C
	EIS 4F	(PURPOSE) 228D
	ENDEIKNUMI 1	DEMONSTRATE 262A
	EXEGEIRW 4	CAUSE TO APPEAR 273B
	ONOMA 14B	NAME 575A
	PAS 1Cα	ALL 637B
	PHARAW	PHARAOH 861B
17A	HOPWS 2Aα	IN ORDER THAT 580C
17B	HOPWS 2Aα	IN ORDER THAT 580C
18	ARA 4	THEN 103C
	ELEEW	HAVE MERCY 249B
	SKL8RUNW 1B	HARDEN 763C
18A	THELW 2	WISH 355D
18B	THELW 2	WISH 355D
19	ANTHIST8MI 2	SET AGAINST 66C
	BOUL8MA	INTENTION 145C
	EIPON 2B	SAY 225C
	ETI 2C	STILL 316B
	MEMPHOMAI	FIND FAULT WITH 503C
19B	TIS, TI 1Aα	WHICH 826B
20	ANTHRWPOS 1Aᵧ	MAN 67C
	ANTAPOKRINOMAI	ANSWER IN TURN 72C
	GE 3E	OF COURSE 152B
	MENOUNGE	RATHER 504C
	M8 C1	NOT 519A
	HOUTW 1B	THUS 602C
	PLASMA	IMAGE 672B
	PLASSW 1A	FORM 672B
	W 1	O 903B
21	ATIMIA	DISHONOR 119D
	AUTOS 4A	THE SAME 123B
	EIS 4D	FOR 228C
	EK 3H	BY 235A
	EXOUSIA 1	RIGHT 277C
	KERAMEUS	POTTER 430A
	MEN 1C	(PARTICLE) 504A
	HOS,H8,HO II2	THIS (ONE) 589B
	P8LOS 1A	CLAY 662A
	PLASMA	IMAGE 672B
	POIEW IIAα	DO 687B
	SKEUOS 1B	THING 761D
	TIM8 2B	HONOR 825B
	PHURAMA	THAT WHICH IS MIXED 877A
22	APWLEIA 2	DESTRUCTION 103A
	DUNATOS 2D	POSSIBLE 208B
	ENDEIKNUMI 1	DEMONSTRATE 262A
	KATARTIZW 2A	PREPARE 419A
	MAKROTHUMIA 2Bα	PATIENCE 489B
	HO,H8,TO II2C	THE 553C
	POLUS II8β	MANY 694C
	SKEUOS 2	THING 761D
	PHERW 1C	BEAR 862D
22A	ORG8 2B	ANGER 583A
22B	ORG8 2B	ANGER 583A
22F	GNWRIZW 1	MAKE KNOWN 162C
22F	EIS 4D	FOR 228C
23	DOXA 1A	GLORY 202D
	ELEOS 2B	MERCY 249D
	EPI IIII8ɛ	TOWARD 289A

#	Greek	Gloss	Ref
23	PLOUTOS 2	WEALTH	680B
	PROETOIMAZW		712C
	PREPARE BEFOREHAND		
	SKEUOS 2	THING	761D
	CHR8STOT8S 2B	GOODNESS	894D
24	ALLA IA	BUT, YET	37C
	ETHNOS 2	GENTILES	217C
	EK IB	AWAY FROM	233C
	KAI II6		394C
	KALEW 2	CALL	400C
25	AGAPAW ID	LOVE	5A
	EN IID	IN	257D
	KALEW IAβ	CALL	399D
	LAOS 38	PEOPLE	468B
	LEGW I7	SAY	470A
	HWS II4A	SO	906B
	HWS8E	HOSEA	908A
25A	OU 2A	NO	594B
25B	OU 3C	NO	594D
26	EIMI I4	TO BE	222C
	ZAW IAε	LIVE	336D
	KALEW IAβ	CALL	399D
	TOPOS 2D	PLACE	831A
	HUIOS ICγ	SON	841D
27	AMMOS	SAND	45D
	ARITHMOS I	NUMBER	106A
	8SAIAS	ISAIAH	349C
	THALASSA IA	SEA	350D
	KATALEIMMA	REMNANT	414C
	KRAZW 2Bα	CALL	449A
	SUNTEMNW	SHORTEN	800A
	SWZW 3	SAVE	806C
	HUIOS IBα	SON	841C
	HUPER IF	IN BEHALF OF	847A
	HUPOLEIMMA	REMNANT	853B
	HWS II3B	SO	906A
27A	ISRA8L 2	ISRAEL	382B
27B	ISRA8L I	ISRAEL	382B
28	G8 5B	EARTH	156D
	DIKAIOSUN8 I	RIGHTEOUSNESS	195C
	LOGOS IBα	COMMAND	479A
	SUNTELEW 2	COMPLETE	799D
	SUNTEMNW	SHORTEN	800A
29	AN IBβ	(PARTICLE)	48A
	GOMORRA	GOMORRAH	164A
	EGKATALEIPW I	LEAVE BEHIND	214D
	8SAIAS	ISAIAH	349C
	KURIOS 2A	LORD	460C
	HOMOIOW I	MAKE LIKE	570B
	HOMOIOW	MAKE LIKE	570B
	PROEIPON I	FORETELL	711D
	SABAWTH	LORD OF HOSTS	746A
	SODOMA	SODOM	766B
	SPERMA 2A	SEED	769B
29A	HWS II3B	SO	906A
30	DE 2	BUT, AND	170D
	DIKAIOSUN8 2B	RIGHTEOUSNESS	195D
	*DIKAIOSUN8 3	RIGHTEOUSNESS	196A
	DIWKW 4B	PURSUE	200B
	EIPON I	SAY	225B
	KATALAMBANW IA	SEIZE	413D
	OUN ICβ	THEREFORE	597C
	PISTIS 2Dα	FAITH	669B

#	Greek	Gloss	Ref
30	TIS, TI IBε	WHICH	827A
31	DIWKW 4B	PURSUE	200B
	PHTHANW 2	COME	864D
32	DIA BII2	WHY	180B
	ERGON ICβ	DEED	308B
	NOMOS 3	LAW	544D
	HOTI 3A	THAT	593D
	PISTIS 2Dα	FAITH	669B
	PROSKOPTW 2A	TAKE OFFENSE	723C
	HWS III3	SO	906D
32F	LITHOS 2	STONE	475D
32F	PROSKOMMA IA	STUMBLING	723B
33	GRAPHW 2C	WRITE	165D
	EPI IIIBγ	ON	287A
	KATAISCHUNW 3B	DISAPPOINT	411D
	PETRA 2	ROCK	660C
	PISTEUW 2Aγ	BELIEVE	667B
	SIWN 2B	ZION	760A
	SKANDALON 2	TRAP	760C
	TITH8MI IIAα	PUT	823C

ROMANS 10

#	Greek	Gloss	Ref
I	DE8SIS	PRAYER	171A
	EMOS IAα	MY	255A
	EUDOKIA 3	WISH	320A
	KARDIA IBε	HEART	405A
	MEN 2A	(PARTICLE)	504B
	PROS IIIIF	TOWARD	717A
	SWT8RIA 2	DELIVERANCE	809B
2	EPIGNWSIS	KNOWLEDGE	291C
	ECHW I2Eβ	HAVE	333A
	Z8LOS I	ZEAL	338B
	KATA II5Aγ	ACCORDING TO	408B
	MARTUREW IA	BEAR WITNESS	493D
3	AGNOEW 2	NOT TO KNOW	IIB
	*DIKAIOSUN8 3	RIGHTEOUSNESS	196A
	Z8TEW 2Bγ	SEEK	339C
	IDIOS IAβ	ONES OWN	370B
	HIST8MI IIBα	PUT	383A
	HUPOTASSW IBβ	SUBJECT	855D
4	DIKAIOSUN8 3	RIGHTEOUSNESS	196A
	NOMOS 3	LAW	544D
	PAS ICγ	WHOEVER	637B
	PISTEUW 2B	BELIEVE	667C
	TELOS IA	END	819A
	TELOS IC	END	819B
5	ANTHRWPOS 3B	MAN	68D
	GRAPHW 2C	WRITE	166A
	DIKAIOSUN8 3	RIGHTEOUSNESS	196A
	ZAW 2Bβ	LIVE	337B
	NOMOS 3	LAW	544D
6	ANABAINW IAβ	GO UP	50A
	DIKAIOSUN8 3	RIGHTEOUSNESS	196A
	EIMI II3	TO BE	222D
	EIPON 5	SAY	225D
	KARDIA IBβ	HEART	404C
	KATAGW	LEAD	411A
	OURANOS 2B	HEAVEN	599B
	HOUTOS IBε	THIS	601D
	HOUTW 2	THUS	602C
	PISTIS 2Dα	FAITH	669B
7	ABUSSOS 2	ABYSS	2B

7   ANAGW I   LEAD   52D
    EK IB   AWAY FROM 233C
    KATABAINW IA6   COME DOWN 409C
    NEKROS 2A   DEAD 537A
    HOUTOS IBᴄ   THIS 601D
8   EGGUS 3   NEAR 213C
    EIMI II3   TO BE 222D
    EIMI II9A   TO BE 223D
    KARDIA IBα   HEART 404C
    K8RUSSW 2Bβ   ANNOUNCE 432D
    HOUTOS IBᴄ   THIS 601D
    PISTIS 2Dα   FAITH 669B
    STOMA IA   MOUTH 777B
    TIS, TI IBα   WHICH 826D
8A   R8MA I   WORD   743A
8B   R8MA I   WORD   743A
9   EGEIRW IAβ   RAISE 213D
    KURIOS 2A   LORD 460B
    KURIOS 2Cγ   LORD 461B
    NEKROS 2A   DEAD 537A
    HOMOLOGEW 4   CONFESS 571B
    PISTEUW IAβ   BELIEVE 666A
    SWZW 2B   SAVE 806B
9F   KARDIA IBα   HEART 404C
10 DIKAIOSUN8 3   RIGHTEOUSNESS 196A
    EIS 4E   SO THAT 228D
    HOMOLOGEW 4   CONFESS 571D
    PISTEUW ID   BELIEVE 666D
    SWT8RIA 2   DELIVERANCE 809B
11 GRAPH8 2Bβ   SCRIPTURE 165B
    EPI IIIBγ   ON 287A
    KATAISCHUNW 3B   DISAPPOINT 411D
    LEGW I7   SAY 470A
    PAS ICγ   WHOEVER 637B
    PISTEUW 2Aγ   BELIEVE 667B
12 DIASTOL8   DIFFERENCE 188A
    EIS 4G   FOR 229A
    HELL8N 2A   GENTILE 251C
    EPIKALEW 2B   CALL UPON 294B
    IOUDAIOS 2A   JEWISH 380B
    KURIOS 2Cγ   LORD 461B
    PLOUTEW 2   BE RICH 679D
13 EPIKALEW 2B   CALL UPON 294B
    KURIOS 2Cα   LORD 460C
    ONOMA I4B   NAME 575A
    PAS ICγ   WHOEVER 637C
    SWZW 2B   SAVE 806B
14 AKOUW IBα   HEAR   31B
    EPIKALEW 2B   CALL UPON 294B
    K8RUSSW 2Bβ   ANNOUNCE 432D
    OUN ICγ   THEREFORE 597C
    OUN 4   THEREFORE 597D
    CHWRIS 2Aβ   APART 899A
14A   HOS,H8,HO I2Bβ   (REL PRON) 587C
14A   PISTEUW 2Aα   BELIEVE 667A
14A   PISTEUW 2Aβ   BELIEVE 667B
14A   PWS IE   HOW 739D
14B   HOS,H8,HO I2Bγ   (REL PRON) 587C
14B   PISTEUW 2Aα   BELIEVE 667A
14B   PWS IE   HOW 739D
14C   PWS IE   HOW 739D
15 AGATHOS 2Bγ   GOOD   3C
    GRAPHW 2C   WRITE 165D

15 EAN I3B   IF 210D
    EIR8N8 3   PEACE 226D
    EUAGGELIZW 2Aβ   PREACH 317D
    KATHAPER   JUST AS 387D
    K8RUSSW 2Bβ   ANNOUNCE 432D
    POUS IB   FOOT 703C
    PWS IE   HOW 739D
    HWRAIOS   BEAUTIFUL 905B
    HWS IV6   WHEN 907C
16 EUAGGELION IA   GOSPEL 318A
    8SAIAS   ISAIAH 349C
    LEGW I7   SAY 470A
    OU 2A   NO 594B
    PAS 2Aγ   ALL 638B
    PISTEUW IA6   BELIEVE 666B
    TIS, TI IAα   WHICH 826C
    HUPAKOUW I   LISTEN TO 845B
16F   AK08 2B   REPORT   30C
17 ARA 4   THEN 103C
    PISTIS 2Dα   FAITH 669B
    R8MA I   WORD 742D
18 AKOUW 3A   LEARN   31D
    GE 3E   OF COURSE 152B
    EXERCHOMAI 2Bα   GO OUT 274C
    MENOUNGE   RATHER 504C
    OIKOUMEN8 IA   THE WORLD 564A
    OU 6B   NO 595B
    PERAS I   END 649D
    R8MA I   WORD 742D
    PHTHOGGOS   SOUND 865B
18F   ALLA 2   BUT, YET   37D
18F   M8 CI   NOT 519B
19 ASUNETOS I   FOOLISH 118B
    EPI IIIBγ   ON 287B
    LEGW I7   SAY 470A
    OU 2A   NO 594B
    OU 6B   NO 595B
    PARAZ8LOW PROVOKE TO JEALOUSY 621B
    PARORGIZW   MAKE ANGRY 635A
    PRWTOS IA   FIRST 732D
20 APOTOLMAW   BE BOLD 101A
    EMPHAN8S   VISIBLE 257A
    EPERWTAW IC   ASK 285A
    HEURISKW 2   FIND 325D
    Z8TEW IAβ   SEEK 339B
    8SAIAS   ISAIAH 349C
    KAI IIE   AND 393A
    LEGW I7   SAY 470A
21 ANTILEGW 2   OPPOSE 74B
    APEITHEW 2   DISOBEY 82A
    EKPETANNUMI   SPREAD 243A
    H8MERA 2   DAY 347A
    ISRA8L 2   ISRAEL 382B
    HOLOS 2A   WHOLE 567C
21A   PROS III5A   TOWARD 717C

ROMANS 11

1   ABRAAM   ABRAHAM   1D
    BENIAMIN   BENJAMIN 139A
    GAR IB   FOR 151A
    GINOMAI I3A   TAKE PLACE 157D
    EK 3B   FROM 234B

```
1   EK   3B                    FROM 234B        8  HO,H8,TO II4Bγ              THE 554A
    ISRA8LIT8S           ISRAELITE 382C             OUS 2                      EAR 600B
    KL8RONOMIA 4       INHERITANCE 436B             OPHTHALMOS 2              EYE 604C
    M8   AIII2                NOT 518C              PNEUMA 7                SPIRIT 684B
    SPERMA 2B                SEED 769B              S8MERON                 TODAY 756C
    PHUL8 I                 TRIBE 876D        9  ANTAPODOMA           REPAYMENT  72C
1F    APWTHEW 2            REJECT 103A             GINOMAI I4A            BECOME 158D
2   GRAPH8 2A           SCRIPTURE 165B             DAUID                   DAVID 170B
    EN IID                     IN 257D             TH8RA                     NET 361B
    ENTUGCHANW I            MEET 269C              LEGW I7                   SAY 470A
    8   IDα                    OR 343A             PAGIS 2                  TRAP 607A
    8LIAS                  ELIJAH 345D             SKANDALON I              TRAP 760C
    ISRA8L 2               ISRAEL 382B             TRAPEZA 2               TABLE 832B
    KATA I2Bβ               DOWN 406D        10 BLEPW IB                    SEE 143A
    LEGW I7                  SAY 470A              DIA AIIIA             THROUGH 178D
    OIDA IF                 KNOW 558C              NWTOS                    BACK 549D
    PROGINWSKW   KNOWS BEFOREHAND 710C             SKOTIZW 2         BECOME DARK 764D
    HWS I2D                   AS 905D              SUGKAMPTW     (CAUSE TO) BEND 781A
3   Z8TEW 2Bδ               SEEK 339C        11 GINOMAI I3A           TAKE PLACE 157D
    THUSIAST8RION IC       ALTAR 367B              M8   AIII2               NOT 518C
    KATASKAPTW         TEAR DOWN 419B              PARAZ8LOW PROVOKE TO JEALOUSY 621B
    MONOS IΔα               ONLY 529C              PIPTW 2Aβ                FALL 665C
    HUPOLEIPW            BE LEFT 853B              PTAIW I               STUMBLE 734C
    PSUCH8 IAβ         SOUL LIFE 901C              SWT8RIA 2         DELIVERANCE 809B
4   BAAL                    BAAL 129A        11F   PARAPTWMA 2Aβ                 627B
    GONU                    KNEE 164B                        TRANSGRESSION
    HEPTAKISCHILIOI              306B         12 H8TT8MA                 DEFEAT 350C
              SEVEN THOUSAND                       KOSMOS 4A               WORLD 447A
    KAMPTW I                BEND 403A              MALLON 2B                MORE 490C
    KATALEIPW IC     LEAVE BEHIND 414C             PL8RWMA 4   THAT WHICH FILLS 678B
    HOSTIS IB             WHOEVER 590D             PLOUTOS 2              WEALTH 680B
    CHR8MATISMOS DIVINE STATEMENT 894A             POSOS I             HOW GREAT 701A
5   GINOMAI II5            EXIST 159D         13 APOSTOLOS 3           APOSTLES  99B
    EKLOG8 I           SELECTION 242C             DIAKONIA 3             SERVICE 183C
    KAIROS I                TIME 395C             DOXAZW I                PRAISE 203D
    KATA II5A6       ACCORDING TO 408B            EPI III3                    ON 289C
    LEIMMA               REMNANT 471C             MEN 2B              (PARTICLE) 504B
    NUN 3A                   NOW 548A        14 EI VII2B                     IF 219B
    OUN IA             THEREFORE 597B             PARAZ8LOW PROVOKE TO JEALOUSY 621B
    HOUTW IB                THUS 602B             SARX 4                    BODY 751B
    CHARIS 2A              FAVOR 885C             SWZW 2Aβ                  SAVE 806B
6   EI  IIA                   IF 218A        15 APOBOL8 I            REJECTION  88C
    EK   3F                   BY 234D             EK IC               AWAY FROM 233D
    EPEI 2               BECAUSE 283D             ZW8 2Bβ                   LIFE 341C
    ERGON ICβ               DEED 308B             KATALLAG8       RECONCILIATION 415A
6A    OUKETI 2          NO LONGER 597A            KOSMOS 4A               WORLD 447A
6A    CHARIS 2A             FAVOR 885C            PROSL8MPSIS         ACCEPTANCE 724D
6B    CHARIS 2A             FAVOR 885C       16 APARCH8 I           FIRST FRUITS  80D
6C    CHARIS 2A             FAVOR 885C            PHURAMA  THAT WHICH IS MIXED 877A
7   EKLOG8 2           SELECTION 242C        16A   HAGIOS IAβ   WORTHY OF GOD   9C
    EPIZ8TEW 2A        STRIVE FOR 292D       16FF  KLADOS               BRANCH 434A
    EPITUGCHANW            OBTAIN 304A       16=18 RIZA IB              ROOT 743B
    LOIPOS 2Bα         THE OTHERS 481A       17 AGRIELAIOS    WILD OLIVE TREE  I3B
    OUN ICβ             THEREFORE 597C            EGKENTRIZW                GRAFT 215B
    P8ROW                DISABLE 662C             EKKLAW                BREAK OFF 240A
    PWROW                 HARDEN 739B             ELAIA I              OLIVE TREE 247B
    TIS, TI I8c            WHICH 827A             PIOT8S                RICHNESS 664D
8   BLEPW 2                  SEE 143A             SU IC                       YOU 780A
    GRAPHW 2C              WRITE 165D             SUGKOINWNOS         PARTICIPANT 782A
    H8MERA 2                 DAY 347A        18 BASTAZW 2A               CARRY 137A
    KATHAPER             JUST AS 387D             EI  IIA                    IF 218A
    KATANUXIS       STUPEFACTION 416B             M8   AIII3B              NOT 518D
    M8   AIIIDβ              NOT 518A             SU   2                     YOU 780A
```

18B	KATAKAUCHAOMAI I	BOAST 412B
19	EGKENTRIZW	GRAFT 215B
	EIPON 2B	SAY 225C
	EKKLAW	BREAK OFF 240A
20	APISTIA 2B	UNBELIEF 85A
	EKKLAW	BREAK OFF 240A
	HIST8MI II2Cα	STAND 383C
	KALWS 4C	WELL 402B
	M8 AIII3B	NOT 518D
	PISTIS 2Dα	FAITH 669B
	HUPS8LOS 2	HIGH 857C
	HUPS8LOPHRONEW	BE PROUD 857D
	PHRONEW I	THINK 874B
21	EI IIA	IF 218A
	KATA II7A	(ADJ PHRASE) 408D
	KLADOS	BRANCH 434A
	M8PWS IB	LEST SOMEHOW 521C
	OU 5B	NO 595A
	OUDE 2	AND NOT 595D
	PHUSIS I	NATURE 877C
21A	PHEIDOMAI I	SPARE 862C
21B	PHEIDOMAI I	SPARE 862C
22	APOTOMIA	SEVERITY 101A
	EIDON 3	NOTICE 220A
	EKKOPTW I	CUT OFF 241B
	EPEI 2	BECAUSE 283D
	EPI IIII8ε	TOWARD 289A
	EPI IIII8ε	TOWARD 289A
	EPIMENW 2	CONTINUE 296B
	PIPTW 2AB	FALL 665C
22A	CHR8STOT8S 2B	GOODNESS 894D
22B	CHR8STOT8S 2B	GOODNESS 894D
22C	CHR8STOT8S 2B	GOODNESS 894D
23	APISTIA 2B	UNBELIEF 85A
	DUNATOS IAB	POWERFUL 208A
	EGKENTRIZW	GRAFT 215B
	EPIMENW 2	CONTINUE 296B
	KAKEINOS IB	AND HE 397C
	PALIN IB	AGAIN 611C
24	AGRIELAIOS	WILD OLIVE TREE 138
	*EGKENTRIZW	GRAFT 215B
	EKKOPTW I	CUT OFF 241B
	ELAIA I	OLIVE TREE 247B
	IDIOS IAB	ONES OWN 370B
	KALLIELAIOS	400D
	CULTIVATED OLIVE TREE	
	MALLON 2B	MORE 490C
	HOUTOS 2A	THIS 601D
	POSOS I	HOW GREAT 701A
24A	PHUSIS I	NATURE 877C
24B	PHUSIS I	NATURE 877C
24C	PHUSIS I	NATURE 877C
25	AGNOEW I	BE IGNORANT 11B
	ACHRI 2A	UNTIL 128C
	EISERCHOMAI 2A	COME 232B
	THELW I	WISH 355C
	MEROS IC	IN PART 507B
	M8 AI2	NOT 517C
	MUST8RION 2	MYSTERY 532A
	HOS,H8,HO IIIF	(REL PRON) 589A
	PARA II23	BESIDE 615C
	PL8RWMA 3A	THAT WHICH FILLS 678B
	PWRWSIS	HARDENING 739B
25	PHRONIMOS	THOUGHTFUL 874D
25F	ISRA8L 2	ISRAEL 382B
26	APOSTREPHW IAB	TURN AWAY 100A
	ASEBEIA	GODLESSNESS 114A
	H8KW IA	HAVE COME 345B
	IAKWB I	JACOB 368B
	HOUTW 2	THUS 602C
	PAS IAε	ALL 637A
	RUOMAI	SAVE 745A
	SIWN 2B	ZION 760A
	SWZW 2B	SAVE 806B
27	APHAIREW 3	TAKE AWAY 124A
	DIATH8K8 2	182B
	LAST WILL AND TESTAMENT	
	HO,H8,TO IIIG	THE 553A
	HOUTOS IAη	THIS 601B
	PARA I4A	FROM 615A
28	AGAP8TOS 2	BELOVED 6C
	EKLOG8 I	SELECTION 242C
	EUAGGELION IA	GOSPEL 318A
	ECHTHROS I	HOSTILE 331C
	KATA II6	WITH RESPECT TO 408D
29	AMETAMEL8TOS I	WITHOUT REGRET 44D
	KL8SIS I	CALL 436D
	CHARISMA I	A GIFT 887A
30	APEITHEIA	DISOBEDIENCE 81D
	APEITHEW I	DISOBEY 82A
	NUN IC	NOW 547D
	NUNI IC	NOW 548C
	POTE I	ONCE 701D
30F	ELEEW	HAVE MERCY 249B
30F	KAI II3	ALSO 394B
31	APEITHEW 2	DISOBEY 82A
	ELEOS 2B	MERCY 249D
	HINA IV	IN ORDER THAT 379B
	NUN IAγ	NOW 547C
	HUMETEROS 2	YOUR 844A
31F	HINA II2	IN ORDER THAT 378D
32	APEITHEIA	DISOBEDIENCE 81D
	EIS 4A	INTO 228B
	ELEEW	HAVE MERCY 249B
	SUGKLEIW 2	ENCLOSE 781C
32A	PAS 2Bα	IN ALL RESPECTS 638C
32B	PAS 2Bα	IN ALL RESPECTS 638C
33	ANEXERAUN8TOS	UNFATHOMABLE 64B
	ANEXICHNIASTOS	INSCRUTABLE 64C
	BATHOS 2	DEPTH 129D
	GNWSIS I	KNOWLEDGE 162D
	KAI I6	AND 394A
	KRIMA 2	DECISION 451C
	HODOS 2B	WAY 557A
	SOPHIA 3B	WISDOM 767B
	W 3A	O 903B
	HWS IV6	WHEN 907C
34	NOUS 4	THE MIND 547A
	SUMBOULOS	ADVISER 785D
34A	TIS, TI IAα	WHICH 826C
34B	TIS, TI IAα	WHICH 826C
35	ANTAPODIDWMI I	REPAY 72B
	PRODIDWMI I	GIVE IN ADVANCE 711B
36	AIWN IB	TIME 26D
	AM8N I	AMEN 45A
	DIA AIII28B	BY 179D

36	DOXA 3	FAME 203B
	EK 3C	FROM 234B
	PAS 2Bβ	ALL THINGS 638D

ROMANS 12

1	HAGIOS IAβ	WORTHY OF GOD 9C
	DIA AIIIIF	BY 179C
	EUARESTOS I	PLEASING 319A
	ZAW 4B	LIVE 337C
	THUSIA 2B	SACRIFICE 367A
	LATREIA	SERVICE 468C
	LOGIKOS	SPIRITUAL 477C
	OIKTIRMOS	PITY 564C
	PARAKALEW 2	APPEAL TO 622C
	PARIST8MI ID	PRESENT 633B
	*SWMA IB	BODY 807A
2	AIWN 2A	AGE 27A
	ANAKAINWSIS	RENEWAL 55A
	DOKIMAZW 2B	APPROVE 201D
	EURESTOS I	PLEASING 319A
	THEL8MA ICγ	WILL 355A
	METAMORPHOW 2	TRANSFORM 513B
	NOUS 3A	THE MIND 546D
	SUSCH8MATIZW	FORMED LIKE 803B
	TELEIOS IAβ	816D
		HAVING ATTAINED THE END
3	GAR 4	INDEED 151D
	DIA AIIIIE	BY 179C
	HEKASTOS 2	EACH 236A
	MERIZW 2B	ASSIGN 505D
	METRON 2B	MEASURE 516D
	M8 AIIIBβ	NOT 517D
	HOS,H8,HO I2A	(REL PRON) 587B
	PARA III3	IN COMPARISON 616B
	PISTIS 2Dα	FAITH 669B
	SWPHRONEW 2	SOUND MIND 809D
	HUPERPHRONEW	BE HAUGHTY 850A
	CHARIS 4	FAVOR 886C
	HWS I2C	AS 905D
3A	PHRONEW I	THINK 874B
3B	PHRONEW 2	THINK 874B
4	EN I5C	IN 259A
	KATHAPER	JUST AS 387D
	POLUS IIAα	MANY 694A
	PRAXIS I	ACTING 704C
	SWMA IB	BODY 806D
4A	ECHW I2Cα	HAVE 332D
4A	MELOS I	MEMBER 502D
4B	ECHW I2I	HAVE 333C
4B	MELOS I	MEMBER 502D
4F	HOUTW IA	THUS 602B
5	ALL8LWN	EACH OTHER 38D
	HEIS IB	ONE 230A
	HEIS 5E	ONE 231B
	KATA II3A	(DISTRIBUTIVE) 407D
	MELOS 3	MEMBER 503A
	POLUS I2Aβ	MANY 694D
	SWMA 5	BODY 807C
6	ANALOGIA	IN AGREEMENT 56D
	DIAPHOROS I	DIFFERENT 190A
	PISTIS 2Dα	FAITH 669B
	PISTIS 3	FAITH 670A

6	PROPH8TEIA 2	PROPHECY 730A
	CHARIS 4	FAVOR 886C
	CHARISMA 2	A GIFT 887A
6-8	EI VII3B	IF 219B
7	DIAKONIA 5	OFFICE OF A DEACON 183C
	DIDASKALIA I	TEACHING 190C
8	HAPLOT8S 2	GENEROSITY 85B
	ELEEW	HAVE MERCY 249B
	EN III2	BY 260C
	HILAROT8S	CHEERFULNESS 376A
	METADIDWMI	SHARE 512B
	PARAKALEW 2	APPEAL TO 622C
	PARAKALEW 4	IMPLORE 623A
	PARAKL8SIS I	ENCOURAGEMENT 623B
	PROIST8MI I	RULE 714A
	SPOUD8 2	DILIGENCE 771B
9	AGATHOS 2Aα	GOOD 3B
	AGAP8 IIA	LOVE 5C
	AGAP8 IIA	LOVE 5D
	ANUPOKRITOS	GENUINE 76A
	APOSTUGEW	HATE 100A
	DIDWMI IBα	GIVE 192A
	KOLLAW 2C	UNITE 442C
	PON8ROS 2C	WICKED 698A
10	ALL8LWN	EACH OTHER 39A
	PRO8GEOMAI	GO BEFORE 712D
	TIM8 2A	HONOR 825B
	PHILADELPHIA	BROTHERLY LOVE 866B
	PHILOSTORGOS	LOVING DEARLY 869B
11	DOULEUW 2B	SERVE 204C
	ZEW	BOIL 338A
	KURIOS 2Cγ	LORD 460D
	M8 AIII6	NOT 519A
	OKN8ROS I	IDLE 565D
	PNEUMA 5Dα	SPIRIT 683A
	SPOUD8 2	DILIGENCE 771B
12	ELPIS 2B	HOPE 252C
	THLIPSIS I	TRIBULATION 362D
	PROSEUCH8 I	PRAYER 720C
	PROSKARTEREW 2A	ADHERE TO 722D
	HUPOMENW 2	REMAIN 853D
	CHAIRW I	REJOICE 881D
13	HAGIOS 2Dβ	SAINTS 10A
	DIWKW 4B	PURSUE 200C
	KOINWNEW IBγ	SHARE 439D
	MNEIA I	REMEMBRANCE 526B
	CHREIA 2	NEED 893B
14	DIWKW 2	PERSECUTE 200B
	KATARAOMAI	CURSE 418B
14A	EULOGEW 2A	BLESS 322C
14B	EULOGEW 2A	BLESS 322C
15	KLAIW I	WEEP 434B
15A	META AII2	WITH 510C
15A	CHAIRW I	REJOICE 881B
15B	META AII2	WITH 510C
15B	CHAIRW I	REJOICE 881B
16	EIS 4Cβ	(GOAL) 228C
	PARA II2B	BESIDE 615C
	SUNAPAGW	LEAD AWAY 792C
	TAPEINOS I	LOW 811D
	HUPS8LOS 2	HIGH 857D
	PHRONIMOS	THOUGHTFUL 874D
16A	PHRONEW I	THINK 874B

```
16B   PHRONEW 2              THINK 874B
17 ANTI 2                    FOR 73A
   APODIDWMI 3               RECOMPENSE 90A
   KAKOS 3                   EVIL 399A
   KALOS 2B                  GOOD 401B
   M8DEIS 2A                 NO 520A
   PAS 1B                    ALL 637A
   PRONOEW 2                 TAKE CARE 715C
18 DUNATOS 2A                POSSIBLE 208A
   EIR8NEUW 2B               KEEP IN PEACE 226B
   EK 3F                     BY 234D
   META AII3B                WITH 510C
   HO,H8,TO II5              THE 554B
   PAS 1B                    ALL 637A
19 AGAP8TOS 2                BELOVED 6C
   ANTAPODIDWMI 2            REPAY 72B
   GRAPHW 2C                 WRITE 165D
   EKDIKEW 1                 AVENGE SOMEONE 238A
   EKDIK8SIS                 VENGEANCE 238B
   ORG8 2A                   ANGER 582D
   ORG8 2B                   ANGER 583A
  *TOPOS 2C                  PLACE 831A
20 ANTHRAX                   CHARCOAL 67A
   DIPSAW 1                  THIRST 199C
   ECHTHROS 2B?             THE ENEMY 331C
   KEPHAL8 1A                HEAD 431B
   PEINAW 1                  HUNGER 645D
   POTIZW 1                  GIVE TO DRINK 702C
   PUR 1A                    FIRE 737B
   SWREUW 1                  HEAP 808A
   PSWMIZW 1                 FEED 903A
21 HUPO 1A?                  BY 850D
21A KAKOS 3                  EVIL 399A
21A NIKAW 2B                 BE CONQUERED 541C
21B KAKOS 3                  EVIL 399A
21B NIKAW 2A                 CONQUER 541C

            ROMANS 13

1 EIMI V                     TO BE 225A
  EXOUSIA 4C?                AUTHORITY 278B
  TASSW 1A                   PLACE 813C
  HUPERECHW 2A               SURPASS 848D
  HUPOTASSW 1B?              SUBJECT 855D
  PSUCH8 2                   SOUL LIFE 902C
2 ANTHIST8MI 2              SET AGAINST 66C
  ANTHIST8MI 3              SET AGAINST 66D
  ANTITASSW                  OPPOSE 75B
  DIATAG8                    ORDINANCE 188B
  EXOUSIA 4C?                AUTHORITY 278B
  KRIMA 4B                   VERDICT 451D
  LAMBANW 2                  RECEIVE 466C
  HWSTE 1A                   THEREFORE 908B
3 AGATHOERGOS                DOING GOOD 2B
  ARCHWN 2                   AUTHORITIES 113B
  EXOUSIA 4C?                AUTHORITY 278B
  EPAINOS 1A?                PRAISE 281B
  ERGON 1C?                  DEED 308A
  KAKOS 1B                   BAD 398C
  M8 AII16?                  NOT 517D
  POIEW 11B?                 DO 687D
  PHOBEW 1B?                 BE AFRAID 871A
  PHOBOS 1                   CAUSING OF FEAR 871B

3B   AGATHOS 2A?            GOOD 3B
4 AGATHOS 2A?               GOOD 3B
  DIAKONOS 2A                AUTHORITIES 184A
  EAN IIA                    IF 210B
  EIK8 3                     TO NO PURPOSE 221A
  EIS 4E                     SO THAT 228D
  EKDIKOS                    THE AVENGER 238B
  MACHAIRA 2                 SWORD 497C
  POIEW 11B?                 DO 687D
  PRASSW 1A                  DO 705B
  PHOREW 1                   WEAR 872D
4A   KAKOS 1C               EVIL 398D
4B   KAKOS 1C               EVIL 398D
4F   ORG8 2A                ANGER 582D
5 ALLA 1A                   BUT, YET 37C
  ANAGK8 1                   NECESSITY 52A
  DIO                        THEREFORE 197D
  SUNEID8SIS 2               CONSCIOUSNESS 794B
  HUPOTASSW 1B?              SUBJECT 855D
6 AUTOS 1H                  EVEN 122D
  LEITOURGOS 1               SERVANT 472C
  PROSKARTEREW 2A            ADHERE TO 722D
  TELEW 3                    PAY 818D
  PHOROS                     TAX 872D
7 APODIDWMI 1               GIVE AWAY 90A
  HO,H8,TO II9A              THE 554D
  OPHEIL8 2A                 DEBT 603B
  TIM8 2B                    HONOR 825B
  PHOROS                     TAX 872D
7A   PHOBOS 2B?             FEAR 871D
7B   TELOS 3                TAX 819D
7B   PHOBOS 2B?             FEAR 871D
8 AGAPAW 1A?                LOVE 4B
  AGAPAW 1A?                 LOVE 4B
  ALL8LWN                    EACH OTHER 39A
  HETEROS 1B?                ANOTHER 315C
  M8DEIS 2B?                 NOTHING 520A
  NOMOS 3                    LAW 544D
  HO,H8,TO II4A              THE 553D
  OPHEILW 2A?                OWE 603C
  PL8ROW 4B                  MAKE FULL 677D
9 AGAPAW 1A?                LOVE 4B
  ANAKEPHALAIOW              SUM UP 55C
  HEAUTOU 2                  ONESELF 211C
  ENTOL8 2A?                 COMMAND 268C
  EPITHUMEW                  DESIRE 293A
  HETEROS 1B?                ANOTHER 315B
  KLEPTW                     STEAL 435C
  LOGOS 1B?                  COMMAND 479B
  MOICHEUW 1      COMMIT ADULTERY 528B
  HO,H8,TO II8A              THE 554D
  OU 4B                      NO 594D
  PL8SION 1B                 NEAR 678D
  PHONEUW                    MURDER 872C
  PSEUDOMARTUREW                    900A
          BEAR FALSE WITNESS
10 AGAP8 11A                 LOVE 5B
  ERGAZOMAI 2A               WORK 307A
  KAKOS 3                    EVIL 399A
  NOMOS 3                    LAW 544D
  OUN 1A                     THEREFORE 597B
  PL8RWMA 4        THAT WHICH FILLS 678C
  PL8SION 1B                 NEAR 678D
```

11	EGGUS 2A	NEAR 213C
	EGEIRW 2A	AWAKEN 214A
	EK IC	AWAY FROM 233D
	KAI I3	AND 393D
	KAIROS I	TIME 395C
	NUN IC	NOW 547D
	HO,H8,TO IIIAα	THE 552C
	HOTE IB	WHEN 592C
	HOUTOS IBγ	THIS 601D
	PISTEUW 2B	BELIEVE 667C
	SWT8RIA 2	DELIVERANCE 809B
	HUPNOS	SLEEP 850D
	HWRA 3	TIME OF DAY 905A
12	APOBALLW 4	TAKE AWAY 88C
	APOTITH8MI IB	LAY ASIDE 100C
	EGGIZW 5B	APPROACH 212D
	ENDUW 2A	DRESS 263C
	ERGON ICβ	DEED 308B
	NUX 2	NIGHT 549A
	HOPLON 2B	WEAPON 579A
	PROKOPTW I	GO FORWARD 714D
	SKOTOS 2B	DARKNESS 765B
	PHWS 3A	LIGHT 880C
12F	H8MERA IB	DAY 346D
13	ASELGEIA	LICENTIOUSNESS 114C
	*ERIS	STRIFE 309C
	EUSCH8MONWS	DECENTLY 327B
	Z8LOS 2	JEALOUSY 338B
	KOIT8 2A	BED 440D
	KWMOS	CAROUSING 462D
	METH8	DRUNKENNESS 500A
	PERIPATEW 2Aβ	GO ABOUT 655B
	PERIPATEW 2Aα	GO ABOUT 655B
	HWS I2A	AS 905C
14	EIS 4E	SO THAT 228D
	ENDUW 2B	DRESS 263D
	EPITHUMIA 3	DESIRE 293D
	KURIOS 2Cγ	LORD 461A
	PRONOIA 2	FORESIGHT 715D
	SARX 7	BODY 751D

ROMANS 14

1	ASTHENEW 2	WEAK 115A
	DE IC	BUT, AND 170C
	DIAKRISIS 2	QUARREL 184C
	DIALOGISMOS I	THOUGHT 185A
	M8 AIII6	NOT 519A
	PISTIS 2Dα	FAITH 669B
	PROSLAMBANW 2B	TAKE 724C
2	ASTHENEW 2	WEAK 115A
	LACHANON	VEGETABLE 468D
	MEN IC	(PARTICLE) 504A
	HOS,H8,HO II2	THIS (ONE) 589B
	PISTEUW 4	BELIEVE 667D
2B	ESTHIW IA	EAT 312C
3	EXOUTHENEW I	DESPISE 277B
	PROSLAMBANW 2B	TAKE 724C
3F	KRINW 6B	JUDGE 453B
4	ALLOTRIOS IA	TO ANOTHER 40A
	DUNATEW 2	BE STRONG 207D
	DUNATOS IAβ	POWERFUL 208A
	EIMI II6C	TO BE 223C

4	8 IAα	OR 342B
	HIST8MI IIBβ	PUT 383A
	OIKET8S	HOUSE SLAVE 559C
	PIPTW 2Aβ	FALL 665C
	ST8KW 2	STAND 775C
	TIS, TI IAβ	WHICH 826D
4A	HIST8MI IIID	STAND 383B
4A	KURIOS IAβ	LORD 460A
4F	IDIOS IAβ	ONES OWN 370B
5	GAR 4	INDEED 151D
	HEKASTOS 2	EACH 236A
	H8MERA 2	DAY 347C
	MEN IC	(PARTICLE) 504A
	NOUS 4	THE MIND 547A
	HOS,H8,HO II2	THIS (ONE) 589B
	PARA III3	IN COMPARISON 616B
	PL8ROPHOREW 2	FILL 676B
5A	KRINW I	SEPARATE 452B
5B	KRINW I	SEPARATE 452B
6	EUCHARISTEW 2	GIVE THANKS 328C
	H8MERA 2	DAY 347C
	PHRONEW 2	THINK 874B
7	ZAW 3B	LIVE 337C
7A	OUDEIS 2A	NO ONE 596B
7B	OUDEIS 2A	NO ONE 596B
8	APOTHN8SKW IAα	DIE 91A
	EAN IIA	IF 210B
	EAN I3D	IF 211A
	KURIOS 2Cγ	LORD 460D
	OUN 5	THEREFORE 597D
8A	ZAW IAα	LIVE 336B
8A	TE 2	AND 815B
8B	ZAW 3B	LIVE 337C
8B	TE 2	AND 815B
9	ANAZAW IA COME TO LIFE AGAIN	53B
	EIS 4F	(PURPOSE) 228D
	HINA I5	IN ORDER THAT 378A
	KURIEUW I	RULE 459D
	NEKROS 2A	DEAD 536D
	HOUTOS IBβ	THIS 601C
9A	ZAW IAβ	LIVE 336C
9B	ZAW IAα	LIVE 336C
10	B8MA 2	TRIBUNAL 139D
	GAR IE	FOR 151C
	EXOUTHENEW I	DESPISE 277B
	8 IAβ	OR 342D
	KRINW 6B	JUDGE 453B
	PARIST8MI 2Aα	APPROACH 633C
11	GLWSSA IA	TONGUE 161B
	GONU	KNEE 164B
	GRAPHW 2C	WRITE 165D
	EXOMOLOGEW 2C	CONFESS 276D
	ZAW IAε	LIVE 336D
	KAMPTW 2	BEND 403B
12	APODIDWMI I	GIVE AWAY 90A
	ARA 4	THEN 103C
	DIDWMI 4	GIVE 192D
	HEKASTOS 2	EACH 236A
	LOGOS 2A	ACCOUNT 479C
12A	ESTHIW IA	EAT 312D
13	8 IAβ	OR 342D
	MALLON 3Aα	RATHER 490C
	M8 AIIIG	NOT 518B

13	M8KETI 6C	NO LONGER 520C
	PROSKOMMA 2B	STUMBLING 723B
	SKANDALON 2	TRAP 760C
	TITH8MI IIAα	PUT 823C
13A	KRINW 6B	JUDGE 453B
13B	KRINW 3	DECIDE 452C
13B	KRINW 6B	JUDGE 453B
14	HEAUTOU IB	ONESELF 211B
	EKEINOS IB	THAT 239A
	EN I5D	IN 259B
	LOGIZOMAI 3	THINK 477B
	PEITHW 4	OBEY 645C
14A	KOINOS 2	COMMON 439B
14B	KOINOS 2	COMMON 439B
14C	KOINOS 2	COMMON 439B
15	AGAP8 IIA	LOVE 5C
	APOTHN8SKW IAα	DIE 90D
	APOLLUMI IAα	RUIN 94B
	EKEINOS ID	THAT 239A
	LUPEW 2B	BE GRIEVED 483A
	OUKETI 2	NO LONGER 597A
	PERIPATEW 2Aδ	GO ABOUT 655B
	HUPER IAε	IN BEHALF OF 846C
15A	BRWMA I	FOOD 147C
15B	BRWMA I	FOOD 147C
16	AGATHOS 2Aγ	GOOD 3B
	BLASPH8MEW 2Bε	BLASPHEME 142B
17	BASILEIA 3B	KINGDOM 134D
	BASILEIA 3G	KINGDOM 135B
	BRWSIS I	EATING 147C
	DIKAIOSUN8 2B	RIGHTEOUSNESS 195D
	EIR8N8 3	PEACE 227A
	PNEUMA 5Cβ	SPIRIT 683A
	POSIS I	DRINKING 701A
	CHARA I	JOY 883D
18	DOKIMOS 2	RESPECTED 202A
	DOULEUW 2B	SERVE 204B
	EUARESTOS I	PLEASING 319A
19	ARA 4	THEN 103C
	DIWKW 4B	PURSUE 200C
	EIR8N8 IB	PEACE 226C
	HO,H8,TO II7	THE 554C
	OIKODOM8 IBα	BUILDING 561C
20	ALLA IB	BUT, YET 37D
	ANTHRWPOS 3B	MAN 68D
	DIA AIIIC	THROUGH 179B
	HENEKA	BECAUSE OF 264B
	ERGON 3	WORK 308C
	ESTHIW IC	EAT 313A
	KATHAROS 2	CLEAN 388D
	KAKOS IC	EVIL 398D
	KAKOS 2	EVIL 398D
	KATALUW IBβ	DESTROY 415C
	MEN IAβ	(PARTICLE) 503D
	PROSKOMMA IB	STUMBLING 723B
21	ASTHENEW 2	WEAK 115A
	EN IV6C	IN 261A
	ESTHIW IA	EAT 312C
	KALOS 3C	GOOD 401D
	KREAS	MEAT 450D
	M8 AIIIC	NOT 518A
	M8DE IB	AND NOT 519D
	OINOS I	WINE 565A
21	HOS,H8,HO I2Bβ	(REL PRON) 587B
	PINW I	DRINK 664B
	PROSKOPTW 2A	TAKE OFFENSE 723C
	SKANDALIZW IB	CAUSE TO FALL 760B
22	DOKIMAZW 2B	APPROVE 201D
	EN IV6A	IN 261A
	ENWPION 2B	BEFORE 270B
	ECHW I2Eβ	HAVE 333A
	KATA IIIC	BY 407B
	KRINW 6B	JUDGE 453C
	MAKARIOS IB	BLESSED 488A
	M8 AII2A	NOT 518B
	PISTIS 2Dε	FAITH 669D
23	DIAKRINW 2B	WAVER 184B
	EK 3Gγ	BY 235A
	KATAKRINW	CONDEMN 413A
	PAS ICγ	WHOEVER 637C
	PISTIS 2Dε	FAITH 669D
23A	PISTIS 2Dα	FAITH 669B
23B	PISTIS 2Dα	FAITH 669B

ROMANS 15

1	ADUNATOS IB	POWERLESS 18D
	ARESKW I	ACCOMMODATE 105A
	ASTHEN8MA	WEAKNESS 115A
	BASTAZW 2Bβ	ENDURE 137A
	DUNATOS IAβ	POWERFUL 208A
	OPHEILW 2Aβ	OWE 603D
2	AGATHOS 2Aβ	GOOD 3B
	ARESKW I	ACCOMMODATE 105A
	OIKODOM8 IBα	BUILDING 561C
	PL8SION IB	NEAR 678C
	PROS III3A	TOWARD 717A
3	ARESKW I	ACCOMMODATE 105A
	GAR IB	FOR 151A
	EPI IIIBγ	ON 289A
	EPIPIPTW 2	FALL UPON 297C
	ONEIDIZW I	REPROACH 573A
	ONEIDISMOS	REPROACH 573C
4	GRAPH8 2Bα	SCRIPTURE 165B
	DIDASKALIA I	TEACHING 190C
	EIS 4D	FOR 228C
	ELPIS 2B	HOPE 252D
	ECHW I2Eβ	HAVE 333A
	H8METEROS	OUR 348C
	PARAKL8SIS 3	COMFORT 623C
	PROGRAPHW IB	WRITE BEFORE 711A
4F	HUPOMON8 I	PATIENCE 854A
5	ALL8LWN	EACH OTHER 39A
	DIDWMI	GIVE 191D
	EN I4A	IN 258B
	KATA II5Aα	ACCORDING TO 408A
	PARAKL8SIS 3	COMFORT 623C
	PHRONEW I	THINK 874B
6	DOXAZW I	PRAISE 203C
	HEIS 2A	ONE 230A
	THEOS 3D	GOD 358A
	KURIOS 2Cγ	LORD 461B
	HO,H8,TO II10B	THE 555A
	HOMOTHUMADON	WITH ONE MIND 569C
	PAT8R 3Dβ	FATHER 641D
	STOMA IA	MOUTH 777C

7	KATHWS I	JUST AS 392A
	KAI II3	ALSO 394B
7A	PROSLAMBANW 2B	TAKE 724C
7B	PROSLAMBANW 2B	TAKE 724C
8	AL8THEIA I	TRUTHFULNESS 35A
	BEBAIOW I	ESTABLISH 138A
	DIAKONOS IB	HELPER 183D
	EPAGGELIA 2A	PROMISE 280B
	LEGW IIIE	DECLARE 471A
	PERITOM8 4A	CIRCUMCISION 658D
	HUPER IB	IN BEHALF OF 846D
9	DOXAZW I	PRAISE 203C
	ELEOS 2B	MERCY 249D
	EXOMOLOGEW 2C	CONFESS 276D
	ONOMA I4B	NAME 575A
	HUPER ID	IN BEHALF OF 847A
	PSALLW	SING 899B
10	ETHNOS 2	GENTILES 217C
	EUPHRAINW 2	GLADDEN 328A
	LAOS 3A	PEOPLE 468A
	LEGW I7	SAY 470A
	META AII2	WITH 510C
10-12	PALIN 3	AGAIN 611D
11	AINEW	TO PRAISE 23A
	EPAINEW	PRAISE 281B
	LAOS 3A	PEOPLE 468B
	PAS IDα	ALL 637C
12	ANIST8MI 2A	RISE 69C
	ARCHW I	RULE II3A
	ELPIZW 3	HOPE 252B
	EPI IIIBγ	ON 287A
	8SAIAS	ISAIAH 349C
	IESSAI	JESSE 374B
	LEGW I7	SAY 470A
	RIZA 2	ROOT 743C
13	DUNAMIS I	POWER 206D
	EIR8N8 3	PEACE 227A
	ELPIS 2B	HOPE 252C
	ELPIS 2B	HOPE 252D
	PERISSEUW IBα	BE LEFT OVER 656D
	PISTEUW 2B	BELIEVE 667C
	PL8ROW IB	MAKE FULL 676D
	PNEUMA 5Cβ	SPIRIT 683A
	CHARA I	JOY 883C
	CHARA I	JOY 883D
14	AGATHWSUN8	GOODNESS 3D
	AUTOS IAβ	SELF 122B
	MESTOS 2A	FULL 509C
	NOUTHETEW	ADMONISH 546B
	PEITHW 4	OBEY 645C
15	GRAPHW 2D	WRITE 166A
	DIA BIII	BECAUSE OF 180A
	EPANAMIMN8SKW	REMIND 282C
	MEROS IC	IN PART 507B
	*TOLM8ROS	BOLD 829D
	CHARIS 4	FAVOR 886C
	HWS I2A	AS 905C
16	HAGIAZW 2	CONSECRATE 8D
	HAGIAZW 4	PURIFY 9A
	EUAGGELION 2Bα	GOSPEL 318B
	EUAGGELION 2Bβ	GOSPEL 318B
	EUPROSDEKTOS I	ACCEPTABLE 324D

16	HIEROURGEW	374A
	PERFORM HOLY SERVICE	
	LEITOURGOS 2	SERVANT 472D
	PNEUMA 5Cβ	SPIRIT 683A
	PROSPHORA 2	PRESENTING 727D
17	EN I5D	IN 259B
	THEOS 3A	GOD 357D
	KAUCH8SIS I	BOASTING 427C
	HO,H8,TO II5	THE 554B
	PROS III5B	TOWARD 717D
18	ERGON IA	DEED 307D
	KATERGAZOMAI I	ACHIEVE 422D
	LOGOS IAα	WORD 478A
	HOS,H8,HO I4A	(REL PRON) 587D
	TIS, TI IBα	ANY ONE 828A
	TOLMAW IB	DARE 829C
	HUPAKO8 IB	OBEDIENCE 844D
19	APO II2B	FROM 86C
	DUNAMIS I	POWER 206D
	EUAGGELION 2Bα	GOSPEL 318B
	HIEROSOLUMA IA	JERUSALEM 373D
	ILLURIKON	ILLYRICUM 376D
	KUKLW IA	AROUND 458A
	MECHRI IA	UNTIL 517A
	PL8ROW 3	MAKE FULL 677B
	PNEUMA 5Cβ	SPIRIT 683A
	S8MEION 2A	SIGN 755D
	HWSTE 2Aβ	THEREFORE 908C
20	ALLOTRIOS IA	TO ANOTHER 40A
	EUAGGELIZW 2Aδ	PREACH 318A
	THEMELIOS 2A	FOUNDATION 356B
	M8 AI2	NOT 517C
	OIKODOMEW 2	BUILD 561A
	ONOMAZW 3	NAME 577C
	HOPOU IAα	WHERE 579C
	PHILOTIMEOMAI	ASPIRE 869C
21	ANAGGELLW 2	DISCLOSE 51A
	HORAW ICβ	SEE 582A
	HOS,H8,HO I2Bα	(REL PRON) 587B
	OU 5A	NO 595A
	SUNI8MI	UNDERSTAND 798A
22	DIO	THEREFORE 197D
	EGKOPTW	HINDER 215C
	HO,H8,TO II4Bδ	THE 554A
	POLUS I2Bβ	MANY 695B
23	EPIPOTHIA	LONGING 298A
	ETOS	YEAR 317B
	HIKANOS IB	SUFFICIENT 375A
	KLIMA	DISTRICT 437B
	M8KETI 3	NO LONGER 520B
	NUNI IA	NOW 548B
	HO,H8,TO II4Bβ	THE 553D
	POLUS IIAα	MANY 694A
	TOPOS 2C	PLACE 831A
23B	ECHW I2Eβ	HAVE 333A
24	AN 3D	(PARTICLE) 48C
	DIAPOREUOMAI	GO THROUGH 186D
	EIS IAα	INTO 227C
	EKEI 2	THERE 238D
	ELPIZW 2	HOPE 252A
	EMPI(M)PL8MI 3	FILL 255C
	THEAOMAI IB	SEE 353D
	MEROS IC	IN PART 507B

24 POREUW I   PROCEED 699A   32 CHARA I   JOY 883C
   PROPEMPW 2   ACCOMPANY 716B   33 AM8N I   AMEN 45A
   PRWTOS 2A   FIRST 733D   EIR8N8 3   PEACE 226D
   SPANIA   SPAIN 768A   THEOS 3E   GOD 358B
   HWS IVIC∝   WHEN 907A   META AIIIC8   WITH 510A
25 HAGIOS 2D8   SAINTS 10A   PAS IE∝   ALL 637D
   DIAKONEW 4   HELP 183B
   EIS IA∝   INTO 227C   ROMANS 16
   NUNI IA   NOW 548B
   POREUW I   PROCEED 699A   I ADELPH8 3   SISTER 15C
   PTWCHOS IA BEGGING POOR 735C   DIAKONOS 2B   DEACONESS 184A
25F HIEROSOLUMA IA JERUSALEM 373D   EKKL8SIA 4B   CHURCH 240C
26 ACHAIA   ACHAIA 127D   KEGCHREAI   CENCHREAE 427D
   EIS 4G   FOR 229A   HO,H8,TO II5   THE 554B
   EUDOKEW I   WELL PLEASED 319C   SUNIST8MI IIB   UNITE 798B
   KOINWNIA I   ASSOCIATION 440A   PHOIB8   PHOEBE 872A
   KOINWNIA 3   ASSOCIATION 440B   2 AXIWS   WORTHILY 78A
   MAKEDONIA   MACEDONIA 488B   GAR IB   FOR 151A
   POIEW III   DO 689C   EN I5D   IN 259B
   PTWCHOS IA BEGGING POOR 735C   KATARGEW IB MAKE INEFFECTIVE 418B
27 GAR 3   CERTAINLY 151D   KURIOS 2Cɣ   LORD 461A
   EI III   IF 218C   PARASTATIS   HELPER 627D
   EUDOKEW I   WELL PLEASED 319C   PARIST8MI 2Aɣ   HELP 633C
   KOINWNEW IB∝   SHARE 439C   POLUS I2A∝   MANY 694D
   LEITOURGEW 3   SERVE 472A   PRAGMA 2   DEED 703D
   OPHEILET8S 2B   DEBTOR 603A   PROSDECHOMAI IA   RECEIVE 719B
   OPHEILW 2A8   OWE 603D   PROSTATIS   PROTECTRESS 726A
   PNEUMATIKOS 2B∝ SPIRITUAL 685C   CHR8ZW   NEED 893D
   SARKIKOS I   FLESHLY 750B   3 AKULAS   AQUILA 33C
28 APERCHOMAI 2   GO 83D   ASPAZOMAI IA   GREET 116B
   DIA AII   THROUGH 178B   *PRISKA   PRISCILLA 708B
   EIS IA∝   INTO 227C   SUNERGOS   WORKING WITH 795C
   EPITELEW I   END 302B   4 ETHNOS 2   GENTILES 217C
   KARPOS 2A   RESULT 406A   EKKL8SIA 4E6   CHURCH 240D
   HOUTOS 2B   THIS 601D   EUCHARISTEW I   BE THANKFUL 328B
   SPANIA   SPAIN 768A   MONOS IAɣ   ONLY 529C
   SPHRAGIZW 2D   SEAL 804B   HOSTIS 2B   WHOEVER 591A
29 EN I4C8   IN 258C   PAS ID∝   ALL 637C
   ERCHOMAI IIA8   COME 310C   TRACH8LOS   NECK 832D
   EULOGIA 3B∝   BLESSING 323B   HUPER IA∈   IN BEHALF OF 846C
   PL8ROPHORIA   CERTAINTY 676C   HUPOTITH8MI I   RISK 856A
   PL8RWMA 3B THAT WHICH FILLS 678B   PSUCH8 IA8   SOUL LIFE 901C
30 AGAP8 IIA   LOVE   5D   5 AGAP8TOS 2   BELOVED   6C
   DIA AIIIIF   BY 179C   APARCH8 2A   FIRST FRUITS 80D
   KURIOS 2Cɣ   LORD 461B   ASIA   ASIA 115C
   PARAKALEW 2   APPEAL TO 622C   ACHAIA   ACHAIA 127D
   PNEUMA 5D∝   SPIRIT 683A   EKKL8SIA 4C   CHURCH 240C
   PROS IIIIF   TOWARD 717A   EPAINETOS   EPAENETUS 281A
   PROSEUCH8 I   PRAYER 720C   KATA IIIC   BY 407B
   SUNAGWNIZOMAI   HELP 791A   OIKOS IA∝   HOUSE 563A
31 APEITHEW 2   DISOBEY 82A   5FF ASPAZOMAI IA   GREET 116B
   APEITHEW 3   DISOBEY 82A   6 *KOPIAW 2   BECOME WEARY 444B
   DIAKONIA 4   SUPPORT 183C   MARIA 7   MARY 493B
   DWROPHORIA BRINGING OF A GIFT 210C   HOSTIS 2B   WHOEVER 591A
   EUPROSDEKTOS I ACCEPTABLE 324D   POLUS I2B8   MANY 695B
   IOUDAIA I   JUDAEA 379D   7 ANDRONIKOS   ANDRONICUS 63C
   RUOMAI   SAVE 745A   APOSTOLOS 3   APOSTLES 99B
32 ANAPSUCHW 2   REVIVE 63B   GINOMAI II4A   BE 159C
   DIA AIIIID   THROUGH 179C   EPIS8MOS I   PROMINENT 298B
   EN III2   BY 260B   IOULIA   JULIA 381A
   ERCHOMAI IIA8   COME 310C   IOUNIAS   JUNIAS 381A
   THEL8MA 2B   WILL 355A   HOSTIS 2B   WHOEVER 591A
   SUNANAPAUOMAI REST (WITH) 792A   PRO 2   BEFORE 708D

7 SUGGEN8S	RELATED	780B
SUNAICHMALWTOS		791B
FELLOW PRISONER		
8 AMPLIATOS	AMPLIATUS	46C
8F AGAP8TOS 2	BELOVED	6C
9 OURBANOS	URBANUS	600A
STACHUS	STACHYS	773B
SUNERGOS	WORKING WITH	795C
10 APELL8S	APELLES	83A
ARISTOBOULOS	ARISTOBULUS	106B
DOKIMOS I	GENUINE	202A
EN I5D	IN	259B
IOF EK 3D	FROM	234C
IOF HO,H8,TO II7	THE	554C
II EN I5D	IN	259B
H8RWDIWN	HERODION	349C
NARKISSOS	NARCISSUS	536A
SUGGEN8S	RELATED	780B
12 AGAP8TOS 2	BELOVED	6C
EN I5D	IN	259B
HOSTIS 2B	WHOEVER	591A
PERSIS	PERSIS	659D
POLUS I28P	MANY	695B
TRUPHAINA	TRYPHAENA	836B
TRUPHWSA	TRYPHOSA	836C
12A KOPIAW 2	BECOME WEARY	444B
12A KURIOS 2Cy	LORD	461A
12B *KOPIAW 2	BECOME WEARY	444B
12B KURIOS 2Cy	LORD	461A
13 EKLEKTOS 2	CHOSEN	242B
EN I5D	IN	259B
M8T8R 3	MOTHER	522A
ROUPHOS 2	RUFUS	744D
14 ASUGKRITOS	ASYNCRITUS	II8A
HERMAS I	HERMAS	309D
HERM8S 2	HERMES	3I0A
PATROBAS	PATROBAS	642C
SUN IC	WITH	789B
PHLEGWN	PHLEGON	869D
15 ADELPH8 I	SISTER	I5C
IOULIA	JULIA	38IA
N8REUS	NEREUS	539D
OLUMPAS	OLYMPAS	568A
PAS IFP	ALL	638A
SUN IC	WITH	789B
PHILOLOGOS	PHILOLOGUS	868B
16 ASPAZOMAI IA	GREET	II6C
EKKL8SIA 4B	CHURCH	240C
EKKL8SIA 4EP	CHURCH	240D
PAS ID«	ALL	637C
PHIL8MA	A KISS	867B
17 DIDACH8 2	TEACHING	I9IB
DICHOSTASIA	DISSENSION	I99B
EKKLINW	TURN AWAY	24IA
MANTHANW I	LEARN	49IB
PARA III6	AGAINST	6I6C
PARAKALEW 2	APPEAL TO	622C
POIEW II3y	DO	687C
SKANDALON 2	TRAP	760C
SKOPEW	NOTICE	764A
18 AKAKOS	INNOCENT	28D
DOULEUW 2C	SERVE	204C
DOULEUW 2B	SERVE	204C
18 EXAPATAW	DECEIVE	272C
EUGLWTTIA	GLIBNESS	3I9B
EULOGIA 2	PRAISE	323A
KARDIA I8P	HEART	404D
KOILIA I	BELLY	438B
KURIOS 2Cy	LORD	46IB
TOIOUTOS 3A«	SUCH A KIND	829B
CHR8STOLOGIA	SMOOTH SPEECH	894C
19 AGATHOS 2A«	GOOD	3B
AKERAIOS	PURE	29D
APHIKNEOMAI	REACH	I26A
EPI IIIBy	ON	287B
THELW I	WISH	355C
KAKOS IC	EVIL	398D
*MEN	(PARTICLE)	503C
OUN IA	THEREFORE	597B
SOPHOS 3	LEARNED	767D
HUPAKO8 IB	OBEDIENCE	844D
CHAIRW I	REJOICE	88IB
CHAIRW I	REJOICE	88ID
20 EIR8N8 3	PEACE	226D
EN III2	BY	260C
POUS IB	FOOT	703C
SATAN	ADVERSARY	752C
SUNTRIBW IB	SHATTER	80IA
TACHOS	SPEED	8I4D
HUPO 2A«	UNDER	85IB
CHARIS 2C	FAVOR	885D
21 IASWN 2	JASON	369C
LOUKAS	LUKE	48IC
LOUKIOS 2	LUCIUS	48ID
SUGGEN8S	RELATED	780B
SUNERGOS	WORKING WITH	795C
SWSIPATROS	SOSIPATER	808A
TIMOTHEOS	TIMOTHY	826A
22 ASPAZOMAI IA	GREET	II6C
EPISTOL8	LETTER	300D
KURIOS 2Cy	LORD	46IA
TERTIOS	TERTIUS	820C
23 ADELPHOS 2	BROTHER	I6A
GAIOS 3	GAIUS	I49A
ERASTOS I	ERASTUS	306C
KOUARTOS	QUARTUS	448B
XENOS 2C	THE HOST	550C
24 AM8N I	AMEN	45A
CHARIS 2C	FAVOR	885D
25 AIWNIOS I	ETERNAL	27D
APOKALUPSIS I	REVELATION	9ID
EUAGGELION 28P	GOSPEL	3I8C
K8RUGMA 2	PROCLAMATION	432A
MUST8RION 2	MYSTERY	532B
SIGAW 2	BE SILENT	757B
ST8RIZW 2	ESTABLISH	775D
CHRONOS	TIME	896C
25A KATA II5A«	ACCORDING TO	408A
26 AIWNIOS 2	ETERNAL	27D
GNWRIZW I	MAKE KNOWN	I62D
GRAPH8 2B«	SCRIPTURE	I65B
EIS ID	IN	227D
EPITAG8	COMMAND	302A
KATA II5A6	ACCORDING TO	408B
NUN IAy	NOW	547D
PISTIS 2D«	FAITH	669B

26	PROPH8TIKOS	PROPHETIC 731C
	HUPAKO8 1B	OBEDIENCE 845A
	PHANEROW 1B	REVEAL 860C
27	AIWN 1B	TIME 26D
	AM8N 1	AMEN 45A
	THEOS 31	GOD 358C
	MONOS 1A6	ONLY 529C
	SOPHOS 4	LEARNED 767D

I CORINTHIANS 1

1	ADELPHOS 2	BROTHER 16A
	APOSTOLOS 3	APOSTLES 99B
	DIA AIIIID	THROUGH 179C
	THEL8MA 2B	WILL 355A
	KL8TOS	CALLED 437B
	PAULOS	PAUL 643A
	SWSTHEN8S 2	SOSTHENES 808A
2	HAGIAZW 2	CONSECRATE 8D
	HAGIAZW 4	PURIFY 9A
	HAGIOS 2D9	SAINTS 10A
	EKKL8SIA 4B	CHURCH 240C
	EKKL8SIA 4E«	CHURCH 240D
	EN 15D	IN 259D
	EPIKALEW 2B	CALL UPON 294B
	KL8TOS	CALLED 437A
	KORINTHOS	CORINTH 445C
	KURIOS 2Cy	LORD 461B
	ONOMA 14B	NAME 575A
	PAS 1D9	ALL 637D
	TE 3A	AND 815B
	TOPOS 1A	PLACE 830A
	CHRISTOS 2	ANOINTED ONE 895D
3	APO V4	FROM 87C
	EIR8N8 2	PEACE 226D
	THEOS 3D	GOD 358A
	KURIOS 2Cy	LORD 461A
	PAT8R 3C9	FATHER 641C
	CHARIS 2C	FAVOR 885D
4	EPI IIIBy	ON 287B
	EUCHARISTEW 2	GIVE THANKS 328C
	THEOS 3C	GOD 358A
	PANTOTE	ALWAYS 614A
	CHARIS 3B	FAVOR 886B
	CHRISTOS 2	ANOINTED ONE 895D
4F	EUCHARISTEW 2	GIVE THANKS 328C
5	GNWSIS 2	KNOWLEDGE 163A
	LOGOS 1A«	WORD 478A
	PAS 2A9	EVERY RESPECT 638A
	PLOUTIZW 2	MAKE RICH 680A
5B	PAS 1A9	EVERY EACH 636D
6	BEBAIOW 1	ESTABLISH 138A
	KATHWS 3	AS 392B
	MARTURION 1B	TESTIMONY 495A
	CHRISTOS 1	ANOINTED ONE 895C
7	APEKDECHOMAI	AWAIT 82D
	APOKALUPSIS 3	REVELATION 92A
	M8 AI3	NOT 517C
	M8DEIS 1	NO 520A
	HUSTEREW 2	TO MISS 857A
	CHARISMA 1	A GIFT 887A
	HWSTE 2A9	THEREFORE 908C
7F	KURIOS 2Cv	LORD 461B

8	ANEGKL8TOS	BLAMELESS 63C
	BEBAIOW 2	ESTABLISH 138A
	HEWS IIIA	UNTIL 335B
	H8MERA 3B9	DAY 347D
	PAROUSIA 2B«	COMING 635C
	TELOS 1D9	END 819C
9	DIA AIII2B9	BY 179D
	KALEW 2	CALL 400C
	KOINWNIA 1	ASSOCIATION 439D
	KOINWNIA 4	ASSOCIATION 440B
	KURIOS 2Cy	LORD 461B
	PISTOS 1A9	TRUSTWORTHY 670C
	HUIOS 2B	SON 842D
10	AUTOS 4A	THE SAME 123B
	AUTOS 4B	THE SAME 123B
	GNWM8 !	MIND 162B
	DIA AIIIF	BY 179C
	EIMI 14	TO BE 222B
	HINA IIIAy	IN ORDER THAT 378B
	KATARTIZW 1B	RESTORE 418D
	KURIOS 2Cy	LORD 461B
	LEGW 11A	SAY 469B
	NOUS 3B	THE MIND 547A
	ONOMA 14C«	NAME 575C
	PARAKALEW 2	APPEAL TO 622C
	SCHISMA 2	SPLIT 805D
11	D8LOW	REVEAL 177C
	EIMI 14	TO BE 222C
	ERIS	STRIFE 309C
	HO,H8,TO III7	THE 554C
	HUPO 1A«	BY 850D
	CHLO8	CHLOE 890D
12	APOLLWS	APOLLOS 95A
	EIMI IV2	TO BE 225A
	HEKASTOS 2	EACH 236A
	K8PHAS	CEPHAS 432D
	MEN 1B	(PARTICLE) 504A
	HOUTOS 1B9	THIS 601C
12A	LEGW 12B	SAY 469D
12F	PAULOS	PAUL 643A
13	BAPTIZW 2B9	BAPTIZE 131C
	8 1C	NOR 343A
	MERIZW 1A	DIVIDE 505D
	M8 C1	NOT 519B
	ONOMA 14C9	NAME 576A
	PERI 1F	ABOUT 650C
	STAUROW 1	CRUCIFY 773A
	HUPER 1A«	IN BEHALF OF 846C
	CHRISTOS 1	ANOINTED ONE 895C
14	GAIOS 3	GAIUS 149A
	EUCHARISTEW 2	GIVE THANKS 328C
	KRISPOS	CRISPUS 454B
	OUDEIS 2A	NO ONE 596B
14=17	BAPTIZW 2B«	BAPTIZE 131C
15	BAPTIZW 2B9	BAPTIZE 131C
	EIPON 2C	SAY 225C
	ONOMA 14C9	NAME 576A
	TIS, TI 1Ay	ANY ONE 827D
16	ALLOS 1D	OTHER 39C
	LOIPOS 3B	THE REST 481B
	OIDA 5	KNOW 559A
	OIKOS 2	HOUSEHOLD 563C
	STEPHANAS	STEPHANAS 774C

Verse	Word	Gloss	Code
16	TIS, TI 2AY	ANY ONE	828B
17	APOSTELLW 1BY	SEND AWAY	98B
	GAR 1B	FOR	151B
	EUAGGELIZW 2A6	PREACH	318A
	KENOW 2	MAKE EMPTY	429C
	LOGOS 1AB	WORD	478C
	SOPHIA 1	WISDOM	766D
	STAUROS 3	THE CROSS	772C
	CHRISTOS 1	ANOINTED ONE	895C
18	APOLLUMI 2AA	PERISH	94D
	GAR 1E	FOR	151C
	DUNAMIS 1	POWER	206C
	LOGOS 1BB	WORD	479C
	MEN 1B	(PARTICLE)	504A
	MWRIA	FOOLISHNESS	533A
	HO,H8,TO III6	THE	553A
	STAUROS 3	THE CROSS	772C
	SWZW 2B	SAVE	806C
19	ATHETEW 1A	SET ASIDE	20C
	APOLLUMI 1AB	RUIN	94C
	GRAPHW 2C	WRITE	165D
	SOPHIA 1	WISDOM	766D
	SOPHOS 2	LEARNED	767D
	SUNESIS 1	INTELLIGENCE	796A
	SUNETOS	INTELLIGENT	796C
20	AIWN 2A	AGE	27A
	GRAMMATEUS 2	SCRIBES	165A
	MWRAINW 1	SHOW TO BE FOOLISH	533A
	HOUTOS 2B	THIS	601D
	OUCHI 3	NOT	603A
	SOPHIA 1	WISDOM	766D
	SOPHOS 2	LEARNED	767D
	SUZ8T8T8S	DISPUTANT	783C
20A	POU 1A	WHERE	702D
20B	POU 1A	WHERE	702D
20C	POU 1A	WHERE	702D
21	DIA AIIIID	THROUGH	179B
	EPEID8 2	SINCE	284A
	EUDOKEW 1	WELL PLEASED	319C
	K8RUGMA 2	PROCLAMATION	432A
	MWRIA	FOOLISHNESS	533B
	PISTEUW 2B	BELIEVE	667C
	SWZW 2AA	SAVE	806A
21A	SOPHIA 3B	WISDOM	767B
21B	SOPHIA 1	WISDOM	766D
22	AITEW	ASK	25B
	HELL8N 2A	GENTILE	251C
	EPEID8 2	SINCE	284A
	Z8TEW 2C	SEEK	339C
	KAI 16	AND	394A
	SARX 6	BODY	751C
	S8MEION 2A	SIGN	755D
	SOPHIA 1	WISDOM	766D
23	K8RUSSW 2BB	ANNOUNCE	432C
	MEN 1B	(PARTICLE)	504A
	MWRIA	FOOLISHNESS	533A
	SKANDALON 3	TRAP	760D
	STAUROW 1	CRUCIFY	773A
24	DUNAMIS 1	POWER	206C
	HELL8N 2A	GENTILE	251C
	IOUDAIOS 2C	JEWISH	380B
	KL8TOS	CALLED	437A
	SOPHIA 3B	WISDOM	767B
24	TE 3A	AND	815C
25	ASTHEN8S 2A	WEAK	115B
	THEOS 3FA	GOD	358B
	ISCHUROS 1A	STRONG	384A
	MWROS 2	FOOLISH	533B
	HO,H8,TO II2A	THE	553B
	HOTI 3B	THAT	594A
	SOPHOS 4	LEARNED	767D
26	BLEPW 4B	SEE	143B
	DUNATOS 1AA	POWERFUL	207D
	EUGEN8S 1	WELL BORN	319B
	KL8SIS 1	CALL	437A
	SARX 6	BODY	751C
	SOPHOS 2	LEARNED	767D
26A	POLUS IIAA	MANY	694B
27	ASTHEN8S 2A	WEAK	115B
	ISCHUROS 1B	STRONG	384A
	KATAISCHUNW 2	DISHONOR	411D
	MWROS 1	FOOLISH	533B
	HO,H8,TO II2A	THE	553B
	SOPHOS 2	LEARNED	767D
27F	EKLEGOMAI 3B	CHOOSE	241D
27F	KOSMOS 5A	WORLD	447B
27F	HO,H8,TO II2A	THE	553B
28	AGEN8S	LOW	8C
	EIMI II	TO BE	222A
	EXOUTHENEW 1	DESPISE	277B
	KATARGEW 1B	MAKE INEFFECTIVE	418B
	M8 AII2D	NOT	518C
	HO,H8,TO II3A	THE	553C
29	ENWPION 2B	BEFORE	270B
	KAUCHAOMAI 1	BOAST	427A
	M8 AI2	NOT	517C
	HOPWS 2AA	IN ORDER THAT	580C
	PAS IAA	EVERY EACH	636D
	SARX 3	BODY	751B
30	HAGIASMOS	HOLINESS	9B
	APO V4	FROM	87C
	APOLUTRWSIS 2B	REDEEMER	95D
	EN 15D	IN	259B
	SOPHIA 3A	WISDOM	767B
	TE 3A	AND	815C
	CHRISTOS 2	ANOINTED ONE	895D
31	HINA III3	IN ORDER THAT	379A
	KURIOS 2CA	LORD	460C
	KURIOS 2CY	LORD	461A
31A	KAUCHAOMAI 1	BOAST	427A
31B	KAUCHAOMAI 1	BOAST	426D

I CORINTHIANS 2

Verse	Word	Gloss	Code
1	KATAGGELLW 1	PROCLAIM	410C
	LOGOS 1AB	WORD	478C
	MARTURION 1B	TESTIMONY	495A
	MUST8RION 2	MYSTERY	532B
	SOPHIA 1	WISDOM	766D
	HUPEROCH8 1	PROMINENCE	849C
2	KAI 13	AND	393D
	KRINW 3	DECIDE	452C
	HOUTOS 2A	THIS	601A
	STAUROW 1	CRUCIFY	773A
	CHRISTOS 2	ANOINTED ONE	895C
3	ASTHENEIA 2	TIMIDITY	114D

3	GINOMAI 14Cα	COME, GO	159A
	GINOMAI 14A	BE	159C
	POLUS 11Bβ	MANY	694D
	TROMOS	TREMBLING	834D
	PHOBOS 2Aα	FEAR	871C
4	ANTHRWPINOS 3	HUMAN	67B
	APODEIXIS	PROOF	89B
	APOKALUPSIS 2	REVELATION	91D
	K8RUGMA 2	PROCLAMATION	432A
	PEITHOS	PERSUASIVE	644C
	PEITHW	PERSUASIVENESS	644C
	PNEUMA 6A	SPIRIT	683D
	SOPHIA 1	WISDOM	766D
4A	LOGOS 1Aβ	WORD	478B
4B	LOGOS 1A6	WORD	478D
5	EIMI III4	TO BE	224C
	PISTIS 2Dα	FAITH	669B
	SOPHIA 1	WISDOM	766D
6	AIWN 2A	AGE	27A
	AIWN 2A	AGE	27B
	EN I3	IN	258A
	KATARGEW 2	ABOLISH	418C
	LALEW 2	SPEAK	464D
	HOUTOS 2B	THIS	601D
	TELEIOS 2Aβ	MATURE	817A
6A	SOPHIA 2	WISDOM	767A
6B	SOPHIA 1	WISDOM	766D
6F	LALEW 2B	SPEAK	464C
6=8	ARCHWN 2	AUTHORITIES	113B
6=8	ARCHWN 3	AUTHORITIES	113C
7	AIWN 1A	TIME	26C
	APOKRUPTW	CONCEAL	93B
	DOXA 1Bβ	GLORY	203A
	EN III2	BY	260C
	MUST8RION 2	MYSTERY	532B
	PRO 2	BEFORE	708C
	PROORIZW		716A
	DECIDE UPON BEFOREHAND		
	SOPHIA 2	WISDOM	767A
8	AIWN 2A	AGE	27B
	AN 1Bβ	(PARTICLE)	47D
	GINWSKW 3A	UNDERSTAND	160B
	DOXA 1A	BRIGHTNESS	202D
	STAUROW 1	CRUCIFY	773A
9	AGAPAW 1Aβ	LOVE	4C
	ANABAINW 2	GO UP	50B
	EIDON 1A	SEE	219C
	HETOIMAZW 3	PREPARE	316C
	KARDIA 1Bβ	HEART	404C
	OUS 1	EAR	600A
	OPHTHALMOS 1	EYE	604B
10	APOKALUPTW 2	REVEAL	91C
	BATHOS 2	DEPTH	129D
	ERAUNAW	SEARCH	306C
	KAI II2	EVEN	394B
	PAS 2A6	EVERYTHING	638B
10A	PNEUMA 5A	SPIRIT	682C
10A	PNEUMA 6C	SPIRIT	684A
10B	PNEUMA 6C	SPIRIT	684A
11	ANTHRWPOS 3Aζ	MAN	68C
	GINWSKW 3A	UNDERSTAND	160B
	THEOS 3Fγ	GOD	358B
	HO,H8,TO II7	THE	554C

11	OIDA 4	KNOW	559A
	OUDEIS 2A	NO ONE	596B
11B	PNEUMA 5A	SPIRIT	682B
12	KOSMOS 7	WORLD	447D
	LAMBANW 2	RECEIVE	466B
	OIDA 4	KNOW	559A
	PNEUMA 5G	SPIRIT	683C
	CHARIZOMAI 1	GIVE FREELY	884D
12B	PNEUMA 5A	SPIRIT	682C
13	ANTHRWPINOS 3	HUMAN	67B
	DIDAKTOS 2	TAUGHT	190C
	LOGOS 1A6	WORD	478D
	PNEUMA 5Gγ	SPIRIT	683D
	PNEUMATIKOS 2Bα	SPIRITUAL	685C
	PNEUMATIKOS 2Bβ	SPIRITUAL	685C
	PNEUMATIKWS 2	SPIRITUALLY	685D
	SOPHIA 1	WISDOM	766D
	SUGKRINW 1	COMBINE	782B
	SUGKRINW 3	COMPARE	782C
	SUGKRINW 2B	COMPARE	782C
14	GINWSKW 3A	UNDERSTAND	160B
	DECHOMAI 3B	ACCEPT	176C
	MWRIA	FOOLISHNESS	533B
	PNEUMA 5A	SPIRIT	682B
	PNEUMATIKOS 2Aγ	SPIRITUAL	685B
	PNEUMATIKWS 2	SPIRITUALLY	685D
	PSUCHIKOS 1		902D
	PERTAINING TO THE SOUL		
14F	ANAKRINW 2	QUESTION	56A
14F	ANTHRWPOS 2Cβ	MAN	68A
15	ANAKRINW 2	QUESTION	56A
	AUTOS 1C	SELF	122C
	DE 1A	BUT, AND	170C
	MEN	(PARTICLE)	503C
	PNEUMATIKOS 2Aγ	SPIRITUAL	685B
16	HOS,H8,HO I8	(REL PRON)	588D
	SUMBIBAZW 4	UNITE	785C
16A	NOUS 4	THE MIND	547A
16B	NOUS 4	THE MIND	547A

1 CORINTHIANS 3

1	EN I5D	IN	259B
	LALEW 2A6	SPEAK	464B
	N8PIOS 1Bα	CHILDREN	539C
	PNEUMATIKOS 2Bβ	SPIRITUAL	685C
	SARKIKOS 3	FLESHLY	750B
	SARKINOS 2	FLESHY	750C
	TELEIOS 2Aβ	MATURE	817A
1A	HWS IIIIA	SO	906C
1B	HWS IIIIA	SO	906C
1C	HWS IIIIA	SO	906C
2	ALLA 3	BUT, YET	38A
	BRWMA 1	FOOD	147C
	GALA 2	MILK	149A
	DUNAMAI 2	ABLE	206B
	ETI 1Bα	STILL	315D
	NUN 1C	NOW	547D
	OUDE 3	NOT EVEN	596A
	OUPW	NOT YET	597D
	OUTE	NOT	600C
	POTIZW 1	GIVE TO DRINK	702C
3	ANTHRWPOS 1C	HUMAN	67D

3	ERIS	STRIFE 309C
	ETI IAα	STILL 315D
	Z8LOS 2	JEALOUSY 338B
	KATA II5Bβ	ACCORDING TO 408C
	HOPOU 2B	WHERE 580A
	PERIPATEW 2A6	GO ABOUT 655B
	TELEIOS 2B	THE INITIATE 817A
3A	SARKIKOS 3	FLESHLY 750B
3B	SARKIKOS 3	FLESHLY 750B
4	AN 3A	(PARTICLE) 48B
	EIMI IV2	TO BE 225A
	SARKIKOS 3	FLESHLY 750B
	TIS, TI IAε .	ANY ONE 828A
4F	PAULOS	PAUL 643A
4→6	APOLLWS	APOLLOS 95A
5	DIAKONOS IA	SERVANT 183D
	KAI I3	AND 393D
	OUN ICβ	THEREFORE 597C
	OUN 3	THEREFORE 597D
	PISTEUW 2B	BELIEVE 667C
	HWS I2C	AS 905D
5A	TIS, TI IAβ	WHICH 826D
5B	TIS, TI IAβ	WHICH 826D
6F	AUXANW I	GROW 121B
6→8	POTIZW 3	GIVE TO DRINK 702C
6→8	PHUTEUW	PLANT 878A
7	EIMI II6B	TO BE 223C
	OUTE	NOT 600C
	TIS, TI IBε	ANY ONE 828A
	HWSTE IA	THEREFORE 908B
8	EIMI II7	TO BE 223D
	HEIS IB	ONE 230A
	IDIOS IAβ	ONES OWN 370B
	KATA II5Aβ	ACCORDING TO 408A
	KOPOS 2	WORK 444C
	LAMBANW 2	RECEIVE 466B
	MISTHOS 2A	REWARD 525B
	HO,H8,TO IIIOC	THE 555A
9	GEWRGION	CULTIVATED LAND 156B
	OIKODOM8 2B	BUILDING 561D
	SUNERGOS	WORKING WITH 795C
10	ARCHITEKTWN	MASTER BUILDER 112D
	BLEPW 4C	SEE 143B
	EPOIKODOMEW IB	BUILD ON TO 305B
	THEMELIOS 2A	FOUNDATION 356B
	PWS 2A	HOW 739D
	SOPHOS I	CLEVER 767D
	CHARIS 4	FAVOR 886C
	HWS IIIIA	SO 906B
IOF	TITH8MI IIAα	PUT 823C
II	ALLOS IEβ	ANOTHER 39C
	THEMELIOS 2B	FOUNDATION 356C
	KEIMAI IB	LIE 428A
	OUDEIS 2A	NO ONE 596B
	PARA III3	IN COMPARISON 616B
	CHRISTOS I	ANOINTED ONE 895C
12	ARGURION I	SILVER 104B
	ARGUROS 2	SILVER 104C
	EPOIKODOMEW IB	BUILD ON TO 305C
	THEMELIOS 2A	FOUNDATION 356B
	KALAM8	STRAW 399C
	LITHOS IB	STONE 475B
	LITHOS IC	STONE 475C
12	XULON I	WOOD 551B
	TIMIOS IA	VALUABLE 825D
	CHORTOS	GRASS 892B
	CHRUSION	GOLD 896D
	CHRUSOS	GOLD 897A
13	APOKALUPTW 4	REVEAL 91D
	GINOMAI I4B	BECOME 158D
	D8LOW	REVEAL 177C
	DOKIMAZW 2A	EXAMINE 201C
	EIMI II6D	TO BE 223D
	ERGON 3	WORK 308C
	H8MERA 3Bβ	DAY 348A
	HO,H8,TO IIIAα	THE 552D
	HOPOIOS	WHAT SORT 579B
	PHANEROS I	CLEAR 860B
13A	PUR IB	FIRE 737C
13B	PUR IB	FIRE 737C
14	EPOIKODOMEW IB	BUILD ON TO 305B
	ERGON 3	WORK 308C
	LAMBANW 2	RECEIVE 466B
	MENW ICβ	REMAIN 505C
	MISTHOS 2A	REWARD 525B
15	AUTOS IC	SELF 122C
	DIA AI2	THROUGH 178C
	ERGON 3	WORK 308C
	Z8MIOW 2	BE PUNISHED 339A
	KATAKAIW	CONSUME 412A
	HOUTW 2	THUS 602C
	PUR IA	FIRE 737B
	SWZW 3	SAVE 806C
	HWS II	AS 905B
16	EN I5A	IN 258D
	NAOS 2	TEMPLE 535D
	HO,H8,TO IIII	THE 555A
	OIDA IE	KNOW 558C
	OIKEW I	DWELL 559C
	PNEUMA 5A	SPIRIT 682B
16F	OIKOPHTHOROS	564B
	DESTROYING HOUSES	
17	HAGIOS IAβ	WORTHY OF GOD 9C
	HOUTOS IAε	THIS 601B
17A	NAOS 2	TEMPLE 535D
17A	PHTHEIRW IB	RUIN 865A
17B	NAOS 2	TEMPLE 535D
17B	PHTHEIRW 2C	RUIN 865B
18	AIWN 2A	AGE 27A
	GINOMAI I4A	BECOME 158C
	DOKEW IB	THINK 200D
	EXAPATAW	DECEIVE 272C
	KENOS 2Aα	EMPTY 429A
	M8DEIS 2A	NO 520A
	MWROS I	FOOLISH 533B
18A	SOPHOS 3	LEARNED 767D
18B	SOPHOS 3	LEARNED 767D
19	DRASSOMAI	CATCH 205D
	KOSMOS 7	WORLD 447D
	MWRIA	FOOLISHNESS 533A
	PANOURGIA	CUNNING 613A
	PARA II2B	BESIDE 615C
	SOPHIA I	WISDOM 766D
	SOPHOS 2	LEARNED 767D
20	GINWSKW 6C	KNOW 160D
	DIALOGISMOS I	THOUGHT 185B

20 MATAIOS — IDLE 496C
HOTI IB[— THAT 593A
PALIN 3 — AGAIN 611D
SOPHOS 2 — LEARNED 767D
21 KAUCHAOMAI 1 — BOAST 426D
PAS 2A6 — EVERYTHING 638C
HWSTE IB — THEREFORE 9088
22 APOLLWS — APOLLOS 95A
EI VII3B — IF 219B
ENIST8MI 1 — BE PRESENT 266B
ZW8 1A — LIFE 340D
THANATOS 1A — DEATH 351B
K8PHAS — CEPHAS 432D
KOSMOS 2 — WORLD 446D
MELLW 2 — IS DESTINED 502D
PAS 2A6 — EVERYTHING 638C
PAULOS — PAUL 643A
23 EIMI IVI — TO BE 225A

I CORINTHIANS 4

1 ANTHRWPOS 3AY — MAN 68B
LOGIZOMAI IB — CONSIDER 477B
MUST8RION 2 — MYSTERY 532B
OIKONOMOS 2 — MANAGER 562D
HOUTW 2 — THUS 602C
*HUP8RET8S — SERVANT 850C
HWS IIIIC — SO 906D
2 EN I2 — IN 258A
HEURISKW 2 — FIND 326A
Z8TEW 2C — SEEK 339D
HINA IIIA« — IN ORDER THAT 378A
LOIPOS 3B — THE REST 481B
OIKONOMOS 1A — MANAGER 562C
PISTOS IA« — TRUSTWORTHY 670B
HWDE 2B — HERE 903D
3 ALLA 3 — BUT, YET 38A
ANAKRINW IB — QUESTION 56A
ANTHRWPINOS 3 — HUMAN 67B
EIMI III2 — TO BE 224B
ELACHISTOS 2A — SMALLEST 248B
H8MERA 3B« — DAY 347D
HINA IIIB — IN ORDER THAT 378C
OUDE 3 — NOT EVEN 596A
3F ANAKRINW IB — QUESTION 56A
4 DIKAIOW — JUSTIFY 196C
*DIKAIOW 3A — JUSTIFY 196D
EMAUTOU 2 — MYSELF 253B
EN III3A — BECAUSE OF 260C
KURIOS 2CY — LORD 460D
PARA III5 — BECAUSE OF 616C
SUNOIDA 2 — SHARE KNOWLEDGE 799A
5 APO V4 — FROM 87C
BOUL8 1 — PURPOSE 145A
GINOMAI I3BY — TAKE PLACE 158B
EPAINOS IA« — PRAISE 281B
ERCHOMAI IIAη — COME 311A
HEWS IIB — UNTIL 334D
KAIROS 4 — TIME 396B
KARDIA IBY — HEART 404D
KRINW 6B — JUDGE 453B
KRUPTOS 2A — HIDDEN 455A
M8 AI3 — NOT 517C

5 PRO 2 — BEFORE 708C
SKOTOS 2A — DARKNESS 765B
TOTE 2 — AT THAT TIME 831D
PHANEROW IA — REVEAL 860C
PHWTIZW 2C — SHINE 881C
HWSTE IB — THEREFORE 908B
6 APOLLWS — APOLLOS 95A
GRAPHW 2C — WRITE 166A
EMAUTOU 3 — MYSELF 253B
EN I2 — IN 258A
HETEROS IA — OTHER 315A
HINA I3 — IN ORDER THAT 377D
KATA I2B« — DOWN 406C
MANTHANW 1 — LEARN 491C
METASCH8MATIZW — TRANSFORM 515A
HUPER IA6 — IN BEHALF OF 846C
HUPER 2 — BEYOND 847A
HUPER 3 — BEYOND 847C
PHRONEW 1 — THINK 874B
PHUSIOW — BLOW UP 877B
7 DIAKRINW IB — DIFFERENTIATE 184B
EI VI2 — BUT IF 218D
ECHW I2A — HAVE 332B
KAUCHAOMAI 1 — BOAST 427A
LAMBANW 2 — RECEIVE 466B
M8 AII2C — NOT 518B
HWS III2 — SO 906D
7B TIS, TI IB« — WHICH 826D
7C TIS, TI 3A — WHICH 827B
8 BASILEUW 2 — BECOME KING 136B
GE 3H — INDEED 152C
KORENNUMI 2 — SATIATE 445C
OPHELON — O THAT 604A
PLOUTEW 2 — BE RICH 680A
SUMBASILEUW RULE WITH SOMEONE 785B
CHWRIS 2A« — APART 898D
9 AGGELOS 2B — ANGEL 8A
ANTHRWPOS IAß — MAN 67C
APODEIKNUMI 1 — MAKE 89A
APOSTOLOS 3 — APOSTLES 99B
GINOMAI I4A — BECOME 158C
DOKEW IE — THINK 201A
DOKEW ID — THINK 201A
EPITHANATIOS — 292D
CONDEMNED TO DEATH
ESCHATOS 2 — LAST 314A
THEATRON 2 — SPECTACLE 354A
KOSMOS 3 — WORLD 446D
HOTI 3B — THAT 594A
SUMBASILEUW RULE WITH SOMEONE 785B
10 ASTHEN8S 2A — WEAK 115B
ATIMOS 1 — DISHONORED 119D
EN I5D — IN 259B
ENDOXOS 1 — HONORED 262D
ISCHUROS IB — STRONG 384A
MWROS 1 — FOOLISH 533B
PHRONIMOS — THOUGHTFUL 874C
PHRONIMOS — THOUGHTFUL 874D
10A SU IA — YOU 779D
10B SU IA — YOU 779D
10C SU IA — YOU 779D
11 ARTI 3 — NOW 110A
ASTATEW — BE UNSTEADY 117A

11	ACHRI IA	UNTIL	128B
	GUMNITEUW	BE POORLY CLOTHED	166D
	DIPSAW I	THIRST	199C
	KOLAPHIZW I	STRIKE	441D
	PEINAW I	HUNGER	645D
	HWRA 2B	TIME OF DAY	904D
12	ANECHW IC	ENDURE	65B
	DIWKW 2	PERSECUTE	200B
	ERGAZOMAI I	WORK	306D
	EULOGEW 2A	BLESS	322C
	IDIOS 2A	ONES OWN	370C
	KOPIAW 2	BECOME WEARY	444B
	LOIDOREW	REVILE	480C
	CHEIR I	HAND	888B
13	ARTI 3	NOW	110A
	BLASPH8MEW I	DEFAME	142A
	GINOMAI III	BE	159B
	DUSPH8MEW	SLANDER	209A
	HEWS IIIC	UNTIL	335C
	KOSMOS 5A	WORLD	447B
	PARAKALEW 5	IMPLORE	623A
	PERIKATHARMA	DIRT	653C
	PERIPS8MA	DIRT	659C
	HWS II3B	SO	906A
	HWSPEREI	LIKE	908B
14	AGAP8TOS 2	BELOVED	6C
	ENTREPW IA	MAKE ASHAMED	269B
	NOUTHETEW	ADMONISH	546B
	TEKNON 2B	CHILD	816B
	HWS IIIIA	SO	906C
15	ALLA 4	BUT, YET	38B
	GENNAW IB	BEGET	154D
	DIA AIIIID	THROUGH	179B
	EN I5D	IN	259B
	EN I5D	IN	259C
	EUAGGELION IA	GOSPEL	318A
	ECHW I2Bβ	HAVE	332D
	MURIOS	INNUMERABLE	531C
	PAIDAGWGOS	ATTENDANT	608B
	PAT8R 2A	FATHER	640D
	POLUS IIAα	MANY	694B
16	EGW	I	213C
	MIM8T8S I	IMITATOR	524A
	OUN IA	THEREFORE	597B
	PARAKALEW 2	APPEAL TO	622C
17	AGAP8TOS 2	BELOVED	6C
	ANAMIMN8SKW	REMIND	57C
	DIDASKW I	TEACH	191A
	EKKL8SIA 4B	CHURCH	240B
	EN I5D	IN	259B
	KATHWS I	JUST AS	392B
	KURIOS 2Cγ	LORD	461A
	HODOS 2C	WAY	557B
	HOS,H8,HO I8	(REL PRON)	588D
	PANTACHOU I	EVERYWHERE	613B
	PEMPW I	SEND	647C
	PISTOS IAα	TRUSTWORTHY	670B
	TEKNON 2B	CHILD	816B
	TIMOTHEOS	TIMOTHY	826A
18	DE 4B	BUT, AND	170D
	M8 AII2C	NOT	518B
	TIS, TI IAβ	ANY ONE	827D
	HWS III2	SO	906D

18F	PHUSIOW	BLOW UP	877B
19	THELW 2	WISH	355D
	KURIOS 2D	LORD	461B
	LOGOS IAα	WORD	478B
	TACHEWS IA	QUICKLY	814B
19F	DUNAMIS I	POWER	207A
20	BASILEIA 3B	KINGDOM	134D
	BASILEIA 3G	KINGDOM	135B
	LOGOS IAα	WORD	478B
21	AGAP8 IIA	LOVE	5C
	EN I4Cβ	IN	258C
	ERCHOMAI IIAβ	COME	310C
	8 IDγ	OR	343A
	THELW I	WISH	355B
	PNEUMA 3C	SPIRIT	681D
	PRAUT8S	HUMILITY	705D
	RABDOS	ROD	740D
	TE IB	AND	815B
	TIS, TI IBγ	WHICH	827A

I CORINTHIANS 5

I	AKOUW 3B	LEARN	31D
	GUN8 2	WIFE	167C
	ECHW I2Bα	HAVE	332C
	HOLWS	GENERALLY SPEAKING	568A
	ONOMAZW 3	NAME	577C
	OUDE 3	NOT EVEN	596A
	PAT8R IA	FATHER	640C
	TOIOUTOS 2Aγ	SUCH A KIND	829A
	HWSTE 2Aβ	THEREFORE	908C
IA	PORNEIA I	PROSTITUTION	699D
IB	PORNEIA I	PROSTITUTION	699D
2	AIRW 4	TAKE AWAY	24B
	EK IB	AWAY FROM	233C
	EXAIRW	REMOVE	271C
	ERGON ICβ	DEED	308A
	KAI I2G	AND	393C
	MALLON 3B	RATHER	490D
	MESOS 2	THE MIDDLE	509A
	OUCHI I	NOT	603A
	PENTHEW I	BE SAD	648B
	POIEW IIBα	DO	687C
	PRASSW IA	DO	705A
	PHUSIOW	BLOW UP	877B
3	APEIMI I	BE ABSENT	82C
	*GAR IE	FOR	151C
	KATERGAZOMAI I	ACHIEVE	422C
	HOUTW IB	THUS	602B
	SWMA IB	BODY	806D
	SWMA IB	BODY	807A
3A	PAREIMI IA	BE PRESENT	629C
3B	PAREIMI IA	BE PRESENT	629C
3=5	KRINW 3	DECIDE	452C
3=5	PNEUMA 3A	SPIRIT	681B
4	DUNAMIS I	POWER	206C
	KURIOS 2Cγ	LORD	461B
	ONOMA I4Cγ	NAME	576B
	SUNAGW 2	GATHER	790B
5	H8MERA 3Bβ	DAY	347D
	OLETHROS	DESTRUCTION	566A
	PARADIDWMI IB	GIVE OVER	620B
	SARX 2	BODY	751A

5   SATAN   ADVERSARY 752C
    SWZW 2B   SAVE 806B
    TOIOUTOS 3Aα   SUCH A KIND 829B
6   DOLOW   FALSIFY 202C
    ZUMB I   LEAVEN 340C
    ZUMOW   FERMENT 340C
    KALOS 2B   GOOD 401C
    KAUCH8MA I   BOAST 427B
    MIKROS 2A   SMALL 523B
    OIDA IE   KNOW 558C
    PHURAMA   THAT WHICH IS MIXED 877A
7   AZUMOS 2   UNLEAVENED BREAD 19C
    GAR IB   FOR 151A
    EKKATHAIRW I   CLEANSE 239D
    ZUMB 2   LEAVEN 340C
    THUW 2   SACRIFICE 367D
    KATHWS 3   AS 392B
    NEOS IAα   NEW 537D
    PALAIOW 2   MAKE OLD 611A
    PASCHA 2   THE PASCHAL LAMB 639A
    HUPER IAγ   IN BEHALF OF 846B
    PHURAMA   THAT WHICH IS MIXED 877A
7F PALAIOS 2   OLD 610D
8   AZUMOS IA   UNLEAVENED BREAD 19C
    AL8THEIA I   TRUTHFULNESS 35A
    EILIKRINEIA   SINCERITY 221D
    EN I4Cβ   IN 258C
    HEORTAZW   CELEBRATE 279D
    KAKIA IA   BADNESS 397C
    M8 AIIII   NOT 518C
    M8DE IA   AND NOT 519C
    PON8RIA   WICKEDNESS 697A
    HWSTE IB   THEREFORE 908B
9   EN IID   IN 257D
    EPISTOL8   LETTER 300D
    M8 AIIIBβ   NOT 517D
    HO,H8,TO IIIAα   THE 552B
    PORNOS   FORNICATOR 700B
    SUNANAMEIGNUMI   MINGLE 792A
10 ARA I   THEN 103B
    EIDWLOLATR8S   IDOLATER 220C
    EXERCHOMAI IB6   GO OUT 274C
    EPEI 2   BECAUSE 283D
    OU 2A   NO 594B
    OPHEILW 2Aβ   OWE 603D
    PANTWS 5B   NOT AT ALL 614B
    PORNOS   FORNICATOR 700B
10A KOSMOS 7   WORLD 447D
10B KOSMOS 4B   WORLD 447A
10F HARPAX 2   SWINDLER 108D
10F PLEONEKT8S   673C
    A COVETOUS PERSON
11 ADELPHOS 2   BROTHER 16A
    EIDWLOLATR8S   IDOLATER 220C
    8   IAβ   OR 342D
    LOIDOROS   REVILER 480D
    METHUSOS   DRUNKARD 500C
    M8 AIIIBβ   NOT 517D
    M8DE 2   NOT EVEN 519D
    NUN 2   NOW 548A
    NUNI 2B   NOW 548C
    ONOMAZW I   NAME 577B
    PLEONEKT8S   A COVETOUS PERSON 673C

11 PORNOS   FORNICATOR 700B
    SUNANAMEIGNUMI   MINGLE 792A
    SUNESTHIW   EAT WITH 796A
12 ESW 2   IN 314C
    ESWTHEN 2   INSIDE 314C
    TIS, TI IBε   WHICH 827B
12A KRINW 4Aα   JUDGE 452D
12B KRINW 4Aα   JUDGE 452D
12F EXW IAβ   OUTSIDE 279A
13 EXAIRW   REMOVE 271C
    KRINW 4Bα   JUDGE 452D
    PON8ROS 2A   WICKED 697D

            I CORINTHIANS 6

I   ADIKOS I   UNJUST 18A
    EPI IIA6   BEFORE 286A
    HETEROS IBε   ANOTHER 315C
    ECHW I7A   HAVE 334B
    OUCHI I   NOT 602D
    PRAGMA 5   LAW SUIT 704A
    PROS III4A   TOWARD 717C
    TIS, TI IAα   ANY ONE 827C
    TOLMAW IB   DARE 829C
1F HAGIOS 2Dβ   SAINTS 10A
2   ANAXIOS   UNWORTHY 58B
    ELACHISTOS 2A   SMALLEST 248B
    EN I3   IN 258B
    EN IIIB   BY 260B
    KRIT8RION I   LAWCOURT 454B
2A KOSMOS 5A   WORLD 447B
2A KRINW 4Bβ   JUDGE 453B
2B KOSMOS 5A   WORLD 447B
2B KRINW 4Bβ   JUDGE 453B
2F OIDA IE   KNOW 558C
3   AGGELOS 2C   ANGEL   8B
    GE 3F   LET ALONE 152B
    M8TIGE   LET ALONE 522B
4   BIWTIKOS   BELONGING TO LIFE 141C
    EAN I   IF 210B
    EKKL8SIA 4D   CHURCH 240C
    EXOUTHENEW I   DESPISE 277B
    KATHIZW IB   APPOINT 390D
    KRIT8RION I   LAWCOURT 454B
    MEN 2E   (PARTICLE) 504C
    HOUTOS IAε   THIS 601B
5   ANA IB   AMONG 49B
    DIAKRINW ID   JUDGE 184B
    ENI   THERE IS NOT 265D
    ENTROP8 I   SHAME 269C
    LEGW IIIF   DECLARE 471A
    MESOS 2   THE MIDDLE 508C
    OUDEIS 2A   NO ONE 596B
    HOUTW IB   THUS 602C
    PROS III3A   TOWARD 717A
    SOPHOS I   CLEVER 767D
6   ALLA IA   BUT, YET 37C
    APISTOS 2   FAITHLESS 85A
    KAI I3   AND 393D
    KRINW 4Aβ   JUDGE 452D
    META AII3A   WITH 510C
    HOUTOS IBγ   THIS 601D
7   ADIKEW 2A   DO WRONG 17B

7	APOSTEREW	STEAL 98D	15 OUN ICα	THEREFORE 597B
	DIA BII2	WHY 180B	POIEW IIB₁	DO 688B
	ECHW I7A	HAVE 334A	PORN8 I	PROSTITUTE 700B
	8D8 2	ALREADY 344D	15F OIDA IE	KNOW 558C
	H8TT8MA	DEFEAT 350C	16 DUO ID	TWO 208B
	KRIMA I	DISPUTE 451C	EAN I3B	IF 210D
	MEN 2A	(PARTICLE) 504B	EIMI III2	TO BE 224A
	HOLWS	GENERALLY SPEAKING 568A	HEIS IB	ONE 230A
7A	MALLON 3B	RATHER 490D	8 IDα	OR 343A
7A	OUCHI 3	NOT 603A	KOLLAW 2Bα	UNITE 442C
7B	MALLON 3B	RATHER 490D	PORN8 I	PROSTITUTE 700B
7B	OUCHI 3	NOT 603A	SARX 2	BODY 751A
8	ADIKEW 2A	DO WRONG 17B	SWMA IB	BODY 807B
	APOSTEREW	STEAL 98C	PH8MI IC	SAY 864B
	KAI I3	AND 393D	16F HEIS 2A	ONE 230B
	HOUTOS IBɣ	THIS 601D	17 KOLLAW 2Bα	UNITE 442C
9	ADIKOS I	UNJUST 18A	KURIOS 2Cɣ	LORD 460D
	ARSENOKOIT8S	109B	PNEUMA 5D3	SPIRIT 683B
	A MALE HOMOSEXUAL		18 HAMARTANW 4B	SIN 42A
	BASILEIA 3B	KINGDOM 134D	HAMART8MA	SIN 42B
	EIDWLOLATR8S	IDOLATER 220C	EIMI II9A	TO BE 223D
	8 IDα	OR 343A	EKTOS 2A	OUTSIDE 245C
	MALAKOS 2	EFFEMINATE 490A	IDIOS 2C	ONES OWN 370C
	M8 AIII3A	NOT 518C	PAS IAβ	EVERY EACH 636D
	MOICHOS I	ADULTERER 528C	POIEW IICɣ	DO 688C
	OIDA IE	KNOW 558C	PORNEIA I	PROSTITUTION 700A
	PLANAW 2Cɣ	DECEIVE 671C	PORNEUW I	TO PROSTITUTE 700B
	PORNOS	FORNICATOR 700C	PHEUGW 3	FLEE 863D
9F	BASILEIA 3G	KINGDOM 135A	18A SWMA IB	BODY 806D
9F	BASILEIA 3G	KINGDOM 135B	18B SWMA IB	BODY 806D
9F	KL8RONOMEW 2	INHERIT 435D	19 APO V4	FROM 87C
9F	OUTE	NOT 600C	EIMI IVI	TO BE 224D
10	HARPAX 2	SWINDLER 108D	8 IDα	OR 343A
	BASILEIA 3B	KINGDOM 134D	NAOS 2	TEMPLE 535D
	KLEPT8S	THIEF 435C	OIDA IE	KNOW 558C
	LOIDOROS	REVILER 480D	OIKOPHTHOROS	564B
	METHUSOS	DRUNKARD 500C	DESTROYING HOUSES	
	PLEONEKT8S	A COVETOUS PERSON 673C	HOS,H8,HO I4A	(REL PRON) 587D
11	HAGIAZW 2	CONSECRATE 8D	PNEUMA 5Cα	SPIRIT 682D
	APOLOUW	WASH ONESELF 95C	20 AGORAZW 2	BUY 12D
	DIKAIOW 3C	MAKE FREE 197A	D8 2	NOW 177B
	KURIOS 2Cɣ	LORD 461B	DOXAZW I	PRAISE 203C
	ONOMA I4Cɣ	NAME 576D	THEOPHOROS	INSPIRED 359B
	HOUTOS IBζ	THIS 601D	SWMA IB	BODY 807A
	PNEUMA 5A	SPIRIT 682B	TIM8 I	VALUE 825A
	TIS, TI IAα	ANY ONE 827D		
12	EXESTI 2	IT IS POSSIBLE 274C	I CORINTHIANS 7	
	EXOUSIAZW	ONE IN AUTHORITY 278C		
	SUMPHERW 2A	HELP 787D	I ANTHRWPOS 2Bα	MAN 67D
	TIS, TI IAɣ	ANY ONE 827D	HAPTW 2A	TOUCH 102B
13	ALLA IB	BUT, YET 37D	GRAPHW 2D	WRITE 166B
	KATARGEW 2	ABOLISH 418B	DE IC	BUT, AND 170C
	KOILIA I	BELLY 438B	KALOS 3B	GOOD 401C
	PORNEIA I	PROSTITUTION 699D	M8 AIIIC	NOT 518A
13A	BRWMA I	FOOD 147C	HOS,H8,HO I4A	(REL PRON) 587D
13B	BRWMA I	FOOD 147C	PERI IH	ABOUT 650D
13F	KURIOS 2Cɣ	LORD 460D	2 PORNEIA I	PROSTITUTION 700A
14	EGEIRW IAβ	RAISE 213D	2A ECHW I2Bα	HAVE 332C
	EXEGEIRW 2	RAISE 273B	2B ECHW I2Bα	HAVE 332C
15	AIRW 4	TAKE AWAY 24B	2FF AN8R I	MAN 65D
	GINOMAI I3A	TAKE PLACE 157D	2FF GUN8 2	WIFE 167C
	MELOS 3	MEMBER 503A	3 APODIDWMI I	GIVE AWAY 90A
	M8 AIII2	NOT 518C	EUNOIA I	FAVOR 323C

Verse	Word	Meaning	No.
3	OPHEIL8 2A	DEBT	603B
	OPHEILW 2Aα	OWE	603C
3F	HOMOIWS	LIKEWISE	570D
4	EXOUSIAZW	ONE IN AUTHORITY	278C
4A	IDIOS 1B	ONES OWN	370B
4A	SWMA 1B	BODY	806D
4B	IDIOS 1B	ONES OWN	370B
4B	SWMA 1B	BODY	806D
5	AKRASIA	SELF INDULGENCE	32B
	AN 6	(PARTICLE)	49A
	APOSTEREW	STEAL	98C
	EI VI9	UNLESS INDEED	219A
	EIMI III5C	TO BE	224C
	EK 6C	FROM	235D
	EPI IIIIAζ	ON	288C
	HINA IIC	IN ORDER THAT	377C
	KAIROS I	TIME	395C
	M8 AIII3A	NOT	518C
	N8STEIA 2B	FASTING	540A
	PALIN IB	AGAIN	611C
	PEIRAZW 2D	TRY	646B
	PROS III2B	TOWARD	717A
	PROSEUCH8 I	PRAYER	720C
	SATAN	ADVERSARY	752B
	SUMPHWNOS 2	AGREEING	789A
	SUNERCHOMAI IB	ASSEMBLE	796A
	SCHOLAZW I	HAVE TIME	805C
6	EPITAG8	COMMAND	302A
	KATA II5Bβ	ACCORDING TO	408C
	LEGW I5	SAY	470A
	LEGW IIIF	DECLARE	471A
	SUGGNWM8	CONCESSION	780C
7	ALLA 2	BUT, YET	38A
	ANTHRWPOS 3Aζ	MAN	68C
	EK 3C	FROM	234B
	EMAUTOU 3	MYSELF	253B
	THELW I	WISH	355C
	IDIOS IAβ	ONES OWN	370B
	KAI II3	ALSO	394B
	MEN IC	(PARTICLE)	504A
	HO,H8,TO I2	THE	552A
	HOUTW IB	THUS	602C
	PAS IB	ALL	637A
	CHARISMA 2	A GIFT	887A
7F	HWS II3B	SO	906A
8	AGAMOS	UNMARRIED	4A
	KAGW 3C	I	387A
	KALOS 3B	GOOD	401C
	KALOS 3C	GOOD	401D
	MENW IB	REMAIN	505B
	CH8RA	THE WIDOW	889D
9	EGKRATEUOMAI	ABSTAIN	215D
	EI IIA	IF	218A
	KREITTWN 2	BETTER	451A
	PUROW IB	SET ON FIRE	738C
9F	GAMEW 2	MARRY	150A
10	ALLA IB	BUT, YET	37D
	KURIOS 2Cγ	LORD	460D
	PARAGGELLW	GIVE ORDERS	618C
	CHWRIZW 2A	DIVIDE	898C
IOF	M8 AIIIBβ	NOT	517D
IOFF	AN8R I	MAN	65D
II	AGAMOS	UNMARRIED	4A

Verse	Word	Meaning	No.
II	EAN IIB	IF	210B
	EAN I3A	IF	210D
	8 IAα	OR	342B
	KATALLASSW 2B	RECONCILE	415B
	MENW IB	REMAIN	505B
	CHWRIZW 2A	DIVIDE	898C
IIFF	APHI8MI IB	DIVORCE	125C
12	APISTOS 2	FAITHLESS	85A
	ECHW I2Bα	HAVE	332C
	KURIOS 2Cγ	LORD	460D
	LOIPOS 2Bα	THE OTHERS	481A
12F	M8 AIII3A	NOT	518C
12F	OIKEW I	DWELL	559C
12F	SUNEUDOKEW	AGREE WITH	796C
13	ECHW I2Bα	HAVE	332C
13F	APISTOS 2	FAITHLESS	85A
14	HAGIAZW 2	CONSECRATE	8D
	HAGIOS IBα	DEDICATED TO GOD	9D
	AKATHARTOS I	IMPURE	28C
	APISTOS 2	FAITHLESS	85A
	ARA I	THEN	103B
	EN III3A	BECAUSE OF	260C
	EPEI 2	BECAUSE	283D
	NUN 2	NOW	548A
	TEKNON IAα	CHILD	816A
15	ADELPH8 3	SISTER	15C
	APISTOS 2	FAITHLESS	85A
	DOULOW 2	ENSLAVE	205B
	EIR8N8 IC	PEACE	226C
	KALEW 2	CALL	400D
	TOIOUTOS 3Aβ	SUCH A KIND	829B
15A	CHWRIZW 2A	DIVIDE	898C
15B	CHWRIZW 2A	DIVIDE	898C
16	EI V2A	WHETHER	218D
	8 ID6	OR	343B
	OIDA	KNOW	558A
16A	OIDA IF	KNOW	558C
16A	SWZW 2Aβ	SAVE	806B
16B	OIDA IF	KNOW	558C
16B	SWZW 2Aβ	SAVE	806B
17	DIATASSW	ORDER	188D
	EKKL8SIA 4B	CHURCH	240C
	KURIOS 2D	LORD	461B
	MERIZW 2B	ASSIGN	506A
	M8 AII	NOT	517C
	PAS IDα	ALL	637C
	PERIPATEW 2Aγ	GO ABOUT	655B
17A	HOUTW IA	THUS	602B
17A	HWS I2C	AS	905D
17B	HWS I2C	AS	905D
17F	KALEW 2	CALL	400C
18	EPISPAOMAI 3	CONCEAL CIRCUMCISION	299D
	M8 AIII3A	NOT	518C
18A	PERITEMNW I	CUT AROUND	658A
18B	PERITEMNW I	CUT AROUND	658A
18F	AKROBUSTIA I	UNCIRCUMCISED	33A
19	ENTOL8 2B	COMMAND	268D
	PERITOM8 2	CIRCUMCISION	658D
	T8R8SIS 3	OBSERVANCE	823A
19A	OUDEIS 2Bβ	WORTHLESS	596C
19B	OUDEIS 2Bβ	WORTHLESS	596C
20	KL8SIS 2	CALL	437A

20	MENW IB	REMAIN	505B
	HOUTOS IAε	THIS	601B
20≈2	KALEW 2	CALL	400C
21	ALLA IA	BUT, YET	37C
	EI VI4	EVEN IF	219A
	ELEUTHEROS I	FREE	250A
	MALLON 2A	RATHER	490B
	MELEI 4	IT IS A CONCERN	501B
	CHRAOMAI IA	USE	892C
21F	DOULOS IB	SLAVE	204D
22	APELEUTHEROS	FREEDMAN	83A
	DOULOS 4	SLAVE	205B
	ELEUTHEROS I	FREE	250B
22A	KURIOS 2Cγ	LORD	461A
22B	KURIOS 2Cγ	LORD	460D
23	AGORAZW 2	BUY	12D
	ANTHRWPOS IAβ	MAN	67C
	DOULOS 3	SLAVE	205A
	TIM8 I	VALUE	825A
24	KALEW 2	CALL	400C
	PARA II2E	BESIDE	615D
25	GNWM8 2	JUDGMENT	162B
	DIDWMI IBα	GIVE	192A
	ELEEW	HAVE MERCY	249B
	EPITAG8	COMMAND	302A
	ECHW I2I	HAVE	333D
	PARTHENOS I	VIRGIN	632B
	PERI IH	ABOUT	650D
	PISTOS IAα	TRUSTWORTHY	670C
	HWS IIIIA	SO	906C
25B	KURIOS 2Cγ	LORD	461A
26	ANAGK8 2	DISTRESS	52B
	ANTHRWPOS 3Aγ	MAN	68B
	ENIST8MI 2	BE IMMINENT	266B
	NOMIZW 2	THINK	543B
	OUN IA	THEREFORE	597B
	HOUTW IB	THUS	602B
	HUPARCHW 2	BE	846A
26A	KALOS 3A	GOOD	401C
26B	KALOS 3B	GOOD	401C
26B	KALOS 3C	GOOD	401D
27	DEW 3	BIND	177A
	LUSIS	A DIVORCE	483C
	LUW 2B	RELEASE	485A
27A	Z8TEW 2Bα	SEEK	339C
27B	Z8TEW 2A	SEEK	339C
28	HAMARTANW I	SIN	41D
	GAMEW IB	MARRY	150A
	EAN I3A	IF	210D
	ECHW I2Eα	HAVE	333A
	THLIPSIS I	TRIBULATION	363A
	PARTHENOS I	VIRGIN	632B
	SARX 5	BODY	751B
	TOIOUTOS 3Aα	SUCH A KIND	829B
	PHEIDOMAI I	SPARE	862C
28B	GAMEW 3Aβ	MARRY	150B
29	EIMI II4A	TO BE	223A
	ECHW I2Bα	HAVE	332C
	HINA II2	IN ORDER THAT	379A
	HINA IV	IN ORDER THAT	379B
	KAIROS 4	TIME	396B
	LOIPOS 3Aα	THE REST	481B
	HO,H8,TO II6	THE	554C

29	HOUTOS IBβ	THIS	601C
	SUSTELLW I	LIMIT	802D
	PH8MI 2	SAY	864B
29≈31	HWS II3B	SO	906A
30	AGORAZW I	BUY	12C
	KATECHW IBγ	KEEP	424A
	KLAIW I	WEEP	434B
30A	CHAIRW I	REJOICE	881B
30B	CHAIRW I	REJOICE	881B
31	KATACHRAOMAI	USE	421D
	PARAGW 2Aβ	BRING IN	619A
	PARACHRAOMAI	MISUSE	629B
	SCH8MA 2	BEARING	805A
	CHRAOMAI IA	USE	892C
	CHRAOMAI IB	USE	893A
31A	KOSMOS 6	WORLD	447C
31B	KOSMOS 7	WORLD	447D
32	AMERIMNOS I	FREE FROM CARE	44C
	ARESKW 2A	BE PLEASING	105A
	THELW I	WISH	355C
	MERIMNAW 2	BE CONCERNED ABOUT	506B
	PWS 2B	HOW	740A
32≈4	PWS 2B	HOW	740A
33	ARESKW 2A	BE PLEASING	105A
	GAMEW IB	MARRY	150A
	MERIMNAW 2	BE CONCERNED ABOUT	506B
	PWS 2B	HOW	740A
33F	KOSMOS 6	WORLD	447C
33F	HO,H8,TO II7	THE	554C
34	AGAMOS	UNMARRIED	4A
	ARESKW 2A	BE PLEASING	105A
	GAMEW 3Aβ	MARRY	150B
	MERIZW IA	DIVIDE	505D
	PARTHENOS I	VIRGIN	632B
	PNEUMA 3A	SPIRIT	681B
	PWS 2B	HOW	740A
	SWMA IB	BODY	806D
34A	MERIMNAW 2		506B
		BE CONCERNED ABOUT	
34B	MERIMNAW 2		506B
		BE CONCERNED ABOUT	
35	APERISPASTWS		83C
		WITHOUT DISTRACTION	
	BROCHOS	NOOSE	147B
	EPIBALLW IA	THROW OVER	289D
	EUPAREDROS	CONSTANT	324B
	EUPERISPASTOS		324B
		EASILY DISTRACTING	
	EUPROSEDROS	CONSTANT	324D
	EUSCH8MWN I	PRESENTABLE	327B
	HO,H8,TO II2C	THE	553C
	SUMPHERW 2Bγ	ADVANTAGE	788A
	SUMPHOROS	PROFITABLE	788B
35A	PROS III3A	TOWARD	717A
35B	PROS III3A	TOWARD	717A
36	HAMARTANW I	SIN	41D
	ASCH8MONEW 2		118D
		FEEL SHOULD BE ASHAMED	
	ASCH8MONEW I		118D
		BEHAVE DISGRACEFULLY	
	GAMEW 2	MARRY	150B
	EPI IIIIBε	TOWARD	289A
	THELW 2	WISH	355D

36 NOMIZW 2	THINK	543B
OPHEILW 2Aβ	OWE	603D
HUPERAKMOS	PAST ONES PRIME	847D
36-38 GAMIZW I	GIVE IN MARRIAGE	150C
36-8 PARTHENOS I	VIRGIN	632C
37 ANAGK8 I	NECESSITY	52A
HEDRAIOS	FIRM	217A
EXOUSIA I	RIGHT	277C
THEL8MA 2A	WILL	355A
HIST8MI II2Cα	STAND	383C
KARDIA 18γ	HEART	404D
KRINW 3	DECIDE	452C
HOUTOS 18β	THIS	601C
PERI IE	ABOUT	650B
POIEW I24α	DO	689A
T8REW 2B	KEEP	822C
37A ECHW 12I	HAVE	333C
37A IDIOS 2C	ONES OWN	370C
37B IDIOS 2C	ONES OWN	370C
37F KALWS 4A	WELL	402B
38 GAMIZW I	GIVE IN MARRIAGE	150B
EKGAMIZW	MARRY	237C
KREITTWN 3	BETTER	451A
HWSTE IA	THEREFORE	908B
38A POIEW I2Aα	DO	689A
38B POIEW I2Aα	DO	689A
39 GAMEW 3C	MARRY	150B
DEW 3	BIND	177A
EAN IIB	IF	210B
EN I5D	IN	259B
EPI III2B	ON	289B
ZAW IAα	LIVE	336B
KOIMAW 2A	SLEEP	438D
NOMOS 3	LAW	545A
HOSOS I	HOW GREAT	590B
CHRONOS	TIME	896B
40 GNWM8 2	JUDGMENT	162B
DOKEW IA	THINK	200D
KAGW 3A	I ALSO	387A
MAKARIOS IA	BLESSED	487C
MENW IB	REMAIN	505B
HOUTW IB	THUS	602C
PNEUMA 5A	SPIRIT	682C

I CORINTHIANS 8

I AGAP8 IIA	LOVE	5B
GNWSIS I	KNOWLEDGE	162D
DE IC	BUT, AND	170C
EIDWLOTHUTOS		220C
MEAT OFFERED TO AN IDOL		
ECHW I2Eβ	HAVE	333A
*OIKODOMEW 3	BUILD	561A
OUN 2A	THEREFORE	597C
PERI IH	ABOUT	650D
PHUSIOW	BLOW UP	877B
2 KATHWS I	JUST AS	392A
OUPW	NOT YET	597D
2A GINWSKW 6Aα	KNOW	160C
3 AGAPAW IAβ	LOVE	4C
GINWSKW 7	ACKNOWLEDGE	160D
HOUTOS IAε	THIS	601B
4 BRWSIS I	EATING	147D

4 EIDWLOTHUTOS		220C
MEAT OFFERED TO AN IDOL		
EIDWLON 2	IDOL	220D
HEIS 2B	ONE	230B
THEOS I	GOD	357B
KOSMOS 2	WORLD	446D
OUN 2A	THEREFORE	597C
PERI IH	ABOUT	650D
4A OUDEIS I	NO	596B
4B OUDEIS 2A	NO ONE	596B
5 EI VII3B	IF	219B
EI VIII	IF	219B
EIMI II	TO BE	222A
EIMI II	TO BE	222B
KURIOS 2Eβ	LORD	461C
LEGW II3	CALL	471B
OURANOS IAβ	HEAVEN	598B
HWSPER 2	(JUST) AS	908A
5A THEOS I	GOD	357B
5A POLUS IIAα	MANY	694A
5B THEOS I	GOD	357B
5B POLUS IIAα	MANY	694A
6 ALLA 4	BUT, YET	38B
AUTOS 3E	(OBLIQUE CASE)	123B
DIA AIII2A	BY	179D
HEIS 2B	ONE	230B
EK 3C	FROM	234B
THEOS 3D	GOD	358A
KURIOS 2Cγ	LORD	461B
6A PAS 2Bβ	ALL THINGS	638D
6B PAS 2Bβ	ALL THINGS	638D
7 ARTI 3	NOW	110A
ASTHEN8S 2B	WEAK	115C
GNWSIS I	KNOWLEDGE	162D
EIDWLOTHUTOS		220C
MEAT OFFERED TO AN IDOL		
EIDWLON 2	IDOL	220D
EIMI II8	TO BE	223D
ESTHIW IA	EAT	312C
HEWS IIIC	UNTIL	335C
MOLUNW 2	DEFILE	528D
SUNEID8SIS 2	CONSCIOUSNESS	794B
SUNEID8SIS 2	CONSCIOUSNESS	794C
SUN8THEIA 2A	HABIT	797B
TIS, TI IAα	ANY ONE	827C
HWS IIIIA	SO	906C
7A SUNEID8SIS I	CONSCIOUSNESS	794A
8 BRWMA I	FOOD	147C
EAN IIB	IF	210B
OUTE	NOT	600C
PARIST8MI IE	BRING BEFORE	633B
PERISSEUW IBα	BE LEFT OVER	656D
HUSTEREW 2	TO MISS	857A
9 BLEPW 6	SEE	143B
GINOMAI III	BE	159B
EXOUSIA I	RIGHT	277C
M8PWS IB	LEST SOMEHOW	521C
PROSKOMMA 2B	STUMBLING	723C
9F ASTHEN8S 2B	WEAK	115C
10 EIDWLEION	AN IDOLS TEMPLE	220B
EIDWLOTHUTOS		220C
MEAT OFFERED TO AN IDOL		
ESTHIW IA	EAT	312C

```
10  ECHW I2Eβ              HAVE 333A      7  EK  4Aε                    FROM 235B
    KATAKEIMAI 3       LIE DOWN 412C          ESTHIW IBβ                 EAT 313A
    OIKODOMEW 3          BUILD 561B       8   ID6                        OR 343B
    SUNEID8SIS 2  CONSCIOUSNESS 794B          IDIOS IAβ             ONES OWN 370B
    TIS, TI IAγ       ANY ONE 827D           KARPOS IA                 FRUIT 405C
11  APOLLUMI 2Aα        PERISH 94D           OPSWNION IA               WAGES 607A
    GNWSIS I         KNOWLEDGE 162D          POIMAINW I                 TEND 690B
    SOS I              YOURS 766C            POTE I                     ONCE 701D
11F   ASTHENEW 2         WEAK 115A           STRATEUW I                      778A
12  HAMARTANW 4B          SIN 42A                    DO MILITARY SERVICE
    AUTOS 3A     (OBLIQUE CASE) 123A         PHUTEUW                   PLANT 878A
    HOUTW IB            THUS 602B       7A    POIMN8                   FLOCK 691A
    SUNEID8SIS 2  CONSCIOUSNESS 794B    7A    TIS, TI IAα              WHICH 826C
    TUPTW 2           STRIKE 838B       7B    POIMN8                   FLOCK 691A
13  AIWN IB             TIME 26D        7B    TIS, TI IAα              WHICH 826C
    BRWMA I             FOOD 147C       7C    TIS, TI IAα              WHICH 826C
    DIOPER         THEREFORE 198A       8   ANTHRWPOS IC               HUMAN 67D
    ESTHIW IA            EAT 312C             LALEW 2B                  SPEAK 464D
    KREAS              MEAT 450D             NOMOS 4A                    LAW 545A
    M8 DIA              NOT 519B        8F    M8 CI                      NOT 519B
13A   SKANDALIZW IA         760B       9   ALOAW                      THRESH 40C
          CAUSE TO FALL                     BOUS                         OX 146A
13B   SKANDALIZW IA         760B           GAR IE                       FOR 151C
          CAUSE TO FALL                     K8MOW                     MUZZLE 431D
                                            MELEI I        IT IS A CONCERN 501B
        I CORINTHIANS 9                     NOMOS 4A                    LAW 545A
                                            OU 4B                        NO 594D
1   ELEUTHEROS 2         FREE 250B          PHIMOW I                TIE SHUT 869D
    EN I5D                IN 259C      10  ALOAW                      THRESH 40C
    ERGON 3             WORK 308C           AROTRIAW                 TO PLOW 108A
    KURIOS 2Cγ          LORD 461B           GAR 4                    INDEED 151D
    HORAW IAα            SEE 581C          *GRAPHW 2C                 WRITE 166A
1F    APOSTOLOS 3     APOSTLES 99B          EPI IIIBγ                   ON 287A
2   ALLA 4          BUT, YET 38B            METECHW                   SHARE 515C
    APOSTOL8     APOSTLESHIP 98D            HO,H8,TO II4Bβ              THE 553D
    EI IIA                IF 218A           OPHEILW 2Aβ                 OWE 603D
    EIMI II2           TO BE 222D           PANTWS I           BY ALL MEANS 614B
    KURIOS 2Cγ          LORD 461A      10A   ELPIS I                   HOPE 252B
    SPHRAGIS 2A         SEAL 804C      10B   ELPIS I                   HOPE 252B
3   ANAKRINW IB      QUESTION 56A      11  THERIZW 2A                  REAP 360A
    APOLOGIA I        DEFENSE 95B          MEGAS 2Bβ                  GREAT 499C
    HOUTOS IAη           THIS 601B          PNEUMATIKOS 2Bα       SPIRITUAL 685C
4   ESTHIW IEα           EAT 313B           SARKIKOS I              FLESHLY 750B
    OU 6B                NO 595B            SPEIRW IBβ                  SOW 768D
4F    M8 CI              NOT 519B      12  ALLA 2                   BUT, YET 38A
4FF   EXOUSIA I        RIGHT 277C           DIDWMI IBα                 GIVE 192A
5   ADELPH8 3         SISTER 15C            EGKOP8                HINDRANCE 215C
    ADELPHOS I       BROTHER 15D            EXOUSIA I                 RIGHT 277C
    APOSTOLOS 3     APOSTLES 99B            EUAGGELION 2Bα           GOSPEL 318B
    GUN8 2             WIFE 167C            HINA IIA          IN ORDER THAT 377C
    KAI II3            ALSO 394B            MALLON 2B                  MORE 490C
    K8PHAS           CEPHAS 432D            METECHW                   SHARE 515C
    LOIPOS 2A         OTHER 481A            STEGW 2                   COVER 773C
    OU 6B                NO 595B            CHRAOMAI IA                 USE 892C
    PERIAGW I    LEAD AROUND 651B           CHRISTOS I        ANOINTED ONE 895C
    PETROS            PETER 660C      13  EK 3Gα                        BY 234D
    PETROS            PETER 661A            ERGAZOMAI 2B            PRACTISE 307B
6   BARNABAS       BARNABAS 133C            ESTHIW IA                   EAT 312D
    ERGAZOMAI I         WORK 307A           OIDA IE                    KNOW 558C
    8  IDβ                OR 343A           PAREDREUW            SIT BESIDE 629C
    MONOS IAβ           ONLY 529C           PROSEDREUW               ATTEND 719D
7   AMPELWN         VINEYARD 46B            SUMMERIZW            SHARE WITH 786B
    GALA I              MILK 149A      13A   THUSIAST8RION IA          ALTAR 367B
```

13B	THUSIAST8RION 1A	ALTAR	367B
14	DIATASSW	ORDER	188C
	EK 3Gα	BY	234D
	EUAGGELION 1C	GOSPEL	318B
	ZAW 1C	LIVE	336D
	KATAGGELLW 1	PROCLAIM	410C
15	GINOMAI I2B	MAY BE	157D
	EN I2	IN	257D
	8 2A	THAN	343B
	8	TRULY	343C
	KALOS 3C	GOOD	401C
	KAUCH8MA 1	BOAST	427B
	KENOW 2	MAKE EMPTY	429C
	MALLON 1	MORE	490B
	MALLON 3C	RATHER	490D
	CHRAOMAI 1A	USE	892C
15A	OUDEIS 2Bα	NOTHING	596C
15=17	GAR 1C	FOR	151B
16	ANAGK8 1	NECESSITY	52A
	EPIKEIMAI 2C	BE IMPOSED	294C
	EUAGGELIZW 2A6	PREACH	318A
	KAUCH8MA 1	BOAST	427B
	OUAI 2	WOE	595D
	CHARIS 2B	FAVOR	885D
17	AKWN	UNWILLING	33D
	GAR IE	FOR	151C
	HEKWN	WILLING	247A
	MISTHOS 2A	REWARD	525B
	OIKONOMIA 1B	MANAGEMENT	562B
	PISTEUW 3	BELIEVE	667D
18	ADAPANOS	FREE OF CHARGE	15B
	EXOUSIA 1	RIGHT	277C
	EUAGGELIZW 2A6	PREACH	318A
	EUAGGELION 1A	GOSPEL	318A
	HINA I2	IN ORDER THAT	377D
	HINA IIICα	IN ORDER THAT	378C
	HINA IIIE	IN ORDER THAT	378C
	KATACHRAOMAI	USE	421D
	TITH8MI I2Aβ	MAKE	824A
19	GAR 3	CERTAINLY	151D
	DOULOW 2	ENSLAVE	205B
	EK ID	AWAY FROM	233D
	ELEUTHEROS 2	FREE	250B
	EMAUTOU 2	MYSELF	253B
	POLUS II2Aα	MANY	695D
	POLUS II2Aγ	MANY	696A
19=22	KERDAINW 1B	TO GAIN	430C
20	M8 AII2B	NOT	518B
	NOMOS 3	LAW	544D
20A	HUPO 2B	UNDER	851B
20B	HUPO 2B	UNDER	851B
20C	HUPO 2B	UNDER	851B
20D	HUPO 2B	UNDER	851B
20F	GINOMAI III	BE	159B
20F	HWS II3B	SO	906A
21	ANOMOS 3	LAWLESS	71C
	ANOMOS 2A	LAWLESS	71C
	ENNOMOS	LEGAL	266D
	HINA I2	IN ORDER THAT	377D
22	ASTHEN8S 2B	WEAK	115C
	PANTWS 4	AT LEAST	614B
	PAS 2Bα	IN ALL RESPECTS	638C
	SWZW 2Aβ	SAVE	806B

22	TIS, TI 1Aα	ANY ONE	827C
22B	HINA IIB	IN ORDER THAT	377C
23	EUAGGELION 1A	GOSPEL	318A
	POIEW IIBε	DO	687D
	SUGKOINWNOS	PARTICIPANT	782A
24	BRABEION 1	PRIZE	146B
	HEIS 2B	ONE	230C
	KATALAMBANW 1A	SEIZE	413D
	MEN 1Aα	(PARTICLE)	503D
	OIDA 1E	KNOW	558C
	HOUTW 2	THUS	602C
	STADION 2	ARENA	771D
24A	TRECHW 1	RUN	833C
24B	TRECHW 1	RUN	833C
24C	TRECHW 2A	RUN	833C
24F	LAMBANW 2	RECEIVE	466B
24=6	THEODROMOS	GODS RUNNER	356D
25	AGWNIZOMAI 1		15A
		ENGAGE IN A CONTEST	
	APHTHARTOS	IMPERISHABLE	125A
	EGKRATEUOMAI	ABSTAIN	215D
	EKEINOS 1A	THAT	238D
	MEN 1Aα	(PARTICLE)	503D
	OUN 5	THEREFORE	597D
	PAS 1Cγ	WHOEVER	637B
	STEPHANOS 1	WREATH	774D
	PHTHARTOS	PERISHABLE	864D
25B	PAS 2A6	EVERYTHING	638C
26	AD8LWS	UNCERTAINLY	16C
	A8R	AIR	19D
	DERW	BEAT	174D
	OU 2C	NO	594D
	PUKTEUW	FIGHT WITH FISTS	736C
	TOINUN	HENCE	828D
	TRECHW 2A	RUN	833C
26A	HOUTW 2	THUS	602C
26A	HWS I2A	AS	905C
26B	HOUTW 2	THUS	602C
26B	HWS I2A	AS	905C
27	ADOKIMOS	UNQUALIFIED	18B
	ALLOS 1A	OTHER	39B
	DOULAGWGEW	ENSLAVE	204A
	K8RUSSW 2Bβ	ANNOUNCE	432C
	M8PWS 1A	LEST SOMEHOW	521C
	HUPWPIAZW 2		856C
		STRIKE UNDER THE EYE	

I CORINTHIANS 10

1	AGNOEW 1	BE IGNORANT	11B
	GAR 4	INDEED	151D
	DIERCHOMAI 1Bα	GO THROUGH	193C
	EIMI III12	TO BE	224D
	THELW 1	WISH	355C
	NEPHEL8	CLOUD	538D
	PAT8R 2E	FATHERS	641A
	HUPO 2Aβ	UNDER	851B
1F	THALASSA 1Bα	SEA	350D
2	BAPTIZW 3A	BAPTIZE	131D
3	BRWMA 1	FOOD	147C
	PNEUMATIKOS 2Aβ	SPIRITUAL	685B
3F	AUTOS 4A	THE SAME	123B
4	AKOLOUTHEW 1	FOLLOW	30C

4	EK IA	AWAY FROM	233C
	PINW	DRINK	664B
	POMA 2	A DRINK	696D
	CHRISTOS I	ANOINTED ONE	895C
4A	PETRA IA	ROCK	660B
4A	PNEUMATIKOS 2Aβ SPIRITUAL		685B
4B	PETRA IA	ROCK	660B
4B	PINW I	DRINK	664C
4B	PNEUMATIKOS 2Aβ SPIRITUAL		685B
5	ER8MOS 2	DESERT	309A
	EUDOKEW 2A	WELL PLEASED	319C
	KATASTRWNNUMI I	KILL	420B
	OU 7C	NO	595B
	POLUS II2Aα	MANY	695D
6	EPITHUMEW	DESIRE	293A
	EPITHUM8T8S	ONE WHO DESIRES	293B
	KATHWS I	JUST AS	392A
	KAKEINOS IB	AND HE	397C
	KAKOS IC	EVIL	398D
	M8 AIIIE	NOT	518A
	TUPOS 6	MARK	838A
7	ANIST8MI 2A	RISE	69C
	EIDWLOLATR8S	IDOLATER	220C
	ESTHIW IEβ	EAT	313B
	KATHIZW 2Aα	SIT DOWN	390D
	PAIZW	PLAY	609C
7=10	M8DE IB	AND NOT	519D
7=10	TIS, TI IAα	ANY ONE	827C
8	EIKOSI	TWENTY	221A
	H8MERA 2	DAY	346D
	PIPTW IBα	FALL	665B
	CHILIAS	THOUSAND	890B
8A	PORNEUW I	TO PROSTITUTE	700A
8B	PORNEUW I	TO PROSTITUTE	700A
9	APOLLUMI 2Aα	PERISH	94D
	EKPEIRAZW	PUT TO THE TEST	243A
	OPHIS I	SNAKE	604D
	PEIRAZW 2E	TRY	646C
9F	HUPO IB	BY	851A
10	APOLLUMI 2Aα	PERISH	94D
	GOGGUZW I	MURMUR	163D
	KATHAPER	JUST AS	387D
	OLOTHREUT8S	THE DESTROYER	567A
11	AIWN 2B	AGE	27B
	GRAPHW 2C	WRITE	166A
	DE 2	BUT, AND	170D
	KATANTAW 2B	ARRIVE	416B
	NOUTHESIA	ADMONITION	546B
	PROS III3A	TOWARD	717A
	SUMBAINW	MEET	784D
	TELOS IB	END	819A
	TELOS 3	TAX	819D
	TUPIKWS	TYPOLOGICALLY	837C
	TUPOS 6	MARK	838A
12	BLEPW 6	SEE	143B
	HIST8MI II2Cα	STAND	383C
	M8 BIB	NOT	519A
	PIPTW 2Aβ	FALL	665C
	HWSTE IB	THEREFORE	908B
13	ANTHRWPINOS I	HUMAN	67A
	DUNAMAI 2	ABLE	206B
13	EAW I	LET	211D
	EKBASIS	END	237B
	LAMBANW IC	TAKE	465D
	HO,H8,TO II4Bγ	THE	554A
	HOS,H8,HO I2A	(REL PRON)	587B
	PEIRAZW 2B	TRY	646A
	PISTOS IAβ	TRUSTWORTHY	670C
	POIEW IIBγ	DO	687C
	SUN 4A	WITH	789D
	HUPER 2	BEYOND	847A
	HUPOPHERW	ENDURE	856B
13A	PEIRASMOS 2B	TEST	646D
13B	PEIRASMOS 2B	TEST	646D
14	AGAP8TOS 2	BELOVED	6C
	DIOPER	THEREFORE	198A
	EIDWLOLATRIA	IDOLATRY	220C
	PHEUGW 3	FLEE	863D
15	KRINW 2	JUDGE	452C
	PH8MI 2	SAY	864B
	PHRONIMOS	THOUGHTFUL	874C
	HWS IIIIA	SO	906C
16	HAIMA 2B	BLOOD	22C
	EULOGEW 2B	BLESS	322D
	EULOGIA 4	CONSECRATION	323B
	EUCHARISTIA 3	EUCHARIST	329A
	KLAW	BREAK	434D
	KOINWNIA 4	ASSOCIATION	440B
	HOS,H8,HO I4D	(REL PRON)	588A
	POT8RION I	CUP	702A
	SWMA IB	BODY	807B
	CHRISTOS I	ANOINTED ONE	895C
16A	KOINWNIA 3	ASSOCIATION	440B
16B	KOINWNIA 3	ASSOCIATION	440B
16F	ARTOS IC	BREAD	110B
17	HEIS 2A	ONE	230B
	EK 4Aα	FROM	235B
	METECHW	SHARE	515C
	HOTI 3B	THAT	594A
	PAS 2Bα	IN ALL RESPECTS	638C
	POLUS I2Aβ	MANY	694D
	SWMA 5	BODY	807C
18	BLEPW 4B	SEE	143B
	ESTHIW IA	EAT	312C
	THUSIA 2A	SACRIFICE	366D
	THUSIAST8RION IA	ALTAR	367B
	ISRA8L 3	ISRAEL	382C
	KOINWNOS IBα	COMPANION	440C
	SARX 4	BODY	751B
19	EIDWLOTHUTOS MEAT OFFERED TO AN IDOL		220C
	EIDWLON 2	IDOL	220D
	EIMI II6B	TO BE	223C
	OUN ICβ	THEREFORE	597C
	TIS, TI IBα	WHICH	827A
	*PH8MI 2	SAY	864B
20	ALLA 3	BUT, YET	38A
	THELW I	WISH	355C
	THUW I	SACRIFICE	367D
	KOINWNOS IAβ	COMPANION	440C
20F	DAIMONION 2	DEMON	168C
21	METECHW	SHARE	515C
	PINW I	DRINK	664B
	TRAPEZA 2	TABLE	832B

21	TRAPEZA 2		TABLE	832B
21A	KURIOS 2Cγ		LORD	460D
21A	POT8RION 1		CUP	702A
21B	KURIOS 2Cγ		LORD	460D
21B	POT8RION 1		CUP	702A
22 8	1Dα		OR	343A
	ISCHUROS 1A		STRONG	384A
	M8 C1		NOT	519B
	PARAZ8LOW	PROVOKE TO JEALOUSY		621B
23	EXESTI 1	IT IS POSSIBLE		274D
	OIKODOMEW 3		BUILD	561B
	OU 7C		NO	595B
	SUMPHERW 2A		HELP	787D
24	HETEROS 1Bє		ANOTHER	315C
	Z8TEW 2Bα		SEEK	339C
	M8DEIS 2A		NO	520A
25	ANAKRINW 1A		QUESTION	56A
	ESTHIW 1A		EAT	312D
	THUW 2		SACRIFICE	367D
	MAKELLON		MEAT MARKET	488C
	M8DEIS 2Bα		NOTHING	520A
	PAS 1Cγ		WHOEVER	637C
	PWLEW		SELL	739A
	SUNEID8SIS 2	CONSCIOUSNESS		794B
26	PL8RWMA 1A	THAT WHICH FILLS		678A
27	ANAKRINW 1A		QUESTION	56A
	APISTOS 2		FAITHLESS	85A
	DEIPNON 2		DINNER	172B
	ESTHIW 1A		EAT	312D
	KALEW 1B		INVITE	400B
	M8DEIS 2Bα		NOTHING	520A
	PARATITH8MI 1A	PLACE BESIDE		628B
	PAS 1Cγ		WHOEVER	637C
	POREUW 1		PROCEED	699B
27F	SUNEID8SIS 2	CONSCIOUSNESS		794B
28	EIDWLOTHUTOS			220C
		MEAT OFFERED TO AN IDOL		
	HIEROTHUTOS			373A
		SACRIFICED TO A DIVINITY		
	M8NUW		REVEAL	521A
	TIS, TI 1Aγ		ANY ONE	827D
29	ALLOS 1A		OTHER	39B
	ELEUTHERIA		FREEDOM	250A
	HETEROS 1Bє		ANOTHER	315C
	HINATI		WHY	379B
	KRINW 6B		JUDGE	453C
	LEGW 12B		SAY	469D
	OUCHI 1		NOT	603A
	HUPO 1Aβ		BY	850D
29A	SUNEID8SIS 2	CONSCIOUSNESS		794B
29B	SUNEID8SIS 2	CONSCIOUSNESS		794B
30	BLASPH8MEW 1		DEFAME	142A
	EUCHARISTEW 2	GIVE THANKS		328C
	METECHW		SHARE	515C
	HOS, H8, HO 12A	(REL PRON)		587B
	TIS, TI 3A		WHICH	827B
	HUPER 1D	IN BEHALF OF		846D
	CHARIS 5		FAVOR	886D
31	DOXA 3		FAME	203B
	EIS 4D		FOR	228C
	OUN 1B		THEREFORE	597B
	OUN 5		THEREFORE	597D
	TIS, TI 1Bα		ANY ONE	828A

31B	POIEW 11Bє		DO	687D
32	APROSKOPOS 2			102A
		GIVING NO OFFENSE		
	GINOMAI III		BE	159B
	EKKL8SIA 4Eα		CHURCH	240D
	HELL8N 2A		GENTILE	251C
	IOUDAIOS 2C		JEWISH	380B
33	ARESKW 1	ACCOMMODATE		105A
	EMAUTOU 1		MYSELF	253B
	Z8TEW 2Bα		SEEK	339C
	KAGW 3C		I	387A
	PAS 2A6		EVERYTHING	638C
	POLUS 12Aβ		MANY	694D
	SUMPHERW 2Bγ		ADVANTAGE	788A
	SUMPHOROS		PROFITABLE	788B
	SWZW 2B		SAVE	806B

I CORINTHIANS II

1	KAGW 3C		I	387A
	*MIM8T8S 1		IMITATOR	524A
2	EPAINEW		PRAISE	281A
	KATECHW 1Bβ	HOLD FAST		424A
	MIMN8SKOMAI 1Aβ	REMEMBER		524B
	PARADIDWMI 3	GIVE OVER		620D
	PARADOSIS 2	TRADITION		621B
	PAS 2A6		EVERYTHING	638C
3	AN8R 1		MAN	65D
	GUN8 1		WOMAN	167C
3A	KEPHAL8 2A		HEAD	431C
3B	KEPHAL8 2A		HEAD	431C
3C	*KEPHAL8 2A		HEAD	431C
4	ECHW 11B		HAVE	332B
	ECHW 17A		HAVE	334A
	KATA 11A		DOWN	406B
4A	KEPHAL8 1A		HEAD	431B
4B	KEPHAL8 1A		HEAD	431A
4F	KATAISCHUNW 1	DISHONOR		411D
4F	PROSEUCHOMAI		PRAY	721A
4F	PROPH8TEUW 1	PROPHESY		730B
5	AKATAKALUPTOS	UNCOVERED		29B
	AUTOS 4B	THE SAME		123C
	GAR 1A		FOR	151A
	XURAW	HAVE ONESELF SHAVED		551D
	HO, H8, TO III F		THE	553A
5A	KEPHAL8 1A		HEAD	431A
5B	KEPHAL8 1A		HEAD	431A
5FF	GUN8 1		WOMAN	167C
6	AISCHROS		SHAMEFUL	24D
	EI 11A		IF	218A
	XURAW	HAVE ONESELF SHAVED		551D
6A	KEIRW		CUT	428B
6B	KEIRW		CUT	428B
7	GAR 1E		FOR	151C
	DOXA 1C		GLORY	203A
	EIKWN 1B		IMAGE	221B
	KEPHAL8 1A		HEAD	431A
	MEN 1Aα	(PARTICLE)		503D
	OPHEILW 2Aβ		OWE	603D
	HUPARCHW 2		BE	846A
7FF	AN8R 1		MAN	65D
8	EIMI III3		TO BE	224D
9	GAR 1B		FOR	151B

9	KTIZW	CREATE	456C
10	AGGELOS 2C	ANGEL	88
	EXOUSIA 5	AUTHORITY	278B
	EPI IIAα	ON	285D
	KEPHAL8 IA	HEAD	431A
	OPHEILW 2Aβ	OWE	603D
11	KURIOS 2Cγ	LORD	461A
	OUTE	NOT	600C
	PL8N IC	BUT	675B
	CHWRIS 2Aα	APART	898D
12	EK 3C	FROM	234B
	EK 3H	BY	235A
	KAI II3	ALSO	394B
13	AKATAKALUPTOS	UNCOVERED	29B
	AUTOS IAβ	SELF	122B
	EIMI II4D	TO BE	223B
	KRINW 2	JUDGE	452C
	PREPW	BE FITTING	706A
	PROSEUCHOMAI	PRAY	721A
14	ATIMIA	DISHONOR	119D
	AUTOS IG	EVEN	122C
	DIDASKW 2E	TEACH	191B
	EAN I	IF	210B
	KOMAW	WEAR LONG HAIR	443C
	MEN IAα	(PARTICLE)	503D
	OUDE 3	NOT EVEN	596A
	PHUSIS 3	NATURE	877D
15	ANTI 2	FOR	73A
	KOMAW	WEAR LONG HAIR	443C
	KOM8	HAIR	443C
	PERIBOLAION	COVERING	652B
16	DOKEW IB	THINK	200D
	EKKL8SIA 4Eα	CHURCH	240D
	SUN8THEIA 2B	HABIT	797B
	TOIOUTOS 2Aβ	SUCH A KIND	829A
	PHILON(E)IKOS I	QUARRELSOME	868C
17	ALLA IB	BUT, YET	37D
	EPAINEW	PRAISE	281A
	H8SSWN	LESSER	349D
	KREITTWN 2	BETTER	451A
	PARAGGELLW	GIVE ORDERS	618C
	SUNERCHOMAI IA	ASSEMBLE	795D
18	EKKL8SIA 4A	CHURCH	240B
	MEN 2C	(PARTICLE)	504B
	MEROS ID	IN PART	507C
	PISTEUW ID	BELIEVE	666D
	PRWTOS 2B	FIRST	733D
	SUNERCHOMAI IA	ASSEMBLE	795D
	SCHISMA 2	SPLIT	805B
	TIS, TI 2C	ANY ONE	828B
	HUPARCHW I	BE	845D
19	HAIRESIS IC	DISSENSION	23C
	DEI 5	IT IS NECESSARY	171B
	DOKIMOS I	GENUINE	202A
	EIMI I4	TO BE	222C
	*PHANEROS I	CLEAR	860B
20	AUTOS 4B	THE SAME	123B
	DEIPNON I	DINNER	172B
	EIMI I7	TO BE	222C
	EPI IIIIAζ	ON	288C
	ESTHIW IA	EAT	312D
	KURIAKOS		459C
	BELONGING TO THE LORD		

20	OUN 2A	THEREFORE	597C
	SUNERCHOMAI IA	ASSEMBLE	795D
21	DEIPNON I	DINNER	172B
	ESTHIW ID	EAT	313B
	IDIOS IAβ	ONES OWN	370B
	METHUW I	BE DRUNK	500C
	MEN IC	(PARTICLE)	504A
	HOS,H8,HO II2	THIS (ONE)	589B
	PEINAW I	HUNGER	645D
	PROLAMBANW 2A	TAKE BEFORE	715B
22	GAR IF	WHAT	151C
	EIPON I	SAY	225B
	EKKL8SIA 4Eα	CHURCH	240D
	ESTHIW IEβ	EAT	313B
	ECHW I2A	HAVE	332C
	ECHW I2D	HAVE	332D
	8 IDβ	OR	343A
	KATAISCHUNW 2	BE HUMILIATED	411D
	KATAPHRONEW I	SCORN	421C
	M8 CI	NOT	519B
	OIKIA IA	HOUSE	559D
	OU 6B	NO	595B
22A	EPAINEW	PRAISE	281A
22B	EPAINEW	PRAISE	281A
23	APO V4	FROM	87C
	ARTOS IC	BREAD	110B
	KAI II6		394C
	KURIOS 2Cγ	LORD	461A
	NUX IC	NIGHT	549A
	PARALAMBANW 2Bγ	TAKE	625B
23A	PARADIDWMI 3	GIVE OVER	620D
23B	PARADIDWMI	GIVE OVER	619D
23B	PARADIDWMI IB	GIVE OVER	620A
24	EIS 4D	FOR	228C
	EUCHARISTEW 2	GIVE THANKS	328C
	THRUPTW	BREAK IN PIECES	365A
	KLAW	BREAK	434D
	HOUTOS IAα	THIS	600D
	SWMA IB	BODY	807B
	HUPER IAε	IN BEHALF OF	846C
24F	ANAMN8SIS	REMINDER	57C
24F	EMOS IAβ	MY	255A
24F	POIEW IIBε	DO	687D
25	HAIMA 2B	BLOOD	22C
	AN 3C	(PARTICLE)	48C
	DEIPNEW	EAT	172B
	DIATH8K8 2	COVENANT	182B
	KAI II3	ALSO	394B
	KAINOS 3B	NEW	395B
	LEGW I8A	SAY	470B
	META BII4B	AFTER	511D
	HWSAUTWS	SIMILARLY	907D
25A	POT8RION I	CUP	702A
25B	POT8RION I	CUP	702A
25F	HOSAKIS	AS OFTEN AS	589B
26	AN 3D	(PARTICLE)	48C
	AN 3C	(PARTICLE)	48C
	ACHRI 2A	UNTIL	128C
	ERCHOMAI IIAη	COME	311A
	THANATOS IBβ	DEATH	351C
	KATAGGELLW I	PROCLAIM	410C
	HOS,H8,HO IIIF	(REL PRON)	589A
	HOUTOS 2B	THIS	601D

26 POTBRION I   CUP 702A
26F PINW I   DRINK 664B
26FF ARTOS IC   BREAD 110B
27 AN 2A   (PARTICLE) 48A
   ANAXIWS   CARELESS 58B
   ENOCHOS 2BY   GUILTY 267C
   POTBRION I   CUP 702A
   SWMA IB   BODY 807B
   HWSTE IA   THEREFORE 908B
28 ANTHRWPOS 3AY   MAN 68B
   DOKIMAZW I   EXAMINE 201C
   EK IA   AWAY FROM 233C
   EK 4AE   FROM 235B
   ESTHIW IBB   EAT 313A
   PINW I   DRINK 664C
29 DIAKRINW ICB   JUDGE 184B
   KRIMA 4B   VERDICT 451D
   SWMA IB   BODY 807B
29B PINW I   DRINK 664C
30 ARRWSTOS   SICK 109B
   ASTHENBS IA   SICK 115B
   HIKANOS IC   SUFFICIENT 375A
   KOIMAW 2A   SLEEP 438D
   POLUS IIAα   MANY 694A
31 AN IBα   (PARTICLE) 47D
   DIAKRINW ICB   JUDGE 184B
   HEAUTOU 2   ONESELF 211C
31F KRINW 4Bα   JUDGE 453A
32 KATAKRINW   CONDEMN 413B
   KOSMOS 7   WORLD 447D
   PAIDEUW 2Bα   INSTRUCT 608D
   SUN 2B   WITH 789C
33 EKDECHOMAI   WAIT 237D
   SUNERCHOMAI IA   ASSEMBLE 795D
   HWSTE IB   THEREFORE 908B
34 AN 3D   (PARTICLE) 48C
   DIATASSW   ORDER 188D
   EIS 4E   SO THAT 228D
   ERCHOMAI IIAα   COME 310B
   HINA IIC   IN ORDER THAT 377C
   KRIMA 4B   VERDICT 451D
   LOIPOS 2BB   THE REST 481A
   OIKOS IAα   HOUSE 563A
   PEINAW I   HUNGER 645D
   SUNERCHOMAI IA   ASSEMBLE 795D
   HWS IVICα   WHEN 907A

I CORINTHIANS 12

I AGNOEW I   BE IGNORANT 11B
   DE IC   BUT, AND 170C
   THELW I   WISH 355C
   PERI IH   ABOUT 650D
   PNEUMATIKOS 2Bα   SPIRITUAL 685C
   PNEUMATIKOS 2BB   SPIRITUAL 685C
2 AGW 3   LEAD 14C
   AMORPHOS   MISSHAPEN 46A
   AN IA   (PARTICLE) 47D
   ANAGW I   LEAD 52D
   APAGW 4   LEAD AWAY 79A
   APHWNOS I   SILENT 127C
   EIDWLON I   IDOL 220D
   HOTE IA   WHEN 592C

3 GNWRIZW I   MAKE KNOWN 162C
   *EN I5D   IN 259C
   KURIOS 2CY   LORD 461B
   LEGW IIBα   SAY 469C
   PNEUMA 6E   SPIRIT 684A
3A   PNEUMA 5A   SPIRIT 682C
3B   PNEUMA 5CB   SPIRIT 683A
4 DIAIRESIS I   APPORTIONMENT 182D
   PNEUMA 6D   SPIRIT 684A
   CHARISMA 2   A GIFT 887A
4FF   AUTOS 4A   THE SAME 123B
4FF   EIMI II   TO BE 222B
5 DIAIRESIS I   APPORTIONMENT 182D
   DIAKONIA 3   SERVICE 183C
5F   KAI I2B   AND 393A
6 ANATHEMA 2A   ACCURSED 53D
   DIAIRESIS I   APPORTIONMENT 182D
   EN I5A   IN 258D
   ENERGEW 2   WORK 265A
   ENERGBMA I   ACTIVITY 265A
7 PNEUMA 6D   SPIRIT 684A
   SUMPHERW 2BY   ADVANTAGE 788A
   PHANERWSIS   ANNOUNCEMENT 861A
8 GAR ID   FOR 151B
   GNWSIS 2   KNOWLEDGE 163A
   KATA II5Aδ   ACCORDING TO 408B
   SOPHIA 2   WISDOM 767A
8A   LOGOS IAβ   WORD 478C
8FF   ALLOS IC   OTHER 39B
8FF   MEN IC   (PARTICLE) 504A
8=10 HOS,H8,HO II2   THIS (ONE) 589B
8=10 PNEUMA 6D   SPIRIT 684A
9 HEIS 2A   ONE 230B
   HETEROS IBδ   ANOTHER 315B
   IAMA   HEALING 368D
   PISTIS 2Dζ   FAITH 669D
   CHARISMA 2   A GIFT 887A
10 GENOS 4   CLASS 155C
   GLWSSA 3   TONGUE 161C
   DIAKRISIS I   DISTINGUISHING 184C
   DIERMBNEIA   EXPLANATION 193B
   DUNAMIS 4   MIRACLE 207B
   ENERGEIA I   WORKING 264C
   ENERGBMA I   ACTIVITY 265A
   HERMBNEIA   TRANSLATION 309D
   HETEROS IBδ   ANOTHER 315B
   PNEUMA 7   SPIRIT 684B
   PROPHBTEIA 2   PROPHECY 730A
11 AUTOS 4B   THE SAME 123C
   BOULOMAI 2B   DESIRE 146A
   DIAIRESIS I   APPORTIONMENT 182D
   DIAIRE   DISTRIBUTE 182D
   HEIS 2A   ONE 230B
   IDIOS 4   PRIVATELY 370D
   KATHWS 2   AS 392B
   PAS IEβ   ALL 637D
   PNEUMA 6D   SPIRIT 684A
12 HEIS IB   ONE 230A
   ECHW I2Cα   HAVE 332D
   KATHAPER   JUST AS 387D
   MELOS 3   MEMBER 503A
   HOUTW IA   THUS 602B
12A MELOS I   MEMBER 502D

12A	POLUS IIAα	MANY 694A	
12A	SWMA IB	BODY 806D	
12B	MELOS I	MEMBER 502D	
12B	SWMA IB	BODY 806D	
12C	SWMA IB	BODY 806D	
13	BAPTIZW 2Bβ	BAPTIZE 131C	
	BAPTIZW 3B	BAPTIZE 131D	
	DOULOS IB	SLAVE 204D	
	HEIS 2A	ONE 230B	
	ELEUTHEROS I	FREE 250A	
	HELL8N 2A	GENTILE 251C	
	IOUDAIOS 2C	JEWISH 380B	
	PNEUMA 5Dβ	SPIRIT 683B	
	POMA 2	A DRINK 696D	
	POTIZW I	GIVE TO DRINK 702C	
	SWMA 5	BODY 807C	
13A	PNEUMA 6D	SPIRIT 684A	
13B	PNEUMA 6D	SPIRIT 684A	
14	ALLA IB	BUT, YET 37D	
	MELOS I	MEMBER 502D	
14=20	SWMA IB	BODY 806D	
15	OU 6B	NO 595A	
	POUS IA	FOOT 703B	
15F	EIMI III3	TO BE 224B	
15F	EK 4A6	FROM 235B	
15F	HOTI 3A	THAT 593D	
15F	PARA III5	BECAUSE OF 616C	
16	OUS I	EAR 600A	
16F	OPHTHALMOS I	EYE 604B	
17	AKO8 IA	HEARING 30B	
	OSPHR8SIS	SENSE OF SMELL 591D	
17A	POU IA	WHERE 702D	
17B	POU IA	WHERE 702D	
18	HEKASTOS 2	EACH 236A	
	THELW 2	WISH 355D	
	KATHWS 2	AS 392B	
	NUN 2	NOW 548A	
	NUNI 2B	NOW 548C	
	TITH8MI IIIA	ESTABLISH 824B	
18=20	MELOS I	MEMBER 502D	
19	PAS 2Bβ	ALL THINGS 638D	
	POU IA	WHERE 702D	
20	HEIS IB	ONE 230A	
	MEN	(PARTICLE) 503C	
	MEN IAα	(PARTICLE) 503D	
	NUN 2	NOW 548A	
	POLUS IIAα	MANY 694A	
21	ECHW I2I	HAVE 333C	
	KEPHAL8 IA	HEAD 431A	
	PALIN 4	AGAIN 611D	
	POUS IA	FOOT 703B	
21A	CHREIA I	NEED 893B	
21B	CHREIA I	NEED 893B	
22	ANAGKAIOS I	NECESSARY 51D	
	ASTHEN8S 2A	WEAK 1158	
	DOKEW 2A	SEEM 201A	
	MALLON I	MORE 490B	
	MELOS I	MEMBER 502D	
	POLUS I2Cα	MANY 695C	
	HUPARCHW 2	BE 846A	
23	ASCH8MWN	UNPRESENTABLE 119A	
	ATIMOS 2	LESS HONORED 119D	
	DOKEW IC	THINK 200D	

23	EUSCH8MOSUN8	PROPRIETY 327B	
	PERITITH8MI 2	PLACE AROUND 658C	
	TIM8 2B	HONOR 825B	
23A	PERISSOTEROS I	GREATER 657B	
23B	PERISSOTEROS I	GREATER 657B	
24	EUSCH8MWN I	PRESENTABLE 327B	
	PERISSOTEROS I	GREATER 657B	
	SUGKERANNUMI 2	BLEND 781B	
	TIM8 2B	HONOR 825B	
	HUSTEREW 2	TO MISS 857A	
	HUSTEREW IC	TO MISS 857A	
	CHREIA I	NEED 893B	
25	ALL8LWN	EACH OTHER 380	
	EIMI I4	TO BE 222B	
	MERIMNAW 2	BE CONCERNED ABOUT 506B	
	SCHISMA 2	SPLIT 805B	
25F	MELOS I	MEMBER 502D	
26	DOXAZW I	PRAISE 203D	
	EI VII3A	IF 219B	
	PASCHW 3Aα	SUFFER 639C	
	SUGCHAIRW I	REJOICE WITH 782D	
	SUMPASCHW	SUFFER WITH 787A	
26A	PAS IDα	ALL 637C	
26B	PAS IDα	ALL 637C	
27	EK 6C	FROM 235D	
	MELOS 3	MEMBER 503A	
	MEROS IC	IN PART 507B	
	SWMA 5	BODY 807C	
28	ANTIL8MPSIS	HELPFUL DEEDS 74B	
	GENOS 4	CLASS 155C	
	GLWSSA 3	TONGUE 161C	
	DEUTEROS 4	SECOND 176B	
	EITA I	THEN 233A	
	EKKL8SIA 4D	CHURCH 240C	
	EPEITA 2B	THEN 284B	
	IAMA	HEALING 368D	
	KUBERN8SIS	ADMINISTRATION 457C	
	HOS,H8,HO II2	THIS (ONE) 589B	
	PRWTOS 2B	FIRST 733D	
	TITH8MI II2B	MAKE 824B	
	TRITOS 3	THIRD 834C	
	CHARISMA 2	A GIFT 887A	
28F	APOSTOLOS 3	APOSTLES 99B	
28F	DIDASKALOS	TEACHER 190D	
28F	DUNAMIS I	POWER 206D	
28F	DUNAMIS 4	MIRACLE 207B	
28F	PROPH8T8S 5	PROPHET 731B	
30	GLWSSA 3	TONGUE 161C	
	DIERM8NEUW 2	EXPLAIN 193C	
	IAMA	HEALING 368D	
	CHARISMA 2	A GIFT 887A	
31	DEIKNUMI IB	SHOW 171D	
	EI VII	219B	
	Z8LOW IA	STRIVE 338C	
	KATA II5Bβ	ACCORDING TO 408D	
	KREITTWN I	BETTER 450D	
	MEGAS 2Bβ	GREAT 499C	
	HUPERB(L8	EXCESS 848B	
	CHARISMA 2	A GIFT 887A	

I CORINTHIANS 13

I	AGGELOS 2A	ANGEL 7C	

```
 1  ALALAZW      A CLASHING CYMBAL   348      8  KATARGEW 2              ABOLISH  418C
    ANTHRWPOS IAβ              MAN    67C         OUDEPOTE                 NEVER  596D
    GLWSSA 3               TONGUE    161C         PAUW 2                    STOP  643D
    8   IAβ                    OR    342D         PIPTW 2B6                 FALL  665D
    8CHEW                   SOUND    350C        *PROPH8TEIA 2         PROPHECY  730A
    KUMBALON                CYMBAL   458C      9  GINWSKW IA                KNOW  159D
    CHALKOS 2               COPPER   883B         PROPH8TEUW I          PROPHESY  730B
IFF    EAN IIA                  IF   210B      9A  MEROS IC              IN PART  507B
IFF    ECHW I2Eβ              HAVE   333A      9B  MEROS IC              IN PART  507B
I-3    AGAP8 IIA              LOVE     5C      10 ERCHOMAI I2B              COME  311C
 2  GNWSIS 2            KNOWLEDGE    163A         KATARGEW 2             ABOLISH  418C
    ECHW I2Eβ               HAVE    333A         MEROS IC               IN PART  507C
    ECHW I2Eβ               HAVE    333A         HO,H8,TO II6               THE  554B
    METHIST8MI I          REMOVE    500A         TELEIOS IAβ                      816D
    MUST8RION 2          MYSTERY    532B           HAVING ATTAINED THE END
    OIDA IB                 KNOW    558B      11 AN8R 2                     MAN   66A
    OROS                MOUNTAIN    586C         GINOMAI I4A             BECOME  158C
    OUDEIS 2Bβ         WORTHLESS    596C         KATARGEW 2             ABOLISH  418B
    PISTIS 2Dς             FAITH    669D         LALEW 2Aε                SPEAK  464C
    PROPH8TEIA 2        PROPHECY    730A         LOGIZOMAI 2           CONSIDER  477B
    HWSTE 2Aβ           THEREFORE   908C         HO,H8,TO II7               THE  554C
2A  PAS IDα                  ALL    637C         PHRONEW I                THINK  874A
2B  PAS ICα                  ALL    637B     IIA  N8PIOS IA             CHILDREN  539C
2C  PAS ICα                  ALL    637B     IIA  HOTE IA                  WHEN  592C
2F  KAN I                 AND IF    403B     IIA  HWS I2A                    AS  905C
 3  HINA I2         IN ORDER THAT   377D     IIB  N8PIOS IA             CHILDREN  539C
    KAIW 2                  BURN    397B     IIB  HOTE IC                  WHEN  592C
    KAUCHAOMAI I           BOAST    427A     IIB  HWS I2A                    AS  905C
    OUDEIS 2Bγ     IN NO RESPECT    596C     IIC  N8PIOS IA             CHILDREN  539C
    PARADIDWMI IA      GIVE OVER    619D     IIC  HWS I2A                    AS  905C
    PAS IDβ                 ALL    637D     IID  N8PIOS IA             CHILDREN  539C
    HUPARCHW I               BE    845D     IIE  N8PIOS IA             CHILDREN  539C
    PSWMIZW 2              FEED    903C      12 AINIGMA               INDISTINCT   23A
    WPHELEW IA            HELP    909A         ARTI 3                     NOW  109D
 4  AGAP8 IIA             LOVE      5B         BLEPW IC                   SEE  143A
    Z8LOW 2                       338C         GINWSKW IA                KNOW  159D
     BE FILLED WITH JEALOUSY                   ESOPTRON                MIRROR  313C
    MAKROTHUMEW 2   HAVE PATIENCE   489B         KAI II3                   ALSO  394B
    PERPEREUOMAI          BOAST    659D         MEROS IC               IN PART  507B
    PHUSIOW             BLOW UP    877B         PROSWPON IB               FACE  728B
    CHR8STEUOMAI        BE KIND    894B     12A  EPIGINWSKW IA            KNOW  291A
 5  ASCH8MONEW I                  118D     12A  TOTE IB          AT THAT TIME  831C
     BEHAVE DISGRACEFULLY                   12B  EPIGINWSKW IA            KNOW  291A
    EUSCH8MONEW                   327B     12B  TOTE IB          AT THAT TIME  831C
     BEHAVE WITH DIGNITY                    13 AGAP8 IIA                 LOVE    5C
    Z8TEW 2Bα              SEEK    339C         ELPIS 2B                  HOPE  252C
    KAKOS IC                EVIL    398D         MEGAS 2Bβ                GREAT  499C
    LOGIZOMAI IA          RECKON    477A         MENW ICβ               REMAIN  505C
    HO,H8,TO II7             THE    554C         NUNI 2A                    NOW  548C
    PAROXUNW            IRRITATE    634D         PISTIS 2Dγ               FAITH  669C
 6  ADIKIA 2    UNRIGHTEOUSNESS     17C         TREIS                    THREE  833A
    AL8THEIA 2B            TRUTH     35B
    SUGCHAIRW I      REJOICE WITH   782D                | CORINTHIANS 14
    CHAIRW I            REJOICE    881B
 7  ELPIZW 2               HOPE    252A      1  AGAP8 IIA                 LOVE    5C
    PISTEUW IAα          BELIEVE   666A         DIWKW 4B                PURSUE  200C
    STEGW 2                COVER    773C         Z8LOW IA                STRIVE  338C
    STEGW I                COVER    773C         HINA IIIAα       IN ORDER THAT  378A
    HUPOMENW 2            REMAIN    853D         PNEUMATIKOS 2Bα      SPIRITUAL  685C
 8  AGAP8 IIA              LOVE      5B         PROPH8TEUW I          PROPHESY  730B
    GLWSSA 3              TONGUE    161C     I=27  GLWSSA 3              TONGUE  161C
    GNWSIS 2           KNOWLEDGE    163A      2  AKOUW 7             UNDERSTAND   32B
    EKPIPTW 3B             FAIL    243B         LALEW 2B                 SPEAK  464D
```

2	MUST8RION 2	MYSTERY 532B
	PNEUMA 6E	SPIRIT 684A
3	LALEW 2B	SPEAK 464D
	OIKODOM8 1Bα	BUILDING 561C
	PARAKL8SIS 1	ENCOURAGEMENT 623B
	PARAMUTHIA	COMFORT 626B
3=5	PROPH8TEUW 1	PROPHESY 730B
4	OIKODOMEW 3	BUILD 561B
	TOPOS 1E	PLACE 830C
4F	EKKL8SIA 4A	CHURCH 240B
5	DIERM8NEUW 2	EXPLAIN 193C
	EKTOS 1	OUTSIDE 245C
	THELW 1	WISH 355C
	HINA III Aα	IN ORDER THAT 378A
	LAMBANW 2	RECEIVE 466C
	MEGAS 2Bα	GREAT 499B
	OIKODOM8 1Bβ	BUILDING 561C
6	APOKALUPSIS 2	REVELATION 91D
	GNWSIS 2	KNOWLEDGE 163A
	DIDACH8 1	TEACHING 191B
	EAN I3B	IF 210D
	8 1B	OR 342D
	NUNI 2A	NOW 548C
	PROPH8TEIA 3B	PROPHECY 730B
	WPHELEW 1A	HELP 908D
7	AULEW	PLAY THE FLUTE 120D
	AULOS	FLUTE 121B
	APSUCHOS	INANIMATE 129C
	DIASTOL8	DIFFERENCE 188A
	KITHARA	LYRE 433A
	KITHARIZW	PLAY 433A
	HO,H8,TO II3A	THE 553C
	HOMWS	ALL THE SAME 572D
	PWS 1D	HOW 739D
	PHTHOGGOS	SOUND 865B
7F	DIDWMI 1Bγ	GIVE 192C
7F	PHWN8 1	SOUND 878D
8	AD8LOS 2	INDISTINCT 16C
	PARASKEUAZW 2	PREPARE 627C
	POLEMOS 1B	ARMED CONFLICT 691D
	SALPIGX 1	TRUMPET 748B
9	A8R	AIR 19D
	GAR 1E	FOR 151C
	GLWSSA 1A	TONGUE 161B
	GLWSSA 3	TONGUE 161C
	DIA AIII1A	BY MEANS OF 179A
	DIDWMI I3α	GIVE 192A
	EUS8MOS	CLEAR 326D
	LALEW 2Aε	SPEAK 464C
	LOGOS 1Aβ	WORD 478C
	HO,H8,TO II3A	THE 553C
	HOMWS	ALL THE SAME 572D
	PWS 1D	HOW 739D
10	APHWNOS 2	127C
	INCAPABLE OF SPEECH	
	GENOS 4	CLASS 155C
	EI I3	IF 218B
	KOSMOS 4A	WORLD 447A
	TOSOUTOS 1B	SO GREAT 831B
	TUGCHANW 2B	HAPPEN 837B
10F	PHWN8 3	LANGUAGE 879C
11	BARBAROS 1	UNINTELLIGIBLE 132D
	DUNAMIS 3	MEANING 207A
11	EN I3	IN 258A
	EN IV4A	IN 260D
11A	LALEW 2Aγ	SPEAK 464B
11B	LALEW 2Aγ	SPEAK 464B
12	EPEI 2	BECAUSE 283D
	Z8LWT8S 1Aβ	ZEALOT 338D
	Z8TEW 2Bγ	SEEK 339C
	HINA III Aα	IN ORDER THAT 378A
	OIKODOM8 1Bα	BUILDING 561C
	PERISSEUW 1Bα	BE LEFT OVER 656D
	PNEUMA 6D	SPIRIT 684A
	PROS III3B	TOWARD 717B
13	DIERM8NEUW 2	EXPLAIN 193C
	DIOPER	THEREFORE 198A
	HINA III Aγ	IN ORDER THAT 378B
14	AKARPOS 2	UNFRUITFUL 29B
	NOUS 1 THE	UNDERSTANDING 546C
14A	PROSEUCHOMAI	PRAY 721A
14B	PROSEUCHOMAI	PRAY 721A
14=16	PNEUMA 6E	SPIRIT 684A
15	OUN ICβ	THEREFORE 597C
	PROSEUCHOMAI	PRAY 721A
	TIS, TI IBε	WHICH 827A
	PSALLW	SING 899B
15A	NOUS 1 THE	UNDERSTANDING 546C
15B	NOUS 1 THE	UNDERSTANDING 546C
16	AM8N 1	AMEN 45A
	AM8N 3	AMEN 45B
	ANAPL8ROW 4	FILL 59B
	EPEI 2	BECAUSE 283D
	EPEID8 2	SINCE 284A
	EPI III Bβ	TO 286D
	EULOGEW 1	SPEAK WELL 322C
	EUCHARISTIA 2	THANKFULNESS 329A
	IDIWT8S 2	LAYMAN 371B
	LEGW II A	SAY 469B
	OIDA 4	KNOW 559A
	PWS 1D	HOW 739D
	SOS 1	YOURS 766C
	TOPOS 1E	PLACE 830C
17	ALLA 1B	BUT, YET 37D
	HETEROS 1Bε	ANOTHER 315C
	EUCHARISTEW 2	GIVE THANKS 328D
	KALWS 1	WELL 402A
	MEN 1Aβ	(PARTICLE) 503D
	OIKODOMEW 3	BUILD 561B
18	EUCHARISTEW 2	GIVE THANKS 328C
	EUCHARISTEW 2	GIVE THANKS 328D
	MALLON 1	MORE 490A
19	DIA AIII1A	BY MEANS OF 179A
	EKKL8SIA 4A	CHURCH 240B
	8 2Bα	THAN 343B
	THELW 1	WISH 355C
	KAT8CHEW 2A	TEACH 425A
	LALEW 2B	SPEAK 464D
	NOUS 1 THE	UNDERSTANDING 546C
19A	LOGOS 1A6	WORD 478D
19B	LOGOS 1A6	WORD 478D
20	KAKIA 1A	BADNESS 397D
	N8PIAZW	BE AS A CHILD 539C
	PAIDION 3A	CHILD 609B
	TELEIOS 2Aα	MATURE 817A
20A	PHR8N	THINKING 873D

20B PHR8N — THINKING 873D
21 EISAKOUW I — LISTEN TO 231C
   EN IIIIB — BY 260B
   HETEROGLWSSOS — 314D
      SPEAKING FOREIGN TONGUE
   HETEROS 2 — ANOTHER 315C
   NOMOS 4B — LAW 545A
   HOTI 2 — THAT 593D
   OUDE 3 — NOT EVEN 596A
   CHEILOS I — LIP 887C
22 APISTOS 2 — FAITHLESS 85A
   GLWSSA 3 — TONGUE 161C
   EIMI III2 — TO BE 224A
   EIS 4D — FOR 228C
   PROPH8TEIA 2 — PROPHECY 730A
   S8MEION I — SIGN 755B
   HWSTE IA — THEREFORE 908B
22A PISTEUW 2B — BELIEVE 667C
22B PISTEUW 2B — BELIEVE 667C
23 AUTOS 4B — THE SAME 123B
   EAN IIC — IF 210C
   EIPON 2C — SAY 225C
   EPI IIIIAς — ON 288C
   MAINOMAI BE OUT OF ONES MIND 487C
   SUNERCHOMAI IA — ASSEMBLE 795D
23F ANAPL8ROW 4 — FILL 59B
23F APISTOS 2 — FAITHLESS 85A
23F EISERCHOMAI IA6 — COME 232A
23F IDIWT8S 2 — LAYMAN 371B
24 ANAKRINW 2 — QUESTION 56A
   EAN IIC — IF 210C
   ELEGCHW 2 — EXPOSE 248D
   PROPH8TEUW I — PROPHESY 730B
25 APAGGELLW 2 — PROCLAIM 78D
   GINOMAI I4B — BECOME 158D
   EIMI III4 — TO BE 224C
   EPI IIIIA8 — ON 288A
   KARDIA I8α — HEART 404B
   KRUPTOS 2A — HIDDEN 455A
   ONTWS I — REALLY 577C
   HOUTW IB — THUS 602C
   PIPTW I8α — FALL 665B
   PROSKUNEW 2A — DO REVERENCE 724A
   PROSWPON IA — FACE 728B
   PHANEROS I — CLEAR 860B
26 APOKALUPSIS 2 — REVELATION 91D
   DIDACH8 2 — TEACHING 191B
   HEKASTOS 2 — EACH 236A
   HERM8NEIA — TRANSLATION 309D
   OIKODOM8 I8α — BUILDING 561C
   OUN ICβ — THEREFORE 597C
   PROS III3B — TOWARD 717B
   SUNERCHOMAI IA — ASSEMBLE 795D
   TIS, TI I9α — WHICH 827A
   PSALMOS 2 — PSALM 899B
27 ANA 2 — IN TURN 49B
   DIERM8NEUW 2 — EXPLAIN 193C
   DUO 5 — TWO 208C
   EI VII3B — IF 219B
   KATA II3A — (DISTRIBUTIVE) 407D
   MEROS IC — IN SUCCESSION 507B
   HO,H8,TO II6 — THE 554C
   POLUS III28β — MANY 696C

28 DIERM8NEUT8S — INTERPRETER 193B
   EKKL8SIA 4A — CHURCH 240B
   HERM8NEUT8S — TRANSLATOR 309D
   SIGAW IA — BE SILENT 757A
29 ALLOS IC — OTHER 39B
   DIAKRINW ICα — JUDGE 184B
   DUO IC — TWO 208B
   LALEW 2Aγ — SPEAK 464B
   PROPH8T8S 5 — PROPHET 731B
30 APOKALUPTW 2 — REVEAL 91C
   KATH8MAI IAγ — SIT 390B
   PRWTOS IA — FIRST 732D
   SIGAW IB — BE SILENT 757B
31 HEIS 5E — ONE 231B
   KATA II3A — (DISTRIBUTIVE) 407D
   MANTHANW I — LEARN 491B
   PARAKALEW 2 — APPEAL TO 622C
   PROPH8TEUW I — PROPHESY 730B
32 PNEUMA 6D — SPIRIT 684A
   PROPH8T8S 5 — PROPHET 731B
   HUPOTASSW I8β — SUBJECT 855D
33 AKATASTASIA 2 — DISTURBANCE 29C
   EIR8N8 IC — PEACE 226C
   EKKL8SIA 4E6 — CHURCH 240D
   THEOS 3E — GOD 358B
34 EKKL8SIA 4A — CHURCH 240B
   EPITREPW I — ALLOW 303C
   LEGW I7 — SAY 470A
   NOMOS 4A — LAW 545A
   HUPOTASSW I8β — SUBJECT 855D
34F GUN8 I — WOMAN 167B
35 AISCHROS — SHAMEFUL 24D
   AN8R I — MAN 65D
   EKKL8SIA 4A — CHURCH 240B
   EPERWTAW IA — ASK 284D
   MANTHANW I — LEARN 491B
   OIKOS IAα — HOUSE 563A
36 EXERCHOMAI 28α — GO OUT 274C
   KATANTAW 2B — ARRIVE 416B
   LOGOS I8β — WORD 479B
   MONOS IAβ — ONLY 529C
37 GRAPHW 2D — WRITE 166A
   DOKEW IB — THINK 200D
   ENTOL8 2D — COMMAND 268D
   EPIGINWSKW 2A — KNOW 291A
   PNEUMATIKOS 28β — SPIRITUAL 685C
   PROPH8T8S 5 — PROPHET 731B
38 AGNOEW 2 — NOT TO KNOW IIC
39 GLWSSA 3 — TONGUE 161C
   Z8LOW IA — STRIVE 338C
   KWLUW 2 — HINDER 462C
   PROPH8TEUW I — PROPHESY 730B
   HWSTE IB — THEREFORE 908B
40 EUSCH8MONWS — DECENTLY 327B
   KATA II58β — ACCORDING TO 408C
   TAXIS 2 — FIXED ORDER 811C

I CORINTHIANS 15

I GNWRIZW I — MAKE KNOWN 162D
   DE IC — BUT, AND 170C
   EUAGGELIZW 2Aα — PREACH 317D
   EUAGGELION IC — GOSPEL 318B

1	HIST8MI II2Cβ	STAND 383C	12	EGEIRW 2C	RISE 214A
	PARALAMBANW 3B	TAKE 625B		EIMI II	TO BE 222B
2	EIK8 4	TO NO PURPOSE 221A		K8RUSSW 2Bβ	ANNOUNCE 432D
	EKTOS I	OUTSIDE 245C		LEGW IIIE	DECLARE 471A
	EUAGGELIZW 2AY	PREACH 317D		HOTI IBζ	THAT 593A
	KATECHW IBα	HOLD FAST 424A		PWS IC	HOW 739C
	LOGOS IAβ	WORD 478C		TIS, TI IAα	ANY ONE 827D
	PISTEUW 2B	BELIEVE 667C	12A	NEKROS 2A	DEAD 537A
	SWZW 2B	SAVE 806B	12B	NEKROS 2A	DEAD 537A
	TIS, TI 2	WHICH 827B	12F	ANASTASIS 2B	RESURRECTION 60A
3	APOTHN8SKW IAα	DIE 90D	12FF	ANASTASIS 2B	RESURRECTION 60A
	KATA II5Aα	ACCORDING TO 408A	13	NEKROS 2A	DEAD 537A
	PARADIDWMI 3	GIVE OVER 620D		OUDE 2	AND NOT 595D
	PARALAMBANW 2BY	TAKE 625A	13FF	EI IIA	IF 218A
	PRWTOS ICα	FIRST 733B	14	ARA 3	THEN 103C
	HUPER IAε	IN BEHALF OF 846C		K8RUGMA 2	PROCLAMATION 432A
3F	GRAPH8 2Bβ	SCRIPTURE 165C		PISTIS 2Dα	FAITH 669B
4	ANIST8MI 2A	RISE 69C	14A	KENOS 2Aα	EMPTY 429A
	H8MERA 2	DAY 346D	14B	KENOS 2Aα	EMPTY 429A
	THAPTW	BURY 352C	15	ARA I	THEN 103B
	TRITOS I	THIRD 834B		DE 4A	BUT, AND 170D
5	DWDEKA	TWELVE 209B		EI VIII	IF 219B
	HENDEKA	ELEVEN 262B		HEURISKW 2	FIND 326A
	K8PHAS	CEPHAS 432D		KATA I2Bβ	DOWN 406D
	PETROS	PETER 661A		MARTUREW IA	BEAR WITNESS 493D
5=8	HORAW IAδ	SEE 582A		PSEUDOMARTUS	A FALSE WITNESS 900B
6	ARTI 3	NOW 110A	15F	NEKROS 2A	DEAD 537A
	EK 4Aα	FROM 235B	15FF	EGEIRW IAβ	RAISE 213D
	EPANW IB	MORE THAN 283A	16	OUDE 2	AND NOT 595D
	EPEITA 2A	THEN 284B	17	ARA 3	THEN 103C
	EPHAPAX I	AT ONCE 330B		ETI IAα	STILL 315D
	HEWS IIIC	UNTIL 335C		KENOS 2Aα	EMPTY 429A
	KOIMAW 2A	SLEEP 438D		MATAIOS	IDLE 496C
	MENW ICα	REMAIN 505C	18	APOLLUMI 2Aα	PERISH 94D
	PENTAKOSIOI	FIVE HUNDRED 648D		ARA 3	THEN 103C
	POLUS II2Aα	MANY 695D		EN I5D	IN 259B
7	APOSTOLOS 3	APOSTLES 99B		KOIMAW 2A	SLEEP 438D
	EITA I	THEN 233B	19	EIMI II4A	TO BE 223A
	IAKWBOS 3	JAMES 368C		ELEEINOS	MISERABLE 249A
	PAS IDα	ALL 637C		ELPIZW 3	HOPE 252A
8	EKTRWMA	UNTIMELY BIRTH 246A		ZW8 IA	LIFE 340D
	ESCHATOS 3B	LAST 314B		MONOS 2A	ONLY 529D
	HWSPEREI	LIKE 908B		PAS IB	ALL 637A
9	APOSTOLOS 3	APOSTLES 99B	20	APARCH8 2A	FIRST FRUITS 80D
	DIOTI I	BECAUSE 198C		EGEIRW 2C	RISE 214A
	DIWKW 2	PERSECUTE 200B		KOIMAW 2B	SLEEP 438D
	EKKL8SIA 4Eα	CHURCH 240D		NEKROS 2A	DEAD 537A
	ELACHISTOS I	SMALLEST 248B		NUNI 2B	NOW 548C
	HIKANOS 2	APPROPRIATE 375B	21	ANTHRWPOS 2D	MAN 68A
	KALEW IAδ	CALL 400B		EPEID8 2	SINCE 284A
10	KENOS 2Aβ	EMPTY 429A		THANATOS IBγ	DEATH 351D
	KOPIAW 2	BECOME WEARY 444B		NEKROS 2A	DEAD 537A
	PAS IEα	ALL 637D	22	ADAM	ADAM 15B
	PERISSOTEROS 2	GREATER 657B		EN I5D	IN 259B
	PTWCHOS 2	BEGGING POOR 735D		EN I5D	IN 259C
	SUN 3	WITH 789C		ZWOPOIEW I	MAKE ALIVE 342C
10A	CHARIS 4	FAVOR 886C		KAI II3	ALSO 394B
10B	CHARIS 4	FAVOR 886C	23	APARCH8 2A	FIRST FRUITS 80D
10C	CHARIS 4	FAVOR 886C		EN II2	WHILE 259D
11	K8RUSSW 2Bβ	ANNOUNCE 432D		EPEITA 2A	THEN 284B
	OUN 5	THEREFORE 597D		IDIOS IB	ONES OWN 370B
	PISTEUW ID	BELIEVE 666D		HO,H8,TO II7	THE 554C
12	ANASTASIS 2B	RESURRECTION 60B		PAROUSIA 2Bα	COMING 635C

Ref	Greek	Gloss
23F	TAGMA 1B	GROUP 810C
24	ARCH8 3	RULER 112A
	BASILEIA 1	KINGDOM 134C
	DUNAMIS 6	POWER 207B
	EXOUSIA 4C?	AUTHORITY 278B
	THEOS 3D	GOD 358A
	KAI 11A	AND 392C
	KATARGEW 2	ABOLISH 418B
	PARADIDWMI	GIVE OVER 619C
	PARADIDWMI 1A	GIVE OVER 619D
	PAS 1A?	EVERY EACH 636C
	PAT8R 3D?	FATHER 641D
	TELOS 1B	END 819A
	TELOS 1D?	END 819C
	TELOS 2	REMAINDER 819D
25	AN 3D	(PARTICLE) 48C
	ACHRI 2A	UNTIL 128C
	BASILEUW 1B?	RULE 136B
	ECHTHROS 2B?	THE ENEMY 331D
	POUS 1B	FOOT 703C
	TITH8MI 11A?	PUT 823D
	HUPO 2A?	UNDER 851B
26	ESCHATOS 3B	LAST 314A
	ECHTHROS 2B?	THE ENEMY 331D
	THANATOS 1F	DEATH 352A
	KATARGEW 2	ABOLISH 418B
27	D8LOS	CLEAR 177B
	EKTOS 2B	OUTSIDE 245C
	POUS 1B	FOOT 703C
	HUPO 2A?	UNDER 851B
27A	PAS 2A6	EVERYTHING 638B
27A	HUPOTASSW 1A	SUBJECT 855C
27B	HUPOTASSW 1B?	SUBJECT 855D
27C	HUPOTASSW 1A	SUBJECT 855C
28	HINA 11D	IN ORDER THAT 377C
	HOTAN 1B	WHEN 592B
	TOTE 2	AT THAT TIME 831D
	HUIOS 2B	SON 842D
28A	PAS 2B?	ALL THINGS 638D
28A	HUPOTASSW 1B?	SUBJECT 855D
28B	PAS 2B?	ALL THINGS 638D
28B	HUPOTASSW 1B?	SUBJECT 855D
28C	PAS 2A6	EVERYTHING 638B
28C	HUPOTASSW 1A	SUBJECT 855C
28D	PAS 2A6	EVERYTHING 638B
29	EI 11A	IF 218A
	EPEI 2	BECAUSE 283D
	KAI 115	STILL 394C
	HOLWS	GENERALLY SPEAKING 568A
	POIEW 11B?	DO 688A
29A	BAPTIZW 2B?	BAPTIZE 131C
29A	NEKROS 2A	DEAD 537A
29A	HUPER 1C	IN BEHALF OF 846D
29B	BAPTIZW 2B?	BAPTIZE 131C
29B	NEKROS 2A	DEAD 537A
29B	TIS, TI 3A	WHICH 827C
30	KAI 115	STILL 394C
	KINDUNEUW	RUN A RISK 433B
	TIS, TI 3A	WHICH 827C
	HWRA 2B	TIME OF DAY 904C
31	APOTHN8SKW 2	BE ABOUT TO DIE 91A
	EN 15D	IN 259B
	H8MERA 2	DAY 347B
31	KATA 112C	EVERY 407C
	KAUCH8SIS 1	BOASTING 427C
	KURIOS 2C?	LORD 461B
	N8	BY 539B
	HUMETEROS 2	YOUR 844A
32	ANTHRWPOS 1C	HUMAN 67D
	AURION 2	SOON 121D
	EI 11A	IF 218A
	ESTHIW 1D	EAT 313A
	ESTHIW 1E?	EAT 313B
	EPHESOS	EPHESUS 330B
	TH8RIOMACHEW	361B
	FIGHT WITH WILD ANIMALS	
	TH8RIOMACHEW	361C
	FIGHT WITH WILD ANIMALS	
	NEKROS 2A	DEAD 537A
	OPHELOS	BENEFIT 604A
33	8THOS	CUSTOM 345A
	KAKOS 1B	BAD 398C
	HOMILIA 1	ASSOCIATION 568C
	PLANAW 2C6	DECEIVE 671C
	PHTHEIRW 2B	RUIN 865B
	CHR8STOS 1A?	USEFUL 894C
34	AGNWSIA	IGNORANCE 12A
	DIKAIWS 1B	JUSTLY 197C
	EKN8PHW	BECOME SOBER 242D
	ENTROP8 1	SHAME 269C
	ECHW 12E?	HAVE 333A
	TIS, TI 1A?	ANY ONE 827D
35	ALLA 2	BUT, YET 38A
	EIPON 2B	SAY 225C
	NEKROS 2A	DEAD 537A
	POIOS 1A?	OF WHAT KIND 691B
	PWS 1A	HOW 739C
	SWMA 3	BODY 807B
	TIS, TI 1A?	ANY ONE 827C
36	APOTHN8SKW 1A?	DIE 91A
	APHRWN	FOOLISH 127B
	ZWOPOIEW 2C	MAKE ALIVE 342D
	SPEIRW 1A?	SOW 768C
37	GINOMAI 11A	BE BORN 157B
	GUMNOS 4	BARE 167A
	EI 13	IF 218B
	KOKKOS 1	SEED 441B
	LOIPOS 2B?	THE REST 481A
	SITOS	WHEAT 759D
	TUGCHANW 2B	HAPPEN 837B
37A	SPEIRW 1A?	SOW 768C
37B	SPEIRW 1A?	SOW 768C
37F	SWMA 3	BODY 807B
38	HEKASTOS 2	EACH 236A
	THELW 2	WISH 355D
	IDIOS 1A?	ONES OWN 370B
	KATHWS 2	AS 392B
	KAI 13	AND 393D
	SPERMA 1A	SEED 769A
39	ANTHRWPOS 1A?	MAN 67C
	AUTOS 4A	THE SAME 123B
	ICHTHUS	FISH 385A
	KT8NOS	ANIMAL 456B
	MEN 1C	(PARTICLE) 504A
	OU 2A	NO 594B
	PT8NOS	WINGED 734D

39A	SARX I	FLESH	750C
39B	SARX I	FLESH	750C
39C	SARX I	FLESH	750C
39D	SARX I	FLESH	750C
39FF	ALLOS IEα	OTHER	39C
40	EPIGEIOS I	EARTHLY	290C
	EPOURANIOS IB	HEAVENLY	306A
	HETEROS 2	ANOTHER	315C
	MEN IC	(PARTICLE)	504A
	SWMA 3	BODY	807B
40F	DOXA IA	BRIGHTNESS	202C
41	AST8R	STAR	117B
	DIAPHERW 2A	DIFFER	189C
	H8LIOS	THE SUN	346B
	SEL8N8	MOON	754A
42	ATIMIA	DISHONOR	119D
	APHTHARSIA	INCORRUPTIBILITY	124D
	EN 14D	IN	258C
	NEKROS 2A	DEAD	537A
	PHTHORA I	RUIN	865D
42=4	SPEIRW I86	SOW	768D
43	ASTHENEIA IB	WEAKNESS	114D
	DOXA IA	BRIGHTNESS	202D
44A	PNEUMATIKOS 2Aβ SPIRITUAL		685B
44A	PNEUMATIKOS 2Aγ SPIRITUAL		685C
44A	SWMA I8	BODY	807B
44A	PSUCHIKOS I PERTAINING TO THE SOUL		902D
44B	PNEUMATIKOS 2Aβ SPIRITUAL		685B
44B	SWMA I8	BODY	807B
44B	PSUCHIKOS I PERTAINING TO THE SOUL		902D
44C	SWMA I8	BODY	807B
45	ADAM	ADAM	15B
	ANTHRWPOS 2D	MAN	68A
	ESCHATOS 3A	LAST	314A
	ZAW IAα	LIVE	336B
	ZWOPOIEW I	MAKE ALIVE	342C
	PNEUMA 5F	SPIRIT	683C
	PSUCH8 2	SOUL LIFE	902C
45FF	ANTHRWPOS 2D	MAN	68B
46	EPEITA 2A	THEN	284B
	PNEUMATIKOS 2Bα	SPIRITUAL	685C
	PRWTOS 2A	FIRST	733D
	PSUCHIKOS 2A PERTAINING TO THE SOUL		902D
47	ANTHRWPOS 2D	MAN	68A
	DEUTEROS 3	SECOND	176A
	EK 3H	BY	235A
	ESCHATOS 3A	LAST	314A
	OURANIOS	HEAVENLY	598A
	OURANOS 2B	HEAVEN	599B
	PNEUMATIKOS 2Aα	SPIRITUAL	685A
	CHOIKOS	EARTHY	891B
48	EPOURANIUS IAγ	HEAVENLY	306A
	KAI II3	ALSO	394B
48A	HOIOS	OF WHAT SORT	565C
48A	TOIOUTOS I	SUCH A KIND	829A
48B	HOIOS	OF WHAT SORT	565C
48B	TOIOUTOS I	SUCH A KIND	829A
48F	EPOURANIOS IAβ	HEAVENLY	306A
49	EIKWN IB	IMAGE	221B
	KATHWS I	JUST AS	392A
	KAI II3	ALSO	394B
49A	PHOREW 2	WEAR	872D
49B	PHOREW 2	WEAR	872D
50	HAIMA IA	BLOOD	22A
	APHTHARSIA	INCORRUPTIBILITY	124D
	BASILEIA 3B	KINGDOM	134D
	BASILEIA 3G	KINGDOM	135A
	BASILEIA 3G	KINGDOM	135B
	HOUTOS I8β	THIS	601C
	SARX 3	BODY	751B
	PH8MI 2	SAY	864B
	PHTHORA I	RUIN	865D
50A	KL8RONOMEW 2	INHERIT	435D
50B	KL8RONOMEW 2	INHERIT	436A
51	ANIST8MI 2A	RISE	69C
	IDOU IA	BEHOLD	371C
	KOIMAW 2A	SLEEP	438D
	LEGW IIA	SAY	469B
	LEGW-IIIF	DECLARE	471A
	MUST8RION 2	MYSTERY	532A
	OU 2A	NO	594B
51F	ALLASSW I	CHANGE	38C
52	ATOMOS	INDIVISIBLE	120A
	APHTHARTOS	IMPERISHABLE	125A
	EN II2	WHILE	259D
	ESCHATOS 3B	LAST	314A
	NEKROS 2A	DEAD	537A
	OPHTHALMOS I	EYE	604C
	RIP8	THROWING	743D
	ROP8	TWINKLING OF AN EYE	744C
	SALPIGX 2	TRUMPET	748B
53	DEI I	IT IS NECESSARY	171A
53F	ATHANASIA	IMMORTALITY	20A
53F	APHTHARSIA INCORRUPTIBILITY		124D
53F	ENDUW 2B	DRESS	263C
53F	THN8TOS	MORTAL	363B
53F	PHTHARTOS	PERISHABLE	864D
54	GRAPHW 2C	WRITE	165D
	KATAPINW 2	SWALLOW	417C
	LOGOS IAζ	MATTER	479A
	NIKOS I	VICTORY	542A
	HOTAN I8	WHEN	592B
	TOTE 2	AT THAT TIME	831D
54=6	THANATOS IF	DEATH	352A
55	HAD8S 2	HADES	16D
	NIKOS I	VICTORY	541D
55A	POU IA	WHERE	702D
55B	POU IA	WHERE	702D
55F	KENTRON I	STING	429C
56	DE 2	BUT, AND	170D
	DUNAMIS 7	POWER	207C
	NOMOS 3	LAW	544C
57	KURIOS 2Cγ	LORD	461B
	NIKOS I	VICTORY	542A
	CHARIS 5	FAVOR	886D
58	AGAP8TOS 2	BELOVED	6C
	AMETAKIN8TOS	IMMOVABLE	44D
	GINOMAI I4B	BECOME	158D
	HEDRAIOS	FIRM	217A

58	ERGON 2	WORK	308B
	KENOS 2Aβ	EMPTY	429A
	KOPOS 2	WORK	444C
	PANTOTE	ALWAYS	614A
	PERISSEUW IBβ	BE LEFT OVER	656D
	HWSTE IB	THEREFORE	908B

I CORINTHIANS 16

1	GALATIA	GALATIA	149B
	DE IC	BUT, AND	170C
	DIATASSW	ORDER	188C
	EIS 4G	FOR	229A
	EKKL8SIA 4B	CHURCH	240C
	LOGEIA	COLLECTION	476D
	PERI IH	ABOUT	650D
	POIEW I2Aα	DO	689A
2	AN 2A	(PARTICLE)	48A
	HEAUTOU IG	ONESELF	211C
	HEIS 4	ONE	231A
	HEKASTOS 2	EACH	236A
	EUODOW	PROSPER	324A
	TH8SAURIZW I	STORE UP	362A
	KATA II2C	EVERY	407C
	LOGEIA	COLLECTION	476D
	HOSTIS IEα	WHOEVER	591A
	PARA III8α	BESIDE	615C
	SABBATON 2A	WEEK	746D
	SABBATON 2B	WEEK	746D
	TITH8MI IIBγ	DEPOSIT	823D
	TOTE 2	AT THAT TIME	831D
3	AN 2A	(PARTICLE)	48A
	APOPHERW IB	TAKE	101B
	ATIMOS I	DISHONORED	119D
	DIA AIII1B	BY MEANS OF	179B
	DOKIMAZW 2B	APPROVE	201C
	EPISTOL8	LETTER	300D
	PARAGINOMAI I	COME	618D
	PEMPW I	SEND	647D
	CHARIS 3A	FAVOR	886A
4	AXIOS IC	WORTHY	77C
	HO,H8,TO II4Bα	THE	553D
	POREUW I	PROCEED	699B
4B	POREUW I	PROCEED	699A
5	DIERCHOMAI IA	GO THROUGH	193C
5A	MAKEDONIA	MACEDONIA	488B
5B	MAKEDONIA	MACEDONIA	488B
6	EAN II	IF	211A
	8 IAβ	OR	342D
	KATAMENW	STAY	415D
	HOU 2	WHERE	594B
	PARAMENW IB	REMAIN	626A
	PARACHEIMAZW	SPEND THE WINTER	629A
	POREUW I	PROCEED	699B
	PROPEMPW 2	ACCOMPANY	716B
	PROS III7	TOWARD	718A
	TUGCHANW 2C	HAPPEN	837B
7	ARTI 3	NOW	109D
	GAR IC	FOR	151B
	EIDON 6	VISIT	220A
	ELPIZW 2	HOPE	252A
	EPIMENW I	REMAIN	296B
	EPITREPW I	ALLOW	303C

7	THELW 2	WISH	355D
	PARODOS 2	PASSING BY	634A
	PROS III7	TOWARD	718A
	TIS, TI 2C	ANY ONE	828B
	CHRONOS	TIME	896B
8	EPIMENW I	REMAIN	296A
	EPHESOS	EPHESUS	330B
	HEWS IIIA	UNTIL	335A
	PENT8KOST8	FIFTIETH	648D
9	ANOIGW IA	OPEN	70C
	ANOIGW 2	OPEN	70D
	ANTIKEIMAI	BE OPPOSED	73D
	ENARG8S	EVIDENT	261C
	ENERG8S	EFFECTIVE	265B
	THURA 2C	DOOR	366C
	MEGAS IB	LARGE	498D
10	APHOBWS I	FEARLESSLY	126C
	BLEPW 4D	SEE	143B
	GINOMAI II4A	BE	159C
	ERGAZOMAI 2A	WORK	307A
	ERGON 2	WORK	308B
	HINA IIIAβ	IN ORDER THAT	378B
	TIMOTHEOS	TIMOTHY	826A
11	EIR8N8 2	PEACE	226C
	EKDECHOMAI	WAIT	237D
	EXOUTHENEW I	DESPISE	277B
	META AII4	WITH	510D
	M8 AIII5A	NOT	518D
	PROPEMPW 2	ACCOMPANY	716B
	TIS, TI IAγ	ANY ONE	827D
12	ADELPHOS 2	BROTHER	16A
	APOLLWS	APOLLOS	95A
	DE 2	BUT, AND	170D
	EUKAIREW	OPPORTUNITY	321C
	THEL8MA IB	WILL	354D
	NUN IAγ	NOW	547D
	PANTWS 5A	NOT AT ALL	614B
	PARAKALEW 3	IMPLORE	622D
	PERI IH	ABOUT	650D
	POLUS I2Bβ	MANY	695B
12B	HINA IIICα		378C
		IN ORDER THAT	
13	ANDRIZOMAI	BEHAVE AS A MAN	63C
	GR8GOREW 2	BE AWAKE	166C
	KRATAIOW	STRENGTHEN	449C
	PISTIS 2Dα	FAITH	669B
	ST8KW 2	STAND	775C
14	AGAP8 IIA	LOVE	5C
	PAS 2Aδ	EVERYTHING	638C
15	APARCH8 2A	FIRST FRUITS	80D
	ACHAIA	ACHAIA	127D
	DIAKONIA I	SERVICE	183B
	OIDA IC	KNOW	558B
	OIKIA 2	HOUSEHOLD	560A
	HOTI IBζ	THAT	593A
	STEPHANAS	STEPHANAS	774C
	TASSW IB	PLACE	813D
	PHORTOUNATOS I	FORTUNATUS	873A
15F	PARAKALEW 2	APPEAL TO	622C
16	HINA III2	IN ORDER THAT	379A
	KOPIAW 2	BECOME WEARY	444B
	SUNERGEW	WORK WITH	795B
	TOIOUTOS 3Aα	SUCH A KIND	829B

16	HUPOTASSW 1Bβ	SUBJECT 855D
17	ANAPL8ROW 3	REPLACE 59B
	ACHAIKOS	ACHAICUS 127D
	DE 2	BUT, AND 170D
	PAROUSIA 1	PRESENCE 635B
	HUMETEROS 1	YOUR 843D
	HUMETEROS 2	YOUR 844A
	HUSTER8MA 1	NEED 857A
	PHORTOUNATOS 1	FORTUNATUS 873A
18	ANAPAUW 1	CAUSE TO REST 58C
	APOLLWS	APOLLOS 95A
	EPIGINWSKW 1C	ACKNOWLEDGE 291A
	PNEUMA 3B	SPIRIT 681C
19	AKULAS	AQUILA 33C
	ASIA	ASIA 115C
	ASPAZOMAI 1A	GREET 116C
	EKKL8SIA 4B	CHURCH 240C
	EKKL8SIA 4C	CHURCH 240C
	EN 15D	IN 259B
	KATA 111C	BY 407B
	KURIOS 2Cγ	LORD 461A
	XENIZW 1 RECEIVE AS A GUEST	550A
	OIKOS 1Aα	HOUSE 563A
	POLUS 12Bβ	MANY 695A
	PRISKA	PRISCILLA 708B
19F	ASPAZOMAI 1A	GREET 116B
20	ASPAZOMAI 1A	GREET 116C
	PAS 1Dα	ALL 637C
	PHIL8MA 1	A KISS 867B
21	ASPASMOS 2	GREETING 116D
	EMOS 1Aα	MY 255A
	PAULOS	PAUL 643A
	CHEIR 1	HAND 888B
22	ANATHEMA 2A	ACCURSED 2A
	EI 11A	IF 218A
	MARAN ATHA	LORD COME 492B
	OU 2D	NO 594C
	PHILEW 1A	LOVE LIKE 867A
23	KURIOS 2Cγ	LORD 461A
	KURIOS 2Cγ	LORD 461A
	META A111Cγ	WITH 510A
	CHARIS 2C	FAVOR 885D
24	AGAP8 11Bβ	LOVE 5D
	AM8N 1	AMEN 45B
	GINOMAI 13A	TAKE PLACE 158A
	META A111Cγ	WITH 510B

2 CORINTHIANS 1

1	HAGIOS 2Dβ	SAINTS 10A
	ADELPHOS 2	BROTHER 16A
	APOSTOLOS 3	APOSTLES 99B
	ACHAIA	ACHAIA 127D
	DIA A111D	THROUGH 179C
	EKKL8SIA 4B	CHURCH 240C
	EKKL8SIA 4Eα	CHURCH 240D
	THEL8MA 2B	WILL 355A
	KORINTHOS	CORINTH 445C
	PAULOS	PAUL 643A
	TIMOTHEOS	TIMOTHY 826A
2	APO V4	FROM 87C
	EIR8N8 2	PEACE 226D
	THEOS 3D	GOD 358A

2	KURIOS 2Cγ	LORD 461A
	PAT8R 3Cβ	FATHER 641C
	CHARIS 2C	FAVOR 885D
3	EPOURANIOS 2Aα	HEAVENLY 306A
	EULOG8TOS	BLESSED 323A
	THEOS 3D	GOD 358A
	KAI 11A	AND 392C
	KURIOS 2Cγ	LORD 461B
	HO,H8,TO 111OB	THE 555A
	OIKTIRMOS	PITY 564C
	PARAKL8SIS 3	COMFORT 623C
3A	PAT8R 3Dβ	FATHER 641D
3B	THEOS 3E	GOD 358B
3B	PAT8R 3Cβ	FATHER 641C
4	EPI 112	AT 287D
	HOS,H8,HO 14B	(REL PRON) 588A
	PARAKL8SIS 3	COMFORT 623C
	HUPO 1Aα	BY 850D
4A	THLIPSIS 1	TRIBULATION 362D
4A	PARAKALEW 4	IMPLORE 623A
4A	PAS 1Aγ	EVERY EACH 637A
4A	PAS 1Cβ	ALL 637B
4B	THLIPSIS 1	TRIBULATION 362D
4B	PARAKALEW 4	IMPLORE 623A
4B	PAS 1Aγ	EVERY EACH 637A
4B	PAS 1Cβ	ALL 637B
4C	PARAKALEW 4	IMPLORE 623A
5	ANTANAPL8ROW	FILL UP 72B
	KATHWS 1	JUST AS 392A
	HOUTW 1A	THUS 602B
	PATH8MA 1	SUFFERING 607B
5A	PERISSEUW 1Aβ BE LEFT OVER	656C
5B	PERISSEUW 1Aβ BE LEFT OVER	656C
6	EI V113A	IF 219B
	ENERGEW 1B	WORK 264D
	THLIBW 3	OPPRESS 362C
	HOS,H8,HO 14A	(REL PRON) 587D
	PARAKALEW 4	IMPLORE 623A
	PASCHW 3B	ENDURE 639D
	SWT8RIA 2	DELIVERANCE 809B
	HUPOMON8 1	PATIENCE 854B
6A	HUPER 1B	IN BEHALF OF 846D
6B	HUPER 1B	IN BEHALF OF 846D
6F	PATH8MA 1	SUFFERING 607B
7	BEBAIOS 2	FIRM 137D
	ELPIS 1	HOPE 252B
	KOINWNOS 1Bα	COMPANION 440C
	PARAKL8SIS 3	COMFORT 623C
	HUPER 1F	IN BEHALF OF 847A
	HWS 111	SO 905D
8	AGNOEW 1	BE IGNORANT 11B
	ASIA	ASIA 115C
	BAREW	BURDEN 133B
	GAR 1B	FOR 151B
	DUNAMIS 2	POWER 207A
	EXAPOREW BE IN GREAT DIFFICULTY	272C
	ZAW 1Aα	LIVE 336B
	THELW 1	WISH 355C
	THLIPSIS 1	TRIBULATION 362D
	KAI 112	EVEN 394B

8	HO,H8,TO II4Bα	THE 553D
	HUPER 2	BEYOND 847A
	HUPER IF	IN BEHALF OF 847A
	HUPERBOL8	EXCESS 848B
	HWSTE 2Aβ	THEREFORE 908C
9	APOKRIMA	OFFICIAL REPORT 92D
	HEAUTOU IC	ONESELF 211B
	HEAUTOU 2	ONESELF 211C
	EPI IIIBγ	ON 287A
	ECHW I2J	HAVE 333C
	THANATOS IA	DEATH 351B
	THANATOS IBα	DEATH 351C
	NEKROS 2A	DEAD 537A
	PEITHW 2A	CONVINCE 645B
10	ELPIZW 3	HOPE 252A
	ETI IAγ	STILL 315D
	THANATOS IC	DEATH 351D
	T8LIKOUTOS 2	SO GREAT 822B
10A	RUOMAI	SAVE 745A
10B	RUOMAI	SAVE 745A
11	DE8SIS	PRAYER 171A
	DIA AIII2Bα	BY 179D
	EK 3Eα	BY 234C
	EUCHARISTEW 2	GIVE THANKS 328C
	EUCHARISTEW 2	GIVE THANKS 328D
	PROSWPON IE	FACE 729A
	SUNUPOURGEW	COOPERATE WITH 801B
	CHARISMA I	A GIFT 887A
11A	HUPER IAδ	IN BEHALF OF 846C
11B	HUPER IAδ	IN BEHALF OF 846C
12	HAGIOT8S	HOLINESS 10B
	ANASTREPHW 2Bδ	LIVE 61A
	GAR 4	INDEED 151D
	EILIKRINEIA	SINCERITY 221D
	KAUCH8SIS 2	BOASTING 427C
	KOSMOS 5A	WORLD 447C
	MARTURION IB	TESTIMONY 495A
	PERISSOTERWS 2	MORE 657C
1	PROS III7	TOWARD 718A
	SARKIKOS 3	FLESHLY 750B
	SARKINOS 2	FLESHY 750C
	SOPHIA I	WISDOM 766D
	*SUNEID8SIS 2	CONSCIOUSNESS 794B
	CHARIS 4	FAVOR 886C
13	ALLA IA	BUT, YET 37C
	ALLOS IEβ	ANOTHER 39C
	ANAGINWSKW I	READ 51B
	GAR IB	FOR 151B
	GAR IE	FOR 151C
	GRAPHW 2D	WRITE 166A
	ELPIZW 2	HOPE 252A
	TELOS IDβ	END 819C
13B	8 IAβ	OR 342D
13F	EPIGINWSKW 2D	KNOW 291B
14	H8MERA 3Bβ	DAY 347D
	KATHAPER	JUST AS 387D
	KATHWS I	JUST AS 392A
	*KAI II3	ALSO 394B
	KAUCH8MA I	BOAST 427B
	KURIOS 2Cγ	LORD 461B
	MEROS IC	IN PART 507B
15	BOULOMAI 2Aβ	DESIRE 145D
	DEUTEROS 2	SECOND 176A
15	PEPOITH8SIS I	TRUST 649A
	PROTEROS IBα	EARLIER 729B
	CHARA I	JOY 883D
	CHARIS 3A	FAVOR 886A
16	APERCHOMAI 2	GO 83D
	DIA AII	THROUGH 178B
	DIERCHOMAI IBα	GO THROUGH 193C
	IOUDAIA I	JUDAEA 379D
	PALIN IA	BACK 611B
	PROPEMPW 2	ACCOMPANY 716B
16A	MAKEDONIA	MACEDONIA 488B
16B	MAKEDONIA	MACEDONIA 488B
17	ARA 2	THEN 103C
	BOULEUW 2	DECIDE 145A
	BOULOMAI 2Aα	DESIRE 145D
	ELAPHRIA	FICKLE 248A
	HINA II2	IN ORDER THAT 378D
	KATA II5Bβ	ACCORDING TO 408C
	M8TI	PERHAPS 522A
	NAI 5	YES 535A
	OU I	NO 594B
	PARA II2D	BESIDE 615D
	SARX 7	BODY 752A
	CHRAOMAI 2	USE 893A
18	LOGOS IAβ	WORD 478C
	NAI 5	YES 535A
	HOTI IBα	THAT 592D
	PISTOS IAβ	TRUSTWORTHY 670C
	PROS IIIF	TOWARD 717A
19	K8RUSSW 28β	ANNOUNCE 432D
	SILOUANOS	SILVANUS 758B
	TIMOTHEOS	TIMOTHY 826A
	HUIOS 2B	SON 842D
19A	NAI 5	YES 535A
19B	NAI 5	YES 535A
20	AM8N 3	AMEN 45B
	DIA AIII2Bγ	BY 179D
	DIO	THEREFORE 197D
	EPAGGELIA 2A	PROMISE 280B
	NAI 5	YES 535A
	PROS III3C	TOWARD 717B
21	BEBAIOW 2	ESTABLISH 138A
	THEOS 3B	GOD 357D
	SUN 2C	WITH 789C
	CHRIW 4	ANOINT 896A
22	ARRABWN	DOWN PAYMENT 109A
	DIDWMI IBβ	GIVE 192A
	KARDIA IB θ	HEART 405B
	PNEUMA 5Dα	SPIRIT 683A
	SPHRAGIZW 2B	SEAL 804A
23	EPI IIIIBε	TOWARD 289A
	EPIKALEW 2Aα	CALL UPON 294A
	KORINTHOS	CORINTH 445C
	MARTUS 2A	WITNESS 495C
	HOTI IBα	THAT 592D
	OUKETI I	NO LONGER 596D
	PHEIDOMAI I	SPARE 862C
	PSUCH8 IC	SOUL LIFE 902B
	PSUCH8 IF	SOUL LIFE 902C
24	HIST8MI II2Cβ	STAND 383C
	KURIEUW I	RULE 459C
	HOTI IC	THAT 593A
	SUNERGOS	WORKING WITH 795C

24 CHARA I	JOY	883C
24A PISTIS 2Dα	FAITH	669B
24B PISTIS 2Dα	FAITH	669B

2 CORINTHIANS 2

1 KRINW 3	DECIDE	452C
LUP8	GRIEF	483B
M8 AIIIG	NOT	518B
HOUTOS 18β	THIS	601C
2 EK 3Eα	BY	234C
EUPHRAINW I	GLADDEN	328A
KAI I2H	AND	393D
M8 AIIIE	NOT	518A
2A LUPEW I	GRIEVE	482D
2B LUPEW 2B	BE GRIEVED	483A
3 AUTOS IH	EVEN	122D
DEI 6B	IT IS NECESSARY	171C
EPI IIIIBє	TOWARD	289A
ECHW I2Eβ	HAVE	333A
LUP8	GRIEF	483B
HOS,H8,HO I2A	(REL PRON)	587B
PEITHW 2A	CONVINCE	645B
CHAIRW I	REJOICE	881D
CHARA I	JOY	883C
4 AGAP8 IIBβ	LOVE	5D
GINWSKW IA	KNOW	159D
GRAPHW 2D	WRITE	166A
DAKRUON	TEAR	169A
DIA AIIIIC	THROUGH	179B
EIS 4Cβ	(GOAL)	228C
EK 3Gγ	BY	235A
ECHW I2Eβ	HAVE	333A
THLIPSIS 2	TRIBULATION	363A
HINA IV	IN ORDER THAT	379B
KARDIA IBє	HEART	405A
LUPEW 2A	GRIEVE	483A
PERISSOTERWS 2	MORE	657C
SUNOCH8 2	DISTRESS	799C
4A POLUS IIBβ	MANY	694C
5 EPIBAREW	BURDEN	290B
LUPEW I	GRIEVE	482D
MEROS IC	IN PART	507B
TIS, TI IAβ	ANY ONE	827D
6 EPITIMIA	PUNISHMENT	303B
HIKANOS IA	SUFFICIENT	375A
POLUS II2Aα	MANY	695D
POLUS II2Aγ	MANY	696A
HUPO IC	BY	851A
6F TOIOUTOS 3Aα	SUCH A KIND	829B
7 ENANTION 2	BEFORE	261B
KATAPINW IC	SWALLOW	417C
LUP8	GRIEF	483A
MALLON 3Aβ	RATHER	490C
M8PWS IA	LEST SOMEHOW	521C
PARAKALEW 4	IMPLORE	623A
PERISSOTEROS I	GREATER	657B
CHARIZOMAI 2	GIVE FREELY	885A
HWSTE 2Aβ	THEREFORE	908C
8 AGAP8 IIBβ	LOVE	5D
EIS 4Cβ	(GOAL)	228C
KUROW 2	CONFIRM	462A
PARAKALEW 2	APPEAL TO	622C
9 GAR IB	FOR	151B
GRAPHW 2D	WRITE	166A
DOKIM8 I	CHARACTER	201D
EIS 4F	(PURPOSE)	228D
HINA I5	IN ORDER THAT	378A
KAI II4	ALSO	394C
HOUTOS 18β	THIS	601C
PAS 2A6	IN ALL RESPECTS	638C
HUP8KOOS	OBEDIENT	850B
10 GAR IB	FOR	151A
PROSWPON ICγ	FACE	728D
10A CHARIZOMAI 2	GIVE FREELY	885A
10B CHARIZOMAI 2	GIVE FREELY	885A
10C CHARIZOMAI 2	GIVE FREELY	885A
11 AGNOEW I	BE IGNORANT	11B
NO8MA 2	DESIGN	543A
OU 2D	NO	594C
PLEONEKTEW IB	OUTWIT	673C
SATAN	ADVERSARY	752B
12 ANOIGW IA	OPEN	70C
EUAGGELION 2Bα	GOSPEL	318B
THURA 2C	DOOR	366C
KURIOS 2Cγ	LORD	461A
TRWAS	TROAS	836D
CHRISTOS I	ANOINTED ONE	895C
13 ANESIS 2	REST	64D
APOTASSW I	SAY FAREWELL	100B
AUTOS 3B	(OBLIQUE CASE)	123A
EXERCHOMAI IAє	GO OUT	274B
HEURISKW IA	FIND	325A
MAKEDONIA	MACEDONIA	488B
M8 AIIIF	NOT	518A
PNEUMA 3B	SPIRIT	681C
TITOS I	TITUS	828C
14 GNWSIS 2	KNOWLEDGE	163A
THRIAMBEUW I	TRIUMPH OVER	364B
OSM8 2	ODOR	590A
PANTOTE	ALWAYS	614A
TOPOS IA	PLACE	830A
PHANEROW IA	REVEAL	860C
CHARIS 5	FAVOR	886D
15 APOLLUMI 2Aα	PERISH	94D
EUWDIA	FRAGRANCE	330A
SWZW 2B	SAVE	806C
16 EIS 4E	SO THAT	228D
EK 6D	FROM	236A
ZW8 2Bα	LIFE	341B
THANATOS 2B	DEATH	352A
HIKANOS 2	APPROPRIATE	375B
HOS,H8,HO II2	THIS (ONE)	589B
OSM8 2	ODOR	590A
PROS III3C	TOWARD	717B
17 EILIKRINEIA	SINCERITY	221D
EK 3Gγ	BY	235A
EN I5D	IN	259B
KAP8LEUW	PEDDLE	404A
KATENANTI 2B	IN THE SIGHT OF	422B
LOGOS I8β	WORD	479B
HO,H8,TO IIII	THE	555A
POLUS I2Aβ	MANY	695A
17B HWS IIIIA	SO	906C
17C HWS IIIIA	SO	906C

2 CORINTHIANS 3

	Greek	English	No.
1	EPISTOL8	LETTER	300D
	EPISTOL8	LETTER	301A
	8 ID8	OR	343D
	SUNIST8MI IIB	UNITE	798B
	SUSTATIKOS	INTRODUCING	802C
	TIS, TI IA8	ANY ONE	827D
	CHR8ZW	NEED	893D
2	ANAGINWSKW I	READ	51B
	EGGRAPHW 2	RECORD	213A
	EIMI II2	TO BE	222D
	EPISTOL8	LETTER	300D
	PAS IB	ALL	637A
	PROEIPON 2B	FORETELL	711D
2F	KARDIA IBy	HEART	404D
3	DIAKONEW 3	CARE FOR	183B
	EN IIB	IN	257D
	EPISTOL8	LETTER	300D
	ZAW IAe	LIVE	336D
	LITHINOS I	STONE	475A
	MELAS	BLACK	501A
	PLAX	FLAT STONE	672B
	PNEUMA 5A	SPIRIT	682C
	SARKINOS I	FLESHY	750C
	PHANEROW 2B«	REVEAL	860D
4	ECHW I2E8	HAVE	333A
	PEPOITH8SIS 2	TRUST	649B
	PROS III4B	TOWARD	717C
	TOIOUTOS 2A8	SUCH A KIND	829A
5	APO V5	OF	87D
	HEAUTOU IA	ONESELF	211B
	HEAUTOU IE	ONESELF	211B
	THEOS 3A	GOD	357D
	HIKANOS 2	APPROPRIATE	375B
	HIKANOT8S	FITNESS	375B
	LOGIZOMAI 2	CONSIDER	477B
	HOTI IC	THAT	593A
6	APOKTEINW IB	KILL	93C
	GRAMMA 2C	WRITING	164D
	DIATH8K8 2	COVENANT	182B
	DIAKONOS IA	SERVANT	183D
	ZWOPOIEW I	MAKE ALIVE	342C
	HIKANOW	MAKE SUFFICIENTLY	375C
	KAINOS 3B	NEW	395B
6A	PNEUMA 5Gy	SPIRIT	683C
6B	PNEUMA 5Gy	SPIRIT	683C
7	ATENIZW	LOOK INTENTLY AT	119C
	GINOMAI II4A	BE	159C
	GRAMMA I	LETTER	164C
	DIAKONIA 3	SERVICE	183C
	ENTUPOW	CARVE	269D
	KATARGEW 2	ABOLISH	418C
	LITHOS IE	STONE	475C
	M8 AI3	NOT	517C
	MWUS8S	MOSES	533D
	PNEUMA 5Gy	SPIRIT	683C
	PROSWPON IA	FACE	728A
	HUIOS IB«	SON	841C
	HWSTE 2A8	THEREFORE	908C
7FF	DOXA IA	BRIGHTNESS	202D
8	DIAKONIA 3	SERVICE	183C
	EIMI III4	TO BE	224B
8	MALLON 2B	MORE	490C
	PNEUMA 5Gy	SPIRIT	683C
	PWS ID	HOW	739D
9	DIAKONIA 3	SERVICE	183C
	DIKAIOSUN8 3	RIGHTEOUSNESS	196A
	KATAKRISIS	CONDEMNATION	413B
	MALLON 2B	MORE	490C
	PERISSEUW IAy	BE LEFT OVER	656D
	POLUS I2C«	MANY	695C
9=11	GAR IC	FOR	151B
10	GAR IE	FOR	151C
	DOXAZW 2	GLORIFY	203D
	HEINEKEN	ON ACCOUNT OF	225A
	HENEKA	BECAUSE OF	264B
	MEROS IBθ	MATTER	507B
	HUPERBALLW	SURPASS	848A
11	KATARGEW 2	ABOLISH	418C
	MALLON 2B	MORE	490C
	MENW IC8	REMAIN	505C
	POLUS I2C«	MANY	695C
12	ELPIS 2B	HOPE	252D
	ECHW I2E8	HAVE	333A
	OUN IA	THEREFORE	597B
	*PARR8SIA I	PLAINLY	636A
	POLUS IIB8	MANY	694D
	TOIOUTOS 2A8	SUCH A KIND	829A
	CHRAOMAI 2	USE	893A
13	ATENIZW	LOOK INTENTLY AT	119C
	KATHAPER	JUST AS	387D
	KALUMMA I	COVERING	401D
	KATARGEW 2	ABOLISH	418C
	M8 AIIIE	NOT	518A
	MWUS8S	MOSES	533D
	PROS III3A	TOWARD	717A
	PROSWPON IA	FACE	728A
	TELOS IA	END	819A
	TITH8MI IIA8	PUT	823D
	HUIOS IB«	SON	841C
14	ANAGNWSIS I	READING	52A
	ANAKALUPTW	UNCOVER	55B
	ACHRI IA	UNTIL	128B
	DIATH8K8 2	COVENANT	182B
	KALUMMA 2	COVERING	401D
	KATARGEW 2	ABOLISH	418C
	MENW IA«	REMAIN	505A
	NO8MA I	THOUGHT	542D
	PALAIOS I	OLD	610C
	*PWROW	HARDEN	739B
	S8MERON	TODAY	756C
15	AN 3B	(PARTICLE)	48C
	ANAGINWSKW 2	READ	51C
	EPI IIIIAζ	ON	288C
	HEWS IIIC	UNTIL	335C
	H8NIKA	WHEN	349A
	KALUMMA 2	COVERING	401D
	KARDIA IB8	HEART	404D
	KEIMAI IB	LIE	427D
	MWUS8S	MOSES	533D
	S8MERON	TODAY	756C
16	AN 3B	(PARTICLE)	48C
	EPISTREPHW IB8	TURN	301B
	H8NIKA	WHEN	349A
	KALUMMA 2	COVERING	401D

16	KURIOS 2Cγ	LORD 461A
	PERIAIREW 1	TAKE AWAY 651C
16FF	PNEUMA 5Dα	SPIRIT 683B
17	ELEUTHERIA	FREEDOM 250A
	HOU 1B	WHERE 594A
	PNEUMA 5Dα	SPIRIT 683B
17A	PNEUMA 5Dα	SPIRIT 683B
17B	PNEUMA 5B	SPIRIT 682C
18	ANAKALUPTW	UNCOVER 55B
	APO 113B	FROM 86C
	APO V4	FROM 87C
	EIKWN 2	FORM 221C
	KATHAPER	JUST AS 387D
	KATHWSPER	AS 392C
	KATOPTRIZW	CONTEMPLATE 426A
	METAMORPHOW 2	TRANSFORM 513A
	PAS 1Eα	ALL 637D
	PNEUMA 5B	SPIRIT 682C
	PROSWPON 1A	FACE 728A

2 CORINTHIANS 4

1	DIAKONIA 3	SERVICE 183C
	EGKAKEW 2	DESPAIR 214C
	EKKAKEW	LOSE HEART 240A
	ELEEW	HAVE MERCY 249B
	ECHW 121	HAVE 333C
	HOUTOS 2B	THIS 601D
2	AISCHUN8 1	SHAME 24D
	AL8THEIA 2B	TRUTH 35C
	ANTHRWPOS 1Aα	MAN 67C
	APEIPON	DISOWN 82D
	DOLOW	FALSIFY 202C
	EN 14D	IN 258C
	ENWPION 2B	BEFORE 270B
	KRUPTOS 2A	HIDDEN 455A
	LOGOS 1Bβ	WORD 479B
	M8DE 1B	AND NOT 519D
	HO,H8,TO 112A	THE 553B
	PANOURGIA	CUNNING 613A
	PAS 1Aα	EVERY EACH 636C
	PERIPATEW 2Aδ	GO ABOUT 655B
	PROS 1115B	TOWARD 717D
	SUNEID8SIS 2	CONSCIOUSNESS 794B
	SUNIST8MI 11B	UNITE 798B
	PHANERWSIS	ANNOUNCEMENT 861A
3	APOLLUMI 2Aα	PERISH 94D
	EI VI2	BUT IF 218D
	EUAGGELION 2Bβ	GOSPEL 318C
	KALUPTW 2B	HIDE 402A
4	AIWN 2A	AGE 27B
	APISTOS 2	FAITHLESS 85B
	AUGAZW 1	SEE 120B
	AUGAZW 2	SHINE FORTH 120B
	DIAUGAZW 1	SHINE THROUGH 189B
	EIKWN 1B	IMAGE 221B
	EUAGGELION 2Bα	GOSPEL 318B
	EUAGGELION 2Bα	GOSPEL 318B
	THEOS 5	GOD 358D
	KATAUGAZW	ILLUMINATE 420D
	M8 AII1E	NOT 518A
	NO8MA 1	THOUGHT 542D
	TUPHLOW	TO BLIND 838D

4	PHWTISMOS 1	ILLUMINATION 881C
	CHRISTOS 1	ANOINTED ONE 895C
5	DOULOS 1Eα	SLAVE 204D
	K8RUSSW 2Bβ	ANNOUNCE 432C
	KURIOS 2Cγ	LORD 461A
6	GNWSIS 2	KNOWLEDGE 163A
	KARDIA 1Bβ	HEART 404C
	HOTI 3B	THAT 594A
	PROS 1113A	TOWARD 717A
	PROSWPON 1A	FACE 728A
	PROSWPON 1Cγ	FACE 728D
	SKOTOS 1	DARKNESS 765A
	PHWS 1A	LIGHT 879C
	PHWTISMOS 2	ILLUMINATION 881C
6A	LAMPW 1B	SHINE OUT 467B
6B	LAMPW 2	SHINE 467B
7	DE 2	BUT, AND 170D
	EIMI IV5	TO BE 225A
	TH8SAUROS 2Bγ	TREASURE 362B
	OSTRAKINOS	MADE OF EARTH 591C
	HOUTOS 2B	THIS 601D
	SKEUOS 2	THING 761D
	HUPERBOL8	EXCESS 848B
8	APOREW	UNCERTAIN 97A
	EXAPOREW	272C
	BE IN GREAT DIFFICULTY	
	THLIBW 3	OPPRESS 362C
	OU 3A	NO 594C
	PAS 2Aβ	EVERY RESPECT 638A
	STENOCHWREW	CRAMP 774A
9	DIWKW 2	PERSECUTE 200B
	EGKATALEIPW 2	FORSAKE 214D
	KATABALLW 1	THROW DOWN 409D
	OU 3A	NO 594C
10	ANTANAPL8ROW	FILL UP 72B
	NEKRWSIS 1	DEATH 537C
	PERIPHERW 1	CARRY ABOUT 659A
10A	SWMA 1B	BODY 807A
10B	SWMA 1B	BODY 807A
10F	ZW8 1A	LIFE 340D
10F	PHANEROW 1B	REVEAL 860C
11	AEI 3	ALWAYS 19A
	EIS 4A	INTO 228B
	ZAW 1Aα	LIVE 336C
	THANATOS 1C	DEATH 351D
	THN8TOS	MORTAL 363B
	PARADIDWMI 1B	GIVE OVER 620B
	SARX 5	BODY 751B
12	ENERGEW 1B	WORK 264D
	ZW8 2Bα	LIFE 341B
	THANATOS 1C	DEATH 351D
	HWSTE 1A	THEREFORE 908B
13	GRAPHW 2C	WRITE 166A
	PISTIS 2Dα	FAITH 669B
	PNEUMA 5E	SPIRIT 683C
13A	PISTEUW 2C	BELIEVE 667D
13B	PISTEUW 2C	BELIEVE 667D
14	EGEIRW 1Aβ	RAISE 213D
	KURIOS 2Cγ	LORD 461A
	PARIST8MI 1E	BRING BEFORE 633B
	SUN 2C	WITH 789C
15	DOXA 3	FAME 203B
	EUCHARISTIA 2	THANKFULNESS 329A

15	PAS 2Bβ	ALL THINGS 638D
	PERISSEUW 2A	BE LEFT OVER 656D
	PLEONAZW 1A	INCREASE 673B
	POLUS II2Aβ	MANY 695D
	CHARIS 3B	FAVOR 886B
16	ALLA 4	BUT, YET 38B
	ANAKAINOW	RENEW 55A
	ANTHRWPOS 2Cα	MAN 68A
	ANTHRWPOS 2Cα	MAN 68A
	DIAPHTHEIRW 1	SPOIL 189D
	EGKAKEW 2	DESPAIR 214C
	EI VI4	EVEN IF 219A
	EKKAKEW	LOSE HEART 240A
	EXW 1Aγ	OUTSIDE 279A
	ESW 2	IN 314C
	H8MERA 2	DAY 347C
17	AIWNIOS 3	ETERNAL 28B
	BAROS 3	FULNESS 133C
	DOXA 1Bβ	GLORY 203A
	EIS 3	COMPLETELY 228B
	ELAPHROS 1	LIGHT 248A
	THLIPSIS 1	TRIBULATION 362D
	KATA II5Bβ	ACCORDING TO 408D
	KATERGAZOMAI 2	ACHIEVE 422D
	PARAUTIKA	628D
	SLIGHT MOMENTARY TROUBLE	
	HUPERBOL8	EXCESS 848B
18	AIWNIOS 3	ETERNAL 28B
	BLEPW 1B	SEE 143A
	PROSKAIROS	TEMPORARY 722C
	SKOPEW	NOTICE 764A
18A	M8 AII2D	NOT 518C
18B	M8 AII2D	NOT 518C

2 CORINTHIANS 5

1	AIWNIOS 3	ETERNAL 28A
	ACHEIROPOI8TOS	127D
	NOT MADE BY HAND	
	EK 3C	FROM 234B
	EPIGEIOS 1	EARTHLY 290C
	THEOS 3B	GOD 357D
	KATALUW 1Bβ	DESTROY 415B
	OIDA 1E	KNOW 558C
	OIKODOM8 2B	BUILDING 562A
1A	OIKIA 1B	HOUSE 560A
1B	OIKIA 1B	HOUSE 560A
1F	OURANOS 2D	HEAVEN 599D
2	GAR 1E	FOR 151C
	EPENDUOMAI	PUT ON 284C
	EPIPOTHEW	DESIRE 297D
	OIK8T8RION 2	DWELLING 559D
	STENAZW	SIGH 773D
3	GE 3A (EMPHASIZING PARTICLE)	152A
	GUMNOS 4	BARE 167A
	EKDUW 2	STRIP 238C
	ENDUW 2A	DRESS 263C
	HEURISKW 2	FIND 326A
4	BAREW	BURDEN 133B
	BARUNW	BURDEN 133D
	GAR 3	CERTAINLY 151D
	EKDUW 2	STRIP 238C
	EPENDUOMAI	PUT ON 284C

4	EPI III8γ	ON 287C
	ZW8 IA	LIFE 340D
	THN8TOS	MORTAL 363B
	KATAPINW 2	SWALLOW 417C
	HO,H8,TO II2A	THE 553B
	HOS,H8,HO III0	(REL PRON) 589A
	SK8NOS	TENT 762C
	STENAZW	SIGH 773D
	HUPO IAβ	BY 850D
5	ARRABWN	DOWN PAYMENT 109A
	AUTOS 1H	EVEN 122D
	EIS 4F	(PURPOSE) 228D
	KATERGAZOMAI 3	ACHIEVE 423A
	PNEUMA 5Dα	SPIRIT 683A
6	APOD8MEW 2	BE AWAY 89C
	END8MEW	BE AT HOME 262C
	THARREW	BE CONFIDENT 352C
	KURIOS 2Cγ	LORD 460D
	SWMA 1B	BODY 807A
7	EIDON 1A	SEE 219D
	EIDOS 3	SIGHT 220B
	PERIPATEW 2B	GO ABOUT 655C
	PISTIS 2Dβ	FAITH 669C
8	APOLUTRWSIS 2A	REDEMPTION 95D
	EKD8MEW 1	LEAVE 237D
	END8MEW	BE AT HOME 262C
	EUDOKEW 1	WELL PLEASED 319C
	KURIOS 2Cγ	LORD 460D
	SWMA 1B	BODY 807A
9	DIO	THEREFORE 197D
	END8MEW	BE AT HOME 262C
	EUARESTOS 1	PLEASING 319A
	PHILOTIMEOMAI	ASPIRE 869C
10	B8MA 2	TRIBUNAL 139D
	DEI 1	IT IS NECESSARY 171A
	EI VI13B	IF 219B
	EMPROSTHEN 2B	IN FRONT 256C
	KOMIZW 2A	BRING 443D
	HOS,H8,HO I2A	(REL PRON) 587B
	PAS 1Eα	ALL 637D
	PRASSW 1A	DO 705A
	PROS III5D	TOWARD 717D
	*SWMA 1B	BODY 807A
	PHANEROW 2Bβ	REVEAL 860D
	PHAULOS 2	WORTHLESS 862B
	PHOBOS 1	CAUSING OF FEAR 871B
11	ELPIZW 2	HOPE 252A
	EN IIE	IN 257D
	PEITHW 1B	CONVINCE 644D
	SUNEID8SIS 2	CONSCIOUSNESS 794B
	PHOBOS 1	CAUSING OF FEAR 871B
	PHOBOS 2Bα	FEAR 871D
11A	PHANEROW 2Bα	REVEAL 860D
11B	PHANEROW 2Bα	REVEAL 860D
12	APHORM8	PRETEXT 127A
	DIDWMI 1Bα	GIVE 192A
	KARDIA 1Bα	HEART 404C
	KAUCHAOMAI 1	BOAST 427A
	KAUCH8MA 2	BOAST 427B
	PROSWPON 1D	FACE 729A
	SUNIST8MI II1B	UNITE 798B
	HUPER IF	IN BEHALF OF 847A
13	EXIST8MI 2A	LOSE ONES MIND 276A

13	THEOS 3Gα	GOD	358C
	SWPHRONEW I	SOUND MIND	809C
14	AGAP8 I2A	LOVE	6A
	APOTHN8SKW IBβ	DIE	91A
	ARA 3	THEN	103C
	HEIS 2B	ONE	230C
	KRINW 2	JUDGE	452C
	SUNECHW 7	URGE ON	797A
	HUPER IC	IN BEHALF OF	846D
14B	PAS 2Bα	IN ALL RESPECTS	638C
14F	APOTHN8SKW IAα	DIE	90D
15	ZAW 3B	LIVE	337C
	M8KETI I	NO LONGER	520B
15A	HUPER IC	IN BEHALF OF	846D
15B	HUPER IC	IN BEHALF OF	846D
16	ALLA 4	BUT, YET	38B
	GINWSKW IB	KNOW	160A
	OIDA 2	KNOW	558D
	SARX 6	BODY	751C
16A	KATA II5Bβ	ACCORDING TO	408C
16A	NUN 3B	NOW	548B
16B	KATA II5Bβ	ACCORDING TO	408C
16B	KATA II7A	(ADJ PHRASE)	408D
16B	NUN IC	NOW	547D
16B	SARX 6	BODY	751C
16F	HWSTE IA	THEREFORE	908B
17	ARCHAIOS 2	ANCIENT	111A
	IDOU IA	BEHOLD	371C
	KTISIS IBα	CREATION	457A
	HOTI IDβ	THAT	593C
	PARERCHOMAI IBα	PASS AWAY	631C
17A	KAINOS 3B	NEW	395B
17B	KAINOS 3B	NEW	395B
18	DIAKONIA 3	SERVICE	183C
	THEOS 3A	GOD	357C
	KATALLAG8	RECONCILIATION	415A
	KATALLASSW I	RECONCILE	415A
	HOTI IDβ	THAT	593C
19	AUTOS 3Fβ	(OBLIQUE CASE)	123B
	EIMI II4F	TO BE	223B
	THEOS 3B	GOD	357D
	KATALLAG8	RECONCILIATION	415A
	KATALLASSW I	RECONCILE	415A
	KATALUW IBβ	DESTROY	415C
	KOSMOS 5A	WORLD	447C
	KOSMOS 7	WORLD	447D
	LOGIZOMAI IA	RECKON	477A
	LOGOS IBβ	WORD	479C
	HOTI IDβ	THAT	593B
	HOTI IDβ	THAT	593C
	PARAPTWMA 2B	TRANSGRESSION	627B
	TITH8MI III A	ESTABLISH	824B
20	DEOMAI 3	ASK	174B
	KATALLASSW 2A	RECONCILE	415A
	PARAKALEW 2	APPEAL TO	622C
	PRESBEUW	BE AN AMBASSADOR	706B
20B	HUPER IA6	IN BEHALF OF	846C
21	HAMARTIA 3	SIN	43A
	GINWSKW 6Aα	KNOW	160C
	DIKAIOSUN8 3	RIGHTEOUSNESS	196A
	M8 AII2D	NOT	518C
	POIEW IIB¹	DO	688B
	HUPER IC	IN BEHALF OF	846D

2 CORINTHIANS 6

1	DECHOMAI 3B	ACCEPT	176C
	EIS 4E	SO THAT	228D
	KENOS 2Aβ	EMPTY	429A
	PARAKALEW 2	APPEAL TO	622C
	SUNERGEW	WORK WITH	795B
2	DEKTOS	ACCEPTABLE	173B
	EPAKOUW I	HEAR	282A
	EUPROSDEKTOS I	ACCEPTABLE	324D
	H8MERA 4A	TIME	348A
	IDOU 2	THERE IS	371D
	LEGW I7	SAY	470A
2A	KAIROS I	TIME	395C
2A	SWT8RIA 2	DELIVERANCE	809A
2B	SWT8RIA 2	DELIVERANCE	809A
3	DIAKONIA 3	SERVICE	183C
	DIDWMI IBα	GIVE	192A
	M8DEIS I	NO	520A
	M8DEIS 2B6	NOTHING	520B
	PROSKOP8		723C
		TIME FOR TAKING OFFENCE	
4	ANAGK8 2	DISTRESS	52B
	DIAKONOS IA	SERVANT	183D
	THLIPSIS I	TRIBULATION	362D
	STENOCHWRIA	DISTRESS	774A
	SUNIST8MI IIB	UNITE	798D
	HUPOMON8 I	PATIENCE	854A
	HWS III A	SO	906C
5	AGRUPNIA I	WAKEFULNESS	14A
	AKATASTASIA I	DISTURBANCE	29C
	KOPOS 2	WORK	444A
	N8STEIA I	FASTING	540A
	PL8G8 I	BLOW	674A
	PHULAK8 3	GUARD	875C
6	AGAP8 II A	LOVE	5C
	AGAP8 II A	LOVE	5D
	HAGNOT8S	PURITY	12A
	ANUPOKRITOS	GENUINE	76A
	GNWSIS 2	KNOWLEDGE	163A
	MAKROTHUMIA 2A	PATIENCE	489B
	PNEUMA 5Cβ	SPIRIT	683A
	CHR8STOT8S 2A	GOODNESS	894D
7	AL8THEIA 2A	TRUTH	35B
	ARISTEROS	WEAPONS	106B
	DEXIOS I	RIGHT	173C
	DIKAIOSUN8 2B	RIGHTEOUSNESS	195D
	LOGOS IAβ	WORD	478C
	HOPLON 2B	WEAPON	579A
8	AL8TH8S I	TRUE	36A
	ATIMIA	DISHONOR	119D
	DUSPH8MIA	SLANDER	209A
	EUPH8MIA	GOOD REPUTE	327D
	PLANOS 2	DECEITFUL	672A
9	AGNOEW 2	NOT TO KNOW	11B
	APOTHN8SKW 2	BE ABOUT TO DIE	91B
	EPIGINWSKW IA	KNOW	291A
	THANATOW I	PUT TO DEATH	352B
	IDOU IBβ	BEHOLD	371C
	KAI I2G	AND	393C
	PAIDEUW 2Bα	INSTRUCT	608D
10	AEI I	ALWAYS	19A
	ECHW I2A	HAVE	332B

10	KATECHW 1Bγ	KEEP	424A
	PAS 2A6	EVERYTHING	638C
	PLOUTIZW 2	MAKE RICH	680A
	PTWCHOS 1A	BEGGING POOR	735C
	CHAIRW 1	REJOICE	882A
11	ANOIGW 2	OPEN	70D
	KARDIA 1Bα	HEART	404C
	KORINTHIOS	CORINTHIAN	445C
	PLATUNW 2	ENLARGE	673A
	PROS III4A	TOWARD	717C
12	EPOURANIOS 2Aα	HEAVENLY	306A
	PROEIPON 2B	FORETELL	711D
	SPLAGCHNON 1B	INWARD PARTS	770C
	STENOCHWREW	CRAMP	774A
	CHWREW 3Bα	HAVE ROOM FOR	898B
13	ANTIMISTHIA	PENALTY	74C
	LEGW 19	SAY	470C
	LEGW IIIF	DECLARE	471A
	PLATUNW 2	ENLARGE	673A
	TEKNON 2B	CHILD	816B
	HWS IIIIA	SO	906C
14	ANOMIA 1	LAWLESSNESS	71A
	DIKAIOSUN8 2B	RIGHTEOUSNESS	195C
	HETEROZUGEW	BE MISMATED	315A
	KOINWNIA 1	ASSOCIATION	440A
	METOCH8	SHARING	516A
	PROS III4B	TOWARD	717C
	SKOTOS 2B	DARKNESS	765B
14F	APISTOS 2	FAITHLESS	85A
14-16	TIS, TI 2	WHICH	827B
15	BELIAR	BELIAL	138D
	MERIS 2	SHARE	506C
	PISTOS 2	TRUSTWORTHY	671A
	PROS III4B	TOWARD	717C
	SUMPHWN8SIS	AGREEMENT	788D
16	EIDWLON 2	IDOL	220D
	EIMI II2	TO BE	222D
	EMPERIPATEW	WALK ABOUT	255B
	ENOIKEW	LIVE	267A
	ZAW 1Aε	LIVE	336D
	THEOS 3C	GOD	358A
	SUGKATATHESIS	AGREEMENT	781A
16A	NAOS 2	TEMPLE	535D
16B	NAOS 2	TEMPLE	535D
17	AKATHARTOS 1	IMPURE	28C
	HAPTW 2A	TOUCH	102B
	APHORIZW 1	SEPARATE	126D
	EISDECHOMAI	WELCOME	231C
	EK 1B	AWAY FROM	233C
	EXERCHOMAI 1B8	GO OUT	274C
	MESOS 2	THE MIDDLE	509A
18	EIMI III2	TO BE	224A
	EIS 8A8		229C
	THUGAT8R 2C	DAUGHTER	365C
	PANTOKRATWR	ALMIGHTY	613D
	PAT8R 3C8	FATHER	641C
	HUIOS 1Cγ	SON	841D

2 CORINTHIANS 7

1	AGAP8TOS 2	BELOVED	6C
	HAGIWSUN8	HOLINESS	10C
	EPAGGELIA 2A	PROMISE	280A

1	EPITELEW 2	PERFORM	302B
	KATHARIZW 2Bα	CLEANSE	388B
	MOLUSMOS	DEFILEMENT	528D
	OUN 1B	THEREFORE	597B
	PAS 1A8	EVERY EACH	636D
	PNEUMA 3A	SPIRIT	681B
	SARX 2	BODY	751A
	PHOBOS 2Bα	FEAR	871D
2	ADIKEW 2A	DO WRONG	17B
	PLEONEKTEW 1A	OUTWIT	673B
	PHTHEIRW 2A	RUIN	865A
	PHTHEIRW 1A	RUIN	865A
	CHWREW 3Bα	HAVE ROOM FOR	898B
3	KARDIA 1B5	HEART	405B
	KATAKRISIS	CONDEMNATION	413B
	PROEIPON 2B	FORETELL	711D
	PROS III3A	TOWARD	717A
	SUZAW	LIVE WITH	783B
	SUNAPOTHN8SKW	DIE WITH	792C
4	THLIPSIS 1	TRIBULATION	362D
	KAUCH8SIS 1	BOASTING	427B
	PARAKL8SIS 3	COMFORT	623C
	PARR8SIA 3A	COURAGE	636A
	PAS 1C8	ALL	637B
	PL8ROW 1B	MAKE FULL	677A
	PROS III4B	TOWARD	717C
	HUPER 1F	IN BEHALF OF	847A
	HUPERPERISSEUW 2	BE ABUNDANT	849D
	CHARA 1	JOY	883D
4A	POLUS 11B8	MANY	694D
4B	POLUS 11B8	MANY	694C
5	ANESIS 2	REST	64D
	EXWTHEN 1Bα	OUTSIDE	279B
	ESWTHEN 2	INSIDE	314C
	THLIBW 3	OPPRESS	362C
	MAKEDONIA	MACEDONIA	488B
	MACH8	BATTLE	497C
	PAS 2A8	EVERY RESPECT	638A
	PHOBOS 2Aα	FEAR	871C
6	TAPEINOS 1	LOW	811D
	TITOS 1	TITUS	828C
6A	PARAKALEW 4	IMPLORE	623A
6B	PARAKALEW 4	IMPLORE	623A
6F	PAROUSIA 2A	COMING	635B
7	ANAGGELLW 1	TO REPORT	50D
	EN IIIIA	BY	260B
	EPI IIIA6	AT	286D
	EPIPOTH8SIS	LONGING	297D
	Z8LOS 1	ZEAL	338B
	MALLON 1	MORE	490B
	MONOS 2C	ONLY	529D
	ODURMOS	LAMENTATION	557C
	PARAKALEW 4	IMPLORE	623A
	PARAKL8SIS 3	COMFORT	623C
	CHAIRW 1	REJOICE	882A
	HWSTE 2A8	THEREFORE	908C
8	BLEPW 7B	SEE	143C
	EI VI4	EVEN IF	219A
	EPISTOL8	LETTER	300D
	KAIROS 1	TIME	395C
	METAMELOMAI	REPENT	513A
	HOTI 3B	THAT	594A
	PROS III2B	TOWARD	717A

8	HWRA 2Aß	TIME OF DAY 904C
8A	LUPEW I	GRIEVE 482D
8A	METAMELOMAI	REPENT 513A
8B	LUPEW I	GRIEVE 482D
8B	METAMELOMAI	REPENT 513A
9	EIS 4E	SO THAT 228D
	EK 3E«	BY 234C
	Z8MIOW I	SUFFER DAMAGE 339A
	METANOIA	REPENTANCE 514B
	M8DEIS 2B6	NOTHING 520A
	CHAIRW I	REJOICE 881D
9A	LUPEW 2A	GRIEVE 483A
9B	LUPEW 2A	GRIEVE 483A
9C	LUPEW 2A	GRIEVE 483A
9FF	THEOS 3B	GOD 358A
9=11	KATA II5A«	ACCORDING TO 408A
10	AMETAMEL8TOS I	WITHOUT REGRET 44D
	ERGAZOMAI 2C	BRING ABOUT 307B
	THANATOS 2B	DEATH 352A
	KATERGAZOMAI 2	ACHIEVE 422D
	KOSMOS 7	WORLD 447D
	METANOEW	CHANGE ONES MIND 513D
	METANOIA	REPENTANCE 514B
	SWT8RIA 2	DELIVERANCE 809A
	SWT8RIA 2	DELIVERANCE 809B
10A	LUP8	GRIEF 483B
10B	LUP8	GRIEF 483B
11	AGANAKT8SIS	INDIGNATION 4B
	HAGNOS I	PURE IID
	ALLA 5	BUT, YET 38B
	APOLOGIA 2B	DEFENSE 95C
	AUTOS IH	EVEN 122D
	GAR IB	FOR 151A
	EKDIK8SIS	VENGEANCE 238B
	EPIPOTH8SIS	LONGING 297D
	Z8LOS I	ZEAL 338A
	IDOU IC	REMEMBER 371D
	KATERGAZOMAI 2	ACHIEVE 422D
	LUPEW 2A	GRIEVE 483A
	PAS 2Aß	EVERY RESPECT 638A
	POSOS I	HOW GREAT 701A
	PRAGMA I	DEED 703D
	SPOUD8 2	DILIGENCE 771B
	SUNIST8MI IIC	UNITE 798C
	PHOBOS 2A«	FEAR 871B
12	ARA 4	THEN 103C
	GRAPHW 2D	WRITE 166A
	HENEKA	BECAUSE OF 264B
	HENEKA	BECAUSE OF 264C
	ENWPION 4	BEFORE 270C
	PROS III7	TOWARD 718A
	SPOUD8 2	DILIGENCE 771B
	PHANEROW IB	REVEAL 860C
12A	ADIKEW 2A	DO WRONG 17B
12B	ADIKEW 2A	DO WRONG 17B
13	ANAPAUW I	CAUSE TO REST 58C
	EPI IIIBß	TO 286D
	MALLON I	MORE 490B
	PARAKALEW 4	IMPLORE 623A
	PARAKL8SIS 3	COMFORT 623C
	PERISSOTERWS 2	MORE 657C
	PNEUMA 3B	SPIRIT 681C
	CHAIRW I	REJOICE 881B

13	CHARA I	JOY 883C
13F	TITOS I	TITUS 828C
14	AL8THEIA I	TRUTHFULNESS 35A
	EPI IIA6	BEFORE 286A
	KATAISCHUNW 2	BE HUMILIATED 411D
	KAUCHAOMAI 2	BOAST 427A
	KAUCH8SIS I	BOASTING 427C
	LALEW 2B	SPEAK 464D
	HOTI 3B	THAT 594A
	HOUTW IA	THUS 602B
	HUPER IF	IN BEHALF OF 847A
	HWS III	SO 905D
15	ANAMIMN8SKW	REMIND 57C
	DECHOMAI I	RECEIVE 176C
	EIMI II9B	TO BE 224A
	EIMI III2	TO BE 224A
	META AIIII	WITH 511A
	PAS IE«	ALL 637D
	PERISSOTERWS 2	MORE 657C
	SPLAGCHNON IB	INWARD PARTS 770C
	TROMOS	TREMBLING 834D
	HUPAKO8 IB	OBEDIENCE 844D
	PHOBOS 2A«	FEAR 871C
	HWS I2D	AS 905D
16	THARREW	BE CONFIDENT 352C
	PAS 2Aß	EVERY RESPECT 638A
	CHAIRW I	REJOICE 881D

2 CORINTHIANS 8

1	GNWRIZW I	MAKE KNOWN 162C
	DE 2	BUT, AND 170D
	EKKL8SIA 4B	CHURCH 240C
	MAKEDONIA	MACEDONIA 488B
	CHARIS 4	FAVOR 886B
2	HAPLOT8S 2	GENEROSITY 85B
	BATHOS 2	DEPTH 129D
	DOKIM8 2	TEST 201D
	THLIPSIS I	TRIBULATION 362D
	KATA IIB	DOWN 406C
	PERISSEIA	SURPLUS 656B
	PERISSEUW IAɣ	BE LEFT OVER 656D
	PLOUTOS	WEALTH 680A
	PLOUTOS 2	WEALTH 680B
	POLUS IIBß	MANY 694C
	PTWCHEIA	(EXTREME) POVERTY 735C
	CHARA I	JOY 883C
3	AUTHAIRETOS	120C
		OF ONES OWN ACCORD
	MARTUREW IA	BEAR WITNESS 493D
	PARA III3	IN COMPARISON 616B
	HUPER 2	BEYOND 847A
3A	DUNAMIS 2	POWER 207A
3B	DUNAMIS 2	POWER 207A
4	DEOMAI 2	ASK 174A
	DIAKONIA 4	SUPPORT 183C
	EIS 4G	FOR 229A
	KOINWNIA 4	ASSOCIATION 440B
	META AIII2	WITH 511A
	HO,H8,TO IIIG	THE 553A
	PARAKL8SIS 2	APPEAL 623C
	POLUS IIBß	MANY 694C
	CHARIS 3A	FAVOR 886A

5	DIA AIIIID	THROUGH 179C
	DIDWMI 6	GIVE 192D
	ELPIZW I	HOPE 252A
	THEL8MA 2B	WILL 355A
	PRWTOS 2C	FIRST 734A
6	EPITELEW I	END 302B
	HOUTOS 2B	THIS 601D
	PARAKALEW 2	APPEAL TO 622C
	PROENARCHOMAI	BEGIN 712A
	TITOS I	TITUS 828C
6F	CHARIS 3A	FAVOR 886A
7	AGAP8 IIB8	LOVE 5D
	ALLA 6	NOW 38B
	EK 3C	FROM 234B
	HINA III2	IN ORDER THAT 379A
	LOGOS IA8	WORD 478C
	PAS 2A8	EVERY RESPECT 638A
	PISTIS 2DY	FAITH 669C
	SPOUD8 2	DILIGENCE 771B
	HWSPER I	(JUST) AS 908A
7A	PERISSEUW IB8	656D
	BE LEFT OVER	
7B	PERISSEUW IB8	656D
	BE LEFT OVER	
8	AGAP8 IIA	LOVE 5C
	GN8SIOS 2	GENUINE 162A
	DOKIMAZW 2B	APPROVE 201D
	EPITAG8	COMMAND 302A
	KATA II58B	ACCORDING TO 408C
	LEGW I5	SAY 470A
	LEGW IIIF	DECLARE 471A
	HO,H8,TO II2C	THE 553C
	SPOUD8 2	DILIGENCE 771B
	HUMETEROS I	YOUR 843D
9	GINWSKW 6AA	KNOW 160C
	HINA IIE	IN ORDER THAT 377C
	KURIOS 2CY	LORD 461B
	PLOUSIOS 2	RICH 679C
	PLOUTEW 2	BE RICH 680A
	PTWCHEIA	(EXTREME) POVERTY 735C
	PTWCHEUW	BE (EXTREMELY) POOR 735C
	CHARIS 2A	FAVOR 885C
10	ALLA IA	BUT, YET 37C
	APO II2A	FROM 86B
	GNWM8 2	JUDGMENT 162B
	DIDWMI IB8	GIVE 192A
	THELW 2	WISH 355D
	HO,H8,TO II4A	THE 553D
	PERUSI	LAST YEAR 659D
	PROENARCHOMAI	BEGIN 712A
	SUMPHERW 2A	HELP 787D
10F	POIEW I2C	DO 689B
11	EK 3I	BY 235A
	ECHW I2A	HAVE 332C
	KATHAPER	JUST AS 387D
	KAI II3	ALSO 394B
	NUNI IC	NOW 548C
	HO,H8,TO II4A	THE 553D
	HO,H8,TO II4B8	THE 554A
	HOPWS 2AA	IN ORDER THAT 580C
	HOUTW IA	THUS 602B
	PROENARCHOMAI	BEGIN 712A
	PROTHUMIA	WILLINGNESS 713C
11A	EPITELEW I	END 302B
11B	EPITELEW I	END 302B
12	PROTHUMIA	WILLINGNESS 713C
	PROKEIMAI 2	BE SET BEFORE 714C
12A	KATHO 2	IN SO FAR AS 391C
12B	KATHO 2	IN SO FAR AS 391C
13	ANESIS 2	REST 64D
	EK 3I	BY 235A
	THLIPSIS I	TRIBULATION 363A
	HINA III3	IN ORDER THAT 379A
	ISOT8S I	EQUALITY 382A
14	GINOMAI I4CA	COME, GO 158D
	EKEINOS IA	THAT 238D
	ISOT8S I	EQUALITY 382A
	KAIROS I	TIME 395C
	NUN 3A	NOW 548A
	HOPWS 2AA	IN ORDER THAT 580C
14A	PERISSEUMA I	ABUNDANCE 656B
14A	HUSTER8MA I	NEED 857A
14B	PERISSEUMA I	ABUNDANCE 656B
14B	HUSTER8MA I	NEED 857A
15	ELATTONEW	HAVE LESS 247D
	HO,H8,TO II9A	THE 554D
	OLIGOS 2A	LITTLE 566C
	PLEONAZW IB	INCREASE 673B
	POLUS I2CA	MANY 695C
16	DIDWMI IB8	GIVE 192A
	SPOUD8 2	DILIGENCE 771B
	TITOS I	TITUS 828C
	CHARIS 5	FAVOR 886D
17	AUTHAIRETOS	120C
	OF ONES OWN ACCORD	
	DECHOMAI 3B	ACCEPT 176C
	EXERCHOMAI IAE	GO OUT 274B
	PARAKL8SIS I	ENCOURAGEMENT 623B
	PARAKL8SIS 2	APPEAL 623C
	SPOUDAIOS	EAGER 771A
	HUPARCHW 2	BE 846A
18	DIA AI2	THROUGH 178C
	EPAINOS IAA	PRAISE 281B
	EUAGGELION IA	GOSPEL 318A
	META AII4	WITH 510D
	PAS IDA	ALL 637C
	SUMPEMPW	SEND (WITH) 787A
18F	EKKL8SIA 4B	CHURCH 240C
19	ALLA IA	BUT, YET 37C
	DIAKONEW 2	SERVE 183A
	MONOS 2C	ONLY 530A
	PROTHUMIA	WILLINGNESS 713B
	SUNEKD8MOS	794D
	TRAVELING COMPANION	
	CHARIS 3A	FAVOR 886A
	CHEIROTONEW	CHOOSE 889B
20	HADROT8S	ABUNDANCE 18C
	DIAKONEW 2	SERVE 183A
	M8 BIB	NOT 519A
	MWMAOMAI	FIND FAULT 532D
	STELLW 2	KEEP AWAY 773C
	TIS, TI IAY	ANY ONE 827D
21	ALLA IA	BUT, YET 37C
	KALOS 2B	GOOD 401B
	KURIOS 2D	LORD 461B
	PRONOEW 2	TAKE CARE 715C

21 PRONOEW 2 TAKE CARE 715C
21B ENWPION 3 BEFORE 270B
22 DOKIMAZW 2B APPROVE 201D
   EIS 4Cβ (GOAL) 228C
   NUNI 1A NOW 548B
   PEPOITH8SIS 1 TRUST 649A
   POLLAKIS OFTEN 693B
   SUMPEMPW SEND (WITH) 787A
22A POLUS I2Bα MANY 695A
22A SPOUDAIOS EAGER 771A
22B POLUS I2Cα MANY 695B
22B SPOUDAIOS EAGER 771A
22C POLUS I1Bβ MANY 694D
23 APOSTOLOS 1 MESSENGER 99A
   KOINWNOS 1D COMPANION 440D
   HO,H8,TO III1D THE 552D
   SUNERGOS WORKING WITH 795C
   TITOS 1 TITUS 828C
   HUPER 1F IN BEHALF OF 847A
23F EKKL8SIA 4B CHURCH 240C
24 AGAP8 II1A LOVE 5C
   ENDEIKNUMI 1 DEMONSTRATE 262A
   ENDEIXIS 2 PROOF 262A
   KAUCH8SIS 1 BOASTING 427B
   PROSWPON 1Cβ FACE 728D
   HUPER 1F IN BEHALF OF 847A

2 CORINTHIANS 9

1 GAR 1B FOR 151B
   GAR 1E FOR 151C
   GRAPHW 2D WRITE 166B
   DIAKONIA 4 SUPPORT 183C
   EIS 4G FOR 229A
   PERI 1H ABOUT 650D
   PERISSOS 2B EXTRAORDINARY 657B
2 APO II2A FROM 86B
   ACHAIA ACHAIA 127D
   EK 3C FROM 234B
   ERETHIZW IRRITATE 308D
   Z8LOS 1 ZEAL 338A
   KAUCHAOMAI 2 BOAST 427A
   MAKEDWN MACEDONIAN 488B
   PERUSI LAST YEAR 659D
   POLUS II2Aα MANY 695D
   POLUS II2Aγ MANY 696A
   PROTHUMIA WILLINGNESS 713B
2F PARASKEUAZW 2 PREPARE 627C
2F HUPER 1F IN BEHALF OF 847A
3 KATHWS 1 JUST AS 392A
   KAUCH8MA 2 BOAST 427B
   KENOW 3 MAKE EMPTY 429C
   MEROS 1B θ MATTER 507B
   PEMPW 1 SEND 647B
4 APARASKEUASTOS UNPREPARED 80B
   HEURISKW 1Cβ FIND 325C
   KATAISCHUNW 2 BE HUMILIATED 411D
   MAKEDWN MACEDONIAN 488B
   M8PWS 1A LEST SOMEHOW 521C
   SUN 1B WITH 789B
   HUPOSTASIS 2 CONFIDENCE 854D
5 ANAGKAIOS 1 NECESSARY 51D
   HETOIMOS 1 READY 316D

5 H8GEOMAI 2 CONSIDER 344B
   PARAKALEW 3 IMPLORE 622D
   PLEONEXIA GREEDINESS 673D
   PROEPAGGELLW PROMISE BEFORE 712A
   PROERCHOMAI 3 GO FORWARD 712B
   PROKATAGGELLW FORETELL 714B
   PROKATARTIZW GET READY 714B
5A EULOGIA 3Bβ BLESSING 323A
5A EULOGIA 5 BOUNTY 323B
5B EULOGIA 5 BOUNTY 323B
6 EPI III1B⌠ ON 287C
   THERIZW 2A REAP 360A
6A EULOGIA 5 BOUNTY 323B
6A SPEIRW 1Bα SOW 768D
6A PHEIDOMENWS SPARINGLY 862C
6B EULOGIA 5 BOUNTY 323B
6B SPEIRW 1Bα SOW 768D
7 AGAPAW 1Bα LOVE 4D
   ANAGK8 1 NECESSITY 52B
   DOT8S GIVER 204A
   EK 6C FROM 235D
   HILAROS CHEERFUL 376A
   KARDIA 1Bγ HEART 404D
   LUP8 GRIEF 483B
   PROAIREW 2 PREFER 709B
8 AGATHOS 1Bβ GOOD 3B
   AUTARKEIA 1 SUFFICIENCY 121D
   DUNATEW 2 BE STRONG 207D
   DUNATOS 1Aβ POWERFUL 208A
   EIS 5 FOR 229B
   ERGON 1Cβ DEED 308A
   CHARIS 4 FAVOR 886B
8A PERISSEUW 2A BE LEFT OVER 657A
8B PAS 1Aβ EVERY EACH 636D
8B PAS 1Aδ ALL 637A
8B PAS 2Aβ EVERY RESPECT 638A
8B PERISSEUW 1Bα BE LEFT OVER 656D
8C PAS 1Aβ EVERY EACH 636D
9 DIKAIOSUN8 2A RIGHTEOUSNESS 195C
   MENW 1Cβ REMAIN 505C
   PEN8S POOR 648A
   SKORPIZW 2 SCATTER 764B
10 ARTOS 1A BREAD 110A
   AUXANW 1 GROW 121B
   BRWSIS 1 EATING 147D
   GEN8MA PRODUCT 154B
   EPICHOR8GEW 2 GIVE 305A
   PL8THUNW 1A INCREASE 674D
   SPEIRW 1Aα SOW 768C
   SPERMA 1A SEED 769A
   CHOR8GEW PROVIDE 892A
10A SPOROS 2 SEED 770D
10B SPOROS 2 SEED 771A
11 HAPLOT8S 2 GENEROSITY 85B
   EUCHARISTIA 2 THANKFULNESS 329A
   KATERGAZOMAI 2 ACHIEVE 422D
   PAS 2Aβ EVERY RESPECT 638A
   PLOUTIZW 2 MAKE RICH 680A
12 ALLA 1A BUT, YET 37C
   DIAKONIA 4 SUPPORT 183C
   EIMI II4Bα TO BE 223A
   EUCHARISTIA 2 THANKFULNESS 329A

12	LEITOURGIA 2	SERVICE	472B
	PERISSEUW IAɤ	BE LEFT OVER	656C
	PROSANAPL8ROW	FILL UP	718D
	HUSTER8MA I	NEED	857A
13	HAPLOT8S 2	GENEROSITY	85B
	DIA ΔIV	BECAUSE OF	180A
	DIAKONIA 4	SUPPORT	183C
	DOKIM8 I	CHARACTER	201D
	DOXΑZW I	PRAISE	203C
	EIS 4G	FOR	229A
	EPI IIIBɤ	ON	287B
	EUAGGELION 2Bα	GOSPEL	318B
	KOINWNIA 2	ASSOCIATION	440A
	HOMOLOGIA I	CONFESSION	571D
	HUPOTAG8	SUBJECTION	855C
14	DE8SIS	PRAYER	171A
	EPIPOTHEW	DESIRE	297D
	HUPERBALLW	SURPASS	848A
	CHARIS 4	FAVOR	886B
15	ANEKDI8G8TOS	INDESCRIBABLE	63D
	DWREA	GIFT	209C
	EPI IIIBɤ	ON	287B
	CHARIS 5	FAVOR	886D

2 CORINTHIANS 10

I	APEIMI I	BE ABSENT	82B
	AUTOS IAβ	SELF	122B
	DIA AIIIIF	BY	179C
	EIS 4Cα	AGAINST	228B
	EPIEIKEIA	CLEMENCY	292C
	THARREW	BE CONFIDENT	352C
	KATA IIIB	TO	407B
	PARAKALEW 2	APPEAL TO	622B
	PAULOS	PAUL	643A
	PRAUT8S	HUMILITY	705D
	PROSWPON IC6	FACE	728D
	TAPEINOS 2A	LOW	811D
2	DE 3	BUT, AND	170D
	DEOMAI 2	ASK	174A
	EPI IIIIBℰ	TOWARD	289A
	THARREW	BE CONFIDENT	352C
	M8 AIIIG	NOT	518B
	PAREIMI IA	BE PRESENT	629C
	PEPOITH8SIS 2	TRUST	649B
	PERIPATEW 2A6	GO ABOUT	655B
	SARX 7	BODY	752A
	TIS, TI IA6	ANY ONE	828A
	TOLMAW 2	DARE	829C
	HWS IIIIC	SO	906D
	HWS III3	SO	906D
2A	LOGIZOMAI 2	CONSIDER	477B
2B	LOGIZOMAI IB	CONSIDER	477B
3	PERIPATEW 2B	GO ABOUT	655C
	STRATEUW 2		778A
	DO MILITARY SERVICE		
3A	SARX 5	BODY	751C
3B	SARX 7	BODY	752A
4	DUNATOS IB	POWERFUL	208A
	THEOS 3Gα	GOD	358C
	THEOS 3Gβ	GOD	358C
	KATHAIRESIS I	DESTRUCTION	387B
	KATHAIREW 2B	DESTROY	387C

4	LOGISMOS I	THOUGHT	478A
	HOPLON 2B	WEAPON	579A
	OCHURWMA	STRONGHOLD	606A
	PROS III3C	TOWARD	717B
	SARKIKOS 3	FLESHLY	750B
	STRATEIA	CAMPAIGN	777D
	STRATIA 2	ARMY	778B
5	AICHMALWTIZW 2	CAPTURE	26C
	GNWSIS 2	KNOWLEDGE	163A
	EIS 4A	INTO	228B
	EPAIRW 2Bα	RAISE UP	281C
	KATA I2Bα	DOWN	406C
	NO8MΑ 2	DESIGN	543A
	HUPAKO8 IB	OBEDIENCE	845A
	HUPSWMA 2	HEIGHT	858D
5A	PAS IAβ	EVERY EACH	636D
5B	PAS IAβ	EVERY EACH	636D
6	EKDIKEW 2	AVENGE SOMEONE	238A
	EN I4D	IN	258C
	HETOIMOS 2	READY	316D
	ECHW I7A	HAVE	334A
	ECHW III	BE	334B
	PARAKO8	DISOBEDIENCE	624B
	PL8ROW 3	MAKE FULL	677B
	HUPAKO8 IB	OBEDIENCE	844D
7	BLEPW 5	SEE	143B
	EIMI IV2	TO BE	225A
	EPI IIBβ	ON	286B
	KATHWS I	JUST AS	392A
	KATA IIIB	TO	407B
	LOGIZOMAI 2	CONSIDER	477B
	HOUTW IA	THUS	602B
	PALIN 4	AGAIN	611D
	PEITHW 2B	CONVINCE	645B
	PROSWPON IC6	FACE	728D
	TIS, TI IAβ	ANY ONE	827D
8	AISCHUNW 2	BE ASHAMED	25A
	EXOUSIA 3	AUTHORITY	278A
	KATHAIRESIS 2	DESTRUCTION	387B
	KAUCHAOMAI 2	BOAST	427A
	OIKODOM8 IBα	BUILDING	561C
	HOS,H8,HO I4A	(REL PRON)	587D
	PERISSOTEROS 2	GREATER	657B
9	AN 6	(PARTICLE)	49A
	DOKEW 2A	SEEM	201A
	EKPHOBEW	FRIGHTEN	246C
	EPISTOL8	LETTER	300D
	HWSAN	AS IF	907C
10	ASTHEN8S IB	SICK	115B
	BARUS 2A	BURDENSOME	134A
	EXOUTHENEW I	DESPISE	277B
	EPISTOL8	LETTER	300D
	ISCHUROS 2	STRONG	384B
	LOGOS IAβ	WORD	478C
	MEN IAα	(PARTICLE)	503D
	PAROUSIA I	PRESENCE	635B
	SWMA IB	BODY	807A
	PH8MI	SAY	864A
	PH8MI IC	SAY	864B
11	DIA AIIIIB	BY MEANS OF	179B
	EIMI II6D	TO BE	223C
	EPISTOL8	LETTER	300D
	ERGON IA	DEED	307D

11	LOGIZOMAI 2	CONSIDER 477B
	LOGOS 1Aα	WORD 478A
	HOIOS	OF WHAT SORT 565C
	PAREIMI 1A	BE PRESENT 629C
11A	TOIOUTOS 3Aα	SUCH A KIND 829B
11B	TOIOUTOS 1	SUCH A KIND 829A
12	GAR 4	INDEED 151D
	EGKRINW	TO CLASS 215D
	METREW 1B	MEASURE 516B
	*SUNI8MI	UNDERSTAND 797D
	SUNI8MI	UNDERSTAND 798A
	SUNIST8MI IIB	UNITE 798B
	TOLMAW 1B	DARE 829C
12A	SUGKRINW 2A	COMPARE 782B
12B	SUGKRINW 2A	COMPARE 782B
13	AMETROS	IMMEASURABLE 45A
	EIS 3	COMPLETELY 228A
	EPHIKNEOMAI	REACH 330D
	KANWN 2	SPHERE 403D
	KAUCHAOMAI 1	BOAST 427A
	MERIZW 2B	ASSIGN 505D
	METRON 2B	MEASURE 516D
	HOS,H8,HO I4A	(REL PRON) 587D
	OUCHI 1	NOT 603A
	SUNI8MI	UNDERSTAND 798A
13F	ACHRI 1B	AS FAR AS 128C
14	EN I4Cβ	IN 258C
	EUAGGELION 2Bα	GOSPEL 318B
	EPHIKNEOMAI	REACH 330D
	HUPEREKTEINW	OVEREXTEND 848C
	PHTHANW 2	COME 864C
15	ALLOTRIOS 1A	TO ANOTHER 40A
	AMETROS	IMMEASURABLE 45A
	AUXANW 2	GROW 121B
	*EIS 3	COMPLETELY 228A
	ELPIS 2B	HOPE 252D
	ECHW I2Eβ	HAVE 333A
	*KAUCHAOMAI 1	BOAST 427A
	KOPOS 2	WORK 444C
	MEGALUNW 1	MAKE LARGE 498B
	PERISSEIA	SURPLUS 656B
	PISTIS 2Dα	FAITH 669B
15F	KANWN 2	SPHERE 403D
16	ALLOTRIOS 1A	TO ANOTHER 40A
	EIS IDβ	IN 227D
	HETOIMOS 1	READY 316D
	EUAGGELIZW 2Aγ	PREACH 317D
	KAUCHAOMAI 1	BOAST 427A
	HUPEREKEINA	BEYOND 848B
17A	KAUCHAOMAI 1	BOAST 427A
17B	KAUCHAOMAI 1	BOAST 426D
18	DOKIMOS 1	GENUINE 202A
18A	SUNIST8MI IIB	UNITE 798B
18B	SUNIST8MI IIB	UNITE 798B

2 CORINTHIANS 11

1	APHROSUN8	FOOLISHNESS 127B
	OPHELON	O THAT 604A
1A	ANECHW 1B	ENDURE 65B
1B	ANECHW 1A	ENDURE 65B
2	HAGNOS 1	PURE 11D
	HARMOZW 3	BETROTH 107B
2	Z8LOS 1	ZEAL 338B
	Z8LOW 1B	STRIVE 338C
	PARTHENOS 1	VIRGIN 632C
	PARIST8MI 1Bα	PRESENT 633A
3	HAGNOT8S	PURITY 12A
	HAPLOT8S 1	SIMPLICITY 85B
	APO 15	FROM 86A
	EXAPATAW	DECEIVE 272C
	HEUA	EVE 317C
	M8PWS 1B	LEST SOMEHOW 521C
	NO8MA 1	THOUGHT 542D
	OPHIS 3	SNAKE 605A
	PANOURGIA	CUNNING 613A
	PHTHEIRW 2B	RUIN 865B
	PHOBEW 1A	BE AFRAID 870D
	HWS III	SO 905D
4	ALLOS 1Eα	OTHER 39C
	ANECHW 1C	ENDURE 65B
	GAR 1B	FOR 151B
	DECHOMAI 1	TAKE 176B
	EI VI5	FOR IF 219A
	ERCHOMAI IIAθ	COME 311B
	HETEROS 1Bγ	ANOTHER 315B
	EUAGGELION 2A	GOSPEL 318B
	KALWS 6	WELL 402C
	K8RUSSW 2Bβ	ANNOUNCE 432C
	LAMBANW 2	RECEIVE 466B
	PNEUMA 7	SPIRIT 684B
5	APOSTOLOS 3	APOSTLES 99C
	GAR 4	INDEED 151D
	LOGIZOMAI 3	THINK 477C
	M8DEIS 2Bβ	NOTHING 520A
	HUPERLIAN	EXCEEDINGLY 849B
	HUSTEREW 1C	TO MISS 856D
6	ALLA 4	BUT, YET 38B
	GNWSIS 2	KNOWLEDGE 163A
	EI VI2	BUT IF 218D
	IDIWT8S 1	LAYMAN 371B
	LOGOS 1Aα	WORD 478B
	PHANEROW 1A	REVEAL 860C
	PHANEROW 2Bα	REVEAL 860D
6A	PAS 2Aβ	EVERY RESPECT 638A
7	HAMARTIA 1	SIN 42B
	DWREAN 1	GRATIS 209D
	EUAGGELIZW 2Aα	PREACH 317D
	EUAGGELION 1C	GOSPEL 318B
	EUAGGELION 2Bβ	GOSPEL 318B
8	1Dα	OR 343A
	POIEW IICγ	DO 688C
	TAPEINOW 2A	LOWER 812B
	HUPSOW 2	LIFT UP 858D
8	DIAKONIA 1	SERVICE 183B
	OPSWNION 1B	WAGES 607A
	PROS III3A	TOWARD 717A
	SULAW	ROB 784B
9	ABAR8S	LIGHT IN WEIGHT 1B
	ERCHOMAI IIAβ	COME 310B
	KAI I2F	AND 393C
	KATANARKAW	BURDEN 415D
	MAKEDONIA	MACEDONIA 488B
	OU 6A	NO 595A
	PAREIMI 1A	BE PRESENT 629C
	PAS 2Aβ	EVERY RESPECT 638A

Verse	Word	Gloss	Ref
9	PROS III7	TOWARD	718A
	PROSANAPL8ROW	FILL UP	718D
	T8REW 2B	KEEP	822C
	HUSTEREW 2	TO MISS	857A
	HUSTER8MA I	NEED	857A
10	ACHAIA	ACHAIA	127D
	EIMI III4	TO BE	224D
	KAUCH8SIS I	BOASTING	427B
	KLIMA	DISTRICT	437B
	HOTI 1B«	THAT	592D
	HOUTOS 2B	THIS	601D
	PHRASSW 1B	SHUT	873C
	PHRASSW 2	SHUT	873C
11	DIA BII2	WHY	180B
	OIDA II	KNOW	558D
	HOTI 3A	THAT	593D
12	APHORM8	PRETEXT	127A
	EKKOPTW 2	REMOVE	241B
	EN IV6A	IN	261A
	HEURISKW ICY	FIND	325C
	THELW I	WISH	355B
	KATHWS I	JUST AS	392A
	KAUCHAOMAI I	BOAST	427A
	HOS,H8,HO I2A	(REL PRON)	587B
13	APOSTOLOS 3	APOSTLES	99B
	DOLIOS	DECEITFUL	202B
	ERGAT8S 1B	WORKMAN	307D
	METASCH8MATIZW	TRANSFORM	515A
	PSEUDAPOSTOLOS	FALSE APOSTLE	899D
13F	EIS 4B	TO	228B
14	AGGELOS 2A	ANGEL	7C
	THAUMA IA	A WONDER	352D
	THAUMASTOS 2	WONDERFUL	353C
	METASCH8MATIZW	TRANSFORM	515A
	SATAN	ADVERSARY	752C
	PHWS IA	LIGHT	879D
15	DIAKONOS IA	SERVANT	183D
	DIKAIOSUN8 2B	RIGHTEOUSNESS	195D
	EI II	IF	218C
	ERGON ICP	DEED	308A
	MEGAS 2BP	GREAT	499C
	METASCH8MATIZW	TRANSFORM	515A
	TELOS IC	END	819C
16	APHRWN	FOOLISH	127B
	GE 3BP	OTHERWISE	152B
	DECHOMAI 3A	TOLERATE	176C
	DOKEW IC	THINK	200D
	KAN 3	AT LEAST	403B
	KAUCHAOMAI 2	BOAST	427A
	M8 AIII5A	NOT	518D
	MIKROS 3A	A LITTLE	523B
16A	TIS, TI IAY	ANY ONE	827D
17	APHROSUN8	FOOLISHNESS	127B
	KATA II5A«	ACCORDING TO	408A
	KAUCH8SIS I	BOASTING	427B
	KURIOS 2CY	LORD	461A
	LALEW 2A«	SPEAK	464C
	HUPOSTASIS 2	CONFIDENCE	854D
	HWS III3	SO	906D
18	EPEI 2	BECAUSE	283D
	POLUS I2A«	MANY	694D
	SARX 6	BODY	751C
18A	KAUCHAOMAI I	BOAST	427A
18B	KAUCHAOMAI I	BOAST	427A
19	ANECHW IA	ENDURE	65B
	APHRWN	FOOLISH	127B
	H8DEWS	GLADLY	344C
	PHRONIMOS	THOUGHTFUL	874C
19F	GAR IC	FOR	151B
20	DERW	BEAT	174D
	EPAIRW 2BP	RAISE UP	281D
	KATADOULOW	ENSLAVE	411C
	KATESTHIW 2	DESTROY	423C
	LAMBANW IC	TAKE	465D
	PROSWPON IA	FACE	728B
	TIS, TI IA«	ANY ONE	827C
21	ASTHENEW IB	WEAK	115A
	ATIMIA	DISHONOR	119D
	APHROSUN8	FOOLISHNESS	127B
	KAGW 3A	I ALSO	387A
	KATA II4	FOR (PURPOSE)	407D
	HOTI IDP	THAT	593C
	TIS, TI IAP	ANY ONE	827D
	TOLMAW 2	DARE	829C
21B	LEGW I9	SAY	470C
22	ABRAAM	ABRAHAM	ID
	HEBRAIOS I	HEBREW	212B
	ISRA8LIT8S	ISRAELITE	382C
	SPERMA 2B	SEED	769B
22A	KAGW 3A	I ALSO	387A
22B	KAGW 3A	I ALSO	387A
22C	KAGW 3A	I ALSO	387A
23	DIAKONOS IA	SERVANT	183D
	THANATOS IC	DEATH	351D
	KOPOS 2	WORK	444C
	PARAPHRONEW	BE BESIDE ONESELF	628D
	PERISSOTERWS I	MORE	657C
	PL8G8 I	BLOW	674A
	POLLAKIS	OFTEN	693B
	HUPER 3	BEYOND	847C
	HUPERBALLONTWS	EXCEEDINGLY	848A
	PHULAK8 3	GUARD	875C
23G9	TH8RIOMACHEW		361B
	FIGHT WITH WILD ANIMALS		
24	LAMBANW 2	RECEIVE	466C
	PARA III7	LESS	616C
	PENTAKIS	FIVE TIMES	648C
	TESSARAKONTA	FORTY	820D
	HUPO 1B	BY	851A
25	HAPAX I	ONCE	80A
	BUTHOS	DEPTH	148A
	LITHAZW	STONE	475A
	NAUAGEW I	SUFFER SHIPWRECK	536A
	NUCHTH8MERON		549C
	A DAY AND A NIGHT		
	POIEW IIE6	DO	689A
	RABDIZW	BEAT WITH A ROD	740C
25A	TRIS	THRICE	834A
25B	TRIS	THRICE	834A
26	GENOS 3	NATION	155C
	ER8MIA	DESERT	308D
	THALASSA IA	SEA	350D
	L8ST8S I	ROBBER	474B
	HODOIPORIA	JOURNEY	556A
	POLIS I	CITY	692A
	POLLAKIS	OFTEN	693B

26	POTAMOS I	RIVER	701B
	PSEUDADELPHOS	FALSE BROTHER	899B
26A	KINDUNOS	DANGER	433B
26B	KINDUNOS	DANGER	433B
27	AGRUPNIA I	WAKEFULNESS	14A
	GUMNOT8S 2	DESTITUTION	167B
	DIPSOS	THIRST	199D
	KOPOS 2	WORK	444C
	LIMOS I	HUNGER	476B
	MOCHTHOS	LABOR	530C
	N8STEIA I	FASTING	540A
	PSUCHOS	COLD	902D
27A	POLLAKIS	OFTEN	693B
27B	POLLAKIS	OFTEN	693B
28	EPISTASIS	PRESSURE	300B
	EPISUSTASIS	UPRISING	301D
	H8MERA 2	DAY	347B
	KATA II2C	EVERY	407C
	MERIMNA	ANXIETY	506A
	PAREKTOS I	OUTSIDE	630C
	PAS ID«	ALL	637C
	CHWRIS 2B«	APART	899C
29	ASTHENEW 2	WEAK	115A
	PUROW IB	SET ON FIRE	738C
	SKANDALIZW IA	CAUSE TO FALL	760B
	SKANDALIZW 2	CAUSE TO FALL	760C
29A	TIS, TI IA«	WHICH	826C
29B	TIS, TI IA«	WHICH	826C
30	ASTHENEIA IB	WEAKNESS	114D
	DEI 4	IT IS NECESSARY	171B
	HO,H8,TO II7	THE	554C
30A	KAUCHAOMAI I	BOAST	427A
30B	KAUCHAOMAI 2	BOAST	427A
31	AIWN IB	TIME	26D
	EULOG8TOS	BLESSED	323A
	KAI IIA	AND	392C
	KURIOS 2CY	LORD	461A
	HO,H8,TO III0B	THE	555A
	PAT8R 3D«	FATHER	641D
	PSEUDOMAI I	LIE	900A
32	HARETAS	ARETAS	105B
	BASILEUS I	KING	135D
	DAMASKOS	DAMASCUS	169C
	DAMASK8NOS	DAMASCENE	169C
	ETHNARCH8S	GOVERNOR	217B
	PIAZW 2A	GRASP	662D
	POLIS I	CITY	692A
	PHROUREW I	GUARD	875A
32F	HARETAS	ARETAS	105B
33	DIA AI2	THROUGH	178C
	EKPHEUGW 2B«	RUN AWAY	246C
	THURIS	WINDOW	366D
	SARGAN8	BASKET	749D
	TEICHOS	WALL	815C
	CHALAW	LET DOWN	882C
	CHEIR 2B	HAND	888D

2 CORINTHIANS 12

I	APOKALUPSIS 2	REVELATION	91D
	ERCHOMAI I2C	COME	311C
	KAUCHAOMAI I	BOAST	427A
	KURIOS 2CY	LORD	461A

I	OPTASIA I	A VISION	580A
	SUMPHERW 2A	HELP	787D
	SUMPHERW 2B«	PROFITABLE	788A
2	HARPAZW 2B	SNATCH	108D
	DEKATESSARES	FOURTEEN	173A
	EKTOS 2A	OUTSIDE	245C
	EN I5D	IN	259B
	EPOURANIOS 2A«	HEAVENLY	306A
	ETOS	YEAR	317B
	HEWS II2A	AS FAR AS	335C
	OIDA IC	KNOW	558B
	OURANOS IE	HEAVEN	599A
	TOIOUTOS 2A«	SUCH A KIND	829A
	TOIOUTOS 3A«	SUCH A KIND	829B
	TRITOS I	THIRD	834B
2F	OIDA IF	KNOW	558C
2F	SWMA IB	BODY	807A
3	TOIOUTOS 2A«	SUCH A KIND	829A
	CHWRIS 2B«	APART	899A
3F	OURANOS IE	HEAVEN	599A
4	AGGELOS 2A	ANGEL	7C
	AKOUW IB«	HEAR	31B
	HARPAZW 2B	SNATCH	108D
	ARR8TOS 2	INEXPRESSIBLE	109B
	*PARADEISOS 2	PARADISE	619B
	R8MA I	WORD	742D
5	ASTHENEIA IB	WEAKNESS	114D
	ASTHENEIA IA	WEAKNESS	114D
	EMAUTOU 3	MYSELF	253B
	TOIOUTOS 3A«	SUCH A KIND	829B
5A	KAUCHAOMAI I	BOAST	427A
5A	HUPER IF	IN BEHALF OF	847A
5B	KAUCHAOMAI I	BOAST	427A
5B	HUPER IF	IN BEHALF OF	847A
6	AKOUW IB«	HEAR	31C
	AL8THEIA 2A	TRUTH	35B
	APHRWN I	FOOLISH	127B
	BLEPW IA	SEE	143A
	EIPON I	SAY	225B
	KAUCHAOMAI I	BOAST	427A
	LOGIZOMAI IA	RECKON	477A
	M8 B2	NOT	519A
	HOS,H8,HO I2A	(REL PRON)	587B
	PHEIDOMAI 2	SPARE	862C
7	AGGELOS 2C	ANGEL	8A
	APOKALUPSIS 2	REVELATION	91D
	KOLAPHIZW 2	STRIKE	442A
	SARX I	FLESH	750D
	SATAN	ADVERSARY	752B
	SATAN	ADVERSARY	752C
	SKOLOPS	STAKE	763D
	HUPERBOL8	EXCESS	848B
7A	HUPERAIRW	RISE UP	847C
7B	HUPERAIRW	RISE UP	847C
8	APHIST8MI 2B	KEEP AWAY	126C
	PARAKALEW IC	INVITE	622B
	TRIS	THRICE	834A
	HUPER ID	IN BEHALF OF	847A
9	ARKEW I	BE ENOUGH	106D
	ASTHENEIA IB	WEAKNESS	114D
	EPI IIIIBY	ON	288D
	EPISK8NOW	TAKE UP QUARTERS	298C
	H8DEWS	GLADLY	344C

Ref	Greek	Meaning	No.
9	KAUCHAOMAI 1	BOAST	427A
	MALLON 3Aβ	RATHER	490C
	TELEIOW 2Eβ	MAKE PERFECT	817D
	TELEW 1	FINISH	818D
	CHARIS 4	FAVOR	886C
9F	ASTHENEIA 1A	WEAKNESS	114D
9F	ASTHENEIA 1B	WEAKNESS	114D
10	ANAGK8 2	DISTRESS	52B
	ANAGK8 3	TORTURE	52B
	ASTHENEW 1B	WEAK	115A
	DIWGMOS	PERSECUTION	200A
	DUNATOS 1Aα	POWERFUL	207D
	EUDOKEW 2B	WELL PLEASED	319C
	HOTAN 1A	WHEN	592A
	STENOCHWRIA	DISTRESS	774A
	TOTE 1C	AT THAT TIME	831C
	HUBRIS 2	SHAME	839D
	HUPER 1D	IN BEHALF OF	846D
11	APOSTOLOS 3	APOSTLES	99C
	APHRWN	FOOLISH	127B
	EI VI4	EVEN IF	219A
	OPHEILW 2Aβ	OWE	603D
	SUNIST8MI 11B	UNITE	798C
	HUPERLIAN	EXCEEDINGLY	849B
	HUSTEREW 1C	TO MISS	856D
11A	OUDEIS 2Bγ	IN NO RESPECT	596C
11B	OUDEIS 2Bβ	WORTHLESS	596C
12	APOSTOLOS 3	APOSTLES	99B
	DUNAMIS 4	MIRACLE	207B
	KATERGAZOMAI 1	ACHIEVE	422D
	MEN 2A	(PARTICLE)	504B
	HO,H8,TO IIIAβ	THE	552C
	PAS 1Aδ	ALL	637A
	HUPOMON8 1	PATIENCE	854A
12A	S8MEION 1	SIGN	755C
12B	S8MEION 2A	SIGN	755D
13	ADIKIA 1	WRONGDOING	17C
	AUTOS 1C	SELF	122C
	ELATTOW 2A	INFERIOR	247D
	HESSOOMAI	BE DEFEATED	313D
	H8TTAOMAI	SUCCUMB	350C
	KATANARKAW	BURDEN	415D
	LOIPOS 2A	OTHER	481A
	HUPER 2	BEYOND	847B
	CHARIZOMAI 2	GIVE FREELY	885A
14	GONEUS	PARENTS	164B
	HETOIMWS	BE READY	317A
	ECHW III1	BE	334B
	Z8TEW 2A	SEEK	339C
	TH8SAURIZW 1	STORE UP	362A
	IDOU 1Bε	BEHOLD	371C
	KATANARKAW	BURDEN	415D
	HO,H8,TO II7	THE	554C
	HOUTOS 2C	THIS	602A
	OPHEILW 2Aβ	OWE	603D
14A	TEKNON 1Aα	CHILD	816A
14B	TEKNON 1Aε	CHILD	816A
15	AGAPAW 1Aα	LOVE	4C
	DAPANAW 1	SPEND	170A
	EKDAPANAW	BE SPENT	237C
	H8DEWS	GLADLY	344C
	H8SSWN	LESSER	349D
	PERISSOTERWS 1	MORE	657C
15	HUPER 1Aε	IN BEHALF OF	846C
	PSUCH8 1C	SOUL LIFE	902A
	PSUCH8 1F	SOUL LIFE	902C
16	DOLOS	DECEIT	202B
	KATABAREW	BURDEN	409D
	LAMBANW 1C	TAKE	465D
	PANOURGOS	CLEVER	613A
	HUPARCHW 2	BE	846A
17	HOS,H8,HO I4A	(REL PRON)	587D
18	ICHNOS	FOOTPRINT	385A
	M8TI	(INTERROG PARTICLE)	522A
	PARAKALEW 3	IMPLORE	622D
	PERIPATEW 2Aβ	GO ABOUT	655B
	PLEONEKTEW 1A	OUTWIT	673B
	PNEUMA 5Dα	SPIRIT	683A
	SUNAPOSTELLW	SEND WITH	792D
	TITOS 1	TITUS	828C
19	AGAP8TOS 2	BELOVED	6C
	APOLOGEOMAI	DEFEND ONESELF	95B
	DOKEW 1D	THINK	201A
	EN 15D	IN	259B
	KATENANTI 2B	IN THE SIGHT OF	422B
	HODE 3	THIS	555D
	OIKODOM8 1Bα	BUILDING	561C
	PALAI 2A	LONG AGO	610C
	HUPER 1B	IN BEHALF OF	846D
20	AKATASTASIA 2	DISTURBANCE	29C
	ERITHEIA	SELFISHNESS	309C
	ERIS	STRIFE	309C
	ERCHOMAI IIAζ	COME	310D
	HEURISKW 1Cγ	FIND	325C
	*Z8LOS 2	JEALOUSY	338B
	THUMOS 2	ANGER	366A
	KAGW 1	AND I	387A
	KATALALIA	SLANDER	413D
	PHOBEW 1A	BE AFRAID	870D
	PHUSIWSIS	PRIDE	877D
	PSITHURISMOS	GOSSIP	901B
20A	M8PWS 1B	LEST SOMEHOW	521C
20A	HOIOS	OF WHAT SORT	565C
20B	M8PWS 1B	LEST SOMEHOW	521C
20B	HOIOS	OF WHAT SORT	565C
21	AKATHARSIA 2	IMPURITY	28B
	ASELGEIA	LICENTIOUSNESS	114C
	EPI IIIBγ	ON	287B
	THEOS 3C	GOD	358A
	METANOEW	CHANGE ONES MIND	513C
	PENTHEW 2	BE SAD	648C
	POLUS I2Aα	MANY	694D
	PORNEIA 1	PROSTITUTION	699D
	PRASSW 1A	DO	705A
	PROAMARTANW	SIN BEFOREHAND	709C
	PROS III7	TOWARD	718A
	TAPEINOW 2A	LOWER	812B

2 CORINTHIANS 13

Ref	Greek	Meaning	No.
1	DUO 1C	TWO	208B
	EPI IIBβ	ON	286B
	ERCHOMAI IIAβ	COME	310C
	HETOIMWS	BE READY	317A
	HIST8MI IIID	STAND	383B
	KAI IIB	AND	392D

1	MARTUS 1	WITNESS	495B
	HOUTOS 2C	THIS	602A
	R8MA 2	WORD	743A
	STOMA 1A	MOUTH	777C
2	APEIMI 1	BE ABSENT	82B
	DEUTEROS 4	SECOND	176B
	EIS 2AY	UNTIL	228A
	LOIPOS 2Bα	THE OTHERS	481A
	NUN 1Aα	NOW	547C
	HO,H8,TO II6	THE	554B
	PALIN 2	AGAIN	611D
	PAREIMI 1A	BE PRESENT	629C
	PROAMARTANW	SIN BEFOREHAND	709C
	PROEIPON 1	FORETELL	711D
	PROLEGW 1	TELL BEFOREHAND	715B
	PHEIDOMAI 1	SPARE	862C
	HWS III	SO	905D
3	ASTHENEW 1B	WEAK	115A
	DOKIM8 2	TEST	201D
	DUNATEW 1	BE STRONG	207D
	EIS 5	FOR	229B
	EPEI 2	BECAUSE	283D
	Z8TEW 2C	SEEK	339C
4	ASTHENEIA 1C	WEAKNESS	114D
	ASTHENEW 1B	WEAK	115A
	GAR 1E	FOR	151C
	EK 3F	BY	234D
	ZAW 2A	LIVE	337A
	STAUROW 1	CRUCIFY	773A
	SUN 2B	WITH	789C
4A	ZAW 1Aβ	LIVE	336C
5	DOKIMAZW 1	EXAMINE	201C
	EI V2A	WHETHER	218D
	EI V19	UNLESS INDEED	219A
	EIMI III4	TO BE	224C
	EN I5A	IN	258D
	EPIGINWSKW 2A	KNOW	291A
	PEIRAZW 2A	TRY	646A
	PISTIS 2Dα	FAITH	669B
5-7	ADOKIMOS	UNQUALIFIED	18B
6	GINWSKW 3C	UNDERSTAND	160B
	ELPIZW 2	HOPE	252A
7	DOKIMOS 1	GENUINE	202A
	*EUCHOMAI 1	PRAY	329C
	KAKOS 1C	EVIL	398D
	KALOS 2B	GOOD	401B
	M8 AIIIBβ	NOT	518A
	M8DEIS 1	NO	520A
	PROS IIIIF	TOWARD	717A
	PHAINW 2D	APPEAR	859D
	HWS III3	SO	906D
7A	POIEW IIBε	DO	687D
7B	POIEW IIBε	DO	687D
8	DUNAMAI 3	ABLE	206B
	KATA I2BY	DOWN	406D
9	ASTHENEW 1B	WEAK	115A
	DUNATOS 1Aα	POWERFUL	207D
	EUCHOMAI 1	PRAY	329C
	KATARTISIS	COMPLETION	419A
	HOUTOS 1Bβ	THIS	601C
	SU 1A	YOU	779D
	CHAIRW 1	REJOICE	881D
10	APEIMI 1	BE ABSENT	82B

10	APOTOMWS	SEVERELY	101A
	DIA BII2	FOR THIS REASON	180B
	DIDWMI 1Bβ	GIVE	192B
	EXOUSIA 3	AUTHORITY	278A
	HINA I5	IN ORDER THAT	378A
	KATHAIRESIS 2	DESTRUCTION	387B
	OIKODOM8 1Bα	BUILDING	561C
	HOUTOS 1Bβ	THIS	601C
	PAREIMI 1A	BE PRESENT	629C
	CHRAOMAI 2	USE	893A
11	AGAP8 I2A	LOVE	5D
	EIR8NEUW 2B	KEEP IN PEACE	226A
	EIR8N8 3	PEACE	226D
	THEOS 3E	GOD	358B
	KATARTIZW 1A	RESTORE	418D
	LOIPOS 3B	THE REST	481B
	META AIIICY	WITH	510A
	PARAKALEW 4	IMPLORE	623A
	PHRONEW 1	THINK	874B
	CHAIRW 1	REJOICE	882A
12	ASPAZOMAI 1A	GREET	116B
	ASPAZOMAI 1A	GREET	116C
	*PHIL8MA	A KISS	867B
13	AGAP8 I2A	LOVE	5D
	AM8N 1	AMEN	45B
	KOINWNIA 1	ASSOCIATION	439D
	KOINWNIA 4	ASSOCIATION	440B
	KURIOS 2CY	LORD	461A
	META AIIICY	WITH	510B
	PNEUMA 5Cα	SPIRIT	682D
	PNEUMA 8	SPIRIT	684B
	CHARIS 2C	FAVOR	885D

GALATIANS 1

1	ANTHRWPOS 1B	MAN	67D
	APO V4	FROM	87C
	APOSTOLOS 3	APOSTLES	99B
	DIA AII2A	BY	179C
	EGEIRW 1Aβ	RAISE	213D
	NEKROS 2A	DEAD	537A
	OUDE 1	AND NOT	595D
	PAULOS	PAUL	643A
2	GALATIA	GALATIA	149B
	EKKL8SIA 4B	CHURCH	240C
	PAS 1Fβ	ALL	638A
	SUN 1C	WITH	789B
3	APO V4	FROM	87C
	EIR8N8 2	PEACE	226D
	*THEOS 3D	GOD	358B
	KURIOS 2CY	LORD	461A
	PAT8R 3Cβ	FATHER	641C
	*CHARIS 2C	FAVOR	885D
4	AIWN 2A	AGE	27B
	DIDWMI 6	GIVE	192D
	ENIST8MI 1	BE PRESENT	266B
	EXAIREW 2A	DELIVER	271C
	THEL8MA 2B	WILL	355B
	THEOS 3D	GOD	358A
	HOPWS 2Aα	IN ORDER THAT	580C
	PAT8R 3Cβ	FATHER	641C
	PERI 1G	ABOUT	650C
	PON8ROS 1Bβ	WICKED	697D

Verse	Greek	Gloss	Ref
4	HUPER 1B	IN BEHALF OF	846C
5	AIWN 1B	TIME	260
	AMBN 1	AMEN	45A
	DOXA 3	FAME	203B
6	ALLOS 1Eβ	ANOTHER	39C
	EIS 4A	INTO	228B
	EN III2	BY	260C
	HETEROS 2	ANOTHER	315C
	EUAGGELION 2A	GOSPEL	318B
	THAUMAZW 1Aγ	WONDER	353A
	KALEW 2	CALL	400C
	METATITH8MI 2B	CHANGE	515B
	HOUTW 3	THUS	602D
	TACHEWS 1B	QUICKLY	814B
	CHARIS 3B	FAVOR	886B
6F	HETEROS 1Bγ	ANOTHER	315B
7	ALLOS 1Eβ	ANOTHER	39C
	ALLOS 1Eα	OTHER	39C
	EI VI8B	BUT	219A
	EUAGGELION 2Bα	GOSPEL	318B
	METASTREPHW	CHANGE	514D
	HO,H8,TO II3B	THE	553C
	TARASSW 2	STIR UP	813A
	TIS, TI 1Aβ	ANY ONE	827D
	TIS, TI 1A6	ANY ONE	828A
	CHRISTOS 1	ANOINTED ONE	895C
8	AGGELOS 2A	ANGEL	7C
	HOS,H8,HO I2A	(REL PRON)	587B
	OURANOS 2C	HEAVEN	599C
8A	EUAGGELIZW 2Aγ	PREACH	317D
8B	EUAGGELIZW 2Aα	PREACH	317D
8F	ANATHEMA 2A	ACCURSED	53D
8F	PARA III6	AGAINST	616C
9	EUAGGELIZW 2Aγ	PREACH	317D
	KAI II3	ALSO	394B
	PALIN 2	AGAIN	611C
	PARALAMBANW 2Bγ	TAKE	625B
	PROEIPON 2A	FORETELL	711D
	HWS III	SO	905D
9F	ARTI 3	NOW	109D
10	AN 1Bα	(PARTICLE)	47D
	ANTHRWPARESKEW	MAN PLEASER	67A
	ANTHRWPOS 1Aβ	MAN	67C
	ARESKW 1	ACCOMMODATE	105A
	ARESKW 2A	BE PLEASING	105A
	DOULOS 1	SLAVE	205B
	ETI 1Aα	STILL	315D
	Z8TEW 2Bγ	SEEK	339C
	8 1Dγ	OR	343A
	PEITHW 1B	CONVINCE	644D
	PEITHW 1C	CONVINCE	645A
11	ANTHRWPOS 1C	HUMAN	67D
	GAR 4	INDEED	151D
	GNWRIZW 1	MAKE KNOWN	162C
	EIMI III6B	TO BE	224D
	EUAGGELIZW 2Bα	PREACH	318A
	EUAGGELION 1C	GOSPEL	318B
	HUPO 1Aα	BY	850D
11F	ANTHRWPOS 1B	MAN	67D
12	APOKALUPSIS 2	REVELATION	91D
	GAR 1B	FOR	151B
	DIDASKW 2C	TEACH	191A
	OUDE 2	AND NOT	596A
12*	OUTE	NOT	600C
	PARA 13B	FROM	614D
	PARALAMBANW 2Bγ	TAKE	625B
13	AKOUW 3B	LEARN	31D
	ANASTROPH8	CONDUCT	61B
	DIWKW 2	PERSECUTE	200B
	EKKL8SIA 4Eα	CHURCH	240D
	POLEMEW 2	FIGHT	691C
	PORTHEW	PILLAGE	699D
	POTE 1	ONCE	701D
	HUPERBOL8	EXCESS	848B
13F	IOUDAISMOS	JUDAISM	380C
14	GENOS 3	NATION	155C
	EN I4A	IN	258B
	Z8LWT8S 1Aβ	ZEALOT	338D
	PARADOSIS 2	TRADITION	621B
	PATRIKOS	PATERNAL	642B
	PERISSOTERWS 1	MORE	657C
	PROKOPTW 2	GO FORWARD	714D
	SUN8LIKIWT8S	CONTEMPORARY	797C
	HUPARCHW 2	BE	846A
	HUPER 2	BEYOND	847B
15	APHORIZW 2	SET APART	127A
	DIA AIIIE	BY	179C
	EUDOKEW 1	WELL PLEASED	319C
	KALEW 2	CALL	400C
	KOILIA 2	BELLY	438B
	HOTE 1B	WHEN	592C
	CHARIS 2A	FAVOR	885C
16	HAIMA 1A	BLOOD	22A
	APOKALUPTW 2	REVEAL	91C
	EN IV4A	IN	260D
	EUAGGELIZW 2Aα	PREACH	317D
	EUTHEWS	IMMEDIATELY	320D
	PROSANATITH8MI 2	CONSULT	718D
	SARX 3	BODY	751B
	HUIOS 2B	SON	842D
17	APERCHOMAI 2	GO	83D
	APOSTOLOS 3	APOSTLES	99C
	ARABIA	ARABIA	103D
	DAMASKOS	DAMASCUS	169C
	PALIN 1A	BACK	611C
	PRO 2	BEFORE	708D
	HUPOSTREPHW	RETURN	855B
17F	ANERCHOMAI	GO UP	64C
17F	HIEROSOLUMA 1A	JERUSALEM	373D
18	DEKAPENTE	FIFTEEN	173A
	EPEITA 1	THEN	284B
	EPIMENW 1	REMAIN	296A
	EPIMENW 1	REMAIN	296B
	ETOS	YEAR	317B
	H8MERA 2	DAY	347A
	HISTOREW	VISIT	383D
	K8PHAS	CEPHAS	432D
	META BIII	AFTER	511C
	PETROS	PETER	661A
	PROS III7	TOWARD	718A
19	ADELPHOS 1	BROTHER	15D
	APOSTOLOS 3	APOSTLES	99B
	EI VI8A	IF NOT	219A
	HETEROS 1Bα	ANOTHER	315A
	IAKWBOS 3	JAMES	368C
	KURIOS 2Cγ	LORD	460D

20	GRAPHW 2D	WRITE 166A
	ENWPION 2B	BEFORE 270B
	HOTI 1Bα	THAT 592D
	PSEUDOMAI 1	LIE 900A
21	EPEITA 1	THEN 284B
	KILIKIA	CILICIA 433B
	KLIMA	DISTRICT 437B
	SURIA	SYRIA 801D
22	AGNOEW 2	NOT TO KNOW 11C
	EKKL8SIA 4B	CHURCH 240C
	EN 15D	IN 259B
	IOUDAIA 1	JUDAEA 379D
	PROSWPON 1B	FACE 728C
23	DIWKW 2	PERSECUTE 200B
	EUAGGELIZW 2Aβ	PREACH 317D
	MONOS 2A	ONLY 529D
	NUN 1Aα	NOW 547C
	PISTIS 2Dα	FAITH 669C
	PISTIS 3	FAITH 669D
	PORTHEW	PILLAGE 699D
	POTE 1	ONCE 701D
24	DOXAZW 1	PRAISE 203C

GALATIANS 2

1	ANABAINW 1Aα	GO UP 49D
	BARNABAS	BARNABAS 133C
	DEKATESSARES	FOURTEEN 173A
	DIA ΛII2	AFTER 179A
	EPEITA 1	THEN 284B
	ETOS	YEAR 317B
	HIEROSOLUMA 1A	JERUSALEM 373D
	META ΔII1A	WITH 509D
	PALIN 1A	BACK 611B
	SUMPARALAMBANW	TAKE ALONG 786D
	TITOS 1	TITUS 828C
1-10	PETROS	PETER 661A
2	ANATITH8MI 2	DECLARE 61D
	APOKALUPSIS 2	REVELATION 91D
	DOKEW 2B	SEEM 201B
	EIS 4E	SO THAT 228D
	EUAGGELION 1A	GOSPEL 318A
	IDIOS 4	PRIVATELY 371A
	KATA II5Aδ	ACCORDING TO 408B
	KENOS 2Aβ	EMPTY 429A
	K8RUSSW 2Bβ	ANNOUNCE 432C
	M8PWS 2	LEST SOMEHOW 521C
	TRECHW 2A	RUN 833C
3	ALLA 3	BUT, YET 38A
	ANAGKAZW 1	COMPEL 51D
	EIMI II8	TO BE 223D
	HELL8N 2A	GENTILE 251C
	OUDE 3	NOT EVEN 596A
	PERITEMNW 1	CUT AROUND 658A
	SUN 1C	WITH 789B
	TITOS 1	TITUS 828C
3-5	HWRA 2Aβ	TIME OF DAY 904C
4	ELEUTHERIA	FREEDOM 250A
	EN 15D	IN 259A
	ECHW I2G	HAVE 333B
	HINA I2	IN ORDER THAT 377D
	KATADOULOW	ENSLAVE 411C
	KATASKOPEW	SPY OUT 419D

4	HOSTIS 2B	WHOEVER 591A
	PAREISAKTOS	SNEAKED IN 630A
	PAREISERCHOMAI 2	SLIP IN 630B
	PSEUDADELPHOS	FALSE BROTHER 899D
5	AL8THEIA 2B	TRUTH 35B
	DIAMENW	REMAIN 185D
	EIKW	YIELD 221B
	EUAGGELION 1B	GOSPEL 318B
	KAIROS 1	TIME 395C
	HUPOTAG8	SUBJECTION 855C
	HWRA 2Aβ	TIME OF DAY 904C
5A	PROS III2B	TOWARD 717A
5B	PROS III7	TOWARD 718A
6	DIAPHERW 2C	189C
	MAKES NO DIFFERENCE	
	EIMI II6B	TO BE 223C
	EIMI II6D	TO BE 223C
	THEOS 3A	GOD 357D
	LAMBANW 1Eβ	RECEIVE 466A
	HOPOIOS	WHAT SORT 579B
	OUDEIS 2Bγ	IN NO RESPECT 596C
	POTE 3	ONCE 702A
	PROSANATITH8MI 1	ADD 718D
	PROSWPON 1B	FACE 728C
	TIS, TI 1Bε	ANY ONE 828A
6A	DOKEW 2B	SEEM 201B
6A	HOPOIOS	WHAT SORT 579B
6B	DOKEW 2B	SEEM 201B
7	AKROBUSTIA 3	HEATHENISM 33B
	EIDON 3	NOTICE 220A
	ENANTION 2	BEFORE 261B
	EUAGGELION 2Bα	GOSPEL 318B
	PISTEUW 3	BELIEVE 667D
7F	PETROS	PETER 661A
7-9	PERITOM8 4A	CIRCUMCISION 658D
8	APOSTOL8	APOSTLESHIP 98D
	EIS 4G	FOR 229A
	ENERGEW 1A	WORK 264D
	PETROS	PETER 661A
9	BARNABAS	BARNABAS 133C
	DEXIOS 2A	RIGHT 173D
	DOKEW 2B	SEEM 201B
	IAKWBOS 3	JAMES 368C
	HINA III3	IN ORDER THAT 379A
	IWAN(N)8S 2	JOHN 385C
	K8PHAS	CEPHAS 432D
	KOINWNIA 1	ASSOCIATION 440A
	PETROS	PETER 661A
	STULOS	PILLAR 779C
	CHARIS 4	FAVOR 886C
10	AUTOS 1H	EVEN 122D
	HINA III2	IN ORDER THAT 379A
	HINA IV	IN ORDER THAT 379B
	KAI II6	394C
	MN8MONEUW 1A	REMEMBER 527A
	MONOS 2B	ONLY 529D
	HOS,H8,HO I7B	(REL PRON) 588C
	POIEW II8ε	DO 687D
	PTWCHOS 1A	BEGGING POOR 735D
	SPOUDAZW 2	HASTEN 771A
11	ANTHIST8MI 1	SET AGAINST 66C
	ANTIOCHEIA 1	ANTIOCH 74D
	KATA III1B	TO 407B

11 KATAGINWSKW	CONDEMN 410D	17 M8 A1112	NOT 518C
K8PHAS	CEPHAS 432D	18 KATALUW 1B9	DESTROY 415B
HOTE 1B	WHEN 592C	OIKODOMEW 2	BUILD 561A
PROSWPON 1C6	FACE 728D	PALIN 1B	AGAIN 611C
11FF PETROS	PETER 660D	PARABAT8S	TRANSGRESSOR 617A
12 APHORIZW 1	SEPARATE 126D	SUNIST8MI	UNITE 798B
ETHNOS 2	GENTILES 217C	SUNIST8MI 11C	UNITE 798C
EK 3D	FROM 234C	19 APOTHN8SKW 1B¥	DIE 91A
ERCHOMAI 11A9	COME 310B	DIA A111D	THROUGH 179B
IAKWBOS 3	JAMES 368C	ZAW 2A	LIVE 337A
META A112	WITH 510C	ZAW 3B	LIVE 337C
PERITOM8 4A	CIRCUMCISION 658D	THEOS 3B	GOD 357D
PRO 2	BEFORE 708D	SUSTAUROW 2	CRUCIFY WITH 802C
SUNESTHIW	EAT WITH 796A	19A NOMOS 3	LAW 544C
TIS, TI 1A«	ANY ONE 827C	19B NOMOS 3	LAW 544C
HUPOSTELLW 1	WITHDRAW 855A	20 AGAPAW 1B«	LOVE 4D
PHOBEW 1B«	BE AFRAID 870D	EN 15A	IN 258D
13 BARNABAS	BARNABAS 133C	EN 15D	IN 259A
IOUDAIOS 2D	JEWISH 380B	ZAW 1B	LIVE 336D
LOIPOS 2A	OTHER 481A	HOS,H8,HO 17C	(REL PRON) 588D
SUNAPAGW	LEAD AWAY 792C	OUKETI 1	NO LONGER 596D
SUNUPOKRINOMAI	801B	PARADIDWMI 1B	GIVE OVER 620B
JOIN IN PRETENDING		PISTIS 2B9	FAITH 668D
HUPOKRISIS	HYPOCRISY 852D	SARX 5	BODY 751C
14 AL8THEIA 2B	TRUTH 35B	HUIOS 2B	SON 842D
ANAGKAZW 1	COMPEL 51C	HUPER 1A«	IN BEHALF OF 846C
ETHNIKWS	LIKE THE HEATHEN 217B	20A ZAW 2A	LIVE 337A
ETHNOS 2	GENTILES 217C	20B ZAW 2A	LIVE 337A
EIDON 3	NOTICE 220A	20D ZAW 3A	LIVE 337B
EMPROSTHEN 2B	IN FRONT 256C	21 ATHETEW 1A	SET ASIDE 20C
EUAGGELION 1B	GOSPEL 318B	ARA 3	THEN 103C
ZAW 3A	LIVE 337B	DIKAIOSUN8 3	RIGHTEOUSNESS 196A
IOUDAIKWS	IN A JEWISH MANNER 380A	DWREAN 3	IN VAIN 209D
IOUDAIZW	LIVE AS A JEW 380A	NOMOS 3	LAW 544C
IOUDAIOS 2A	JEWISH 380B	CHARIS 3B	FAVOR 886C
K8PHAS	CEPHAS 432D		
ORTHOPODEW	WALK STRAIGHT 583D	GALATIANS 3	
PROS 1115D	TOWARD 717D		
PWS 1C	HOW 739C	1 ANO8TOS 1	UNINTELLIGENT 70A
SU 1C	YOU 779D	BASKAINW 1	BEWITCH 136D
HUPARCHW 2	BE 846A	GALAT8S	GALATIAN 149B
15 HAMARTWLOS 2	SINNER 43D	KATA 111B	TO 407B
EK 3B	FROM 234B	OPHTHALMOS 2	EYE 604D
PHUSIS 1	NATURE 877C	PEITHW 3B	OBEY 645C
16 ANTHRWPOS 3A¥	MAN 68B	PROGRAPHW 2	WRITE BEFORE 711A
DIA A111D	THROUGH 179C	STAUROW 1	CRUCIFY 773A
DIOTI 3	FOR 198C	W 1	O 903B
EK 3F	BY 234D	2 AKO8 2B	REPORT 30C
ERGON 1C9	DEED 308B	APO 1V2B	FROM 87A
NOMOS 3	LAW 544D	EK 3F	BY 234D
PAS 1A«	EVERY EACH 636D	ERGON 1C9	DEED 308B
PISTEUW 2A9	BELIEVE 667B	8 1D¥	OR 343A
SARX 3	BODY 751B	THELW 1	WISH 355C
16A PISTIS 2B9	FAITH 668D	MANTHANW 3	FIND OUT 491C
16B PISTIS 2B9	FAITH 668D	MONOS 2B	ONLY 529D
16F DIKAIOW 3A	JUSTIFY 196D	NOMOS 3	LAW 544D
17 ARA	(PARTICLE) 103C	PISTIS 2D«	FAITH 669C
GINOMAI 13A	TAKE PLACE 157D	PNEUMA 5D«	SPIRIT 683A
DIAKONOS 1B	HELPER 183D	3 ANO8TOS 1	UNINTELLIGENT 70A
EN 15D	IN 259B	ENARCHOMAI	BEGIN 261D
HEURISKW 2	FIND 326A	EPITELEW 1	END 302B
Z8TEW 2B¥	SEEK 339C	HOUTW 3	THUS 602D
KAI 112	EVEN 394B	PNEUMA 5D9	SPIRIT 683B

3	PNEUMA 5Gα	SPIRIT 683C
	SARX 7	BODY 751D
4	GE 3A (EMPHASIZING PARTICLE)	152A
	EIK8 2	IN VAIN 221A
	PASCHW 1	EXPERIENCE 639B
	TOSOUTOS 2Aβ	SO GREAT 831B
5	AKO8 2B	REPORT 30C
	DUNAMIS 1	POWER 206D
	DUNAMIS 4	MIRACLE 207B
	EK 3F	BY 234D
	ENERGEW 2	WORK 265A
	EPICHOR8GEW 2	GIVE 305A
	ERGON 1Cβ	DEED 308B
8	1Dγ	OR 343A
	NOMOS 3	LAW 544D
	PISTIS 2Dα	FAITH 669C
	PNEUMA 5Dα	SPIRIT 683A
6	ABRAAM	ABRAHAM 1D
	DIKAIOSUN8 3	RIGHTEOUSNESS 196A
	KATHWS 1	JUST AS 392B
	LOGIZOMAI 1A	RECKON 477A
	PISTEUW 1B	BELIEVE 666C
7	ARA 1	THEN 103B
	EK 3D	FROM 234C
	HOUTOS 1Aε	THIS 601B
	PISTIS 2Dα	FAITH 669C
	HUIOS 1Cγ	SON 841D
7-26	PISTIS 2Dα	FAITH 669B
8	*ABRAAM	ABRAHAM 1D
	GRAPH8 2Bβ	SCRIPTURE 165C
	DIKAIOW 3B	JUSTIFY 196D
	ENEULOGEW	BLESS 265B
	PROEUAGGELIZOMAI	712C
	PROCLAIM IN ADVANCE	
	PROORAW 2	SEE PREVIOUSLY 716A
9	ABRAAM	ABRAHAM 1D
	EK 3D	FROM 234C
	EULOGEW 3	BLESS 322D
	PISTIS 2Dα	FAITH 669C
	PISTOS 2	TRUSTWORTHY 670D
	SUN 2B	WITH 789C
	HWSTE 1A	THEREFORE 908B
10	BIBLION 1	BOOK 140D
	EIMI III3	TO BE 224B
	EIMI III12	TO BE 224D
	EMMENW 2	PERSEVERE IN 254D
	EPIKATARATOS	CURSED 294C
	ERGON 1Cβ	DEED 308B
	KATARA	CURSE 418A
	HO,H8,TO II4Bζ	THE 554A
	OU 5A	NO 595A
	PAS 1Cγ	WHOEVER 637C
	POIEW IICα	DO 688C
	HUPO 2B	UNDER 851B
10A	NOMOS 3	LAW 544D
10B	NOMOS 4A	LAW 545A
11	D8LOS	CLEAR 177B
	DIKAIOS 1B	UPRIGHT 195A
	DIKAIOW 3A	JUSTIFY 196D
	ZAW 2Bβ	LIVE 337B
	NOMOS 3	LAW 544D
	PARA II2B	BESIDE 615C
12	EIMI III3	TO BE 224B
12	ZAW 2Bβ	LIVE 337B
	POIEW IICα	DO 688C
12F	NOMOS 3	LAW 544C
13	GINOMAI I4A	BECOME 158C
	EK 1C	AWAY FROM 233D
	EXAGORAZW 1	REDEEM 271A
	EPI IIAβ	ON 285D
	EPIKATARATOS	CURSED 294C
	KATATHEMA	ACCURSED THING 411D
	KREMANNUMI 2A	HANG 451A
	XULON 2C	CROSS 551C
	PAS 1Cγ	WHOEVER 637B
	HUPER IAε	IN BEHALF OF 846C
13A	KATARA	CURSE 418A
13B	KATARA	CURSE 418A
14	*ABRAAM	ABRAHAM 1D
	GINOMAI I4Cα	COME, GO 158D
	DIA AIIIID	THROUGH 179C
	EPAGGELIA 2B	PROMISE 280B
	EULOGIA 3Bα	BLESSING 323B
	LAMBANW 2	RECEIVE 466B
	PNEUMA 5Dα	SPIRIT 683A
15	ATHETEW 1A	SET ASIDE 20C
	ANTHRWPOS 1C	HUMAN 67D
	DIATH8K8 1	182A
	LAST WILL AND TESTAMENT	
	EPIDIATASSOMAI	ADD A CODICIL 292A
8	1C	NOR 343A
	KUROW 1	CONFIRM 462A
	LEGW I5	SAY 470A
	HOMWS	ALL THE SAME 572D
16	*ABRAAM	ABRAHAM 1D
	EIPON 1	SAY 225B
	EPAGGELIA 2A	PROMISE 280A
	EPI IIBγ	ON 286B
	LEGW I7	SAY 470A
	HOS,H8,HO I4C	(REL PRON) 588A
	POLUS I2Aα	MANY 694D
	SPERMA 2B	SEED 769C
	HWS I2A	AS 905C
17	AKUROW	MAKE VOID 33D
	DIATH8K8 1	182A
	LAST WILL AND TESTAMENT	
	EPAGGELIA 2A	PROMISE 280A
	ETOS	YEAR 317B
	KATARGEW 1B	MAKE INEFFECTIVE 418B
	LEGW I2B	SAY 469D
	META BIII	AFTER 511C
	NOMOS 3	LAW 544C
	HOUTOS 1Bβ	THIS 601C
	PROKUROW	RATIFY PREVIOUSLY 715A
	TETRAKOSIOI	FOUR HUNDRED 821B
18	*ABRAAM	ABRAHAM 1D
	DIA AIIIE	BY 179C
	KL8RONOMIA 3	INHERITANCE 436A
	NOMOS 3	LAW 544C
	OUKETI 2	NO LONGER 597A
	CHARIZOMAI 1	GIVE FREELY 884D
	CHARIZOMAI 3	GIVE FREELY 885A
18A	EPAGGELIA 2A	PROMISE 280A
18B	EPAGGELIA 2A	PROMISE 280A
19	AGGELOS 2A	ANGEL 7D
	AN 3D	(PARTICLE) 48D

	Word	Gloss
19	ACHRI 2B	UNTIL 128C
	ACHRI 2A	UNTIL 128C
	DIA AIII2A	BY 179C
	DIATAG8	ORDINANCE 188B
	DIATASSW	ORDER 188C
	EPAGGELLOMAI 1B	ANNOUNCE 280C
	MESIT8S	MEDIATOR 508A
	NOMOS 3	LAW 544C
	HOS,H8,HO IIIF	(REL PRON) 589A
	OUN ICβ	THEREFORE 597C
	PARABASIS	OVERSTEPPING 617A
	PROSTITH8MI 1A	ADD 726B
	SPERMA 2B	SEED 769C
	TITH8MI IIBζ	GIVE 824A
	TIS, TI 3A	WHICH 827B
	CHARIN 1	FOR THE SAKE OF 885A
	CHEIR 1	HAND 888C
20	EIMI II7	TO BE 223D
	HEIS 2B	ONE 230B
	HEIS 2B	ONE 230C
	MESIT8S	MEDIATOR 508A
21	AN 1Bα	(PARTICLE) 47D
	GINOMAI I3A	TAKE PLACE 157D
	DIKAIOSUN8 3	RIGHTEOUSNESS 196A
	EPAGGELIA 2A	PROMISE 280B
	ZWOPOIEW 1	MAKE ALIVE 342C
	M8 AIII2	NOT 518C
	ONTWS 1	REALLY 577C
	OUN ICα	THEREFORE 597B
21A	NOMOS 3	LAW 544C
21C	NOMOS 3	LAW 544C
21C	NOMOS 3	LAW 544D
22	HAMARTIA 3	SIN 43A
	GRAPH8 2Bβ	SCRIPTURE 165C
	EPAGGELIA 2C	PROMISE 280B
	PAS 2Bβ	ALL THINGS 638D
	PISTEUW 2B	BELIEVE 667C
	PISTIS 2Bβ	FAITH 668D
	SUGKLEIW 2	ENCLOSE 781D
	HUPO 2B	UNDER 851B
23	APOKALUPTW 4	REVEAL 91D
	DE 2	BUT, AND 170D
	ERCHOMAI I2B	COME 311C
	MELLW 1Bβ	BE DESTINED 502A
	NOMOS 3	LAW 544D
	PRO 2	BEFORE 708D
	SUGKLEIW 2	ENCLOSE 781D
	HUPO 2B	UNDER 851B
	PHROUREW 2	GUARD 875A
23-5	PISTIS 3	FAITH 669D
24	DIKAIOW 3A	JUSTIFY 196D
	EK 3F	BY 234D
	NOMOS 3	LAW 544C
	PAIDAGWGOS	ATTENDANT 608B
	HWSTE 1A	THEREFORE 908B
24F	TELOS 1C	END 819C
25	EIMI III12	TO BE 224D
	ERCHOMAI I2B	COME 311C
	PAIDAGWGOS	ATTENDANT 608B
	HUPO 2B	UNDER 851B
26	DIA AIIIID	THROUGH 179C
	PISTIS 2Bβ	FAITH 669A
	HUIOS ICγ	SON 841D

	Word	Gloss
27	BAPTIZW 2Bβ	BAPTIZE 131C
	ENDUW 2B	DRESS 263D
28	HAPAS 2	ALL 81A
	ARS8N	MALE 109C
	DOULOS 1B	SLAVE 204D
	EIMI II7	TO BE 223D
	HEIS 1B	ONE 230A
	ELEUTHEROS 1	FREE 250B
	HELL8N 2A	GENTILE 251C
	ENI	THERE IS NOT 265D
	TH8LUS	FEMALE 361B
	IOUDAIOS 2A	JEWISH 380B
	PAS 1Eα	ALL 637D
28A	OUDE 1	AND NOT 595D
28B	OUDE 1	AND NOT 595D
29	ABRAAM	ABRAHAM 1D
	ARA 3	THEN 103C
	EPAGGELIA 2A	PROMISE 280A
	KL8RONOMOS 2B	HEIR 436B
	SPERMA 2B	SEED 769B

GALATIANS 4

	Word	Gloss
1	DIAPHERW 2A	DIFFER 189C
	DOULOS 1B	SLAVE 204D
	EPI III2B	ON 289B
	KL8RONOMOS 1	HEIR 436B
	LEGW III E	DECLARE 471A
	N8PIOS 2	MINOR 539D
	HO,H8,TO IIIAβ	THE 552C
	HOSOS 1	HOW GREAT 590B
	OUDEIS 2Bγ	IN NO RESPECT 596C
	PAS 2Aδ	EVERYTHING 638C
	CHRONOS	TIME 896B
2	ACHRI 1A	UNTIL 128B
	EPITROPOS 3	GUARDIAN 303D
	OIKONOMOS 1A	MANAGER 562D
	PROTHESMIA	APPOINTED DAY 713B
	HUPO 2B	UNDER 851B
3	DOULOW 2	ENSLAVE 205B
	N8PIOS 2	MINOR 539D
	STOICHEION 3	FUNDAMENTAL PRINCIPLES 776C
	STOICHEION 4	FUNDAMENTAL PRINCIPLES 777A
	HUPO 2B	UNDER 851B
4	GINOMAI IIA	BE BORN 157B
	GINOMAI II4A	BE 159C
	EK 3A	FROM 234A
	EXAPOSTELLW 1B	SEND OUT 272D
	ERCHOMAI II8α	COME 311B
	PL8RWMA 5	THAT WHICH FILLS 678C
	HUIOS 2B	SON 842D
	HUPO 2B	UNDER 851B
	CHRONOS	TIME 896B
4F	NOMOS 3	LAW 544D
5	APOLAMBANW 1	RECEIVE 93D
	EXAGORAZW 1	REDEEM 271A
	HUIOTHESIA 2	ADOPTION 841B
	HUPO 2B	UNDER 851C
6	ABBA	FATHER 1B
	EXAPOSTELLW 18	SEND OUT 272D
	KARDIA 1Bθ	HEART 405B

6	KRAZW 2Bα	CALL	449A
	PAT8R 3Cβ	FATHER	641C
	PNEUMA 5B	SPIRIT	682C
6A	HUIOS ICγ	SON	841D
7	DOULOS IC	SLAVE	204D
	KL8RONOMOS 2B	HEIR	436B
	HWSTE IA	THEREFORE	908B
7A	HUIOS ICγ	SON	841D
7B	HUIOS ICγ	SON	841D
8	DOULEUW 2B	SERVE	204C
	OIDA IA	KNOW	558B
	OU 3B	NO	594C
	TOTE IA	AT THAT TIME	831C
	PHUSIS 2	NATURE	877C
8B	THEOS I	GOD	357C
8F	THEOS 3B	GOD	357D
9	ANWTHEN 3	AGAIN	76D
	ASTHEN8S IB	SICK	115B
	GINWSKW IB	KNOW	160A
	GINWSKW 7	ACKNOWLEDGE	160D
	DOULEUW 2B	SERVE	204C
	EPI IIIB6	TOWARD	289A
	EPISTREPHW IBβ	TURN	301B
	THELW 2	WISH	355D
	MALLON 3D	RATHER	490D
	NUN IC	NOW	548A
	PTWCHOS 2	BEGGING POOR	735D
	PWS IB	HOW	739C
	STOICHEION 3		776C
	FUNDAMENTAL PRINCIPLES		
	STOICHEION 4		777A
	FUNDAMENTAL PRINCIPLES		
9A	PALIN IA	BACK	611C
9B	PALIN 2	AGAIN	611D
10	ENIAUTOS 3	YEAR	266A
	H8MERA 2	DAY	346D
	H8MERA 2	DAY	347C
	KAIROS 3	TIME	396A
	M8N 2	NEW MOON	520D
	PARAT8REW 3	WATCH	628A
11	KOPIAW 2	BECOME WEARY	444B
	M8PWS IB	LEST SOMEHOW	521C
	PHOBEW IA	BE AFRAID	870D
12	ADIKEW 2A	DO WRONG	17B
	GINOMAI III	BE	159B
	DEOMAI 3	ASK	174B
	OUDEIS 2Bγ	IN NO RESPECT	596C
	SU IA	YOU	779D
13	ASTHENEIA IA	WEAKNESS	114D
	DIA BII	BECAUSE OF	180A
	EUAGGELIZW 2Aγ	PREACH	317D
	HO,H8,TO II6	THE	554C
	PROTEROS IBβ	EARLIER	729C
	SARX 2	BODY	751A
14	AGGELOS 2A	ANGEL	7C
	BASKAINW I	BEWITCH	136D
	DECHOMAI I	RECEIVE	176C
	EKPTUW	SPIT	244A
	EXOUTHENEW I	DESPISE	277B
	EXOUTHENEW 2	REJECT	277C
	PEIRASMOS 2B	TEST	646D
	SARX 2	BODY	751A
15	DUNATOS 2A	POSSIBLE	208A

15	EXORUSSW	TEAR OUT	277A
	MAKARISMOS	BLESSING	488B
	MARTUREW IA	BEAR WITNESS	493D
	OUN ICα	THEREFORE	597C
	POU IA	WHERE	702D
16	AL8THEUW	BE TRUTHFUL	36A
	ECHTHROS 2Bβ	THE ENEMY	331D
	HWSTE IA	THEREFORE	908B
17	EKKLEIW I	EXCLUDE	240A
	HINA I3	IN ORDER THAT	377D
	KALWS 2	WELL	402B
17A	Z8LOW IB	STRIVE	338C
17B	Z8LOW IB	STRIVE	338C
18	Z8LOW IC	MANIFEST ZEAL	338C
	M8 AIIIC	NOT	518A
	MONOS 2C	ONLY	529D
	PAREIMI IA	BE PRESENT	629C
	PROS III7	TOWARD	718A
18A	KALOS 3C	GOOD	401D
18B	KALOS 2B	GOOD	401B
19	EN I5A	IN	258D
	MECHRI 2	UNTIL	517B
	MORPHOW	TO FORM	530B
	HOS,H8,HO I3Bγ	(REL PRON)	587D
	HOS,H8,HO IIIF	(REL PRON)	589A
	TEKNION	CHILD	815D
	TEKNON 2B	CHILD	816B
	WDINW	SUFFER BIRTH PANGS	904A
20	ALLASSW I	CHANGE	38C
	APOREW	UNCERTAIN	97A
	ARTI 3	NOW	109D
	THELW I	WISH	355B
	PAREIMI IA	BE PRESENT	629C
	PROS III7	TOWARD	718A
	PHWN8 2B	VOICE	879A
21	AKOUW 7	UNDERSTAND	328B
	HUPO 2B	UNDER	851B
21A	NOMOS 3	LAW	544D
21B	NOMOS 4A	LAW	545A
22	HEIS 5A	ONE	231A
	ECHW I2Bα	HAVE	332C
	M8T8R 4	MOTHER	522A
	HUIOS IAα	SON	841B
22F	EK 3A	FROM	234A
22F	ELEUTHEROS I	FREE	250B
22F	HO,H8,TO IIIAα	THE	552B
22F	PAIDISK8	MAID	609B
23	GENNAW IA	BEGET	154C
	DIA AIIIIE	BY	179C
	EPAGGELIA 2A	PROMISE	280A
	MEN	(PARTICLE)	503C
	MEN IC	(PARTICLE)	504A
	HO,H8,TO I2	THE	552A
	SARX 4	BODY	751B
24	HAGAR	HAGAR	6D
	ALL8GOREW SPEAK ALLEGORICALLY		38D
	GENNAW 2	BEAR	154D
	DIATH8K8 2	COVENANT	182B
	DOULEIA 2	SLAVERY	204B
	HOUTOS IAη	THIS	601B
24F	OROS	MOUNTAIN	586B
24F	SINA	SINAI	759A
24=6	SIWN I	ZION	759D

25 HAGAR — HAGAR 6D
ARABIA — ARABIA 103D
DOULEUW 1A — BE A SLAVE 204B
META AII2 — WITH 510C
NUN 3A — NOW 548A
HO,H8,TO IIIC — THE 552D
HO,H8,TO II8B — THE 554D
SUSTOICHEW — CORRESPOND 803A
TEKNON 2Fα — CHILD 816C
25 HIEROSOLUMA — JERUSALEM 373D
25F HIEROSOLUMA 2 — JERUSALEM 374A
26 ANW 1 — ABOVE 76B
ELEUTHEROS 3 — FREE 250B
M8T8R 4 — MOTHER 522A
27 AN8R 1 — MAN 65D
BOAW 1 — SHOUT 143D
ER8MOS 1B — DESOLATE 309A
EUPHRAINW 2 — GLADDEN 328A
ECHW I28α — HAVE 332C
MALLON 1 — MORE 490B
MALLON 3C — RATHER 490D
OU 3C — NO 594D
POLUS I1Aα — MANY 694B
R8GNUMI 2 — TEAR 742C
STEIRA — BARREN 773C
TIKTW 1 — GIVE BIRTH 824C
WDINW — SUFFER BIRTH PANGS 904A
28 EPAGGELIA 2A — PROMISE 280B
ISAAK — ISAAC 381C
KATA II58α — ACCORDING TO 408C
29 GENNAW 1A — BEGET 154C
DIWKW 2 — PERSECUTE 200B
KAI II3 — ALSO 394B
NUN 1C — NOW 548A
PNEUMA 5D8 — SPIRIT 683B
SARX 4 — BODY 751B
TOTE 1A — AT THAT TIME 831C
30 GAR 1B — FOR 151B
GRAPH8 2B8 — SCRIPTURE 165B
EKBALLW 1 — DRIVE OUT 237A
KL8RONOMEW 1 — INHERIT 435D
LEGW I7 — SAY 470A
META AII2 — WITH 510C
M8 D2 — NOT 519C
30A PAIDISK8 — MAID 609B
30A HUIOS 1Aα — SON 841B
30B PAIDISK8 — MAID 609B
30B HUIOS 1Aα — SON 841B
30C HUIOS 1Aα — SON 841B
31 TEKNON 2C — CHILD 816B

GALATIANS 5

1 DOULEIA 2 — SLAVERY 204B
ELEUTHERIA — FREEDOM 250A
ELEUTHEROW 2 — SET FREE 250C
ENECHW 2 — BE LOADED DOWN 265B
ZUGOS 1 — YOKE 340B
OUN 1B — THEREFORE 597B
PALIN 1B — AGAIN 611C
ST8KW 2 — STAND 775C
2 IDE 1 — SEE 369D
LEGW IIIF — DECLARE 471A

2 PAULOS — PAUL 643A
WPHELEW 1A — HELP 908D
2F PERITEMNW 1 — CUT AROUND 658A
3 MARTUROMAI 1 — TESTIFY 495B
NOMOS 3 — LAW 544C
NOMOS 3 — LAW 544D
HOTI 1B8 — THAT 592D
OPHEILET8S 2B — DEBTOR 603B
PAS 1Aα — EVERY EACH 636C
POIEW IICα — DO 688C
4 DIKAIOW 3A — JUSTIFY 196D
EKPIPTW 3A — LOSE 243B
KATARGEW 3 — BE RELEASED 418C
HOSTIS 1A — WHOEVER 590D
CHARIS 3B — FAVOR 886B
5 APEKDECHOMAI — AWAIT 82D
DIKAIOSUN8 3 — RIGHTEOUSNESS 196B
ELPIS 2B — HOPE 252C
PISTIS 2Dα — FAITH 669B
PNEUMA 5D8 — SPIRIT 683B
6 AGAP8 I1A — LOVE 5C
AKROBUSTIA 2 — UNCIRCUMCISED 33A
DIA AIIIID — THROUGH 179C
ENERGEW 1B — WORK 265A
ISCHUW 4 — BE VALID 384D
OUTE — NOT 600C
PERITOM8 2 — CIRCUMCISION 658D
PISTIS 2Dα — FAITH 669B
7 AL8THEIA 2B — TRUTH 358
ANAKOPTW — HINDER 55D
EGKOPTW — HINDER 215C
THEODROMOS — GODS RUNNER 356D
KALWS 1 — WELL 402A
M8 AII1A — NOT 517D
PEITHW 3B — OBEY 645C
TRECHW 2A — RUN 833C
8 EK 3C — FROM 234B
KALEW 2 — CALL 400C
HO,H8,TO IIIAα — THE 552C
PEISMON8 — PERSUASION 647A
9 ZUMOW — FERMENT 340C
ZUM8 1 — LEAVEN 340C
MIKROS 2A — SMALL 523B
PHURAMA — THAT WHICH IS MIXED 877A
10 BASTAZW 2B8 — ENDURE 137A
EIMI II6D — TO BE 223C
EN 15D — IN 259B
KRIMA 4B — VERDICT 451C
KURIOS 2Cγ — LORD 461A
HOSTIS 1Eα — WHOEVER 591A
PEITHW 2A — CONVINCE 645B
TARASSW 2 — STIR UP 813A
PHRONEW 1 — THINK 874B
11 ARA 3 — THEN 103C
GINWSKW 1B — KNOW 160A
DIWKW 2 — PERSECUTE 200B
KATARGEW 2 — ABOLISH 418C
K8RUSSW 2B8 — ANNOUNCE 432C
PERITOM8 1 — CIRCUMCISION 658C
SKANDALON 3 — TRAP 760D
STAUROS 3 — THE CROSS 772C
11A ETI 1Aα — STILL 315D
11B ETI 2C — STILL 316B

12 ANASTATOW	DISTURB	60C
APOKOPTW 2	CASTRATE	92C
KAI II2	EVEN	394B
OPHELON	O THAT	604A
13 AGAP8 IIA	LOVE	5C
APHORM8	PRETEXT	127A
GAR 4	INDEED	151D
DOULEUW 2C	SERVE	204C
EPI IIIB€	ON	287C
KALEW 2	CALL	400D
M8 AIII6	NOT	519A
MONOS 2C	ONLY	529D
SARX 7	BODY	751D
13A ELEUTHERIA	FREEDOM	250A
13B ELEUTHERIA	FREEDOM	250A
14 AGAPAW IA«	LOVE	4B
HEIS 2B	ONE	230B
LOGOS IB«	COMMAND	479B
NOMOS 3	LAW	544C
NOMOS 3	LAW	544D
HO,H8,TO II8A	THE	554D
PAS IF«	WHOLE	638A
PL8ROW 3	MAKE FULL	677B
PL8ROW 4B	MAKE FULL	677C
PL8SION IB	NEAR	678D
15 ALL8LWN	EACH OTHER	38D
ANALISKW	CONSUME	56D
BLEPW 6	SEE	143B
DAKNW 2	BITE	169A
KATESTHIW 2	DESTROY	423C
M8 BIB	NOT	519A
16 EPITHUMIA 3	DESIRE	293D
PERIPATEW 2AÞ	GO ABOUT	655B
PNEUMA 5DÞ	SPIRIT	683B
PNEUMA 6B	SPIRIT	683D
*SARX 7	BODY	751D
TELEW 2	PERFORM	818D
17 ALL8LWN	EACH OTHER	38D
ANTIKEIMAI	BE OPPOSED	73D
EPITHUMEW	DESIRE	293B
THELW 2	WISH	355D
HINA II2	IN ORDER THAT	378D
KATA I2Bγ	DOWN	406D
POIEW IIB€	DO	687D
17A PNEUMA 5G«	SPIRIT	683C
17A SARX 7	BODY	751D
17B HOUTOS IA€	THIS	601B
17B PNEUMA 5G«	SPIRIT	683C
17B SARX 7	BODY	751D
18 AGW 3	LEAD	14B
NOMOS 3	LAW	544D
PNEUMA 5DÞ	SPIRIT	683B
HUPO 2B	UNDER	851B
19 AKATHARSIA 2	IMPURITY	28B
ASELGEIA	LICENTIOUSNESS	114C
EIMI II6D	TO BE	223C
ERGON ICÞ	DEED	308B
MOICHEIA	ADULTERY	528A
PORNEIA I	PROSTITUTION	699D
SARX 7	BODY	751D
PHANEROS I	CLEAR	860A
20 HAIRESIS IC	DISSENSION	23C
DICHOSTASIA	DISSENSION	199B

20 EIDWLOLATRIA	IDOLATRY	220C
ERITHEIA	SELFISHNESS	309C
ERIS	STRIFE	309C
*Z8LOS 2	JEALOUSY	338B
THUMOS 2	ANGER	366A
PHARMAKEIA	SORCERY	861D
21 BASILEIA 3B	KINGDOM	134D
BASILEIA 3G	KINGDOM	135B
KL8RONOMEW 2	INHERIT	435D
KWMOS	CAROUSING	462D
METH8	DRUNKENNESS	500A
HOMOIOS I	LIKE	569C
PRASSW IA	DO	705A
PROEIPON I	FORETELL	711D
PROLEGW I	TELL BEFOREHAND	715B
TOIOUTOS 3AÞ	SUCH A KIND	829B
PHTHONOS	ENVY	865C
22 AGATHWSUN8	GOODNESS	3D
AGAP8 IIA	LOVE	5D
EIR8N8 IB	PEACE	226C
KARPOS 2A	RESULT	405D
MAKROTHUMIA 2A	PATIENCE	489B
PISTIS IA	FAITH	668B
PNEUMA 6B	SPIRIT	683D
CHARA I	JOY	883C
CHR8STOT8S 2A	GOODNESS	894D
23 EGKRATEIA	SELF CONTROL	215C
EIMI III6A	TO BE	224C
NOMOS 3	LAW	544C
PRAUT8S	HUMILITY	705D
24 EPITHUMIA 3	DESIRE	293C
HO,H8,TO II7	THE	554C
PATH8MA 2	PASSION	607D
SARX 7	BODY	751D
STAUROW 2	CRUCIFY	773A
SUN 4B	WITH	789D
25 ZAW 2	LIVE	337A
PNEUMA 5DÞ	SPIRIT	683B
PNEUMA 6B	SPIRIT	683D
STOICHEW	BE IN LINE WITH	777A
26 KENODOXOS	CONCEITED	428D
M8 AIII	NOT	518C
PROKALEW	PROVOKE	714B
PHTHONEW	ENVY	865C

GALATIANS 6

1 EAN I3A	IF	210D
KATARTIZW IA	RESTORE	418D
M8 BIB	NOT	519A
PARAPTWMA 2A«	TRANSGRESSION	627B
PEIRAZW 2D	TRY	646B
PNEUMA 3C	SPIRIT	681D
PNEUMATIKOS 2BÞ	SPIRITUAL	685C
PRAUT8S	HUMILITY	705D
PROLAMBANW 2B	TAKE BEFORE	715B
SEAUTOU 3	YOURSELF	753A
SKOPEW	NOTICE	764A
SU IC	YOU	779D
TOIOUTOS 3A«	SUCH A KIND	829B
2 ALL8LWN	EACH OTHER	38D
ANAPL8ROW 2	MAKE COMPLETE	59B
BAROS I	WEIGHT	133C

2 BASTAZW 2Bα   CARRY 137A
   NOMOS 5   LAW 545B
   CHRISTOS 1   ANOINTED ONE 895C
3 DOKEW 1B   THINK 200D
   EIMI 116β   TO BE 223C
   M8DEIS 2Bγ   NOTHING 520A
   TIS, TI 1Bε   ANY ONE 828A
   PHRENAPATAW   DECIEVE 873D
4 DOKIMAZW 1   EXAMINE 201C
   ERGON 1Cβ   DEED 308A
   HETEROS 1Bε   ANOTHER 315C
   KAUCH8MA 1   BOAST 427B
   TOTE 2   AT THAT TIME 831D
5 BASTAZW 2Bα   CARRY 137A
   IDIOS 1Aβ   ONES OWN 370B
   PHORTION 2   LOAD 873A
6 AGATHOS 2Bβ   GOOD 3C
   KOINWNEW 2   SHARE 439D
   LOGOS 1Bβ   WORD 479C
6A KAT8CHEW 2A   TEACH 425A
6B KAT8CHEW 2A   TEACH 425A
7 ANTHRWPOS 3Aγ   MAN 68B
   THERIZW 2A   REAP 359D
   MUKT8RIZW   TREAT WITH CONTEMPT 531A
   HOUTOS 1Aε   THIS 601B
   PLANAW 2Cγ   DECEIVE 671C
   SPEIRW 1Bα   SOW 768D
8 ZW8 2Bβ   LIFE 341C
   THERIZW 2A   REAP 360A
   PNEUMA 5Gα   SPIRIT 683C
   PHTHORA 4   RUIN 865D
8A SARX 7   BODY 751D
8A SPEIRW 1Bα   SOW 768D
8B SARX 7   BODY 751D
8B SPEIRW 1Bα   SOW 768D
9 EGKAKEW 1   BECOME WEARY 214C
   EKKAKEW   LOSE HEART 240A
   EKLUW   BECOME WEARY 242C
   THERIZW 2A   REAP 360A
   KAIROS 3   TIME 396A
   KALOS 2B   GOOD 401B
   M8 AII2B   NOT 518B
   M8 AIII1   NOT 518C
   POIEW 11Bε   DO 687D
10 AGATHOS 2Aα   GOOD 3B
   ARA 4   THEN 103C
   ERGAZOMAI 2A   WORK 307A
   MALISTA 1   ABOVE ALL 490A
   OIKEIOS 2   559B
       MEMBERS OF THE HOUSEHOLD
   PISTIS 2Dα   FAITH 669B
   HWS IV1B   WHEN 907A
10A PROS III4B   TOWARD 717C
10B PROS III4B   TOWARD 717C
11 GRAMMA 1   LETTER 164C
   GRAPHW 1   WRITE 165C
   EIDON 1C   SEE 219D
   EMOS 1Aα   MY 255A
   H8LIKOS   HOW GREAT 346A
   P8LIKOS 1   HOW LARGE 662A
   CHEIR 1   HAND 888B
12 ANAGKAZW 1   COMPEL 51D
   DIWKW 2   PERSECUTE 200B

12 EUPROSWPEW   324D
       MAKE A GOOD SHOWING
   HINA 13   IN ORDER THAT 377D
   HOSOS 2   HOW GREAT 590B
   HOUTOS 1Aε   THIS 601B
   PERITEMNW 1   CUT AROUND 658A
   SARX 6   BODY 751C
   STAUROS 3   THE CROSS 772C
13 THELW 1   WISH 355C
   HINA 11A   IN ORDER THAT 377C
   KAUCHAOMAI 1   BOAST 427A
   NOMOS 3   LAW 544D
   SARX 1   FLESH 750D
   HUMETEROS 1   YOUR 843D
   PHULASSW 1F   WATCH 876C
13A *PERITEMNW 1   CUT AROUND 658A
13B PERITEMNW 1   CUT AROUND 658A
14 GINOMAI 13A   TAKE PLACE 157D
   KAGW 1   AND I 387A
   KAUCHAOMAI 1   BOAST 427A
   KOSMOS 7   WORLD 447D
   KURIOS 2Cγ   LORD 461B
   M8 AIII2   NOT 518C
   STAUROS 3   THE CROSS 772C
   STAUROW 2   CRUCIFY 773A
15 AKROBUSTIA 2   UNCIRCUMCISED 33A
   EIMI 116B   TO BE 223C
   KAINOS 3B   NEW 395B
   KTISIS 1Bα   CREATION 457A
   OUTE   NOT 600C
   PERITOM8 2   CIRCUMCISION 658D
16 EIR8N8 2   PEACE 226D
   ELEOS 2A   MERCY 249D
   ISRA8L 3   ISRAEL 382C
   KANWN 1   RULE 403D
   HOSOS 2   HOW GREAT 590B
   SARX 4   BODY 751B
   STOICHEW   BE IN LINE WITH 777D
17 BASTAZW 2C   CARRY 137A
   KOPOS 1   TROUBLE 444C
   LOIPOS 3Aβ   THE REST 481B
   M8DEIS 2A   NO 520A
   PARECHW 1C   CAUSE 632C
   STIGMA   MARK 776A
   SWMA 1B   BODY 807A
18 AM8N 1   AMEN 45A
   KURIOS 2Cγ   LORD 461B
   META AIIICγ   WITH 510A
   PNEUMA 3B   SPIRIT 681C
   CHARIS 2C   FAVOR 885D

EPHESIANS 1

1 APOSTOLOS 3   APOSTLES 99B
   DIA AIIIID   THROUGH 179C
   EPHESOS   EPHESUS 330B
   THEL8MA 2B   WILL 355C
   PAULOS   PAUL 643A
   PISTOS 2   TRUSTWORTHY 671A
2 APO V4   FROM 87C
   EIR8N8 2   PEACE 226D
   THEOS 3D   GOD 358B
   KURIOS 2Cγ   LORD 461A

2	PAT8R 3Cβ	FATHER 641C
	CHARIS 2C	FAVOR 885D
3	EN IIIIA	BY 260B
	EULOGEW 3	BLESS 322D
	EULOG8TOS	BLESSED 323A
	EULOGIA 3Bα	BLESSING 323B
	THEOS 3D	GOD 358A
	KAI IIA	AND 392C
	KURIOS 2Cγ	LORD 461B
	HO,H8,TO IIIOB	THE 555A
	PAS IAβ	EVERY EACH 636D
	PAT8R 3Dβ	FATHER 641D
	PNEUMATIKOS 2Aβ	SPIRITUAL 685B
4	HAGIOS IBα DEDICATED TO GOD	9D
	AMWMOS 2A	BLAMELESS 47B
	EKLEGOMAI 3C	CHOOSE 241D
	KATHWS 3	AS 392B
	KATABOL8 I	FOUNDATION 410A
	KATENWPION B	422C
	IN THE PRESENCE OF	
	KOSMOS 2	WORLD 446D
	PRO 2	BEFORE 708C
4F	AGAP8 I2A	LOVE 5D
5	EUDOKIA 2	FAVOR 320A
	THEL8MA 2B	WILL 355A
	KATA II5A6	ACCORDING TO 408B
	PROORIZW	716A
	DECIDE UPON BEFOREHAND	
	HUIOTHESIA 2	ADOPTION 841B
6	AGAPAW ID	LOVE 4D
	DOXA IA	GLORY 202D
	EPAINOS IB	PRAISE 281B
	HOS,H8,HO I4B	(REL PRON) 588A
	CHARITOW	FAVOR HIGHLY 887B
6F	CHARIS 2A	FAVOR 885C
7	HAIMA 2B	BLOOD 22C
	APOLUTRWSIS 2A	REDEMPTION 95D
	APHESIS 2	PARDON 124C
	DIA AIIIIA	BY MEANS OF 179A
	PARAPTWMA 2B	TRANSGRESSION 627B
	PLOUTOS	WEALTH 680A
	PLOUTOS 2	WEALTH 680B
8	PAS IAβ	EVERY EACH 636D
	PERISSEUW 2A	BE LEFT OVER 657A
	*SOPHIA 2	WISDOM 767A
	PHRON8SIS 2	WAY OF THINKING 874C
9	GNWRIZW I	MAKE KNOWN 162C
	EUDOKIA 2	FAVOR 320A
	THEL8MA IB	WILL 354D
	MUST8RION 2	MYSTERY 532B
	PROTITH8MI 2B	PLAN 729C
10	ANAKEPHALAIOW	SUM UP 55C
	EPI IIIAα	ON 286C
	KAIROS 4	TIME 396B
	OIKONOMEW	BE MANAGER 562A
	OIKONOMIA 2a	PLAN 562C
	PAS 2Bβ	ALL THINGS 638D
	PL8RWMA 5	THAT WHICH FILLS 678C
11	BOUL8 2B	WILL 145B
	ENERGEW 2	WORK 265A
	THEL8MA 2B	WILL 355A
	KATA II5A6	ACCORDING TO 408B
	KL8ROW I	APPOINT BY LOT 436D

11	PROTHESIS 2B	SETTING FORTH 713B
	PROORIZW	716A
	DECIDE UPON BEFOREHAND	
12	EPAINOS IB	PRAISE 281B
	KL8ROW I	APPOINT BY LOT 436D
	PROORIZW	716A
	DECIDE UPON BEFOREHAND	
13	AL8THEIA 2B	TRUTH 35B
	EPAGGELIA 2A	PROMISE 280B
	EUAGGELION 2Bα	GOSPEL 318B
	LOGOS IBβ	WORD 479C
	PISTEUW 2Aε	BELIEVE 667B
	PISTEUW 2B	BELIEVE 667C
	PNEUMA 5Cα	SPIRIT 682D
	SPHRAGIZW 2B	SEAL 804A
	SWT8RIA 2	DELIVERANCE 809A
14	APOLUTRWSIS 2A	REDEMPTION 95D
	ARRABWN	DOWN PAYMENT 109A
	EPAINOS IB	PRAISE 281B
	KL8RONOMIA 3	INHERITANCE 436A
	NOUS 3A	THE MIND 546D
	HOS,H8,HO I4C	(REL PRON) 588A
	PERIPOI8SIS 3	KEEPING SAFE 656A
15	AGAP8 IIBβ	LOVE 5D
	AKOUW 3B	LEARN 31D
	KAGW 3C	I 387A
	KATA II7B	(POSSESSIVE) 409A
	KURIOS 2Cγ	LORD 461A
	PISTIS 2Bβ	FAITH 669A
16	EPI I2	UNDER 286C
	EUCHARISTEW 2	GIVE THANKS 328C
	MNEIA 2	MENTION 526B
	PAUW 2	STOP 643C
	POIEW III	DO 689C
	PROSEUCH8 I	PRAYER 720C
16F	HINA IIIAγ	378B
	IN ORDER THAT	
17	APOKALUPSIS I	REVELATION 91D
	DIDWMI	GIVE 191D
	EPIGNWSIS	KNOWLEDGE 291C
	THEOS 3C	GOD 358A
	HINA I4	IN ORDER THAT 377D
	PAT8R 3E	FATHER 642A
	PNEUMA 5E	SPIRIT 683C
	SOPHIA 2	WISDOM 767A
18	DOXA IA	GLORY 202D
	ELPIS 2B	HOPE 252D
	KARDIA IBβ	HEART 404C
	KL8RONOMIA 3	INHERITANCE 436A
	KL8SIS I	CALL 436D
	OIDA 4	KNOW 559A
	OPHTHALMOS 2	EYE 604C
	PLOUTOS 2	WEALTH 680B
	PHWTIZW 2B	SHINE 881C
19	DUNAMIS I	POWER 206D
	EIS 4G	FOR 229A
	ENERGEIA I	WORKING 264C
	ISCHUS	STRENGTH 384B
	KRATOS 3	POWER 450B
	MEGETHOS 2	GREATNESS 499D
	PISTEUW 2B	BELIEVE 667C
	TIS, TI IBβ	WHICH 827A
	HUPERBALLW	SURPASS 848A

20 DEXIOS 2A   RIGHT 173D
  EGEIRW 1AB   RAISE 213D
  EN IIC   IN 257D
  ENERGEW 2   WORK 265A
  EPOURANIOS 2Aα   HEAVENLY 306A
  KATHIZW IA   SET 390D
  NEKROS 2A   DEAD 537A
21 AIWN 2B   AGE 27B
  ALLA IA   BUT, YET 37C
  ARCH8 3   RULER 112A
  DUNAMIS 6   POWER 207B
  EXOUSIA 4CB   AUTHORITY 278B
  KURIOT8S 3   LORDSHIP 461D
  MELLW 2   IS DESTINED 502C
  MONOS 2C   ONLY 529D
  ONOMAZW 2   NAME 577C
  HUPERANW   ABOVE 847D
21A   PAS 1AB   EVERY EACH 636D
22 DIDWMI 5   GIVE 192D
  EKKL8SIA 4D   CHURCH 240C
  KEPHAL8 2A   HEAD 431C
  POUS 1B   FOOT 703C
  HUPER 2   BEYOND 847A
  HUPO 2Aα   UNDER 851B
  HUPOTASSW IA   SUBJECT 855C
22A   PAS 2A6   EVERYTHING 638B
23 PL8ROW IA   MAKE FULL 676D
  PL8RWMA IB   THAT WHICH FILLS 678A
  SWMA 5   BODY 807C
23B   PAS 2A6   IN ALL RESPECTS 638C

EPHESIANS 2

1 NEKROS 18α   DEAD 536D
  PARAPTWMA 2B   TRANSGRESSION 627B
2 A8R   AIR 20A
  AIWN 4   THE AEON 27D
  APEITHEIA   DISOBEDIENCE 81D
  ARCHWN 3   AUTHORITIES 113D
  EN 15A   IN 258D
  ENERGEW IA   WORK 264D
  ENERGEW 2   WORK 265A
  EXOUSIA 4B   AUTHORITY 278B
  KOSMOS 7   WORLD 447D
  PERIPATEW 2A6   GO ABOUT 655B
  PNEUMA 5G   SPIRIT 683C
  HUIOS IC6   SON 842A
2F   POTE I   ONCE 701D
3 ANASTREPHW 2BB   LIVE 61A
  DIANOIA 5   SENSES 186B
  EPITHUMIA 3   DESIRE 293C
  EPITHUMIA 3   DESIRE 293D
  THEL8MA IC6   WILL 355A
  LOIPOS 2Bα   THE OTHERS 481A
  ORG8 2B   ANGER 583A
  PAS IEα   ALL 637D
  POIEW IICα   DO 688C
  TEKNON 2FB   CHILD 816C
  PHUSIS I   NATURE 877C
3A   SARX 7   BODY 751D
4 AGAPAW 2   LOVE 5A
  AGAP8 I2A   LOVE 5D
  DIA BIII   BECAUSE OF 180B

4 ELEOS 2B   MERCY 249D
  EN IVIA   IN 260C
  PLOUSIOS 2   RICH 679C
  POLUS IIBB   MANY 694C
5 NEKROS 18α   DEAD 536D
  PARAPTWMA 2B   TRANSGRESSION 627B
  SUZWOPOIEW   783D
   MAKE ALIVE TOGETHER
  SWZW 2B   SAVE 806B
  CHARIS 2A   FAVOR 885C
  CHRISTOS I   ANOINTED ONE 895C
6 EPOURANIOS 2Aα   HEAVENLY 306A
  SUGKATHIZW I   780D
   CAUSE TO SIT DOWN WITH
  SUNEGEIRW 2   RISE UP WITH 793C
7 AIWN 2B   AGE 27B
  ENDEIKNUMI I   DEMONSTRATE 262A
  EPERCHOMAI IBα   COME 284D
  EPI IIIIBε   TOWARD 289A
  PLOUTOS   WEALTH 680A
  PLOUTOS 2   WEALTH 680B
  HUPERBALLW   SURPASS 848A
  CHARIS 2A   FAVOR 885C
  CHR8STOT8S 2B   GOODNESS 894D
8 DIA AIIIID   THROUGH 179C
  DWRON I   GIFT 210C
  KAI I3   AND 394A
  HOUTOS IBγ   THIS 601D
  PISTIS 2Dα   FAITH 669B
  SWZW 2B   SAVE 806C
  CHARIS 2A   FAVOR 885C
9 ERGON ICB   DEED 308B
  KAUCHAOMAI I   BOAST 427A
  TIS, TI IAγ   ANY ONE 827D
10 EPI IIIBε   ON 287C
  ERGON ICB   DEED 308A
  KTIZW   CREATE 456C
  HOS,H8,HO I4A   (REL PRON) 587D
  PERIPATEW 2A6   GO ABOUT 655B
  POI8MA   WORK 689D
  PROETOIMAZW   712C
   PREPARE BEFOREHAND
11 AKROBUSTIA 3   HEATHENISM 33B
  LEGW II3   CALL 471B
  MN8MONEUW IC   REMEMBER 527A
  PERITOM8 4A   CIRCUMCISION 658D
  HUPO IAα   BY 850D
  CHEIROPOI8TOS   889A
   MADE BY HUMAN HANDS
11B   SARX I   FLESH 750D
12 ATHEOS I   GODLESS 20B
  APALLOTRIOW   ESTRANGE 79C
  DIATH8K8 2   182B
   LAST WILL AND TESTAMENT
  ELPIS 2B   HOPE 252D
  EPAGGELIA 2A   PROMISE 280B
  ECHW I2EB   HAVE 333A
  ISRA8L 2   ISRAEL 382B
  KAIROS I   TIME 395D
  XENOS 18α   STRANGE 550B
  POLITEIA I   CITIZENSHIP 692D
  CHWRIS 2Aα   APART 898D
13 HAIMA 2B   BLOOD 22C

13 GINOMAI I4Cη	COME, GO	159B
EGGUS ID	NEAR	213B
EIMI II9A	TO BE	223D
MAKRAN IAβ	FAR	488D
NUNI IC	NOW	548C
14 AMPHOTEROI I	BOTH	47A
EIR8N8 3	PEACE	226D
HEIS IB	ONE	230A
LUW 3	DESTROY	485A
MESOTOICHON	DIVIDING WALL	509A
POIEW II8ι	DO	688B
SARX 2	BODY	751A
PHRAGMOS 2	FENCE	873C
15 DOGMA I	DECREE	200C
EIR8N8 IB	PEACE	226D
HEIS IB	ONE	230A
EN IV3	IN	260D
ENTOL8 2Ay	COMMAND	268C
KAINOS 3B	NEW	395B
KATARGEW IB	MAKE INEFFECTIVE	418B
KTIZW	CREATE	456C
POIEW II8y	DO	687C
16 AMPHOTEROI I	BOTH	47A
APOKATALLASSW	RECONCILE	92A
APOKTEINW 2	PUT TO DEATH	93C
DIA AIIIIA	BY MEANS OF	179A
STAUROS 3	THE CROSS	772C
SWMA 5	BODY	807C
17 EGGUS 3	NEAR	213C
EIR8N8 3	PEACE	226D
EUAGGELIZW 2Aα	PREACH	317C
MAKRAN IAβ	FAR	488D
18 AMPHOTEROI I	BOTH	47A
PAT8R 3E	FATHER	641D
PNEUMA 5Dβ	SPIRIT	683B
PROS IIIIA	TOWARD	716D
PROSAGWG8	APPROACH	718C
19 HAGIOS 2Dβ	SAINTS	10A
ARA 4	THEN	103C
XENOS 2A	THE STRANGER	550B
OIKEIOS 2		559B
MEMBERS OF THE HOUSEHOLD		
OUKETI I	NO LONGER	596D
PAROIKOS 2	STRANGER	634C
SUMPOLIT8S	FELLOW CITIZEN	787C
20 AKROGWNIAIOS	CORNERSTONE	33B
APOSTOLOS 3	APOSTLES	99B
APOSTOLOS 3	APOSTLES	99C
EPI IIIAβ	ON	286D
EPOIKODOMEW IB	BUILD ON TO	305C
THEMELIOS 2B	FOUNDATION	356C
PROPH8T8S 5	PROPHET	731B
21 HAGIOS IAβ	WORTHY OF GOD	9C
AUXANW 3	GROW	121C
EIS 4E	SO THAT	228C
NAOS 2	TEMPLE	535D
OIKODOM8 2B	BUILDING	561D
PAS IAε	ALL	637A
SUNARMOLOGEW	JOIN TOGETHER	792D
22 KATOIK8T8RION	DWELLING PLACE	425D
PNEUMA 5Dβ	SPIRIT	683B
SUNOIKODOMEW I	BUILT UP	799B

EPHESIANS 3

1 DESMIOS	PRISONER	175A
ETHNOS 2	GENTILES	217C
PAULOS	PAUL	643A
HUPER IAε	IN BEHALF OF	846C
CHARIN 2	FOR THE SAKE OF	885B
2 AKOUW 3B	LEARN	31D
GE 3A (EMPHASIZING PARTICLE)		152A
OIKONOMIA IB	MANAGEMENT	562B
CHARIS 4	FAVOR	886C
3 APOKALUPSIS 2	REVELATION	91D
GNWRIZW I	MAKE KNOWN	162C
KATA II5A6	ACCORDING TO	408B
OLIGOS 3B	LITTLE	566D
PROGRAPHW IA	WRITE BEFORE	710D
3FF MUST8RION 2	MYSTERY	532B
4 ANAGINWSKW I	READ	51C
MUST8RION 2	MYSTERY	532B
PROS III5D	TOWARD	717D
SUNESIS 2	INTELLIGENCE	796B
5 HAGIOS I8α	DEDICATED TO GOD	9C
ANTHRWPOS IAδ	PEOPLE	67D
APOKALUPTW 2	REVEAL	91C
APOSTOLOS 2	MESSENGER	99A
GENEA 3B	AGE	153C
GNWRIZW I	MAKE KNOWN	162C
HETEROS I8β	ANOTHER	315B
NUN IAy	NOW	547C
PNEUMA 5Dβ	SPIRIT	683B
PROPH8T8S 5	PROPHET	731B
HUIOS ICβ	SON	841D
6 EPAGGELIA 2C	PROMISE	280B
EUAGGELION IA	GOSPEL	318A
SUGKL8RONOMOS		781D
INHERITING TOGETHER		
SUMMETOCHOS	SHARING WITH	786B
SUSSWMOS		802B
BELONGING TO SAME BODY		
7 DIAKONOS IA	SERVANT	183D
DWREA	GIFT	209C
ENERGEIA I	WORKING	264C
7F CHARIS 4	FAVOR	886C
8 HAGIOS 2Dβ	SAINTS	10A
ANEXICHNIASTOS	INSCRUTABLE	64C
ELACHISTOS 2B	SMALLEST	248B
EUAGGELIZW 2Aα	PREACH	317D
HOUTOS 2B	THIS	601D
PLOUTOS	WEALTH	680A
PLOUTOS 2	WEALTH	680B
9 AIWN 4	THE AEON	27D
APOKRUPTW	CONCEAL	93B
KTIZW	CREATE	456C
OIKONOMIA 2B	PLAN	562C
PAS 2Bβ	ALL THINGS	638D
PHWTIZW 2B	SHINE	881C
PHWTIZW 2C	SHINE	881C
9FF MUST8RION 2	MYSTERY	532B
10 ARCH8 3	RULER	112A
GNWRIZW I	MAKE KNOWN	162C
EKKL8SIA 4D	CHURCH	240C
EXOUSIA 4Cβ	AUTHORITY	278B
EPOURANIOS 2Aα	HEAVENLY	306A

```
10 NUN IAY              NOW 547C        20 HOS,H8,HO I4A   (REL PRON) 587D
   POLUPOIKILOS    MANY SIDED 694B         HUPER 2            BEYOND 847B
   SOPHIA 3B          WISDOM 767B          HUPEREKPERISSOU            848C
11 AIWN IB               TIME 27A               BEYOND ALL MEASURE
   KURIOS 2CY            LORD 461B        21 AIWN IB             TIME 26D
   POIEW II86             DO 687C            AM8N I             AMEN 45A
   PROTHESIS 2B  SETTING FORTH 713B         GENEA 3B            AGE 153C
12 DIA AIIIID         THROUGH 179C          EKKL8SIA 4D      CHURCH 240C
   PARR8SIA 3B        COURAGE 636B          PAS IDC            ALL 637C
   PEPOITH8SIS I        TRUST 649A
   PISTIS 28B           FAITH 668D
   PROSAGWG8         APPROACH 718C                   EPHESIANS 4
13 AITEW                 ASK 25C
   EGKAKEW 2          DESPAIR 214C        1 AXIWS           WORTHILY 78A
   EKKAKEW        LOSE HEART 240A           DESMIOS         PRISONER 175A
   THLIPSIS I      TRIBULATION 362D         EN I5D                IN 259B
   M8 AIII8B              NOT 518A          KALEW 2             CALL 400C
   HUPER IAC    IN BEHALF OF 846C           KL8SIS I            CALL 436D
14 GONU                 KNEE 164B           HOS,H8,HO I4B  (REL PRON) 588A
   KAMPTW I             BEND 403A           OUN IA          THEREFORE 597B
   HOUTOS 18C           THIS 601C           PARAKALEW 2     APPEAL TO 622C
   PAT8R 3E           FATHER 641D           PERIPATEW 2AC    GO ABOUT 655A
   CHARIN 2   FOR THE SAKE OF 885B        2 AGAP8 IIA            LOVE 5C
14F PATRWNUMOS                642C          ANECHW IA           ENDURE 65B
      NAMED AFTER THE FATHER                MAKROTHUMIA 2A     PATIENCE 489B
15 ONOMAZW I            NAME 577B           PAS IA6               ALL 637A
   OURANOS 2C         HEAVEN 599C           PRAUT8S            HUMILITY 705D
   PATRIA 3           PEOPLE 642B           TAPEINOPHROSUN8    HUMILITY 812A
16 ANTHRWPOS 2CC        MAN 68A         2A   META AIIII          WITH 511A
   DUNAMIS I           POWER 206D       2B   META AII6           WITH 510D
   ESW 2                  IN 314C       3 EIR8N8 IB             PEACE 226B
   KRATAIOW        STRENGTHEN 449C         HENOT8S              UNITY 267A
   PLOUTOS            WEALTH 680A          PNEUMA 5DC          SPIRIT 683A
   PLOUTOS 2          WEALTH 680B          SPOUDAZW 2          HASTEN 771A
   PNEUMA 5A          SPIRIT 682C          SUNDESMOS IB          BOND 793A
17 AGAP8 IIA            LOVE 5C            T8REW 3               KEEP 822D
   DIA AIIIID         THROUGH 179C       4 ELPIS 2B              HOPE 252D
   THEMELIOW 2A     ESTABLISH 356C         KALEW 2              CALL 400D
   KARDIA 13θ          HEART 405B          *KL8SIS I            CALL 436D
   KATOIKEW IB          LIVE 425C          PNEUMA 5DB          SPIRIT 683B
   PISTIS 2DC          FAITH 669B          SWMA 5               BODY 807C
   RIZOW           FIX FIRMLY 743C       5 BAPTISMA 2         BAPTISM 132B
   CHRISTOS I   ANOINTED ONE 895C          PISTIS 2DC          FAITH 669B
18 BATHOS I            DEPTH 129D       5F HEIS 2A               ONE 230B
   EXISCHUW          BE ABLE 276B       6 EPI II8C              OVER 286B
   KATALAMBANW 2       GRASP 414B          PAT8R 3CB          FATHER 641C
   M8KOS              LENGTH 520C       7 DWREA                 GIFT 209C
   PLATOS I          BREADTH 672D          HEKASTOS 2           EACH 236A
   PLATOS            BREADTH 672D          KATA II5AY    ACCORDING TO 408B
   SUN 4B               WITH 789D          METRON 2B          MEASURE 516D
   TIS, TI 18B         WHICH 827A          CHARIS 4             FAVOR 886C
   HUPSOS IA          HEIGHT 858B       8 AICHMALWSIA 2 PRISONER OF WAR 26B
19 AGAP8 I2A            LOVE 6A            AICHMALWTEUW       CAPTURE 26B
   EIS 4E             SO THAT 228D         DIDWMI I8B           GIVE 192A
   PAS ICC               ALL 637B          DOMA                 GIFT 202C
   PL8ROW IB       MAKE FULL 677A          LEGW I7               SAY 470A
   PL8RWMA 3B THAT WHICH FILLS 678B        HUPSOS IB          HEIGHT 858B
   TE IB                  AND 815B      8F   ANABAINW IAB       GO UP 50A
   HUPERBALLW        SURPASS 848A       9 EIMI II3             TO BE 222D
20 AITEW                 ASK 25B           KATABAINW IA6    COME DOWN 409C
   DUNAMIS I           POWER 206D          KATWTEROS           LOWER 426B
   ENERGEW IB           WORK 264D          MEROS I8Y            PART 507A
   NOEW 3            IMAGINE 542D          HO,H8,TO II8B         THE 554D
                                        10 ANABAINW IAB        GO UP 50A
```

10 KATABAINW IAᵧ	COME DOWN	409C
OURANOS IE	HEAVEN	599A
PAS IDα	ALL	637C
PL8ROW IA	MAKE FULL	676D
HUPERANW	ABOVE	847D
10B PAS 28β	ALL THINGS	638D
11 DIDASKALOS	TEACHER	190D
DIDWMI 5	GIVE	192D
EUAGGELIST8S	EVANGELIST	318C
MEN IC	(PARTICLE)	504A
HO,H8,TO I2	THE	552A
POIM8N 28ᵧ	SHEPHERD	690D
PROPH8T8S 5	PROPHET	731B
12 DIAKONIA I	SERVICE	183B
ERGON IB	MANIFESTATION	307D
KATARTISMOS	EQUIPMENT	419A
OIKODOM8 IBβ	BUILDING	561C
PROS III3A	TOWARD	717A
SWMA 5	BODY	807C
13 AN8R 2	MAN	66A
HENOT8S	UNITY	267C
EPIGNWSIS	KNOWLEDGE	291C
H8LIKIA ICα	AGE	346A
H8LIKIA 2	BODILY STATURE	346A
KATANTAW 2A	ARRIVE	416B
METRON 28	MEASURE	516D
PAS 28α	IN ALL RESPECTS	638C
PISTIS 20α	FAITH	669B
PL8RWMA 3B	THAT WHICH FILLS	678B
TELEIOS 2Aα	MATURE	817A
HUIOS 28	SON	842D
14 ANEMOS 2	WIND	648
DIDASKALIA 2	TEACHING	190C
KLUDWNIZOMAI	BE TOSSED	437D
KUBEIA	CRAFTINESS	457C
METHODEIA	CRAFTINESS	500B
M8KETI I	NO LONGER	520B
N8PIOS I8α	CHILDREN	539C
PANOURGIA	CUNNING	613A
PAS IAᵧ	EVERY EACH	636D
PERIPHERW 2	CARRY ABOUT	659B
PLAN8	WANDERING	671D
15 AGAP8 IIA	LOVE	5C
AL8THEUW	BE TRUTHFUL	36A
AUXANW 3	GROW	121C
DE ID	BUT, AND	170C
KEPHAL8 2A	HEAD	431C
PAS 28β	ALL THINGS	638D
16 AGAP8 IIA	LOVE	5C
AUX8SIS	CAUSE GROWTH	121C
HAPH8	LIGAMENT	124D
HEIS 5C	ONE	231B
EN III2	BY	260C
ENERGEIA I	WORKING	264C
EPICHOR8GIA	SUPPORT	305B
MELOS 3	MEMBER	503A
MEROS IBβ	PART	507A
METRON 28	MEASURE	516D
OIKODOM8 IBβ	BUILDING	561C
PAS ICα	ALL	637B
POIEW III	DO	689C
SUMBIBAZW IA	UNITE	785B
SUNARMOLOGEW	JOIN TOGETHER	792D

16 SWMA 5	BODY	807C
17 EN I5D	IN	259B
KATHWS I	JUST AS	392A
KAI II3	ALSO	394B
KURIOS 2Cᵧ	LORD	461A
MARTUROMAI 2	AFFIRM	495B
MATAIOT8S	FUTILITY	496D
M8KETI 4	NO LONGER	520B
NOUS 3A	THE MIND	546D
OUN IA	THEREFORE	597B
HOUTOS IBβ	THIS	601C
PERIPATEW 2Aᵧ	GO ABOUT	655B
18 AGNOIA 2	IGNORANCE	IID
APALLOTRIOW	ESTRANGE	79C
DIANOIA I	UNDERSTANDING	186A
EIMI III4	TO BE	224C
ZW8 28α	LIFE	341A
KARDIA IBβ	HEART	404D
PWRWSIS	HARDENING	739B
SKOTIZW 2	BECOME DARK	764D
SKOTOW 2	DARKEN	765B
19 AKATHARSIA 2	IMPURITY	28B
APALGEW	LANGUISH	79B
ASELGEIA	LICENTIOUSNESS	114C
ERGASIA I	PRACTICE	307C
HOSTIS 28	WHOEVER	591A
PARADIDWMI IB	GIVE OVER	620C
PAS IAβ	EVERY EACH	636D
PLEONEXIA	GREEDINESS	673D
20 MANTHANW I	LEARN	491B
21 GE 3A (EMPHASIZING PARTICLE)		152A
22 ANASTROPH8	CONDUCT	61B
ANTHRWPOS 2Cβ	MAN	68A
APOTITH8MI IB	LAY ASIDE	100C
EPITHUMIA 3	DESIRE	293C
PALAIOS 2	OLD	610D
PROTEROS IA	EARLIER	729B
PHTHEIRW 2A	RUIN	865A
22B KATA II5A6	ACCORDING TO	408B
23 ANANEOW I	RENEW	57D
NOUS 3A	THE MIND	546D
PNEUMA 3C	SPIRIT	681D
24 AL8THEIA 2B	TRUTH	35B
ANTHRWPOS 2Cβ	MAN	68A
ENDUW 2B	DRESS	263D
KAINOS 3B	NEW	395B
KATA II58α	ACCORDING TO	408C
KTIZW	CREATE	456C
HOSIOT8S	DEVOUTNESS	589D
25 AL8THEIA 2A	TRUTH	35B
ALL8LWN	EACH OTHER	38D
HEKASTOS 2	EACH	236B
*LALEW 2B	SPEAK	464D
MELOS 3	MEMBER	503A
PL8SION IB	NEAR	678C
PSEUDOS	LIE	900B
26 HAMARTANW I	SIN	41D
EPI II2	AT	287D
EPIDUW	SET	292C
H8LIOS	THE SUN	346B
M8 AIII3A	NOT	518C
ORGIZW	BE ANGRY	583B
PARORGISMOS	ANGER	635A

27	DIABOLOS 2	THE SLANDERER	181A	3	PAS 1Aβ	EVERY EACH	636D
	DIDWMI 1Bα	GIVE	192A		PLEONEXIA	GREEDINESS	673D
	M8TE	AND NOT	521C		PORNEIA 1	PROSTITUTION	699D
	TOPOS 2C	PLACE	831A		PREPW	BE FITTING	706A
28	AGATHOS 2Aα	GOOD	3B	4	AISCHROT8S	UGLINESS	24D
	ERGAZOMAI 2A	WORK	307A		AN8KW 2	IT IS PROPER	65D
	KLEPTW	STEAL	435C		EUTRAPELIA	BUFFOONERY	327D
	KOPIAW 2	BECOME WEARY	444B		EUCHARISTIA 2	THANKFULNESS	329A
	MALLON 3Aα	RATHER	490C		MALLON 3Aα	RATHER	490C
	METADIDWMI	SHARE	512B		MWROLOGIA	SILLY TALK	533B
	M8KETI 6A	NO LONGER	520B		OU 3D	NO	594D
	CHEIR 1	HAND	888B	5	AKATHARTOS 2	IMPURE	28C
	CHREIA 2	NEED	893B		BASILEIA 3B	KINGDOM	134D
28A	ECHW 16A	CAN	333D		BASILEIA 3G	KINGDOM	135B
28B	ECHW 12I	HAVE	333C		GINWSKW 6C	KNOW	160D
29	AGATHOS 1Aβ	GOOD	2D		EIDWLOLATR8S	IDOLATER	220C
	EKPOREUOMAI 2	GO OUT	244A		EIDWLOLATRIA	IDOLATRY	220C
	OIKODOM8 1Bα	BUILDING	561C		ECHW 12A	HAVE	332B
	PAS 1Aα	EVERY EACH	636D		KL8RONOMIA 3	INHERITANCE	436B
	PROS III3C	TOWARD	717B		OIDA	KNOW	558A
	SAPROS 2	DECAYED	749C		HOS,H8,HO 17A	(REL PRON)	588C
	STOMA 1A	MOUTH	777B		PAS 1Aα	EVERY EACH	636D
	CHARIS 3A	FAVOR	886A		PLEONEKT8S	A COVETOUS PERSON	673C
	CHREIA 3	NEED	893C		PORNOS	FORNICATOR	700B
30	APOLUTRWSIS 2A	REDEMPTION	950	6	APATAW 1	DECEIVE	81B
	EIS 2Aβ	FOR	228A		APEITHEIA	DISOBEDIENCE	81D
	H8MERA 38β	DAY	348A		EPI III1Bγ	ON	289A
	LUPEW 1	GRIEVE	482D		ERCHOMAI I2C	COME	311D
	PNEUMA 5Cα	SPIRIT	682D		KENOS 2Aα	EMPTY	429A
	SPHRAGIZW 2B	SEAL	804A		LOGOS 1A6	WORD	478D
31	AIRW 4	TAKE AWAY	248		M8DEIS 2A	NO	520A
	BLASPH8MIA 1	SLANDER	142C		ORG8 2B	ANGER	583A
	KAKIA 1B	MALICE	397D		HUIOS 1C6	SON	842A
	KRAUG8 1A	SHOUT	450C	7	SUMMETOCHOS	SHARING WITH	786B
	ORG8 1	ANGER	582C	8	KURIOS 2Cγ	LORD	461A
	PIKRIA 2	BITTERNESS	663B		NUN 1C	NOW	547D
	SUN 4B	WITH	789D		PERIPATEW 2Aγ	GO ABOUT	655B
32	HEAUTOU 3	ONESELF	211D		SKOTOS 2B	DARKNESS	765B
	EIS 4Cβ	(GOAL)	228C		TEKNON 2Fβ	CHILD	816C
	EUSPLAGCHNOS	COMPASSIONATE	327A		HWS I2A	AS	905C
	KATHWS 3	AS	392B	8A	PHWS 3C	LIGHT	880C
	CHR8STOS 1Bα	USEFUL	894C	8B	PHWS 3A	LIGHT	880C
32A	CHARIZOMAI 2	GIVE FREELY	885A	9	AGATHWSUN8	GOODNESS	3D
32B	CHARIZOMAI 2	GIVE FREELY	885A		AL8THEIA 1	TRUTHFULNESS	35A
					DIKAIOSUN8 2B	RIGHTEOUSNESS	195D

EPHESIANS 5

					KARPOS 2A	RESULT	405D
					PHWS 3A	LIGHT	880C
1	AGAP8TOS 2	BELOVED	6C	10	DOKIMAZW 1	EXAMINE	201C
	MIM8T8S 1	IMITATOR	524A		EUARESTOS 1	PLEASING	319A
	TEKNON 2E	CHILD	816C	11	AKARPOS 2	UNFRUITFUL	29B
	HWS IIIIA	SO	906C		ERGON 1Cβ	DEED	308B
2	AGAPAW 1Bα	LOVE	4D		ERGON 1Cβ	DEED	308B
	AGAP8 IIA	LOVE	5C		MALLON 3Aα	RATHER	490C
	EUWDIA	FRAGRANCE	330A		SKOTOS 2B	DARKNESS	765B
	THUSIA 2A	SACRIFICE	367A		SUGKOINWNEW 1	BE CONNECTED	781D
	OSM8 2	ODOR	590A	12	AISCHROS	SHAMEFUL	24D
	PARADIDWMI 1B	GIVE OVER	620B		AUTOS 3B	(OBLIQUE CASE)	123A
	PERIPATEW 2A6	GO ABOUT	655B		GINOMAI I2A	CREATED	157C
	PROSPHORA 2	PRESENTING	727C		KAI II2	EVEN	394B
	HUPER 1Aγ	IN BEHALF OF	846B		KRUPH8	IN SECRET	455D
3	AKATHARSIA 2	IMPURITY	288		LEGW II2	SPEAK	471A
	M8DE 2	NOT EVEN	519D		HUPO 1B	BY	851A
	ONOMAZW 2	NAME	577C	13	PHWS 3A	LIGHT	880B

13F	PHANEROW 1B	REVEAL	860C
14	ANIST8MI 2A	RISE	69C
	EGEIRW 1B	RAISE UP	214A
	EPIPHAUSKW	ARISE	304B
	EPIPSAUW	ATTAIN	305B
	KATHEUDW 2B	SLEEP	389D
	LEGW 17	SAY	470A
	NEKROS 2B	DEAD	537B
	PAS 1Cγ	WHOEVER	637C
	PHWS 1Bβ	LIGHT	880A
	CHRISTOS 1	ANOINTED ONE	895C
15	AKRIBWS	ACCURATELY	32C
	ASOPHOS	UNWISE	116B
	BLEPW 4C	SEE	143B
	PERIPATEW 2Aγ	GO ABOUT	655B
	PWS 2A	HOW	739D
	SOPHOS 3	LEARNED	767D
16	EXAGORAZW 2	REDEEM	271A
	H8MERA 4B	TIME	348B
	KAIROS 2	TIME	395D
	PON8ROS 1Bβ	WICKED	697D
17	APHRWN	FOOLISH	127B
	THEL8MA 1Cγ	WILL	355A
*	SUNI8MI	UNDERSTAND	797D
	SUNI8MI	UNDERSTAND	798A
18	ASWTIA	DEBAUCHERY	119A
	EIMI III4	TO BE	224C
	METHUSKW	GET DRUNK	500B
	OINOS 1	WINE	565A
	PL8ROW 1B	MAKE FULL	677A
	PNEUMA 5Dβ	SPIRIT	683B
19	ADW	SING	19A
	LALEW 2Aε	SPEAK	464C
	PNEUMATIKOS 2Aβ	SPIRITUAL	685B
	HUMNOS	HYMN	844B
	PSALLW	SING	899B
	PSALMOS 2	PSALM	899B
	WD8	SONG	903D
20	EUCHARISTEW 2	GIVE THANKS	328C
	THEOS 3D	GOD	358A
	KURIOS 2Cγ	LORD	461B
	HO,H8,TO III0B	THE	555A
	ONOMA 14Cγ	NAME	576B
	PAT8R 3E	FATHER	641D
	HUPER 1D	IN BEHALF OF	846D
21	HUPOTASSW 1Bβ	SUBJECT	855D
	PHOBOS 2Bα	FEAR	871D
22	IDIOS 2B	ONES OWN	370C
	HUPOTASSW 1Bβ	SUBJECT	855D
	HWS III1A	SO	906C
22FF	AN8R 1	MAN	65D
22FF	GUN8 2	WIFE	167C
23	SWMA 5	BODY	807C
	SWT8R 2	SAVIOR	808D
23A	KEPHAL8 2A	HEAD	431C
23B	KEPHAL8 2A	HEAD	431C
23FF	EKKL8SIA 4D	CHURCH	240C
24	ALLA 6	NOW	38B
	PAS 2Aβ	EVERY RESPECT	638A
	HUPOTASSW 1Bβ	SUBJECT	855D
25	AGAPAW 1Aα	LOVE	4B
	PARADIDWMI 1B	GIVE OVER	620B
	HUPER 1Aε	IN BEHALF OF	846C

26	HAGIAZW 2	CONSECRATE	8D
	KATHARIZW 2Bα	CLEANSE	388C
	LOUTRON	WASHING	481D
	R8MA 1	WORD	743A
	HUDWR 1	WATER	840D
27	HAGIOS 1Bα	DEDICATED TO GOD	9D
	AMWMOS 2A	BLAMELESS	47B
	EKKL8SIA 4D	CHURCH	240C
	ENDOXOS 2	GLORIOUS	262D
	PARIST8MI 1C	RENDER	633B
	RUTIS	WRINKLE	745C
	SPILOS	SPOT	770B
	TIS, TI 1Bα	ANY ONE	828A
	TOIOUTOS 3Aβ	SUCH A KIND	829B
28	AGAPAW 1Aα	LOVE	4B
	OPHEILW 2Aβ	OWE	603D
	SWMA 1B	BODY	807A
	HWS II	AS	905C
29	EKKL8SIA 4D	CHURCH	240C
	EKTREPHW 1	NOURISH	246A
	THALPW	CHERISH	351A
	MISEW 2	HATE	524D
	POTE 1	ONCE	701D
	SARX 2	BODY	751A
30	MELOS 3	MEMBER	503A
*	OSTEON	BONE	590D
	SARX 1	FLESH	750D
	SWMA 5	BODY	807C
31	ANTHRWPOS 2Bα	MAN	67D
	ANTI 3	FOR	73B
	DUO 1D	TWO	208B
	EIMI III2	TO BE	224A
	KATALEIPW 1A	LEAVE BEHIND	414C
	PROSKOLLAW	ADHERE CLOSELY TO	723B
	SARX 2	BODY	751A
32	DE 2	BUT, AND	170D
	EKKL8SIA 4D	CHURCH	240C
	LEGW 12A	SAY	469C
	LEGW IIIE	DECLARE	471A
	MUST8RION 2	MYSTERY	532B
	MUST8RION 4B	MYSTERY	532C
	HOUTOS 2B	THIS	601D
33	AGAPAW 1Aα	LOVE	4B
	HEIS 5E	ONE	231B
	HINA III2	IN ORDER THAT	379A
	HOUTW 2	THUS	602C
	PL8N 1C	BUT	675B
	PHOBEW 2B	BE AFRAID	871B
	HWS II	AS	905B

EPHESIANS 6

1	GONEUS	PARENTS	164B
	DIKAIOS 5	RIGHTEOUS	195B
	EN 15D	IN	259B
	KURIOS 2Cγ	LORD	461A
	TEKNON 1Aα	CHILD	816A
	HUPAKOUW 1	LISTEN TO	845A
2	ENTOL8 2Aγ	COMMAND	268C
	EPAGGELIA 2A	PROMISE	280A
	PRWTOS 1Cα	FIRST	733B
	TIMAW 2	HONOR	824D
3	G8 5B	EARTH	156D

3	GINOMAI I3Bβ	TAKE PLACE 158A	12	HAIMA IA	BLOOD 22A
	EU	WELL 317C		ARCH8 3	RULER II2A
	MAKROCHRONIOS	LONG LIVED 489C		EXOUSIA 4Cβ	AUTHORITY 278B
4	EKTREPHW 2	NOURISH 246A		KOSMOKRATWR	WORLD RULER 446C
	NOUTHESIA	ADMONITION 546A		METHODEIA	CRAFTINESS 500B
	PAIDEIA I	TRAINING 608B		PAL8	STRUGGLE 611A
	PARORGIZW	MAKE ANGRY 635A		PNEUMATIKOS 3	SPIRITUAL 685C
	TEKNON IAα	CHILD 816A		PON8RIA	WICKEDNESS 697B
5	HAPLOT8S I	SIMPLICITY 85B		PROS III4A	TOWARD 717B
	DOULOS IA	SLAVE 204D		SARX 3	BODY 751B
	KARDIA I3η	HEART 405B		SKOTOS 2B	DARKNESS 765B
	KATA II7A	(ADJ PHRASE) 408D	13	ANALAMBANW 2	TAKE UP 56C
	KURIOS IAβ	LORD 460A		ANTHIST8MI 3	SET AGAINST 66D
	META AIIII	WITH 511A		H8MERA 4A	TIME 348A
	SARX 6	BODY 751C		HIST8MI IIIC	STAND 383B
	TROMOS	TREMBLING 834D		KATERGAZOMAI I	ACHIEVE 422D
	HUPAKOUW I	LISTEN TO 845A		KATERGAZOMAI 4	ACHIEVE 423A
	PHOBOS 2Bβ	FEAR 871D		PANOPLIA 2	FULL ARMOR 612D
	HWS IIIIA	SO 906C		PON8ROS I8β	WICKED 697D
6	ANTHRWPARESKOS	MEN PLEASER 67A	14	AL8THEIA 2B	TRUTH 35B
	DOULOS 4	SLAVE 205B		DIKAIOSUN8 2B	RIGHTEOUSNESS 195D
	EK 3Gγ	BY 234D		ENDUW 2A	DRESS 263C
	THEL8MA ICγ	WILL 355A		THWRAX I	BREASTPLATE 368C
	KATA II58β	ACCORDING TO 408C		HIST8MI IIID	STAND 383B
	M8 AIII6	NOT 519A		OSPHUS I	WAIST 591D
	POIEW IICα	DO 688D		PERIZWNNUMI 2C	GIRD ABOUT 653B
	PSUCH8 IBγ	SOUL LIFE 901D	15	EIR8N8 3	PEACE 226D
6A	HWS I2A	AS 905C		HETOIMASIA	PREPARATION 316C
6B	HWS I2A	AS 905C		EUAGGELION IB	GOSPEL 318A
6F	OPHTHALMODOULIA	604B		EUAGGELION 2Bα	GOSPEL 318B
	EYE SERVICE			POUS IA	FOOT 703B
7	DOULEUW 2A	SERVE 204B		HUPODEW	TIE 852A
	EUNOIA 2	ZEAL 323D	16	ANALAMBANW 2	TAKE UP 56C
	KURIOS 2A	LORD 460B		BELOS	ARROW I38D
	META AIIII	WITH 511A		THUREOS	SHIELD 366C
	HWS IIIIA	SO 906C		HO,H8,TO II2A	THE 553B
8	DOULOS I8	SLAVE 204D		PISTIS 2Dα	FAITH 669B
	ELEUTHEROS I	FREE 250B		PON8ROS 2B	WICKED 698A
	KOMIZW 2A	BRING 443D		PUROW IA	SET ON FIRE 738C
	KURIOS 2Cγ	LORD 461A		SBENNUMI	EXTINGUISH 752D
	PARA I3B	FROM 614D	16B	PAS IDα	ALL 637C
9	ANI8MI 3	ABANDON 69A	17	DECHOMAI 2	GRASP 176C
	APEIL8	THREAT 82B		MACHAIRA 2	SWORD 497C
	AUTOS 4B	THE SAME I23B		HOS,H8,HO I4C	(REL PRON) 588A
	EIMI III4	TO BE 224B		PERIKEPHALAIA	HELMET 653D
	EIMI III8B	TO BE 224D		PNEUMA 5Dα	SPIRIT 683A
	OURANOS 2A	HEAVEN 599A		R8MA I	WORD 743A
	PARA II2D	BESIDE 615D		SWT8RIOS 2	SAVING 809C
	PROSWPOL8MPSIA	PARTIALITY 728A	18	AGRUPNEW 2	GUARD I4A
9A	KURIOS IAβ	LORD 460A		*DE8SIS	PRAYER 171A
10	DUNAMOW	STRENGTHEN 207C		DIA AIIIIB	BY MEANS OF 179B
	ENDUNAMOW 2B	BECOME STRONG 263B		KAIROS I	TIME 395C
	ISCHUS	STRENGTH 384C		PNEUMA 5Dβ	SPIRIT 683B
	KRATOS 3	POWER 450B		PROSEUCH8 I	PRAYER 720B
	KURIOS 2Cγ	LORD 461A		PROSEUCHOMAI	PRAY 721A
	LOIPOS 3Aβ	THE REST 481B		PROSKARTER8SIS	PATIENCE 723A
	PANOPLIA 2	FULL ARMOR 612D	18C	PAS IA6	ALL 637A
11	DIABOLOS 2	THE SLANDERER I81A	19	ANOIXIS	OPENING 71A
	ENDUW 2A	DRESS 263C		GNWRIZW I	MAKE KNOWN 162C
	HIST8MI IIIC	STAND 383B		EUAGGELION IB	GOSPEL 318A
	METHODEIA	CRAFTINESS 500B		HINA IIICα	IN ORDER THAT 378C
	PANOPLIA 2	FULL ARMOR 612D		LOGOS IAβ	WORD 478C
11A	PROS III3A	TOWARD 717A		MUST8RION 2	MYSTERY 532B

19	PARR8SIA 3A	COURAGE	636A
	STOMA IA	MOUTH	777C
20	HALUSIS 2	IMPRISONMENT	40D
	EN II3	WHILE	259D
	PARR8SIAZOMAI I	SPEAK FREELY	636B
	PRESBEUW	BE AN AMBASSADOR	706B
	HWS II	AS	905C
21	AGAP8TOS 2	BELOVED	6C
	GNWRIZW I	MAKE KNOWN	162C
	DIAKONOS I8	HELPER	183D
	EN I5D	IN	259B
	KATA II6	WITH RESPECT TO	408D
	KURIOS 2Cγ	LORD	461A
	HO,H8,TO II5	THE	554B
	PISTOS IAα	TRUSTWORTHY	670B
	PRASSW 2B	DO	705C
	TUCHIKOS	TYCHICUS	839C
22	AUTOS IH	EVEN	122D
	EIS 4F	(PURPOSE)	228D
	HINA I5	IN ORDER THAT	378A
	KARDIA I8ε	HEART	405A
	PARAKALEW 4	IMPLORE	623A
	PEMPW I	SEND	647C
	PEMPW I	SEND	647D
	PEMPW I	SEND	648A
	PERI II	ABOUT	650D
23	AGAP8 IIA	LOVE	5C
	ADELPHOS 2	BROTHER	16A
	APO V4	FROM	87C
	EIR8N8 2	PEACE	226D
	THEOS 3D	GOD	358B
	KURIOS 2Cγ	LORD	461A
	META AII6	WITH	510D
	PAT8R 3E	FATHER	641D
	PISTIS 2Dγ	FAITH	669C
24	APHTHARSIA	INCORRUPTIBILITY	124D
	KURIOS 2Cγ	LORD	461B
	META AIIICγ	WITH	510A
	PAS ID8	ALL	637D
	CHARIS 2C	FAVOR	885D

PHILIPPIANS I

I	DIAKONOS IC	DEACON	183D
	DOULOS 4	SLAVE	205B
	EN I5D	IN	259B
	EPISKOPOS 2	OVERSEER	299C
	PAULOS	PAUL	643A
	SUN 4B	WITH	789D
	TIMOTHEOS	TIMOTHY	826A
	PHILIPPOI	PHILIPPI	867D
2	APO V4	FROM	87C
	THEOS 3D	GOD	358B
	KURIOS 2Cγ	LORD	461A
	PAT8R 3Cꞵ	FATHER	641C
	CHARIS 2C	FAVOR	885D
3	EPI II2	AT	287D
	EUCHARISTEW 2	GIVE THANKS	328C
	THEOS 3C	GOD	358A
	MNEIA 2	MENTION	526B
	PAS ICꞵ	ALL	637B
4	*DE8SIS	PRAYER	171A
	PAS IEα	ALL	637D

4	POIEW III	DO	689C
	CHARA I	JOY	883C
5	APO II2B	FROM	86C
	ACHRI IA	UNTIL	128B
	EIS 4Cꞵ	(GOAL)	228C
	EUAGGELION IA	GOSPEL	318A
	H8MERA 2	DAY	347A
	KOINWNIA I	ASSOCIATION	440A
	NUN 3B	NOW	548B
	PRWTOS IA	FIRST	732D
6	AUTOS IH	EVEN	122D
	ACHRI IA	UNTIL	128B
	ENARCHOMAI	BEGIN	261D
	EPITELEW I	END	302B
	ERGON ICꞵ	DEED	308A
	H8MERA 3Bꞵ	DAY	347D
	PEITHW 2B	CONVINCE	645B
7	APOLOGIA 2B	DEFENSE	95C
	BEBAIWSIS	CONFIRMATION	138B
	DESMOS I	FETTER	175B
	DIKAIOS 5	RIGHTEOUS	195B
	EUAGGELION IB	GOSPEL	318A
	ECHW I2J	HAVE	333C
	KATHWS 3	AS	392B
	KARDIA IBζ	HEART	405B
	SUGKOINWNOS	PARTICIPANT	782A
	HUPER IAδ	IN BEHALF OF	846C
	PHRONEW I	THINK	874A
	CHARIS 4	FAVOR	886C
7A	PAS IEα	ALL	637D
7B	PAS IEα	ALL	637D
8	EPIPOTHEW	DESIRE	297D
	MARTUS 2A	WITNESS	495B
	PAS IEα	ALL	637D
	SPLAGCHNON IC	AFFECTION	770C
	HWS IV4	WHEN	907B
9	AGAP8 IIA	LOVE	5B
	AISTH8SIS	INSIGHT	24C
	EPIGNWSIS	KNOWLEDGE	291C
	ETI 2B	STILL	316A
	HINA IIIE	IN ORDER THAT	378D
	MALLON I	MORE	490A
	PAS IAꞵ	EVERY EACH	636D
	PERISSEUW IAδ	BE LEFT OVER	656D
	PROSEUCHOMAI	PRAY	721A
10	APROSKOPOS I	BLAMELESS	102A
	DIAPHERW 2B	BE SUPERIOR	189C
	DOKIMAZW 2B	APPROVE	201D
	EILIKRIN8S	SINCERE	221D
	EIS 2Aα	UNTIL	228A
	H8MERA 3Bꞵ	DAY	347D
11	DIKAIOSUN8 2B	RIGHTEOUSNESS	195D
	DOXA 3	FAME	203B
	EPAINOS IB	PRAISE	281B
	KARPOS 2A	RESULT	405D
	PL8ROW IB	MAKE FULL	677A
12	BOULOMAI 2Aδ	DESIRE	145D
	GINWSKW 6C	KNOW	160D
	ERCHOMAI I2C	COME	311C
	EUAGGELION IB	GOSPEL	318A
	KATA II6	WITH RESPECT TO	408D
	MALLON I	MORE	490A
	HO,H8,TO II5	THE	554B

12	PROKOP8	PROGRESS	714D
13	GINOMAI 14B	BECOME	158D
	LOIPOS 28α	THE OTHERS	481A
	*PRAITWRION	THE PRAETORIUM	704B
	PHANEROS 1	CLEAR	860B
	HWSTE 2Aβ	THEREFORE	908C
13F	DESMOS 1	FETTER	175B
14	APHOBWS 1	FEARLESSLY	126C
	EN 15D	IN	259B
	KURIOS 2Cγ	LORD	461A
	LALEW 2B	SPEAK	465A
	LOGOS 1Bβ	WORD	479B
	PEITHW 2A	CONVINCE	645B
	PERISSOTERWS 1	MORE	657C
	POLUS II2Aα	MANY	695D
	POLUS II2Aγ	MANY	696A
	TOLMAW 1A	DARE	829C
15	DIA BII1	BECAUSE OF	180B
	ERIS	STRIFE	309C
	EUDOKIA 1	GOOD WILL	319D
	K8RUSSW 2Bβ	ANNOUNCE	432C
	MEN 1C	(PARTICLE)	504A
	TIS, TI 1Aε	ANY ONE	828A
	PHTHONOS	ENVY	865C
	CHRISTOS 1	ANOINTED ONE	895C
16	AGAP8 IIA	LOVE	5C
	APOLOGIA 2B	DEFENSE	95C
	EUAGGELION 1B	GOSPEL	318A
	KEIMAI 2A	SET	428A
	MEN 1C	(PARTICLE)	504A
16F	HO,H8,TO 12	THE	552A
17	HAGNWS	PURELY	12A
	DESMOS 1	FETTER	175B
	EGEIRW 1Aε	RAISE UP	214A
	EPIPHERW 2B	BRING OVER	304C
	ERITHEIA	SELFISHNESS	309B
	THLIPSIS 2	TRIBULATION	363A
	KATAGGELLW 2	PROCLAIM	410C
	OIOMAI	THINK	565B
	OU 2B	NO	594C
18	AL8THEIA 3	REALITY	35D
	ALLA 3	BUT, YET	38A
	GAR 1F	WHAT	151C
	KATAGGELLW 2	PROCLAIM	410C
	PL8N 1C	BUT	675B
	PL8N 1D	BUT	675C
	PROPHASIS 2	ACTUAL MOTIVE	730A
	TIS, TI 1Bε	WHICH	827A
	TROPOS 1	MANNER	835B
18A	CHAIRW 1	REJOICE	881D
18B	CHAIRW 1	REJOICE	881D
19	APOBAINW 2	TURN OUT	88A
	DE8SIS	PRAYER	171A
	EPICHOR8GIA	SUPPORT	305B
	PNEUMA 5B	SPIRIT	682C
	SU 3	YOU	780A
	SWT8RIA 2	DELIVERANCE	809B
	CHAIRW 1	REJOICE	881D
20	AISCHUNW 2	BE ASHAMED	25A
	APOKARADOKIA		92A
		EAGER EXPECTATION	
	ELPIS 2B	HOPE	252C
	ELPIS 2B	HOPE	252D
20	EN III2	BY	260C
	ZW8 1A	LIFE	340D
	THANATOS 1A	DEATH	351B
	KAI II3	ALSO	394B
	KARADOKIA	EAGER EXPECTATION	404B
	MEGALUNW 2	EXALT	498B
	NUN 1B	NOW	547D
	NUN 1C	NOW	547D
	OUDEIS 2Bγ	IN NO RESPECT	596C
	PARR8SIA 2	OPENLY	636A
	PAS 1A6	ALL	637A
	*SWMA 1B	BODY	807A
	HWS III	SO	905D
21	APOTHN8SKW 1Aα	DIE	90D
	ZAW 28α	LIVE	337A
	KERDOS	GAIN	430D
22	HAIREW 2	CHOOSE	23C
	GNWRIZW 2	KNOW	162D
	ERGON 2	WORK	308D
	ZAW 1B	LIVE	336D
	KAI I2H	AND	393D
	KARPOS 2B	GAIN	406A
	HOUTOS 1Aε	THIS	601B
	SARX 5	BODY	751C
	TIS, TI 1Bγ	WHICH	827A
23	ANALUW 2	DEPART	57A
	EPITHUMIA 2	DESIRE	293B
	ECHW I2Eβ	HAVE	333A
	KREITTWN 2	BETTER	451A
	MALLON 1	MORE	490B
	POLUS I2Cα	MANY	695C
	SUN 1C	WITH	789B
	SUNECHW 5	DISTRESS	797A
24	ANAGKAIOS 1	NECESSARY	52A
	EPIMENW 1	REMAIN	296B
	SARX 5	BODY	751C
25	MENW 1Cα	REMAIN	505C
	PARAMENW 1B	REMAIN	626A
	PEITHW 2B	CONVINCE	645B
	PISTIS 2Dα	FAITH	669B
	PROKOP8	PROGRESS	714D
	SU 3	YOU	780A
	SUMPARAMENW	STAY WITH	786D
	CHARA 1	JOY	883D
26	HINA IID	IN ORDER THAT	377C
	KAUCH8MA 1	BOAST	427B
	PALIN 1A	BACK	611C
	PAROUSIA 2A	COMING	635B
	PERISSEUW 1Aβ	BE LEFT OVER	656C
	PROS III7	TOWARD	718A
27	AXIWS	WORTHILY	78A
	APEIMI 1	BE ABSENT	82B
	EIDON 1A	SEE	219C
	HEIS 2A	ONE	230B
	ERCHOMAI IIAζ	COME	310D
	EUAGGELION 1B	GOSPEL	318B
	EUAGGELION 2Bα	GOSPEL	318B
	HO,H8,TO II5	THE	554B
	PERI II	ABOUT	650D
	PISTIS 2C	FAITH	669A
	PNEUMA 3A	SPIRIT	681B
	POLITEUOMAI 3	LIVE	693A
	ST8KW 2	STAND	775C

27	SUNATHLEW	STRUGGLE WITH	791A
	PSUCH8 18γ	SOUL LIFE	901D
28	ANTIKEIMAI	BE OPPOSED	73D
	APO V4	FROM	87C
	APWLEIA 2	DESTRUCTION	103A
	ENDEIXIS I	SIGN	262A
	M8DEIS 28α	NOTHING	520A
	M8DEIS 286	NOTHING	520B
	PTURW	FRIGHTEN	735A
	*SWT8RIA 2	DELIVERANCE	809A
29	ALLA IA	BUT, YET	37C
	PASCHW 3A6	SUFFER	639C
	PISTEUW 2A6	BELIEVE	667D
	CHARIZOMAI I	GIVE FREELY	884D
29A	HUPER ID	IN BEHALF OF	846D
29B	HUPER ID	IN BEHALF OF	846D
30	AGWN 2	STRUGGLE	14D
	AUTOS 4A	THE SAME	123B
	EIDON	SEE	219C
	EIDON IA	SEE	219C
	EN I2	IN	258A
	ECHW I2I	HAVE	333C
	NUN IC	NOW	547D
	HOIOS	OF WHAT SORT	565C

PHILIPPIANS 2

I	AGAP8 IIA	LOVE	5C
	KOINWNIA I	ASSOCIATION	440A
	KOINWNIA 2	ASSOCIATION	440A
	OIKTIRMOS	PITY	564C
	PARAKL8SIS I	ENCOURAGEMENT	623B
	PARAKL8SIS 3	COMFORT	623C
	PARAMUTHION	ENCOURAGEMENT	626B
	PNEUMA 5D6	SPIRIT	683B
	SPLAGCHNON IB	INWARD PARTS	770C
2	AGAP8 IIA	LOVE	5C
	HEIS 2A	ONE	230B
	ECHW I2E6	HAVE	333A
	*PL8ROW 3	MAKE FULL	677B
	CHARA I	JOY	883D
2A	PHRONEW I	THINK	874B
2B	PHRONEW I	THINK	874B
3	ERITHEIA	SELFISHNESS	309B
	H8GEOMAI 2	CONSIDER	344B
	KATA II586	ACCORDING TO	408C
	KENODOXIA I	VANITY	428D
	TAPEINOPHROSUN8	HUMILITY	812A
	HUPERECHW 2B	SURPASS	848C
4	HEKASTOS 2	EACH	236B
	HETEROS 18ε	ANOTHER	315C
	HO,H8,TO II7	THE	554C
	PELAS	NEAR	647B
	SKOPEW	NOTICE	764A
5	PHRONEW 3	THINK	874C
6	HARPAGMOS I	ROBBERY	108A
	H8GEOMAI 2	CONSIDER	344B
	ISOS	EQUAL	382A
	MORPH8	FORM	530B
	HUPARCHW 2	BE	846A
7	ANTHRWPOS IA6	MAN	67C
	GINOMAI II4A	BE	159C
	DOULOS IE6	SLAVE	205A

7	HEURISKW 2	FIND	326A
	KENOW I	MAKE EMPTY	429B
	LAMBANW IA	TAKE	465C
	MORPH8	FORM	530B
	HOMOIWMA 4	LIKENESS	570D
	SCH8MA I	BEARING	805A
	HWS IIIIC	SO	906D
8	DE 2	BUT, AND	170D
	MECHRI IC	UNTIL	517B
	STAUROS I	THE CROSS	772B
	TAPEINOW 2A	LOWER	812B
	HUP8KOOS	OBEDIENT	850A
8A	THANATOS 186	DEATH	351C
8B	THANATOS ID	DEATH	351D
9	ONOMA I4C6	NAME	576A
	HUPER 2	BEYOND	847B
	HUPERUPSOW I		849D
	RAISE TO LOFTIEST HEIGHT		
	CHARIZOMAI I	GIVE FREELY	884D
10	EPIGEIOS 2B	EARTHLY	290D
	EPOURANIOS 2B	HEAVENLY	306A
	HINA I2	IN ORDER THAT	377D
	KAMPTW 2	BEND	403B
	KATACHTHONIOS	UNDER THE EARTH	421D
	ONOMA I4Cγ	NAME	576B
11	GLWSSA 2	LANGUAGE	161C
	DOXA 3	FAME	203B
	EXOMOLOGEW 2B	CONFESS	276D
	THEOS 3D	GOD	358A
	KURIOS 2Cγ	LORD	461B
	PAT8R 3E	FATHER	642A
12	AGAP8TOS 2	BELOVED	6C
	APOUSIA	ABSENCE	101B
	EN II2	WHILE	259D
	*KATERGAZOMAI 2	ACHIEVE	422D
	MALLON 2A	RATHER	490B
	META AIIII	WITH	511A
	MONOS 2C	ONLY	530A
	PAROUSIA I	PRESENCE	635B
	POLUS I2Cα	MANY	695C
	SWT8RIA 2	DELIVERANCE	809B
	TROMOS	TREMBLING	834D
	HUPAKOUW I	LISTEN TO	845A
	PHOBOS 28α	FEAR	871D
	HWSTE IB	THEREFORE	908B
13	EN I5A	IN	258D
	EUDOKIA I	GOOD WILL	319D
	THELW 2	WISH	355D
	KAI I6	AND	394A
	HUPER IE	IN BEHALF OF	847A
13A	ENERGEW 2	WORK	265A
13B	ENERGEW IA	WORK	264D
14	GOGGUSMOS I	COMPLAINT	163D
	DIALOGISMOS 2	DOUBT	185B
	PAS 2A6	EVERYTHING	638C
	CHWRIS 2B6	APART	899A
15	AKERAIOS	PURE	29D
	AMEMPTOS	BLAMELESS	44C
	AMWMOS 2A	BLAMELESS	47B
	AMWM8TOS	BLAMELESS	47B
	GENEA 2	GENERATION	153B
	DIASTREPHW I8	PERVERT	188A
	KOSMOS 2	WORLD	446C

15	KOSMOS 2	WORLD 446D	25	H8GEOMAI 2	CONSIDER 344B
	MESOS 3B	THE MIDDLE 509A		LEITOURGOS 3	SERVANT 472D
	HOS,H8,HO I3Bγ	(REL PRON) 587D		PEMPW I	SEND 647C
	SKOLIOS 2	CROOKED 763D		SUNERGOS	WORKING WITH 795C
	TEKNON 2E	CHILD 816C		SUSTRATIWT8S	FELLOW SOLDIER 803A
	PHAINW 2A	SHINE 859B		CHREIA 2	NEED 893B
	PHWST8R I	LIGHT GIVING BODY 880D	26	AD8MONEW	TROUBLED 16C
16	EIS 2Aβ	FOR 228A		DIOTI I	BECAUSE 198C
	EIS 4E	SO THAT 228D		EPEID8 2	SINCE 284A
	EPECHW I	HOLD FAST 285B		EPIPOTHEW	DESIRE 297D
	ZW8 2Bα	LIFE 341B	26F	ASTHENEW IA	BE SICK 115A
	H8MERA 3Bβ	DAY 347D	27	GAR IE	FOR 151C
	KAUCH8MA I	BOAST 427B		ELEEW	HAVE MERCY 249B
	KOPIAW 2	BECOME WEARY 444B		EPI III1Bβ	TO 286D
	LOGOS I8β	WORD 479C		EPI III1Bβ	TO 288D
	TRECHW 2A	RUN 833C		ECHW I2Eβ	HAVE 333A
16A	KENOS 2Aβ	EMPTY 429A		THANATOS IA	DEATH 351C
16B	KENOS 2Aβ	EMPTY 429A		LUP8	GRIEF 483B
17	EI VI4	EVEN IF 219A		MONOS 2C	ONLY 529D
	EPI II2	AT 287D		PARAPL8SIOS	COMING NEAR 627A
	THUSIA I	ACT OF OFFERING 366D	28	ALUPOS	FREE FROM ANXIETY 40D
	THUSIA 2B	SACRIFICE 367A		OUN IA	THEREFORE 597B
	LEITOURGIA 2	SERVICE 472B		PALIN IB	AGAIN 611C
	PISTIS 2Dα	FAITH 669B		PEMPW I	SEND 647B
	SPENDW	OFFER A LIBATION 769A		PEMPW I	SEND 648A
17F	SUGCHAIRW I	REJOICE WITH 782C		SPOUDAIWS I	WITH HASTE 771B
17F	SUGCHAIRW 2	REJOICE WITH 782D		CHAIRW I	REJOICE 881D
17F	CHAIRW I	REJOICE 882A	29	EN I5D	IN 259B
19	ELPIZW 2	HOPE 252A		ENTIMOS IB	HONORED 268C
	EN I5D	IN 259B		ECHW I5	CONSIDER 333D
	EUPSUCHEW	BE GLAD 330A		KURIOS 2Cγ	LORD 461A
	PEMPW I	SEND 647C		META AIII1	WITH 511A
	TACHEWS IA	QUICKLY 814B		OUN IB	THEREFORE 597B
	TIMOTHEOS	TIMOTHY 826A		PAS IAδ	ALL 637A
19F	PERI II	ABOUT 650D		PROSDECHOMAI IA	RECEIVE 719B
20	GN8SIWS	SINCERELY 162B		CHARA I	JOY 883C
	ECHW I2D	HAVE 333A	30	ANAPL8ROW 3	REPLACE 59B
	ISOPSUCHOS	OF LIKE SOUL 382A		EGGIZW 4	APPROACH 212D
	MERIMNAW 2	BE CONCERNED ABOUT 506B		ERGON 2	WORK 308B
	HOSTIS 2B	WHOEVER 591A		THANATOS IC	DEATH 351D
21	Z8TEW 2Bα	SEEK 339C		LEITOURGIA 2	SERVICE 472B
	HO,H8,TO II7	THE 554C		MECHRI IC	UNTIL 517B
	PAS 2Bα	IN ALL RESPECTS 638C		PARABOLEUOMAI	RISK 617B
22	DOKIM8 I	CHARACTER 201D		PARABOULEUOMAI	BE CARELESS 618B
	DOULEUW 2C	SERVE 204C		HUSTER8MA I	NEED 857A
	EUAGGELION IA	GOSPEL 318A		PSUCH8 IAβ	SOUL LIFE 901C
	SUN 2A	WITH 789C			
	TEKNON IAβ	CHILD 816A			
	HWS I2A	AS 905C		**PHILIPPIANS 3**	
23	AN 3D	(PARTICLE) 48C			
	APHORAW 2	SEE 126D	1	ASPHAL8S 2	SAFE 118C
	ELPIZW 2	HOPE 252A		EN I5D	IN 259B
	EXAUT8S	AT ONCE 273B		LOIPOS 3B	THE REST 481B
	HO,H8,TO II5	THE 554B		MEN IB	(PARTICLE) 504A
	PEMPW I	SEND 647B		HO,H8,TO II6	THE 554C
	HWS IVICα	WHEN 907A		OKN8ROS 2	CAUSING FEAR 565D
24	KURIOS 2Cγ	LORD 461A		CHAIRW 2A	REJOICE 882A
	PEITHW 2A	CONVINCE 645B		*CHAIRW I	REJOICE 882A
	TACHEWS IA	QUICKLY 814B	2	BLEPW 6	SEE 143B
25	ADELPHOS 2	BROTHER 16A		ERGAT8S IB	WORKMAN 307D
	ANAGKAIOS I	NECESSARY 51D		KAKOS IA	BAD 398C
	APOSTOLOS I	MESSENGER 99A		KUWN 2	DOG 462B
	EPAPHRODITOS	EPAPHRODITUS 283C	3	KAUCHAOMAI I	BOAST 426D
				LATREUW	SERVE 468D

3	OU 3B	NO	594C
	PERITOM8 4B	CIRCUMCISION	658D
	PNEUMA 5A	SPIRIT	682C
3F	PEITHW 2A	CONVINCE	645B
3F	SARX 6	BODY	751C
4	ALLOS ID	OTHER	39C
	DOKEW IA	THINK	200D
	ECHW I2E8	HAVE	333A
	KAIPER	ALTHOUGH	395B
	MALLON I	MORE	490A
	PEPOITH8SIS I	TRUST	649A
	TIS, TI 2AY	ANY ONE	828B
	HUPER 3	BEYOND	847C
5	BENIAMIN	BENJAMIN	139A
	GENOS 3	NATION	155C
	HEBRAIOS I	HEBREW	212B
*EK 3B		FROM	234B
	ISRA8L I	ISRAEL	382A
	KATA II6	WITH RESPECT TO	408D
	NOMOS 3	LAW	544D
	OKTA8MEROS	ON THE EIGHTH DAY	565D
*PHARISAIOS		PHARISEE	861C
	PHUL8 I	TRIBE	876D
6	AMEMPTOS	BLAMELESS	44B
	DIKAIOSUN8 2A	RIGHTEOUSNESS	195C
	DIWKW 2	PERSECUTE	200B
	EKKL8SIA 4D	CHURCH	240C
	Z8LOS I	ZEAL	338A
	NOMOS 3	LAW	544D
6A	KATA II58	ACCORDING TO	408C
6B	KATA II6	WITH RESPECT TO	408D
7	Z8MIA	LOSS	339A
	H8GEOMAI 2	CONSIDER	344B
	HOUTOS IAε	THIS	601B
8	ALLA 3	BUT, YET	38A
	GE 3E	OF COURSE	152B
	GNWSIS 2	KNOWLEDGE	163B
	Z8MIA	LOSS	339A
	Z8MIOW I	SUFFER DAMAGE	339A
	HINA IIA	IN ORDER THAT	377C
	KERDAINW IB	TO GAIN	430C
	KURIOS 2CY	LORD	461B
	MENOUNGE	RATHER	504C
	SKUBALON	REFUSE	765B
	HUPERECHW 2C	SURPASS	848D
8A	H8GEOMAI 2	CONSIDER	344B
8B	H8GEOMAI 2	CONSIDER	344B
8B	PAS 28ß	ALL THINGS	638D
9	DIKAIOSUN8 3	RIGHTEOUSNESS	196A
	EK 3C	FROM	234B
	EN I5D	IN	259D
	EPI IIIBY	ON	287A
	HEURISKW IB	FIND	325C
	THEOS 3B	GOD	358A
	NOMOS 3	LAW	544D
9A	PISTIS 2Bß	FAITH	668D
9B	PISTIS 2Dα	FAITH	669B
10	ANASTASIS 2A	RESURRECTION	59D
	ANASTASIS 2B	RESURRECTION	60B
	THANATOS IBß	DEATH	351C
	KOINWNIA 4	ASSOCIATION	440B
	HO,H8,TO II48ς	THE	554A
	PATH8MA I	SUFFERING	607B

10	SUMMORPHIZW	GRANT	786B
	SUMMORPHOW	GIVE THE SAME FORM	786C
	SUMPHORTIZW	BURDEN TOGETHER	788B
11	EI VII2B	IF	219B
	EXANASTASIS	RESURRECTION	272B
	KATANTAW 2A	ARRIVE	416B
	NEKROS 2A	DEAD	537A
12	DIWKW I	HASTEN	200B
	EI V2B	WHETHER	218D
	EPI IIIBY	ON	287C
	8 IC	NOR	343A
	LAMBANW IG	MAKE ONES OWN	466A
	HOS,H8,HO IIID	(REL PRON)	589A
	HOTI IC	THAT	593A
	TELEIOW 2Eα	MAKE PERFECT	817D
	TELEIOW 3	CONSECRATE	818A
	HUPO IAα	BY	850D
12A	KATALAMBANW IA	SEIZE	413D
12B	KATALAMBANW IA	SEIZE	413D
13	HEIS 2B	ONE	230C
	EMPROSTHEN IA	AHEAD	256C
	EPEKTEINOMAI	STRAIN	284C
	EPILANTHANOMAI I	FORGET	295B
	KATALAMBANW IA	SEIZE	413D
	LOGIZOMAI 3	THINK	477B
	OPISW IA	BEHIND	578C
	OUPW	NOT YET	597D
14	ANEGKL8SIA	BLAMELESSNESS	63C
	ANW 2	UPWARDS	76B
	BRABEION 2	PRIZE	146B
	DIWKW I	HASTEN	200B
	KATA IIIB	TO	407A
	KL8SIS I	CALL	436D
	SKOPOS	GOAL	764A
15	APOKALUPTW 2	REVEAL	91C
	HETERWS	DIFFERENTLY	315D
	TELEIOS 2B	THE INITIATE	817A
15A	PHRONEW I	THINK	874B
16	KANWN I	RULE	403D
	PL8N IC	BUT	675B
*STOICHEW		BE IN LINE WITH	777A
	PHTHANW 2	COME	864D
	PHRONEW I	THINK	874B
17	ECHW I28ß	HAVE	332D
	HOUTW	THUS	602B
	HOUTW 2	THUS	602C
	PERIPATEW 2AY	GO ABOUT	655B
	SKOPEW	NOTICE	764A
	SUMMIM8T8S	FELLOW IMITATOR	786B
	TUPOS 5B	MARK	837D
18	KLAIW I	WEEP	434B
	LEGW II2	SPEAK	471A
	NUN IC	NOW	548A
	PERIPATEW 2AY	GO ABOUT	655B
	POLLAKIS	OFTEN	693B
	STAUROS 3	THE CROSS	772D
19	AISCHUN8 2	SHAME	24D
	APWLEIA 2	DESTRUCTION	103A
	EPIGEIOS 2A	EARTHLY	290D
	THEOS 4B	GOD	358D
	KOILIA I	BELLY	438B
	TELOS IC	END	819C
	PHRONEW 2	THINK	874B

20 APEKDECHOMAI   AWAIT 82D
   KURIOS 2Cγ   LORD 461A
   HOS,H8,HO I3Bα   (REL PRON) 587C
   OURANOS 2B   HEAVEN 599C
   OURANOS 2D   HEAVEN 599D
   POLITEUMA   STATE 692D
   SWT8R 2   SAVIOR 808C
   HUPARCHW I   BE 845D
21 DOXA IA   BRIGHTNESS 202D
   ENERGEIA I   WORKING 264C
   METASCH8MATIZW   TRANSFORM 514D
   HO,H8,TO II48β   THE 554A
   PAS 2Bβ   ALL THINGS 638D
   SUMMORPHOS   SAME FORM 786B
   SWMA IB   BODY 807B
   TAPEINWSIS 2   HUMILIATION 812D
   HUPOTASSW IA   SUBJECT 855C

PHILIPPIANS 4

1 AGAP8TOS 2   BELOVED 6C
   EN I5D   IN 259B
   EPIPOTH8TOS   LONGED FOR 298A
   KURIOS 2Cγ   LORD 461A
   STEPHANOS 2B   WREATH 775A
   ST8KW 2   STAND 775C
   CHARA 2A   JOY 883D
   HWSTE IB   THEREFORE 908B
2 EN I5D   IN 259B
   EUODIA   EUODIA 324A
   KURIOS 2Cγ   LORD 461A
   PARAKALEW 2   APPEAL TO 622C
   SUNTUCH8   SYNTYCHE 801B
   PHRONEW I   THINK 874B
3 BIBLOS 2   BOOK 141A
   GN8SIOS I   LEGITIMATE 162A
   ERWTAW 2   ASK 312A
   EUAGGELION IA   GOSPEL 318A
   ZW8 2Bβ   LIFE 341C
   KAI II7A   394C
   KL8M8S I   CLEMENT 435D
   LOIPOS 2A   OTHER 481A
   NAI 3   CERTAINLY 535A
   ONOMA II   NAME 574A
   SU 2   YOU 780A
   SUZUGOS   TRUE COMRADE 783C
   SULLAMBANW 2B   SEIZE 784C
   SUNATHLEW   STRUGGLE WITH 791A
   SUNERGOS   WORKING WITH 795C
4 EN I5D   IN 259B
   PALIN 2   AGAIN 611C
   CHAIRW 2A   REJOICE 882A
4A *CHAIRW I   REJOICE 882A
4B   CHAIRW I   REJOICE 882A
5 EGGUS 2A   NEAR 213B
   EPIEIK8S   GENTLE 292C
   HO,H8,TO II2C   THE 553C
   PAS IB   ALL 637A
6 AIT8MA   REQUEST 25C
   GNWRIZW I   MAKE KNOWN 162D
   DE8SIS   PRAYER 171A
   EUCHARISTIA 2   THANKFULNESS 329A
   MERIMNAW I   HAVE ANXIETY 506A

6 META AIIII   WITH 511A
   M8DEIS 2Bβ   NOTHING 520A
   PAS 2Aβ   EVERY RESPECT 638A
   PROS IIIIF   TOWARD 717A
   PROSEUCH8 I   PRAYER 720B
7 EIR8N8 3   PEACE 226D
   NO8MA I   THOUGHT 542D
   NOUS I   THE UNDERSTANDING 546C
   HUPERECHW 2B   SURPASS 848D
   PHROUREW 2   GUARD 875B
8 HAGNOS 2   PURE IID
   AL8TH8S 2   TRUE 36B
   ARET8 I   VIRTUE 105C
   DIKAIOS 5   RIGHTEOUS 195B
   EPAINOS 2   PRAISE 281B
   EPIST8M8   KNOWLEDGE 300C
   EUPH8MOS   AUSPICIOUS 327D
   LOGIZOMAI 2   CONSIDER 477B
   LOIPOS 3B   THE REST 481B
   HOSOS 2   HOW GREAT 590C
   HOUTOS IAε   THIS 601B
   PROSPHIL8S   PLEASING 727C
   SEMNOS 2   NOBLE 754C
9 EIDON IA   SEE 219C
   EIR8N8 3   PEACE 226D
   MANTHANW I   LEARN 491C
   META AIIICγ   WITH 510A
   HOUTOS IAε   THIS 601B
   PARALAMBANW 3B   TAKE 625B
10 AKAIREOMAI   NO OPPORTUNITY 28D
   ANATHALLW 2   BLOOM AGAIN 53D
   EN I5D   IN 259B
   EPI IIIBγ   ON 287C
   8D8 IC   ALREADY 344D
   HOS,H8,HO IIID   (REL PRON) 589A
   POTE I   ONCE 701D
   HUPER IAδ   IN BEHALF OF 846C
   CHAIRW I   REJOICE 881D
   CHAIRW I   REJOICE 882A
10A   PHRONEW I   THINK 874A
11 AUTARK8S   CONTENT 122A
   EIMI III4   TO BE 224B
   KATA II5Aδ   ACCORDING TO 408B
   LEGW I5   SAY 470A
   LEGW IIIF   DECLARE 471A
   MANTHANW 4   LEARN 491D
   HOS,H8,HO I2A   (REL PRON) 587B
   HOTI IC   THAT 593A
   HUSTER8SIS   NEED 857B
12 KAI I6   AND 394C
   MUEW   INITIATE 530D
   OIDA 3   KNOW 558D
   PEINAW I   HUNGER 645D
   TAPEINOW 2C   LOWER 812C
   HUSTEREW 2   TO MISS 857A
   CHORTAZW 2A   FEED 892B
12A   PERISSEUW IBα   656D
   BE LEFT OVER
12B   PERISSEUW IBα   656D
   BE LEFT OVER
13 ENDUNAMOW I   STRENGTHEN 263A
   ISCHUW 2A   BE STRONG 384C
14 THLIPSIS I   TRIBULATION 363A

14 KALWS 4A	WELL 402B	23 META AIIICY	WITH 510A
PL8N IC	BUT 675B	PNEUMA 3B	SPIRIT 681C
POIEW I2AY	DO 689B	CHARIS 2C	FAVOR 885D
SUGKOINWNEW I	BE CONNECTED 781D		
15 ARCH8 IB	BEGINNING IIIC	**COLOSSIANS I**	
DOSIS 2	GIVING 204A		
EIS 4G	FOR 229A	1 ADELPHOS 2	BROTHER 16A
EKKL8SIA 4B	CHURCH 240B	APOSTOLOS 3	APOSTLES 99B
EXERCHOMAI IAα	GO OUT 274A	DIA AIIIID	THROUGH 179C
EUAGGELION IB	GOSPEL 318B	THEL8MA 2B	WILL 355A
KOINWNEW 2	SHARE 439D	PAULOS	PAUL 643A
L8MPSIS	RECEIVING 474A	TIMOTHEOS	TIMOTHY 826A
LOGOS 2B	SETTLEMENT 479D	2 APO V4	FROM 87C
MAKEDONIA	MACEDONIA 488B	EIR8N8 2	PEACE 226D
MONOS IAY	ONLY 529C	THEOS 3D	GOD 358B
OUDEIS I	NO 596B	KOLOSSAI	COLOSSAE 443A
PHILIPP8SIOS	THE PHILIPPIAN 867C	PAT8R 3Cβ	FATHER 641C
16 HAPAX I	ONCE 80A	PISTIS 2	TRUSTWORTHY 671A
DIS	TWICE 198D	CHARIS 2C	FAVOR 885D
EIS 4D	FOR 228C	3 EUCHARISTEW 2	GIVE THANKS 328C
THESSALONIK8	THESSALONICA 360C	THEOS 3D	GOD 358A
KAI I6	AND 394A	KURIOS 2CY	LORD 461B
PEMPW 2	SEND 648A	PAT8R 3Dβ	FATHER 641D
CHREIA 2	NEED 893B	PERI IF	ABOUT 650C
17 DOMA	GIFT 202C	PROSEUCHOMAI	PRAY 721A
EPIZ8TEW 2A	STRIVE FOR 292D	4 AGAP8 IIBβ	LOVE 5D
KARPOS 2B	GAIN 406A	HAGIOS 2Dβ	SAINTS I0A
LOGOS 2B	SETTLEMENT 479D	AKOUW 3B	LEARN 31D
PLEONAZN IA	INCREASE 673B	EIS 4Cβ	(GOAL) 228C
18 APECHW I	RECEIVE IN FULL 848	PISTIS 2Bβ	FAITH 669A
DEKTOS	ACCEPTABLE 173B	4F AGAP8 IIA	LOVE 5C
DECHOMAI I	TAKE 176B	4F PISTIS 2DY	FAITH 669C
EPAPHRO])ITOS	EPAPHRODITUS 283C	5 AL8THEIA 2B	TRUTH 35B
EUARESTOS I	PLEASING 319A	APOKEIMAI 2	BE PUT AWAY 92B
EUWDIA	FRAGRANCE 330A	ELPIS 4	HOPE 252D
THUSIA 2B	SACRIFICE 367A	EUAGGELION IB	GOSPEL 318B
OSM8 2	ODOR 590A	LOGOS IBβ	WORD 479C
PERISSEUW IBα	BE LEFT OVER 656D	OURANOS 2D	HEAVEN 599D
PL8ROW IB	MAKE FULL 677A	PROAKOUW	HEAR BEFOREHAND 709C
18A PARA I3B	FROM 614D	6 AL8THEIA 3	REALITY 35D
18B PARA I4Bα	FROM 615A	APO II2C	SINCE 86C
19 DOXA IA	GLORY 202D	AUXANW 2	GROW 121B
THEOS 3C	GOD 358A	EPIGINWSKW IA	KNOW 291A
PL8ROW IA	MAKE FULL 676D	H8MERA 2	DAY 347A
PLOUTOS	WEALTH 680A	KARPOPHOREW 2	BEAR FRUIT 406A
PLOUTOS 2	WEALTH 680B	KOSMOS 4A	WORLD 447A
CHREIA 2	NEED 893B	HOS,H8,HO I5Cα	(REL PRON) 588B
20 AIWN IB	TIME 26D	PAREIMI IB	BE PRESENT 629D
AM8N I	AMEN 45A	PAS ICα	ALL 637B
THEOS 3D	GOD 358A	CHARIS 3B	FAVOR 886B
HO,H8,TO III0B	THE 555A	7 AGAP8TOS 2	BELOVED 6C
PAT8R 3Cβ	FATHER 641C	APO IV2B	FROM 87A
21 PAS IAα	EVERY EACH 636C	DIAKONOS IA	SERVANT 183D
SUN IC	WITH 789B	EPAPHRAS	EPAPHRAS 283C
21F ASPAZOMAI IA	GREET 116B	KOLOSSAI	COLOSSAE 443A
22 HAGIOS 2Dβ	SAINTS I0A	MANTHANW I	LEARN 491B
EK 3D	FROM 234C	PISTOS IAα	TRUSTWORTHY 670B
KAISAR	EMPEROR 396C	SUNDOULOS 3	FELLOW SLAVE 793C
MALISTA I	ABOVE ALL 490A	HUPER IAβ	IN BEHALF OF 846B
HO,H8,TO II5	THE 554B	CHRISTOS I	ANOINTED ONE 895C
*OIKIA 3	HOUSEHOLD 560B	8 AGAP8 IIA	LOVE 5C
23 AM8N I	AMEN 45A	AGAP8 IIA	LOVE 5D
KURIOS 2CY	LORD 461A	D8LOW	REVEAL 177C

8 PNEUMA 5Dβ   SPIRIT 683B   16 HORATOS   VISIBLE 581B
9 AITEW   ASK 25C   OURANOS IE   HEAVEN 599A
   APO II2C   SINCE 86C   16A KTIZW   CREATE 456C
   EPIGNWSIS   KNOWLEDGE 291B   16A PAS 2Bβ   ALL THINGS 638D
   H8MERA 2   DAY 347A   16B KTIZW   CREATE 456C
   THEL8MA ICγ   WILL 355A   16B PAS 2Bβ   ALL THINGS 638D
   HINA IIIAγ   IN ORDER THAT 378B   17 PRO 2   BEFORE 708C
   HOS,H8,HO I5Cα   (REL PRON) 588B   SUNIST8MI II3   UNITE 798D
   PAUW 2   STOP 643C   17B PAS 2Bβ   ALL THINGS 638D
   PL8ROW IB   MAKE FULL 677A   18 ARCH8 ID   BEGINNING IIID
   PNEUMATIKOS 2Aβ   SPIRITUAL 685B   EKKL8SIA 4D   CHURCH 240C
   PROSEUCHOMAI   PRAY 721A   KEPHAL8 IB   HEAD 431B
   SOPHIA 2   WISDOM 767A   NEKROS 2A   DEAD 537A
   SUNESIS 2   INTELLIGENCE 796B   PRWTEUW   BE FIRST 732C
10 AGATHOS IBβ   GOOD   3B   PRWTOTOKOS 2A   FIRSTBORN 734B
   AXIWS   WORTHILY 78A   SWMA 5   BODY 807C
   ARESKEIA   DESIRE TO PLEASE I05A   19 EUDOKEW I   WELL PLEASED 319C
   AUXANW 2   GROW 121B   KATOIKEW IB   LIVE 425C
   EPIGNWSIS   KNOWLEDGE 291C   PAS ICα   ALL 637D
   ERGON ICβ   DEED 308A   PL8RWMA 3B THAT WHICH FILLS 678B
   KARPOPHOREW 2   BEAR FRUIT 406A   20 HAIMA 2B   BLOOD 22C
   KURIOS 2Cγ   LORD 460D   APOKATALLASSW   RECONCILE 92A
   PERIPATEW 2Aα   GO ABOUT 655A   DIA AIIIIA   BY MEANS OF 179A
11 DOXA IA   GLORY 202D   EIR8NOPOIEW   MAKE PEACE 227A
   DUNAMIS I   POWER 206D   OURANOS IE   HEAVEN 599A
   DUNAMOW   STRENGTHEN 207C   PAS 2Bβ   ALL THINGS 638D
   KRATOS I   POWER 450B   STAUROS 3   THE CROSS 772C
   MAKROTHUMIA I   PATIENCE 489B   21 APALLOTRIOW   ESTRANGE 79C
   META AII6   WITH 510D   DIANOIA 2   MIND 186B
   HUPOMON8 I   PATIENCE 854A   ERGON ICβ   DEED 308B
   CHARA I   JOY 883C   ECHTHROS 2Bα   THE ENEMY 331D
IIA   PAS IA6   ALL 637A   PON8ROS IBβ   WICKED 697D
IIB   PAS IA6   ALL 637A   22 HAGIOS IBα   DEDICATED TO GOD   90
12 EIS 5   FOR 229B   AMWMOS 2A   BLAMELESS 47B
   EUCHARISTEW 2   GIVE THANKS 328C   ANEGKL8TOS   BLAMELESS 63C
   HIKANOW   MAKE SUFFICIENTLY 375C   APOKATALLASSW   RECONCILE 92A
   KL8ROS 2   LOT 436C   DE IE   BUT, AND 170C
   MERIS 2   SHARE 506C   DIA AIIIIA   BY MEANS OF 179A
   PHWS 3A   LIGHT 880B   THANATOS IBβ   DEATH 351C
13 AGAP8 I2B   LOVE   6A   KATENWPION B   422C
   BASILEIA 3D   KINGDOM 134D   IN THE PRESENCE OF
   BASILEIA 3G   KINGDOM 135A   NUNI IC   NOW 548C
   EXOUSIA 4B   AUTHORITY 278B   PARIST8MI IC   RENDER 633B
   METHIST8MI I HE TRANSFERRED 500A   SARX 5   BODY 751B
   RUOMAI   SAVE 745A   SWMA IB   BODY 807B
   SKOTOS 2B   DARKNESS 765B   23 GE 3A (EMPHASIZING PARTICLE) 152A
   HUIOS 2B   SON 842D   GINOMAI I4A   BECOME 158C
14 HAIMA 2B   BLOOD 22C   DIAKONOS IA   SERVANT 183D
   APOLUTRWSIS 2A   REDEMPTION 95D   HEDRAIOS   FIRM 217A
   APHESIS 2   PARDON 124C   ELPIS 2B   HOPE 252D
15 EIKWN IB   IMAGE 221B   EPIMENW 2   CONTINUE 296B
   KTISIS IBα   CREATION 456D   EUAGGELION IB   GOSPEL 318B
   MONOGEN8S   ONLY 529A   THEMELIOW 2A   ESTABLISH 356C
   PAS IAα   EVERY EACH 636C   K8RUSSW 2Bβ   ANNOUNCE 432C
   PRWTOTOKOS 2A   FIRSTBORN 734B   KTISIS IBα   CREATION 456D
16 AORATOS   UNSEEN 78B   METAKINEW   SHIFT 512C
   ARCH8 3   RULER II2A   OURANOS IB   HEAVEN 598C
   G8 5A   EARTH 156D   PAS IAα   EVERY EACH 636C
   DIA AIII2A   BY 179D   PAULOS   PAUL 643A
   EN I5A   IN 258D   PISTIS 2Dα   FAITH 669B
   EXOUSIA 4Cβ   AUTHORITY 278B   HUPO 2Aβ   UNDER 851B
   THRONOS 2B   THRONE 365A   24 ANTANAPL8ROW   FILL UP 72B
   KURIOT8S 3   LORDSHIP 461D   EKKL8SIA 4D   CHURCH 240C

24	THLIPSIS I	TRIBULATION	363A
	HOS,H8,HO I7A	(REL PRON)	588C
	PATH8MA I	SUFFERING	607B
	SARX 5	BODY	751B
	SWMA 5	BODY	807C
	HUSTER8MA I	NEED	857A
	CHAIRW I	REJOICE	882A
24A	HUPER IAε	IN BEHALF OF	846C
25	DIAKONOS IA	SERVANT	183D
	EIS 4G	FOR	229A
	LOGOS I8β	WORD	479B
	OIKONOMIA IB	MANAGEMENT	562B
	PL8ROW 3	MAKE FULL	677B
26	HAGIOS 2D8	SAINTS	IOA
	AIWN 4	THE AEON	27D
	APOKRUPTW	CONCEAL	93B
	GENEA 3B	AGE	153C
	MUST8RION 2	MYSTERY	532B
	NUN IC	NOW	547D
	PHANEROW IB	REVEAL	860C
27	GNWRIZW I	MAKE KNOWN	162C
	DOXA IA	GLORY	202D
	ELPIS 2B	HOPE	252C
	ELPIS 3	HOPE	252D
	THELW 2	WISH	355D
	MUST8RION 2	MYSTERY	532B
	PLOUTOS	WEALTH	680A
	PLOUTOS 2	WEALTH	680B
	TIS, TI I8β	WHICH	827A
28	KATAGGELLW 2	PROCLAIM	410C
	NOUTHETEW	ADMONISH	546B
	PARIST8MI IC	RENDER	633B
	SOPHIA 2	WISDOM	767A
	TELEIOS 2B	THE INITIATE	817A
28A	PAS IAα	EVERY EACH	636C
29	DUNAMIS I	POWER	206D
	EIS 4F	(PURPOSE)	228D
	EN III2	BY	260B
	ENERGEIA I	WORKING	264C
	ENERGEW IB	WORK	264D
	KAI II6		394C
	KOPIAW 2	BECOME WEARY	448B
	HOS,H8,HO I7B	(REL PRON)	588C

COLOSSIANS 2

I	AGWN 2	STRUGGLE	14D
	ECHW I2I	HAVE	333C
	H8LIKOS	HOW GREAT	346A
	LAODIKEIA	LAODICEA	467D
	OIDA IF	KNOW	558C
	HORAW IAγ	SEE	581D
	PERI IF	ABOUT	650C
	PROSWPON IB	FACE	728C
	SARX 2	BODY	751A
2	AGAP8 IIA	LOVE	5C
	EPIGNWSIS	KNOWLEDGE	291B
	MUST8RION 2	MYSTERY	532B
	PARAKALEW 4	IMPLORE	623A
	*PL8ROPHORIA	CERTAINTY	676C
	PLOUTOS	WEALTH	680A
	PLOUTOS 2	WEALTH	680B
	SUMBIBAZW IB	UNITE	785B

2	SUMBIBAZW 4	UNITE	785C
	SUNESIS 2	INTELLIGENCE	796B
3	APOKRUPHOS	HIDDEN	93B
	GNWSIS 2	KNOWLEDGE	163A
	EN I5A	IN	258D
	TH8SAUROS 2Bγ	TREASURE	362B
	SOPHIA 3A	WISDOM	767B
4	LEGW IIIF	DECLARE	471A
	PARALOGIZOMAI I	DECEIVE	625C
	PITHANOLOGIA		663A
	PERSUASIVE SPEECH		
5	APEIMI I	BE ABSENT	82C
	BLEPW 4B	SEE	143B
	EI VI4	EVEN IF	219A
	EIS 4Cβ	(GOAL)	228C
	KAI IIE	AND	393A
	PISTIS 2Bβ	FAITH	669A
	PNEUMA 3A	SPIRIT	681B
	SARX 2	BODY	751A
	STEREWMA 2	FIRMNESS	774C
	SUN IC	WITH	789B
	TAXIS 2	FIXED ORDER	811C
	CHAIRW I	REJOICE	881D
6	KURIOS 2Cγ	LORD	461A
	PARALAMBANW 2Bγ	TAKE	625B
	PERIPATEW 2A8	GO ABOUT	655B
7	BEBAIOW 2	ESTABLISH	138A
	EPOIKODOMEW 2	BUILD ON TO	305C
	EUCHARISTIA 2	THANKFULNESS	329A
	PERISSEUW I8β	BE LEFT OVER	656D
	PISTIS 2Dα	FAITH	669B
	RIZOW	FIX FIRMLY	743C
8	ANTHRWPOS IB	MAN	67D
	APAT8 I	DECEPTION	81C
	BLEPW 6	SEE	143B
	KENOS 2Aα	EMPTY	429A
	KOSMOS 7	WORLD	447D
	M8 BIC	NOT	519A
	HO,H8,TO II3B	THE	553D
	PARADOSIS 2	TRADITION	621B
	STOICHEION 3		776C
	FUNDAMENTAL PRINCIPLES		
	STOICHEION 3		776D
	FUNDAMENTAL PRINCIPLES		
	STOICHEION 4		777A
	FUNDAMENTAL PRINCIPLES		
	SULAGWGEW	CARRY OFF AS BOOTY	784B
	TIS, TI IA8	ANY ONE	828A
	PHILOSOPHIA	PHILOSOPHY	869A
9	EN I5A	IN	258D
	THEIOT8S	DIVINITY	354C
	THEOT8S	DEITY	359A
	KATOIKEW IB	LIVE	425C
	PAS ICα	ALL	637B
	PL8RWMA 3B	THAT WHICH FILLS	678B
	SWMATIKWS	BODILY	807D
10	ARCH8 3	RULER	112A
	EXOUSIA 4Cβ	AUTHORITY	278B
	KEPHAL8 2A	HEAD	431C
	PL8ROW IB	MAKE FULL	677A
11	HAMARTIA 3	SIN	43A
	APEKDUSIS	REMOVAL	83A

```
11  ACHEIROPOI8TOS              127D     18  HORAW IAʏ                        SEE 581D
        NOT MADE BY HAND                     OU  5A                           NO  595A
    PERITEMNW 2A      CUT AROUND 658A         PL8SMON8         SATISFACTION 679A
    SARX 7                  BODY 751D         SARX 7                   BODY 751D
    SWMA 1B                 BODY 807A         TAPEINOPHROSUN8      HUMILITY 812A
11A   PERITOM8 3    CIRCUMCISION 658D         HUPO IAβ                   BY 850D
12  BAPTISMOS            WASHING 132B         PHUSIOW         .     BLOW UP 877B
    BAPTISMA 2          BAPTISM 132B     19  AUXANW 3                  GROW 121C
    EGEIRW IAβ            RAISE 213D          AUX8SIS        CAUSE GROWTH 121C
    ENERGEIA I         WORKING 264C          HAPH8              LIGAMENT 124D
    NEKROS 2A              DEAD 537A          EPICHOR8GEW 3       SUPPORT 305A
    PERITOM8 3     CIRCUMCISION 658D          EPICHOR8GIA         SUPPORT 305B
    PISTIS 2A             FAITH 668D          KEPHAL8 1B             HEAD 431B
    SUNEGEIRW 2    RISE UP WITH 793C          KRATEW 2Eβ             HOLD 449D
    SUNTHAPTW         BURY WITH 797C          HOS,H8,HO 13Bʏ  (REL PRON) 587D
13  AKROBUSTIA 2   UNCIRCUMCISED  33A         OU  3B                   NO  594D
    NEKROS 1Bα             DEAD 536D          PAS ICα                 ALL 637B
    PAS IDα                ALL 637C          SUMBIBAZW IA          UNITE 785B
    SARX I               FLESH 750D          SUNDESMOS IA          BOND 793A
    SUZWOPOIEW                  783D          SWMA 5                 BODY 807C
        MAKE ALIVE TOGETHER              20  APO I5                  FROM  86A
    SUN 2C                 WITH 789C          APOTHN8SKW IBʏ          DIE  91A
    CHARIZOMAI 2   GIVE FREELY 885A          DOGMATIZW    SUBMIT TO RULES 200D
13A   PARAPTWMA 2B             627B          EI III                    IF 218C
        TRANSGRESSION                        ZAW 1B                  LIVE 336D
13B   PARAPTWMA 2B             627B          KOSMOS 7               WORLD 447D
        TRANSGRESSION                        STOICHEION 3               776C
14  AIRW 4            TAKE AWAY  24B             FUNDAMENTAL PRINCIPLES
    DOGMA I             DECREE 200C          STOICHEION 4               777A
    EXALEIPHW 2         REMOVE 272A             FUNDAMENTAL PRINCIPLES
    KATA I28β             DOWN 406D          SUN 2B                  WITH 789C
    MESOS 2        THE MIDDLE 509A          TIS, TI 3A             WHICH 827B
    PROS8LOW         NAIL FAST 722A     21  HAPTW 2A               TOUCH 102B
    STAUROS 3        THE CROSS 772C          HAPTW 2A               TOUCH 102C
    HUPENANTIOS        OPPOSED 846A          GEUOMAI I              TASTE 156A
    CHEIROGRAPHON     DOCUMENT 889A          THIGGANW               TOUCH 362B
15  APEKDUOMAI 2        DISARM  82D          M8  AIII5A               NOT 518D
    ARCH8 3              RULER 112A          M8DE 1B             AND NOT 519D
    DEIGMATIZW         EXPOSE 171D     22  ANTHRWPOS 1B             MAN  67D
    THRIAMBEUW I   TRIUMPH OVER 364B          APOCHR8SIS        CONSUMING 101C
    PARR8SIA 2        PUBLICLY 636A          DIDASKALIA 2        TEACHING 190C
16  BRWSIS I           EATING 147C          EIMI III2                TO BE 224A
    HEORT8           FESTIVAL 279D          EIS 4D                   FOR 228C
    KRINW 6B            JUDGE 453B          ENTALMA         COMMANDMENT 267D
    MEROS IC          IN PART 507C          HO,H8,TO III0A           THE 555A
    NEOM8NIA         NEW MOON 537D          PHTHORA I               RUIN 865D
    OUN 1B           THEREFORE 597B     23  APHEIDIA  SEVERE TREATMENT 124C
    POSIS I          DRINKING 701A          ETHELOTHR8SKIA             217A
    SABBATON 1Bβ       SABBATH 746C             SELF=MADE RELIGION
17  MELLW 2        IS DESTINED 502D          LOGOS IAβ               WORD 478C
    SKIA 2              SHADE 763A          MEN 2A          (PARTICLE) 504B
    SWMA 4               BODY 807C          PL8SMON8         SATISFACTION 679A
    SWMATIKWS          BODILY 807D          PROS III3B           TOWARD 717B
    CHRISTOS I    ANOINTED ONE 895C          SARX 7                  BODY 751D
18  AGGELOS 2A          ANGEL   8A          SOPHIA 2              WISDOM 767B
    EIK8 I      WITHOUT CAUSE 221A          *TAPEINOPHROSUN8     HUMILITY 812A
    EMBATEUW 3     ENTER INTO 253D          TIM8 2E                HONOR 825C
    THELW 4B             WISH 356A
    THR8SKEIA        RELIGION 364A                    COLOSSIANS 3
    KATABRABEUW        CONDEMN 410B
    KENEMBATEUW  MAKE A MISSTEP 428D      I  ANW I                 ABOVE  76B
    M8  AI5               NOT 517D          DEXIOS 2A              RIGHT 173D
    NOUS 3A         THE MIND 547A          EI VII0                   IF 219A
```

1	Z8TEW 2A	SEEK 339C		11	IOUDAIOS 2A	JEWISH 380B	
	KATH8MAI 1Aα	SIT 390B			HOPOU 2A	WHERE 579D	
	SUNEGEIRW 2	RISE UP WITH 793C			PERITOM8 4A	CIRCUMCISION 658D	
1F	HO,H8,TO 116	THE 554B			SKUTH8S	SCYTHIAN 765C	
2	ANW 1	ABOVE 76B		12	AGAPAW 1D	LOVE 5A	
	G8 5A	EARTH 156D			EKLEKTOS 1B	CHOSEN 242B	
	PHRONEW 2	THINK 874B			ENDUW 2B	DRESS 263D	
3	APOTHN8SKW 1Bβ	DIE 91A			MAKROTHUMIA 2A	PATIENCE 489B	
	EN 15A	IN 258D			OIKTIRMOS	PITY 564C	
	ZW8 2Bα	LIFE 341B			PRAUT8S	HUMILITY 705D	
	THEOS 3A	GOD 357D			SPLAGCHNON 1B	INWARD PARTS 770C	
	KRUPTW 2C	HIDE 455D			TAPEINOPHROSUN8	HUMILITY 812A	
	SUN 2B	WITH 789C			CHR8STOT8S 2A	GOODNESS 894D	
4	DOXA 1A	BRIGHTNESS 202D			HWS IIIIA	SO 906C	
	ZW8 2Aβ	LIFE 341A		13	ALL8LWN	EACH OTHER 38D	
	HOTAN 1B	WHEN 592B			ANECHW 1A	ENDURE 65B	
	TOTE 2	AT THAT TIME 831D			HEAUTOU 3	ONESELF 211D	
4A	PHANEROW 2Bβ	REVEAL 860D			ECHW 17A	HAVE 334B	
4B	PHANEROW 2Bβ	REVEAL 860D			KATHWS 1	JUST AS 392A	
5	AKATHARSIA 2	IMPURITY 28B			KAI 113	ALSO 394B	
	G8 5A	EARTH 156D			MEMPSIS	REASON FOR COMPLAINT 503C	
	EIDWLOLATRIA	IDOLATRY 220C			MOMPH8	COMPLAINT 528D	
	EPITHUMIA 3	DESIRE 293C			HOUTW 1A	THUS 602B	
	KAKOS 1B	BAD 398C			PROS III4A	TOWARD 717B	
	MELOS 2	MEMBER 502D		13A	TIS, TI 1Aγ	ANY ONE 827D	
	NEKROW	PUT TO DEATH 537B		13A	CHARIZOMAI 2	GIVE FREELY 885A	
	PATHOS 2	PASSION 608A		13B	CHARIZOMAI 2	GIVE FREELY 885A	
	PLEONEXIA	GREEDINESS 673D		14	AGAP8 11A	LOVE 5C	
	PORNEIA 1	PROSTITUTION 699D			HENOT8S	UNITY 267A	
6	APEITHEIA	DISOBEDIENCE 81D			EPI II1Bβ	TO 286D	
	ERCHOMAI 12C	COME 311D			HOS,H8,HO 17A	(REL PRON) 588C	
	ORG8 2B	ANGER 583A			PAS 1Eβ	ALL 637D	
	HUIOS 1C6	SON 842A			SUNDESMOS 1B	BOND 793A	
7	ZAW 3A	LIVE 337B			TELEIOT8S	MATURITY 817B	
	PERIPATEW 2Aδ	GO ABOUT 655B		15	BRABEUW	RULE 146B	
8	AISCHROLOGIA	EVIL SPEECH 24C			EIR8N8 3	PEACE 226D	
	APOTITH8MI 1B	LAY ASIDE 100C			EUCHARISTOS	THANKFUL 329B	
	BLASPH8MIA 1	SLANDER 142C			KALEW 2	CALL 400D	
	THUMOS 2	ANGER 366A			SWMA 5	BODY 807C	
	KAKIA 1B	MALICE 397D		16	ADW	SING 18D	
	NUNI 1C	NOW 548C			DIDASKW 2F	TEACH 191B	
	ORG8 1	ANGER 582C			HEAUTOU 3	ONESELF 211D	
	PAS 2Bβ	ALL THINGS 638D			EN 15A	IN 258D	
	STOMA 1A	MOUTH 777B			ENOIKEW	LIVE 267A	
9	ANTHRWPOS 2Cβ	MAN 68A			LOGOS 1Bβ	WORD 479B	
	APEKDUOMAI 1	TAKE OFF 82D			NOUTHETEW	ADMONISH 546B	
	EIS 4Cα	AGAINST 228B			PLOUSIWS	RICHLY 679D	
	PALAIOS 2	OLD 610D			PNEUMATIKOS 2Aβ	SPIRITUAL 685B	
	PRAXIS 4B	ACTING 704D			SOPHIA 2	WISDOM 767A	
	PSEUDOMAI 1	LIE 900A			HUMNOS	HYMN 844B	
10	ANAKAINOW	RENEW 55A			CHARIS 5	FAVOR 886D	
	EIKWN 2	FORM 221C			PSALMOS 2	PSALM 899B	
	ENDUW 2B	DRESS 263D			WD8	SONG 903D	
	EPIGNWSIS	KNOWLEDGE 291C		17	DIA AIII2A	BY 179D	
	KATA II5Bα	ACCORDING TO 408C			ERGON 1A	DEED 307D	
	KTIZW	CREATE 456D			EUCHARISTEW 2	GIVE THANKS 328C	
	NEOS 1Aβ	NEW 537D			LOGOS 1Aα	WORD 478A	
11	AKROBUSTIA 3	HEATHENISM 33B			ONOMA 14Cγ	NAME 576A	
	BARBAROS 2B	FOREIGN 133A			HOSTIS 1Eα	WHOEVER 591A	
	DOULOS 1B	SLAVE 204D			PAS 1Cγ	WHOEVER 637C	
	ELEUTHEROS 1	FREE 250B			PAT8R 3E	FATHER 642A	
	HELL8N 2A	GENTILE 251C		18	AN8KW 2	IT IS PROPER 65D	
	ENI	THERE IS NOT 265D			HUPOTASSW 1Bβ	SUBJECT 855D	

18 HWS II   AS 905C
18F   AN8R I   MAN 650
18F   GUN8 2   WIFE 167C
19 AGAPAW IAα   LOVE 4B
   PIKRAINW 2   MAKE BITTER 663A
20 GONEUS   PARENTS 164B
   EN   I5D   IN 259B
   EUARESTOS I   PLEASING 319A
   KATA II6   WITH RESPECT TO 408D
   TEKNON IAα   CHILD 816A
   HUPAKOUW I   LISTEN TO 845A
21 ATHUMEW   LOSE HEART 21A
   ERETHIZW   IRRITATE 308D
   PARORGIZW   MAKE ANGRY 635A
   TEKNON IAα   CHILD 816A
22 ANTHRWPARESKOS   MEN PLEASER 67A
   HAPLOT8S I   SIMPLICITY 85B
   DOULOS IA   SLAVE 204D
   KARDIA IBη   HEART 405B
   KURIOS IAβ   LORD 460A
   OPHTHALMODOULIA EYE SERVICE 604B
   SARX 6   BODY 751C
   HUPAKOUW I   LISTEN TO 845A
   PHOBEW 2A   BE AFRAID 871B
   HWS I2A   AS 905C
22A   KATA II6   WITH RESPECT TO 408D
22B   KURIOS 2D   LORD 461B
23 EK   3Gγ   BY 234D
   ERGAZOMAI 2A   WORK 307A
   OU   2C   NO 594C
   PSUCH8 IBγ   SOUL LIFE 901D
   HWS IIIIA   SO 906C
24 ANTAPODOSIS   REPAYING 72C
   APOLAMBANW I   RECEIVE 93D
   DOULEUW 2B   SERVE 204C
   KL8RONOMIA 3   INHERITANCE 436A
   KURIOS 2Cγ   LORD 461A
25 KOMIZW 2A   BRING 443D
   PROSWPOL8MPSIA   PARTIALITY 728A
25A   ADIKEW IA   DO WRONG 17A
25B   ADIKEW IA   DO WRONG 17A

                 COLOSSIANS 4

 I DIKAIOS 5   RIGHTEOUS 195B
    ECHW I2Bβ   HAVE 332D
    ISOT8S 2   EQUALITY 382A
    KURIOS IAβ   LORD 460A
    OURANOS 2A   HEAVEN 599A
    PARECHW 2B   GRANT 632B
    TEKNON IAα   CHILD 816A
 2 GR8GOREW 2   BE AWAKE 166C
    EN   II3   WHILE 259D
    EUCHARISTIA 2   THANKFULNESS 329A
    PROSEUCH8 I   PRAYER 720C
    PROSKARTEREW 2A   ADHERE TO 722D
 3 HAMA IA   TOGETHER 41B
    ANOIGW IA   OPEN 70C
    DEW IB   BIND 176D
    THURA 2C   DOOR 366C
    LALEW 2B   SPEAK 464D
    LOGOS IBβ   WORD 479C
    MUST8RION 2   MYSTERY 532B

 3 PERI IF   ABOUT 650C
    PROSEUCHOMAI   PRAY 721A
 4 PHANEROW IA   REVEAL 860C
    HWS II   AS 905C
 5 EXAGORAZW 2   REDEEM 271A
    EXW IAβ   OUTSIDE 279A
    KAIROS 2   TIME 395D
    PERIPATEW 2A6   GO ABOUT 655B
    PROS III4B   TOWARD 717C
    SOPHIA 2   WISDOM 767A
 6 HALAS 2   SALT 34C
    ARTUW   SEASON 110C
    LOGOS IAβ   WORD 478C
    OIDA IF   KNOW 558C
    PWS 2A   HOW 739D
    CHARIS I   GRACIOUSNESS 885B
 7 AGAP8TOS 2   BELOVED   6C
    ADELPHOS 2   BROTHER 16A
    GNWRIZW I   MAKE KNOWN 162C
    DIAKONOS IB   HELPER 183D
    KATA II6   WITH RESPECT TO 408D
    HO,H8,TO II5   THE 554B
    PISTOS IAα   TRUSTWORTHY 670B
    SUNDOULOS 3   FELLOW SLAVE 793C
    TUCHIKOS   TYCHICUS 839C
 8 AUTOS IH   EVEN 122D
    GINWSKW 2A   FIND OUT 160A
    EIS 4F   (PURPOSE) 228D
    HINA I5   IN ORDER THAT 378A
    KARDIA IBє   HEART 405A
    PARAKALEW 4   IMPLORE 623A
    PEMPW I   SEND 647C
    PEMPW I   SEND 647D
    PEMPW I   SEND 648A
    PERI II   ABOUT 650D
 9 AGAP8TOS 2   BELOVED   6C
    ADELPHOS 2   BROTHER 16A
    GNWRIZW I   MAKE KNOWN 162C
    EIMI III3   TO BE 224B
    HO,H8,TO II6   THE 554B
    ON8SIMOS I   ONESIMUS 573C
    PISTOS IAα   TRUSTWORTHY 670B
    HWDE 2A   HERE 903D
10 ANEPSIOS   COUSIN 65C
    ARISTARCHOS   ARISTARCHUS 106B
    ASPAZOMAI IA   GREET 116B
    BARNABAS   BARNABAS 133C
    DECHOMAI I   RECEIVE 176B
    ENTOL8 IB   COMMAND 268C
    MARKOS   MARK 493C
    PERI IE   ABOUT 650B
    SUNAICHMALWTOS   791B
                 FELLOW PRISONER
11 EK   3D   FROM 234C
    I8SOUS 5   JESUS CHRIST 374D
    IOUSTOS 3   JUSTUS 381B
    LEGW II3   CALL 471B
    PAR8GORIA   COMFORT 632B
    PERITOM8 4A   CIRCUMCISION 658D
    SUNERGOS   WORKING WITH 795C
12 AGWNIZOMAI 2B   STRUGGLE 15A
    ASPAZOMAI IA   GREET 116B
    DOULOS 4   SLAVE 205B

12	EPAPHRAS	EPAPHRAS 283C
	THEL8MA 1A	WILL 354D
	KOLOSSAI /	COLOSSAE 443A
	PL8ROPHOREW 2	FILL 676B
	PL8ROPHOREW 1B	FILL 676B
	PL8ROW 1B	MAKE FULL 677A
	PL8ROW 3	MAKE FULL 677B
	PROSEUCH8 1	PRAYER 720C
	TELEIOS 2D	PERFECT 817B
13	HIERAPOLIS	HIERAPOLIS 372B
	LAODIKEIA	LAODICEA 467D
	MARTUREW 1A	BEAR WITNESS 493D
	POLUS 11B8	MANY 694D
	PONOS 1	TOIL 698B
14	AGAP8TOS 2	BELOVED 6C
	D8MAS	DEMAS 177C
	IATROS 1	PHYSICIAN 369C
	LOUKAS	LUKE 481C
14F	ASPAZOMAI 1A	GREET 116B
15	EKKL8SIA 4C	CHURCH 240C
	OIKOS 1Aα	HOUSE 563A
15F	LAODIKEIA	LAODICEA 467D
16	ANAGINWSKW 1	READ 51B
	ANAGINWSKW 1	READ 51C
	ANAGINWSKW 2	READ 51C
	EK 6A	FROM 235D
	EPISTOL8	LETTER 300D
	HINA 111Ac	IN ORDER THAT 378B
	LAODIKEUS	A LAODICEAN 467D
	PARA 111B8	BESIDE 615C
	POIEW 11B θ	DO 688B
16B	HINA IV	IN ORDER THAT 379B
17	ARCHIPPOS	ARCHIPPUS 112D
	BLEPW 4B	SEE 143B
	DIAKONIA 3	SERVICE 183C
	KURIOS 2CY	LORD 461A
	PARALAMBANW 2Bα	TAKE 625A
	PL8ROW 4B	MAKE FULL 677D
18	ASPASMOS 2	GREETING 116D
	DESMOS 1	FETTER 175B
	EMOS 1Aα	MY 255A
	META A111CY	WITH 510A
	MN8MONEUW 1A	REMEMBER 527A
	PAULOS	PAUL 643A
	CHARIS 2C	FAVOR 885D
	CHEIR 1	HAND 888B

1 THESSALONIANS 1

1	APO V4	FROM 87C
	EIR8N8 2	PEACE 226D
	EKKL8SIA 4B	CHURCH 240C
	EKKL8SIA 4EY	CHURCH 240D
	THESSALONIKEUS	THESSALONIAN 360B
	KURIOS 2CY	LORD 461A
	PAT8R 3E	FATHER 642A
	PAULOS	PAUL 643A
	SILOUANOS	SILVANUS 758B
	TIMOTHEOS	TIMOTHY 826A
	*CHARIS 2C	FAVOR 885D
2	ADIALEIPTWS	CONSTANTLY 17A
	EPI 12	UNDER 286C
	MNEIA 2	MENTION 526B

2	MNEIA 2	MENTION 526B
	PAS 1Eα	ALL 637D
	POIEW 111	DO 689C
	PROSEUCH8 1	PRAYER 720C
3	*AGAP8 11A	LOVE 5C
	ELPIS 2B	HOPE 252D
	EMPROSTHEN 2B	IN FRONT 256C
	ERGON 1B	MANIFESTATION 307D
	THEOS 3D	GOD 358A
	KOPOS 2	WORK 444C
	KURIOS 2CY	LORD 461B
	MN8MONEUW 1A	REMEMBER 527A
	HO,H8,TO 11108	THE 555A
	PAT8R 3C8	FATHER 641C
	PISTIS 2Dα	FAITH 669C
	PISTIS 2DY	FAITH 669C
	HUPOMON8 1	PATIENCE 854A
4	AGAPAW 1D	LOVE 4D
	ADELPHOS 2	BROTHER 16A
	EKLOG8 1	SELECTION 242C
	HUPO 1Aα	BY 850D
5	ALLA 1A	BUT, YET 37C
	DUNAMIS 1	POWER 207A
	EUAGGELION 2B8	GOSPEL 318C
	LOGOS 1Aα	WORD 478B
	OIDA 1F	KNOW 558C
	HOIOS	OF WHAT SORT 565C
	PL8ROPHORIA	CERTAINTY 676C
	PNEUMA 5C8	SPIRIT 683A
	PNEUMA 6A	SPIRIT 683D
	POLUS 11B8	MANY 694D
6	DECHOMAI 3B	ACCEPT 176C
	THLIPSIS 1	TRIBULATION 362D
	LOGOS 1B8	WORD 479C
	META A1111	WITH 511A
	MIM8T8S 1	IMITATOR 524A
	PNEUMA 5C8	SPIRIT 683A
	POLUS 11B8	MANY 694C
	CHARA 1	JOY 883D
7	PAS 1D8	ALL 637D
	PISTEUW 2B	BELIEVE 667C
	TUPOS 5B	MARK 837D
	HWSTE 2A8	THEREFORE 908C
7F	ACHAIA	ACHAIA 127D
7F	MAKEDONIA	MACEDONIA 488B
8	APO 111	FROM 86B
	EN 16	IN 259C
	EXERCHOMAI 2Bα	GO OUT 274C
	EX8CHEW	RESOUND 275D
	ECHW 121	HAVE 333C
	LOGOS 1B8	WORD 479B
	M8 A13	NOT 517C
	HO,H8,TO 111G	THE 553A
	PISTIS 2A	FAITH 668C
	PROS 111 4B	TOWARD 717C
	TOPOS 1A	PLACE 830A
	CHREIA 1	NEED 893B
	HWSTE 2A8	THEREFORE 908C
9	AL8THINOS 3	GENUINE 36C
	APAGGELLW 1	REPORT 78C
	AUTOS 1C	SELF 122C
	DOULEUW 2B	SERVE 204B
	EIDWLON 2	IDOL 220D

9 EISODOS I　　　　　　ENTRANCE 232C
　EPISTREPHW IBβ　　　　　　TURN 301B
　ZAW IAє　　　　　　　　　LIVE 336D
　HOPOIOS　　　　WHAT SORT 579B
　PWS 2A　　　　　　　　　HOW 739D
9A　PROS IIIIA　　　　　TOWARD 716D
10 ANAMENW 2　　　　　　EXPECT 57B
　EGEIRW IAβ　　　　　　　RAISE 213D
　ERCHOMAI IIBβ　　　　　　COME 311B
　NEKROS 2A　　　　　　　　DEAD 537A
　ORG8 2A　　　　　　　　ANGER 582D
　ORG8 2B　　　　　　　　ANGER 583A
　OURANOS 2B　　　　　　HEAVEN 599C
　RUOMAI　　　　　　　　　SAVE 745A
　HUIOS 2B　　　　　　　　　SON 842D

　　　I THESSALONIANS 2

1 EISODOS I　　　　　　ENTRANCE 232C
　KENOS 2Aβ　　　　　　　EMPTY 429A
　HOTI IBʃ　　　　　　　　THAT 593A
　OU 5B　　　　　　　　　　NO 595A
2 AGWN 2　　　　　　STRUGGLE 14D
　EN 14D　　　　　　　　　IN 258C
　EUAGGELION 2Bβ　　　GOSPEL 318B
　LALEW 2B　　　　　　SPEAK 464D
　OIDA II　　　　　　　　KNOW 558D
　PARRθSIAZOMAI 2　　VENTURE 636C
　POLUS IIBβ　　　　　　MANY 694C
　PROPASCHW　SUFFER PREVIOUSLY 716B
　HUBRIZW　　　　　MISTREAT 839B
　PHILIPPOI　　　　　PHILIPPI 867C
3 AKATHARSIA 2　　　IMPURITY 28B
　DOLOS　　　　　　　DECEIT 202C
　OUDE I　　　　　AND NOT 595D
　OUTE　　　　　　　　NOT 600C
　PARAKLθSIS I　ENCOURAGEMENT 623B
　PLANθ　　　　　WANDERING 671D
4 ARESKW I　　　　ACCOMMODATE 105A
　EUAGGELION IA　　　　GOSPEL 318A
　KARDIA IBα　　　　　　HEART 404B
　OU 7A　　　　　　　　　NO 595B
　HOUTW IA　　　　　　　THUS 602B
　PISTEUW 3　　　　　BELIEVE 667D
　HWS IIIIA　　　　　　　SO 906C
4A　DOKIMAZW 2B　　　APPROVE 201D
4B　DOKIMAZW I　　　EXAMINE 201C
5 GAR IB　　　　　　　　　FOR 151B
　KOLAKEIA　　　　　FLATTERY 441C
　MARTUS 2A　　　　　WITNESS 495B
　OIDA II　　　　　　　　KNOW 558D
　PLEONEXIA　　　GREEDINESS 673D
　POTE I　　　　　　　　ONCE 701D
　PROPHASIS 2　ACTUAL MOTIVE 730A
5F　OUTE　　　　　　　　NOT 600C
6 APO IV2A　　　　　　　FROM 87A
　DOXA 3　　　　　　　　FAME 203A
7 APOSTOLOS 3　　　APOSTLES 99B
　BAROS 2　　　　　　WEIGHT 133C
　EIMI III4　　　　　　TO BE 224C
　8PIOS　　　　　　　GENTLE 349A
　THALPW　　　　　　CHERISH 351A
　MESOS 2　　　　THE MIDDLE 509A

7 NθPIOS 2　　　　　　　MINOR 539D
　TEKNON IAα　　　　　　CHILD 816A
　TROPHOS　　　　　　　NURSE 835D
7A　HWS IIIIA　　　　　　　SO 906C
8 AGAPθTOS 2　　　　BELOVED 6C
　ALLA IA　　　　　　BUT, YET 37C
　GINOMAI III　　　　　　　BE 159B
　DIOTI I　　　　　　BECAUSE 198C
　EUAGGELION 2Bβ　　　GOSPEL 318B
　EUDOKEW I　　WELL PLEASED 319C
　METADIDWMI　　　　　SHARE 512B
　HOMEIROMAI　　　　　　　568B
　　HAVE A KINDLY FEELING
　PSUCHθ IBγ　　　SOUL LIFE 901D
9 EIS IDβ　　　　　　　　IN 227D
　EIS 4G　　　　　　　　FOR 229A
　EPIBAREW　　　　　BURDEN 290B
　ERGAZOMAI I　　　　　WORK 306D
　EUAGGELION 2Bβ　　　GOSPEL 318B
　HθMERA IA　　　　　　　DAY 346C
　KθRUSSW 2Bβ　　　ANNOUNCE 432C
　KOPOS 2　　　　　　　WORK 444C
　Mθ AIIIE　　　　　　　NOT 518A
　MNθMONEUW IB　　REMEMBER 527A
　MOCHTHOS　　　　　LABOR 530C
　NUX IB　　　　　　　NIGHT 548D
　PROS III3A　　　　　TOWARD 717A
　TIS, TI IAγ　　　ANY ONE 827D
10 AMEMPTWS　　BLAMELESSLY 44C
　GINOMAI III　　　　　　　BE 159B
　DIKAIWS IB　　　　　JUSTLY 197B
　MARTUS 2A　　　　　WITNESS 495B
　MARTUS 2B　　　　　WITNESS 495C
　HOSIWS　　　　　　DEVOUTLY 590A
　PISTEUW 2B　　　　BELIEVE 667C
　HWS IV4　　　　　　　WHEN 907B
11 HEKASTOS 2　　　　　EACH 236A
　KATHAPER　　　　　JUST AS 387D
　TEKNON IAα　　　　　　CHILD 816A
11A　HWS IV4　　　　　　　WHEN 907B
12 AXIWS　　　　　　WORTHILY 78A
　BASILEIA 3G　　　KINGDOM 135B
　DOXA IA　　　　　　GLORY 202D
　DOXA IBβ　　　　　　GLORY 203A
　MARTUROMAI 2　　　AFFIRM 495B
　PARAKALEW 2　　APPEAL TO 622B
　PARAKALEW 5　　　IMPLORE 623A
　PARAMUTHEOMAI　ENCOURAGE 626B
　PERIPATEW 2Aα　　GO ABOUT 655B
13 ADIALEIPTWS　CONSTANTLY 17A
　AKOθ 2B　　　　　　REPORT 30C
　ALθTHWS 2　　　　　TRULY 37A
　ANTHRWPOS IAβ　　　　MAN 67C
　DECHOMAI 3B　　　ACCEPT 176C
　ENERGEW IB　　　　　WORK 264D
　EUCHARISTEW 2　GIVE THANKS 328D
　KATHWS I　　　　　JUST AS 392B
　HO,Hθ,TO IIII　　　　　THE 555A
　PARA I3B　　　　　　FROM 614D
　PARALAMBANW 2Bγ　　TAKE 625B
　PISTEUW 2B　　　　BELIEVE 667C
13A　LOGOS IBβ　　　　　WORD 479B
13B　LOGOS IBβ　　　　　WORD 479B

14	EKKL8SIA 4B	CHURCH 240C
	EKKL8SIA 4Eα	CHURCH 240D
	EN I5D	IN 259B
	IDIOS 2B	ONES OWN 370C
	IOUDAIA 2	JUDAEA 379D
	IOUDAIOS 2C	JEWISH 380B
	KATHWS I	JUST AS 392A
	KAI II3	ALSO 394B
	MIM8T8S 2	IMITATOR 524A
	PASCHW 3B	ENDURE 639D
	SUMPHULET8S	COMPATRIOT 788B
14A	HUPO IB	BY 851A
14B	HUPO IB	BY 851A
15	EKDIWKW	PERSECUTE SEVERELY 238B
	ENANTIOS 2	OPPOSED 261C
	KURIOS 2Cγ	LORD 461A
	PAS IB	ALL 637A
	PROPH8T8S I	PROPHET 730D
	PROPH8T8S 4	PROPHET 731B
16	HAMARTIA I	SIN 42B
	ANAPL8ROW I	MAKE COMPLETE 59B
	EIS 3	COMPLETELY 228A
	KWLUW I	HINDER 462C
	LALEW 2A6	SPEAK 464B
	ORG8 2A	ANGER 582D
	SWZW 2B	SAVE 806B
	TELOS IDγ	FOREVER 819D
	PHTHANW 2	COME 864C
17	APORPHANIZW	MAKE AN ORPHAN 97B
	EIDON 6	VISIT 220A
	EPITHUMIA 2	DESIRE 293B
	KAIROS I	TIME 395C
	KARDIA IBα	HEART 404C
	PERISSOTERWS 2	MORE 657C
	POLUS IIBβ	MANY 694C
	PROS III2B	TOWARD 717A
	SPOUDAZW 2	HASTEN 771A
	HWRA 2Aβ	TIME OF DAY 904C
17A	PROSWPON IB	FACE 728C
17B	PROSWPON IB	FACE 728C
18	HAPAX I	ONCE 80A
	DIOTI 3	FOR 198C
	DIS	TWICE 198D
	EGKOPTW	HINDER 215C
	THELW 2	WISH 355D
	KAI I2G	AND 393C
	KAI I6	AND 394A
	MEN 2A	(PARTICLE) 504B
	PAULOS	PAUL 643A
	SATAN	ADVERSARY 752B
19	ELPIS 3	HOPE 252D
	EMPROSTHEN 2B	IN FRONT 256C
	EN II2	WHILE 259D
	KAUCH8SIS I	BOASTING 427B
	KURIOS 2Cγ	LORD 461B
	PAROUSIA 2Bα	COMING 635C
	STEPHANOS 2B	WREATH 775A
19F	CHARA 2A	JOY 884A
20	GAR 4	INDEED 151D
	DOXA 3	FAME 203B

I THESSALONIANS 3

1	ATH8NAI	ATHENS 20D
	EUDOKEW I	WELL PLEASED 319C
	KATALEIPW IA	LEAVE BEHIND 414C
	M8KETI 3	NO LONGER 520B
	MONOS IAα	ONLY 529C
2	ADELPHOS 2	BROTHER 16A
	DIAKONOS IB	HELPER 183D
	DIAKONOS IA	SERVANT 183D
	EIS 4D	FOR 228C
	EUAGGELION 2Bα	GOSPEL 318B
	EUAGGELION 2Bα	GOSPEL 318B
	PARAKALEW 4	IMPLORE 623A
	PEMPW I	SEND 647D
	PISTIS 2Dα	FAITH 669B
	ST8RIZW 2	ESTABLISH 775D
	*SUNERGOS	WORKING WITH 795C
	TIMOTHEOS	TIMOTHY 826A
	HUPER IB	IN BEHALF OF 846D
3	ANTANAPL8ROW	FILL UP 72B
	THLIPSIS I	TRIBULATION 362D
	KEIMAI 2A	SET 428A
	SAINW	FLATTER 747B
4	GAR IE	FOR 151C
	THLIBW 3	OPPRESS 362C
	MELLW IC6	IS DESTINED 502C
	OIDA II	KNOW 558D
	PROLEGW I	TELL BEFOREHAND 715B
	PROS III7	TOWARD 718A
5	GINOMAI I4A	BECOME 158D
	GINWSKW 2A	FIND OUT 160A
	EIS 4D	FOR 228C
	EIS 4E	SO THAT 228D
	KAGW 3C	I 387A
	KAI I2E	AND 393C
	KENOS 2Aβ	EMPTY 429A
	KOPOS 2	WORK 444C
	M8KETI 3	NO LONGER 520B
	M8PWS IB	LEST SOMEHOW 521C
	HO.H8.TO II3A	THE 553C
	PEMPW I	SEND 647D
	PISTIS 2Dα	FAITH 669B
	STEGW 2	COVER 773C
5A	PEIRAZW 2D	TRY 646B
5B	PEIRAZW 2D	TRY 646B
6	AGATHOS IBβ	GOOD 3A
	AGAP8 IIA	LOVE 5C
	ARTI 3	NOW 109D
	EPIPOTHEW	DESIRE 297D
	ERCHOMAI IIAβ	COME 310C
	EUAGGELIZW I	317C
		ANNOUNCE GOOD NEWS
	ECHW I2Eβ	HAVE 333A
	KATHAPER	JUST AS 387D
	MNEIA I	REMEMBRANCE 526B
	PISTIS 2Dγ	FAITH 669C
	TIMOTHEOS	TIMOTHY 826A
7	ANAGK8 2	DISTRESS 52B
	*THLIPSIS I	TRIBULATION 362D
	PARAKALEW 4	IMPLORE 623A
	PAS ICβ	ALL 637B
	PISTIS 2Dα	FAITH 669B

7A	EPI III8γ	ON 287B
7B	EPI II2	AT 287D
8	EAN I2B	IF 210D
	ZAW IAγ	LIVE 336C
	KURIOS 2Cγ	LORD 461A
	NUN 2	NOW 548A
	ST8KW 2	STAND 775C
9	ANTAPODIDWMI I	REPAY 72B
	EMPROSTHEN 2B	IN FRONT 256C
	EPI III8γ	ON 287B
	EUCHARISTIA 2	THANKFULNESS 329A
	*CHAIRW I	REJOICE 881B
	CHARA I	JOY 883D
10	DEOMAI 4	ASK 174B
	EIDON 6	VISIT 220A
	H8MERA IA	DAY 346C
	KATARTIZW IB	RESTORE 4|8D
	NUX IB	NIGHT 548D
	PISTIS 2D∝	FAITH 669B
	PROSWPON IB	FACE 728C
	HUPEREKPERISSOU	848C
	BEYOND ALL MEASURE	
	HUSTER8MA 2	NEED 857B
11	THEOS 3D	GOD 358A
	KATEUTHUNW	LEAD 423C
	KURIOS 2Cγ	LORD 461B
	HO,H8,TO III0B	THE 555A
	HODOS IA	WAY 556B
	PAT8R 3C8	FATHER 641C
12	AGAP8 II88	LOVE 5D
	EIS 4C8	(GOAL) 228C
	KATHAPER	JUST AS 387D
	PERISSEUW 2B	BE LEFT OVER 657A
	PLEONAZW 2B	INCREASE 673B
13	HAGIOS 2D∝	THE HOLY ONES 10A
	HAGIWSUN8	HOLINESS 10C
	AMEMPTOS	BLAMELESS 44B
	EIS 4E	SO THAT 228D
	EMPROSTHEN 2B	IN FRONT 256C
	EN II2	WHILE 259D
	THEOS 3D	GOD 358A
	KARDIA IB6	HEART 404D
	KURIOS 2Cγ	LORD 461B
	META AIIIA	WITH 509D
	HO,H8,TO III0B	THE 555A
	PAROUSIA 2B∝	COMING 635C
	PAT8R 3C8	FATHER 641C
	ST8RIZW 2	ESTABLISH 775D

I THESSALONIANS 4

1	ARESKW I	ACCOMMODATE 105A
	DEI 2	IT IS NECESSARY 171B
	EN I5D	IN 259B
	ERWTAW 2	ASK 312B
	MALLON I	MORE 490B
	HO,H8,TO II8A	THE 554D
	PARA I3B	FROM 614D
	PARAKALEW 2	APPEAL TO 622C
	PARALAMBANW 2Bγ	TAKE 625B
	PERISSEUW IB8	BE LEFT OVER 656D
	PWS 2A	HOW 740A
1A	PERIPATEW 2Aγ	GO ABOUT 655B

1B	PERIPATEW 2Aγ	GO ABOUT 655B
2	DIDWMI I8∝	GIVE 192A
	KURIOS 2Cγ	LORD 461A
	OIDA IF	KNOW 558C
	PARAGGELIA	ORDER 618B
	TIS, TI 2	WHICH 827B
3	HAGIASMOS	HOLINESS 9A
	APECHW 3	KEEP AWAY 84C
	THEL8MA ICγ	WILL 355A
	PORNEIA I	PROSTITUTION 700A
4	HAGIASMOS	HOLINESS 9A
	KTAOMAI I	GET 456A
	OIDA 3	KNOW 558D
	SKEUOS 2	THING 761D
	SKEUOS 2	THING 762A
	TIM8 2C	HONOR 825C
5	EPITHUMIA 3	DESIRE 293C
	KATHAPER	JUST AS 387D
	OIDA IA	KNOW 558B
	PATHOS 2	PASSION 608A
6	DIAMARTUROMAI 2	TESTIFY 185C
	DIOTI I	BECAUSE 198C
	EKDIKOS	THE AVENGER 238B
	KURIOS 2D	LORD 461B
	M8 AIIIG	NOT 518B
	PAS IE8	ALL 637D
	PLEONEKTEW IA	OUTWIT 673C
	PRAGMA 2	DEED 703D
	PROEIPON 2A	FORETELL 711D
	HUPERBAINW 2	OVERSTEP 848A
7	HAGIASMOS	HOLINESS 9A
	AKATHARSIA 2	IMPURITY 28B
	EPI III8∝	ON 287C
	KALEW 2	CALL 400D
8	ATHETEW IB	REJECT 20C
	DIDWMI I88	GIVE 192A
	PNEUMA 5A	SPIRIT 682C
	TOIGAROUN	THEREFORE 828D
9	AGAP8 IA∝	LOVE 4C
	ALL8LWN 2	EACH OTHER 39A
	GRAPHW 2D	WRITE 166B
	ECHW I2I	HAVE 333C
	THEODIDAKTOS	TAUGHT BY GOD 356D
	PERI IH	ABOUT 650D
	PHILADELPHIA	BROTHERLY LOVE 866B
	CHREIA I	NEED 893B
10	GAR IE	FOR 151C
	EIS 4G	FOR 229A
	MAKEDONIA	MACEDONIA 488B
	MALLON I	MORE 490B
	PERISSEUW IB8	BE LEFT OVER 656D
	POIEW IID8	DO 688D
11	ERGAZOMAI I	WORK 306D
	H8SUCHAZW I	REST 349D
	IDIOS 3B	ONES OWN 370D
	PARAGGELLW	GIVE ORDERS 618B
	PRASSW IA	DO 705D
	PHILOTIMEOMAI	ASPIRE 869C
	CHEIR I	HAND 888B
12	EXW IA8	OUTSIDE 279B
	EUSCH8MONWS	DECENTLY 327B
	PERIPATEW 2A∝	GO ABOUT 655B
	CHREIA I	NEED 893B

13	AGNOEW I	BE IGNORANT 11B	3	TOTE 2	AT THAT TIME 831D
	ELPIS 2B	HOPE 252D		WDIN I	BIRTH PAIN 904A
	THELW I	WISH 355C		HWSPER 2	(JUST) AS 908A
	KOIMAW 2B	SLEEP 438D	4	EIMI III4	TO BE 224B
	LOIPOS 2Bα	THE OTHERS 481A		H8MERA 3Bβ	DAY 348A
14	AGW IA	LEAD 14A		HINA II2	IN ORDER THAT 378D
	ANIST8MI 2A	RISE 69C		KATALAMBANW IB	SEIZE 414A
	PISTEUW IAβ	BELIEVE 666A		KLEPT8S	THIEF 435C
	SUN 2C	WITH 789C	4F	SKOTOS 2B	DARKNESS 765B
14F	KOIMAW 2A	SLEEP 438D	5	EIMI IV2	TO BE 225A
15	ZAW IAα	LIVE 336C		H8MERA IB	DAY 346D
	LOGOS IAγ	WORD 478C		NUX 2	NIGHT 549A
	PAROUSIA 2Bα	COMING 635C		OUDE I	AND NOT 595D
	PERILEIPOMAI	REMAIN 654B		HUIOS IC6	SON 842A
	PHTHANW I	PRECEDE 864C		PHWS 3A	LIGHT 880B
15A	KURIOS 2Cγ	LORD 461A	6	ARA 4	THEN 103C
15B	KURIOS 2Cγ	LORD 460D		GR8GOREW 2	BE AWAKE 166C
16	ANIST8MI 2A	RISE 69C		KATHEUDW 2B	SLEEP 389D
	ARCHAGGELOS	ARCHANGEL 110D		LOIPOS 2Bα	THE OTHERS 481A
	EN I5D	IN 259B		M8 AIIII	NOT 518C
	KATABAINW IAγ	COME DOWN 409C		N8PHW	BE SELF CONTROLLED 540D
	KELEUSMA	SIGNAL 428C	7	KATHEUDW I	SLEEP 389C
	OURANOS 2B	HEAVEN 599C		METHUSKW	GET DRUNK 500B
	PRWTOS 2A	FIRST 733D		METHUW I	BE DRUNK 500C
	SALPIGX 2	TRUMPET 748B	7A	NUX IB	NIGHT 548D
17	A8R	AIR 19D	7B	NUX IB	NIGHT 548D
	HAMA 2	TOGETHER 41C	8	*AGAP8 IIA	LOVE 5C
	APANT8SIS	MEETING 79D		EIMI IV2	TO BE 225A
	HARPAZW 2B	SNATCH 108D		ELPIS 2B	HOPE 252C
	EPEITA 2A	THEN 284B		ENDUW 2A	DRESS 263C
	ZAW IAα	LIVE 336C		H8MERA IB	DAY 346D
	NEPHEL8	CLOUD 538D		THWRAX I	BREASTPLATE 368C
	HOUTW IB	THUS 602C		N8PHW	BE SELF CONTROLLED 540D
	PERILEIPOMAI	REMAIN 654B		PERIKEPHALAIA	HELMET 653D
	SUN 6	WITH 789D		PISTIS 2Dγ	FAITH 669C
17B	KURIOS 2Cγ	LORD 461A		PISTIS 2Dγ	FAITH 669C
18	LOGOS IBβ	WORD 479C		SWT8RIA 2	DELIVERANCE 809A
	PARAKALEW 4	IMPLORE 623A	9	KURIOS 2Cγ	LORD 461B
	HWSTE IB	THEREFORE 908B		ORG8 2B	ANGER 583A
				PERIPOI8SIS 2	KEEPING SAFE 656A

I THESSALONIANS 5

1	GRAPHW 2D	WRITE 166B		*SWT8RIA 2	DELIVERANCE 809A
	ECHW I2I	HAVE 333C		TITH8MI II2C	APPOINT 824B
	KAIROS 4	TIME 396B	10	HAMA 2	TOGETHER 41C
	PERI IH	ABOUT 650D		GR8GOREW 2	BE AWAKE 166C
	CHRONOS	TIME 896C		EI VII3A	IF 219B
2	AKRIBWS	ACCURATELY 32D		ZAW 2Bβ	LIVE 337B
	ERCHOMAI IIBα	COME 311B		KATHEUDW 2A	SLEEP 389C
	H8MERA 3Bβ	DAY 347D		SUN 2B	WITH 789C
	KLEPT8S	THIEF 435C		SUN 6	WITH 789D
	NUX IC	NIGHT 549A		HUPER IAε	IN BEHALF OF 846C
	HO,H8,TO IIII	THE 555A	11	HEIS 5A	ONE 231A
	HWS II	AS 905C		OIKODOMEW 3	BUILD 561B
3	AIPHNIDIDS	SUDDEN 26A		PARAKALEW 2	APPEAL TO 622B
	ASPHALEIA 2	SAFETY 118C		POIEW I2Aα	DO 689A
	GAST8R 2	WOMB 152A	12	EN I5D	IN 259B
	EIR8N8 IB	PEACE 226C		ERWTAW 2	ASK 312B
	EKPHEUGW 2A	RUN AWAY 246B		KOPIAW 2	BECOME WEARY 444B
	EPHIST8MI IB	STAND BY 331A		KURIOS 2Cγ	LORD 461A
	ECHW I2J	HAVE 333C		NOUTHETEW	ADMONISH 546B
	OLETHROS	DESTRUCTION 566A		OIDA 5	KNOW 559A
	HOTAN IA	WHEN 592A		PROIST8MI I	RULE 714A
			13	AGAP8 IIA	LOVE 5C
				HEAUTOU 3	ONESELF 211D

13 EIR8NEUW 2B　　KEEP IN PEACE 226A
ERGON 2　　WORK 308C
H8GEOMAI 2　　CONSIDER 344C
PROIST8MI 2　　RULE 714A
HUPEREKPERISSOU　　848C
　　BEYOND ALL MEASURE
HUPEREKPERISSWS　　848C
　　BEYOND ALL MEASURE
14 ANTECHW 2　　HELP 72D
ASTHEN8S 2B　　WEAK 115C
ASAKTOS　　DISORDERLY 119B
MAKROTHUMEW 2　　HAVE PATIENCE 489B
NOUTHETEW　　ADMONISH 546B
OLIGOPSUCHOS　　FAINT HEARTED 567A
PARAKALEW 2　　APPEAL TO 622C
PARAMUTHEOMAI　　ENCOURAGE 626B
PROS III4B　　TOWARD 717C
15 AGATHOS 2Aα　　GOOD 3B
ANTI 2　　FOR 73A
APODIDWMI 3　　RECOMPENSE 90A
DIWKW 4B　　PURSUE 200C
EIS 4G　　FOR 229A
KAKOS 3　　EVIL 399A
M8 8IB　　NOT 519A
HORAW 2B　　SEE 582B
TIS, TI IAγ　　ANY ONE 827D
16 CHAIRW I　　REJOICE 882A
17 ADIALEIPTWS　　CONSTANTLY 17A
PROSEUCHOMAI　　PRAY 721A
18 EUCHARISTEW 2　　GIVE THANKS 328C
THEL8MA ICγ　　WILL 355A
PAS 2Aβ　　EVERY RESPECT 638A
19 M8 AIII3B　　NOT 518D
PNEUMA 6D　　SPIRIT 684A
SBENNUMI 2　　EXTINGUISH 752D
20 EXOUTHENEW 2　　REJECT 277B
PNEUMA 6D　　SPIRIT 684A
PROPH8TEIA 2　　PROPHECY 730A
PROPH8TEIA 3B　　PROPHECY 730B
21 DOKIMAZW I　　EXAMINE 201C
KALOS 2Cβ　　GOOD 401C
KATECHW IBβ　　HOLD FAST 424A
PAS 2A6　　EVERYTHING 638C
22 APECHW 3　　KEEP AWAY 84C
EIDOS 2　　FORM 220B
PON8ROS 2C　　WICKED 698A
23 HAGIAZW 4　　PURIFY 9A
HAGIAZW 2　　CONSECRATE 9A
AMEMPTWS　　BLAMELESSLY 44C
EIR8N8 3　　PEACE 226D
THEOS 3E　　GOD 358B
KURIOS 2Cγ　　LORD 461B
HOLOKL8ROS　　WHOLE 567B
HOLOTEL8S　　QUITE COMPLETE 567D
PAROUSIA 2Bα　　COMING 635C
PNEUMA 3A　　SPIRIT 681B
SWMA IB　　BODY 806D
T8REW 2B　　KEEP 822C
PSUCH8 IE　　SOUL LIFE 902B
24 KALEW 2　　CALL 400C
PISTOS IAβ　　TRUSTWORTHY 670C
POIEW I2C　　DO 689B
25 PERI IF　　ABOUT 650C

25 PROSEUCHOMAI　　PRAY 721A
26 ASPAZOMAI IA　　GREET 116C
PAS IDα　　ALL 637C
PHIL8MA　　A KISS 867B
27 ANAGINWSKW 2　　READ 51C
ENORKIZW　　ADJURE 267A
EPISTOL8　　LETTER 300D
HORKIZW　　ADJURE 585A
28 KURIOS 2Cγ　　LORD 461B
META AIIICγ　　WITH 510A
CHARIS 2C　　FAVOR 885D

2 THESSALONIANS I

1 EKKL8SIA 4B　　CHURCH 240C
THESSALONIKEUS　　THESSALONIAN 360B
PAULOS　　PAUL 643A
SILOUANOS　　SILVANUS 758B
TIMOTHEOS　　TIMOTHY 826A
2 APO V4　　FROM 87C
EIR8N8 2　　PEACE 226D
THEOS 3D　　GOD 358B
KURIOS 2Cγ　　LORD 461A
PAT8R 3Cβ　　FATHER 641C
CHARIS 2C　　FAVOR 885D
3 AGAP8 IIBβ　　LOVE 5D
AXIOS IC　　WORTHY 77C
HEKASTOS 2　　EACH 236A
EUCHARISTEW 2　　GIVE THANKS 328C
OPHEILW 2Aβ　　OWE 603D
PISTIS 2Dα　　FAITH 669B
PLEONAZW IA　　INCREASE 673B
HUPERAUXANW　　847D
　　INCREASE ABUNDANTLY
4 ANECHW IB　　ENDURE 65B
DIWGMOS　　PERSECUTION 200A
EGKAUCHAOMAI　　BOAST 215A
EKKL8SIA 4Eα　　CHURCH 240D
ENECHW 2　　BE LOADED DOWN 265B
THLIPSIS I　　TRIBULATION 362D
HOS,H8,HO I4A　　(REL PRON) 587D
PISTIS IA　　FAITH 668B
HUPER IF　　IN BEHALF OF 847A
HUPOMON8 I　　PATIENCE 854A
HWSTE 2Aβ　　THEREFORE 908C
5 BASILEIA 3G　　KINGDOM 135A
DIKAIOKRISIA　　194C
　　RIGHTEOUS JUDGMENT
DIKAIOS 4　　RIGHTEOUS 195B
ENDEIGMA　　EVIDENCE 262A
KATAXIOW I　　CONSIDER WORTHY 416C
KRISIS IAα　　JUDGING 453C
PASCHW 3Aβ　　SUFFER 639C
HUPER ID　　IN BEHALF OF 846D
6 ANTAPODIDWMI 2　　REPAY 72B
DIKAIOS 5　　RIGHTEOUS 195B
EI VIII　　IF 219B
THLIBW 3　　OPPRESS 362C
THLIPSIS I　　TRIBULATION 362D
PARA II2B　　BESIDE 615C
7 AGGELOS 2A　　ANGEL 7D
ANESIS 2　　REST 64D
APOKALUPSIS 3　　REVELATION 92A

7	DUNAMIS I	POWER 206D	I	PAROUSIA 2Bα	COMING 635C
	EN II2	WHILE 259D		HUPER IF	IN BEHALF OF 847A
	THLIBW 3	OPPRESS 362C	2	DIA AIIIIB	BY MEANS OF 179B
	KURIOS 2Cɣ	LORD 461A		ENIST8MI I	BE PRESENT 266B
	META AIIIA	WITH 509D		EPISTOL8	LETTER 300D
	META AII4	WITH 510D		H8MERA 3Bβ	DAY 347D
	OURANOS 2B	HEAVEN 599C		THROEW	BE DISTURBED 364C
8	DIDWMI IBβ	GIVE 192B		LOGOS IAα	WORD 478B
	EKDIK8SIS	VENGEANCE 238B		M8TE	AND NOT 521D
	EUAGGELION 2Bα	GOSPEL 318B		NOUS I	THE UNDERSTANDING 546D
	THEOS 3B	GOD 357D		HO,H8,TO IIII	THE 555A
	KURIOS 2Cɣ	LORD 461B		HOTI IDβ	THAT 593C
	OIDA 2	KNOW 558D		PARA I3C	FROM 615A
	PUR IB	FIRE 737C		PNEUMA 7	SPIRIT 684B
	HUPAKOUW I	LISTEN TO 845B		SALEUW 2	SHAKE 748A
	PHLOX	FLAME 870A		TACHEWS IB	QUICKLY 814B
9	AIWNIOS 3	ETERNAL 28A	2A	HWS III3	SO 906D
	APO III	AWAY FROM 86D	3	ANTHRWPOS 2A	MAN 67D
	DIK8 I	PENALTY 197C		ANOMIA I	LAWLESSNESS 71B
	DOXA IA	BRIGHTNESS 202C		ANOMIA 2	LAWLESSNESS 71B
	ISCHUS	STRENGTH 384C		APOKALUPTW 4	REVEAL 91D
	OLETHROS	DESTRUCTION 566A		APOSTASIA	REBELLION 97D
	OLETHRIOS	DESTRUCTIVE 566A		APWLEIA 2	DESTRUCTION 103B
	PROSWPON ICα	FACE 728C		EXAPATAW	DECEIVE 272C
	TINW	PAY 826C		ERCHOMAI I2B	COME 311C
10	HAGIOS 2Dα	THE HOLY ONES 10A		KATA II5Bα	ACCORDING TO 408C
	EKEINOS 2Bβ	THAT 239B		M8 AIII5A	NOT 518D
	ENDOXAZOMAI	HONORED 262D		M8DEIS I	NO 520A
	EPI IIIIAς	ON 288C		TROPOS I	MANNER 835A
	ERCHOMAI IIAη	COME 311A		HUIOS IC6	SON 842A
	H8MERA 38β	DAY 348A	4	ANTIKEIMAI	BE OPPOSED 73D
	THAUMAZW IBβ	WONDER 353A		APODEIKNUMI I	MAKE 89A
	MARTURION IB	TESTIMONY 495A		EIS IAα	INTO 227B
	PAS IDβ	ALL 637D		EPI IIIIBα	OVER 288D
10A	PISTEUW 2B	BELIEVE 667C		THEOS I	GOD 357B
10B	PISTEUW IAα	BELIEVE 666A		KATHIZW 2Aα	SIT DOWN 390D
11	AGATHWSUN8	GOODNESS 3D		NAOS IA	TEMPLE 535B
	AXIOW IB	CONSIDER WORTHY 78A		PAS IAα	EVERY EACH 636C
	DUNAMIS I	POWER 206D		SEBASMA	OBJECT OF WORSHIP 753A
	EIS 4F	(PURPOSE) 228D		HUPERAIRW	RISE UP 847C
	EN III2	BY 260B		HWSTE 2Aβ	THEREFORE 908C
	ERGON IB	MANIFESTATION 307D	5	ETI IAβ	STILL 315D
	EUDOKIA I	GOOD WILL 319D		LEGW IIA	SAY 469B
	EUDOKIA 3	WISH 320A		MN8MONEUW IC	REMEMBER 527A
	KL8SIS I	CALL 436D		PROS IIII7	TOWARD 718A
	HOS,H8,HO IIIB	(REL PRON) 589A	6	APOKALUPTW 4	REVEAL 91D
	PERI IF	ABOUT 650C		KAIROS 3	TIME 396A
	PISTIS 2Dα	FAITH 669B		KATECHW IAɣ	HOLD BACK 423D
	PISTIS 2Dα	FAITH 669C	7	ANOMIA I	LAWLESSNESS 71B
	PL8ROW 3	MAKE FULL 677B		ARTI 3	NOW 109D
	PROSEUCHOMAI	PRAY 721A		GINOMAI I4Cα	COME, GO 159A
11F	HOPWS 2Aα	IN ORDER THAT 580C		ENERGEW IB	WORK 265A
12	ENDOXAZOMAI	HONORED 262D		HEWS IIB	UNTIL 334D
	ONOMA I4B	NAME 575A		MESOS 2	THE MIDDLE 509A
	CHARIS 2A	FAVOR 885C		MUST8RION 2	MYSTERY 532B
12B	KURIOS 2Cɣ	LORD 461A	8	ANAIREW IA	DO AWAY WITH 54C
13	PARA I3C	FROM 615A		ANALISKW	CONSUME 56D
				ANOMOS 4	LAWLESS 71D
				APOKALUPTW 4	REVEAL 91D
				EPIPHANEIA I	APPEARING 304B
				KATARGEW 2	ABOLISH 418B
				KURIOS 2Cɣ	LORD 461A
				PAROUSIA 2Bα	COMING 635C

2 THESSALONIANS 2

I	EPISUNAGWG8 2	MEETING 301D
	ERWTAW 2	ASK 312A
	KURIOS 2Cɣ	LORD 461B

8	PNEUMA 13	BREATH	680D
	STOMA 1A	MOUTH	777B
	TOTE 2	AT THAT TIME	831D
9	DUNAMIS 4	MIRACLE	207B
	ENERGEIA 1	WORKING	264C
	KATA II15A6	ACCORDING TO	408B
	PAROUSIA 2By	COMING	635D
	SATAN	ADVERSARY	752B
	S8MEION 2B	SIGN	755D
	PSEUDOS	LIE	900C
10	AGAP8 II8α	LOVE	5D
	ADIKIA 2	UNRIGHTEOUSNESS	17D
	AL8THEIA 2B	TRUTH	35C
	ANTI 3	FOR	73B
	APAT8 1	DECEPTION	81C
	APOLLUMI 2Aα	PERISH	94D
	DECHOMAI 3B	ACCEPT	176C
	HOS,H8,HO I11A	(REL PRON)	589A
	PLAN8	WANDERING	671D
	SWZW 2B	SAVE	806B
10F	EIS 4E	SO THAT	228D
11	ENERGEIA 1	WORKING	264C
	PEMPW 1	SEND	647D
	PISTEUW 1A6	BELIEVE	666B
	PLAN8	WANDERING	671D
	PSEUDOS	LIE	900C
12	ADIKIA 2	UNRIGHTEOUSNESS	17D
	AL8THEIA 2B	TRUTH	35B
	EUDOKEW 2B	WELL PLEASED	319C
	KRINW 4B«	JUDGE	453A
	M8 AII2A	NOT	518B
	PISTEUW 1A6	BELIEVE	666B
	PSEUDOS	LIE	900C
13	AGAPAW 1D	LOVE	4D
	HAGIASMOS	HOLINESS	9B
	HAIREW 2	CHOOSE	23C
	AL8THEIA 2B	TRUTH	35B
	APARCH8 2A	FIRST FRUITS	80D
	ARCH8 1C	BEGINNING	111D
	EIS 4D	FOR	228C
	EN I111A	BY	260B
	EUCHARISTEW 2	GIVE THANKS	328C
	KURIOS 2Cy	LORD	461A
	OPHEILW 2A8	OWE	603D
	PISTIS 2C	FAITH	669A
	PNEUMA 508	SPIRIT	683B
	SWT8RIA 2	DELIVERANCE	809B
14	EUAGGELION 2B8	GOSPEL	318C
	KALEW 2	CALL	400C
	KURIOS 2Cy	LORD	461B
	PERIPOI8SIS 2	KEEPING SAFE	656A
15	ARA 4	THEN	103C
	DIA AIII1B	BY MEANS OF	179A
	DIA AIII1B	BY MEANS OF	179B
	DIDASKW 2C	TEACH	191A
	EPISTOL8	LETTER	300D
	KRATEW 2E8	HOLD	449D
	LOGOS 1Aα	WORD	478B
	PARADOSIS 2	TRADITION	621B
	ST8KW 2	STAND	775D
16	AGATHOS I88	GOOD	3B
	AGAPAW I8«	LOVE	4D
	AIWNIOS 3	ETERNAL	28A
16	ELPIS 2B	HOPE	252C
	EN III2	BY	260C
	KURIOS 2Cy	LORD	461B
	PARAKL8SIS 3	COMFORT	623C
	PAT8R 3C8	FATHER	641C
	CHARIS 2A	FAVOR	885C
17	AGATHOS I88	GOOD	3B
	ERGON 1A	DEED	307D
	LOGOS 1Aα	WORD	478A
	PARAKALEW 4	IMPLORE	623A
	PAS 1A8	EVERY EACH	636D
	ST8RIZW 2	ESTABLISH	775D

2 THESSALONIANS 3

1	DOXAZW 2	GLORIFY	203D
	KURIOS 2Cy	LORD	460D
	LOGOS 1B8	WORD	479B
	LOIPOS 3B	THE REST	481B
	PERI 1F	ABOUT	650C
	PROS III7	TOWARD	718A
	PROSEUCHOMAI	PRAY	721A
	TRECHW 2B	RUN	833D
2	ATOPOS 2	IMPROPER	120A
	PISTIS 2Dα	FAITH	669B
	PON8ROS 18α	WICKED	697C
	RUOMAI	SAVE	745A
3	KURIOS 2A	LORD	460B
	PISTOS 1A8	TRUSTWORTHY	670D
	PON8ROS 2B	WICKED	698A
	ST8RIZW 2	ESTABLISH	775D
	PHULASSW 1C	WATCH	876B
4	EN I5D	IN	259B
	EPI IIII8«	TOWARD	289A
	KURIOS 2Cy	LORD	461A
	PARAGGELLW	GIVE ORDERS	618C
	PEITHW 2A	CONVINCE	645B
5	AGAP8 II8y	LOVE	5D
	KATEUTHUNW	LEAD	423C
	HUPOMON8 2	PATIENCE	854B
	HUPOMON8 1	PATIENCE	854B
	CHRISTOS 1	ANOINTED ONE	895C
6	ATAKTWS 2	LIVE IN IDLENESS	119B
	KURIOS 2Cy	LORD	461A
	ONOMA 14Cy	NAME	576A
	PARA 13B	FROM	614D
	PARAGGELLW	GIVE ORDERS	618C
	PARADOSIS 2	TRADITION	621B
	PARALAMBANW 2By	TAKE	625B
	PERIPATEW 2Aα	GO ABOUT	655B
	STELLW 1	KEEP AWAY	773C
7	ASAKTEW	BE IDLE	119B
	MIMEOMAI	IMITATE	523D
	OIDA 1F	KNOW	558C
	PWS 2A	HOW	739D
8	ARTOS 2	FOOD	110B
	DWREAN 1	GRATIS	209D
	EPIBAREW	BURDEN	290B
	ERGAZOMAI 1	WORK	306D
	ESTHIW 1A	EAT	312D
	H8MERA 1A	DAY	346C
	KOPOS 2	WORK	444C
	M8 AII1E	NOT	518A

8	MOCHTHOS	LABOR	530C
	NUX 1B	NIGHT	548D
	PARA 13B	FROM	615A
	PROS III3A	TOWARD	717A
9	EXOUSIA 1	RIGHT	277C
	MIMEOMAI	IMITATE	523D
	HOTI 1C	THAT	593A
	TUPOS 5B	MARK	837D
10	ERGAZOMAI 1	WORK	307A
	THELW 2	WISH	355D
	M8DE 1C	AND NOT	519D
	HOTI 2	THAT	593D
	OU 2D	NO	594C
	PARAGGELLW	GIVE ORDERS	618C
	PROS III7	TOWARD	718A
11	ATAKTWS 2	LIVE IN IDLENESS	119B
	ERGAZOMAI 2A	WORK	307A
	PERIERGAZOMAI	BE A BUSYBODY	652C
	PERIPATEW 2Aα	GO ABOUT	655B
	TIS, TI 1Aα	ANY ONE	827C
12	ARTOS 2	FOOD	110C
	ERGAZOMAI 1	WORK	307A
	ESTHIW 1A	EAT	312D
	H8SUCHIA 1	QUIETNESS	350A
	PARAGGELLW	GIVE ORDERS	618C
	PARAKALEW 2	APPEAL TO	622C
13	EGKAKEW 1	BECOME WEARY	214C
	EKKAKEW	LOSE HEART	240A
	KALOPOIEW	DO WHAT IS RIGHT	401A
14	ENTREPW 2A	BE ASHAMED	269B
	EPISTOL8	LETTER	300D
	OU 2D	NO	594C
	S8MEIOW 2	MARK	756B
	SUNANAMEIGNUMI	MINGLE	792A
	HUPAKOUW 1	LISTEN TO	845B
15	ECHTHROS 2Bα	THE ENEMY	331D
	H8GEOMAI 2	CONSIDER	344C
	NOUTHETEW	ADMONISH	546B
15A	HWS IIIIC	SO	906D
15B	HWS IIIIC	SO	906D
16	DIA AIIIA	THROUGH	178D
	DIDWMI	GIVE	191D
	EIR8N8 2	PEACE	226D
	EIR8N8 3	PEACE	226D
	KURIOS 2D	LORD	461B
	META AIIICγ	WITH	510A
	TOPOS 1A	PLACE	830A
	TROPOS 1	MANNER	835A
16C	PAS 1Eα	ALL	637D
17	ASPASMOS 2	GREETING	116D
	GRAPHW 1	WRITE	165C
	EMOS 1Aα	MY	255A
	EPISTOL8	LETTER	300D
	PAULOS	PAUL	643A
	S8MEION 1	SIGN	755B
	CHEIR 1	HAND	888B
18	KURIOS 2Cγ	LORD	461B
	META AIIICγ	WITH	510A
	PAS 1Eα	ALL	637D
	CHARIS 2C	FAVOR	885D

| TIMOTHY |

1	APOSTOLOS 3	APOSTLES	99B
	ELPIS 3	HOPE	252D
	EPAGGELIA 2A	PROMISE	280B
	EPITAG8	COMMAND	302A
	KATA II5A6	ACCORDING TO	408B
	PAULOS	PAUL	643A
	SWT8R 1	SAVIOR	808C
2	APO V4	FROM	87C
	GN8SIOS 1	LEGITIMATE	162A
	EIR8N8 2	PEACE	226D
	ELEOS 2A	MERCY	249D
	KURIOS 2Cγ	LORD	461B
	PAT8R 3Cβ	FATHER	641C
	PISTIS 2Dα	FAITH	669B
	TEKNON 2B	CHILD	816B
	TIMOTHEOS	TIMOTHY	826A
	CHARIS 2C	FAVOR	885D
3	HETERODIDASKALEW		314D

DIFFERENT DOCTRINE

	EPHESOS	EPHESUS	330C
	KATHWS 1	JUST AS	392B
	MAKEDONIA	MACEDONIA	488B
	M8 AIIIBβ	NOT	518A
	PARAGGELLW	GIVE ORDERS	618C
	PROSMENW 2	REMAIN	724D
	TIS, TI 1Aβ	ANY ONE	827D
4	APERANTOS	ENDLESS	83C
	GENEALOGIA	GENEALOGY	153C
	EKZ8T8SIS	USELESS SPECULATION	239D
	MALLON 3C	RATHER	490D
	M8DE 1B	AND NOT	519D
	OIKODOMIA	BUILDING	562A
	OIKONOMIA 3	TRAINING	562C
	HOSTIS 2B	WHOEVER	591A
	PARECHW 1C	CAUSE	632A
	PISTIS 2Dα	FAITH	669B
	PROSECHW 1Aβ		721C

PAY ATTENTION TO

5	AGATHOS 18β	GOOD	3B
	AGAP8 IIA	LOVE	5C
	ANUPOKRITOS	GENUINE	76A
	EK 3Gγ	BY	235A
	KATHAROS 3B	CLEAN	389A
	KARDIA 1Bα	HEART	404B
	PISTIS 2Dα	FAITH	669B
	SUNEID8SIS 2	CONSCIOUSNESS	794B
	TELOS 1C	END	819B
6	ASTOCHEW	MISS THE MARK	117D
	EKTREPW	TURN AWAY	245D
	MATAIOLOGIA	FRUITLESS TALK	496C
7	DIABEBAIOOMAI		180D

SPEAK CONFIDENTLY

	LEGW IIA	SAY	469B
	M8TE	AND NOT	521D
	NOMODIDASKALOS		543D

TEACHER OF THE LAW

	HOS,H8,HO 19A	(REL PRON)	588D
	TIS, TI 1Bζ	WHICH	827B
8	KALOS 2B	GOOD	401C
	NOMIMWS		543D

ACCORDING TO THE RULES

8	NOMOS 3	LAW 544C
	OIDA IE	KNOW 558C
	TIS, TI IAv	ANY ONE 827D
	CHRAOMAI	USE 892C
	CHRAOMAI IA	USE 892C
9	HAMARTWLOS 2	SINNER 43C
	ANDROPHONOS	MURDERER 63C
	ANOMOS 3	LAWLESS 71C
	ANOSIOS I	UNHOLY 71D
	ANUPOTAKTOS 2	UNDISCIPLINED 76A
	ASEB8S I	GODLESS 114B
	BEB8LOS 2	PROFANE 138B
	DIKAIOS IA	UPRIGHT 194C
	DIKAIOS IB	UPRIGHT 194D
	KEIMAI 2B	EXIST 428A
	M8TRALWAS	A MATRICIDE 522B
	NOMOS 3	LAW 544C
	OIDA IE	KNOW 558C
	HOUTOS I8ß	THIS 601C
	PATROLWAS	A PARRICIDE 642C
10	ANDRAPODIST8S	SLAVE DEALER 63B
	ANTIKEIMAI	BE OPPOSED 73D
	ARSENOKOIT8S	109B
	A MALE HOMOSEXUAL	
	DIDASKALIA 2	TEACHING 190C
	EPIORKOS	PERJURED 296D
	HETEROS I8α	ANOTHER 315B
	PORNOS	FORNICATOR 700B
	*HUGIAINW 2	BE HEALTHY 840A
	PSEUST8S	LIAR 900D
11	EUAGGELION 2Bα	GOSPEL 318B
	MAKARIOS 2	BLESSED 488A
	PISTEUW 3	BELIEVE 667D
12	DIAKONIA 3	SERVICE 183B
	ENDUNAMOW I	STRENGTHEN 263A
	ECHW I2E8	HAVE 333B
	H8GEOMAI 2	CONSIDER 344B
	KURIOS 2Cv	LORD 461B
	PISTOS IAø	TRUSTWORTHY 670B
	TITH8MI II2C	APPOINT 824B
	CHARIS 5	FAVOR 886C
13	AGNOEW I	BE IGNORANT 11B
	APISTIA 2B	UNBELIEF 85A
	BLASPH8MOS	SLANDEROUS 142D
	DIWKT8S	PERSECUTOR 200A
	ELEEW	HAVE MERCY 249B
	PROTEROS I8α	EARLIER 729B
	PROTEROS I8ß	EARLIER 729C
	HUBRIST8S	INSOLENT MAN 839D
14	AGAP8 IIA	LOVE 5C
	KURIOS 2A	LORD 460B
	META AII6	WITH 510D
	PISTIS 2Dv	FAITH 669C
	HUPERPLEONAZW	BE ABUNDANT 849D
	CHARIS 2A	FAVOR 885C
15	HAMARTWLOS 2	SINNER 43C
	ANTHRWPINOS I	HUMAN 67A
	AXIOS IB	WORTHY 77C
	APODOCH8	ACCEPTANCE 90C
	ERCHOMAI IIAη	COME 311A
	KOSMOS 4C	WORLD 447B
	LOGOS I8ß	WORD 479C
	PISTOS I8	TRUSTWORTHY 670D

15	PRWTOS ICß	FIRST 733C
	SWZW 2Aα	SAVE 806A
16	DIA BII2	FOR THIS REASON 180B
	ELEEW	HAVE MERCY 249B
	ENDEIKNUMI I	DEMONSTRATE 262A
	ZW8 2Bß	LIFE 341C
	HINA I5	IN ORDER THAT 378A
	MAKROTHUMIA 2B8	PATIENCE 489C
	MELLW ICß	BE ABOUT TO 502B
	HOUTOS I8ß	THIS 601C
	PISTEUW 2Av	BELIEVE 667B
	PRWTOS IA	FIRST 733A
	HUPOTUPWSIS	MODEL 856A
17	AIWN IB	TIME 26D
	AIWN 3	THE WORLD 27C
	AM8N I	AMEN 45A
	APHTHARTOS	IMPERISHABLE 125A
	BASILEUS 2B	KING 136A
	THEOS 3I	GOD 358C
	MONOS IA6	ONLY 529C
	SOPHOS 4	LEARNED 767D
	TIM8 2B	HONOR 825C
18	EPI IIIIBζ	ON 289B
	KALOS 2Cß	GOOD 401C
	HOUTOS 2A	THIS 601D
	PANOPLIA 2	FULL ARMOR 612D
	PARAGGELIA	ORDER 618B
	PARATITH8MI 2Bα	628C
	PLACE BESIDE	
	PROAGW 2B	LEAD 709A
	PROPH8TEIA 3B	PROPHECY 730B
	STRATEIA	CAMPAIGN 777D
	STRATEUW 2	778A
	DO MILITARY SERVICE	
	TEKNON 2B	CHILD 816B
	TIMOTHEOS	TIMOTHY 826A
19	AGATHOS I8ß	GOOD 3B
	APWTHEW 2	REJECT 102D
	ECHW I2E8	HAVE 333A
	ECHW I2E8	HAVE 333B
	NAUAGEW 2	SUFFER SHIPWRECK 536A
	PERI 2D	ABOUT 651A
	PISTIS 3	FAITH 669D
	SUNEID8SIS 2	CONSCIOUSNESS 794B
	TIS, TI IA8	ANY ONE 827D
19A	PISTIS 2Dα	FAITH 669B
19B	PISTIS 2Dα	FAITH 669B
20	ALEXANDROS 4	ALEXANDER 35A
	BLASPH8MEW 2Bα	BLASPHEME 142A
	EIMI IV2	TO BE 225A
	PAIDEUW 2Bα	INSTRUCT 609A
	PARADIDWMI IB	GIVE OVER 620C
	SATAN	ADVERSARY 752C
	HUMENAIOS	HYMENAEUS 843D

I TIMOTHY 2

I	*DE8SIS	PRAYER 171A
	ENTEUXIS 2A	PRAYER 268B
	EUCHARISTIA 2	THANKFULNESS 329A
	PARAKALEW 2	APPEAL TO 622C
	PAS 2A6	EVERYTHING 638C
	POIEW III	DO 689C

I	PROSEUCH8 I	PRAYER	720B	
	PRWTOS 2C	FIRST	734A	
IF	DE8SIS	PRAYER	171A	
IF	HUPER IAα	IN BEHALF OF	846B	
2	BASILEUS I	KING	135D	
	BIOS I	LIFE	141B	
	DIAGW	SPEND ONES LIFE	181D	
	EN I4D	IN	258C	
	EUSEBEIA	GODLINESS	326B	
	8REMOS	TRANQUIL	349A	
	H8SUCHIOS	QUIET	350A	
	SEMNOT8S I	REVERENCE	754C	
	HUPEROCH8 2	PROMINENCE	849C	
2B	PAS IA6	ALL	637A	
3	APODEKTOS	ACCEPTABLE	89B	
	ENWPION 3	BEFORE	270B	
	KALOS 2B	GOOD	401C	
	SWT8R I	SAVIOR	808C	
4	AL8THEIA 2B	TRUTH	35C	
	*EPIGNWSIS	KNOWLEDGE	291B	
	ERCHOMAI I2C	COME	311C	
	PAS IB	ALL	637A	
	SWZW 2B	SAVE	806B	
5	ANTHRWPOS IAβ	MAN	67C	
	ANTHRWPOS 2D	MAN	68A	
	GAR 4	INDEED	151D	
	MESIT8S	MEDIATOR	508A	
6	ANTILUTRON	RANSOM	74C	
	DIDWMI 6	GIVE	192D	
	IDIOS IB	ONES OWN	370B	
	KAIROS 3	TIME	396A	
	MARTURION IA	TESTIMONY	495A	
	POLUS I24α	MANY	694D	
	HUPER IAε	IN BEHALF OF	846C	
7	AL8THEIA 2A	TRUTH	35B	
	APOSTOLOS 3	APOSTLES	99B	
	K8RUX 2	HERALD	432B	
	LEGW IIA	SAY	469B	
	TITH8MI I2Aα	MAKE	824A	
	PSEUDOMAI I	LIE	900A	
8	BOULOMAI 2A6	DESIRE	145D	
	DIALOGISMOS 2	DOUBT	185B	
	EPAIRW I	LIFT UP	281C	
	ORG8 I	ANGER	582C	
	HOSIOS	PIOUS	589B	
	HOSIOS IA	PIOUS	589C	
	CHWRIS 2Bβ	APART	899A	
	HWSAUTWS	SIMILARLY	907D	
9	AIDWS I	MODESTY	21D	
	HIMATISMOS	CLOTHING	377B	
	KATASTOL8	DEPORTMENT	420A	
	KOSMEW 2Aα	DECORATE	445D	
	KOSMIOS 2	RESPECTABLE	446B	
	KOSMIWS	MODESTLY	446B	
	MARGARIT8S I	PEARL	492C	
	META AIIII	WITH	511A	
	PLEGMA	WOVEN	673A	
	POLUTEL8S	COSTLY	696C	
	SWPHROSUN8 2	REASONABLENESS	810A	
	CHRUSION	GOLD	896D	
	CHRUSOS	GOLD	897A	
	HWSAUTWS	SIMILARLY	907D	
10	AGATHOS IBβ	GOOD	3B	

10	EPAGGELLOMAI 2	ANNOUNCE	280D	
	ERGON ICβ	DEED	308A	
	THEOSEBEIA	REVERENCE FOR GOD	358D	
	PREPW	BE FITTING	706A	
11	MANTHANW I	LEARN	491B	
	PAS IA6	ALL	637A	
	HUPOTAG8	SUBJECTION	855C	
IIF	GUN8 I	WOMAN	167B	
IIF	H8SUCHIA 2	SILENCE	350A	
12	AUTHENTEW	HAVE AUTHORITY	120C	
	EPITREPW I	ALLOW	303C	
13	ADAM	ADAM	15B	
	EITA I	THEN	233A	
	HEUA	EVE	317C	
	PLASSW IBα	FORM	672C	
	PRWTOS IA	FIRST	733A	
14	ADAM	ADAM	15B	
	APATAW I	DECEIVE	81B	
	EXAPATAW	DECEIVE	272C	
	PARABASIS	OVERSTEPPING	617A	
15	AGAP8 IIA	LOVE	5C	
	HAGIASMOS	HOLINESS	9B	
	DIA AIIIIC	THROUGH	179B	
	EN I4D	IN	258C	
	MENW IAβ	REMAIN	505A	
	META AII6	WITH	510D	
	PISTIS 2Dγ	FAITH	669C	
	SWZW 2B	SAVE	806B	
	TEKNOGONIA		815D	

BEARING OF CHILDREN

I TIMOTHY 3

I	ANTHRWPINOS I	HUMAN	67A	
	EI VII		219B	
	EPITHUMEW	DESIRE	293A	
	ERGON 2	WORK	308C	
	ERGON 4	THING	308C	
	KALOS 2Cβ	GOOD	401C	
	LOGOS IBβ	WORD	479C	
	OREGW	ASPIRE TO	583C	
	PISTOS IB	TRUSTWORTHY	670D	
2	ANEPIL8MPTOS	IRREPROACHABLE	64C	
	AN8R I	MAN	65D	
	DIDAKTIKOS		190B	

SKILFUL IN TEACHING

	HEIS 2B	ONE	230C	
	EPISKOPOS 2	OVERSEER	299C	
	KOSMIOS I	RESPECTABLE	446B	
	N8PHALIOS	TEMPERATE	540D	
	SWPHRWN	PRUDENT	810C	
	PHILOXENOS	HOSPITABLE	868C	
3	AMACHOS	PEACEABLE	44A	
	APHILARGUROS	NOT GREEDY	126B	
	EPIEIK8S	GENTLE	292C	
	PAROINOS	DRUNKEN	634D	
	PL8KT8S	BULLY	675A	
4	ECHW I2Bα	HAVE	332C	
	KALWS I	WELL	402A	
	OIKOS 2	HOUSEHOLD	563C	
	PAS IA6	ALL	637A	
	SEMNOT8S I	REVERENCE	754C	
	TEKNON IAα	CHILD	816A	

4	HUPOTAG8	SUBJECTION	855C
4F	IDIOS IB	ONES OWN	370B
4F	OIKOS 2	HOUSEHOLD	563D
4F	PROIST8MI I	RULE	713D
5	EI VII		219B
	EKKL8SIA 4Eα	CHURCH	240D
	EPIMELEOMAI	CARE FOR	296A
	OIDA 3	KNOW	558D
	PWS ID	HOW	739D
6	EMPIPTW 2	FALL	255D
	KRIMA 4B	VERDICT	451D
	NEOPHUTOS	NEWLY CONVERTED	538C
	TUPHOW I	CONCEITED	838D
6F	EIS 4A	INTO	228B
7	APO V4	FROM	87C
	DIABOLOS 2	THE SLANDERER	181A
	EMPIPTW 2	FALL	255D
	EXWTHEN 18β	OUTSIDE	279B
	KALOS 2B	GOOD	401B
	MARTURIA 2C	TESTIMONY	494C
	ONEIDISMOS	REPROACH	573B
	PAGIS 2	TRAP	607B
	PRESBUTEROS 28γ	OLDER	707C
8	AISCHROKERD8S		24C
		FOND OF DISHONEST GAIN	
	DIAKONOS IC	DEACON	183D
	DILOGOS	INSINCERE	197D
	OINOS I	WINE	565A
	PROSECHW IC	PAY ATTENTION TO	721D
	SEMNOS IA	NOBLE	754B
	HWSAUTWS	SIMILARLY	907D
9	ECHW IICβ	KEEP	332B
	KATHAROS 3B	CLEAN	389A
	MUST8RION 2	MYSTERY	532B
	PISTIS 2Dα	FAITH	669B
	SUNEID8SIS 2	CONSCIOUSNESS	794B
10	ANEGKL8TOS	BLAMELESS	63C
	DE 4B	BUT, AND	170D
	DIAKONEW 5	HELP	183B
	DOKIMAZW I	EXAMINE	201C
	EITA I	THEN	233A
	PRWTOS 2A	FIRST	733D
11	DIABOLOS I	SLANDEROUS	181A
	N8PHALIOS	TEMPERATE	540D
	PAS 2A6	IN ALL RESPECTS	638C
	PISTIS 14α	TRUSTWORTHY	670C
	SEMNOS IA	NOBLE	754B
	HWSAUTWS	SIMILARLY	907D
12	AN8R I	MAN	65D
	DIAKONOS IC	DEACON	183D
	HEIS 2B	ONE	230C
	IDIOS IB	ONES OWN	370B
	KALWS I	WELL	402A
	OIKOS 2	HOUSEHOLD	563D
	OIKOS 2	HOUSEHOLD	563D
	PROIST8MI I	RULE	713D
	TEKNON I4α	CHILD	816A
13	BATHMOS	RANK	129C
	DIAKONEW 5	HELP	183B
	KALOS 2Cβ	GOOD	401C
	KALWS I	WELL	402B
	PARR8SIA 3B	CONFIDENCE	636B
	PERIPOIEW 2	SAVE	655D

13	PISTIS 2Bβ	FAITH	669A
	POLUS IIBβ	MANY	694D
14	ELPIZW 2	HOPE	252A
	TACHEWS 2B	QUICKLY	814C
	TACHOS	SPEED	814D
15	ANASTREPHW 2Bβ	LIVE	61A
	BRADUNW	DELAY	146B
	HDRAIWMA	FOUNDATION	217A
	EKKL8SIA 4Eα	CHURCH	240D
	EN IIA	IN	257C
	ZAW IAc	LIVE	336D
	OIDA IF	KNOW	558C
	OIKOS I8α	HOUSE	563C
	STULOS	PILLAR	779C
16	AGGELOS 2A	ANGEL	7C
	ANALAMBANW I	TAKE UP	56B
	DIKAIOW 3D	MAKE FREE	197A
	EN I4B	IN	258B
	EUSEBEIA	GODLINESS	326C
	K8RUSSW 2Bβ	ANNOUNCE	432C
	KOSMOS 4C	WORLD	447B
	MEGAS 2Bβ	GREAT	499C
	MUST8RION 2	MYSTERY	532B
	HOMOLOGOUMENWS	CONFESSEDLY	572A
	HORAW IA6	SEE	582A
	PISTEUW 2Aα	BELIEVE	667A
	PNEUMA 2	SPIRIT	681B
	SARX 2	BODY	751A
	PHANEROW 2Bβ	REVEAL	860D
16A	DIKAIOW 3C	MAKE FREE	197A

I TIMOTHY 4

I	APHIST8MI 2A	FALL AWAY	126C
	DAIMONION 2	DEMON	168C
	DIDASKALIA 2	TEACHING	190C
	KAIROS 4	TIME	396B
	PISTIS 2Dα	FAITH	669B
	PISTIS 3	FAITH	669D
	PLANOS I	DECEITFUL	672A
	PROSECHW IAα		721C
		PAY ATTENTION TO	
	R8TWS	EXPRESSLY	743B
	HUSTEROS IB	THE LATTER	857B
IA	PNEUMA 5Dα	SPIRIT	683A
2	IDIOS IB	ONES OWN	370B
	KAUST8RIAZW	SEAR	426D
	SUNEID8SIS 2	CONSCIOUSNESS	794B
	HUPOKRISIS	HYPOCRISY	852D
	PSEUDOLOGOS	LIAR	899D
3	AL8THEIA 2B	TRUTH	35C
	APECHW 3	KEEP AWAY	84C
	BRWMA I	FOOD	147C
	GAMEW 2	MARRY	150B
	EPIGINWSKW 2A	KNOW	291A
	KTIZW	CREATE	456C
	KWLUW 2	HINDER	462C
	METAL8MPSIS	RECEIVE	512D
	HOS,H8,HO I4E	(REL PRON)	588B
	PISTOS 2	TRUSTWORTHY	671A
3F	EUCHARISTIA 2	THANKFULNESS	329A
3F	META AIIIi	WITH	511A
4	APOBL8TOS	REJECTED	88C

4	KALOS 2Cβ	GOOD 401C	12	PISTOS 2	TRUSTWORTHY 671A
	KTISMA	CREATURE 457B		SU 3	YOU 780A
	LAMBANW IA	TAKE 465C		TUPOS 5B	MARK 837D
	LAMBANW 2	RECEIVE 466B	13	ANAGNWSIS I	READING 52C
5	HAGIAZW I	CONSECRATE 8D		DIDASKALIA I	TEACHING 190C
	ENTEUXIS 2C	PRAYER 268B		ERCHOMAI I2C	COME 311D
	LOGOS IBα	COMMAND 479B		HEWS IIC	UNTIL 334D
6	DIAKONOS IB	HELPER 183D		PARAKL8SIS I	ENCOURAGEMENT 623B
	DIAKONOS IA	SERVANT 183D		*PROSECHW IC	PAY ATTENTION TO 721D
	DIDASKALIA 2	TEACHING 190C	14	AMELEW	TO NEGLECT 44B
	ENTREPHW	BRING UP 269B		EN I5A	IN 258D
	LOGOS IBβ	WORD 479C		EPITHESIS	LAYING ON 293A
	HOS,H8,HO I4B	(REL PRON) 588A		META AIII2	WITH 511A
	PARAKOLOUTHEW 2	FOLLOW 624C		PRESBUTERION 2	706B
	PISTIS 20α	FAITH 669B			COUNCIL OF ELDERS
	PISTIS 3	FAITH 669D		PROPH8TEIA 3B	PROPHECY 730B
	HUPOTITH8MI 2	SUGGEST 856A		CHARISMA 2	A GIFT 887A
6A	KALOS 2Cα	GOOD 401C	15	EIMI III4	TO BE 224C
7	BEB8LOS I	PROFANE 138B		HINA IIC	IN ORDER THAT 377C
	GRAW08S	166B		MELETAW 2	PRACTISE 501C
	LIKE AN OLD WOMAN			PROKOP8	PROGRESS 714D
	GUMNAZW	TRAIN 166D		PHANEROS I	CLEAR 860A
	MUTHOS	FABLE 531A	16	DIDASKALIA I	TEACHING 190C
	PARAITEOMAI 2B	REFUSE 622A		EPECHW 2A	AIM AT 285B
	PROS III3B	TOWARD 717B		EPIMENW 2	CONTINUE 296B
7F	EUSEBEIA	GODLINESS 326B	16A	SWZW 2Aβ	SAVE 806B
8	GUMNASIA	TRAINING 166D	16B	SEAUTOU 3	YOURSELF 753A
	EPAGGELIA 2A	PROMISE 280B	16B	SWZW 2Aβ	SAVE 806B
	ZW8 IA	LIFE 340D			
	MELLW 2	IS DESTINED 502C		I TIMOTHY 5	
	NUN 3A	NOW 548A			
	OLIGOS 3B	LITTLE 566D	I	EPIPL8SSW	REBUKE 297D
	SWMATIKOS 2	BODILY 807D		NEOS 2Bβ	NOVICE 538A
8A	PROS III3C	TOWARD 717B		PARAKALEW 2	APPEAL TO 622B
8A	WPHELIMOS	USEFUL 909C		PARAKALEW 5	IMPLORE 623A
8B	PROS III3C	TOWARD 717B		PRESBUTEROS IA	OLDER 706B
8B	WPHELIMOS	USEFUL 909C	2	HAGNEIA	PURITY 10D
9	AXIOS IB	WORTHY 77C		ADELPH8 I	SISTER 15C
	APODOCH8	ACCEPTANCE 90C		NEOS 2Bβ	NOVICE 538B
	LOGOS IBβ	WORD 479C		PAS IA6	ALL 637A
	PAS IA6	ALL 637A		PRESBUTEROS IA	OLDER 706C
	PISTOS IB	TRUSTWORTHY 670D	3	ONTWS 2	REAL 577D
10	AGWNIZOMAI 2B	STRUGGLE I5A		TIMAW 2	HONOR 824D
	ELPIZW 3	HOPE 252B		CH8RA 2	THE WIDOW 890A
	EPI IIIBγ	ON 287A	3B	CH8RA	THE WIDOW 889D
	ZAW IAε	LIVE 336D	4	AMOIB8	RECOMPENSE 46A
	KOPIAW 2	BECOME WEARY 444B		APODEKTOS	ACCEPTABLE 89B
	MALISTA I	ABOVE ALL 490A		APODIDWMI 3	RECOMPENSE 90A
	ONEIDIZW I	REPROACH 573B		EI VII	219B
	PAS IB	ALL 637A		EKGONOS	GRANDCHILDREN 237C
	PISTOS 2	TRUSTWORTHY 671A		EUSEBEW 2	BE REVERENT 326C
	SWT8R I	SAVIOR 808C		ECHW I2Bα	HAVE 332C
11	DIDASKW I	TEACH 191A		IDIOS IB	ONES OWN 370B
	DIDASKW 2F	TEACH 191B		MANTHANW 4	LEARN 491C
	PARAGGELLW	GIVE ORDERS 618C		OIKOS 2	HOUSEHOLD 563D
12	AGAP8 IIA	LOVE 5C		PROGONOS	ANCESTORS 710D
	HAGNEIA	PURITY 10D		TEKNON IAα	CHILD 816A
	ANASTROPH8	CONDUCT 61B		CH8RA	THE WIDOW 889D
	KATAPHRONEW I	SCORN 421C	5	DE8SIS	PRAYER 171A
	LOGOS IAα	WORD 478B		ELPIZW 3	HOPE 252B
	M8DEIS 2A	NO 520A		EPI IIIBε	TOWARD 289A
	NEOT8S	YOUTH 538B		MONOW	BE LEFT ALONE 530A
	PISTIS 2Dγ	FAITH 669C		NUX IB	NIGHT 548D

Ref	Greek	English	No.
5	ONTWS 2	REAL	577D
	PROSEUCH8 I	PRAYER	720B
	PROSMENW IB	REMAIN	724D
	CH8RA	THE WIDOW	889D
6	ZAW IAα	LIVE	336C
	THN8SKW 2	DIE	363B
	SPATALAW	LIVE LUXURIOUSLY	768B
7	ANEPIL8MPTOS	IRREPROACHABLE	64C
	PARAGGELLW	GIVE ORDERS	618C
8	APISTOS 2	FAITHLESS	85A
	ARNEOMAI 3D	DENY	107D
	EI VII		219B
	IDIOS 3A	ONES OWN	370D
	MALISTA I	ABOVE ALL	490A
	OIKEIOS I		559B
		MEMBERS OF THE HOUSEHOLD	
	PISTIS 2Dα	FAITH	669B
	PRONOEW I	TAKE CARE	715C
	CHEIRWN	WORSE	889C
9	AN8R I	MAN	65D
	GINOMAI II2B	BE	159C
	HEIS 2B	ONE	230C
	ELASSWN	SMALLER	247C
	ELASSWN	SMALLER	247D
	HEX8KONTA	SIXTY	275C
	ETOS	YEAR	317A
	KATALEGW	ENLIST	414B
	CH8RA 2	THE WIDOW	890A
10	AGATHOS I8β	GOOD	3B
	HAGIOS 2Dβ	SAINTS	10A
	EPAKOLOUTHEW 2	FOLLOW	282A
	EPARKEW	HELP	283B
	THLIBW 3	OPPRESS	362C
	KALOS 2B	GOOD	401B
	MARTUREW 2B	BE APPROVED	494B
	NIPTW I	WASH	542B
	XENODOCHEW	SHOW HOSPITALITY	550A
	POUS IA	FOOT	703C
	TEKNOTROPHEW		816C
		BRING UP CHILDREN	
10A	ERGON IC8	DEED	308A
11	GAMEW 3Aβ	MARRY	150B
	KATASTR8NIAW		420B
		BECOME WANTON AGAINST	
	NEOS I8β	YOUNG	538A
	PARAITEOMAI 2A	REFUSE	621D
	CH8RA	THE WIDOW	889D
	CHRISTOS I	ANOINTED ONE	895C
12	ATHETEW IA	SET ASIDE	20C
	KRIMA 4B	VERDICT	451D
	PISTIS I8	FAITH	668D
	PRWTOS IA	FIRST	733A
13	HAMA IA	TOGETHER	41B
	DEI 6	IT IS NECESSARY	171C
	LALEW 2B	SPEAK	464D
	MANTHANW 4	LEARN	491D
	M8 AII2D	NOT	518C
	PERIERCHOMAI	GO AROUND	652C
	PERIERGOS I	MEDDLESOME	652C
	PHLUAROS	GOSSIPY	870A
13A	ARGOS 2	IDLE	104C
13B	ARGOS 2	IDLE	104A
14	ANTIKEIMAI	BE OPPOSED	73D
14	APHORM8	PRETEXT	127A
	BOULOMAI 2A6	DESIRE	145D
	GAMEW 3Aβ	MARRY	150B
	LOIDORIA	ABUSE	480D
	M8DEIS I	NO	520A
	NEOS I8β	YOUNG	538A
	OIKODESPOTEW	KEEP HOUSE	560B
	TEKNOGONEW	BEAR CHILDREN	815D
	CHARIN I	FOR THE SAKE OF	885A
15	EKTREPW	TURN AWAY	245D
	OPISW 2Aβ	AFTER	578D
	SATAN	ADVERSARY	752B
16	BAREW	BURDEN	133B
	EI VII		219B
	EKKL8SIA 4D	CHURCH	240C
	ECHW I28β	HAVE	332D
	ONTWS 2	REAL	577D
	PISTOS 2	TRUSTWORTHY	671A
16A	CH8RA	THE WIDOW	889D
16B	CH8RA	THE WIDOW	889D
17	AXIOW IA	CONSIDER WORTHY	77D
	DIDASKALIA 2	TEACHING	190C
	DIPLOUS	DOUBLE	198C
	KALWS I	WELL	402B
	KOPIAW 2	BECOME WEARY	444B
	LOGOS IAβ	WORD	478B
	MALISTA I	ABOVE ALL	490A
	PRESBUTEROS 2Bα	OLDER	707A
	PROIST8MI I	RULE	714A
	TIM8 2E	HONOR	825C
17FF	PRESBUTEROS 2B	OLDER	706D
18	ALOAW	THRESH	40C
	AXIOS 2A	WORTHY	77C
	BOUS	OX	146A
	GRAPH8 2Bβ	SCRIPTURE	165B
	ERGAT8S IA	WORKMAN	307C
	LEGW I7	SAY	470A
	MISTHOS I	WAGES	525A
	PHIMOW I	TIE SHUT	869D
19	EKTOS I	OUTSIDE	245C
	EPI II8β	ON	286B
	KAT8GORIA	ACCUSATION	424C
	MARTUS I	WITNESS	495B
	PARADECHOMAI I	ACCEPT	619C
	PRESBUTEROS 2Bα	OLDER	707A
20	ELEGCHW 3	EXPOSE	249A
	ENWPION 2A	BEFORE	270B
	ECHW I2E8	HAVE	333B
	LOIPOS 2Bα	THE OTHERS	481A
	PHOBOS 2Aα	FEAR	871C
21	AGGELOS 2A	ANGEL	7C
	DIAMARTUROMAI I	CHARGE	185C
	EKLEKTOS IA	CHOSEN	242A
	ENWPION 2B	BEFORE	270B
	HINA IIIA6	IN ORDER THAT	378B
	KATA II5A6	ACCORDING TO	408B
	PROKRIMA	DISCRIMINATION	715A
	PROSKLISIS	INCLINATION	723B
	PHULASSW IF	WATCH	876C
	CHWRIS 2Bβ	APART	899A
22	HAGNOS I	PURE	11D
	ALLOTRIOS IA	TO ANOTHER	40A
	HAMARTIA I	SIN	42B

22	EPITITH8MI IAα	PUT UPON	302D
	KOINNNEW IBβ	SHARE	439C
	M8DE IB	AND NOT	519D
	TACHEWS IB	QUICKLY	814B
	T8REW 2B	KEEP	822C
23	ASTHENEIA IA	WEAKNESS	114D
	M8KETI 6A	NO LONGER	520B
	OINOS I	WINE	565A
	OLIGOS 2A	LITTLE	566C
	PUKNOS	FREQUENT	736B
	STOMACHOS	STOMACH	777D
	HUDROPOTEW	DRINK WATER	840B
	CHRAOMAI IA	USE	892C
24	ANTHRWPOS 3Aα	MAN	68B
	EPAKOLOUTHEW 2	FOLLOW	282A
	KRISIS IAα	JUDGING	453D
	PROAGW 2B	LEAD	709A
24F	PROD8LOS	CLEAR	711A
25	ALLWS	OTHERWISE	40B
	ERGON ICβ	DEED	308A
	ECHW II2	BE	334B
	KALOS 2B	GOOD	401B
	KRUPTW 2A	HIDE	455C
	HWSAUTWS	SIMILARLY	907D

I TIMOTHY 6

I	AXIOS 2A	WORTHY	77C
	BLASPH8MEW 2Bβ	BLASPHEME	142B
	DIDASKALIA 2	TEACHING	190C
	DOULOS IA	SLAVE	204D
	ZUGOS I	YOKE	340B
	H8GEOMAI 2	CONSIDER	344B
	IDIOS 2C	ONES OWN	370C
	TIM8 2A	HONOR	825A
	HUPO 2Aβ	UNDER	851B
IF	DESPOT8S	MASTER	175C
2	AGAP8TOS 2	BELOVED	6C
	ADELPHOS 2	BROTHER	16A
	ANTILAMBANW 3	ENJOY	74A
	ANTILAMBANW 2	PRACTISE	74A
	DIDASKW I	TEACH	191A
	DIDASKW 2F	TEACH	191B
	DOULEUW 2A	SERVE	204B
	EUERGESIA I	KINDNESS	320A
	ECHW I2Bβ	HAVE	332D
	KATAPHRONEW I	SCORN	421C
	MALLON 2A	RATHER	490B
	PARAKALEW 2	APPEAL TO	622C
2A	PISTOS 2	TRUSTWORTHY	671A
2B	PISTOS 2	TRUSTWORTHY	671A
3	DIDASKALIA 2	TEACHING	190C
	HETERODIDASKALEW		314D

DIFFERENT DOCTRINE

	EUSEBEIA	GODLINESS	326C
	KATA II7A	(ADJ PHRASE)	408D
	KURIOS 2Cγ	LORD	461B
	LOGOS IBβ	WORD	479B
	PROSERCHOMAI 2B	APPROACH	720B
	PROSECHW 2	PAY ATTENTION TO	721D
	HUGIAINW 2	BE HEALTHY	840A
4	BLASPH8MIA I	SLANDER	142C
	GINOMAI IIBβ	COME ABOUT	157B

4	EPISTAMAI I	UNDERSTAND	300A
	ERIS	STRIFE	309C
	Z8T8SIS I	INVESTIGATION	339D
	Z8T8SIS 2	CONTROVERSY	339D
	LOGOMACHIA		478A

DISPUTE ABOUT WORDS

	NOSEW	HAVE A MORBID CRAVING	545C
	PERI 2D	ABOUT	651B
	PON8ROS IBβ	WICKED	697D
	TUPHOW I	CONCEITED	838D
	HUPONOIA	SUSPICION	854C
	PHTHONOS	ENVY	865C
5	AL8THEIA 2B	TRUTH	35C
	APOSTEREW	STEAL	98C
	DIAPARATRIB8		186C

MUTUAL IRRITATION

	DIAPHTHEIRW 2	SPOIL	189D
	NOMIZW 2	THINK	543B
	NOUS 3A	THE MIND	547A
	PARADIATRIB8		619C

USELESS OCCUPATION

	PORISMOS	MEANS OF GAIN	699D
5F	EUSEBEIA	GODLINESS	326B
6	AUTARKEIA 2	CONTENTMENT	122A
	MEGAS 2Aβ	GREAT	498D
	META AII6	WITH	510D
	PORISMOS	MEANS OF GAIN	699D
7	D8LOS	CLEAR	177B
	EISPHERW I	BRING IN	233A
	EKPHERW I	CARRY	246B
	KOSMOS 4B	WORLD	447B
	HOTI IDγ	THAT	593C
	TIS, TI IBβ	ANY ONE	828A
8	ARKEW 2	BE SATISFIED	106D
	DIATROPH8	SUSTENANCE	189B
	SKEPASMA	COVERING	761B
9	ANO8TOS 2	UNINTELLIGENT	70A
	ANON8TOS	USELESS	71D
	APWLEIA 2	DESTRUCTION	103A
	BLABEROS	HARMFUL	141C
	BOULOMAI I	DESIRE	145D
	BUTHIZW 2	SINK	148A
	EIS 4A	INTO	228B
	EMPIPTW 2	FALL	255D
	EPITHUMIA 3	DESIRE	293C
	OLETHROS	DESTRUCTION	566A
	PAGIS 2	TRAP	607B
	PEIRASMOS 2B	TEST	646C
	PLOUTEW I	BE RICH	679D
10	APOPLANAW	MISLEAD	96D
	ARCH8 IC	BEGINNING	111D
	KAKOS IC	EVIL	398D
	ODUN8	PAIN	557C
	OREGW	ASPIRE TO	583C
	PAS IDα	ALL	637C
	PERIPEIRW	PIERCE THROUGH	655C
	PISTIS 2Dα	FAITH	669B
	PISTIS 3	FAITH	669D
	RIZA IB	ROOT	743C
	TIS, TI IAδ	ANY ONE	828A
	PHILARGURIA	LOVE OF MONEY	866D
11*	AGAP8 IIA	LOVE	5C
	ANTHRWPOS 2A	MAN	67D

11 DIKAIOSUN8 2B RIGHTEOUSNESS 195D
DIWKW 4B PURSUE 200B
EUSEBEIA GODLINESS 326B
PISTIS 2Dv FAITH 669C
PISTIS 2Dv FAITH 669D
PRAUPATHEIA GENTLENESS 705C
SU 1B YOU 779D
HUPOMON8 1 PATIENCE 854A
PHEUGW 3 FLEE 863D
12 AGWN 2 STRUGGLE 14D
AGWNIZOMAI 2B STRUGGLE 15A
ENWPION 2A BEFORE 270B
EPILAMBANOMAI 2B GRASP 295A
ZW8 2B8 LIFE 341C
KALEW 2 CALL 400C
MARTUS 2B WITNESS 495C
HOMOLOGEW 4 CONFESS 571C
HOMOLOGIA 2 CONFESSION 571D
PISTIS 2D8 FAITH 669B
POLUS IIA8 MANY 694A
12A KALOS 2C8 GOOD 401C
12B KALOS 2C8 GOOD 401C
13 ENWPION 2B BEFORE 270B
EPI IIA8 BEFORE 286A
ZWOGONEW 1 GIVE LIFE 342A
ZWOPOIEW 1 MAKE ALIVE 342C
KALOS 2C8 GOOD 401C
MARTUREW 1D TESTIFY 494A
HOMOLOGIA 2 CONFESSION 571D
PAS 2B8 ALL THINGS 638D
PILATOS PILATE 663C
PONTIOS PONTIUS 698C
13F PARAGGELLW GIVE ORDERS 618C
14 ANEPIL8MPTOS IRREPROACHABLE 64C
ASPILOS 2 WITHOUT BLEMISH 116D
ENTOL8 2F COMMAND 268D
EPIPHANEIA 1 APPEARING 304B
KURIOS 2Cv LORD 461B
MECHRI 1B UNTIL 517B
T8REW 2B KEEP 822C
15 BASILEUS 2B KING 136A
BASILEUW 1A RULE 136B
DEIKNUMI 1A SHOW 171D
DUNAST8S 1A RULER 207D
IDIOS 1B ONES OWN 370B
KAIROS 3 TIME 396A
KURIEUW 1 RULE 459D
KURIOS 2A LORD 460B
MAKARIOS 2 BLESSED 488A
MONOS 1A8 ONLY 529D
16 ATHANASIA IMMORTALITY 20A
AIWNIOS 3 ETERNAL 28A
AM8N 1 AMEN 45A
APROSITOS UNAPPROACHABLE 102A
KRATOS 4 POWER 450B
MONOS 1A8 ONLY 529D
OIKEW 2 DWELL 559C
TIM8 2B HONOR 825C
PHWS 2 LIGHT 880A
17 AD8LOT8S UNCERTAINTY 16C
AIWN 2A AGE 27B
APOLAUSIS ENJOYMENT 94A
ELPIZW 3 HOPE 252B

17 EPI IIIBv ON 287A
M8 AIIIB8 NOT 518A
M8DE 1B AND NOT 519D
NUN 3A NOW 548A
PARAGGELLW GIVE ORDERS 618C
PARECHW 1B GRANT 632A
PLOUSIOS 1 RICH 679C
PLOUSIWS RICHLY 679D
PLOUTOS 1 WEALTH 680B
HUPS8LOS 2 HIGH 857C
HUPS8LOPHRONEW BE PROUD 857D
PHRONEW 1 THINK 874B
18 AGATHOERGEW DO GOOD 2B
ERGON 1C8 DEED 308A
EUMETADOTOS GENEROUS 323C
KALOS 2B GOOD 401B
KOINWNIKOS LIBERAL 440C
PLOUTEW 2 BE RICH 679D
19 APOTH8SAURIZW STORE UP 90C
EIS 2A8 FOR 228A
EPILAMBANOMAI 2B GRASP 295A
ZW8 2B8 LIFE 341C
ZW8 2B8 LIFE 341C
THEMELIOS 2C FOUNDATION 356C
KALOS 2C8 GOOD 401C
MELLW 2 IS DESTINED 502D
ONTWS 2 REAL 577D
20 ANTITHESIS OPPOSITION 73C
BEB8LOS 1 PROFANE 138B
GNWSIS 3 GNOSIS 163B
KENOPHWNIA CHATTER 429B
PARATH8K8 ENTRUSTED 621C
PARAKATATH8K8 DEPOSIT 623B
TIMOTHEOS TIMOTHY 826A
PHULASSW 1C WATCH 876B
PSEUDWNUMOS FALSELY CALLED 900C
W 1 O 903B
21 ASTOCHEW MISS THE MARK 117D
EPAGGELLOMAI 2 ANNOUNCE 280D
META AIIICv WITH 510A
PERI 2D ABOUT 651A
TIS, TI 1A8 ANY ONE 828A
CHARIS 2C FAVOR 885D

2 TIMOTHY 1

1 APOSTOLOS 3 APOSTLES 99B
DIA AIIIID THROUGH 179C
EPAGGELIA 2A PROMISE 280A
ZW8 2B8 LIFE 341A
THEL8MA 2B WILL 355A
PAULOS PAUL 643A
2 AGAP8TOS 2 BELOVED 6C
APO V4 FROM 87C
EIR8N8 2 PEACE 226D
ELEOS 2A MERCY 249D
THEOS 3D GOD 358B
KURIOS 2Cv LORD 461B
PAT8R 3C8 FATHER 641C
TEKNON 2B CHILD 816B
TIMOTHEOS TIMOTHY 826A
CHARIS 2C FAVOR 885D
3 ADIALEIPTOS UNCEASING 17A

3	DE8SIS	PRAYER 171A
	ECHW I2Eβ	HAVE 333B
	KATHAROS 3B	CLEAN 389A
	LATREUW	SERVE 468D
	MNEIA I	REMEMBRANCE 526B
	NUX IB	NIGHT 548D
	PROGONOS	ANCESTORS 710D
	SUNEID8SIS 2	CONSCIOUSNESS 794D
	CHARIS 5	FAVOR 886C
4	DAKRUON	TEAR 169A
	EPIPOTHEW	DESIRE 297D
	MIMN8SKOMAI IA«	REMEMBER 524B
	PL8ROW IB	MAKE FULL 677A
	CHARA I	JOY 883D
5	ANUPOKRITOS	GENUINE 76A
	ENOIKEW	LIVE 267A
	EUNIK8	EUNICE 323C
	LAMBANW 2	RECEIVE 466C
	LWIS	LOIS 485C
	MAMM8	GRANDMOTHER 491A
	M8T8R I	MOTHER 521D
	PEITHW 4	OBEY 645C
	PISTIS 2D«	FAITH 669B
	TIMOTHEOS	TIMOTHY 826A
	HUPOMN8SIS 2	REMEMBERING 854A
6	AITIA I	CAUSE 25D
	ANAZWPUREW I	REKINDLE 53C
	ANAMIMN8SKW	REMIND 57C
	EN I5A	IN 258D
	EPITHESIS	LAYING ON 293A
	CHARISMA 2	A GIFT 887A
7	AGAP8 IIA	LOVE 5C
	DEILIA	COWARDICE 172A
	DUNAMIS I	POWER 206D
	PNEUMA 5E	SPIRIT 683C
	SWPHRONISMOS I	ADVICE 809D
8	DESMIOS	PRISONER 175A
	EPAISCHUNOMAI I	BE ASHAMED 281D
	EUAGGELION IA	GOSPEL 318A
	KURIOS 2Cγ	LORD 461B
	MARTURION IB	TESTIMONY 495A
	SUGKAKOPATHEW	SUFFER TOGETHER WITH 780D
9	HAGIOS IA«	DEDICATED TO GOD 9C
	AIWNIOS I	ETERNAL 27D
	KALEW 2	CALL 400C
	KATA II5A6	ACCORDING TO 408B
	KL8SIS I	CALL 436D
	PRO 2	BEFORE 708C
	PROTHESIS 2B	SETTING FORTH 713B
	SWZW 2A«	SAVE 806A
	CHARIS 2A	FAVOR 885C
	CHRONOS	TIME 896C
10	APHTHARSIA	INCORRUPTIBILITY 124D
	EPIPHANEIA 2	APPEARING 304B
	EUAGGELION IA	GOSPEL 318A
	ZW8 2Bβ	LIFE 341B
	ZW8 2B«	LIFE 341B
	THANATOS 2B	DEATH 352A
	KATARGEW 2	ABOLISH 418B
	NUN IAγ	NOW 547D
	SWT8R	SAVIOR 808B
	SWT8R 2	SAVIOR 808D
10	PHANEROW IB	REVEAL 860C
	PHWTIZW 2C	SHINE 881C
11	APOSTOLOS 3	APOSTLES 993
	DIDASKALOS	TEACHER 190D
	K8RUX 2	HERALD 432B
	TITH8MI I2A«	MAKE 824A
12	AITIA I	CAUSE 25D
	DUNATOS IAβ	POWERFUL 208A
	EIS 2A«	UNTIL 228A
	EKEINOS 2Bβ	THAT 239B
	EPAISCHUNOMAI 4	BE ASHAMED 281D
	H8MERA 3Bβ	DAY 348A
	OIDA IG	KNOW 558C
	HOS,H8,HO I2Bβ	(REL PRON) 587B
	PARATH8K8	ENTRUSTED 621C
	PASCHW 3B	ENDURE 639D
	PEITHW 4	OBEY 645C
	PISTEUW 2A«	BELIEVE 667A
	PHULASSW IC	WATCH 876B
13	AGAP8 IIA	LOVE 5C
	AKOUW IBβ	HEAR 31C
	ECHW IICβ	KEEP 332B
	LOGOS IBβ	WORD 479C
	PISTIS 2Dγ	FAITH 669C
	HUGIAINW 2	BE HEALTHY 840A
	HUPOTUPWSIS	MODEL 856A
14	EN I5A	IN 258D
	ENOIKEW	LIVE 267A
	KALOS 2Cβ	GOOD 401C
	PARATH8K8	ENTRUSTED 621C
	PARAKATATH8K8	DEPOSIT 623B
	PNEUMA 5Cβ	SPIRIT 682D
	PHULASSW IC	WATCH 876B
15	APOSTREPHW 3A	TURN AWAY 100A
	ASIA	ASIA 115C
	HERMOGEN8S	HERMOGENES 310A
	OIDA IE	KNOW 558C
	PAS IDγ	ALL 637D
	PHUGELOS	PHYGELUS 875C
16	HALUSIS 2	IMPRISONMENT 40D
	ANAPSUCHW I	REVIVE 63A
	DIDWMI	GIVE 191D
	EPAISCHUNOMAI I	BE ASHAMED 281D
	KURIOS 2A	LORD 460B
	OIKOS 2	HOUSEHOLD 563C
	ON8SIPHOROS	ONESIPHORUS 573C
	POLLAKIS	OFTEN 693B
17	GINOMAI II4A	BE 159C
	HEURISKW IA	FIND 325A
	Z8TEW IAβ	SEEK 339B
	RWM8	ROME 745D
	SPOUDAIOS	EAGER 771A
	*SPOUDAIWS 2	DILIGENTLY 771B
18	BELTIWN	BETTER 139A
	DIAKONEW 2	SERVE 183A
	DIDWMI	GIVE 191D
	EKEINOS 2Bβ	THAT 239B
	HEURISKW 3	FIND 326A
	EPHESOS	EPHESUS 330C
	H8MERA 3Bβ	DAY 348A
	KURIOS 2A	LORD 460B
	HOSOS 2	HOW GREAT 590C
	PARA I3B	FROM 614D

2 TIMOTHY 2

1	ENDUNAMOW 2B	BECOME STRONG	263B
	TEKNON 2B	CHILD	816B
	CHARIS 3B	FAVOR	886B
2	AKOUW 1Bβ	HEAR	31C
	DIA AIII2A	BY	179D
	HETEROS 1Bβ	ANOTHER	315B
	HIKANOS 2	APPROPRIATE	375B
	MARTUS 2B	WITNESS	495C
	HOUTOS 1Aε	THIS	601B
	PARATITH8MI 2Bα		628C
	PLACE BESIDE		
	PISTOS 1Aα	TRUSTWORTHY	670B
	POLUS IIAα	MANY	694A
3	KALOS 2Cα	GOOD	401C
	STRATIWT8S 2	SOLDIER	778B
	SUGKAKOPATHEW		780D
	SUFFER TOGETHER WITH		
4	ARESKW 2A	BE PLEASING	105A
	BIOS 1	LIFE	141B
	EMPLEKW 2	ENTANGLE	256A
	PRAGMATEIA	ACTIVITY	704A
	STRATEUW 1		778A
	DO MILITARY SERVICE		
	STRATOLOGEW	ENLIST SOLDIERS	778C
5	ATHLEW	COMPETE	20D
	EAN IIC	IF	210C
	EAN I3A	IF	210D
	NOMIMWS		543C
	ACCORDING TO THE RULES		
	STEPHANOW 1	WREATHE	775B
	TIS, TI 1Aγ	ANY ONE	827D
6	GEWRGOS 1	FARMER	156B
	DEI 6	IT IS NECESSARY	171B
	KARPOS 1A	FRUIT	405C
	KOPIAW 2	BECOME WEARY	444B
	METALAMBANW 1	RECEIVE	512C
7	LEGW IIA	SAY	469B
	NOEW 2	CONSIDER	542D
	PAS 2Aδ	IN ALL RESPECTS	638C
	*SUNESIS 2	INTELLIGENCE	796B
8	DAUID	DAVID	170B
	EGEIRW 2C	RISE	214A
	EUAGGELION 2Bβ	GOSPEL	318C
	KATA II5Aα	ACCORDING TO	408A
	MN8MONEUW 1B	REMEMBER	527A
	SPERMA 1B	SEED	769A
	SPERMA 2B	SEED	769B
9	DESMOS 1	FETTER	175B
	DEW 1B	BIND	176D
	KAKOPATHEW 1		398B
	SUFFER MISFORTUNE		
	KAKOURGOS	CRIMINAL	399B
	LOGOS 1Bβ	WORD	479B
	MECHRI 1C	UNTIL	517B
10	AIWNIOS 3	ETERNAL	28A
	DOXA 1Bβ	GLORY	203A
	EKLEKTOS 1B	CHOSEN	242B
	PAS 2Aδ	EVERYTHING	638C
	SWT8RIA 2	DELIVERANCE	809B
	TUGCHANW 1	MEET	837A
	HUPOMENW 2	REMAIN	853D

11	LOGOS 1Bβ	WORD	479C
	PISTOS 1B	TRUSTWORTHY	670D
	SUZAW	LIVE WITH	783B
	SUNAPOTHN8SKW	DIE WITH	792C
12	ARNEOMAI 3C	DENY	107D
	EI IIA	IF	218A
	SUMBASILEUW RULE WITH SOMEONE		785B
	HUPOMENW 2	REMAIN	853C
13	APISTEW 2	BE UNFAITHFUL	84D
	ARNEOMAI 4	DENY	107D
	MENW 1B	REMAIN	505B
	PISTOS 1Aβ	TRUSTWORTHY	670D
14	DIAMARTUROMAI 1	CHARGE	185C
	ENWPION 2B	BEFORE	270B
	EPI III8ε	ON	287C
	KATASTROPH8	RUIN	420B
	LOGOMACHEW		478A
	DISPUTE ABOUT WORDS		
	HUPOMIMN8SKW 1B	REMIND	854A
	CHR8SIMOS	USEFUL	894B
15	AL8THEIA 2B	TRUTH	35B
	ANEXICHNIASTOS	INSCRUTABLE	64C
	DOKIMOS 1	GENUINE	202A
	ERGAT8S 1B	WORKMAN	307D
	LOGOS 1Bβ	WORD	479C
	ORTHOTOMEW		584A
	GUIDE ON A STRAIGHT PATH		
	PARIST8MI 1C	RENDER	633B
	SPOUDAZW 2	HASTEN	771A
16	ASEBEIA	GODLESSNESS	114A
	BEB8LOS 1	PROFANE	138B
	KENOPHWNIA	CHATTER	429B
	PERIIST8MI 2	AVOID	653B
	POLUS II2C	MANY	696A
	PROKOPTW 2	GO FORWARD	714D
17	GAGGRAINA	CANCER	148B
	NOM8 2	SPREADING	543A
	HUMENAIOS	HYMENAEUS	843D
	PHIL8TOS	PHILETUS	867C
	HWS II2	SO	906A
18	ANASTASIS 2B	RESURRECTION	60B
	ANATREPW 2	OVERTURN	62B
	ASTOCHEW	MISS THE MARK	117D
	LEGW IIIE	DECLARE	471A
	HOSTIS 3	WHOEVER	591B
	PERI 2D	ABOUT	651A
	PISTIS 2Dα	FAITH	669B
	PISTIS 3	FAITH	670A
19	ADIKIA 2	UNRIGHTEOUSNESS	17D
	APHIST8MI 2B	KEEP AWAY	126C
	GINWSKW 6Aβ	KNOW	160C
	EIMI IVI	TO BE	225A
	THEMELIOS 2B	FOUNDATION	356C
	HIST8MI II2Cα	STAND	383C
	MENTOI 2	THOUGH	504C
	ONOMA I4B	NAME	575A
	ONOMAZW 2	NAME	577C
	HOUTOS 2B	THIS	601D
	PAS 1Cγ	WHOEVER	637B
	STEREOS 1	FIRM	774B
	SPHRAGIS 1C	SEAL	804C
20	ARGUROUS	(MADE OF) SILVER	104C
	ATIMIA	DISHONOR	119D

20	MEGAS 1B	LARGE 498D
	MEN 1C	(PARTICLE) 504A
	XULINOS	WOODEN 551A
	HOS,H8,HO 112	THIS (ONE) 589B
	OSTRAKINOS	MADE OF EARTH 591C
	SKEUOS 1B	THING 761D
	CHRUSOUS	GOLDEN 897B
20F	EIS 4D	FOR 228C
20F	TIM8 2B	HONOR 825B
21	AGATHOS 1Bβ	GOOD 3B
	HAGIAZW 2	CONSECRATE 8D
	DESPOT8S	MASTER 175C
	EIS 5	FOR 229A
	EKKATHAIRW 2	CLEANSE 240A
	HETOIMAZW 1	PREPARE 316B
	EUCHR8STOS	USEFUL 329D
	OUN 5	THEREFORE 597D
	SKEUOS 1B	THING 761D
22*	AGAP8 11A	LOVE 5C
	DIKAIOSUN8 2B	RIGHTEOUSNESS 195D
	DIWKW 4B	PURSUE 200B
	EIR8N8 1B	PEACE 226C
	EK 3Gγ	BY 235A
	EPITHUMIA 3	DESIRE 293C
	EPIKALEW 2B	CALL UPON 294B
	KATHAROS 3B	CLEAN 389A
	KARDIA 1Bα	HEART 404B
	META AII3B	WITH 510C
	NEWTERIKOS	YOUTHFUL 539B
	PISTIS 2Dγ	FAITH 669C
	PHEUGW 3	FLEE 863D
23	APAIDEUTOS	UNINSTRUCTED 79A
	GENNAW 3	BRING FORTH 155A
	Z8T8SIS 1	INVESTIGATION 339D
	MACH8	BATTLE 497C
	MWROS 2	FOOLISH 533B
	PARAITEOMAI 2B	REFUSE 622A
24	ANEXIKAKOS	PATIENT 64C
	*DEI 6	IT IS NECESSARY 171B
	DIDAKTIKOS	190B
	SKILFUL IN TEACHING	
	DOULOS 4	SLAVE 205B
	8PIOS	GENTLE 349A
	KURIOS 2Cγ	LORD 461A
	MACHOMAI 2	DISPUTE 497D
	PROS III4B	TOWARD 717C
25	AL8THEIA 2B	TRUTH 35C
	ANTIDIATITH8MI	BE OPPOSED 73C
	DIDWMI	GIVE 191D
	EPIGNWSIS	KNOWLEDGE 291B
	METANOIA	REPENTANCE 514A
	M8POTE 3Bβ	WHETHER PERHAPS 521B
	PAIDEUW 2A	INSTRUCT 608D
	PRAUT8S	HUMILITY 705D
26	ANAN8PHW	BECOME SOBER 57D
	DIABOLOS 2	THE SLANDERER 181A
	EK 1D	AWAY FROM 233D
	EKEINOS 1B	THAT 239A
	ZWGREW	CAPTURE ALIVE 340D
	THEL8MA 1Cβ	WILL 355A
	PAGIS 2	TRAP 607B

2 TIMOTHY 3

1	ENIST8MI 2	BE IMMINENT 266B
	ESCHATOS 3B	LAST 314B
	H8MERA 4B	TIME 348B
	KAIROS 1	TIME 395C
	HOUTOS 1Bβ	THIS 601C
	CHALEPOS	HARD 882C
2	ALAZWN	BOASTER 34A
	ANOSIOS 1	UNHOLY 71D
	APEITH8S 1	DISOBEDIENT 82B
	ACHARISTOS	UNGRATEFULLY 127D
	BLASPH8MOS	SLANDEROUS 142D
	GONEUS	PARENTS 164B
	HUPER8PHANOS	PROUD 849A
	PHILAUTOS	SELFISH 866D
	PHILARGUROS	FOND OF MONEY 866D
3	AKRAT8S	DISSOLUTE 32B
	AN8MEROS	SAVAGE 65D
	ASPONDOS	IRRECONCILABLE 116D
	ASTORGOS	UNLOVING 117C
	DIABOLOS 1	SLANDEROUS 181A
4	MALLON 3C	RATHER 490D
	PRODOT8S	TRAITOR 711B
	PROPET8S	RECKLESS 716B
	TUPHOW 1	CONCEITED 838D
	PHIL8DONOS	LOVING PLEASURE 867B
	PHILOTHEOS	LOVING GOD 868B
5	APOTREPW	AVOID 101A
	ARNEOMAI 4	DENY 107D
	DUNAMIS 1	POWER 207A
	EUSEBEIA	GODLINESS 326B
	MORPHWSIS 2	OUTWARD FORM 530C
	HOUTOS 1Aβ	THIS 601A
6	AGW 3	LEAD 14B
	AICHMALWTEUW	CAPTURE 26B
	AICHMALWTIZW 3	MISLEAD 26C
	HAMARTIA 1	SIN 42D
	GUNAIKARION	SILLY WOMAN 167B
	ENDUNW 1	ENTER 263B
	EPITHUMIA 3	DESIRE 293D
	HOUTOS 1Aβ	THIS 601A
	POIKILOS 1	DIVERSIFIED 690A
	SWREUW 2	HEAP 808A
7	AL8THEIA 2B	TRUTH 35C
	*EPIGNWSIS	KNOWLEDGE 291B
	ERCHOMAI I2C	COME 311C
	MANTHANW 1	LEARN 491B
	M8DEPOTE	NEVER 520B
8	ADOKIMOS	UNQUALIFIED 18B
	AL8THEIA 2B	TRUTH 35C
	ANTHIST8MI 1	SET AGAINST 66C
	ANTHIST8MI 2	SET AGAINST 66C
	IANN8S	JANNES 368D
	KAI II3	ALSO 394B
	KATAPHTHEIRW 2	RUIN 421B
	MWUS8S	MOSES 533D
	NOUS 3A	THE MIND 547A
	HOUTOS 1Aβ	THIS 601A
	HOUTW 1A	THUS 602B
	PISTIS 2Dα	FAITH 669B
	TROPOS 1	MANNER 835B
9	ANOIA	FOLLY 70A

9	GINOMAI I4B	BECOME	158D		17	ARTIOS	CAPABLE	110A
	EKD8LOS	PLAIN	237D			EXARTIZW 2	EQUIP	273A
	EPI III3	ON	289C			PROS III3C	TOWARD	717B
	POLUS II2C	MANY	696A					
	PROKOPTW 2	GO FORWARD	714D			**2 TIMOTHY 4**		
10	AGAP8 IIA	LOVE	5C					
	AGWG8	CONDUCT	14D		1	BASILEIA 3G	KINGDOM	135B
	DIDASKALIA 2	TEACHING	190C			DIAMARTUROMAI I	CHARGE	185C
	MAKROTHUMIA I	PATIENCE	489B			ENWPION 2B	BEFORE	270B
	PARAKOLOUTHEW 2	FOLLOW	624C			EPIPHANEIA I	APPEARING	304B
	PISTIS 2Dγ	FAITH	669C			ZAW IAα	LIVE	336C
	PISTIS 2Dγ	FAITH	669D			KRINW 4Bα	JUDGE	453A
	PROTHESIS 2A	SETTING FORTH	713A			MELLW ICβ	BE ABOUT TO	502B
	SU IC	YOU	780A			NEKROS 2A	DEAD	536D
	HUPOMON8 I	PATIENCE	854A		2	AKAIRWS	OUT OF SEASON	28D
11	ANTIOCHEIA 2	ANTIOCH	74D			DIDACH8 I	TEACHING	191B
	*DIWGMOS	PERSECUTION	200A			ELEGCHW 3	EXPOSE	249A
	THEKLA	THECLA	354D			EPITIMAW I	REBUKE	303B
	IKONION	ICONIUM	375D			EUKAIRWS	CONVENIENTLY	321D
	LUSTRA	LYSTRA	483D			EPHIST8MI IA	STAND BY	331A
	PATH8MA I	SUFFERING	607B			K8RUSSW 28β	ANNOUNCE	432C
	RUOMAI	SAVE	745A			LOGOS IBβ	WORD	479C
	HUPOPHERW	ENDURE	856B			MAKROTHUMIA 2A	PATIENCE	489B
11A	HOIOS	OF WHAT SORT	565C			PARAKALEW 2	APPEAL TO	622C
11B	HOIOS	OF WHAT SORT	565C		3	AK08 IC	HEARING	30C
12	DE 4B	BUT, AND	170D			ANECHW 2	ENDURE	65B
	DIWKW 2	PERSECUTE	200B			DIDASKALIA 2	TEACHING	190C
	EUSEBWS	A GODLY MANNER	326D			EPITHUMIA 3	DESIRE	293C
	ZAW 3A	LIVE	337B			EPISWREUW	HEAP UP	302A
	PAS IDβ	ALL	637D			KAIROS I	TIME	395C
13	GO8S	SWINDLER	164A			KN8THW	ITCH	438A
	EPI III3	ON	289C			HOTE 2Aα	WHEN	592C
	PLANAW 2C6	DECEIVE	671C			OU 5B	NO	595A
	PON8ROS IBα	WICKED	697C			HUGIAINW 2	BE HEALTHY	840A
	PROKOPTW 2	GO FORWARD	715A		4	AK08 IC	HEARING	30C
	CHEIRWN	WORSE	889C			AL8THEIA 2B	TRUTH	35C
13A	PLANAW IB	DECEIVE	671B			APOSTREPHW IAα	TURN AWAY	99D
14	MENW IAβ	REMAIN	505A			EKTREPW	TURN AWAY	245D
	OIDA IF	KNOW	558C			MUTHOS	FABLE	531A
	PARA I3C	FROM	615A		5	DIAKONIA 3	SERVICE	183C
	PISTOW 2	FEEL CONFIDENCE	671A			ERGON 2	WORK	308C
	TIS, TI IAα	WHICH	826C			EUAGGELIST8S	EVANGELIST	318D
14A	MANTHANW I	LEARN	491B			KAKOPATHEW 2		398B
14B	MANTHANW I	LEARN	491B			BEAR HARDSHIP PATIENTLY		
15	BREPHOS 2	INFANT	147A			N8PHW	BE SELF CONTROLLED	540D
	GRAMMA 2C	WRITING	164C			PAS 2A6	IN ALL RESPECTS	638C
	HIEROS I	HOLY	373B			PL8ROPHOREW IA	FILL	676A
	PISTIS 28β	FAITH	669A			POIEW IIBα	DO	687C
	SOPHIZW IA	· MAKE WISE	767C		6	ANALUSIS	DEPARTURE	57A
	SWT8RIA 2	DELIVERANCE	809D			EPHIST8MI 2B	STAND BY	331B
16	GRAPH8 2A	SCRIPTURE	165B			KAIROS 3	TIME	396A
	DIDASKALIA I	TEACHING	190C			SPENDW	OFFER A LIBATION	769A
	DIKAIOSUN8 2B	RIGHTEOUSNESS	195D		7	AGWN 2	STRUGGLE	14D
	ELEGMOS	CONVICTION	248C			AGWNIZOMAI 2B	STRUGGLE	15A
	ELEGCHOS 3	PROOF	248D			DROMOS I	COURSE	206A
	EPANORTHWSIS	IMPROVEMENT	282D			THEODROMOS	GODS RUNNER	356D
	THEOPNEUSTOS	INSPIRED BY GOD	357A			KALOS 2Cβ	GOOD	401C
	PAIDEIA I	TRAINING	608C			PISTIS IA	FAITH	668B
	PAS IAα	EVERY EACH	636C			PISTIS 3	FAITH	670A
	PROS III3C	TOWARD	717B			TELEW I	FINISH	818C
	WPHELIMOS	USEFUL	909C			T8REW 3	KEEP	822D
17	AGATHOS IBβ	GOOD	3B		8	AGAPAW 2	LOVE	5A
	ANTHRWPOS 2A	MAN	67D			APODIDWMI I	GIVE AWAY	89D

```
8  APOKEIMAI 2        BE PUT AWAY   92B     16 SUMPARAGINOMAI 2              786D
   DIKAIOS 2          RIGHTEOUS    195A        COME TOGETHER
   DIKAIOSUN8 2B      RIGHTEOUSNESS 196A   17 ENDUNAMOW 1      STRENGTHEN  263A
   EPIPHANEIA I       APPEARING    304B       K8RUGMA 2        PROCLAMATION 432A
   H8MERA 3B          DAY          348A       LEWN 2           LION        474A
   KRIT8S IAB         JUDGE        454C       PARIST8MI 2AY    HELP        633C
   LOIPOS 3Aα         THE REST     481B       RUOMAI           SAVE        745A
   PAS IDB            ALL          637D       STOMA IC         MOUTH       777C
   STEPHANOS 2A       WREATH       775A    18 AIWN IB          TIME         26D
9  SPOUDAZW I         HASTEN       771A       AM8N I           AMEN         45A
   TACHEWS IA         QUICKLY      814B       BASILEIA 3F      KINGDOM     135A
10 AGAPAW 2           LOVE           5A       EIS 7            TO          229B
   AIWN 2A            AGE           27B       EPOURANIOS IAY   HEAVENLY    306A
   GALATIA            GALATIA      149B       PON8ROS IBB      WICKED      697D
   DALMATIA           DALMATIA     169B       RUOMAI           SAVE        745A
   D8MAS              DEMAS        177C       SWZW 2Aα         SAVE        806A
   EGKATALEIPW 2      FORSAKE      214D    19 AKULAS           AQUILA       33C
   THESSALONIK8       THESSALONICA 360C       ASPAZOMAI IA     GREET       116B
   KR8SK8S            CRESCENS     451B       Z8NWN            ZENO        339A
   KRISPOS            CRISPUS      454B       LEKTRA           LECTRA      472D
   NUN 3A             NOW          548A       OIKOS 2          HOUSEHOLD   563C
   TITOS I            TITUS        828C       ON8SIPHOROS      ONESIPHORUS 573C
11 AGW IB             BRING         14B       PRISKA           PRISCILLA   708B
   ANALAMBANW 4       TAKE ALONG    56C       SIMAIAS          SILOAM      758C
   DIAKONIA I         SERVICE      183B    20 APOLEIPW I       LEAVE BEHIND 94B
   EIS 5              FOR          229A       ASTHENEW IA      BE SICK     115A
   EUCHR8STOS         USEFUL       330A       ERASTOS 2        ERASTUS     306C
   LOUKAS             LUKE         481C       KORINTHOS        CORINTH     445C
   MARKOS             MARK         493C       MENW IAα         REMAIN      504D
   META AIIIB         WITH         509D       TROPHIMOS        TROPHIMUS   835C
   MONOS IAα          ONLY         529B    21 ASPAZOMAI IA     GREET       116B
   SEAUTOU I          YOURSELF     753A       EUBOULOS         EUBULUS     319A
12 EPHESOS            EPHESUS      330C       KLAUDIA          CLAUDIA     434C
   TUCHIKOS           TYCHICUS     839C       LINOS            LINUS       476C
13 APOLEIPW I         LEAVE BEHIND  94B       PAS IDα          ALL         637C
   BIBLION I          BOOK         140D       POUD8S           PUDENS      703B
   KARPOS             CARPUS       405C       PRO 2            BEFORE      708C
   MALISTA I          ABOVE ALL    490A       SPOUDAZW I       HASTEN      771A
   MEMBRANA           PARCHMENT    503B       CHEIMWN 2        WINTER      888A
   PARA IIIBα         BESIDE       615C    22 META AIIICY      WITH        510A
   TRWAS              TROAS        836D       PNEUMA 3B        SPIRIT      681C
   PHAILON8S          CLOAK        859B       CHARIS 2C        FAVOR       885D
   PHERW 4Aα          BEAR         863A
14 ALEXANDROS 4       ALEXANDER     35A                    TITUS I
   APODIDWMI 3        RECOMPENSE    90A
   ENDEIKNUMI 2       DEMONSTRATE  262A    I  AL8THEIA 2B     TRUTH        35C
   ERGON ICB          DEED         308A       APOSTOLOS 3     APOSTLES     99B
   ERGON ICB          DEED         308A       DOULOS 4        SLAVE       205B
   KAKOS 3            EVIL         399A       EKLEKTOS IB     CHOSEN      242B
   KATA II5AB         ACCORDING TO 408A       EPIGNWSIS       KNOWLEDGE   291B
   CHALKEUS           COPPERSMITH  882D       EUSEBEIA        GODLINESS   326C
15 ANTHIST8MI 2       SET AGAINST   66C       KATA II4        FOR (PURPOSE) 407D
   H8METEROS          OUR          348C       PAULOS          PAUL        643A
   LIAN I             VERY         474C       PISTIS 2Dα      FAITH       669B
   LOGOS IA6          WORD         478D    1B    KATA II7A    (ADJ PHRASE) 408D
   PHULASSW 2A        WATCH        876C    2  AIWNIOS I       ETERNAL      27D
16 APOLOGIA 2A        DEFENSE       95C       APSEUD8S        TRUTHFUL    128D
   EGKATALEIPW 2      FORSAKE      214D       ELPIS 2B        HOPE        252C
   LOGIZOMAI IA       RECKON       477A       ELPIS 2A        HOPE        252C
   M8  AIII2          NOT          518C       EPAGGELLOMAI IB ANNOUNCE    280C
   PARAGINOMAI 3      COME         619A       EPI IIIBY       ON          287A
 *PRWTOS IA           FIRST        732D       ZW8 2BB         LIFE        341C
                                             HOS,H8,HO I4E   (REL PRON)   588B
```

2 PRO 2 — BEFORE 708C
  CHRONOS — TIME 896C
3 EPITAG8 — COMMAND 302A
  IDIOS IB — ONES OWN 370B
  KAIROS 3 — TIME 396A
  KATA II5A6 — ACCORDING TO 408B
  K8RUGMA 2 — PROCLAMATION 432A
  LOGOS IBβ — WORD 479B
  PISTEUW 3 — BELIEVE 667D
  SWT8R I — SAVIOR 808C
  PHANEROW IA — REVEAL 860C
4 APO V4 — FROM 87C
  GN8SIOS I — LEGITIMATE 162A
  EIR8N8 2 — PEACE 226D
  THEOS 3D — GOD 358B
  KOINOS IA — COMMON 439A
  PAT8R 3Cβ — FATHER 641C
  PISTIS 2Dα — FAITH 669B
  SWT8R 2 — SAVIOR 808D
  TEKNON 2B — CHILD 816B
  TITOS I — TITUS 828C
  CHARIS 2C — FAVOR 885D
5 APOLEIPW I — LEAVE BEHIND 94B
  DIATASSW — ORDER 188C
  EPIDIORTHOW — SET RIGHT 292B
  HINA I5 — IN ORDER THAT 378A
  KATHIST8MI 2B — APPOINT 391B
  KATA IIID — (DISTRIBUTIVE) 407B
  KATALEIPW IA — LEAVE BEHIND 414C
  KR8T8 — CRETE 451C
  LEIPW 2 — LACK 471D
  POLIS I — CITY 692B
  PRESBUTEROS 2Bα — OLDER 707A
  TITOS I — TITUS 828C
  CHARIN I — FOR THE SAKE OF 885A
  HWS II — AS 905C
6 AN8R I — MAN 65D
  ANUPOTAKTOS 2 — UNDISCIPLINED 76B
  ASWTIA — DEBAUCHERY 119A
  HEIS 2B — ONE 230C
  ECHW I2Bα — HAVE 332C
  KAT8GORIA — ACCUSATION 424C
  PISTOS 2 — TRUSTWORTHY 671A
6F ANEGKL8TOS — BLAMELESS 63C
7 AISCHROKERD8S — 24C
  FOND OF DISHONEST GAIN
  AUTHAD8S — SELF WILLED 120C
  EPISKOPOS 2 — OVERSEER 299C
  OIKONOMOS 2 — MANAGER 562D
  ORGILOS — INCLINED TO ANGER 583B
  PAROINOS — DRUNKEN 634D
  PL8KT8S — BULLY 675A
  HWS IIIIA — SO 906C
8 DIKAIOS IA — UPRIGHT 194C
  EGKRAT8S — SELF CONTROLLED 215D
  HOSIOS IA — PIOUS 589C
  SWPHRWN — PRUDENT 810C
  PHILAGATHOS — LOVING GOOD 866A
  PHILOXENOS — HOSPITABLE 868C
9 ADIKOKRIT8S — UNJUST JUDGE 17D
  ANELE8MWN — UNMERCIFUL 63D
  ANTECHW I — CLING TO 72D
  ANTILEGW I — CONTRADICT 74A

9 HARPAX 2 — SWINDLER 108D
  ARCHWN 2 — AUTHORITIES 113B
  DIAKONOS IA — SERVANT 183D
  DIAKONOS IC — DEACON 183D
  DIGAMOS 2 — SECOND MARRIAGE 190B
  DIGAMIA — SECOND MARRIAGE 190B
  DIDASKALIA 2 — TEACHING 190C
  DIDACH8 2 — TEACHING 191B
  DUNATOS IAβ — POWERFUL 208A
  ELEGCHW 2 — EXPOSE 248D
  THEIOS IB — DIVINE 354C
  LEITOURGEW I — 471D
  PERFORM A PUBLIC SERVICE
  LOGOS IAβ — WORD 478C
  PARAKALEW 2 — APPEAL TO 622C
  PARAKALEW 4 — IMPLORE 623A
  PISTOS IB — TRUSTWORTHY 670D
  HUGIAINW 2 — BE HEALTHY 840A
  CHEIROTONEW — CHOOSE 889B
  PSEUST8S — LIAR 900D
10 ANUPOTAKTOS 2 — UNDISCIPLINED 76A
  EK 3D — FROM 234C
  KAI I4 — AND 394A
  MALISTA I — ABOVE ALL 490A
  MATAIOLOGOS — IDLE TALKER 496C
  PERITOM8 4A — CIRCUMCISION 658D
  POLUS I2Aα — MANY 694D
  PHRENAPAT8S — DECEIVER 873D
11 AISCHROS — SHAMEFUL 24D
  ANATREPW 2 — OVERTURN 62B
  GONEUS — PARENTS 164B
  DEI 2 — IT IS NECESSARY 171B
  DEI 6 — IT IS NECESSARY 171B
  EPISTOMIZW — STOP THE MOUTH 301A
  KERDOS — GAIN 430D
  M8 AI5 — NOT 517D
  NOUTHETEW — ADMONISH 546B
  OIKOS 2 — HOUSEHOLD 563C
  HOLOS I — WHOLE 567C
  HOSTIS 2B — WHOEVER 591A
  OU 5A — NO 595A
  TUPTW I — STRIKE 838A
  HUBRIZW — MISTREAT 839B
  CHARIN I — FOR THE SAKE OF 885A
12 AEI 2 — ALWAYS 19A
  ARGOS 2 — IDLE 104A
  GAST8R IB — GLUTTON 151D
  TH8RION 2 — BEAST 361D
  IDIOS IAβ — ONES OWN 370B
  KAKOS 2 — EVIL 398D
  KR8S — A CRETAN 451B
  PROPH8T8S 6 — PROPHET 731C
  PSEUST8S — LIAR 900D
13 AITIA I — CAUSE 25D
  AL8TH8S 2 — TRUE 36B
  APOTOMWS — SEVERELY 101A
  ELEGCHW 2 — EXPOSE 248D
  MARTURIA 2C — TESTIMONY 494C
  PISTIS 2Dα — FAITH 669B
  HUGIAINW 2 — BE HEALTHY 840A
14 APOSTREPHW 3A — TURN AWAY 100A
  ENTOL8 IB — COMMAND 268C
  IOUDAIKOS — JEWISH 380A

14 MUTHOS FABLE 531A
   PROSECHW IAβ 721C
     PAY ATTENTION TO
15 APISTOS 2 FAITHLESS 85A
   NOUS 3A THE MIND 547A
   PAS 2A6 EVERYTHING 638C
   SUNEID8SIS 2 CONSCIOUSNESS 794C
15A KATHAROS 2 CLEAN 388D
15A MIAINW 2 DEFILE 522D
15B KATHAROS 3A CLEAN 389A
15B MIAINW 2 DEFILE 522D
15C KATHAROS 2 CLEAN 388D
16 AGATHOS IBβ GOOD 3B
   ADOKIMOS UNQUALIFIED 18B
   APEITH8S 2 DISOBEDIENT 82B
   ARNEOMAI 3B DENY 107C
   BDELUKTOS I ABOMINABLE 137C
   THEOS 3B GOD 357D
   OIDA 2 KNOW 558D
   HOMOLOGEW 4 CONFESS 571B
   PAS IAβ EVERY EACH 636D
   PROS III3C TOWARD 717B
16A ERGON IA DEED 307D

TITUS 2

1 DIDASKALIA 2 TEACHING 190C
   PREPW BE FITTING 706A
   HUGIAINW 2 BE HEALTHY 840A
2 AGAP8 IIA LOVE 5C
   N8PHALIOS TEMPERATE 540D
   PISTIS 2Dγ FAITH 669C
   PISTIS 2Dγ FAITH 669D
   PRESBUT8S OLD MAN 707C
   SEMNOS IA NOBLE 754B
   SWPHRWN PRUDENT 810C
   HUGIAINW 2 BE HEALTHY 840A
   HUPOMON8 I PATIENCE 854A
3 DIABOLOS I SLANDEROUS 181A
   DOULOW 2 ENSLAVE 205C
   EN IVIA IN 260C
   HIEROPREP8S 373B
     WORTHY OF REVERENCE
   KALODIDASKALOS 401A
     TEACHING WHAT IS GOOD
   KATAST8MA BEHAVIOR 420A
   OINOS I WINE 565A
   PRESBUTIS ELDERLY LADY 707C
   HWSAUTWS SIMILARLY 907D
4 HINA I3 IN ORDER THAT 377D
   NEOS 2Bα NOVICE 538A
   PHILANDROS LOVING HER HUSBAND 866B
   PHILOTEKNOS 869B
     LOVING ONES CHILDREN
4F SWPHRONIZW ENCOURAGE 809D
5 AGATHOS IAα GOOD 2D
   HAGNOS I PURE IID
   AN8R I MAN 66A
   BLASPH8MEW 2Bε BLASPHEME I42B
   IDIOS 2C ONES OWN 370C
   LOGOS IBβ WORD 479B
   OIKOURGOS WORKING AT HOME 564B
   OIKOUROS STAYING AT HOME 564B

5 SWPHRWN PRUDENT 810C
   HUPOTASSW IBβ SUBJECT 855D
6 NEOS 2Bβ NOVICE 538A
   PARAKALEW 2 APPEAL TO 622C
   SWPHRONEW 2 SOUND MIND 809C
   HWSAUTWS SIMILARLY 907D
7 ADIAPHTHORIA SINCERITY I7A
   APHTHONIA WILLINGNESS 125A
   APHTHARSIA INCORRUPTIBILITY 125A
   APHTHORIA SOUNDNESS 125B
   DIDASKALIA 2 TEACHING 190C
   ERGON ICβ DEED 308A
   KALOS 2B GOOD 401B
   PARECHW 2A SHOW ONESELF 632B
   PERI 2D ABOUT 651B
   SEMNOT8S I REVERENCE 754C
   TUPOS 5B MARK 837D
8 AKATAGNWSTOS BEYOND REPROACH 29B
   EK 2 AWAY FROM 234A
   ENANTIOS 3B THE OPPONENT 261C
   ENTREPW 2A BE ASHAMED 269B
   ECHW I6A CAN 333D
   LEGW I4 SAY 469D
   LOGOS IBβ WORD 479C
   HUGIAINW 2 BE HEALTHY 840A
   HUGI8S 2 HEALTHY 840B
   PHAULOS I WORTHLESS 862B
9 ANTILEGW I CONTRADICT 74A
   DESPOT8S MASTER 175C
   DOULOS IA SLAVE 204D
   EURESTOS 2 PLEASING 319A
   IDIOS 2C ONES OWN 370C
   PAS 2A6 IN ALL RESPECTS 638C
   HUPOTASSW IBβ SUBJECT 855D
10 DIDASKALIA 2 TEACHING 190C
   ENDEIKNUMI I DEMONSTRATE 262A
   KOSMEW 2Bβ DECORATE 446A
   PISTIS IA FAITH 668B
   SWT8R I SAVIOR 808C
10B PAS 2A6 IN ALL RESPECTS 638C
11 EPIPHAINW 2 APPEAR 304A
   PAS IB ALL 637A
   SWT8RIOS I SAVING 809C
   CHARIS 2A FAVOR 885C
12 AIWN 2A AGE 27B
   ARNEOMAI 4 DENY 107D
   ASEBEIA GODLESSNESS I14A
   DIKAIWS IB JUSTLY 197B
   EPITHUMIA 3 DESIRE 293D
   EUSEBWS A GODLY MANNER 326D
   ZAW 3A LIVE 337B
   KOSMIKOS 2 EARTHLY 446B
   NUN 3A NOW 548A
   PAIDEUW 2A INSTRUCT 608D
   SWPHRONWS SOBERLY 809D
13 ELPIS 4 HOPE 252D
   EPIPHANEIA I APPEARING 304B
   THEOS 2 GOD 357C
   MAKARIOS 3C BLESSED 488A
   MEGAS 2Bα GREAT 499B
   HO,H8,TO III0B THE 555A
   PROSDECHOMAI 2B RECEIVE 719C
   SWT8R 2 SAVIOR 808D

14 ANOMIA 2 — LAWLESSNESS 71B
   DIDWMI 6 — GIVE 192D
   ERGON 1Cβ — DEED 308A
   Z8LWT8S 1Aβ — ZEALOT 338D
   KATHARIZW 2Bα — CLEANSE 388C
   KALOS 2B — GOOD 401B
   LAOS 3B — PEOPLE 468B
   LUTROW 2 — REDEEM 484A
   PAS 1Aβ — EVERY EACH 636D
   PERIOUSIOS — CHOSEN 654C
   SWT8R 2 — SAVIOR 808D
   HUPER 1Aε — IN BEHALF OF 846C
   CHARIS 2A — FAVOR 885C
15 ELEGCHW 1 — EXPOSE 248D
   EPITAG8 — COMMAND 302A
   KATAPHRONEW 1 — SCORN 421C
   M8DEIS 2A — NO 520A
   PARAKALEW 2 — APPEAL TO 622C
   PAS 1A6 — ALL 637A
   PERIPHRONEW — DISREGARD 659B

TITUS 3

1 AGATHOS 1Bβ — GOOD 3B
   ARCH8 3 — RULER 112A
   EXOUSIA 4Cα — AUTHORITY 278B
   HETOIMOS 2 — READY 316D
   PAS 1Aβ — EVERY EACH 636D
   PEITHARCHEW — OBEY 644C
   PROS III3C — TOWARD 717B
   HUPOMIMN8SKW 1A — REMIND 853D
   HUPOTASSW 1Bβ — SUBJECT 855D
2 AMACHOS — PEACEABLE 44A
   BLASPH8MEW 1 — DEFAME 142A
   ENDEIKNUMI 1 — DEMONSTRATE 262A
   EPIEIK8S — GENTLE 292C
   PRAUT8S — HUMILITY 705D
   PROS III4B — TOWARD 717C
3 ANO8TOS 1 — UNINTELLIGENT 70A
   APEITH8S 2 — DISOBEDIENT 82B
   DIAGW — SPEND ONES LIFE 181C
   DOULEUW 2C — SERVE 204C
   EPITHUMIA 3 — DESIRE 293D
   H8DON8 1 — PLEASURE 345A
   KAKIA 1B — MALICE 397D
   MISEW 1 — HATE 524D
   PLANAW 2Cα — DECEIVE 671C
   POIKILOS 1 — DIVERSIFIED 690A
   STUG8TOS — HATED 779B
   PHTHONOS — ENVY 865C
4 EPIPHAINW 2 — APPEAR 304A
   HOTE 1B — WHEN 592C
   SWT8R 1 — SAVIOR 808C
   PHILANTHRWPIA — 866C
   LOVE FOR MANKIND
   CHR8STOT8S 2B — GOODNESS 894D
5 ANAKAINWSIS — RENEWAL 55A
   DIKAIOSUN8 2B — RIGHTEOUSNESS 195D
   ELEOS 2B — MERCY 249D
   ERGON 1Cβ — DEED 308A
   KATA II5A6 — ACCORDING TO 408B
   LOUTRON — WASHING 481D
   PALIGGENESIA 2 — REBIRTH 611B

5 PNEUMA 5Cβ — SPIRIT 683A
   SWZW 2Aα — SAVE 806A
6 EKCHEW 2 — POUR OUT 246D
   EPI IIIIBγ — ON 288D
   PLOUSIWS — RICHLY 679D
   SWT8R 2 — SAVIOR 808D
7 DIKAIOW 3A — JUSTIFY 196D
   EKEINOS 1B — THAT 239A
   ELPIS 2B — HOPE 252C
   ZW8 2Bβ — LIFE 341C
   KL8RONOMOS 2B — HEIR 436B
   CHARIS 2A — FAVOR 885C
8 BOULOMAI 2A6 — DESIRE 145D
   DIABEBAIOOMAI — 180D
   SPEAK CONFIDENTLY
   ERGON 1Cβ — DEED 308A
   THEOS 3B — GOD 357D
   LOGOS 1Bβ — WORD 479C
   PISTEUW 2Aα — BELIEVE 667A
   PISTOS 1B — TRUSTWORTHY 670D
   PROIST8MI 2 — RULE 714A
   PHRONTIZW — THINK OF 874D
   WPHELIMOS — USEFUL 909C
8A KALOS 2B — GOOD 401B
8B KALOS 2B — GOOD 401B
9 ANWPHEL8S 2 — HARMFUL 77A
   GENEALOGIA — GENEALOGY 153D
   *ERIS — STRIFE 309C
   Z8T8SIS 1 — INVESTIGATION 339D
   LOGOMACHIA — 478A
   DISPUTE ABOUT WORDS
   MATAIOS — IDLE 496C
   MACH8 — BATTLE 497C
   MWROS 2 — FOOLISH 533B
   NOMIKOS 1 — ABOUT THE LAW 543B
   PERIIST8MI 2 — AVOID 653B
10 HAIRETIKOS — FACTIOUS 23C
   ANTHRWPOS 3Aε — MAN 68C
   DEUTEROS 2 — SECOND 176A
   HEIS 4 — ONE 231A
   META BII3 — AFTER 511C
   NOUTHESIA — ADMONITION 546A
   PARAITEOMAI 2A — REFUSE 621D
11 HAMARTANW 1 — SIN 41D
   AUTOKATAKRITOS — SELF CONDEMNED 122A
   EKSTREPHW — TURN ASIDE 244C
   TOIOUTOS 3Aα — SUCH A KIND 829B
12 ARTEMAS — ARTEMAS 109C
   KRINW 3 — DECIDE 452C
   NIKOPOLIS — NICOPOLIS 541D
   PARACHEIMAZW — SPEND THE WINTER 629A
   PEMPW 1 — SEND 647D
   SPOUDAZW 1 — HASTEN 771A
   TUCHIKOS — TYCHICUS 839C
13 APOLLWS — APOLLOS 95A
   Z8NAS — ZENAS 339D
   HINA IIC — IN ORDER THAT 377C
   LEIPW 2 — LACK 471D
   NOMIKOS 2 — LAWYER 543C
   PROPEMPW 2 — ACCOMPANY 716B
   SPOUDAIWS 2 — DILIGENTLY 771B
14 AKARPOS 2 — UNFRUITFUL 29B
   ANAGKAIOS 1 — NECESSARY 51D

14	H8METEROS	OUR 348C
	KALOS 2B	GOOD 401B
	MANTHANW 4	LEARN 491C
	NIKOPOLIS	NICOPOLIS 541D
	CHREIA 2	NEED 893B
15	ASPAZOMAI 1A	GREET 116B
	ASPAZOMAI 1A	GREET 116C
	META AIIICγ	WITH 510B
	PISTIS 2Dα	FAITH 669B
	PHILEW 1A	LOVE LIKE 866D
	CHARIS 2C	FAVOR 885D
15A	PAS 1Dγ	ALL 637D
15B	PAS 1Eα	ALL 637D

PHILEMON

1	AGAP8TOS 2	BELOVED 6C
	ADELPHOS 2	BROTHER 16A
	DESMIOS	PRISONER 175A
	PAULOS	PAUL 643A
	SUNERGOS	WORKING WITH 795C
	TIMOTHEOS	TIMOTHY 826A
	PHIL8MWN	PHILEMON 867B
2	ADELPH8 3	SISTER 15C
	APPHIA	APPHIA 102D
	ARCHIPPOS	ARCHIPPUS 112D
	EKKL8SIA 4C	CHURCH 240C
	OIKOS 1Aα	HOUSE 563A
	SUSTRATIWT8S	FELLOW SOLDIER 803A
3	APO V4	FROM 87C
	EIR8N8 2	PEACE 226D
	THEOS 3D	GOD 358B
	PAT8R 3Cβ	FATHER 641C
	CHARIS 2C	FAVOR 885D
4	EPI I2	UNDER 286C
	EUCHARISTEW 2	GIVE THANKS 328C
	THEOS 3C	GOD 358A
	MNEIA 2	MENTION 526B
	POIEW III	DO 689C
	PROSEUCH8 I	PRAYER 720C
5	AGAP8 IIA	LOVE 5C
	AKOUW 3B	LEARN 31D
	KURIOS 2Cγ	LORD 461A
	PISTIS 2Dγ	FAITH 669C
	PROS III4B	TOWARD 717C
6	ENARG8S	EVIDENT 261C
	ENERG8S	EFFECTIVE 265B
	EPIGNWSIS	KNOWLEDGE 291B
	KOINWNIA 4	ASSOCIATION 440B
	PISTIS 2Dα	FAITH 669B
7	AGAP8 IIA	LOVE 5C
	ANAPAUW I	CAUSE TO REST 58C
	EPI IIIBγ	ON 287B
	ECHW I2Eβ	HAVE 333B
	PARAKL8SIS 3	COMFORT 623C
	POLUS IIBβ	MANY 694D
	SPLAGCHNON IB	INWARD PARTS 770C
	CHARA I	JOY 883C
	CHARA I	JOY 883D
	CHARIS 5	FAVOR 886D
8	AN8KW 2	IT IS PROPER 65D
	EN I5D	IN 259B
	EPITASSW	COMMAND 302A

8	ECHW I2Eβ	
	PARR8SIA 3A	
	POLUS IIBβ	
9	AGAP8 IIA	
	DESMIOS	
	EIMI II6A	
	MALLON 3Aβ	
	NUNI IA	
	PARAKALEW 3	
	PAULOS	
	PRESBUT8S	
	TOIOUTOS 2B	
10	GENNAW IB	
	DESMOS I	
	ON8SIMOS I	
	HOS,H8,HO I3Bγ	
	HOS,H8,HO I4E	
	PARAKALEW 3	
	TEKNON 2B	
11	EUCHR8STOS	
	NUNI IA	
	ON8SIMOS	
12	ANAPEMPW 2	
	EIMI II3	
	HOUTOS IBε	
	PROSLAMBANW 2B	
	SPLAGCHNON IC	
13	BOULOMAI I	
	DESMOS I	
	DIAKONEW 2	
	EMAUTOU 3	
	EN I4D	
	EUAGGELION IB	
	KATECHW IAα	
	PROS III7	
	HUPER IC	
14	ANAGK8 I	
	GNWM8 3	
	HEKOUSIOS	
	KATA II5A6	
	SOS I	
	CHWRIS 2Bβ	
	CHWRIS 2Bγ	
15	AIWNIOS 3	
	APECHW I	
	DIA BII2	
	HINA I5	
	KAIROS I	
	HOUTOS IBβ	
	PROS III2B	
	TACHA	
	CHWRIZW 2B	
	HWRA 2Aβ	
16	AGAP8TOS 2	
	DOULOS ID	
	KURIOS 2Cγ	
	MALISTA I	
	MALLON 2B	
	OUKETI I	
	POSOS I	
	SARX 6	
	HUPER 2	
	HWS IIIIA	

HAVE 333A	
COURAGE 636A	
MANY 694D	
LOVE 5C	
PRISONER 175A	
TO BE 223C	
RATHER 490C	
NOW 548B	
IMPLORE 622D	
PAUL 643A	
OLD MAN 707C	
SUCH A KIND 829A	
BEGET 154D	
FETTER 175B	
ONESIMUS 573C	
(REL PRON) 587D	
(REL PRON) 588B	
IMPLORE 622D	
CHILD 816B	
USEFUL 329D	
NOW 548B	
ONESIMUS 573C	
SEND 58D	
TO BE 222D	
THIS 601D	
TAKE 724C	
AFFECTION 770C	
DESIRE 145D	
FETTER 175B	
SERVE 183A	
MYSELF 253B	
IN 258C	
GOSPEL 318B	
HOLD BACK 423D	
TOWARD 718A	
IN BEHALF OF 846D	
NECESSITY 52B	
CONSENT 162C	
VOLUNTARY 242D	
ACCORDING TO 408B	
YOURS 766C	
APART 899A	
APART 899C	
ETERNAL 28A	
RECEIVE IN FULL 84B	
FOR THIS REASON 180B	
IN ORDER THAT 378A	
TIME 395C	
THIS 601C	
TOWARD 717A	
PERHAPS 814B	
DIVIDE 898C	
TIME OF DAY 904C	
BELOVED 6C	
SLAVE 204D	
LORD 461A	
ABOVE ALL 490A	
MORE 490C	
NO LONGER 596D	
HOW GREAT 701A	
BODY 751C	
BEYOND 847B	
SO 906C	

17	EI VI10	IF 219A
	KOINWNOS 1D	COMPANION 440D
	PROSLAMBANW 2B	TAKE 724C
18	ADIKEW 2B	INJURE 178
	ELLOGEW	251D
	CHARGE TO ONES ACCOUNT	
	OPHEILW 1	OWE 603C
19	APOTINW	PAY THE DAMAGES 100D
	GRAPHW 1	WRITE 165C
	EMOS 1Aα	MY 255A
	PAULOS	PAUL 643A
	PROSOPHEILW	OWE BESIDES 725A
	CHEIR 1	HAND 888B
20	ANAPAUW 1	CAUSE TO REST 58C
	NAI 3	CERTAINLY 535A
	ONIN8MI	BENEFIT 573D
	SPLAGCHNON 1B	INWARD PARTS 770C
21	GRAPHW 2D	WRITE 166A
	KAI II2	EVEN 394B
	LEGW IIA	SAY 469B
	LEGW IIIF	DECLARE 471A
	HOS,H8,HO I2A	(REL PRON) 587B
	PEITHW 2A	CONVINCE 645B
	HUPAKO8 1B	OBEDIENCE 844D
	HUPER 2	BEYOND 847B
22	HAMA 1A	TOGETHER 41B
	DIA AIII1E	BY 179C
	ELPIZW 2	HOPE 252A
	XENIA	GUEST ROOM 549D
	CHARIZOMAI 1	GIVE FREELY 884D
23	ASPAZOMAI 1A	GREET 116B
	EPAPHRAS	EPAPHRAS 283C
	SUNAICHMALWTOS	791B
	FELLOW PRISONER	
24	ARISTARCHOS	ARISTARCHUS 106B
	D8MAS	DEMAS 177C
	LOUKAS	LUKE 481C
	MARKOS	MARK 493C
	SUNERGOS	WORKING WITH 795C
25	KURIOS 2Cγ	LORD 461A
	META AIIICγ	WITH 510A
	CHARIS 2C	FAVOR 885D

HEBREWS 1

1	KAI IIA	AND 392C
	PALAI 1	LONG AGO 610B
	PAT8R 1B	FOREFATHERS 640D
	POLUMERWS	IN MANY WAYS 693D
	POLUTROPWS	IN VARIOUS WAYS 696D
	PROPH8T8S 1	PROPHET 731A
1F	LALEW 2A6	SPEAK 464B
2	AIWN 3	THE WORLD 27C
	EPI I2	UNDER 286C
	ESCHATOS 3B	LAST 314B
	H8MERA 4B	TIME 348B
	KL8RONOMOS 2A	HEIR 436B
	POIEW IIAβ	DO 687B
	TITH8MI I2Aα	MAKE 824A
	HUIOS 2B	SON 842D
3	HAMARTIA 1	SIN 42C
	APAUGASMA	RADIANCE 81D
	DEXIOS 2A	RIGHT 173D

3	DOXA 1A	GLORY 202D
	DUNAMIS 1	POWER 206D
	EN IIC	IN 257D
	KATHARISMOS 2	PURIFICATION 388C
	KATHIZW 2Aα	SIT DOWN 390D
	MEGALWSUN8	GREATNESS 498C
	PAS 2Bβ	ALL THINGS 638D
	POIEW III1	DO 689C
	R8MA 1	WORD 742D
	TE 1B	AND 815B
	HUPOSTASIS 1	ESSENCE 854D
	HUPS8LOS 1	HIGH 857C
	PHERW 1B	BEAR 862D
	CHARAKT8R 1B	FORM 884B
4	DIAPHOROS 2	OUTSTANDING 190A
	KL8RONOMEW 2	INHERIT 436A
	KREITTWN 1	BETTER 450D
	ONOMA I2A	NAME 574B
	ONOMA I4A	NAME 574D
	HOSOS 3	HOW GREAT 590C
	PARA III3	IN COMPARISON 616B
	TOSOUTOS 2Bγ	SO GREAT 831B
4FF	AGGELOS 2A	ANGEL 7D
5	GENNAW 1B	BEGET 154D
	EIMI III2	TO BE 224A
	EIS 8Aβ	229C
	PALIN 3	AGAIN 611D
	PAT8R 3Dβ	FATHER 641D
	POTE 1	ONCE 701D
	S8MERON	TODAY 756B
	TIS, TI 1Aα	WHICH 826C
5A	HUIOS 2B	SON 842B
5B	HUIOS 2B	SON 842B
6	AGGELOS 2A	ANGEL 7C
	AN 3A	(PARTICLE) 488
	EISAGW	BRING 231C
	OIKOUMEN8 1A	THE WORLD 564A
	PAS 1B	ALL 637B
	PRWTOTOKOS 2A	FIRSTBORN 734A
7	AGGELOS 2A	ANGEL 7C
	LEGW I2A	SAY 469B
	LEITOURGOS 1	SERVANT 472D
	PNEUMA 1A	WIND 680D
	POIEW IIB1	DO 688B
	PUR 1B	FIRE 737C
	PHLOX	FLAME 870A
7F	PROS III5A	TOWARD 717C
8	AIWN 1B	TIME 26D
	BASILEIA 1	KINGDOM 134C
	EUTHUT8S	STRAIGHTNESS 321C
	THEOS 3H	GOD 358C
	THRONOS IC	THRONE 364D
	RABDOS	ROD 740D
	HUIOS 2B	SON 842D
8,9	THEOS 2	GOD 357C
9	AGALLIASIS	EXULTATION 3D
	AGAPAW 2	LOVE 5A
	ADIKIA 1	WRONGDOING 17C
	ANOMIA 1	LAWLESSNESS 71B
	ANOMIA 2	LAWLESSNESS 71B
	DIKAIOSUN8 2B	RIGHTEOUSNESS 195C
	ELAION 2	OLIVE OIL 247B
	METOCHOS 2	PARTNER 516A

9	MISEW 2	HATE 524D
	PARA III3	IN COMPARISON 616B
	CHRIW I	ANOINT 896A
10	ARCH8 IC	BEGINNING IIID
	G8 5A	EARTH 156D
	ERGON 3	WORK 308C
	THEMELIOW I	356C
	LAY THE FOUNDATION OF	
	KATA II2A	DURING 407C
	KURIOS 2Cα	LORD 460C
	OURANOS IE	HEAVEN 599A
	CHEIR 2Aα	HAND 888C
11	APOLLUMI 2Aβ	PASS AWAY 94D
	DIAMENW	REMAIN 185D
	PALAIOW 2	MAKE OLD 610D
	SU IA	YOU 779D
IIF	HIMATION I	GARMENT 377A
12	ALLASSW I	CHANGE 38C
	AUTOS 4B	THE SAME 123C
	EKLEIPW	FAIL 242A
	HELISSW	ROLL UP 250D
	ETOS	YEAR 317A
	PERIBOLAION	COVERING 652B
	HWSEI I	AS 907D
13	DEXIOS 2B	RIGHT 174A
	ECHTHROS 2Bβ	THE ENEMY 331D
	HEWS IIB	UNTIL 334D
	KATH8MAI 2	SIT DOWN 390C
	POTE I	ONCE 701D
	POUS IB	FOOT 703C
	TITH8MI I2Aα	MAKE 824A
	TIS, TI IAα	WHICH 826D
	HUPOPODICN	FOOTSTOOL 854D
14	AGGELOS 2A	ANGEL 7C
	APOSTELLW IBγ	SEND AWAY 98B
	DIAKONIA I	SERVICE 183B
	EIS 4D	FOR 228C
	KL8RONOMEW 2	INHERIT 436A
	LEITOURGIKOS	SERVICE 472C
	MELLW IC6	IS DESTINED 502C
	OUCHI 3	NOT 603A
	PNEUMA 4B	SPIRIT 682A
	SWT8RIA 2	DELIVERANCE 809B

HEBREWS 2

1	AKOUW IBα	HEAR 31B
	M8POTE 2Bα	(NEG PARTICLE) 521A
	PARARREW	DRIFT AWAY 627B
	PERISSOTERWS I	MORE 657C
	PROSECHW IAβ	721C
	PAY ATTENTION TO	
2	AGGELOS 2A	ANGEL 7D
	BEBAIOS 2	FIRM 137D
	DIA AIII2A	BY 179C
	DIATAG8	ORDINANCE 188B
	ENDIKOS	DESERVED 262C
	LALEW 2B	SPEAK 464D
	LOGOS IBα	COMMAND 479A
	MISTHAPODOSIA	PUNISHMENT 525A
	PARABASIS	OVERSTEPPING 617A
	PARAKO8	DISOBEDIENCE 624B
3	AMELEW	TO NEGLECT 44B

3	ARCH8 IB	BEGINNING IIIC
	BEBAIOW I	ESTABLISH 138A
	EKPHEUGW 2A	RUN AWAY 246B
	KURIOS 2Cγ	LORD 460D
	LALEW 2B	SPEAK 464D
	LAMBANW 2	RECEIVE 466C
	PWS ID	HOW 739D
	SWT8RIA 2	DELIVERANCE 809B
	T8LIKOUTOS 2	SO GREAT 822B
4	DUNAMIS 4	MIRACLE 207B
	THEL8SIS	WILL 355B
	MERISMOS 2	DISTRIBUTION 506D
	PNEUMA 5Cβ	SPIRIT 682D
	POIKILOS I	DIVERSIFIED 690A
	S8MEION 2A	SIGN 755D
	SUNEPIMARTUREW	TESTIFY 795A
	TE 3A	AND 815C
5	LALEW 2Aδ	SPEAK 464C
	MELLW 2	IS DESTINED 502C
	OIKOUMEN8 3	THE WORLD 564B
	HUPOTASSW IA	SUBJECT 855C
6	DIAMARTUROMAI 2	TESTIFY 185C
	EPISKEPTOMAI 3	VISIT 298C
	MIMN8SKOMAI IC	REMEMBER 524B
	HO,H8,TO IIII	THE 555A
	HOTI IDγ	THAT 593C
	POU I	SOMEWHERE 703A
	TIS, TI IB6	WHICH 827A
	HUIOS 2C	SON 843B
6A	ANTHRWPOS 2D	MAN 68A
7	BRACHUS 2	SHORT 146D
	DOXA IA	GLORY 202D
	ELATTOW I	INFERIOR 247D
	EPI IIIIBα	OVER 288D
	KATHIST8MI 2A	APPOINT 391B
	PARA III3	IN COMPARISON 616B
	STEPHANOW 2	WREATHE 775B
	TIM8 2B	HONOR 825C
	TIS, TI 2Bβ	ANY ONE 828B
	CHEIR 2Aα	HAND 888C
8	ANUPOTAKTOS I	INDEPENDENT 76A
	APHI8MI 3A	LEAVE 125D
	EN IIIIB	BY 260B
	NUN IC	NOW 547D
	HORAW ICα	SEE 582A
	OUPW	NOT YET 598A
	POUS IB	FOOT 703C
	HUPOKATW	UNDER 852C
8A	HUPOTASSW IA	SUBJECT 855C
8B	HUPOTASSW IA	SUBJECT 855C
8C	HUPOTASSW IBα	SUBJECT 855D
9	BLEPW IA	SEE 143A
	GEUOMAI 2	COME TO KNOW SOMETH 156A
	ELATTOW I	INFERIOR 247D
	THANATOS IBβ	DEATH 351C
	HOPWS 2Aα	IN ORDER THAT 580C
	PATH8MA I	SUFFERING 607C
	PARA III3	IN COMPARISON 616B
	STEPHANOW 2	WREATHE 775B
	TIM8 2B	HONOR 825C
	TIS, TI 2Bβ	ANY ONE 828B
	HUPER IAε	IN BEHALF OF 846C
	CHARIS 2A	FAVOR 885C

9	CHWRIS 2Aα	APART 898D
9B	THANATOS 1A	DEATH 351B
10	AGW 1C	LEAD 14B
	ARCH8GOS 3	ORIGINATOR 112B
	DIA AIII1A	BY MEANS OF 179A
	DOXA 1Bβ	GLORY 203A
	*EIS 4A	INTO 228B
	PATH8MA 1	SUFFERING 607B
	POLUS 11Aα	MANY 694A
	PREPW	BE FITTING 706A
	SWT8RIA 2	DELIVERANCE 809B
	TELEIOW 2A	COMPLETE 817C
	TELEIOW 3	CONSECRATE 818A
	HUIOS 1Cγ	SON 841D
10A	DIA BIII	BECAUSE OF 180B
10A	PAS 2Bβ	ALL THINGS 638D
10B	DIA AIII2Bβ	179D
	BY	
10B	PAS 2Bβ	ALL THINGS 638D
11	HAGIAZW 2	CONSECRATE 8D
	AITIA 1	CAUSE 25D
	GAR 1B	FOR 151B
	EPAISCHUNOMAI 3	BE ASHAMED 281D
	KALEW 1Aβ	CALL 399D
	TE 3A	AND 815C
12	ADELPHOS 2	BROTHER 16A
	APAGGELLW 2	PROCLAIM 78C
	EKKL8SIA 3	ASSEMBLY 240B
	ONOMA 14B	NAME 575B
	HUMNEW 1	SING THE PRAISE OF 844A
13	DIDWMI 3	GIVE 192C
	EPI 111Bγ	ON 287A
	PEITHW 2A	CONVINCE 645B
13A	PALIN 3	AGAIN 611D
13B	PALIN 3	AGAIN 611D
13F	PAIDION 3B	CHILD 609B
14	HAIMA 1A	BLOOD 22A
	DIA AIII1A	BY MEANS OF 179A
	DIABOLOS 2	THE SLANDERER 181A
	EPEI 2	BECAUSE 283D
	HINA IIE	IN ORDER THAT 377C
	KATARGEW 2	ABOLISH 418C
	KOINWNEW 1A	SHARE 439C
	KRATOS 4	POWER 450B
	METECHW	SHARE 515C
	HOUTOS 1Bε	THIS 601D
	PARAPL8SIWS	SIMILARLY 627A
	SARX 4	BODY 751B
14A	THANATOS 1Bβ	DEATH 351C
14B	THANATOS 2B	DEATH 352A
15	DIA AIII1A	THROUGH 178D
	DOULEIA 2	SLAVERY 204A
	ENOCHOS 1	SUBJECT TO 267B
	ZAW 1Aα	LIVE 336B
	THANATOS 1A	DEATH 351C
	HOSOS 2	HOW GREAT 590C
	PHOBOS 2Aα	FEAR 871C
16	ABRAAM	ABRAHAM 1D
	D8POU	SURELY 178B
	EPILAMBANOMAI 2C	GRASP 295A
	SPERMA 2B	SEED 769B
17	ADELPHOS 2	BROTHER 16A
	HAMARTIA 4	SIN 43A

17	ARCHIEREUS 2A	HIGH PRIEST 112C
	ELE8MWN	MERCIFUL 249C
	THEOS 3A	GOD 357D
	HILASKOMAI 2	PROPITIATE 376B
	KATA II6	WITH RESPECT TO 408D
	LAOS 1Cγ	PEOPLE 467D
	HO,H8,TO II5	THE 554B
	HOTHEN 3	FROM WHICH 558A
	HOMOIOW 1	MAKE LIKE 570B
	OPHEILW 2Aβ	OWE 603D
	PISTOS 1Aα	TRUSTWORTHY 670B
	PROS III5B	TOWARD 717D
18	BO8THEW 2	AID 144A
	EN IV6D	IN 261A
	PASCHW 3Aα	SUFFER 639C
18A	PEIRAZW 2B	TRY 646A
18A	PEIRAZW 2D	TRY 646B
18B	PEIRAZW 2B	TRY 646A

HEBREWS 3

1	HAGIOS 1Bα	DEDICATED TO GOD 9D
	APOSTOLOS 2	MESSENGER 99A
	ARCHIEREUS 2A	HIGH PRIEST 112C
	EPOURANIOS 1A6	HEAVENLY 306D
	KATANOEW 3	NOTICE 416A
	KL8SIS 1	CALL 436D
	METOCHOS 1	SHARING 516A
	HOTHEN 3	FROM WHICH 558A
	HOMOLOGIA 2	CONFESSION 571D
2	PISTOS 1Aα	TRUSTWORTHY 670B
	POIEW IIAβ	DO 687B
2≂6	OIKOS 2	HOUSEHOLD 563C
3	AXIOW 1A	CONSIDER WORTHY 77D
	KATA II5A6	ACCORDING TO 408B
	HOSOS 3	HOW GREAT 590C
	PARA III3	IN COMPARISON 616B
	TIM8 2B	HONOR 825B
3A	POLUS IIIB	MANY 695D
3B	POLUS IIIB	MANY 695D
3F	KATASKEUAZW 2	BUILD 419C
4	GAR 2	FOR 151C
	THEOS 3B	GOD 357D
	PAS 1Aα	EVERY EACH 636C
	TIS, TI 1Aα	ANY ONE 827C
4B	KATASKEUAZW 2	BUILD 419C
5	EIS 4D	FOR 228C
	THERAPWN	SERVANT 359D
	MARTURION 1A	TESTIMONY 495A
	MEN 1Aα	(PARTICLE) 503D
	MWUS8S	MOSES 533D
	PISTOS 1Aα	TRUSTWORTHY 670B
	PISTOS 2	TRUSTWORTHY 670D
6	BEBAIOS 2	FIRM 137D
	ELPIS 2B	HOPE 252D
	EPI III1Bβ	OVER 288D
	KATECHW 1Bβ	HOLD FAST 424A
	KAUCH8MA 1	BOAST 427B
	MECHRI 1B	UNTIL 517B
	PARR8SIA 3B	CONFIDENCE 636B
	TELOS 1Dδ	END 819C
	CHRISTOS 2	ANOINTED ONE 895D
7	EAN II0	IF 210D

7	LEGW 17		SAY 470A	16	DIA AIII2A		BY 179C
	HO,H8,TO IIIF		THE 553A		EXERCHOMAI 1Aα		GO OUT 273D
	PNEUMA 5Cα		SPIRIT 682D		PARAPIKRAINW 2	BE DISOBEDIENT	626C
	PHWN8 2A		VOICE 878D	16=18	TIS, TI 1Aα		WHICH 826C
8	ER8MOS 2		DESERT 309A	17	ER8MOS 2		DESERT 309A
	KARDIA 1Bγ		HEART 404D		KWLON		CORPSE 462B
	KATA II2A		DURING 407C		PIPTW 1Bα		FALL 665B
	M8 AIII5A		NOT 518D		PROSOCHTHIZW	BE ANGRY	725A
	PARAPIKRASMOS		REBELLION 626D		TESSARAKONTA		FORTY 820D
	PEIRASMOS 3		TEST 646D	18	APEITHEW 2		DISOBEY 82A
	SKL8RUNW 1A		HARDEN 763C		EISERCHOMAI 2A		COME 232B
9	DOKIMAZW 1		EXAMINE 201C		KATAPAUSIS 2	PLACE OF REST	416D
	DOKIMASIA	PUT TO THE TEST	201D		M8 AIIIBα		NOT 517D
	KAI I2G		AND 393C		OMNUW	TAKE AN OATH	569B
	PEIRAZW 2E		TRY 646C	19	APISTIA 2B		UNBELIEF 85A
	PEIRASMOS 3		TEST 646D		BLEPW 7B		SEE 143C
10	AEI 3		ALWAYS 19A		KAI I2F		AND 393C
	GENEA 2		GENERATION 153B				
	GINWSKW 3A		UNDERSTAND 160B			HEBREWS 4	
	HODOS 2B		WAY 557A				
	PLANAW 2Cα		DECEIVE 671C	1	DOKEW 2A		SEEM 201B
	PROSOCHTHIZW	BE ANGRY	725A		EISERCHOMAI 2A		COME 232B
	TESSARAKONTA		FORTY 820D		EPAGGELIA 2A		PROMISE 280B
11	EI IV		IF 218C		KATALEIPW 2F	LEAVE BEHIND	414D
	EISERCHOMAI 2A		COME 232B		KATAPAUSIS 2	PLACE OF REST	416D
	KATAPAUSIS 2	PLACE OF REST	416D		M8POTE 2Aβ	(NEG PARTICLE)	521A
	OMNUW	TAKE AN OATH	569A		HUSTEREW 1A		TO MISS 856D
	ORG8 2A		ANGER 582D		PHOBEW 1A	BE AFRAID	870D
	HWS IV2		WHEN 907B	2	AK08 2B		REPORT 30C
12	APISTIA 2B		UNBELIEF 85A		EUAGGELIZW 2Bβ		PREACH 318A
	APHIST8MI 2A		FALL AWAY 126C		KATHAPER		JUST AS 387D
	ZAW 1Aε		LIVE 336D		LOGOS 1Bα		COMMAND 479A
	KARDIA 1Bδ		HEART 404D		PISTIS 2Dβ		FAITH 669C
	M8 BIC		NOT 519A		SUGKERANNUMI 2		BLEND 781B
	M8POTE 2Aγ	(NEG PARTICLE)	521A		WPHELEW 1A		HELP 908D
	PON8ROS 1Bβ		WICKED 697D	3	EI IV		IF 218C
13	HAMARTIA 4		SIN 43A		EIPON 4		SAY 225D
	APAT8 1		DECEPTION 81B		EISERCHOMAI 2A		COME 232B
	ACHRI 2A	AS LONG AS	128C		ERGON 1A		DEED 307D
	HEKASTOS 1		EACH 236A		KAITOI	AND YET	396D
	H8MERA 2		DAY 347B		KATABOL8 1		FOUNDATION 410A
	KALEW 1A6		CALL 400B		KATAPAUSIS 2	PLACE OF REST	416D
	KATA II2C		EVERY 407C		KOSMOS 2		WORLD 446D
	PARAKALEW 2		APPEAL TO 622B		OMNUW	TAKE AN OATH	569A
	S8MERON		TODAY 756C		ORG8 2A		ANGER 582D
	SKL8RUNW 2		HARDEN 763C		PISTEUW 2B		BELIEVE 667C
	TIS, TI 1Aα		ANY ONE 827C		HWS IV2		WHEN 907B
14	ARCH8 1B		BEGINNING 111C	4	ERGON 1A		DEED 307D
	BEBAIOS 2		FIRM 137D		H8MERA 2		DAY 347B
	EAN 13C		IF 211A		KATAPAUW 2		STOP 417A
	KATECHW 1Bβ	HOLD FAST	424A		HOUTW 2		THUS 602C
	METOCHOS 1		SHARING 516A		PAS 1Dα		ALL 637C
	MECHRI 1B		UNTIL 517B		POU 1		SOMEWHERE 703A
	TELOS 1Dβ		END 819C	4A	HEBDOMOS		SEVENTH 212A
	HUPOSTASIS 2		CONFIDENCE 854D	4B	HEBDOMOS		SEVENTH 212A
	CHRISTOS 1	ANOINTED ONE	895C	5	EI IV		IF 218C
15	M8 AIII5A		NOT 518D		KATAPAUSIS 2	PLACE OF REST	416D
	PARAPIKRASMOS		REBELLION 626D		PALIN 3		AGAIN 611D
	PROEIPON 2B		FORETELL 711D	5F	EISERCHOMAI 2A		COME 232B
	SKL8RUNW 1A		HARDEN 763C	6	APEITHEIA	DISOBEDIENCE	81D
	PHWN8 2A		VOICE 878D		APOLEIPW 2		REMAIN 94B
16	AIGUPTOS		EGYPT 21C		EPEI 2		BECAUSE 283D
	ALLA 2		BUT, YET 38A		EUAGGELIZW 2Bβ		PREACH 318A

6	PROTEROS 1Bα	EARLIER 729B	14	OURANOS 1E	HEAVEN 599A
7	EN 11D	IN 257D		HUIOS 2B	SON 842D
	H8MERA 3A	DAY 347D	15	ASTHENEIA 2	TIMIDITY 114D
	LEGW 17	SAY 470A		DE 1D	BUT, AND 170C
	META B111	AFTER 511B		KATA 115Bβ	ACCORDING TO 408D
	HORIZW 1Aα	DETERMINE 584C		HOMOIOT8S	LIKENESS 570A
	PROEIPON 2B	FORETELL 711D		OU 7B	NO 595B
	SKL8RUNW 1A	HARDEN 763C		PEIRAZW 2B	TRY 646A
	TIS, TI 2Aα	ANY ONE 828A		PEIRAZW 2D	TRY 646B
	TOSOUTOS 1Aα	SO GREAT 831A		PEIRAW 2	TRY 646D
	PHWN8 2A	VOICE 878D		SUMPATHEW	SYMPATHIZE WITH 786C
	CHRONOS	TIME 896B		CHWRIS 2Bβ	APART 899A
8	AN 1Bα	(PARTICLE) 47D	15A	KATA 116	WITH RESPECT TO 408D
	I8SOUS 1	JOSHUA 374C	16	808THEIA	HELP 144A
	KATAPAUW 1Bβ	BRING TO REST 417A		EIS 4E	SO THAT 228D
	LALEW 2A6	SPEAK 464C		ELEOS 2B	MERCY 249D
9	APOLEIPW 2	REMAIN 94B		EUKAIROS	WELL TIMED 321D
	ARA 4	THEN 103C		HEURISKW 3	FIND 326A
	LAOS 3B	PEOPLE 468B		THRONOS 1B	THRONE 364D
	SABBATISMOS	SABBATH REST 746A		HINA 11C	IN ORDER THAT 377C
10	IDIOS 1Aβ	ONES OWN 370B		LAMBANW 2	RECEIVE 466B
	KATAPAUW 2	STOP 417A		META A111I	WITH 511A
	HWSPER 2	(JUST) AS 908A		OUN 1B	THEREFORE 597B
10F	EISERCHOMAI 2A	COME 232B		PARR8SIA 3B	CONFIDENCE 636B
10F	KATAPAUSIS 2	PLACE OF REST 416D		PROSERCHOMAI 2A	APPROACH 720B
11	APEITHEIA	DISOBEDIENCE 81D	16A	CHARIS 2A	FAVOR 885C
	PIPTW 2Aβ	FALL 665C	16B	CHARIS 2B	FAVOR 885D
	SPOUDAZW 2	HASTEN 771A			
	TIS, TI 1Aγ	ANY ONE 827D			
	HUPODEIGMA 1	EXAMPLE 851D			**HEBREWS 5**
12	HARMOS	JOINT 107B			
	ACHRI 1B	AS FAR AS 128C	1	HAMARTIA 4	SIN 43A
	DIIKNEOMAI	PIERCE 194B		DWRON 2	GIFT 210C
	DISTOMOS	DOUBLE EDGED 199A		THEOS 3A	GOD 357D
	ENARG8S	EVIDENT 261C		THUSIA 2A	SACRIFICE 366D
	ENERG8S	EFFECTIVE 265B		HINA 11A	IN ORDER THAT 377C
	ENTHUM8SIS	THOUGHT 265D		KATHIST8MI 2B	APPOINT 391B
	ENNOIA	THOUGHT 266C		LAMBANW 1F	CHOOSE 466A
	ZAW 4B	LIVE 337C		HO,H8,TO 115	THE 554B
	KRITIKOS	ABLE TO DISCERN 454D		PROS 115B	TOWARD 717D
	MACHAIRA 1	SWORD 497C		PROSPHERW 2A	BRING (TO) 727B
	MACHAIRA 2	SWORD 497C		TE 3A	AND 815B
	MERISMOS 1A	SEPARATION 506D	1B	HUPER 1B	IN BEHALF OF 846C
	MUELOS	MARROW 530D	2	AGNOEW 4	DO WRONG 11C
	PNEUMA 3A	SPIRIT 681B		ASTHENEIA 1C	WEAKNESS 114D
	TOMOS	CUTTING 829D		EPEI 2	BECAUSE 283D
	HUPER 2	BEYOND 847B		METRIOPATHEW	DEAL GENTLY 516C
	PSUCH8 1E	SOUL LIFE 902B		PERIKEIMAI 2B	653D
13	APHAN8S	INVISIBLE 124A			BE PLACED AROUND
	GUMNOS 4	BARE 167A		PLANAW 2Cα	DECEIVE 671C
	DE 1D	BUT, AND 170C	3	HAMARTIA 4	SIN 43A
	ENWPION 4	BEFORE 270C		LAOS 1Cγ	PEOPLE 467D
	KTISIS 1Bα	CREATION 456D		OPHEILW 2Aβ	OWE 603D
	LOGOS 2E	REASON 480A		PROSPHERW 2A	BRING (TO) 727B
	OU 7B	NO 595B	3C	PERI 1G	ABOUT 650C
	OPHTHALMOS 1	EYE 604C	4	AARWN	AARON 1A
	TRACH8LIZW	TO WOUND 832C		KATHWSPER	AS 392C
14	ARCHIEREUS 2A	HIGH PRIEST 112C		KALEW 2	CALL 400D
	DIERCHOMAI 1A	GO THROUGH 193C		LAMBANW 1C	TAKE 465C
	ECHW 12Bβ	HAVE 332D		TIM8 2D	HONOR 825C
	KRATEW 2Eβ	HOLD 450A	5	GENNAW 1B	BEGET 154D
	MEGAS 2Bα	GREAT 499B		GINOMAI 14A	BECOME 158C
	HOMOLOGIA 2	CONFESSION 571D		DOXAZW 2	GLORIFY 203D
				S8MERON	TODAY 756B

5	HUIOS 2B	SON	842B
6	HETEROS 18ζ	ANOTHER	315C
	KATA II5Bα	ACCORDING TO	408C
	LEGW 17	SAY	470A
	MELCHISEDEK	MELCHIZEDEK	503A
	TAXIS 4	FIXED ORDER	811C
7	APO VI	BECAUSE OF	87B
	DAKRUON	TEAR	169A
	DE8SIS	PRAYER	171A
	EISAKOUW 2A	LISTEN TO	231C
	EK IC	AWAY FROM	233D
	EULABEIA	AWE	322A
	H8MERA 4B	TIME	348B
	THANATOS IC	DEATH	351D
	HIKET8RIA	PRAYER	375D
	ISCHUROS 2	STRONG	384A
	KRAUG8 IB	SHOUT	450C
	META AIIII	WITH	511A
	PROSPHERW 2B	BRING (TO)	727B
	SWZW IB	SAVE	805D
	TE 3A	AND	815B
8	KAIPER	ALTHOUGH	395B
	MANTHANW 4	LEARN	491C
	HOS,H8,HO I4A	(REL PRON)	587D
	PASCHW 3B	ENDURE	639D
	HUIOS 2B	SON	842D
	HUPAKO8 IB	OBEDIENCE	844D
9	AITIOS I	SOURCE	26A
	AIWNIOS 3	ETERNAL	28B
	PAS ID8	ALL	637D
	SWT8RIA 2	DELIVERANCE	809A
	*TELEIOW 2A	COMPLETE	817C
	TELEIOW 3	CONSECRATE	818A
	HUPAKOUW I	LISTEN TO	845A
10	ARCHIEREUS 2A	HIGH PRIEST	112C
	MELCHISEDEK	MELCHIZEDEK	503A
	PROSAGOREUW 2	CALL	718B
	TAXIS 4	FIXED ORDER	811C
11	AKO8 IC	HEARING	30B
	DUSERM8EUTOS	HARD TO EXPLAIN	208D
	EPEI 2	BECAUSE	283D
	LOGOS IAζ	MATTER	479A
	NWTHROS	LAZY	549D
	POLUS II8α	MANY	694C
12	ARCH8 IB	BEGINNING	111B
	GAR IB	FOR	151A
	DIA BIII	BECAUSE OF	180A
	DIDASKALOS	TEACHER	190D
	DIDASKW 2C	TEACH	191A
	LOGION	A SAYING	477D
	HO,H8,TO II4B8	THE	553D
	OPHEILW 2A8	OWE	603D
	PALIN IB	AGAIN	611C
	STEREOS I	FIRM	774B
	STOICHEICN I		776C
	FUNDAMENTAL PRINCIPLES		
	TROPH8 2	FOOD	835C
	CHRONOS	TIME	896B
12A	CHREIA I	NEED	893B
12B	CHREIA I	NEED	893B
12F	GALA 2	MILK	149A
13	AKM8N	STILL	30B
	APEIROS I	UNACQUAINTED	82D

13	DIKAIOSUN8 4	RIGHTEOUSNESS	196C
	LOGOS IB8	WORD	479C
	METECHW	SHARE	515C
	N8PIOS IB	CHILDREN	539C
	PAS ICγ	WHOEVER	637B
14	AISTH8T8RION	SENSE	24C
	GUMNAZW	TRAIN	166D
	DIAKRISIS I	DISTINGUISHING	184B
	HEXIS	EXERCISE	275D
	KAKOS IC	EVIL	398D
	KALOS 2B	GOOD	401B
	PROS III3C	TOWARD	717B
	STEREOS I	FIRM	774B
	TELEIOS 2A8	MATURE	817A
	TROPH8 2	FOOD	835C

HEBREWS 6

1	APHI8MI 3B	ABANDON	125D
	EPI IIIIBε	TOWARD	289A
	EPI IIIIBη	ON	289B
	ERGON IC8	DEED	308B
	THEMELIOS 2A	FOUNDATION	356B
	KATABALLW 2	FOUND	409D
	LOGOS IB8	WORD	479B
	METANOIA	REPENTANCE	513D
	NEKROS IB8	DEAD	536D
	PISTIS 2A	FAITH	668C
	TELEIOT8S	MATURITY	817B
	PHERW 3C-	BEAR	863A
2	AIWNIOS 3	ETERNAL	28A
	ANASTASIS 2B	RESURRECTION	60A
	BAPTISMOS	WASHING	132B
	DIDACH8 2	TEACHING	191B
	EPITHESIS	LAYING ON	293A
	KRIMA 3	JUDGING	451D
3	EAN I3C	IF	210D
	EPITREPW I	ALLOW	303C
4	ADUNATOS 2A	IMPOSSIBLE	18D
	HAPAX I	ONCE	80A
	GEUOMAI 2 COME TO KNOW SOMETH		156A
	DWREA	GIFT	209C
	EPOURANIOS IA6	HEAVENLY	306A
	METOCHOS I	SHARING	516A
	PNEUMA 5C8	SPIRIT	682D
	TE IB	AND	815B
	PHWTIZW 2B	SHINE	881C
5	AIWN 2B	AGE	27B
	GEUOMAI 2 COME TO KNOW SOMETH		156A
	DUNAMIS 4	MIRACLE	207B
	KALOS 2C8	GOOD	401C
	MELLW 2	IS DESTINED	502C
	OIKOUMEN8 3	THE WORLD	564B
	R8MA I	WORD	743A
	TE IB	AND	815B
6	ANAKAINIZW	RENEW	55A
	ANASTAUROW	CRUCIFY	60C
	EIS 4A	INTO	228B
	METANOIA	REPENTANCE	514A
	PALIN IB	AGAIN	611C
	PARADEIGMATIZW	EXPOSE	619A
	PARAPIPTW	GO ASTRAY	626D
	HUIOS 2B	SON	842D

7	BOTAN8 1	PLANT	144D
	GEWRGEW	CULTIVATE	156B
	G8 1	EARTH	156C
	EPI IIAβ	ON	285D
	ERCHOMAI IIC«	COME	311B
	EUTHETOS	SUITABLE	320C
	EULOGIA 3B«	BLESSING	323C
	EULOGIA 5	BOUNTY	323B
	METALAMBANW 1	RECEIVE	512C
	PINW 2A	DRINK	664C
	POLLAKIS	OFTEN	693B
	TIKTW 2	BRING FORTH	824C
	HUETOS	RAIN	841A
8	ADOKIMOS	UNQUALIFIED	18B
	AKANTHA	THORN PLANT	29A
	EGGUS 3	NEAR	213C
	KATARA	CURSE	418A
	KAUSIS	BURNING	426C
	TELOS 1C	END	819C
	TRIBOLOS	THISTLE	833D
9	AGAP8TOS 2	BELOVED	6C
	EI VI4	EVEN IF	219A
	ECHW III1	HOLD FAST	334C
	KREITTWN 2	BETTER	450D
	PEITHW 4	OBEY	645C
	SWT8RIA 2	DELIVERANCE	809B
10	AGAP8 IIBγ	LOVE	5D
	HAGIOS 2Dβ	SAINTS	10A
	ADIKOS 1	UNJUST	18A
	DIAKONEW 4	HELP	183B
	ENDEIKNUMI 1	DEMONSTRATE	262A
	EPILANTHANOMAI 2	NEGLECT	295B
	ERGON 1Cβ	DEED	308A
	ONOMA 14Cβ	NAME	575D
11	ELPIS 2B	HOPE	252C
	ENDEIKNUMI 1	DEMONSTRATE	262A
	EPITHUMEW	DESIRE	293A
	*PL8ROPHORIA	CERTAINTY	676C
	PROS III5B	TOWARD	717D
	SPOUD8 2	DILIGENCE	771B
	TELOS 1Dβ	END	819C
12	DE 1D	BUT, AND	170C
	EPAGGELIA 2C	PROMISE	280B
	HINA IIA	IN ORDER THAT	377C
	KL8RONOMEW 2	INHERIT	436A
	MAKROTHUMIA 1	PATIENCE	489B
	MIM8T8S 1	IMITATOR	524A
	NWTHROS	LAZY	549C
	PISTIS 2D«	FAITH	669B
13	*ABRAAM	ABRAHAM	1D
	EPAGGELLOMAI 1B	ANNOUNCE	280C
	EPEI 2	BECAUSE	283D
	ECHW I6A	CAN	334A
	KATA I2A	DOWN	406C
	MEGAS 2B«	GREAT	499B
	OMNUW	TAKE AN OATH	569A
14	EI M8N	SURELY	219C
	EULOGEW 3	BLESS	322D
	8	TRULY	343C
	PL8THUNW 1A	INCREASE	674D
15	EPAGGELIA 2C	PROMISE	280B
	EPITUGCHANW	OBTAIN	303D
	MAKROTHUMEW 1	HAVE PATIENCE	489A

16	ANTILOGIA 1	CONTRADICTION	74C
	BEBAIWSIS	CONFIRMATION	138B
	KATA I2A	DOWN	406C
	OMNUW	TAKE AN OATH	569A
	PERAS 2	END	649D
17	BOUL8 2B	WILL	145B
	BOULOMAI 2B	DESIRE	146A
	EN IV6D	IN	261A
	EPAGGELIA 2C	PROMISE	280B
	EPIDEIKNUMI 2B	SHOW	291D
	KL8RONOMOS 2B	HEIR	436B
	MESITEUW	MEDIATE	507D
	HORKOS	OATH	585B
	PERISSOTEROS 3	GREATER	657C
18	ADUNATOS 2A	IMPOSSIBLE	18D
	AMETATHETOS 1	UNCHANGEABLE	44D
	ISCHUROS 2	STRONG	384A
	KATAPHEUGW 2	FLEE	421A
	KRATEW 2Eβ	HOLD	450A
	PARAKL8SIS 1	ENCOURAGEMENT	623C
	PRAGMA 1	DEED	703D
	PROKEIMAI 2	BE SET BEFORE	714C
	PSEUDOMAI 1	LIE	900A
19	AGKURA 2	ANCHOR	10C
	BEBAIOS 1	FIRM	137D
	EISERCHOMAI 2B	COME	232C
	ESWTEROS	INNER	314C
	KATAPETASMA	CURTAIN	417B
	TE 3A	AND	815B
	PSUCH8 1C	SOUL LIFE	902A
	HWS III1A	SO	906C
20	ARCHIEREUS 2A	HIGH PRIEST	112C
	EISERCHOMAI 1H	COME	232B
	MELCHISEDEK	MELCHIZEDEK	503A
	PRODROMOS	GOING	711C
	TAXIS 4	FIXED ORDER	811C
	HUPER 1A∈	IN BEHALF OF	846C

HEBREWS 7

1	AICHMALWSIA 2	PRISONER OF WAR	26B
	EULOGEW 2A	BLESS	322C
	KOP8	SLAUGHTER	444B
	MELCHISEDEK	MELCHIZEDEK	503A
	HOUTOS 2A	THIS	601D
	SUNANTAW 1	MEET	792B
	HUPOSTREPHW	RETURN	855B
	HUPSISTOS 2	HIGHEST	858B
1F	BASILEUS 1	KING	135D
1F	SAL8M	SALEM	748A
2	DEKATOS 2B	TENTH	173A
	DIKAIOSUN8 2B	RIGHTEOUSNESS	195D
	EIMI II3	TO BE	222D
	EIR8N8 1B	PEACE	226B
	EPEITA 2B	THEN	284B
	HERM8NEUW 2	TRANSLATE	310A
	MEN 1C	(PARTICLE)	504A
	MERIZW 2B	ASSIGN	506A
	HOS,H8,HO I7A	(REL PRON)	588C
	PRWTOS 2B	FIRST	733D
3	AGENEALOG8TOS	WITHOUT GENEALOGY	8C
	AM8TWR	WITHOUT A MOTHER	45C

3	APATWR	FATHERLESS 81C
	ARCH8 1B	BEGINNING 111B
	APHOMOIOW	RESEMBLE 126D
	DI8NEK8S	CONTINUOUS 194B
	EIS 2B	FOR 228A
	ECHW I2F	HAVE 333B
	ZW8 IA	LIFE 340D
	H8MERA 4B	DAY 348C
	MENW IB	REMAIN 505B
	M8TE	AND NOT 521D
	TELOS IA	END 819A
	HUIOS 2B	SON 842D
4	AKROTHINION	BOOTY 33B
	DEKATOS 2B	TENTH 173A
	THEWREW 2A	OBSERVE 360D
	MELCHISEDEK	MELCHIZEDEK 503B
	PATRIARCH8S	PATRIARCH 642B
	P8LIKOS 2	HOW LARGE 662A
5	APODEKATOW 2	COLLECT A TITHE 89B
	EIMI II3	TO BE 222D
	EXERCHOMAI I8α	GO OUT 274C
	ECHW I2I	HAVE 333C
	HIERATEIA	PRIESTLY OFFICE 372B
	KAIPER	ALTHOUGH 395B
	KATA I15Aα	ACCORDING TO 408A
	LAOS ICγ	PEOPLE 467D
	NOMOS 3	LAW 544C
	OSPHUS 2	LOINS 591D
	HUIOS I8α	SON 841C
5F	HO,H8,TO I2	THE 552A
6	GENEALOGEW	TRACE DESCENT 153C
	DEKATOW	RECEIVE TITHES 173B
	EPAGGELIA 2A	PROMISE 280A
6F	EULOGEW 2A	BLESS 322C
7	ANTILOGIA I	CONTRADICTION 74C
	*ELASSWN	SMALLER 247C
	KREITTWN I	BETTER 450D
	HO,H8,TO II2A	THE 553B
	PAS IAα	EVERY EACH 636C
	CHWRIS 2Bβ	APART 899A
8	APOTHN8SKW 2	BE ABOUT TO DIE 91B
	ZAW IAε	LIVE 336D
	MARTUREW 2A	BE WITNESSED 494B
	HWDE 2B	HERE 903D
8F	DEKATOS 2B	TENTH 173B
8F	LAMBANW ID	RECEIVE 465D
9	DEKATOW	RECEIVE TITHES 173B
	EPOS	WORD 305D
	LEUI I	LEVI 473B
	HWS IV3B	WHEN 907B
10	ETI IAβ	STILL 315D
	OSPHUS 2	LOINS 591D
	HOTE IB	WHEN 592C
	SUNANTAW I	MEET 792B
IOF	MELCHISEDEK	MELCHIZEDEK 503A
11	AARWN	AARON IA
	ANIST8MI 2C	RISE 69C
	DIA AIIIID	THROUGH 179B
	EI VI6	IF 219A
	EPI IIBβ	ON 286B
	ETI 2C	STILL 316B
	HIERWSUN8	PRIESTLY OFFICE 374B
	LEUITIKOS	LEVITICAL 473C
11	MEN 2E	(PARTICLE) 504C
	NOMOTHETEW I	RECEIVE LAW 544A
	TELEIWSIS I	PERFECTION 818A
	CHREIA I	NEED 893B
IIA	TAXIS 4	FIXED ORDER 811C
12	ANAGK8 I	NECESSITY 52B
	METATITH8MI 2	CHANGE 515B
	NOMOS 3	LAW 544D
13	EPI IIIIB[	ON 289B
	THUSIAST8RION IA	ALTAR 367B
	LEGW I2A	SAY 469C
	METECHW	SHARE 515C
	HOS,H8,HO I2Bα	(REL PRON) 587B
	PROSECHW IC	PAY ATTENTION TO 721D
	PHUL8 I	TRIBE 876D
14	ANATELLW 2	RISE 61C
	HIEREUS I8α	PRIEST 372C
	IOUDAS IB	JUDAH 38CC
	KURIOS 2Cγ	LORD 461B
	PROD8LOS	CLEAR 711B
	PHUL8 I	TRIBE 876D
15	EI III	IF 218C
	ETI 2B	STILL 316A
	KATAD8LOS	VERY CLEAR 411B
	MELCHISEDEK	MELCHIZEDEK 503A
	HOMOIOT8S	LIKENESS 570A
	PERISSOTEROS 3	GREATER 657C
16	AKATALUTOS	INDESTRUCTIBLE 29B
	DUNAMIS I	POWER 206D
	ENTOL8 2Aα	COMMAND 268C
	ZW8 IA	LIFE 340D
	KATA I15A6	ACCORDING TO 408B
	NOMOS 2	A RULE 544B
	SARKIKOS 3	FLESHLY 750B
	SARKINOS 2	FLESHY 750C
17	MARTUREW 2A	BE WITNESSED 494B
	MELCHISEDEK	MELCHIZEDEK 503A
	TAXIS 4	FIXED ORDER 811C
18	ATHET8SIS I	ANNULMENT 20D
	ANWPHEL8S I	USELESS 76D
	ASTHEN8S 2A	WEAK 115B
	GAR IB	FOR 151B
	GAR IE	FOR 151C
	ENTOL8 2Aα	COMMAND 268C
	PROAGW 2B	LEAD 709A
19	EGGIZW I	APPROACH 212D
	ELPIS 2B	HOPE 252C
	EPEISAGWG8	INTRODUCTION 284B
	KREITTWN I	BETTER 450D
	NOMOS 3	LAW 544C
	TELEIOW I	COMPLETE 817C
	TELEIOW 2Eα	MAKE PERFECT 817D
20	GAR IB	FOR 151B
	HIEREUS I8α	PRIEST 372C
	KATA I15A6	ACCORDING TO 408B
	HOSOS 3	HOW GREAT 590C
20A	CHWRIS 2Bβ	APART 899A
20B	CHWRIS 2Bβ	APART 899A
20F	HO,H8,TO I2	THE 552A
20F	HORKWMOSIA	OATH 585B
20=2	TOSOUTOS 2Bγ	SO GREAT 831C
21	KURIOS 2A	LORD 460B
	METAMELOMAI	REPENT 513A

21	OMNUW	TAKE AN OATH 569A
	TAXIS 4	FIXED ORDER 811C
22	DIATH8K8 2	COVENANT 182B
	EGGUOS	GUARANTEE 213A
	KATA II5A6	ACCORDING TO 408B
	KREITTWN 1	BETTER 450D
	HOSOS 3	HOW GREAT 590C
23	THANATOS 1A	DEATH 351B
	HIEREUS 18α	PRIEST 372C
	KWLUW 1	HINDER 462C
	PARAMENW 2	REMAIN 626A
	POLUS III4	MANY 695C
24	APARABATOS	80A
	WITHOUT A SUCCESSOR	
	MENW 1Cα	REMAIN 505B
25	EIS 3	COMPLETELY 228B
	ENTUGCHANW 1	MEET 269C
	KAI II2	EVEN 394B
	KAI II4	ALSO 394C
	HOTHEN 3	FROM WHICH 558A
	PANTEL8S 1	COMPLETE 613B
	PANTEL8S 3	COMPLETE 613C
	PANTOTE	ALWAYS 614A
	PROSERCHOMAI 2A	APPROACH 720B
	SWZW 2Aα	SAVE 806A
26	AKAKOS	INNOCENT 28D
	HAMARTWLOS 2	SINNER 43D
	AMIANTOS 2	UNDEFILED 45C
	ARCHIEREUS 2A	HIGH PRIEST 112C
	HOSIOS 1B	PIOUS 589C
	OURANOS 1E	HEAVEN 599A
	PREPW	BE FITTING 706A
	TOIOUTOS 2Aβ	SUCH A KIND 829A
	HUPS8LOS 1	HIGH 857C
	CHWRIZW 2C	DIVIDE 898C
27	ANAGK8 1	NECESSITY 52A
	*ANAPHERW 2	OFFER UP 62D
	EPHAPAX 2	ONCE FOR ALL 330B
	ECHW I21	HAVE 333C
	H8MERA 2	DAY 347B
	THUSIA 2A	SACRIFICE 366D
	IDIOS 1Aβ	ONES OWN 370B
	KATA II2C	EVERY 407C
	LAOS 1Cγ	PEOPLE 467D
	PROSPHERW 2A	BRING (TO) 727B
	PROTEROS 1Bα	EARLIER 729B
	HUPER 1B	IN BEHALF OF 846C
	HWSPER 2	(JUST) AS 908A
28	ASTHENEIA 1C	WEAKNESS 114D
	ECHW I2Eβ	HAVE 333A
	KATHIST8MI 2B	APPOINT 391B
	LOGOS 1Bα	COMMAND 479A
	NOMOS 3	LAW 544C
	HORKWMOSIA	OATH 585B
	TELEIOW 2A	COMPLETE 817C
	TELEIOW 3	CONSECRATE 818A
	HUIOS 2B	SON 842D

HEBREWS 8

1	ARCHIEREUS 2A	HIGH PRIEST 112C
	DEXIOS 2A	RIGHT 173D
	EN IIC	IN 257D

	EPI IIIBβ	TO 286D
	ECHW I2Bβ	HAVE 332D
	KATHIZW 2Aα	SIT DOWN 390D
	KEPHALAION 1	MAIN THING 431A
	MEGALWSUN8	GREATNESS 498C
	OURANOS 2A	HEAVEN 599A
	TOIOUTOS 2Aγ	SUCH A KIND 829A
2	HAGIOS 2B	SANCTUARY 10A
	AL8THINOS 3	GENUINE 36C
	KURIOS 2A	LORD 460B
	LEITOURGOS 2	SERVANT 472C
	HOS,H8,HO I4E	(REL PRON) 588B
	P8GNUMI 2	BUILD 661D
	SK8N8	TENT 762B
3	ANAGKAIOS 1	NECESSARY 51D
	THUSIA 2A	SACRIFICE 366D
	KATHIST8MI 2B	APPOINT 391B
	HOTHEN 3	FROM WHICH 558A
	HOUTOS 1Aβ	THIS 601A
3F	DWRON 2	GIFT 210C
3F	PROSPHERW 2A	BRING (TO) 727A
4	AN 1Bα	(PARTICLE) 47D
	EI VI5	FOR IF 219A
	EIMI I6	TO BE 222C
	HIEREUS 18α	PRIEST 372C
	MEN 2E	(PARTICLE) 504C
	NOMOS 3	LAW 544D
	OUDE 3	NOT EVEN 596A
5	DEIKNUMI 1A	SHOW 171D
	EN IIB	IN 257D
	EPITELEW 2	PERFORM 302B
	EPOURANIOS 2Aβ	HEAVENLY 306A
	KATA II5Bα	ACCORDING TO 408C
	LATREUW	SERVE 468D
	MELLW 1Cγ	INTEND 502B
	HORAW 2B	SEE 582B
	OROS	MOUNTAIN 586B
	HOSTIS 2B	WHOEVER 591A
	POIEW IIAα	DO 687A
	POIEW IIAα	DO 687A
	SK8N8	TENT 762A
	SKIA 2	SHADE 763A
	TUPOS 5A	MARK 837D
	HUPODEIGMA 2	EXAMPLE 851D
	PH8MI 1C	SAY 864C
	CHR8MATIZW 1Bα	894A
	IMPART A WARNING	
6	DIATH8K8 2	COVENANT 182B
	DIAPHOROS 2	OUTSTANDING 190A
	EPAGGELIA 2A	PROMISE 280A
	EPI IIIBγ	ON 287A
	KAI II3	ALSO 394B
	KREITTWN 1	BETTER 450D
	LEITOURGIA 1	SERVICE 472B
	MESIT8S	MEDIATOR 508A
	NOMOTHETEW 2	ORDAIN 544A
	NUNI	NOW 548B
	NUNI 2B	NOW 548C
	HOSOS 3	HOW GREAT 590C
	TUGCHANW 1	MEET 837A
7	AMEMPTOS	BLAMELESS 44B
	AN 1Bα	(PARTICLE) 47D
	DEUTEROS 2	SECOND 176A

7   TOIOUTOS 2Aɣ   SUCH A KIND 829A
    TOPOS IF   PLACE 830C
8   DIATH8K8 2   COVENANT 182B
    ERCHOMAI IIBα   COME 311B
    H8MERA 4B   TIME 348B
    IOUDAS IC   JUDAH 380C
    ISRA8L I   ISRAEL 382B
    KAI I2C   AND 393B
    KAINOS 3B   NEW 395B
    MEMPHOMAI   FIND FAULT WITH 503C
    OIKOS 3   NATION 563D
    SUNTELEW 2   COMPLETE 799D
8A   LEGW I8D   SAY 470C
8=I0   DIATH8K8 2   182B
       LAST WILL AND TESTAMENT
8=I0   LEGW I7   SAY 470A
9   AIGUPTOS   EGYPT 21C
    AMELEW   TO NEGLECT 44B
    AUTOS 3B   (OBLIQUE CASE) 123A
    G8 4   LAND 156C
    EMMENW 2   PERSEVERE IN 254D
    EXAGW I   LEAD OUT 271A
    EPILAMBANOMAI I   GRASP 295A
    H8MERA 4A   TIME 348A
    KATA II5Bα   ACCORDING TO 408C
    PAT8R IB   FOREFATHERS 640D
    POIEW IIB6   DO 687C
I0 DIANOIA I   UNDERSTANDING 186A
    DIATITH8MI I   DECREE 188D
    DIDWMI I8β   GIVE 192A
    EIS 8Aβ   229C
    EPIGRAPHW 2   WRITE ON 291D
    ISRA8L I   ISRAEL 382B
    KARDIA IBɣ   HEART 404D
    NOMOS 3   LAW 544D
    OIKOS 3   NATION 563D
II DIDASKW 2A   TEACH 191A
    HEKASTOS 2   EACH 236B
    HEWS II3   AS FAR AS 335D
    MEGAS 2Aα   GREAT 498D
    MIKROS IB   SMALL 523A
    OIDA   KNOW 558A
    POLIT8S 2   CITIZEN 693B
I2 ADIKIA I   WRONGDOING 17C
    ANOMIA 2   LAWLESSNESS 71B
    ETI I8β   STILL 316A
    HILEWS   MERCIFUL 376C
    M8 DIA   NOT 519B
    MIMN8SKOMAI IC   REMEMBER 524B
I3 APHANISMOS   DESTRUCTION 124B
    G8RASKW   GROW OLD 157A
    EGGUS 3   NEAR 213C
    EN IIIIB   BY 260B
    KAINOS 3B   NEW 395B
I3A   PALAIOW I   MAKE OLD 610D
I3B   PALAIOW 2   MAKE OLD 611A

           HEBREWS 9

I   HAGIOS 2Aβ   WHAT IS HOLY IOA
    DIKAIWMA I   REGULATION 197B
    KOSMIKOS I   EARTHLY 446B
    LATREIA   SERVICE 468C

I   MEN 2E   (PARTICLE) 504C
    TE IB   AND 815B
2   HAGIOS 2B   SANCTUARY IOA
    ARTOS IB   BREAD 110B
    KATASKEUAZW 3   FURNISH 419C
    LUCHNIA   LAMPSTAND 484B
    HOSTIS 3   WHOEVER 591B
    PROTHESIS I   SETTING FORTH 713A
    PRWTOS ID   FIRST 733B
    SK8N8   TENT 762A
    TE 3A   AND 815C
    TRAPEZA I   TABLE 832A
3   HAGIOS 2B   SANCTUARY IOA
    DEUTEROS 4   SECOND 176B
    KATAPETASMA   CURTAIN 417A
    LEGW II3   CALL 471B
    META BI   BEHIND 511B
4   AARWN   AARON IA
    BLASTANW 2   SPROUT 141D
    DIATH8K8 3   COVENANT 182C
    KIBWTOS 2   BOX 433A
    MANNA I   MANNA 492A
    PANTOTHEN FROM ALL DIRECTIONS 613C
    PERIKALUPTW   COVER 653C
    PLAX   FLAT STONE 672A
    RABDOS   ROD 740D
    STAMNOS   JAR 771D
    CHRUSION   GOLD 896D
4A   CHRUSOUS   GOLDEN 897B
4B   CHRUSOUS   GOLDEN 897B
5   DOXA IA   BRIGHTNESS 202C
    EIMI I7   TO BE 222C
    HILAST8RION   376B
         THAT WHICH PROPITIATES
    KATA II3B   (DISTRIBUTIVE) 407D
    KATASKIAZW   OVERSHADOW 419D
    MEROS IC   IN PART 507C
    HUPERANW   ABOVE 847D
    CHEROUB   CHERUB 889C
6   DIA AIIIA   THROUGH 178D
    EISEIMI   GO IN 231C
    EPITELEW 2   PERFORM 302C
    HIEREUS IBα   PRIEST 372C
    LATREIA   SERVICE 468C
    MEN IAα   (PARTICLE) 503D
    PRWTOS ID   FIRST 733C
    SK8N8   TENT 762A
7   AGNO8MA   IIC
        SIN DONE IN IGNORANCE
    HAIMA IB   BLOOD 22B
    HAPAX I   ONCE 80A
    DEUTEROS 4   SECOND 176B
    ENIAUTOS I   YEAR 266A
    MONOS IAβ   ONLY 529C
    HOS,H8,HO I4E   (REL PRON) 588B
    PROSPHERW 2A   BRING (TO) 727B
    SK8N8   TENT 762A
    HUPER IAɣ   IN BEHALF OF 846B
    HUPER IB   IN BEHALF OF 846C
    CHWRIS 2Bβ   APART 899A
8   D8LOW   REVEAL 177C
    ETI IAβ   STILL 315D
    M8PW   NOT YET 521B

8	HO,H8,TO IIIF	THE	553A
	HODOS IA	WAY	556C
	PNEUMA 5Cα	SPIRIT	682D
	PRWTOS ID	FIRST	733C
	SK8N8	TENT	762A
	STASIS I	EXISTENCE	771D
	PHANEROW IB	REVEAL	860C
9	DWRON 2	GIFT	210C
	ENIST8MI I	BE PRESENT	266B
	THUSIA 2A	SACRIFICE	366D
	KAIROS I	TIME	395D
	LATREUW	SERVE	468D
	HOSTIS 3	WHOEVER	591B
	PARABOL8 I	COMPARISON	617C
	PROSPHERW 2A	BRING (TO)	727B
	SUNEID8SIS 2	CONSCIOUSNESS	794C
	TELEIOW 2Eα	MAKE PERFECT	817D
9B	KATA II6	WITH RESPECT TO	408D
10	BAPTISMOS	WASHING	132B
	BRWMA I	FOOD	147C
	DIAPHOROS I	DIFFERENT	190A
	DIKAIWMA I	REGULATION	197B
	DIORTHWSIS	NEW ORDER	198B
	EPI IIIBγ	ON	287A
	EPIKEIMAI 2C	BE IMPOSED	294C
	KAIROS 3	TIME	396A
	MECHRI IB	UNTIL	517B
	MONOS 2B	ONLY	529D
	POMA I	A DRINK	696D
	SARX 2	BODY	751A
11	AGATHOS 2Bγ	GOOD	3C
	ARCHIEREUS 2A	HIGH PRIEST	112C
	KTISIS IBβ	CREATION	457A
	MELLW 2	IS DESTINED	502C
	PARAGINOMAI 2	COME	619A
	TELEIOS IAα		816D
		HAVING ATTAINED THE END	
	CHEIROPOI8TOS		889A
		MADE BY HUMAN HANDS	
	CHRISTOS 2	ANOINTED ONE	895D
IIF	SK8N8	TENT	762B
12	HAGIOS 2B	SANCTUARY	IOA
	*HAIMA IB	BLOOD	22B
	HAIMA 2B	BLOOD	22C
	AIWNIOS 3	ETERNAL	28A
	DE ID	BUT, AND	170C
	EISERCHOMAI IAβ	COME	231D
	HEURISKW 3	FIND	326A
	EPHAPAX 2	ONCE FOR ALL	330B
	IDIOS IAβ	ONES OWN	370B
	LUTRWSIS I	REDEMPTION	484B
	MOSCHOS	CALF	530C
12F	TRAGOS	HE GOAT	831D
13	HAGIAZW 2	CONSECRATE	8D
	HAIMA IB	BLOOD	22B
	DAMALIS	HEIFER	169B
	KATHAROT8S	PURITY	389B
	KOINOW IA	DEFILE	439B
	RANTIZW I	SPRINKLE	741C
	SARX 2	BODY	751A
	SPODOS	ASHES	770D
	TAUROS	BULL	813D
14	HAIMA 2B	BLOOD	22C
14	AIWNIOS 2	ETERNAL	28A
	AMWMOS I	UNBLEMISHED	47B
	ARCHIEREUS 2A	HIGH PRIEST	112C
	ERGON ICβ	DEED	308B
	ZAW IAε	LIVE	336D
	KATHARIZW 2Bα	CLEANSE	388B
	LATREUW	SERVE	468C
	MALLON 2B	MORE	490C
	NEKROS IBβ	DEAD	536D
	PNEUMA 5Cβ	SPIRIT	683A
	POSOS I	HOW GREAT	701A
	PROSPHERW 2A	BRING (TO)	727B
	SARX 2	BODY	751A
	SUNEID8SIS 2	CONSCIOUSNESS	794B
	SUNEID8SIS 2	CONSCIOUSNESS	794C
15	APOLUTRWSIS 2A	REDEMPTION	95D
	GINOMAI I3A	TAKE PLACE	157D
	DIA BII2	FOR THIS REASON	180B
	EPAGGELIA 2A	PROMISE	280B
	EPI IIIBγ	ON	287A
	EPI II2	AT	287C
	KAINOS 3B	NEW	395B
	KALEW 2	CALL	400C
	KL8RONOMIA 3	INHERITANCE	436A
	MESIT8S	MEDIATOR	508A
	HOPWS 2Aα	IN ORDER THAT	580C
	PARABASIS	OVERSTEPPING	617A
	PRWTOS IA	FIRST	732D
15A	DIATH8K8 2	COVENANT	182B
15B	DIATH8K8 2	COVENANT	182B
15F	THANATOS IA	DEATH	351B
16	ANAGK8 I	NECESSITY	52A
	HOPOU 2A	WHERE	579D
	PHERW 4Aβ	BEAR	863B
16F	DIATH8K8 I		182A
		LAST WILL AND TESTAMENT	
16F	DIATITH8MI 3	MAKE A WILL	189A
17	BEBAIOS 2	FIRM	137D
	EPEI 2	BECAUSE	283D
	EPI IIIBγ	ON	287A
	ISCHUW 4	BE VALID	384D
	M8POTE I	(NEG PARTICLE)	521A
	HOTE ID	WHEN	592C
18	HAIMA IB	BLOOD	22B
	EGKAINIZW 2	DEDICATE	214C
	HOTHEN 3	FROM WHICH	558A
	CHWRIS 2Bβ	APART	899A
19	HAIMA IB	BLOOD	22B
	BIBLION I	BOOK	140D
	ENTOL8 2Aα	COMMAND	268C
	ERION	WOOL	309C
	KOKKINOS	SCARLET	441A
	LALEW 2B	SPEAK	464D
	LAMBANW IA	TAKE	465B
	MOSCHOS	CALF	530C
	NOMOS 4A	LAW	545A
	RANTIZW I	SPRINKLE	741C
	TRAGOS	HE GOAT	831D
	HUSSWPOS	HYSSOP	856C
19B	PAS ICα	ALL	637B
19C	PAS ICα	ALL	637B
20	DIATH8K8 2	COVENANT	182B
	ENTELLW	COMMAND	268A

21	LEITOURGIA I	SERVICE	472B
	PAS IDα	ALL	637C
	RANTIZW I	SPRINKLE	741C
	SKEUOS IA	THING	761C
	SK8N8	TENT	762A
22	HAIMATEKCHUSIA		22D
	SHEDDING OF BLOOD		
	HAIMA 2B	BLOOD	22D
	APHESIS 2	PARDON	124C
	EN IIIIA	BY	260A
	NOMOS 3	LAW	544C
	SCHEDON	NEARLY	804D
	CHWRIS 2Bβ	APART	899A
22F	KATHARIZW 2C	CLEANSE	388C
23	ANAGK8 I	NECESSITY	52A
	AUTOS IAβ	SELF	122B
	EPOURANIOS 2Aβ	HEAVENLY	306A
	THUSIA 2A	SACRIFICE	367A
	KREITTWN I	BETTER	450D
	OURANOS IE	HEAVEN	599A
	PARA III3	IN COMPARISON	616B
	HUPODEIGMA 2	EXAMPLE	851D
23FF	HAMARTIA 4	SIN	43A
24	AL8THINOS 3	GENUINE	36D
	ANTITUPOS 2	COPY	75C
	EMPHANIZW IA	MAKE VISIBLE	257A
	OURANOS IE	HEAVEN	599A
	PROSWPON IB	FACE	728B
	CHEIROPOI8TOS		889A
	MADE BY HUMAN HANDS		
24F	HAGIOS 2B	SANCTUARY	10A
24F	EISERCHOMAI IAB	COME	231D
25	HAIMA IB	BLOOD	22B
	ALLOTRIOS IA	TO ANOTHER	40A
	EN I4Cβ	IN	258C
	ENIAUTOS I	YEAR	266A
	KATA II2C	EVERY	407C
	OUDE I	AND NOT	595D
	PROSPHERW 2A	BRING (TO)	727B
	HWSPER 2	(JUST) AS	908A
25F	POLLAKIS	OFTEN	693B
26	ATHET8SIS 2	ANNULMENT	20D
	AIWN 2A	AGE	27B
	HAPAX I	ONCE	80A
	DIA AIIIIA	BY MEANS OF	179A
	EPEI 2	BECAUSE	283D
	EPI II2	AT	287D
	THUSIA 2A	SACRIFICE	367A
	KATABOL8 I	FOUNDATION	410A
	KOSMOS 2	WORLD	446D
	NUNI	NOW	548B
	NUNI 2B	NOW	548C
	PASCHW 3Aα	SUFFER	639C
	SUNTELEIA	CLOSE	799C
	PHANEROW 2Bβ	REVEAL	860D
27	ANTHRWPOS IB	MAN	67D
	HAPAX I	ONCE	80A
	APOTHN8SKW IAα	DIE	90D
	APOKEIMAI 2	BE PUT AWAY	92B
	KATA II5Bα	ACCORDING TO	408C
	KRISIS IAα	JUDGING	453D
	META BII3	AFTER	511C
27F	HOSOS 3	HOW GREAT	590C

27F	HOUTW IA	THUS	602B
28	ANAPHERW 3	TAKE AWAY	62D
	HAPAX I	ONCE	80A
	APEKDECHOMAI	AWAIT	82D
	DEUTEROS 4	SECOND	176B
	HORAW IAδ	SEE	582A
	PROSPHERW 2A	BRING (TO)	727B
	SWT8RIA 2	DELIVERANCE	809B
	CHRISTOS I	ANOINTED ONE	895C
	CHWRIS 2Bδ	APART	899C

HEBREWS 10

I	AGATHOS 2Bγ	GOOD	3C
	DI8NEK8S	CONTINUOUS	194B
	EIKWN 2	FORM	221C
	EIS 2B	FOR	228A
	ENIAUTOS I	YEAR	266A
	THUSIA 2A	SACRIFICE	366D
	KATA II2C	EVERY	407C
	NOMOS 3	LAW	544C
	OUDEPOTE	NEVER	596D
	PRAGMA 4	DEED	703D
	PROSERCHOMAI 2A	APPROACH	720B
	PROSPHERW 2A	BRING (TO)	727A
	SKIA 2	SHADE	763A
	TELEIOW	COMPLETE	817B
	TELEIOW 2Eα	MAKE PERFECT	817D
2	HAMARTIA 4	SIN	43A
	AN IBβ	(PARTICLE)	48A
	HAPAX 2	ONCE	80A
	EPEI 2	BECAUSE	283D
	ECHW I2Eβ	HAVE	333B
	KATHARIZW 2Bα	CLEANSE	388B
	LATREUW	SERVE	468D
	M8DEIS I	NO	520A
	PAUW 2	STOP	643D
	PROSPHERW 2A	BRING (TO)	727A
	SUNEID8SIS I	CONSCIOUSNESS	794A
3	HAMARTIA 4	SIN	43A
	ANAMN8SIS	REMINDER	57C
	ENIAUTOS I	YEAR	266A
	KATA II2C	EVERY	407C
4	ADUNATOS 2A	IMPOSSIBLE	18D
	HAMARTIA I	SIN	42C
	APHAIREW I	CUT OFF	123D
	TAUROS	BULL	813D
	TRAGOS	HE GOAT	831D
5	EISERCHOMAI IAγ	COME	231D
	THUSIA 2A	SACRIFICE	366D
	KATARTIZW 2B	PREPARE	419A
	KOSMOS 4C	WORLD	447B
	PROSPHORA 2	PRESENTING	727C
	SWMA IB	BODY	807B
6	HAMARTIA 4	SIN	43A
	EUDOKEW 2B	WELL PLEASED	319C
	HOLOKAUTWMA I		567B
	WHOLE BURNT OFFERING		
	PERI IG	ABOUT	650C
	PROSPHORA 2	PRESENTING	727D
7	BIBLION I	BOOK	140D
	H8KW IC	HAVE COME	345B
	THEL8MA ICγ	WILL	355A

7 THEOS 3H .... GOD 358C
   KEPHALIS .... ROLL OF A BOOK 431D
   HO,H8,TO II4B⟨ .... THE 554B
   POIEW IICα .... DO 688C
8 HAMARTIA 4 .... SIN 43A
   EUDOKEW 2B .... WELL PLEASED 319C
   THUSIA 2A .... SACRIFICE 366D
   NOMOS 3 .... LAW 544D
   HOLOKAUTWMA I 567B
      WHOLE BURNT OFFERING
   PERI IG .... ABOUT 650C
   PROSPHORA 2 .... PRESENTING 727C
9 ANAIREW IB .... DO AWAY WITH 54D
   DEUTEROS 2 .... SECOND 176A
   H8KW IC .... HAVE COME 345B
   THEL8MA ICγ .... WILL 355A
   HIST8MI IIBα .... PUT 383A
   POIEW IICα .... DO 688C
   PRWTOS IB .... FIRST 733A
10 HAGIAZW 2 .... CONSECRATE 8D
   DIA AIIIIA .... BY MEANS OF 179A
   EN III3A .... BECAUSE OF 260C
   EPHAPAX 2 .... ONCE FOR ALL 330B
   THEL8MA IA .... WILL 354D
   PROSPHORA I .... PRESENTING 727C
   SWMA IB .... BODY 807B
   CHRISTOS 2 .... ANOINTED ONE 895C
11 HAMARTIA I .... SIN 42C
   H8MERA 2 .... DAY 347B
   THUSIA 2A .... SACRIFICE 366D
   HIEREUS IBα .... PRIEST 372C
   KATA II2C .... EVERY 407C
   LEITOURGEW I 471D
      PERFORM A PUBLIC SERVICE
   HOSTIS 2B .... WHOEVER 591A
   OUDEPOTE .... NEVER 596D
   POLLAKIS .... OFTEN 693B
   PROSPHERW 2A .... BRING (TO) 727A
12 HAMARTIA 4 .... SIN 43A
   DEXIOS 2A .... RIGHT 173D
   DI8NEK8S .... CONTINUOUS 194B
   EIS 2B .... FOR 228A
   THUSIA 2A .... SACRIFICE 367A
   KATHIZW 2Aα .... SIT DOWN 390D
   PROSPHERW 2A .... BRING (TO) 727B
   HUPER IB .... IN BEHALF OF 846D
13 EKDECHOMAI .... WAIT 237D
   ECHTHROS 2Bβ .... THE ENEMY 331D
   HEWS IIB .... UNTIL 334D
   LOIPOS 3Aα .... THE REST 481B
   POUS IB .... FOOT 703C
   TITH8MI I2Aα .... MAKE 824A
   HUPOPODIUN .... FOOTSTOOL 854D
14 HAGIAZW 2 .... CONSECRATE 8D
   ANASWZW .... SAVE 61B
   DI8NEK8S .... CONTINUOUS 194B
   EIS 2B .... FOR 228A
   PROSPHORA I .... PRESENTING 727C
   TELEIOW 2Eα .... MAKE PERFECT 817D
15 MARTUREW IA .... BEAR WITNESS 493D
   META BII4B .... AFTER 511D
   HO,H8,TO IIIF .... THE 553A
   PNEUMA 5Cα .... SPIRIT 682D

15 PROEIPON 2A .... FORETELL 711D
16 DIATH8K8 2 .... 182B
      LAST WILL AND TESTAMENT
   DIANOIA I .... UNDERSTANDING 186A
   DIATITH8MI I .... DECREE 189A
   DIDWMI IBβ .... GIVE 192A
   EPIGRAPHW 2 .... WRITE ON 291D
   NOMOS 3 .... LAW 544D
17 ANOMIA 2 .... LAWLESSNESS 71B
   ETI IBβ .... STILL 316A
   M8 D2 .... NOT 519C
   MIMN8SKOMAI IC .... REMEMBER 524B
18 HAMARTIA 4 .... SIN 43A
   APHESIS 2 .... PARDON 124C
   HOPOU 2A .... WHERE 579D
   PERI IG .... ABOUT 650C
   PROSPHORA I .... PRESENTING 727C
19*HAGIOS 2B .... SANCTUARY IOA
   HAIMA 2B .... BLOOD 22C
   EISODOS I .... ENTRANCE 232C
   ECHW I2Eβ .... HAVE 333A
   PARR8SIA 3B .... CONFIDENCE 636B
20 EGKAINIZW I .... RENEW 214C
   ZAW 4B .... LIVE 337C
   KATAPETASMA .... CURTAIN 417B
   PROSPHATOS .... NEW 726D
   SARX 2 .... BODY 751A
21 EPI IIIBα .... OVER 288D
   OIKOS IAβ .... HOUSE 563B
22 AL8THINOS I .... TRUE 36B
   KATHAROS I .... CLEAN 388D
   KARDIA IB6 .... HEART 404D
   KARDIA IBε .... HEART 405A
   LOUW 2B .... BATHE 482B
   PISTIS 2Dα .... FAITH 669B
  *PL8ROPHORIA .... CERTAINTY 676C
   PON8ROS IBβ .... WICKED 697D
   PROSERCHOMAI 2A .... APPROACH 720B
   RANTIZW 2B .... CLEANSE 741C
   SUNEID8SIS 2 ..... CONSCIOUSNESS 794C
   HUDWR I .... WATER 840D
23 AKLIN8S .... WITHOUT WAVERING 30A
   ELPIS 2B .... HOPE 252C
   EPAGGELLOMAI IB .... ANNOUNCE 280C
   KATECHW IBβ .... HOLD FAST 424A
   HOMOLOGIA 2 .... CONFESSION 571D
   PISTOS IAβ .... TRUSTWORTHY 670C
24 AGAP8 IIA .... LOVE 5C
   ERGON ICβ .... DEED 308A
   KALOS 2B .... GOOD 401B
   KATANOEW 3 .... NOTICE 416A
   PAROXUSMOS I .... STIRRING UP 634D
25 EGGIZW 5B .... APPROACH 212D
   EGKATALEIPW 2 .... FORSAKE 214D
   ETHOS I .... HABIT 217C
   EPISUNAGWG8 I .... MEETING 301D
   H8MERA 3Bβ .... DAY 348A
   MALLON 2A .... RATHER 490D
   HO,H8,TO IIIAα .... THE 552C
   HOSOS 3 .... HOW GREAT 590C
   PARAKALEW 2 .... APPEAL TO 622C
   TOSOUTOS 2Bγ .... SO GREAT 831B
26 AL8THEIA 2B .... TRUTH 35C

26 HAMARTANW 3	SIN 41D	33 TE 3A	AND 815B
APOLEIPW 2	REMAIN 94B	34 HARPAG8 I	ROBBERY 108A
HEKOUSIWS	WILLINGLY 242D	GINWSKW 6B	KNOW 160C
EPIGNWSIS	KNOWLEDGE 291B	DESMIOS	PRISONER 175A
THUSIA 2A	SACRIFICE 366D	KREITTWN I	BETTER 450D
META 8II4B	AFTER 511D	MENW IC8	REMAIN 505C
PERI IG	ABOUT 650C	META AIIII	WITH 511A
27 EKDOCH8	EXPECTATION 238C	PROSDECHOMAI IB	RECEIVE 719B
ESTHIW 2	CONSUME 313C	SUMPATHEW	SYMPATHIZE WITH 786C
Z8LOS I	ZEAL 338B	HUPARXIS 2	PROPERTY 845D
KRISIS IA8	JUDGING 453D	HUPARCHW I	BE 845D
MELLW IC8	BE ABOUT TO 502B	CHARA I	JOY 883C
PUR IB	FIRE 737C	35 APOBALLW 2	LOSE 88B
TIS, TI 2B8	ANY ONE 828B	ECHW I4	HAVE 333D
HUPENANTIOS	OPPOSED 846A	MEGAS 2A8	GREAT 498D
PHOBEROS	FEARFUL 870A	MISTHAPODOSIA	REWARD 525A
28 ATHETEW IA	SET ASIDE 20C	PARR8SIA 3B	CONFIDENCE 636B
APOTHN8SKW IA«	DIE 90D	36 EPAGGELIA 2B	PROMISE 280B
DUO 3	TWO 208C	ECHW I2I	HAVE 333C
EPI IIIBγ	ON 287A	THEL8MA ICγ	WILL 355A
MARTUS I	WITNESS 495B	KOMIZW 2A	BRING 443D
NOMOS 3	LAW 544C	HUPOMON8 I	PATIENCE 854A
OIKTIRMOS	PITY 564C	CHREIA I	NEED 893B
TIS, TI IA6	ANY ONE 828A	37 ERCHOMAI IIAη	COME 310D
CHWRIS 2B8	APART 899A	ETI IC	STILL 316A
29 HAGIAZW 2	CONSECRATE 8D	H8KW IC	HAVE COME 345B
HAIMA 2B	BLOOD 22C	MIKROS 3E	A LITTLE WHILE 523C
AXIOW IA	CONSIDER WORTHY 77D	HOSOS I	HOW GREAT 590B
DIATH8K8 2	COVENANT 182B	CHRONIZW I	TAKE TIME 896A
DOKEW IE	THINK 201A	CHRONIZW I	TAKE TIME 896A
ENUBRIZW	INSULT 269D	38 DIKAIOS IB	UPRIGHT 195A
H8GEOMAI 2	CONSIDER 344B	EUDOKEW 2A	WELL PLEASED 319C
KATAPATEW 2	TRAMPLE 416D	ZAW 2B8	LIVE 337B
KOINOS 2	COMMON 439B	PISTIS 2A	FAITH 668D
PNEUMA 5E	SPIRIT 683C	PISTIS 2D«	FAITH 669B
POSOS I	HOW GREAT 701A	HUPOSTELLW 2A	WITHDRAW 855A
TIMWRIA	PUNISHMENT 826B	PSUCH8 IBγ	SOUL LIFE 901D
HUIOS 2B	SON 842D	39 APWLEIA 2	DESTRUCTION 103A
CHARIS 3B	FAVOR 886B	EIMI IV4	TO BE 225A
30 ANTAPODIDWMI 2	REPAY 72B	EIS 4E	SO THAT 228D
EKDIK8SIS	VENGEANCE 238B	PERIPOI8SIS I	KEEPING SAFE 656A
KRINW 4B«	JUDGE 453A	PISTIS 2D«	FAITH 669B
OIDA IA	KNOW 558B	HUPOSTOL8	TIMIDITY 855A
PALIN 3	AGAIN 611D	PSUCH8 IC	SOUL LIFE 902A
31 EMPIPTW 2	FALL 255D		
ZAW IA«	LIVE 336D		
PHOBEROS	FEARFUL 870A	HEBREWS II	
CHEIR 2Aγ	HAND 888D		
32 ATHL8SIS	CONTEST 21A	I ELEGCHOS I	PROOF 248C
ANAMIMN8SKW	REMIND 57C	ELPIZW I	HOPE 252A
H8MERA 4B	TIME 348B	OU 3A	NO 594C
PATH8MA I	SUFFERING 607B	PISTIS 2D8	FAITH 669C
POLUS IIB8	MANY 694C	PRAGMA 4	DEED 703D
PROTEROS IB8	EARLIER 729C	HUPOSTASIS 2	CONFIDENCE 854D
HUPOMENW 2	REMAIN 853D	HUPOSTASIS 2	CONFIDENCE 855A
PHWTIZW 2B	SHINE 881C	2 MARTUREW 2B	BE APPROVED 494B
33 ANASTREPHW 2B6	LIVE 61A	PRESBUTEROS IB	OLDER 706C
THEATRIZW	PUT TO SHAME 354A	3 AIWN 3	THE WORLD 27C
THLIPSIS I	TRIBULATION 362D	EIS 4E	SO THAT 228D
KOINWNOS IA8	COMPANION 440C	KATARTIZW 2A	PREPARE 418D
MEN IC	(PARTICLE) 504A	NOEW IC	UNDERSTAND 542C
ONEIDISMOS	REPROACH 573C	PISTIS 2A	FAITH 668D
HOUTOS IB6	THIS 601D	R8MA I	WORD 742D
		PHAINW 2B	APPEAR 859C

4	HABEL	ABEL	1C
	DIKAIOS 1B	UPRIGHT	194D
	DWRON 2	GIFT	210C
	EPI III B6	ON	287C
	ETI 1Aα	STILL	315D
	THUSIA 2A	SACRIFICE	366D
	KAIN	CAIN	394D
	LALEW I	SOUND	464B
	PARA III3	IN COMPARISON	616B
	POLUS III B	MANY	695D
	PROSPHERW 2A	BRING (TO)	727A
4A	MARTUREW 2B	BE APPROVED	494B
4B	MARTUREW 1A	BEAR WITNESS	493D
4=33	PISTIS 2A	FAITH	668C
5	DIOTI I	BECAUSE	198C
	EIDON 5	SEE	220A
	ENWCH	ENOCH	270D
	EUARESTEW I	PLEASE	318D
	HEURISKW 1A	FIND	325B
	THANATOS 1A	DEATH	351B
	MARTUREW 2B	BE APPROVED	494B
	METATHESIS I	REMOVAL	512B
	HO,H8,TO 114Bζ	THE	554B
5A	METATITH8MI I	TRANSLATED	515B
5B	METATITH8MI I	TRANSLATED	515B
6	ADUNATOS 2A	IMPOSSIBLE	18D
	GINOMAI III	BE	159B
	EIMI II	TO BE	222A
	EKZ8TEW I	SEEK OUT	239C
	MISTHAPODOT8S	REWARDER	525A
	PISTEUW 1Aβ	BELIEVE	666A
	PROSERCHOMAI 2A	APPROACH	720B
	CHWRIS 28γ	APART	899C
7	DIKAIOSUN8 3	RIGHTEOUSNESS	196A
	EULABEOMAI I	BE AFRAID	322B
	KATA II7C	(GENITIVE)	409A
	KATAKRINW	CONDEMN	413B
	KATASKEU4ZW 2	BUILD	419C
	KIBWTOS I	BOX	433B
	KL8RONOMOS 2B	HEIR	436B
	M8DEPW	NOT YET	520B
	NWE	NOAH	549C
	SWT8RIA I	DELIVERANCE	808D
	CHR8MATIZW 1Bα		894A
	IMPART A WARNING		
8	EXERCHOMAI 1Aβ	GO OUT	274A
	EPISTAMAI 2	KNOW	300A
	ERCHOMAI II Aγ	COME	310C
	KALEW 1D	CALL	400C
	KL8RONOMIA 2	INHERITANCE	436A
	MELLW 1C6	IS DESTINED	502C
	POU 2B	WHERE	703A
	HUPAKOUW I	LISTEN TO	845B
9	ALLOTRIOS 1A	TO ANOTHER	40A
	EIS 9A	IN	229D
	EPAGGELIA 2A	PROMISE	280B
	IAKWB I	JACOB	368B
	ISAAK	ISAAC	381C
	KATOIKEW 1A	LIVE	425B
	PAROIKEW 1C	MIGRATE	634B
	SK8N8	TENT	762A
	SUGKL8RONOMOS		781D
	INHERITING TOGETHER		
9	HWS IIIIA	SO	906C
9B	EPAGGELIA 2C	PROMISE	280B
10	D8MIOURGOS	CREATOR	178A
	EKDECHOMAI	WAIT	237D
	ECHW I2Cβ	HAVE	332D
	POLIS 2	CITY	692C
	TECHNIT8S	CRAFTSMAN	821D
11	HAIMA 1A	BLOOD	22A
	AUTOS 1G	EVEN	122C
	EPAGGELLOMAI 1B	ANNOUNCE	280C
	EPEI 2	BECAUSE	283D
	H8GEOMAI 2	CONSIDER	344B
	H8LIKIA 1Cα	AGE	346A
	KAIROS 3	TIME	396A
	KATABOL8 I	FOUNDATION	410B
	KATABOL8 2	FOUNDATION	410B
	PARA III3	IN COMPARISON	616B
	PISTOS 1Aα	TRUSTWORTHY	670B
	PISTOS 1Aβ	TRUSTWORTHY	670C
	SARRA	SARAH	752B
	SPERMA 1B	SEED	769A
	SPERMA 2B	SEED	769B
	TEKNOW	BEGET	816D
12	AMMOS	SAND	45D
	ANARITHM8TOS	INNUMERABLE	59C
	APO V4	FROM	87C
	ASTRON	STAR	118A
	GENNAW 1A	BEGET	154C
	THALASSA 1A	SEA	350D
	KAI I3	AND	394A
	NEKROW	PUT TO DEATH	537C
	OURANOS 1C	HEAVEN	598C
	HOUTOS 1Bγ	THIS	601D
	PARA III1D	ALONG	616A
	PL8THOS I	QUANTITY	674B
	CHEILOS 2	SHORE	887D
	HWS II3Aα	SO	906A
13	ASPAZOMAI 2	GREET	116C
	G8 5A	EARTH	156D
	EPAGGELIA 2B	PROMISE	280B
	KOMIZW 2A	BRING	443D
	XENOS 2A	THE STRANGER	550B
	HOMOLOGEW 2	ADMIT	571B
	PAREPID8MOS	EXILE	631B
	PAS 1Eβ	ALL	637D
	PEITHW 3A	BELIEVE	645B
	PORRWTHEN	FROM A DISTANCE	700C
14	EMPHANIZW 2	MAKE VISIBLE	257A
	EPIZ8TEW 2A	STRIVE FOR	292D
	LEGW IIA	SAY	469B
	PATRIS I	FATHERLAND	642C
	TOIOUTOS 3B	SUCH A KIND	829C
15	AN 1Bα	(PARTICLE)	47D
	ANAKAMPTW 1A	RETURN	55B
	EKBAINW	GO OUT	236C
	EKEINOS 1D	THAT	239A
	KAIROS 2	TIME	395D
	MEN 1Aα	(PARTICLE)	503D
	MN8MONEUW 1A	REMEMBER	527A
16	EPAISCHUNOMAI 3	BE ASHAMED	281D
	EPIKALEW 1Bα	NAME	294A
	EPOURANIOS 1Aγ	HEAVENLY	306A
	HETOIMAZW 3	PREPARE	316C

16 THEOS 3C	GOD	358A
KREITTWN I	BETTER	450D
NUN 2	NOW	548A
NUNI 2B	NOW	548C
OREGW	ASPIRE TO	583C
POLIS 2	CITY	692C
17 ANADECHOMAI I	RECEIVE	53B
EPAGGELIA 2A	PROMISE	280A
ISAAK	ISAAC	381C
MONOGEN8S	ONLY	529A
PEIRAZW 2B	TRY	646A
PROSPHERW	BRING (TO)	726D
PROSPHERW 2A	BRING (TO)	727B
18 EN III3A	BECAUSE OF	260C
ISAAK	ISAAC	381C
HOTI 2	THAT	593D
SPERMA 2B	SEED	769B
19 DUNATOS IAß	POWERFUL	208A
EGEIRW IAß	RAISE	213D
EK IB	AWAY FROM	233C
KAI II4	ALSO	394C
KOMIZW 2B	BRING	443D
LOGIZOMAI 2	CONSIDER	477B
HOTHEN 3	FROM WHICH	558A
PARABOL8 I	COMPARISON	617C
20 8SAU	ESAU	349C
ISAAK	ISAAC	381C
PERI IE	ABOUT	650B
TAPEINWSIS 2	HUMILIATION	812D
20F IAKWB I	JACOB	368B
21 AKRON	TOP	33B
PROSKUNEW 2A	DO REVERENCE	724A
RABDOS	ROD	740D
21F IWS8PH I	JOSEPH	386C
22 ENTELLW	COMMAND	268A
EXODOS I	GOING OUT	276B
MN8MONEUW IC	REMEMBER	527A
OSTEON	BONE	590D
TELEUTAW	DIE	818B
HUIOS IBα	SON	841C
23 AIGUPTIOS	EGYPTIAN	21B
ASTEIOS I	BEAUTIFUL	117A
DIATAGMA	EDICT	188C
DIOTI I	BECAUSE	198C
DOGMA I	DECREE	200C
KRUPTW IA	HIDE	455B
PAIDION I	INFANT	609A
PAT8R IA	PARENTS	640C
TRIM8NOS	THREE MONTHS	834A
PHOBEW IBγ	BE AFRAID	871A
24 ARNEOMAI I	REFUSE	107C
THUGAT8R I	DAUGHTER	365B
LEGW II3	CALL	471B
MEGAS 2Aα	GREAT	498D
PHARAW	PHARAOH	861B
25 HAIREW 2	CHOOSE	23C
APOLAUSIS	ENJOYMENT	94A
ECHW I2G	HAVE	333B
LAOS 3A	PEOPLE	468A
MALLON 3C	RATHER	490D
PROSKAIROS	TEMPORARY	722C
SUGKAKOUCHEOMAI	SUFFER	780D
26 APOBLEPW	LOOK	88C
26 H8GEOMAI 2	CONSIDER	344B
TH8SAUROS 2A	TREASURE	362B
MISTHAPODOSIA	REWARD	525A
ONEIDISMOS	REPROACH	573B
PLOUTOS 2	WEALTH	680C
26F AIGUPTOS	EGYPT	21C
27 THUMOS 2	ANGER	366A
KARTEREW	ENDURE	406B
KATALEIPW 2B	LEAVE BEHIND	414D
HORAW IAα	SEE	581C
PHOBEW IBγ	BE AFRAID	871A
28 HAIMA IB	BLOOD	22B
THIGGANW	TOUCH	362B
HO,H8,TO III3A	THE	553C
OLOTHREUW	DESTROY	567A
OLOTHREUT8S	THE DESTROYER	567A
PASCHA 3	PASSOVER MEAL	639A
POIEW IIBς	DO	688A
PROSCHUSIS	POURING	727D
PRWTOTOKOS I	FIRSTBORN	734A
29 AIGUPTIOS	EGYPTIAN	21C
DIA AII	THROUGH	178B
DIABAINW	GO THROUGH	180C
ERUTHROS	RED	310B
HEURISKW 3	FIND	326A
THALASSA IBα	SEA	350D
KATAPINW IC	SWALLOW	417C
LAMBANW IH	TAKE	466A
X8ROS I	DRY	550D
PEIRA I	TRIAL	645D
HWS I2A	AS	905C
30 EPI III2B	ON	289B
H8MERA 2	DAY	347B
IERICHW	JERICHO	372D
KUKLOW 2	SURROUND	457D
PIPTW IBß	FALL	665C
TEICHOS	WALL	815D
31 APEITHEW 2	DISOBEY	82A
DECHOMAI I	RECEIVE	176B
EIR8N8 IB	PEACE	226C
KATASKOPOS	A SPY	419D
META AIIII	WITH	511A
PORN8 I	PROSTITUTE	700B
RAAB	RAHAB	740A
SUNAPOLLUMI	DESTROY WITH	792D
32 BARAK	BARAK	132C
GEDEWN	GIDEON	152C
DI8GEOMAI	TELL	194A
EPILEIPW	FAIL	295C
IEPHTHAE	JEPHTHAH	374B
LEGW IIA	SAY	469B
PROPH8T8S I	PROPHET	730D
SAMOU8L	SAMUEL	749B
SAMPSWN	SAMSON	749B
TE 3A	AND	815C
CHRONOS	TIME	896B
33 BASILEIA I	KINGDOM	134C
DIKAIOSUN8 I	RIGHTEOUSNESS	195C
EPAGGELIA 2C	PROMISE	280B
EPITUGCHANW	OBTAIN	303D
ERGAZOMAI 2A	WORK	307A
KATAGWNIZOMAI	CONQUER	411A
STOMA IC	MOUTH	777C

33	PHRASSW 1A	SHUT 873C
34	ALLOTRIOS 3	ENEMY 40B
	ASTHENEIA 1B	WEAKNESS 114D
	DUNAMIS 1	POWER 207A
	DUNAMOW	STRENGTHEN 207C
	KLINW 1D	TURN TO FLIGHT 437C
	MACHAIRA 1	SWORD 497C
	PAREMBOL8 3	A CAMP 630D
	POLEMOS 1A	ARMED CONFLICT 691D
	SBENNUMI 1	EXTINGUISH 752D
	STOMA 2	MOUTH 777D
	PHEUGW 2	FLEE 863C
35	ANASTASIS 2A	RESURRECTION 60A
	ANASTASIS 2B	RESURRECTION 60A
	APOLUTRWSIS 1	RELEASE 95D
	EK 3F	BY 234D
	HINA IIE	IN ORDER THAT 377C
	KREITTWN 1	BETTER 450D
	LAMBANW 2	RECEIVE 466D
	OU 3B	NO 594C
	PROSDECHOMAI 1B	RECEIVE 719B
	TUGCHANW 1	MEET 837A
	TUMPANIZW	TORTURE 837C
35F	ALLOS 1C	OTHER 39B
36	DESMOS 1	FETTER 175A
	EMPAIGMOS	SCORN 255B
	HETEROS 1B6	ANOTHER 315C
	ETI 2B	STILL 316A
	LAMBANW 2	RECEIVE 466C
	MASTIX 1	WHIP 496B
	PEIRA 2	TRIAL 646A
	PHULAK8 3	GUARD 875C
37	AIGEIOS	GOATSKINS 21B
	DERMA	SKIN 174C
	DICHOTOMEW	CUT IN TWO 199C
	THLIBW 3	OPPRESS 362C
	KAKOUCHEW	MALTREAT 399B
	MACHAIRA 1	SWORD 497B
	PEIRAZW 2B	TRY 646A
	PERIERCHOMAI	GO AROUND 652C
	PRIZW	SAW 707D
	HUSTEREW 2	TO MISS 857A
	PHONOS	MURDER 872C
38	AXIOS 2A	WORTHY 77C
	ER8MIA	DESERT 308D
	OP8	HOLE 578B
	OROS	MOUNTAIN 586C
	PLANAW 2A	DECEIVE 671B
	PLANAW 2B	DECEIVE 671C
	SP8LAION	CAVE 769D
39	EPAGGELIA 2B	PROMISE 280B
	KOMIZW 2A	BRING 443D
	MARTUREW 2B	BE APPROVED 494B
	PAS 1E8	ALL 637D
	PISTIS 2A	FAITH 668C
40	KREITTWN 1	BETTER 450D
	PROBLEPW	FORESEE 710B
	TELEIOW 1	COMPLETE 817C
	TELEIOW 2D	PERFECTION 817D
	TIS, TI 2AY	ANY ONE 828B
	CHWRIS 2Aα	APART 898D

HEBREWS 12

1	AGWN 1	CONTEST 14D
	APOTITH8MI 1B	LAY ASIDE 100C
	EUPERISPASTOS	324B
	EASILY DISTRACTING	
	EUPERISTATOS EASILY ENSNARING 324B	
	ECHW 12A	HAVE 332B
	MARTUS 2B	WITNESS 495C
	NEPHOS	CLOUD 539A
	OGKOS	IMPEDIMENT 555B
	PERIKEIMAI 1B	653C
	BE PLACED AROUND	
	PROKEIMAI 3	BE SET BEFORE 714C
	TOIGAROUN	THEREFORE 828D
	TOSOUTOS 1A8	SO GREAT 831B
	TRECHW 2A	RUN 833C
	HUPOMON8 1	PATIENCE 854B
2	AISCHUN8 2	SHAME 24D
	ANTI 1	OPPOSITE 73A
	ARCH8GOS 3	ORIGINATOR 112B
	APHORAW 1	FIX ONES EYES 126D
	DEXIOS 2A	RIGHT 173D
	THRONOS 1B	THRONE 364D
	KATHIZW 2Aα	SIT DOWN 390D
	KATAPHRONEW 2	DISREGARD 421C
	PISTIS 2A	FAITH 668D
	PROKEIMAI 2	BE SET BEFORE 714C
	STAUROS 1	THE CROSS 772B
	TE 1A	AND 815A
	TELEIWT8S	PERFECTER 818A
	HUPOMENW 2	REMAIN 853D
	CHARA 2B	JOY 884A
3	ANALOGIZOMAI	CONSIDER 56D
	ANTILOGIA 2	HOSTILITY 74C
	GAR 3	CERTAINLY 151D
	KAMNW 1	BE WEARY 403A
	HUPO 1B	BY 851A
	HUPOMENW 2	REMAIN 853D
	PSUCH8 1BY	SOUL LIFE 901D
4	HAIMA 2A	BLOOD 22B
	ANTAGWNIZOMAI	STRUGGLE 72A
	ANTIKATHIST8MI	OPPOSE 73D
	MECHRI 1C	UNTIL 517B
	OUPW	NOT YET 598A
5	DIALEGOMAI 2	SPEAK 184D
	EKLANTHANOMAI	FORGET 241C
	EKLUW	BECOME WEARY 242C
	ELEGCHW 4	DISCIPLINE 249A
	M8DE 1B	AND NOT 519D
	OLIGWREW	THINK LIGHTLY 567A
	PAIDEIA 1	TRAINING 608B
	PARAKL8SIS 1	ENCOURAGEMENT 623B
	HUIOS 1Cα	SON 841C
	HWS II1IA	SO 906C
5-8	HUIOS 1CY	SON 841D
6	AGAPAW 1B«	LOVE 4D
	KURIOS 2A	LORD 460B
	MASTIGOW 2A	PUNISH 496A
	PARADECHOMAI 2	ACCEPT 619C
7	PAIDEIA 1	TRAINING 608C
	PROSPHERW 3	BRING (TO) 727C
	HUPOMENW 2	REMAIN 853C

7	HUPOMENW 2	REMAIN 853D	15	ENOCHLEW	TROUBLE 267B
8	ARA 3	THEN 103C		EPISKOPEW I	LOOK AT 299A
	EIMI II9A	TO BE 223D		KAI I2E	AND 393C
	METOCHOS I	SHARING 516A		M8 BIA	NOT 519A
	NOTHOS	ILLEGITIMATE 543A		MIAINW 2	DEFILE 522D
	PAIDEIA I	TRAINING 608C		PIKRIA I	BITTERNESS 663B
	CHWRIS 2By	APART 899C		POLUS I2Aβ	MANY 695A
9	EITA 2	THEN 233B		RIZA IB	ROOT 743C
	ENTREPW 2B	RESPECT 269B		HUSTEREW IA	TO MISS 856D
	ZAW 2Bα	LIVE 337A		PHUW	GROW 878B
	MALLON 2A	RATHER 490C		CHARIS 3B	FAVOR 866B
	PAIDEUT8S	INSTRUCTOR 608D	16	ANTI 3	FOR 73B
	PNEUMA 4B	SPIRIT 682A		APODIDWMI 4B	GIVE UP 90B
	POLUS I2Cα	MANY 695B		BEB8LOS 2	PROFANE 138B
	SARX 4	BODY 751B		BRWSIS 3A	FOOD 147D
	HUPOTASSW IBβ	SUBJECT 855D		8SAU	ESAU 349C
9A	PAT8R IA	FATHER 640C		PORNOS	FORNICATOR 700B
9B	PAT8R 3B	FATHER 641B		PRWTOTOKIA	BIRTHRIGHT 734A
10	HAGIOT8S	HOLINESS 10B	17	APODOKIMAZW 2	DECLARE USELESS 90B
	GAR IB	FOR 151B		DAKRUON	TEAR 169A
	DOKEW 3A	SEEM 201B		EKZ8TEW I	SEEK OUT 239C
	EPI IIIIBη	ON 289B		EULOGIA 38α	BLESSING 323B
	H8MERA 4B	TIME 348B		EULOGIA 3Aα	BLESSING 323B
	METALAMBANW I	RECEIVE 512C		HEURISKW 3	FIND 326A
	OLIGOS IA	FEW 566B		KAIPER	ALTHOUGH 395B
	PROS III2B	TOWARD 717A		KL8RONOMEW 2	INHERIT 436A
	SUMPHERW 2By	ADVANTAGE 788A		META AIII	WITH 511A
10B	PAIDEUW 2Bα	INSTRUCT 608D		METANOIA	REPENTANCE 514A
11	APODIDWMI I	GIVE AWAY 90A		METEPEITA	AFTERWARDS 515C
	GUMNAZW	TRAIN 166D		OIDA	KNOW 558A
	DIKAIOSUN8 2B	RIGHTEOUSNESS 195D		TOPOS 2C	PLACE 830D
	DOKEW 2A	SEEM 201A	18	GNOPHOS	DARKNESS 162B
	EIMI IV4	TO BE 225A		ZOPHOS I	DARKNESS 340A
	EIR8NIKOS	PEACEABLE 227A		THUELLA	STORM 365C
	KARPOS 2A	RESULT 405D		KAIW IA	LIGHT 397A
	KARPOS IA	FRUIT 405D		PROSERCHOMAI I	APPROACH 720A
	LUP8	GRIEF 483B		PUR IA	FIRE 737B
	PAIDEIA I	TRAINING 608B		SKOTOS	DARKNESS 765A
	PAREIMI IB	BE PRESENT 629D		*PS8LAPHAW	TOUCH 900D
	PAS IAα	EVERY EACH 636C	19	8CHOS I	SOUND 350C
	PROS III2B	TOWARD 717A		LOGOS IBα	COMMAND 479A
	HUSTEROS 2A	LATER 857B		M8 AIIIA	NOT 517D
	CHARA I	JOY 883C		PARAITEOMAI 2C	BEGGED 622A
	CHARA I	JOY 883D		PROSTITH8MI IA	ADD 726B
12	ANORTHOW	REBUILD 71D		R8MA I	WORD 742D
	GONU	KNEE 164B		SALPIGX I	TRUMPET 748B
	PARALUW	WEAKEN 625D		PHWN8 I	SOUND 878D
	PARI8MI 2A	WEAKENED 632D	20	BOLIS	MISSILE 144B
13	DE ID	BUT, AND 170C		DIASTELLW	ORDER 187D
	EKTREPW	TURN AWAY 245D		TH8RION IAα	BEAST 361C
	IAOMAI 2	HEAL 369A		THIGGANW	TOUCH 362B
	MALLON 3Aα	RATHER 490C		KAN 2	EVEN IF 403B
	ORTHOS IB	UPRIGHT 584A		KATATOXEUW	SHOOT DOWN 420D
	TROCHIA	COURSE 835D		LITHOBOLEW 2	STONE 475B
	CHWLOS	LAME 897C		OROS	MOUNTAIN 586B
14	HAGIASMOS	HOLINESS 9B		PHERW IC	BEAR 862D
	DIWKW 4B	PURSUE 200C	21	EKTROMOS	TREMBLING 246A
	EIR8N8 IB	PEACE 226C		EKPHOBOS	TERRIFIED 246C
	META AII3B	WITH 510D		ENTROMOS	TREMBLING 269B
	HORAW IAy	SEE 581D		HOUTW	THUS 602B
	CHWRIS 2	APART 898D		HOUTW 3	THUS 602D
	CHWRIS 2By	APART 899C		PHANTAZW	APPEAR 861A
15	ANW 2	UPWARDS 76B		PHOBEROS	FEARFUL 870A

22 AGGELOS 2A   ANGEL   7D
   EPOURANIOS IAY   HEAVENLY 306A
   ZAW IAᴇ   LIVE 336D
   HIEROSOLUMA 2   JERUSALEM 374A
   MURIAS 2   MYRIADS 531C
   HO,H8,TO IIIC   THE 552D
   OROS   MOUNTAIN 586B
   PAN8GURIS   FESTAL GATHERING 612C
   POLIS 2   CITY 692C
   PROSERCHOMAI I   APPROACH 720A
   SIWN I   ZION 759D
23 APOGRAPHW 2   REGISTER 89A
   DIKAIOS IB   UPRIGHT 194D
   KRIT8S IAᵦ   JUDGE 454C
   OURANOS 2D   HEAVEN 599D
   PNEUMA 2   SPIRIT 681A
   PRWTOTOKOS 2Bᵅ   FIRSTBORN 734B
   TELEIOW 2D   PERFECTION 817D
24 HABEL   ABEL   IC
   HAIMA IB   BLOOD 22B
   DIATH8K8 2   COVENANT 182B
   KREITTWN 3   BETTER 451A
   LALEW I   SOUND 464B
   MESIT8S   MEDIATOR 508A
   NEOS IAᵅ   NEW 537D
   PARA III3   IN COMPARISON 616B
   RANTISMOS   SPRINKLING 741D
25 APOSTREPHW 3A   TURN AWAY 100A
   BLEPW 6   SEE 143B
   EKEINOS IA   THAT 238D
   EKPHEUGW 2A   RUN AWAY 246B
   MALLON 2B   MORE 490C
   M8 BIB   NOT 519A
   OU 5B   NO 595A
   POLUS I2Cᵅ   MANY 695B
   PHEUGW 2   FLEE 863C
   CHR8MATIZW IA   894A
        IMPART A WARNING
25A PARAITEOMAI 2A   REFUSE 621D
25B PARAITEOMAI 2A   REFUSE 621D
26 ALLA IA   BUT, YET 37C
   EPAGGELLOMAI IB   ANNOUNCE 280C
   NUN IC   NOW 548A
   OURANOS IAᵦ   HEAVEN 598B
   SALEUW I   SHAKE 747D
   SALEUW 2   SHAKE 748A
   SEIW I   SHAKE 754A
   TOTE IA   AT THAT TIME 831C
26F   HAPAX I   ONCE 80A
26F   ETI 2B   STILL 316A
27 D8LOW   REVEAL 177C
   METATHESIS I   REMOVAL 512B
   M8 AII2D   NOT 518C
   HO,H8,TO II8B   THE 554D
   POIEW   DO 687A
   POIEW IIAᵦ   DO 687B
   HWS IIIIA   SO 906C
27A   SALEUW 2   SHAKE 748A
27B   SALEUW 2   SHAKE 748A
28 AIDWS 2   REVERENCE 21D
   ASALEUTOS 2   IMMOVABLE 113D
   DEOS   AWE 174B

28 EUARESTWS   319A
        AN ACCEPTABLE MANNER
   EULABEIA   AWE 322A
   LATREUW   SERVE 468D
   PARALAMBANW 2Bᵦ   TAKE 625A
   SALEUW 2   SHAKE 748A
   CHARIS 5   FAVOR 886D
29 GAR IB   FOR 151A
   KATANALISKW   CONSUME 415D
   PUR IB   FIRE 737D

                 HEBREWS 13

1 MENW ICᵦ   REMAIN 505C
   PHILADELPHIA   BROTHERLY LOVE 866B
2 EPILANTHANOMAI 2   NEGLECT 295B
   LANTHANW   ESCAPE NOTICE 467C
   XENIZW I   RECEIVE AS A GUEST 550A
   PHILOXENIA   HOSPITALITY 868C
3 DESMIOS   PRISONER 175A
   KAKOUCHEW   MALTREAT 399B
   SUNDEW   BIND 793B
   SWMA IB   BODY 807A
4 AMIANTOS I   UNDEFILED 45C
   GAMOS 2   WEDDING 150D
   KOIT8 IB   BED 440D
   KRINW 4Bᵅ   JUDGE 453A
   MOICHOS I   ADULTERER 528C
   PAS 2A6   IN ALL RESPECTS 638C
   PORNOS   FORNICATOR 700C
   TIMIOS IC   VALUABLE 825D
5 ANI8MI 2   ABANDON 69A
   ARKEW 2   BE SATISFIED 106D
   AUTOS IB   SELF 122B
   APHILARGUROS   NOT GREEDY 126B
   EGKATALEIPW 2   FORSAKE 214D
   M8 DIA   NOT 519B
   M8 DIB   NOT 519C
   OU 6D   NO 595B
   PAREIMI 2   BE PRESENT 630A
   TROPOS 2   MANNER 835B
6 ANTHRWPOS IAᵦ   MAN 67C
   BO8THOS 2   HELPER 144A
   THARREW   BE CONFIDENT 352C
   POIEW IIDʸ   DO 688D
   HWSTE 2Aᵦ   THEREFORE 908C
7 ANATHEWREW 2   EXAMINE 54B
   ANASTROPH8   CONDUCT 61B
   EKBASIS   END 237B
   H8GEOMAI I   LEAD 344B
   LOGOS IBᵦ   WORD 479B
   MIMEOMAI   IMITATE 523D
   MN8MONEUW IA   REMEMBER 526D
   HOSTIS 2B   WHOEVER 591A
   PISTIS 2A   FAITH 668D
8 AIWN IB   TIME 26D
   AUTOS 4B   THE SAME 123C
   ECHTHES   YESTERDAY 331C
   S8MERON   TODAY 756C
   CHRISTOS 2   ANOINTED ONE 895C
9 BEBAIOW I   ESTABLISH 138A
   BRWMA I   FOOD 147C
   DIDACH8 2   TEACHING 191C

	Greek	Gloss	Ref
9	KALOS 3B	GOOD	401C
	XENOS 1A	STRANGE	550B
	PARAPHERW 2B	TAKE AWAY	628D
	PERIPATEW 2A6	GO ABOUT	655B
	PERIPHERW 2	CARRY ABOUT	659B
	POIKILOS 1	DIVERSIFIED	690A
	CHARIS 3B	FAVOR	886B
	WPHELEW 1A	HELP	909A
10	EK 1A	AWAY FROM	233C
	EXOUSIA 1	RIGHT	277C
	ESTHIW 1B?	EAT	313A
	THUSIAST8RION 2D	ALTAR	367C
	LATREUW	SERVE	468D
	SK8N8	TENT	762A
10A	ECHW I2A	HAVE	332B
11	HAGIOS 2B	SANCTUARY	10A
	HAIMA 1B	BLOOD	22B
	HAMARTIA 4	SIN	43A
	EISPHERW 1	BRING IN	233A
	EXW 2A	OUTSIDE	279B
	ZWON 2	ANIMAL	342A
	KATAKAIW	CONSUME	412A
	PAREMBOL8 1	A CAMP	630D
	PERI 1G	ABOUT	650C
	SWMA 1A	BODY	806D
12	HAGIAZW 2	CONSECRATE	8D
	EXW 2A	OUTSIDE	279B
	IDIOS 1AB	ONES OWN	370B
	KAI II4	ALSO	394C
	PAREMBOL8 1	A CAMP	630D
	PASCHW 3AB	SUFFER	639D
	PUL8 1	GATE	736C
13	EXERCHOMAI 1Aa	GO OUT	274A
	EXW 2B	OUTSIDE	279B
	ONEIDISMOS	REPROACH	573B
	PAREMBOL8 1	A CAMP	630D
	TOINUN	HENCE	828D
	PHERW 1C	BEAR	862D
14	EPIZ8TEW 2A	STRIVE FOR	292D
	MELLW 2	IS DESTINED	502C
	MENW 1CB	REMAIN	505C
	POLIS 2	CITY	692C
	HWDE 2A	HERE	903D
15	AINESIS	PRAISE	23A
	ANAPHERW 2	OFFER UP	62D
	DIA AIIIA	THROUGH	178D
	THUSIA 2B	SACRIFICE	367A
	KARPOS 2C	GAIN	406A
	HOMOLOGEW 5	CONFESS	571D
	ONOMA I4B	NAME	575A
	CHEILOS 1	LIP	887C
16	EPILANTHANOMAI 2	NEGLECT	295B
	EUARESTEW 2B	PLEASE	318D
	EUPOIIA 1	DOING OF GOOD	324B
	THUSIA 2B	SACRIFICE	367A
	KOINWNIA 2	ASSOCIATION	440A
	TOIOUTOS 2AB	SUCH A KIND	829A
17	AGRUPNEW 2	GUARD	14A
	ALUSITEL8S	UNPROFITABLE	40D
	APODIDWMI 1	GIVE AWAY	90A
	H8GEOMAI 1	LEAD	344B
	LOGOS 2A	ACCOUNT	479C
	META AIIII	WITH	511A

	Greek	Gloss	Ref
17	PEITHW 3B	OBEY	645C
	STENAZW	SIGH	773D
	HUPEIKW	YIELD	846A
	CHARA 1	JOY	883C
	PSUCH8 1C	SOUL LIFE	902A
	PSUCH8 1F	SOUL LIFE	902C
18	ECHW I2EB	HAVE	333B
	KALOS 2B	GOOD	401B
	KALWS 2	WELL	402B
	PAS 2A6	IN ALL RESPECTS	638C
	PEITHW 3A	BELIEVE	645B
	PEITHW 2B	CONVINCE	645B
	PERI 1F	ABOUT	650C
	PROSEUCHOMAI	PRAY	721A
	SUNEID8SIS 2	CONSCIOUSNESS	794B
19	APOKATHIST8MI 3	GIVE BACK	91C
	PERISSOTERWS 1	MORE	657C
	TACHEWS 2A	QUICKLY	814C
20	HAIMA 2B	BLOOD	22C
	AIWNIOS 3	ETERNAL	28A
	ANAGW 1	LEAD	52D
	ARCHIPOIM8N	CHIEF SHEPHERD	112C
	DIATH8K8 2	COVENANT	182B
	EIR8N8 3	PEACE	226D
	KURIOS 2CY	LORD	461B
	MEGAS 2Ba	GREAT	499B
	NEKROS 2A	DEAD	537A
	POIM8N 2BB	SHEPHERD	690D
	PROBATON 2	SHEEP	710A
21	AIWN 1B	TIME	26D
	AM8N 1	AMEN	45A
	EN IVIB	IN	260C
	ENWPION 3	BEFORE	270B
	EUARESTOS 1	PLEASING	319A
	THEL8MA 1CY	WILL	355A
	KATARTIZW 1B	RESTORE	418D
	PAS 1AB	EVERY EACH	636D
	CHRISTOS 2	ANOINTED ONE	895C
21B	POIEW 11Ba	DO	687D
22	ANECHW 2	ENDURE	65B
	BRACHUS 3	LITTLE	146D
	DIA AIIIB	BY MEANS OF	179B
	EPISTELLW	WRITE	300C
	LOGOS 1A	MATTER	479A
	PARAKALEW 2	APPEAL TO	622C
	PARAKL8SIS 1	ENCOURAGEMENT	623B
23	APOLUW 2B	SEND AWAY	96B
	GINWSKW 6AB	KNOW	160C
	HORAW 1Aa	SEE	581C
	TACHEWS 2B	QUICKLY	814C
	TIMOTHEOS	TIMOTHY	826A
24	APO IVIB	FROM	86D
	ASPAZOMAI 1A	GREET	116B
	H8GEOMAI 1	LEAD	344B
	ITALIA	ITALY	384D
	HO,H8,TO II5	THE	554B
	PAS 1DB	ALL	637D
25	AM8N 1	AMEN	45A
	META AIIICY	WITH	510B
	PAS 1Ea	ALL	637D
	CHARIS 2C	FAVOR	885D

JAMES I

1	DIASPORA 2	DISPERSION	187D
	DOULOS 4	SLAVE	205B
	IAKWBOS 3	JAMES	368C
	KURIOS 2Cy	LORD	461A
	PHUL8 I	TRIBE	876D
	CHAIRW 2B	REJOICE	882B
	CHRISTOS 2	ANOINTED ONE	895C
2	H8GEOMAI 2	CONSIDER	344C
	PAS IA6	ALL	637A
	PEIRASMOS 2B	TEST	646D
	PERIPIPTW 2	FALL IN WITH	655C
	POIKILOS I	DIVERSIFIED	690A
	CHARA I	JOY	883C
	CHARA I	JOY	883D
3	GINWSKW 6C	KNOW	160D
	DOKIMION I	TESTING	202A
	KATERGAZOMAI 2	ACHIEVE	422D
	PISTIS 2Dα	FAITH	669B
	PISTIS 2Dy	FAITH	669D
3F	HUPOMON8 I	PATIENCE	854A
4	EN IVIB	IN	260C
	ERGON IB	MANIFESTATION	307D
	ECHW 14	HAVE	333D
	LEIPW IA	LEAVE	471C
	M8DEIS 2B6	NOTHING	520A
	HOLOKL8ROS	WHOLE	567C
4A	TELEIOS IAα		816D
	HAVING ATTAINED THE END		
4B	TELEIOS 2D	PERFECT	817B
5	AITEW	ASK	25B
	HAPLWS 2	GENEROUSLY	85D
	LEIPW IB	BE IN NEED	471C
	ONEIDIZW I	REPROACH	573B
	PARA I3A	FROM	614D
	*SOPHIA 2	WISDOM	767A
6	ADIAKRITOS	UNWAVERING	16D
	AITEW	ASK	25C
	ANEMIZW	MOVED BY THE WIND	64A
	DIAKRINW 2B	WAVER	184B
	EOIKA	BE LIKE	279D
	THALASSA IA	SEA	350D
	KLUDWN	ROUGH WATER	437D
	M8DEIS 28β	NOTHING	520A
	PISTIS 2A	FAITH	668D
	RIPIZW	TOSS	743D
7	ANTHRWPOS 4B	MAN	68D
	GAR IB	FOR	151B
	GAR 3	CERTAINLY	151C
	KURIOS 2A	LORD	460B
	LAMBANW 2	RECEIVE	466C
	OIOMAI	THINK	565B
	PARA I3B	FROM	614D
8	AKATASTATOS	UNSTABLE	29C
	AN8R 4	MAN	66B
	DIPSUCHOS	DOUBLE MINDED	200A
	EN IVIA	IN	260C
	HODOS 2B	WAY	557A
	PAS IDα	ALL	637C
	POREIA I	GOING	698D
9	KAUCHAOMAI I	BOAST	427A
	TAPEINOS I	LOW	811D
9	HUPSOS 2A	HEIGHT	858B
10	ANTHOS I	BLOSSOM	66D
	PARERCHOMAI IBα	PASS AWAY	631C
	TAPEINWSIS I	HUMILIATION	812D
	CHORTOS	GRASS	892B
IOF	PLOUSIOS I	RICH	679C
11	ANATELLW 2	RISE	61C
	ANTHOS I	BLOSSOM	66D
	APOLLUMI 2Aβ	PASS AWAY	94D
	EKPIPTW I	FALL OFF	243B
	EUPREPEIA	BEAUTY	324C
	H8LIOS	THE SUN	346B
	KAUSWN	HEAT	426D
	MARAINW	FADE	492B
	X8RAINW I	DRY	550C
	POREIA 2	GOING	698D
	POREIA I	GOING	698D
	PROSWPON ID	FACE	729A
	SUN 4B	WITH	789D
	CHORTOS	GRASS	892B
12	AN8R 6	MAN	66B
	GINOMAI I4B	BECOME	158D
	DOKIMOS I	GENUINE	202A
	EPAGGELLOMAI IB	ANNOUNCE	280C
	ZW8 2Bβ	LIFE	341D
	LAMBANW 2	RECEIVE	466B
	MAKARIOS IB	BLESSED	487D
	PEIRASMOS 2B	TEST	646C
	STEPHANOS 2A	WREATH	775A
	HUPOMENW 2	REMAIN	853D
13	APEIRASTOS	WITHOUT TEMPTATION	82C
	APO V6	BY	88A
	KAKOS IC	EVIL	398D
	M8DEIS 2A	NO	520A
13A	PEIRAZW 2D	TRY	646B
13B	PEIRAZW 2D	TRY	646B
14	DELEAZW	LURE	173B
	EXELKW	DRAG AWAY	273C
	IDIOS 2C	ONES OWN	370C
	PEIRAZW 2D	TRY	646B
	HUPO IAβ	BY	850D
I4F	EPITHUMIA 3	DESIRE	293C
15	APOKUEW	GIVE BIRTH	93C
	APOTELEW I	FINISH	100C
	EITA I	THEN	233A
	THANATOS 2A	DEATH	352A
	SULLAMBANW IB	SEIZE	784C
	TIKTW 2	BRING FORTH	824C
16	AGAP8TOS 2	BELOVED	6C
	PLANAW 2Cy	DECEIVE	671C
17	AGATHOS IAβ	GOOD	2D
	ANWTHEN I	FROM ABOVE	76C
	APOSKIASMA	SHADOW	97C
	DOSIS I	GIFT	204A
	DWR8MA	GIFT	210A
	ENI	THERE IS NOT	265D
	KATABAINW IB	COME DOWN	409C
	PARA II2D	BESIDE	615D
	PARALLAG8	CHANGE	625C
	PAS IAβ	EVERY EACH	636D
	PAT8R 3A	FATHER	641B
	TELEIOS IAα		816D
	HAVING ATTAINED THE END		

17	TROP8 2	TURN 834D
	PHWS 1Bα	LIGHT 880A
18	AL8THEIA 2B	TRUTH 35B
	APARCH8 2A	FIRST FRUITS 80D
	APOKUEW	GIVE BIRTH 93C
	BOULOMAI 2B	DESIRE 146A
	KTISMA	CREATURE 457B
	LOGOS 1Bβ	WORD 479C
	TIS, TI 2Bα	ANY ONE 828C
19	AGAP8TOS 2	BELOVED 6C
	ANTHRWPOS 3Aʓ	MAN 68C
	BRADUS	SLOW 146C
	LALEW 2Aβ	SPEAK 464B
	OIDA	KNOW 558A
	OIDA II	KNOW 558D
	ORG8 I	ANGER 582C
	PAS 1Aα	EVERY EACH 636C
	TACHUS I	QUICK 814D
	HWSTE 1B	THEREFORE 908B
20	DIKAIOSUN8 2B	RIGHTEOUSNESS 195D
	ERGAZOMAI 2A	WORK 307A
	ERGAZOMAI 2C	BRING ABOUT 307B
	ORG8 I	ANGER 582C
21	APOTITH8MI 1B	LAY ASIDE 100C
	DECHOMAI 3B	ACCEPT 176C
	EMPHUTOS	IMPLANTED 257C
	KAKIA 1A	BADNESS 397D
	LOGOS 1Bβ	WORD 479C
	PAS 1Aβ	EVERY EACH 636D
	PERISSEIA	SURPLUS 656B
	PRAUT8S	HUMILITY 705D
	RUPARIA	DIRT 745B
	SWZW 2Aγ	SAVE 806B
	PSUCH8 IC	SOUL LIFE 902A
22	AKROAT8S	A HEARER 33A
	MONOS 2C	ONLY 529D
	PARALOGIZOMAI I	DECEIVE 625C
22F	POI8T8S 2	MAKER 690A
23	AKROAT8S	A HEARER 33A
	GENESIS 2	EXISTENCE 154A
	EOIKA	BE LIKE 279D
	ESOPTRON	MIRROR 313C
	KATANOEW 2	NOTICE 416A
	HOUTOS 1Aα	THIS 601B
	PROSWPON 1A	FACE 728B
23F	PARAKUPTW 2	LOOK INTO 624D
24	APERCHOMAI 1A	GO AWAY 83D
	EPILANTHANOMAI I	FORGET 295B
	EUTHEWS	IMMEDIATELY 320D
	KATANOEW 2	NOTICE 416A
	HOPOIOS	WHAT SORT 579B
	TELEIOS 1Aα	816D
	HAVING ATTAINED THE END	
25	AKROAT8S	A HEARER 33A
	ELEUTHERIA	FREEDOM 250A
	EPIL8SMON8	FORGETFULNESS 295C
	ERGON 1A	DEED 307D
	MAKARIOS 1B	BLESSED 487D
	NOMOS 5	LAW 545B
	PARAKUPTW 2	LOOK INTO 624D
	PARAMENW 2	REMAIN 626A
	POI8SIS I	DOING 689D
	POI8T8S 2	MAKER 690A

26	APATAW I	DECEIVE 81B
	DOKEW 1A	THINK 200D
	THR8SKEIA	RELIGION 364A
	THR8SKOS	RELIGIOUS 364B
	KARDIA 1Bβ	HEART 404D
	MATAIOS	IDLE 496C
	CHALINOW	BRIDLE 882D
	CHALINAGWGEW	BRIDLE 882D
27	AMIANTOS I	UNDEFILED 45C
	ASPILOS 2	WITHOUT BLEMISH 116D
	EIMI II6A	TO BE 223C
	EPISKEPTOMAI 2	VISIT 298C
	THEOS 3D	GOD 358A
	THLIPSIS I	TRIBULATION 363A
	THR8SKEIA	RELIGION 364A
	KATHAROS 3B	CLEAN 389A
	KAI IIA	AND 392C
	KOSMOS 7	WORLD 447D
	ORPHANOS I	ORPHANED 586D
	HOUTOS 1A6	THIS 601A
	PARA II2B	BESIDE 615C
	PAT8R 3E	FATHER 642A
	T8REW 2B	KEEP 822D
	CH8RA	THE WIDOW 889D

JAMES 2

1	DOXA 1A	GLORY 202D
	KURIOS 2Cγ	LORD 461B
	M8 AII13B	NOT 518D
	PISTIS 2Bβ	FAITH 668D
	PROSWPOL8MPSIA	PARTIALITY 728A
	CHRISTOS 2	ANOINTED ONE 895C
2	EISERCHOMAI 1Aβ	COME 231D
	HO,H8,TO III1Aα	THE 552B
	RUPAROS I	DIRTY 745B
	SUNAGWG8 5	PLACE OF ASSEMBLY 790D
	SUNAGWG8 2B	790D
		PLACE OF ASSEMBLY
	CHRUSODAKTULIOS	896D
		GOLD RING ON FINGER
2F	ESTH8S	CLOTHING 312B
2F	LAMPROS 3	BRIGHT 467A
2F	PTWCHOS 1A	BEGGING POOR 735D
3	EPIBLEPW	LOOK AT 290B
	HIST8MI III1A	STAND 383B
	KATH8MAI 2	SIT DOWN 390C
	KALWS I	WELL 402A
	HO,H8,TO III1Aα	THE 552B
	HUPO 2Aα	UNDER 851A
	HUPOPODION	FOOTSTOOL 854D
	PHOREW I	WEAR 872D
	HWDE 2A	HERE 903D
4	DIAKRINW 2B	WAVER 184B
	DIALOGISMOS I	THOUGHT 185B
	KRIT8S 1B	JUDGE 454C
	PON8ROS 1Bβ	WICKED 697C
5	AGAP8TOS 2	BELOVED 6C
	BASILEIA 3G	KINGDOM 135A
	EKLEGOMAI 3C	CHOOSE 242A
	EPAGGELLOMAI 1B	ANNOUNCE 280C
	KL8RONOMOS 2B	HEIR 436B
	KOSMOS 5A	WORLD 447C

Ref	Greek	English	No.
5	PISTIS 2Dα	FAITH	669B
	PLOUSIOS 2	RICH	679C
	PTWCHOS 1A	BEGGING POOR	735D
6	ATIMAZW	DISHONOR	119C
	HELKW 1A	DRAG	251A
	KATADUNASTEUW	OPPRESS	411C
	KRIT8RION 1	LAWCOURT	454B
	PLOUSIOS 1	RICH	679C
	PTWCHOS 1A	BEGGING POOR	735D
	SU 1C	YOU	780A
7	AUTOS 2	THEY	122D
	BLASPH8MEW 2B6	BLASPHEME	142B
	EPI IIIIA(	ON	288C
	EPIKALEW 1Bβ	NAME	294A
	KALOS 2Cβ	GOOD	401C
	ONOMA 14B	NAME	575A
8	AGAPAW 1Aα	LOVE	4B
	BASILIKOS	ROYAL	136C
	GRAPH8 2A	SCRIPTURE	165B
	GRAPH8 2Bβ	SCRIPTURE	165C
	EI VI7	IF	219A
	KALWS 4A	WELL	402B
	KATA II5Aα	ACCORDING TO	408A
	MENTOI 1	REALLY	504C
	NOMOS 5	LAW	545B
	PL8SION 1B	NEAR	678D
	POIEW I2Aα	DO	689A
	POIEW I2Ay	DO	689B
	TELEW 2	PERFORM	818D
9	HAMARTIA 1	SIN	42C
	ELEGCHW 2	EXPOSE	248C
	ERGAZOMAI 2A	WORK	307B
	NOMOS 5	LAW	545B
	PARABAT8S	TRANSGRESSOR	617A
	PROSWPOL8MPTEW	SHOW PARTIALITY	728A
	HWS IIIIC	SO	906D
10	AN 2B	(PARTICLE)	48B
	ENOCHOS 2By	GUILTY	267C
	NOMOS 3	LAW	544D
	HOSTIS 1D	WHOEVER	590D
	PTAIW 1	STUMBLE	734C
	T8REW 5	KEEP	822D
11	APOSTAT8S	APOSTATE	97D
	NOMOS 3	LAW	544D
	PARABAT8S	TRANSGRESSOR	617A
11A	MOICHEUW 1	COMMIT ADULTERY	528B
11A	PHONEUW	MURDER	872C
11B	MOICHEUW 1	COMMIT ADULTERY	528B
11B	PHONEUW	MURDER	872C
12	ELEUTHERIA	FREEDOM	250A
	KRINW 4Bα	JUDGE	453A
	LALEW 2Aβ	SPEAK	464B
	NOMOS 5	LAW	545B
	HOUTW 2	THUS	602C
	POIEW I2Aα	DO	689A
	HWS I2A	AS	905C
13	ANELEOS	MERCILESS	64A
	ANILEWS	MERCILESS	69A
	*ELEOS 1	MERCY	249C
	KATAKAUCHAOMAI 2	TRIUMPH OVER	412B
	POIEW IICβ	DO	688C
13A	KRISIS 1Aβ	JUDGING	453D
13B	KRISIS 1Aβ	JUDGING	453D
14	LEGW 11Bβ	SAY	469C
	SWZW 2Ay	SAVE	806B
	TIS, TI 1Ay	ANY ONE	827D
14A	PISTIS 2D6	FAITH	669B
14B	PISTIS 2D6	FAITH	669D
14=26	ERGON 1A	DEED	307D
15	ADELPH8 3	SISTER	15C
	GUMNOS 3	POORLY DRESSED	167A
	EPH8MEROS	FOR THE DAY	330D
	LEIPW 1B	BE IN NEED	471C
	TROPH8 1	FOOD	835C
	HUPARCHW 2	BE	846A
16	EIR8N8 2	PEACE	226C
	EPIT8DEIOS	PROPER	302C
	THERMAINW	WARM ONESELF	360B
	OPHELOS	BENEFIT	604A
	TIS, TI 1Aα	ANY ONE	827C
	HUPAGW 1	GO AWAY	844B
	CHORTAZW 2A	FEED	892B
17	HEAUTOU 1F	ONESELF	211B
	ECHW 14	HAVE	333D
	KATA IIIC	BY	407B
	NEKROS 1Bβ	DEAD	536D
	PISTIS 2D6	FAITH	669D
18	ALLA 2	BUT, YET	38A
	*DEIKNUMI 2	EXPLAIN	171D
	EIPON 2B	SAY	225C
	EK 3Gβ	BY	234D
	SU 1A	YOU	779D
	TIS, TI 1Aα	ANY ONE	827C
	CHWRIS 2Bβ	APART	899A
18A	KAGW 2	BUT I	387A
18A	PISTIS 2D6	FAITH	669D
18B	PISTIS 2D6	FAITH	669D
18C	PISTIS 2D6	FAITH	669D
19	DAIMONION 2	DEMON	168C
	EIMI I17	TO BE	223D
	HEIS 2B	ONE	230B
	KALWS 4A	WELL	402B
	POIEW I2Aα	DO	689A
	PHRISSW	SHUDDER	874A
19A	PISTEUW 1Aβ	BELIEVE	666A
19B	PISTEUW 1D	BELIEVE	666D
20	ANTHRWPOS 1Ay	MAN	67C
	ARGOS 3	USELESS	104B
	GINWSKW 3C	UNDERSTAND	160B
	THELW 1	WISH	355C
	KENOS 2B	EMPTY	429B
	NEKROS 1Bβ	DEAD	536D
	PISTIS 2D6	FAITH	669D
	CHWRIS 2Bβ	APART	899A
	W 1	O	903B
21	ABRAAM	ABRAHAM	1D
	ANAPHERW 2	OFFER UP	62D
	DIKAIOW 3A	JUSTIFY	196D
	THUSIAST8RION 1C	ALTAR	367B
	ISAAK	ISAAC	381C
	PAT8R 2E	FATHERS	641A
	HUIOS 1Aα	SON	841B
22	BLEPW 7B	SEE	143C
	SUNERGEW	WORK WITH	795B
	TELEIOW 2Eβ	MAKE PERFECT	817D

22A	PISTIS 2D6	FAITH 669D	
22B	PISTIS 2D6	FAITH 669D	
23	ABRAAM	ABRAHAM 1D	
	GRAPH8 2A	SCRIPTURE 165B	
	DIKAIOSUN8 3	RIGHTEOUSNESS 196A	
	KALEW 1AB	CALL 399D	
	LEGW 17	SAY 470A	
	LOGIZOMAI 1A	RECKON 477A	
	PISTEUW 1B	BELIEVE 666C	
	PL8ROW 4A	MAKE FULL 677C	
	PHILOS 2AB	LOVING 869A	
24	ANTHRWPOS 3Aγ	MAN 68B	
	MONOS 2C	ONLY 529D	
	HORAW 1Cα	SEE 582A	
	PISTIS 2D6	FAITH 669D	
	TOINUN	HENCE 828D	
24F	DIKAIOW 3A	JUSTIFY 196D	
25	AGGELOS 1A	MESSENGER 7A	
	EKBALLW 2	SEND OUT 237A	
	HETEROS 2	ANOTHER 315C	
	KATASKOPOS	A SPY 419D	
	HOMOIWS	LIKEWISE 570D	
	PORN8 1	PROSTITUTE 700B	
	RAAB	RAHAB 740A	
	HUPODECHOMAI	RECEIVE 852A	
26	PISTIS 2D6	FAITH 669D	
	PNEUMA 2	SPIRIT 680D	
	SWMA 1B	BODY 806D	
	HWSPER 1	(JUST) AS 908A	
26A	NEKROS 1Aα	DEAD 536C	
26A	CHWRIS 2Bγ	APART 899C	
26B	NEKROS 1BB	DEAD 536D	
26B	CHWRIS 2BB	APART 899A	

JAMES 3

1	DIDASKALOS	TEACHER 190D	
	KRIMA 4B	VERDICT 451D	
	LAMBANW 2	RECEIVE 466C	
	POLULALOS	TALKATIVE 693D	
2	AN8R 2	MAN 66A	
	HAPAS 2	ALL 81A	
	DUNATOS 1AB	POWERFUL 208A	
	LOGOS 1AB	WORD 478C	
	OU 2D	NO 594C	
	HOUTOS 1Aε	THIS 601B	
	POLUS I2BB	MANY 695B	
	TELEIOS 2D	PERFECT 817B	
	CHALINAGWGEW	BRIDLE 882D	
2A	PTAIW 1	STUMBLE 734C	
2B	PTAIW 1	STUMBLE 734C	
3	BALLW 2B	PUT 130D	
	HIPPOS	HORSE 381B	
	METAGW 1	GUIDE 512A	
	PEITHW 3B	OBEY 645C	
	PROS III3A	TOWARD 717A	
	STOMA 1C	MOUTH 777C	
	SWMA 1B	BODY 806D	
	CHALINOS	BIT 882D	
4	ANEMOS 1A	WIND 64A	
	BOULOMAI 2Aς	DESIRE 145D	
	EIMI II6A	TO BE 223C	
	ELAUNW	DRIVE 248A	

4	ELACHISTOS 2A	SMALLEST 248B	
	EUTHUNW 2	STRAIGHTEN 321B	
	METAGW 1	GUIDE 512A	
	HOPOU 1Bα	WHERE 579D	
	HORM8	IMPULSE 585C	
	P8DALION	RUDDER 661D	
	PLOION 1	SHIP 679B	
	SKL8ROS 1B	HARD 763B	
	T8LIKOUTOS 1	SO GREAT 822A	
4A	HUPO 1AB	BY 850D	
4B	HUPO 1AB	BY 850D	
4F	IDOU 1C	REMEMBER 371D	
5	ANAPTW	KINDLE 59C	
	AUCHEW	BOAST 123D	
	H8LIKOS	HOW GREAT 346A	
	MEGALAUCHEW	BOAST 497D	
	MELOS 1	MEMBER 502D	
	MIKROS 2A	SMALL 523B	
	OLIGOS 2A	LITTLE 566C	
	HUL8 1	WOOD 843C	
5F	GLWSSA 1A	TONGUE 161B	
6	ADIKIA 2	UNRIGHTEOUSNESS 17D	
	GEENNA	HELL 152C	
	GENESIS 4		154A
	WHEEL OF HUMAN ORIGIN		
	KATHIST8MI 3	CAUSE 391C	
	KOSMOS 8	TOTALITY 448A	
	MELOS 1	MEMBER 502D	
	PUR 2	FIRE 737D	
	SPILOW	STAIN 770B	
	SWMA 1B	BODY 806D	
	TROCHOS	WHEEL 835D	
6A	PHLOGIZW	SET ON FIRE 869D	
7	ANTHRWPINOS 2	HUMAN 67B	
	DAMAZW 1	SUBDUE 169B	
	ENALIOS	SEA CREATURES 261A	
	HERPETON	REPTILE 310B	
	TH8RION 1AB	BEAST 361C	
	PETEINON	BIRD 660A	
	TE 3A	AND 815C	
7A	PHUSIS 4	NATURE 877D	
7B	PHUSIS 2	NATURE 877C	
7B	PHUSIS 4	NATURE 877D	
8	AKATASCHETOS	UNCONTROLLABLE 29D	
	AKATASTATOS	UNSTABLE 29D	
	DAMAZW 2	TAME 169B	
	THANAT8PHOROS	DEATH BRINGING 351B	
	IOS 1B	POISON 379C	
	KAKOS 2	EVIL 398D	
	MESTOS 1	FULL 509B	
9	EULOGEW 1	SPEAK WELL 322C	
	KAI II A	AND 392C	
	KATA II5Bα	ACCORDING TO 408C	
	KATARAOMAI	CURSE 418A	
	HOMOIWSIS	LIKENESS 571A	
	PAT8R 3E	FATHER 642A	
10	GINOMAI III	BE 159B	
	EXERCHOMAI 2BB	GO OUT 274D	
	EULOGIA 3Aα	BLESSING 323B	
	KATARA	CURSE 418A	
	STOMA 1A	MOUTH 777B	
	CHR8	IT IS NECESSARY 893C	
11	BRUW	POUR FORTH 147C	

11 M8TI   (INTERROG PARTICLE) 522A
    OP8   HOLE 578B
    P8G8 I   FOUNTAIN 661C
    PIKROS I   BITTER 663B
11F GLUKUS   SWEET 161B
12 HALUKOS   SALTY 40C
    AMPELOS I   VINE 46A
    ELAIA 2   OLIVE TREE 247B
    8 IC   NOR 343A
    OUTE   NOT 600C
    OUTE   NOT 600D
    P8G8 I   FOUNTAIN 661C
    SUK8   FIG TREE 783D
    SUKON   RIPE FIG 784A
    HUDWR I   WATER 840C
12A POIEW IIBη   DO 688A
12B POIEW IIBη   DO 688A
13 ANASTROPH8   CONDUCT 61B
    DEIKNUMI 2   EXPLAIN 171D
    EPIST8MWN   EXPERT 300C
    ERGON ICβ   DEED 308A
    KALOS 2B   GOOD 401B
    PRAUT8S   HUMILITY 705D
    SOPHIA 2   WISDOM 767A
    SOPHOS 3   LEARNED 767D
    TIS, TI IAδ   WHICH 826D
14 AL8THEIA 2A   TRUTH 35B
    ERITHEIA   SELFISHNESS 309B
    ECHW I2Eβ   HAVE 333A
    Z8LOS 2   JEALOUSY 338B
    KARDIA IBε   HEART 405A
    KATA I2Bβ   DOWN 406D
    KATAKAUCHAOMAI I BOAST 412B
    PIKROS 2   BITTER 663B
    PSEUDOMAI I   LIE 900A
15 ANWTHEN I   FROM ABOVE 76C
    DAIMONIWD8S   DEMONIC 168D
    EPIGEIOS I   EARTHLY 290C
    KATERCHOMAI 2 COME DOWN 423B
    SOPHIA I   WISDOM 767A
    PSUCHIKOS I   902D
            PERTAINING TO THE SOUL
16 AKATASTASIA 2 DISTURBANCE 29C
    ERITHEIA   SELFISHNESS 309B
    Z8LOS 2   JEALOUSY 338B
    HOPOU 2A   WHERE 579D
    PRAGMA 4   DEED 704A
    PHAULOS I   WORTHLESS 862B
17 AGATHOS IAβ   GOOD 2D
    HAGNOS 2   PURE 12A
    ADIAKRITOS   UNWAVERING 16D
    ANUPOKRITOS   GENUINE 76A
    ANWTHEN I   FROM ABOVE 76C
    EIR8NIKOS   PEACEABLE 227A
    ELEOS I   MERCY 249C
    EPEITA 2B   THEN 284B
    EUPEITH8S   OBEDIENT 324B
    KARPOS 2A   RESULT 406A
    MEN 2C   (PARTICLE) 504B
    MESTOS 2A   FULL 509C
    PRWTOS 2B   FIRST 733D
   *SOPHIA 2   WISDOM 767A
18 DIKAIOSUN8 2B RIGHTEOUSNESS 195D

18 EIR8N8 IB   PEACE 226C
    KARPOS 2A   RESULT 405D
    POIEW IIBγ   DO 687C
    SPEIRW IBγ   SOW 768D

                JAMES 4

1   ENTEUTHEN 2   FROM HERE 268A
    H8DON8 I   PLEASURE 345A
    MACH8   BATTLE 497C
    MELOS I   MEMBER 502D
    POLEMOS 2   ARMED CONFLICT 691D
    STRATEUW 2   778A
            DO MILITARY SERVICE
1A POTHEN 2   FROM WHERE 686D
1B POTHEN 2   FROM WHERE 686D
2   EPITHUMEW   DESIRE 293A
    EPITUGCHANW   OBTAIN 304A
    Z8LOW 2   338C
            BE FILLED WITH JEALOUSY
    M8 AIIIE   NOT 518A
    PHONEUW   MURDER 872C
2F AITEW   ASK 25B
3   AITEW   ASK 25C
   *DAPANAW I   SPEND 170A
    DIOTI I   BECAUSE 198C
    H8DON8 I   PLEASURE 345A
    KAKWS 2   BADLY 399B
3B AITEW   ASK 25C
4   AN 2B   (PARTICLE) 48B
    BOULOMAI I   DESIRE 145D
    ECHTHRA   ENMITY 331C
    KATHIST8MI 3 CAUSE 391C
    MOICHALIS 2B ADULTEROUS 528A
    MOICHOS 2   ADULTERER 528C
    OUN 5   THEREFORE 597D
    PHILOS 2Aα   LOVING 869A
4A KOSMOS 7   WORLD 447D
4B KOSMOS 7   WORLD 447D
5   GRAPH8 2Bβ   SCRIPTURE 165B
    DOKEW ID   THINK 201A
    EPIPOTHEW   DESIRE 297D
    KATOIKIZW   CAUSE TO DWELL 425D
    KENWS   IDLY 429D
    LEGW 17   SAY 470A
    PNEUMA 5Dα   SPIRIT 683A
    PROS III6   TOWARD 718A
    PHTHONOS   ENVY 865C
6   ANTITASSW   OPPOSE 75B
    DIDWMI IBβ   GIVE 192B
    TAPEINOS 2B   LOW 812A
    HUPER8PHANOS PROUD 849A
6A CHARIS 3B   FAVOR 886A
6B CHARIS 3B   FAVOR 886A
7   ANTHIST8MI I SET AGAINST 66C
    DIABOLOS 2   THE SLANDERER 181A
    KAI I2F   AND 393C
    HUPOTASSW IBβ SUBJECT 855D
    PHEUGW I   FLEE 863C
8   HAGNIZW IB   PURIFY 11A
    DIPSUCHOS   DOUBLE MINDED 200A
    EGGIZW I   APPROACH 212D
    KATHARIZW 2Bα CLEANSE 388B

8 KARDIA IB∂	HEART	404D
9 GELWS	LAUGHTER	152D
EIS 4B	TO	228B
KAT8PHEIA	GLOOMINESS	424D
KLAIW I	WEEP	434B
METASTREPHW	CHANGE	514D
METATREPW	TURN AROUND	515B
PENTHEW I	BE SAD	648B
PENTHOS	GRIEF	648C
TALAIPWREW IB	LAMENT	810D
CHARA I	JOY	883C
10 ENWPION 5B	BEFORE	270C
KAI I2F	AND	393C
TAPEINOW 2B	LOWER	812C
HUPSOW 2	LIFT UP	858D
11 ALL8LWN	EACH OTHER	38D
KRINW 6B	JUDGE	453B
KRIT8S IB	JUDGE	454C
POI8T8S 2	MAKER	689D
11A KATALALEW	SPEAK AGAINST	413C
11B KATALALEW	SPEAK AGAINST	413C
11C KATALALEW	SPEAK AGAINST	413C
11D NOMOS 3	LAW	544D
12 APOLLUMI IAα	RUIN	94C
HEIS 2B	ONE	230C
KRINW 6B	JUDGE	453B
KRIT8S IAβ	JUDGE	454C
NOMOTHET8S	LAWGIVER	544B
PL8SION IB	NEAR	678C
SWZW 2Aα	SAVE	806A
TIS, TI IAβ	WHICH	826D
13 AGE	COME	8C
AURION I	TOMORROW	121D
EMPOREUOMAI I	BUY AND SELL	256A
ENIAUTOS I	YEAR	266A
KAI IIB	AND	392D
KERDAINW IA	TO GAIN	430C
LEGW II8α	SAY	469C
HODE 3	THIS	555C
POIEW IIE6	DO	689A
POLIS I	CITY	692A
S8MERON	TODAY	756B
14 ATMIS	MIST	120A
AURION I	TOMORROW	121D
APHANIZW	RENDER INVISIBLE	124A
APHANIZW	RENDER INVISIBLE	124B
GAR IF	WHAT	151C
EPEITA I	THEN	284B
EPISTAMAI 2	KNOW	300A
ZW8 IA	LIFE	340D
OLIGOS 3B	LITTLE	566D
POIA	GRASS	687A
POIOS IAγ	OF WHAT KIND	691B
PROS II12B	TOWARD	717A
PHAINW 2B	APPEAR	859B
15 ANTI 3	FOR	73B
EKEINOS IA	THAT	238D
ZAW IA6	LIVE	336D
THELW 2	WISH	355D
KURIOS 2A	LORD	460B
HOUTOS	THIS	600D
16 ALAZONEIA	PRETENSION	34A
KATAKAUCHAOMAI I	BOAST	412B

16 KAUCHAOMAI I	BOAST	427A
KAUCH8SIS I	BOASTING	427B
NUN 2	NOW	548A
PON8ROS IB∂	WICKED	697D
TOIOUTOS 2A∂	SUCH A KIND	829A
17 AUTOS 3C	(OBLIQUE CASE)	123A
KALOS 2B	GOOD	401B
OIDA 3	KNOW	558D
POIEW IIB∉	DO	687D

JAMES 5

1 AGE	COME	8C
EPERCHOMAI IB∂	COME	284D
EPI IIIBγ	ON	287B
KLAIW I	WEEP	434B
OLOLUZW	CRY OUT	567C
PLOUSIOS I	RICH	679C
TALAIPWRIA	DISTRESS	811A
2 HIMATION I	GARMENT	377A
PLOUTOS I	WEALTH	680B
S8TOBRWTOS	MOTHEATEN	756D
S8PW	CAUSE TO ROT	756D
3 ARGUROS 2	SILVER	104C
EIMI III2	TO BE	224A
EIS 4D	FOR	228C
ESTHIW 2	CONSUME	313D
ESCHATOS 3B	LAST	314B
H8MERA 4B	TIME	348B
TH8SAURIZW I	STORE UP	362A
IOS 2	RUST	379D
KATIOW	BECOME RUSTY	425A
MARTURION IA	TESTIMONY	495A
PUR IA	FIRE	737B
SARX I	FLESH	750D
CHRUSOS	GOLD	897A
4 AMAW	MOW	44A
APOSTEREW	STEAL	98D
APHUSTEREW	WITHHOLD	127C
BO8	CRY	144A
EISERCHOMAI 2B	COME	232C
ERGAT8S IA	WORKMAN	307C
THERIZW I	REAP	359D
IDOU IC	REMEMBER	371D
KRAZW 2B∂	CALL	449A
KURIOS 2A	LORD	460C
MISTHOS I	WAGES	525A
OUS I	EAR	600B
SABAWTH	LORD OF HOSTS	746A
CHWRA 4	COUNTRY	897D
5 G8 5B	EARTH	156D
H8MERA 3B∂	DAY	348B
KARDIA IA	HEART	404B
SPATALAW	LIVE LUXURIOUSLY	768B
SPHAG8	SLAUGHTER	803C
TREPHW I	FEED	833B
TRUPHAW	REVEL	836B
6 ANTITASSW	OPPOSE	75B
KATADIKAZW	CONDEMN	411B
PHONEUW	MURDER	872C
7 AN 3D	(PARTICLE)	48C
GEWRGOS I	FARMER	156B
G8 I	EARTH	156C

7   EKDECHOMAI   WAIT 237D
     EPI IIIBγ   ON 287B
     HEWS IIB   UNTIL 334D
     IDOU IC   REMEMBER 371D
     KARPOS IA   FRUIT 405C
     LAMBANW 2   RECEIVE 466B
     OPSIMOS   LATE 606C
     PROIMOS   EARLY RAIN 713D
     TIMIOS IB   VALUABLE 825D
     HUETOS   RAIN 841A
7A   MAKROTHUMEW I   489A
             HAVE PATIENCE
7B   MAKROTHUMEW I   489A
             HAVE PATIENCE
7F   KURIOS 2Cγ   LORD 460D
7F   PAROUSIA 2Bα   COMING 635C
8   EGGIZW 5B   APPROACH 212D
     KARDIA IBε   HEART 405A
     MAKROTHUMEW I   HAVE PATIENCE 489A
     ST8RIZW 2   ESTABLISH 775D
9   ALL8LWN   EACH OTHER   38D
     THURA 2A   DOOR 366C
     IDOU IA   BEHOLD 371C
     KATA I2Bβ   DOWN 406D
     KRINW 4Bα   JUDGE 453A
     KRIT8S IAβ   JUDGE 454C
     PRO I   BEFORE 708C
     STENAZW   SIGH 773D
10   KAKOPATHEIA   SUFFERING 398B
     KALOKAGATHIA   EXCELLENCE 401A
     LAMBANW IA   TAKE 465C
     MAKROTHUMIA I   PATIENCE 489B
     ONOMA I4Cγ   NAME 576A
     PROPH8T8S I   PROPHET 730D
     HUPODEIGMA I   EXAMPLE 851D
11   AKOUW 3B   LEARN   31D
     EIDON IA   SEE 219C
     IDOU IC   REMEMBER 371D
     IWB   JOB 385D
     MAKARIZW   CONSIDER BLESSED 487C
     OIKTIRMWN   MERCIFUL 564C
     POLUEUSPLAGCHNOS   693C
             RICH IN COMPASSION
     POLUSPLAGCHNOS   SYMPATHETIC 696C
     TELOS IA   END 819A
     TELOS IC   END 819B
     HUPOMENW 2   REMAIN 853C
     HUPOMON8 I   PATIENCE 854A
12   ALLOS ID   OTHER   39C
     KRISIS IAβ   JUDGING 453D
     M8TE   AND NOT 521D
     NAI 5   YES 535A
     OMNUW   TAKE AN OATH 568D
     HORKOS   OATH 585B
     OU I   NO 594B
     OURANOS IAβ   HEAVEN 598B
     PAS 2A6   IN ALL RESPECTS 638C
     PIPTW 2Aγ   FALL 665C
     PRO 3   BEFORE 708D
     TIS, TI 2Aγ   ANY ONE 828B
     HUPOKRISIS   HYPOCRISY 852D
13   EUTHUMEW   BE CHEERFUL 321A

13   KAKOPATHEW I   398B
             SUFFER MISFORTUNE
     PROSEUCHOMAI   PRAY 721A
     PSALLW   SING 899B
13A   TIS, TI IAα   ANY ONE 827D
14   ALEIPHW I   ANOINT   34C
     ASTHENEW IA   BE SICK 115A
     ELAION I   OLIVE OIL 247B
     EPI IIIIAζ   ON 288D
     ONOMA I4Cγ   NAME 576A
     PRESBUTEROS 2Bα   OLDER 707A
     PROSEUCHOMAI   PRAY 721A
     PROSKALEW IA   SUMMON 722C
     TIS, TI IAα   ANY ONE 827D
15   HAMARTIA I   SIN   42B
     APHI8MI 2   FORGIVE 125C
     EGEIRW IAβ   RAISE 213D
     EUCH8 I   PRAYER 329C
     KAMNW 2   BE ILL 403A
     KAN I   AND IF 403B
     PISTIS 2A   FAITH 668D
     POIEW IICγ   DO 688C
     SWZW IC   SAVE 806A
16   HAMARTIA I   SIN   42D
     DE8SIS   PRAYER 171A
     DIKAIOS IB   UPRIGHT 195A
     ENERGEW IB   WORK 265A
     EXOMOLOGEW 2A   CONFESS 276C
     EUCHOMAI I   PRAY 329D
     IAOMAI 2   HEAL 369A
     ISCHUW 2A   BE STRONG 384C
     HOPWS 2B   IN ORDER THAT 580D
     PARAPTWMA 2B   TRANSGRESSION 627B
     POLUS I2Cα   MANY 695B
     PROSEUCHOMAI   PRAY 721A
17   ANTHRWPOS IB   MAN   67D
     BRECHW 2B   RAIN 147A
     ENIAUTOS I   YEAR 265D
     8LIAS   ELIJAH 345D
     M8N I   MONTH 520D
     HO,H8,TO II48ε   THE 554A
     HOMOIOPATH8S   569C
             WITH THE SAME NATURE
     PROSEUCH8 I   PRAYER 720C
     *PROSEUCHOMAI   PRAY 721A
18   BLASTANW I   SPROUT 141D
     DIDWMI IBγ   GIVE 192B
     KARPOS IA   FRUIT 405C
     OURANOS IB   HEAVEN 598C
     PALIN 2   AGAIN 611C
     PROSEUCHOMAI   PRAY 721A
     HUETOS   RAIN 841A
19   AL8THEIA 2B   TRUTH   35C
     EPISTREPHW IA   TURN 301A
     HODOS 2B   WAY 557A
     PLANAW 2Cβ   DECEIVE 671C
     TIS, TI IAα   ANY ONE 827D
20   HAMARTIA I   SIN   42B
     HAMARTWLOS 2   SINNER   43C
     EK IA   AWAY FROM 233C
     EK IC   AWAY FROM 233D
     EPISTREPHW IA   TURN 301A
     THANATOS 2A   DEATH 352A

20	KALUPTW 2A	COVER	402A
	HO,H8,TO IIID	THE	552D
	HODOS 2B	WAY	557A
	PLAN8	WANDERING	671D
	PL8THOS 2A	QUANTITY	674B
	SWZW 2AB	SAVE	806B
	PSUCH8 IC	SOUL LIFE	902A

I PETER I

1	APOSTOLOS 3	APOSTLES	99B
	ASIA	ASIA	115C
	BITHUNIA	BITHYNIA	141A
	GALATIA	GALATIA	149B
	DIASPORA 2	DISPERSION	187D
	EKLEKTOS IB	CHOSEN	242B
	KAPPADOKIA	CAPPADOCIA	404A
	PAREPID8MOS	EXILE	631A
	PETROS	PETER	661A
	PONTOS	PONTUS	698C
1=3	CHRISTOS 2	ANOINTED ONE	895C
2	HAGIASMOS	HOLINESS	9B
	HAIMA 2B	BLOOD	22C
	EIR8N8 2	PEACE	226D
	EN IIIIA	BY	260B
	THEOS 3D	GOD	358A
	PL8THUNW IB	INCREASE	675A
	PNEUMA 50B	SPIRIT	683B
	PROGNWSIS	FOREKNOWLEDGE	710D
	RANTISMOS	SPRINKLING	741D
	HUPAKO8 IB	OBEDIENCE	845A
	CHARIS 2C	FAVOR	885D
3	ANAGENNAW	BEGET AGAIN	51A
	ANASTASIS 2A	RESURRECTION	60A
	EK IB	AWAY FROM	233C
	ELEOS 2B	MERCY	249D
	ELPIS 2B	HOPE	252C
	EULOG8TOS	BLESSED	323A
	ZAW 4B	LIVE	337C
	THEOS 3D	GOD	358A
	KATA II5A6	ACCORDING TO	408B
	KURIOS 2CY	LORD	461B
	HO,H8,TO II10B	THE	555A
	PAT8R 3DB	FATHER	641D
	POLUS IIBB	MANY	694C
4	AMARANTOS 2	UNFADING	4ID
	AMIANTOS I	UNDEFILED	45C
	APHTHARTOS	IMPERISHABLE	125A
	KL8RONOMIA 3	INHERITANCE	436A
	OURANOS 2D	HEAVEN	599D
	T8REW 2A	KEEP	822C
5	APOKALUPTW 4	REVEAL	91D
	HETOIMOS I	READY	316D
	KAIROS 4	TIME	396B
	PISTIS 2Da	FAITH	669B
	SWT8RIA 2	DELIVERANCE	809B
	PHROUREW 2	GUARD	875B
6	AGALLIAW	BE GLAD	3D
	ARTI 3	NOW	109D
	DEI 6	IT IS NECESSARY	171B
	EIMI II4D	TO BE	223B
	EN I4D	IN	258C
	LUPEW 2A	GRIEVE	483A

6	OLIGOS 3A	LITTLE	566C
	PEIRASMOS 2B	TEST	646D
	POIKILOS I	DIVERSIFIED	690A
7	APOKALUPSIS 3	REVELATION	92A
	APOLLUMI 2AB	PASS AWAY	94D
	DIA AIIIIA	BY MEANS OF	179A
	DOKIMAZW 2A	EXAMINE	201C
	DOKIMION 2	GENUINE	202A
	EIS 4E	SO THAT	228D
	EN II2	WHILE	259D
	EPAINOS IAB	PRAISE	281B
	HEURISKW 2	FIND	326A
	HO,H8,TO II3B	THE	553D
	PISTIS 2Da	FAITH	669B
	POLUS I2Ca	MANY	695B
	POLUTIMOS	VALUABLE	696D
	PUR IA	FIRE	737B
	TIM8 2B	HONOR	825C
	TIMIOS IB	VALUABLE	825D
	CHRISTOS 2	ANOINTED ONE	895C
	CHRUSION	GOLD	896D
8	AGALLIAW	BE GLAD	3D
	AGALLIAW	BE GLAD	4A
	AGAPAW IAB	LOVE	4C
	ANEKLAL8TOS	INEXPRESSIBLE	63D
	ARTI 3	NOW	109D
	DOXAZW 2	GLORIFY	203D
	HORAW IAa	SEE	581C
	OU 3B	NO	594C
	PISTEUW 2AB	BELIEVE	667B
	CHARA I	JOY	883D
9	KOMIZW 2A	BRING	443D
	PISTIS 2Da	FAITH	669B
	SWT8RIA 2	DELIVERANCE	809A
	TELOS IC	END	819C
	PSUCH8 IC	SOUL LIFE	902A
10	EIS 4D	FOR	228C
	EKZ8TEW I	SEEK OUT	239C
	EXERAUNAW	INQUIRE CAREFULL	273D
	PROPH8TEUW 3	PROPHESY	730C
	PROPH8T8S I	PROPHET	730D
	PROPH8T8S 5	PROPHET	731C
	SWT8RIA 2	DELIVERANCE	809A
	CHARIS 3B	FAVOR	886B
11	D8LOW	REVEAL	177C
	DOXA I8a	GLORY	203A
	EIS 4H	OF	229A
	ERAUNAW	SEARCH	306D
	8 IAB	OR	342D
	KAIROS I	TIME	395C
	PATH8MA I	SUFFERING	607B
	PNEUMA 5B	SPIRIT	682C
	POIOS IAa	OF WHAT KIND	691A
	PROMARTUROMAI	PREDICT	715B
12	AGGELOS 2A	ANGEL	7C
	ANAGGELLW 2	DISCLOSE	51A
	APOKALUPTW 2	REVEAL	91C
	APOSTELLW IBd	SEND AWAY	98B
	APOSTELLW IC	SEND AWAY	98B
	DIAKONEW 2	SERVE	183A
	EPITHUMEW	DESIRE	293A
	EUAGGELIZW 2AY	PREACH	317D
	NUN IAY	NOW	547D

12	OURANOS 2A	HEAVEN	599B
	PARAKUPTW 2	LOOK INTO	624D
	PNEUMA 5CB	SPIRIT	682D
	PNEUMA 5CB	SPIRIT	683A
13	ANAZWNNUMI	BIND UP	53C
	APOKALUPSIS 3	REVELATION	92A
	DIANOIA 2	MIND	186B
	ELPIZW 3	HOPE	252B
	EN II2	WHILE	259D
	EPI IIIIBc	TOWARD	289A
	N8PHW	BE SELF CONTROLLED	540D
	OSPHUS I	WAIST	591D
	TELEIWS	PERFECTLY	818A
	PHERW 4AB	BEAR	863B
	CHARIS 3B	FAVOR	886B
14	AGNOIA 2	IGNORANCE	11D
	EPITHUMIA 3	DESIRE	293C
	PROTEROS 1BB	EARLIER	729C
	SUSCH8MATIZW	FORMED LIKE	803B
	TEKNON 2FB	CHILD	816C
	HUPAKO8 1B	OBEDIENCE	845A
	HWS IIIIA	SO	906C
15	HAGIOS 1Bc	DEDICATED TO GOD	9D
	ANASTROPH8	CONDUCT	61B
	KALEW 2	CALL	400C
	KATA II5Ac	ACCORDING TO	408A
16	DIOTI 3	FOR	198C
16A	HAGIOS 1Bc DEDICATED TO GOD		9D
16B	HAGIOS 1B6	HOLY	9D
17	ANASTREPHW 2BB	LIVE	61A
	APROSWPOL8MPTWS	IMPARTIALLY	102A
	EI III	IF	218C
	EPIKALEW 2B	CALL UPON	294B
	ERGON 1CB	DEED	308A
	KATA II54AB	ACCORDING TO	408B
	KRINW 4Bc	JUDGE	453A
	PAROIKIA 1B	SOJOURN	634B
	PAT8R 3CB	FATHER	641C
	PHOBOS 2Ac	FEAR	871B
	PHOBOS 2B8c	FEAR	871D
	CHRONOS	TIME	896B
18	ANASTROPH8	CONDUCT	61B
	ARGURION 2A	SILVER	104B
	EK IC	AWAY FROM	233D
	LUTROW 1B	REDEEM	484A
	MATAIOS	IDLE	496D
	PATROPARADOTOS	INHERITED	642C
	PHTHARTOS	PERISHABLE	864D
	CHRUSION	GOLD	896D
19	HAIMA 2B	BLOOD	22C
	AMNOS	LAMB	45D
	AMWMOS I	UNBLEMISHED	47B
	ASPILOS I	WITHOUT BLEMISH	116D
	PATROPARADOTOS	INHERITED	642C
	TIMIOS 1B	VALUABLE	825D
	HWS IIIIA	SO	906C
20	EPI I2	UNDER	286C
	ESCHATOS 3B	LAST	314B
	KATABOL8 I	FOUNDATION	410A
	KOSMOS 2	WORLD	446D
	MEN IAc	(PARTICLE)	503D
	PRO 2	BEFORE	708C
20	PROGINWSKW	KNOWS BEFOREHAND	710C
	PHANEROW 2BB	REVEAL	860D
	CHRONOS	TIME	896C
21	EGEIRW IAB	RAISE	213D
	EIMI III2	TO BE	224A
	ELPIS 2B	HOPE	252D
	NEKROS 2A	DEAD	537A
	PISTEUW 2AB	BELIEVE	667B
	PISTIS 2A	FAITH	668C
	PISTIS 2BB	FAITH	669A
	PISTOS 2	TRUSTWORTHY	671A
	HWSTE 2AB	THEREFORE	908C
22	HAGNIZW 1B	PURIFY	11A
	AL8THEIA 2B	TRUTH	35C
	ANUPOKRITOS	GENUINE	76A
	EK 3Gy	BY	234D
	KATHAROS 3B	CLEAN	389A
	KARDIA 1Bc	HEART	404B
	PNEUMA 5DB	SPIRIT	683B
	HUPAKO8 1B	OBEDIENCE	845A
	PHILADELPHIA	BROTHERLY LOVE	866B
	PSUCH8 1C	SOUL LIFE	902A
23	AIWN 1B	TIME	26D
	ANAGENNAW	BEGET AGAIN	51A
	APHTHARTOS	IMPERISHABLE	125A
	ZAW 4B	LIVE	337C
	LOGOS 1BB	WORD	479B
	MENW 1CB	REMAIN	505C
	SPORA	SOWING	770D
	PHTHARTOS	PERISHABLE	864D
24	DIOTI 3	FOR	198C
	DOXA 2	MAGNIFICENCE	203A
	EKPIPTW I	FALL OFF	243B
	X8RAINW 2A	DRY UP	550D
	SARX 3	BODY	751A
	HWS II3B	SO	906A
24A	ANTHOS I	BLOSSOM	66D
24A	CHORTOS	GRASS	892B
24B	ANTHOS I	BLOSSOM	66D
24B	CHORTOS	GRASS	892B
24C	CHORTOS	GRASS	892B
25	AIWN 1B	TIME	26D
	EIS 1DB	IN	227D
	EUAGGELIZW 2AY	PREACH	317D
	EUAGGELIZW 2B8c	PREACH	318A
	KURIOS 2A	LORD	460B
	MENW 1CB	REMAIN	505C
25A	R8MA I	WORD	743A
25B	R8MA I	WORD	743A

1 PETER 2

1	APOTITH8MI 1B	LAY ASIDE	100C
	DOLOS	DECEIT	202B
	KAKIA 1B	MALICE	397D
	KATALALIA	SLANDER	413D
	PETROS	PETER	661A
	HUPOKRISIS	HYPOCRISY	852D
	PHTHONOS	ENVY	865C
1A	PAS 1AB	EVERY EACH	636C
1B	PAS 1AB	EVERY EACH	636D
2	ADOLOS	WITHOUT DECEIT	18B
	ANAGENNAW	BEGET AGAIN	51A

	Greek	Gloss	Ref		Greek	Gloss	Ref
2	ARTIGENN8TOS	NEW BORN	110A	8	PETRA 2	ROCK	660C
	AUXANW 2	GROW	121B		PROSKOMMA IA	STUMBLING	723B
	BREPHOS 2	INFANT	147A		PROSKOPTW 2A	TAKE OFFENSE	723C
	GALA 2	MILK	149A		SKANDALON 2	TRAP	760C
	EIS 4E	SO THAT	228D		TITH8MI I2B	MAKE	824A
	EPIPOTHEW	DESIRE	297D	9	HAGIOS IAα	DEDICATED TO GOD	9C
	LOGIKOS	SPIRITUAL	477C		ARET8 2	PRAISE	105C
	SWT8RIA 2	DELIVERANCE	809B		BASILEIOS	ROYAL	135C
	HWS IIIIA	SO	906B		GENOS 3	NATION	155C
3	GEUOMAI 2 COME TO KNOW SOMETH		156B		EK IA	AWAY FROM	233C
	KURIOS 2Cα	LORD	460C		EKLEKTOS 1B	CHOSEN	242B
	PROSERCHOMAI 2A	APPROACH	720B		EXAGGELLW	PROCLAIM	270D
	CHR8STOS 1Bβ	USEFUL	894C		THAUMASTOS 2	WONDERFUL	353B
4	APODOKIMAZW I DECLARE USELESS		90B		HIERATEUMA	PRIESTHOOD	372C
	EKLEKTOS 2	CHOSEN	242B		KALEW 2	CALL	400C
	ENTIMOS 2	HONORED	268C		LAOS 3B	PEOPLE	468B
	ZAW 4B	LIVE	337C		HOPWS 2Aα	IN ORDER THAT	580C
	LITHOS 2	STONE	475D		PERIPOI8SIS 3	KEEPING SAFE	656A
	PARA II2H	BESIDE	615C		SKOTOS 2B	DARKNESS	765B
5	HAGIOS IAα	DEDICATED TO GOD	9C		PHWS 3A	LIGHT	880B
	ANAPHERW 2	OFFER UP	62D	10	ELEEW	HAVE MERCY	249B
	EPOIKODOMEW 1B	BUILD ON TO	305C		LAOS 3B	PEOPLE	468B
	EUPROSDEKTOS I	ACCEPTABLE	324D		NUN IC	NOW	547D
	ZAW 4B	LIVE	337C		OU 2A	NO	594B
	THUSIA 2B	SACRIFICE	367A		OU 3C	NO	594D
	HIERATEUMA	PRIESTHOOD	372B	10B	NUN IAγ	NOW	547D
	LITHOS 2	STONE	475D	11	AGAP8TOS 2	BELOVED	6C
	OIKODOMEW 2	BUILD	561A		APECHW 3	KEEP AWAY	84C
	OIKOS 1Bα	HOUSE	563C		EPITHUMIA 3	DESIRE	293C
5A	PNEUMATIKOS 2Aβ SPIRITUAL		685B		KATA I2Bα	DOWN	406C
					HOSTIS 2B	WHOEVER	591A
5B	PNEUMATIKOS 2Aβ SPIRITUAL		685B		PAROIKOS 2	STRANGER	634C
6	AKROGWNIAIOS	CORNERSTONE	33B		SARKIKOS 3	FLESHLY	750B
	GRAPH8 2Bβ	SCRIPTURE	165B		STRATEUW 2		778A
	DIOTI 3	FOR	198C		DO MILITARY SERVICE		
	EKLEKTOS 2	CHOSEN	242B		PSUCH8 IC	SOUL LIFE	902A
	ENTIMOS 2	HONORED	268C		HWS IIIIA	SO	906C
	EPI III8γ	ON	287A	12	ANASTROPH8	CONDUCT	61B
	KATAISCHUNW 3B	DISAPPOINT	411D		EK 3Gβ	BY	234D
	LITHOS 2	STONE	475D		EPISKOP8 I	A VISITATION	299A
	M8 DIA	NOT	519B		EPISKOP8 2	A VISITATION	299A
	PERIECHW 2B	SEIZE	652D		EPOPTEUW	OBSERVE	305C
	PISTEUW 2Aγ	BELIEVE	667B		ERGON ICβ	DEED	308A
	SIWN 2B	ZION	760A		H8MERA 3Bβ	DAY	348A
	TITH8MI 11Aα	PUT	823C		KAKOPOIOS	CRIMINAL	398C
7	APISTEW 18	DISBELIEVE	84D		*KALOS 2B	GOOD	401B
	APODOKIMAZW I DECLARE USELESS		90B		KATALALEW	SPEAK AGAINST	413C
	GINOMAI I4A	BECOME	158D		HOS,H8,HO I2A	(REL PRON)	587B
	GWNIA	CORNER	167D	13	ANTHRWPINOS 3	HUMAN	67B
	KEPHAL8 2B	HEAD	431C		BASILEUS I	KING	135D
	LITHOS 2	STONE	475D		KTISIS 2	INSTITUTION	457B
	OIKODOMEW 1Bβ	BUILD	560D		HUPERECHW 2A	SURPASS	848D
	HOS,H8,HO I4D	(REL PRON)	588A		HUPOTASSW 1Bβ	SUBJECT	855D
	OUN IA	THEREFORE	597B	13F	HWS IIIIA	SO	906C
	PISTEUW 2B	BELIEVE	667C	14	AGATHOPOIOS	DOING GOOD	2C
	TIM8 2B	HONOR	825B		EKDIK8SIS	VENGEANCE	238B
8	APEITHEW I	DISOBEY	82A		EPAINOS IAα	PRAISE	281B
	APEITHEW 3	DISOBEY	82A		H8GEMWN 2	GOVERNORS	344A
	LITHOS 2	STONE	475D		KAKOPOIOS	CRIMINAL	398C
	LOGOS 1Bβ	WORD	479C		*PEMPW I	SEND	647D
	HOS,H8,HO I7B	(REL PRON)	588C	15	AGATHOPOIEW 2	DO GOOD	2C
	PARASKEUAZW I	PREPARE	627C		AGNWSIA	IGNORANCE	12A
					APHRWN	FOOLISH	127B

```
15 THEL8MA ICɣ              WILL 355A      24 APOGINOMAI                     DIE  88C
   HOUTW 2                  THUS 602C         ZAW 3B                        LIVE 337C
   PHIMOW 2             TIE SHUT 869D         IAOMAI 2                      HEAL 369A
16 DOULOS 4                SLAVE 205B         MWLWPS                       WOUND 532D
   ELEUTHERIA           FREEDOM 250A          XULON 2C                     CROSS 551C
   ELEUTHEROS 3            FREE 250B          HOS,H8,HO I3A          (REL PRON) 587C
   EPIKALUMMA             COVER 294B          SWMA IB                       BODY 807B
   KAKIA IA             BADNESS 397D      25 EPI IIIIB6                   TOWARD 289A
17 ADELPHOT8S I       BROTHERHOOD  16B         EPISKOPOS I               OVERSEER 299B
   BASILEUS I              KING 135D          EPISTREPHW 2B                 TURN 301C
   PHOBEW 2A          BE AFRAID 871A          NUN IAɣ                        NOW 547D
17A   TIMAW 2              HONOR 824D          PLANAW 2B                   DECEIVE 671B
17B   TIMAW 2              HONOR 824D          PLANAW 2A                   DECEIVE 671B
18 AGATHOS IB∝             GOOD   3A          POIM8N 2B∂                 SHEPHERD 690D
   ALLA IA            BUT, YET  37C           PROBATON 2                   SHEEP 710A
   DESPOT8S              MASTER 175C          PSUCH8 IC                SOUL LIFE 902A
   EPIEIK8S             GENTLE 292C
   OIKET8S          HOUSE SLAVE 559C
   SKOLIOS 2           CROOKED 763D                         | PETER 3
   HUPOTASSW IB∂       SUBJECT 855D
   PHOBOS 2B∂             FEAR 871D      I  ANASTROPH8                  CONDUCT  61B
19 ADIKWS             UNJUSTLY  18A         ANEU 2                      WITHOUT  65A
   LUP8                  GRIEF 483B         AN8R I                          MAN  66A
   PASCHW 3A∂           SUFFER 639D         APEITHEW I                  DISOBEY  82A
   SUNEID8SIS I   CONSCIOUSNESS 794A        APEITHEW 3                  DISOBEY  82A
   HUPOPHERW            ENDURE 856B         IDIOS 2B                  ONES OWN 370C
   CHARIS 2B             FAVOR 885D         HINA I2             IN ORDER THAT 377D
20 AGATHOPOIEW 2       DO GOOD   2C         KERDAINW IB                TO GAIN 430C
   HAMARTANW I             SIN  41D         LOGOS IB∂                     WORD 479C
   GAR IF                 WHAT 151C         HOMOIWS                   LIKEWISE 571A
   EI IIA                   IF 218A         HUPOTASSW IB∂              SUBJECT 855D
   KLEOS                  FAME 435B      IB  LOGOS IA∝                   WORD 478B
   KOLAPHIZW I          STRIKE 441D      2  HAGNOS 2                      PURE  I2A
   PARA II2B            BESIDE 615C         ANASTROPH8                 CONDUCT  61B
   PASCHW 3A∝           SUFFER 639C         EPOPTEUW                   OBSERVE 305C
   POIOS IA∂     OF WHAT KIND 691B          PHOBOS 2B∂                    FEAR 871D
   CHARIS 2B             FAVOR 885D      3  EMPLOK8                    BRAIDING 256A
20A   HUPOMENW 2        REMAIN 853D         ENDUSIS I              PUTTING ON 263B
20B   HUPOMENW 2        REMAIN 853D         EXWTHEN IBɣ                OUTSIDE 279C
21 EPAKOLOUTHEW I       FOLLOW 282A         THRIX 2                       HAIR 364C
   ICHNOS            FOOTPRINT 385B         HIMATION I                 GARMENT 377A
   KALEW 2                CALL 400D         KOSMOS I                  ADORNMENT 446C
   PASCHW 3A∂           SUFFER 639C         PERITHESIS             PUTTING ON 653B
   HUPER IA∈    IN BEHALF OF 846C           PLOK8                        BRAID 679B
   HUPOGRAMMOS          PATTERN 851C         CHRUSION                      GOLD 896D
   HUPOLIMPANW           LEAVE 853B      4  ANTHRWPOS 2C∝                  MAN  68A
   CHRISTOS 2     ANOINTED ONE 895D         APHTHARTOS              IMPERISHABLE 125A
22 HAMARTIA I              SIN  42B         BATHUS 2                      DEEP 130A
   DOLOS                DECEIT 202B         EIMI II9A                    TO BE 223D
   HEURISKW IB            FIND 325C         ENWPION 3                   BEFORE 270B
   OUDE I             AND NOT 595D          H8SUCHIOS                    QUIET 350A
   POIEW IICɣ               DO 688C         KARDIA IB∝                   HEART 404B
   STOMA IA              MOUTH 777C         KRUPTOS I                   HIDDEN 455A
23 ADIKWS             UNJUSTLY  18A         PNEUMA 3C                    SPIRIT 681D
   ANTILOIDOREW REVILE IN RETURN  74C       POLUTEL8S                   COSTLY 696C
   APEILEW             THREATEN  82B         PRAUS                       HUMBLE 705D
   DIKAIWS IA           JUSTLY 197B      5  HAGIOS IB∝      DEDICATED TO GOD   9C
   KRINW 4B∝             JUDGE 453A         AN8R I                         MAN  66A
   LOIDOREW             REVILE 480C         ELPIZW 3                      HOPE 252A
   PARADIDWMI        GIVE OVER 619C         IDIOS 2C                  ONES OWN 370C
   PARADIDWMI 2      GIVE OVER 620D         KOSMEW 2B∝                DECORATE 446A
   PASCHW 3A∝           SUFFER 639C         HUPOTASSW IB∂              SUBJECT 855D
24 ANAPHERW 2         OFFER UP  62D      6  AGATHOPOIEW 2              DO GOOD   2C
                                            KALEW IA∂                     CALL 399D
```

6	KURIOS IR	LORD	460A
	M8DEIS I	NO	520A
	PTO8SIS 2	FEAR	735A
	SARRA	SARAH	752B
	TEKNON 2D	CHILD	816C
	HUPAKOUW I	LISTEN TO	845A
	PHOBEW IA	BE AFRAID	870D
	PHOBEW IBγ	BE AFRAID	871A
	HWS II4A	SO	906B
7	AN8R I	MAN	66A
	APONEMW	SHOW	96C
	ASTHEN8S IB	SICK	1158
	GNWSIS 2	KNOWLEDGE	163A
	GUNAIKEIOS	WOMAN	167B
	EGKOPTW	HINDER	215C
	ZW8 2Bα	LIFE	341B
	M8 AIIIE	NOT	518A
	HOMOIWS	LIKEWISE	571A
	PROSEUCH8 I	PRAYER	720B
	SKEUOS 2	THING	761D
	SUGKL8RONOMOS		781D
	INHERITING TOGETHER		
	SUNOIKEW	LIVE WITH	799A
	SUNOMILEW	TALK	799B
	TIM8 2B	HONOR	825B
	CHARIS 3B	FAVOR	886B
7A	HWS IIIIA	SO	906C
7B	HWS IIIIA	SO	906C
8	EUSPLAGCHNOS	COMPASSIONATE	327A
	HOMOPHRWN	LIKE MINDED	572C
	SUMPATH8S	SYMPATHETIC	786C
	TAPEINOPHRWN	HUMBLE	812B
	TELOS IDα	END	819C
	PHILADELPHOS		866B
	LOVING ONES BROTHER		
	PHILOPHRWN	FRIENDLY	869C
9	ANTI 2	FOR	73A
	APODIDWMI 3	RECOMPENSE	90A
	ENANTION 2	BEFORE	261B
	EULOGEW 2A	BLESS	322C
	EULOGIA 3Bα	BLESSING	323B
	HINA I5	IN ORDER THAT	378A
	KAKOS 3	EVIL	399A
	KALEW 2	CALL	400D
	KL8RONOMEW 2	INHERIT	436A
	LOIDORIA	ABUSE	480C
10	AGATHOS IAβ	GOOD	2D
	AGAPAW 2	LOVE	5A
	GLWSSA IA	TONGUE	161B
	DOLOS	DECEIT	202B
	EIDON 5	SEE	220A
	ZW8 2Bβ	LIFE	341C
	H8MERA 4B	TIME	348B
	THELW I	WISH	355C
	M8 AIIIDα	NOT	518A
	HO,H8,TO II4B6	THE	554A
	PAUW I	STOP	643C
	CHEILOS I	LIP	887C
IOF	KAKOS IC	EVIL	398D
11	DIWKW 4B	PURSUE	200C
	EIR8N8 IB	PEACE	226C
	EKKLINW	TURN AWAY	241A
	Z8TEW 2A	SEEK	339C
11	POIEW IIBε	DO	667D
12	DE8SIS	PRAYER	171A
	DIKAIOS IB	UPRIGHT	194D
	KAKOS IC	EVIL	398D
	OUS I	EAR	600A
	OPHTHALMOS I	EYE	604C
	POIEW IIBε	DO	687D
	PROSWPON IB	FACE	728B
13	AGATHOS 2Aα	GOOD	3B
	Z8LWT8S IAβ	ZEALOT	338D
	KAKOW I	HARM	399B
	MIM8T8S 2	IMITATOR	524A
14	AUTOS 3B	(OBLIQUE CASE)	123A
	DIKAIOSUN8 4	RIGHTEOUSNESS	196C
	EI I3	IF	218B
	MAKARIOS IB	BLESSED	487D
	M8DE IB	AND NOT	519D
	PASCHW 3Aβ	SUFFER	639C
	TARASSW 2	STIR UP	813A
	PHOBEW IA	BE AFRAID	870D
	PHOBEW IBγ	BE AFRAID	871A
	PHOBOS I	CAUSING OF FEAR	871B
	PHOBOS 2Aα	FEAR	871C
15	HAGIAZW 3	TO REVERENCE	9A
	AEI I	ALWAYS	19A
	AITEW	ASK	25B
	APAITEW 2	DEMAND	79B
	APOLOGIA 2B	DEFENSE	95C
	ELPIS 2B	HOPE	252C
	HETOIMOS 2	READY	316D
	KURIOS 2Cα	LORD	460C
	LOGOS 2A	ACCOUNT	479D
	PROS III3C	TOWARD	717B
16	AGATHOS IBβ	GOOD	3B
	AGATHOS IBβ	GOOD	3B
	ANASTROPH8	CONDUCT	61B
	EP8REAZW	MISTREAT	285C
	ECHW I2Eβ	HAVE	333B
	KATAISCHUNW 2	BE HUMILIATED	411D
	KATALALEW	SPEAK AGAINST	413C
	META AIII1	WITH	511A
	HOS,H8,HO I2A	(REL PRON)	587B
	PRAUT8S	HUMILITY	705D
	SUNEID8SIS 2	CONSCIOUSNESS	794B
17	AGATHOPOIEW 2	DO GOOD	2C
	EI I3	IF	218B
	THEL8MA 2B	WILL	355A
	KAKOPOIEW I	DO WRONG	398B
	KREITTWN 2	BETTER	451A
	PASCHW 3Aα	SUFFER	639C
18	ADIKOS I	UNJUST	17D
	HAMARTIA 4	SIN	43A
	HAPAX I	ONCE	80A
	DIKAIOS IB	UPRIGHT	194D
	ZWOPOIEW I	MAKE ALIVE	342C
	THANATOW I	PUT TO DEATH	352B
	PASCHW 3Aβ	SUFFER	639C
	PERI IG	ABOUT	650C
	PROSAGW IBα	BRING	718B
	SARX 2	BODY	751A
	HUPER IAε	IN BEHALF OF	846C
	CHRISTOS 2	ANOINTED ONE	895D
18F	PNEUMA 2	SPIRIT	681A

19 EN IV6E	IN	261A
ENWCH	ENOCH	270D
K8RUSSW 2Bβ	ANNOUNCE	432C
PNEUMA 2	SPIRIT	681A
PNEUMA 4C	SPIRIT	682A
PHULAK8 3	GUARD	875D
20 APEITHEW 2	DISOBEY	82A
APEITHEW 3	DISOBEY	82A
APEKDECHOMAI	AWAIT	82D
DIA AI2	THROUGH	178C
*DIASWZW	SAVE	186B
EIS 7	TO	229B
H8MERA 4B	TIME	348B
KATASKEUAZW 2	BUILD	419C
KIBWTOS I	BOX	433A
MAKROTHUMIA 2Bα	PATIENCE	489B
NWE	NOAH	549C
OKTW	EIGHT	565D
OLIGOS IB	FEW	566C
PNEUMA 2	SPIRIT	681A
HUDWR I	WATER	840C
PSUCH8 2	SOUL LIFE	902C
21 AGATHOS IBβ	GOOD	3B
ANASTASIS 2A	RESURRECTION	59D
ANTITUPOS I	CORRESPONDING TO	75B
APOTHESIS	REMOVAL	90C
BAPTISMA 2	BAPTISM	132B
EPERWT8MA 2	REQUEST	285B
NUN IAα	NOW	547C
RUPOS I	DIRT	745C
SARX 2	BODY	751A
SUNEID8SIS 2	CONSCIOUSNESS	794B
SWZW 2Aγ	SAVE	806B
22 AGGELOS 2A	ANGEL	7D
DEXIOS 2A	RIGHT	173D
DUNAMIS 6	POWER	207B
EXOUSIA 4Cβ	AUTHORITY	278B
OURANOS 2B	HEAVEN	599C
HUPOTASSW IBα	SUBJECT	855D

I PETER 4

1 ENNOIA	THOUGHT	266C
HOPLIZW	EQUIP	579A
PAUW 2	STOP	643D
1A PASCHW 3Aβ	SUFFER	639D
1A SARX 2	BODY	751A
1B PASCHW 3Aβ	SUFFER	639D
1B SARX 2	BODY	751A
2 BIOW	LIVE	141C
EPITHUMIA 3	DESIRE	293C
EPILOIPOS	REMAINING	295D
THEL8MA ICγ	WILL	355A
M8KETI 2	NO LONGER	520B
SARX 5	BODY	751C
CHRONOS	TIME	896B
3 ATHEMITOS	UNLAWFUL	20B
ARKETOS	SUFFICIENT	106C
ASELGEIA	LICENTIOUSNESS	114C
BIOS I	LIFE	141A
BOUL8MA	INTENTION	145B
EIDWLOLATRIA	IDOLATRY	220C
EPITHUMIA 3	DESIRE	293C

3 EPITHUMIA 3	DESIRE	293D
KATERGAZOMAI I	ACHIEVE	422D
KWMOS	CAROUSING	462D
OINOPHLUGIA	DRUNKENNESS	565B
PARERCHOMAI IAβ	GO BY	631B
POREUW 2C	PROCEED	699C
POTOS	DRINKING	702D
CHRONOS	TIME	896C
4 ANACHUSIS	POURING OUT	62D
ASWTIA	DEBAUCHERY	119A
BLASPH8MEW 2Bα	BLASPHEME	142A
SUNTRECHW 2	RUN TOGETHER	800D
5 APODIDWMI I	GIVE AWAY	90A
ECHW III	BE	334B
ZAW IAα	LIVE	336C
KRINW 4Bα	JUDGE	453A
LOGOS 2A	ACCOUNT	479D
NEKROS 2A	DEAD	536D
6 ANTHRWPOS IC	HUMAN	67D
EUAGGELIZW 2Bα	PREACH	318A
ZAW 2Bβ	LIVE	337B
HINA I5	IN ORDER THAT	378A
KRINW 4Bα	JUDGE	453A
PNEUMA 5Dβ	SPIRIT	683B
SARX 2	BODY	751A
7 EGGIZW 5B	APPROACH	212D
N8PHW	BE SELF CONTROLLED	540D
PROSEUCH8 I	PRAYER	720C
SWPHRONEW 2	SOUND MIND	809C
TELOS IA	END	819A
8 AGAP8 IIBβ	LOVE	5D
AGAP8 IIA	LOVE	5D
HAMARTIA I	SIN	42B
EKTEN8S	EARNEST	245A
ECHW I2Eβ	HAVE	333A
KALUPTW 2A	COVER	402A
PAS 2Aδ	IN ALL RESPECTS	638B
PL8THOS 2A	QUANTITY	674B
PRO 3	BEFORE	708D
9 ANEU 2	WITHOUT	65A
GOGGUSMOS I	COMPLAINT	163D
EIS 4Cβ	(GOAL)	228C
PHILOXENOS	HOSPITABLE	868C
10 DIAKONEW 2	SERVE	183A
KATHWS 2	AS	392B
KALOS 2Cα	GOOD	401C
OIKONOMOS 2	MANAGER	562D
POIKILOS I	DIVERSIFIED	690A
CHARIS 4	FAVOR	886C
CHARISMA 2	A GIFT	887C
11 AIWN IB	TIME	26D
AM8N I	AMEN	45A
DIAKONEW 2	SERVE	183A
ISCHUS	STRENGTH	384B
KRATOS 4	POWER	450B
PAS 2Aδ	IN ALL RESPECTS	638C
CHOR8GEW	PROVIDE	892A
11A HWS IIIIA	SO	906C
11B HWS IIIIA	SO	906C
12 AGAP8TOS 2	BELOVED	6C
XENIZW 2	SURPRISE	550A
XENOS IBβ	STRANGE	550B
PEIRASMOS I	TEST	646C

12 PROS III3C	TOWARD 717B
PURWSIS 2	BURNING 738D
SUMBAINW	MEET 784D
13 AGALLIAW	BE GLAD 3D
APOKALUPSIS 3	REVELATION 92A
EN II2	WHILE 259D
KATHO 2	IN SO FAR AS 391C
KOINWNEW IBα	SHARE 439C
PATH8MA I	SUFFERING 607B
CHRISTOS I	ANOINTED ONE 895C
13A CHAIRW I	REJOICE 882A
13B CHAIRW I	REJOICE 881B
13B CHAIRW I	REJOICE 882A
14 ANAPAUW 2	REST 58C
DOXA IBβ	GLORY 203A
EPI IIIIBγ	ON 289A
MAKARIOS IB	BLESSED 487D
ONEIDIZW I	REPROACH 573A
ONOMA II	TITLE 577A
PNEUMA 5A	SPIRIT 682C
PNEUMA 5E	SPIRIT 683C
15 ALLOTRIEPISKOPOS	A BUSYBODY 39D
GAR 3	CERTAINLY 151D
8 IAβ	OR 342D
KAKOPOIOS	CRIMINAL 398C
KLEPT8S	THIEF 435C
PASCHW 3Aβ	SUFFER 639D
PHONEUS	MURDERER 872B
15A HWS IIIIA	SO 906C
15B HWS IIIIA	SO 906C
16 AISCHUNW I	BE ASHAMED 25A
DOXAZW I	PRAISE 203C
MEROS IBθ	MATTER 507B
ONOMA II	TITLE 577A
CHRISTIANOS	THE CHRISTIAN 895A
HWS IIIIA	SO 906C
17 APEITHEW I	DISOBEY 82A
APEITHEW 3	DISOBEY 82A
ARCHW 2C	BEGIN 113B
EUAGGELION 2Bβ	GOSPEL 318B
KAIROS 3	TIME 396A
KRIMA 3	JUDGING 451D
HO,H8,TO II4Bβ	THE 553D
OIKOS IBα	HOUSE 563C
TELOS IC	END 819C
18 HAMARTWLOS 2	SINNER 43C
ASEB8S I	GODLESS 114B
*DIKAIOS IB	UPRIGHT 194D
MOLIS I	WITH DIFFICULTY 528C
POU IA	WHERE 702D
SWZW 2B	SAVE 806B
PHAINW	CLOAK 859B
PHAINW 2B	APPEAR 859B
19 AGATHOPOIIA	DOING GOOD 2C
THEL8MA 2B	WILL 355B
KAI II4	ALSO 394C
KTIST8S	CREATOR 457C
PARATITH8MI 28β	628C
PLACE BESIDE	
PASCHW 3Aβ	SUFFER 639D
PISTOS IAβ	TRUSTWORTHY 670C
PSUCH8 IC	SOUL LIFE 902A
HWSTE IB	THEREFORE 908B

I PETER 5

1 APOKALUPTW 4	REVEAL 91D
DOXA IBβ	GLORY 203A
KOINWNOS IBα	COMPANION 440C
MARTUS 2C	WITNESS 495C
MELLW ICα	BE ABOUT TO 502A
PATH8MA I	SUFFERING 607B
PARAKALEW 2	APPEAL TO 622C
PRESBUTEROS 28α	OLDER 707A
SUMPRESBUTEROS	787D
FELLOW PRESBYTER	
2 AISCHROKERDWS	24C
FOND OF DISHONEST GAIN	
ANAGKASTWS	BY COMPULSION 52A
HEKOUSIWS	WILLINGLY 242D
EPISKOPEW 2	OVERSEE 299A
POIMAINW 2Aα	TEND 690B
POIMNION 2B	FLOCK 691A
PROTHUMWS	WILLINGLY 713C
3 KATAKURIEUW 2	RULE 413C
KL8ROS 2	LOT 436C
POIMNION 2B	FLOCK 691A
TUPOS 5B	MARK 837D
HWS I2A	AS 905C
4 AMARANTINOS	UNFADING 41C
ARCHIPOIM8N	CHIEF SHEPHERD 112C
DOXA IBβ	GLORY 203A
KOMIZW 2A	BRING 443D
STEPHANOS 2A	WREATH 775A
PHANEROW 2Bβ	REVEAL 860D
5 ANTITASSW	OPPOSE 75B
DIDWMI IBβ	GIVE 192B
EGKOMBOOMAI	PUT ON 215B
NEOS 2Bβ	NOVICE 538A
HOMOIWS	LIKEWISE 571A
PRESBUTEROS IA	OLDER 706C
PRESBUTEROS 28α	OLDER 707A
TAPEINOS 2B	LOW 812A
TAPEINOPHROSUN8	HUMILITY 812A
HUPER8PHANOS	PROUD 849A
HUPOTASSW IBβ	SUBJECT 855D
CHARIS 3B	FAVOR 886A
5B HUPOTASSW IBβ	SUBJECT 855D
6 KAIROS 4	TIME 396B
KRATAIOS	POWERFUL 449B
TAPEINOW 2B	LOWER 812C
HUPO 2B	UNDER 851B
HUPSOW 2	LIFT UP 858D
CHEIR 2Aβ	HAND 888D
7 EPI IIIIBγ	ON 289A
EPIR(R)IPTW 2	THROW 298A
MELEI 2	IT IS A CONCERN 501B
MERIMNA	ANXIETY 506A
PAS ICβ	ALL 637B
8 ANTIDIKOS	OPPONENT 73C
GR8GOREW 2	BE AWAKE 166C
DIABOLOS 2	THE SLANDERER 181A
KATAPINW IB	SWALLOW 417B
LEWN I	LION 473D
N8PHW	BE SELF CONTROLLED 540D
PERIPATEW IC	GO ABOUT 655A
WRUOMAI	ROAR 905B

8	HWS II2	SO	906A
9	ADELPHOT8S I	BROTHERHOOD	16B
	ANTHIST8MI I	SET AGAINST	66C
	AUTOS 4B	THE SAME	123C
	EPITELEW 4	LAY UPON	302C
	KOSMOS 4A	WORLD	447A
	OIDA ID	KNOW	558B
	PATH8MA I	SUFFERING	607B
	PISTIS 2Dα	FAITH	669B
	STEREOS 2	FIRM	774B
10	DOXA IA	GLORY	202D
	THEMELIOW 2A	ESTABLISH	356C
	THEOS 3E	GOD	358B
	KALEW 2	CALL	400C
	KATARTIZW IB	RESTORE	418D
	OLIGOS 3A	LITTLE	566C
	PASCHW 3Aβ	SUFFER	639D
	STHENOW	STRENGTHEN	756D
	ST8RIZW 2	ESTABLISH	775D
	CHARIS 3B	FAVOR	886A
II	AIWN IB	TIME	26D
	AM8N I	AMEN	45A
	KRATOS 4	POWER	450B
12	ADELPHOS 2	BROTHER	16A
	AL8TH8S 3	REAL	36B
	GRAPHW 2D	WRITE	166A
	GRAPHW 2D	WRITE	166B
	DIA AIIIIB	BY MEANS OF	179B
	DIA AIII2A	BY	179C
	EIS 9A	IN	229D
	EPIMARTUREW	BEAR WITNESS	295C
	HIST8MI IIID	STAND	383B
	LOGIZOMAI 3	THINK	477C
	OLIGOS IB	FEW	566C
	HOUTOS IA6	THIS	601A
	PARAKALEW 2	APPEAL TO	622C
	PISTOS IAα	TRUSTWORTHY	670B
	SILOUANOS	SILVANUS	758B
	CHARIS 3B	FAVOR	886B
	HWS II4B	SO	906B
13	BABULWN	BABYLON	129B
	MARKOS	MARK	493C
	RWM8	ROME	745D
	SUNEKLEKTOS	CHOSEN TOGETHER	794D
	HUIOS ICα	SON	841C
13F	ASPAZOMAI IA	GREET	116B
14	AGAP8 IIA	LOVE	5C
	ASPAZOMAI IA	GREET	116C
	EIR8N8 2	PEACE	226D
	EN I5D	IN	259B
	PAS IDγ	ALL	637D
	PHIL8MA	A KISS	867B

2 PETER I

I	APOSTOLOS 3	APOSTLES	99B
	DIKAIOSUN8 2B	RIGHTEOUSNESS	195D
	THEOS 2	GOD	357C
	ISOTIMOS	EQUAL IN VALUE	382A
	LAGCHANW I	RECEIVE	463B
	PETROS	PETER	661A
	PISTIS 2Dα	FAITH	669B
	SUMEWN 5	SYMEON	786A

I	SWT8R 2	SAVIOR	808D
IA	CHRISTOS 2	ANOINTED ONE	895C
IB	CHRISTOS 2	ANOINTED ONE	895C
2	EIR8N8 2	PEACE	226D
	*EPIGNWSIS	KNOWLEDGE	291C
	PL8THUNW IB	INCREASE	675A
	CHARIS 2C	FAVOR	885D
3	ARET8 3	MIRACLE	105D
	DIA AIIIIE	BY	179C
	DOXA IA	GLORY	202D
	DUNAMIS I	POWER	206C
	DWREOMAI	GIVE	209D
	EPIGNWSIS	KNOWLEDGE	291C
	EUSEBEIA	GODLINESS	326B
	ZW8 2Bα	LIFE	341B
	THEIOS IA	DIVINE	354B
	KALEW 2	CALL	400C
	PROS III5B	TOWARD	717D
	HWS IIIIB	SO	906C
3F	DE IE	BUT, AND	170C
4	APOPHEUGW	ESCAPE	101C
	DWREOMAI	GIVE	209D
	EPAGGELMA 2	PROMISE	280D
	EPITHUMIA 3	DESIRE	293C
	THEIOS IA	DIVINE	354B
	KOINWNOS IBα	COMPANION	440C
	KOSMOS 7	WORLD	447D
	MEGAS 2Bβ	GREAT	499C
	TIMIOS IB	VALUABLE	825D
	PHTHORA 3	RUIN	865D
	PHUSIS 2	NATURE	877C
5	ARET8 I	VIRTUE	105C
	AUTOS IH	EVEN	122D
	DE IE	BUT, AND	170C
	EPICHOR8GEW I	FURNISH	305A
	PAREISPHERW	APPLY	630B
	PAS IA6	ALL	637A
	SPOUD8 2	DILIGENCE	771B
5F	PISTIS 2Dγ	FAITH	669C
5F	PISTIS 2Dγ	FAITH	669D
5FF	GNWSIS 2	KNOWLEDGE	163A
5=8	DE IC	BUT, AND	170C
6	EGKRATEIA	SELF CONTROL	215C
6A	HUPOMON8 I	PATIENCE	854A
6B	HUPOMON8 I	PATIENCE	854A
6F	EUSEBEIA	GODLINESS	326B
7	AGAP8 IIA	LOVE	5C
7A	PHILADELPHIA	BROTHERLY LOVE	866B
7B	PHILADELPHIA	BROTHERLY LOVE	866B
8	AKARPOS 2	UNFRUITFUL	29B
	ARGOS 3	USELESS	104B
	EPIGNWSIS	KNOWLEDGE	291C
	KATHIST8MI 3	CAUSE	391C
	KURIOS 2Cγ	LORD	461B
	PLEONAZW IA	INCREASE	673B
	HUPARCHW I	BE	845D
9	HAMART8MA	SIN	42B
	KATHARISMOS 2	PURIFICATION	388D
	LAMBANW 2	RECEIVE	466C
	L8TH8	FORGETFULNESS	474A
	M8 AI5	NOT	517D

9	MUWPAZW	BE SHORTSIGHTED	532D
	HOS,H8,HO I2B«	(REL PRON)	587B
	OU 5A	NO	595A
	PALAI I	LONG AGO	610B
	PAREIMI 2	BE PRESENT	630A
	TUPHLOS 2Aβ	BLIND	838C
10	BEBAIOS 2	FIRM	137D
	EKLOG8 I	SELECTION	242C
	KL8SIS I	CALL	436D
	POIEW II2	DO	689D
	POTE I	ONCE	701D
	PTAIW 2	STUMBLE	734C
	SPOUDAZW 2	HASTEN	771A
10B	POIEW IIB«	DO	687D
11	AIWNIOS 3	ETERNAL	28A
	BASILEIA 3G	KINGDOM	135A
	EISODOS I	ENTRANCE	232C
	EPICHOR8GEW 2	GIVE	305A
	KURIOS 2Cγ	LORD	461A
	HO,H8,TO II10B	THE	555A
	HOUTW IB	THUS	602C
	PLOUSIWS	RICHLY	679D
	SWT8R 2	SAVIOR	808D
12	AEI 3	ALWAYS	19A
	KAIPER	ALTHOUGH	395B
	MELLW ICγ	INTEND	502B
	OIDA II	KNOW	558D
	PAREIMI 2	BE PRESENT	630A
	ST8RIZW 2	ESTABLISH	775D
	HUPOMIMN8SKW IA	REMIND	853D
13	DIEGEIRW	AROUSE	193A
	DIKAIOS 5	RIGHTEOUS	195B
	EPI III2B	ON	289B
	H8GEOMAI 2	CONSIDER	344B
	HOSOS I	HOW GREAT	590B
	SK8NWMA 2	DWELLING	762D
	HUPOMN8SIS I	REMEMBERING	854A
14	APOTHESIS	REMOVAL	90C
	D8LOW	REVEAL	177C
	KURIOS 2Cγ	LORD	461B
	SK8NWMA 2	DWELLING	762D
	TACHINOS 2	QUICKLY	814C
15	HEKASTOTE	ALWAYS	236B
	EXODOS 2	GOING OUT	276B
	ECHW 16A	CAN	334A
	MN8M8 I	REMEMBRANCE	526D
	POIEW III	DO	689C
	SPOUDAZW 2	HASTEN	771A
16	GNWRIZW I	MAKE KNOWN	162C
	EXAKOLOUTHEW I	FOLLOW	271D
	EPOPT8S 2	EYEWITNESS	305D
	KURIOS 2Cγ	LORD	461B
	MEGALEIOT8S	GRANDEUR	498A
	MUTHOS	FABLE	530D
	PAROUSIA 2B«	COMING	635C
	PAROUSIA 2Bβ	ADVENT	635D
	SOPHIZW 2	MAKE WISE	767C
17	AGAP8TOS I	BELOVED	6C
	DOXA IA	BRIGHTNESS	202C
	EIS 5	FOR	229B
	EUDOKEW 2A	WELL PLEASED	319C
	THEOS 3D	GOD	358B
	MEGALOPREP8S	MAGNIFICENT	498A

17	HOUTOS IA«	THIS	600D
	PARA I3B	FROM	614D
	PAT8R 3E	FATHER	642A
	TIM8 2B	HONOR	825B
	TOIOSDE	SUCH AS THIS	828D
	HUIOS 2B	SON	842C
	PHERW	BEAR	862D
	PHERW 4Aβ	BEAR	863B
	PHWN8 2C	VOICE	879A
18	HAGIOS IA«	DEDICATED TO GOD	9C
	SUN IC	WITH	789B
	PHERW 4Aβ	BEAR	863B
	PHWN8 2C	VOICE	879A
19	ANATELLW 2	RISE	61C
	AUCHM8ROS	DRY	123D
	BEBAIOS 2	FIRM	137D
	DIAUGAZW 2	DAWN	189B
	HEWS IIIB«	UNTIL	335C
	H8MERA IA	DAY	346C
	KAI I2F	AND	393C
	KALWS 4A	WELL	402B
	KARDIA I8β	HEART	404C
	LOGOS IAζ	MATTER	479A
	LUCHNOS I	LAMP	484C
	POIEW I2Aγ	DO	689B
	PROSECHW IAβ		721C
		PAY ATTENTION TO	
	PROPH8TIKOS	PROPHETIC	731C
	PHAINW I	SHINE	859B
	PHWSPHOROS	GIVING LIGHT	880D
	HWS IIIIA	SO	906C
20	GINOMAI II2A	BE	159C
	GINWSKW 6C	KNOW	160D
	GRAPH8 2Bβ	SCRIPTURE	165B
	GRAPH8 2B«	SCRIPTURE	165B
	EPILUSIS	EXPLANATION	295D
	IDIOS IAβ	ONES OWN	370B
	HOUTOS IBβ	THIS	601C
	PAS IA«	EVERY EACH	636D
	PRWTOS 2C	FIRST	734A
20F	PROPH8TEIA 3A	PROPHECY	730B
21	ANTHRWPOS 2A	MAN	67D
	THEL8MA 2A	WILL	355A
	PNEUMA 5Cβ	SPIRIT	683A
	PNEUMA 6C	SPIRIT	683D
	POTE I	ONCE	701D
21A	PHERW	BEAR	862D
21A	PHERW 4Aβ	BEAR	863B
21B	PHERW 3B	BEAR	863A

2 PETER 2

1	AGORAZW 2	BUY	12D
	HAIRESIS 2	OPINION	23C
	APWLEIA 2	DESTRUCTION	103A
	APWLEIA 2	DESTRUCTION	103B
	ARNEOMAI 3A	DENY	107C
	GINOMAI II5	EXIST	159D
	DESPOT8S	MASTER	175C
	EPAGW	BRING ON	280D
	LAOS 3A	PEOPLE	468A
	PAREISAGW	BRING IN	630A
	TACHINOS 2	QUICKLY	814C

1	PSEUDODIDASKALOS		899D
	FALSE TEACHER		
	PSEUDOPROPH8T8S	FALSE PROPHET	900B
2	AL8THEIA 2B	TRUTH	35C
	ASELGEIA	LICENTIOUSNESS	114C
	BLASPH8MEW 2Bc	BLASPHEME	142B
	EXAKOLOUTHEW 1	FOLLOW	271D
	HODOS 2C	WAY	557B
	POLUS I2Aα	MANY	694D
3	APWLEIA 2ᴸ	DESTRUCTION	103A
	ARGEW	BE IDLE	104A
	AUTOS 3E	(OBLIQUE CASE)	123B
	EKPALAI	FOR A LONG TIME	242D
	EMPOREUOMAI 2	BUY AND SELL	256B
	KRIMA 4B	VERDICT	451D
	LOGOS IA6	WORD	478D
	NUSTAZW 2	ASLEEP	549C
	PLASTOS	MADE UP	672C
	PLEONEXIA	GREEDINESS	673D
4	AGGELOS 2C	ANGEL	8A
	HAMARTANW I	SIN	41D
	ZOPHOS 2	DARKNESS	340B
	KRISIS IAα	JUDGING	453D
	SEIRA	CORD	753D
	SIROS	PIT	759C
	TARTAROW	HOLD CAPTIVE	813C
	T8REW 2A	KEEP	822C
4F	PHEIDOMAI I	SPARE	862C
5	ARCHAIOS 2	ANCIENT	111A
	ASEB8S I	GODLESS	114B
	DIKAIOSUN8 2B	RIGHTEOUSNESS	196A
	EPAGW	BRING ON	280D
	KATAKLUSMOS	FLOOD	412D
	K8RUX 2	HERALD	432B
	NWE	NOAH	549C
	OGDOOS	THE EIGHTH	555B
	PHULASSW IC	WATCH	876B
5A	KOSMOS 5A	WORLD	447C
5B	KOSMOS 5A	WORLD	447C
6	ASEBEW	ACT IMPIOUSLY	114B
	GOMORRA	GOMORRAH	164A
	KATAKRINW	CONDEMN	413A
	KATASTROPH8	RUIN	420B
	MELLW ICᵝ	BE ABOUT TO	502B
	POLIS I	CITY	692B
	SODOMA	SODOM	766B
	TEPHROW	REDUCE TO ASHES	821D
	TITH8MI IIAα	PUT	823C
	HUPODEIGMA I	EXAMPLE	851D
7	ATHESMOS	LAWLESS	20C
	ANASTROPH8	CONDUCT	61B
	ASELGEIA	LICENTIOUSNESS	114C
	DIKAIOS IB	UPRIGHT	194D
	KATAPONEW	SUBDUE	417D
	LWT	LOT	485C
	RUOMAI	SAVE	744D
8	AKO8 IB	HEARING	30B
	ANOMOS 3	LAWLESS	71C
	BASANIZW 2B	TORMENT	134B
	GAR 2	FOR	151C
	DIKAIOS 4	RIGHTEOUS	195A
	EGKATOIKEW	LIVE	215A
	EK 5Bα	FROM	235C
8	ERGON ICᵝ	DEED	308B
	H8MERA 2	DAY	347A
	PSUCH8 IBγ	SOUL LIFE	901D
9	ADIKOS I	UNJUST	18A
	EUSEB8S	DEVOUT	326D
	H8MERA 3Bᵝ	DAY	347D
	KOLAZW	PUNISH	441C
	KRISIS IAα	JUDGING	453C
	KRISIS IAα	JUDGING	453D
	KURIOS 2A	LORD	460B
	OIDA 3	KNOW	558D
	*PEIRASMOS 2B	TEST	646D
	RUOMAI	SAVE	745A
	T8REW 2A	KEEP	822C
10	AUTHAD8S	SELF WILLED	120C
	BLASPH8MEW 2C	BLASPHEME	142B
	DOXA 4		203B
	GLORIOUS ANGELIC BEINGS		
	EPITHUMIA 3	DESIRE	293C
	KATAPHRONEW I	SCORN	421C
	KURIOT8S 2	LORDSHIP	461D
	MALISTA I	ABOVE ALL	490A
	MIASMOS	POLLUTION	522D
	OPISW 2Aᵝ	AFTER	578D
	POREUW 2B	PROCEED	699C
	SARX I	FLESH	750D
	TOLM8T8S	BOLD	829D
	TREMW	TREMBLE	833B
11	BLASPH8MOS	SLANDEROUS	142D
	DUNAMIS I	POWER	207A
	ISCHUS	STRENGTH	384B
	KRISIS IBᵝ	JUDGING	454A
	MEGAS 2Bα	GREAT	499B
	HOPOU 2A	WHERE	580A
	PARA II2A	BESIDE	615C
	PHERW 4Aᵝ	BEAR	863B
12	AGNOEW 3	BE IGNORANT	IIC
	ALOGOS I	WITHOUT REASON	40C
	HALWSIS	CAPTURE	41B
	BLASPH8MEW 2C	BLASPHEME	142B
	GENNAW 2	BEAR	154D
	ZWON 2	ANIMAL	342C
	KATAPHTHEIRW I	DESTROY	421A
	HOS,H8,HO I2Bᵝ	(REL PRON)	587B
	PHTHEIRW 2C	RUIN	865B
	PHUSIKOS 2	NATURAL	877A
12A	PHTHORA I	RUIN	865D
12B	PHTHORA 4	RUIN	865D
12B	PHTHORA 3	RUIN	865D
13	AGAP8 II	LOVE FEAST	6B
	ADIKEW 2B	INJURE	17C
	ADIKIA 2	UNRIGHTEOUSNESS	17D
	APAT8 2	PLEASURE	81C
	ENTRUPHAW	REVEL	269C
	H8GEOMAI 2	CONSIDER	344B
	H8DON8 I	PLEASURE	344D
	H8MERA IA	DAY	346D
	KOMIZW 2A	BRING	443D
	MISTHOS I	WAGES	525B
	MWMOS 2	BLEMISH	533D
	SPILAS 2	STAIN	770A
	SPILOS	SPOT	770B
	SUNEUWCHEOMAI	FEAST TOGETHER	796D

13	TRUPH8 I	INDULGENCE	836C
14	AKAT4PAUSTOS	UNCEASING	29C
	AST8RIKTOS	UNSTABLE	117C
	GUMNAZW	TRAIN	166D
	DELEAZW	LURE	173B
	KARDIA 136	HEART	405A
	KATARA	CURSE	418A
	MESTOS 2B	FULL	509C
	MOICHALIS I	ADULTERESS	527D
	OPHTHALMOS I	EYE	604C
	PLEONEXIA	GREEDINESS	673D
	TEKNON 2F3	CHILD	816C
	PSUCH8 IC	SOUL LIFE	902A
15	AGAPAW 2	LOVE	5A
	ADIKIA 2	UNRIGHTEOUSNESS	17D
	BALAAM	BALAAM	130B
	BEWR	BEOR	139A
	BOSOR	BOSOR	144D
	EXAKOLOUTHEW 2	FOLLOW	271D
	EUTHUS 2A	STRAIGHT	321B
	KATALEIPW 2B	LEAVE BEHIND	414D
	MISTHOS I	WAGES	525B
	PLANAW 2B	DECEIVE	671B
16	ANTHRWPOS IA3	MAN	67C
	APHWNOS 2		127C
	INCAPABLE OF SPEECH		
	ELEGXIS	REBUKE	248C
	KWLUW 2	HINDER	462C
	PARANOIA	MADNESS	626B
	PARANOMI4	EVIL DOING	626C
	PARAPHRONIA	MADNESS	628D
	PARAPHROSUN8	MADNESS	628D
	PROPH8T8S I	PROPHET	730D
	HUPOZUGION	PACK ANIMAL	852C
	PHTHEGGOMAI	SPEAK	864D
	PHWN8 3	LANGUAGE	879C
17	ANUDROS	WATERLESS	76A
	ELAUNW	DRIVE	248A
	ZOPHOS 2	DARKNESS	340B
	LAILAPS	HURRICANE	463D
	NEPHEL8	CLOUD	538C
	HOMICHL8	MIST	568C
	HOUTOS IA3	THIS	601A
	P8G8 I	FOUNTAIN	661C
	SKOTOS I	DARKNESS	765A
	T8REW 2A	KEEP	822C
	HUPO IA3	BY	850D
18	ANASTREPHW 2B3	LIVE	61A
	APOPHEUGW	ESCAPE	101B
	ASELGEIA	LICENTIOUSNESS	114C
	DELEAZW	LURE	173B
	EPITHUMIA 3	DESIRE	293C
	MATAIOT8S	FUTILITY	496D
	OLIGWS	SCARCELY	567A
	ONTWS 2	REAL	577D
	PLAN8	WANDERING	671D
	SARX 7	BODY	751D
	HUPEROGKOS	HAUGHTY	849C
	PHTHEGGOMAI	SPEAK	864D
19	DOULOS 3	SLAVE	205A
	DOULOW I	ENSLAVE	205B
	ELEUTHERIA	FREEDOM	249D
	EPAGGELLOMAI IA	ANNOUNCE	280C

19	H8TTAOMAI	SUCCUMB	350C
	TIS, TI IA«	ANY ONE	827C
	HUPARCHW 2	BE	846A
	PHTHORA 3	RUIN	865D
20	APOPHEUGW	ESCAPE	101B
	EMPLEKW 2	ENTANGLE	256A
	EPIGNWSIS	KNOWLEDGE	291C
	ESCHATOS 3A	LAST	314A
	H8TTAOMAI	SUCCUMB	350C
	KOSMOS 7	WORLD	447D
	KURIOS 2Cγ	LORD	461A
	MIASMA	DEFILEMENT	522D
	HO,H8,TO III0B	THE	555A
	PALIN IB	AGAIN	611C
	PRWTOS IA	FIRST	732D
	SWT8R 2	SAVIOR	808D
	CHEIRWN	WORSE	889C
21	HAGIOS IA«	DEDICATED TO GOD	9C
	ANAKAMPTW 2	RETURN	55B
	*DIKAIOSUN8 2B	RIGHTEOUSNESS	195D
	EK IA	AWAY FROM	233C
	ENTOL8 2F	COMMAND	268D
	EPISTREPHW IB3	TURN	301B
	KREITTWN 2	BETTER	451A
	M8 AIIIC	NOT	518A
	HODOS 2B	WAY	557A
	PARADIDWMI 3	GIVE OVER	620D
	HUPOSTREPHW	RETURN	855B
21A	EPIGINWSKW 2E	KNOW	291B
21B	EPIGINWSKW 2E	KNOW	291B
22	AL8TH8S 2	TRUE	36A
	BORBOROS 2	MUD	144C
	EXERAMA	VOMIT	273D
	EPI IIIA6	TO	288B
	EPISTREPHW IB«	TURN	301B
	IDIOS 2C	ONES OWN	370C
	KULISMOS	ROLLING	458B
	KUWN I	DOG	462B
	LOUW 2A«	BATHE	482A
	HO,H8,TO II7	THE	554C
	PAROIMIA I	PROVERB	634C
	SUMBAINW	MEET	784D
	HUS	SOW	856C

2 PETER 3

1	AGAP8TOS 2	BELOVED	6C
	GRAPHW 4	WRITE	166B
	DEUTEROS 3	SECOND	176A
	DIANOIA 2	MIND	186B
	DIEGEIRW	AROUSE	193A
	EILIKRIN8S	SINCERE	221D
	EPISTOL8	LETTER	300D
	HOS,H8,HO I38 3	(REL PRON)	587D
	HUPOMN8SIS I	REMEMBERING	854A
2	HAGIOS IB«	DEDICATED TO GOD	9C
	HAGIOS IB«	DEDICATED TO GOD	9C
	APOSTOLOS 3	APOSTLES	99B
	ENTOL8 2F	COMMAND	268D
	KURIOS 2Cγ	LORD	461A
	MIMN8SKOMAI IA«	REMEMBER	524B
	PROEIPON I	FORETELL	711C
	PROPH8T8S I	PROPHET	730D

2	R8MA 1	WORD 742D
	SWT8R 2	SAVIOR 808D
3	GINWSKW 6C	KNOW 160D
	EMPAIGMON8	MOCKING 255A
	EMPAIKT8S	MOCKER 255B
	EPI I2	UNDER 286C
	EPITHUMIA 3	DESIRE 293D
	ERCHOMAI IIAθ	COME 311B
	ESCHATOS 3B	LAST 314B
	H8MERA 4B	TIME 348B
	HOUTOS IBβ	THIS 601C
	POREUW 2D	PROCEED 699C
	PRWTOS 2C	FIRST 734A
4	APO II2C	SINCE 86C
	ARCH8 IC	BEGINNING 111D
	DIAMENW	REMAIN 185D
	EPAGGELIA 2A	PROMISE 280B
	KOIMAW 2A	SLEEP 438D
	KTISIS IBβ	CREATION 457A
	HOS,H8,HO IIIF	(REL PRON) 589A
	PAROUSIA 2Bα	COMING 635C
	PAT8R 2D	FATHER 640D
	POU IA	WHERE 702D
5	G8 5A	EARTH 156D
	EKPALAI	FOR A LONG TIME 242D
	THELW 5	WISH 356A
	LANTHANW	ESCAPE NOTICE 467C
	LOGOS IAβ	WORD 478B
	OURANOS IE	HEAVEN 599A
	SUNIST8MI II3	UNITE 798C
	HUDWR I	WATER 840C
6	KATAKLUZW	FLOOD 412D
	KOSMOS 5A	WORLD 447C
	TOTE IA	AT THAT TIME 831C
	HUDWR I	WATER 840C
7	APWLEIA 2	DESTRUCTION 103A
	ASEB8S I	GODLESS 114B
	G8 5A	EARTH 156D
	H8MERA 3Bβ	DAY 347D
	TH8SAURIZW 2C	STORE UP 362A
	KRISIS IAα	JUDGING 453C
	LOGOS IAβ	WORD 478B
	NUN 3A	NOW 548A
	OURANOS IE	HEAVEN 599A
	PUR IB	FIRE 737C
	T8REW 2A	KEEP 822C
8	AGAP8TOS 2	BELOVED 6C
	HEIS IAα	ONE 230A
	HEIS 2B	ONE 230C
	ETOS	YEAR 317A
	KURIOS 2A	LORD 460C
	LANTHANW	ESCAPE NOTICE 467C
	PARA II2B	BESIDE 615C
8A	CHILIOI	THOUSAND 890B
8A	HWS II3B	SO 906A
8B	CHILIOI	THOUSAND 890B
8B	HWS II3B	SO 906A
9	APOLLUMI 2Aα	PERISH 94D
	BOULOMAI 2B	DESIRE 146A
	BRADUT8S	SLOWNESS 146C
	BRADUNW	DELAY 146C
	EIS 4Cβ	(GOAL) 228C
	EPAGGELIA 2A	PROMISE 280A

9	H8GEOMAI 2	CONSIDER 344B
	MAKROTHUMEW 2	HAVE PATIENCE 489B
	METANOIA	REPENTANCE 514A
	CHWREW IB	GO 898A
9A	TIS, TI IAβ	ANY ONE 827D
9B	TIS, TI IAα	ANY ONE 827C
10	APHANIZW	RENDER INVISIBLE 124B
	G8 5A	EARTH 156D
	EKPUROW	SET ON FIRE 244B
	ERGON 3	WORK 308C
	HEURISKW IA	FIND 325B
	H8KW 2	HAVE COME 345C
	H8MERA 3Bβ	DAY 347D
	KATAKAIW	CONSUME 412A
	*KAUSOW	BURN UP 426C
	KLEPT8S	THIEF 435C
	NUX IC	NIGHT 549A
	OURANOS IE	HEAVEN 599A
	PARERCHOMAI IBα	PASS AWAY 631C
	ROIZ8DON	W. GREAT SUDDENNESS 744B
	STOICHEION 2	776C

FUNDAMENTAL PRINCIPLES

10a12	LUW 3	DESTROY 485A
11	HAGIOS IAβ	WORTHY OF GOD 9C
	ANASTROPH8	CONDUCT 61B
	EUSEBEIA	GODLINESS 326C
	PAS IEβ	ALL 638A
	POTAPOS	WHAT SORT 701C
	HUPARCHW 2	BE 846A
12	H8MERA 3Bβ	DAY 347D
	KAUSOW	BURN UP 426C
	PAROUSIA 2Bα	COMING 635C
	PUROW IA	SET ON FIRE 738C
	SPEUDW 2	HURRY 769D
	STOICHEION 2	776C

FUNDAMENTAL PRINCIPLES

	T8KW	BE MELTED 822A
12F	OURANOS IE	HEAVEN 599A
12a14	PROSDOKAW 2	EXPECT 719C
13	G8 5A	EARTH 156D
	DIKAIOSUN8 2B	RIGHTEOUSNESS 195D
	EPAGGELMA I	PROMISE 280D
	KAINOS 3B	NEW 395B
	KATOIKEW IB	LIVE 425C
14	AGAP8TOS 2	BELOVED 6C
	AMWM8TOS	BLAMELESS 47B
	AMWMOS 2A	BLAMELESS 47B
	ASPILOS 2	WITHOUT BLEMISH 116D
	EIR8N8 3	PEACE 227A
	HEURISKW 2	FIND 326A
	SPOUDAZW 2	HASTEN 771A
15	AGAP8TOS 2	BELOVED 6C
	ADELPHOS 2	BROTHER 16A
	GRAPHW 2D	WRITE 166A
	H8GEOMAI 2	CONSIDER 344B
	KURIOS 2A	LORD 460B
	MAKROTHUMIA 2Bβ	PATIENCE 489C
	PAULOS	PAUL 643A
	SOPHIA 2	WISDOM 767A
	SWT8RIA 2	DELIVERANCE 809B
16	AMATH8S	IGNORANT 41C
	APWLEIA 2	DESTRUCTION 103A
	GRAPH8 2Bα	SCRIPTURE 165B

16	DUSNO8TOS	HARD TO UNDERSTAND	209A	5	HOUTOS IA6	THIS	601A
	EPISTOL8	LETTER	300D		SKOTIA 2	DARKNESS	764D
	LOIPOS 2A	OTHER	481A		PHWS 2	LIGHT	880A
	STREBLOW 2	TWIST	778D	6	AL8THEIA 2B	TRUTH	35D
17	AGAP8TOS 2	BELOVED	6C		EIPON 2C	SAY	225C
	ATHESMOS	LAWLESS	20C		KOINWNIA I	ASSOCIATION	440A
	EKPIPTW 3A	LOSE	243B		PERIPATEW ID	GO ABOUT	655A
	IDIOS 2B	ONES OWN	370C		POIEW IICβ	DO	688C
	HINA IIIAβ	IN ORDER THAT	378B		SKOTOS 2B	DARKNESS	765B
	PLAN8	WANDERING	671D		PSEUDOMAI I	LIE	900A
	PROGINWSKW	KNOWS BEFOREHAND	710C	7	HAIMA 2B	BLOOD	22C
	ST8RIGMOS	FIRMNESS	775C		KATHARIZW 2Bα	CLEANSE	388B
	SUNAPAGW	LEAD AWAY	792C		KOINWNIA I	ASSOCIATION	440A
	PHULASSW 2A	WATCH	876D		META AII3B	WITH	510D
18	AUXANW 3	GROW	121C		HUIOS 2B	SON	842D
	EIS 2B	FOR	228A	7A	PHWS 3A	LIGHT	880B
	H8MERA 3Bβ	DAY	348A	7B	PHWS 2	LIGHT	880A
	HO,H8,TO IIIOB	THE	555D	8	HAMARTIA 2	SIN	42D
	SWT8R 2	SAVIOR	808D		EIPON 2C	SAY	225C
	CHARIS 3B	FAVOR	886B		PLANAW IB	DECEIVE	671B
	CHARIS 4	FAVOR	886C	9	ADIKIA 2	UNRIGHTEOUSNESS	17D
					HAMARTIA I	SIN	42D
	I JOHN I				APHI8MI 2	FORGIVE	125C
					DIKAIOS 2	RIGHTEOUS	195A
I	AKOUW IBα	HEAR	31B		HINA II2	IN ORDER THAT	378D
	ARCH8 IC	BEGINNING	111D		KATHARIZW 2Bα	CLEANSE	388B
	DIABLEPW 2	SEE CLEARLY	180D		HOMOLOGEW 3B	CONFESS	571B
	ZW8 2Aβ	LIFE	341A		PISTOS IAβ	TRUSTWORTHY	670C
	THEAOMAI IA	SEE	353C	10	EIPON 2C	SAY	225C
	LOGOS 3	THE LOGOS	480A		EN I5A	IN	258D
	OPHTHALMOS I	EYE	604B		LOGOS IBβ	WORD	479B
	PS8LAPHAW	TOUCH	900D		POIEW IIB:	DO	688D
I-3	HORAW IAβ	SEE	581D		PSEUST8S	LIAR	900D
2	AIWNIOS 3	ETERNAL	28A				
	APAGGELLW 2	PROCLAIM	78C		**I JOHN 2**		
	ZW8 2Aβ	LIFE	341A				
	ZW8 2Bα	LIFE	341C	I	DIKAIOS 3	RIGHTEOUS	195A
	MARTUREW IB	BEAR WITNESS	494A		ECHW I2D	HAVE	333A
	HO,H8,TO IIIF	THE	553A		PARAKL8TOS	HELPER	624A
	PAT8R 3E	FATHER	641D		PAT8R 3E	FATHER	641D
	PROS III7	TOWARD	718A		PROS III7	TOWARD	718A
2A	PHANEROW 2Bβ	REVEAL	860D		TEKNION	CHILD	815D
2B	PHANEROW 2Bβ	REVEAL	860D		TIS, TI IAγ	ANY ONE	827D
3	AKOUW IBα	HEAR	31B		CHRISTOS 2	ANOINTED ONE	895C
	APAGGELLW 2	PROCLAIM	78C	2	DE 4B	BUT, AND	170D
	*DE 4B	BUT, AND	170D		H8METEROS	OUR	348C
	H8METEROS	OUR	348C		HILASMOS I	EXPIATION	376B
	HINA IIA	IN ORDER THAT	377C		KOSMOS 5A	WORLD	447C
	HO,H8,TO IIIE	THE	553A	3	GINWSKW IB	KNOW	160A
	PAT8R 3Dα	FATHER	641D		GINWSKW IC	KNOW	160A
	HUIOS 2B	SON	842D		HOUTOS IBβ	THIS	601C
	CHRISTOS 2	ANOINTED ONE	895C	3F	GINWSKW IB	KNOW	160A
3A	KOINWNIA I	ASSOCIATION	440A	3F	T8REW 5	KEEP	822D
3A	META AII3B	WITH	510D	4	LEGW IIIE	DECLARE	471A
3B	KOINWNIA I	ASSOCIATION	440A		PSEUST8S	LIAR	900D
4	PL8ROW 3	MAKE FULL	677B	5	AGAP8 IIBγ	LOVE	5D
	CHARA I	JOY	883D		AL8THWS I	TRULY	36D
5	AGGELIA I	MESSAGE	7A		GINWSKW IC	KNOW	160A
	AKOUW IBβ	HEAR	31C		EIMI III4	TO BE	224C
	ANAGGELLW 2	DISCLOSE	51A		LOGOS IBβ	WORD	479B
	APO V4	FROM	87C		TELEIOW 2Eβ	MAKE PERFECT	817D
	EIMI II6A	TO BE	223C		T8REW 5	KEEP	823A
	HOTI IA	THAT	592D	6	EKEINOS IC	THAT	239A

6	KATHWS 1	JUST AS 392A	
	LEGW IIBβ	SAY 469C	
	MENW IAβ	REMAIN 505A	
	OPHEILW 2Aβ	OWE 603D	
	PERIPATEW 2Aγ	GO ABOUT 655B	
7	AGAPθTOS 2	BELOVED 6C	
	ARCHθ IB	BEGINNING IIIC	
	ECHW I2I	HAVE 333C	
	LOGOS IBβ	WORD 479C	
7A	PALAIOS 1	OLD 610C	
7B	PALAIOS 1	OLD 610C	
7F	GRAPHW 4	WRITE 166B	
7F	KAINOS 2	NEW 395A	
8	ALθTHINOS 3	GENUINE 36C	
	PALIN 4	AGAIN 611D	
	PARAGW IB	BRING IN 619A	
	SKIA IA	SHADE 763A	
	PHAINW 1	SHINE 859B	
	PHWS 3A	LIGHT 880B	
8F	SKOTIA 2	DARKNESS 764D	
9	ARTI 3	NOW 110A	
	EIMI III4	TO BE 224B	
	HEWS IIIC	UNTIL 335C	
	LEGW IIBβ	SAY 469C	
	MISEW 1	HATE 524C	
	PHWS 3A	LIGHT 880B	
10	AGAPAW IAα	LOVE 4B	
	MENW IAβ	REMAIN 505A	
	SKANDALON 3	TRAP 760D	
	PHWS 3A	LIGHT 880B	
11	EIMI III4	TO BE 224B	
	MISEW 1	HATE 524C	
	PERIPATEW ID	GO ABOUT 655A	
	POU 2B	WHERE 703A	
	TUPHLOW	TO BLIND 838D	
	HUPAGW 3	GO AWAY 844D	
11A	SKOTIA 2	DARKNESS 764D	
11B	SKOTIA 2	DARKNESS 764D	
11C	SKOTIA 2	DARKNESS 764D	
12	APHIθMI 2	FORGIVE 125C	
	ONOMA I4Cα	NAME 575C	
	TEKNION	CHILD 815D	
12FF	GRAPHW 2D	WRITE 166A	
13	GINWSKW IB	KNOW 160A	
	PATθR 2C	FATHER 640D	
13F	ARCHθ IC	BEGINNING IIID	
13F	NEANISKOS 1	YOUTH 536C	
13F	NIKAW 2A	CONQUER 541B	
13F	PONθROS 2B	WICKED 698A	
14	ISCHUROS IB	STRONG 384A	
	LOGOS IBβ	WORD 479B	
	MENW IAβ	REMAIN 505B	
	PAIDION 2A	CHILD 609B	
14B	PATθR 2C	FATHER 640D	
15	AGAPAW 2	LOVE 5A	
	AGAPθ IIBγ	LOVE 5D	
	MθDE IA	AND NOT 519C	
	PATθR 3E	FATHER 641D	
	TIS, TI IAγ	ANY ONE 827D	
15F	KOSMOS 6	WORLD 447D	
15F	KOSMOS 7	WORLD 448A	
16	ALAZONEIA	PRETENSION 34A	
	BIOS 3	LIFE 141B	

16	EK 3B	FROM 234B	
	EK 3C	FROM 234B	
*EPITHUMIA 3		DESIRE 293C	
	OPHTHALMOS 1	EYE 604C	
	SARX 7	BODY 751D	
17	AIWN IB	TIME 26D	
	EPITHUMIA 3	DESIRE 293C	
	THELθMA ICγ	WILL 355A	
	KOSMOS 7	WORLD 448A	
	MENW ICα	REMAIN 505B	
	PARAGW IB	BRING IN 619A	
	POIEW IICα	DO 688C	
18	*ANTICHRISTOS	ANTICHRIST 75C	
	GINOMAI II5	EXIST 159D	
	GINWSKW IC	KNOW 160A	
	ERCHOMAI IIAθ	COME 311B	
	ESCHATOS 3B	LAST 314B	
	KATHWS 1	JUST AS 392A	
	NUN IAβ	NOW 547C	
	HOTHEN 2	FROM WHICH 557D	
	PAIDION 3C	CHILD 609B	
18A	HWRA 3	TIME OF DAY 905B	
18B	HWRA 3	TIME OF DAY 905B	
19	AN IBβ	(PARTICLE) 48A	
	EXERCHOMAI IBα	GO OUT 274C	
	MENW IB	REMAIN 505B	
	META AIIIA	WITH 509D	
	PHANEROW 2Bα	REVEAL 860D	
20	HAGIOS 2Cα	THE HOLY ONE 10A	
	APO V4	FROM 87C	
	CHRISMA	ANOINTING 894D	
21	ALθTHEIA 2B	TRUTH 35D	
	EIMI III3	TO BE 224B	
	EK 3C	FROM 234B	
	PAS IAα	EVERY EACH 636D	
	PSEUDOS	LIE 900C	
22	ANTICHRISTOS	ANTICHRIST 75C	
	ARNEOMAI 3B	DENY 107C	
	ARNEOMAI 2	DENY 107C	
	OU 5B	NO 595A	
	TIS, TI IAα	WHICH 826C	
	CHRISTOS 1	ANOINTED ONE 895B	
	PSEUSTθS	LIAR 900D	
22=4	PATθR 3Dα	FATHER 641D	
22=4	HUIOS 2B	SON 842D	
23	ARNEOMAI 3A	DENY 107C	
	ECHW I2Bβ	HAVE 332D	
	HOMOLOGEW 4	CONFESS 571C	
	PAS ICγ	WHOEVER 637C	
24	ARCHθ IB	BEGINNING IIIC	
	EN I5D	IN 259A	
24A	MENW IAβ	REMAIN 505B	
24B	MENW IAβ	REMAIN 505B	
24C	MENW IAβ	REMAIN 505A	
24C	MENW IAβ	REMAIN 505A	
25	AIWNIOS 3	ETERNAL 28A	
	EPAGGELIA 2B	PROMISE 280B	
	EPAGGELLOMAI IB	ANNOUNCE 280C	
	ZWθ 2Bα	LIFE 341C	
	HO,Hθ,TO IIIF	THE 553A	
	HOS,Hθ,HO I4D	(REL PRON) 588A	
26	GRAPHW 2D	WRITE 166B	
	PLANAW IB	DECEIVE 671B	

27	AL8TH8S 2	TRUE	36B
	DIDASKW 2C	TEACH	191A
	HINA IIICα	IN ORDER THAT	378C
	LAMBANW 2	RECEIVE	466C
	MENW IAβ	REMAIN	505B
	PAS 2A6	EVERYTHING	638C
	CHREIA I	NEED	893B
	PSEUDOS	LIE	900C
27A	CHRISMA	ANOINTING	894D
27B	CHRISMA	ANOINTING	894D
27F	MENW IAβ	REMAIN	505A
28	AISCHUNW 2	BE ASHAMED	25A
	EAN IID	IF	210D
	EN II2	WHILE	259D
	ECHW I2Eβ	HAVE	333A
	NUN 2	NOW	548A
	HOTAN I	WHEN	592A
	PAROUSIA 2Bα	COMING	635C
	PARR8SIA 3B	CONFIDENCE	636B
	TEKNION	CHILD	815D
	PHANEROW 2Bβ	REVEAL	860D
29	GENNAW IB	BEGET	154D
	GINWSKW 6C	KNOW	160D
	DIKAIOSUN8 2B	RIGHTEOUSNESS	195D
	PAS ICγ	WHOEVER	637C
	POIEW IICβ	DO	688C

I JOHN 3

1	AGAP8 I2A	LOVE	5D
	GINWSKW IB	KNOW	160A
	DIA BII2	THEREFORE	180B
	EIDON 4	CONSIDER	220A
	EIMI III	TO BE	222D
	HINA IIIE	IN ORDER THAT	378C
	KALEW IA6	CALL	400B
	KOSMOS 7	WORLD	448A
	HOTI 3A	THAT	593D
	PAT8R 3E	FATHER	641D
	POTAPOS	WHAT SORT	701C
IF	TEKNON 2E	CHILD	816C
2	AGAP8TOS 2	BELOVED	6C
	EIMI II9B	TO BE	224A
	KATHWS I	JUST AS	392B
	NUN IAα	NOW	547C
	OIDA IE	KNOW	558C
	HOMOIOS I	LIKE	569D
	HORAW IAγ	SEE	581D
	OUPW	NOT YET	598A
	TIS, TI 186	WHICH	827A
2A	PHANEROW IB	REVEAL	860C
2B	PHANEROW 2Bβ	REVEAL	860D
3	HAGNIZW IB	PURIFY	IIA
	HAGNOS I	PURE	IID
	EKEINOS IC	THAT	239A
	ELPIS 2B	HOPE	252D
	EPI IIIBγ	ON	287A
	ECHW I2Eβ	HAVE	333A
4	*HAMARTIA I	SIN	42B
	ANOMIA I	LAWLESSNESS	71A
	ANOMIA 2	LAWLESSNESS	71B
4A	POIEW IICγ	DO	688C
4B	POIEW IICγ	DO	688C
5	AIRW 4	TAKE AWAY	24B
	HAMARTIA 2	SIN	42D
	EIMI III4	TO BE	224C
	EKEINOS IC	THAT	239A
	HINA IIE	IN ORDER THAT	377C
	OIDA IE	KNOW	558C
	PARR8SIA 3B	CONFIDENCE	636B
	PHANEROW 2Bβ	REVEAL	860D
6	GINWSKW IB	KNOW	160A
	MENW IAβ	REMAIN	505A
	HORAW ICβ	SEE	582B
7	DIKAIOS IA	UPRIGHT	194D
	DIKAIOS 3	RIGHTEOUS	195A
	DIKAIOSUN8 2B	RIGHTEOUSNESS	195D
	EKEINOS IC	THAT	239A
	M8DEIS 2A	NO	520A
	PAIDION 3C	CHILD	609B
	PLANAW IB	DECEIVE	671B
	POIEW IICβ	DO	688C
	TEKNION	CHILD	815D
8	HAMARTANW I	SIN	41D
	HAMARTIA I	SIN	42C
	ARCH8 IC	BEGINNING	IIID
	DIABOLOS 2	THE SLANDERER	181B
	EIMI III3	TO BE	224B
	EIS 4F	(PURPOSE)	228D
	EK 3A	FROM	234B
	ERGON 3	WORK	308C
	HINA I5	IN ORDER THAT	378A
	LUW 4	DESTROY	485A
	POIEW IICγ	DO	688C
	HUIOS 2B	SON	842D
	PHANEROW 2Bβ	REVEAL	860D
9	*GENNAW IB	BEGET	154D
	EK 3A	FROM	234B
	MENW IAβ	REMAIN	505B
	POIEW IICγ	DO	688C
	SPERMA 2C	SEED	769C
9F	THEOS 3A	GOD	357D
10	AGAPAW IAα	LOVE	4B
	DIABOLOS 2	THE SLANDERER	181B
	DIKAIOSUN8 2B	RIGHTEOUSNESS	195D
	POIEW IICβ	DO	688C
	PHANEROS I	CLEAR	860A
10A	M8 AII2A	NOT	518B
10A	TEKNON 2E	CHILD	816C
10B	M8 AII2A	NOT	518B
10B	TEKNON 2E	CHILD	816C
11	AGAPAW IAα	LOVE	4B
	AGGELIA 2	COMMAND	7A
	ALL8LWN	EACH OTHER	39A
	ARCH8 IB	BEGINNING	IIIC
	*EIMI II6A	TO BE	223C
	HINA IIIE	IN ORDER THAT	378C
	HOUTOS IA6	THIS	601A
IIF	KATHWS I	JUST AS	392B
12	DIKAIOS 4	RIGHTEOUS	195A
	EIMI III3	TO BE	224B
	ERGON ICβ	DEED	308A
	ERGON ICβ	DEED	308B
	KAIN	CAIN	394D
	HOTI 3A	THAT	593D
	SPHAZW	SLAUGHTER	803C

```
12 TIS, TI  1Bα                           WHICH 827A
   CHARIN            FOR THE SAKE OF 885A
   CHARIN 2          FOR THE SAKE OF 885B
12A PON8ROS 2B                          WICKED 698A
12B PON8ROS 1Bβ                         WICKED 697D
13 EI  II                                   IF 218C
   THAUMAZW 1Aγ                         WONDER 353A
   KOSMOS 7                              WORLD 447D
   MISEW 1                                HATE 524C
14 AGAPAW 1Aα                             LOVE   4B
   EK  1C                             AWAY FROM 233D
   EN  14D                                  IN 258C
   ZW8 2Bα                                LIFE 341C
   THANATOS 2A                           DEATH 352A
   MENW 1Aβ                             REMAIN 505A
   METABAINW 2A                           PASS 512A
   PARR8SIA 3B                      CONFIDENCE 636B
15 ANTHRWPOKTONOS                      MURDERER 67B
   ZW8 2Bα                                LIFE 341B
   ZW8 2Bα                                LIFE 341C
   MENW 1Aβ                             REMAIN 505B
   MISEW 1                                HATE 524C
15B PAS 1Aα                         EVERY EACH 636D
16 EKEINOS 1C                            THAT 239A
   HOTI 1A                                THAT 592D
   HOUTOS 1Bβ                             THIS 601C
   OPHEILW 2Aβ                             OWE 603D
16A  TITH8MI 11B6                     LAY DOWN 823D
16A  HUPER 1Aε                  IN BEHALF OF 846C
16A  PSUCH8 1Aβ                     SOUL LIFE 901C
16B  TITH8MI 11B6                     LAY DOWN 823D
16B  HUPER 1Aε                  IN BEHALF OF 846C
16B  PSUCH8 1Aβ                     SOUL LIFE 901C
17 AGAP8 11Bγ                            LOVE   5D
   BIOS 3                                 LIFE 141B
   ECHW 12A                                HAVE 332B
   THEWREW 1                           OBSERVE 360C
   KLEIW 2                                SHUT 435B
   KOSMOS 6                              WORLD 447D
   MENW 1Aβ                             REMAIN 505B
   PWS 1D                                  HOW 739D
   SPLAGCHNON 1B              INWARD PARTS 770C
   CHREIA 2                               NEED 893B
18 AGAPAW 1C                             LOVE   4D
   GLWSSA 1A                            TONGUE 161B
   ERGON 1A                               DEED 307D
   LOGOS 1Aα                              WORD 478A
   M8DE 1A                            AND NOT 519C
   TEKNION                               CHILD 815D
18FF OIDA 1E                             KNOW 558C
19 AL8THEIA 2B                          TRUTH  35D
   EMPROSTHEN 2B                    IN FRONT 256C
   EN  12                                   IN 258A
   KAI 12F                                 AND 393C
   HOUTOS 1Bα                             THIS 601C
   PEITHW 1D                          CONVINCE 645A
20 GINWSKW 6Aα                          KNOW 160C
   KARDIA 1Bε                            HEART 405A
   KATAGINWSKW                         CONDEMN 410D
   MEGAS 2Bα                             GREAT 499B
21 AGAP8TOS 2                         BELOVED   6C
   ECHW 12Eβ                             HAVE 333A
   KARDIA 1Bε                            HEART 405A

21 KATAGINWSKW                        CONDEMN 410D
   PARR8SIA 3B                     CONFIDENCE 636B
   PROS III4B                         TOWARD 717C
22 AITEW                                  ASK  25B
   ARESTOS                           PLEASING 105B
   ENWPION 3                           BEFORE 270B
   LAMBANW 2                          RECEIVE 466C
   POIEW 11Bε                              DO 687D
   T8REW 5                                KEEP 822D
22=4 ENTOL8 2B                        COMMAND 268D
23 AGAPAW 1Aα                            LOVE   4B
   DIDWMI 1Bα                            GIVE 192A
   EIMI II6A                            TO BE 223C
   HINA III E                   IN ORDER THAT 378D
   ONOMA 14B                             NAME 575B
   HOUTOS 1A6                            THIS 601A
   PISTEUW 2Aα                        BELIEVE 667A
   HUIOS 2B                               SON 842D
   CHRISTOS 2                ANOINTED ONE 895C
24 GINWSKW 1C                           KNOW 160A
   EK  3Gβ                                 BY 234D
   EN  15D                                  IN 259A
   MENW 1Aβ                             REMAIN 505A
   HOUTOS 1Bβ                             THIS 601C
   PNEUMA 5Dα                           SPIRIT 683A
   T8REW 5                                KEEP 822D
24A  MENW 1Aβ                          REMAIN 505A


                  I JOHN 4

 1 AGAP8TOS 2                         BELOVED   6C
   DOKIMAZW 1                          EXAMINE 201C
   EI  V2A                             WHETHER 218D
   EXERCHOMAI 1Aε                      GO OUT 274B
   KOSMOS 5A                            WORLD 447C
   PAS 1Aγ                         EVERY EACH 636D
   PISTEUW 1B                          BELIEVE 666C
   POLUS 11Aα                             MANY 694B
   PSEUDOPROPH8T8S   FALSE PROPHET 900B
 1B   PNEUMA 7                         SPIRIT 684B
 1FF  THEOS 3A                            GOD 357D
 1=3  PNEUMA 7                         SPIRIT 684B
 2 GINWSKW 1A                           KNOW 159D
   EN  14B                                  IN 258B
   ERCHOMAI 11Aη                         COME 311A
  *HOMOLOGEW 4                        CONFESS 571C
   SARX 2                                 BODY 751A
 2A   PNEUMA 5A                        SPIRIT 682B
 3 ANTICHRISTOS               ANTICHRIST  75C
   8D8 1A                             ALREADY 344D
   KOSMOS 5A                            WORLD 447C
   LUW 4                               ABOLISH 485C
   M8 AI5                                  NOT 517D
   NUN 1C                                  NOW 547D
   HOMOLOGEW 4                         CONFESS 571C
   OU 5A                                    NO 595A
 4 EK  3A                                FROM 234B
   KOSMOS 7                              WORLD 447D
   MEGAS 2Bα                             GREAT 499B
   NIKAW 2A                            CONQUER 541B
   TEKNION                               CHILD 815D
 5 EIMI III3                            TO BE 224B
   EK  3B                                FROM 234B
```

5 KOSMOS 7	WORLD	448A
6 AL8THEIA 2B	TRUTH	35C
GINWSKW IA	KNOW	159D
EK 3A	FROM	234B
EK 3G8	BY	234D
PLAN8	WANDERING	671D
PNEUMA 5E	SPIRIT	683B
6F THEOS 3A	GOD	357D
6FF GINWSKW IB	KNOW	160A
7 AGAPAW IA«	LOVE	4B
AGAPAW IA«	LOVE	4C
AGAP8 I2A	LOVE	5D
AGAP8TOS 2	BELOVED	6C
GENNAW IB	BEGET	154D
EK 3A	FROM	234B
8 AGAPAW IA«	LOVE	4C
AGAP8 I2A	LOVE	5D
9 AGAP8 I2A	LOVE	5D
ZAW 2B8	LIVE	337B
KOSMOS 4C	WORLD	447B
MONOGEN8S	ONLY	529B
HOTI IA	THAT	592D
HOUTOS IB8	THIS	601C
PHANEROW IB	REVEAL	860C
9F HUIOS 2B	SON	842D
10 AGAPAW IB«	LOVE	4D
APOSTELLW IBy	SEND AWAY	98B
HILASMOS I	EXPIATION	376B
HOTI IA	THAT	592D
HOUTOS IB8	THIS	601C
11 AGAP8TOS 2	BELOVED	6C
EI III	IF	218C
HOUTW 3	THUS	602D
OPHEILW 2A8	OWE	603D
11F AGAPAW IA«	LOVE	4B
12 AGAP8 IIBy	LOVE	5D
THEAOMAI IA	SEE	353C
PWPOTE	EVER	739B
TELEIOW 2E8	MAKE PERFECT	817D
12F MENW IA8	REMAIN	505A
13*GINWSKW IC	KNOW	160A
DIDWMI IB8	GIVE	192A
EK 4A«	FROM	235B
EN I5D	IN	259A
MENW IA8	REMAIN	505A
HOTI IA	THAT	592D
PNEUMA 5A	SPIRIT	682C
14 APOSTELLW IBy	SEND AWAY	98B
THEAOMAI 2	SEE	354A
KOSMOS 5A	WORLD	447B
MARTUREW IA	BEAR WITNESS	493D
SWT8R 2	SAVIOR	808D
14F HUIOS 2B	SON	842D
15 MENW IA8	REMAIN	505A
HOMOLOGEW 4	CONFESS	571C
15F EN I5D	IN	259A
16*AGAP8 I2A	LOVE	5D
ECHW I2E8	HAVE	333A
MENW IA8	REMAIN	505A
PISTEUW IA«	BELIEVE	666A
16B AGAP8 IIA	LOVE	5C
17 EIMI II9B	TO BE	224A
EKEINOS IA	THAT	238D

17 EKEINOS IC	THAT	239A
ENANTHRWPEW		261B
	TAKE ON HUMAN FORM	
ECHW I2E8	HAVE	333A
H8MERA 3B8	DAY	347D
HINA IIIE	IN ORDER THAT	378C
KATHWS I	JUST AS	392A
KOSMOS 7	WORLD	447D
KRISIS IA«	JUDGING	453C
HOUTOS IB8	THIS	601C
PARR8SIA 3B	CONFIDENCE	636B
TELEIOW 2E8	MAKE PERFECT	817D
18 BALLW IB	THROW	130C
EXW IB	OUTSIDE	279A
ECHW I4	HAVE	333D
KOLASIS 2	PUNISHMENT	441D
TELEIOS IA«		816D
	HAVING ATTAINED THE END	
TELEIOW 2E«	MAKE PERFECT	817D
18A PHOBOS 2A8	FEAR	871D
18B PHOBOS 2A8	FEAR	871D
18C PHOBOS 2A8	FEAR	871D
19 AGAPAW IA«	LOVE	4C
AGAPAW IB«	LOVE	4D
PRWTOS IA	FIRST	733A
20 MISEW I	HATE	524C
HOTI 2	THAT	593D
PWS ID	HOW	739D
TIS, TI IAy	ANY ONE	827C
PSEUST8S	LIAR	900D
20A HORAW IA«	SEE	581C
20B HORAW IA«	SEE	581C
20F AGAPAW IA«	LOVE	4B
21 APO V4	FROM	87C
ECHW I2I	HAVE	333A
HINA IIIE	IN ORDER THAT	378C
HOUTOS 2A	THIS	601D

I JOHN 5

1 *GENNAW IB	BEGET	154D
EK 3A	FROM	234B
THEOS 3A	GOD	357D
PISTEUW IA8	BELIEVE	666A
CHRISTOS I	ANOINTED ONE	895B
2 AGAPAW IA«	LOVE	4B
GINWSKW IA	KNOW	160A
HOUTOS IB8	THIS	601C
TEKNON 2E	CHILD	816C
3 AGAP8 IIBy	LOVE	5D
BARUS 2A	BURDENSOME	134A
EIMI II6A	TO BE	223C
HINA IIIE	IN ORDER THAT	378C
HOUTOS IA6	THIS	601A
T8REW 5	KEEP	822D
4 GENNAW IB	BEGET	154D
EK 3A	FROM	234B
THEOS 3A	GOD	357D
NIK8	VICTORY	541C
HOUTOS IA6	THIS	601A
PAS ICy	WHOEVER	637C
PISTEUW	BELIEVE	666A
PISTIS 2D«	FAITH	669B

4B	NIKAW 2A	CONQUER 541B
4F	KOSMOS 7	WORLD 448A
4F	NIKAW 2A	CONQUER 541B
5	PISTEUW IA∅	BELIEVE 666A
	TIS, TI IA∝	WHICH 826C
	HUIOS 2B	SON 842D
6	HAIMA 2B	BLOOD 22C
	AL8THEIA 2B	TRUTH 35C
	DIA AII	THROUGH 178C
	DIA AIIIIC	THROUGH 179B
	EN I4C∅	IN 258C
	ERCHOMAI IIAη	COME 311A
	MONOS 2C	ONLY 529D
	HOUTOS IA∅	THIS 601A
	CHRISTOS I	ANOINTED ONE 895C
6A	PNEUMA 5D∝	SPIRIT 683A
6A	HUDWR I	WATER 840D
6B	PNEUMA 5D∝	SPIRIT 683A
6B	HUDWR I	WATER 840D
6C	HUDWR I	WATER 840D
6F	MARTUREW IA	BEAR WITNESS 493C
7	LOGOS 3	THE LOGOS 480B
	PNEUMA 5C∝	SPIRIT 682D
	TREIS	THREE 833A
8	HAIMA 2B	BLOOD 22C
	EIMI III2	TO BE 224A
	HEIS IB	ONE 230A
	PNEUMA 5D∝	SPIRIT 683A
	HUDWR I	WATER 840D
9	MARTUREW IA	BEAR WITNESS 493D
	MEGAS 2B∅	GREAT 499C
9A	MARTURIA 2C	TESTIMONY 494C
9B	MARTURIA 2D∅	TESTIMONY 494D
9C	MARTURIA 2D∅	TESTIMONY 494D
9-13	HUIOS 2B	SON 842D
10	ECHW I2J	HAVE 333C
	MARTUREW IB	BEAR WITNESS 494A
	POIEW IIB:	DO 688B
	PSEUST8S	LIAR 900D
10A	MARTURIA 2D∅	TESTIMONY 494D
10A	PISTEUW 2A∅	BELIEVE 667B
10B	MARTURIA 2D∅	TESTIMONY 494D
10B	PISTEUW IB	BELIEVE 666C
10C	PISTEUW IA∝	BELIEVE 666B
11	EIMI II6A	TO BE 223C
	ZW8 2B∝	LIFE 341B
	ZW8 2B∝	LIFE 341C
	MARTURIA 2D∅	TESTIMONY 494D
	HOTI IA	THAT 592D
	HOUTOS IA6	THIS 601A
11B	ZW8 2A∅	LIFE 341A
12A	ZW8 2B∝	LIFE 341B
12B	ZW8 2B∝	LIFE 341B
12FF	AITEW	ASK 25B
13	ZW8 2B∝	LIFE 341B
	ZW8 2B∝	LIFE 341C
	ONOMA I4C∅	NAME 576A
	PISTEUW 2A∅	BELIEVE 667B
14	AITEW	ASK 25C
	ECHW I2E∅	HAVE 333A
	THEL8MA 2B	WILL 355B
	HOUTOS IA6	THIS 601A
	PROS III4B	TOWARD 717C
14F	AKOUW 5	LISTEN 32A
15	AITEW	ASK 25B
	AIT8MA	REQUEST 25C
	EAN I2B	IF 210D
	ECHW I2G	HAVE 333B
	PARA I3A	FROM 614D
16	AITEW	ASK 25C
	HAMARTIA I	SIN 42C
	HAMARTIA 5	SIN 43A
	EIMI II	TO BE 222B
	ERWTAW 2	ASK 312A
	ZW8 2B∝	LIFE 341B
	LEGW IIIC	ORDER 470D
16A	HAMARTANW 3	SIN 41D
16B	HAMARTANW 5	SIN 42A
16F	THANATOS 2B	DEATH 352A
16F	PROS III3B	TOWARD 717B
17	ADIKIA 2	UNRIGHTEOUSNESS 17C
	HAMARTIA I	SIN 42B
	HAMARTIA 5	SIN 43A
18	HAPTW 2D	TOUCH 102D
	GENNAW IB	BEGET 154D
	GENN8SIS	BIRTH 155A
	EK 3A	FROM 234B
	PON8ROS 2B	WICKED 698A
	T8REW 2B	KEEP 822C
	T8REW 3	KEEP 822D
19	EK 3A	FROM 234B
	EN I5D	IN 259C
	KEIMAI 2D	FIND ONESELF 428B
	KOSMOS 7	WORLD 447A
	HOLOS 2B	WHOLE 567D
	PON8ROS 2B	WICKED 698A
20	AL8THINOS 3	GENUINE 36C
	GINWSKW IB	KNOW 160A
	DIANOIA I	UNDERSTANDING 186A
	EIMI III4	TO BE 224C
	ZW8 2A∝	LIFE 340D
	ZW8 2B∝	LIFE 341C
	H8KW IC	HAVE COME 345B
	THEOS 2	GOD 357C
	HINA I3	IN ORDER THAT 377D
	HUIOS 2B	SON 842D
21	EIDWLON 2	IDOL 220D
	TEKNION	CHILD 815D
	PHULASSW IC	WATCH 876B

2 JOHN

1	AL8THEIA 2B	TRUTH 35D
	AL8THEIA 3	REALITY 35D
	GINWSKW 6A∝	KNOW 160C
	EKLEKTOS IB	CHOSEN 242B
	KURIA I	LADY 459B
	MONOS IA∀	ONLY 529C
	HOS,H8,HO I3B∀	(REL PRON) 587D
	PAS ID∅	ALL 637D
	PRESBUTEROS 2B∅	OLDER 707A
	TEKNON 2C	CHILD 816B
2	AIWN IB	TIME 26D
3	EIR8N8 2	PEACE 226D
	ELEOS 2A	MERCY 249D
	THEOS 3D	GOD 358B

3	META AIIICγ	WITH	5I0B
	PARA I3B	FROM	6I4D
	HUIOS 2B	SON	842D
	CHARIS 2C	FAVOR	885D
3A	PAT8R 3Cβ	FATHER	64IC
4	AL8THEIA 2B	TRUTH	35B
	EK 4Aγ	FROM	235B
	LAMBANW 2	RECEIVE	466C
	LIAN I	VERY	474C
	PARA I3B	FROM	6I4D
	PERIPATEW 2A6	GO ABOUT	655B
	TEKNON 2C	CHILD	8I6B
	CHAIRW I	REJOICE	88ID
5	AGAPAW IAα	LOVE	4B
	ALL8LWN	EACH OTHER	39A
	GRAPHW 4	WRITE	I66B
	ERWTAW 2	ASK	3I2B
	ECHW I2I	HAVE	333C
	KAINOS 2	NEW	395A
	KURIA I	LADY	459B
	NUN 2	NOW	548A
5F	ARCH8 IB	BEGINNING	IIIC
6A	HINA IIIE	IN ORDER THAT	378C
6A	HOUTOS IA6	THIS	60IA
6A	PERIPATEW 2A6	GO ABOUT	655B
6B	HOUTOS IA6	THIS	60IA
6B	PERIPATEW 2A6	GO ABOUT	655B
7	ANTICHRISTOS	ANTICHRIST	75C
	EN I4B	IN	258B
	EXERCHOMAI IAε	GO OUT	274B
	ERCHOMAI IIAη	COME	3IIA
	KOSMOS 4B	WORLD	447B
	HO,H8,TO II3B	THE	553D
	HOMOLOGEW 4	CONFESS	57IC
	HOUTOS IAγ	THIS	60IA
	POLUS IIAα	MANY	694A
	SARX 2	BODY	75IA
	CHRISTOS 2	ANOINTED ONE	895C
7B	PLANOS 2	DECEITFUL	672A
8	APOLAMBANW I	RECEIVE	93D
	APOLLUMI IB	LOSE	94C
	BLEPW 6	SEE	I43B
	ERGAZOMAI 2A	WORK	307A
	MISTHOS 2A	REWARD	525B
	PL8R8S 2	FULL	675D
9	ECHW I2Bβ	HAVE	332D
	M8 AII2A	NOT	5I8B
	PARABAINW 2B	GO ASIDE	6I6D
	PAS ICγ	WHOEVER	637C
	PAT8R 3Dα	FATHER	64ID
	PROAGW 2A	LEAD	709A
	HUIOS 2B	SON	842D
	CHRISTOS I	ANOINTED ONE	895C
9A	MENW IAβ	REMAIN	505A
9B	MENW IAβ	REMAIN	505A
9F	DIDACH8 2	TEACHING	I9IB
10	LAMBANW IEα	RECEIVE	465D
	OIKIA IA	HOUSE	559D
	PHERW 4Aβ	BEAR	863B
IOF	LEGW IIIC	ORDER	470D
IOF	CHAIRW 2A	REJOICE	882A
II	ERGON ICβ	DEED	308B
	KOINWNEW IBβ	SHARE	439D

II	PON8ROS I8β	WICKED	697D
12	BOULOMAI 2Aζ	DESIRE	I45D
	GINOMAI I4Cε	COME, GO	I59A
	DIA AIIIIA	BY MEANS OF	I79A
	ELPIZW 2	HOPE	252A
	ECHW I6B	MUST	334A
	LALEW 2Aε	SPEAK	464C
	MELAS	BLACK	50IA
	PL8ROW 3	MAKE FULL	677B
	STOMA IA	MOUTH	777C
	CHARA I	JOY	883D
	CHART8S	PAPYRUS	887C
I2B	PROS IIIIE	TOWARD	7I6D
I3	ADELPH8 4	SISTER	I5C
	ASPAZOMAI IA	GREET	II6B
	EKLEKTOS IB	CHOSEN	242B
	TEKNON 2C	CHILD	8I6B

3 JOHN

I	AGAP8TOS 2	BELOVED	6C
	AL8THEIA 3	REALITY	35D
	GAIOS 4	GAIUS	I49A
	PRESBUTEROS 2Bβ	OLDER	707A
2	AGAP8TOS 2	BELOVED	6C
	EUODOW	PROSPER	324A
	EUCHOMAI 2	WISH	329D
	PAS 2A6	IN ALL RESPECTS	638C
	HUGIAINW I	BE HEALTHY	840A
	PSUCH8 IC	SOUL LIFE	902A
	PSUCH8 IF	SOUL LIFE	902C
3	AL8THEIA 2B	TRUTH	35D
	ERCHOMAI IIAζ	COME	3I0D
	KATHWS 5	HOW	392C
	LIAN I	VERY	474C
	MARTUREW IA	BEAR WITNESS	493D
	CHAIRW I	REJOICE	88ID
3F	AL8THEIA 2B	TRUTH	35B
3F	PERIPATEW 2A6	GO ABOUT	655B
4	AKOUW 3F	LEARN	32A
	HINA IIIE	IN ORDER THAT	378C
	TEKNON 2B	CHILD	8I6B
	CHARA I	JOY	883D
5	AGAP8TOS 2	BELOVED	6C
	EIS 4G	FOR	229A
	ERGAZOMAI 2A	WORK	307A
	XENOS 2A	THE STRANGER	550B
	PISTOS IB	TRUSTWORTHY	670D
6	AXIWS	WORTHILY	78A
	EKKL8SIA 4A	CHURCH	240B
	ENWPION 2A	BEFORE	270B
	KALWS 4A	WELL	402B
	MARTUREW IA	BEAR WITNESS	493D
	POIEW I2Aγ	DO	689B
	PROPEMPW 2	ACCOMPANY	7I6B
7	APO IV2A	FROM	87A
	ETHNIKOS	GENTILE	2I7B
	ONOMA I4Cθ	NAME	576D
	ONOMA I4D	NAME	576D
	HUPER IB	IN BEHALF OF	846D
8	AL8THEIA 2B	TRUTH	35D
	APOLAMBANW 4	WELCOME	94A
	OUN IA	THEREFORE	597B

8 OPHEILW 2Aß   OWE 603D
   SUNERGOS   WORKING WITH 795C
   HUPOLAMBANW 2   TAKE UP 853A
9 GRAPHW 2D   WRITE 166A
   EPIDECHOMAI 2   RECEIVE 292A
   PHILOPRWTEUW WISH TO BE FIRST 868D
10 ARKEW 2   BE SATISFIED 107A
   BOULOMAI 2A⟨   DESIRE 145D
   EKBALLW 1   DRIVE OUT 237A
   EPI IIIBy   ON 287A
   EPIDECHOMAI 1   RECEIVE 292A
   ERGON 1Cß   DEED 308A
   KAI I2E   AND 393B
   KWLUW 1   HINDER 462C
   LOGOS 1A6   WORD 478D
   OUTE   NOT 600D
   PON8ROS 1Bß   WICKED 697D
   HUPOMIMN8SKW 1B   REMIND 854A
   PHLUAREW   870A
        TALK NONSENSE (ABOUT)
11 AGATHOPOIEW 2   DO GOOD   2C
   AGAP8TOS 2   BELOVED   6C
   KAKOPOIEW 1   DO WRONG 398B
   KAKOS 1C   EVIL 398D
   MIMEOMAI   IMITATE 523D
   HORAW 1Cß   SEE 582B
12 AL8TH8S 2   TRUE 368
   D8M8TRIOS 1   DEMETRIUS 177D
   MARTURIA 2C   TESTIMONY 494C
12A   MARTUREW 2B BE APPROVED 494B
12B   MARTUREW 1C   494A
        TESTIFY FAVORABLY
13 GRAPHW 2D   WRITE 166A
   DIA AIIIIA   BY MEANS OF 179A
   ECHW 16B   MUST 334A
   KALAMOS 4   PEN 399C
   MELAS   BLACK 501A
14 ELPIZW 2   HOPE 252A
   EUTHEWS   IMMEDIATELY 320D
   LALEW 2A⊄   SPEAK 464C
   PROS IIIIE   TOWARD 716D
   STOMA 1A   MOUTH 777C
15 ASPAZOMAI 1A   GREET 116B
   ASPAZOMAI 1A   GREET 116C
   EIR8N8 2   PEACE 226D
   KATA II3B   (DISTRIBUTIVE) 407D
   ONOMA I3   NAME 574C
15A   PHILOS 2A⊄   LOVING 868D
15B   PHILOS 2A⊄   LOVING 868D

                JUDE

1 AGAPAW 1D   LOVE   5A
   DOULOS 4   SLAVE 205B
   EN I3   IN 258A
   IAKWBOS 3   JAMES 368C
   IOUDAS 8   JUDAS 381A
   KL8TOS   CALLED 437A
   PAT8R 3E   FATHER 642A
   T8REW 2B   KEEP 822D
1A   CHRISTOS 2 ANOINTED ONE 895C
1B   CHRISTOS 2 ANOINTED ONE 895C
2 AGAP8 I2A   LOVE   5D

2 EIR8N8 2   PEACE 226D
   ELEOS 2A   MERCY 249D
3 AGAP8TOS 2   BELOVED   6C
   ANAGK8 1   NECESSITY 52A
   HAPAX 2   ONCE 80A
   GRAPHW 2D   WRITE 166B
   EPAGWNIZOMAI   FIGHT 281A
   KOINOS 1A   COMMON 439A
   PARADIDWMI 3   GIVE OVER 620D
   PARAKALEW 2   APPEAL TO 622C
   PAS 1A6   ALL 637A
   PISTIS 3   FAITH 669D
   POIEW III   DO 689C
   SPOUD8 2   DILIGENCE 771C
   SWT8RIA 2   DELIVERANCE 809A
4 ARNEOMAI 3A   DENY 107C
   ASEB8S 1   GODLESS 114B
   ASELGEIA   LICENTIOUSNESS 114C
   DESPOT8S   MASTER 175C
   EIS 4D   FOR 228C
   KRIMA 4B   VERDICT 451D
   KURIOS 2Cy   LORD 461B
   METATITH8MI 2   CHANGE 515B
   MONOS 1A6   ONLY 529D
   HO,H8,TO II3B   THE 553D
   PALAI 1   LONG AGO 610B
   PALAI 2A   LONG AGO 610C
   PAREISDU(N)W   SNEAK IN 630A
   PROGRAPHW 1B   WRITE BEFORE 711A
   CHARIS 3B   FAVOR 886B
5 AIGUPTOS   EGYPT 21C
   HAPAX 2   ONCE 80A
   APOLLUMI 1A⊄   RUIN 94C
   BOULOMAI 2A6   DESIRE 145D
   DEUTEROS 4   SECOND 176B
   EK 1A   AWAY FROM 233C
   KURIOS 2A   LORD 460B
   LAOS 3A   PEOPLE 468A
   PISTEUW 1D   BELIEVE 666D
   SWZW 1B   SAVE 805D
   HUPOMIMN8SKW 1A   REMIND 853D
6 AGGELOS 2C   ANGEL   8A
   AIDIOS   ETERNAL 21C
   APOLEIPW 3   DESERT 94B
   ARCH8 4   RULE 112A
   DESMOS 1   FETTER 175A
   IDIOS 2C   ONES OWN 370C
   KRISIS 1A⊄   JUDGING 453C
   MEGAS 2Bß   GREAT 499C
   OIK8T8RION 1   DWELLING 559D
   TE 1A   AND 815A
   HUPO 2Aß   UNDER 851B
6A   T8REW 3   KEEP 822D
6B   T8REW 2A   KEEP 822C
7 AIWNIOS 3   ETERNAL 28A
   APERCHOMAI 4   GO AFTER 84A
   GOMORRA   GOMORRAH 164A
   DEIGMA 2   EXAMPLE 171C
   DIK8 1   PENALTY 197C
   EKPORNEUW   244A
        INDULGE IN IMMORALITY
   HOMOIOS 1   LIKE 569D
   OPISW 2Aß   AFTER 578D

7	PERI 2Aγ	ABOUT 650D
	POLIS I	CITY 692B
	PROKEIMAI I BE SET BEFORE	714C
	PUR 1B	FIRE 737C
	SARX I	FLESH 750D
	SODOMA	SODOM 766B
	TROPOS I	MANNER 835A
	HUPECHW UNDERGO PUNISHMENT	850A
8	ATHETEW 1B	REJECT 20C
	BLASPH8MEW 2C BLASPHEME	142B
	DOXA 4	203B
	GLORIOUS ANGELIC BEINGS	
	ENUPNAZOMAI	TO DREAM 270A
	KAI II3	ALSO 394B
	KURIOT8S 2	LORDSHIP 461D
	MIAINW 2	DEFILE 522C
	HOMOIWS	LIKEWISE 570D
9	BLASPH8MIA 2Aβ	SLANDER 142C
	DIAKRINW 2A	TAKE ISSUE 184B
	DIALEGOMAI I	DISCUSS 184D
	EPITIMAW I	REBUKE 303B
	EPIPHERW 3	BRING 304C
	KRISIS 1Bβ	JUDGING 454A
	KURIOS 2A	LORD 460B
	MICHA8L	MICHAEL 526A
	MWUS8S	MOSES 533D
	SWMA IA	BODY 806D
	TOLMAW 1B	DARE 829C
10	ALOGOS I WITHOUT REASON	40C
	BLASPH8MEW 2C BLASPHEME	142B
	EPISTAMAI 2	KNOW 300A
	ZWON 2	ANIMAL 342C
	PHTHEIRW 2C	RUIN 865B
	PHUSIKWS	NATURALLY 877B
11	ANTILOGIA 2	HOSTILITY 74C
	BALAAM	BALAAM 130B
	KAIN	CAIN 394D
	KORE	KORAH 445B
	MISTHOS I	WAGES 525B
	HODOS 2B	WAY 557A
	OUAI IA	WOE 595C
	PLAN8	WANDERING 671D
	POREUW 2C	PROCEED 699C
11C	APOLLUMI 2Aα	PERISH 94D
12	AGAP8 II	LOVE FEAST 6B
	AKARPOS I	UNFRUITFUL 29A
	ANEMOS IA	WIND 64A
	ANUDROS	WATERLESS 76A
	APOTHN8SKW IAβ	DIE 91A
	APHOBWS I	FEARLESSLY 126C
	DIS	TWICE 198D
	EKRIZOW I	UPROOT 244B
	EUWCHIA	BANQUET 330B
	NEPHEL8	CLOUD 538C
	PARAPHERW 2A	TAKE AWAY 628D
	SPILAS I	REEF 770A
	SUNEUWCHEOMAI FEAST TOGETHER	796D
	HUPO IAβ	BY 850D
	PHTHINOPWRINOS LATE AUTUMN	865B
13	AGRIOS 2	WILD 13C
	AISCHUN8 3 SHAMEFUL DEED	25A
	APAPHRIZW CAST OFF LIKE FOAM	81D
	AST8R	STAR 117C

13	EPAPHRIZW CAUSE TO SPLASH UP	283C
	ZOPHOS 2	DARKNESS 340B
	THALASSA IA	SEA 350D
	KUMA	WAVE 458C
	PLAN8T8S	WANDERER 672A
	SKOTOS I	DARKNESS 765A
	T8REW 2A	KEEP 822C
14	HAGIOS 1Bβ	HOLY 9D
	ADAM	ADAM 15B
	APO II3A	FROM 86C
	HEBDOMOS	SEVENTH 212A
	EN I4Cα	IN 258C
	ENWCH	ENOCH 270D
	ERCHOMAI IIAβ	COME 310C
	IDOU IA	BEHOLD 371C
	MURIAS 2	MYRIADS 531C
	PROPH8TEUW 3	PROPHESY 730C
15	HAMARTWLOS 2	SINNER 43D
	ASEBEIA	GODLESSNESS 114A
	ASEBEW	ACT IMPIOUSLY 114B
	*ASEB8S I	GODLESS 114B
	ELEGCHW 2	EXPOSE 248D
	EXELEGCHW	CONVICT 273C
	ERGON ICβ	DEED 308B
	KATA I2Bβ	DOWN 406D
	KRISIS IAβ	JUDGING 453D
	HOS,H8,HO I4A	(REL PRON) 587D
	POIEW IIB6	DO 687C
	SKL8ROS IB	HARD 763B
15A	KATA I2Bβ	DOWN 406D
16	GOGGUST8S	GRUMBLER 163D
	EPITHUMIA 3	DESIRE 293D
	THAUMAZW IBα	WONDER 353A
	LALEW 2B	SPEAK 464D
	MEMPSIMOIROS	COMPLAINING 503C
	POREUW 2C	PROCEED 699C
	PROSWPON IB	FACE 728C
	HUPEROGKOS	HAUGHTY 849C
	CHARIN I FOR THE SAKE OF	885A
	WPHELEIA	USE 908D
17	AGAP8TOS 2	BELOVED 6C
	APOSTOLOS 3	APOSTLES 99B
	KURIOS 2Cγ	LORD 461B
	MIMN8SKOMAI IAα	REMEMBER 524B
	PROEIPON I	FORETELL 711C
	R8MA I	WORD 742D
18	ASEBEIA	GODLESSNESS 114A
	EMPAIKT8S	MOCKER 255B
	EPI I2	UNDER 286C
	EPITHUMIA 3	DESIRE 293D
	EPITHUMIA 3	DESIRE 293D
	ESCHATOS 3B	LAST 314B
	POREUW 2C	PROCEED 699C
	CHRONOS	TIME 896C
19	APODIORIZW	DIVIDE 90B
	PNEUMA 5Dβ	SPIRIT 683B
	PSUCHIKOS 2B	902D
	PERTAINING TO THE SOUL	
20	AGAP8TOS 2	BELOVED 6C
	HAGIOS IAα DEDICATED TO GOD	9C
	EPOIKODOMEW 2 BUILD ON TO	305C
	PISTIS 3	FAITH 669D
	PNEUMA 5Cβ	SPIRIT 683A

20 PROSEUCHOMAI — PRAY 721A
21 ELEOS 3 — MERCY 249D
   ZW8 2Bβ — LIFE 341C
   KURIOS 2Cγ — LORD 461B
   PROSDECHOMAI 2B — RECEIVE 719C
   T8REW 2B — KEEP 822C
22 DIAKRINW 2B — WAVER 184B
   ELEAW — HAVE MERCY ON 248C
   ELEGCHW 2 — EXPOSE 248D
   MEN IC — (PARTICLE) 504A
22F HOS,H8,HO II2 — THIS (ONE) 589B
23 HARPAZW 2A — SNATCH 108D
   ELEAW — HAVE MERCY ON 248C
   KAI II2 — EVEN 394B
   MISEW 2 — HATE 524D
   PUR IA — FIRE 737B
   SARX 7 — BODY 751D
   SPILOW — STAIN 770B
   SWZW 2Aβ — SAVE 806B
   PHOBOS 2Aα — FEAR 871C
   CHITWN — SHIRT 890C
24 AGALLIASIS — EXULTATION 3D
   AMWMOS 2A — BLAMELESS 47B
   APTAISTOS — WITHOUT STUMBLING 102A
   HIST8MI IIAα — PUT 382D
   KATENWPION A — 422C IN THE PRESENCE OF
   PHULASSW IC — WATCH 876B
25 AM8N I — AMEN 45A
   EXOUSIA 2 — ABILITY 277D
   THEOS 31 — GOD 358C
   KRATOS 4 — POWER 450B
   KURIOS 2Cγ — LORD 461B
   MEGALWSUN8 — GREATNESS 498C
   MONOS IAδ — ONLY 529C
   SOPHOS 4 — LEARNED 767D
   SWT8R I — SAVIOR 808C
25A AIWN IA — TIME 26C
25B AIWN IB — TIME 26D

REVELATION I

1 APOKALUPSIS 2 — REVELATION 91D
  APOSTELLW ID — SEND AWAY 98C
  DEI I — IT IS NECESSARY 171A
  DEIKNUMI IA — SHOW 171D
  DOULOS 4 — SLAVE 205B
  EN III2 — BY 260C
  IWAN(N)8S 3 — JOHN 385C
  S8MAINW I — MAKE KNOWN 755D
  TACHOS — SPEED 814D
  CHRISTOS 2 — ANOINTED ONE 895C
2 EIDON — SEE 219C
  LOGOS I8β — WORD 479B
  MARTUREW IB — BEAR WITNESS 494A
  MARTURIA 2Dβ — TESTIMONY 494D
  CHRISTOS 2 — ANOINTED ONE 895C
3 ANAGINWSKW I — READ 51B
  DIDACH8 2 — TEACHING 191B
  EGGUS 2A — NEAR 213B
  KAIROS 4 — TIME 396B
  MAKARIOS IB — BLESSED 488A
  PROPH8TEIA 3B — PROPHECY 730B

3 T8REW 5 — KEEP 823A
4 APO V4 — FROM 87C
  ASIA — ASIA 115C
  EIMI II — TO BE 222A
  EIR8N8 2 — PEACE 226D
  EKKL8SIA 4B — CHURCH 240C
  ENWPION I — BEFORE 270A
  HEPTA — SEVEN 306B
  ERCHOMAI IIBβ — COME 311B
  THRONOS IB — THRONE 364D
  IWAN(N)8S 3 — JOHN 385C
  PNEUMA 4B — SPIRIT 682A
  CHARIS 2C — FAVOR 885D
5 HAIMA 2B — BLOOD 22C
  ARCHWN I — RULER 113B
  BASILEUS I — KING 135C
  LOUW I — BATHE 482A
  LUW 2B — RELEASE 485A
  MARTUS 3 — WITNESS 495D
  NEKROS 2A — DEAD 537A
  PISTOS IAα — TRUSTWORTHY 670B
  PRWTOTOKOS 2A — FIRSTBORN 734B
  CHRISTOS 2 — ANOINTED ONE 895C
6 AIWN IB — TIME 26D
  AM8N I — AMEN 45A
  BASILEIA I — KINGDOM 134C
  HIEREUS 2B — PRIEST 372D
  KRATOS 4 — POWER 450B
  PAT8R 3Dβ — FATHER 641D
  POIEW IIBι — DO 688B
7 AM8N I — AMEN 45A
  EKKENTEW — PIERCE 240A
  EPI IIIBε — TOWARD 289A
  IDOU IA — BEHOLD 371C
  KOPTW 2 — BEAT 445A
  META AI — WITH 509D
  NAI 4 — CERTAINLY 535A
  NEPHEL8 — CLOUD 538D
  HORAW IAα — SEE 581C
  HOSTIS IB — WHOEVER 590D
  OPHTHALMOS I — EYE 604B
  PHUL8 2 — NATION 876D
7A PAS IAα — EVERY EACH 636C
7B PAS IDα — ALL 637C
8 A — ALPHA IA
  ARCH8 ID — BEGINNING 111D
  EIMI II — TO BE 222A
  ERCHOMAI IIBβ — COME 311B
  KURIOS 2A — LORD 460B
  PANTOKRATWR — ALMIGHTY 613D
  TELOS IB — END 819B
  W — OMEGA 903A
9 ADELPHOS 2 — BROTHER 16A
  GINOMAI II4A — BE 159C
  THLIPSIS I — TRIBULATION 362D
  IWAN(N)8S 3 — JOHN 385C
  KALEW IAγ — CALL 400A
  LOGOS I8β — WORD 479B
  MARTURIA 2Dβ — TESTIMONY 494D
  N8SOS — ISLAND 540A
  PATMOS — PATMOS 642A
  SUGKOINWNOS — PARTICIPANT 782A
  HUPOMON8 2 — PATIENCE 854B

10 GINOMAI II4A	BE	159C	
EN I5D	IN	259C	
H8MERA 2	DAY	347C	
KURIAKOS		459C	
BELONGING TO THE LORD			
MEGAS 2Aγ	GREAT	498D	
OPISTHEN 2A	FROM BEHIND	578B	
OPISW 2Aα	BEHIND	578C	
PNEUMA 6E	SPIRIT	684A	
SALPIGX I	TRUMPET	748B	
HWS II3B	SO	906B	
11 A	ALPHA	1A	
BIBLION I	BOOK	140D	
GRAPHW 2B	WRITE	165D	
HEPTA	SEVEN	306B	
EPHESOS	EPHESUS	330C	
THUATIRA	THYATIRA	365B	
LAODIKEIA	LAODICEA	467D	
PEMPW 2	SEND	648A	
PERGAMOS	PERGAMUS	650A	
SARDEIS	SARDIS	749D	
SMURNA	SMYRNA	766B	
PHILADELPHEIA	PHILADELPHIA	866A	
W	OMEGA	903A	
11F BLEPW IA	SEE	142D	
12 HEPTA	SEVEN	306B	
LALEW 2A6	SPEAK	464C	
HOSTIS 3	WHOEVER	591B	
PHWN8 2E	VOICE	879C	
12A EPISTREPHW IBα	TURN	301B	
12B EPISTREPHW IBα	TURN	301A	
12F LUCHNIA	LAMPSTAND	484B	
12F CHRUSOUS	GOLDEN	897B	
13 ENDUW 2A	DRESS	263C	
ZWN8	BELT	342A	
MAZOS I	BREAST	486C	
MASTOS I	BREAST	496B	
MESOS 2	THE MIDDLE	509A	
HOMOIOS 3	LIKE	570A	
PERIZWNNUMI I	GIRD ABOUT	653A	
PERIZWNNUMI 2B	GIRD ABOUT	653A	
POD8R8S REACHING TO THE FEET		686C	
PROS III	NEAR	716C	
HUIOS 2C	SON	843B	
CHRUSOUS	GOLDEN	897A	
14 ERION	WOOL	309C	
THRIX 2	HAIR	364C	
KEPHAL8 IA	HEAD	431A	
OPHTHALMOS I	EYE	604B	
PUR IA	FIRE	737B	
PHLOX	FLAME	870A	
CHIWN	SNOW	890C	
14A LEUKOS 2	WHITE	473C	
14B LEUKOS 2	WHITE	473C	
15 KAMINOS	FURNACE	402D	
HOMOIOS I	LIKE	569C	
POLUS IIAβ	MANY	694B	
PUROW 2	SET ON FIRE	738C	
HUDWR I	WATER	840D	
CHALKOLIBANON	BRONZE	883A	
15B PHWN8 I	SOUND	878C	
16 AST8R	STAR	117B	
DISTOMOS	DOUBLE EDGED	199A	

16 EKPOREUOMAI 2	GO OUT	244A	
HEPTA	SEVEN	306B	
ECHW IIA	HAVE	332A	
H8LIOS	THE SUN	346B	
OXUS I	SHARP	578A	
OPSIS 3	APPEARANCE	606D	
OPSIS 2	APPEARANCE	606D	
ROMPHAIA	SWORD	744C	
STOMA IA	MOUTH	777B	
PHAINW I	SHINE	859B	
16F DEXIOS I	RIGHT	173C	
17 DEXIOS 2A	RIGHT	173D	
ESCHATOS 3B	LAST	314A	
NEKROS IAα	DEAD	536C	
PIPTW IBα	FALL	665B	
POUS I	FOOT	703B	
PRWTOS IA	FIRST	732D	
TITH8MI IIAβ	PUT	823D	
18 HAD8S I	HADES	16C	
EIMI II4F	TO BE	223B	
ECHW I2H	HAVE	333C	
THANATOS IF	DEATH	352A	
KLEIS I	KEY	435A	
NEKROS IAα	DEAD	536C	
19 GRAPHW 2B	WRITE	165D	
EIMI II6D	TO BE	223C	
MELLW IC6	IS DESTINED	502C	
20 AGGELOS 2A	ANGEL	7D	
AST8R	STAR	117B	
DEXIOS 2A	RIGHT	173D	
HEPTA	SEVEN	306B	
MUST8RION 3	MYSTERY	532C	
HOS,H8,HO I4E	(REL PRON)	588B	
CHRUSOUS	GOLDEN	897B	
20A LUCHNIA	LAMPSTAND	484B	
20B LUCHNIA	LAMPSTAND	484B	

REVELATION 2

I AGGELOS 2A	ANGEL	7D	
AST8R	STAR	117B	
GRAPHW 2D	WRITE	166A	
DEXIOS 2A	RIGHT	173D	
EKKL8SIA 4B	CHURCH	240C	
HEPTA	SEVEN	306B	
EPHESOS	EPHESUS	330C	
KRATEW 2B	HOLD	449D	
LEGW IIIC	ORDER	470D	
LUCHNIA	LAMPSTAND	484B	
MESOS 2	THE MIDDLE	509A	
HODE I	THIS	555C	
PERIPATEW IA	GO ABOUT	654D	
CHRUSOUS	GOLDEN	897A	
2 APOSTOLOS 2	MESSENGER	99A	
BASTAZW 2Bβ	ENDURE	137A	
ERGON ICβ	DEED	308A	
HEURISKW 2	FIND	325D	
KAKOS IA	BAD	398C	
KOPOS 2	WORK	444C	
PEIRAZW 2A	TRY	646A	
PHASKW	SAY	862B	
PSEUD8S I	FALSE	899D	
2F HUPOMON8 I	PATIENCE	854A	

3	BASTAZW 2Bβ	ENDURE	137A
	ECHW I2Eβ	HAVE	333B
	KOPIAW I	BECOME WEARY	444B
	ONOMA I4Cα	NAME	575C
4	APHI8MI 3B	ABANDON	125D
	ECHW I7A	HAVE	334A
	KATA I2Bβ	DOWN	406C
	HOTI IA	THAT	592D
	PRWTOS IA	FIRST	733A
5	EI VI3A	IF NOT	218D
	ERCHOMAI IIA6	COME	310C
	KINEW I	MOVE	433C
	LUCHNIA	LAMPSTAND	484B
	MN8MONEUW IC	REMEMBER	527A
	PIPTW	FALL	664D
	PIPTW 2Aβ	FALL	665C
	POTHEN I	FROM WHERE	686D
	POIEW IIBα	DO	687C
	PRWTOS IA	FIRST	732D
	TACHOS	SPEED	814D
	TACHUS 2B	QUICK	815A
	TOPOS IF	PLACE	830C
5A	METANOEW	CHANGE ONES MIND	513C
5B	METANOEW	CHANGE ONES MIND	513C
6	ECHW I7B	HAVE	334B
	MISEW 2	HATE	524D
	NIKOLAIT8S	NICOLAITAN	541D
	HOTI IA	THAT	592D
	HOUTOS IBβ	THIS	601C
7	AKOUW IA	HEAR	31B
	AUTOS 3C	(OBLIQUE CASE)	123A
	EK 4Aα	FROM	235B
	ESTHIW IBβ	EAT	313A
	ESTHIW ID	EAT	313B
	ECHW I2Cα	HAVE	332D
	ZW8 2Bβ	LIFE	341D
	NIKAW IA	BE VICTOR	541A
	XULON 3	TREE	551C
	OUS 2	EAR	600B
	PARADEISOS 2	PARADISE	619B
	PNEUMA 5Dα	SPIRIT	683A
8	AGGELOS 2A	ANGEL	7D
	GRAPHW 2D	WRITE	166A
	EKKL8SIA 4B	CHURCH	240C
	ESCHATOS 3B	LAST	314A
	ZAW IAβ	LIVE	336D
	LEGW IIIC	ORDER	470D
	NEKROS IAα	DEAD	536C
	HODE I	THIS	555C
	PRWTOS IA	FIRST	732D
	PRWTOTOKOS 2A	FIRSTBORN	734B
	SMURNA	SMYRNA	766B
	SMURNAIOS	SMYRNAEN	766B
9	BLASPH8MIA 2Aα	SLANDER	142C
	EK 3C	FROM	234B
	THLIPSIS I	TRIBULATION	362D
	PLOUSIOS 2	RICH	679C
	SATAN	ADVERSARY	752C
	SUNAGWG8 4	PLACE OF ASSEMBLY	790D
9F	SATAN	ADVERSARY	752B
10	ACHRI IC	AS FAR AS	128C
	BALLW IB	THROW	130C
	DEKA	TEN	172D
10	ECHW I2Eα	HAVE	333A
	ZW8 2Bβ	LIFE	341D
	THANATOS IA	DEATH	351C
	THLIPSIS I	TRIBULATION	363A
	M8DEIS 2Bβ	NOTHING	520A
	PASCHW 3B	ENDURE	639D
	PEIRAZW 2D	TRY	646B
	PISTOS IAα	TRUSTWORTHY	670C
	STEPHANOS 2A	WREATH	775A
	PHULAK8 3	GUARD	875D
11	ADIKEW 2B	INJURE	17C
	AKOUW IA	HEAR	31B
	DEUTEROS 2	SECOND	176A
	EK 3Eα	BY	234C
	ECHW I2Cα	HAVE	332D
	THANATOS 2B	DEATH	352B
	M8 DIA	NOT	519B
	NIKAW IA	BE VICTOR	541A
	OUS 2	EAR	600B
	PNEUMA 5Dα	SPIRIT	683A
12	AGGELOS 2A	ANGEL	7D
	GRAPHW 2D	WRITE	166A
	DISTOMOS	DOUBLE EDGED	199A
	EKKL8SIA 4B	CHURCH	240C
	LEGW IIIC	ORDER	470D
	HODE I	THIS	555C
	OXUS I	SHARP	578A
	PERGAMOS	PERGAMUS	650A
	ROMPHAIA	SWORD	744C
13	ANTIPAS	ANTIPAS	75A
	ARNEOMAI 3D	DENY	107D
	THRONOS IE	THRONE	365A
	KRATEW 2Eβ	HOLD	449D
	MARTUS 3	WITNESS	495C
	ONOMA I4B	NAME	575B
	PARA IIIBβ	BESIDE	615C
	PISTIS 2Bβ	FAITH	668D
	PISTOS IAα	TRUSTWORTHY	670B
	POU IB	WHERE	702D
13A	KATOIKEW IA	LIVE	425C
13A	HOPOU IAα	WHERE	579C
13A	SATAN	ADVERSARY	752C
13B	KATOIKEW IA	LIVE	425C
13B	HOPOU IAα	WHERE	579C
13B	SATAN	ADVERSARY	752C
14	BALAAM	BALAAM	130B
	BALAK	BALAK	130B
	BALLW 2B	PUT	131A
	DIDASKW 2D	TEACH	191B
	EIDWLOTHUTOS	MEAT OFFERED TO AN IDOL	220C
	ENWPION I	BEFORE	270B
	ESTHIW IA	EAT	312C
	ECHW I7A	HAVE	334A
	KATA I2Bβ	DOWN	406C
	OLIGOS IB	FEW	566C
	PORNEUW I	TO PROSTITUTE	700B
	SKANDALON 2	TRAP	760C
14F	DIDACH8 2	TEACHING	191C
14F	KRATEW 2Eβ	HOLD	449D
15	NIKOLAIT8S	NICOLAITAN	541D
16	EI VI3A	IF NOT	218D
	ERCHOMAI IIA6	COME	310C

16	META ΔII3Δ	WITH	510C
	METANOEW	CHANGE ONES MIND	513C
	POLEMEW IΔ	FIGHT	691C
	ROMPHAIA	SWORD	744C
	STOMA IΔ	MOUTH	777B
	TACHUS 2B	QUICK	815A
17	AKOUW IΔ	HEAR	31B
	AUTOS 3C	(OBLIQUE CASE)	123A
	GRAPHW 2Δ	WRITE	165D
	DIDWMI IBβ	GIVE	192A
	KAINOS 2	NEW	395A
	KRUPTW IΔ	HIDE	455B
	LEUKOS 2	WHITE	473C
	MANNA 2	MANNA	492A
	NIKAW IΔ	BE VICTOR	541A
	OUDEIS 2Δ	NO ONE	596B
	OUS 2	EAR	600B
	PNEUMA 5Dα	SPIRIT	683A
17A	PS8PHOS 2		901A
	CAST A VOTE AGAINST		
17B	PS8PHOS 2		901A
	CAST A VOTE AGAINST		
18	AGGELOS 2Δ	ANGEL	7D
	GRAPHW 2D	WRITE	166A
	EKKL8SIΔ 4B	CHURCH	240C
	THUATIRA	THYATIRA	365B
	LEGW IIIC	ORDER	470D
	HODE I	THIS	555C
	HOMOIOS I	LIKE	569C
	OPHTHALMOS I	EYE	604B
	PUR IΔ	FIRE	737B
	HUIOS 2B	SON	842C
	PHLOX	FLAME	870A
	CHALKOLIBANON	BRONZE	883A
19	AGAP8 IIΔ	LOVE	5C
	DIAKONIA I	SERVICE	183B
	ERGON ICβ	DEED	308A
	ESCHATOS 3Δ	LAST	314A
	PISTIS 2Dγ	FAITH	669C
	POLUS IIIΔ	MANY	695D
	HUPOMON8 I	PATIENCE	854A
20	APHI8MI 4	TOLERATE	125D
	DOULOS 4	SLAVE	205B
	EAW 2	LET	212A
	EIDWLOTHUTOS		220C
	MEAT OFFERED TO AN IDOL		
	ESTHIW IΔ	EAT	312C
	ECHW I7Δ	HAVE	334A
	IEZABEL	JEZEBEL	372B
	KATA I2Bβ	DOWN	406C
	LEGW II3	CALL	471B
	PLANAW IB	DECEIVE	671B
	PORNEUW I	TO PROSTITUTE	700B
	PROPH8TIS	PROPHETESS	731D
21	HINA IIID	IN ORDER THAT	378C
	METANOEW	CHANGE ONES MIND	513C
	PORNEIA 2	PROSTITUTION	700A
	CHRONOS	TIME	896C
21B	METANOEW	CHANGE ONES MIND	513C
21F	EK IC	AWAY FROM	233D
22	BALLW IB	THROW	130C
	EAN I38	IF	210D
	EIS 4Δ	INTO	228B

22	THLIPSIS I	TRIBULATION	362D
	KLIN8	COUCH	437C
	MEGAS 2Aγ	GREAT	499A
	META ΔII3B	WITH	510D
	METANOEW	CHANGE ONES MIND	513C
	MOICHEUW 2C	COMMIT ADULTERY	528B
23	HEKASTOS 2	EACH	236B
	ERAUNAW	SEARCH	306C
	ERGON ICβ	DEED	308A
	THANATOS IE	DEATH	352A
	KARDIA IBα	HEART	404B
	KATA II5Aβ	ACCORDING TO	408A
	NEPHROS	MIND	539A
	TEKNON 2B	CHILD	816B
24	BATHOS 2	DEPTH	129D
	BATHUS 2	DEEP	130A
	BALLW 2B	PUT	130D
	BAROS I	WEIGHT	133C
	DIDACH8 2	TEACHING	191B
	THUATIRA	THYATIRA	365B
	LOIPOS 2Bα	THE OTHERS	481A
	HOSTIS 2B	WHOEVER	591A
	HOUTOS 2B	THIS	601D
	SATAN	ADVERSARY	752C
25	AN 3D	(PARTICLE)	48C
	ACHRI 2A	UNTIL	128C
	H8KW IC	HAVE COME	345B
	KRATEW 2Eγ	HOLD	450A
	PL8N IC	BUT	675B
26	ACHRI IA	UNTIL	128B
	EXOUSIA 3	AUTHORITY	278A
	EPI II8α	OVER	286A
	ERGON ICβ	DEED	308A
	NIKAW IA	BE VICTOR	541A
	TELOS IDβ	END	819C
	T8REW 5	KEEP	823A
27	EN IIIIA	BY	260A
	KERAMIKOS		430A
	BELONGING TO THE POTTER		
	POIMAINW 2Aγ	TEND	690B
	RABDOS	ROD	740D
	SID8ROUS	IRON	757C
	SKEUOS IB	THING	761D
	SUNTRI8W IA	SHATTER	801A
28	LAMBANW 2	RECEIVE	466C
	PARA I3B	FROM	614D
	PAT8R 3Dα	FATHER	641D
	PRWINOS	EARLY	732B
29	AKOUW IA	HEAR	31B
	OUS 2	EAR	600B
	PNEUMA 5Dα	SPIRIT	683A

REVELATION 3

I	AGGELOS 2A	ANGEL	7D
	AST8R	STAR	117B
	GRAPHW 2D	WRITE	166A
	EKKL8SIA 4B	CHURCH	240C
	ZAW 2A	LIVE	337A
	KAI I2G	AND	393C
	LEGW IIIC	ORDER	470D
	NEKROS I8α	DEAD	536D
	HODE I	THIS	555C

1	ONOMA IV	FAME	577B
	PNEUMA 4B	SPIRIT	682A
	SARDEIS	SARDIS	749D
1B	ONOMA I2A	NAME	574B
2	APOTHN8SKW IB«	DIE	91A
	ENWPION 3	BEFORE	270B
	ERGON ICβ	DEED	308A
	HEURISKW 2	FIND	325D
	LOIPOS 2Bβ	THE REST	481A
	MELLW IB«	BE ABOUT TO	502A
	PL8ROW 3	MAKE FULL	677B
	ST8RIZW 2	ESTABLISH	775D
2F	GR8GOREW 2	BE AWAKE	166C
3	EPI IIIIBy	ON	289A
	KLEPT8S	THIEF	435C
	METANOEW	CHANGE ONES MIND	513C
	MN8MONEUW IC	REMEMBER	527A
	POIOS 2Aβ	OF WHAT KIND	691B
	PWS 2A	HOW	739D
	T8REW 5	KEEP	823A
	HWRA I	TIME OF DAY	904B
3A	H8KW IC	HAVE COME	345B
3B	H8KW IB	HAVE COME	345B
3B	OUN 5	THEREFORE	597D
4	AXIOS 2A	WORTHY	77D
	LEUKOS 2	WHITE	473D
	MOLUNW I	DEFILE	528D
	OLIGOS IA	FEW	566B
	ONOMA III	PEOPLE	577A
	HOS,H8,HO I3By	(REL PRON)	587D
	PERIPATEW IB	GO ABOUT	654D
	SARDEIS	SARDIS	749D
5	BIBLOS 2	BOOK	141A
	EK IA	AWAY FROM	233C
	EN I4B	IN	258B
	ENWPION 2B	BEFORE	270B
	EXALEIPHW IB	WIPE AWAY	272A
	ZW8 2Bβ	LIFE	341C
	HIMATION I	GARMENT	377A
	LEUKOS 2	WHITE	473D
	NIKAW IA	BE VICTOR	541A
	HOMOLOGEW 4	CONFESS	571D
	PAT8R 3D«	FATHER	641D
	PERIBALLW IBy	THROW AROUND	651D
5A	ONOMA I2A	NAME	574B
6	AKOUW IA	HEAR	31B
	OUS 2	EAR	600B
	PNEUMA 5D«	SPIRIT	683A
7	AGGELOS 2A	ANGEL	7D
	HAGIOS 2Cβ	THE HOLY ONE	10A
	AL8THINOS I	TRUE	36B
	GRAPHW 2D	WRITE	166A
	DAUID	DAVID	170B
	EKKL8SIA 4B	CHURCH	240C
	ECHW I2H	HAVE	333C
	KLEIS I	KEY	435A
	LEGW IIIC	ORDER	470D
	HODE I	THIS	555C
	PHILADELPHEIA	PHILADELPHIA	866A
7A	KLEIW I	SHUT	435B
7B	KLEIW I	SHUT	435B
7F	ANOIGW IA	OPEN	70B
8	ARNEOMAI 3D	DENY	107D
8	AUTOS 3D	(OBLIQUE CASE)	123B
	DUNAMIS 5	RESOURCES	207B
	ENWPION I	BEFORE	270A
	THURA 2B	DOOR	366C
	KLEIW I	SHUT	435A
	LOGOS IBβ	WORD	479B
	MIKROS 2C	SMALL	523B
	HOS,H8,HO I3A	(REL PRON)	587C
	T8REW 5	KEEP	823A
9	DIDWMI	GIVE	191D
	ENWPION I	BEFORE	270A
	H8KW IC	HAVE COME	345B
	HINA I2	IN ORDER THAT	377D
	HINA IIIA«	IN ORDER THAT	378B
	POIEW IIBθ	DO	688B
	POUS IA	FOOT	703B
	PROSKUNEW I	DO REVERENCE	724A
	SATAN	ADVERSARY	752C
	SUNAGWG8 4	PLACE OF ASSEMBLY	790D
	PSEUDOMAI I	LIE	900A
10	EK IC	AWAY FROM	233D
	EPI IIAβ	ON	285D
	KAGW 3B	I	387A
	KATOIKEW IA	LIVE	425C
	LOGOS IBβ	WORD	479C
	OIKOUMEN8 IA	THE WORLD	564A
	HOLOS 2B	WHOLE	567D
	PEIRAZW 2B	TRY	646A
	PEIRASMOS 2B	TEST	646D
	HUPOMON8 2	PATIENCE	854B
	HUPOMON8 I	PATIENCE	854B
	HWRA 3	TIME OF DAY	905A
10A	T8REW 5	KEEP	823A
10B	T8REW 4	KEEP	822D
11	KRATEW 2Ey	HOLD	450A
	LAMBANW IB	TAKE	465C
	M8DEIS 2A	NO	520A
	STEPHANOS 2A	WREATH	775A
	TACHUS 2B	QUICK	815A
12	GRAPHW 2A	WRITE	165D
	EXERCHOMAI IAβ	GO OUT	274A
	EXW IB	OUTSIDE	279A
	HIEROSOLUMA	JERUSALEM	373D
	HIEROSOLUMA 2	JERUSALEM	374A
	KAINOS 2	NEW	395A
	KAINOS 3B	NEW	395B
	KATABAINW IB	COME DOWN	409C
	M8 DIA	NOT	519B
	NAOS IB	TEMPLE	535C
	NIKAW IA	BE VICTOR	541A
	HO,H8,TO IIIC	THE	552D
	OURANOS 2D	HEAVEN	599D
	POIEW IIBι	DO	688B
	POLIS 2	CITY	692D
	STULOS	PILLAR	779C
13	AKOUW IA	HEAR	31B
	OUS 2	EAR	600B
	PNEUMA 5D«	SPIRIT	683A
14	AGGELOS 2A	ANGEL	7D
	AL8THINOS I	TRUE	36B
	AM8N 4	AMEN	45B
	ARCH8 2	THE FIRST CAUSE	112A
	GRAPHW 2D	WRITE	166A

14 EKKL8SIA 4B	CHURCH	240C
KTISIS IBβ	CREATION	457A
LAODIKEIA	LAODICEA	467D
LEGW IIIC	ORDER	470D
MARTUS 3	WITNESS	495D
HO,H8,TO II9C	THE	554D
HODE I	THIS	555C
PISTOS IAα	TRUSTWORTHY	670B
15 8 IAα	OR	342B
OPHELON	O THAT	604A
15A PSUCHROS 2	COLD	903A
15B PSUCHROS 2	COLD	903A
15F ZESTOS	HOT	337D
15F OUTE	NOT	600C
16 EMEW	SPIT OUT	254B
MELLW IBα	BE ABOUT TO	502A
HOUTW IB	THUS	602C
STOMA IA	MOUTH	777B
CHLIAROS	LUKEWARM	890D
PSUCHROS 2	COLD	903A
17 GUMNOS I	NAKED	166D
ELEEINOS	MISERABLE	249A
OUDEIS 2Bγ	IN NO RESPECT	596D
PLOUSIOS 2	RICH	679C
PLOUTEW 2	BE RICH	680A
PTWCHOS IC	BEGGING POOR	735D
TALAIPWROS	MISERABLE	811A
TUPHLOS 2Aβ	BLIND	838C
CHREIA 2	NEED	893B
18 AGORAZW I	BUY	12D
AISCHUN8 2	SHAME	24D
BLEPW 2	SEE	143A
GUMNOT8S I	NAKEDNESS	167B
EGCHRIW	RUB ON	216A
EK 3Eβ	BY	234C
HIMATION I	GARMENT	377A
KOLLOURION	EYE SALVE	442D
LEUKOS 2	WHITE	473D
PARA I3B	FROM	615A
PERIBALLW IBε	THROW AROUND	651D
PLOUTEW 2	BE RICH	680A
PUR IA	FIRE	737B
PUROW 2	SET ON FIRE	738C
SUMBOULEUW I	ADVISE	785C
PHANEROW IB	REVEAL	860C
CHRUSION	GOLD	896D
19 ELEGCHW 4	DISCIPLINE	249A
Z8LEUW	BE EAGER	338A
METANOEW	CHANGE ONES MIND	513C
PAIDEUW 2Bα	INSTRUCT	608D
PHILEW IA	LOVE LIKE	867A
20 ANOIGW IA	OPEN	70B
DEIPNEW	EAT	172B
EISERCHOMAI IC	COME	232A
*EPI IIIIAʒ	ON	288C
HIST8MI II2Bβ	BEING	383C
KAI I2D	AND	393B
KROUW	STRIKE	454D
META AII2	WITH	510C
TIS,TI IAγ	ANY ONE	827D
PHWN8 2A	VOICE	879A
20A THURA 2A	DOOR	366C
20B THURA 2A	DOOR	366C

21 NIKAW IA	BE VICTOR	541B
PAT8R 3Dα	FATHER	641D
21A THRONOS IC	THRONE	364D
21A KATHIZW 2Aα	SIT DOWN	391A
21B THRONOS IB	THRONE	364D
21B THRONOS IC	THRONE	364D
21B KATHIZW 2Aα	SIT DOWN	391A
21B NIKAW IA	BE VICTOR	541A
22 AKOUW IA	HEAR	31B
OUS 2	EAR	600B
PNEUMA 5Dα	SPIRIT	683A

REVELATION 4

1 ANABAINW IAβ	GO UP	50A
DEI I	IT IS NECESSARY	171A
DEIKNUMI IA	SHOW	171D
EIDON	SEE	219C
THURA IB	ENTRANCE	366B
IDOU 2	THERE IS	371D
KAI I2F	AND	393C
LALEW I	SOUND	464A
LALEW 3	SPEAK	465A
SALPIGX I	TRUMPET	748B
HWDE I	HERE	903B
HWS II3B	SO	906B
1F EIDON IA	SEE	219D
2 GINOMAI II4A	BE	159C
EN I5D	IN	259C
EUTHEWS	IMMEDIATELY	320D
KATH8MAI IAα	SIT	390B
KEIMAI IB	LIE	428A
PNEUMA 6E	SPIRIT	684A
2FF THRONOS IB	THRONE	364D
3 IASPIS	JASPER	369B
IRIS 2	HALO	381C
*SARDION	CARNELIAN	750A
SMARAGDINOS	EMERALD	765D
3A HOMOIOS I	LIKE	569C
3A HORASIS 2A	APPEARANCE	581A
3B HOMOIOS		569C

LIKE

3B HOMOIOS I	LIKE	569C
3B HORASIS 2A	APPEARANCE	581A
3F KUKLOTHEN 2	ALL AROUND	457D
4 EIKOSI	TWENTY	221A
EN I4B	IN	258B
EPI IIIIAʒ	ON	288C
THRONOS IE	THRONE	365A
HIMATION I	GARMENT	377A
KATH8MAI IAα	SIT	390B
KEPHAL8 IA	HEAD	431A
LEUKOS 2	WHITE	473D
PERIBALLW IBγ	THROW AROUND	651D
PRESBUTEROS 2Bγ	OLDER	707B
STEPHANOS I	WREATH	774D
CHRUSOUS	GOLDEN	897A
4A TESSARES	FOUR	821A
4B TESSARES	FOUR	821A
5 ASTRAP8	LIGHTNING	117D
BRONT8	THUNDER	147A
EKPOREUOMAI 2	GO OUT	244A
HEPTA	SEVEN	306B

5	KAIW IA	LIGHT 397A
	LAMPAS I	TORCH 466D
	HOS,H8,HO I4C	(REL PRON) 588A
	PNEUMA 4B	SPIRIT 682A
	PUR IB	FIRE 737C
	PHWN8 I	SOUND 878D
5F	ENWPION I	BEFORE 270A
6	GEMW I	BE FULL 153A
	EMPROSTHEN IA	AHEAD 256B
	KRUSTALLOS	ROCK CRYSTAL 455D
	KUKLW 2	AROUND 458A
	MESOS 2	THE MIDDLE 508D
	OPISTHEN IB	FROM BEHIND 578B
	OPHTHALMOS I	EYE 604B
	TESSARES	FOUR 821A
	HUALINOS	OF GLASS 839B
	HWS II3Aα	SO 906A
6F	HOMOIOS I	LIKE 569C
6=9	ZWON I	LIVING THING 342B
7	AETOS	EAGLE 19B
	DEUTEROS 3	SECOND 176A
	ECHW I2Cα	HAVE 332D
	LEWN I	LION 474A
	MOSCHOS	CALF 530C
	PETOMAI	FLY 660A
	PROSWPON IA	FACE 728A
	PRWTOS IB	FIRST 733A
	TETARTOS	FOURTH 821A
	TRITOS I	THIRD 834B
8	HAGIOS IB6	HOLY 9D
	ANA 3	EACH 49C
	ANAPAUSIS I	STOPPING 58B
	GEMW I	BE FULL 153A
	EIMI II	TO BE 222A
	HEIS 5E	ONE 231B
	ERCHOMAI IIB9	COME 311B
	ESWTHEN 2	INSIDE 314C
	ECHW I2Cα	HAVE 332D
	ECHW I2G	HAVE 333B
	KUKLOTHEN I	ALL AROUND 457D
	KURIOS 2A	LORD 460C
	NUX IB	NIGHT 548D
	OPHTHALMOS I	EYE 604B
	PANTOKRATWR	ALMIGHTY 613D
	PTERUX	WING 734D
9	DIDWMI I	GIVE 191D
	DIDWMI IA	GIVE 191D
	EPI IIIAα	ON 286C
	EUCHARISTIA 2	THANKFULNESS 329A
	ZAW IAε	LIVE 336D
	THRONOS IB	THRONE 364D
	HOTAN 2A	WHEN 592B
	TIM8 2B	HONOR 825B
9F	AIWN IB	TIME 27A
9F	KATH8MAI IAα	SIT 390B
10	BALLW 2B	PUT 131A
	EIKOSI	TWENTY 221A
	*ENWPION I	BEFORE 270A
	PIPTW IB	FALL 665B
	PRESBUTEROS 2Bγ	OLDER 707B
	PROSKUNEW 2A	DO REVERENCE 724A
	STEPHANOS I	WREATH 774D
II	AXIOS 2A	WORTHY 77C

II	DIA BIII	BECAUSE OF 180A
	DUNAMIS I	POWER 206C
	THEL8MA 2B	WILL 355A
	THEOS 3C	GOD 358A
	PAS 2Bβ	ALL THINGS 638D
	TIM8 2B	HONOR 825B
IIA	KTIZW	CREATE 456C
IIB	KTIZW	CREATE 456C

REVELATION 5

I	GRAPHW 3	WRITE 166B
	DEXIOS 2A	RIGHT 173D
	EXWTHEN IBα	OUTSIDE 279B
	EPI IIIIAζ	ON 288C
	ESWTHEN 2	INSIDE 314C
	THRONOS IB	THRONE 364D
	KATH8MAI IAα	SIT 390B
	KATASPHRAGIZW	SEAL 420C
	OPISTHEN IB	FROM BEHIND 578B
	SPHRAGIS IA	SEAL 804B
IFF	BIBLION I	BOOK 140D
2	AGGELOS 2A	ANGEL 7C
	AXIOS 2A	WORTHY 77C
	ISCHUROS IA	STRONG 384A
	K8RUSSW I	ANNOUNCE 432B
	LUW IA	LOOSE 484D
	MEGAS 2Aγ	GREAT 498D
	SPHRAGIS IA	SEAL 804B
	PHWN8 2B	VOICE 878D
2FF	ANOIGW IC	OPEN 70C
3	OUDE I	AND NOT 595D
	OURANOS IAβ	HEAVEN 598B
	OUTE	NOT 600C
	HUPOKATW	UNDER 852C
3F	BLEPW IA	SEE 142D
3F	BLEPW 3	SEE 143B
4	AXIOS 2A	WORTHY 77C
	HEURISKW 2	FIND 326A
	KLAIW I	WEEP 434A
	*OUTE	NOT 600C
	OUTE	NOT 600D
	POLUS I2C9	MANY 695D
5	DAUID	DAVID 170B
	IOUDAS IB	JUDAH 380C
	KLAIW I	WEEP 434A
	LEWN 2	LION 474A
	NIKAW IA	BE VICTOR 541A
	RIZA 2	ROOT 743C
	SPHRAGIS IA	SEAL 804B
	PHUL8 I	TRIBE 876D
5=14	PRESBUTEROS 2Bγ	OLDER 707B
6	*ARNION	SHEEP 107D
	ECHW I2Cα	HAVE 332D
	ZWON I	LIVING THING 342C
	HIST8MI II2Bγ	BEING 383C
	KERAS I	HORN 430B
	PNEUMA 4B	SPIRIT 682A
	SPHAZW	SLAUGHTER 803C
	HWS II3B	SO 906A
6A	MESOS 2	THE MIDDLE 508D
6B	MESOS 2	THE MIDDLE 508D
6F	THRONOS IB	THRONE 364D

7	DEXIOS 2A	RIGHT 173D
	ERCHOMAI IIAζ	COME 310D
	KATH8MAI IAα	SIT 390B
8	ARNION	SHEEP 107D
	GEMW I	BE FULL 153A
	EIKOSI	TWENTY 221A
	HEKASTOS 2	EACH 236B
	ENWPION I	BEFORE 270A
	ECHW IIA	HAVE 332A
	ZWON I	LIVING THING 342C
	THUMIAMA IB	INCENSE 365D
	KITHARA	LYRE 433A
	HOS,H8,HO I4C	(REL PRON) 588A
	PIPTW IBα	FALL 665B
	PROSEUCH8 I	PRAYER 720B
	PHIAL8	BOWL 866A
	CHRUSOUS	GOLDEN 897A
8F	LAMBANW IA	TAKE 465B
9	AGORAZW 2	BUY 12D
	ADW	SING 19A
	HAIMA 2B	BLOOD 22C
	ANOIGW ID	OPEN 70C
	AXIOS 2A	WORTHY 77C
	GLWSSA 2	LANGUAGE 161C
	EN IIIIA	BY 260B
	KAINOS 2	NEW 395A
	LAOS 2	PEOPLE 468A
	SPHAZW	SLAUGHTER 803D
	SPHRAGIS IA	SEAL 804B
	PHUL8 2	NATION 876D
	WD8	SONG 903D
10	BASILEIA I	KINGDOM 134C
	BASILEUW IB6	RULE 136B
	EPI IIBα	OVER 286A
	HIERATEIA	PRIESTLY OFFICE 372B
	HIEREUS 2B	PRIEST 372D
11	AGGELOS 2A	ANGEL 7D
	ARITHMOS I	NUMBER 105D
	ZWON I	LIVING THING 342C
	THRONOS IB	THRONE 364D
	KUKLW 2	AROUND 458A
	MURIAS 2	MYRIADS 531C
	POLUS IIAα	MANY 694A
	CHILIAS	THOUSAND 890B
11F	AGGELOS 2A	ANGEL 7D
12	AXIOS 2A	WORTHY 77C
	ISCHUS	STRENGTH 384B
	LEGW I6	SAY 470A
	MEGAS 2Aγ	GREAT 498D
	PLOUTOS 2	WEALTH 680B
	SOPHIA 3A	WISDOM 767B
	SPHAZW	SLAUGHTER 803C
	TIM8 2B	HONOR 825B
12F	ARNION	SHEEP 107D
12F	EULOGIA I	PRAISE 323A
13	AIWN IB	TIME 26D
	AKOUW IC	HEAR 31D
	EPI IIIAα	ON 286C
	THALASSA IA	SEA 350D
	THRONOS IB	THRONE 364D
	KATH8MAI IAα	SIT 390B
	KRATOS 4	POWER 450B
	KTISMA	CREATURE 457B

13	OURANOS IAβ	HEAVEN 598B
	TIM8 2B	HONOR 825C
	HUPOKATW	UNDER 852C
13A	PAS IAα	EVERY EACH 636C
14	AM8N I	AMEN 45A
	ZWON I	LIVING THING 342C
	PIPTW IBα	FALL 665B
	PROSKUNEW 2A	DO REVERENCE 724A

REVELATION 6

1	ARNION	SHEEP 107D
	BRONT8	THUNDER 147A
	DIDACH8 2	TEACHING 191B
	HEPTA	SEVEN 306B
	ZWON I	LIVING THING 342C
	SPHRAGIS IA	SEAL 804B
	PHWN8 I	SOUND 878C
1FF	EIDON	SEE 219C
1=12	ANOIGW ID	OPEN 70C
2	*EXERCHOMAI IAζ	GO OUT 274B
	EPI IIIIAζ	ON 288C
	IDOU 2	THERE IS 371D
	HIPPOS	HORSE 381B
	KATH8MAI IAα	SIT 390B
	NIKAW IA	BE VICTOR 541A
	STEPHANOS I	WREATH 775A
	TOXON	THE BOW 829D
3	DEUTEROS 3	SECOND 176A
	ZWON I	LIVING THING 342C
	SPHRAGIS IA	SEAL 804B
4	AUTOS 3C	(OBLIQUE CASE) 123A
	DIDWMI IBβ	GIVE 192B
	EIR8N8 IA	PEACE 226B
	HINA I2	IN ORDER THAT 377D
	HIPPOS	HORSE 381B
	LAMBANW IB	TAKE 465C
	MACHAIRA I	SWORD 497B
	MEGAS IA	LARGE 498C
	PURROS	RED (AS FIRE) 738D
	SPHAZW	SLAUGHTER 803D
4F	KATH8MAI IAα	SIT 390B
5	ECHW IIA	HAVE 332A
	ZUGOS 2	YOKE 340B
	IDOU 2	THERE IS 371D
	HIPPOS	HORSE 381B
	MELAS	BLACK 501A
	SPHRAGIS IA	SEAL 804B
5A	TRITOS I	THIRD 834B
5B	TRITOS I	THIRD 834B
5=7	ZWON I	LIVING THING 342C
6	ADIKEW 2B	INJURE 17B
	D8NARION	DENARIUS 178B
	ELAION 3	OLIVE OIL 247B
	KRITH8	BARLEY 451C
	MESOS 2	THE MIDDLE 508D
	OINOS 3	WINE 565B
	SITOS	WHEAT 759D
6A	CHOINIX	QUART 891C
6B	CHOINIX	QUART 891C
6F	PHWN8 2D	VOICE 879C
7	SPHRAGIS IA	SEAL 804B
8	HAD8S 2	HADES 16D

8	AKOLOUTHEW 2	ACCOMPANY 30D	12 TRICHINOS
	APOKTEINW IA	KILL 93C	12A HWS II3B
	EN IIIIA	BY 260A	12B HWS II3B
	EXOUSIA 3	AUTHORITY 278A	12F SEL8N8
	EPANW 2A	ON 283A	12FF KAI I2B
	EPI IIIIBα	OVER 288D	13 ANEMOS IA
	TH8RION IAβ	BEAST 361D	AST8R
	IDOU 2	THERE IS 371D	BALLW IC
	HIPPOS	HORSE 381B	MEGAS 2Aγ
	KATH8MAI IAα	SIT 390B	OLUNTHOS
	LIMOS 2	FAMINE 476B	OURANOS IC
	META AIIIA	WITH 509D	PIPTW IA
	ONOMA II	NAME 574A	SALEUW I
	ROMPHAIA	SWORD 744C	SEIW I
	TETARTOS	QUARTER 821A	SUK8
	HUPO ID	BY 851A	HUPO IAβ
	CHLWROS 2	PALE 891A	13F HEKTOS
8A	THANATOS IF	DEATH 352A	14 APOCHWRIZW
8B	THANATOS IE	DEATH 352A	BIBLION I
9	HEKTOS	SIXTH 245C	EK IA
	ECHW IICβ	KEEP 332B	HELISSW
	THUSIAST8RION IBβ	ALTAR 367B	N8SOS
	LOGOS IBβ	WORD 479B	OROS
	MARTURIA 2Dγ	TESTIMONY 494D	TOPOS IF
	PEMPTOS	FIFTH 647B	15 BASILEUS I
	SPHAZW	SLAUGHTER 803D	DOULOS IB
	SPHRAGIS IA	SEAL 804B	DUNATOS IAα
	HUPOKATW	UNDER 852C	ELEUTHEROS I
	PSUCH8 IAα	SOUL LIFE 901C	ISCHUROS IB
10	HAGIOS IB6	HOLY 9D	KRUPTW IB
	HAIMA 2A	BLOOD 22B	OROS
	HAIMA 2A	BLOOD 22C	PETRA IA
	AL8THINOS I	TRUE 36B	PLOUSIOS I
	DESPOT8S	MASTER 175C	SP8LAION
	EKDIKEW 2	AVENGE SOMEONE 238A	CHILIARCHOS
	HEWS IIIC	UNTIL 335C	16 ARNION
	KATOIKEW IA	LIVE 425C	EPI IIAα
	KRAZW 2A	CALL 448D	KATH8MAI IAα
	KRINW 4Bα	JUDGE 452D	KRUPTW IA
	MEGAS 2Aγ	GREAT 498D	ORG8 2B
	POTE	WHEN 701D	OROS
	PHWN8 2A	VOICE 878D	PETRA IA
11	ANAPAUW 2	REST 58C	PIPTW IA
	*HEKASTOS 2	EACH 236B	PROSWPON ICα
	HEWS IIB	UNTIL 334D	17 ERCHOMAI IIBα
	HINA I2	IN ORDER THAT 377D	H8MERA 3Bβ
	LEUKOS 2	WHITE 473D	HIST8MI IIID
	MIKROS 2D	SHORT 523B	MEGAS 2Bβ
	PL8ROW 5	MAKE FULL 677D	ORG8 2B
	PL8ROW 6	MAKE FULL 678A	
	STOL8	ROBE 777B	
	SUNDOULOS 3	FELLOW SLAVE 793C	REVELATION 7
	CHRONOS	TIME 896B	
12	HAIMA 3	BLOOD 22D	1 AGGELOS 2A
	GINOMAI IIBα	COME ABOUT 157B	*ANEMOS IA
	HEKTOS	SIXTH 245C	GWNIA
	H8LIOS	THE SUN 346B	DENDRON
	KAI I2B	AND 393A	EPI IIIIAβ
	MELAS	BLACK 501A	HIST8MI II2Bβ
	SAKKOS	SACK 747C	KRATEW 2D
	SEISMOS	SHAKING 753D	META BIII3
	SEL8N8	MOON 754B	M8TE
	SPHRAGIS IA	SEAL 804B	PAS IAα
			PNEW IA

MADE OF HAIR	834C
SO	906A
SO	906A
MOON	754A
AND	393A
WIND	64A
STAR	117B
LET FALL	130D
GREAT	499A
SUMMER FIG	568A
HEAVEN	598C
FALL	665A
SHAKE	747D
SHAKE	754A
FIG TREE	783D
BY	850D
SIXTH	245C
SEPARATE	101D
BOOK	140C
AWAY FROM	233C
ROLL UP	251A
ISLAND	540A
MOUNTAIN	586A
PLACE	830C
KING	135C
SLAVE	204D
POWERFUL	207D
FREE	250B
STRONG	384A
HIDE	455C
MOUNTAIN	586A
ROCK	660A
RICH	679C
CAVE	769D
TRIBUNE	890A
SHEEP	107D
ON	285D
SIT	390B
HIDE	455B
ANGER	583A
MOUNTAIN	586A
ROCK	660A
FALL	665A
FACE	728C
COME	311B
DAY	348A
STAND	383B
GREAT	499C
ANGER	583A

REVELATION 7

ANGEL	7D
WIND	64A
CORNER	167D
TREE	173C
ON	288A
BEING	383C
HOLD	449D
AFTER	511C
AND NOT	521D
EVERY EACH	636D
BLOW	686A

1-3	THALASSA 1A	SEA	350D
2	ANATOL8 2A	EAST	62A
	AUTOS 3D	(OBLIQUE CASE)	123B
	DIDWMI 18β	GIVE	192B
	ZAW 1A∈	LIVE	336D
	H8LIOS	THE SUN	346B
	KRAZW 2A	CALL	449A
	HOS,H8,HO I3A	(REL PRON)	587C
	SPHRAGIS 1B	SEAL	804B
	PHWN8 2A	VOICE	878D
2F	ADIKEW 2B	INJURE	17B
3	ACHRI 2B	UNTIL	128C
	DENDRON	TREE	173C
	DOULOS 4	SLAVE	205B
	EPI IIA∝	ON	285D
	METWPON	FOREHEAD	517A
	M8TE	AND NOT	521D
	SPHRAGIZW 2B	SEAL	804A
4	ARITHMOS I	NUMBER	106A
	EK 4A∝	FROM	235B
	HEKATON	ONE HUNDRED	236B
	ISRA8L 2	ISRAEL	382C
	TESSARAKONTA	FORTY	820D
	PHUL8 I	TRIBE	876D
	CHILIAS	THOUSAND	890B
4A	SPHRAGIZW 2B	SEAL	804A
4B	SPHRAGIZW 2B	SEAL	804A
4-8	CHILIAS	THOUSAND	890B
5	GAD	GAD	148B
	DAN	DAN	169C
	IOUDAS 1B	JUDAH	380C
	ROUB8N	REUBEN	744C
	SPHRAGIZW 2B	SEAL	804A
5A	CHILIAS	THOUSAND	890B
5-8	PHUL8 I	TRIBE	876D
6	AS8R	ASHER	114C
	IWS8PH I	JOSEPH	386C
	MANASS8S I	MANASSEH	491B
	NEPHTHALIM	NAPHTALI	538D
7	ISSACHAR	ISSACHAR	382C
	LEUI I	LEVI	473B
	SUMEWN I	SYMEON	786A
8	BENIAMIN	BENJAMIN	139A
	ZABOULWN	ZEBULUN	336A
	IWS8PH I	JOSEPH	386C
	SPHRAGIZW 2B	SEAL	804A
8C	CHILIAS	THOUSAND	890B
9	ARITHMEW	COUNT	105D
	GLWSSA 2	LANGUAGE	161C
	ENWPION I	BEFORE	270A
	IDOU 2	THERE IS	371D
	HIST8MI II2Bβ	BEING	383C
	LAOS 2	PEOPLE	468A
	LEUKOS 2	WHITE	473D
	HOS,H8,HO I3A	(REL PRON)	587C
	PERIBALLW 1B∝	THROW AROUND	651D
	POLUS II8∝	MANY	694C
	STOL8	ROBE	777B
	PHOINIX I2	PALM TREE	872B
	PHUL8 2	NATION	876D
9F	ARNION	SHEEP	107D
10	EPI IIIA∝	ON	286C
	KRAZW 2A	CALL	448D

10	SWT8RIA 2	DELIVERANCE	809B
	PHWN8 2A	VOICE	878D
11	ENWPION I	BEFORE	270A
	EPI IIIA β	ON	288A
	ZWON I	LIVING THING	342C
	HIST8MI II2Bβ	BEING	383C
	KUKLW 2	AROUND	458A
	PAS ID∝	ALL	637C
	PIPTW 1B∝	FALL	665B
	PIPTW 1B∝	FALL	665B
	PRESBUTEROS 2Bγ	OLDER	707B
	PROSKUNEW 2A	DO REVERENCE	724A
	PROSWPON IA	FACE	728B
12	AIWN 1B	TIME	26D
	AM8N I	AMEN	45A
	AM8N I	AMEN	45B
	DUNAMIS I	POWER	206C
	EULOGIA I	PRAISE	323A
	EUCHARISTIA 2	THANKFULNESS	329A
	ISCHUS	STRENGTH	384B
	SOPHIA 3B	WISDOM	767B
	TIM8 2B	HONOR	825C
13	ERCHOMAI I1Aγ	COME	310C
	LEUKOS 2	WHITE	473D
	PERIBALLW 1B∝	THROW AROUND	651B
	POTHEN I	FROM WHERE	686D
	PRESBUTEROS 2Bγ	OLDER	707B
	STOL8	ROBE	777B
	TIS, TI IA∝	WHICH	826C
14	HAIMA 2B	BLOOD	22C
	ARNION	SHEEP	107D
	EN IIIIA	BY	260A
	ERCHOMAI I2C	COME	311C
	THLIPSIS I	TRIBULATION	362D
	KURIOS 1B	LORD	460B
	LEUKAINW 2	MAKE WHITE	473D
	MEGAS 2Aγ	GREAT	499A
	PLUNW I	WASH	680C
	STOL8	ROBE	777A
15	EIMI II9A	TO BE	223D
	ENWPION I	BEFORE	270A
	EPI IIIIA ζ	ON	288C
	THRONOS 1B	THRONE	364D
	LATREUW	SERVE	468C
	NAOS 1B	TEMPLE	535C
	NUX 1B	NIGHT	548D
	SK8NOW	LIVE	762D
16	DIPSAW I	THIRST	199C
	H8LIOS	THE SUN	346B
	KAUMA	HEAT	426C
	OUDE I	AND NOT	595D
	*OUTE	NOT	600C
	PAS IA∝	EVERY EACH	636C
	PEINAW I	HUNGER	645D
	PIPTW 2B∝	FALL	665D
17	ANA 1B	AMONG	49B
	ARNION	SHEEP	107D
	DAKRUON	TEAR	169A
	EXALEIPHW IA	WIPE AWAY	272A
	ZW8 2Bβ	LIFE	341D
	MESOS 2	THE MIDDLE	508C
	HOD8GEW I	LEAD	555D
	OPHTHALMOS I	EYE	604B

17	P8G8 2	FOUNTAIN 661D
	POIMAINW 2B	TEND 690B
	HUDWR 2	WATER 841A

REVELATION 8

1	ANOIGW 1D	OPEN 70C
	GINOMAI IIBβ	COME ABOUT 157B
	HEBDOMOS	SEVENTH 212A
	H8MIWRON	A HALF HOUR 348D
	HOTAN 2D	WHEN 592B
	SIG8	SILENCE 757B
	SPHRAGIS IA	SEAL 804B
	HWS IV5	WHEN 907C
2	AGGELOS 2A	ANGEL 7D
	ENWPION I	BEFORE 270A
	HEPTA	SEVEN 306B
	HIST8MI II2Bβ	BEING 383C
	SALPIGX I	TRUMPET 748B
3	DIDWMI	GIVE 191D
	ENWPION I	BEFORE 270A
	ERCHOMAI IIAα	COME 310B
	ECHW IIA	HAVE 332A
	THUSIAST8RION IBβ	ALTAR 367B
	HINA I2	IN ORDER THAT 377C
	LIBANWTOS	CENSER 474D
	HO,H8,TO IIIF	THE 553A
	PAS ID α	ALL 637C
	POLUS IIAβ	MANY 694B
3A	CHRUSOUS	GOLDEN 897B
3B	CHRUSOUS	GOLDEN 897B
3F	THUMIAMA IB	INCENSE 365D
3F	PROSEUCH8 I	PRAYER 720B
4	ANABAINW IB	GO UP 50A
	ENWPION I	BEFORE 270A
	KAPNOS	SMOKE 404A
	CHEIR I	HAND 888B
5	ASTRAP8	LIGHTNING 117D
	BRONT8	THUNDER 147A
	GEMIZW 2	FILL 152D
	GINOMAI IIBα	COME ABOUT 157B
	EK 4Aζ	FROM 235C
	THUSIAST8RION IBβ	ALTAR 367B
	LIBANWTOS	CENSER 474D
	PUR IB	FIRE 737C
	SEISMOS	SHAKING 753D
	PHWN8 I	SOUND 878D
6	AGGELOS 2A	ANGEL 7D
	HEPTA	SEVEN 306B
	HETOIMAZW 2	PREPARE 316C
	ECHW IIA	HAVE 332A
	SALPIGX I	TRUMPET 748B
6=13	SALPIZW SOUND THE TRUMPET	748C
7	HAIMA 3	BLOOD 22D
	GINOMAI IIBα	COME ABOUT 157B
	DENDRON	TREE 173C
	MEIGNUMI I	MIX 500D
	PAS IAβ	EVERY EACH 636D
	PRWTOS IB	FIRST 733A
	PUR IB	FIRE 737C
	CHALAZA	HAIL 882B
	CHLWROS I	YELLOWISH GREEN 891A
	CHORTOS	GRASS 892B
7A	KATAKAIW	CONSUME 412A
7B	KATAKAIW	CONSUME 412A
7C	KATAKAIW	CONSUME 412A
7F	BALLW IB	THROW 130C
7=12	TRITOS 2	THIRD 834C
8	HAIMA 3	BLOOD 22D
	KAIW IA	LIGHT 397A
	MEGAS IA	LARGE 498C
	OROS	MOUNTAIN 586B
	PUR IA	FIRE 737B
	HWS II3Aα	SO 906A
8F	THALASSA IA	SEA 350B
9	DIAPHTHEIRW I	SPOIL 189D
	ECHW I2Cα	HAVE 332D
	KTISMA	CREATURE 457B
	PLOION I	SHIP 679B
	PSUCH8 IAα	SOUL LIFE 901C
10	AST8R	STAR 117B
	KAIW IA	LIGHT 397A
	LAMPAS I	TORCH 466D
	MEGAS IA	LARGE 498C
	OURANOS IC	HEAVEN 598C
	P8G8 I	FOUNTAIN 661C
	POTAMOS I	RIVER 701B
	HUDWR I	WATER 840C
10A	PIPTW IA	FALL 665A
10A	TRITOS I	THIRD 834B
10B	PIPTW IA	FALL 665A
11	ANTHRWPOS IB	MAN 67D
	APOTHN8SKW IAα	DIE 91A
	GINOMAI I4A	BECOME 158D
	EIS 8Aα	229C
	EK 3Eβ	BY 234C
	LEGW II3	CALL 471B
	ONOMA I2A	NAME 574B
	PIKRAINW I	MAKE BITTER 663A
	POLUS I2Aα	MANY 694D
11A	APSINTHION	WORMWOOD 129A
11A	HUDWR I	WATER 840C
11B	APSINTHION	WORMWOOD 129A
11B	HUDWR I	WATER 840C
12	AST8R	STAR 117B
	H8LIOS	THE SUN 346B
	H8MERA IA	DAY 346C
	NUX IA	NIGHT 548C
	PL8SSW 2	STRIKE 679A
	SKOTIZW I	BECOME DARK 764D
	PHAINW I	SHINE 859B
13	AETOS	EAGLE 19B
	HEIS 3B	SOMEONE 230D
	EK 3F	BY 234D
	KATOIKEW IA	LIVE 425C
	LEGW I6	SAY 470A
	LOIPOS IA	REMAINING 481A
	MESOURAN8MA	IN MIDHEAVEN 509B
	OUAI IC	WOE 595C
	OUAI IA	WOE 595C
	PETOMAI	FLY 660A
	SALPIGX I	TRUMPET 748B
13B	PHWN8 I	SOUND 878C

REVELATION 9

1	AST8R	STAR	117B
	KLEIS 1	KEY	435A
	OURANOS 1C	HEAVEN	598C
	PEMPTOS	FIFTH	647B
	PIPTW 1A	FALL	665A
	SALPIZW	SOUND THE TRUMPET	748C
	PHREAR	A WELL	873D
1F	ABUSSOS 2	ABYSS	2B
1FF	KAI 12B	AND	393A
2	A8R	AIR	19D
	ANABAINW 1B	GO UP	50A
	ANOIGW 1B	OPEN	70C
	EK 3E8	BY	234C
	H8LIOS	THE SUN	346B
	KAMINOS	FURNACE	402D
	MEGAS 1A	LARGE	498C
	SKOTOW 1	DARKEN	765B
2A	KAPNOS	SMOKE	404A
2A	PHREAR	A WELL	873D
2B	KAPNOS	SMOKE	404A
2B	PHREAR	A WELL	873D
2C	PHREAR	A WELL	873D
2F	KAPNOS	SMOKE	404A
3	DIDWMI 1B8	GIVE	192B
	EXOUSIA 2	ABILITY	277D
	SKORPIOS 1	THE SCORPION	764C
4	ADIKEW 2B	INJURE	17B
	ANTHRWPOS 1A8	MAN	67C
	DENDRON	TREE	173C
	EPI 11A∝	ON	285D
	HINA 12	IN ORDER THAT	377D
	METWPON	FOREHEAD	517A
	MONOS 1AY	ONLY	529C
	OUTE	NOT	600C
	PAS 1A∝	EVERY EACH	636D
	SPHRAGIS 1C	SEAL	804B
	CHLWROS 1	YELLOWISH GREEN	891A
	CHORTOS	GRASS	892B
5	APOKTEINW 1A	KILL	93C
	BASANIZW 2A	TORMENT	134A
	DIDWMI 1B8	GIVE	192B
	HINA 12	IN ORDER THAT	377D
	HINA 111A∫	IN ORDER THAT	378B
	M8N 1	MONTH	520D
	PAIW 1	STRIKE	610B
	SKORPIOS 1	THE SCORPION	764C
5A	BASANISMOS 2	TORMENTING	134B
5B	BASANISMOS 1	TORMENTING	134B
6	EKEINOS 2B8	THAT	239B
	EPITHUMEW	DESIRE	293A
	HEURISKW 1A	FIND	325A
	Z8TEW 2B∝	SEEK	339C
	THANATOS 1A	DEATH	351B
	PHEUGW 1	FLEE	863C
7	ANTHRWPOS 1A8	MAN	67C
	HETOIMAZW 1	PREPARE	316B
	HIPPOS	HORSE	381B
	KEPHAL8 1A	HEAD	431B
	HOMOIOS 1	LIKE	569C
	HOMOIWMA 3	LIKENESS	570C
	POLEMOS 1B	ARMED CONFLICT	691D

7	STEPHANOS 1	WREATH	775A
	CHRUSOS	GOLD	897A
7A	PROSWPON 1A	FACE	728A
7A	HWS 113A∝	SO	906A
7B	PROSWPON 1A	FACE	728A
8	ECHW 12C∝	HAVE	332D
	THRIX 1	HAIR	364C
	LEWN 1	LION	474A
	ODOUS	TOOTH	557B
	HWS 113B	SO	906A
8B	HWS 113B	SO	906B
9	HARMA	CARRIAGE	107A
	ECHW 11B	HAVE	332B
	HIPPOS	HORSE	381B
	POLEMOS 1B	ARMED CONFLICT	691D
	POLUS 11A∝	MANY	694A
	PTERUX	WING	734D
	SID8ROUS	IRON	757C
	TRECHW 1	RUN	833C
9A	PHWN8 1	SOUND	878C
9B	THWRAX 1	BREASTPLATE	368A
10	ADIKEW 2B	INJURE	17B
	EXOUSIA 2	ABILITY	277D
	KENTRON 1	STING	429C
	M8N 1	MONTH	520D
	HOMOIOS 1	LIKE	569D
	OURA	TAIL	598A
	SKORPIOS 1	THE SCORPION	764C
11	ABADDWN	ABADDON	1B
	ABUSSOS 2	ABYSS	2B
	AGGELOS 2C	ANGEL	8A
	APOLLUWN	APOLLYON	95A
	BASILEUS 2C	KING	136A
	HEBRAISTI	IN HEBREW	212C
	HELL8NIKOS	GREEK	251C
	HOS,H8,HO 13A	(REL PRON)	587C
11A	ONOMA 11	NAME	574A
11B	ONOMA 12A	NAME	574B
12	APERCHOMAI 1B	GO AWAY	83D
	HEIS 4	ONE	231A
	ETI 2A	STILL	316A
	IDOU 1A	BEHOLD	371C
	HO,H8,TO 119C	THE	554D
12A	OUAI 2	WOE	595D
12B	OUAI 2	WOE	595D
13	HEIS 2A	ONE	230B
	ENWPION 1	BEFORE	270A
	THUSIAST8RION 1B8	ALTAR	367B
	KERAS 2	HORN	430B
	HO,H8,TO 111F	THE	553A
	SALPIZW	SOUND THE TRUMPET	748C
	PHWN8 2D	VOICE	879C
	CHRUSOUS	GOLDEN	697B
14	DEW 2	BIND	177A
	EPI 111A6	AT	286D
	EUPHRAT8S	EUPHRATES	328B
	POTAMOS 1	RIVER	701B
	SALPIGX 1	TRUMPET	748B
14F	LUW 2A	LOOSE	484D
15	EIS 2A8	FOR	228A
	ENIAUTOS 1	YEAR	265D
	HETOIMAZW 2	PREPARE	316C
	H8MERA 2	DAY	346D

15	H8MERA 2	DAY 347A
	M8N 1	MONTH 520D
	TRITOS 2	THIRD 834C
	HWRA 2Aα	TIME OF DAY 904B
16	ARITHMOS 1	NUMBER 106A
	DISMURIAS	A DOUBLE MYRIAD 198D
	DIS	TWICE 198D
	HIPPIKOS	CAVALRY 381B
	MURIAS 2	MYRIADS 531C
	STRATEUMA	ARMY 778A
17	EIDON 1A	SEE 219D
	EPI IIAα	ON 285D
	ECHW IIB	HAVE 332B
	THEIWD8S	SULPHUROUS 354D
	THWRAX 1	BREASTPLATE 368A
	HIPPOS	HORSE 381B
	KATH8MAI 1Aα	SIT 390B
	KEPHAL8 1A	HEAD 431B
	LEWN 1	LION 474A
	HORASIS 3	APPEARANCE 581B
	HOUTW 5	THUS 602D
	PURINOS	FIERY 738B
	HUAKINTHINOS	HYACINTH-COLORED 839A
17F	EKPOREUOMAI 2	GO OUT 244A
17F	THEION	SULPHUR 354B
17F	KAPNOS	SMOKE 404A
17F	PUR 1B	FIRE 737C
17-19	STOMA 1C	MOUTH 777C
18	APOKTEINW 1A	KILL 93C
	PL8G8 3	BLOW 674B
	TRITOS 2	THIRD 834C
19	ADIKEW 2B	INJURE 17C
	EXOUSIA 2	ABILITY 277D
	HIPPOS	HORSE 381B
	KEPHAL8 1A	HEAD 431B
	HOMOIOS 1	LIKE 569C
	OURA	TAIL 598A
	OPHIS 1	SNAKE 604D
20	ARGUROUS	(MADE OF) SILVER 104C
	BLEPW 1B	SEE 143A
	DAIMONION 2	DEMON 168C
	EIDWLON 1	IDOL 220D
	HINA I2	IN ORDER THAT 377D
	HINA II2	IN ORDER THAT 378D
	LOIPOS 1B	REMAINING 481A
	XULINOS	WOODEN 551A
	*OUTE	NOT 600C
	PERIPATEW 1C	GO ABOUT 655A
	PL8G8 3	BLOW 674B
	PROSKUNEW	DO REVERENCE 723B
	PROSKUNEW 3	DO REVERENCE 724B
	*CHALKOUS	MADE OF COPPER 883B
	CHEIR 1	HAND 888B
	CHRUSOUS	GOLDEN 897B
20F	EK 1C	AWAY FROM 233D
20F	METANOEW	CHANGE ONES MIND 513C
21	KLEMMA	THEFT 435B
	OUTE	NOT 600A
	PORNEIA 2	PROSTITUTION 700A
	PHARMAKEIA	SORCERY 861D
	PHARMAKON 2	MAGIC POTION 862A
	PHONOS	MURDER 872C

REVELATION 10

1	H8LIOS	THE SUN 346B
	IRIS 1	RAINBOW 381C
	ISCHUROS 1A	STRONG 384A
	KATABAINW 1Aγ	COME DOWN 409C
	KEPHAL8 1A	HEAD 431B
	NEPHEL8	CLOUD 538D
	OURANOS 2C	HEAVEN 599C
	PERIBALLW 1Bα	THROW AROUND 651D
	POUS 1A	FOOT 703C
	PROSWPON 1A	FACE 728A
	STULOS	PILLAR 779C
2	ANOIGW 1C	OPEN 70C
	BIBLARIDION	LITTLE BOOK 140C
	DEXIOS 1	RIGHT 173C
	EUWNUMOS	LEFT 330A
	ECHW IIA	HAVE 332A
	TITH8MI IIAβ	PUT 823D
3	KRAZW 1	CRY OUT 448D
	LALEW 1	SOUND 464A
	LEWN 1	LION 474A
	MUKAOMAI	ROAR 531A
	HWSPER 2	(JUST) AS 908A
3B	PHWN8 2C	VOICE 879A
3F	BRONT8	THUNDER 147A
3F	HEPTA	SEVEN 306B
4	MELLW 1Cα	BE ABOUT TO 502A
	SPHRAGIZW 2A	SEAL 804A
	PHWN8 2D	VOICE 879C
4A	LALEW 1	SOUND 464A
4B	LALEW 1	SOUND 464A
5	AIRW 1A	LIFT UP 23D
	DEXIOS 1	RIGHT 173C
	EPI IIAα	ON 285D
	HIST8MI II2Bβ	BEING 383C
6	AIWN 1B	TIME 27A
	EN IV5	IN 260D
	THALASSA 1A	SEA 350D
	KTIZW	CREATE 456C
	OMNUW	TAKE AN OATH 569A
	HOTI 1Bα	THAT 592D
	OUKETI 1	NO LONGER 596D
	CHRONOS	TIME 896C
6F	OMNUW	TAKE AN OATH 569A
7	DOULOS 4	SLAVE 205A
	HEBDOMOS	SEVENTH 212A
	EUAGGELIZW 1	317C
	ANNOUNCE GOOD NEWS	
	H8MERA 4B	TIME 348B
	MELLW 1Cα	BE ABOUT TO 502B
	MUST8RION 3	MYSTERY 532C
	SALPIZW	SOUND THE TRUMPET 748C
	TELEW 1	FINISH 818D
	PHWN8 1	SOUND 878C
8	ANOIGW 1C	OPEN 70C
	BIBLARIDION	LITTLE BOOK 140C
	BIBLION 1	BOOK 140D
	EPI IIAα	ON 285D
	HIST8MI II2Bβ	BEING 383C
	LALEW 2Aδ	SPEAK 464C
	HUPAGW 2	GO AWAY 844C
	PHWN8 2D	VOICE 879C

9	APERCHOMAI 2	GO 84A	6	EAN II	IF 211A
	KOILIA 1	BELLY 438B		EIS 4B	TO 228B
	KOILIA 3	BELLY 438B		EXOUSIA 2	ABILITY 277D
	LEGW III C	ORDER 470D		H8MERA 4B	TIME 348B
	PIKRAINW 1	MAKE BITTER 663A		THELW 2	WISH 355D
9F	BIBLARIDION	LITTLE BOOK 140C		KLEIW 2	SHUT 435B
9F	GLUKUS	SWEET 161B		HOSAKIS	AS OFTEN AS 589B
9F	KATESTHIW 1	EAT UP 423B		OURANOS 1B	HEAVEN 598C
9F	MELI	HONEY 501C		PATASSW 2	STRIKE 640B
9F	STOMA 1A	MOUTH 777B		PL8G8 3	BLOW 674B
10	GEMIZW 3	FILL 153A		PROPH8TEIA 1	PROPHECY 730A
	ESTHIW 1A	EAT 312D		STREPHW 1Aβ	TURN 778D
	KOILIA 1	BELLY 438B		HUETOS	RAIN 841A
	PIKRAINW 1	MAKE BITTER 663A	6B	EXOUSIA 3	AUTHORITY 278A
	CHEIR 1	HAND 888B	7	ABUSSOS 2	ABYSS 2B
11	GLWSSA 2	LANGUAGE 161C		ANABAINW 1Aβ	GO UP 50A
	EPI III B6	ON 287C		TH8RION 1B	BEAST 361D
	LAOS 2	PEOPLE 468A		MARTURIA 1	TESTIMONY 494C
	POLUS II Aα	MANY 694A		META AII3A	WITH 510C
	PROPH8TEUW 3	PROPHESY 730C		NIKAW 2A	CONQUER 541B
				POIEW II B6	DO 687C
	REVELATION 11			POLEMOS 1A	ARMED CONFLICT 691D
				TELEW 1	FINISH 818C
1	EGEIRW 1B	RAISE UP 214A	8	AIGUPTOS	EGYPT 21C
	THUSIAST8RION 1A	ALTAR 367B		KALEW 1Aγ	CALL 400A
	KALAMOS 3	MEASURING ROD 399C		KURIOS 2Cγ	LORD 461B
	METREW 1A	MEASURE 516A		HOPOU 1Aα	WHERE 579C
	METREW 1A	MEASURE 516B		HOSTIS 3	WHOEVER 591B
	NAOS 1A	TEMPLE 535B		PLATEIA	WIDE ROAD 672D
	HOMOIOS 1	LIKE 569C		PNEUMATIKWS 2	SPIRITUALLY 685D
	PROSKUNEW 2A	DO REVERENCE 724A		POLIS 1	CITY 692B
	RABDOS	ROD 740D		SODOMA	SODOM 766B
2	HAGIOS 1Aα	DEDICATED TO GOD 9B		STAUROW 1	CRUCIFY 773A
	AUL8 3	COURT 121A	8F	PTWMA	CORPSE 735B
	EKBALLW 3	TAKE OUT 237B	9	APHI8MI 4	TOLERATE 126A
	METREW 1A	MEASURE 516A		GLWSSA 2	LANGUAGE 161C
	M8N 1	MONTH 520D		EK 4Aγ	FROM 235B
	NAOS 1A	TEMPLE 535B		H8MERA 2	DAY 347A
	PATEW 1Aγ	TRAMPLE 640C		H8MISUS 2	HALF 348D
	POLIS 1	CITY 692B		LAOS 2	PEOPLE 468A
2A	EXWTHEN 2B	OUTSIDE 279C		MN8MA	TOMB 526C
2B	EXWTHEN 1C	OUTSIDE 279C		TITH8MI II Aβ	PUT 823C
3	HEX8KONTA	SIXTY 275C		PHUL8 2	NATION 876D
	H8MERA 2	DAY 347A	9A	PTWMA	CORPSE 735B
	MARTUS 2C	WITNESS 495C	9B	PTWMA	CORPSE 735B
	PERIBALLW 1Bα	THROW AROUND 651D	10	BASANIZW 2A	TORMENT 134A
	PROPH8TEUW 1	PROPHESY 730B		DWRON 1	GIFT 210A
	SAKKOS	SACK 747C		EUPHRAINW 2	GLADDEN 328A
	CHILIOI	THOUSAND 890B		KATOIKEW 1A	LIVE 425C
4	ELAIA 1	OLIVE TREE 247B		PEMPW 2	SEND 648A
	ENWPION 1	BEFORE 270A		PROPH8T8S 4	PROPHET 731B
	HIST8MI II2Bβ	BEING 383C		*CHAIRW 1	REJOICE 881B
	LUCHNIA	LAMPSTAND 484B	11	EISERCHOMAI 1Bβ	COME 232A
5	ADIKEW 2B	INJURE 17B		EN 16	IN 259C
	EI 12	IF 218B		EPI III Bγ	ON 289A
	EI VII	219B		EPIPIPTW 2	FALL UPON 297C
	EKPOREUOMAI 2	GO OUT 244A		ZW8 1A	LIFE 340D
	THELW 2	WISH 355D		H8MISUS 2	HALF 348D
	KATESTHIW 2	DESTROY 423B		HIST8MI III E	STAND 383B
	PUR 1B	FIRE 737C		PIPTW 2Bγ	FALL 665D
	STOMA 1A	MOUTH 777B		PNEUMA 2	SPIRIT 680D
6	HAIMA 3	BLOOD 22D		PHOBOS 2Aα	FEAR 871C
	BRECHW 1	WET 147A	11F	THEWREW 1	OBSERVE 360C

12	ANABAINW I Aβ	GO UP 50A
	ANABAINW I Aβ	GO UP 50A
	NEPHEL8	CLOUD 538D
	PHWN8 2D	VOICE 879C
	HWDE I	HERE 903B
13	GINOMAI IIBα	COME ABOUT 157B
	DEKATOS 2A	TENTH 173A
	DOXA 3	FAME 203B
	EKEINOS 2Bγ	THAT 239B
	EMPHOBOS	AFRAID 257B
	LOIPOS IB	REMAINING 481A
	ONOMA III	PEOPLE 577A
	OURANOS 2A	HEAVEN 599A
	POLIS I	CITY 692A
	*CHILIAS	THOUSAND 890B
	HWRA 3	TIME OF DAY 905A
13A	SEISMOS	SHAKING 753D
13B	SEISMOS	SHAKING 753D
14	APERCHOMAI IB	GO AWAY 83D
	DEUTEROS 2	SECOND 176A
	IDOU IA	BEHOLD 371C
	HO,H8,TO II9C	THE 554D
	TACHUS 2B	QUICK 815A
	TRITOS I	THIRD 834B
14A	OUAI 2	WOE 595D
14B	OUAI 2	WOE 595D
15	BASILEUW IBγ	RULE 136B
	GINOMAI IIBβ	COME ABOUT 157B
	GINOMAI I3C	TAKE PLACE 158B
	HEBDOMOS	SEVENTH 212A
	KOSMOS 4A	WORLD 447A
	KURIOS 2A	LORD 460B
	SALPIZW	SOUND THE TRUMPET 748C
	CHRISTOS I	ANOINTED ONE 895B
16	EIKOSI	TWENTY 221A
	ENWPION I	BEFORE 270A
	EPI IIIIAζ	ON 288C
	THRONOS IE	THRONE 365A
	KATH8MAI IAα	SIT 390B
	PIPTW IBα	FALL 665B
	PRESBUTEROS 2Bγ	OLDER 707B
	PROSKUNEW 2A	DO REVERENCE 724A
	PROSWPON IA	FACE 728B
17	BASILEUW IBα	RULE 136B
	BASILEUW 2	BECOME KING 136B
	EIMI II	TO BE 222A
	EUCHARISTEW 2	GIVE THANKS 328D
	PANTOKRATWR	ALMIGHTY 613D
18	DIDWMI 4	GIVE 192C
	DOULOS 4	SLAVE 205A
	KAIROS 3	TIME 396A
	KRINW 4Bα	JUDGE 452D
	MEGAS 2Aα	GREAT 498D
	MIKROS IB	SMALL 523A
	MISTHOS 2A	REWARD 525B
	ONOMA I4B	NAME 575B
	ORG8 2B	ANGER 583A
	ORGIZW	BE ANGRY 583B
	PROPH8T8S 5	PROPHET 731C
	PHOBEW 2A	BE AFRAID 871B
18A	DIAPHTHEIRW I	SPOIL 189D
18B	DIAPHTHEIRW 2	SPOIL 189D
19	ANOIGW IB	OPEN 70C

19	ASTRAP8	LIGHTNING 117D
	BRONT8	THUNDER 147A
	GINOMAI IIBα	COME ABOUT 157B
	DIATH8K8 3	COVENANT 182C
	KIBWTOS 2	BOX 433A
	MEGAS 2Aγ	GREAT 499A
	HORAW IA6	SEE 581D
	SEISMOS	SHAKING 753D
	PHWN8 I	SOUND 878D
	CHALAZA	HAIL 882B
19A	NAOS IB	TEMPLE 535C
19B	NAOS IB	TEMPLE 535C

REVELATION 12

I	AST8R	STAR 117B
	EN IIA	IN 257D
	EPI IIAα	ON 285D
	H8LIOS	THE SUN 346B
	KEPHAL8 IA	HEAD 431A
	HORAW IA6	SEE 581D
	OURANOS IB	HEAVEN 598C
	PERIBALLW IBα	THROW AROUND 651D
	SEL8N8	MOON 754A
	S8MEION 2C	SIGN 755D
	STEPHANOS I	WREATH 775A
	HUPOKATW	UNDER 852C
I=17	GUN8 4	WOMAN 167C
2	BASANIZW 2A	TORMENT 134A
	GAST8R 2	WOMB 152A
	ECHW I2J	HAVE 333C
	KRAZW I	CRY OUT 448D
	TIKTW I	GIVE BIRTH 824C
	WDINW	SUFFER BIRTH PANGS 904A
3	DEKA	TEN 172D
	DIADECHOMAI	DIADEM 181D
	DRAKWN	DRAGON 205D
	ECHW I2Cα	HAVE 332D
	IDOU 2	THERE IS 371D
	KERAS I	HORN 430B
	KEPHAL8 IA	HEAD 431B
	MEGAS IA	LARGE 498C
	HORAW IA6	SEE 581D
	OURANOS IB	HEAVEN 598C
	PURROS	RED (AS FIRE) 738D
	S8MEION 2C	SIGN 755D
4	BALLW IB	THROW 130C
	DRAKWN	DRAGON 205C
	ENWPION I	BEFORE 270A
	HIST8MI II2Bβ	BEING 383C
	KATESTHIW I	EAT UP 423B
	MELLW IBα	BE ABOUT TO 502A
	OURA	TAIL 598A
	OURANOS IC	HEAVEN 598C
	ST8KW I	STAND 775C
	SURW	DRAG 802A
	TEKNON IAα	CHILD 815D
	TRITOS 2	THIRD 834C
4A	TIKTW I	GIVE BIRTH 824C
4B	TIKTW I	GIVE BIRTH 824C
5	HARPAZW 2B	SNATCH 108D
	ARS8N	MALE 109C
	EN IIIIA	BY 260A

5 THRONOS 1B THRONE 364D
  MELLW 1C6 IS DESTINED 502C
  POIMAINW 2Aγ TEND 690B
  RABDOS ROD 740D
  SID8ROUS IRON 757C
  TEKNON 1Aβ CHILD 816A
  TIKTW 1 GIVE BIRTH 824C
6 APO V6 BY 88A
  EKEI 1 THERE 238D
  HEX8KONTA SIXTY 275C
  ER8MOS 2 DESERT 309A
  HETOIMAZW 3 PREPARE 316C
  HINA I3 IN ORDER THAT 377D
  HOPOU 1Aα WHERE 579C
  *TOPOS 1E PLACE 830C
  TREPHW 1 FEED 833B
  PHEUGW 1 FLEE 863C
  CHILIOI THOUSAND 890B
7 AGGELOS 2A ANGEL 7D
  AGGELOS 2C ANGEL 8A
  GINOMAI 11Bβ COME ABOUT 157B
  DRAKWN DRAGON 205C
  META AII3A WITH 510C
  MICHA8L MICHAEL 526A
  POLEMOS 1B ARMED CONFLICT 691D
7A POLEMEW 1A FIGHT 691C
7B POLEMEW 1A FIGHT 691C
7F OURANOS 1D HEAVEN 598D
8 ETI 1Bβ STILL 316A
  HEURISKW 1B FIND 325B
  ISCHUW 3 BE STRONG 384C
  *OUTE NOT 600C
  TOPOS 1F PLACE 830C
9 AGGELOS 2C ANGEL 8A
  ARCHAIOS 1 ANCIENT 110D
  BALLW 1B THROW 130C
  DRAKWN DRAGON 205C
  KALEW 1Aγ CALL 400A
  MEGAS 1A LARGE 498C
  OIKOUMEN8 1B THE WORLD 564A
  OPHIS 3 SNAKE 605A
  PLANAW 1B DECEIVE 671B
  SATAN ADVERSARY 752B
10 ADELPHOS 2 BROTHER 16A
  ANTIDIKOS OPPONENT 73C
  ARTI 1 NOW 109D
  ENWPION 2B BEFORE 270B
  EXOUSIA 3 AUTHORITY 278A
  KATABALLW 1 THROW DOWN 409D
  KAT8GOREW 1B BRING CHARGES 424C
  KAT8GWR ACCUSER 424D
  KAT8GOROS ACCUSER 424D
  NUX 1B NIGHT 548D
  SWT8RIA 2 DELIVERANCE 809B
  PHWN8 2D VOICE 879C
  CHRISTOS 1 ANOINTED ONE 895B
11 AGAPAW 2 LOVE 5A
  HAIMA 2B BLOOD 22C
  ARNION SHEEP 107D
  ACHRI 1C AS FAR AS 128C
  DIA 8II4A BY 180C
  THANATOS 1A DEATH 351C
  MARTURIA 2Dα TESTIMONY 494C

11 NIKAW 2A CONQUER 541B
  PSUCH8 1Aβ SOUL LIFE 901C
12 EUPHRAINW 2 GLADDEN 328A
  ECHW I2E8 HAVE 333A
  THUMOS 2 ANGER 366A
  KAIROS 2 TIME 395D
  KATABAINW 1A6 COME DOWN 409C
  MEGAS 2Aγ GREAT 499A
  OLIGOS 2C LITTLE 566C
  OUAI 1C WOE 595C
  OURANOS 1E HEAVEN 598D
  OURANOS 2E HEAVEN 599D
  SK8NOW LIVE 762D
13 ARS8N MALE 109C
  BALLW 1B THROW 130C
  DIWKW 2 PERSECUTE 200B
  DRAKWN DRAGON 205C
  EIDON 1D SEE 219D
  HOSTIS 3 WHOEVER 591B
  TIKTW 1 GIVE BIRTH 824C
14 AETOS EAGLE 19B
  APO III AWAY FROM 86D
  EKEI 1 THERE 238D
  ER8MOS 2 DESERT 309A
  H8MISUS 2 HALF 348D
  KAIROS 4 TIME 396B
  MEGAS 1A LARGE 498C
  HOPOU 1Aα WHERE 579C
  PETOMAI FLY 660A
  PROSWPON 1Cα FACE 728C
  PTERUX WING 734D
  TOPOS 1E PLACE 830C
  TREPHW 1 FEED 833B
14F OPHIS 3 SNAKE 605A
15 OPISW 2Aβ AFTER 578C
  POIEW 11B1 DO 688B
  POTAMOPHOR8TOS 701C
     SWEPT AWAY BY A RIVER
  STOMA 1C MOUTH 777C
15F BALLW 1B THROW 130C
15F POTAMOS 1 RIVER 701B
16 ANOIGW 1Eα OPEN 70D
  B08THEW 2 AID 144A
  KATAPINW 1A SWALLOW 417B
16A STOMA 1D MOUTH 777C
16B STOMA 1C MOUTH 777C
16F DRAKWN DRAGON 205C
17 ENTOL8 2B COMMAND 268D
  EPI IIIBγ ON 287B
  ECHW IIC8 KEEP 332B
  LOIPOS 2Bα THE OTHERS 481A
  MARTURIA 2Dγ TESTIMONY 494D
  META AII3A WITH 510C
  ORGIZW BE ANGRY 583B
  POIEW 11B6 DO 687C
  POLEMOS 1A ARMED CONFLICT 691D
  SPERMA 2B SEED 769C
  T8REW 5 KEEP 822D
18 AMMOS SAND 45D
  HIST8MI III1B STAND 383B

REVELATION 13

1	ANABAINW 1Aβ	GO UP 50A
	BLASPH8MIA 2B	SLANDER 142C
	DIADECHOMAI	DIADEM 181D
	KERAS 1	HORN 430B
	KEPHAL8 1A	HEAD 431B
1FF	TH8RION 1B	BEAST 361D
2	ARKOS	BEAR 107A
	DRAKWN	DRAGON 205C
	EXOUSIA 2	ABILITY 277D
	THRONOS 1E	THRONE 365A
	LEWN 1	LION 474A
	HOMOIOS 1	LIKE 569C
	PARDALIS	LEOPARD 629B
	STOMA 1C	MOUTH 777C
2A	HWS 1I3B	SO 906B
3	EIS 4E	SO THAT 228D
	THAUMAZW 2	WONDER 353A
	THERAPEUW 2	HEAL 359D
	KEPHAL8 1A	HEAD 431B
	OPISW 2Aβ	AFTER 578D
	SPHAZW	SLAUGHTER 803D
3A	THANATOS 1A	DEATH 351C
3B	THANATOS 1A	DEATH 351C
4	DRAKWN	DRAGON 205C
	EXOUSIA 2	ABILITY 277D
	META AII3A	WITH 510C
	HOMOIOS 1	LIKE 569D
	POLEMEW 1A	FIGHT 691C
4A	PROSKUNEW 3	DO REVERENCE 724B
4B	PROSKUNEW 3	DO REVERENCE 724B
5	BLASPH8MOS	SLANDEROUS 142C
	BLASPH8MIA 2B	SLANDER 142C
	EXOUSIA 1	RIGHT 277C
	LALEW 2B	SPEAK 464D
	MEGAS 2Bβ	GREAT 499C
	M8N 1	MONTH 520D
	POIEW 12C	DO 689B
6	ANOIGW 1Eα	OPEN 70D
	BLASPH8MEW 2Bβ	BLASPHEME 142B
	BLASPH8MIA 2B	SLANDER 142C
	ONOMA 14B	NAME 574D
	PROS III4A	TOWARD 717C
	SK8N8	TENT 762B
	SK8NOW	LIVE 762D
7	GLWSSA 2	LANGUAGE 161C
	DIDWMI 1Bβ	GIVE 192B
	EXOUSIA 3	AUTHORITY 278A
	LAOS 2	PEOPLE 468A
	META AII3A	WITH 510C
	NIKAW 2A	CONQUER 541B
	POIEW 11B6	DO 687C
	POLEMOS 1A	ARMED CONFLICT 691D
	PHUL8 2	NATION 876D
8	ARNION	SHEEP 107D
	BIBLION 1	BOOK 140D
	BIBLOS 2	BOOK 141A
	GRAPHW 2B	WRITE 165D
	KATABOL8 1	FOUNDATION 410A
	KATOIKEW 1A	LIVE 425C
	KOSMOS 2	WORLD 446D
	ONOMA 12A	NAME 574B
8	HOS,H8,HO 13A	(REL PRON) 587C
	PAS 1Dβ	ALL 637D
	SPHAZW	SLAUGHTER 803C
9	AKOUW 1A	HEAR 31B
	OUS 2	EAR 600B
10	AICHMALWSIA 1	CAPTIVITY 26B
	MACHAIRA 1	SWORD 497B
	PISTIS 2Dγ	FAITH 669C
	SUNAGW 2	GATHER 790A
	HUPAGW 2	GO AWAY 844C
	HUPOMON8 1	PATIENCE 854B
	HWDE 2B	HERE 903D
11	ANABAINW 1Aβ	GO UP 50A
	ARNION	SHEEP 107D
	DRAKWN	DRAGON 205C
	KERAS 1	HORN 430B
	LALEW 2Aε	SPEAK 464C
	HOMOIOS 1	LIKE 569D
11F	TH8RION 1B	BEAST 361D
12	AUTOS 3D	(OBLIQUE CASE) 123B
	ENWPION 5C	BEFORE 270C
	EXOUSIA 2	ABILITY 277D
	THANATOS 1A	DEATH 351C
	THERAPEUW 2	HEAL 359D
	HINA 12	IN ORDER THAT 377D
	KATOIKEW 1A	LIVE 425B
	HOS,H8,HO 13A	(REL PRON) 587C
	PAS 1Cα	ALL 637B
	PROSKUNEW 3	DO REVERENCE 724B
12A	POIEW 11Cα	DO 688B
12B	POIEW 11Bθ	DO 688B
13	ENWPION 2A	BEFORE 270B
	HINA II2	IN ORDER THAT 378D
	KATABAINW 1B	COME DOWN 409D
13A	POIEW 11Bβ	DO 687D
13B	POIEW 11Bθ	DO 688B
13F	S8MEION 2B	SIGN 755D
14	DIA BII4A	BY 180C
	EMOS 2	MY 255A
	ENWPION 5C	BEFORE 270C
	ECHW 12Eα	HAVE 333A
	LEGW III1C	ORDER 470D
	MACHAIRA 1	SWORD 497C
	HOS,H8,HO 13Bγ	(REL PRON) 587D
	PLANAW 1B	DECEIVE 671B
	PL8G8 2	BLOW 674B
14A	KATOIKEW 1A	LIVE 425C
14B	KATOIKEW 1A	LIVE 425C
14B	POIEW 11Aα	DO 687A
14F	DIDWMI 1Bβ	GIVE 192B
14F	EIKWN 1A	IMAGE 221B
14F	TH8RION 1B	BEAST 361D
15	M8 AI1	NOT 517C
	PNEUMA 2	SPIRIT 680D
	POIEW 11Bθ	DO 688B
	PROSKUNEW 3	DO REVERENCE 724B
16	DEXIOS 1	RIGHT 173C
	DOULOS 1B	SLAVE 204D
	ELEUTHEROS 1	FREE 250B
	HINA IIIAε	IN ORDER THAT 378B
	MEGAS 2Aα	GREAT 498D
	METWPON	FOREHEAD 517A
	MIKROS 1B	SMALL 523A

16	PLOUSIOS I	RICH 679C
	POIEW IIBθ	DO 688B
	PTWCHOS IA	BEGGING POOR 735C
	CHARAGMA I	A MARK 884A
17	AGORAZW I	BUY 12D
	8 IC	NOR 343A
	HINA I3	IN ORDER THAT 377D
	PWLEW	SELL 739A
	CHARAGMA I	A MARK 884A
17F	ARITHMOS I	NUMBER 106A
17F	TH8RION IB	BEAST 361D
18	ANTHRWPOS IAβ	MAN 67C
	DEKAHEX	SIXTEEN 172D
	HEXAKOSIOI	SIX HUNDRED 271D
	HEX8KONTA	SIXTY 275C
	NOUS I	THE UNDERSTANDING 546C
	SOPHIA 2	WISDOM 767A
	CHXZ	SIX HUNDRED SIXTY SIX 891A
	PS8PHIZW	COUNT 901A
	HWDE 2B	HERE 903D

REVELATION 14

I	ARNION	SHEEP 107D
	GRAPHW 2A	WRITE 165D
	HEKATON	ONE HUNDRED 236B
	EPI IIIIAζ	ON 288C
	HIST8MI II2Bβ	BEING 383C
	METWPON	FOREHEAD 517A
	OROS	MOUNTAIN 586B
	SIWN I	ZION 759D
	CHILIAS	THOUSAND 890B
2	BRONT8	THUNDER 147A
	KITHARA	LYRE 433A
	KITHARIZW	PLAY 433A
	KITHARWDOS	HARPIST 433A
	MARTUS 3	WITNESS 495D
	MEGAS 2Aγ	GREAT 499A
	POLUS IIAβ	MANY 694B
	HUDWR I	WATER 840D
	PHWN8 2D	VOICE 879C
2B	PHWN8 I	SOUND 878C
2C	PHWN8 I	SOUND 878C
2C	HWS II3B	SO 906B
2D	PHWN8 I	SOUND 878C
2F	AGGELOS 2A	ANGEL 7C
3	AGORAZW 2	BUY 12D
	ADW	SING 19A
	G8 5B	EARTH 156D
	HEKATON	ONE HUNDRED 236B
	ENWPION 2A	BEFORE 270B
	ZWON I	LIVING THING 342C
	KAINOS 2	NEW 395A
	MANTHANW 5	LEARN 491D
	OUDEIS 2A	NO ONE 596B
	PRESBUTEROS 2Bγ	OLDER 707B
	CHILIAS	THOUSAND 890B
	HWS II3Aβ	SO 906A
3A	WD8	SONG 903D
3B	WD8	SONG 903D
4	AGORAZW 2	BUY 12D
	APARCH8 2A	FIRST FRUITS 80D
	ARNION	SHEEP 107D

4	META ΔII3B	WITH 510D
	MOLUNW 2	DEFILE 528D
	HOPOU IBβ	WHERE 579D
	PARTHENOS 2	CHASTE MAN 632D
	HUPAGW 2	GO AWAY 844C
5	AMWMOS 2A	BLAMELESS 47B
	DOLOS	DECEIT 202B
	HEURISKW IB	FIND 325C
	STOMA IA	MOUTH 777C
	PSEUDOS	LIE 900C
6	AIWNIOS 3	ETERNAL 28A
	GLWSSA 2	LANGUAGE 161C
	EUAGGELIZW I	317C
		ANNOUNCE GOOD NEWS
	EUAGGELION 2A	GOSPEL 318B
	KATH8MAI IB	RESIDE 390C
	LAOS 2	PEOPLE 468A
	MESOURAN8MA	IN MIDHEAVEN 509B
	PETOMAI	FLY 660A
	PHUL8 2	NATION 876D
7	DOXA 3	FAME 203B
	ERCHOMAI IIBα	COME 311B
	THALASSA IA	SEA 350D
	KRISIS IAα	JUDGING 453C
	LEGW I6	SAY 470A
	OURANOS IAα	HEAVEN 598B
	P8G8 I	FOUNTAIN 661C
	POIEW IIAβ	DO 687B
	PROSKUNEW 2A	DO REVERENCE 724A
	HUDWR I	WATER 840C
	PHOBEW 2A	BE AFRAID 871A
	PHWN8 2A	VOICE 878D
	HWRA 3	TIME OF DAY 905A
8	AKOLOUTHEW I	FOLLOW 30C
	BABULWN	BABYLON 129B
	THUMOS I	PASSION 366A
	THUMOS 2	ANGER 366A
	OINOS I	WINE 565B
	PORNEIA 2	PROSTITUTION 700A
	POTIZW I	GIVE TO DRINK 702C
9	EIKWN IA	IMAGE 221B
	TH8RION IB	BEAST 361D
	LAMBANW 2	RECEIVE 466C
	LEGW I6	SAY 470A
	METWPON	FOREHEAD 517A
	TRITOS 2	THIRD 834C
	CHARAGMA I	A MARK 884A
10	AGGELOS 2A	ANGEL 7C
	HAGIOS IBβ	HOLY 9D
	AKRATOS	UNMIXED 32C
	ARNION	SHEEP 107D
	ACHRI IB	AS FAR AS 128C
	BASANIZW 2A	TORMENT 134A
	EK 4Aε	FROM 235B
	ENWPION 2A	BEFORE 270B
	THEION	SULPHUR 354B
	THUMOS 2	ANGER 366A
	KERANNUMI I	MIX 430B
	OINOS 2	WINE 565B
	ORG8 2B	ANGER 583A
	PINW 2Bα	DRINK 664C
	POT8RION 2	CUP 702B
	PUR IB	FIRE 737D

11	ANAPAUSIS 1	STOPPING 58B	18	AKMAZW	BE RIPE 30A
	BASANISMOS 2	TORMENTING 134B		BOTRUS	GRAPES 145A
	EIKWN 1A	IMAGE 221B		EXOUSIA 3	AUTHORITY 278A
	ECHW I2G	HAVE 333B		THUSIAST8RION 2A	ALTAR 367B
	TH8RION 1B	BEAST 361D		THUSIAST8RION 1Bβ	ALTAR 367B
	KAPNOS	SMOKE 404A		KRAUG8 1B	SHOUT 450C
	LAMBANW 2	RECEIVE 466C		PEMPW 2	SEND 648A
	NUX 1B	NIGHT 548D		STAPHUL8	BUNCH OF GRAPES 773A
	PROSKUNEW 3	DO REVERENCE 724B		TRUGAW	PICK (GRAPES) 836A
	CHARAGMA 1	A MARK 884A		PHWNEW 1B	CRY OUT 878B
12	ENTOL6 2B	COMMAND 268D	18B	DREPANON	SICKLE 205D
	PISTIS 2Bβ	FAITH 668D	18F	AMPELOS 1	VINE 46A
	T8REW 5	KEEP 822D	19	BALLW 1B	THROW 130C
	HUPOMON8 1	PATIENCE 854B		BALLW 2B	PUT 130D
	HWDE 2B	HERE 903D		THUMOS 2	ANGER 366A
13	AKOLOUTHEW 2	ACCOMPANY 30D		L8NOS	WINE PRESS 474B
	ANAPAUW 2	REST 58C		MEGAS 1B	LARGE 498D
	APARTI	EXACTLY 80C		TRUGAW	PICK (GRAPES) 836A
	APOTHN8SKW 1Aα	DIE 91A	20	HAIMA 3	BLOOD 22D
	ARTI 3	NOW 109D		APO III	AWAY FROM 86D
	GRAPHW 2A	WRITE 165C		HEXAKOSIOI	SIX HUNDRED 271D
	EK 1C	AWAY FROM 233D		EXERCHOMAI 2A	GO OUT 274C
	EN 15D	IN 259B		EXWTHEN 2B	OUTSIDE 279C
	ERGON 1Cβ	DEED 308A		HIPPOS	HORSE 381B
	HINA I2	IN ORDER THAT 377D		L8NOS	WINE PRESS 474B
	HINA III2	IN ORDER THAT 379A		PATEW 1Aα	TREAD 640B
	KOPOS 2	WORK 444C		STADION 1	STADE 771C
	KURIOS 2Cγ	LORD 461A		CHALINOS	BIT 882D
	MAKARIOS 1B	BLESSED 488A		CHILIOI	THOUSAND 890B
	META AIIIA	WITH 509D	20B	L8NOS	WINE PRESS 474B
	NAI 2	CERTAINLY 534D			
	PNEUMA 5Dα	SPIRIT 683A			REVELATION 15
	PHWN8 2D	VOICE 879C			
14	IDOU 2	THERE IS 371D	1	AGGELOS 2A	ANGEL 7D
	KEPHAL8 1A	HEAD 431A		*HEPTA	SEVEN 306B
	LEUKOS 2	WHITE 473D		ESCHATOS 3B	LAST 314A
	HOMOIOS 3	LIKE 570A		THAUMASTOS 2	WONDERFUL 353C
	OXUS 1	SHARP 578A		THUMOS 2	ANGER 366A
	STEPHANOS 1	WREATH 774D		HO,H8,TO IIIAα	THE 552B
	HUIOS 2C	SON 843B		PL8G8 3	BLOW 674B
	CHRUSOUS	GOLDEN 897B		S8MEION 2C	SIGN 755D
14A	NEPHEL8	CLOUD 538C		TELEW 1	FINISH 818D
14B	NEPHEL8	CLOUD 538D	2	ARITHMOS 1	NUMBER 106A
15	HARPAGMOS 2	ROBBERY 108B		EIKWN 1A	IMAGE 221B
	DREPANON	SICKLE 205D		EK 1D	AWAY FROM 233D
	EXERCHOMAI 1Aα	GO OUT 273D		TH8RION 1B	BEAST 361D
	ERCHOMAI IIBα	COME 311B		HIST8MI II2Bβ	BEING 383C
	THERIZW 2B	REAP 360A		KITHARA	LYRE 433A
	THERISMOS 2B	HARVEST 360A		MARTUS 3	WITNESS 495D
	KATH8MAI 1Aα	SIT 390B		MEIGNUMI 1	MIX 500D
	KRAZW 2A	CALL 448D		CHARAGMA 1	A MARK 884A
	KRAZW 2A	CALL 449A	2A	HUALINOS	OF GLASS 839B
	NAOS 1B	TEMPLE 535C	2B	HUALINOS	OF GLASS 839B
	X8RAINW 2A	DRY UP 550D	3	ADW	SING 19A
	PEMPW 2	SEND 648A		AL8THINOS 2	TRUE 36C
	HWRA 3	TIME OF DAY 905A		ARNION	SHEEP 107D
15F	NEPHEL8	CLOUD 538D		*BASILEUS 2B	KING 136A
16	THERIZW 2B	REAP 360A		DIKAIOS 4	RIGHTEOUS 195B
17	ECHW IIA	HAVE 332A		DOULOS 4	SLAVE 205A
	NAOS 1B	TEMPLE 535C		ERGON 1Cα	DEED 308A
17F	EXERCHOMAI 1Aα	GO OUT 273D		THAUMASTOS 2	WONDERFUL 353B
17F	OXUS 1	SHARP 578A		KURIOS 2A	LORD 460C
18	AGGELOS 2A	ANGEL 7D		MEGAS 2Aγ	GREAT 499A

3	MWUS8S	MOSES 533D	2	GINOMAI 14Cγ	COME, GO 159A
	HODOS 2B	WAY 557A		EIKWN 1A	IMAGE 221B
	PANTOKRATWR	ALMIGHTY 613D		HELKOS	SORE 251A
	WD8	SONG 903D		TH8RION 1B	BEAST 361D
4	DIKAIWMA 2	RIGHTEOUS DEED 197B		KAKOS 2	EVIL 398D
	ENWPION 1	BEFORE 270A		MARTUS 3	WITNESS 495D
	H8KW 1Dβ	HAVE COME 345C		PON8ROS 1Aβ	SICK 697C
	M8 DIA	NOT 519B		PROSKUNEW 3	DO REVERENCE 724B
	MONOS 1A6	ONLY 529D		CHARAGMA 1	A MARK 884A
	ONOMA 14B	NAME 575A	3	DEUTEROS 3	SECOND 176A
	HOSIOS 1B	PIOUS 589C		ZW8 1A	LIFE 340D
	PAS 1Dα	ALL 637C		NEKROS 2A	DEAD 537B
	PROSKUNEW 2A	DO REVERENCE 724A		PSUCH8 2	SOUL LIFE 902C
	PHANEROW 1B	REVEAL 860C		HWS 113B	SO 906B
5	ANOIGW 1B	OPEN 70C	3F	HAIMA 3	BLOOD 22D
	MARTURION 2	TESTIMONY 495A	4	P8G8 1	FOUNTAIN 661C
	NAOS 1B	TEMPLE 535C		POTAMOS 1	RIVER 701B
	SK8N8	TENT 762B		TRITOS 1	THIRD 834B
6	AGGELOS 2A	ANGEL 7D		HUDWR 1	WATER 840C
	ENDUW 2A	DRESS 263C	5	AGGELOS 2A	ANGEL 7D
	HEPTA	SEVEN 306B		AKOUW 1C	HEAR 31C
	ZWN8	BELT 342A		DIKAIOS 2	RIGHTEOUS 195A
	KATHAROS 1	CLEAN 388D		EIMI II	TO BE 222A
	LAMPROS 3	BRIGHT 467A		KRINW 4Bα	JUDGE 453B
	LITHOS 1C	STONE 475C		HOSIOS 2B	PIOUS 589D
	LINON 2	LINEN GARMENT 476C	6	*HAIMA 2A	BLOOD 22B
	NAOS 1B	TEMPLE 535C		AXIOS 2A	WORTHY 77D
	HO,H8,TO IIIAα	THE 552B		DIDWMI 2	GIVE 192C
	PERI 2Aβ	ABOUT 650D		EKCHEW 1	POUR OUT 246D
	PERIZWNNUMI 1	GIRD ABOUT 653A		PROPH8T8S 5	PROPHET 731C
	PERIZWNNUMI 2B	GIRD ABOUT 653A	7	AKOUW 1C	HEAR 31C
	PL8G8 3	BLOW 674B		AL8THINOS 2	TRUE 36C
	ST8THOS	CHEST 775B		DIKAIOS 4	RIGHTEOUS 195B
	CHRUSOUS	GOLDEN 897B		THUSIAST8RION 1Bβ	ALTAR 367B
6F	HEPTA	SEVEN 306B		KRISIS 1Aβ	JUDGING 454A
7	AIWN 1B	TIME 27A		KURIOS 2A	LORD 460C
	GEMW 1	BE FULL 153A		NAI 2	CERTAINLY 534D
	HEPTA	SEVEN 306B		PANTOKRATWR	ALMIGHTY 613D
	ZAW 1A∈	LIVE 336D	8	EKCHEW 1	POUR OUT 246D
	ZWON 1	LIVING THING 342C		H8LIOS	THE SUN 346B
	THUMOS 2	ANGER 366A		KAUMATIZW	BURN 426C
	PHIAL8	BOWL 866A		PUR 1B	FIRE 737C
8	ACHRI 2B	UNTIL 128C		PHIAL8	BOWL 866A
	GEMIZW 1	FILL 152D	9	BLASPH8MEW 2Bβ	BLASPHEME 142B
	DOXA 1A	BRIGHTNESS 202C		DOXA 3	FAME 203B
	EISERCHOMAI 1Aβ	COME 231D		EXOUSIA 2	ABILITY 277D
	EK 3C	FROM 234B		EPI IIIIBα	OVER 288D
	KAPNOS	SMOKE 404A		KAUMATIZW	BURN 426C
	PL8G8 3	BLOW 674B		KAUMA	HEAT 426C
	TELEW 1	FINISH 818D		MEGAS 2Aγ	GREAT 499A
8A	NAOS 1B	TEMPLE 535C		METANOEW	CHANGE ONES MIND 513C
8B	NAOS 1B	TEMPLE 535C		ONOMA 14B	NAME 574D
				PL8G8 3	BLOW 674B
	REVELATION 16		10	GLWSSA 1A	TONGUE 161B
				EK 3F	BY 234D
1	AGGELOS 2A	ANGEL 7D		EKCHEW 1	POUR OUT 246D
	HEPTA	SEVEN 306B		TH8RION 1B	BEAST 361D
	THUMOS 2	ANGER 366A		THRONOS 1E	THRONE 365A
	NAOS 1B	TEMPLE 535C		MASAOMAI	BITE 496A
	HUPAGW 2	GO AWAY 844C		PEMPTOS	FIFTH 647B
	PHWN8 2D	VOICE 879C		PONOS 2	PAIN 698B
1FF	EKCHEW 1	POUR OUT 246D		SKOTOW 1	DARKEN 765B
1=4	PHIAL8	BOWL 866A		PHIAL8	BOWL 866A

11 BLASPH8MEW 2Bα   BLASPHEME 142A
   EK 1C   AWAY FROM 233D
   EK 3F   BY 234D
   HELKOS   SORE 251A
   ERGON 1Cβ   DEED 308A
   METANOEW   CHANGE ONES MIND 513C
   OURANOS 2A   HEAVEN 599A
   PONOS 2   PAIN 698B
12 ANATOL8 2A   EAST 62A
   HEKTOS   SIXTH 245C
   EKCHEW 1   POUR OUT 246D
   HETOIMAZW 1   PREPARE 316B
   EUPHRAT8S   EUPHRATES 328B
   H8LIOS   THE SUN 346B
   X8RAINW 2A   DRY UP 550D
   HODOS 1A   WAY 556B
   POTAMOS 1   RIVER 701B
   HUDWR 1   WATER 840C
   PHIAL8   BOWL 866A
13 AKATHARTOS 2   IMPURE 28C
   BATRACHOS   FROG 137B
   DRAKWN   DRAGON 205C
   TH8RION 1B   BEAST 361D
   PNEUMA 4C   SPIRIT 682A
   PSEUDOPROPH8T8S FALSE PROPHET 900B
13A STOMA 1C   MOUTH 777C
13B STOMA 1C   MOUTH 777C
13C STOMA 1C   MOUTH 777C
14 DAIMONION 2   DEMON 168C
   DAIMWN   DEMON 168D
   EKPOREUOMAI 1C   GO OUT 244A
   H8MERA 3Bβ   DAY 347D
   H8MERA 3Bβ   DAY 348A
   MEGAS 2Bβ   GREAT 499C
   OIKOUMEN8 1A   THE WORLD 564A
   PANTOKRATWR   ALMIGHTY 613D
   PNEUMA 4C   SPIRIT 682A
   POIEW 11Bβ   DO 687C
   POLEMOS 1 ARMED CONFLICT 691D
   S8MEION 2B   SIGN 755D
   SUNAGW 2   GATHER 790A
15 ASCH8MOSUN8 2   SHAME 119A
   BLEPW 1A   SEE 142D
   GR8GOREW 2   BE AWAKE 166C
   GUMNOS 1   NAKED 166D
   KAI I2E   AND 393C
   KLEPT8S   THIEF 435C
   MAKARIOS 1B   BLESSED 488A
   PERIPATEW 1C   GO ABOUT 655A
   T8REW 3   KEEP 822D
16 HARMAGED(D)WN   ARMAGEDDON 107A
   HEBRAISTI   IN HEBREW 212C
   KALEW 1Aγ   CALL 400A
   SUNAGW 2   GATHER 790A
   TOPOS 1C   PLACE 830B
17 A8R   AIR 19D
   HEBDOMOS   SEVENTH 212A
   EKCHEW 1   POUR OUT 246D
   EXERCHOMAI 2Bα   GO OUT 274C
   NAOS 1B   TEMPLE 535C
   PHIAL8   BOWL 866A
   PHWN8 2D   VOICE 879B
18 APO 112C   SINCE 86C

18 ASTRAP8   LIGHTNING 117D
   BRONT8   THUNDER 147A
   GINOMAI 11Bα   COME ABOUT 157B
   GINOMAI 115   EXIST 159D
   HOIOS   OF WHAT SORT 565C
   HOS,H8,HO 111F   (REL PRON) 589A
   HOUTW   THUS 602B
   HOUTW 3   THUS 602D
   T8LIKOUTOS 2   SO GREAT 822B
   PHWN8 1   SOUND 878D
18A   SEISMOS   SHAKING 753D
18B   SEISMOS   SHAKING 753D
19 BABULWN   BABYLON 129B
   EIS 8Aα   229C
   ENWPION 5A   BEFORE 270C
   THUMOS 1   PASSION 366A
   THUMOS 2   ANGER 366A
   MEROS 1A   PART 507A
   MIMN8SKOMAI 2A BE MENTIONED 524C
   MIMN8SKOMAI 2B   524C
        BE CALLED TO REMEMBRANCE
   OINOS 2   WINE 565B
   ORG8 2B   ANGER 583A
   POT8RION 2   CUP 702B
19A   POLIS 1   CITY 692B
19B   POLIS 1   CITY 692A
20 HEURISKW 1A   FIND 325B
   N8SOS   ISLAND 540A
   OROS   MOUNTAIN 586A
   PHEUGW 5   FLEE 863D
21 BLASPH8MEW 2Bα   BLASPHEME 142A
   EPI 111Aβ   ON 288A
   KATABAINW 1B   COME DOWN 409D
   OURANOS 1B   HEAVEN 598C
   SPHODRA   GREATLY 803D
   TALANTIAIOS WEIGHING A TALENT 811A
21A   MEGAS 2Aγ   GREAT 499A
21A   PL8G8 3   BLOW 674B
21A   CHALAZA   HAIL 882B
21B   MEGAS 2Aγ   GREAT 499A
21B   PL8G8 3   BLOW 674B
21B   CHALAZA   HAIL 882B

            REVELATION 17

1 AGGELOS 2A   ANGEL 7D
   DEIKNUMI 1A   SHOW 171D
   DEURO 1   COME 175C
   ERCHOMAI 11Aζ   COME 310D
   KRIMA 4B   VERDICT 451D
   LALEW 2A6   SPEAK 464C
   LALEW 3   SPEAK 465A
   HO,H8,TO 111F   THE 553A
   POLUS 11Aβ   MANY 694B
   PORN8 2   PROSTITUTE 700B
   HUDWR 1   WATER 840C
   PHIAL8   BOWL 866A
2 KATOIKEW 2   LIVE 425C
   METHUSKW   GET DRUNK 500B
   META A113B   WITH 510D
   OINOS 2   WINE 565B
   PORNEIA 2   PROSTITUTION 700A
   PORNEUW 2   TO PROSTITUTE 700B

3 APOPHERW IAα   TAKE AWAY 101B
   BLASPH8MIA 2B   SLANDER 142C
   GEMW 3   BE FULL 153A
   DEKA   TEN 172D
   EIDON   SEE 219C
   EN I5D   IN 259C
   ER8MOS 2   DESERT 309A
   TH8RION IB   BEAST 361D
   KATH8MAI IAα   SIT 390B
   KERAS I   HORN 430B
   KEPHAL8 IA   HEAD 431B
   KOKKINOS   SCARLET 441A
   MARTUS 3   WITNESS 495D
   PNEUMA 6E   SPIRIT 684A
4 AKATHART8S   UNCLEANNESS 28B
   AKATHARTOS 2   IMPURE 28C
   GEMW I   BE FULL 153A
   ECHW IIA   HAVE 332A
   KOKKINOS   SCARLET 441A
   LITHOS IC   STONE 475C
   MARGARIT8S I   PEARL 492C
   PERIBALLW IBα   THROW AROUND 651D
   PERIBALLW IBβ   THROW AROUND 651D
   PORNEIA 2   PROSTITUTION 700A
   PORPHURA   PURPLE 700D
   PORPHUROUS   A PURPLE CLOAK 700D
   POT8RION I   CUP 702A
   TIMIOS IA   VALUABLE 825D
   CHRUSION   GOLD 896D
   CHRUSOS   GOLD 897A
   CHRUSOW   MAKE. GOLDEN 897B
   CHRUSOUS   GOLDEN 897B
4F   BDELUGMA 2   ABOMINATION 137C
5 BABULWN   BABYLON 129B
   METWPON   FOREHEAD 517A
   M8T8R 5   MOTHER 522A
   MUST8RION 3   MYSTERY 532C
   PORN8 2   PROSTITUTE 700B
6 HAIMA 2A   BLOOD 22B
   EIDON   SEE 219C
   THAUMA 2   A WONDER 352D
   THAUMAZW IAα   WONDER 352D
   MARTUS 3   WITNESS 495D
   METHUW 2   BE DRUNK 500C
7 BASTAZW 2A   CARRY 136D
   DEKA   TEN 172D
   DIA BII2   WHY 180B
   THAUMAZW IAα   WONDER 352D
   KERAS I   HORN 430B
   KEPHAL8 IA   HEAD 431B
   MUST8RION 3   MYSTERY 532C
7F   TH8RION IB   BEAST 361D
8 ABUSSOS 2   ABYSS 2B
   ANABAINW IAβ   GO UP 50A
   APWLEIA 2   DESTRUCTION 103A
   BIBLION I   BOOK 140D
   BLEPW IA   SEE 142D
   GRAPHW 2B   WRITE 165D
   EIMI II   TO BE 222A
   EIS 4A   INTO 228B
   ZW8 2Bβ   LIFE 341C
   THAUMAZW 2   WONDER 353A
   KATABOL8 I   FOUNDATION 410A

8 KATOIKEW IA   LIVE 425C
   KOSMOS 2   WORLD 446D
   ONOMA I2A   NAME 574B
   HOTI IBζ   THAT 593A
   PAREIMI IA   BE PRESENT 629C
   PIPTW 2Aα   FALL 665C
   HUPAGW   GO AWAY 844C
9 BASILEUS I   KING 135D
   HEPTA   SEVEN 306B
   ECHW I2Eβ   HAVE 333B
   KATH8MAI IAβ   SIT 390B
   KEPHAL8 IA   HEAD 431B
   NOUS I   THE UNDERSTANDING 546C
   HOPOU IAα   WHERE 579C
   OROS   MOUNTAIN 586B
   SOPHIA 2   WISDOM 767A
   HWDE 2B   HERE 903D
10 ALLOS IC   OTHER 39B
   HEIS 5D   ONE 231B
   MENW ICα   REMAIN 505C
   HO,H8,TO II2D   THE 553C
   OLIGOS 3A   LITTLE 566C
   OUPW   NOT YET 598A
   PIPTW 2Aδ   FALL 665D
11 APWLEIA 2   DESTRUCTION 103A
   AUTOS IC   SELF 122C
   EIS 4A   INTO 228B
   OGDOOS   THE EIGHTH 555B
   HUPAGW 2   GO AWAY 844C
11FF TH8RION IB   BEAST 361D
12 BASILEIA I   KINGDOM 134C
   *DEKA   TEN 172D
   KERAS I   HORN 430B
   OUPW   NOT YET 598A
   HWRA 2Aβ   TIME OF DAY 904C
12F   EXOUSIA 4A   AUTHORITY 278A
13 GNWM8 I   MIND 162B
   DIADIDWMI   DISTRIBUTE 181D
14 ARNION   SHEEP 107D
   BASILEUS 2A   KING 136A
   EKLEKTOS IB   CHOSEN 242B
   KL8T0S   CALLED 437B
   KURIOS 2Cγ   LORD 461B
   META AII3A   WITH 510C
   NIKAW 2A   CONQUER 541B
   POLEMEW IA   FIGHT 691C
15 GLWSSA 2   LANGUAGE 161C
   KATH8MAI IAβ   SIT 390B
   LAOS 2   PEOPLE 468A
   OCHLOS 4   CROWD 606A
15F   PORN8 2   PROSTITUTE 700B
16 GUMNOS I   NAKED 166D
   DEKA   TEN 172D
   *EN IIIIA   BY 260A
   ER8MOW   LAY WASTE 309A
   ESTHIW IA   EAT 312D
   KATAKAIW   CONSUME 412A
   KERAS I   HORN 430B
   MISEW I   HATE 524C
   PUR IA   FIRE 737B
   SARX I   FLESH 750D
16F   TH8RION IB   BEAST 361D
17 ACHRI 2B   UNTIL 128C

17 ACHRI 2B
   BASILEIA 1
   GNWM8 4
   DIDWMI 1Bβ
   KARDIA 1Bγ
   TELEW 1
18 BASILEIA 1
   EPI 11Bα
   POLIS 1

REVELATION 18

1 EK 3Eβ
  EXOUSIA 2
  KATABAINW 1Aγ
  OURANOS 2C
  PHWTIZW 2A
2 AKATHARTOS 2
  AKATHARTOS 1
  ANUDROS
  BABULWN
  DAIMONION 2
  DAIMWN
  ISCHUROS 2
  KATOIK8T8RION
  KRAZW 2A
  MISEW 3
  ORNEON
  PIPTW 2Aα
  PNEUMA 4C
  PHWN8 2A
2A   PHULAK8 3
2B   PHULAK8 3
3 DUNAMIS 5
  EMPOROS
  THUMOS 1
  THUMOS 2
  META AII3B
  OINOS 2
  PINW 2Bα
  PIPTW
  PLOUTEW 1
  PORNEIA 2
  PORNEUW 2
  STR8NOS
4 EK 4Aε
  LAOS 3B
  PL8G8 3
  SUGKOINWNEW 1
  PHWN8 2D
5 ADIK8MA
  ACHRI 1B
  KOLLAW 2Aβ
  MN8MONEUW 1B
6 APODIDWMI 3
  DIPLOW
  ERGON 1Cβ
  KERANNUMI 1
  HOS,H8,HO 16
  POT8RION 2
6A   DIPLOUS
7 BASANISMOS 2
  BASILISSA

UNTIL 128C
KINGDOM 134C
DECISION 162C
GIVE 192A
HEART 404D
FINISH 818D
KINGDOM 134C
OVER 286A
CITY 692B

BY 234C
ABILITY 277D
COME DOWN 409C
HEAVEN 599C
SHINE 881A
IMPURE 28C
IMPURE 28C
WATERLESS 76A
BABYLON 129B
DEMON 168B
DEMON 168D
STRONG 384A
DWELLING PLACE 425D
CALL 448D
HATE 524D
BIRD 585C
FALL 665C
SPIRIT 682A
VOICE 878D
GUARD 875D
GUARD 875D
RESOURCES 207B
MERCHANT 256B
PASSION 366A
ANGER 366A
WITH 510D
WINE 565B
DRINK 664C
FALL 664D
BE RICH 679D
PROSTITUTION 700A
TO PROSTITUTE 700B
SENSUALITY 779A
FROM 235B
PEOPLE 468B
BLOW 674B
BE CONNECTED 781D
VOICE 879C
A WRONG 17C
AS FAR AS 128C
UNITE 442B
REMEMBER 527A
RECOMPENSE 90A
TO DOUBLE 198D
DEED 308A
MIX 430B
(REL PRON) 588C
CUP 702B
DOUBLE 198C
TORMENTING 134B
QUEEN 136C

7 DIDWMI 1Bβ
  EIDON 5
  KATH8MAI 1Aε
  KARDIA 1Bβ
  LEGW 16
  HOSOS 3
  STR8NIAW
  TOSOUTOS 1Aα
  CH8RA
7A   PENTHOS
7B   PENTHOS
8 HEIS 2A
  H8KW 2
  THANATOS 1A
  THANATOS 1E
  ISCHUROS 1A
  KATAKAIW
  KRINW 4Bα
  LIMOS 2
  PENTHOS
  PL8G8 3
  PUR 1A
9 BLEPW 1A
  EPI 111Bε
  KAPNOS
  KLAIW 1
  KLAIW 2
  KOPTW 2
  META AII3B
  PORNEUW 2
  PURWSIS 1
10 BABULWN
  BASANISMOS 2
  ERCHOMAI 11Bβ
  HIST8MI 112Bα
  ISCHUROS 2
  KRISIS 1Aβ
  MAKROTHEN
  OUAI 1B
  POLIS 1
  PHOBOS 2Aα
  HWRA 2Aβ
11 AGORAZW 1
  GOMOS
  EMPOROS
  KLAIW 1
  OUDEIS 2A
  OUKETI 1
  PENTHEW 1
12 ARGUROS 2
  BUSSOS
  BUSSINOS
  GOMOS
  EK 3H
  ELEPHANTINOS
  THUINOS
  LITHOS 1C
  MARGARIT8S 1
  MARMAROS
  PORPHURA
  SIRIKOS
  CHALKOS 1
  CHRUSOS

GIVE 192B
SEE 220A
SIT 390B
HEART 404C
SAY 470A
HOW GREAT 590C
LIVE IN LUXURY 779A
SO GREAT 831B
THE WIDOW 889D
GRIEF 648C
GRIEF 648C
ONE 230B
HAVE COME 345C
DEATH 351B
DEATH 352A
STRONG 383D
CONSUME 412A
JUDGE 453A
FAMINE 476B
GRIEF 648C
BLOW 674B
FIRE 737B
SEE 142D
TOWARD 289A
SMOKE 404A
WEEP 434A
WEEP 434B
BEAT 445A
WITH 510D
TO PROSTITUTE 700B
BURNING 738D
BABYLON 129B
TORMENTING 134B
COME 311B
BEING 383C
STRONG 384A
JUDGING 453D
FROM FAR AWAY 489A
WOE 595C
CITY 692B
FEAR 871C
TIME OF DAY 904C
BUY 12C
CARGO 164A
MERCHANT 256B
WEEP 434B
NO ONE 596B
NO LONGER 597A
BE SAD 648C
SILVER 104C
LINEN 148C
LINEN 148C
CARGO 164A
BY 235A
MADE OF IVORY 250C
CITRON WOOD 365C
STONE 475C
PEARL 492C
MARBLE 493C
PURPLE 700D
SILK 759B
COPPER 883A
GOLD 897A

12A	XULON I	WOOD	551B
12A	SKEUOS IA	THING	761C
12A	TIMIOS IA	VALUABLE	825D
12B	XULON I	WOOD	551B
12B	SKEUOS IA	THING	761C
12B	TIMIOS IA	VALUABLE	825D
13	AMWMON	AMOMUM	47B
	ELAION I	OLIVE OIL	247B
	THUMIAMA IB	INCENSE	365D
	HIPPOS	HORSE	381B
	KINNAMWMON	CINNAMON	433D
	KT8NOS	ANIMAL	456B
	LIBANOS	FRANKINCENSE	474D
	MURON	OINTMENT	531D
	OINOS I	WINE	565A
	PROBATON I	SHEEP	710A
	RED8	CARRIAGE	742B
	SEMIDALIS	FINE FLOUR	754B
	SITOS	WHEAT	759D
	SWMA 2	BODY	807B
	PSUCH8 IE	SOUL LIFE	902B
14	APERCHOMAI IB	GO AWAY	83D
	APOLLUMI 2Aβ	PASS AWAY	94D
	EPITHUMIA I	DESIRE	293B
	LAMPROS 5	SPLENDOR	467A
	LIPAROS 2	LUXURY	476C
	M8 D2	NOT	519C
	OPWRA	FRUIT	580B
	OUKETI I	NO LONGER	597A
	PSUCH8 IBα	SOUL LIFE	901D
	PSUCH8 IF	SOUL LIFE	902C
15	APO V2	WITH	87B
	BASANISMOS 2	TORMENTING	134B
	EMPOROS	MERCHANT	256B
	HIST8MI IIIA	STAND	383A
	KLAIW I	WEEP	434B
	MAKROTHEN	FROM FAR AWAY	489A
	PENTHEW I	BE SAD	648B
	PLOUTEW I	BE RICH	679D
	PHOBOS 2Aα	FEAR	871C
16	BUSSINOS	LINEN	148C
	KOKKINOS	SCARLET	441A
	LITHOS IC	STONE	475C
	MARGARIT8S I	PEARL	492C
	OUAI IB	WOE	595C
	PERIBALLW IBα	THROW AROUND	651D
	POLIS I	CITY	692B
	PORPHUROUS	A PURPLE CLOAK	700D
	TIMIOS IA	VALUABLE	825D
	CHRUSION	GOLD	896D
	CHRUSOS	GOLD	897A
	CHRUSOW	MAKE GOLDEN	897B
17	ERGAZOMAI 2D	WORK	307B
	ER8MOW	LAY WASTE	309B
	THALASSA IA	SEA	350D
	HIST8MI IIIA	STAND	383A
	KUBERN8T8S I	STEERSMAN	457C
	MAKROTHEN	FROM FAR AWAY	489A
	NAUT8S	SAILOR	536B
	HOMILOS	CROWD	568C
	PLEW	SAIL	674A
	PLOUTOS I	WEALTH	680B
	PONTOS	SEA	698C

17	TOPOS IA	PLACE	830A
	TOSOUTOS IAα	SO GREAT	831A
	HWRA 2Aβ	TIME OF DAY	904C
18	KAPNOS	SMOKE	404A
	HOMOIOS I	LIKE	569D
	PURWSIS I	BURNING	738D
18F	KRAZW 2A	CALL	448D
18F	POLIS I	CITY	692B
19	BALLW IB	THROW	130C
	ER8MOW	LAY WASTE	309A
	ECHW I2A	HAVE	332B
	KEPHAL8 IA	HEAD	431A
	KLAIW I	WEEP	434B
	OUAI IB	WOE	595C
	PENTHEW I	BE SAD	648B
	PLOION I	SHIP	679B
	PLOUTEW I	BE RICH	679D
	TIMIOT8S	COSTLINESS	826A
	CHOUS	SOIL	892C
	HWRA 2Aβ	TIME OF DAY	904C
20	HAGIOS 2Dγ	DEDICATED TO GOD	10B
	APOSTOLOS 2	MESSENGER	99A
	EK 6B	FROM	235D
	EPI III Bγ	ON	287B
	EUPHRAINW 2	GLADDEN	328A
	KRIMA 5	JUDGMENT	452A
	KRINW 4Bα	JUDGE	453B
	OURANOS 2E	HEAVEN	599D
	PROPH8T8S 5	PROPHET	731C
21	AGGELOS 2A	ANGEL	7C
	AIRW IA	LIFT UP	23D
	BABULWN	BABYLON	129B
	BALLW IB	THROW	130C
	HEIS 3B	SOMEONE	230D
	ETI IBβ	STILL	316A
	HEURISKW IA	FIND	325B
	ISCHUROS IA	STRONG	384A
	LITHOS ID	STONE	475C
	MULIKOS	MILLSTONE	531A
	MULINOS	MILLSTONE	531A
	MULOS 2	MILLSTONE	531B
	HORM8MA	WITH VIOLENCE	585C
	POLIS I	CITY	692B
21A	BALLW IC	LET FALL	130D
21=3	M8 DIA	NOT	519D
22	AKOUW IBα	HEAR	31B
	AUL8T8S	FLUTE PLAYER	121A
	ETI IBβ	STILL	316A
	HEURISKW IB	FIND	325B
	KITHARWDOS	HARPIST	433A
	MOUSIKOS	THE MUSICIAN	530C
	MULOS I	MILL	531A
	PAS IAα	EVERY EACH	636D
	SALPIST8S	TRUMPETER	748C
	TECHN8	TRADE	821D
	TECHNIT8S	CRAFTSMAN	821D
22A	PHWN8 I	SOUND	878C
22B	PHWN8 I	SOUND	878C
23	EMPOROS	MERCHANT	256B
	ETI IBβ	STILL	316A
	LUCHNOS I	LAMP	484C
	MEGISTAN	GREAT MAN	499D
	NUMPH8 I	BRIDE	547B

23 NUMPHIOS   BRIDEGROOM 547B
   PLANAW 2C6   DECEIVE 671C
   PHAINW 2A   SHINE 859B
   PHAINW 1   SHINE 859B
   PHARMAKEIA   SORCERY 861D
   PHWN8 2A   VOICE 879A
   PHWS 1A   LIGHT 879D
24 HAGIOS 2Dy   DEDICATED TO GOD 10B
   HAIMA 2A   BLOOD 22B
   AUTOS 3Fα   (OBLIQUE CASE) 123B
   HEURISKW 1B   FIND 325B
   PAS 1D8   ALL 637D
   PROPH8T8S 5   PROPHET 731C
   SPHAZW   SLAUGHTER 803D

              REVELATION 19

1 HALL8LOUIA   HALLELUJAH 38D
  DOXA 1A   BRIGHTNESS 202C
  DUNAMIS 1   POWER 206C
  MARTUS 3   WITNESS 495D
  POLUS IIBα   MANY 694C
  SWT8RIA 2   DELIVERANCE 809B
  PHWN8 1   SOUND 878D
  HWS II3A8   SO 906A
2 HAIMA 2A   BLOOD 22B
  HAIMA 2A   BLOOD 22C
  AL8THINOS 2   TRUE 36C
  DIAPHTHEIRW 2   SPOIL 189D
  DIKAIOS 4   RIGHTEOUS 195B
  DOULOS 4   SLAVE 205B
  EK 6B   FROM 235D
  KRINW 4B«   JUDGE 453A
  KRISIS 1A8   JUDGING 454A
  PORNEIA 2   PROSTITUTION 700A
  PORN8 2   PROSTITUTE 700B
  PHTHEIRW 2A   RUIN 865A
3 HALL8LOUIA   HALLELUJAH 38D
  ANABAINW 1B   GO UP 50A
  DEUTEROS 4   SECOND 176B
  KAPNOS   SMOKE 404A
4 HALL8LOUIA   HALLELUJAH 38D
  AM8N 1   AMEN 45B
  EIKOSI   TWENTY 221A
  ZWON 1   LIVING THING 342C
  PIPTW 1B«   FALL 665B
  PRESBUTEROS 2By   OLDER 707B
  PROSKUNEW 2A   DO REVERENCE 724A
5 AINEW   TO PRAISE 23A
  DOULOS 4   SLAVE 205B
  EXERCHOMAI 2B«   GO OUT 274C
  MEGAS 2A«   GREAT 498D
  MIKROS 1B   SMALL 523A
  PHOBEW 2A   BE AFRAID 871A
  PHWN8 2D   VOICE 879B
6 HALL8LOUIA   HALLELUJAH 38D
  BASILEUW 2   BECOME KING 136B
  BASILEUW 1B«   RULE 136B
  BRONT8   THUNDER 147A
  ISCHUROS 2   STRONG 384A
  KURIOS 2A   LORD 460C
  PANTOKRATWR   ALMIGHTY 613D
  POLUS IIB«   MANY 694C

6   HUDWR 1   WATER 840D
6A PHWN8 1   SOUND 878D
6A HWS II3A8   SO 906A
6B POLUS IIA8   MANY 694B
6B PHWN8 1   SOUND 878C
6B HWS II3A8   SO 906A
6C PHWN8 1   SOUND 878C
6C HWS II3A8   SO 906A
7   AGALLIAW   BE GLAD 3D
    ARNION   SHEEP 107D
    GAMOS 1B   WEDDING 150D
    GUN8 3   BRIDE 167C
    DOXA 3   FAME 203B
    ERCHOMAI IIB8   COME 311B
    HETOIMAZW 2   PREPARE 316C
    CHAIRW 1   REJOICE 881B
8   BUSSINOS   LINEN 148C
    DIDWMI 1B8   GIVE 192B
    DIKAIWMA 2   RIGHTEOUS DEED 197B
    KATHAROS 1   CLEAN 388D
    LAMPROS 3   BRIGHT 467A
    PERIBALLW 1B«   THROW AROUND 651D
9   AL8THINOS 2   TRUE 36B
    ARNION   SHEEP 107D
    GAMOS 1B   WEDDING 150D
    DEIPNOS   DINNER 172C
    DEIPNON 2   DINNER 172C
    KALEW 1B   INVITE 400B
    MAKARIOS 1B   BLESSED 488A
    HOUTOS 2A   THIS 601D
10 EMPROSTHEN 2A   IN FRONT 256C
    ECHW IIC8   KEEP 332B
    M8 8IB   NOT 519A
    HORAW 2B   SEE 582B
    PIPTW 1B«   FALL 665B
    PNEUMA 6D   SPIRIT 684A
    POUS 1A   FOOT 703B
    PROPH8TEIA 2   PROPHECY 730B
    SUNDOULOS 4   FELLOW SLAVE 793C
10A   MARTURIA 2Dy   TESTIMONY 494D
10A   PROSKUNEW 4   DO REVERENCE 724B
10B   MARTURIA 2Dy   TESTIMONY 494D
10B   PROSKUNEW 2A   DO REVERENCE 724A
11 AL8THINOS 1   TRUE 36B
    ANOIGW 1B   OPEN 70C
    DIKAIOSUN8 1   RIGHTEOUSNESS 195C
    EN III2   BY 260B
    IDOU 2   THERE IS 371D
    HIPPOS   HORSE 381D
    KATH8MAI 1A«   SIT 390B
    KALEW 1Ay   CALL 400A
    KRINW 4B«   JUDGE 453A
    PISTOS 1A«   TRUSTWORTHY 670B
    POLEMEW 1A   FIGHT 691C
12 AUTOS 1C   SELF 122C
    DIADECHOMAI   DIADEM 181D
    KEPHAL8 1A   HEAD 431A
    OUDEIS 2A   NO ONE 596B
    OPHTHALMOS 1   EYE 604B
    PUR 1A   FIRE 737B
    STEPHANOS 1   WREATH 774D
    PHLOX   FLAME 870A
13 BAPTW 1   DIP 132B

```
13 BAPTW 2           DIP 132C
   HIMATION 2        GARMENT 377B
   KALEW 1AY         CALL 400A
   LOGOS 3           THE LOGOS 480A
   ONOMA 12A         NAME 574B
   PERIBALLW 1Bα     THROW AROUND 651D
   PERI(R)RAINW      SPRINKLE 656A
   RAINW             SPRINKLE 741A
   RANTIZW 1         SPRINKLE 741C
14 BUSSINOS          LINEN 148C
   ENDUW 2A          DRESS 263C
   EPI III1Aα        ON 286C
   HIPPOS            HORSE 381B
   KATHAROS 1        CLEAN 388D
   OURANOS 2C        HEAVEN 599C
   STRATEUMA         ARMY 778A
14B   LEUKOS 2       WHITE 473D
15 DISTOMOS          DOUBLE EDGED 199A
   EKPOREUOMAI 2     GO OUT 244A
   EN III1A          BY 260A
   THUMOS 1          PASSION 366A
   THUMOS 2          ANGER 366A
   L8NOS             WINE PRESS 474B
   OINOS 2           WINE 565B
   OXUS 1            SHARP 578A
   ORG8 2B           ANGER 583A
   PANTOKRATWR       ALMIGHTY 613D
   PATASSW 2         STRIKE 640B
   PATEW 1Aα         TREAD 640B
   POIMAINW 2AY      TEND 690B
   RABDOS            ROD 740D
   ROMPHAIA          SWORD 744C
   SID8ROUS          IRON 757C
   STOMA 1A          MOUTH 777B
16 BASILEUS 2A       KING 136A
   GRAPHW 2A         WRITE 165D
   HIMATION 2        GARMENT 377A
   KURIOS 2CY        LORD 461B
   M8ROS             THIGH 521C
17 DEIPNOS           DINNER 172C
   DEIPNON 2         DINNER 172C
   DEUTE 1           COME 175D
   HEIS 3B           SOMEONE 230D
   H8LIOS            THE SUN 346B
   HIST8MI II2Bβ     BEING 383C
   KRAZW 2A          CALL 448D
   MESOURAN8MA       IN MIDHEAVEN 509B
   ORNEON            BIRD 585C
   PETOMAI           FLY 660A
   SUNAGW 2          GATHER 790A
18 DOULOS 1B         SLAVE 204D
   ELEUTHEROS 1      FREE 250B
   ESTHIW 1A         EAT 312D
   HIPPOS            HORSE 381B
   ISCHUROS 1B       STRONG 384A
   MEGAS 2Aα         GREAT 498D
   MIKROS 1B         SMALL 523A
   SARX 1            FLESH 750D
   CHILIARCHOS       TRIBUNE 890A
19 HIPPOS            HORSE 381B
   META AII3A        WITH 510C
   POLEMOS 1A        ARMED CONFLICT 691D
   SUNAGW 2          GATHER 790B

19A   STRATEUMA      ARMY 778A
19B   STRATEUMA      ARMY 778A
19F   TH8RION 1B     BEAST 361D
20 BALLW 1B          THROW 130C
   EIKWN 1A          IMAGE 221B
   ENWPION 5C        BEFORE 270C
   ZAW 1Aα           LIVE 336B
   THEION            SULPHUR 354B
   KAIW 1A           LIGHT 397A
   LAMBANW 2         RECEIVE 466C
   LIMN8 1           LAKE 476A
   PIAZW 2B          GRASP 662D
   PLANAW 1B         DECEIVE 671B
   POIEW IIBβ        DO 687C
   PROSKUNEW 3       DO REVERENCE 724B
   PUR 1B            FIRE 737C
   S8MEION 2B        SIGN 755D
   CHARAGMA 1        A MARK 884A
   PSEUDOPROPH8T8S   FALSE PROPHET 900B
21 EK  4Aα           FROM 235B
   EXERCHOMAI 2Bβ    GO OUT 274D
   HIPPOS            HORSE 381B
   LOIPOS 2Bα        THE OTHERS 481A
   ORNEON            BIRD 585C
   ROMPHAIA          SWORD 744C
   SARX 1            FLESH 750D
   STOMA 1A          MOUTH 777B
   CHORTAZW 1        FEED 892B
```

REVELATION 20

```
1  ABUSSOS 2         ABYSS  2B
   KATABAINW 1AY     COME DOWN 409C
   KLEIS 1           KEY 435A
   MEGAS 1A          LARGE 498C
   OURANOS 2C        HEAVEN 599C
   CHEIR 1           HAND 888B
1F    HALUSIS 1      CHAIN  40D
2  ARCHAIOS 1        ANCIENT 110D
   DRAKWN            DRAGON 205C
   KRATEW 1A         ARREST 449C
   OPHIS 3           SNAKE 605A
   SATAN             ADVERSARY 752B
2=7   CHILIOI        THOUSAND 890B
3 *ABUSSOS 2         ABYSS  2B
   ACHRI 2B          UNTIL 128C
   BALLW 1B          THROW 130C
   EPANW 2A          ON 283A
   KLEIW 1           SHUT 435B
   LUW 2A            LOOSE 484D
   MIKROS 2D         SHORT 523B
   PLANAW 1B         DECEIVE 671B
   PLATOS 1          BREADTH 672D
   SPHRAGIZW 1       SEAL 804A
   TELEW 1           FINISH 818C
   CHRONOS           TIME 896B
3=7   ETOS           YEAR 317A
4  BASILEUW 1B6      RULE 136B
   EIKWN 1A          IMAGE 221B
   ZAW 1Aβ           LIVE 336C
   TH8RION 1B        BEAST 361D
   THRONOS 1D        THRONE 365A
   KATHIZW 2Aα       SIT DOWN 391A
```

4	KRIMA 3	JUDGING 451C
	LAMBANW 2	RECEIVE 466C
	MARTURIA 2Dγ	TESTIMONY 494D
	META ΔII2	WITH 510B
	METWPON	FOREHEAD 517A
	HOSTIS 1B	WHOEVER 590D
	*OUTE	NOT 600C
	PELEKIZW	BEHEAD 647B
	PROSKUNEW 3	DO REVERENCE 724B
	CHARAGMA 1	A MARK 884A
	CHRISTOS 1	ANOINTED ONE 895C
	PSUCH8 1Aα	SOUL LIFE 901C
5	ANAZAW 1A	COME TO LIFE AGAIN 53B
	ACHRI 2B	UNTIL 128C
	ZAW 1Aβ	LIVE 336C
	LOIPOS 2Bα	THE OTHERS 481A
	TELEW 1	FINISH 818C
5F	ANASTASIS 2B	RESURRECTION 60B
5F	PRWTOS 1A	FIRST 732D
6	BASILEUW 1B6	RULE 136B
	EXOUSIA 2	ABILITY 277D
	EPI 11Bα	OVER 286A
	ECHW I2A	HAVE 332B
	THANATOS 2B	DEATH 352B
	HIEREUS 2B	PRIEST 372D
	MAKARIOS 1B	BLESSED 488A
	MEROS 2	SHARE 507C
	META ΔII2	WITH 510C
7	LUW 2A	LOOSE 484D
	PLATOS 1	BREADTH 672D
	SATAN	ADVERSARY 752C
	TELEW 1	FINISH 818C
	PHULAK8 3	GUARD 875D
8	AMMOS	SAND 45D
	ARITHMOS 1	NUMBER 106A
	GWNIA	CORNER 167D
	GWG	GOG 167D
	EXERCHOMAI 1Aζ	GO OUT 274B
	MAGWG	MAGOG 486B
	HOS,H8,HO I3A	(REL PRON) 587C
	PLANAW 1B	DECEIVE 671B
	PLATOS 1	BREADTH 672D
	POLEMOS 1B	ARMED CONFLICT 691D
	SUNAGW 2	GATHER 790A
9	AGAPAW 1D	LOVE 4D
	ANABAINW 1Aβ	GO UP 50A
	KATABAINW 1B	COME DOWN 409D
	KATESTHIW 2	DESTROY 423B
	KUKLEUW	SURROUND 457D
	OURANOS 1B	HEAVEN 598C
	PAREMBOL8 1	A CAMP 630D
	PLATOS 1	BREADTH 672D
	POLIS 1	CITY 692B
	PUR 1B	FIRE 737C
10	BALLW 1B	THROW 130C
	BASANIZW 2A	TORMENT 134A
	THEION	SULPHUR 354B
	TH8RION 1B	BEAST 361D
	LIMN8 1	LAKE 476A
	NUX 1B	NIGHT 548D
	HOPOU 1Aα	WHERE 579C
	PLANAW 1B	DECEIVE 671B
	PUR 1B	FIRE 737C
10	PSEUDOPROPH8T8S	FALSE PROPHET 900B
11	LEUKOS 2	WHITE 473D
	OURANOS 1Aα	HEAVEN 598B
	PROSWPON 1Cα	FACE 728C
	PROSWPON 1Cα	FACE 728C
	TOPOS 1F	PLACE 830C
	PHEUGW 5	FLEE 863D
12	ANOIGW 1C	OPEN 70C
	BIBLION 1	BOOK 140D
	GRAPHW 2B	WRITE 165D
	EK 3I	BY 235A
	ENWPION 1	BEFORE 270A
	ZW8 2Bβ	LIFE 341C
	HIST8MI II2Bβ	BEING 383C
	KRINW 4Bα	JUDGE 453A
	MEGAS 2Aα	GREAT 498D
	MIKROS 1B	SMALL 523A
12F	ERGON 1Cβ	DEED 308A
13	DIDWMI 4	GIVE 192C
	HEKASTOS 2	EACH 236B
	KRINW 4Bα	JUDGE 453A
13F	HAD8S 2	HADES 16D
13F	THANATOS 1F	DEATH 352A
14	DEUTEROS 2	SECOND 176A
	HOUTOS 2A	THIS 601D
14A	LIMN8 1	LAKE 476A
14A	PUR 1B	FIRE 737D
14B	THANATOS 2B	DEATH 352B
14B	LIMN8 1	LAKE 476A
14B	PUR 1B	FIRE 737D
14F	BALLW 1B	THROW 130C
15	BIBLOS 2	BOOK 141A
	GRAPHW 2B	WRITE 165D
	HEURISKW 1A	FIND 325B
	ZW8 2Bβ	LIFE 341C
	LIMN8 1	LAKE 476A
	PUR 1B	FIRE 737D

REVELATION 21

1	APERCHOMAI 1B	GO AWAY 83D
	G8 5A	EARTH 156D
	KAINOS 3B	NEW 395B
	OURANOS 1Aβ	HEAVEN 598B
	PARERCHOMAI 1Bα	PASS AWAY 631C
2	HAGIOS 1Aα	DEDICATED TO GOD 9C
	AN8R 1	MAN 66A
	HETOIMAZW 2	PREPARE 316C
	*HIEROSOLUMA 2	JERUSALEM 374A
	KAINOS 3B	NEW 395B
	KATABAINW 1B	COME DOWN 409C
	KOSMEW 2Aα	DECORATE 445D
	NUMPH8 1	BRIDE 547B
	OURANOS 2D	HEAVEN 599D
	POLIS 2	CITY 692C
3	AUTOS 1Aβ	SELF 122B
	IDOU 2	THERE IS 371D
	LAOS 3B	PEOPLE 468B
	SK8N8	TENT 762B
	SK8NOW	LIVE 762D
	PHWN8 2D	VOICE 879C
3A	META AI	WITH 509D
4	APERCHOMAI 1B	GO AWAY 83D

4	DAKRUON	TEAR	169A
	EIMI I4	TO BE	222C
	EXALEIPHW IA	WIPE AWAY	272A
	THANATOS IF	DEATH	352A
	KRAUGB IA	SHOUT	450C
	OUTE	NOT	600C
	OPHTHALMOS I	EYE	604B
	PENTHOS	GRIEF	648C
	PONOS 2	PAIN	698B
5	ALBTHINOS 2	TRUE	36B
	KAINOS 3B	NEW	395B
	LOGOS IBß	WORD	479C
	PAS 2A6	EVERYTHING	638B
	PISTOS IB	TRUSTWORTHY	670D
	POIEW II8ı	DO	688B
6	A	ALPHA	IA
	ARCHB ID	BEGINNING	IIID
	DIPSAW 2	THIRST	199C
	DWREAN I	GRATIS	209D
	ZWB 2Bß	LIFE	341D
	PBGB 2	FOUNTAIN	661D
	TELOS IB	END	819B
	HUDWR 2	WATER	841A
	W	OMEGA	903A
7	KLBRONOMEW 2	INHERIT	436A
	NIKAW IA	BE VICTOR	541B
	HUIOS ICγ	SON	841D
8	HAMARTWLOS 2	SINNER	43C
	APISTOS 2	FAITHLESS	85A
	BDELUSSOMAI	ABHORE	137D
	DEILOS	COWARDLY	172A
	DEUTERCS 2	SECOND	176A
	EIDWLOLATRBS	IDOLATER	220C
	THANATOS 2B	DEATH	352B
	THEION	SULPHUR	354B
	KAIW IA	LIGHT	397A
	LIMNB I	LAKE	476A
	MEROS 2	SHARE	507C
	HOS,HB,HO I7B	(REL PRON)	588C
	PORNOS	FORNICATOR	700B
	PUR IB	FIRE	737D
	PHARMAKEUS	MAGICIAN	861D
	PHARMAKOS	POISONER	862A
	PHONEUS	MURDERER	872B
	PSEUDBS I	FALSE	899D
9	AGGELOS 2A	ANGEL	7D
	ARNION	SHEEP	107D
	GEMW I	BE FULL	153A
	GUNB 3	BRIDE	167C
	DEURO I	COME	175C
	*HEPTA	SEVEN	306B
	ERCHOMAI IIAζ	COME	310D
	ESCHATOS 3B	LAST	314A
	LALEW 2A6	SPEAK	464C
	NUMPHB I	BRIDE	547B
	PLBGB 3	BLOW	674B
	PHIALB	BOWL	866A
9F	DEIKNUMI IA	SHOW	171D
10	HAGIOS IAα	DEDICATED TO GOD	9C
	APOPHERW IAα	TAKE AWAY	101B
	EN I5D	IN	259C
	HIEROSOLUMA 2	JERUSALEM	374A
	KATABAINW IB	COME DOWN	409C

10	OROS	MOUNTAIN	586B
	OURANOS 2D	HEAVEN	599D
	PNEUMA 6E	SPIRIT	684A
	POLIS 2	CITY	692C
	HUPSBLOS I	HIGH	857C
11	DOXA IA	BRIGHTNESS	202C
	IASPIS	JASPER	369B
	KRUSTALLIZW		455D
	SHINE LIKE CRYSTAL		
	LITHOS IC	STONE	475C
	HOMOIOS I	LIKE	569C
	TIMIOS IA	VALUABLE	825D
	PHWSTBR 2	LIGHT GIVING BODY	880D
12	EPI IIIA6	AT	286D
	EPIGRAPHW I	WRITE ON	291C
	TEICHOS	WALL	815D
	HUPSBLOS I	HIGH	857C
	PHULB I	TRIBE	876D
12A	PULWN I	GATE	736D
12B	PULWN I	GATE	736D
13	ANATOLB 2A	EAST	62A
	APO III	FROM	86B
	BORRAS	NORTH	144D
	DUSMB	WEST	209A
	NOTOS 2	SOUTH	546A
13A	PULWN I	GATE	736D
13B	PULWN I	GATE	736D
13C	PULWN I	GATE	736D
13D	PULWN I	GATE	736D
14	APOSTOLOS 3	APOSTLES	99B
	ARNION	SHEEP	107D
	ECHW I2Cβ	HAVE	332D
	THEMELIOS IA	FOUNDATION	356B
	ONOMA II	NAME	573D
14F	TEICHOS	WALL	815D
14=16	POLIS 2	CITY	692C
15	LALEW 2A6	SPEAK	464C
	METREW IA	MEASURE	516A
	METRON IB	MEASURE	516D
	PULWN I	GATE	736D
	CHRUSOUS	GOLDEN	897B
15F	KALAMOS 3	MEASURING ROD	399C
16	EPI IIIIAα	ACROSS	287D
	ISOS	EQUAL	381D
	KEIMAI IB	LIE	428A
	*METREW IA	MEASURE	516B
	HOSOS I	HOW GREAT	590B
	STADION I	STADE	771C
	TETRAGWNOS	LIKE A CUBE	821B
	TETRAGWNOS	SQUARE	821B
	TOSOUTOS IAα	SO GREAT	831A
	HUPSOS IA	HEIGHT	858B
	CHILIAS	THOUSAND	890B
16A	MBKOS	LENGTH	520C
16A	PLATOS I	BREADTH	672D
16B	MBKOS	LENGTH	520C
16B	PLATOS I	BREADTH	672D
17	ANTHRWPOS IAα	MAN	67C
	HEKATON	ONE HUNDRED	236B
	METREW IA	MEASURE	516B
	METRON IB	MEASURE	516D
	PBCHUS	FOREARM	662D
17=19	TEICHOS	WALL	815D

18	ENDWM8SIS	CONSTRUCTION 263D
	HOMOIOS I	LIKE 569C
	HUALOS	GLASS 839B
	CHRUSION	GOLD 896D
18A	KATHAROS I	CLEAN 388D
18B	KATHAROS I	CLEAN 388D
18F	IASPIS	JASPER 369B
18F	POLIS 2	CITY 692C
18FF	LITHOS IC	STONE 475C
19	DEUTEROS 3	SECOND 176A
	KOSMEW 2Aβ	DECORATE 446A
	LITHOS IC	STONE 475C
	PRWTOS IB	FIRST 733A
	SAPPHIROS	SAPPHIRE 749D
	SMARAGDOS	EMERALD 766A
	TIMIOS IA	VALUABLE 825D
	TRITOS I	THIRD 834C
	HUAKINTHOS	HYACINTH 839B
	CHALK8DWN	CHALCEDONY 882D
19A	THEMELIOS IA	FOUNDATION 356B
19B	THEMELIOS IA	FOUNDATION 356B
20	AMETHUSTOS	AMETHYST 44A
	B8RULLOS	BERYL 140A
	DWDEKATOS	TWELFTH 209B
	HEBDOMOS	SEVENTH 212A
	HEKTOS	SIXTH 245D
	ENATOS	NINTH 261D
	OGDOOS	THE EIGHTH 555B
	PEMPTOS	FIFTH 647B
	SARDION	CARNELIAN 750A
	SARDONUX	THE SARDONYX 750A
	TOPAZION	TOPAZ 830A
	HUAKINTHOS	HYACINTH 839B
	CHRUSOPRASOS	CHRYSOPRASE 897A
	CHRUSOLITHOS	CHRYSOLITE 897A
21	ANA 3	EACH 49C
	DIAUG8S	TRANSPARENT 189B
	DIAPHAN8S	TRANSPARENT 189B
	HEIS 5E	ONE 231B
	EK 3H	BY 235A
	HEKASTOS 2	EACH 236A
	KATHAROS I	CLEAN 388D
	MARGARIT8S I	PEARL 492C
	PLATEIA	WIDE ROAD 672D
	POLIS 2	CITY 692C
	HUALOS	GLASS 839B
	CHRUSION	GOLD 896D
21A	PULWN I	GATE 736D
21B	PULWN I	GATE 736D
22	KURIOS 2A	LORD 460C
	PANTOKRATWR	ALMIGHTY 613D
22A	NAOS IB	TEMPLE 535C
22B	NAOS IB	TEMPLE 535C
22F	ARNION	SHEEP 107D
23	DOXA IA	BRIGHTNESS 202C
	H8LIOS	THE SUN 346B
	LUCHNOS 2	LAMP 484C
	OUDE I	AND NOT 595D
	OUTE	NOT 600C
	POLIS 2	CITY 692C
	SEL8N8	MOON 754A
	PHAINW I	SHINE 859B
	PHWTIZW 2A	SHINE 881A
23	CHREIA I	NEED 893B
24	DIA AII	THROUGH 178C
	DOXA 2	MAGNIFICENCE 203A
	PERIPATEW IC	GO ABOUT 654D
	PHERW 4Aα	BEAR 863A
	PHWS IA	LIGHT 879D
25	H8MERA IA	DAY 346C
	KLEIW I	SHUT 435A
	NUX IA	NIGHT 548C
	PULWN I	GATE 736D
26	DOXA 2	MAGNIFICENCE 203A
	TIM8 2B	HONOR 825C
	PHERW	BEAR 862D
	PHERW 4Aα	BEAR 863A
27	ARNION	SHEEP 107D
	BDELUGMA 2	ABOMINATION 137C
	BIBLION I	BOOK 140D
	GRAPHW 2B	WRITE 165D
	ZW8 2Bβ	LIFE 341C
	KOINOS 2	COMMON 439B
	KOINOW IC	DEFILE 439B
	PAS IAα	EVERY EACH 636D
	POIEW IICγ	DO 688C
	PSEUDOS	LIE 900C

REVELATION 22

1	ARNION	SHEEP 107D
	DEIKNUMI IA	SHOW 171D
	EKPOREUOMAI 2	GO OUT 244A
	ZW8 2Bβ	LIFE 341D
	THRONOS IB	THRONE 364D
	THRONOS IC	THRONE 364D
	LAMPROS 2	CLEAR 467A
	POTAMOS I	RIVER 701C
	HUDWR 2	WATER 841A
2	APODIDWMI I	GIVE AWAY 90A
	EIS 4D	FOR 228C
	HEKASTOS I	EACH 236A
	ENTEUTHEN I	FROM HERE 268A
	ZW8 2Bβ	LIFE 341D
	THERAPEIA IB	SERVING 359C
	KATA II2C	EVERY 407C
	MESOS 2	THE MIDDLE 508D
	M8N I	MONTH 520D
	PLATEIA	WIDE ROAD 672D
	POIEW IIBη	DO 688A
	POTAMOS I	RIVER 701C
	PHULLON	FOLIAGE 877A
2A	KARPOS IA	FRUIT 405C
2A	XULON 3	TREE 551C
2B	KARPOS IA	FRUIT 405D
2B	XULON 3	TREE 551C
3	ARNION	SHEEP 107D
	*DOULOS 4	SLAVE 205B
	THRONOS IB	THRONE 364D
	THRONOS IC	THRONE 364D
	KATATHEMA	ACCURSED THING 411C
	LATREUW	SERVE 468C
4	METWPON	FOREHEAD 517A
	HORAW IAγ	SEE 581D
	PROSWPON IB	FACE 728B
5	BASILEUW IBδ	RULE 136B

5	H8LIOS	THE SUN 346B
	LUCHNOS I	LAMP 484C
	NUX IA	NIGHT 548C
	PHWTIZW 2A	SHINE 881A
	PHWTIZW I	SHINE 881A
	CHREIA I	NEED 893B
5A	PHWS IA	LIGHT 879D
5B	PHWS IA	LIGHT 879D
6	AL8THINOS 2	TRUE 36B
	APOSTELLW IBγ	SEND AWAY 98B
	DEI I	IT IS NECESSARY 171A
	DEIKNUMI IA	SHOW 171D
	DOULOS 4	SLAVE 205B
	EN III2	BY 260C
	LOGOS IBß	WORD 479C
	PISTOS IB	TRUSTWORTHY 670D
	PNEUMA 6D	SPIRIT 684A
	PROPH8T8S 5	PROPHET 731B
	TACHOS	SPEED 814D
7	BIBLION I	BOOK 140D
	MAKARIOS IB	BLESSED 488A
	PROPH8TEIA 3B	PROPHECY 730B
	TACHUS 2B	QUICK 815A
	T8REW 5	KEEP 823A
8	BLEPW IA	SEE 142D
	DEIKNUMI IA	SHOW 171D
	EMPROSTHEN 2A	IN FRONT 256C
	IWAN(N)8S 3	JOHN 385C
	PIPTW IBα	FALL 665B
	POUS IA	FOOT 703B
	PROSKUNEW 4	DO REVERENCE 724B
9	M8 BIB	NOT 519A
	HORAW 2B	SEE 582B
	SUNDOULOS 4	FELLOW SLAVE 793C
	T8REW 5	KEEP 823A
9F	BIBLION I	BOOK 140D
10	EGGUS 2A	NEAR 213B
	KAIROS 4	TIME 396B
	PROPH8TEIA 3B	PROPHECY 730B
	SPHRAGIZW 2A	SEAL 804A
11	HAGIAZW 3	TO REVERENCE 9A
	ADIKEW IA	DO WRONG 17A
	DIKAIOS IA	UPRIGHT 194D
	DIKAIOSUN8 2B	RIGHTEOUSNESS 195D
	DIKAIOW 3A	JUSTIFY 196D
	POIEW IICß	DO 688C
	RUPAREUW	DEFILE 745B
	RUPAROS 2	DIRTY 745B
	RUPAINW	DEFILE 745B
	RUPOW	DEFILE 745C
12	APODIDWMI 3	RECOMPENSE 90A
	ERGON ICß	DEED 308A
	META AIIICα	WITH 510A
	MISTHOS 2C	REWARD 525C
	TACHUS 2B	QUICK 815A
	HWS I2C	AS 905D
13	A	ALPHA IA
	ARCH8 ID	BEGINNING 111D
	ESCHATOS 3B	LAST 314A
	PRWTOS IA	FIRST 732D
	TELOS IB	END 819B
	W	OMEGA 903A
14	EXOUSIA I	RIGHT 277C

14	EPI IIIIBα	OVER 288D
	ZW8 2Bß	LIFE 341D
	HINA I2	IN ORDER THAT 377D
	MAKARIOS IB	BLESSED 488A
	XULON 3	TREE 551C
	PLUNW I	WASH 680C
	POLIS 2	CITY 692C
	PULWN I	GATE 736D
	STOL8	ROBE 777A
15	EIDWLOLATR8S	IDOLATER 220C
	EXW IAα	OUTSIDE 279A
	KUWN 2	DOG 462B
	PORNOS	FORNICATOR 700B
	PHARMAKOS	POISONER 862A
	PHILEW IB	LOVE LIKE 867A
	PHONEUS	MURDERER 872B
	PSEUDOS	LIE 900C
16	GENOS I	DESCENDANTS 155B
	DAUID	DAVID 170B
	EPI III8δ	ON 287C
	LAMPROS I	BRIGHT 467A
	MARTUREW IB	BEAR WITNESS 494A
	ORTHRINOS	584B
		EARLY IN THE MORNING
	PEMPW I	SEND 647D
	PRWINOS	EARLY 732B
	RIZA 2	ROOT 743C
17	DIPSAW 2	THIRST 199C
	DWREAN I	GRATIS 209D
	ZW8 2Bß	LIFE 341D
	LAMBANW 2	RECEIVE 466B
	NUMPH8 I	BRIDE 547B
	PNEUMA 5Dα	SPIRIT 683A
	HUDWR 2	WATER 841A
18	MARTUREW IA	BEAR WITNESS 493D
	PAS ICγ	WHOEVER 637C
	PL8G8 3	BLOW 674B
	PROPH8TEIA 3B	PROPHECY 730B
	SUMMARTUREW	TESTIFY 786A
18A	EPI IIIIBß	TO 288D
18A	EPITITH8MI IB	ADD 303C
18B	EPITITH8MI IAß	303A
		INFLICT BLOWS
18F	BIBLION I	BOOK 140D
18F	GRAPHW 2B	WRITE 165D
18F	TIS, TI IAγ	ANY ONE 827D
19	HAGIOS IAα	DEDICATED TO GOD 9C
	ZW8 2Bß	LIFE 341D
	MEROS 2	SHARE 507C
	XULON 3	TREE 551C
	POLIS 2	CITY 692C
	PROPH8TEIA 3B	PROPHECY 730B
19A	APHAIREW I	TAKE AWAY 124A
19B	APHAIREW I	TAKE AWAY 124A
20	AM8N I	AMEN 45B
	KURIOS 2Cγ	LORD 461B
	MARTUREW IB	BEAR WITNESS 494A
	NAI 4	CERTAINLY 535A
	TACHUS 2B	QUICK 815A
20B	NAI 2	CERTAINLY 534D
21	CHARIS 2C	FAVOR 885D